THE OXFORD HANDBOOK OF

IMPROVISATION IN DANCE

THE OXFORD HANDBOOK OF

IMPROVISATION

IN DANCE

Edited by

VIDA L. MIDGELOW

OXFORD
UNIVERSITY PRESS

Oxford University Press is a department of the University of Oxford. It furthers
the University's objective of excellence in research, scholarship, and education
by publishing worldwide. Oxford is a registered trade mark of Oxford University
Press in the UK and certain other countries.

Published in the United States of America by Oxford University Press
198 Madison Avenue, New York, NY 10016, United States of America.

CIP data is on file at the Library of Congress
ISBN 978-0-19-939698-6

1 3 5 7 9 8 6 4 2

Printed by Sheridan Books, Inc., United States of America

Contents

Acknowledgements

THIS handbook has been a long time in the making. It draws together authors to speak of the presence of improvisation in diverse dance forms and in a myriad of contexts, many considering improvisation anew.

Throughout I have had the privilege of being surrounded by colleagues that have supported my work and thinking. In particular, my fellow artist-researchers in the Transdisciplinary Improvisation Network at Middlesex University, my home institution, have given me delightful spaces in which to practice and share ideas. It was this Network, too, that co-curated the event *What's in a Name?*, a cross-disciplinary conference bringing together an international group of researchers to articulate the nature and significance of improvisation. More recently, it was my pleasure to be invited to engage with the work of the International Institute of Critical Studies in Improvisation at Regina University, Regina, Canada. Such gatherings, like this handbook, bring together artists and scholars in ways that enrich our understanding of improvisation and highlight its significance as part of arts practice, creativity, and human interaction.

I would particularly like to thank each of the authors for their contributions and also for their patience in the process. It is their insights that have shaped the final form of the book. Many are improviser-researchers who reflect on findings emerging from their own physical experiences—be that as performers, teachers, or participants. Many, too, have been inspired by the work of other improvisers, and so, too, it is important to thank these dancers and dance-makers, whose practices and experiences are discussed in these pages.

There are a few people I would like to thank by name. Jane Bacon, a longstanding collaborator and friend, generously read early versions of the introduction and, through our joint work on the Creative Articulation Process, helped me develop tools through which it became possible to articulate my own movement practice. Deep thanks also go to Courtney Hopf and Katherine Hall—two assistants who, at the start and end of the project, worked in the background to ensure that communications, tracking, and iteration control of the many chapters was maintained.

Finally, this project would not have happened but for the ongoing support of Norm Hirschy at Oxford University Press. Both Norm and Assistant Editor Lauralee Yeary were paragons of patience and kindness throughout. As indeed were my colleagues at Middlesex University and my family, who are scattered across the globe. As always, my family has gently supported my endeavours, enabling time spent in studios, at the laptop, and travelling to international conferences and workshops—without this support, nothing would be possible.

Contributors

Tamara Ashley's research investigates the practices of dance improvisation in the context of environmental change. Her work has included several durational site-responsive performances, including a thirty-one-day performance on the Pennine Way National Trail with fellow artist Simone Kenyon. She is particularly interested in the ethical dimensions of ecological dance practices. Tamara's work also draws on her work as a yoga teacher and somatic practitioner, with a strong emphasis on encouraging rigorous practices of first person enquiry for cultivating well-being and human development. She recently served as a guest editor for the *Journal of Dance and Somatic Practices* and chaired the Well-being and Mindfulness Group as part of the Climate Change Collaborations Conference. She directs the MA programme in Dance Performance and Choreography at the University of Bedfordshire.

Fiona Bannon (PhD) is Senior Lecturer at the School of Performance and Cultural Industries at the University of Leeds, where she teaches courses in research practice, performance, and collaborative enterprise and choreography. Fiona is currently Chair of DanceHE, the representative body for dance in higher education in the United Kingdom. As Chair of World Dance Alliance-Europe, she is also a member of the Global Executive of World Dance Alliance. Her career includes time working as a dance animateur in the United Kingdom and Australia and, more recently, as Head of the School of Arts, University of Hull. She is now based at the University of Leeds; her research interests include exploration of creative practice, collaboration in art-making, and learning through arts.

Robert Bingham is an improviser, scholar, and teacher living in Philadelphia,. His dances have been presented throughout the eastern United States, Canada, and Mexico, and he has studied with and performed in works by Ishmael Houston-Jones, Jennifer Monson, Diego Piñon, and Merián Soto. His articles on dance and somatics appear in *Moving Consciously, Dance and the Quality of Life*, and elsewhere. In 2013 he received a Fulbright Scholar Award to initiate an interdisciplinary arts laboratory in Berlin. Robert completed his PhD dissertation, *Improvising Meaning in the Age of Humans* at Temple University, 2017.

Melinda Buckwalter is the author of *Composing While Dancing: An Improviser's Companion* (University of Wisconsin Press) and coeditor (since 2005) of the dance and improvisation journal *Contact Quarterly*. At Earthdance, an artist-run dance workshop and retreat centre, she co-curated the SEEDS Festival of Arts and Ecology (Somatic

Experiments in Earth, Dance + Science). She studied somatics and improvisation with Anatomical Release Technique pioneer Nancy Topf and received her MFA in dance from Bennington College. Currently, she is a Fulbright postgraduate scholar in dance anthropology at Roehampton University in London. Her website is www.melindabuckwalter.com.

Jane Carr trained and worked as a ballet dancer before studying at Laban Centre for Movement and Dance and later at Roehampton University. A founder member of quiet, a collaborative artists' group, Jane also worked for over fifteen years at Morley College, southeast London, to provide opportunities for adults and young people to participate in dance. More recently Jane was Head of Studies at Central School of Ballet and lectured at the Laban Centre and the University of Lincoln before moving to the University of Bedford, where she is Principal Lecturer in Dance.

Kerry Chappell (PhD) is a Senior Lecturer at the University of Exeter, UK, where she is MA Education: Creative Arts Pathway Leader and Secondary Dance PGCE Deputy Programme Leader. As part of coleading the Centre for Creativity, Sustainability and Educational Futures, her research focuses on creativity in education, specifically in the arts (prioritizing dance), and on how creativity contributes to educational futures debates, for example in digital environments and science education (e.g., she is Principal Investigator for the EU-funded H2020 CREATIONs project). Kerry is also interested in the development of methodologies for participatory research. She is a Trustee of the regional organization Dance in Devon. Her work is informed by her current practice as a dance artist with Devon-based Dancelab Collective, her past work as an education manager, and her ongoing experience of being a mum to her two children.

Ann Cooper Albright is Professor and Chair of Dance at Oberlin College and former President of the Society of Dance History Scholars. Combining her interests in movement and cultural theory, she is involved in teaching a variety of courses and workshops that seek to engage participants in both practices and theories of the body. She is the author of *How to Land: Finding Ground in an Unstable World* (2019); *Engaging Bodies: The Politics and Poetics of Corporeality* (2013), which won the Selma Jeanne Cohen Prize from the American Society for Aesthetics; *Modern Gestures: Abraham Walkowitz Draws Isadora Duncan Dancing* (2010); *Traces of Light: Absence and Presence in the Work of Loie Fuller* (2007); and *Choreographing Difference: The Body and Identity in Contemporary Dance* (1997). The book *Encounters with Contact Improvisation* (2010) is the product of one of her adventures in writing and dancing and dancing and writing with others.

Kent De Spain is a US-based movement/multimedia artist who has taught workshops and intensives in the United States, Europe, Asia, and Latin America. He has performed internationally and toured to such venues as Judson Memorial Church, Jacob's Pillow, and the Painted Bride. He is particularly recognized for his research and writing on movement improvisation, including his essay in the book *Taken by Surprise* (edited by Ann Cooper Albright and David Gere); his feature-length documentary film *A Moving Presence: Ruth Zaporah and Action Theater*; his book *Landscape of the*

Now: A Topography of Movement Improvisation; and essays in *Contact Quarterly* and *Choreographic Practices*.

Thomas F. DeFrantz is Director of SLIPPAGE: Performance, Culture, Technology. He has authored many books, including *Dancing Many Drums: Excavations in African American Dance* (2002), *Dancing Revelations Alvin Ailey's Embodiment of African American Culture* (2004), *Black Performance Theory*, coedited with Anita Gonzalez (2014), and *Choreography and Corporeality: Relay in Motion*, coedited with Philipa Rothfield (2016). His creative work has included *Queer Theory! An Academic Travesty*, commissioned by the Theater Offensive of Boston and the Flynn Center for the Arts; *fastDANCEpast*, created for the Detroit Institute for the Arts; and *reVERSE-gesture-reVIEW*, commissioned by the Nasher Museum in response to the work of Kara Walker, January 2017. He has served as Convenor for the conferences Black Performance Theory and Collegium for African Diaspora Dance. He has curated afroFUTUREqu##r, with niv ACOSTA at Jack, October 2015, and National Black Arts Festival Dance Focus, 2015. He has taught at the American Dance Festival, ImPulsTanz, and the New Waves Dance Institute, as well as the Massachusetts Institute of Technology, Stanford University, Yale University, New York University, Hampshire College, and the University of Nice.

Evan D. Dorn received his PhD in computation and neural systems from the California Institute of Technology in 2005, performing original research in astrobiology, artificial life, and the mathematics of chemical evolution. His work has been published in *Icarus, Journal of Molecular Evolution, and Astrobiology*. He was the founder and, for twenty years, the CEO of the software development company Logical Reality Design, Inc., and is interested in applying his background in perception and neuroscience to other fields.

Sally Doughty has choreographed, taught, and performed since the early 1990s in the United States, Latvia, Mexico, Berlin, Brussels, Paris, Estonia, and the United Kingdom. She is published variously and has developed an international reputation as a facilitator and performer of improvisational practices, representing the United Kingdom in an on-line conversation with improvisers from Australia and India. Sally is produced by Dance4 (UK) and is funded by Arts Council England to make improvised dance performances for middle-scale venues; she hosted the symposium Dance Improvisation: The Estranged Cousin (2016), which explored the status of and challenges involved in making impro-vised dance for larger venues. She is Co-researcher in the project The Identity of Hybrid Dance Artist-Academics Working across Academia and the Professional Arts Sector and in the project Body of Knowledge, which promotes the dancer's body as a living archive. Sally is Associate Professor Dance, Reader in Dance and Improvisation, and Head of Dance at De Montfort University, Leicester, UK.

Lisa Dowler (MA, SME) is an in independent dance artist, researcher, and Somatic Movement Educator. She has twenty years' experience in facilitating dance, movement, and performance in diverse contexts, including community, professional, and higher education and is the Artistic Director of Small Things Dance Collective. In 2006 she was invited to be the first Dance Artist in Residence at Alder Hey Children's Hospital,

Liverpool, one of the largest children's hospitals in Europe. The success of this work has led to a long-term relationship with Alder Hey in both practice development and research. Her practice is underpinned by her studies in the experiential anatomy of Body-Mind Centering* and relational movement practices, including contact improvisation and capoeira. Lisa is fascinated by the developmental process, and her experience and discovery about movement, creativity, and perception is greatly enhanced by witnessing this fluid process through her two daughters.

Colleen Dunagan, PhD, is Professor of Dance at California State University, Long Beach. Her research has been published in *Dance Research Journal, The Oxford Handbook of Dance and Theatre* (2015), and the *International Journal of Arts in Society*. With Roxane Fenton, she has contributed chapters to *The Oxford Handbook of Dance and the Popular Screen* (2014) and *Movies, Moves and Music* (2016). Her current book manuscript examines intersections of dance, affect, and identity in television advertising. Dunagan has studied contact improvisation with artists such as KJ Holmes and Carolyn Stuart.

Alison (Ali) East (MPHED) is a New Zealand dance artist and educator at the University of Otago, New Zealand, teaching choreography, contemporary dance history, somatics, and community dance. In 1980, with poet and musician Denys Trussell, she founded Origins Dance Theatre and has made more than twenty-five interdisciplinary ecopolitical dance works. Ali is Coordinator of Dancespeak Dunedin and of the annual Shared Agendas Improvised Performance Events—celebrating their twentieth year. In 1989–1996 she founded and directed New Zealand's first choreographic programme, now Bachelor of Performing and Screen Arts (Unitec, Auckland), training many of New Zealand's dance artists. A regular conference presenter, she has published several journal articles and book chapters, including her book *Teaching Dance As If the World Matters: A Design for Teaching Dance-Making in the 21st Century* (2011). Her research interests include intuitive dance processes and teaching; dance and transdisciplinarity; translocational (situated) teaching and learning; and dance, place, and identity.

Hilary Elliott was born in Adelaide, Australia, and grew up in Canberra, where she studied ballet and contemporary dance, worked with the Canberra Dance Theatre, and earned a BA (Hons) in English and drama from the Australian National University. She was the recipient of Australia's prestigious Pilkington/Leeds University/Commonwealth Office Scholarship in 1992 and went on to achieve a master's in theatre studies, with distinction, at the University of Leeds. In 2013 she achieved her practice-led doctorate, which investigated the role of vision in understanding solo performance improvisation. She has directed, choreographed, and performed in dozens of productions in small-scale touring and educational contexts in England and Australia. Whilst living in Melbourne, she encountered improvisation as a performance form and went on to study with Al Wunder, Peter Trotman, and Andrew Morrish. She has performed regularly in Australia and overseas in solo, duet, and ensemble formats and has written and presented on improvisatory practices in a range of international contexts. She is currently writing a book on Al Wunder.

Roxane L. Fenton received her PhD from the University of California, Riverside. She has coauthored articles discussing the films Dirty Dancing (1987) and Across the Universe (2007) with Colleen Dunagan. She has taught dance history and appreciation at several colleges and universities in the United States. She has studied improvisation with Susan Rose, Susan Foster, and Wendy Rodgers and contact improvisation with Caroline Waters and has taught dance improvisation at California State University, Long Beach. She has performed improvisationally in Los Angeles and Riverside, California.

April Flakne is Associate Professor of Philosophy at the New College of Florida. Her work centres on phenomenology, with special attention to ethics, politics, and dance theory. Her articles have appeared in journals such as *Hypatia, New German Critique*, and *Philosophy Today*, and she is completing a monograph on intercorporeity and ethical life.

Sondra Fraleigh is Professor Emeritus at the State University of New York (SUNY), Brockport, a Fulbright Scholar, and an award-winning author of eight books, including *Moving Consciously: Somatic Transformations through Dance, Yoga, and Touch* (2015), *BUTOH: Metamorphic Dance and Global Alchemy* (2010), *Land to Water Yoga* (2008), *Hijikata Tatsumi and Ohno Kazuo* (2006), *Dancing Identity: Metaphysics in Motion* (2004), *Dancing into Darkness: Butoh, Zen, and Japan* (1999), *Researching Dance: Evolving Modes of Inquiry* (1998), and *Dance and the Lived Body* (1987). She has published numerous chapters on culture, ecology, and cognitive psychology. Fraleigh was Chair of the Department of Dance at SUNY Brockport and later Head of Graduate Dance Studies and was selected as a university-wide Faculty Exchange Scholar. She received the Outstanding Service to Dance Award from the Congress on Research in Dance in 2003. Her choreography has been shown internationally. She has held teaching fellowships at Ochanomizu University in Tokyo and the University of Baroda in India. She is the founder of Eastwest Somatics Institute.

Doran George, PhD, who tragically died in November 2017, was a cultural historian writing on sexual culture, avant-garde dance, and performance art. As a performance artist and choreographer their work deconstructs sociopolitical identity categories, stages work that builds microcommunities, and cultivates radical practices of intimacy. George's artwork and scholarship is represented in art books, Oxford University Press anthologies, and journals. George also was an LGBT activist and mentor of artists through organizations such as the California's Choreographers in Mentorship Exchange program and London's Wellcome Trust.

Ivar Hagendoorn is a freelance choreographer, photographer, and researcher. His research applies insights from philosophy, cognitive neuroscience, psychology, mathematics, and sociology to the study of art in general and dance and choreography in particular. In 2004 he created an evening-long production for the Ballett Frankfurt. He holds an MSc in econometrics and an MA in philosophy (both from Erasmus University, Rotterdam), an MA in Latin American literature from University College, London, and a PhD in cognitive neuroscience from Tilburg University. His website is www.ivarhagendoorn.com.

Stephanie Hanna is a visual artist and performer. She is researching the range of possible meanings and interpretations of objects and images through shifting their constellations. Stephanie's artistic works and interventions most often take place in public space, in surprising, unannounced, and unframed ways. These works include curating a big and previously unused window space in the back wall of a department store in the heart of Berlin-Neukölln with nonchalant artistic installations and performances that are accessible for a diverse public of passers-by. She has realized works in collaboration with art institutions, such as Haus der Kulturen der Welt in Berlin, Akademie Remscheid, and Autostadt Wolfsburg, and with established art festivals and art spaces across Berlin and Europe.

Victoria Hunter is a practitioner-researcher in dance and Reader in Dance at the University of Chichester, UK. Her practice-based research explores site-specific dance performance and the body-self's relationship with space and place, encountered through corporeal, material, spatial, and kinetic engagement with lived environments. Her writing on site-dance has been published in *New Theatre Quarterly, Performance Research, Literary Geographies,* and *Contemporary Theatre Review.* She edited *Moving Sites: Investigating Site-Specific Dance Performance* (Routledge, 2015). She is a coauthor of *(Re)Positioning Site-Dance* (Intellect, forthcoming 2019) with Melanie Kloetzel (Canada) and Karen Barbour (New Zealand).

Dimitris Karalis studied music at the Ateneum Conservatory (flute class of Stella Gadedi) and Nakas Conservatory. He holds a BA in history and archaeology from the National and Kapodistrian University of Athens and an MA in advanced theatre practice from the Royal Central School of Speech and Drama. As a theatre and sound director, he has worked with many international artists, including with Lee Breuer to produce Aeschylus's *Libation Bearers* (commissioned by Patras Cultural Capital of Europe 2006). He has worked as music director and composer for Theatre enCorps's new circus project *We Implicated and Complicated,* choreographed by Ana Sanchez-Colberg and developed with the Circus Department of the University of the Arts, Stockholm (2007).

Michael Kimmel is a full-time researcher at the University of Vienna, where he earned his PhD in 2002. Trained in cognitive linguistics and cognitive anthropology, he has published extensively on metaphor, imagery, sociocultural embodiment, and gesture. Over the past ten years he has turned to interaction research, taking interest in the prerequisites of successful joint improvisation and creativity in fields as diverse as aikido, tango argentino, contact improvisation dance, shiatsu, and the Feldenkrais Method. He has developed methods that have helped experts explicate their perception, action, and decision-making skills, aided by think-alouds, video feedback, and an on-site experimental dialogue between researchers and experts. This work is situated with the '4E' (enactive, embodied, extended, and embedded) cognition paradigm; it focuses on the ways in which experts coordinate, build synergies, adapt, invite novelty, and cope with complexity and on the comparison of skill systems. Kimmel also explores convergences between first-person data and biomechanics.

Larry Lavender is Professor of Interdisciplinary Arts at the School of Visual and Performing Arts, and Faculty Fellow in the Lloyd International Honors College, at the University of North Carolina, Greensboro. His areas of research and teaching are choreography, dance criticism, creativity theories and practices, and critical animal studies in the arts. He has presented artistic and scholarly works throughout the United States and in many parts of the world.

Amy LaViers is Assistant Professor in Systems and Information Engineering at the University of Virginia. She studies movement and dance through the lens of robotics and control theory. In particular, she has developed a quantitative definition of 'style' for movement and a way of interpreting this notion of style for robotic implementation. Her framework identifies specific parameters that, when varied, change the high-level style of the movement produced by the framework. She completed her PhD at Georgia Institute of Technology in 2013, and her research first began with a senior thesis at Princeton University, where she earned a certificate in dance and a bachelor's degree in mechanical and aerospace engineering. She is also a dancer and choreographer and creates work in this vein synergistically with her research, for example a contemporary dance show, *Automaton*, which was presented in Atlanta as part of her dissertation, and a movement score, *A Dance Score for the Downtown Mall*, which was used for a performance in Charlottesville, Virginia.

Irven Lewis's initial experience of dancing was through his local community in Leeds, where he experimented with improvisational street jazz styles. He later auditioned for the Urdang Academy in London, winning a three-year scholarship. At college, while further developing his reputation as a jazz dancer, he was awarded the Choreographic Cup by David Bintley. Irven was a founder member of the company Brothers in Jazz, which combined jazz with ballet, contemporary, and a range of other dance forms. After touring extensively with Brothers in Jazz, his formation of Irven Lewis Dance Theatre led to further choreographic exploration, for which he received a Dance UK/ADAD Trailblazer Fellowship in 2004–2005. In addition to his work as a dancer and choreographer, Irven is also a dance photographer.

Josephine Machon is Associate Professor in Contemporary Performance at Middlesex University, London. She is the author of *The Punchdrunk Encyclopaedia* (2018), *Immersive Theatres: Intimacy and Immediacy in Contemporary Performance* (2013) and *(Syn)aesthetics: Redefining Visceral Performance* (2009, 2011) and has published widely on experiential and immersive performance. Josephine is Joint Editor of the Palgrave Macmillan Series in Performance and Technology. Her broad research interests address the audience in immersive theatres and the creative intersections of theory and practice in experiential performance.

Louise McDowall is a dance artist and academic whose interest concerns transdisciplinary ways of working that open avenues of knowledge that advocate and critically engage with dance and body-based practices. In 2014, she completed her PhD dissertation, *Experiencing Dance Improvisation as a 'Conversational Dynamic,* at the University of Leeds, and she continues to explore the inclusion of hybrid writing practices and 'languaging' in dance pedagogical training. Louise's current research explores the impact of movement and physical activity interventions on the health and well-being of young and elderly people from deprived communities, and within palliative care settings, through ethnographic and qualitative approaches. She also has a strong inclusive community dance practice honed over twelve years of working in educational, outreach, and community settings. She specializes in dance work with children, adults with learning/physical disabilities, and elderly people (including people living with dementia/care home residents) and in the development of cultural exchanges through performance projects between Alderney and France.

Vida L. Midgelow, dance artist and academic, is Professor of Choreographic Practice at Middlesex University, London. She has over twenty years' experience facilitating and lecturing on performance. Her movement and video work has been shown internationally, and she publishes her research in professional, online, and academic journals. As a movement artist, her work focuses on somatic approaches to dance training; improvisation; and articulating choreographic processes. Recent works include *Scratch, Home (a replacing); Skript; ScreenBody* and *Voice (a retracing).* Some relevant essays include 'Nomadism and Ethics in/as Improvised Movement Practices' (*Critical Studies in Improvisation,* 2012), 'Sensualities: Dancing/Writing/Experiencing' (*New Writing: The International Journal for the Practice and Theory of Creative Writing,* 2013), and 'Improvisation as Paradigm for Phenomenologies' in the edited collection *Back to the Dance Itself*(University of Illinois, 2018) She also enjoys mentoring and undertakes dramaturgical, curatorial, and consultancy roles for artists and organizations. These facilitative activities combine with her own research within the framework of the Choreographic Lab, of which she is Codirector (with Jane Bacon). Extending these interests, Midgelow and Bacon also coedit the hybrid peer-reviewed journal *Choreographic Practices,* published with *Intellect.* The summer 2014 issue of this journal includes a coauthored essay (with Bacon) that outlines the authors' Creative Articulations Process, which is designed to support artistic practices and (self)-reflexivity.

Clare Parfitt is Reader in Popular Dance at the University of Chichester, UK. Her research focuses on the cultural histories of popular dance practices, particularly the cancan. She is Chair of PoP Moves UK, an international network to develop research into popular performance. From 2014 to 2016 Clare was an AHRC Leadership Fellow directing the project Dancing with Memory, which explored the relationships between popular dance and cultural memory via the case study of the cancan. Clare has coauthored *Planning Your PhD* (Palgrave, 2010) and *Completing Your PhD* (Palgrave, 2011) and has published in *The Oxford Handbook of Dance and the Popular Screen* (2014) and *Bodies of Sound: Studies across Popular Music and Dance* (Ashgate, 2013).

Gary Peters was until recently Professor of Philosophy and Performance at the School of Performance and Media Production at York St John University. His main area of research is continental philosophy and aesthetics with particular reference to improvisation and performance. His is the author of *Irony and Singularity: Aesthetic Education from Kant to Levinas* (Routledge 2005), *The Philosophy of Improvisation* (University of Chicago Press, 2009), and *Improvising Improvisation: From Out Of Music, Dance and Literature* (University of Chicago Press, 2017). Other recent publications include 'Improvisation and Time Consciousness', in *The Oxford Handbook of Critical Improvisation Studies* (2016), and 'Certainty, Contingency and Improvisation', in *Journal of Critical Improvisation Studies* (2013). He is a multiinstrumentalist, improviser, and composer working across a broad range of genres.

Susanne Ravn is Associate Professor and Head of the research unit Body, Culture and Society at the Department of Sport Science and Biomechanics, University of Southern Denmark. In her research, she critically explores the embodied insights of different movement practices—especially dance practices—and actively deals with the interdisciplinary challenges of employing phenomenological thinking in the analysis of these practices. She is the author of several books in Danish and English and has published her research in journals related to phenomenology; qualitative research methods in sports, exercise, and health; dance research; and sociological analysis of embodied experiences. She has published in journals related to phenomenology, dance, sports, and sociology. She has been President of the Nordic Forum for Dance Research and since 2014 a member of the executive board of the Society of Dance History Scholars.

Allison Robbins is Assistant Professor of Music at the University of Central Missouri, where she teaches courses in musicology and ethnomusicology. Her articles on music and dance in Hollywood musicals appear in *Journal of the Society for American Music* and *Studies in Musical Theatre*. Her current book project focuses on the mediatization of Broadway song and dance in the Hollywood studios.

Janice Ross is Professor in the Theatre and Performance Studies Department and Faculty Director of ITALIC, a residential arts immersion program, at Stanford University. Her research interests focus on the role of dance in shaping and mediating social change globally, historically, and in the contemporary moment. She is the author of four books, including *Like A Bomb Going Off: Leonid Yakobson and Ballet as Resistance in Soviet Russia* (Yale University Press, 2015), which was named one of the ten best dance books of 2015. Her previous books include *San Francisco Ballet at 75* (Chronicle Books, 2007), *Anna Halprin: Experience as Dance* (University of California Press, 2007), and *Moving Lessons: Margaret H'Doubler and the Beginning of Dance in American Education* (University of Wisconsin Press, 2001). Her essays on dance studies have been published in numerous anthologies. She is the winner of the Award for Outstanding Scholarly Research in Dance (Congress on Research in Dance, 2015). Her awards also include a Guggenheim Fellowship, a Fulbright Scholar Fellowship to Israel, and two Stanford Humanities Center Fellowships.

Philipa Rothfield (PhD) is Adjunct Professor in Philosophy of the Body and Dance at the University of Southern Denmark and honorary Senior Lecturer in Philosophy and Politics at La Trobe University, Melbourne, Australia. She writes on philosophy of the body in relation to dance through the work of Merleau-Ponty, Nietzsche, Klossowski, Ravaisson, and Deleuze. She is co-author of *Practising with Deleuze, Design, Dance, Art, Writing, Philosophy* (Edinburgh University Press, 2017). She has recently published chapters on dance and philosophy in *The Routledge Dance Studies Reader,* 2nd ed. (Routledge), *Somatechnics* (Ashgate), *Performance and Phenomenology* (Routledge), *and Art and Ethics* (Springer). Alongside these commitments, she has engaged in an ongoing but intermittent performance project with Russell Dumas (Director of Dance Exchange, Australia). Her recent forays into dance improvisation have been facilitated and guided by Alice Cummins. She is Coconvenor, with Aoife McGrath and Prarthana Purkayastha, of the Choreography and Corporeality working group of the International Federation of Theatre Research. She is a dance reviewer for *RealTime Magazine*, an Australian arts magazine and *Momm Magazine* (Korea), Head of the editorial board of *Dancehouse Diary*, and Creative Advisor for Dancehouse, Melbourne.

Ana Sánchez-Colberg , BA (Hons), MFA, PhD, is a choreographer, dancer, and scholar with an extensive track record of dance production and academic publications. She is Director of the award-winning dance theatre company Theatre enCorps, with which she has toured internationally since its establishment in 1989. She has served as Coordinator of the MA European Dance Theatre Practice at Trinity/ Laban (2002–2005), Course Leader of the MA Performance Practices and Research degrees and the PhD and Research degrees at Royal Central School of Speech and Drama (2005–2009) and (Visiting) Professor of Choreography and Composition at University Dance and Circus Stockholm (2007–2013).

Malaika Sarco-Thomas (PhD) is a dance artist researching the potential of improvisation technologies to facilitate skills in environmental perception. She lectures in Dance in the Department of Performing Arts at the University of Chester (UK). Previously she was Head of Department of Dance Studies at the University of Malta, and coordinated courses in Dance Performance and Choreography at Falmouth University, formerly Dartington College of Arts (UK). With Richard Sarco-Thomas, she has co-organised Contact Festival Dartington, an international gathering and platform for exchange in practices of contact and improvisation, with several associated conferences. Publications include 'On Contact [and] Improvisation', a special issue of the *Journal of Dance and Somatic Practices* (2014), with Misri Dey; *Performance and Interdisciplinarity: Contemporary Perspectives*, with Stefan Aquilina (2018) and *Thinking Touch: Artistic, Scientific and Philosophical Perspectives on Partnering and Contact Improvisation* (forthcoming). Malaika curates *touch + talk*, a series of contact improvisation performance dialogues, which have been presented at numerous European festivals (2011–2018).

Barbara Sellers-Young is Senior Scholar and Professor Emerita at York University, where she has served as Dean of the School of Arts, Media, Performance and Design and Professor in the Department of Dance. She has been Professor in and former Chair of the Department of Theatre and Dance at the University of California, Davis. She has also taught at universities in England, China, and Australia. Recent publications include *Belly Dance, Pilgrimage and Identity* and a volume edited with Anthony Shay, *The Oxford Handbook of Dance and Ethnicity*.

Anthony Shay is Associate Professor of Dance and Cultural Studies at Pomona College in Claremont, California. He received his PhD in dance history and theory from the University of California, Riverside, an MA in anthropology from California State University, Los Angeles, and an MA in folklore and mythology and an MLS from the University of California, Los Angles. He is the author of six monographs and editor or coeditor of four others—most recently *The Oxford Handbook of Dance and Ethnicity*, edited with Barbara Sellers-Young—and two monographs, *The Dangerous Lives of Public Performers: Dance, Sex, and Entertainment in the Middle East* (Palgrave Macmillan, 2014) and *Ethno Identity Dance for Sex Fun and Profit* (Palgrave Macmillan, 2016). His book *Choreographic Politics: State Folk Dance Companies, Representation and Power* (Wesleyan University Press, 2002) was chosen as the Outstanding Publication in Dance of 2002 by the Congress on Research in Dance. As a choreographer and dancer, he founded UCLA Village Dancers, whose name he changed in 1963 to AMAN Folk Ensemble. In 1977, he founded the AVAZ International Dance Theatre, which was closed in 2007. He created over two hundred choreographies for these companies, as well as several others.

Stephanie Skura, 'major American experimentalist' and Bessie Award–winner, is a choreographer, director, performer, teacher, teacher-trainer, and writer. She has performed and taught movement and performance for three decades in sixteen countries. She researches boundaries and intersections of dance, poetry, and performance, with a deep respect for individual diversity and subconscious realms. Her current work integrates a radically visceral approach to language and voice. In 2008, she instigated Open Source Forms, a practice and teacher certification program that addresses deep commonalities and cross-fertilizations of Skinner Releasing Technique and creative process. A BFA and MFA graduate of The New York University Tisch School of the Arts, and a former New Yorker directing a touring dance company, she now lives near Seattle and travels frequently. Her website is www.stephanieskura@com.

Nigel Stewart is a dance artist and scholar. He is Senior Lecturer at the Institute for Contemporary Arts at Lancaster University and Artistic Director of Sap Dance and has been Principal Investigator at the Arts and Humanities Research Council-funded project *Re-enchantment and Reclamation: New Perceptions of Morecambe Bay through Dance, Film and Sound* (2006–2008). He has published many essays on contemporary dance, dance phenomenology, and environmental dance and is coeditor of *Performing Nature: Explorations in Ecology and the Arts* (Peter Lang, 2005). He has danced as a solo artist and for various UK and European choreographers, including Thomas Lehmen, and was a member of the improvisation collective Grace & Danger. Apart from his choreography for Sap Dance, he has worked as a choreographer and director for Artevents, Louise Ann Wilson Company, National Theatre Wales, Theatre Nova, Theatreworks Ltd., Triangle, and many other UK companies, as well as Odin Teatret in Denmark.

Lizzie Swinford is a dance practitioner based in Exeter, UK, with background as a dance artist and teacher working with children and adults in further and higher education. She trained at the London Contemporary Dance School. In the last few years she has begun to focus on dance with early years children. Her playful, interactive, and interdisciplinary approach has developed through her work with the Devon Carousel Project, involved her in action research, and guided her MA studies at the University of Exeter, St Lukes. Lizzie loves to use stories in her practice. This has grown through her work in libraries in her independent project Flim Flam, *ExploraTale* in collaboration with the visual artist Tamsin Pender for The Carousel Project, and her collaboration with Pip Jones in their dance work *Paper Capers*. This webpage has more about Lizzie's activities: https://www.facebook.com/flimflam1234/.

Robert Vesty is an artist-scholar based in London. He is Senior Lecturer in Theatre Arts at Middlesex University, London, a doctoral candidate (Royal Holloway, University of London), and a performer who draws on a training in acting and a practice in dance. His performance uses improvisation as a tool to make instant compositions, and his research is looking at improvised speech in dance- or movement-based performance practices. He is a practitioner of the Feldenkrais Method. He is a founder member of TransDisciplinary Improvisation Network, a research cluster based at Middlesex University. His performance work includes *A Piece for Two (Lovers),* with Antonio de la Fe (London, 2015); *Sand and Vision,* directed by Julyen Hamilton (Brussels, 2016); and ongoing collaboration with a group of dance-artists working as *anthologyofamess.*

Nalina Wait is Lecturer at Australian College of Physical Education and current PhD candidate at the University of New South Wales (UNSW), researching the nexus of improvised performance practice and somatic intelligence. She coauthored a chapter with Erin Brannigan, '(Non) competitive Body States: Corporeal Freedom and Innovation in Contemporary Dance' (Oxford University Press, 2018). She has presented her research at the following symposia: Dance as Experience (at Centre de recherché sur les arts et le language, at Ecole des hautes études en sciences sociales, Paris, 2015); (at Sydney University, 2015); Improvisational Practices Symposium (at Critical Path, Sydney 2014); and Cultures of Change (at UNSW, Sydney 2013). She worked as a professional performer for twenty-five years in award-winning works by Sue Healey, as well as with Hans Van Den Broeck, Danceworks, Nikki Haywood, Devastation Menu, Sydney Performance Group, Rosalind Crisp, Marina Abramović, and Joan Jonas and in many improvisational settings.

Christopher J. Wells is Assistant Professor of Musicology at Arizona State University's Herberger Institute School of Music and Managing Editor of the *Journal of Jazz Studies.*

A social jazz dancer for over a decade, Wells is currently writing a book about the history of jazz music's ever-shifting relationship with popular dance and has a chapter in the *Oxford Handbook of Dance and Ethnicity* (2016).

Sarah Whatley is Director of the Centre for Dance Research at Coventry University, UK. Her research interests extend to dance and new technologies, intangible cultural heritage, somatic dance practice and pedagogy, dance documentation, and inclusive dance practice; she has published widely on these themes. Her current research projects, funded by the Arts and Humanities Research Council, the European Commission, the Leverhulme Trust, and the Wellcome Trust, focus on the creative reuse of digital cultural content, smart learning environments for dancers, reimagining dance archives and dance documentation, the generative potential of error in dance and Human-Computer Interaction, dance and disability, and dancer imagery. She is also Founding Editor of the *Journal of Dance and Somatic Practices* and sits on the editorial boards of several other Journals.

Libby Worth, Reader in Contemporary Performance in the Department of Drama, Theatre and Dance at Royal Holloway, University of London, is a movement practitioner who has trained in the Feldenkrais Method and in dance with Anna Halprin. She coedited the book *Ninette de Valois: Adventurous Traditionalist* with Richard Cave; has published on Mabel Todd, Caryl Churchill, and Jenny Kemp; and has coauthored books on Anna Halprin and on the work of Jasmin Vardimon (2017). She codevised the performance *Step Feather Stitch* (2012) with visual artist Julie Brixey-Williams (see *Choreographic Practices* 3 [2012]) and a new dance film duet, *Moving Between Folds* (2017). Current research includes interests in time/temporality in performer training, with a coedited book planned for 2018, and in 'folk' dance in border regions, and in the issues raised for training in relation to amateur practices. She is coeditor with Jonathan Pitches of the journal *Theatre, Dance and Performance Training*.

S. Ama Wray is Associate Professor of Dance at the University of California, Irvine; she received her PhD from the University of Surrey in 2016. Within the realm of contemporary dance, she was a dancer with flagship dance companies in the United Kingdom—London Contemporary Dance Theatre and Rambert Dance Company—and she continues to be the custodian of Jane Dudley's timeless solo *Harmonica Breakdown,* created in 1938. Alongside her scholarly purpose in developing her neo-African improvisation praxis, Embodiology, she continues her longstanding artistic practice as a choreographer and director, choosing the term 'neo-African performance architect' to describe her professional role. Her collaborators include Gary Grosby, Julian Joseph, Zoe Rahman, and Wynton Marsalis. Beyond dance, she directs and choreographs Mojisola Adebayo's work and cocreates Texterritory with Fleeta Siegel, a cellphone-based interactive performance platform that stimulates audience participation in performance.

I-Ying Wu is an improvisation practitioner and researcher. She received her PhD from the University of Northampton, UK, in 2014 and pursued her postdoctoral research at the Improvisation Studies Centre, based in the Faculty of Media, Art and Performance at the University of Regina, Canada, during 2016–2017. She developed an improvisational movement practice in her practice-led doctoral research, starting from a Daoist perspective of qi—a pathway towards formlessness and Dao understood through improvised movement. Informed by Chinese traditional qigong and Daoist philosophy, her improvisation practice focuses on subtle awareness of the very moment when an improvisational phenomenon emerges.

Norah Zuniga Shaw is an artist, creative director, and facilitator focusing on choreographic ideas as catalysts for interdisciplinary and intercultural discovery. She is best known for her award-winning collaborations with animator Maria Palazzi and choreographers William Forsythe, Thomas Hauert, and Bebe Miller integrating art and science research. The project Synchronous Objects flows from dance to data to objects to visualize counterpoint in a masterwork by Forsythe; Motion Bank visualizes the thinking body and dancing mind in performance improvisation. Shaw tours extensively and since 2004 has been based at Ohio State University, where she is Professor and Director for Dance and Technology at the Advanced Computing Center for the Arts and Design and the Department of Dance. Improvisation has been central to Shaw's dancing life since her upbringing in 1970s North American children's dance contexts and serves as the primary mode of investigation and expression in all of her teaching and research.

INTRODUCTION

Improvising Dance: A Way of Going about Things

VIDA L. MIDGELOW

THIS handbook encompasses dance practices across forms, styles, and contexts. It asks: What are the features and practices of improvisation in dance? How might we articulate and understand improvisation from differing perspectives? What is the significance of improvisation in aesthetic, social, and political terms? How might dance improvisation have an impact in and beyond performance contexts?

Discussing improvisatory activities in dance, this handbook attests to the presence of improvisation in many forms of dance and to the ways improvisation has been developed and employed for far-reaching purposes. The handbook recognizes that improvisation has been a long-standing and central approach within the choreographic process for many dance makers; while for others it is a performance form in its own right. It is also a key, although often implicit and overlooked, feature of most social dance forms and is widely used within therapeutic, educational, and other applied contexts. Accordingly, throughout the handbook examples of improvised dancing from tango to therapy and contact to ballet are discussed. This breadth has been important in gathering this collection, foregrounding improvisation in dance as it occurs in a wide range of contexts—be it in theatres, community halls, or hospitals. This very breadth also expands our vision, such that the nature and significance of the improvisatory can be better understood.

DISCOURSES IN IMPROVISATION

Addressing this wide agenda, this handbook comes at a significant moment in the development of improvisation as a critical practice and emergent discourse. This handbook is part of an increasing body of writing that positions improvisation as a critical area of study, reaching beyond the arts to wider inter/transdisciplinary concerns (see for example Hallam and Ingold 2007; Heble and Caines 2015; Lewis and Piekut 2016). It seems important in this context that the *Handbook* acknowledges this inter/ transdisciplinary discourse, while at the same time positioning the improvisatory insights of dance at the centre, for, despite what might be assumed if we only look only to Western theatre dance, most movement is improvised. Improvisation is a prevalent and implicit feature of most movement activity—taking place as part of everyday actions, in nightclubs, at weddings, on our streets, and in our homes. Indeed movement improvisation can be seen to be an important part of our everyday existence as humans, for 'there is no script for social and cultural life. People have to work it out as they go along', since, Elizabeth Hallam and Tim Ingold argue, life is fundamentally 'unscriptable' (2007: 1).

Yet, whilst ever present, improvisation in dance, in its many manifestations, has often been hidden in the shadows, often going unmarked in writings about dance practice. As Susan Foster noted, improvised events have been 'frequently omitted from the historical record or glossed over as insubstantial or indescribable' (2003a: 196). In the same year David Gere similarly noted a gap in the scholarship, pointing out that little consideration had been given to 'improvisation in social dance forms, from salsa to goth', and encouraged scholars to take up research in this territory (Albright and Gere 2003: xix).

Thankfully, some of these gaps have started to be filled, and there has been a marked increase in the number of publications about dance improvisation, such as the full-length studies by Melinda Buckwalter (2010), Daniel Goldman (2010), and Kent De Spain (2014). These sit alongside books by artists, such as *Caught Falling*, by David Koteen and Nancy Stark Smith (2008), *This Very Moment*, by Barbara Dilley (2015), and *Improvisation on the Edge*, by Ruth Zaporah (2014). Further, as noted, there has also been an increasing interdisciplinary discourse about improvisation as a critical area of study. Recent collections which incorporate chapters on dance include the *Improvisation Studies Reader* (with its excellent thematic introductions) (Heble and Caines 2015) and the extensive double volume *Oxford Handbook of Critical Improvisation Studies* (Lewis and Piekut 2016). Also pertinent here are the more explicitly philosophically oriented texts by writers such as Gary Peters (2009) and Edgar Landgraf (2014). These two authors focus on improvisation in discourse rather than in practice—while giving prominence to music and visual arts, respectively. They each emphasize how notions of aesthetic autonomy, subjectivity, and genius have informed contemporary understandings of improvisation, with Landgraf connecting improvisation to the beginnings of modern aesthetics and Peters developing a sophisticated meeting between continental philosophy and improvisatory concepts.

These practice-led, theoretical, and interdisciplinary collections enrich the preceding monographs in dance on American postmodern improvised practices by writers such as Sally Banes (1987, 1993), Cynthia Novack (1990), Susan Foster (2002), and, beyond the Western canon, investigations such as the study of solo improvised Iranian dance by Anthony Shay (1999) and the insightful discussions of an Africanist presence in improvised practices by Brenda Dixon Gottschild (1998). These monographs sit alongside the 2003 reader by David Gere and Ann Cooper Albright *Taken by Surprise*, interview-based collections such as the *On the Edge* (1997), and historically descriptive books such as Margaret Hupp Ramsey's on the Grand Union (1991). These accounts enrich the comparatively larger number of experiential guides for improvisers that include inspiring texts by Tufnell and Crickmay (1990, 2004), Pallent's *Introduction to Contact Improvisation* (2006), and Daniel Nagrin's *Dance and the Specific Image* (1994).

To turn first to some of the scholarly works; Cynthia Novack's 1990 book *Sharing the Dance* is an early example of ethnographically based writing about contact improvisation. It was one of the first texts to offer critically informed insights into this form, placing it in a historical and cultural context. This book, inspirational on many levels (and one I have used with my students for many years), offers an analysis of dance as culture, interrogating what she calls the 'responsive body' at an intersection with communality and equality. As such, the ideological and social nature of contact improvisation is revealed alongside its aesthetic and the physical properties. Here improvisation is conceived as a social action in which American individualism was both framed and challenged by the context of noncompetitive and collaborative activity, for she notes that improvisational dancers often 'share the dance for ethical reasons, because they believe they can model certain moral and social aspects of their lives on this noncompetitive, collaborative form of dancing' (1990: 191). Further, Novack writes: 'in addition to the dynamic of individual and collective action in improvisation, the concept of spontaneity is central, both aesthetically and ideologically. Improvisational dancers believe that they are making art while being spontaneous, a contrast to the worked-out, predetermined nature of traditional modern dance' (191). Novack goes on to explain that the ideological significance of spontaneity meant that the dancers understood improvisation to be more ' "real," "playful," and "natural," joining the making of art to everyday action' (191). Conceived in counterpoint to modern dance traditions of expressive individualism, contact improvisers placed an emphasis on the conjoining of 'natural' everyday behaviours with culture, such that the dance was artful and natural, structured and spontaneous.

American postmodern dance in this era emphasized the liberatory potential of improvising, exploring alternative ways to make dances that were social and emancipatory. As Foster writes in her excellent book on Richard Bull, 'improvisation functioned both to catalyze and to sustain democratic action' (2002: 62). These perceived democratic and emancipatory potentialities can still be felt as the foundation for improvisation practices today, albeit current artists are perhaps less ideologically driven and perhaps more cynically pragmatic.

Reflecting on the shifts in postmodern dance, Sally Banes uses the term 'abundance' to describe the context and quality of improvised dance in the 1960s and 1970s—where there was a feeling of time to play and explore. She sets this in contradistinction to the 1990s, when the dances, whilst explicitly exploring politics of identity, evidence a more frenetic sense of urgency. 'If dancers in the sixties saw open choreography as a way of expressing freedom and creating community, cultural critics [and dancers] in the eighties and nineties questioned the meaning of freedom and community' (Banes 2003: 81). For, Banes notes, in the latter period, 'spontaneity, resourceful-ness and attitudes toward time and bodies ... all had added layers of significance in a world of urban homelessness and violence' (83). Improvised dancing and touch was further complicated by the AIDS crisis—adding to the sense that improvised contact was both an implicit statement of resistance to a culture seized by the need to restrict and control the body and at the same time a symbol of danger and excess.

This essay by Banes appeared in the much-referenced collection *Taken by Surprise,* edited by Ann Cooper Albright and David Gere (2003). As an edited book, it emerged from a couple of conference gatherings and brings together a diverse set of writings arranged in terms of their relationship to postmodern dance (so we have sections titled 'Improvising Body, Improvising Mind', 'A Duet with Postmodern Dance', Expanding the Canon', 'Reconsidering Contact improvisation', and 'Improvisation in Everyday Life'). The collection includes writings that focus on or are written by artists such as Ruth Zaporah, Simone Forte, Anna Halprin, Steve Paxton, and Nancy Stark Smith. In addition, it incorporates a few reflections on popular dance, as well as less US-centric dance forms; for example, tap, by Constance Vais Hill, flamenco, by Michelle Heffner Hayes, and Bharatanatyam, by Avanthi Meduri. Through the collection, improvisation is variously described in terms of consciousness and physicality, historically and culturally specific situations, disability and daily life. As such, it both offers insights into significant artists/practices of the postmodern era and lays down a challenge to expand the canon, pointing to the lack of writings on improvisation beyond ones that refer to the largely white concert dance scene.

In many ways Danielle Goldman (2010) picks up these challenges, addressing the recurring myths of improvisatory freedom and the lack of cultural and ethnic diversity in writings on improvisation. Her work is grounded in an analysis of the Mambo as danced at the New York Palladium ballroom in the mid-1950s and the work of artists such as Judith Dunn, Bill Dixon, Dianne McIntyre, and Bill T. Jones. She reveals the deeply charged racial, social, and political contexts of each dance's/dancer's circumstance and considers improvisation beyond the discourses of freedom, replacing this instead with a more circumspect perspective in her elaboration of 'tight spaces'. This phrase arises from literature scholar Houston Baker, who writes of the African American experience and the struggle through slavery, incarceration, and social exclusion to find socially mobile space. 'Tight spaces', Baker suggests, are 'the always ambivalent cultural compromises of occupancy, differentially affected by contexts of situations' (cited in Goldman 2010: 7).

Several authors in this handbook pick up Goldman's critique of freedom. One such author is Clare Parfitt (chapter 14), writing on the cancan in the early 1800s. She usefully elaborates the 'practice of freedom' (after Foucault) within the 'tight spaces' of postrevolutionary France. In response to laws and restrictions, she argues, 'cancan dancers attempted to prise open improvisatory moments within the otherwise fixed choreography of the quadrille' (chapter 14 here). Tactically creating improvisation-within-structure, the dancers made their physical protest difficult to ignore by creating alternative definitions of liberty through their bodies.

These academically focused texts sit within the framework of the long-standing US-based magazine *Contact Quarterly Dance Journal* (https://contactquarterly.com), which—since 1978—has published artists' writings about contact improvisation and improvisation more broadly. *Contact Quarterly* has been key to shaping a shared understanding of improvisation in dance and enabling languages about improvisation to develop. Indeed Albright and Gere acknowledge the influence of this magazine in their own collection (2003: ix), as does Buckwalter in her book *Composing Whilst Dancing: An Improvisers Companion* (2010).

Buckwalter's book, like the pages of *Contact Quarterly*, is filled with inspirational insights. Organizing her book through core performative elements (time, space, music partnering, eyes, etc.), Buckwalter articulates the practices of a series of largely East Coast American dance artists. She explicitly references her experiences of dancing with each of the chosen artists and includes both 'field notes' and 'interludes' through which she shares her own embodied stories and notes. Similarly, in *Landscape of the Now*, Kent De Spain offers detailed insights into the practice of eight well-established artists: Anna Halprin, Barbara Dilley, Simone Fortie, Deborah Hay, Lisa Nelson, Steve Paxton, Nancy Stark Smith, and Ruth Zaporah. Forming this book through the corralling of extended interviews, De Spain elaborates common issues such as verbal/nonverbal awareness, intentionality, and the transpersonal in improvisation.

These accounts, replete as they are with intimate and embodied knowledge, provide some very useful source materials and are written through very direct methodologies. This might best be described as a practice-based approach to research, and many instances of this are evident in the contributions that make up this handbook. Indeed Buckwalter's chapter continues this approach, as does Ashley's narration of ecologically driven improvisation, as informed by her work as a contact improviser. Her practice-based approach brings insights not possible through other modalities, for by improvising, walking and moving in contact with her subjects, she develops connectivities and enables differences to be negotiated through the shared 'memories in muscles and minds of the contours and weather of the land, and of the conversations and journeys between us' (chapter 33 here).

Taking this approach a step further are contributions by Norah Zuniga Shaw and the collaborative chapter by Robert Bingham and Stephanie Hanna. Bingham and Hanna's contribution is both a reflection on dancing and a practice in and of itself. Through an email conversation, which falls in and out of sync, they discuss 'what remains' and a dance work by the same name. They recall memories and allow their associations to surface, enabling 'what remains' to resonate as a concept through which improvisation might be considered. Fragmented and partial, this poetic and playful offering is something akin to a duet that has been thrown off balance through the time/space disjunctures of the digital exchange and the written word (chapter 19). Norah Zuniga Shaw creates a fictional exchange with artists who have influenced (her own) improvisatory practices, using memories to form a playful narrative (chapter 18).

Understandings of improvisation have also been greatly enriched by the capacities of digitization, such as the resources developed by William Forsythe and his collaborators. His animated videos, which make up the basis of the innovative CD-ROM *Improvisation Technologies* (1996), offer detailed demonstrations of specific improvisation strategies, such as 'room writing' and 'imaging lines'. As Forsythe explains and demonstrates each strategy, the movement explorations are simultaneously made evident through the addition of white drawn lines to allow the viewer to graphically visualize the improvised actions. These lines make manifest the geometric and spatial concerns of each strategy. Furthering this approach, the websites *Synchronous Objects* (2009) and *Motion Bank* (2010–2013) make physical thinking evident in visual and digital forms (see Zuniga Shaw 2014). Investigating the use of dance scores and creative strategies, the visual documentation in *Motion Bank Two* (Palazzi et al. 2013) of Bebe Miller and Thomas Hauert is of particular interest here, as it articulates two improvisation practices. Documenting and analysing how these two artists work, they reveal the use of habit, tendency, impulse, and memory in the making of improvised dances.

These texts and online documents reveal multifaceted improvisatory approaches and richly complex discourses that are far from any stereotypical definition of improvisation as a make-do, anything-goes, or unprepared phenomenon. Similarly, this handbook includes an expanded notion of improvisation, seeking out the presence, practices, and significance of the improvisatory as it appears in many dance forms and contexts.

A Way of Going About Things

As a basis for understanding shared concerns across such diverse practices and contexts, I propose that improvisation might be broadly understood as a way of going about things, for it has no inherent content. If you will allow this perhaps at first sight slightly odd thought, what I mean by this is that unless we align improvisation with, say, contact improvisation or salsa, improvisation is a process that has no predetermined or inherent movement style or context. Dancer Lisa Nelson describes it this way: 'improvisational dance is an idea. It has no inherent substance, cannot put a picture in your head' (Nelson 2008: n.p.).

Taken in the abstract, and away from any particular dance form, improvisation is, especially in its intentional modes, not a 'style' but an approach, a practised process. A process that provides ways of working. As Hallam and Ingold observe, improvisation is 'the way we work' (2007: 1); crescented rather than created, they continue, improvisation 'is "always in the making" (Jackson 1996: 4) rather than ready made' (Hallam and Ingold 2007: 3). Waxing and waning, improvisation is always in the process of emerging into the world.

They continue: 'Because improvisation is generative, it is not conditional upon judgments of novelty or otherwise of the forms it yields. Because is it relational, it does not pit the individual against either nature or society. Because it is temporal, it inheres in the onward propulsion of life rather than being broken off, as a new present, from a past that is already over. And because it is the way we work, the creativity of our imaginative reflections is inseparable from our engagements with the materials that surround us' (3). It is these generative and relational features of improvisation as a creative force for new thinking which is to the fore in fields beyond the arts. In areas such as management studies (Vera and Crossan 2004; Kamoche et al. 2003), law (Ramshaw 2013), and education (Corbett and Vibert 2016), as well as in work in cognition, including scientific studies on brain activity during the improvisation of music (Donnay et al. 2014), improvisation has become a topic for study and debate. Whilst it is fair to say that many, if not most, of these studies draw upon music, particularly jazz (often used as a poor short-hand for improvisation per se) as a way to understand improvisation, this increased attention to improvisation in general might be seen as a counter to contemporary life, which is tainted by uncertainty and unrest. In offering other ways of going about things, the move towards improvisation is connected to similar shifts towards the embodied, situated, and performative in other fields. Here, themes of communication, creativity, adaptability, and innovation have come into focus around improvisation.

The resistant impulse in improvisation to mainstream society is not altogether new or specific to dance. Daniel Belgrad, in his book *The Culture of Spontaneity* (1998), argued that the art of spontaneity 'constituted a distinct third alternative, opposed to both the mass culture and established high culture of the postwar period' (1998: 1). Discussing American post-war artists, he wrote that they 'embraced spontaneity as a style ... [and] assumed a more actively confrontational stance toward the dominant ethnocentrism and continued to believe in the social role of art' (2). Artists, he observed, developed an alternative worldview, rooted in 'intersubjectivity and body-mind holism' (3).

This link between improvisation as an arts practice and improvisation as a part of living carries within an understanding that improvisation is central to human inter-action and social action. It is this dynamic potential of improvisation that drives of the music-focused International Institute for Critical Studies in Improvisation (http:// improvisationinstitute.ca), as directed by musician Ajay Heble, and its associated on-line journal *Critical Studies in Improvisation* (www.criticalimprov.com). This institute grew out of the Improvisation, Community and Social Practice project and has begun to richly document the power of improvisation as part of social change, and to articulate the ways improvisation has been instrumental in forming identities, histories, and communities (Fischlin et al. 2013; Siddal et al. 2016; Heble and Wallace 2013). Whilst acknowledging that improvisation is certainly not automatically inclusive or emancipatory, it can, Fischlin et al. note, teach 'us to make "a way" out of "no way" by cultivating that capacity to discern hidden elements of possibility, hope, and promise in even the most discouraging circumstances' (2013: xii).

These words in turn resonate with Ann Cooper Albright, who in her epilogue to *Taken by Surprise* elaborates ways in which improvisation might prepare us for traumatic situations, teaching 'us to be patient, to see a future in the hole' (2003: 258). Continuing this thinking, her contribution to this handbook suggests that rather than 'what *is* improvisation?'—we might ask 'what *if* improvisation?' (chapter 1). This 'what if' carries within it the implication that improvisation as a 'practice of dwelling in possibility can be ... both personally useful and politically profound'. This 'what if' question, which raises the significance of improvisation beyond the arts to our very ways of being in the world—to improvisation as a philosophy of life—is worthy of more attention.

To think this through, let's go back to my suggestion that improvisation is a way of going about things, as it has no content—for it might be that in this 'what is' question, we might also begin to see the ways in which 'what if' is activated in our lives. What might be seen to be the recurring and inherent features of all purposeful and consciously engaged improvisatory acts? What is it that people are doing when they are improvising? What does improvisation entail? What does improvisation as a way of going about things enable?

Such question reach beyond the specifics of any single form or dance artist's approach, for whilst each approach to improvised dance has its own histories, movement forms, organizational tendencies and conventions, and aesthetic priorities and purposes, improvisatory approaches, as a way of going about things, can be seen to share a nexus of concerns, whatever the 'thingness' of the practice may be. These improvisatory *ways of going about things* can be broadly said to coalesce under the following themes: *convergence, irreversibility, receptivity, memory, processuality*, and *emergent-construction*. In what follows, I reach towards connectivity, crossing between forms and practices in an undulating landscape so as to elaborate these themes.

Entailing the manifesting of actions in real time, improvisations are contexts in which process and its realization is one and the same generative act, wherein making and interpreting become simultaneous. As Sheets-Johnstone states, 'in dance improvisation, the process of creating is not the means of realizing *a* dance; it is *the* dance itself' (2009: 30, italics in original). Improvisation is then a place of *convergence*, in which the narrower the duration is between (and extent of) known, preplanned events and the realization of events, the greater the degree of improvisation is at work.

This convergence requires that planning and acting, thinking and doing (Sheets-Johnstone 2009: 30) are happening in the same moment, for decisions happen in action. Improviser Katie Duck has said: 'improvisation means choice' (Duck n.d.). Indeed, stressing the significance of decision-making, she extorts dancers to 'choose, choose, choose', often yelling these words across the space. Choosing 'what' is not always defined by Duck: it could be any element of performance; rather she emphasizes the importance of continually and purposefully choosing to be in the moment, choosing to be present and decisive in every movement, choosing to make your actions meaningful in the space and in relation to your fellow dancers.

In a dance performance context, of course, this choosing takes place in front of an audience, and this in-the-moment blurring of process and realization leads inevitably to the *irreversibility of improvisation*. There can be no regrets, no going over, retouching, reshaping, when improvising—it is all part of the mix! Embracing such irreversibility, when one is improvising, 'mistakes' become openings—for they cannot be crossed out. Being able to respond to openings, improvisers may work to see what happens when you amplify the 'mistakes'. Let them grow; see where that trip, fall, or awkward gesture takes you when extended, repeated, enlarged. It cannot be corrected after its end, as it were, from the outside.

It is this irreversibility that makes improvisation feel risky and brings the question of failure to the fore; so how might we consider failure in improvisation? Of course, to ask this question requires us to address the value systems at work in an improvisation—values embedded in the prevailing cultural and aesthetic norms and/or concerns. Accordingly, failure might be found in any number of shortcomings—including limited technical proficiency, lack of innovation, poor responsiveness, failure in style, or simply failure to avoid being boring.

Musician Ellen Waterman (2015) picks up the question of failure and risk in her writing on the theme of trust. Stressing the relational features of improvisation, she aligns risk and trust, for 'what seems like virtuosic risk-taking in improvisation is actually the skillful exercise of trust' (2015: 60). This balance of trust and risk is understood through social interaction and accountability. As such, Waterman suggests that failure in improvisation is found not so much in the performed outcomes, which may of course be more or less interesting or in accord or not with our aesthetic preferences, as in a lack of empathy—be it with others or with conventions. She writes: 'in the end, improvisers may not reach agreement but, arguably, even a "failed" improvisation in that sense may be redeemed by its mindfulness. Improvisation models the social relations that both structure and animate our wider lives: "good improvisation" is conducted in "good faith." However, if we fail to empathize with others in the process of improvising, then we close ourselves off to the possibility of transformation, and that constitutes a considerable loss' (2015: 61). Notions of mindfulness and empathy are also very present in somatically informed improvisatory forms. The 'rightness' of particular movement choices in this way of going about things is predicated less upon a predetermined organization of the body and more upon the ability to 'faithfully' attend to an internal awareness and the ways your presence, your movement choices, are shaped by and, in turn, shape those around you. Such mindful awareness is more broadly founded upon *receptivity*, wherein improvisations are enabled through being open and responsive to interior and exterior worlds—to the ideas, sounds, actions, and impressions both within and around us. Engaging receptively requires effort and needs to be purposefully pursued. Receptivity enables dancers to operate, for example, as an ensemble, to work closely with music or their environment—be that a downtown shopping district, a theatre, or a field—while noting and attending to their own moving. As such, receptivity encompasses the dancers' interior proprioception and extends out to exterior worlds, such that the improvisers work within the circumstances in which they find themselves.

Hilary Elliott (chapter 36) reflects on the ways that in her own practice (as informed by improviser Al Wunder) she generates movement material from her spatial environment. Grasping her external bodily situation and responding to its idiosyncrasies, she describes a process of 'reading space', 'wielding vision as a tool of awareness'. While Elliott emphasizes sight and site, Ali East (chapter 26) asks her students to connect to their ' "creaturely knowing" (Sheets-Johnstone, 2009) and somaesthetic sensing (Shusterman, 2008)'. East proposes that through somatic sensing, we might be 'encouraged to "dig down" beneath the intellect to a place so instinctual, so beneath any strategy or rationale that a move may happen as or before one becomes aware of it as an event'.

It is in such receptive states that the improviser is able to draw most fluently on her available embodied, material, and critical resources. It is here when those elusive moments of originality are possible. This requires a willingness to be open and vulnerable to, and perhaps assailable by, that which is present in order for the improviser to follow routes, take opportunities, and note emerging pathways; to catch that which becomes apparent and to spark or reframe the dance as it emerges.

Dancers have used different terms to describe this receptive state: lindy artist Norma Miller describes the link between dance and music as being in 'perfect attunement' (in Dixon Gottschild 2000, 73), while Novack, for example, describes contact improvisers as operating with a 'responsive' body (1990, 3) that needs to 'yield rather than resit' (8) while dancer Eva Karczag writes in poem form:

> Listening
> To myself,
> and to my surroundings,
> To the song that rises from this moment
> in which I am contained—
> These dances rise up inside me
> and spin out beneath me,
> And it's as if I stand back, inside myself
> and observe…
>
> (Karczag in Tufnell and Crickmay 1990: 48)

Here, listening as described by Karczag reflects a process by which the improviser draws upon her interior and exterior environment as a basis from which material emerges and is developed. Similarly, writing about music, George Lipsitz notes that a 'jazz musician has to listen carefully, to recognize not only what the music being played *is*, but also what it *could* be' (2015: 9, italics in original). This imaginative engagement in 'what could be', he writes, 'questions surface appearances' and cultivates the 'capacity to view things from all sides before making a judgment' (91–0).

Being receptive is not a sponge-like process wherein everything is absorbed without discrimination; rather, it is a process that enables new ways of considering and acting. The ability to listen, Lipsitz suggests, 'creates new understandings of previousness and futurity in order to explore hidden possibilities' (2015: 11). Being between the reference points of previousness and futurity, and thereby being available to possibilities, is similar to what Nancy Stark Smith describes as being 'in the gap'. She writes:

> Where you are when you don't know where you are is one of the most precious spots offered by improvisation. It is a place from which more directions are possible than anywhere else. I call this place the Gap. The more I improvise, the more I am convinced that it is through the medium of these gaps—this momentary suspension of reference point—that comes the unexpected and much sought after 'original' material.… Being in the gap is like being in a fall before you touch bottom. You're suspended—in time and space—and you don't really know how long it'll take to get 'back'.
>
> (Stark Smith 1987: 3)

The sensation of falling described here has clear and direct references to Stark Smith's practice as a contact improviser—as one body falls and flows with and into another, two mutually dependent bodies reach moments of support and suspension. Rolling off-balance, tipping, and veering, senses of direction are reframed. Upside down, the relationship to the vertical and horizontal is experienced anew, offering perhaps a 'pathway to curiosity—falling to fly' (Claid and Allsopp 2013: 3).

To continue the metaphor of falling to describe the 'gap', and to take it a little further—expanding the gap by not taking the first or even second impulse that comes (as Stark Smith [1987] through reference to Katie Duck proposes)—what might emerge? Through the metaphor and process of falling, we might just be able to re-frame our perspectives and question our preconceived politics of space (Albright 2013: 38). Perhaps, as Claid and Allsopp suggest, 'in the practice of falling we face fear, here-and-now uncertainty and a realisation that a sense of self emerges in re-lationship with the environment and that letting go (falling out) of a fixed identity taps into a potential for unknown possibilities' (2013: 1). Riffing off this notion of 'un-known possibilities' reminds me of Susan Foster's discussion of knows and unknowns in improvisation. What (un)knowns reside in the fall, in the widening the gap? Foster writes: 'the improvising dancer tacks back and forth between the *known* and the *un-known*, between the familiar and the unanticipated/unpredictable' (2003b: 3). She goes on to describe the known as the context and any predetermined structural choices, the individual's body and its movement, as established through training, as well as what-ever has occurred previously in the performance of improvising (4). The unknown, Foster writes, is 'that which we could not have thought of doing next', concluding that 'we could never accomplish this encounter with the unknown without engaging the known' (4).

It is clear, then, that improvisation doesn't happen in a vacuum but relationally to the known, with that which has gone before. Improvising entails entering into a relationship with previous practices and the dancer's body *memory*. So whilst it is self-evident that we don't engage in improvisation as if in a tabula rasa, the awareness of how we might be in an encounter with embodied memory, whilst valuing and promoting the occurrence of the novel, is a recurring question in practice.

Investigating the processes and languages used by improvisers, dancer-writer Kent De Spain (2003) proposes that memory in improvisation can be seen to operate in two modes: associational and kinaesthetic. He writes that associational memory re-fers to images, facts, qualities, situations, and places—those past experiences that are stored in memory and triggered by an act of dancing—sparking an associated memory. Kinaesthetic memory, De Spain writes, relates to the ability of the body to (re)produce patterns and habitual movement responses. Both these modalities speak to the signifi-cance of preknowledge in improvisation and lead to a consideration of the way in which the improvised both draws upon and shifts beyond that which is in memory—such that improvisers are always at once operating with/in (deeply embedded in) and with/out (brushing along the edges of) embodied memory.

In my own writing I have described the importance of embodied memory in im-provisation, suggesting that it enables 'us to move away from a model of improvisation that takes its ontological basis solely from spontaneity and innovation' (Midgelow 2015a: 120). For as musician and philosopher Gary Peters reminds us, an improvisatory gesture is 'not just a question of remembering "at the last moment" the possibilities made available by the "countless generations" of codes and rules, but rather, of making aesthetic judgements that, to recall Kant, bring into conjunction the individual act and its universal communicative force, subjective feeling, and common sense' (2009: 98). The relationship between improvisation and embodied preknowledge—those 'countless generations' of codes and rules' (Peters 2009: 98)—particularly as engrained in the form of dance techniques has received much attention across disciplines. Santi and Illetterati (2010), in the edited collection *Improvisation: Between Technique and Spontaneity,* write that 'if improvisation is transcendence of the rules, those very rules are the conditions that enable this transcendence to occur'. Improvisation 'grasps and transforms elements into actions that, without technique, would otherwise be lost' (2010: 3).

In a related fashion Hallam and Ingold note: 'fluent response [in improvisation] calls for a degree of precision in the co-ordination of perception and action that can only be achieved through practice. But it is this, rather than a knowledge of the rules, that distinguishes the skilled practitioner from the novice. And in this too, we find the essence of improvisation' (2007: 12). So whilst the significance of established codes and techniques is more or less valued in different dance forms, it is clear that improvisation doesn't stand apart from known forms and the embodiment, and in-the-moment utilization, of established skills. We can see the significance of the known in diverse forms such as Kathak and freestyle hip-hop. In Kathak, for instance, the ability to operate skilfully within the form is critical to acceptance as a performer. The guru-based training is long and repetitive (not unlike that of ballet). Yet here the traditional solo form is mainly improvised, and success in the solo form is considered the highest level of accomplishment. It is risk-taking, utterly dynamic—simultaneously in-the-moment and honouring the legacy from which it comes. The solo is performed in series of specific sections, ranging from invocational to pure dance and to fiery rhythmic exchanges and to dramatic stories in which the soloist portrays all of the characters. So whilst dancers are clearly generating the movement improvisationally, discourses of the new and the novel, of freedom and resistance, are contrary to this practice, which instead seeks complex, intricate, and expressive gesture that prioritizes preknown technical skills and dancers' characterizations. In this context, it is the ability to improvise within the frame of the codified forms, structures, and narratives, rather than to resist them, that is evident.

Similarly, to take another example, in freestyle hip-hop there is also an emphasis on established practices. Operating through tropes of authenticity, hip-hop dancer place high value on issues of legitimacy, emphasizing the pioneers of the style and highlighting the need to understand the foundations of the form. Here the ability to skilfully reference the movement signatures of key figures, those renowned for specific actions or styles, and to respond in innovative, often ever more daring ways is the aim. Dance scholar Sherril Dodds notes that hip-hop dancers use processes of borrowing, quoting, and rearticulating (2016: 64). As b-boy Rukkus says: 'everything is recycled. People will hate on you because you think you've done a move that they did. But in essence you're just taking off a move that was created far beyond and you're just implicating it in your style now, and claiming that it's yours. But really, everything is really recycled. Everybody takes ideas from something. If you really think about it, breaking is a dance that grabs from everything' (in Dodds 2016: 64). The referenced and recycled foundational movement is elaborated and made individual in informal jams in which the dancers improvise in a cipher form and in response to the music as selected by DJs (Dodds 2016). Improvisation here, then, operates through reference to 'imagined affinities' (Fogerty 2012: 453) such that the 'dancers imagine a commonality with each other' through a sense of shared knowledge of b-boying/b-girling as embodied in the dancer's ability and competence in particular styles (453). At the same time, dancers carve out individual identities through their improvised choices and the reimagining of possibilities. For as DeFrantz writes, 'improvisation in this realm, then, reaches back in order to cast forward, confirming affiliation among movements from a lively past of dancing while reimagining possibilities of gesture' (2014: 3).

Improvisation thereby entails mimicry and emulation as well as exploration and the possibility of the novel. This double gaze—to the known and the unknown—can clarify and reinforce established paradigms, as well as promoting skill development and extending the boundaries of a field.

Improviser Julyen Hamilton describes his process this way: 'every movement has within it seeds of another movement—it is like any life form—it has within it a living structure . . . it is a strong discipline to follow—which life has to be manifested at that moment and to not lose it' (Hamilton 1994). The following of this 'living structure' means that improvisations are *processual* in an essential sense. It is a process that unfolds while being invented, that occurs here and now and vanishes even while it's occurring. The ongoing and developing actions involve accepting a state of continual change, for improvisations are ephemeral, irreversible, unrepeatable events. It arises, it is developed, while being experienced, and then it disappears, never to be repeated.

Jane Bacon suggests that in a processual approach, 'attention always drifts to the processes of engagement, of lived experience or direct experience' (2013: 118). Similarly here, in the course of the improvisation the improviser is continually attending to the process itself and to the 'how' of the engagement. Through feedback loops, the improviser tracks back and forth, making choices and changes of direction—choosing to stay with something or initiate anew, to change location or relate to others. These emergences, and the tracking of them, are the basis of a construction process. So whilst many discussions of improvisation seek to articulate the relationship between improvisation and choreography—either decrying improvisation's lack of choreographic discipline or emphasizing the essential skill of the improviser as the making of choreographic choices in the moment (in the manner of a 'speeded-up' choreographic process)—I want to open up these and other related debates somewhat further and so refer instead to *emergent-construction*.

Perhaps by articulating improvisation in terms of emergent-construction, a more encompassing framework of and for improvisation is possible. This seems important, as the repeated recourse to the choreographic tends to reveal a particular hegemony in which choreography is valued over improvisation (and thereby improvisation only becomes valued as a form of choreography). This problematic overwriting of improvisation by choreography continues the reification of particular forms of dancing and dance-making. This becomes particularly significant when we note that while choreographic concepts and choreographic thinking are part of the practice and discourse in certain types of improvised performance, it is not a particularly helpful paradigm in other contexts (even noting the ever expanding concept of the choreographic). In using the term 'emergent-construction', I mark out a way of dancing improvisationally that can be inclusive of, as well as other than, the choreographic (in an affirmation of alterity rather than of a second cousin defined by lack).

In a related move, musician and educator Edward Sarath has argued that viewing improvisation as 'accelerated composition' misses much of the specificity of the improvisatory experience. He points to the differing cognitive mechanics of improvisation and composition that render them 'contrasting expressive vehicles' (2013: 173). He points out that the surface conditions of time and context as evident within the processes of improvisation and composition require us to rethink prevailing notions that seek to draw improvisation into the frame of composition. Self-evidently, for example, improvisation happens in a 'single continuous episode', whereas composition occurs over 'a series of discontinuous creative episodes' (173). 'Thus', he writes, we 'begin to see how vastly differing surface conditions might give rise to significantly different expressive results that might correlate with different cultural sensibilities' (173). The sensibilities, or musical worldview, of the improviser are underscored, Sarath proposes, by tendencies toward: 'inner-directed temporality' (178), the importance of flow, the 'heightened experience of the localized present' (178), collectivity, and a differing state of consciousness (181).

This resonates with me, as in my own dancing I am often improvising across performance and experientially focused contexts. Here the movement itself is generated from interior impulse. The focus is upon the individual exploration of anatomical and image-based metaphors, attained via a process of interior sensing. In this context, the processes of choreography and compositional form are not given prominence. Instead, the values, meanings, and structures of the dancing are found: the inner felt sense of moving alone and with others, which might or might not always also attend to compositional concerns.

Moreover, if we consider the expanded range of improvised practices, as described in this book, it is clear that choreographic or, indeed, compositional concerns are not key to all forms or even particularly important in many. In this wider framing of improvisation, which includes social dance and non-Western forms, the connection between improvisation and choreography can be seen to reinforce the privileging of the choreographic over the improvised and, in turn, of Western dance styles in relation to non-Western ones. As such, the experience of dancing and the features of improvisation, such as interior flow (as described earlier) and communion (discussed later), are often overlooked.

As Thomas DeFrantz points out, in the context of black social dance, the assertion of the choreographed (which he aligns with the written) over the improvised (aligned with spontaneous oration) overwrites important aspects of improvised dancing such as social exchange: 'this line of argumentation tends to restabilize choreography, or writing, as the ideal model for dance practice. But improvisation, especially in black social dance circumstances, conveys its own pleasures and urgencies without necessary recourse to translatable signs and symbols that characterize writing. The improvisational practices of these dances complete themselves without an insistence on translation into language or visual mark' (2014: 2). DeFranz notes how operating outside of language relates to questions of pleasure, communion, and sexuality and, in doing so, importantly points to the emergence of self in communion with others. Poetically, DeFrantz writes: '*I want my dance to confirm me in this moment. To validate our communion as people in relationship, in the space of the dance, in the process of discovery. When we dance we wonder at what is possible, we appreciate how impulse turns into gesture and gesture reveals desire and intellect*' (3, italics in original).

Such concerns—the confirmation of self, the communicative encounter, the willingness to accept risk, the potential of discovery—circulate us back to Albright's question 'What if improvisation?' and, too, to US dance artist Deborah Hay, who centres her practices around questions, asking: 'What if every cell in the body had the potential to get what it needs, while surrendering the habit of a singular facing, and inviting being seen?' 'What if where I am is what I need, cellularly?' 'What if alignment is everywhere?' or 'What if Now is Here is Harmony?' These questions invite us to consider possibilities rather than formulate answers. They seek to cultivate an awareness of the bodily at a microcellular level as well as wider curiosities that are part philosophical and part ecological in nature. These are unanswerable questions that, when explored through/as improvisation, bring about shifts in perception and assert the body as part of the world.

Extending the significance of improvisation from dance to the human experience, we might go on to ask: What if improvisation can teach us how to go about things differently? What if improvisation can enable adaptability, fluidity, and openness to change? What if improvisation can show us ways of being that are sensitive to environments and to each other? These questions are physical, intellectual, social, and ethical. They highlight the ways that improvisation, as 'a way of going about things' entails responsibilities to those we are improvising with and to audiences, carrying the potential of alterity through which we might reenvisage ourselves and others, pasts and futures.

Writing Improvisation and the Organization of the Handbook

The complexities and distinctiveness of improvised acts and the process-oriented nature of improvisation mean it is hard to see and more difficult to articulate. Indeed the musician Stephen Nachmanovitch (1990) has said that improvisation refuses to lie flat upon the page, and dancer Steve Paxton (1987a, 1987b) has noted that written language cannot capture the inherently prelingual form of improvised dance, saying: 'I feel it is a difficult situation you have caught yourselves in with this issue on improvisation. You are requesting articles in *language* (that most civilizing, consciousness "raising" medium, requiring so much formal effort), about a prelingual and probably largely unconscious arousal of manifested physical imagery which, by its nature, resists definition because whatever you claim it is it is immediately not; definition (by definition) pinning down the immanent and turning it into available techniques and thus into history' (1987: 4). Here Paxton expresses his concerns about the relationship between language and improvisation. He continues: 'improvisation is a word for something which can't keep a name: if it does stick around long enough to acquire a name, it has begun to move toward fixity' (19).

More recently, as noted, Thomas DeFrantz has considered related issues, writing: 'dance literature, or choreography, might be work that could be recorded on paper or via technologies of visual media, while improvisation might be more akin to structures of spontaneous oration and rhetoric' (2014: 2). His argument not only questions the rarefication of writing practices but also cogently argues that the valorization of the literary/choreographic undermines the experiential, physical, and relational nature of improvisation in black social dance (and, we might argue, all improvised [social] dance). Accordingly, we can see that the articulation in words is particularly problematic for improvisatory forms; yet this is the endeavour all the authors in this collection have undertaken.

While the difficulties of translating movement into (written) language exist across dance forms, in improvisation the stakes are particularly present, and the difference between what might be described as the semiotics of languages and the phenomenological experience of improvised movement is notably difficult to overcome. Yet we need to find ways to speak of improvisation if its significance is to be understood. Indeed I am acutely aware of the language and structural choices in my writing and the tendencies they reveal—I speak of emergence rather than riffing and emphasize a sense of organic connectivity (or perhaps a drifting flow) rather than structural breaks or the clarity of the singular gesture. These choices implicitly reinforce my own dance and cultural background whilst explicitly trying to give voice to more diverse possibilities. Given the limited range of documentation and writing about improvisation, the responsibility to give voice to a diverse range of approaches is all the more pressing. Furthermore, as the words become affixed for publication, the distance from dancing to the tap of the fingers on the keyboard, and from the thought action that such a touch entails to the ink mark on the page, increases. I wonder about the nature of the writing as artefact. When developing an academic argument that sifts through previous moments of dancing, what is being created? Can it be more than a 'retro-entrail'? (with thanks again to Paxton [1993: 84] for this image).

In a book review in *Dance Research*, Paxton writes: 'the findings were then sorted to create patterns and cemented into place. This cementing creates mosaics from what was once in flux.... the translation of one medium into another, and life into print. Life was more complete and fluid than history is. And the historians have the responsibility for the last cementing of the artifacts' (84). How might this 'cementing' be undone, or at least done in a manner more akin to the life of an improvisation? How might a collection such as this handbook take its responsibility seriously by retaining a sense of flux? Perhaps, short of creating an ever-changing book in which words can move around the page, re-forming themselves on each reading, all we can do is point to the organic processes of construction such that the artefact in print reveals itself, acknowledging itself as a thoughtful mosaic rather than a truly crescent life-world.

And so, on that note, I turn to the materials in this collection.

This handbook contains writing by both established and emerging writers and locates dance as an important form within the emergent discipline of critical improvisation studies. Reflecting the influence of this emergent discipline, the handbook encompasses a wealth of methodologies and perspectives, including authors who find their first disciplinary home in dance scholarship as well as those coming to dance from other disciplines. Rather than focusing on ways of doing improvisation, as a 'how to' book might (although there is certainly discussion of pedagogy), this book incorporates historiographic, ethnographic, and interview-based approaches alongside perspectives drawn from philosophy, cognition and neuroscience, phenomenology, ecology, human geography, and practice-based research, to name but a few.

In editing and arranging these rich materials, there were many possible options. In accord with the nature of publishing processes, I had, before even seeing any of the chapters, proposed a structure. I thought perhaps a 'useful' model would be to reveal contexts in which improvisation occurs or purposes for which improvisation is employed. As such, I had envisaged sections arranged around performance, education, therapy, and social and popular dance. In this model, it would have been possible to bring together writers Anthony Shay, Michael Kimmel, and Suzannne Ravn, all of whom write about tango in this handbook. The juxtaposition of these chapters would highlight tango as an improvised social dance formed in terms of a reconsideration of the 'traditional' (Shay), intentionality of movement in prereflexive and shared situations (Ravn), and the sensory-motor and interactive features (Kimmel) of tango, respectively. Or, in an imagined section on education, Kerry Chappell and Lizzie Swinford's observations of improvisation with children might have been interesting to read alongside artist Stephanie Skura's own reflections on her workshop practice. Two very different learning contexts—but together illuminating how learning in improvisation can give rise to discoveries and new experiences.

This imagined, context- and purpose-derived structure has the advantage of highlighting from the start the many multifaceted times and places we find improvisation and would certainly be reader friendly—encouraging students and teachers to pick up debates about improvisation in relation to a wide range of situations and making visible the reach of improvisation beyond the theatre and beyond the dance studio and the utility and application of improvisation in many other real-world contexts.

In the end, what I have chosen to do is respond to themes and concerns as framed by the authors themselves, and so this handbook is organized into these eight parts: 'Live

Worlds and Ethics', 'Attunement and Perception', 'Habit, Freedom, and Resistance', 'Memory and Transmission', 'Agency and Transformation', 'Interconnectivity, Emergence, and Technologies', 'Ecology and Environments', and finally 'Techniques, Strategies, and Histories'.

To flesh out these parts just a little: part I brings into focus the generative potential of improvisation and ways in which it rejects individualism in lieu of human connectivity (Fraleigh: chapter 4). As part of everyday life, the authors consider how improvised ways of dancing give us ways of responding to life questions. Part II reflects and extends my earlier openings on receptivity. The authors illuminate how embodied perceptual frameworks operate in improvised practices. Sally Doughty, for example, describes her work arising from Deborah Hay's solo commissioning project to interrogate the processes involved in 'noticing' and how such processes can have a significant impact on the developing improvisation (chapter 7). In a related fashion, Malaika Sarco-Thomas draws upon Maurice Merleau-Ponty's theorizing of sensory perception in bodily movement to reveal enhanced perceptual attentions (chapter 9).

Part III also finds clear connections to the discussions earlier about the complexity of prior skill in improvisation and the question of freedom and expands these ideas to consider various freedoms *to*, rather than freedoms *from*, pointing to the embodied, sociohistorical, and institutional agendas at work in a diverse range of contexts. The close reading by Janice Ross of the work of Leonid Yakobson, the leading modernist at the Kirov Ballet and the Bolshoi Ballet, reveals how improvisation in his rehearsal rooms and the courting of chance carried unique aesthetic force and political risk (chapter 15). Also in part III, Gary Peters counters the dominant antipathy to habit in the discourses on improvisation and argues for a deeper engagement with the habitual as the locus for every event of dance (chapter 12).

Part IV encompasses the ways in which personal and cultural memory operates as a inherent feature of improvising and illuminates the transmission of practice in learning contexts. Part V is opened by Sarah Whatley's chapter, drawing attention to the complex interactions between improvisation and disabilities challenging the rhetoric that surrounds both (chapter 23). Other authors' contributions to part V discuss the transformative power of improvisation for happiness (Sellers Young, chapter 27), humanizing (Chappell and Swinford, chapter 24), knowing (East, chapter 26), and well-being (Dowler, chapter 25).

In part VI, improvisation is discussed in/with technologies that problematize the assumptions of collaboration and intersubjectivity in improvisation (DeFranz, chapter 28, and LaVeirs, chapter 29). Part VI also includes a group of writings that draw on studies in cognition and neuroscience to consider improvisation as a social, self-organizing process.

Part VII considers site-responsive improvisation in a range of ways. Hilary Elliott (chapter 36) and Vicky Hunter both explore strategies for engaging with 'architectural, spatial, and sensory "data" in site-dance processes' (Hunter, chapter 35). Tamara Ashley (chapter 33) and Melinda Buckwalter consider the ecological power of improvisation 'to pull us across the boundary of self toward a fresh experience of integration of self and environment' (Buckwalter, chapter 34). Moving us in a different direction, Josephine Machon (chapter 37) considers the improvisation of audiences within immersive performance forms.

Part VII presents improvisation from a diverse range of contexts, to illuminate particularized strategies and trajectories and to rewrite histories. Anthony Shay (chapter 39), for example, provides a wide overview of dance genres, such as tango and Iranian solo urban dance, to illuminate the ways improvisation informs each of them. Allison Robbins and Christopher J. Wells (chapter 40) focus on tap dance, providing an example of how music studies might contribute more substantively to discourses on Afrocentric improvisation within dance studies.

As you read, I invite you, in the manner of an improviser, to track your processes, being receptive to that which is drawing you. Note your pre-dispositions and attend to how these give you particular ways of going about things, for you might try to read another way and in doing so improvise alternative ways through.

References

Albright, Ann Cooper. (2007) *Traces of Light: Absence and Presence in the Work of Loie Fuller*. Middletown, CT: Wesleyan University Press.

Albright, Ann Cooper. (2013) *Falling*. Performance Research 18(4): 36–41.

Albright, Ann Cooper, and Gere, David (eds.). (2003) *Taken by Surprise: A Dance Improvisation Reader*. Middletown, CT: Wesleyan University Press.

Banes, Sally. (1987) *Terpsichore in Sneakers: Postmodern Dance*. Middletown, CT: Wesleyan University Press.

Banes, Sally. (1993) *Greenwich Village, 1963: Avant-Garde Performance and the Effervescent Body*. Durham, NC: Duke University Press.

Banes, Sally. (2003) Spontaneous Combustion: Notes on Dance Improvisation from the Sixties to the Nineties. In Albright, Ann Cooper, and Gere, David (eds.), *Taken by Surprise: A Dance Improvisation Reader*. Middletown, CT: Wesleyan University Press, 77–89.

Belgrad, Daniel. (1998) *The Culture of Spontaneity: Improvisation and the Arts in Postwar America*. Chicago: University of Chicago Press.

Benoit, Agnès (ed.). (1997) *On the Edge: Dialogues on Dance Improvisation*. Brussels Contredanse/Nouvelles De Dance, #32/33.

Buckwalter, Melinda. (2010) *Composing While Dancing: An Improviser's Companion*. Madison: University of Wisconsin Press.

Carter, Alexandra. (2005) *Dance and Dancers in the Victorian and Edwardian Music Hall Ballet*. Aldershot, UK: Ashgate.

Claid, Emilyn, and Allsopp, Ric. (2013) Editorial: On Falling. *Performance Research* 18(4): 1–3.

Corbett, Michael, and Vibert, Ann. (2016) *Improvising the Curriculum: Negotiating Risky Literacies in Cautious Schools*. London: Routledge.

Crossan, Mary, Cunha, Miguel Pina E., Vera, Dusya, and Cunha, João. (2005) Time and Organizational Improvisation. *Academy of Management Review* 30(1): 129–145.

Csikszentmihalyi, Mihaly. (1991) *Flow: The Psychology of Optimal Experience—Steps toward Enhancing the Quality of Life*. New York: HarperCollins.

Dance Improvisation: The Estranged Cousin. (2016) Dance4.co.uk/artists/project/improvisation/news/2016-05/videos-now-online-dance-improvisation-estranged-cousin-symposium.

DeFrantz, Thomas. (2004) The Black Beat Made Visible: Body Power in Hip Hop Dance. In Lepecki, André (ed.), *Of the Presence of the Body: Essays on Dance and Performance Theory*. Middletown, CT: Wesleyan University Press, 64–81.

DeFrantz, Thomas F. (2016) Improvising Social Exchange: African American Social Dance (2014). In Lewis, George E., and Piekut, Benjamin (eds.), *The Oxford Handbook of Critical Improvisation Studies*, vol. 1, pp. 1–7, Oxford Handbooks Online, www.oxfordhandbooks.com, accessed 23 September 2015.

De Spain, Kent. (2003) The Cutting Edge of Awareness: Reports from the Inside of Improvisation. In Albright, Ann Cooper, and Gere, David (eds.), *Taken by Surprise: A Dance Improvisation Reader*. Middletown, CT: Wesleyan University Press, 27–38.

De Spain, Kent. (2014) *Landscape of the Now: A Topography of Movement Improvisation*. Oxford: Oxford University Press.

Dilley, Barbara. (2015) *This Very Moment: Thinking, Teaching, Dancing*. Boulder: Naropa University Press.

Dixon Gottschild, Barbara. (1998) *Digging the Africanist Presence in American Performance: Dance and Other Contexts*. Westport, CT: Praeger.

Dixon Gottschild, Brenda (2000) *Waltzing in the Dark: African American Vaudeville and Race Politics in the Swing Era*, New York: Palgrave Macmillan.

Dixon Gottschild, Barbara. (2003) *The Black Dancing Body: A Geography from Coon to Cool*. New York: Palgrave Macmillan.

Dodds, Sherril. (2011) *Dancing on the Canon: Embodiments of Value in Popular Dance*. Basingstoke, UK: Palgrave.

Dodds, Sherril. (2016) Hip Hop Battles and Facial Intertexts. *Dance Research* 34(1): 63–83.

Donnay, G. F., Rankin, S. K., Lopez-Gonzalez, M., Jiradejvong, P., and Limb, C. J. (2014) Neural Substrates of Interactive Musical Improvisation: An fMRI Study of 'Trading Fours' in Jazz. *PLoS ONE* 9(2): e88665.

Duck, Katie. (n.d.) Interview: Proximity. http://katieduck.com/about-katie-duck/text/interviews/interview-proximity/.

Fischlin, Daniel. (2009) Improvisation and the Unnameable: On Being Instrumental. *Critical Studies in Improvisation/Études critiques en improvisation* 5(1). http://www.criticalimprov.com/article/view/1121/1638.

Fischlin, Daniel, and Heble, Ajay (eds.). (2004) *The Other Side of Nowhere: Jazz, Improvisation, and Communities in Dialogue*. Middletown, CT: Wesleyan University Press.

Fischlin, Daniel, Heble, Ajay, and Lipsitz, George. (2013) *The Fierce Urgency of Now: Improvisation, Rights, and the Ethics of Cocreation*. Durham, NC: Duke University Press.

Fogarty, Mary. (2012) Breaking Expectations: Imagined Affinities in Mediated Youth Cultures. *Continuum: Journal of Media and Cultural Studies* 26(3): 449–462.

Forsythe, William, with Haffner, Nik, Kuchelmeister, Volker, and Ziegler, Chris (eds.). ([1996] 2011) *Improvisation Technologies: A Tool for the Analytical Dance Eye*. 3rd ZKM digital arts ed. Ostfildern, Germany: Hatje Cantz.

Foster, Susan Leigh. (2002) *Dances That Describe Themselves: The Improvised Choreography of Richard Bull*. Middletown, CT: Wesleyan University Press.

Foster, Susan Leigh. (2003a) Improvising/History. In Worthen, William B., with Holland, Peter (eds.), *Theorizing Practice: Redefining Theatre History*. London: Palgrave, 196–212.

Foster, Susan Leigh. (2003b) Taken by Surprise: Improvisation in Body and Mind. In Albright, Ann Cooper, and Gere, David (eds.), *Taken by Surprise: A Dance Improvisation Reader*. Middletown, CT: Wesleyan, 3–12.

Goldman, Daniel. (2010) *I Want to Be Ready: Improvised Dance as a Practice of Freedom*. Ann Arbor: University of Michigan Press.

Hallam, Elizabeth, and Ingold, Tim (eds.). (2007) *Creativity and Cultural Improvisation*. Oxford: Berg.

Hamilton, Julyen. (1994) *Dance Improvisation*, Arts Archives, Exeter: Exeter Arts Documentation Unit.

Heble, Ajay, and Caines, Rebecca (eds.). (2015) *The Improvisation Studies Reader: Spontaneous Acts*. London: Routledge.

Heble, Ajay, and Wallace, Rob. (2013) *People Get Ready: The Future of Jazz Is Now!* Durham, NC: Duke University Press.

Hupp Ramsey, Margaret. (1991) *The Grand Union (1970–1976), An Improvisational Performance Group*. New York: Peter Lang.

Jackson, Micheal. (1996) *Things as They Are: New Directions in Phenomenolgical Anthropology*, Bloomington: Indiana University Press.

Kamoche, Ken, Pi Cunha and João Vieira da Cunha. (2003) Towards a Theory of Organizational Improvisation: Looking beyond the Jazz Metaphor. *Journal of Management Studies* 40(8) (December): 2023–2050.

Koteen, David, and Stark Smith, Nancy. (2008) *Caught Falling: The Confluence of Contact Improvising, Nancy Stark-Smith, and Other Moving Ideas*. Northampton, MA: Contact Editions.

Landgraf, Edgar. (2014) *Improvisation as Arts: Conceptual Challenges, Historical Perspectives*. New York: Bloomsbury.

Lewis, George E., and Piekut, Benjamin (eds.). (2016) *Handbook of Critical Improvisation Studies*. Vols. 1 and 2. Oxford: Oxford University Press.

Lipsitz, George. (2015) Improvised Listening: Opening Statements. In Heble, Ajay, and Caines, Rebecca (eds.), *The Improvisation Studies Reader: Spontaneous Acts*. London: Routledge, 9–18.

McCarren, Felicia. (2013) *French Moves: The Cultural Politics of Le Hip Hop*. Oxford: Oxford University Press.

Midgelow, Vida L. (2015a) Improvisation Practices and Dramaturgical Consciousness: A Workshop. In Hansan, Pil, and Callison, Darcey (eds.), *Dance Dramaturgy: Modes of Agency, Awareness and Engagement*. Basingstoke, UK: Palgrave Macmillan, 106–123.

Midgelow, Vida L. (2015b) Some Fleshy Thinking: Improvisation and Experience. In George-Graves, Nadine (ed.), *The Oxford Handbook of Dance and Theater*. New York: Oxford University Press, 109–122.

Motion Bank (2010–2013) www.motionbank.org

Nachmanovitch, Stephen. (1990) *Free Play—Improvisation in Life and Art*. New York: Tarcher/Penguin.

Nagrin, Daniel. (1994) *Dance and the Specific Image*. Pittsburgh: University of Pittsburgh Press.

Nelson, Lisa. (2008) Lisa Nelson in Conversation with Lisa Nelson. In *Critical Correspondence*. http://www.movementresearch.org/criticalcorrespondence/blog/?p=2122.

Novack, Cynthia. (1990) *Sharing the Dance: Contact Improvisation and American Culture*. Madison: University of Wisconsin Press.

Palazzi, Maria, and Shaw, Norah Zuniga. (2013) Motion Bank: Two, www.MotionBank.org. http://motionbank.org/de/content/two-bebe-miller-thomas-hauert.

Pallant, Cheryl. (2006) *Contact Improvisation: An Introduction to a Vitalizing Dance Form*. Jefferson, NC: McFarland.

Paxton, Steve. (1987a) Improvisation Issue? *Contact Quarterly* 12(2) (Spring/Summer): 4.

Paxton, Steve. (1987b) Improvisation Is ... *Contact Quarterly* 12(2) (Spring/Summer): 15–19.

Paxton, Steve. (1993) Reviews. *Dance Research: The Journal of the Society for Dance Research* 11(1) (Spring): 82–84.

Peters, Gary. (2009) *The Philosophy of Improvisation*. Chicago: University of Chicago Press.

Ramshaw, Sara. (2013) *Justice as Improvisation: The Law of the Extempore*. London: Routledge.

Robinson, Daniel. (2015) *Modern Moves: Dancing Race during the Ragtime and Jazz Eras*. Oxford: Oxford University Press.

Santi, Marina, and Illetterati, Luca (eds.). (2010) Improvisation between Performance and Lifeworld. In Santi, Marina (ed.), *Improvisation: Between Technique and Spontaneity*. Newcastle upon Tyne, UK: Cambridge Scholars.

Sarath, Edward. (2013) *Improvisation, Creativity and Consciousness: Jazz as Integral Template for Music Education and Society*. Albany: State University of New York Press.

Shay, Anthony. (1999) *Choreophobia: Solo Improvised Dance in the Iranian World*. California: Mazda.

Sheets-Johnstone, Maxine. (2009) Thinking in Movement. In *The Corporeal Turn: An Interdisciplinary Reader*. Exeter, UK: Imprint Academic, 28–63. (Originally published 1999)

Shusterman, R. (2008) *Body Consciousness: A Philosophy of Mindfulness and Somaesthetics*. New York: Cambridge University Press.

Siddall, Gillian, and Waterman, Ellen (eds.). (2016) *Negotiated Moments: Improvisation, Sound and Subjectivity*. Durham, NC: Duke University Press.

Stark Smith, Nancy. (1987) Editor's Note: Taking No for an Answer. *Contact Quarterly* 12(2) (Spring/Summer): 3.

Syncronous Objects (2009) http://synchronousobjects.osu.edu/.

Tufnell, Miranda, and Crickmay, Chris. (1990) *Body, Space, Image*. London: Virago Press.

Tufnell, Miranda, and Crickmay, Chris. (2004) *A Widening Field: Journeys in Body and Imagination*. London: Dance Books.

Valis Hill, Constance. (2010) *Tap Dancing America: A Cultural History*. Oxford: Oxford University Press.

Vera, D., and Crossan, M. (2004) Theatrical Improvisation: Lessons for Organizations. *Organization Studies* 25: 727–749.

Waterman, Ellen. (2015) Improvised Trust: Opening Statements. In Heble, Ajay, and Caines, Rebecca (eds.), *The Improvisation Studies Reader: Spontaneous Acts*. London: Routledge, 59–62.

Zaporah, Ruth. (2014) *Improvisation on the Edge: Notes from On and Off Stage*, Berkeley, CA: North Atlantic Books.

Zuniga Shaw, N. (2014) Animate Inscriptions, Articulate Data and Algorithmic Expressions of Choreographic Thinking. *Choreographic Practices* 5(1): 95–119.

PART I

LIFE WORLDS AND ETHICS

CHAPTER 1

··

LIFE PRACTICES

··

ANN COOPER ALBRIGHT

EVERYBODY'S life is an improvisation, but for those of us who work daily with teaching and performing movement improvisation there is a heightened awareness of how this practice structures our lives. Improvisation, particularly contact improvisation and the many somatic practices that revolve around its physical training, has been the lifeline that has helped me to survive professional disappointment and physical injury, family trauma, and various lapses of imagination. Over the past decade, I have come to realize just how much the physical and psychic state of launching into the unknown has deeply influenced not only my dancing and thinking but also my being-in-the-world. Improvisation is a philosophy of life, albeit not one based on a specific doctrine, or system of beliefs. Rather, it is another way of relating to one's experience—a willingness to explore the realm of possibility, not in order to find the correct solution but simply to *find out*. Over the course of this chapter, I will discuss how my work in improvisation has influenced three main areas of my life: my movement practice and teaching, my intellectual trajectory, and my relationship to my family. Throughout, I suggest that improvisation is best thought of as an approach rather than a subject; a method of inquiry rather than an academic discipline—no matter how cutting-edge. Indeed, I want to propose that instead of asking 'what *is* improvisation?' we ask 'what *if* improvisation?' Implicated in this conditional statement is a practice of dwelling in possibility that I believe can be both personally useful and politically profound.

As many of the chapters in this handbook attest, improvisation can be a highly misunderstood phenomenon, even in our post, post, postmodern society. Notoriously slippery and hard to describe, improvisation often gets defined in terms of what it is not. In modern dance, for instance, improvisation is frequently positioned as the opposite of choreography. It is seen as free, spontaneous, childlike, and wild, as if once improvising, the dancer's previous physical training and aesthetic sensibilities simply evaporate. Similarly, dance improvisation gets figured as a release from constraints—technical, stylistic, or narrative. Within this developmental framework, improvisation is seen as a first step, an opening up of certain movement possibilities that might well provide useful fodder for the more evolved (dare I say mature?) pursuit of dance composition.

Of course, as seasoned improvisers know full well, improvisation requires rigorous and precise training, be it in music, dance, art, or cultural studies. One of these skills is learning to be intentional in the moment. This is made possible by the paradoxically simple yet quite sophisticated ability to be at once internal and external—both open to the world and intensely grounded in an awareness of one's own experience. In dance, a somatic focus on sense perception instead of visual shape can move us beyond our habitual patterns by opening our kinaesthetic curiosity, energizing our physical presence with an attention to a shifting palette of proprioception, gravity, space, time, and other bodies. These improvisational practices not only expand our movement options but also encourage a willingness to cross over into unknown territories, to move in the face of fear, and, most important, to risk failure. In my experience, the psychic state of being open to possibility is grounded in an ongoing kinaesthetic practice that cultivates perceptual awareness and physical mindfulness. This is the corporeal foundation for improvising with, across, through, and beyond one's personal history and cultural expectations.

Ironically and importantly, improvisation can even give us the tools to see past our own tried and true definitions of what we think it is. Dance teachers across the globe typically describe improvisation as a *process* and choreography as the *product*. This is a pretty standard separation of an ongoing, verb-propelled experience that never quite gets to the end of the sentence on the one hand and a direct object that can be authorized to land before the period on the other. This is also a moment when indeterminate statements such as 'I am engaging in a process' shift into the definitive 'I made a dance', locating the choreographer securely within the map of artistic production. But we can plumb the counterintuitive (as improvisers are wont to do) to recognize that these terms are not mutually exclusive. *What if?* What if instead of setting up process as the opposite of product, we invoked an etymologically related word: *produce … produce*. Like process, produce can be both a noun and a verb, depending on one's enunciation or the situation at hand. *Produce/produce* can segue in between process and product to help us realize the mutual interdependence of these activities. Rather than situating choreography as the opposite of improvisation, then, we can begin to see their connectedness— the ways that decision-making in motion is always already both spontaneous and reflective.

I began to study dance at the same time I began to study philosophy, in college in the early 1980s. My budding feminist and political consciousness helped me recognize the ways in which our culture positions certain people as more aligned with the body (women, immigrants, people of colour, and queers) and certain people as more fully of the mind (you get to fill in the blank). Rather than being convinced, however, that the body was completely determined by social proscriptions and written over by cultural identity, I came to see that our bodies are engaged in a fascinating improvisational exchange between what we are told is available and what we feel is possible. Reading Maurice Merleau-Ponty's work *The Phenomenology of Perception* reinforced the intertwined investigations of self and world that I was doing in both the dance and philosophy classes I was taking at the time. Cycling between reading and moving, I found myself increasingly compelled by ideas that accounted for thought as embodied. To understand embodiment as a way of knowing, however, one has to be prepared to navigate the murky waters of ambiguity and the shifting winds of multiple discourses. This in and of itself is already an improvisational impulse, for to live thoughtfully in the body is to refuse any static definition of what it is. Somewhere in the middle of my sophomore year of college, I was introduced to contact improvisation, and I've been deeply engaged in moving with and thinking through this physical and metaphysical practice ever since.

Contact improvisation is a dance form that was developed in the early 1970s by a group of people who were interested in exploring the dancing produced by the exchange of weight between two or more people. The movement in contact improvisation is structured by the changing physics of weight, space, momentum, and force, in addition to the ever-evolving interpersonal dynamics of trust and abandon. The physical techniques of rolling, learning when and when not to give weight, how to accept another person's weight, and how to fall safely, create the movement basis for the improvisation. My three decades of dancing contact have taught me that one of the most important aspects of this form is our training for a responsive body—one that can handle being thrown (sometimes literally) into new situations—a body that can trust fully in the intelligence of its own reflexes.

For me, one of the most enlightening aspects of my training in contact improvisation is the cultivation of an openness and curiosity in the midst of chaos, disorientation, and the inevitable experiences of falling to the ground. In my classes, I speak of this as a kind of responsibility, not as a negative proscriptive state ('Be responsible young lady!') but rather as a cultivation of an ability to respond. The important shift here is replacing the existential panic of losing one's balance with the continuing awareness of physical sensation and the world around one. In describing her early experiments with lofting, catching, and falling, veteran contact improviser Nancy Stark Smith writes: 'The more I fell, the more familiar the sensation of dropping through space became, the less disoriented I was during the fall. Staying awake from the first moment of balance loss, I found that falling was itself a dynamic balance. One in which the forces at play—gravity, momentum, and mass—were all operating in their natural order and if my mind was with me, I could gently guide that fall towards a smooth landing. Confidence came with experience and soon enjoyment took the place of fear and disorientation' (1979: 3). 'Disorientation' is a word that insists on its opposite for meaning. To be disoriented is to be undone, thrown off balance. But it also hints at a deeper knowledge. We rarely think about where we are until we have been lost. In order to understand what orients us, we need to experience disorientation. In the conclusion to her meditation on shifting orientations in *Queer Phenomenology*, Sara Ahmed claims that 'moments of disorientation are vital. They are bodily experiences that throw the world up, or throw the body from its ground. Disorientation as a bodily feeling can be unsettling, and it can shatter one's sense of confidence in the ground or one's belief that the ground on which we reside can support the actions that make a life feel livable. Such a feeling of shattering, or of being shattered, might persist and become a crisis. Or the feeling itself might pass as the ground returns or as we return to the ground' (2006: 157). Thrown off balance, the body skews our sense of direction in ways that may reframe our politics of location or the cultural organization of space. Falling offers a new slant, so to speak, on the binary of up and down. Indeed, we might even posit, following Ahmed's work in phenomenology, that falling insists on a shift of orientation, a different perspective from which we might learn, even once we return to the ground. In order to experience this difference in falling, however, it is important not to shut off sensation, including the sensation of losing one's ground. Embracing disorientation is not the same as feeling totally comfortable with it, of course. As Nancy Stark Smith notes in her early discussion of falling: 'this is not to say that disorientation, confusion and dis-ease have no place in the geometry of balance. They, in fact, stimulate the balancing mechanism. Stimulate us to ask questions' (Smith 1979: 3). Learning to stay responsive in the midst of life's moments of extreme disorientation is a practice that begins with an understanding of our internal balancing mechanisms.

Thus, one of the earliest exercises that I give in my improvisation classes is referred to as 'the small dance' or 'the stand'. First developed by Steve Paxton as he explored the physical skills that would lead towards defining the form of contact improvisation, the stand allows one to focus on the subtle interior motions created by the shifts of bones, muscles, and breath required to stand 'still'. After they have been warming up, moving through the space for awhile with big, vigorous movements, I ask the dancers to choose a spot and stand in a relaxed but active manner. At first, I call their attention to the multiple rhythms of their heartbeat, pulses, and breathing. This is a moment when they are suspended between sky and earth, at once grounded through the feet and extending through the top of their heads. Later, after they have focused on the internal sensations of their bodies, I ask them to play with shifting their balance to the point of almost falling in many different directions. Eventually, this exercise will develop into an exploration that encourages them to initiate a gentle falling off balance that moves them through the space of the studio.

Sometimes, while they are in the stand, I ask the dancers to focus on allowing sounds, light, and air to enter their bodies. Engaging one's peripheral vision is crucial to this process, and I tell the dancers to release the fronts of their eyes, allowing images and colours to come into their head instead of straining their eyes in order to go out and grab the visual image. Then, I ask them to concentrate on opening the pores of their skin so that the world can penetrate their physical awareness. This image helps us to feel our bodies as part and parcel of a whole landscape, rather than the instrument which views, arranges, or destroys that landscape. I have, at times, described this somatic experience as facilitating an ecological consciousness, for in this dialogue between the self and the world one becomes aware of the intriguing possibilities of interdependence. With this comes a deeper sense of responsibility, not as an oppressive duty towards others but as an ability to respond, an ability to be present with the world as a way of being present with oneself. This is the fruit of attention, a mindfulness that prepares one for a variety of improvisations, both physical and metaphysical.

There is also, I believe, a profound psychic reorganization in this exercise as well. By shifting our somatic imagination, we can begin to reorder our cultural notions of selfhood. Rather than the colonialist paradigm of the individual, propelled by his will and determination to go out into the world and stake a claim (stand on one's own two feet, make a mark, etc.), the self becomes an interdependent part that flows through and with the world. The skin no longer operates as the boundary between the world and myself but becomes the sensing organ that opens up an intersubjective space in which the separation of self and other becomes infinitely more fluid. Similar exercises with breath can cultivate a mindfulness of the constant exchange between inhalation and exhalation, teaching us that the air we breathe is not a void or the absence of solid objects but a manifestation of the interchangeability of self and surrounding environment.

In these examples, somatic awareness intersects with imaginative possibility (or is it somatic possibility intersects with imaginative awareness?) such that cultural meaning becomes more fluid, although never abstracted. Another skill that is critical for beginning contact improvisation students is learning how to give and receive weight. Interestingly, this is possible only in the actual practice of a bodily exchange. It is not something that can be visualized or approached on one's own. Rather, one has to feel it in order to comprehend it, and that experience is never automatic, no matter how long one has been dancing the form. Feeling and meeting another's weight requires an intense physical focus and personal vulnerability. It is a kind of sensing and emotional responsiveness that must always be available to adjust at a moment's notice. One of the images I use to teach this skill is that of pouring water from a pitcher into my partner's body. The more weight I pour into my partner, the more they will need to pour of their own weight to meet mine. This two-way exchange is inherently dynamic and unstable, and it can shift from upright to the floor in a split second.

The kind of trust in self and other that is necessary to give someone else one's weight goes against much of our training in contemporary American culture, where we are taught early on to stand on our own two feet and not to be a 'burden' on our families or society. It is not uncommon for people to pretend to give weight but actually be holding most of their own weight in their legs or pelvis. Similarly, a fear of not being able to support another person's weight can make people rigid and stiff as they try to morph into an inanimate object in order to hold their partner up. Practice with lots of differently sized people increases our awareness of this exchange as a dialogue in which bodies learn how to respond. Unlike a scale in which ten pounds on one side needs to be matched by exactly ten pounds on the other side in order to achieve balance, support in contact improvisation is less about the amount of weight and more about the intentionality of one's weight. One of my favourite illustrations of this dynamic is to ask a student who is having a hard time mobilizing their weight if they have a sibling. Usually, once they envision their partner as a sibling, they can activate a push or resistance very quickly. There is a sense of playful, juicy, and fierce but also loving physicality that gets mobilized by childhood memories of wrestling with a brother or a sister.

There is an important cognitive improvisation in this practice as well. In order to highlight the admittedly counterintuitive insight that this practice can give us, I have coined the motto 'Resistance is support.' In the liberal arts college environment in which I teach, 'support' is often seen as lavish praise and superlative compliments. (Remember, this is the generation not only of helicopter parents but also of the mindset that 'everyone is a winner', resulting in lots of childhood trophies for 'effort'.) Yet teachers know well that a little pushback can help a younger person refine her argument or improve her writing. The quality of that resistance is crucial here, of course. We are not talking about thought-less opposition or brute force. Rather, in the practice of giving and receiving weight we find that when I resist you with my weight not only can I support your weight but also I feel my own weight and energy mobilized in exchange. People who attempt to passively support someone else's weight without resisting find their energy burns out quickly. If I offer to support your weight while mobilizing my own, however, we can create a dy-namic exchange that shifts more fluidly back and forth between us, opening up a phys-ical dialogue that refuses any static definition of personality traits or social positioning. As one of my students commented just this past semester, this vital exchange inspires us to think about 'gifting' our weight to one another. That small shift of attitude can create a big change in the buoyancy of the support. The dancing and teaching research that led to the kinds of insights I have been describing is grounded in several decades of improvisa-tional practice, but these acquired skills are not limited to their physical forms. Indeed, over time I have become increasingly curious about the many ways these ideas resonate outside the studio—the 'what if' of movement meeting mind.

As a young scholar, I found that I had to prove that my writing (and by extension dance studies), could have the same academic 'rigor' as any other field of inquiry, espe-cially given the inherent suspicion that academia holds towards bodily ways of knowing. Like many in my position, I spent much of my twenties and thirties shuttling back and forth between dance workshops and academic conferences, worried that I was neither fully a dancer nor fully a scholar. Eventually, a colleague in my writing group (fondly called the Flaming Bitches—but that is another story of improvisation and survival) asked me why I didn't incorporate my focus on contact improvisation into my schol-arly writing. It took a return to professional dancing to finally liberate my imagination enough to pose the question—*what if?* What if I used my dancing to write an academic book? What if I refused the separation of creative activity and critical thinking that is critical to our expectations of academic prose?

It seems to me that academia has traditionally had trouble with conditional state-ments, the 'what if?' instead of the 'what is'. We can mine the past, critique the present, and predict the future, but we are taught to eschew the conditional. 'Define your terms!' is an exhortation we hear again and again. When I first began my doctoral coursework in performance studies at New York University, I was told that I could either dance with a company or write about them, but I couldn't write from the position of dancing. The fear, of course, was that my scholarly objectivity would be compromised if I spent too much time 'inside' rehearsals instead of observing from an appropriate distance and a still body. Interestingly, the first essay I ever published came from my desire to approach an analysis of a dance by way of my embodied experience of improvisation.

'The Mesh in the Mess' was published in the winter 1987 volume of *Contact Quarterly* (and reprinted in *Engaging Bodies: The Politics and Poetics of Corporeality* (2013: 281–287)). Based on a comparative analysis of Pooh Kaye's *Wildfields* (1984) and kids at a local playground, this essay argued that certain activities, such as play, that seem totally chaotic at first glance might in fact have dynamic structuring elements that we adults simply have a hard time perceiving. Inspired by my experiences performing improvisations with the same group of dancers for over a year, I suggested that instead of thinking of choreographic structures as visible forms (a skeleton, a scaffolding, etc.), we might do well to approach structure as a patterning of forces, or a mesh. The essay used studies of play to foreground the ways in which playground activities, choreographed dances, and improvisations all involved moments where various individual and seemingly unconnected movements would distil into an event of group cohesion. I identified kinaesthetic synchrony and movement exchange (including ball passing) as elements of a dynamic structure that disappeared under a chaotic texture only to resurface in moments of spontaneous organization.

Much later in my academic career, I again was inspired to ask 'what if?' What if I used my body to research dance history? What if I were willing to explore the movement techniques of someone whose physicality was rendered historically invisible? The result was my 2007 book on the famous fin-de-siècle dancer Loïe Fuller, *Traces of Light*. I had been thinking about writing a book on Fuller for some time, but it took me awhile to come to terms with how I wanted to respond to the less visible traces of her work. I began with a question: Why do so many critics and historians dismiss the bodily experience of her dancing in their discussions of Fuller's theatrical work? I felt that many scholars covered over the kinaesthetic and material experience of Fuller's body in favour of the image, rather than reading that image as an extension of her dancing. Then, too, there were all those apologies and side notes about how Fuller didn't have a dancer's body, or any dance training really, as if the movement images were solely dependent on the lighting, as if it were all technologically rendered. There was an odd urgency in my response; my whole body revolted with the kinaesthetic knowledge that something else was going on. I first drew on that embodied response to create 'Acts of Passion,' a performance that blended movement and text, with images of Fuller projected onto my spinning body.

The metaphysical conundrum *How is one touched by history?* has, in my case, a very physical complement in my practice of contact improvisation. The meeting point of contact improvisation creates an interconnectedness of weight, momentum, and energy that channels a common destiny. Early on in the research process, I began to think of the physical aspects of my research on Loïe Fuller in terms of a contact improvisation duet. My body was influenced by her dancing as I imagined how she must have used her spine, her head, her chest. When I was spinning with my arms raised high and my head thrown back, historical descriptions of Fuller laid up in bed with excruciating pain and ice packs on her upper back begin to make sense as I literally incorporated into my body some aspects of the physical tolls her nightly performances must have incurred. I realized that Fuller most likely slipped a disc in her cervical spine. Even on an intellectual or metaphysical level, I thought of our interaction as a contact improvisation duet, a somatic meeting set up by the traces of history. I believe that envisioning this relation in terms of an improvisational duet helped to redefine the traditional separation of historical subject (treated as the 'object' of study) and omniscient writer of history.

By 2010, when I published my next monograph, *Modern Gestures,* on Isadora Duncan, and a collection of writings on contact improvisation, *Encounters with Contact,* I had fully committed myself to a practice of scholarship that included my embodied experience as part of an improvisational exchange between reading, writing, and dancing. My most recent book, *How to Land: Finding Ground in an Unstable World,* continues to play back and forth between these improvised spaces of thought and motion, for I am determined to keep both modalities of inquiry available in my life as well as my work. This new book looks at how corporeal experiences are connected to both our personal and public constructions of meaning. Thinking about the generation of students who have grown up in a post-9/11 environment, I asked: How are our bodies affected by images of falling buildings, falling bodies, and descriptions of falling economies or falling governments? I posit this question both in order to underline the importance of embodied experience in constructing theories of cultural meaning and because I want to think seriously about the somatic practices that might help a younger generation (such as my students) survive (and potentially revise) these pervasive cultural metaphors of things falling apart.

I want now to turn to an even more personal arena where I have found my improvisational practice to be particularly useful in navigating moments of crisis: that of my extended family. On the Tuesday after Labor Day in the waning summer of 2008, my elder brother called me. This was highly unusual, since most often I was the one to keep up any semblance of a sibling relationship. John had been plagued by an annoying hernia, which was keeping him from working at his seasonal job waterproofing basements. I had sent him the money to have it fixed, and it was during the pre-op testing that they found the erratic blood sugar levels that eventually led to a diagnosis of pancreatic cancer. In the eight months between that call and the day my brother died, I embarked on an exhausting routine of teaching in Ohio during the week and then driving seven hours to Pennsylvania to care for him and his fifteen-year-old son over the weekend, returning to my place and work late Sunday night.

The first time I walked into his house, I found a sink filled with every dish and pot in the household, no working drains, sewage backed up in the basement, a year's worth of unopened mail, and my brother and his son sleeping on bare mattresses. By the next afternoon, I had organized one set of plumbers who were digging up the side yard and another set who were working in the house to fix the drainage problems. I had also made the first of many trips to Home Depot as well as Bed Bath & Beyond. Duly shaken by his diagnosis, my brother was, at first, deeply grateful for my help and cooperative about planning for the future of his son. As the months passed, however, he would periodically cycle back to his abusive and belligerent self, hiding his emotions under a thick blanket of denial and refusing to deal with his increasingly addicted son, whom I had agreed to adopt.

My brother was seven years older than I was, and while we were more friendly as we got older and both had kids, there was little real communication between us. Over the course of his illness, this tall husky man aged thirty years and went from weighing 235 to 107 pounds. By the end of his life, I was picking him up from the couch and carrying him to the bathroom, supporting him while I pulled down his underpants, lowered him to the toilet and helped him clean himself afterwards. Clearly, this is the kind of deep physical intimacy and emotional complexity for which there is no script. Somehow, despite our history, I was able to walk into his house each weekend to meet the situation at hand. The openness with which I operated in the moment completely dumbfounded me and contradicted every known family scenario to date. Over the course of his devastating illness, my brother and I somehow cut through our differences (I read Jane Austen, he read *Playboy*) to form a sibling bond that absolutely confounded our own expectations about who we were to one another.

While my discussion of this experience may, at first, sound unbelievably Zen, I want to suggest that surviving this familial moment had less to do with my Buddhist nature and much more to do with my improvisational dance practice. The emphasis on sense perception and physical touch in contact improvisation, as well as the psychic training to release expectations about what the next dance will be like, allowed me to keep feeling at the level of an ongoing experience rather than turning my feelings into a static emotional state. Like practice, 'feeling' can be both a verb and a noun. Its meanings span the gamut from the strictly material to the highly cerebral. It can be used to describe a physical sensation (I feel something sticky), an intellectual perception (I have a feeling that), or an emotive state (feeling blue). 'Feeling' can refer to both the surface of the body and the interior self. But as 'feeling' moves from a verb to a noun, it can take on the weight of emotional baggage. I want to argue that my years of working with physical improvisation gave me the option of experiencing my feeling as a bodily sensation (I am feeling) rather than eliding those feelings as a possession (I have feelings). Although it may seem simplistic, the ability to be available to the experience of affect and sensation (especially uncomfortable sensations) without solidifying that experience into an emotion requires a studious willingness to live with a certain amount of ambiguity. Keeping feeling in the present tense allowed me to release a complicated history with my brother that might have kept me from truly being connected to the dying man in front of me.

I believe that there is a deep interconnectedness between how we move through the world and how we think about it. The kind of cognitive flexibility that I have been describing has taught me how to deal with the inevitable complications of contemporary life. The potency of my improvisational practice lies in understanding how to encourage a willingness to experience discomfort, to keep moving without a clear goal. At its best, improvisation refuses the bifurcated realms of creative activity and critical inquiry, home and work, pain and pleasure, love and hate, allowing us to feel 'otherwise'. The improvisation courses that I teach are primarily built on developing technical skills that enable a conscious engaged dancing with one another. From time to time, however, I find myself giving brief expositions detailing the connections between a particular movement practice and its implications in our daily lives. Many of the themes I have outlined so far in this essay are entry points for such discussions. For instance, the experience of opening the pores of one's skin to the world can lead to a conversation about how selfhood is defined, about questions of power and subjectivity, gendered notions of penetration and receptivity, and cultural discourses surrounding disease and contagion.

Given the politicization of police brutality in America during the fall of 2014 and the resultant 'Black Lives Matter' campaign, I found myself returning again and again over those months to a distinction between cultivating a responsive body and engaging a reactive one. As part of a burst of radical fervour sweeping the campus late in the se- mester, some students in the Dance Department put forth a list of demands and sent it to the administration. The tone was strident, the concerns were all-encompassing (curriculum, staffing, and issues with the physical plant), and the line between pro- gressive collective action and a strident self-righteousness got pretty thin as other students were bullied over social media into signing the letter. As chair of my depart- ment, I found myself in the dean's office soon afterwards. Before beginning to discuss the students' actions, I showed him one of my favourite aikido exercises. This is one I use all the time in classes to demonstrate the difference between responsiveness and reactiveness. Facing a partner, one person extends their arm to the partner's shoulder. The partner tries to 'break' that arm by putting pressure on the inside of the elbow in order to bend it. The one extending their arm tries to resist, most often right at the place of most pressure. It is hard work and serves to illustrate how futile it is to resist only at the place of pressure. Instead, I offer an alternative method as I show the stu- dents how to energize their arms through space, imagining their arms as hoses with water shooting out of both ends. The palpable result is that they find how easy it is to keep one's arms from bending if one extends across the point of pressure rather than resisting it. For me, this is an example of how to stay responsive in the midst of a crisis, how to be available to dealing with the students' concerns without becoming reac- tionary or defensive in the moment of pressure. I felt as if the dean understood this experience when I demonstrated it to him, and I found out later that he showed it to others later that day.

I have titled this chapter 'Life Practices', not 'Life Lessons', because even though I am an increasingly old fart, I am not interested in teaching anyone specific lessons about life—either mine or theirs. Nonetheless, I do believe there is a pedagogical value to understanding the importance of improvisational practices for living in this unpredictable world. I want to embrace, maybe even celebrate, the potential of these practices to vibrate between states of knowing and not knowing. Like so many of the concepts I am drawn to, including *pro*duce (pro*duce*), practice is both a noun and a verb. Yet there is an intriguing tension between these two uses of the word. I find that whenever I attempt to define my practice, it slips out of my grasp, leaving me with the trace of an experience that only exists in my ongoing efforts to describe it. I like that elusiveness, for it pushes me to replace my ambition to codify the 'what is?' with a curiosity about the 'what if?' For me, the practice implicated in that question is something to live for.

REFERENCES

Ahmed, Sara. (2006) *Queer Phenomenology*. Durham, NC: Duke University Press.

Albright, Ann Cooper. (2013) *Engaging Bodies: The Politics and Poetics of Corporeality*. Middletown, CT: Wesleyan University Press.

Smith, Nancy Stark. (1979). Editor's Note. *Contact Quarterly* 5 (1): 3.

_____. (1987) Editor's Note. *Contact Quarterly* 12(2): 3.

CHAPTER 2

ETHICO-AESTHETIC PRACTICE OF IMPROVISING

Relations through Motion

FIONA BANNON

□□□

moving through provisional thought filled scores
offers opportunities for distillation

In the process we move away from a
singularity, of an autonomous 'I'
and towards a social reality of *resolutions*, a
subjective being in an objectively viewed world

(Bannon and Holt 2013)

THE intention in the following discussion is to explore the ethical practice that is arguably emerging in the work of a range of practitioners who are investigating the generation of knowledge through movement-based improvisation. The aim is to establish an argument for considering ethics as an identifying feature of the practice of embodiment. This idea alludes to practice that maintains a sense of complementarity whilst being aligned with relations that are generated through individual 'bodily-dwelling'. Beginning from the premise that our bodies are 'our centre of activity in the world' (Schenck 1986: 44), the discussion considers the significant contributions that physicalized experiences make to the ways we each express ourselves. With this said, it is important to remain aware of the continuing inadequacies of our reinforced habits of thinking, where our cultural tradition resists any change in the idea that each of us lives as selves divided; between body and mind.

In considering the ethical potential of relations made in and through movement, the discussion includes incidences where we might utilize experience of spatial location and interaction, and where ideas might be generated through a nexus of rational and emotional responses. Ultimately it is our facility to persevere in terms of exploring co-incidences of experience that informs our approaches to personal practice, and to the practice of working with others. This may not be considered anything new, for arguably dance has always been concerned with situated spatial relations. What is perhaps distinct is the attentive consideration for mingling affective and cognitive relations in terms of experience found moving together. What can be recognized is that within an extending range of practice, the previously reinforced distinctions between choreographer and performer, or between performers and audiences, are collapsing and that the affect of social intermingling experienced in 'doing performance' is becoming a source of attention.

SHIFTING TO A SOCIAL FOCUS

Included in these attentions are the considerations given to the nature of the labour involved in performance creation, with particular respect given to collectivity, dialogue, and embodied interaction. These approaches towards the creation of work are significant when considered in terms of identifying collaborative practice. This heightening of attention to what are social relations is not new for those of us who live and work as dancing persons. This is particularly the case for those familiar with the politics of the participatory arts practice evidenced in the British 'New Dance' of the 1970s, where practitioners—including Mary Prestidge, Fergus Early, and Jacky Lansley—explored ways to realize bodily languages in order to renew art making through nonhierarchic movement strategies.

A similar debate intertwining social, political, aesthetic, and ethical affect has surfaced during the last ten years, shifting the focus to the manner of intent in terms of the making of performance. In a range of current practice, focus more readily shifts towards concern for modes of collaboration, giving specific attention to the labour involved in such collective endeavours. This 'new' situation may well have evolved from the earlier challenges to authorship in terms of what identifies a dance work.

However, it is engagement with mutuality, and complementarity, that now occupies a significant place in terms of an investment in individual and shared improvisational practice. Arguably the shift can be traced through a direction of theorizing by Georgio Agamben, where he addresses ethics in terms of our individual potential to determine our futures. Agamben argues that 'the only ethical experience ... is the experience of being (one's own) potentiality, of being (one's own) possibility' (1993: 43). What we might appreciate from this stance, in terms of human 'becomings', is awareness of the benefits found by investing in joint activity, wherein we might come to recognize the wealth of opportunity to be revealed in social coexistence. In terms of experiments in performance making, there has been an increase in examples of performance that prioritizes the live exploration of what we can recognise as social scores. Examples include performance works including, *These Associations,* by Tino Seghal (2012); *Schreibstuck* (2002) and *Functionen* (2004) by Thomas Lehmen; and the documentary film work entitled, *Vera Mantero: Let's Talk about It Now* (2011). In these examples there is evident impetus to move away from a previous materialist drive that sought to exhibit form, fostering instead a recognition of the singularities of practice each performer brings to the work as a gradual, accumulations of shared possibilities.

In terms of improvisation-based practice and the communities of movers involved, we might do well to follow the idea of apprenticeships favoured by philosopher Gemma Fiumara, in which she argues for the importance of the role our emotions play in our reasoning processes and structures of mind. She argues that 'if we were apprentices of listening rather than masters of discourse we might perhaps promote a different sort of coexistence among humans: not so much in the form of a utopian ideal but rather as an incipient philosophical solidarity capable of envisaging the common destiny of the species' (1990: 57). In terms of such relational and dialogic encounters being realized, the two practitioners discussed later in this chapter make evident the ways in which their processes of handling ideas embrace objective rationality without suppressing their affective emotions or feelings. For choreographer and performer Elizabeth Waterhouse, the experience of working with The Forsythe Company has shaped her consequent practice, in which she works *amidst* ideas with others and where subsequent solutions or responses are found together. Similarly, though working in the field of research and educational theory, Antionette Oberg (2008) fosters what she calls 'inquiry-without-method'. For Oberg this entails working with individuals to unravel and identify their own significant questions for investigation. Her process favours finding ways to work that are suited to the particular instance and purpose, not through the repetition of methods and answers prescribed by previously sanctioned outcomes.

These practitioners and the others mentioned through the chapter represent and echo the sentiment from Fiumara that to value rationality is to appreciate that it 'is not a matter of detached theorizing, but rather a caring way of being rational or searching for rational ways of caring' (2001: 22). If, when improvising, we give little heed to what is happening around us and indeed within us, then we are not open to the potential shifts in our attitudes and understanding; we are not improvising. Both Waterhouse and Oberg, though interestingly working in different fields, seem to focus on delving into ways that might foster fluid, co-creative practice. In so doing they acknowledge the shared responsibilities involved in making socially informed artistic responses, in which emerging ideas become the effective co-creations of material thinking. Such works when made 'in-common' help to promote a view that acknowledges how we each affect and are affected by circumstance. In what feels to be something of a groundswell of apprenticeships by dance practitioners who choose to explore such realms of relational interaction, there is a widening field of sociopolitical debate that questions the idea of in-dependence and co-dependence and echoes the lead from Fiumara in terms of our sharing a 'common destiny'.

Other examples of practice evidencing explorations in this realm can be found in the work of Meg Stuart and Damaged Goods (Peeters 2010); 'artistwin'; deufert&plischke; and the work of social choreographer Michael Klien. These practitioners investigate the social potential of movement improvisation and choreographic encounters in ways that recognize being-together, whether in solo, duet, or group forms. In giving attention to the *in-between* and to the *not-yet* that informs this generative practice resides a potential for renewed understanding in terms of our appreciation for *being-with* others. This reflects a particular stance in terms of ethics as lived experience. These encounters guide us to consider our own ethical position in terms of the ways in which we are available to and identified by our working practice and how we each relate to those with whom we work.

A TURN TO ETHICS

With the intention to realize ethics in practice, as a merging of cocreation, complementarity, and dialogue, it is useful to recognize that when we make reference to ethics, the tendency is often to conjure a series of prohibiting rules that can offer little more than constraint as a form of control. This approach tends to compartmentalize ethics as a trait of culturally enforced behaviour that itself can become part of an implicit, often unexamined background activity. The intention here is to offer an alternate view, fed by the impression that an ostensibly straightforward adherence to prescribed rules can undermine the enrichment that could be found if we were to attend more fully to the effect and affect of relations through ethics. In agreement with cultural theorist Sara Ahmed (2000) it would be more beneficial to think that ethics concerns the ways we each accommodate encounters with others and, more specifically, 'how one can live with what cannot be measured by the regulative force of morality' (138). With ethics being both a subject of philosophical inquiry and a physical way of being-in-the-world, it is worth investigating the ways in which experience found in improvising can enrich our appreciation of social and self-knowledge.

In tracing the etymology of the term *ethics*, we find *ethos* as a reference to concern for our moral character or habit. The idea of *habit* in this context encompasses the repetition of certain traits and attitudes that when brought together foreshadow ideas about what constitutes individual character. In this there is a potential worth to be found in a model of *virtue ethics,* with attention given to the situation(s) wherein we may each find ourselves at any given time. In this way emphasis leads to the ethical sense present in the negotiation of any subsequent situation or dilemma, utilizing an individual's facility to reflect on dialogues as a form of engagement. This approach may in turn go some way in helping us avoid substantiating the critique of Wolfgang Iser in his paradoxical observation that 'human beings have … become unavailable to themselves; we are but do not know what it is to be' (2000: 155–156).

In terms of the experience of improvising, it is important to consider how we relate to difference, variability, chance, interactivity, vulnerability, and power. Learning to dwell-in and rehearse ways to suspend the rush to control or to declare premature solutions implies learning to extend the possibilities inherent in any situation and thereby cultivate sensitivity by identifying with 'ethical generosity and sensitivity (Bennett 2001: 3).

Whilst improvising in a dialogic relation with others can, at times feel like a loss of personal autonomy, it is in such liminal experiences that we source ideas to feed forward in *doing theory*. What becomes evident in such situations is the importance of engaging with the possibilities afforded by a realm of the 'not-yet-known'. Whilst it can at times be an experience of discomfort, something we might prefer to avoid, it is worth remembering the comment made by Deleuze that 'everybody knows very well that in fact men think rarely and more often under the impulse of a shock than in the examination of a taste for thinking' (1995: 132). In receptive approaches to improvising we can access lucid thinking and find responses in-common. When engaged in doing-theory we are engaged in exploring the possibilities of thinking through ideas, without rushing to decisions, and in the process are learning to savour a taste for thinking. Carolyn Ellis (2006) takes this a step further, identifying *relational ethics* as a way to acknowledge our interpersonal bonds whilst taking responsibility for our actions and their consequences. Taken together, these ideas are helpful in identifying an ethical stance that acknowledges the need to deal with reality, as it is experienced. This is an attitude towards ethics that resonates with the idea of fostering a nonexploitative environment, which is a facilitating feature of working in many areas of improvisation.

Through the work of Ahmed, Bennett, and Ellis, there are traces of the philosophical thinking of Baruch Spinoza. What I have found in his works is further support for the practice of relational ethics. In terms of improvisation, this relates to intentionally focusing on what we should do and how we should respond in respect to any given situation or decided action. Spinoza embraces social contexts as political arenas in which we each move between being singular selves and social beings. What becomes evident is that we need to recognize that we live and experience as 'beings' in common. How we each consider ways to live in such relations contributes to our evolving ethical identities. Through his work Spinoza disrupts any illusions of fixity or of there being one existing self over time. Instead we each change, and are changed, through a multiplicity of engagements, which are themselves made evident in our everyday practice of being in relation. Spinoza's argument centres on the notion that every emotional and/or intellectual state is evidenced in the body, for body is what we are and our minds are an idea of our body.

To appreciate relations found through ethics in this context, we need to pay attention to the potential of what we can each achieve in any given situation. This in turn resides within a state that encompasses both the power to affect and to be affected; a merging of consciousness and corporeality. For Deleuze and Guattari, what becomes evident is that if we do not have the facility to give due care and attention to our 'sitatuatedness', we will remain in the position of each having little awareness of our own or our shared capacities. Their clear argument is that 'we know nothing about a body until we know what it can do, in other words, what its affects are, how they can or cannot enter into composition with other affects, with the affects of another body, either to destroy that body or to be destroyed by it, either to exchange actions and passions with it or to join with it in composing a more powerful body' (Deleuze and Guattari 2004: 284).

In Massumi's (2003) readings of both Spinoza and Deleuze and Guattari, we see Massumi emphasizing the call for individuals to work together in the hope of more fully understanding what it means to be in shared situations at any given time. That ethics, in this sense, 'happens in *between* people, in the social gaps.... The ethical value of an action is what it brings out *in* the situation, *for* its transformation, how it breaks sociality open. Ethics is about how we inhabit uncertainty, together' (7). With Spinoza championing such interconnectedness, and Deleuze and Guattari emphasizing the need to understand what is an affective power to act, we can begin to recognize human experience as something indivisible from the world: that it is something that is with the world. Acknowledging this argument as a foundation for relations found through ethics opens the possibility of further exploring the place of ethics in the practice of movement-based improvisation.

With the evident importance of 'dialogue' within these relationships, new opportunities to investigate being-in-common can lead to enhancing our sense of fulfilment in terms of human potential. From philosopher, theologian, and pedagogue Martin Buber, there is further insight to be found through our being in-relation. He argues that individuals develop and realize the complexity of their personalities through the relationships they develop with other people, with their environment, and with their spiritual beings (which, he suggests, are as experiences of art). In the existence of such 'dialogue' resides wholeness in an understanding of self, arguably the only place from which to engage with others. This stance promotes the idea that it is through self-knowledge that we relate to others rather than through what may be the more fashionable idea of identifying with the experiences of others first (Buber 1958; Haim 1986).

Ethics Found in Improvising

Improvisation recognized as a form of material investigation now utilizes a range of approaches to devising, as it gradually shifts from the margins of dance learning to being a central feature of experimental choreographic practice. Into this scenario, the argument for an ethics of participatory practice wherein relations between aesthetics, sociality, and political ideals coalesce might be realized. What is significant here is that it is practice that sustains the accumulations of experience, with practitioners often engaged with context-rich relations that are explicitly ethical encounters. In such scenarios, the ongoing production of self is aligned with continuous coproduction in terms of individuals being-with others. In these social structures in which we live, learn, and thrive resides an inevitably of encounter. It is a situation where we learn to recognize interconnections *amidst* ever-evolving complexities. Rabinow (1997: xix) acknowledges a similar line of thinking in reference to work by Foucault, who argued that we should more fully appreciate that 'who one is ... emerges acutely out of the problems with which one struggles'. In light of this, it might be suggested that it is perhaps more valuable to forge practice that attends to all manner of experience than to restrain exploration to any predicted outcome. More usefully we might acknowledge that in improvisation there is the opportunity to work in a place of continuous formation without the need to conceive of an end. With this focus, we might foster ways in which we each relate through ongoing processes of learning that are not fixed, singular events but instead are realized as multiple iterations of 'ideas'. As Foucault argues, and many of us know from experience found in improvising, 'the challenge is not to replace one certitude (evidence) with another but to cultivate an attention to the conditions under which things become "evident," ceasing to be objects of our attention and therefore seemingly fixed, necessary, and unchangeable' (quoted in Rabinow 1997: xix). In these ways, attention can be given to the local conditions in which one lives and works and the consequences made evident through the continuous changes that ensue during engagement with each other and our ideas. Discussion later in the chapter illustrates this point through the work of Elizabeth Waterhouse, who as a former member of The Forsythe Company has written a series of reflective evaluations of her experience of being embedded within a distinct group and process of making work.

The affective challenges explored in this approach to work include the attentive interplay that exists between rhythm, movement, and spatial design for participants as they create responses in shared contexts. In this sphere and under the banner of a democratic process, such work comes to gradually reveal a collaborative community realizing outcomes together, through what Ruth Zaporah might identify as a 'present mindedness' (1995: 130).

Through this manner of practice, attention is given to sharing a deepening discipline that respects the changing identity of investigative craft. To evolve such engagement requires time being-in-practice, which in turn enhances responses to stimuli and contexts drawn from individual resources and circumstance. It concerns affective dialogue, forged in 'conversations' about the ways in which ideas evolve in movement and in language. This is akin to what an increasing number of movement explorers identify as being *amidst* a living context of art making. It involves a loosening of self-consciousness in favour of evolving something of a differently shared consciousness. In this we might recognize an intertwining of live creation whilst working in association with different artists. It is a fascinating and compelling arena in which there is opportunity for each to engage with changing states of 'being embodied'. Similarities in terms of practice can be traced across experiences of a range of practitioners interested in exploring the potential of reversals in terms of what Bojana Cvejic (2009: n.p.) identifies as 'the economy of ownership and distribution in terms of art products'.

IMPROVISATION: CODETERMINED NIMBLE THINKING

Through an interrelational focus, where participants negotiate in a context of 'an ethical economy of exchange' (Williams 1996), attention is given to the ways in which relatedness might be revealed. Understanding the consequences of how 'movers' engage with such 'potential to knowledge' is probably the most significant thing to learn and to share as a practitioner and teacher. Working through improvisation and collaboration can reveal the value of evolving a deep sense of personal discipline. Through this it is possible to realize that we come to be in relational dialogue, informed by the nexus of aesthetic acuity and ethical sensitivity. Arguably it is through recognition of this inter-weaving of perception and affective response that the emergence of what we can recog-nise as mindful-motion is experienced. This is, after all, where greater attention is given to an intermingling of expertise and connoisseurship. The process inevitably revolves around our abilities to notice and to respond, thereby finding ways to reason through the multiple trajectories that become available and ultimately to articulating resolutions in terms of nuance and affect. Outcomes can include more subtly felt thinking that is realized as a reflexive orchestration of our relations with ideas and with others. For it is movement that shapes consciousness, veined with aesthetic awareness, relational ethics, and critical reflexivity. Where allowed, practice that at times might be deemed chaotic and ambiguous ultimately facilitates coherence and validity. It takes time to learn to sus-pend the deeply embedded rush to answers about how to think or how to move. It takes time to come to recognize the rich benefit to be found in an intertwining of rich, varied speculations and their unknown outcomes.

Forging relations through knowledge making in this way is something that is emer-gent and illuminated through what are sometimes messy and irrational searches for ideas. For writer-artist Emma Cocker (2013: 127) the very situation exhibits per-ceived value, in terms of artistic practices that move towards exploring the realm of not knowing, something she refers to as a 'desirable indeterminacy'. Arguably such moments of flux can be recognized at the very points where new ideas are realized, emerging as a response to new situations that have not previously been experienced. In these terms Cocker reminds us that not-knowing can arrive, unannounced, 'as a space of fleeting liberty or reprieve; a brief interlude of potentiality flanked either side by what is certain' (130). What we need to recognize here is that in the process of being open to not knowing, we enter a transitional state, where we call knowledge into question. It is where what we think we know becomes unsettled by the very act of our unknowing.

In the course of complex movement improvisations, the manner in which we relate to one another will come to frame the incremental changes in our understandings. These fluctuations are constituted by the influx of the 'other', to follow Whitehead's notion of folding our past experiences with our present, towards our future, yet to be known. Equally we might frame this complex realm of individual engagement as 'idea-logics', to borrow a phrase used by William Forsythe via the worlds of design and business man-agement. These ideas insinuate ecology as mindful-motion, recognizing that there is value to be found in keeping things indefinite. The ideas follow a trajectory sketched from Brian Massumi's response to the choreographic explorations of Forsythe, reading Whitehead; all talking of experiences of enlivened space. It is interesting that Forsythe, when speaking of his own working process, identifies his need to learn to allow him-self to 'not know', to practise being frightened and, in the process, to acknowledge the power of being affected by ideas. For as performance theorist Bojana Cvejic suggests in trying to capture dance, it 'works as a metaphor for going beyond contracts, systems, structures, as models of theorizing subjectivity, art, society, and politics … movement operates in the middle of things.… *[It]* expresses the potential of moving relations' (2004: n.p.).

Improvisation evidently can facilitate the exploration of collective thinking in ways that include how we as individuals cope with task-based activities. Indeed, for many, such explorations of everyday interactivity are the materials for performance work itself. Each engagement may start from a given impetus, evolving through the use of less formally agreed mechanisms and towards a yet-undetermined outcome. In what has effectively been a change of attitude towards working processes, products, and the reasons why we might think it beneficial to engage in the first place, philosopher Bojana Kunst alludes to imagining performance itself as something that is open and ongoing. She speaks of 'a continuation of disclosure of lesser acts, acts which do not end in their own finalization, a kind of active present that is intertwined with the unrealized thought of the real' (2009: n.p.). If we accept performance on these terms, improvisation could usefully be seen as a social common, where fluctuations in attention, cooperation, and divergent vocabularies extend the logics of our creative response, and offer us an ensemble of relations through which we might compose.

THE LIVING CONTEXT OF ART MAKING

In her insightful reflections on working as part of the Forsythe Company, Waterhouse (2010: 153) shares experiences that resonate with ideas outlined by Kunst. Waterhouse refers to what she calls 'the living context of … art making' realized by a company who generate performances as a collective of individuals, intertwining both their lives and their dancing. What is revealed is consideration of the potential friction felt by dancers as they encounter each other during improvisations and in their ordinary daily living. What then becomes evident is how this resonates with what she refers to as a 'positive regard to difference'. It is something she feels to be an active phenomenon that arguably holds the company and performance works together. The ideas seem similar to those shared by Elizabeth Ellsworth (2005: 4), who when talking of the drive towards learning experiences asserts that we should consider ourselves to be 'continuously and radically in relation with the world, with others, and with what we can make of them'.

Gradually in the writing a sense of spatial relatedness unfolds. What becomes evident is that apprehending the energetic influence of proximity that operates between individuals, performances, and locations makes a significant difference to the 'codetermining relationship' of working collectively. In terms of explicit and implicit engagement with ethics, what appears most pertinent is the honing of an appreciation for cooperation as a working ethos, particularly when realized as an embodied process of being in relation. It is not about becoming the same people in terms of performance. It is about learning to understand yourself and those you work alongside, taking time to work amidst a range of possibilities that can be felt to be both cohesive and particular. Waterhouse ponders ways that space can be understood as a device to explore relationships of mind, of self, of world, and of community. Ultimately, she argues, choreographic space is a human phenomenon of meaning making in action. Through this manner of engagement with what is a distinct working process, as individuals and as community, the company establishes a communal space that in turn affords further creative investigations. It is in this way that 'meaning is created. It lives amidst spatial coordinates' (Waterhouse 2010: 154).

The complexity of the work involved in learning to recognize varied connections between people becomes evident. Her preference seems to be to talk of 'dancing *amidst*' as an adopted reference to the work of Merleau-Ponty's, 'being of the world'. In this she seeks to clarify her position by arguing that 'to dance amidst implies in the middle of (space) and during (time). Amidst space imbricates space with people (culture), objects (tools), buildings (architectures), and history (events in time)' (Waterhouse 2010: 163). What becomes clear is that sensitivity to the force of spatial dynamics forges connections between individuals. In this there are echoes of Merleau-Ponty speaking of our being of the world, an arena in which we can each coexist without closed boundaries. It is the outcomes of our shared spatial relations that establish the designs and decisions we recognize as performance and that offer windows onto further, future meaning making. The approach relates well with what Nicholas Ridout (2011) refers to as being in a state of 'constant becoming', such that learning to work and to relate offers the potential to nurture engagement through deep investment in human potential. For Waterhouse, dancing is an activity of her whole self, such that the articulation of complex movement resides within a cultural ecosystem. Dancing includes what she refers to as learning to multitask her attention and concentration into 'observing/feedback and anticipation/feed-forward' (2010: 161), a phrase reminiscent of comments made by Steve Paxton, who in referring to his own experience of making art speaks of finding ways to 'knead his thinking' (quoted in T'Jonck 2011: 19).

The attitudes of other practitioners working across a range of fields resonate with these ideas. For example, Antionette Oberg (Chambers 2004), working in the field of educational research and supervision, talks of adopting an approach to investigative and generative learning as 'inquiry without-method'. Effective processes involve churning dialogue through questions about a 'not yet imagined' interest. What becomes evident in the process is a meeting of creativity, artistry, and scholarly endeavour working as a unifying experience.

Similar imaginative processes can be found in the open source performance *Generique*, which is part of the score container in everybodystoolbox. The score elicits opportunity to create a collective postperformance review of a 'not yet presented' performance. What is perhaps most vibrant here is the sense of emergence; that through a process—not of forcing but of 'waiting' and lingering—we might learn to ask questions differently. In the process of exploring method itself, we become part of a reciprocal process that enriches our awareness. It is something quite different from addressing the known or making attempts to prove or disprove in terms of closed answers. Grosz's comment that 'artworks are not so much to be read, interpreted, deciphered as [to be] responded to, touched, engaged, intensified' (2008: 79) is significant here in terms of how we might strive to persevere in our relations and interconnective motivations. With these thoughts in mind, what seems to be important and valuable, in terms of the ethico-aesthetic acuity that is to be honed in improvising, is that we come to understand ourselves, as sensing, thinking, social, and responsible persons.

Whilst embarking on a quest to find words to talk of rich yet illogical processes that are found in improvising may run counter to the practice for some, we may find that in the process of improvising, virtuosity can be revealed by the very waywardness of such a 'fascination'. Blanchot proposes what we might recognize as 'a non-methodological method of progressing [that can] speak from the experience of the artist and an aesthetic that is [foremost] unengaged with the will-to-knowledge' (quoted in Peters 2003: n.p.). Here we find support for a way of sharing ideas about experience that continue rather than complete that experience. For Garry Peters, who references Blanchot in relation to his own work in music improvisation, the importance of this proposal is the call for a mode of engagement that is 'insistent in its sustained articulation of the neutrality of the work'. He references this as he moves to identify what Blanchot considers 'non-systematic coherence (Blanchot 1993: 140). In this, Blanchot alludes to the idea that it is the work of the work to reveal without rushing to answers, or indeed to completions. Instead the work comes to be identified with fragmentary modes of thought and experience that move through and along theoretical perspectives in search of order that can be provisionally affirmed rather than confirmed. These thoughts resonate with comments by choreographer Boris Charmatz, who calls for a new virtuosity, something he sees not as a means to display technical agility or bodies saturated in codified languages but as a continuum of dynamic forces moving between mastery and ordinary ability. Following his argument, it is the potential of action that is key to the experience, for 'what we actually *see* is no thing or action extra ordinary; instead, what we feel is a person or action rife with potential, full of vitality and force that isn't actually visible but sensed. We sense the potential for something extraordinary. We *sense* . . . our own capacity or potential toward ourselves becoming *other*' (cited in Durning 2011: 89–90).

IMPROVISATION AND PATTERNING RELATIONSHIPS

Integrating rhythms and dynamics of our individual and shared experiences entails negotiation and compromise in facilitating reciprocal engagements. In turn, this generates 'foldings' of our sensory somatic selves, such that our histories, experience, ideas, and fabrications can be felt to intertwine. Through experiences found in improvising, we can access bodily-idea-logics that exist between our senses, contexts, interpretation, and relations and in turn embrace an ethico-aesthetic paradigm: a life-world lived in a fluid sense of moments (Guattari 1995). Through this emerge opportunities to realize our sensual, intellectual, emotional, and responsible selves as unitary experience. In adopting this attitude to engagement with improvisation, we might emphasize the inherent virtuosity to be found in fluidly intertwining memory, facility, and adaptability, drawing as we do on a sense of the 'immediate', and of the uncertainties of a future, a yet-to-be-known.

By embracing this trajectory, we might eclipse the continued appropriation of improvisation as 'skilling' in terms of repertory display and thereby bypass 'the danger of creating improvisational clones' (Paxton 1995). For as Blanchot suggests, improvisation may well be tamed as it slides into 'the tranquil discursive continuity' (1993: 8) of so-called evidence-based assessment outcomes inside institutional frameworks. What if the drive could be to generate 'arti-*facts*—crafted *facts* of experience … experiential potentials brought to evolutionary expression' (Massumi 2008: 18)? With Guattari speaking of the need to draw ethics and aesthetics together because of the degeneration of the very fabric of our social awareness, it is evident that experience gained improvising in collective collaborative practices has a contribution to make to 'a new art of living in society' (2006: 20).

Guattari's talk of the need for change in the ways we live and respond to each other and to the world are sentiments he shares through his work in 'chaosmosis' (1992). The furrow is rich and pertinent in terms of engagement with improvisation, where once again we find the wisdom that it is our relationality through ethics that informs embodied cocreation. Guattari reminds us that 'our survival on this planet is not only threatened by environmental damage but by a degeneration in the fabric of social solidarity and in the modes of psychical life, which must literally be reinvented.… The only acceptable finality of human activity is the production of a subjectivity that is auto enriching its relation to the world in a continuous fashion' (2006: 20–21). Improvisation can facilitate an approach to working and learning that is deliberately experimental, deliberately provisional. In terms of the production of material, for many practitioners the sense is of being immersed in a state that is *in-between*, that is speculative. This is an environment where nomadism can facilitate the emergence of a range of possibilities; where affordances are stimulated and made tangible through engaging with the potentials found in shared action and response. Whilst for many a will to seek structural form remains paramount, it is interesting to acknowledge the ways in which creative investigation has come to be embraced more openly. We now see practice that engages with more diverse social practice and that generates thinking through encounters with what is as yet unknown.

In exploring ways to recognize relations formed through ethics as a constitutive feature of movement-based improvisation, we can acknowledge the creative opportunities afforded by giving attention to ethics as something more than the operation of agreed moral codes. In the process, what becomes apparent is a frame of reference that addresses the multiplicity of encounters that also affect and inform our everyday relations in motion. Working in varied forms of improvisation means embracing experiences of working with others in which we each contribute to the realization of shared ideas. This, in turn, affects how we interact in the ongoing negotiation of ourselves both as productive artists and as social, responsive, and responsible persons. In creating elegantly designed frameworks through which to view experience, comprehend ambiguity, appreciate profundity, and enact our essential interconnectedness, we can come to practise a mindful means towards understanding and cohesion that extends 'thought, stretches the mind, and leads us into new and uncharted territory' (Diffey 1986: 11). Within this arena, it is the ability of individuals to function within a series of social and self-regulating processes that offers significance in terms of an evolving ethico-aesthetic practice.

REFERENCES

Agamben, G. (1993). *The Coming Community (Theory Out of Bounds)*. Trans. Michael Hardt. Minneapolis: University of Minnesota Press.

Ahmed, S. (2000). *Strange Encounters: Embodies Others Is Post-Coloniality*. London: Routledge.

Bannon, F., and Holt, D. (2013) Contemplating the Underscore. Unpublished.

Bennett, J. (2001) *The enchantment of modern life*. Princeton: Princeton University Press.

Blanchot, M. (1993) *The Infinite Conversation*. Trans. S. Hanson. Minneapolis: University of Minneapolis Press.

Buber, M. (1958) *I and Thou*. Trans. R. G. Smith. New York: Scribners.

Chambers, C. (2004) Antoinette Oberg: A Real Teacher … and an Organic but Not So Public Intellectual … *Journal of the Canadian Association for Curriculum Studies* 2(1): 245–260.

Charmatz, B. (2009) New Virtuosity. http://www.theoldbrandnew.nl/virtuosity.html. Accessed 9 February 2015.

Cocker, E. (2013) Tactics for Not Knowing: Preparing for the Unexpected. In Fisher, E., and Fortnum, R. (eds.), *On Not Knowing How Artists Think*. London: Black dog publishing, 126–135.

Cvejic, B. (2004) How Open Are You Open? Pre-sentiments, Pre-conceptions, Pro-jections. http://www.sarma.be/text.asp?id=113.

Cvejic, B. (2009) Bojana Cvejić: Learning by Making. Contemporary Choreography in Europe: When Did Theory Give Way to Self-Organization? http://summit.kein.org/node/235.

Deleuze, G. (1995) *Difference and Repetition*. London: Athlone Books.

Deleuze, G., and Guattari, F. (2004) *A Thousand Plateaus: Capitalism and Schizophrenia* Trans. B. Massumi. London: Continuum.

deufert&plischke   artisttwin   berlin.   http://www.deufertandplischke.net/.   Accessed   11 February 2015.

Diffey, T. J. (1986) The Idea of the Aesthetic Experience. In Mitias, M. H. (ed.), *Possibility of Aesthetic Experience*. Dordrecht: Martinus Nijhoff, 3–12.

Durning, J. (2011) Some Things Come to Mind: Imagination, Sensation, Space, and the Body—An Impressionistic Amble after Steve Paxton and the Revision of AveNue. In Fabius, J., and Doruff, S. (eds.), *Paxton AveNue, a Revisioning*. RTRSRCH 3(1). Amsterdam: ARTI, 81–99.

Ellis, C. (2006) Telling Secrets, Revealing Lives: Relational Ethics in Research with Intimate Others. *Qualitative Inquiry* 13(3):3–29.

Ellsworth, E. (2005) *Places of Learning: Media, Architecture, Pedagogy*. New York: Routledge.

Fuimara, G. C. (1990) *The Other Side of Language: A Philosophy of Listening*. New York: Routledge.

Fuimara, G. C. (2001) *The Mind's Affective Life: A Psychoanalytic and Philosophical Inquiry*. Philadelphia: Brunner Routledge.

Grosz, E. (2008). *Chaos, Territory and Art: Deleuze and the Framing of the Earth*. New York: Columbia University Press.

Guattari, F. (1995 [2006]). *Chaosmosis an Ethico-Aesthetic Paradigm*. Trans P. Bains and J. Pefanis. Sydney: Power Publications.

Haim, G. (1986) *Dance, Dialogue and Despair: Existentialist Philosophy and Education for Peace in Israel*. Tuscaloosa: University of Alabama Press.

Iser, W. (2000) *The Range of Interpretation*. New York: Columbia University Press.

Klien, M. http://www.michaelklien.com/index.html. Accessed 9 February 2015.

Kunst, B. (2009) On Potentiality and Future of Performance. (Precise) Woodstock of Thinking, Tanzquarter, Vienna. https://kunstbody.wordpress.com/2009/03/13/on-potentiality-and-the-future-of-performance/

Lansley, J., and Early, F. (eds.). (2011) *The Wise Body*. Bristol: Intellect Books.

Lehmen, T. (2002) *Schreibstuck*. http://www.thomaslehmen.de/schreibstueck-172.html. Accessed 13 July 2012.

Lehmen, T. (2004) *Functionen*. http://www.thomaslehmen.de/funktionen-173.html. Accessed 8 March 2012.

Massumi, B. (2003) Navigating Movements. http://www.brianmassumi.com/interviews/NAVIGATING%20MOVEMENTS.pdf. Accessed 12 August 2009.

Massumi, B. (2008) The Thinking Feeling of What Happens: A Semblance of a Conversation. *Inflexions* 1(1). How Is Research Creation? http://www.inflexions.org/n1_massumihtml.html. Accessed 12 August 2009.

Oberg. A. & Cramner, L. (2008) Mirroring at the borders: strategies for methodless method. In J. G. Knowles, S. Promislow, & A. L. Cole (Eds.) *Creating scholartistry: imaging the arts–informed thesis or dissertation*. (pp.349–361). Halifax, Nova Scotia, & Toronto, Ontario: Backalong Books & Centre for Arts Informed Research.

Paxton, S. (1995) Chaos and Order: Improvisation Taken to the Limit. *Movement Research Performance Journal* 11. http://www.movementresearch.org.

Peeters, J. (ed.) (2010) *Are We Here Yet?* Dijon, France: Les presses du reel.

Peters, G. (2003) The Aestheticization of Research in the Thought of Maurice Blanchot. *International Journal of Education and the Arts* 4(3). http://www.ijea.org/v4n2/.

Peters, G. (2009) *The Philosophy of Improvisation*. Chicago: University of Chicago Press.

Prestidge, M. (2009) What(ever) Happened to British New Dance? https://ciciblumstein.wordpress.com/.

Rabinow, P. (1997) *Michel Foucault: Ethics Subjectivity and Truth*. New York: New York Press.

Ridout, N. (2011) A Prologue. In Matthews, J., and Torevell, D. (eds.), *A Life of Ethics and Performance*. Newcastle Upon Tyne: Cambridge Scholars Press.

Schenck, D. (1986) The Texture of Embodiment: Foundation for Medical Ethics. *Human Studies* 9: 43–54.

Seghal, T. (2012) These Associations. http://www.tate.org.uk/about/press-office/press-releases/tino-sehgal. Press release. Accessed 8 January 2015.

Stuart, M. *Damaged Goods*. www.damagedgoods.be/.

T'Jonck, P. (2011) Other Times, Other Morals. In Fabius, J., and Doruff, S. (eds), *Paxton AveNue, a Revisioning.* RTRSRCH 3(1): 18–29. https://www.ahk.nl/en/research/innovatie-programmas/artists-in-residence/publications/rtrsrch/.

Waterhouse, E. (2010) Dancing amidst The Forsythe Company Space, Enactment and Living Repertory. In Brandstetter, G., and Wiens, B. (eds.), *Theatre without Vanishing Points: The Legacy of Adolphe Appia: Scenography and Choreography in Contemporary Theatre.* Berlin: Alexander Verlag, 153–181.

Williams, D. (1996) Working (in) the In-Between: Contact Improvisation As an Ethical Practice. In Dempster, E., and Gardner, S. (eds.), *Writings on Dance 15, The French Issue,* 23–37. Malvern, Victoria, Aus.

Zaporah, R. (1995). *Action Theater: The Improvisation of Presence.* Berkeley, CA: North Atlantic Books.

CHAPTER 3

....

IMPROVISATION IN DANCE AND THE MOVEMENT OF EVERYDAY LIFE

....

LIBBY WORTH

MOVEMENT improvisation and dance improvisation are closely interlinked but not fully interchangeable categories. For the purposes of this chapter, it is presupposed that the broader frame of the former term applies beyond dance and the performing arts in general to include processes of movement improvisation in everyday life. This is significant for the argument below, which seeks to show how better understanding of both dance improvisation and the more general role of improvisatory strategies in movement communication can be fostered through analysis from diverse perspectives.

Dance improvisation, as it has developed in the UK and US in particular, has become associated with a number of tropes that apparently offer means of best practice. In this chapter, by attending to a few of these, I examine what they might mean and how they might offer insight into dance improvisation. The questions raised stimulated research into ways in which improvisation is a part of everyday life as demonstrated most clearly in examples of infant movement and cognitive development. Taking Henry Montes and Marcus Coates's dance film *A Question of Movement* as a case study example, I consider how their innovative way of dancing responses to life questions connects with the infant's reliance on 'thinking in movement' (Sheets-Johnstone 2009: 28). Finally, I consider what dancers can learn from people living with chronic dementia-related disease who forge ways to live in a perpetual present and, conversely, what insight dancers might offer through integration of dance improvisatory processes in caregiving.

RAISING QUESTIONS

As part of 'Maynard, come home ...' (May 2013), a two-day dance event curated by movement artist Simon Whitehead in Abercych, Wales, a segment from the film A Question of Movement was shown. Each segment of the film, created by dancer Henry Montes and visual artist Marcus Coates, arose through the artists entering selected individuals' home or work spaces and responding in movement to a specific question asked by the host. Touching, thought-provoking, and above all surprising and funny, the short movement improvisations performed by Coates, with Montes behind the camera and facilitating further questioning, proved memorable. Originally this film was part of a curated dance/visual art project titled 'Siobhan Davies Commissions' (November 2011), in which choreographer Davies paired four dancers with four visual artists with a brief to collaborate. Davies 'asked them to peel away the outer edges of their knowledge and reveal some of the small, vital particulars of their practice; to listen to each other and show the things that mattered to them as makers; to look under the surface for those enquiries that stubbornly remain questions' (Davies 2011). This generated a high degree of uncertainty, especially as, within this pairing, Coates, best known for his film, photography, and performance art, took on the role of 'dancer' and dancer/choreographer Montes filmed, whilst the role of choreographer lay with the person who invited the event to their home or work. Their project therefore was riven with questioning, whether stimulated by the brief for collaboration, embedded in the structure/content of each vignette, or coalescing around the dance's production.

In fact, the film raised too many questions relevant to discussions on dance improvisation to hope to be able to address fully here, but some aspects of the work resonated with specific queries that are perplexing to the point of seeming contradictory. For instance, Coates and Montes, when interviewed by Anada Pellerin, explained that they were driven by questions such as 'Does dance have a practical function? Can it be made relevant to people's lives?' Yet underlying these and enmeshed within them were statements that could also readily be reframed as questions. Coates in the same interview suggested: 'What I'm doing is so un-dance; it's just movement, which makes it easier for people to identify with than if it was Henry, the professional dancer, in front of them' (Pellerin 2011). In an instant, this could prompt heated debate on definitions of dance and its relationship to everyday movement, harking back to the concerns in discourse and practice of the early postmodern dancers in US or UK theatre dance. Equally, such discussion could extend globally and comparatively to consider the wide range of dance/movement practices that support a porous and functionally explicit relationship between arts/artists and the communities in which they operate.

For the purposes of this chapter, I am interested in both Coates's statement above and the film segment I watched of his and Montes's work as reference points to ground thoughts on movement improvisation and the quotidian. Dance or movement improvisation always arouses questions driven by its broad range of genealogies, practices, and performances. It can seem more remote to the uninitiated than the most formal dances. By its very nature, it is unpredictable in the responses it initiates in performance—but not entirely so. Its functions are as diverse as the movers who employ them, whether in generation of material, in rehearsal, in teaching, or in performance. Despite so many open perspectives operating within a constantly changing frame, there are recurring apparent imperatives that stubbornly adhere to dance improvisation practices. Being urged to 'stay open', 'be present in the moment', 'be playful', 'do not try to repeat a sequence', 'accept all offers', 'take risks', 'avoid habits', or 'accept mistakes and looking foolish' are just the first that spring to mind. Such an accumulation of clichés threatens to crowd out the opportunity dance improvisation offers to be curious and critical. The Latin root of the term 'improvise' is 'improvisus', meaning 'unforeseen', and in keeping with this, rather than seeking out new, or freshly interpreted, prescriptive requisites for improvisatory practices, I will address several of the tropes mentioned above, reframed as questions. Through attending to the early years of movement development and the problems of memory loss typically found in later life, I argue that human beings are expert in movement improvisation. This expertise, visible from babyhood, can become scaled over if new movement experiences are constricted and the potential for what interdisciplinary scholar and dancer Maxine Sheets-Johnstone calls 'thinking in movement' (2009: 28) is unrecognized or undervalued.

DANCE IMPROVISATION

Before turning to movement development, I need to clarify what I mean by 'dance improvisation' and show where the focus lies within this very broad category of activity. Any live dance performance must of necessity have an element of improvisation within it, however slight that might be. The most formal classical ballet still offers the dancer a space, however constrained by set aesthetic goals supported by intensive training, to respond to the tiny environmental changes experienced during each performance. Part of the artistic outcome and pleasure in this outcome emerges from this sustained ability to respond immediately to shifts in the dancer's conditions. (Fellow dancers offer less weight, there is more space, the stage/studio is warmer, the audience responds differently, etc.) At the point of performance, therefore, the choreographer is no longer available, nor are outside facilitators, directors, or associated devisers, so the performers alone take charge by making instant and active microdecisions as they encounter changes of circumstance. If this is accepted, then two corollary points can be made.

The first point is that dance improvisation, rather than being an entirely separate category of activity within theatre dance, could be seen as being on a continuum ranging from minimal instruction/structure through to operating within highly controlled and formal contexts. Anna Halprin, North American dancer and choreographer now in her late-nineties, offered a useful way to see this when teaching scoring for collectively made improvisations on her trainings. She had students draw a scale from 1 to 10, with 1 representing the most open score (set of instructions) (e.g., 'enter the space and move') and 10 the most tightly closed (a precisely drilled dance sequence for instance). On that scale, the students could then notionally mark where their own scores for dance improvisation sat. Her suggestion was that somewhere in the middle was most satisfying for the performer(s), since it would in all likelihood offer some stimulus and forms of constraint that supported focus without closing down inventiveness. The primary potential for innovative response, she suggested, lay in the interstices or gaps evident between the instructions. (See Worth and Poynor 2010 for discussion on this topic.)

The second point is that the human element within any dance improvisation is never discrete but fluidly moves within and is moved by the environmental conditions around it. So it follows that there is no possibility for a choreographer to control entirely the dance she is making. Anthropologist Tim Ingold suggests that such is the case even when a form or craft is being handed down in a strict mode such that the student or novice copies the expert: 'it is not an iteration. To copy from a master means aligning observation of the master's performance with actions in a world that is itself suspended on movement. And this alignment calls for a good measure of creative improvisation. There is creativity, therefore, even (and perhaps especially) in the maintenance of an established tradition' (2011: 179). Montes and Coates operated towards the more open end of Halprin's proposed scale, but the parameters of the project, that is, the specific question chosen by the host and the limited domestic/work space for movement, brought in constraints as well as stimuli. The term 'dance improvisation' is more usually associated with a high degree of openness, whether in final performance or in the process of generating material that is later set. However, just as it is dangerous to assume that tightly choreographed dance performance is devoid of improvisation, it would be remiss to imagine that seemingly open dance improvisation is without rules, training, or plans. The challenge is that, whereas there is evidence for highly informative and technical training, score setting, and task and theme-based structures for dance improvisation, there are additionally unspoken conventions and forms that hover beneath the surface and are nonetheless determinants of ways of working. A wide variety of methods of incorporating dance improvisation is likely even within one choreographer's practice. At *Yvonne Rainer: Dance Works* (11 July–10 August 2014)—a retrospective exhibition at Raven Row, East London, centred on Rainer's work from 1961 to 1972—this range was evident, both in the scores and notebook writings displayed and in the live performances of several of Rainer's early pieces. The highly open scores she gave workshop participants circa 1969, for instance, were in sharp contrast to the tightly taught movements for some of her performances, reshown during the exhibition. Here are the first three of forty-six workshop instructions (Rainer 2014a):

1. Make a one-minute dance.
2. Make a dance piece for this space.
3. Make a piece for another space and make the getting there part of the piece.

One dance, *Diagonal* (1963), consisted of a series of preset and precise movements, ranging, as Rainer described in an interview, from 'pedestrian movement, to somewhat complicated footwork, to absurd crawling around' (Rainer 2014b). Although the movements were carefully coached and consistently performed by each of the dancers, at any point a dancer could call out a letter and a number that would trigger the designated movement sequence. It appeared that both the caller and those dancers in their immediate vicinity would perform the sequence. The opportunity for improvisation therefore was directed, as far as possible, to spatial, relational, and rhythmic concerns within the whole group rather than to the generation of individual movements. In relooking at this early work, Rainer noted : 'today, watching the series of performances, especially in the work called *Diagonal*, you see them thinking. It's quite wonderful, the physicality and yeah, I did give the instruction "don't freeze when you stand still, you are looking around, you are making decisions" and you see that, it's so visible. [It's] one of the most beautiful things about that particular work. 'In the eyes and in the face' (Rainer 2014b). Rainer's comments on seeing the dancers 'thinking' and 'making decisions' resonates with Montes and Coates's project, which is designed to reveal exactly that element of movement performance. By placing the home or work place host in the role of choreographer who chooses the subject and question for the dance, Montes and Coates not only opened up the potential for anyone to determine a dance performance but also spliced spoken thought with movement to foreground both their interrelatedness and differences.

In the next segment I shift perspective from dance examples to consideration of children's early years of development in order to examine in more detail what might be meant by Rainer's observation of the visibility of the performers' thinking as they danced. Both she and Halprin use task-based activities, in somewhat different formats, to ensure that there is a degree of the 'unforeseen' in the dance environment, but how might this connect with such oft-repeated workshop injunctions as those to, for instance, 'take risks', 'avoid habits', and 'accept mistakes and looking foolish'?

VALLEYS OF UNKNOWING

In babies and very young children this kind of thinking through moving is readily visible. For example, I recollect seeing my three-year-old daughter playing in the bath with three buckets: one a sieve, one a plain bucket, and one with a hole in the side to make a spout. For a long period she played with these but in ways that confounded my assumptions as to what she would do. She paid no special attention to the filling, sieving, or spouting function but moved all three around in apparently random and certainly widely varied manners. She came across sieving, spouting, collecting, but they had no priority over banging, dropping, stacking, emptying, swinging, and so on. In this context, the child had no concept of making a mistake or looking foolish because she played without preconceptions of a correct or singular outcome.

A similarly wide-ranging process of experimentation was noted by Roger Russell and Ulla Schläfke in their highly detailed longitudinal research project employing video of several babies' movement development, observed each week at the Feldenkrais-Zentrum Heidelberg. Russell, a Feldenkrais practitioner/trainer and scientist, in a talk given to students at the Feldenkrais International Training Centre in 2008, discussed how babies learn movement when the brain is at its height of plasticity (Russell 2008). Influenced by the work, for instance, of psychiatrist and developmental psychologist Daniel Stern (1934–2012), Russell spent very many hours watching the stages infants go through leading up to walking. In particular he noted a nonlinear progression, with babies showing how at each significant stage they had to drop familiar habits in order to sense the new experiences and new postures generated and attend to immediate and multiple sensations.

Russell discussed the necessity for the developing infant to discover patterns of movement from the huge range possible, given the permutations generated by the 200 bones and 800 muscles of the body. Even with some inbuilt anatomical restrictions, the task is formidable. One of the babies' major efforts is in finding patterns that are useful and functional. The pattern for walking is not hardwired into the motor cortex of the human brain, unlike that of a herd animal, and must be learnt through a long process of trial and error. Russell described this process not as a singular and steady if uneven progression towards set functional goals but as a gradual development of skills interrupted by 'valleys' (2008). For this reference to a 'landscape' of development, Russell acknowledges his indebtedness to the research undertaken by developmental psychologist Esther Thelen. Her important work on a 'dynamic systems approach' to the understanding of infant movement and, later, cognitive development highlighted the interconnectedness of all aspects of infant movement within a changing environment. In doing so, she recognized the importance of an improvisatory aspect to learning, with the intention to show 'the real process of individual exploration of the natural variability of a system and how adaptive patterns of action are selected from variability' (Thelen and Smith 1994: xxiii).

According to Russell and Schläfke's observations, there were not just learning plateaux but also periods when the infants appeared to unlearn activities with which they had previously shown themselves to be confident. These 'valleys of unknowing' into which they dropped were essential in allowing sufficient physical freedom to discover the next stage in movement development (Russell 2008). Russell described this in some detail in relation to the process of learning to walk that involved several such valleys, including the point at which the children stabilize their hip joints in order to stand but have to venture into destabilizing those same joints if they are to find the motion of walking. This is a familiar sight: toddlers move from a plank-like upright position to uncertain cross-lateral walking, with many tumbles in between.

One of the key elements sought out and recognized in the babies' neurosystem is efficiency, which relates to smoothness of movement that is energy efficient; that is, 'the toddler selects movements that are functional and then optimal' (Russell 2008). Once the pattern is set, then it becomes a habit for a given function (crawling, for example), but to increase learning and range of movement this satisfactory pattern needs to be changed. At these points, Russell observed that the babies went backwards. For instance, they stopped crawling and dropped into a 'wobbly' phase, where they appeared to let go their preferred habit and dropped into a valley of unknowing. They unlearnt a skill in order to gain the physical freedom to experiment more openly again to allow for pulling to standing.

Russell and Schläfke's study and the research undertaken by Thelen on infant development, with her emphasis on dynamic systems theory, have strong resonances with concepts pursued in thinking about dance improvisation. For instance, the question of habits and how to move away from settled patterns in order to discover more fluidly inventive movement responses is familiar terrain for the dance improviser. Yet habits are an essential means by which humans negotiate the world; hard-won, as they are described in infant development research, they create degrees of stability and free up attention. However, significantly, Thelen viewed stability as 'not an end-state, there is always a delicate balance between stability and instability. This allows for improvisation on a theme; for the infant to use stable solutions, and to also discover novel solutions that arise through exploration and often through accident' (Spencer et al. 2006: 1534).

As I watched examples from the videoed records of the babies undertaking these movements, the analysis seemed to me convincing, but equally fascinating was to note the amount of time and attention each child took in exploring. Frustration sometimes set in, leading back to the reliable old habits, but in general, extended periods of time were spent in patient exploration that seemed to be both pleasurable and driven by curiosity. One of the tropes of improvisation mentioned earlier was 'avoid habits'; but to take this seriously, it is perhaps more helpful to ask what your habits are. To actively explore this, and to accept that this will go on changing, necessitates experiencing and paying attention to just the process outlined above in the 'valley of unknowing': that is, how habits are learnt and the functions they enable.

MOVING ANSWERS

Writing on how people 'think in movement', Maxine Sheets-Johnstone reflects on infants' behaviour prior to their ability to communicate through spoken language and asserts that observation shows that 'they are *sensibly* caught up in the primacy of movement and in thinking, not in words, but in movement' (2009: 49). She warns, however, that this unquestioning valuing of movement thinking is fragile. 'When the definitive shift into language takes place, that is, when thinking in words comes to dominate thinking in movement, a foundationally rich and subtle mode of thinking is displaced and typically subdued, commonly to the point that it is no longer even recognized as a mode of thinking' (47). Esther Thelen, both in her many studies of child development and, later in her life, in her fascination with the Feldenkrais Method (she died before she could become a Feldenkrais practitioner) argued forcefully for a dynamic systems approach rather than the enforcing of splits between the different aspects of learning and growth. Spencer et al. suggest that 'rather than viewing development as movement toward the abstract and away from perception–action, Esther [Thelen] believed that, for infants and adults alike, cognition and action are not separate. Instead, cognition is inextricably linked to perception and movement. There is no cognition in the absence of perception and action' (2006: 1529). If Thelen's view is accepted, then the type of dominance of thinking in words that Sheets-Johnstone has suggested is rooted in value systems and taught attitudinal responses that vary across cultures. The tropes so often associated with dance improvisation (mentioned earlier) therefore could be said in part to respond to this kind of imbalance. Setting up open scores for improvisational activities, I suggest, acts as deliberate provocation for privileging just the kind of movement thinking outlined above and is evident in an accessible form in Montes and Coates's *A Question of Movement*. In their film, the familiarity of a home or work space, the conversational tone that leads in to the host's question, and the decision to have the nonprofessional dancer undertake the danced response, all contribute to challenging a conventional view of language thinking dominance.

Within the contract that Montes and Coates set up with their hosts was an agreement that it was worthwhile to initiate a dialogue between someone moving and someone with a burning personal question. That is, they anticipated that the activity of moving in response to a spoken question had the potential to be thoughtful and thought-provoking. Due perhaps to my long experience in the field of dance and movement improvisation, I find the proposition Montes and Coates worked with entirely plausible. However, and given the important barriers to valuing 'thinking in movement' that Sheets-Johnstone has proposed, I also accept that this is not the case for many. Some people, like the reviewer for *London Dance* Katerina Pantelides, might not find it easy to be drawn into such an exchange. She found that at the Bargehouse exhibition of all four pieces commissioned by Siobhan Davies, *A Question of Movement* was the most challenging and commented: 'I confess, I used my prerogative as a mobile exhibition visitor and only stayed for one roughly five-minute extract of the 33-minute long video' (Pantelides 2011). According to her review, however, the audience seemed to find it gripping, and I remain intrigued by what caught their attention.

The ordinariness of the environments (home or work places) in which the dances took place was simultaneously familiar yet strange as a venue for dance. So when Coates responded to the questions, he improvised: that is, he allowed himself to move freely, stimulated by the question's content and perhaps too by the tone, rhythm, or other attribute of the question's delivery. The verbal question, therefore, that would usually anticipate a verbal response was met instead by entirely nonverbal movement sequences. It is these two forms of disjunction, of unexpected activity within both familiar places and forms of social interaction, that direct and sharpen the viewer's focus onto what the movement communicates. In this sense, the dance improvisations are closer to the toddler's explorations, whether in coming to walking or playing with buckets in a bath. The answer to the question proposed by the host was not already known but had to be sought through open dance exploration. Since the hosts were asked to pose a question that was significant for them in their lives, the apparent assumption was that this means of responding was not merely lighthearted but could contribute meaningfully to the dilemma the host expounded.

This intrinsic sense of value accorded to dance improvisation was most clearly illustrated in the varied responses from the hosts after watching Coates's initial movements. A woman in a kitchen asked about how everything keeps turning, the world keeps turning around and around with no stop. Coates turned upside down, with his feet on the counter in the tiny space, and his hands moved feverishly behind his back. The host noted that he seemed to be searching but perhaps could stop being upside down and search upwards. The host's demeanour was calm, almost meditative, as she embraced this form of thinking in movement. Coates went again into movement, with his hands this time turning around each other energetically as if seeking something. He reached up high and in doing so drew attention to the empty spaces in the kitchen rather than counters and cooker, and to the view onto the wider world beyond the window. The host responded again by asking Coates to seek within, not to focus so externally but find something within his heart. As he improvised again, he worked from a more still position, with his fingers seeking in the space, and the host seemed satisfied that this was how she experienced a world that turns, never ceasing.

What was evident in each scenario was a sense of acceptance and understanding of this process by all involved as a means of grappling with the host's urgent question. No doubt this evident sense reflects the skill of the project designers and makers, Montes and Coates, but it also prompts the question as to whether this seemingly strange event is more familiar, and perhaps just less often attended to, than more typical ways of dealing with questions. That is, perhaps there is a familiarity born out of everyday experience that is something like what Jonathan Burrows means when he suggests in *A Choreographer's Handbook* that 'improvisation is a negotiation with the patterns your body is thinking' (2010: 27). This is a statement that could equally apply to everyday decision-making and navigation of the flows and sensations generated in the material world. The difference with dance improvisation is that a specific space and time is set aside in which to privilege movement and attention to movement as a means of communicating thinking with self/others about ideas, stories, or other imaginings.

BEING IN THE PRESENT AND FELLOW-TRAVELLING

In this final section I return to another of the workshop instructions so readily used in dance improvisation: 'stay in the present'. This instruction chimes with the requirements discussed above as to thinking in movement in unforeseen environments but, if taken to an extreme, has other unintended implications.

Recently, I have spent time with elderly people in a care home that specializes in support for those suffering dementia and related illnesses. What I have found striking is that at this end of life, so distant from the infant development discussed earlier, there is nevertheless something similar in the way attention is directed towards the immediate experience of sensations. With the impairment of memory and loss of language, it is immediately obvious that for many who are suffering such chronic brain disease, there is little scope for being goal oriented, comparing past performance with present, or imposing the usual organizing principles to activity. The common dance improvisation advice to 'stay in the present' I have always assumed to be directed at quality of attention and therefore the ability to notice and, importantly, respond to the changing relational and environmental conditions at the very moment such changes take place. We cannot, after all, be anywhere else but in the present. As I listened to those in the care home, however, I became acutely aware of the cruelty of such an injunction if taken at its most extreme. There is choosing to attend to the richness of the flows and dynamic shifts taking place in and around us in conjunction with memories of past experience or learning, and there is an entirely different experience of being locked into the present.

The perpetual present, in this case, is a place of absences, lacunae, caused by the erosion of memories that determined both one's knowledge of the world and one's sense of self. Without the ability to recall immediate past experience or plans for the future, a different terrain opens up. And it is perhaps here that lessons learned from dance improvisation and the idea of thinking in movement can contribute a sensitive and nuanced approach to communicating with people experiencing dementia. In my admittedly limited experience, I noticed a tenacious desire in residents to keep participating as usual, with references to past work and domestic practices being commonplace. But nothing was 'usual', and what became apparent was the degree of ingenuity being employed to fabricate a usual relationship to time and place. The improvisatory nature of such fabrications was immediately noticeable in language, where alternatives were found for words missing from memory: 'hand mirror' for a magnifying glass, or 'a cupboard for the milk' for a fridge. But, as language range declines and even the naming of family members becomes haphazard, or impossible, there were other ways the residents I observed claimed their individuality and navigated their place in the world.

I hazard a guess that at this stage and chronically ill state of life, thinking in movement again takes precedence, as described earlier in infant development. Brain disease might prevent the acquisition of new learning but not necessarily the intensity of sensations experienced in daily movement. It is useful, then, to turn again to Ingold, who hopes 'to shift anthropology in general and the study of material culture in particular, away from the fixation with objects and images, and towards a better appreciation of the material flows and currents of sensory awareness within which both ideas and things reciprocally take shape' (2011:10). His emphasis on process and the fluidity of people's constant engagement with an ever-changing environment leads to the view that knowledge 'is integrated not *up* the levels of classification but *along* paths of movement, and people grow into it by following trails through a meshwork. I call this trail-following *wayfaring,* and conclude that it is through wayfaring and not transmission that knowledge is carried on' (143). This is a helpful and I suggest hopeful image that can validate turning attention to forms of communication that rely less on words and logic and more on the haptic, kinaesthetic, olfactory, and so on. To measure someone's sense of well-being by her adeptness with language or memory skills is to perhaps miss her wayfaring, which has nuances, sensations, and philosophical insights along the way. In the context of the care home, the ability to attend to each person's wayfaring might entail acceptance of the loss of name or family position recall but might provide glimpses instead of other, subtler ways in which a relative's smell or hand grasp, tone of voice, or leaning into proximity might be both familiar and companionable. The textures and tones of communication in this way are afforded value and simultaneously can stimulate forms of interaction requiring close attention, fast interpretation, and a dynamic search for ways of fellow-travelling.

These too are just some of the attitudes and activities associated with dance improvisation. In the case of Montes and Coates's film, the danced response to the question posed was situated in the home or work environment of the host, which was, for the host, crisscrossed with familiar but invisible tracks of habitual movement activity. Coates's movement tore into these, overriding and ignoring them, since they were palpable only for the host. The student in his crowded study bedroom asked why he always became distracted from the important things he needed to do, like revision and essays, by doing the unimportant things. Coates's surprising response was to jump up and down energetically on the bed, land flat on his front on a duvet on the floor, hum, and move one arm with another. When prompted by Montes, the student felt that Coates's dance had chimed with his feeling about the question but had not given the reason why. Montes returned to movement, and in the final sequence, his hand hit the radiator, and the student began to talk about liminal space and how he perhaps needed to be clearer when he was in one state or another. There was no clear answer here but a way of dialoguing that looked to a greater range of interactions where host and dancer might find they could travel together thinking in moving.

References

Burrows, J. (2010) *A Choreographer's Handbook*. Abingdon, UK: Routledge.

Davies, S. (2011) *Siobhan Davies Commissions*. http://www.siobhandavies.com/work/siobhan-davies-commissions/. Accessed 9 November 2015. (Text on process of making the performance event *Siobhan Davies Commissions*)

Ingold, T. (2011) *Being Alive: Essays of Movement, Knowledge and Description*. Abingdon, UK: Routledge.

Montes, H., and Coates, M. (2011) *A Question of Movement*. Film made as part of performance event *Siobhan Davies Commissions*, London, 4–13 November.

Pantelides K. (2011) Review: Siobhan Davies in Commissions at Bargehouse. http://londondance.com/articles/reviews/commissions-at-bargehouse-4100/.   9   November. Accessed 10 November 2015.

Pellerin, A. (2011) *Siobhan Davies Commissions*. http://www.anothermag.com/current/view/1538/Siobhan_Davies_Commissions. 10 November. Accessed 4 November 2015.

Rainer, Y. (2014a) *Yvonne Rainer: Dance Works*. Curated by Catherine Wood. Raven Row, East London, 11 July–10 August. (Exhibition)

Rainer, Y. (2014b) Yvonne Rainer in Conversation with Catherine Wood and Martin Hargreaves. In *Yvonne Rainer: Dance Works*, Exhibition curated by Catherine Wood, Raven Row, East London, 11 July. (Audio recording available at http://www.ravenrow.org/exhibition/yvonne_rainer/)

Russell, R. (2008) Unpublished Lecture on Infant Development delivered at the Feldenkrais Professional Training Program. Feldenkrais International Training Centre, Ditchling, Sussex.

Sheets-Johnstone, M. (2009) Thinking in Movement. In *The Corporeal Turn*. Exeter, UK: Imprint Academic, 28–63.

Spencer, J. P., Clearfield, M., Corbetta, D., Ulrich, B., Buchanan, P., and Schöner, G. (2006) Moving toward a Grand Theory of Development: In Memory of Esther Thelen. *Child Development* 77(6) (November/December): 1521–1538.

Thelen, E., and Smith, L. B. (1994) *A Dynamic Systems Approach to the Development of Cognition and Action*. Cambridge, MA: MIT Press.

Whitehead, S. (curator). (2013) *Maynard, come home …* Abercych, Pembrokeshire, Wales, 11–12 May. (Dance event)

Worth, L., and Poynor, P. (2010) *Anna Halprin*. Routledge Performance Practitioner Series. Abingdon, UK: Routledge.

CHAPTER 4

A PHILOSOPHY OF THE IMPROVISATIONAL BODY

SONDRA FRALEIGH

THIS essay presents a phenomenological analysis and personal history. The first section, 'A Philosophical Approach', develops key terms of the chapter through a philosophy of active embodiment and being seen. The second section, 'Moving through Time', is my story of moving through nine historical phases of dance improvisation. The third section, 'Why Improvise?', inquires into the improvisational body in somatics and human development and reviews ascendant pyramidal conceptions of power in dance improvisation, preferring attributes relative to distinctiveness in motion, intimacy with body and others, inclusive aesthetics, and variables of intentionality. It aims to show how improvisational qualities are both abstract and personal, and that they involve interplays of possibilities—how things draw apart, alternate, disintegrate, or assemble throughout a creative whole. Love and faith both live in dance, stirring the intangibles of dance improvisation.

A PHILOSOPHICAL APPROACH

A philosophy is a coherent school of thought and guiding principles, and it is also, in large measure, a way of life. One's philosophy of life is a way of life. I define philosophy in the above ways for purposes of this essay. In particular, I use phenomenology as a philosophical method for discovering and describing the contents of consciousness. If I am the investigator, my consciousness is on the line, but I also understand the competing view of phenomenology that the individual ego cannot be separated from others or the world. What we suppose to be other is not. My consciousness is more than I am, and even more than it seems to me. We all breathe and share the same air; we share this with every creature on the planet and with every aspect of the ecosystem that sustains or fails us. We are actively involved in our perceptions, not passive recipients of incoming data, and not separate from the perceptions and thoughts of others. Dance improvisation demonstrates such connectivity through intuitive, embodied means. I enter the discussion hereafter with this perspective in mind.

The Lens of Phenomenology and Purpose

Edmund Husserl, the founder of phenomenology, advocated study of the structures of consciousness, and Martin Heidegger added to Husserl's view that one could study the structures of experience in order to understand consciousness. Heidegger shifted concerns in phenomenology from consciousness to existence, rendering phenomenology more personal. Husserl's depictions of consciousness were alien to psychological conceptions, whereas Heidegger described aspects of existence on the periphery of awareness (Nathanson 1973, Safranski 1998). Merleau-Ponty created an ontology of relationships in *The Visible and the Invisible*. His kinaesthetic concepts of flesh and folding hold that perception, however directional, is also reversible and symbiotic (1968: chap. 4).

Phenomenology draws the key terms of our study together. As a method, it is improvisational itself, relying on lateral thought processes, intuitions of phenomena (a phenomenon is anything we are aware of), and the ways we finally make sense of insights through reflection and analysis. Like dance improvisation, phenomenology is not a linear process but develops unpredictably. Phenomenology is the branch of philosophy that takes the body as a key topic, often through its critique of erroneous dualistic views of body and mind. If it doesn't somehow speak to you of transformative possibilities and influence your life, it isn't phenomenology. The philosophy of Husserl questions 'the natural attitude', holding that suspensions of inherited biases and assumptions can bring us closer to phenomenal features of experience. Merleau-Ponty used expressions like 'the lived body' to indicate that features of experience are always being expressed through our embodied presence. His work *The Phenomenology of Perception* (1962) develops a philosophy of the lived body, one that informs my first book, *Dance and the Lived Body* (1987). Phenomenology also holds that philosophical findings are not final, since life itself is a work in process.

The entrance of somatic methods into the field of dance studies draws phenomenology in yet another direction, especially in the context of movement in human development. Core concerns for perception sustain both phenomenology and somatics, as also improvisation; thus, we explore these links. It also occurs to me immediately to ask 'why' one would want to study the improvisational body in dance. What is unique about or valued in the improvisational experience? Do dancers improvise simply for the feeling and sensations of moving spontaneously? This would be an intrinsic 'for itself' value of improvisation, since intrinsic values are experiential, or 'the good' in experience. Or do they improvise to create interest in dance presentations for audiences? This would be an extrinsic use. Extrinsic values are not inferior by definition; they indicate a purpose beyond the experiential per se. Philosopher Paul Taylor, a value theorist, draws these distinctions between intrinsic and extrinsic values (1961). Dancers might also improvise to improve mood or outlook, to unblock sedimented energies held in the body through stress or trauma, or to relate to others through dance. These are matters of connectivity, healing and well-being, which are themselves intrinsic values of experience and personal development. Dancers also explore performative concepts and kinetic complexity improvisationally.

To ask into improvisational experiences and their values is to inquire into active embodiment. In this endeavour, I turn first to my experience, as phenomenologists often do, and I cast a wide net.

Towards Improvisation

I am an improviser. I cultivate spontaneity in life, even within my plans. Sometimes I call my husband 'Mr. Spontaneous', because he isn't. Happily, he is OK with my recognition of his penchant for planning everything down to the last detail. It's how he is. I'm different. I like to pack up everything on a moment's notice and go do something new—without too much thought for the consequences. Sometimes this gets me into trouble. I'm happy I can call my husband when my car runs out of gas. This is when I realize that within my improvisations, there is need for order and foresight, or there should be. I have noticed that resilience comes through *adaptation*, an improvisational principle, and that I get along better with others when I can adapt and not insist.

I like to think I have cultivated resilience through practising improvisation in dance, having time and dedicated space to move freely (within designs of my choosing). Over the many years of being an improviser in dance and life, I have seen how practising spontaneous responsiveness has served my development. It has helped me become a better listener, and when I fail to listen well, it has taught me that self-forgiveness is just a step away. I can always let go and start over.

Improvisation is universal and encompassing; cooking can be as improvisational as dance. I believe that life itself is an improvisation when we see it that way, and that it can be a grand dance, a fun one, or just exceptionally dreary. What we perceive in the everyday can potentially compel us and hold our attention. We can see life as drudgery, or we can appreciate the spontaneous core of ourselves in action.

I distil several experiential values of improvisation from my exploration thus far. These could rightly be called intrinsic values because they arise from the experiential good. Spontaneity, resilience, presence, adaption, readiness, responsiveness, risk, and willingness come to me first, and not in any order; then come somatosensory attentiveness, connectivity, and reversibility. All of these seem very like global perceptual features in awareness, human ways in which intention is directed during improvisatory moments and actions. Temporal perception is abstract and draws forward improvisational features of fleetingness, evanescence, or passing away—momentary dances of death, evaporation, and smoke. What if nothing ever went away or vanished? We would simply be stuck and never heal.

Embodying the Moment and Being Seen

Dance improvisation invites an active engagement of the body and unique ways of being seen. First comes body. 'Body' is a verb when it becomes active in the term 'embodiment'. We could say that we embody an idea or a dance, as we often do, and then body becomes active as lived. I like to speak of 'active embodiment' in order to emphasize that the body is not finished but is ongoing, as anything alive is always coming into being and going away, seemingly at once. To me, this precipice is one of the most fascinating feelings to arise in the dancing body, the body aware of itself in motion, allowing itself to be in the moment, frustrated or just right for the time being, and sometimes at its peak.

Thus, I don't judge my emergent actions. When I improvise in any dance context or compose music improvisationally on my computer, I don't question myself, or what I'm doing in the moment. If I do, I freeze. I need to be alive to potentials and not judge the emerging actions. I spend hours composing music improvisationally on my computer and MIDI keyboard, inputting notes, phrases, chords, and whole lines of music in chosen keys or atonally. I can choose orchestral instruments and synthesizers from hundreds of possibilities I have imported. I listen to my original input, perhaps a long improvised piano phrase, and then improvise other lines of input, maybe overlapping the harp. Thus I build a composition, all through improvisational means. I don't write anything down; rather it gets written as I play what comes to me. I can go back and fix what I don't like, however. I can't do this when dancing. *The first take is it!* The same is true when musicians improvise live. Dancers and musicians alike muddle into situations that aren't working, but if they are good, they can quickly get out of the mire, and make it seem an interesting detour. In dancing, I like to work in somatic improvisational settings where there is no right or wrong, just the moment of emergence, with verbal reflection validating body memory.

The social milieu of dance improvisation is unique. Dancers often improvise in community, except when they are choreographing by themselves, exploring movement that will later become set in choreography. Dancers might also improvise alone for their own enjoyment, as I do when dancing in my kitchen. But I want to address the typical social settings for dance improvisation: classroom and workshop settings, informal performances in community, and staged performances for audiences. In all cases, *being seen* is a factor—dancers see each other perform and are sometimes seen by audiences. Being seen is not usually addressed as a feature of dance improvisation, yet this is a ubiquitous phenomenological feature. Why? And what does being seen have to do with *embodiment*?

We embody being seen experientially (somatically). For instance: Jean Paul Sartre developed a phenomenology of felt helplessness in being seen, which he called 'the look of the other' and 'the gaze' in *Being and Nothingness*. Unable to see ourselves as others do, we are powerless against their glance (Sartre 1965: 340). Somatically, this is a self-conscious, fear-based way of being seen. In his book *Ways of Seeing*, art critic and poet John Berger takes the gender position that men look and act, and women appear. As women envision themselves being looked at, they are captive to the gazes of men. Being seen represents a form of passivity in Berger's analysis (1972). 'The male gaze', a theoretical construct from cinema studies originating with Laura Mulvey in 'Visual Pleasure and Narrative Cinema' (1975), presents a view similar to that of Sartre and Berger. But is being seen passive of necessity? Or is passivity just one of its manifestations, and in any case subject to intentional consciousness? Phenomenology would assert the importance of *intentionality* (orientation and attunement of attention).

Consider also that seeing is more than a visual phenomenon. We commonly say, 'I see' when we understand something. *I see* can mean *I understand*. Still further and in warmer tones, 'seeing' can mean 'appreciating'. Being seen evokes the larger than visual phenomenon of 'seeing' when 'I see' means 'I perceive' or 'I get it'. And when heartfelt, seeing can also be emotionally close to the personal body, enigmatic, and sensitive. In dance, seeing and feeling are related, as all the senses are part of bodily movement as a whole. We typically interpret dance through sense agreements, for instance: 'I sense sadness in your dance' or 'its relentless oppositions are irritating'.

Being seen can be scary, whether in an improvisation or in planned choreography. To show oneself in dance is to feel vulnerable. It might be easier to hide, but not really, because one will be seen in any case. Others see us, and we see them. I know I'm seen, and that I don't really want to be invisible. People generally want to be seen (just not all the time) and are individual in this regard. I have had long spells of shyness and not wanting to be seen. Now I have a secret antidote; I *invite* being seen in dance improvisations and conjure more adventure than fear. I have learned how to absorb the gazes of others with empathy in mind. I make a decision to be assured in the sight of others, and to see them as a mirror of how I would want to be seen. But this doesn't mean I don't have stage fright. I have had bad dreams about blanking out whole sections of memorized choreography; then I slip into an improvisation and wake up happy. What interests me when I reflect on improvisation as social, communal, and performative is how individual people are in their tolerance for being seen.

I facilitate a lot of improvisational dance events in community and on stage, and I notice how people get more comfortable with being seen in these contexts over time and with practice. I have said that performance improvisations, however informal, represent an extrinsic use and that extrinsic uses can be beneficial. One of the values of dance improvisation is that people have a chance to practise being seen (and disappearing) and to improve body image along the way. People can become more comfortable with being seen and less self-conscious. As a teacher, I address students about the importance of letting themselves be seen, because we are seen in many contexts: in job interviews, for instance, in any presentation we make, and daily when we are completely unaware. Being seen is all-encompassing; a little practice can go a long way in terms of confidence.

Seeing and being seen are deeply phenomenological features of active embodiment. Being seen is not necessarily passive in psychological terms, especially if one invites presence. I'm not talking about attention-getting, or acting out. Being present and unafraid of the gaze of others is a choice one can make in being an agent. What others see is in their eyes and hearts. We have no control over how people see or understand us, but we don't have to interpret others as against us. An important part of the aesthetic venture of Authentic Movement practice and the related practice of depth-movement dance lies in this very phenomenon. We get to participate in what others see as witnesses to our improvisations and vice versa. We become connected in an active and nonjudgemental process of improvisational embodiment, which I say more about in the final section.

Moving through Time

Dance improvisation has a history, or maybe several, depending on the genre. The practices and mores of modern/postmodern dance and, still later, contemporary dance have evolved through the years—as my own dance history indicates. My experiences with a variety of practices span a lifetime of seventy-seven years going back to the early modern dance and continuing still, with more than fifty-seven years in community with other dancers. I'm happy to move into old age as an improviser. Thus, I can dance as I like without fear of being wrong. If I fall down, I can stay there, or else someone will help me up, as we make it part of falling down and getting up. In creating my own institute for somatic studies, I have had to invent a lot, to trust and take chances. Fortunately, I have practised inventiveness through dance improvisations of many kinds, as I outline in nine phases here. If they seem linear in the writing, they nevertheless overlap in my experience. Others will likely have different personal histories with dance improvisation. I offer mine as one vantage point.

A Burning Hunger

I started university studies as a music major in 1957 and began dance studies in 1959. Inspired by my dance teachers, LaVeve Whetten (Southern Utah University) and later Joan Woodbury and Shirley Ririe (University of Utah), I learned *how to improvise with images, forms, objects, props, and others*. I had danced since childhood, but not through formal study. I was already an improviser. Woodbury and Ririe taught me technique and composition, and alongside this, how to move without set choreography. Dr. Elizabeth Hayes taught me how to examine dance as art and history. I developed a genuine hunger for learning, dancing, history, aesthetics, and improvisation.

> *Risking,*
> > *Trusting playful instincts,*
> > > *Dancing from inner sources,*
> > > > *Letting my emotional body take shape spontaneously,*
> > > > > *While paying attention to form.*

> > *I was about twenty-one.*
> > > *It was my first improvisation class with Shirley Ririe.*
> > > *I remember rummaging through a box full of props,*
> > > *Coming up with a captain's hat—and making everyone laugh.*
> > > *Performing was mine.*

In love with humour, I played with objects and props, especially through my summers with Hanya Holm and Alwin Nikolais. Hanya prompted improvisational studies on space and the kinaesphere, stories, and pranks. Nik used the abstract relativity of space/time/movement/design as motivation. In widening my vision, I learned how to pay attention to others in the dance.

> Moving together,
> Sensing together.
> Summoning health
> In explosions of cellular retention.
> Our glad knees on the floor,
> Grazing the wounds and
> Mettle of turbulent things.

These ways of improvising extended to my study with Mary Wigman in Germany in 1965–1966. Her improvisation classes often focused on discrete movements such as 'whirling' or 'moving quickly/slowly'. Or they might hold a body focus like 'follow the hands'. She used short narratives and imagery a lot. I remember dancing 'into the depths' and 'up towards the heavens', for instance. Frau Mary (as we called her) encouraged individuality in improvisation:

> Gratitude for life in every detail of dance,
> The face full and shining,
> A fisted presence, throwing it
> to the wind.

> The Creature ... is a created thing, or lower animal
> ... of woods and fields,
> ... or outer space.
> ... a living being
> ... a mortal mammal.
> ... its authenticity, not likely relevant.

When I taught at San Jose State University in California in 1966–1969, my students and I improvised with jazz music, both live and recorded, in syncopated and lyrical styles. Sometimes we performed with musicians onstage. Through my studies in music theory, I knew that jazz was generally improvised within a form and that it could also be free form. I also noticed that much of what we commonly call jazz dance bears no relationship to jazz music and does not include improvisation. Inspired by Marshall Stearns's perspectives on jazz and improvisation in vernacular dance (Stearns 1968), I wrote my first dance research paper on the relationship of jazz dance to jazz music ('Revitalizing Jazz Dance', 1971). Figure 4.1 shows my dancing with live jazz music in an improvised theatre performance of 1971.

FIG. 4.1 Sondra Fraleigh in a jazz improvisation, c. 1971. Photograph courtesy of June Burke.

Yes, my first foray into writing about dance was a study of jazz.
  Instinctive
  Intense
  Cool
    Syncopated
      Torqued
     Flung
       Quickened
       Dropped
   Broken
          Free
           Tight
            Percussive
            Lyric....
          Or, the winged bird could be a
          creature of heights,
          caught mid-air, and
          held on a note....

The Lake between Shifting Grounds

Happenings accept what happens! They open participants to dialogue about the moment and perceptions of place and change.

Happenings arose as loose forms of structured improvisation for large groups, erasing the distance between performer and spectator.

Happenings (I like to write 'happenings happening', over, and over) were first conceived as performance art through the work of Allan Kaprow and were associated with the 'hippie' culture of the 1960s. I organized a few Improvisational happenings in the late 1960s at large conference gatherings and studio installations where everyone present was included, sometimes in mirror relationships with experienced dancers.

Possible-Self-in-a-World *was one of these, performed at San Jose State University in 1969.*

More recently, I led a butoh happening in 2010 in the Kayenta Labyrinth in southwest Utah, called *Plant Us Butoh.* Those who came moved with dancers amidst the rocky landscape and wind sculptures surrounding the labyrinth, and then we all walked the labyrinth in community. Such happenings have vague guidelines that everyone can grasp in a quick explanation, and they often make use of surrounding props, visual art, sculpture, or special landscapes.

When I take people out of the studio to dance with the red-desert earth of Southwest Utah, or in burnt-out trailer homes, or abandoned construction sites, I think of these events in at least three ways—as 'place dances' in the environment, as butoh morphology, and as happenings.

Whatever happens happens.

We accept the happenings of the moment and the place.

And we like to photograph these.

Figures 4.2 and 4.3 below are photographs of *Plant Us Butoh* (2010).

Sentinel Peaks

How about choreographed themes as spur to improvisation?

From about 1975 continuing through 2003, I was teaching both choreography courses and dance improvisation at State University of New York, College at Brockport. This

FIG. 4.2 *Plant Us Butoh* (2010), in Kayenta, Utah, with Japanese and American performers. Photograph courtesy of Teresa Koenig.

juxtaposition taught me about the improvisatory root of choreography. In a phenomenological frame of mind, I came to understand that every dance begins through exploration—read 'improvisation'.

> *Dance as discovery fascinated me then and still does. I like to use short choreographed phrases, easy movement motifs, or images to get people moving; then encourage possible variations. The individual responses are mayhem and magic, streaming character, the self-uncovered—today.*

> *Upholding*
> *The top of a curve,*
> *Today I care.*

Tonight Will Be for Laughter

> *Maybe Dim Candlelight*
> *Scores, Maps,*
> *Some Structure Entailed.*

FIG. 4.3 Community in *Plant Us Butoh* (2010). Kayenta Labyrinth in Kayenta, Utah. Photograph courtesy of Teresa Koenig.

The next stage overlapped the former one and entailed making and performing structures for improvisations called scores or maps. Improvisers could relate to written instructions on when to enter and leave the space, such as, for instance: 'use falling movements'; 'stop in the middle of the stage and wait in silence for sixty seconds'. Structures might provide simple templates for performance, which were easy to grasp and full of open possibility, so that dancers could remember the structure and feel free in the event. These might also be done outdoors, as in a pedestrian and mindful *Walk About*.

Walk About (1989)

I facilitated a two-hour improvisational walk around the town of Brockport, New York, for dance students and community participants using the *I Ching* as a means to structure the event. People walked around, using directions and changes indicated, and they could reflect on images we derived from the book if they chose to. We gathered together at the end to discuss our experiences.

I had been involved with the *I Ching* for many years, having encountered it first in philosophy classes and later through study with Merce Cunningham, eventually using it as a map for two choreographies: *Trigrams of the I Ching* for six dancers (1976) and *He Mounts to Heaven on Six Dragons* for four dancers (1980). These choreographies involved improvisation in performance.

They Had Created a Child

> *And they called it 'contact improvisation'.*

Contact improvisation—giving and taking weight spontaneously in a playful form of dance partnering—overlapped several phases of my dance history. I became aware of it in the 1970s. It remains an influence in my present somatics teaching as impetus for Contact Unwinding. Contact Unwinding is related to contact improvisation, except that in Unwinding, one partner supports and guides the movement of the other using somatic bodywork techniques. The relationship is not symmetrical, in other words. One person moves as she wishes, and with the support and guidance of the other. Either partner can say 'switch' to reverse the roles.

I agonized about the issue of 'touch' in developing my Shin Somatics program. I had used touch techniques from the beginning, but I incorporated them cautiously, improvisationally, into the whole. The methods developing in my teaching and practice began to make sense to me in terms of 'pattern'. I realized that this was nothing new, however. Somatic methods like the Feldenkrais Method and Body-Mind Centering had developed movement patterning as a formative touchstone. My study of Feldenkrais Functional Integration gave me a template for this. I eventually linked pattern to somatic yoga, including five stages of infant movement development. Over time, I saw that Contact Unwinding could also augment my touch methods. In my struggle to find the right words, I came to see 'Contact Repatterning' as the term that would identify Shin Somatics uses of touch. I continue to develop this bodywork practice, which has been evolving improvisationally and structurally since 1990.

> *Listening through touch,*
> *Matching others*
> *In pulsing improvs,*
> *While holding patterns in mind.*
> *Call these models,*
> *But let them go in finding*
> *How pattern repatterns*
> *Travelled paths*
> *In each bossy*
> *Or meekly held body part.*

Her Great Weariness, Her Rheumy Eyes

Butoh grabbed her by the neck
And held her captive.

Butoh represents a distinct phase for me, also relative to somatics. I call it a phase here; it is really a dance genre that implicates strong movement and powerful forces but also finds potency in weakness. Butoh admits weariness and allows aging an honest place. Its improvisatory element is morphic. The butoh body in its morphology is always in process of becoming. Butoh arose in post–World War II Japan as a new genre and very basic form of dance, theatre, and therapy and was later adapted internationally. Power and empowerment have never been butoh goals, and vertical ascent is not its direction. I like it for this reason, among others.

> Butoh is transformational, and thus it probes the margins of consciousness, the places we ignore, misplace, and hide that existential phenomenologists like Heidegger, Merleau-Ponty, Sartre, and Beauvoir explored as *ambiguities* (See especially Beauvoir's *Ethics of Ambiguity* 1948)

When I improvise my embryo-self in butoh,
or become stone, or lightning,
or 'ash pillar';
  when I disappear and reappear,
  or when I become rubbery,
    or hang up a body part,
I let go my conscious thoughts.

Then my 'ancient body' (as we call it in butoh) speaks to me, and I come home to my self. I suspect that when many of us reach this point, we are not so different from each other.

Butoh invites ambiguous dance experiences that morph into light
while holding darkness.

I hold that in its improvisations, butoh is a transformational somatic practice (Fraleigh 2010: 37–62; 2015). I teach butoh for its metamorphic potentials and to encourage ugly beauty or messiness on the margins. Butoh entered my life in 1986. I've been a butoh addict ever since.[1]

The lifeworld of which we are a part inspires my butoh body;
fish and stones, mud and water dance in my scars.

Chunks Coiling

Lately, I am aware of an eighth integrative phase of my story that I call 'Collage Improvisations'. These arise in the moment or with minimal structure and reflect parts

FIG. 4.4 Sondra Fraleigh in her environmental butoh *Butch Cassidy's Cabin* (2008). Photographed by Mark Howe in Circleville, Utah, where Fraleigh was born. Photograph courtesy of Mark Howe ©2008.

of all of the above. Inclusion of everyone present is important, along with the option of moving the performer/audience vantage point, as dancers adopt the audience position whenever they wish. Collage Improvisations also include aspects of the somatic dance practices that I delineate in the next section.

MORPHOSE (June 2014)

In Hannia, on the island of Crete, I facilitated *MORPHOSE*, a somatically inspired collage with international participants. We moved as a single group seamlessly from the indoor studio to the beach, beginning with butoh metamorphosis improvised on edgy imagery and ending with Contact Unwinding partnerships in the sand and water. Performers morphed in and out of the one-hour improvisation, joining the audience when they wished, and in the stairway descent to the beach, the audience joined the dance. It struck me that in the ensemble improvisation of twelve performers, each dancer found distinctiveness.[2]

DUNE

> *Her fair hair flew in lapping coils*
> *As inward—she sank in sand,*
> *Her arms of elemental praise*
> *First burst into that silence.*

Over the last twenty-five years until now, I have continued to explore *somatic dance practices,* the ninth landmark phase of my story, which I will speak about further in the next section. Figures 4.7–4.10 capture images from this phase, especially improvisation influenced by butoh imagery and environmental dance.[3]

FIG. 4.5 *MORPHOSE*, improvised performance in Hannia, Crete. Front to back: Amy Bush (US), Virginia Alizioti (Greece), Hillel Braude (Israel), Kayleigh Crummey (US), Angeliki Rigka (Greece). Photograph courtesy of Kay Nelson.

FIG. 4.6 Contact Unwinding improvisation in Hannia. Ruth Way (UK) and Aliki Hiotaki (Hannia, Crete). Photograph courtesy of Kay Nelson.

FIG. 4.7 *DUNE* (2011). Improvisation in Snow Canyon, Utah. Photograph of Amy Bush courtesy of Sondra Fraleigh

FIG. 4.8 *DUNE* (2011). Photograph of Angela Graff courtesy of Sondra Fraleigh.

FIG. 4.9 *Soft Sandstone Butoh* with Angela Graff (2012). Photograph courtesy of Sondra Fraleigh.

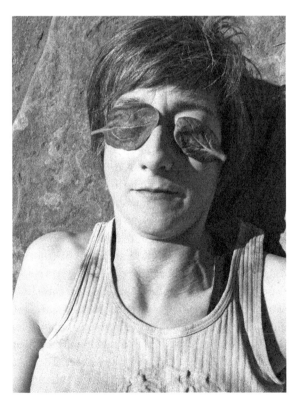

FIG. 4.10 *Be Spinach and Stone Butoh* (2012). Photograph of Kristin Torok courtesy of Sondra Fraleigh.

WHY IMPROVISE?

Somatics, Improvisation, and Human Potential

My experiences with dance improvisation have allowed me to explore several possible-selves and modes of creativity. As a whole, they seed my current concerns with the im-provisational body in somatics, and they lend a perspective on somatic approaches towards improvisation. At their core, somatic processes reflect an ethic of care, not al-ways present in dance improvisation, existing as it does in many differing frameworks. Facilitating safe and encouraging contexts for improvisation is one of the tasks of somatics as a field, whether in education, in therapy, or socially in community. Dance improvisation experiences are not always positive, especially in their social milieu. Moving spontaneously and freely might signal license in the eyes of some or might lead to objectification of participants in negative and exploitive ways. There is no control for this, as in most human undertakings. Dance improvisations are risky and vulnerable ventures. Dance itself is risky, and some forms might invoke sexual objectification and unwanted advances, as one woman explains her experience in a contact improvisation jam (Lee 2014: 34–35).

When we dance, our body is on the line, so to speak, and thus social and sexual boundaries need to be clear. Artists will always question boundaries, but that doesn't mean that just anything goes. Should explicit explorations of sexual acts enter in, for instance, as they have in some contact improvisation jams (Hennessy 2014: 36–38)? The photograph on the back of the Winter/Spring 2014 issue of *Contact Quarterly* shows overt sexual contact as part of contact improvisation, with sexual healing in groups as one of the stated intentions of participants. I'm more apt to ask why people would shift intentionality from dance to sexual behaviour. This seems a sea change. Sex and dance are different acts and activities. For me personally, and as a teacher, the line between sexual contact and dance contact is clear, even as I believe that sexuality as eros (vitality) is part of everything. I like to joke that 'there's no such thing as sex: because everything is sex'. However, we know that wrestling is not sex, even when the contact is sexually close, and dancing is not sex, however sexy it might be or seem.

Somatic approaches to dance court vulnerability in other ways, and this is their strength. How can it be that dance processes turn towards the Greek word *soma*? Soma is body perceived or known by the self and in relation to others. Soma and psyche (vital essence) together indicate ability to commit to an action or emotion. Greeks never use the word 'soma' by itself, except to indicate the organic body, says Aliki Hiotaki, who is a native of Greece and a scholar of somatics. Rather, Greeks use both words: 'soma and psyche' σώμα και ψυχή, to convey a living essence (Hiotaki 2014). Somatics is a field of human development that begins with 'subjective body awareness', a term first expounded in phenomenology. From there it looks outward relationally, cultivating intersubjective awareness and intrasensory, ecofriendly dance experiences. The broad field of somatics lends itself to a variety of perspectives in education, dance, and movement practices.

I cultivate somatics in terms of healing through dance, yoga, and touch. Somatic developments of dance improvisation are also distinct in being intentionally oriented towards personal development and building relationships through sociality, as well as advancing modes of neutral witnessing and nonjudgment. In practice, somatic strategies are focused on change in the person and on participation for all, not on high-tech performance for audiences, even as informal performances can serve somatic goals. Somatic improvisational processes also hold ecological perspectives, envisioning the human in and as nature. (See East 2015.)

Improvisational practices in aesthetic and performance contexts have for years held many of the same developmental values as somatics but have not by design always emphasized these. Somatically inspired improvisations do not in their basic intent aim to be expressive, beautiful, or impressive. Nor do they aim to empower dancers to any given end. To the contrary, they brave vulnerability. In view of perception and process, witnesses to such improvisations accept what happens in the event and in the moment, and they use this consciously, sometimes reflecting back the experience, verbally or in painting. Somatically conceived improvisations often aim towards personal transformations, which are pragmatically open to an array of outcomes.

Such improvisations also intersect with community projects after traumatic events and use somatic tools for healing through group processes. Anna Halprin was famous for facilitating community healing through somatic rituals. The performance details of such events are less important than group cohesion. Somatic dance is autotelic in character, that is, done for the value of the doing, and for no other purpose. Earlier forms of aesthetically conceived improvisation also hold autotelic elements, but not when the dance projects the awareness of participants towards the success of the improvisation in terms of audience reception.

My present work with depth-movement dance (or depth-movement) takes inspiration from Authentic Movement, the improvisational practice that grew out of the work of Mary Whitehouse, but it uses Body Mapping as a therapeutic method. Authentic Movement doesn't generally start with people tracing their partners' body outlines on large body-size pieces of paper as in Body Mapping. In beginning this way, participants have a body outline as a reference point. If it is an outline of my body, I can find places of pain, trauma, and conversely feelings of depth and wholeness in the outline, paint them, and eventually dance them for a witness. Or the witness can dance an aspect of my map for me.

I always feel better when someone else dances my pain as I have painted it, or at least as they see it. I like to join in at the end, improvising the (now doubled) pain away. In another instance, the witness might paint her experience of witnessing my dance. There is also the option that the dancer and the witness might paint on or outside a body outline in tandem. *Intersubjectivity and empathy* develop in Body Mapping depth-movement processes, which can be structured for partners or group connectivity. Depth-movement can also be improvised directly through *dance and response* without visual art intervening. Relating to others creatively is significant to empathic response in what psychologist Abraham Maslow called 'self-actualization' (1954).

The Fluid Self: Flow and Forgiveness

'Why improvise?' has many possible answers. For somatic practices, improvisation is a way of accessing seemingly hidden treasure of human experience, as well as a way of allowing tears to flow. Somatic methods don't replace traditional therapies, but in dance they allow people to know themselves in ways they cannot anticipate or conjure on a therapist's couch. Improvisers get to know themselves not through words, though these may help, but through immediate bodily affectivity. Happiness and sorrow want to surface! Emotions are not bad actors; their expressive flow is needed to sustain physical and mental health. One of the values of improvisation is to provide a safe place for movement expressions, a place to practise, and a way to distance emotional life aesthetically, distilling and reflecting on feeling states through dance. Merleau-Ponty (1968) spoke of 'the flesh of the world' in view of human abilities to reverse sensitivities. Sense perception moves or 'folds' its active and receptive aspects. His idea is dancelike in its creative reciprocities of folding. In being both active and receptive, perceptual life, like dance, is symbiotic and potentially transformative.

As in dance, embodiment is ongoing, as I have said, and never quite complete. This is part of the philosophy we are developing. How we find language for improvisatory values is important, because language is formative in consciousness. Words are formative. We embody them as we speak, write, and communicate. Why improvise? Perhaps one doesn't need a reason, but eventually some understanding or purpose will arise— when we feel better, expand awareness, or understand something we didn't quite get before. The body itself exists in states of feeling, and has inherent reasons to dance.

I like to find words for dance experiences—a daunting task. In looking back over my experiences with dance improvisation, I see how they have been developmental avenues for me. I wouldn't say, however, that improvisation has empowered me to any given end, in or out of somatic contexts. Concerning the latter, I contend that the language of 'empowerment', which has been brewing in dance for several years, does not facilitate the liberation we hope to foster in somatically inspired improvisations. Other terms emerge from my analysis that I believe better define the existentials of human potential, terms like 'encouragement', 'self-realization', 'intersubjective awareness', and 'ecofriendliness', and there are many more.

In distinctions between 'power-over' and 'power-for', the first speaks to control and the second to opportunity. But I believe we can find better words than 'power' and 'empowerment' to value dance experiences. We might cultivate a language of freedom and agency, of self-affirmation and self-knowing, not one that suggests authority. We are sometimes powerful when we improvise, but we are also exposed. Mastery, power, and empowerment all result from pyramidal structures of thought and action. (A critique of mastery is thematic in my book *Dancing Identity: Metaphysics in Motion,* 2006.) They imply an end point of control and solidifying of ego. I imagine that writers on dance don't mean to imply this, but the language is problematic and in repetition becomes clichéd. I think it derives a lot from the early liberation era of feminism when women sought power over their lives, and this is still an important goal today. I have identified with feminist issues since reading Beauvoir in my twenties, often teetering between anger and inspiration; but reasons to improvise are complex and only sometimes hang on issues of empowerment.

Several articles in the 2014 Spring issue of *Dance, Movement & Spiritualities* favour the language of empowerment in articulating values of dance and improvisation. One article examines the term 'empowerment' and places it at the top of a pyramid of learning and experience (Deasy 2014: 131). The author cites several somatic steps leading towards empowerment: freedom, self-discovery, authenticity, and individuality. These words are repeated often in dance writing. 'Individuality' is assumed to be valuable, yet it has so many appearances. To be individual is not a singular somatic value, unless it indicates independence of thought and the ability to act. Sociality is just as important as individuality. Authenticity is also problematic as a human value or movement marker. Antiques can be authentic, but it is very difficult to say what is authentic in emotional and developmental life, or in human movement. All movement is authentically what it is, neither good nor bad until we judge it so.

The word 'authentic' deserves its own article. What seems authentic one moment has veered in another direction the next. If a movement feels good, we might say it feels right (authentic) for that moment, but what about movement that grates against the grain—as in butoh, which pays attention to offbeat affects that don't necessarily feel right or good? Which movements are more and which are less authentic? Freedom is also one of those packed words or ideals that lose meaning without context. In movement, freedom can imply ease of breath and readiness to move in any direction. In improvisation, it often indicates the ability to choose. I have tested freedom as a term extensively in previous works (1987, 2004). The improvisational body implicates *potentials* rather than *power*. Heidegger puts the issue this way: 'greater than actuality stands possibility' (1962: 62–63).

Let us draw a simple distinction between 'empowerment' and 'fluency' and then project this distinction towards a philosophy of the body. After becoming empowered, what comes next? Authority emanates from power and is also an egoistic dead end. Can we find a new language that is more circular, spiralled, and moving, a language that draws ability as 'can do' from a well of potentiality?

The dynamic growth I envision moves towards self-knowing and positive relationships. Confidence might be a result, at least momentarily. I am aware of courting confidence daily, inviting it, losing it, and winning it back in moments. It isn't something I own on any permanent basis. Sometimes I feel strong, even powerful, but the feeling can turn weak. I actually like to do improvisations on 'the weak body' in butoh, which its founder, Hijikata Tatsumi, demonstrated as more true to his dance than strength. Weakness, humility, and strength are all necessary to a full spectrum of feeling. They are movement affects to be explored, and not always singularly. When I improvise, I move through many states, most of which I seldom name. But when I reflect back, I can tease some out, and sometimes say how they mix. Power inflected with love radiates, for instance. It is full, hopeful, and complex.

What language would suffice, then, to speak of the benefits of the improvisational body? I nominate a language of embodied fluency. This might translate in felt terms as 'affective fluidity' or more concretely as *the emotionally fluid body*. I learned from this *fluid body* in outlining phases of my own improvisational dance history, which seemed best summoned in felt imagery and poiesis. In this, I follow the lead of scientist Candace Pert, who explains emotion throughout the body as fluid, tidal, weather-like, and ever changing (Pert 1997). The emotionally fluid body arises existentially from what I think of as 'water logic', a fluid environment in consciousness that can move in any direction. Fluidity generates resilience, forbearance, and a life of 'yes'. 'Yes we can' and 'yes we care' are much more useful as existentials emerging from improvisation than assertion, control, and power.

This 'yes' grows skilful acquaintance with motion that I mentioned in the beginning. This grows through practice, as do particular matters of style in performance. We who improvise for personal development might be less concerned with skill as we cultivate unique opportunities to experience intimacy with body and others, and we surrender a generative flow in relation to strength and will that keeps us moving into the happening of the moment. Not making things happen, we participate in the larger whole. Gratefully, we learn that we are not the doers but that we live in doings and surprises that surpass us. We become more resilient and generous—less forceful. We experience the place of failure in success.

In Figure 4.11, I improvise in performance (circa 1984) about 20 years into my 40-year dance and teaching career at three universities. This performative moment was

FIG. 4.11 Sondra Fraleigh improvises in performance, c. 1984.

photographed at State University of New York in Brockport. It is from a large group work I facilitated in our large studio-theatre with musicians improvising and moving with the dancers. I remember it as a bit chaotic and noisy, an unfinished work in the making, somewhat like life and phenomenology. Now in retirement from university life, I have turned 16 more years of teaching, dancing and writing towards the mysteries of improvisation.

At the beginning of this essay, I rejected individualism in lieu of human connectivity. I've learned as an improviser in life and dance that everyone matters. To have an effect, to project oneself into the future while holding presence, and to be implicated positively in the world are potential benefits arising from fluid processes and conceptions of the improvisational body. When I improvise, I move with others towards my best self. I brim with joy and release past hurts. Sometimes I cry, and find ways to forgive my foibles. I let go of guilt and forgive others. I move, and move more, as one moment dances into the next without dread or anticipation.

NOTES

1. See YouTube video, Sondra Fraleigh in *Ancient Body Butoh in Greece and Utah with Influences from Japan* (2014), video and music by Sondra Fraleigh; video includes explanations of butoh: http://youtu.be/26qQIvyyask.
2. See YouTube video, *MORPHOSE*, performance in Hannia, Crete, June 2014, video and music by Sondra Fraleigh, http://youtu.be/e-7k2Rb3SWQ.
3. See also *DUNE* (2011), YouTube video of group dance improvisation in Snow Canyon, Utah, http://youtu.be/kCCeD3_ZLNQ?list=UUN808Mh6W6ARoFV7ZFGjcUw; YouTube video of *Soft Sandstone Butoh* (2013), video and music by Sondra Fraleigh, http://youtu.be/eUiZw7c_OhQ?list=UUN808Mh6W6ARoFV7ZFGjcUw; YouTube video of *Be Spinach and Stone Butoh* (2013), video and music by Sondra Fraleigh, http://youtu.be/QMjCzcCWQXg?list=UUN808Mh6W6ARoFV7ZFGjcUw.

REFERENCES

Beauvoir, S. (1948) *Ethics of Ambiguity*. Trans. Bernard Frecthman. Reprint, 1994. New York: Carol Publishing.

Berger, J. (1972) *Ways of Seeing*. London, UK: Penguin Books.

Deasy, H. (2014) Freedom to Move, Freedom to Stop. *Dance, Movement & Spiritualities* 1(1): 123–141.

East, A. (2015) Body as Nature. In Fraleigh, S. (ed.), *Moving Consciously: Somatic Transformations through Dance, Yoga, and Touch*. Champaign: University of Illinois Press, 164–179.

Fraleigh, S. (1971) Revitalizing Jazz Dance. Paper presented at Congress on Research in Dance, University of California, Los Angeles, 5 June.

Fraleigh, S. (1987) *Dance and the Lived Body: A Descriptive Aesthetics*. Pittsburgh: University of Pittsburgh Press.

Fraleigh, S. (2004) *Dancing Identity: Metaphysics in Motion*. Pittsburgh: University of Pittsburgh Press.

Fraleigh, S. (2010) *Butoh: Metamorphic Dance and Global Alchemy*. Champaign: University of Illinois Press.

Fraleigh, S. (ed.). (2015) *Moving Consciously: Somatic Transformations through Dance, Yoga, and Touch*. Champaign: University of Illinois Press.

Heidegger, M. (1962) *Being and Time*. Trans. John Macquarrie and Edward Robinson. New York: Harper and Row.

Hennessy, K. (2014) 848 Community Space: Queer, Sex, Performance, and Contact Improvisation in 1990s San Francisco. *Contact Quarterly* 39(1) (Winter/Spring): 36–37.

Hiotaki, A. (2014) Email communication, 15 January.

Lee, R., and CQ. (2014) Contact Improvisation: One Experience. *Contact Quarterly* 39(1) (Winter/Spring): 34–35.

Maslow, A. (1954) *Motivation and Personality*. New York: Harper.

Merleau-Ponty, M. (1962) *Phenomenology of Perception*. Trans. C. Smith. London: Routledge and Kegan Paul.

Merleau-Ponty, M. (1968) *The Visible and the Invisible*. Trans. Alphonso Lingis. Chicago: Northwestern University Press.

Mulvey, L. (1975) Visual Pleasure and Narrative Cinema. *Screen* 16:3: 6–18.

Natanson, M. (1973) *Edmund Husserl: Philosopher of Infinite Tasks*. Evanston, IL: Northwestern University Press.

Pert, C. (1997) *Molecules of Emotion: The Science behind Mind-Body Medicine*. New York: Touchstone Books.

Safranski, R. (1998) *Martin Heidegger: Between Good and Evil*. Cambridge, MA: Harvard University Press.

Sartre, J-P. (1965) *Being and Nothingness*. Trans. Hazel Barnes. 3d ed. New York: Citadel.

Stearns, M. and Jean. (1968) *Jazz Dance: The Story ofr American Vernacular Dance,* New. New York: Macmillan.

Taylor, P. W. (1961) *Normative Discourse*. Englewood Cliffs, NJ: Prentice Hall.

CHAPTER 5

CHANCE ENCOUNTERS, NIETZSCHEAN PHILOSOPHY, AND THE QUESTION OF IMPROVISATION

PHILIPA ROTHFIELD

THIS essay is an attempt to think of dancing per se as a mode of improvisation. It draws on Nietzsche's philosophy as a means to do so, utilizing his emphasis on becoming, a mobile concept which seeks the emergence of things in their origins, but also tracks their comings and goings. Becoming signifies movement. To speak of becoming rather than, say, being allows for a dynamic understanding of the body and therefore of dance itself. Becoming alerts us to the changing nature of dance, its transitoriness. Nietzsche uses the concept of force to trace the becoming in all things. Force is a destabilizing concept. It destabilizes the identity of things, human and nonhuman, discerning the dynamic differences which lie beneath their surface. This is because forces are always plural. There is no single force which is alone responsible for what happens. Forces are found in relation to one another, in the form of contestatory tendencies or impulses: the thrust of the floor, the weight of a limb, the moment before weight is committed, the pull of habit. Dancing lies in between, in the difference between these forces and in their manner of resolution.

The resolution of force does not, for Nietzsche, depend upon a decision or choice, which is made by the dancer in the course of events. We are used to thinking of the dancer as *the one who* makes choices, follows a lead, seizes the opportunity. According to this thought, improvisation is the dancer's achievement. Nietzsche's critique of this sense of the dancer as agent enables a different notion of improvisation, one based upon another kind of agency. Agency in the Nietzschean cosmology is embedded in the event, in the multiple and successive encounters of force with force, which yield new configurations of force. This is in part a matter of chance, to be found in the chance encounter, but it also involves an exertion, an active engagement *with* chance, which for its part generates a shift between relations of force. Such is the agency of the event. It is the driver of change, the inner dynamism of all that happens.

The Nietzschean perspective looks upon the dance as a site of multiple twists and turns, involving choices embedded within the action itself rather than decisions made by some sovereign agent (the dancer). The shift away from sovereign subjectivity (the agent) and towards activity as such generates a different take on improvisation, as well as a different notion of the decision. If not the work of the dancer but the work of the dance itself, improvisation becomes reconceptualized as a shifting play of force. There is an element of chance within this play—chance lays the groundwork, sets the field of possibility, for that which follows. Improvisation is to be found here in relation to the field of possibility, engaging force, shaping it, resisting it, utilizing it, 'drawing force from the universe', from other forces (Lingis 1997: 51). Force can be found in the floor, another body, momentum, even time itself. In each particular instance, one force will make use of the others so as to create a shift. Such are the vicissitudes of movement.

The concept of force invites us to conceive of dance as a dynamic flux, made up of a multiplicity of contestatory forces. Movement may avail itself of the fall or resist it, reshape it, turn it onto a roll, or land bang slap against a wall. Although Nietzsche conceived of force *writ large*, in relation to all events, the idea of force can be oriented towards dance so as to credit the many elements that come together in the constitution of movement. According to Nietzsche, forces resolve into relations of dominance and subordination—in order to move forwards, one force will always take the lead in relation to the others: the foot moulds to the floor, muscles soften to allow gravity to work on bones, breath enables length in the body.[1] In each of these examples, force works with that which lies to hand—other forces—selecting from them so as to move forwards.

The body is a key figure here, the 'fruit' of chance encounters between forces (Deleuze 1983: 40). The body at any time comprises the momentary resolution of the play of forces. It is the shifting field that arises out of relations between force, a midway point between chaos and order.[2] Nietzsche's appeal to the body paves the way for a reformulation of action away from the doer (as animating consciousness) and towards the deed as such (what a body does).[3] The body for Nietzsche is not a fixed agency but is itself composed of multiple forces which are themselves subject to selection and reformulation. The body is less an identity, then, than a transitory mode of organization wherein forces combine to produce that which comes next. Conceived in these terms, dancing can be posed as a kind of improvisation, as the means by which the momentary body (the body at this passing moment) avails itself of that which lies to hand. This may be the thrust of the floor, the forces of gravity, muscular readiness, the give and take of other bodies, or the availability of training and technique in the body. Each of these tendencies can be conceived in terms of force, as possible pathways or factors that arise and inhere in the passing moment and may come together to produce that which follows. Improvisation is the dynamic nexus between these myriad forces, their moment of selection and kinship, constellation, and reformulation.

What follows is a reading of Nietzsche's work on the becomings of movement. Nietzsche's conceptual framework will be utilized to give an account of dance as a shifting series of relations between forces. According to this approach, dancing involves a mode of improvisation which utilizes elements of force. Even fixed choreography calls for an in-the-moment negotiation between the body and its environment. The body must avail itself of that which lies to hand in order to lend itself to the choreographic task. Past training and practice produces a palette of availability in the present. Dancing negotiates these multiple forces in its manner of corporeal becoming. This is the improvisatory task, it is that which gives life to the dance. Even the pirouette, with its signature preparation and predetermined form, must work the floor, keep the body centred, and spin all available forces to become what it is.

This treatment of Nietzsche draws on Deleuze's engagement with Nietzschean philosophy, which is in turn indebted to Klossowski's remarkable interpretation of Nietzsche's life and work (Klossowski 1997; Deleuze 1983). Deleuze's work makes clear the priority of forces in the Nietzschean world of becoming. Underlying the apparent identity of subjects and objects (I, you, the dancer), forces compete with one another for selection. These forces are in contest with one another. The body's becoming arises in virtue of the dominance of one force over the others, through the activity of particular drives or forces which impose themselves upon other drives or forces (Nietzsche 1997, 2003). The body dances this becoming, shifting from moment to moment, enjoying the qualities manifest through this play of contestatory force. Pierre Klossowski depicts the body in Nietzsche as 'the locus of impulses [forces], the locus of their confrontation', a confrontation which for its part yields the successive stages of corporeal becoming that constitute the body (Klossowski 1997: 24). For Klossowski, the body signifies 'the fortuitous encounter of contradictory impulses [forces] temporarily reconciled' (22). The body takes shape through forming a temporary truce between competing tendencies. Impulses contradict one another inasmuch as they represent different directions or pathways, movements not yet formed, which come into being through an emerging movement's resolution of these differences. An impulse does not have an independent identity but takes shape in relation to other impulses as they jointly manifest in movement. This is the plurality of force.

The conception of the body as dynamic, transitional, and transitory breaks with the notion of the body-subject as found in phenomenological philosophy.[4] The body is not a source of intentional activity, consisting of a subject who acts or chooses between forces; rather it emerges through the dynamic confrontation of forces, their multiple struggles and provisional arrangements.[5] The body is itself made up of these competing tendencies, each vying for selection. We as subjects are only (experientially) acquainted with the results of these scenarios, with their outcomes. Furthermore, we tend to claim their resolution as the fruit of our labours, our choices. We claim the deed as our own, supposing that agency belongs to us: 'man believes himself to be cause, doer.... What gives us the extraordinary strength of our belief in causality is *not* the great habit of the succession of occurrences but our *incapacity* to *interpret* what happens other than as happening out of intentions' (Nietzsche 2003: 74). Transposed onto the domain of dance, we might say that we are locked into thinking of the dancer as *the one who* is responsible for the dance. According to this mode of thought, improvisation is the dancer's achievement. Perhaps the dancer is conceived of as an embodied subjectivity, a mode of movement subjectivity (Rothfield 2008, 2015). Nietzschean philosophy critiques this sense of the dancer as agent for another kind of moving body, one which is more provisional and transitory.

According to Nietzsche, the dynamic becoming of the world is not readily apparent because our understanding tends to see the world in terms of subjects and objects whose very identity or fixity is that which undergoes change. It is a feat of human invention and imagination to have imposed and sustained such interpretive stability upon a world of becomings.[6] But that doesn't mean that there isn't this other dimension underlying, nay responsible, for the shape and character of our experiences, which are themselves the manifestation of forces temporarily reconciled. According to this aspect of Nietzschean philosophy, the world is a shifting play of relations between forces. Forces come and go. Always found in relation to one another, they are inherently plural, a dynamic plurality, whose unfolding story is the becoming of the world.

Forces take hold of other forces; they utilize them and draw upon them. Relations between forces are neither mutual nor symmetrical, that is, these relations are formed through force making use of force: using the floor to push off, counterbalancing shifts of weight within the body, holding habit in abeyance, drawing upon traditional idiom in order to stage a contemporary departure. Whenever forces are found in relation to one another, some forces will be dominant, others acquiescent. For example, contemporary reformulations of traditional dance forms make use of the force of tradition for their own ends. A Graham contraction draws upon a counter-tension which sustains length along the spine as the contraction is formed. Rolling down the spine requires a sequence of holding patterns which allow the roll to occur. In each of these events, forces take hold of other forces.

Forces do not exist in the abstract (as preformed, individual entities). They are always found in relation to one another, and once they are, the dominance of one over the others signals a concrete and dynamic difference between them. To say that forces resolve into relations of dominance and subservience is not to say that one force is inherently dominant but that it becomes so in its relation with other forces. This is emergent and contingent. Moreover, relations change. One configuration may over time give way to another. A *plier* becomes a jump and then a landing. What happens, then, is the formation and deformation of shifting sets of relations between forces. Forces emerge, make use of other forces, and then give way to something else, other sets and relations of force. Nietzsche wants to maintain the ontological plurality of forces in relation to one another. A dominant force does not eradicate other forces; rather it makes use of their characteristic tendencies or, for Nietzsche, resistance (2003: 25). Pushing off the floor makes use of the floor's resistance to the push, gravity enables thrust, counterbalancing is made possible through the tug of opposition. The multiplicity of forces represents a kind of flux, such that at any point in time there are several competing yet unformed tendencies. What emerges is a contingent and passing resolution of those potential trends, a resolution between tendencies achieved through the imposition of one tendency upon the others. A snapshot of that resolution reveals one force commanding the others, expressing certain qualities found through forming a relation with, and drawing upon, other forces. Dominance then is not the elimination of pre-given, competing possibilities; rather it is the shaping of possibility itself. New configurations of force emerge through the workings of force upon force. These in turn form the basis of future possibility. Such are the becomings of movement.

Corporeal becoming ensues from this dynamic partnership of differences, a duet that requires a distinction between leading and following. Nothing happens without a kind of driving force, a mode of leadership which drives the difference between forces. Nietzsche's term for this is the will to power.[7] The will to power is a difficult term, but it holds the key to the way in which dancing can be framed as a manner of improvisation. This is because the will to power represents the agency of the passing moment. It is the driver of change and, because of this, must meet and contend with the multiplicity of forces that coalesce in the body and its milieu.

Deleuze locates the will to power alongside the concept of force or, rather, forces in relation with one another.[8] Force and the will to power are companion concepts which together constitute the body's momentary becoming (Deleuze 1983: 53). The will to power speaks to the utilization of force by force in the becoming of movement. As a principle of activity, it is provocative (of change), yet it is also relational, poised between the plurality of forces. The will to power represents the manner in which certain forces make use of others and, in so doing, produce movement. The will to power is the dynamic element of the world's becoming. It is the force of change within and between relations of force, contributing towards the way in which their struggle is resolved. Although it can be theorized as embedded in all becoming, it is also quite specific, a principle of synthesis or relation between particular forces, one which accounts for this particular passing moment. As the driver of change, the will to power is active, expansive, 'willing' to engage the differential structure of force. Nietzsche (2003) writes of the will to power as internal to relations of force, as a kind of inner will or internal dynamism. The will to power is that aspect of change which draws upon the difference between forces so as to produce something new, thereby to become otherwise. It is a principle of change and is implicated in all becomings, human and nonhuman.

Rather than thinking of a human will exerting itself upon an object, the will to power belongs to the multiplicity of forces found within corporeal becoming. It speaks to the ways in which forces resolve so as to become otherwise, that is, to change. It is neither external nor prior to relations of force but rather emerges as an aspect of their becoming, as their embedded and relational mode of agency. As a relational principle of becoming, the will to power has a number of features. While it is dynamic, expansive, and formative, it is also receptive. They say that the leader in tango must be supremely sensitive to his/her partner. Touch must make contact so as to exert its influence. In order to relate to and draw upon the qualities of another force, the will to power must likewise exhibit a certain degree of sensitivity. In Bonnie Bainbridge Cohen's Body-Mind Centering, the notion of *yield* embodies an analogous sense of sensitivity to that posited here. Yield is an element of Body-Mind-Centering's neurocellular patterns, along with push, reach, and pull (see Body-Mind Centering 2017). A body has to yield in order to push. Contact has to be made in order to engage, for example, the floor's resistance. Sensitivity is called for in order to touch another body, to soften into the flatness of a wall, to roll around the ribcage, across the roundness of the pelvis, or to access the weight of another. The difference between a human conception of will and the will to power lies in the intimacy between willing and power, such that the will to power is found within and between relations of force rather than existing as an external driver of change. Nietzsche calls this an inner dynamism; Lingis and Deleuze speak of its *affectivity*.

The notion of affect connotes an ability to be affected, to be touched by, an outside or beyond. The greater the sensitivity to that which lies beyond, the greater the capacity to work with that otherness. Were it not for listening, we would not be able to engage. Affectivity represents this aspect of dynamic change: sensitivity towards that which differs. Meeting other forces and working them requires an *encounter*, with the qualitative difference of those forces. Watching fellow students in class entering a group dance improvisation, it is apparent who is listening and who is inside their own bubble. Those who listen are more capable of taking on elements of their environment, incorporating them into the dance. Greater still is the group which collectively listens, exhibiting a mutuality of feeling amidst innovation. Such sensitivity makes space for surprise, for the emergence of new movement values. The will to power incorporates sensitivity as well as activity, the shaping of difference. Once in play, the will to power works that sensitivity, continually 'drawing force from the universe' (Lingis 1997: 51). Both generative and sensitive, then, the will to power is a principle of synthesis between forces that represents the particular way in which forces come together in the production of movement, that is, in their very moving. If chaos is the multiplicity of impulses, the entire horizon of forces, then the will to power could be thought of as a primal affectivity, the sensitive means by which force partners force.[9]

Although forces come together under the aegis of the will to power, this is not a collective mode of cooperation rather a succession of relations of dominance and subservience: using the floor to push off, shaping the fall, allowing an image to take hold, shutting down vision in order to feel. Forces qualitatively differ, in motion. At any given time, one drive or force will make use of the others so as to produce an event, a becoming, a movement. The will to power varies according to each activity, each moment of the world's becoming. It lies beneath human will. In short, the will to power is the driving force found in any given moment. It is that which produces difference in the body, a dynamic concept which is embedded within and is intertwined with relations of force. The will to power poses the world, and life, as the immanent becoming of forces (Woodward 2011: 16). 'Immanence' means belonging to the same order of things. In this context, immanence suggests a variable sensitivity and agency which is internal to becoming.

The will to power is an odd turn of phrase, almost human in its notion of willing. Nietzsche appropriates and reinterprets the concept, using it to replace human will, which is now a special case of the will to power.[10] Agency does not belong to the individual subject but resides within and between relations of force. Agency is nested in the world's becoming. It is immanent to relations of force but it is also their principle of activity. It is that which generates movement. The will to power is that aspect of the relation between forces which drives, seeks, or shapes that which emerges. It is not a causal factor in the scientific sense of a general law of nature which governs but derives its character from the world.

Deleuze characterizes the will to power as singular, plastic, generative, and synthetic (1983: 50). It binds relations of force (synthetic), varies according to each configuration of forces (plastic, singular) and is that which wills in their becoming (generative). It is, in short, that which produces difference in the body. Taken together, the notion of force and the will to power represent a dynamic conception of bodily becoming, one which is ever in motion. The will to power speaks to the sense in which dancing is the coming together of many factors (forces, drives, impulses, desires, and motivations) but also captures the activity of dancing, the sense in which dancing exhibits a kind of corporeal mastery. Rather than the virtuosity of the subject presumed to know—subjective mastery—the Nietzschean account locates mastery in the momentary reconciliations of force. Forces master other forces. This is how movement happens.

According to this line of thought, dancing results from momentary relations of force. Multiple elements are tied together and pressed into service in the act of dancing, drawing upon that which lies to hand: the floor, space, other bodies, qualities within the body, perceptual flashes, touch, feelings, breath, preparation, memory, you name it. What happens in dancing is the becoming of these arrangements of force, organized in the particular moment through the principle of activity Nietzsche calls the will to power. While the body is the name we might give to a certain set of ongoing activities—the dancing body—the body is not the driver in this scheme of things. The body is a formation in flux, a 'fortuitous encounter of contestatory impulses temporarily reconciled' (Klossowski 1997: 22). Nietzsche writes of the living being as a polyp: 'every moment of our lives sees some of the polyp-arms of our being grow and others of them wither' (1997: 74). So, while the body has a history, and this history impacts upon the subsequent emergence of constellations of force, it is the product of chance: both the work of chance and a working *with* chance.

One way of thinking about chance is to look at the resolution of force as requiring an improvisation with chance. Improvisation is an activity which draws upon a range of available materials, here, the multiplicity of forces as they emerge in the moment. Improvisation is alert to the becomings of force and draws upon them so as to produce that which happens. There is a degree of improvisation in all dancing, in the way a body draws upon a plurality of forces in order to produce movement. The organization implicit in dancing draws upon those forces that cluster around the momentary body. These include the forces that could be said to constitute the body's cultural milieu or kinaesthetic context.[11] The notion of improvisation highlights the momentary aspect of gathering forces so as to generate movement. The floor at this moment is that which enables this roll, the softening of the ribcage as it meets the floor offers the means for the roll, whose nuances themselves arise from years of rolling. Time itself becomes an available force. Even training, a fairly sedimentary notion (something a body has), can be conceived as the inculcation of force(s) in the body so as to become available in the present, alongside environmental and momentary factors. Practice could be likewise conceived as the means by which force is made available in the body. Training equips the momentary body with the capacity to engage force in particular ways. In this sense, even classical technique can be conceived as the capacity to improvise in certain predetermined ways, for a body still needs to reproduce the form by utilizing forces found in the passing moment. Such is the performative demand in all dancing. Every moment of a turn engages and works those forces that come together to produce the turn. The elaboration of contact improvisation ensues from the unfolding arrangement of its constituent bodies as they encounter one another.

The chance encounter offers and produces the force of the future. Improvisation partners chance. It highlights the fact that dancing is an in-the-moment activity, that it is inherently performative. This pertains to the breadth of movement possibilities, from the iconic to the unheralded. In each case, movement will have gathered its forces and given them direction. Even the performance of set choreography requires an in-the-moment (re)configuration of forces towards a certain kind of end. It may feel like bare repetition, but each time is the singular performance of an event which is enriched by a body that differs, the body warmed up and prepped, the well-practised body, the tired body, the body hung-over, in a different space, on a different floor. The performance of set choreography requires the utilization of many elements, corporeal and beyond, an improvisation of sorts, like cooking. You do the shopping, but you still have to make the dish. Spontaneous or free movement equally takes up its own set of forces, according to that which ensues. The foot still needs to meet the floor whether or not it knows what's going to happen next. The work of dancing is an engagement with chance, 'drawing forces from the world' along the way (Lingis 1997: 51).

Thought in this way, the activity of dancing produces new opportunities, new modes of available force which cluster around 'the becoming body' (Manning 2012: 6). How do forces become 'available'? In one sense, availability devolves upon the will to power. The will to power discerns force, and through doing so, renders force available. Deleuze writes: '*in order for the will to power to be able to manifest itself it needs to perceive the things it sees and feel the approach of what is assimilable to it.* The affects of force are active insofar as the force appropriates anything that resists it and compels the obedience of inferior forces' (1983: 63). Relations between forces arise because a force is able to feel another force, to be able to be affected by it so as to affect it. As a principle of synthesis between forces, the will to power must represent this double perspective or bipolarity, one which enables forces to come together through the activity of one force working the others. Another way of putting this is to say that a force utilizes that which lies to hand but that it requires or exhibits a degree of sensitivity in order to do so. The foot needs to feel the floor in order to push off it. Sensitivity or affectivity represents the degree to which a force is able to utilize other forces. So the availability of force is in part the product of sensitivity, a quality of the will to power's synthetic function. The more sensitive, the more fulsome the breadth of relations in play. Deleuze writes: 'it follows that will to power is manifested as a capacity for being affected. This capacity is not an abstract possibility, it is necessarily fulfilled and actualised at each moment by the other forces to which a given force relates' (1983: 62). While some philosophical traditions pose affect as a passive response to sensory input, the attribution of affectivity to the will to power here signals its activity—leading in tango relies upon sensitivity towards those forces that gather within another body. The idea of affective capacity conveys what is at stake in the notion of availability, namely skill. The greater the skill, the greater the available force. Skilful dancing makes (more) force available. This is its active component. A good *plier* makes the ground available for jumping, for maintaining sensitive contact with the ground, whereas a crappy one simply releases the legs. This notion of skill is found in the dancing, in the capacity for being affected, which is simultaneously actualized in the passing moment.

Although skill manifests in action, there is a sense in which it also develops over time as a form of capacity-building. Training is a key component in most, if not all, forms of dance. Although it might seem that training is a kind of predisposition running counter to improvisation, we could equally say that training is the cultivation of a greater ability to improvise, to discern, and to grasp force. The ballet dancer's daily barre enables the reproduction of ballet's lexicon in a wide variety of circumstance. The repetition implicit in training and habitual practice enables the body to encounter difference, to exert a fine grip on the plurality of forces, orienting them towards the desiderata of the form. It represents an even greater encounter with chance, one which turns the forces of the moment into the clear lines of the classical form. This is an art, the art of engaging force.

Clearly, practice and training play a role in the cultivation of fine dancing. There is thus an historical or, rather, genealogical element in the emergence of dance traditions and domains. Nietzsche was very interested in genealogical questions, tracing the origins of value and their temporal establishment as customary forms of practice. The problem with custom, for Nietzsche, is that it accrues a moral dimension. It becomes normative, tending to demand conformity for its own sake. The term he uses to describe this is the morality of custom (*sittlichkeit der sitte*) (Nietzsche 1997). The morality of custom is the propensity for customary practice to assume a kind of authority and expectation for reproduction. Individuals become inculcated with customary values, tending to reproduce them without necessarily discerning why or how a custom was formed in the first place. In contrast to custom, the creation of value requires a legislative sweep, the founding of new values.

Nietzsche lauded the creation of value afforded by artistic practice. The artist, for Nietzsche, is the one who creates (value). He also recognized the conservative tendencies inherent in customary forms of value, felt at the level of (the artist's) subjectivity. The problem with custom is its normative claim upon the subject, forming a predisposition towards reproduction (more of the same). For Nietzsche, art is able to exceed the subjectivity of the artist. The artist is the one who can open up to the force of art itself to forces that lie beyond the artist's conscious understanding. Does this gel from the perspective of improvisational dance practice? There are, I think, certain questions that arise from the point of view of the improviser who finds herself in the midst of the dance; undecidable questions that cluster around the introduction of new material, its adoption and adaptation leading to the question of timing. When is the 'right moment' to abandon established material, transform it, pick up new ideas in motion, or return to something already in play? How are those decisions made? Who or what makes those decisions?

The creation of value within improvisation signals a moment of innovation, the utilization of other forces. This might be temporal, signifying a break with established rhythms or spatial factors, or might involve the production of new movement signatures in solo, duet, or group formation. In the Nietzschean cosmology, value arises because one force takes hold of other forces, producing a certain kind of kinaesthetic variation or difference. Values emerge and pass due to the fluctuations of force, which lead to their adoption, adaptation, and transformation. Nietzsche acknowledges the creation of value that attends the birth of the new. He also recognizes its gravitational pull once custom is established, its tug on the sensibilities of the subject (see earlier: 'the morality of custom'). This is a problem from the dancer's point of view, from the subjectivity of the artist, especially if there is this moral dimension, which is expressed in the tendency to reproduce rather than create value. This might be felt, from the improviser's point of view, as a tension between the dancer's proneness to resort to the familiar alongside a desire to remain open to the unknown.

Nietzsche has a way of posing the problematic that faces the improviser. He supposes a 'wicked dilemma' that confronts the passenger of a ship who 'realizes' that the captain-pilot (the self, bound by the morality of custom) is in the wrong (1997: 186). The question of mutiny (inciting change against the grain of custom) poses a problem of justification for the one inciting mutiny, an 'agonising situation' which pits the past against a potentially different and unknown future (186). When should 'we' rock the boat? When should custom be overturned? What 'justifies' the creation of new values if justification depends on criteria which are rooted in the past?

The thrust of Nietzschean philosophy is to decentre the account away from the subject's perspective and towards activity/dancing per se. It locates decision-making in the dance itself, in its emergent forces. According to this line of thought, the felicity of improvisation lies in 'the good selection' (of force). This may be a surprise to the audience, as well as to the participating dancers. For example, a movement might arise in improvisation for all sorts of accidental reasons—a chance perception, an image, an impulse. This movement may become incorporated within the dance. The practice is transmitted but may be adapted for new reasons, according to new values. Perhaps it adds something or is able to be turned and twisted into something, yet it finds itself repeated. It is open to difference, leaving behind the shell of custom. Ironically, staying *with* material in improvisational dance practice can be more innovative than 'moving on'. The relentless pursuit of the new may become vacuous. Moments of creative felicity can be found in the folds of repetition. Depth, staying with material, opening it up to further possibility, can be productive. Returning to a prior movement signature can be refreshing. The trick is to follow the impulse which makes a good selection and activates a new arrangement of forces. The dancer's conscious impulses may or may not be a good indication. We have a tendency to dance our selves. But we also know the joy that comes when the dancing propels us into new territory.

Nietzsche's movement beyond the surface of subjective experience and towards the plethora of underlying force locates agency in the momentary decision-making inherent in the activity of dancing. His scepticism towards the veracity of the authorial, sovereign subject opens the way for thinking about dance and dance improvisation on its own terms, beyond its being the product of the dancer. There is, I think, an aspect of improvisation that reaches beyond the dancer and into the moment, into the swarming plurality of forces, between and amongst rather than within individual bodies. The good improviser is the one who can open up to these forces, beyond the customary tendencies of his or her movement subjectivity. In the context of her own dance improvisation, Body-Mind Centering practitioner Kim Sargent-Wishart speaks of finding ways to open the self up to the new. Others speak of 'getting out of the way' so as to facilitate the dancing.

Only time will tell. New elements emerge, are taken up singly or collectively, become established, and then give way. Nietzsche supports the impetus to create new value, to pursue a 'legislative' approach to creating new forms, new possibilities, against the moral grain of conformity (affirming difference as against more of the same). Dance improvisation offers a medium for experimentation beyond customary forms of practice, which is not to say that it is immune to the morality of custom within the body of the performer. Improvisers have to find ways to soften the edges of their dancing, to become available and open up to the breadth of possibility. The difficulty for us is that we are always one step behind, listening to a 'distant echo of a battle that has already been fought out' (Haar 1977: 10). For this reason, Nietzsche looks to the body as a cipher of future possibility. The body is a portal, an opening upon the world. Forming relations with other relations, its very identity is in flux. The agency of movement derives from these relations. Force needs force in order to move on. Dance ensues from these eddies and swirls. The action of improvisation represents an encounter with and sensitivity towards the lie of the land. A powerful encounter—Nietzsche would call it affirmative or strong—embraces the diversity and plurality of forces, folding and unfolding over time. That the agency of movement is attributed to the will to power, in conjunction with force, displaces the subjectivity of the dancer, who becomes a player in a bigger picture. The great thing about this lies in the bigger picture, in the beyond of knowing subjectivity, where the encounter and its offspring lead the way.

Not to know how things will turn out is a kind of opening. This is why Nietzsche speaks of the experiment. Experimentation is a process, a facilitation which allows us to listen. To that extent, we might look at the value of the unexpected within improvisation, of openness, and look to the new, to happenstance, and to the emerging moment. One could also speak of making use of that which lies to hand, making use of that which emerges in the present moment, beyond the predictable. There is in improvisation a willingness to play in the present, to create the future from the present rather than knowing all along what that future ought to look like. If there is a sense in which the body is always improvising, the value and practice of improvisation adds a sense of not-knowing to the mix, subtracting what we might call the subject presumed to know: 'so it is that, according to our taste and talent, we live an existence which is either a *prelude* or a *postlude*, and the best we can do in this *interregnum* is to be as far as possible our own *reges* and found little *experimental states*. We are experiments: let us also want to be them!' (Nietzsche 1997: 190–191).

NOTES

The discussion of movement practices in this essay is informed by the understanding and generosity of the artists and practitioners with whom I have worked over many years. This is difficult to make visible according to the conventions of academic acknowledgement but is key to my having anything to say about dance. In the context of this discussion, I would therefore like to acknowledge Margaret Lasica, Russell Dumas, Alice Cummins, Shona Innes, Sally Gardner, Julia Scoglio, and Anneke Hansen; also Eva Karczag, Pam Matt, Lisa Nelson, Deborah Hay, and Joan Skinner.

1. Nietzsche writes: 'every drive is a lust for domination, each has its perspective, which it would like to impose as a norm on all the other drives' (2003: 138). Not all forces can be satisfied at once. If a force characterizes a particular movement, then it will perforce draw on and utilize those other forces which made that movement possible.
2. 'The body is therefore an intermediary between the absolute plural of the world's chaos and the absolute simplification of intellect' (Blondel 1991: 207).
3. ' … there is no 'being' behind the deed, its effect and what becomes of it; 'the doer' is invented as an afterthought, – the doing is everything' (Nietzsche 1994: 28).
4. See for example Merleau-Ponty (1962).
5. Although some phenomenological approaches emphasize corporeal modes of agency, for example Morris (2008), and therefore resonate with Nietzsche's corporeal emphasis, their overall commitment remains with the value of subjectivity, in that intentionality is seen to be embedded within action, and subjects are, for their part, entitled to appropriate action as their own achievement.
6. 'The principle of identity has as its background the 'appearance' that things are the same. A world of becoming could not, in the strict sense, be 'grasped,' be 'known': only inasmuch as the 'grasping' and 'knowing' intellect finds an already created, crude world, cobbled together out of deceptions' (Nietzsche 2003: 26; see also 246–247).
7. 'The triumphant concept of "force" with which our physicists have created God and the world, needs supplementing: it must be ascribed an inner world which I call "will to power," i.e., an insatiable craving to manifest power; or to employ, exercise power, as a creative drive etc.... There is no help for it: one must understand all motion, all "appearances," all "laws" as symptoms of inner events, and use the human analogy consistently to the end. In the case of an animal, all its drives [forces, impulses] can be traced back to the will to power' (Nietzsche 2003: 26–27).
8. 'The will to power in every combination of forces, *resisting what's stronger, attacking what's weaker*' (Nietzsche 2003: 25).
9. Alphonso Lingis writes of the will to power as 'essentially affective', as incorporating a notion of feeling, feeling other forces, relating to them so as to work them (Lingis 1977: 51).
10. Nietzsche's *Daybreak* (1997) offers an alternative way of thinking about human action, in terms of underlying drives (forces) which vie for, and successively achieve dominance. Although prior to his formulation of the will to power, *Daybreak* fleshes out the difference

between the multiplicity of contestatory drives and their ultimate/momentary resolution (which produces that which we experience).

11. The cultural and kinaesthetic everyday consists of multiple practices, preferences, and established factors which together provide a range of forces. These might include cultural modes of bodily organization, established performance values (black box theatre, monthly showings, proscenium arch display), somatic practices (ideokinesis, Feldenkrais, yoga, Alexander Technique), spiritual underpinnings, and so on.

REFERENCES

Blondel, E. (1991) *Nietzsche, The Body and Culture*. Trans. Sean Hand. London: Athlone Press.

Body-Mind Centering. (2017) Bonnie Bainbridge Cohen. www.bodymindcentering.com/course/basic-neurological-patterns-bnp. Accessed 24 March 2017.

Deleuze, G. (1983) *Nietzsche and Philosophy*. Trans. H. Tomlinson. New York: Columbia University Press.

Deleuze, G. (1988) *Spinoza, Practical Philosophy*. Trans. R. Hurley. San Francisco: City Lights Books.

Haar, M. (1977) Nietzsche and Metaphysical Language. In Allison, D. (ed.), *The New Nietzsche*. Cambridge, MA: MIT Press, 5–36.

Klossowski, P. (1997) *Nietzsche and the Vicious Circle*. Trans. D. Smith. London: Continuum Books.

Lingis, A. (1997) The Will to Power. In Allison, D. (ed.), *The New Nietzsche*. Cambridge, MA: MIT Press, 37–63.

Manning, E. (2012) *Relationscapes, Movement, Art, Philosophy*, Cambridge, Massachusetts: MIT Press.

Merleau-Ponty, M. (1962) *Phenomenology of Perception*. Trans. Colin Smith. London: Routledge and Kegan Paul.

Morris, D. (2008) Body. In Diprose, R., and Reynolds, J. (eds.), *Merleau-Ponty, Key Concepts*. Stocksfield, UK: Acumen, pp. 111–120.

Nietzsche, F. (1994) *On the Genealogy of Morality*. Trans. C. Diethe. Ed. K. Ansell-Pearson. Cambridge: Cambridge University Press.

Nietzsche, F. (1997) *Daybreak, Thoughts on the Prejudices of Morality*. Ed. M. Clark and B. Leiter. Cambridge: Cambridge University Press.

Nietzsche, F. (2003) *Writings from the Late Notebooks*. Trans. K. Sturge. Ed. R. Bittner. Cambridge: Cambridge University Press.

Rothfield, P. (2008) Philosophy and the Bodily Arts. *Parallax* 46: 24–35.

Rothfield, P. (2009) Between the Foot and the Floor: Dancing with Nietzsche and Klossowski. In Sullivan, N., and Murray, S. (eds.), *Somatechnics, Queering the Technologisation of Bodies*. Surrey, UK: Ashgate, 207–224.

Rothfield, P. (2015) Playing the Subject Card: Strategies of the Subjective. In Bleeker, Maaike, Nedelkopoulou, Eirini, and Sherman, John (eds.), *Performance and Phenomenology*. London: Routledge, 97–110.

Woodward, A. (2011) *Understanding Nietzscheanism*. Durham, NC: Acumen.

CHAPTER 6

....

MOVING *IN MEDIAS RES*

Towards a Phenomenological Hermeneutics
of Dance Improvisation

....

NIGEL STEWART

SCORE AND UNDERSCORE

....

THIS essay explores ways in which dance improvisation depends on processes of interpretation which are fundamental to human experience. To do this, I evolve an understanding of psychosomatic performance through the phenomenological hermeneutics
of Paul Ricoeur (1913–2005) and, to a lesser extent, Hans Georg Gadamer (1900–2002).
By psychosomatic performance I mean approaches to performance that depend
on some kind of relation between an external 'score' (e.g., choreographed phrases,
sequences of physical action) and an internal 'underscore' (e.g., a subtext of stories, personal associations, poetic images, or sense impressions). I use Ricoeur's critique of the
idealist phenomenology of Edmund Husserl (1859–1938) as the basis of a critique of psychosomatic performance practices that reduce the relation of intention and action to
an idealized essence in order to achieve a state of self-presence. I then argue that improvised dance in general, and the butoh of Marie-Gabrielle Rotie and the site-specific environmental dance of Jennifer Monson in particular, can offer an alternative approach
to psychosomatic performance which exemplifies Ricoeur's phenomenological hermeneutics. I thereby grasp dance improvisation as a practice in which the moving body
unfolds the world of which it is already a part by relating to it through a subtext that it
interprets kinaesthetically.

I start with a typology of relations between score and underscore, external action and
mental image. This can be derived from Vico's four tropes as Susan Foster has applied
them to her 'four modes of representation (1986: 65–67, 234–236 n. 1). *Metonymic* representations are based on relations of *imitation,* in which a part substitutes for the whole,
as in a single movement phrase through which a dancer thinks of a river and delineates

the easily discernible outline of one. *Synecdochic* representations are based on relations of *replication,* in which 'the functionally distinct parts' of the whole are rendered 'as a [self-contained] dynamic system', as in a montage of gestures which draws attention to different qualities, and rhythmical relations between qualities, of key features of a river. An example is provided from my own choreography on the dancer Julia Griffin for a scene performed within a barn near a river as part of Louise Ann Wilson's site-specific work *Ghost Bird* (2012). In one movement phrase, Griffin performed a gesture evoking a purposeful flow of water immediately juxtaposed against a second gesture embodying a helical standing wave and a third signalling a swirling eddy. *Metaphoric* representations are based on relations of *resemblance,* in which the quality of one object substitutes for another, as in a movement phrase in which a dancer imagines a snake to reference the movement of a river. Finally, *ironic* representations are based on *reflection* and involve, for the purpose of Foster's typology, self-referential movement, such as a purely abstract phrase that only accidentally suggests a river to the spectator. Here, then, a continuum exists for the spectator from the transparent to the opaque: if a metonymic or 'imitative representation leaves little doubt about the referent of the movement' (Foster 1986: 65–66), then, at the other end of the continuum, an ironic or reflective representation is ultimately inscrutable. From a phenomenological point of view, I must add that in any of these modes the dancer's *intention* to signify an object will, consciously or unwittingly, be dependent on an *intuition* of that object which is conditioned by one or more of the senses. To intuit the river, the dancer will imaginatively, or even actually, see, hear, smell, taste, or touch the river or, in the instance of resemblance, a snake.

In any of these four modes, the exact relation between physical action and mental image could be evolved through improvisation as much as through predetermined choreography. But does *improvisation* per se have any special value to psychosomatic performance and are there ways of improvising responses to an underscore that reveal the special significance of improvisation in general? To answer these questions I want to examine the philosophical value of the relationship between action and imagination in psychosomatic performance, and to do that it is necessary to provide first a philosophical *critique* of some kinds of psychosomatic practices which do *not* ultimately use improvisation, of which I will provide three examples. The first is the Feldenkrais Method. Many bodywork or somatic practices work through elimination to grasp the body as a psychosomatic idealization independent of historical context and cultural peculiarities. For instance, in Feldenkrais's exploration of 'the dynamic link between standing and rising', the mover is instructed to progressively 'avoid conscious mobilization of the leg ... [and] neck muscles' until she is left with the essential awareness of muscles in the hip joints directing a force through the spine to facilitate a smooth transition (Feldenkrais 1977: 80). Similar examples can be found in the Alexander Technique, Body-Mind Centering, the Klein Technique, and other somatic practices in which any inessential effort is reduced until the subject is fully aware of the ineliminable neuromuscular essence of the action performed in that exercise. Here, ideally, the intentional understanding of the action and the sensuous intuition of the action are identical. Arguably, most bodywork practices are in this way utopian in their drive towards the full awareness of a context-less functional efficiency and an unimpeded relation of self to self, which, Feldenkrais claimed, 'heralds the emergence of the truly human man' (48).

The second example is Ryszard Cieślak's performance as Prince Fernando in *The Constant Prince*, Jerzy Grotowski's adaptation of Calderón's play which focuses on the fortitude of Fernando in the face of his sadistic Moorish captors. Psychosomatic training in Grotowski's Teatr-Laboratorium also worked through a process of elimination known as 'via negativa', specifically through the 'eradication of blocks' that would otherwise cause a 'time-lapse between inner impulse and outer reaction' (Grotowski 1968: 17, 16). Cieślak's performance in *The Constant Prince* provided powerful evidence that this training was efficacious. Such was the 'integration of … [Cieślak's] psychic and bodily powers' (16) that, as Christopher Innes notes, 'Cieślak's body expressed his psychological state in physical reactions that are usually considered involuntary—sweating profusely while remaining still, a red flush spreading over his skin, tears flooding from closed eyes', and paroxysms of laughter (1993: 161). Grotowski assumes that to achieve this state of 'transillumination' or self-transcendence it is first necessary for the actor, through training, to be stripped of socially acquired habits, even the actor's own social persona, in order to 'eliminate' any 'resistance' during rehearsals to the personal associations produced by his role (1968: 16).

The third instance is *Sleep of Stone*, a solo choreographed by Hijikata Tatsumi for Nakajima Natsu according to his own 'double-notation system'. In general this system consists, first, of poetic words which each conjure the kinaesthetic sensation of an individual action, and second, a poetic title which educes the overarching 'energetic quality' or 'space power' of the whole phrase into which those individual actions have been sequenced (Stewart 1998: 45–48). For instance, *Sleep of Stone* consisted of nine phrases: 'Sleep', 'Flower', 'Willow and Wind', 'Sleep of Stone', 'Willow', 'Orchard', 'Willow and Smoke', 'Stuffed Air', and 'The Action of Hands'. 'Stuffed Air' was composed of just two actions. In 'Hands and Nail', the first action, Nakajima's trunk tilted towards forward-high and twisted to the right from her waist. The right arm simultaneously extended to left-side-middle in front of the left arm, which remained flexed as it inclined towards left-forward-low. Nakajima faced forward-middle, baring her teeth. 'Hands and Nail' then slowly mutated into 'A Hawk', in which the whole of her trunk extended further to parallel the floor whilst her arms spread laterally, each to its own side-middle. In Foster's terms, Hijikata's notation system thus works metaphorically. If 'metaphor operates through words composed into full *Gestalts* (phrases or images) that refer us to something beyond the words', stimulating us to take the 'metaphysical leap from the word to the world' (Fraleigh 1987: 171), and if metaphor elides (whereas simile merely compares) one thing (here natural materials and elemental forces) with another (kinaesthetic sensations), then *Sleep of Stone* became a way through which Nakajima (and empathetically the spectator) could experience herself as resembling properties of a natural world beyond herself. But if, by such means, Hijikata's psychosomatic system provides the opportunity for greater self-knowledge, it does so through fixed choreography that controls and reduces, rather than opens up, how the dancer should intuit kinaesthetically the metaphor she intends to represent. In the case of the phrase 'Stuffed

Air', Hijikata's choreography reduces 'Hands and Nail' and 'A Hawk' to the kinaesthetic essence of a 'sustained projection, firm tension, resistant spatial texture, ... bound energy flow, and muscular control with a central inner attitude. These [predatory] qualities ... define the particular "space power" governing the phrase' (Stewart 1998: 45–48).

Inasmuch as these three psychosomatic movement practices are thus concerned with achieving an experience of unmediated self-presence, self-transcendence, and self-knowledge, I propose that they can be compared with the transcendental idealism of Edmund Husserl's eidetic phenomenology. This operates through two moves. First, by virtue of the *epoché* or phenomenological reduction, Husserlian phenomenology suspends belief in the empirical object as such, so as reduce it to my *intuition* of that object as it makes its appearance within my consciousness. If, as in the three examples given, this can include the performer's kinaesthetic consciousness, sensory memory, or somatic imagination of that object, then there is little difference between the intuition of the object in phenomenology and the performer's use of mental images in these psychosomatic movement practices and performances. Second, through eidetic reduction, Husserlian phenomenology reduces that perceived object to its eidetic essence, and ultimately to, the ineliminable and invariable residue and sure foundation of the ego. By thus grasping that object intuitively and without recourse to 'speculative construction' or deduction (Ricoeur 2002: 576), I become—like the Feldenkrais practitioner, Grotowskian actor, or butoh-ka—fully present to my lived experience of the object I imagine. Furthermore, this enables an identity between my *intuition* of the object and what I *intend* towards this object, including the meanings I bestow upon it. This provides, for Husserl, a 'belief in being' (Ricoeur 2002: 581) in which my intention towards what is given in consciousness feels incarnate within the object as it gives itself. Through such a 'belief in being', I become 'master of myself' (576).

Nonetheless, if Husserl's eidetic phenomenology seems to encapsulate the project of the three psychosomatic movement practices I have described, those practices have been roundly criticized in the same way that Husserlian phenomenology has been. Most obviously, Foucauldian historicism, Marxism, gender and cultural studies, and other forms of materialist analysis all contrarily propose that subjectivity is 'discursively constituted' by 'cultural, political and socioeconomic operations' (Garner 1994: 21). Given these operations and the possibility that the relation of self to self will be 'distorted by violence and by the intrusion of structures of domination', phenomenology's goal of self-knowledge seems doubtful (Ricoeur 2002: 585).

DISTANCIATION, CONVERSATION, OCCASION, APPROPRIATION

However, it is not necessary to reject entirely Husserl's eidetic phenomenology any more than it is necessary to adopt completely a materialist, and therefore largely sceptical, stance towards psychosomatic movement practices. Instead, it is possible to follow a third way, namely that of phenomenological hermeneutics, which, as the name suggests, brings together the methods of phenomenology with the objectives of hermeneutics, that is, the philosophy of interpretation. Although it offers a searching critique of Husserlian idealism, the phenomenological hermeneutics of Paul Ricoeur in particular affirms that phenomenology in general, and thus the constitution of the subject in particular, 'remains the unsurpassable presupposition of hermeneutics', whilst insisting that for this to be so, phenomenology must relinquish its desire to establish any sure foundation for subjectivity and should instead focus on a continuous process of interpreting the world through experience. This is what Ricoeur calls 'belonging', an 'original being-involved in the world' in which I express my 'primacy of care' for the world by unfolding it through interpretation (Ricoeur 2002: 583). Belonging is horizonal and finite and never fixed or masterful, that is, it is delimited by my horizon of understanding of the world, which is determined by the intentions (or meanings) I develop through my intuition (or sensory experience) of the objects of which I become conscious.

The contention of this essay is that some forms of improvised psychosomatic dance are grounded in this horizonal and interpretive mode of being. Phenomenological hermeneutics offers four overlapping terms that illuminate such forms of movement practice. They are *distanciation, conversation, occasion*, and *appropriation*. They are all intrinsic to and functions of interpretation. As Ricoeur explains, distanciation is different from Brecht's *Verfremdungseffekt*, for it involves more than just creating a critical distance from what I wish to interpret; rather, it involves a double movement of remoteness and proximity. On the one hand, to interpret is to interrupt some kind of continuity of which I am a part. In phenomenology, the *epoché* is the imaginary act by which I interrupt the natural attitude, or 'lived experience as purely and simply adhered to' or empirically assumed, precisely in order that it might be *intended*, that is, made conscious and meaningful (Ricoeur 2002: 590). Language, in particular, is the act of writing or speaking by which a lingual sign interrupts preconscious experience in order that I can signify it consciously. On the other hand, to understand something anew is to identify with it afresh: 'to interpret is to render near what is far' (586).

ROTIE'S *MUTABILITY*

This double movement is vital to poetic language. If everyday language interrupts preconscious experience by referring to it, then poetic language in turn 'suspends [this] first order referential function [so] that it releases a second order reference', in which the world is intuited anew 'as *Lebenswelt*, as being-in-the-world' (Ricoeur 2002: 587). Now this, I contend, is all the more the case for the dancer whose movement is *improvised* from a poetic text that remains concealed within the texture of the movement it promotes. This is exemplified by the British butoh artist Marie-Gabrielle Rotie and others for whom performance is the work of exploring an underscore of internal images to discover some kind of correspondence between the self and a choreographic form that is in the process of defining itself. In her twenty-three-minute solo *Mutability* (2003–2005), improvisation was dramaturgically and philosophically necessary to a poetic intuition of being-in-the-world. The solo was inspired by Helen Chadwick's *Of Mutability* (1986), a three-part installation at the ICA in which the first part, 'The Oval Court', consisted of a horizontal collage of blue-toned photocopied images of Chadwick's naked and seemingly dead body, 'a macabre Ophelia floating in a pond with fish, lambs, assorted fruit, rotting around her, a distinctly Rubensian image of life on the turn' (Januszczak 1987). Wanting to 'incarnate something of this', Rotie revisioned Chadwick's images as mutant specimens in a bell jar that she wanted to 'unfreeze' as part of her long-term project to explore 'non-essentialist female morphology' (Rotie 2010: 3) and the reconfiguration' of female subjectivity through the 'refusal to be contained, [and] … inscribed' (Stewart 2015). This led to further research into embryology, images of specimens from Lausanne City Museum, and the surrealist paintings of Hans Giger, who designed the eponymous creature of the film *Alien* (1979). As a consequence, Rotie's underscore for *Mutability* was composed of the following imaginary stimuli to which she responded through movement: a dead human foetus and a lively fish swimming to the top of a bell jar; vulnerable human and posthuman states (an old woman, a young child, a puppet with breaking strings, a baby giraffe with weak legs); figures escaping through a hatch or evading capture by a scientist; rapidly metamorphosing untamed animals (a feral cat, a dinosaur, an angry tiger); and then a phantasmagoria through which Rotie returned to the imagined bell jar, consisting of elements that increasingly solidify (frozen water, metal), a seed that fructifies and then shrivels, death postures, and an alien foetus. Whilst these 'image[s] and the ways [they could] travel through the body [were] clear', the precise ways in which those images were realised physically was left until the moment of performance itself (Rotie 2005: 12). The predetermined dramaturgical arc of the whole show, though, set limits on how this was done. Specifically, the underscore of images supported a physical score that transitioned not only from held shapes to more fluid phrases but from metonymic and figurative to metaphoric and abstract modes of representation, and from clearly composed material that was nearly set to loosely conceived movement ideas that put more emphasis on improvisation. Certainly, choreographic ideas for the first of the piece's five sections were well worked. For instance, for the dead foetus, Rotie's left hand clasped her right flank and her right hand clawed her face as she rocked rhythmically left and right, squawking 'like a banshee' (see fig. 6.1); then as the rising fish she undulated lithely, sequencing from pelvis through torso to neck, first in sagittal plane and then, with increasing fluency and rapidity, in lateral and horizontal planes, as if spiralling up around the jar. However, the second section consisted of tentative articulations of, and interconnections between, isolated body parts, such as between incomplete rotations of the left shoulder, wrists, elbows, and a sickled left foot, that synecdochically replicated the functionally distinct parts of the broken puppet. As the unruly animal imagery of the third section took over, Rotie was predatory, drawing attention to micro-movements in the torso, which she seemed to concertina and then telescopically elongate when she crawled as the feral cat. In the fourth

FIG. 6.1. The 'dead foetus' in *Mutability* (2003–2005). Dancer and choreographer: Marie-Gabrielle Rotie. Costume: Anne Fortin. Photograph by Marian Alonso.

section, she morphed through positions that demanded decreasing mobility, as when, as a metaphor for frozen water and then metal, she completed several horizontal turns over the floor with a rigid hyperextended back, or when she coiled into herself and then found the image of a fructifying seed through a shoulder stand. She fought to retain this upward motion even when death pulled her down; so when, for an unplanned number of times, she hurled herself over the floor into a stiff shape, she then rose swiftly into a loose jump, only to hurl herself down again. All that remained, though, when the seed shrivelled and decomposed into an alien foetus as the show drew to a close, were highly provisional articulations: in one performance, knees were hugged, the heel of a sickled foot thuded against the floor, a clawed hand turned out an imaginary light as the show faded to blackout, and banshee squawks pierced the darkness . . .

So if Hijikata 'arrived at a fixed choreographic butoh process through [an] imagistic process', *Mutability* demonstrated through the way it progressed how Rotie, and many other 'butoh performers after Hijikata', are 'much more interested in listening to the interior image that arises' *as* it arises in the moment of performance and in exploring a 'relationship between the [inner] image and [a] somatic reality' that is unfixed (Rotie 2005: 12). As is the case with Husserl's eidetic phenomenology, Hijikata, Grotowski, and Feldenkrais in their different ways experiment with 'free imaginative variation', but only in order to establish what is invariable, that is, the irreducible properties of the mental object of which the performer is conscious. As Bachelard observes, the poetic image is 'essentially *variational*' whilst concepts are '*constitutive*' (1964 [1958]: xv), yet Hijikata ultimately delimits the otherwise infinite variability of the poetic image by predetermining the relationship between external physical action and the kinaesthetic intuition of the poetic image that underscores that action. Accordingly, Hijikata, like Feldenkrais and Grotowski, privileges *immanence* in the manner of Husserl—that is, he invests in what allows for a singular 'coincidence of reflection with what "has just" been experienced' immanently (Ricoeur 2002: 581). Contrarily, Rotie demonstrates, in a way that is closer to Ricoeur's phenomenological hermeneutics, how the dancer can improvise from a poetic underscore to explore endless free imaginative variations on, and radically divergent perceptions of, her own being-in-the-world. As such, she privileges not what is transcendent *about* herself but what she can incarnate of the world *to* transcend herself. Crucially, then, just as 'hermeneutics can be defined no longer as an inquiry into the psychological intentions that are hidden beneath the text, but rather as the explication of being-in-the-world displayed by the text', so here the concern is not with reducing the meaning of an improvisation to the 'hidden truth' of the dancer's subtext or most immanent intuition of an intended image, but with how that subtext is appropriated through improvisation as the *pretext* for a new way of being-in-the-world. In both cases, 'what is to be interpreted in the text is a proposed world which I could inhabit and in which I could project my ownmost possibilities' (587).

But if improvisation from a poetic underscore thus involves the *appropriation* of new possibilities of and for the self, then paradoxically it must first involve a *distanciation* of self from self. This is not just because self-consciousness is always already 'consciousness *of* something [other than itself] *towards which* it [continually] surpasses itself' (Ricoeur 2002: 590; orig. emphasis). Rather, Rotie's butoh practice also indicates that self's sense of self can only be surpassed through the realization of the self as an 'empty space'. If any lingual sign distanciates experience by interrupting it, then, as Ricoeur explains, this is because that sign is in and of itself an 'empty space' waiting to be filled with the significance of the context of the *conversation* in which that sign is used (590). For instance, 'personal pronouns, demonstratives, descriptions introduced by the definite article' have 'fluctuating' and 'occasional meanings' produced by the interlocutors' responses to the circumstance in which they find themselves and through which their *selves are found* (593). In this sense, any genuine conversation—that is, *any* dialogic encounter between self and other—is, by definition, an improvisation. Although Rotie also refers to the choreographic 'form ... as an empty vessel' which is filled by her moving body as it responds to the underscore of images with which she converses during each performance, her ability to respond is preconditioned by her own state of emptiness. This, indeed, is the 'common starting point' for all her 'methods' of work and the raison d'être for what she calls 'the image score': the need to 'remain 'empty' ... to allow impulses arising from the body to move' her and 'access "other selves"' (Rotie 2010: 10, 2). Rotie wants not 'to dance' but 'to be danced' by the underscore (Stewart 2015). She wants not to interpret but to be interpreted by it. If this state of openness necessitates an emptiness close to the 'Japanese ... concept of *ma*'—that is, the space or interval between things—then it manifested itself in *Mutability* not only through

Rotie's general refusal to force movement from one moment to the next but more palpably in her willingness to wait in a state of 'surrender' between one section and another until the next image possessed her (Rotie 2010: 3, 2). As the show progressed, she dared herself to take longer in between sections by meandering across the empty stage, stroking her forearm or hair to remind herself that she was 'human' whilst waiting patiently for that empty 'space to activate the image score' (Stewart 2015). All told, then, *Mutability* was a dance in which the self was lost so that new poetic variations of the self could be found. Here dance is the 'distanciation of self from itself within the interior of appropriation' (Ricoeur 2002: 588).

Monson's Environmental Dance

The four key terms from phenomenological hermeneutics—'distanciation', 'conversation', 'occasion', 'appropriation'—are manifest in different ways and to different degrees in other psychosomatic improvised dance practices. Indeed, these terms could provide a means of comparing and contrasting a wide range of improvisation practices that work with an underscore. As I have explained, Rotie's work exemplifies psychosomatic processes through which new poetic possibilities of the self can be appropriated through distanciation. However, her performance works characteristically integrate those processes with Nick Parkin's prerecorded electro-acoustic compositions, carefully conceived costume designs, and other scenographic elements which, by virtue of being predetermined, inevitably set limits on what is contingent and unforeseen in each performance. In contrast, the environmental improvisation practice of US dance artist Jennifer Monson emphasizes the *occasions* in which those improvisations occur. This is not just because her work is genuinely site-specific and so foregrounds the particular environmental circumstances in which she improvises. Monson's work is occasional also because it heightens consciousness of time by creating a counterpoint between past and present. This can be seen in her exercise Tracing Weight. Here a dancer improvises movement from his sensations of the environment until a witness calls a halt. The witness then traces a finger around the points where the dancer's weight is concentrated and distributed, including not only points where different body parts bring different degrees of weight to bear upon the ground but also points where weight gathers between one body part and another. This process is continued until the dancer has established a score of postures, each with its own particular composition of points where weight is concentrated. The dancer is then ready to perform, not merely by repeating the score of postures but by extemporizing movement from the underscore of weight sensations of which he has become conscious. Monson exemplified this in an improvisation on 1 May 2006 during *Water Log* (2006–2007), a project Monson and I developed intermittently over two years at Aldcliffe Marsh and other locations in the Lune Estuary near Lancaster. Monson rolled slowly over the verge of a gully; as she did so, she softened and folded her face, right arm, and leg into the plump grass yet extended her left arm, splayed her left

FIG. 6.2. Improvisation from weight sensations during *Water Log* (2006–2007). Dancer: Jennifer Monson. Photograph by Nigel Stewart.

hand, and twisted her left leg over and against her right thigh to sickle her left foot into a pocket of earth (see fig. 6.2).

Crucially, whilst improvising from this underscore of remembered weight sensations, the dancer also allows her movement to modulate in response to environmental events as they occur in the present. In this *conversation* between past and present, synchronicities prosper. In developing the score for my own iteration of Tracing Weight at Aldcliffe Marsh, I lunged forward and extended my arms towards the horizon so my foot could smack the edge of a large pond. As I did so, ripples were transmitted to the other side in the same direction as a dark cloud that slid overhead. Later I extemporized on this and other postures. At exactly the point at which my foot smacked the water's edge, swollen raindrops splashed over my face and plopped into the pond. My chest and palms flowered to a rumbling sky . . .

If the underscore of Tracing Weight consists of sense impressions, then Monson's Logging process involves an underscore of more complex and explicit layers of textual information. At timed intervals, each dancer 'logs' perceptions of different layers of his experience of a location. These layers consist of *factual* information, namely the exact 'time' and 'location' in which the logging occurs; *psychosomatic* information concerning the dancer's own immediate 'physical', 'emotional', and 'spiritual' states; and *summative* information in the form of a 'question' to answer, a statement about the total 'experience' acquired, and a 'relation' that has been perceived between two or more environmental features that synecdochically represent the location as a whole. At each location, the dancer then improvises in response to some or all of this data. Having repeated this process a designated number of times across an agreed terrain, the dancer is then able to convert the data which has been logged into an underscore for a performance.

As in Tracing Weight, it is vital that the dancer focuses not only on the movement that arises from this underscore but also the contingencies of the occasion in which that movement is performed. A case in point is an underscore derived from data I logged using the aforementioned categories at hourly intervals during a trek with Monson across the Lune Estuary throughout 30 April 2007, and which I finally performed in the 'golden hour' before dusk on the same day. During that performance, my hands rapidly flicked open and shut in evocation of the diffuse but vigorous birdsong I had heard at 08:09 that morning, my left index finger traced a straight line in memory of the sustained crunch of passing cyclists along a nearby track that I heard at the same time, and my torso jabbed left and right in recall of the cold felt that morning. Taken together, these three movements were the essential 'relation' I perceived at that location in the morning. Yet all three movements came into 'conversation' with something new: my right arm as it rippled and cast shadows in that gorgeous late afternoon sun . . .

Two principle points can be made about this conversation. First, this work deepens our appreciation of *distanciation* as a precondition of environmental knowledge. Again, there is a double movement of remoteness and proximity. To have this conversation though improvisation, I can no longer simply inhabit the environment or myself as other living creatures do. All eight ways of logging a location through writing bring to consciousness, and in a sense constitute, the horizon of understanding which the dancer has of the location at the time at which it is logged. By making this horizon conscious, the dancer is distanced from her otherwise unbroken prereflective experience of the environment, but by virtue of the same, the dancer gains an *orientation* and thus a proximity to it. In this way, language transforms environment into what Gadamer calls 'world'. 'This does not mean that [the human being] leaves his habitat but that he has another posture toward it—a free, distanced orientation—which is always realized [through] language' (Gadamer 1989: 444), including movement informed by language and which is itself language-like, since it is 'articulated' (445). Indeed, as I have shown in Monson's Tracing Weight, this world-bearing, world-creating posture literally involves postures through which a prereflective environment transmutes into an interpreted world.

Second, Monson's work indicates that the interpretation of an environment through improvisation depends on an expanded consciousness of time. If Rotie exemplifies how the self is an unfinished process, then Monson exemplifies how this process is inextricably interwoven with an understanding of the environment in a continuous process of change and, furthermore, how an understanding of that process is considerably enriched through a growing consciousness of how changes in the present do not erase but rather transform events in the past. Tracing Weight and Logging involve neither the slavish repetition of a choreographic score determined in the past nor the chimera of a so-called 'free improvisation' in the present. Rather, traces of an environmental past interlock with an intuition of the environmental present to effect an expanded time-consciousness of the natural world.

I contend that this encapsulates in embryonic form the model that Gadamer has for what he calls 'historically effected consciousness' (Gadamer 1989: xv, 300–307, 341–377). In general, this begins when I acknowledge the prejudgments (presuppositions, fore-knowing, or fore-projections) which constitute my present horizon of understanding of the object of which I am conscious (e.g., a person with whom I converse, text which I read, an item which I handle, a place where I am). For Heidegger, Gadamer, and Ricoeur, this 'structure of anticipation' is of critical importance to what they all call the 'hermeneutic circle'. This circle of understanding is not a 'vicious circle' in which I merely confirm what I think I already know but a 'positive possibility' for new know-ledge in which my prejudgements or 'fore-structures' are 'work[ed] out ... in terms of the things themselves' (Heidegger 1962: 154). This is exactly what Tracing Weight and Logging demand. With the latter, gestures that distilled my kinaesthetic consciousness of that environment in the morning (flicking hands, gliding finger, jabbing torso), and which therefore constituted my somatic prejudgments and fore-structures of knowing that environment later in the day, overlapped with and were transformed by what was new about my kinaesthetic intuition of the same environment in the evening (rippling right arm casting shadows). Thus, my 'fore-projection ... is constantly revised in terms of what emerges ... [from] understanding what is there' (Gadamer 1989: 267).

So if, through Monson's disciplined methods of intuiting and interpreting an environ-ment, I became aware of significant differences between my horizon of understanding that environment *now* (e.g., the Lune Estuary two hours before dusk) from my horizon of understanding that same environment *then* (e.g., the Lune Estuary as I logged it two hours after dawn), those differences of interpretation were mutually inclusive and cru-cial to my growing knowledge of, belonging to, and care for that world. When I com-pleted that benign circle of understanding by returning late in the afternoon to where I began in the morning, I was both back where I began and who I was then and already somewhere else and someone new. All told, then, I experienced a fusion, but never con-flation, between past and present horizons of understanding that led, finally, to an ex-panded, historically effected kinaesthetic consciousness of the natural world. 'What results is neither the collapse of these horizons into an undifferentiated timelessness, nor the solidification of each horizon into a self-alienated consciousness, but rather "the fusion of these horizons"' in and through the dancing body (Stewart 2003: 37). 'The point of fusion is a point of "agreement" in between present and past, self and other' (37), through which both are 'transpos[ed]' to 'a higher universality' of a 'historically effected consciousness' (Gadamer 1989: 306, 305).

Finally, in the improvised dance of Jennifer Monson, this historically effected kin-aesthetic consciousness of, and conversation with, the world can expand indefin-itely. If Rotie projects imaginary new possibilities for herself through the open-ended ways she appropriates a poetic text, then the world into which those possibilities are projected is still, at least in the case of her theatre pieces, what Gadamer calls an 'aesthetically-differentiated' scenic world with clearly defined spatial and temporal parameters (1989: 85–87). With Monson, however, the world into which the dancer projects new possibilities for herself, at least in her site-specific work, is an unlimited aesthetically nondifferentiated world of which the dancer is already a part. If the text from which those possibilities are projected is itself derived from and adds to that world—and if that world is therefore not the environment as objectified by science or the environment as preconsciously experienced but the environment to which I am continually reorientated through conversation; and if, furthermore, this conversation is by definition an exchange in which meanings are determined and transformed by the fluctuating conditions and circumstances of the environment itself—then in these site-specific psychosomatic environmental dances I am no longer the source or 'site-in-life' of my own self but a bodily 'being-in-the-world' to which I belong through a conversation that of necessity involves interpretive 'explication' (Ricoeur 2002: 584, 587). In such improvised conversations, the world and I are equiprimordial, for both are unfinished interpretations of one in the other. In this sense, the improvising dancer is, par excellence, 'the interpreter *in medias res*': in the 'middle of a conversation which has already begun' and in which she is ever trying to orientate herself 'in order to be able to contribute to it' (585).

References

Bachelard, Gaston. (1964 [1958]) *The Poetics of Space*. Trans. Maria Jolas. Boston: Beacon Press.

Barba, Eugenio, and Savarese, Nicola. (2006) *A Dictionary of Theatre Anthropology: The Secret Art of the Performer*. 2nd ed. Trans. Richard Fowler with Judy Barba. Abingdon, UK: Routledge.

Feldenkrais, Moshe. (1977) *Awareness through Movement*. Harmondsworth, UK: Penguin.

Foster, Susan Leigh. (1986) *Reading Dancing: Bodies and Subjects in Contemporary American Dance*. Berkeley: University of California Press.

Fraleigh, Sondra Horton. (1987) *Dance and the Lived Body: A Descriptive Aesthetics*. Pittsburgh: University of Pittsburgh Press.

Gadamer, Hans-Georg. (1989 [1975]) *Truth and Method*. 2nd ed. Trans. W. Glen-Doepel. Rev. trans. Joel Weinsheimer and Donald G. Marshall. London: Sheed and Ward.

Garner, Stanton B. (1994) *Bodied Spaces: Phenomenology and Performance in Contemporary Drama*. Ithaca, NY: Cornell University Press.

Grotowski, Jerzy. (1968) *Towards a Poor Theatre*. Ed. Eugenio Barba. London: Methuen.

Heidegger, Martin. (1962) *Being and Time*. Trans. John Macquarrie and Edward Robinson. San Francisco: Harper and Row.

Januszczak, Waldemar. (1987) Invading Your Space. *Guardian*. 18 November. https://www.theguardian.com/artanddesign/1987/nov/18/20yearsoftheturnerprize.turnerprize. Accessed 29 March 2017.

Ricoeur, Paul. (2002 [1981]) Phenomenology and Hermeneutics. In Moran, Dermot, and Mooney, Timothy (eds.), *The Phenomenology Reader*. London and New York: Routledge, 579–600.

Rotie, Marie-Gabrielle. (2005) Post Performance Discussion. Interviewer Nigel Stewart. 24 May. http://www.rotieproductions.com/articles/4567926104. Accessed 30 March 2017.

Rotie, Marie-Gabrielle. (2010) *Mythic*. Unpublished lecture paper.

Stewart, Nigel. (1998) Re-languaging the Body: Phenomenological Description and the Dance Image. *Performance Research* 3(2): 42–53.

Stewart, Nigel. (2003) To and Fro and In-between: The Ontology of the Image in Thomas Lehmen's *Stations*. In Sven-Thore Kramm (ed.), *Stationen*, Number 3. Berlin: Podewil/Thomas Lehmen, 29–38.

Stewart, Nigel. (2015) *Mutability*. Unpublished paper, including quotations from an interview with Marie Gabrielle Rotie on 13 March 2015.

PART II

ATTUNEMENT AND PERCEPTION

CHAPTER 7

....

I NOTICE THAT
I'M NOTICING . . .

....

SALLY DOUGHTY

EARLIER this year, a friend gave me a T-shirt with a graphic on the front saying 'it's not about how you look, it's about how you see'. I thought it was delightful that she had bought me a present that nods to my improvisational practices and my research into noticing. It was only later, when it was pointed out to me that it could well be referring to 'what we look like' rather than the act of looking 'at' something that I realized my possible misinterpretation. However, it prompted me to think again about the difference between looking and seeing and how they, in turn, differ from the act of *noticing*.

There is a big difference. I will come to this in a bit.

Given that a fundamental premise of movement improvisation is that 'it includes the process of creating and/or choosing your movements as you are doing them' (De Spain 2014: 5), two of the million-dollar questions that are commonly asked in relation to improvisation are: what do artists draw on to inform their improvised material, and how do they do that? This essay therefore considers the concept of noticing in improvisational movement practices from an improviser's in vivo perspective. It specifically interrogates the processes involved in noticing *how* and *what* an improviser notices and how this can have a significant impact on the developing improvisation. In my endeavour to grapple with ideas of noticing in this essay, I draw from my experience of studying with many leading teachers, performers, and researchers of improvisation, including Barbara Dilley, Rosalind Crisp, and Andrew Morrish, to exemplify the significance of noticing in their improvisational practices. However, the primary case study here focuses on my experience of working with American choreographer Deborah Hay in her 2011 Solo Performance Commissioning Project (SPCP) and addresses her orientation to dance, which emphasizes paying attention to specific practices of performance.

I share my experiences of and reflections on improvisation by including extracts from my ongoing personal journal on my practice, as well as from journal entries made whilst working specifically with Hay and other artists. I refer also to dance artists Simon Ellis and Matthias Sperling, who also have engaged in Hay's SPCP, in order to add multiple voices to my own.

And I notice that I am noticing, again.

(Doughty 2011b)

I have long been interested in the spontaneous decisions made when improvising and from where artists source ideas to inform their improvised material. This line of enquiry has underpinned my work as artist, educator, and researcher and is informed by the practices and writings of many artists and scholars (Johnston 2006; De Spain 2014, 1997; Martin 2006, 2007, 2011; Dilley 2011; Crisp 2013). Whilst their improvisational practices are inevitably very personal, one concept that is common across all their work is that they encourage an ability to notice in order to develop one's awareness of engaging in the form.

As I have alluded to already, there is a pronounced difference between looking, seeing, and noticing, and each of these activities demands a different degree of consciousness and awareness. The most immediate difference here is that noticing, unlike looking and seeing, is not restricted to the visual sense but encompasses all manner of sensory activity. However, in order to exemplify the differences in these activities, I offer this visual example: 'looking' merely describes a direction of one's gaze, as in 'she looked out of the window'. 'Seeing' suggests that she sees something or someone but does not register anything of the subject beyond that, as in 'she looked out of the window and saw a cat'. Alva Noë suggests that 'sometimes we see not in order to act, but just in order to know, or to enjoy our experiences of seeing. When you lie back and watch the passing clouds ... you are not using visual skills for purposes of action' (2004: 11). However, in order to act upon what we see, hear, or feel, we must shift from a mode of inactive seeing into one of more active noticing. And so, to conclude this example, if she observes something that she may not have been looking directly *for* or *at* (Perkins 1982: 78) when she saw the cat whilst looking out of the window, then her act of looking becomes more purposeful and shifts into a mode of noticing.

John Mason proposes that 'on the one hand we notice all the time, make choices, and get through the day. On the other hand, there is so much more that we could notice, so many more options we could choose between' (2002: 9). Translating Mason's observations into the context of improvisation, it can be said that the improviser is exposed to countless features that have the potential to be noticed and used as source material in the developing improvised work. Whilst this can certainly offer much inspiration, it can also severely impede the improviser who might feel faced with an overwhelming number of possibilities to choose from that can leave her not knowing what to do (Kraus 1990, cited in Buckwalter 2010: 56). Not knowing what to do in an improvisation can be, at worst, totally debilitating, but at its best can be utterly liberating and is precisely why some artists choose to work with improvisation. Therefore, in my practice I have been working towards developing an understanding of the feature/s I notice when improvising; how that happens ...

why did I notice my breath rather than the shaft of light in that moment?

(Doughty 2011a)

... and how I choose to work with that feature in my improvisation. It is apparent that there are two different kinds of engagement in operation here that inevitably come into play within a split second: the first one deals with noticing the feature, and the second one deals with noticing how I choose to work with that feature in my practice, which directly impacts on my compositional choices.

American dance artist and scholar Kent De Spain has attempted to define these different types of engagement and refers to features as 'operands' that provide much of the 'what' and 'how' of an improvisation, whilst a determinant provides the 'why' and literally determines the improvisation choices that are made (1997: 138). He goes on to suggest that choice-making is 'primarily a conscious acknowledgement of the application of intentions and agendas and structures/delimitations to the sensed multiple possibilities' (139); and I propose that in order for an improviser to begin to develop the ability to shape her improvisation in a conscious way, she must first and foremost develop an ability to notice: to notice *what* she notices (operands) and to notice *how* she chooses to work compositionally with what she notices (determinants).

The phenomenon of noticing in improvisational practices is not new and, indeed, is considered by many to be a fundamental principle of the form. However, whilst artists and scholars concur that a degree of conscious awareness can be present in improvisational practices, when it comes to agreeing on the terminology used to define this phenomenon, we enter a territory that is slippery and tricky. De Spain refers to developing attention and awareness (2014: 168) and 'attending to' something (1997: 131); Meg Stuart calls it 'being absolutely present' (2010: 15); Dilley promotes 'mindfulness' (2011: 15), which Mary Bateson further expands on by suggesting that it is 'being awake to situations, being mindful rather than mindless' (1994, cited in Mason 2002: 38). In her practice, Hay uses the very specific phrase 'here and gone, here and gone, notice and let it go' (2011), which encourages the dancer to stay present and alert in each moment and engenders an acute awareness of one's potentiality in response to operands. However, regardless of the personal semantic preferences cited here, it can be said that all of these terms point to an act of giving 'attention to the action itself' (Tolle 2011: 57) and that the act of noticing whilst improvising is a complex and multilayered experience. Mihalyi Csikszentmihalyi echoes these observations in his concept of 'flow', in which he identifies joy, creativity, and the process of total involvement with life as positive aspects of the human experience (1993: xi). He goes on to observe that 'although the flow experience appears to be effortless, it is far from being so. It often requires strenuous physical exertion, or highly disciplined mental activity. It does not happen without the application of skilled performance. Any lapse in concentration will erase it. And yet whilst it lasts consciousness works smoothly, action follows action seamlessly' (54). Csikszentmihalyi's concept of flow offers a direct and useful parallel for ideas concerning improvisation through its emphasis on self-awareness and action. Developing an awareness of one's spontaneous decision-making process at any moment in an improvisation helps an improviser to understand more about the creative options that are available to her when she improvises and, in doing so, supports her to develop greater understanding and craft in her improvised dancing.

Stephen Nachmanovitch writes about his experience as an improvisational violinist and observes that 'our experience as improvisers is one of direct encounter with what is directly in front of our noses, whatever that may be: our partners when we're improvising together, the unconscious, the room that we're in, the people that we're playing for or with (2006). He cites features that De Spain terms physical operands, which include movement, physicality, effort, sensation, and environment, as well as cognitive operands that include culturally based communication skills, imagination, cognitive skills, emotion, and memory (De Spain 1997: 134). De Spain's codification of the range of physical and cognitive operands available to an improviser is testament to the complexity inherent in being able to notice some, all, or indeed any of them at each and every moment of an improvisation.

> I notice anatomical detail: where my weight is
> and how far my right hand is from my nose.
> Today I feel a bit stiff and my toes are cold.
> This movement
> reminds me of something else;
> it feels like I've just woken up;
> it makes me think of sitting,
> watching seagulls when I was a girl.
>
> (Doughty 2007)

Many artists develop highly personal improvisational practices that engender an ability to develop an awareness of operands and determinants in their work. Ruth Zaporah, initiator of the improvisation form Action Theater, teaches students to notice where their attention is and to use that in their practice. She teaches that the improviser and his improvisation are not separate entities—one cannot exist without the other—so noticing how one is feeling can be the stuff of the improvisation (in De Spain 2014: 170), and she suggests that rather than being distracted about not knowing what to do, 'do a distracted improvisation' (171). Andrew Morrish makes a similar suggestion, advising improvisers to replace the common realization ' "I can't *think* what to do" with "I *notice* what to do" ' (2013; emphasis in original), which suggests a subtle yet significant shift in how one might approach an improvisation. Rosalind Crisp uses a metaphorical 'net' as a framework that is designed to support a dancer's ability to notice whilst improvising. The net uses four ideas—'pouring'; 'unholding'; 'breath' and 'taking care of yourself'—that the dancer can work with at any moment in her practice to bring attention to herself. Crisp acknowledges that they also serve as 'excuses to do what I want!' (2013) and affirms that the more attention she pays to her practice, the more choices she has at her disposal in order to craft her improvised work.

> The net provides some shape for my improvisation, which
> at times, can feel amorphous and
> akin to reining in a difficult dance partner!
>
> (Doughty 2013)

Barbara Dilley collapses together improvisational dance with her practice of Shambhala Buddhism and uses her improvisational structures as 'a laboratory to discover the many ways dancers are influenced—first of all, just noticing that we *are* influenced and then observing who and what influences us as we dance, and how and why they do so' (cited in Buckwalter 2010: 16). In 2011, I participated in a weeklong workshop with Dilley as part of the Lower Left Group's March to Marfa Laboratory. One of the scores we practised daily was *The Red Square*, in which Dilley marked out a large square using red cord to define the performance space. We sat outside the square looking towards it and visualized ourselves in it, either in relation to others in the space or on our own. Once visualized, we entered the space and inhabited our visualization. This structure provided me with space and time to consider my response to *The Red Square* and to other dancers in the space; to notice how I went about constructing my visualization and how I contributed to the practice.

> I noticed that in the early period of working
> I placed primacy on my visual sense,
> seeing and almost predicting how I might physically relate
> to others already in the space.
> However with practice, it became evident that my other senses
> could also determine the nature of my 'visualisation'
> and help inform my decision making process in this practice.
>
> (Doughty 2011a)

Dilley teaches that the simpler the score, the more challenging the practice (2011), which at the risk of sounding like some sort of riddle encourages us to move beyond our habitual movement patterns so as to begin to find more developed and unfamiliar responses to the improvisation task. By having to consciously attend to the simplicity of Dilley's *Red Square* score, I developed an active form of engagement that shifted my practice beyond my more known and familiar responses. Understanding more about my particular habits, preferences, and approaches supports me to more consciously craft my dancing in the moment. Refining my ability to notice helps me to develop new knowledge and skill, but only if I consciously attend to the act of improvising. Otherwise, I risk falling into the trap of revisiting tried and tested methods that, though they potentially serve me well, do not allow me to refine and expand my capacity for spontaneous composition.

If, as Chris Johnston claims, 'the artist who consciously uses improvisation benefits from conjunctions, associations, accidents and impulses' (2006: 6), then it follows that consciousness is key to innovation, and I suggest therefore that engaging consciously with noticing is the bedrock of this activity.

> I notice that the shaft of sunlight on the dance studio floor
> has faded slightly.
> I dip my fingers into that space as the light fades completely.
> I sing a low, soft song.
>
> (Doughty 2012)

In an attempt to develop a degree of conscious awareness of and in my improvisation practices, I have, over time, refined my line of enquiry down to two key questions:

> What do I do?
> Why do I do it?
>
> (Doughty 2006)

These questions have shaped me, rubbed against me and tripped me up in my dancing and in my thinking about dancing for a number of years. In using these questions as a lens through which I interrogate my improvisation practice, I have not found defini-tive answers (nor do I necessarily wish to); instead I use these questions as prompts to stay alert and questioning in my dancing. I am fascinated by the processes that are in-volved in how I pinpoint a particular feature out of all of the operands available to me, at times noticing the micro in the macro, such as the specks of dust in the shaft of sunlight in the expanse of the studio space I am working in. Why is my attention drawn to the dust specks in that moment, over and above the other infinite possibilities in the space? Mason prompts me to consider 'what makes some features salient and others invisible? What is the significance of what I find myself observing? What can be learned about what is not noticed, not marked, not recorded?' (2002: 183), and bringing these ques-tions into my practice helps me to understand more about my particular habits, prefer-ences and compositional choices, so that I can more consciously craft my dancing in the moment. Mason's questions, as well as my own, serve as fuel for my ongoing investiga-tions in to my improvisation practice and inevitably fed into my experience of working with Hay in her 2011 SPCP.

The SPCP works like this: artists commission a solo from Hay and spend an eleven-day residency with her practising her performance practice, learning the solo's choreo-graphic score, and being coached and guided by her in the performance of the solo. Each artist then undertakes a daily performance practice of the solo for between three and nine months to develop a personal adaptation of the work. For each SPCP, Hay proposes an original solo score. The 2011 SPCP score was titled *I Think Not*.

Hay works with a set of performance practices that engage the performer on sev-eral levels of consciousness at once (Buckwalter 2010: 170) and emphasize the ability to notice, see and perceive in order to develop an expansion of one's sensibilities. The concepts of noticing, seeing and perceiving are often used casually and interchangeably in both day-to-day and improvisational contexts, but Hay uses them to refer to very individual specific modes of engagement in her practice. I have already addressed here the differences between seeing and noticing, and the concept of perception offers yet another perspective on how we use our senses to navigate the world around us. Writing about perception and consciousness, Noë claims that 'perceptual experience acquires content thanks to our possession of bodily skills. *What we perceive* is determined by *what we do* [and] by what we are *ready* to do' (2004: 1). He goes on to argue that 'self-movement depends on perceptual modes of self-awareness' (2), which suggests that perception, like noticing, is a mindful, conscious activity that needs to be attended to.

Hay defines the differences between noticing, seeing, and perceiving and how she attends to them in her practice thus: 'I think that it is Deborah who notices, while my whole body is the perceiver and it is my eyes that see.... It is Deborah who must reconfigure her body into her whole body at once' (2014a). Making the distinction between *herself* and *Deborah* suggests that she considers herself to be multifaceted, with each facet being attuned to and serving a particular function in her work that when thought of holistically—or wholly—puts her in a state of readiness in her practice.

Hay's performance practice is not dissimilar to improvisation practices that I have previously engaged in that focus on developing an awareness of oneself and the potential for creativity in any one moment. However, Hay does not conceive of her practice as improvisation, as her experience is that 'there isn't enough time to improvise ... we don't have the time to invent. It's about practising the potential to perceive ... there's just so much to attend to in any one moment' (2011). She refers to it instead as 'practising performance' (2011), yet there are distinct parallels between her practice and that of many artists working with improvisation. Her practice feels like improvisation to me, and Buckwalter observes that because it focuses on presence it is very closely aligned to the practice of the performance of improvisation (2010: 38). The value of focusing on presence or being present cannot be underestimated in improvisational practices, and indeed Johnston encourages improvisers to 'be living entirely moment-to-moment because it's in that spontaneous present that self-discovery is possible and creativity lives. In that present you are more open to receive signals, intuitions and impulses' (2006: 112).

Hay's imperative to develop performer presence is underpinned by an ability to notice, which is developed through practising multiple performance directives and questions that 'focus the performer's attention on presence' (Buckwalter 2010) and 'transform into somatic experiences' (Hay 2011: 38). She is very upfront that these performance directives and questions are not possible to do or answer, and she advises that we should not try to get *it* right because we can't do *it*, and that instead we should play with *it* in the moment that *it* reveals *itself* to us (Hay 2011; emphasis in original). Three of Hay's performance directives in particular resonated for me throughout my experience of the SPCP, into the ensuing three-month adaptation period of *I Think Not* (2011) and beyond into my ongoing personal practice. These are:

Here and gone, here and gone, notice and let it go.

The whole body at once the teacher, bring her with you, bring him with you, no hesitation, no reconsideration.

Turn your fucking head.

(Hay 2011)

These directives posed significant creative challenges for me and prompted me to re-think the potential that noticing might offer me in any one moment of my improvising.

HERE AND GONE, HERE AND GONE, NOTICE AND LET IT GO

On day 1 of the SPCP, we practised walking and noticing. Hay gave the directive 'here and gone, here and gone, notice and let it go' (2011) as a way of encouraging us to not become too attached to what we noticed in any one moment. It acts as a useful reminder to stay present and alert and promotes 'the essential condition that is common to all moments—one unfolds into the next: there is no stopping. Actions take place within a flow, within a continuum' (Zaporah 2002: 52). Hay practises what she refers to as 'the continuity of my discontinuity' (2014b), which directly reflects my experience of engaging in the practice of here and gone. In disattaching myself from what I inhabit in any one moment,

I free myself up to engage in the newness of the next one.
And in dis-attaching myself from this moment
I free myself up to inhabit the next.

(Doughty 2011b)

Practising here and gone does not allow the performer to dwell in any one moment or idea for too long, which Hay defines as being 'before attachment to [the idea] takes hold' (2011). Reflecting on practising here and gone, Simon Ellis (SPCP 2011 participant) said: 'it is about not being seduced by particular sensations or things happening in my visual or auditory field ... there is no particular sensory experience that is more vital or more important than any other' (2014). In improvisational practices, it is easy to over-stay one's welcome with an idea that is being attended to; it can feel like a tough choice to leave it and move on, particularly if the exploration is not yet resolved or there is still scope for more play. Here and gone demands that the improviser moves on sooner than she might prefer or before she is 'seduced' (Ellis 2014) and, as is Hay's wont, provokes a challenge to habitual patterns. Matthias Sperling (SPCP 2012 participant) recalls that here and gone firstly refers to time passing but then goes on to include a more holistic perception. The *here* is about probing my perception of the moment: what is my perception now? By asking that question, I form a perception of time and space in this moment, which I can then use as material. And with *gone*, I dis-attach from the momentarily fixed construct that I've created [with *here*]. I acknowledge that something else is already arriving and acknowledge its nature as a construct. So although there are things that endure and there's a continual passage of time and a continual state of change, there's always a simultaneous condition. Here and gone allows me to attempt to hold them both by alternating my attention to each of them. (2014)

Hay's practice deals largely with 'challenging performers to be hyper-present while moving' (De Spain 2014: 28), and both Ellis and Sperling attest to this in their reflections of working with her. When practising here and gone, I noticed that my pattern of letting go of what I was noticing in order to move on encouraged my phrasing of movement material to become quite staccato. I have never thought of myself as a body-popper, but I was definitely finding that quality in my dancing! I literally took Hay at her word and was engaging in a new movement investigation in response to every new feature that I noticed,

> and I noticed that, overall, I tended to respond to what I see

> (Doughty 2011a)

Csikszentmihalyi considers his concept of flow a means of creativity, and he states that most flow activities 'have their own pace, their own sequence of events marking transitions from one state to another without regard to equal intervals of duration' (1993: 67). Although I was certainly finding my own pace whilst practising here and gone, the constant renewal of information that I was processing in fairly short time frames was reflected in my dancing, producing an effect reminiscent of jump cuts in video editing, due to the fairly drastic shifts I was making to my movement material in response to what I was noticing. Hay fed back that I needed to develop an awareness of the time frame for everything I noticed, and working with this encouraged me to investigate a very different kind of movement aesthetic and vocabulary that challenged the more familiar patterns and phrasing in my dancing. It took me some time before I realized that I did not need to respond to every thing that I was noticing, and as I write this now, this seems very obvious! Ellis likens this observation to having not yet reached a state of object permanence,[1] and so, for example, the door is constantly a new door when the improviser notices it: everything is a new meeting (2014). When practising not responding to *every* new feature I noticed, I did not shift or alter the temporal nature of my engagement with here and gone but instead worked at giving more space to the regularity of my shifting attention in order to notice an operand and make compositional choices in response.

THE WHOLE BODY AT ONCE THE TEACHER, BRING HER WITH YOU, BRING HIM WITH YOU, NO HESITATION, NO RECONSIDERATION

The second of Hay's directives to be impactful on my practice was to consider 'the whole body at once the teacher, bring her with you, bring him with you, no hesitation, no reconsideration' (2011), and it served me in multiple ways. The particularity of Hay's choice of language resonated with me and prompted a reconsideration of what I thought I knew about myself as a rich resource for my improvised material. It particularly emphasized conceiving of myself as a whole animal (Noë 2004: 20) and supported me to not prioritize my visual sense, which I noticed I tended to do.

Bringing this directive into my practice has certainly freed me up from my more habitual movement patterns and behaviours by reaffirming that *all* I have to draw from and use in my improvisations is me—Sally. If I do not have an awareness of myself or an awareness of what I am noticing, then I have nothing. There is a technique used in Action Theatre in which one scans one's body to identify the potential in any areas that are not the main focal point of the activity so that attention may be brought to these to enrich one's material, and this came to mind when working with Hay. Bringing it in to my practising of here and gone, and of my whole body as teacher, assisted me in my attempts to move beyond a purely visual response and to develop a greater ability to notice the potential in all that was available to me. Mason notes 'that it is almost too obvious even to say that what you do not notice you cannot act on; you cannot choose to act if you do not notice an opportunity' (2002: 7), and I conceive of this as noticing the potential in any one moment or, as Hay succinctly puts it, 'I create with everything I perceive' (2011).

> It's all about noticing the potential in where I am,
> what I'm doing,
> what the thing that I'm doing could be.
> Notice the potential.
>
> (Doughty 2011b)

Enhancing my ability to notice with my other senses rather than majoratively with my eyes freed me up to recognize the potential in other operands available to me so that I could practise more acutely a performance question—or tool for the dancer—that Hay outlines in the score for *I Think Not* (2011). She poses the question 'what if how you see while you are dancing, including what you imagine, invent, project, and can and cannot see in a prescribed area near, mid-range, and far, at any given moment, is a means by which movement arises without looking for it?' (2011). Practising bringing my whole body at once the teacher into my dancing supported me in using cognitive and physical operands that were more aligned to internal, imaginative, and sensing mechanisms in my body, which balanced the more regular pattern of how I was using my eyes to source external information.

TURN YOUR FUCKING HEAD

Hay's directive to 'turn your fucking head in order to refresh the body' (2011) has evolved in response to the recognition that we have been choreographed by external factors such as culture, parents, gender, and politics. Hay proposes that in order to rid ourselves of the ways our movement and behaviour is determined by these outside influences, we need to turn our fucking heads to refresh the body's palette and have a whole other experience in the body (2011).

In my practice, turning my fucking head introduced the possibility to experience multiple others in my body rather than being fixed in a singular dimension. I noticed that turning my fucking head refreshed my body's palette primarily through my visual sense again: noticing new material with my eyes allowed me to reconsider, for example, my spatial orientation to what it was I noticed. However, having engaged in Hay's practice over a period of time, I refined my ability to notice that the act of merely turning my (fucking) head from left to right generated enough cellular fire to significantly shift my understanding of where I was at any one moment, as well as noticing the potential in where I was, what I was doing, what I was noticing, and the compositional choices I was making. Sperling makes a similar observation, stating that turning his fucking head refers first to 'seeing, and the literal movement of turning my skull to see something else, but then departs to a much more holistic mobilisation of the boundaries of my perception' (2014).

The primacy of my visual sense when turning my fucking head became very evident for me, and whilst practising *I Think Not* (2011) during the SPCP I noticed that I tended to focus my gaze quite directly at times towards the audience (who were the other participating artists), looking at them in the eyes, perhaps to be a little provocative but also just wanting to bring them in to my work. In much of my performance work, I enjoy a direct relationship with the audience, sometimes through voice but always through my gaze. Hay fedback that I came out of myself a little when taking care of my relationship with my audience and that I attended to them a little more than I needed to (2011). Later, during my three-month daily practice, I wrote:

> I noticed the timing of my head after naming hands:
> I tend to pop my head/focus up to audience—
> try to shift that—it feels predictable and 'known' now.

(Doughty 2011b)

In an attempt to destabilize this predictable pattern in my work, I recalled studying with Dilley (2011) and working with her Five Eye Practices, which she developed in order to 'offer dancers options to a habitual interior or fixed exterior gaze' (Buckwalter 2010: 118). The Five Eye Practices include closed eyes, peripheral seeing, infant eyes, looking between things, and direct looking; playing with these different qualities allowed me to significantly shift how I saw, looked, and noticed in my practice. I became more aware of how I could turn the volume down on my visual sense and up on my whole body, to further reinforce Hay's directive of 'the whole body at once the teacher' (2011).

Hay's proposal to turn my fucking head to refresh the body lets me deal with two possibilities: first, to attend to the new information that I experience (whether visually or otherwise), and second, to refresh my interest in what I am already engaging in. It offers me scope for a different perspective on, for example, my placement in space or my spatial and visual relationship with the audience, and to notice how that impacts on my sensibilities.

> I feel that I can dance like this, with Deborah's questions.
> At times I notice that I am responding
> to the space and using that to inform what I do.
> If I relate my own work to it and use Deborah's idea of space,
> turning my fucking head, notice, let it go, notice, let it go,
> then it feels great.
>
> (Doughty 2011b)

The (newly found) irregularity of rhythm in here and gone, here and gone, and in the act of turning my fucking head before I get too attached to something are very synergistic in my practice and support me in shifting my more familiar patterns. Over time, I noticed that I tended to work with these directives in a linear way, as if I could recall the order of operands that I was noticing and responding to in order to develop a chronological archive of my decision-making processes. In doing so, I engage in what De Spain refers to as a 'tracking feedback loop' (1997: 145), in which the improviser notices significant choices made during the improvisation in order to recall and reincorporate them later on.

> At times there are moments of linearity in which
> I notice the light on the floor
> I turn my fucking head
> Something in the moment of turning my fucking head attracts me
> I work with that
> I turn my fucking head
> I notice an audience member
> I respond to them
> I notice something about what I'm doing in that moment which draws my attention
> I notice that I haven't turned my fucking head for a bit
> So I turn my fucking head and what I notice informs what I do next.
> Yes, there is a certain linearity for me when I am noticing.
>
> (Doughty 2011b)

Sperling also considers this experience to be a continuum (2014), whilst Ellis senses that it operates more like a temporal metaphor that helps him orient his attention to time in many ways: 'to what is about to, to what is, and to what has been' (2014). Here, we are all ostensibly referring to the same experience of noticing, regardless of our semantic preferences: if I am aware of what I have done, where I have been, and how long certain aspects have taken, then I can consciously make choices about where I am in the moment and how that might move me forward into what is still to arise.

Hay developed her performance directives whilst she was dancing; they are borne out of and support her performance practice and are present in her individual scores for performances. In the score for *I Think Not* (2011) she gives the directive 'Fly, but don't know how to do it. Get moving and call it flying. Learn from your body what flying can be' (2011). Many of Hay's directives are representative of riddles that de-mand a high degree of ingenuity from performers, and I very much value the artistic and interpretive freedom that these have presented to me in my adaptation of *I Think Not* (2011). I may not be able to physically realize the directive, but my attention to the endeavour and what I notice whilst practising it engages me profoundly. Sperling cites the performance directive 'turn without turning' from the solo *"Dynamic"* (2012)[2] and reflects:

> I deal with these nonsensical directives in a way that is probably incorrect from Deborah's perspective, because I often take them seriously and I assume that there is an answer and I need to pay attention to notice the answer. And that keeps me really busy and engaged, and I think that is part of Deborah's intention. But then she doesn't intend for me to try and get it right, and that's something that I've al-ways found difficult, but it helps me to invite a response from my nonlinear, less-conscious, more intuitive embodied, felt-sense mind. (2014)

Directives such as 'turn without turning' (2012) and 'fly, but don't know how to do it' (2011) encourage performers to work with a particular attention to their awareness and presence in the moment of grappling with the directive and the ensuing material. Hay constructs these directives as 'tools for re-routing our movement patterns and behav-iour' (Hay 2011) and for challenging our response mechanisms to want to get *it* right (Hay 2014b; emphasis in original). She emphasizes letting go of the ways we have learnt to dance, and she advised me to 'let go of my own attachment to my dancing' (2011) through engaging with her performance practices. Hay's practice can be 'an antidote for habits that no longer serve you' (Millward 2014), and this is certainly true of my ex-perience of practising the performance of *I Think Not* (2011). I have had to let go of the ways I have learnt to dance and instead embrace an idea about Hay's particular practice. Choreographer Meg Stuart talks about a willingness as a performer 'to enter unstable places, and have an ability to go beyond the technical' (2002: 29), and whilst I have been grappling with this in my own practice for a while now, it has been forefronted in *I Think Not* (2011). It has demanded that I do not

> rely on technique, or my tried and tested material,
> or favourite moves or my well worn habits, but instead
> engage in the practice of being in the moment, being receptive
> and able to notice the potential in me and in the work.
> This is not an easy task.
>
> (Doughty 2011b)

Conclusion

A few years ago, I ran a research project called *What do I do and why do I do it?* which focused on developing a framework that engendered critical and reflective skills in artists engaged in movement improvisation (Doughty et al. 2008: 129–146). At the end of the research the participants commented that although the framework supported them in developing their skills, they did not feel as if they were 'dancing' anymore. They thought that this was a negative, but I thought it was great! It suggested to me that they had shifted their understanding and practice in ways that meant they were not relying on habitual patterns and, as a result, their dancing felt and looked different.

This reflects my own experience of grappling with noticing in Hay's practice, in my practising the performance of *I Think Not* (2011) and more generally in my improvised work. I consider myself to be an improviser who works in a conscious way, noticing my operands, my determinants, and my developing improvised material. But engaging in Hay's performance practice blew my mind and my practice, to the extent that having engaged in the daily practice for three months and having publicly performed *I Think Not* (2011), I began to conceive of myself—as a dancer/performer/improviser—as 'Sally Version 2'. Hay's practice heightened my ability to notice with my whole body as teacher (2011) and shifted my reliance on using my visual sense first and foremost. It is evident that Hay's practice has prompted me to reconsider the fundamental principles of my improvised performance practice and to notice the potential in how I engage in the phenomenon that is improvisation.

I suggest therefore that developing an ability to notice and, indeed, to notice what is noticed in improvisation practices offers the artist much scope for creative endeavour and that through the act of noticing, more conscious compositional choices can be made. Enhancing one's ability to notice without placing primacy on one particular sense expands one's potential for creativity and greatly enhances the improviser's ability to carry out spontaneous composition.

Notes

1. Object permanence is used to describe one's ability to know that objects continue to exist even though they can no longer be seen or heard.
2. The title of Hay's 2012 score *"Dynamic"* comes with a movement directive, i.e., with instructions on how to say it to another person: 'first turn your head right or left before turning back to say *"Dynamic"* '. Sperling further notes that 'Deborah additionally coached us in saying it as though you have had too much Botox and can hardly move your face, but are nevertheless very enthusiastic about the title' (Sperling 2014).

References

Buckwalter, M. (2010) *Composing While Dancing: An Improviser's Companion*. Madison: University of Wisconsin Press.

Crisp, R. (2013) First International Laboratory of Improvisation, Falmouth University, Cornwall, 26–28 August 2013.

Csikszentmihalyi, M. (1993) *Flow: The Psychology of Happiness*. London: Rider.

De Spain, K. (1997) *Solo Movement Improvisation: Constructing Understanding through Lived Somatic Experience*. Ann Arbor: University of Michigan Press.

De Spain, K. (2014) *Landscape of the Now: A Topography of Movement Improvisation*. New York: Oxford University Press.

Dilley, B. (2011) *March to Marfa Laboratory*. Marfa, TX. 26 March–2 April 2011.

Doughty, S. (2006) What do I do and why do I do it? Pedagogic Research Project, De Montfort University, Leicester. October 2005–July 2007.

Doughty, S. (2007) Personal Journal. What do I do and why do I do it?, Pedagogic Research Project, De Montfort University, Leicester. October 2005–July 2007.

Doughty, S., et al. (2008) Technological Enhancements in the Teaching and Learning of Reflective and Creative Practice in Dance. *Research in Dance Education* 9 (1): 129–146.

Doughty, S. (2011a) Personal Journal. *March to Marfa* with Barbara Dilley, 26 March–2 April 2011.

Doughty, S. (2011b) Personal Journal. Deborah Hay's Solo Performance Commissioning Project. 24 August 2011–2 September 2011.

Doughty, S. (2012) Personal Journal.

Doughty, S. (2013) Personal Journal.

Ellis, S. (2014) Interview with author. 30 September 2014.

Hay, D. (2011) Solo Performance Commissioning Project. Findhorn, Scotland, 24 August–2 September 2011.

Hay, D. (2014a) Email correspondence with author. 21 September 2014.

Hay, D. (2014b) A Continuity of Discontinuity—Deborah Hay Performative Presentation. London, Siobhan Davies Studios. 6 September 2014.

Johnston, C. (2006) *The Improvisation Game*. London: Nick Hern Books.

Kraus, L. (1990) "At Naropa, 3 Generations: Interviews with Barbara Dilley, Irini Badel Rockwell, and Lisa Kraus". In Buckwalter, M. (2010) *Composing While Dancing: An Improviser's Companion*. Madison: University of Wisconsin Press.

Martin, N. (2006) *March to Marfa Improvisation Laboratory*. Marfa, TX, 19–26 March 2006.

Martin, N. (2007) *March to Marfa Improvisation Laboratory*. Marfa, TX, 25–31 March 2007.

Martin, N. (2011) *March to Marfa Improvisation Laboratory*. Marfa, TX, 26 March–2 April 2011.

Mason, J. (2002) *The Discipline of Noticing*. Abingdon: Routledge.

Millward, F. (2014) *Turn Your F^*ing Head*. Abingdon: Routledge.

Morrish, A. (2013) First International Laboratory of Improvisation. Falmouth University, Cornwall, 29–31 August 2013.

Nachmanovitch, S. (2006) Improvisation as a Tool for Investigating Reality. http://www.freeplay.com/Writings/Nachmanovitch.Ann%20Arbor.Talk.pdf. Accessed 6th September 2018.

Noë, A. (2004) *Action in Perception*. Cambridge, MA: MIT Press.

Perkins, D. (1982) *The Mind's Best Work*. Cambridge, MA: Harvard University Press.

Stuart, M. (2010) in Peters, J. (ed.) (2010) *Are We Here Yet?* Dijon: Les Presses Du Reél.

Sperling, M. (2014) Interview with author. 10 October 2014.

Tolle, E. (2011) *The Power of Now: A Guide to Spiritual Enlightenment*. London: Hodder and Stoughton Ltd.

Zaporah, R. (2002) What's on My Mind Now? *Contact Quarterly* (Winter/Spring) 27 (1): 51–56.

CHAPTER 8

....

EMBODIED CONSCIOUSNESS

....

NALINA WAIT

IN the twenty-first century, improvisation as a mode of Western contemporary performance has blossomed well beyond the impulse to counter the aesthetic values of traditional theatre dance (Banes 1980; Halprin and Kaplan 1995).[1] However, the way that improvisers compose remains undertheorized due to the ephemeral and complex nature of the practice. While artists' practices are diverse (De Spain 2014; Ann Cooper and Gere 2003; Buckwalter 2010), it is possible to identify certain commonalities across a broad aesthetic spectrum. For example, setting tasks is one method many improvisers use: William Forsythe has developed *Improvisation Technologies* (Forsythe 2012), Deborah Hay (Hay 2002) and Lisa Nelson both use scores (Nelson 1995/96), and Steve Paxton has compiled the principles of Contact Improvisation (Paxton 1979). What remains important about tasks is that they offer improvisers the opportunity to compose performance in ways such that even they may be surprised by the outcome.

This qualitative analysis of how an improvisation is composed privileges the articulation of experience-experiments (Dewey 1934; Louppe 2010) with the aim of moving beyond documenting tasks and towards an examination of how an improviser negotiates those tasks.[2] Furthermore, while an improviser in performance is always negotiating a dialogic exchange within a broader spatial, aural, and social context, this chapter excludes other important variables temporarily in order to elucidate the specific processes of an individual body-mind. This analysis of the labour of improvisation seeks to extend the language-based articulation of praxis, without suggesting that there is a 'universal' or ideal experience of improvised performance. In order to attend to this task comprehensively, I've drawn from my own improvised performance practice, which emphasizes somatic awareness (Hannah 1995) while engaging with dance and improvisation theory, biology, and philosophy.[3]

Dance theorist Susan Foster (Foster 2003: 7) has suggested that composing improvisation 'depend[s] on the performer's lucid familiarity with the principles of composition'. While this is certainly true, there is another dimension of improvisation in which compositional choices are not based on the formal logic of 'principles' but on attending to fluctuating, formless 'intensities' (Manning 2009; McCormack 2013), which will be discussed in this chapter. Before a formless compositional approach can be under-stood, the improvisational methodologies informing it must first be examined in detail. Foster (9) has used the term 'embodied consciousness' to describe that which 'enables the making of the dance and the dance's making of itself'. This chapter extends Foster's useful terminology by further examining the practice of embodied consciousness, how it operates in an improvised performance, and how it can be cultivated through practice. The body-mind processes discussed here may not be externally observable, but offer insight into how improvisers 'tune' their body-minds so that they can direct and be dir-ected by the forces that emerge between self and others in a specific space and time.[4]

EMBODIED CONSCIOUSNESS

In a general sense, embodied consciousness involves observing/sensing where move-ment originates from, how that movement is initiated, and how that action unfolds in relation to the time, space, and effort used. An improviser's capacity to be consciously embodied can be enhanced through somatic practices. Observational practices such as somatics refine an improviser's perceptive faculties, allowing her body-mind a greater ability to connect imaginatively with the multidimensions of space-time. This key ac-tivity of somatics can also provide access to a greater range of movement investigations with which to compose improvisation, and can assist in refining an improviser's artistic sensibility.

The approach taken by ideokinesis pioneers, of investigating the lived experience of the dancer in relation to the study of human biology, is useful to this research.[5] Kinaesthesia is integral to embodied consciousness, because it is the means through which we perceive ourselves to be in motion through our biological senses. Kinaesthesia and other sensations are perceived through the sensorium: a network of receptors and processing centres for the sensory modalities. Much of the information collected through the proprioceptive receptors and the sensorium is processed in the region below the cerebral cortex, the subcortical level of the brain, which means that it (usu-ally) goes unnoticed during our everyday activities. However, the activity of embodied consciousness brings a greater conscious awareness to otherwise indiscernible bodily sensations. In this altered state, described by Foster as 'hyperawareness' (Foster 2003: 7), an improviser can cultivate a deeper awareness of his coperceptive condition as a unified body-mind where thought/awareness and sensing/moving interweave, and thoughts/images are felt as sensations.[6]

Part of my research practice involves engaging with particular movement ideas and images that build on the pioneering work of ideokinesis, which will be described in the bulk of this chapter, while paying considerable attention to my sensorium in order to perceive how certain body-mind states motivate the compositional choices I make. To achieve the awareness of an integrated body-mind state from which to begin, I follow 'release' methodologies; such as using the floor to support my weight and deepening my breath to allow the sensation of cellular oxygenation to release any habitual holding of my muscles and/or organs (Bainbridge Cohen 2012).[7] I also move through Bartenieff Fundamental Patterns of Total Body Connectivity (Hackney 2000: 43) to establish co-ordinated movement pathways that integrate connectivity of: breath; the core to what is distal; the head to the tail; the upper to the lower body; the body-halves; and the cross-lateral ends. I do this via a series of locomotive explorations (yielding, pouring, pushing, pulling, and reaching) in order to cultivate a state of global body-mind aware-ness, receptivity, and preparedness. I practice these coordination pathways so that I can be inventive with movement, and anatomically efficient, beyond the range of codified movement pathways that exist in my muscle memory.

Building on the biological framework of embodied consciousness, briefly outlined above, I propose a further bifurcation of embodied consciousness that I have found both commonly reoccurring and crucial to my own improvisational research.[8] These two approaches are what I call 'thinking-through-the-body' (active) and the awareness of 'the body's mind' (passive). These approaches are more accurately described as dif-ferent types of embodied consciousness, distinguished here by their active and passive sates, although they are not entirely active or passive but contain fluctuating elements of both states simultaneously. For example, the passive state is actually active in receiving information, by 'listening' to or feeling through the sensorium. Through the practice of rigorous sensorial self-observation, I have noticed that by enhancing my capacity to switch (or slide along the spectrum of gradients) between these two approaches I am able to activate, or reactivate, my dance impulses and perceive what it is that initiates specific compositional choices.

Thinking-through-the-Body

Thinking-through-the-body is the more commonly experienced type of embodied consciousness of the two, as it includes language-based thoughts. It is used regularly in improvisational methodologies but is also the way that many corporeal knowledges of dance are practiced. To a certain extent, it is the methodology of mimetic training. It is operating when a dancer is able to mentally/physically adjust her movement pathway or position to correctly perform a specific technique using kinaesthetic perception in re-sponse to language-based thought cues. However, this type of embodied consciousness is also operating when exploring a (practical) methodological inquiry through the use of tasks or questions that might generate new movement, rather than the reproduction of known forms.

Tasks are directives that can be used imaginatively to set restrictions or limit the range of movements in order to cultivate specific movement qualities or pathways. The ef-fort of rigorously attending to a task can become a methodology for cultivating diverse and specific movement qualities, therefore ultimately broadening the palate of possible movement materials and compositional choices. Some examples of tasks that I might use are: *swing the bones, press skin surfaces, lead through the ends*, or *fall upwards*. These tasks make it possible to create a sensation-image in the body-mind by locating the parameters of a movement investigation, as will be explained in a moment.

As tasks commonly circulate in language, they require another process to become consciously embodied in order to shift from a word or idea to an image and/or sensation. This requires a self-reflexive dialogue between the sensorium and language-based thinking. Self-reflexive dialogue helps an improviser to perceive any gap between what the task specifies and what is actually happening in the body. For example, a body-mind dialogue about *swinging bones* may include asking, or sensing, 'questions' while dancing such as: 'Which bones am I swinging?' 'What does it mean to swing?' 'Is what I'm doing really swinging?' By that I mean 'Am I allowing the forces of gravity, breath, and momentum to actually swing the weight of my bones or am I adding muscular force to illustrate the "swinging" of bones?' 'How heavy are my bones if I actively switch off the muscles to allow their true weight to be more accurately perceived?' 'Am I continuing to disengage those muscles or are they habitually reengaging?' This example seems heavy in language-based thinking, but actually, all of these tasks are felt-thought through the sensorium and only occasionally are self-reflexive questions voiced cognitively. The resulting quality of the movement that most closely enacts *swinging the bones* (in this case) is very specific and distinct from the movement quality of another task. Thereby, tasks enable an improviser to specify, diversify, and innovate his available palate of movement qualities through a process of inquiry by thinking-through-the-body.

There is no limit to what types of tasks can be used to generate movement, although improvising artists are often very specific about the tasks they use. What is important about most tasks is that they can be sustained, or transformed, for a duration and therefore require a certain endurance of attention. Self-reflexive dialogue allows an improviser to monitor how she feels in relation to a task and can help her refine her response to a task over time. It can also activate a sense of 'aliveness' in a movement inquiry by facilitating an improviser to self-reflexively innovate her responses to the task in real time.[9] The labour of negotiating a task while improvising involves continually refreshing one's attention to the task, approaching it as though for the very first time, every time, all the time. This is not to say that in the context of the performance a recognizable movement won't be repeated, as a habit or as a deliberate compositional choice. For the most part, however, movements need to be enacted without mentally skipping ahead, or holding on to what has passed, so that the improviser is attending to the moment that the movement is performed.

Through the use of tasks, the improviser is also able to transfigure his body-schema (Hawksley 2001). In psychology and phenomenology, the term 'body schema' refers to the sensed kinaesthetic map of a subject's own body (Head and Holms 1911). The 'map' or schema of the body allows one to know one's dimensions, one's shape, and where one is in space. It is a flexible perception of the limits of one's own body that enlarges as the body grows (from childhood) and can be extended deliberately in particular ways to include tools or physical skills that a person may develop. For example, while driving a car one's body schema is extended to sense how large the car is while reversing into a car park. When the body schema is extended through the use of a tool, such as a cane for a blind person, it has been shown to also enlarge the cortical representation of the associated parts in the brain (Noë 2009: 79). Over time, a self-reflexive dialogue can inform the quality or scope of the imaginative body-schemas that can be cultivated, which can also change according to the way the dancer engages with certain tasks.

The way I extend my own body-schema through improvisation not only changes my perception of my dimensions but also imaginatively shifts the quality or textures of my movement. For example, in order to transform my body-schema to embody the image of a 'waterbag' I begin to notice through my sensorium the ways that I am anatomically similar to a waterbag (primarily the fluids contained by skin: blood, lymph, plasma, synovial, and cerebrospinal fluid).[10] Then I connect to the sensation of the weight of those fluids and the pull of gravity on them, and aim to only initiate motion through 'pouring' those fluids: allowing gravity to take my body into motion rather than supporting my locomotion through my musculoskeletal system. Then, to keep myself interested, I might decide that the direction from which gravity moves the waterbag should suddenly shift, so that I can *fall upward*, for example. It is important to use an image based on action rather than stasis because when the body is in motion, stronger or weaker gradients of sensation can be felt more clearly (Bernard, Steinmuller, and Stricker 2006: 59). Furthermore, the specificity of how these actions are described or imaginatively perceived is important, because each word is imbued with its own qualitative associations. For example, 'pouring' is thicker, slower, and more viscous than 'spilling'.

As a task is essentially a linguistic directive embodied imaginatively, it needs to become known corporeally as a 'concrete' sensation if it is to transform an improviser's body-schema. While in the initial stages of learning to improvise, the diligent self-reflexive questioning described earlier can be useful because it brings awareness to the sensory-motor feedback of the sensorium. As improvisational expertise progresses, self-reflexive questioning can become habitual. However, to use a task effectively requires consciously and specifically sensing it with exceptional detail during the self-reflexive process, so that it does not become vague or blur into another task (unless that is the intention). Cultivating a habit of self-reflexivity requires considerable practice over time and can involve working with a broad range of tasks in order to deepen the physical/mental understanding of what a task is, or what it might require one to enact. The types of tasks that can be used are only limited by the imagination of the practitioner. Some possible categories of tasks are those that are qualitative (concerned with textures, and gradients of effort or tone), dimensional (to do with scale, space, time, mathematical, or conceptual), relational (imagining connections or relations, between places/bodies), or poetic (responding to words, images/sensations).

Self-reflexive dialogue in relation to a task transforms the body-schema through the use of imagination similar to the way that using a tool extends the body's capacity to function. After considerable work, this practice can change the habitual way the body-mind thinks/feels through a task. However, a transition to habitual self-reflexivity must occur in its own time, and rushing or truncating this process produces an unclear body-schema that doesn't support a rigorous investigation. When the body-mind is habitually self-reflexive, the dialogic process can occur extremely quickly and sometimes effort-lessly, but it is the specificity with which improvisers attend to a task that enables impro-visation to be a virtuosic choreographic methodology.

Thinking-through-the-body can offer a practitioner a way to deepen her improvisa-tion practice that is far from arbitrary, as it aims to extend the range of possible move-ment investigations through a process of focused limitation. Whatever task is used to focus the movement investigation, it must be deeply established in the body-schema through the self-reflexive process, described above, so that it can be available as a tan-gible method of inquiry. Therefore, rather than arising from 'spontaneous inspiration' a sophisticated improvisation practice can follow an extremely rigorous and technical methodology which can be refined over time. This is true both when improvisation is to be performed in a choreographic situation in which specific limitations have been es-tablished and when the improvisation is completely 'open' and no preset decisions have been made. As with anything, it is the time and attention given to practice that ultim-ately determines the quality of the result in both articulation and inventiveness. There is also great potential for this practice to assist the production of innovative movement material because, even if the tasks appear to only suggest a singular response, through a self-reflexive dialogue this and any other assumption is examined. Tasks require ha-bitual questioning, and the purpose of a task is to provoke creativity rather than to be inexorably obeyed. Therefore, through practice, the body-mind of an improviser can become proficient at interrogating tasks to produce diverse and articulate responses. It is not a process of 'getting it right' but of finding creative and motivating ways to engage with tasks in an ever-changing inquiry.

In addition to generating a tangible body-schema, the endurance and inventiveness of an improviser's attention can be refined in a way that extends improvisation from the level of practice to that of a work of art. Tasks that are movement puzzles or conun-drums have the potential to be particularly engaging for an improviser, as they demand a heightened state of body-mind engagement, described by Foster as 'hyperawareness' (2003: 7). Complex tasks also have the potential to extend the conception of the body-schema in ways that might defy logic or physiological limits but produce an engaging shift in movement quality of an improviser. A task such as *no body part can touch the floor* may not be literally achievable but creates a quality of urgency and levity in an improviser's attempt to produce it. For example, Trisha Brown describes her pro-cess of working from an improvisation task for *Trillium* (1962): '[I was] working in a studio on a movement exploration of traversing the three positions sitting, standing, and lying. I broke those actions down to their basic mechanical structure, finding the places of rest, power, momentum and peculiarity. I went over and over the material, eventually accelerating and mixing up to the degree that lying down was done in air' (Burt 2006: 67). In an improvised performance, the use of tasks enable an improviser to sustain hyperawareness by negotiating the tension between performing the task and considering alternative approaches to it that might offer opportunities to further ex-tend the investigation. As stated earlier, this practice of self-reflexive dialogue is a way of 'tuning' the body-mind instrument that can become a methodology for producing movement (even if there is no task to enact) because approaching all movement with hyperawareness, as an inquiry, is a way that an improviser can develop and refine his practice.

THE BODY'S MIND

The second type of embodied consciousness is more elusive than thinking-through-the-body. It is when the language-based 'voice' of thinking is quiet enough that it is possible to observe the 'mind' of the corporeality. This is experienced as hearing-sensing the intentions of the flesh. This process allows a body to have a mind of its own if by 'mind' we mean intention and desire. What is specific about this level of embodied consciousness is that, first, it does not occur in a language-producing state, and second, it heightens the perception of the resonation of affects (Massumi 1995: 89), to which I shall return.

Over the past seventy years, the humanities have worked to reposition the body in language and as a site of knowing. Yet a persistent problem for dance theory is the articulation of the corporeal knowledges that elude language. This is because, while the issue of language is most apparent, the root cause is the enduring legacy of Cartesian dualism embedded in our structures of language and thought that hierarchize the cognitive over the corporeal.[11] In contrast, somatic-based improvisational theory proposes body-mind integration and erases the hierarchy of dualism by emphasizing the ways mind and body are interconnected. This is because somatic practitioners focus their conscious awareness both on the information circulating in the sensorium and the fact that this information informs patterns of thinking as a two-way flow within a unified system. The body's mind is perceived through the processing and computation activities of the brain, and therefore the body effects what is thought, just as the body-schema can be reshaped through self-reflexive dialogue and imaging, and so thinking also effects sensations of the body. Addressing the problem of language requires not only analysis of this activity by theorists with practical research expertise but also some consideration for the philosophical model that supports the articulation of these practices.

Rolf therapist Hubert Godard (Godard and Rolnik 2008: 178–179), a movement theorist who lucidly articulates haptic bodily states as an extension of his practice, draws on neurophysiologic research that identifies two 'levels of analyzers' effecting the senses in ways that allow the subject to experience objective or subjective senses of self.[12] His example uses the sense of sight, but he explains that any sense can be processed with these two levels of consciousness. Godard explains that 'the first can be qualified as subcortical vision. It is a form of vision in which the person blends into the context. There is no longer a subject and an object but a participation in a general context. That form of vision is not interpreted, therefore, it does not bear meaning.... And then, if we go in the opposite direction of this vision, we have objective, cortical, associative vision ... that is associated with language amongst other things' (178–179).[13] Given the difficulty of articulating some experiences of improvising, it is not surprising that many improvisational sensory experiences are processed at the subcortical level that defies the processing of language. As Godard explains, the subcortical sensory level does not 'bear meaning', so writing about this language-resistant experience is a complex undertaking that is necessarily reductive.[14] Some types of embodied consciousness experienced in the studio, or in performance, are drastically different from those experienced in everyday life. People who have not experienced alternate states of consciousness may not have a reference for what it is like to consciously embody one's sensorium in this way. Conversely, those who practice it regularly increase their capacity to immerse themselves in an experiential sate of subcortical 'formlessness' to the point where they can practice allowing themselves to be directed by the body's mind when improvising.[15]

Phenomena perceptible at this level of the body's mind are 'ideas' that are felt rather than thought as fragments of memory, emotions, and images. Nondancers may also be familiar with these felt ideas that can occur in the form of an inner 'song' or 'story' that arises in one's awareness. The music that is 'heard' by a body-mind may not be sensed aurally but felt as the rise and fall of the 'melody' of movement arising from the breath and the (subtle) shifts in the tonus of the flesh. Similarly, the 'stories' may not have a narrative per se but are rather experienced as body-mind sensations that unfold as a kind of journey through a sensory landscape. These sensations can become threads of interest when felt/listened to, providing an internal source of improvisational material.

When being moved by the body's mind, there is no need for self-reflexive dialogue, because both language-based thoughts and need to achieve an outcome dissolve. The only 'task' is to attend to the thought-feelings that a body-mind expresses, which are felt in the tone of the muscle tissues as desirous and intentional sensations of the flesh. As a simple example, consider the impulses that can be felt during a basic pedagogical exercise: a grid-pattern improvisation. In this pared-back exercise, improvisers are directed to limit the range of movements to only walking, running, standing, or sitting, and they can only travel in the four directions of a grid (upstage, downstage, stage right, and stage left). When performing this exercise, participants invariably feel the impulse to act in response to the rhythm and the spatial composition that is unfolding among the group. It is very common for more than one dancer to make the same choice at the same time because they both feel the impulse that exists in the space that has arisen from a collective attention to composition. Therefore, the impulses that motivate the improvisers originate not only in their individual body-minds, but are circulating in the space and time of the improvisation.

If improvisers train their body-minds to tune into and invest in their impulsive sensations, which are circulating in both the body-mind and circulating in space and time, they might begin to feel the subtle desires of the body's mind and allow these impulses to drive compositional movement choices. These impulses can be directly physicalized— for example, a strong urge to curl inwards, to run, or to suddenly leap—or extended into a whole sequence of movements. This means that rather than being the 'author' of the improvisation, the improviser enters a state where her movements are composed by what is in circulation within the space and time of the improvisation. If the body's mind is attended to, then the impulses can become very clear, whether they feel loud and intense or quiet and diffuse. The impulse or desire of the body's mind can be physicalized directly, which effectively bypasses the process by which these impulses might consolidate into thoughts or be experienced as emotions. An attempt to faithfully articulate this level of embodied consciousness would perhaps sound-feel like a hum of vibrations that are felt as 'intensities', or the effect on the body-mind of the phenomenon that is most commonly described in philosophical terms as affect.

The seventeenth-century monist philosopher Baruch Spinoza first defined the term 'affect' in his *Ethics*: 'By affect I understand affections of the body by which the body's power of acting is increased or diminished, aided or restrained, and at the same time, the ideas of these affections' (Spinoza 1996: 94). Spinoza's definition of affect is useful here as a way to theorize phenomena that has not yet landed in the body-mind as an emotion, or conceptualized cognitively as an idea, but is perceived in the way that it impacts the body's power to act. It is at the subcortical level of embodied consciousness that an improviser is more capable of perceiving the resonation of affects on the body-mind and, aligning with Spinoza's proposition, of noticing the capacity of affect to empower or disempower his body to act.[16] Similarly, impulses are perceptible at the level of the body-mind but can also be felt across the space by different people simultaneously, resulting in the serendipitous moments of complementary action because, importantly, affect is not individualist but is always shared and in circulation.[17] Becoming responsive to impulses is a core feature of improvisation, as it is what propels an improviser into a course of action despite not knowing exactly what that action might lead to. If impulses were to be considered the resonation of the circulation the resonation between and within bodies, then the theorization of improvisation through the lens of affect theory might offer useful models for thinking through a compositional logic that can otherwise be difficult to grasp.[18]

Spinoza's theory of affect enjoyed a revival in the twentieth and twenty-first centuries, becoming a stimulating point of philosophical debate, particularly in relation to encountering art (Deleuze and Guattari 1987; Massumi 1995, 2002). In *A Thousand Plateaus* Gilles Deleuze and Félix Guattari describe affect in relation to the martial arts, which is useful here, as a comparison can be made between improvised dance and martial arts, in that both practices rely on the immediate responsiveness of the practitioner. They say that 'the martial arts do not adhere to a *code* ... but follow *ways*, which are so many paths of the affect: upon these ways, one learns to "unuse" weapons as much as one learns to use them, as if the power and cultivation of the affect were the true goal of the assemblage' (442). Improvisers often emphasize the importance of 'listening' to the space and 'being in the moment' because that is when the resonance of affects on the body-mind can best be perceived. Listening is important because, while affect is a powerful motivator, the perception of the resonation of affects are very subtle and can be easily ignored or overridden by the cognitive 'voice' that can pull the body-subjects consciousness away from the perception of the felt phenomena and towards a conceptual idea. Listening is, for improvisation, one of the 'ways' one learns to approach a performance with an empty hand (without a 'weapon') or, in other words, without conceptualizing how the improvisation will unfold. This is the core 'undisciplined' discipline of consciously embodying the body's mind; suspending a state of subcortical awareness, not through resisting language-based cognition, but through maintaining a physical/ mental space of 'empty-handedness'.

Conclusion

Both types of embodied consciousness operate in a constant state of flux during an improvisation, each providing currency at different moments in the dance, although some methods of improvising preference one state over the other. As these states of embodiment operate on different levels of perception, the distinction between them is subtle, and dancers already completely engaged with the complex task of improvising may or may not notice that they are weaving between different states of embodied consciousness as they dance. These experiential states have become known to me and therefore are identified here because I have observed, investigated, and now employ a bifurcation of embodied consciousness in my practice. For example, by engaging with an external task I can activate the curiosity of my body-mind to 'think-through-the-body' to attend to a movement puzzle, particularly if it is complex or difficult to achieve. At other times, the desire of 'the body's mind' feels stronger, and if I passively allow it to be the source of movement, then my thinking mind 'slips back' or 'swims' in sensorium and observes the dance as it unfolds. Suggesting a bifurcation of embodied consciousness seems to propose, falsely, that the way these states fluctuate is straightforward. In fact this analysis isolates a small section of what is actually a highly complex matrix of interconnected elements; where the hyperawareness of thinking-through-the-body becomes a framework to support the desire of the body's mind to ebb and flow, or surge as 'spontaneous inspiration'. Composing an improvised performance is rarely a matter of drawing from a clearly defined palette of elements or of carefully considering how they might juxtapose or work together to form a coherent whole. In my own experience, improvisation as an art-making practice has more to do with 'holding' the tension along a spectrum of perception, sensing the resonation of affects, and seeking to amplify the affects in circulation in a way that is as authentic to the current space and time as possible.

In my own practice, the passive activity of releasing muscular tension described earlier reduces physical resistance and mental attachment to language-based cognition, which increases my perception of my body's mind. At times, my desire to move is intensified by the effort of performing a specified task in an innovative way (thinking-through-the-body). At other times, my desire for movement is supported by the pleasure of following the 'sensory melody' of the shifting tonus in the flesh (the body's mind). Most often, it is a fluctuating combination of the two, but in all cases, what motivates movement is desire. This includes complicated kinds of desire such as that which seeks the joy of effort, which might not literally be felt as 'joy' but emerges through the thrill of challenging oneself physically-mentally or achieving a state of 'flow' through the balance of effort, challenge, and freedom (Csikszentmihalyi 1992). It is equally possible that aversion can be a motivating impulse for making compositional 'choices' in an improvisation. Although, without intending to devalue any other approach, I choose to focus here on improvised performance that does not deliberately evade the spectacle, or tropes, of dancing and therefore, for me, virtuosity is a valid compositional option.

Desire and aversion, according to Spinoza, are affects that empower or disempower the body-mind's capacity to act. Furthermore, he points out that contrary to Descartes's assertion that humans have 'absolute control over [their] actions, and that [they are] determined solely by [themselves]' (Spinoza 1996: 51) humans are actually motivated, consciously or unconsciously, by affect. Spinoza suggests that 'man's lack of power to moderate and restrain the affects I call bondage' (113). Therefore, his *Ethics* is concerned with ways to be 'free of human bondage' by understanding the power of affect and gaining agency through self-reflection: a conscious awareness of the unification of the body-mind.[19] Similarly, thinking-through-the-body and the body's mind are ways to work with affect as a medium of improvisation, active/passively directing (amplifying) or being directed by its resonance. Allowing the improvisation to be composed by the circulation of affect is a delicate but incredibly useful improvisation 'technique', as it situates improvisers within an immanent context where they can allow the composition and themselves to be danced by the circulation of affect.

Notes

1. Improvisation in a Western theatre dance context gained momentum in the mid-twentieth century as an antiestablishment performance practice among pioneering North American dance artists, such as Anna Halprin (who studied with innovative dance educator Margaret H'Doubler), her mentee Simone Forti, and her student Trisha Brown, as well as Deborah Hay, Steve Paxton, Ruth Zaporah, Barbara Dilley, and Lisa Nelson (De Spain 2014). The global histories of improvised dance, in particular the significant traditions in India and Africa, are beyond the scope of this research. However, the African American traditions were particularly influential on the Western lineage. For more about the influence of the Africanist aesthetic on Western improvised performance see Gottshild (1996, 2003) and Foster (2002).
2. In French, the terms 'experience' and 'experiment' are combined as 'expérience' (Louppe 2010). These terms were also interchangeable in English until the sixteenth century (Williams 1984).
3. My practice as a professional dancer and improvising performer has, for more than twenty-five years, been largely informed by somatic practices of release, Body-Mind Centering, and ideokinesis, as well as contact improvisation and tertiary training in contemporary (predominantly the Cunningham technique) and classical techniques. Philosopher Thomas Hannah (1928–1990) coined the term 'somatics', based on the Greek word *soma*, meaning 'the body as perceived from within by first-person perception' (Hannah 1995: 341), to refer to the philosophical field and practices that aim to unify the body and mind, which have greatly influenced the development of contemporary dance.
4. Influential improvising artist Lisa Nelson also uses the term 'tune' in relation to her improvisational practice. For more details, see http://sarma.be/oralsite/pages/Testpage_Lisa_Nelson_%28general%29/, accessed 17 October 2014.

5. Western somatic practices, such as ideokinesis (Todd 1937, 1953; Sweigard 1974), were originally developed as a form of therapy but have also been instrumental in informing dance and particularly improvised practices. In the early twentieth century, American Mabel Elsworth Todd (1880–1956) developed an approach to improving anatomical alignment using not only self-observation but also visualization of imagery. Her approach would later be called ideokinesis by her mentee Dr. Lulu Sweigard (1895–1974), a composite of *ideo*, image, and *kinesis*, movement.

6. Bonnie Bainbridge Cohen (2012: 1) uses the term 'somatization' to mean 'engage the kinesthetic experience directly, in contrast to "visualization" which utilizes visual imagery to evoke a kinesthetic experience'.

7. Many of the 'release' principles I use are similar to Joan Skinner's Skinner Releasing Technique, which she developed when applying her study of Todd's research to her work as a professional dancer in the Martha Graham and Merce Cunningham companies. I also incorporate principles of Bonnie Bainbridge Cohen's methodology of Body-Mind Centering, such as this example of 'cellular breathing' and ideokinetic imagery. Bartenieff Fundamentals are an extension of Laban Movement Analysis, which was developed by Irmgard Bartenieff (1900–1981) in the second half of the twentieth century.

8. Anna Halprin (De Spain 2014: 176) also describes this dual activity as key to her creative process. She says: 'there were two ways I was working—and still am—one was when the body speaks to the mind and informs the mind, or when the mind informs the body'. She distinguished these states by calling the former 'exploration' and the latter 'improvisation'. Halprin's mentor, Margaret H'Doubler (Brennan, Hagood, and Wilson 2006: 217) taught a methodology of movement inquiry that consisted of three phases. First, the 'feedback' phase is described as bringing information from the muscles, joints, and tendons. The second, or 'associative', phase is said to occur in the brain, and finally the 'feed forward' phase was the process of sending messages back to the muscles. She imparted this cycle as an integration of 'moving, thinking and feeling', and she facilitated this approach to kinaesthetic thinking by leading her students through a movement inquiry into space, time, force, and variations in quality.

9. Constantly producing familiar or habitual movement pathways, which is a function of muscle memory, is a persistent problem for improvisers. This research proposes the rigorous practice of self-reflexivity and unfamiliar tasks to counter this issue.

10. The 'waterbag' image is just one example; for a task to work I do not need to be anatomically similar to the image that is used.

11. The seventeenth-century philosopher and mathematician René Descartes (1596–1650) proposed a relation between mind and matter that has come to be known as Cartesian dualism. His theory was that mind and matter were separate entities and that mind could control matter. For further detail of debates around somatics and dualism, see Bardet and Noceti (2012).

12. Rolfing is a method of structural integration that was developed by Ida Pauline Rolf in New York in the 1930s. See http://www.rolf.com.au/, accessed 27 June 2014.

13. Godard further explains that subcortical sensing 'is beyond objective sight, which is geographic or spatial; vision which is not connected to time or, in any case, is not connected to memory, which is not connected to the history of the subject' (Godard and Rolnik 2008: 178–179).

14. Kent De Spain has developed some useful methods for collecting information about subjective experiences while improvising. See De Spain (2003: 26–29).

15. While becoming an academic I have been far more immobile than ever before in my life. At first, because I was much more 'in my body', remaining in one place for a duration was unbearable. Over time I have become accustomed to it, and my sense of whole embodiment has greatly diminished. I feel that now I understand what it is like to be a nondancer and recognise that it is a very different kind of 'embodiment'.

16. Psychogeographer Dereck McCormack clarifies that 'affective spaces are nonrepresentational: that is, their force does not necessarily cross a threshold of cognitive representation' (2013: 4).

17. Lisa Blackman explains that affect is 'characterised more by reciprocity and co-participation' (2012: 2). See also Manning and Massumi (2014); Stewart (2007).

18. Dance theorist Philipa Rothfield theorizes the ethics of improvisation via the lens of Spinoza's philosophy. She proposes (2014: 91) that with 'nothing to hold onto, striving nevertheless to maximize the body's active affections, dancing could be conceived as an ethical endeavor par excellence'.

19. North American Buddhist meditation practices must also be mentioned here because North American Buddhism was an important influence on pioneering North American improvisers working with both dance and music. For further information, see Larson (2012). However, the aim of, for example, Vipassana meditation is different from improvisation because, while they both practice using the body-mind as an instrument for observing the resonance of the circulation of affects, improvisers aim to act as a conduit for the resonation of affects, whereas meditators attempt to observe them with a detached equanimity. Therefore, while improvisation shares with meditation the practice of observation, the purpose of observation in improvisation is to amplify rather than to mitigate the power of affect. In this sense improvisation deviates from Buddhist spiritual practice, for the purposes of making immediate and affecting art.

References

Albright, Ann Cooper, and Gere, R. (2003) *Taken by Surprise*. Middletown, CT: Wesleyan University Press.

Bainbridge Cohen, B. (2012) *Sensing, Feeling, and Action: The Experiential Anatomy of Body-Mind Centering*, third edition. Northampton, MA: Contact Editions.

Banes, S. (1980) *Democracy's Body: Judson Dance Theatre, 1962–1964*. Michigan: UMI Research Press.

Bardet, M., and Noceti, F. (2012) With Descartes, against Dualism. *Journal of Dance and Somatic Practices* 4(2): 195–209.

Bernard, A., Steinmuller, W., and Stricker, U. (2006) *Ideokinesis: A Creative Approach to Human Movement and Body Alignment*. Berkeley, CA: North Atlantic Books.

Blackman, L. (2012) *Immaterial Bodies: Affect, Embodiment, Mediation*. London: Sage Publications.

Brennan, M., Hagood, T., and Wilson, J. (2006) *Margaret H'Doubler: The Legacy of America's Dance Education Pioneer*. Youngstown, NY: Cambria Press.

Buckwalter, M. (2010) *Composing While Dancing: An Improviser's Companion*. Madison: University of Wisconsin Press.

Burt, R. (2006) *Judson Dance Theatre: Performative Traces*. New York: Routledge.

Csikszentmihalyi, M. (1992) *Optimal Experience: Psychological Studies of Flow in Consciousness*. Cambridge: Cambridge University Press.

Deleuze, G., and Guattari, F. (1987) *A Thousand Plateaus: Capitalism and Schizophrenia*. Trans. Brian Massumi. London: Continuum.

De Spain, K. (2014) *Landscapes of the Now: A Topology of Movement Improvisation*. New York: Oxford University Press.

De Spain, K. (2003) The Cutting Edge of Awareness. In Albright, Ann Cooper, and Gere, D. (eds.), *Taken by Surprise: A Dance Improvisation Reader*. Middletown, CT: Wesleyan University Press, 27–38.

Dewey, J. (1934) *Art as Experience*. New York: Penguin Books.

Forsythe, W. (2012) *Improvisation Technologies: A Tool for the Analytical Dance Eye*. Ostfildern, Germany: Hatje Cantz. (CD-ROM)

Foster, S. (2002) *Dances That Describe Themselves: The Improvised Choreography of Richard Bull*. Middletown, CT: Wesleyan University Press.

Foster, S. (2003) Taken by Surprise: Improvisation in Dance and Mind. In Albright, Ann Cooper, and Gere, D. (eds.), *Taken by Surprise: A Dance Improvisation Reader*. Middletown, CT: Wesleyan University Press, 2–10.

Godard, H., and Rolnik, S. (2008) Blindsight. In *Peripheral Vision and Collective Body*. Bolzano, Italy: Museion Hatje Cantz, 176–219.

Gottshild, B. (1996) *Digging the Africanist Presence in American Performance: Dance and Other Contexts*. Westport, CT: Greenwood Publishing Group.

Gottshild, B. (2003) *The Black Dancing Body: A Geography from Coon to Cool*. New York: Palgrave Macmillan.

Hackney, P. (2000) *Making Connections: Total Body Integration through Bartenieff Fundamentals*. New York: Routledge.

Halprin, A., and Kaplan, R. (eds.). (1995) *Moving towards Life: Five Decades of Transformational Dance*. Middletown, CT: Wesleyan University Press.

Hannah, T. (1995) What Is Somatics? In *Bone, Breath and Gesture: Practices of Embodiment*. Berkeley, CA: North Atlantic Books, 341–351.

Hawksley, S. (2001) Choreographic and Somatic Strategies for Navigating Bodyscapes and Tensegrity Schemata. *Journal of Dance and Somatic Practices* 3(1 and 2): 101–110.

Hay, D. (2002) What If Now Is? *Contact Quarterly* 27(1): 34–37.

Head, H., and Holmes, G. (1911) Sensory Disturbances from Cerebral Lesions. *Brain* 34(2–3): 102.

Larson, K. (2012) *Where the Heart Beats: John Cage, Zen Buddhism, and the Inner Life of Artists*. New York: Penguin Books.

Louppe, L. (2010) *Poetics of Contemporary Dance*. Trans. Sally Gardener. London: Dance Books.

Manning, E. (2009) The Elasticity of the Almost. In Lepeki, A., and Joy, J. (eds.), *Planes of Composition: Dance, Theory, and the Global*. London: Seagull Books, 105–122.

Manning E., and Massumi, B. (2014) *Thought in the Act: Passages in the Ecology of Experience*. Minneapolis: University of Minnesota Press.

Massumi, B. (1995) The Autonomy of Affect. *Cultural Critique* 31: 83–109.

Massumi, B. (2002) *Parables for the Virtual: Movement, Affect, Sensation*. Durham, NC: Duke University Press.

McCormack, D. (2013) *Refrains for Moving Bodies: Experience and Experiment in Affective Spaces*. Durham, NC: Duke University Press.

Nelson, L. (1995) The Sensation Is the Image. *Writings on Dance: Exploring the New Dance Aesthetic* 14: 4–16.

Noë, A. (2009) *Out of Our Heads: Why You Are Not Your Brain, and Other Lessons from the Biology of Consciousness*. New York: Hill and Wang.

Paxton, S. (1979) A Definition. *Contact Quarterly* 4(2): 26.

Rothfield, P. (2014) Embracing the Unknown, Ethics and Dance. In P. Macneill (ed.), *Ethics and the Arts*. Dordrecht, Netherlands: Springer, 89–98.

Spinoza, Baruch de (1996) *Ethics*. Trans. Edwin Curley. New York: Penguin Books.

Stewart, K. (2007) *Ordinary Affects*. Durham, NC: Duke University Press.

Sweigard, L. (1974) *Human Movement Potential: Its Ideokinetic Function*. New York: Harper and Row.

Todd, M. (1937) *The Thinking Body*. New York: Princeton Book Company.

Todd, M. (1953) *The Hidden You: What You Are And What to Do about It*. New York: Dance Horizons.

Williams, R. (1984) *Key Words*. London: Flamingo.

CHAPTER 9

··

'MASS MAY BE THE SINGLE MOST IMPORTANT SENSATION'

Perceptual Philosophies in Dance Improvisation

··

MALAIKA SARCO-THOMAS

GUIDING a group of contact improvisers to tune in to the 'Small Dance' of the act of standing in easy relationship to gravity, Steve Paxton[1] focuses on physical sensations of the body. Transcribed into text, his words should be read with pauses between them, so that each phrase might be sensed as an image:

> Defining the diaphragm in terms of sensation. Bottom of the lung. Two domes of muscle. So with each breath you're massaging the intestine.... What the diaphragm is doing is a signal to the rest of the body. Sky above, earth below....
>
> The head in this work is a limb. It has mass. Mass may be the single most important sensation. The feeling of gravity. Continuing to perceive mass and gravity as you stand. Tension in the muscle masks the sensation of gravity....
>
> You've been swimming in gravity since the day you were born. Every cell knows where down is. Easily forgotten. Your mass and the earth's mass calling to each other. (Paxton 1986: 49)

When received thoughtfully and applied to my breath, to my head, and to the mass of my body (even while seated), Paxton's words have the effect of heightening my awareness of sensation. Italicised passages here are from my own experience.

> *Breath massages intestine, fingers strike plastic keys, wood supports elbows, folded legs rest into wool cushion, my skin reaches softly in every direction and my environment meets me through the activity of sensing mass.*

One might say that by means of my 'tuning in', the opening of my perception reveals my sensation. While deconstructing the relationship between perception and sensation is not within the scope of this essay, for the purposes of my argument, 'sensation' here will refer to sensory impressions, and 'perception' will refer to the activity of extending awareness in order to notice sensation.

If some improvisers subscribe to the notion that 'mass may be the single most important sensation' as a training concept, perhaps it is because sense perception is arguably the most fundamental process by which bodies enter into relationship with an environment. While postmodern dance innovators such as Paxton have cultivated perceptual practices as key aspects of their research, arguments for the importance of sensitizing perception are also made in a number of key philosophical approaches to dwelling in the natural world. The field of ecophenomenology (Brown and Toadvine 2003) and traditions such as deep ecology theorize consciousness of an environment in ways that extend beyond transactional use-value to a 'relational total-field enquiry' of interactions between human and nonhuman (Naess 1973: 95). The potential to analyse and shift perspectives on human-environmental relationships through activating our sensate capacity is articulated by David Abram in his book *Spell of the Sensuous: Perception and Language in a More-Than-Human World*, in which he uses Maurice Merleau-Ponty's work to build a case for an active, sensation-based practice of engaging with our environment. Ecophenomenologist David Wood expands on Merleau-Ponty's (1962: 98) discussion of spatiality and motility of the body to suggest that 'a networked awareness' of multiple bodily skills can be investigated to develop perception (2003b: 24). Monika Langer adds that Merleau-Ponty's work offers a usefully corporeal basis for examining perception of the environment through the body by focusing on the idea of the 'flesh of this world' as formational of our conscious experience (Langer 2003: 116). Recently Alva Noë has theorized that 'perceiving is a kind of skillful bodily activity', which can be developed through thoughtfully moving the body 'as a whole' (2004: 2). If this is the case, then it can be argued that the work of dance improvisation has much to offer towards the development of such skills.

Towards such a claim, this essay looks at some of Merleau-Ponty's work as applied to notions of perception in dance improvisation and ecological thought, developing the idea of 'intelligent flesh' as fundamental to both. It discusses how scores articulated by improvisation artists such as Steve Paxton, Deborah Hay, Jennifer Monson, David Zambrano, Chrysa Parkinson, and Simone Forti indicate how perception can be exercised differently, as a choice, to alter bodily and relational awareness. I look at how their performance-oriented exercises negotiate terrain between imagination, sensation, and activity so as to initiate 'chiasmic', or intertwining, perceptual philosophies of inside-outside, self-other, and body-world. I draw on my own experiences of these practices alongside artist interviews and writings so as to propose that considering perception as an active, purposeful practice rather than a passive event can bring improvisers into a philosophically participatory relationship with their own senses and surroundings.

The first section looks at how, in the phenomenological tradition, perceiving can constitute structured enquiry, and how this thinking has influenced practices in dance improvisation and ecological thought. The second section develops the notion of 'intelligent flesh', whereby perception is harnessed to investigate body and environment as equal, interreliant sources of knowledge. The third section argues that motifs such as 'sensing, feeling, and action' can draw together sensory, imaginative, and cognitive capacities to respond sensitively to environmental others. I conclude by identifying commonalities in these approaches and suggesting how process-based, performance-oriented improvisation can both develop perceptual skills and articulate their associated philosophies, both inside and beyond the dance studio.

Perceiving Perception: Linking Sense and Sensibility

It is not uncommon for a dance teacher today to begin class by inviting students to 'sense your own body; notice how you feel'. Such a simple instruction constitutes an important level of structured enquiry into both subjects and objects of our sensation. Paxton's invitation to sense the mass of the head in the Small Dance equally prioritizes noticing sensation as a means to tuning perception. This training process is used to observe the movement of consciousness throughout the body, as well as to tune into the unconscious movement of the body's reflexes in standing (see Figure 9.1). The exercise links sense, defined by the dictionary as a feeling that something is the case, with sensibility defined as a sensitivity to and appreciation of complex influences.[2] By regarding sensations as sensible—noteworthy—a dancer elevates the status of the sensing body; flesh itself becomes intelligent, and, taken a step further, perception itself, or the process of cognition through sensation, can become an object of dance study. This dual-purpose enquiry invites dancers to recognize both sensation and the mechanisms of consciousness. As Paxton observes, 'the effect of models upon the mind' is significant in the study of improvisation; he references Buddhist frameworks which regard the mind as one of the senses (1987: 16) to illustrate how discourses shape our perception.

Training consciousness of the body as 'one subsystem' of observation of events both inside and outside the body became important in Paxton's work with contact improvisation. He notes that 'consciousness can be felt to change according to what it experiences' and training consciousness to stay open through movement exploration creates an expanded picture of an internal and external world, and hence a 'new ground for moving' (2003: 177).[3]

Such a concept of consciousness that can permeate both internal and external environments echoes views of Merleau-Ponty. In an effort to bypass the subject-object dyad, Merleau-Ponty posits flesh as a continuous surface by which we interface with objects and which also enmeshes the experiencing body in the world (1962: 163), each encroaching upon and altering the other. Later he takes this further into his discussion on the chiasm, or intertwining, which produces an 'intra-ontology' (1968: 227) between

FIG. 9.1 Dance studies students at the University of Malta's School of Performing Arts practise the Small Dance (2015). Photograph by Richard Sarco-Thomas.

objects and bodies.[4] This is useful as a working theme whereby a dancer reflects on the effects of body and place on each other, testing perceptual observations through acts of intentionality, attention to orientation, or in performance practice.

Merleau-Ponty's claim that consciousness is a prereflective act which is always already situated through the body as it is lived in the world recognizes that embodied experience permits insight into 'the things themselves', mapping our own engagement through touch and *movement* with the sensate (1968: 133, emphasis mine). Seen as scores through which to physicalize and articulate perceptions, dance improvisation practices can serve to produce immediate responses to distinctive kinds of orientation.

Examining the relationship of an individual's perception to his own body mass can also be viewed as a basic level of environmental enquiry, acknowledging that perspectives on external environments are always qualified by the windows of our flesh. Paxton says: 'tension in the muscle masks the sensation of gravity' (1986: 49), inviting a release of tension within the body in order to engage more fully with forces beyond it. As Abram and others have argued, how we imagine our environment determines how we perceive and respond to it, even though our preconceptions of an environment are also often contingent upon the discourses through which we define 'an environment' as natural or social. Efforts to represent 'the environment' are always conditioned by the designs of culture (Schama 1996: 6–7).[5] In many cases, these representations can be said to have usurped authority of the sensing body's role in determining 'the real'.

Cultural narratives surrounding machine-based technologies have also been criticized for threatening the utility and agency of the sensing body. Where mediatized information and scientific measurements might call our attention to such 'invisible' threats as nuclear radiation, thus making them more real, the sense-able body can also be undervalued in the wake of such authoritative information (Adam 1995). As Paul Virilio has noted, instantaneous telecommunications collapse space and make bodily movement through space unnecessary (1993: 4), and Erin Manning has argued that bodies often become choreographed by the technologies they use, ironically limiting our embodied, corporeal potential (2009: 63–65). While developments in scientific data-collecting technologies are often justified on the basis of these instruments' potential to enhance or extend the body's sensate capacities, dance improvisation technologies might be said to offer similar potential in developing perception (Sarco-Thomas 2013).

The phenomenological tradition offers philosophical support for foregrounding bodily experience as our primary means of experiencing phenomena, while also enquiring into the structures (corporeal and otherwise) that produce consciousness. In 'Points of Contact, Philosophies of Movement', Philipa Rothfield suggests that philosophies of the body as both perceptive and perceived (body as both sensing subject and sensed object) can be explained through phenomenology as a practice of valuing the kinaesthetic experience of living in a body as knowledge, while recognizing how our social and cultural bodily practices also shape 'the kind of beings we are' (1994: 80). To this end, social and cultural bodily practices such as the Small Dance might also be regarded as technologies through which we shape our experience of consciousness of body and surroundings. If mass is the most important sensation, attention to changes in movement are perceived from the body in contact with another surface, often by sensing beyond that surface into structures it connects to. Crucially, this instruction challenges ownership of sensation. The contact improvisation skill of 'feeling the floor through your partner' or the sense of 'melting into the earth' found in a t'ai chi walk (79) are examples of movement experiences that are not defined by resistance against, but a kind of transitive quality of weight carrying through, and coordinating with, one's surroundings. In practice, such attention to 'feeling support from the floor' can bring efficiency and ease into weight-bearing partnering. Rothfield suggests that Merleau-Ponty's notion of 'reversability—the idea that whenever I touch or look at someone or something, there is a possibility that it could touch me back, that I could be looked at by the object' (86), usurps the active/passive dichotomy in contact improvisation, and furthermore in touch. In such instances, floor, partner, and body are both phenomenal and objective.

If a body is both sensed and sensible, then training body-flesh to skilfully sense its activity in relation to world-flesh can become a complex project. As dance scholarship has recognized, the project of employing phenomenological description to rigorously analyse or describe a dance from the perspective of the dancer poses a distinct challenge: how can I objectively and subjectively describe the effects of a dance which

I am both doing and sensing? How can I make 'sense'—intelligent decisions and sound judgments—out of my 'sensibility', my capacity to engage with a sensory landscape, without reducing my findings to solipsistic relativism? Dance improvisation which features sensation as a starting point often requires physicalizing responses to such sensation; for example, an improviser practicing the Small Dance notices the many tiny 'falls' and shifts of weight that occur in the act of standing, bringing the focus to the body's innate reflexes. These findings can then be amplified or exaggerated through the solo practice of contact improvisation.[6]

Dance phenomenologists Sondra Fraleigh (1999b: 190–191) and Maxine Sheets-Johnstone note that while dance is a means of experiencing phenomena, dance is also a phenomena to be experienced, and they emphasize that consciously experienced and described dancing can be a valuable end in itself (Sheets 1966: 30–31). Fraleigh adds that the process of examining structures of consciousness in movement reveals a diversity of potential locations for consciousness to exist (1999a: 4). Because dance offers a means by which to experience perception through moving in relation to other ideas, structures, and objects—consider Anna Pakes's analogy of riding a bicycle as an example of an embodied knowing *how* to do something as different from recognizing *that* a bicycle works (2009: 11)—studies of perception in dance can be recognized when practised *through* activities of interaction with bodies, scores, and propositions. Such scores can be said to alter and frame our improvisatory and perceptual experience.

INTELLIGENT FLESH

David Wood proposes that in an investigation of boundaries between self and other, body and environment compose the core of ecophenomenological enquiry, where 'imagination is the central connection between space-boundary questions, and boundary/level transformation' (2003b: 23). In Merleau-Ponty's phenomenological approach, however, both the 'seer' and the 'seen' are bound into a fundamental relationship by the 'flesh' of their encounter (1968: 135). Such an image can facilitate boundary explorations in the dance studio.

By proposing that 'mass may be the single most important sensation', Paxton's words sensitize dancers to their interiority and exteriority as a preparation for improvisation. Such focus can be said to 'orient' the improviser's research. Particularly when improvisation is framed by a research question,[7] orientation offers a way to articulate an artist's relationship between movement and thought. Paxton's Small Dance orients dancers towards the sensation of mass, cells, or 'the feeling of gravity'; in doing so, it suggests that the relationship between body and world can be explored through reflective motion. For Merleau-Ponty, enquiring into the body *as* world is an essential component of phenomenological enquiry: 'one can say that we perceive the things themselves, that we are the world that thinks itself—or that the world is at the heart of our flesh. In any case, once a body-world relationship is recognized, there is a ramification of my body and a ramification of the world and a correspondence between its inside and my outside, between my inside and its outside' (1968: 136). The innate intelligence of the body is described by Merleau-Ponty as residing in its powers of recognition and perception *in relationship to the world*, but these skills of perception, as Noë proposes, are honed through exercise. Select improvisation scores offer methods to notice or imagine, and develop, this relational 'intelligence'. Paxton suggests 'your mass and the earth's mass calling to each other', inviting students to cultivate attention to mass and to reciprocal sensations of bodies in relation to other bodies. Merleau-Ponty could have been echoing Paxton's enquiry into gravity when he wrote: 'inside and outside are inseparable. The world is wholly inside and I am wholly outside myself' (1962: 407).

The work of Deborah Hay,[8] Paxton's Judson Dance Theater contemporary, correspondingly exemplifies an enquiry into the intelligence of one's flesh. Hay emphasizes her bodily perceptions by proposing to perform them instantly, as in her score from *O Beautiful*: 'What if every cell in your body has the potential to perceive beauty and to surrender beauty, simultaneously, each and every moment?' (Hay in Rod 2007). Her practice of projecting a hypothetical 'self' as an outside observer further frames the multiple perspectives on an environment made possible through imagined and intertwining sensory positions (2000: xviii). Rather than one entity, Hay proposes 'her body' to be a collection of trillions of cells with the ability to respond to 'everywhere'. Practising her score 'What if [53 trillion cells perceive] alignment is everywhere?' (xiv) initiates a physical dialogue between interior and exterior flesh:

> My whole body, 53 trillion cells at once, perceive alignment is everywhere. This ear, that elbow and this eyebrow bristle, find one another in a spiral chase. Pigeons flap onto the roof above the studio window. Clouds hang heavy on the horizon. Tailbone drops quick to floor, hips open and fold. Walls extend vertical. Eyes see and feel.

Hay creatively practises a physical performance of inquiry into 'intelligence' or 'wisdom' when she dances. For example, a 1987 score—'I imagine every cell in my body has the potential to perceive wisdom every moment, while remaining positionless about what wisdom is or what it looks like' (103)—suggests that the body is capable of perceiving 'wisdom' and conveying this wisdom through movement, regardless of how it appears to a witnessing mind. Hay does not call her work improvisation, but often there is little physical choreographic instruction in her dances. Instead, she choreographs attention. Repeating the instructions, 'ask the question, notice the response, whole body the teacher' (2005), Hay assumes the intelligence of her cells and uses movement to learn from 'the teacher' of her whole body.

Hay, who has been chronicling her inquisitive performance practices since 1970, posits bodily intelligence as an underlying principle in all her work. Rather than quantifying what her 'whole body' is or how it teaches her, she chooses instead to articulate her inquiry in movement. Through acts of moving, Hay researches a bodily perception which accesses both imagination and reality and which is not reducible to any one body part. In an interview with Ann Daly, Hay describes how her attention while improvising transcends divisions of body/mind/spirit:

> [DALY:]   Your bodily practice—your dance—is not just about the physical body, but about the physical/spiritual body.
> [HAY:]   This is crucial. In dance I do not divide the body into physical, spiritual, mental, emotional, psychological parts. I am adamant about this. The whole body is the perceiver of everything imagined, created, invented, not imagined, guessed, faked. (Daly 1999: 15)

Hay's way of seeing 'the body' as unified composite parts enables her to practise 'perception' in a simplified way. She dances by creating conditions for movement and then noticing how her body responds to those conditions. For example, in 2005 as part of the performance O, Hay asked 'What if 53 trillion cells surrender the pattern of facing a single direction?' (2005).

While the request sounds impossible, the result when I use her scores is an incredible lightness and feeling of possibility in my body, as I 'sense'—both imagine and feel—all my cells spinning off into different directions. The dancing that emerges does not come from a body whose organs have swapped places, but the inquiry into the 'what if?' possibility of unpatterned movement creates an eager response in me to try. To my sensate imagination, my body becomes a facility of trillions of intelligences, each possessing and activating the potential to 'dialogue with all that is' (Hay 2000: 104).

Hay does not 'rehearse'; instead she seeks adaptations of her scores through daily performance where every session is a practice of asking the question. In this way, the performer becomes more and more adept at noticing the body's response to the question, and more available to ask the question again. When encountering other dancers or audience, Hay asks her dancers to think 'when I see you, I see you practicing what I'm practicing' (2005). In this way, the dancers become accustomed to accepting all input and output as intelligent, fleshy responses to the 'what if?' question.[9] Hay teaches that the ideosomatic wisdom of the body itself is the site of multiple, profound intelligences which provide insight when enquired into. Privileged to the body's 'subtle forms of knowledge' (Hay 2000: xxv; Drobnick 2006: 44–45) are those who take time to practise inquiring into their bodies through movement. Hay's supplication to her moving body through scores as frameworks for imaginative consciousness creates the conditions for these unquantifiable phenomena of 'knowledge' to arise.

Imaginative consciousness might be said to be a key factor within improvisers' perceptual philosophies but also within aesthetic encounters. Sybil Cohen has argued that a dancer's experience and knowledge manifest through movement and are made visible to a watcher through the medium 'of the lived body' (1984: 164). Though there are significant questions around how far the body offers a medium for a universalized performance experience (see Barba and Savarese 1991; Kuppers 2003; Schechner 2006; Schechner and Schuman 1976), phenomenological interpretations of aesthetics propose that a close communion with a work of art necessarily entails entering into a creatively receptive relationship with its sensible qualities (Ingarden 1975: 260), where perception engenders 'a sympathetic reflection on the aesthetic object' (Dufrenne 1973: 395; see also Freedberg and Gallese 2007). For Maxine Sheets-Johnstone, this experience in dance is grounded in the 'imaginative consciousness' of the dancer so as to recreate forms that align with certain images (1979: 113–114). Thus, this 'knowledge' possessed by movement can be seen as the intention of the dancer to practise awareness of effort and of translating energetic pathways of imagined movement images. Sensation, imagination, and action all feed the project of aligning oneself with images.

'Witnessing' an environment is another example of an imaginative exercise that focuses attention on the intersubjectivity between self and other. Taken from the discipline of Authentic Movement, in which one person silently witnesses a mover who moves in a nondirected way with her eyes closed, witnessing supports movement-based enquiry into sensation and perception. Also referred to as 'the MoverWitness Paradigm' (Goldhahn 2007), Authentic Movement has been used in conjunction with improvisation, dance, therapy, psychology, and arts practices as a way to commit to seeing another in the act of conscious moving (Adler 2002; Goldhahn 2007). Dance artist Jennifer Monson,[10] whose outdoor BIRD BRAIN performances drew inspiration from the activities of migrating birds, and who considers 'improvisation systems as modes of orientation' (Galatea-Wozny 2005: 18), has worked with Authentic Movement as a model through which to improvise in and with a landscape. In her adaptation, Monson witnesses the landscape as a mover before moving with the landscape as witness (Monson 2010). She uses the score to 'bring consciousness of self to a place' and to 'warm up' by focusing energetic and imaginative presence that brings with it awareness of relationship to environment. 'When I'm witnessing, my consciousness moves out; when I'm being witnessed I sense the potential consciousness of place moving in. The energy of consciousness is coming into being with the relationship of myself sensing and perceiving the environment, and the environment sensing or perceiving me' (Monson 2010). In this model, the environment becomes part of an intersubjective relationship of conscious perception. This notion of intersubjectivity is echoed in a model for sensing articulated by dance improviser Lisa Nelson, whose Tuning Scores use compositional tools to heighten performers' sensitivity to space so as 'to illuminate how we compose perception through action' (Galanter 2004). Rather than imagining that 'she' as a subject *does the sensing* of her environment, Nelson 'perceives her consciousness as caused by the environment' and in doing so imagines that the world views itself through the 'permeable (two-way) membrane' of her senses (Paxton in Dymoke 2014: 212). Similarly, Hay proposes her body as an integrated sense structure: she says: 'my game is to be as fully awake as possible. I imagine that I can see with every part of my body—that I have eyes everywhere' (Drobnick 2006: 48).

Improviser David Zambrano[11] asks movers to feel 'little windows and doors' in their fingertips, toes, heels, and elbows while moving quickly. Zambrano uses the phrase 'passing through' to describe how an improviser's body and attention can travel fluidly between self and other, between 'me' and 'you', when performing his technique Flying Low and his improvisation score *Passing Through*. 'Whatever you move through also passes through you' (Zambrano 2005) becomes a score for a philosophy of a body which is never fixed but always negotiating a changing landscape.

Dance artist Chrysa Parkinson[12] asks her students to focus in on kinaesthetically sensing different aspects of moving parts—the moving bodies in the studio space, and the moving bones and muscles in the body—in order to practise nonfrontal, multimodal perception while improvising. In led warmups, Parkinson gives disorienting, challenging instructions: 'Bring perception to the inside of your body.... Feel your eyelids moving.... Register the ways you perceive motion.... Feel your skin.... Notice the bones of your lower leg crossing and uncrossing' (Parkinson 2006a). For Parkinson, defamiliarizing patterns of recognition can help dancers to unlock new sensations and modes of perception as routes towards different ways of authoring their movement experiences (Parkinson 2006b: 43). Her work focuses on shifting our normal way of perceiving bodily movement so that we might understand it more poignantly—with less familiarity. Dancing while blindfolded, imagining the floor as front, or watching dancing from an upside-down vantage point are exercises used to reorient dancers' sensing capacity from its visually dominated patterns and to refine their tactile and spatial perception (2006a). To be skilled and consciously selective in using modes of perception is one of Parkinson's goals as a dancer (Hilton and Parkinson 2014: 12).

As I have investigated within my performances of *Twig Dances,* which use plant structures as starting points for dance improvisations (Sarco-Thomas 2010), another way to defamiliarize perceptual patterns that separate self from environment is to improvise by imitation. In a 2003 workshop, Emilyn Claid placed a red plastic folding chair in the centre of the studio and invited anyone to come up and 'perform the chair'. I responded instantly with an oddly embodied posture.

> *I immediately see the chair like a gaping red mouth leaning backwards on a slanted leg, so I walk up to the chair and assume that position: facing the audience, I lean back on one leg, tilt my head back, open my mouth wide, stick out my tongue and freeze. A sense of familiarity in my own body and sounds of amused recognition from the audience affirm I've performed a likeness.*

By using bodies to emulate postures, shapes, and textures, improvisers practise actively perceiving, and through performing this can come closer to articulating the quality of what they sense. They can also then reflect on the relationship between body and object through perceptual activity. Merleau-Ponty argues for the inherent expressiveness of our own flesh, which extends to comprehend and 'discover' expressions in other objects. Abram translates this 'discovery' to mean our bodily capacity for understanding the language of nonhumans. He argues that perception is always a participatory action (1996: 275–276) and hence is our basic means for inviting relationship with the world around us. As such, improvisation practices that focus on physicalizing bodily perceptions can ground notions of relationship in concrete, sensuous physical efforts.

The notion of intelligent flesh can be both posited and investigated through a range of improvisation scenarios: witnessing paradigms, wise cells, windows in one's whole body, scores for unusual modes of perception, and instantaneous imitation offer potential routes to defamiliarizing the body and its habits within a changing environment. The next section further investigates how enacting responses to objects can be a route towards activating perception.

SENSING, FEELING, ACTION

> I return in my mind's eye to the northern slope of Bald Mountain on which I live. I look around and—pronto! Something happens. I see snow. I jump and curl in air. Hands and feet in air. Heavy rattle winter wind smashes dry sunflower stalks. Again. Again, smash, jump! Snow thud falls from laden roof. Feet slide out, thud. Whole body, thud, flat to floor.
>
> (Forti 2003: 53)

As Simone Forti's[13] words capture, improvisation can be a practice of perceiving and performing simultaneously, or of being inspired by 'movement memory snapshots' we carry (62). Through these 'animations' an improviser can inform his performance with the fullness of his immediate sensations drawn from sense memories. Forti's improvisation practice of 'moving the telling' or 'Logomotion' (57) animates such memories, giving life to sense impressions through enacting them in dance performance. Her exercises ask how movements, textures, and impressions of wild things register in one's memory and can feed performance.

For several years, Simone Forti & Troupe practised 'land portraits', which involved absorbing impressions of a site before performing an improvisation about it. In her writings, Forti reveals that she both moves and is moved by her sense of the natural world: 'reaching into the dirt for the potatoes, my self dives into my fingers and I am the dry crumbly ground. I am the cool round things' (2003: 59). Later she writes, near a waterfall, 'I breathe the falling water and am the soft air smelling of me.... And only by the grace of that which holds me still do I hold still' (63).

Reciprocity with place and delight in the animism of the nonhuman come alive through Forti's words. Abram also urges that to fulfil Merleau-Ponty's project to 'return to things themselves' by 'reawakening the basic experience of the world' (1962: viii–ix, in Abram 1996: 36), we must allow ourselves to be moved by the sensual acts of life all around us: the exploding of a daffodil, a gruesomely wind-slapping hurricane, the unfurling of a fern tentacle, a writhing and flopping pink earthworm. He challenges readers towards sensual empathy with the world, arguing that we can engage meaningfully with an environment via our innate capacity to see, hear, taste, smell, and feel other beings. In her discussion of implications of the perception-based work of artists Eva Karczag, Forti, and Hay for feminist thought, Rachel Fensham argues that such dancing which privileges the senses creates a 'space where the human being might first be seen … as an upright animal with extraordinary conceptual powers vested not in the genitals … but in every part of the body with its unique capacity to provide information and to organise its own movement. This power of the "thinking body" is a power which the dancer may contribute to those theoretical debates that often mask and confuse material (biological) realities' (1993: 37). Fensham suggests that dance which works with the body as a perceptual tool might be seen to offer important perspectives on how 'the' body can be used to identify with 'other' bodies, towards a 'multi-vocal' dance practice. Privileging sensation through writing, speaking, and moving, as in the case of Forti, exemplifies one route towards such a project.

Improvisation methods from Action Theater also encourage performers to recognize the sensations and feelings that objects evoke. Drawing on ideas from Body-Mind Centering[14] and Authentic Movement, the motif 'sense-feel-act'[15] is used by Action Theater teacher Sten Rudstrom[16] to guide improvisers in training themselves to recognize three stages of perception in performance. First, performers are asked to first to notice how an image can manifest as a bodily feeling, by embodying dry leaves, for example. Merleau-Ponty argues that our body responds impulsively to the evocative sensual associations of 'cultural objects like words' (1962: 235). Abram takes up this point as further support for his argument that our responses to things or ideas manifest precognitively in our bodies as (sometimes subtle) resonant sensations (1996: 53). Action Theater assumes likewise; improvisers are trained to be aware of qualities of movement sparked in one's own body by other actors' movements, and by words, sounds, rhythms or feelings/emotions.

Instead of acting out emotions like 'sad' or 'happy',[17] an Action Theater practitioner situates feeling as an act of perception that connects performers to the innate responses of bodies. This can become tricky, because as bodyworker Deane Juhan notes, sensory and mental feelings can be virtually indistinguishable from one another in the ways our bodies recognize and manifest them (1998: xxvii). The complex relationship between sensory feeling and mental feelings can, I propose, become acknowledged and interrogated through the focused inquiry that practices such as sensing-feeling-action offer. Once an improviser distinguishes the informative potential of sensations, there can be greater choice in how to use these sensations to bring about feelings and actions in performance.

Second, the sensing-feeling-action score trains improvisers how to embody a feeling until it becomes an action. 'Pay attention to your feeling. Start from the feeling', instructs Rudstrom (2005). Creating movement from feeling, an actor can then stretch, shrink, repeat, or expand that action in performance.

I feel excited to be performing in front of a small audience, and I sense how my eyes widen and my fingers twitch and my whole body is kind of humming, so I take it further: I really widen my eyes, and twiddle my fingers and totally let my body hum with the actions of feeling excited. The energy of emphasizing these movements eggs me on further: my eyes are popping now, my finger-twiddling is becoming a whole-arm phenomenon, and my 'humming' body is beginning to bounce. I sense myself becoming more excited yet. I feel the associated bodily tensions and flows, and emphasize them. I quickly find myself in a delightfully deepening circle of sensing-feeling-acting-sensing-feeling-acting.

Physicalizing actions in performance give improvisers material to use in response to performance elements, whilst the motif finally asks performers to read all action as sensation. As a whole, the sequence seeks to clarify what a body-subject is perceiving and to make that perception into explicit communication, inviting dialogue with those who see him. Repeating the motif in practice creates a loop that implies the interrelationship of the elements, and the sensible impact of actions.

The exercise might be said to bridge the gap between sensing and participating, exercising what Noë would call an 'enactive approach to perception' (2004). It can be a practice of inviting, as Abram suggests, the body's extension into the whole sensible world as an active participant by 'lending one's sensory imagination to things in order to discover how they alter and transform that imagination, how they reflect us back changed, how they are different from us' (1996: 275–276).

Action Theater's sensing-feeling-action exercise, and Forti's animate writing-speaking-dancing practices make explicit the tangibility of Merleau-Ponty's embodied gestures, or Abram's inseparability between perceiving something and experiencing a bodily feeling which that perception triggers. As performance methods, both work directly with the sensual responses of the body, eliminating steps in which the rational mind judges, corrects, remarks, or qualifies the intensity of a performer's feeling. Seeking swiftness of bodily responses through Forti's animations, and the sensing-feeling-action paradigm, an improviser can practise deepening embodiment, clarification, and communication of her perception.

CONCLUSION: PROCESS AS PRACTICE

This essay has presented examples of improvisation scores that highlight perception as a key component of instant movement composition in performance. As repeatable physicalized enquiries into body-environment relations, Paxton's Small Dance, Hay's 'what if' questions, Monson's landscape witnessing, Forti's animations, and Rudstrom's sense-feel-act motif exemplify practices that seek to develop bodily skills in sensation, and to test philosophies of perception. Their diverse approaches reveal resonant themes: the notion of flesh, both bodily flesh and 'flesh of the world', as an intelligent source for study; the importance of defamiliarization to projects of enhancing and questioning perception; the role of creativity and imagination in orienting perceptual philosophies for dance improvisation; and the centrality of regular practice to building, challenging, and honing perceptual skills.

> *Negotiating down the steep rocky path, I step haltingly, thoughtfully. Then something changes: relaxing, I shift my weight forward, soften, and extend my mind. I let my feet find their place; feeling my improviser's legs sense the ground rising to meet me, foot-holds appear spontaneously.*

These examples show how seeing sensing as a participatory activity, as described in Noë's enactive approach, enables an improviser to engage more fully in practices that tune his skills of perception. They also illustrate how perception can be explored through imagination and movement, and exercised through the heightened attentional states that dance performance offers. Attention-based improvisation scores can be devised and exercised to expand investigation of the body and its possible responses to a multilayered environment.

If these claims hold true, then perception-oriented dance improvisation practice has much to offer as a method of training performers as curious and sensitive movers. Such approaches suggest that developing a philosophy of sensing as an active process can lead a mover to claim response-ability as a sensing, feeling, and acting participant in a larger animate world. As an 'ecological' practice, engaging bodily perception through purposeful sensing brings to view the tangible and direct ways that improvisers can orient their practice towards how human and nonhuman others might impress upon, surprise, shift, and change one another.

NOTES

1. Choreographer, dance innovator, and key founder of the dance form contact improvisation, Steve Paxton has explored multiple ways of investigating the body's potential for movement from its own sense structures in contact improvisation, and through his work on the DVD *Material for the Spine*. His writings regularly feature in *Contact Quarterly*.
2. As found in Dictionary (2005–2014), Apple, Inc. 2.2.1.
3. Used to engage with the world through changing mechanisms, evolving improvisation scores (see Parkinson 2006b) might also be said to evolve to match the unfolding evolutionary processes, which, according to process philosophy developed by Alfred North Whitehead (1926, 1969; see also Bergson 1998; Ingold 2000, 2011), make up the natural world.
4. Merleau-Ponty's writings on phenomenology locate the 'lived body' as the preeminent substance of a subject's sensing universe, challenging the privileging of consciousness over experience implied in Husserlian methods (Merleau-Ponty 1962: xi–xii; Flynn 2004). His notion of the intertwining or the 'chiasm' challenges Husserl's assertion that phenomenological research into an object's essences is possible through a focused attention on an act of consciousness, or *noesis*, in relation to an object of attention, or *noema*.
5. This position is developed by Macnaghten and Urry, who argue in *Contested Natures* that the different 'natures' we understand are a result of various social constructions that are

realized through our everyday performances of dwelling, discourse, transaction, and individual agency (1998: 1–3). Similarly, how we live in and perceive our environment is affected by language, and our experiences of it, to some extent, are also socially constructed (see Evernden 1992; Franklin 2002; Proctor 2001; Rolston 1997; Soper 1995; Smith 2001).

6. Contact improvisation has been described 'as a solo practice' or 'a duet with the floor' by teachers such as Malcolm Manning (2014) and Ray Chung (2014).

7. See for example Lepkoff (2008), as well as Sarco-Thomas (2014).

8. Deborah Hay has investigated many approaches to performance as a means for questioning perception since her work with Judson Dance Theater in the 1960s. Key books include *Lamb at the Altar* (1994), *My Body, The Buddhist* (2000), and *Using the Sky: A Dance* (2015).

9. As Megan Andrews suggests, Hay's scores detail a kind of collaboration between body (cells) and space (environment) that highlights the potential of 'an ethical relation with' (2012: 1).

10. Performer, teacher, and founder of iLAND (interdisciplinary Laboratory for Art, Nature and Dance), Jennifer Monson in her improvisation work has investigated outdoor environments and correlations to internal bodily landscapes through large-scale site performances and theatre works. Monson is based in New York City and Urbana-Champaign, where she teaches at the University of Illinois.

11. David Zambrano is based in Amsterdam and teaches and performs internationally. His movement technique of Flying Low and improvisation score *Passing Through* are taught in intensive workshop situations and have influenced the style of key contemporary choreographers across Europe.

12. Chrysa Parkinson lives in Brussels and regularly teaches at PARTS. She draws on her performance work with artists such as Tere O'Connor, David Zambrano, Thomas Hauert, and Deborah Hay when questioning ways of watching and practicing dance. Key writings include *Self-Interview on Practice* (2009) available on Vimeo, and essays on the Belgian dance forum Sarma, http://sarma.be/pages/Index.

13. Simone Forti has developed improvisation as a means of responding to memories of objects and environments. Her writings appear in *Contact Quarterly* as well as *Handbook in Motion* (1975); key reflections on her work feature in *Terpsichore in Sneakers* (Banes 1987) and *Taken by Surprise* (Ann Cooper and Gere 2003).

14. The initial publication of Bainbridge Cohen (1994) marked a growing exploration of relationships between sensation, perception, and movement for dance educators in the field of somatics. Today Body-Mind Centering practice offers a unique example of sensation- and imagination-based movement explorations of the body. See Zaporah (1995) for more information on Action Theater improvisation.

15. Drawing on Bonnie Bainbridge Cohen and Janet Adler's work, the motif of 'sensing-feeling-action' is used in Rudstrom's Action Theater training to bring about more embodied responses to performance situations (Rudstrom 2015).

16. Performer Sten Rudstrom has been a key player in the development of Ruth Zaporah's Action Theater. Rudstrom teaches and performs improvisation internationally and leads an annual Action Theater training intensive in Berlin, where he is based.

17. For example, if a performer interpreted a vague sense of heaviness in his limbs as 'sad' and then proceeded to make a 'sad' action by turning the corners of his mouth down and furrowing his brow, such an action would be seen as an imitative caricature of 'sad'. In Action Theater, this is seen as a calculated action based on the actor's concept of sad rather than

a specific response to the particular feeling of heaviness in his limbs, that might otherwise be turned into any number of actions which do not necessarily read to an audience as 'sad'.

REFERENCES

Abram, D. (1996) *The Spell of the Sensuous: Perception and Language in a More-Than-Human World*. New York: Vintage Books.

Adam, B. (1995) *Timewatch: The Social Analysis of Time*. Cambridge: Polity Press.

Adler, J. (2002) *Offering from the Conscious Body: The Discipline of Authentic Movement*. Vermont: Inner Traditions.

Andrews, P. M. (2012) Somatic Anacrusis: Towards an Ethics of Being via the Solo Dance Practice of Deborah Hay's *At Once*. PhD Thesis, York University. https://yorkspace.library.yorku.ca/xmlui/handle/10315/32710 Accessed 18 August 2018.

Bainbridge Cohen, B. (1994) *Sensing, Feeling and Action: The Experiential Anatomy of Body-Mind Centering*. Massachusetts: Contact Editions.

Banes, S. (1987) *Terpsichore in Sneakers*. Connecticut: Wesleyan.

Barba, E., and Savarese, N. (1991) *A Dictionary of Theatre Anthropology: The Secret Art of the Performer*. London: Routledge.

Bergson, H. (1998) *Creative Evolution*. New York: Dover Publications.

Brown, C. S., and Toadvine, T. (eds.). (2003) *Eco-phenomenology: Back to the Earth Itself*. Albany: State University of New York Press: 103–120.

Chung, R. (2014) Riding the Curves of Space-Time. Workshop, Contact Festival Vienna, 26 October–2 November.

Claid, E. (2003) Performance workshop. Dartington College of Arts. Hexagon Studio, 4 March.

Cohen, S. S. (1984) Ingarden's Aesthetics and Dance. In Sheets-Johnstone, M. (ed.), *Illuminating Dance: Philosophical Explorations*. London: Associated University Presses, 146–166.

Daly, A. (1999) Horse Rider Woman Playing Dancing: Ann Daly Interviews Deborah Hay. *PAJ: A Journal of Performance and Art* 21(3): 13–23.

Drobnick, J. (2006) Deborah Hay: A Performance Primer. *Performance Research* 11(2): 43–57.

Dufrenne, M. (1973) *The Phenomenology of Aesthetic Experience*. Trans. Edward S. Casey, Albert A. Anderson, Willis Domingo, and Leon Jacobson. Evanston, IL: Northwestern University Press.

Dymoke, K. (2014) Contact Improvisation: The Non-Eroticised Touch in an 'Art-Sport'. *Journal of Dance and Somatic Practices* 6(2): 205–218.

Evernden, N. (1992) *The Social Creation of Nature*. Baltimore: Johns Hopkins University Press.

Fensham, R. (1993) Dancing in and out of Language: A Feminist Dilemma. *Writings on Dance* 9: 22–39.

Flynn, B. (2004) "Maurice Merleau-Ponty", *Stanford Encyclopedia of Philosophy*. Available at: http://plato.stanford.edu/entries/merleau-ponty/ (Accessed: 20 December 2009).

Forti, S. (2003) Animate Dancing: A Practice in Dance Improvisation. In Albright, Ann Cooper, and Gere, D. (eds.), *Taken by Surprise: A Dance Improvisation Reader*. Middletown, CT: Wesleyan University Press, 53–64.

Fraleigh, S. H. (1999a) Family Resemblance. In Hanstein, P., and Fraleigh, S. H. (eds.), *Researching Dance: Evolving Modes of Enquiry*. London: Dance Books, 3–21.

Fraleigh, S. H. (1999b) Witnessing the Frog Pond. In Hanstein, P., and Fraleigh, S. H. (eds.), *Researching Dance: Evolving Modes of Enquiry*. London: Dance Books, 188–224.

Franklin, A. (2002) *Nature and Social Theory*. London: Sage.

Freedberg, D., and Gallese, V. (2007) Motion, Emotion and Empathy in Esthetic Experience. *Trends in Cognitive Sciences* 11 (5): 197–203.

Galanter, M. (2004) Tuning Scores Log. https://tuningscoreslog.wordpress.com/about/. Accessed 20 August 2018.

Galeota-Wozny, N. (2005) Interview with Jennifer Monson on BIRD BRAIN DANCE—A Navigational Dance Project. *Contact Quarterly* (Summer/Fall), 20(2): 12–24.

Goldhahn, E. (2007) *Shared Habitats: The MoverWitness Paradigm*. PhD. Dartington College of Arts.

Hay, D. (2000) *My Body, the Buddhist*. Middletown, CT: Wesleyan University Press.

Hay, D. (2005) *O Performance Project Workshop*, P.A.R.T.S., Brussels, 2–13 May.

Hay, D. (2010) 'What if...? Excerpts from A Lecture on the Performance of Beauty' dancetechtv.

Hilton, R. and Parkinson, C. (2014) Location, Location, Location.in *The Dancer as Agent Collection*, edited by Chrysa Parkinson, DOCH School of Dance and Circus, Stockholm University of the Arts. http://repo.sarma.be/Dancer%20as%20Agent/Hilton%20Parkinson.pdf. Accessed 2 March 2015.

Ingarden, R. (1975) Phenomenological Aesthetics: An Attempt at Defining Its Range. *Journal of Aesthetics and Art Criticism* 33(3): 257–269.

Ingold, T. (2000) *The Perception of the Environment: Essays on Dwelling, Livelihood and Skill*. London: Routledge.

Ingold, T. (2011) *Being Alive: Essays on Movement, Knowledge and Description*. London: Routledge.

Juhan, D. (1998) *Job's Body: A Handbook for Bodywork*. New York: Station Hill Openings.

Kuppers, P. (2003) *Disability and Contemporary Performance: Bodies on Edge*. London: Routledge.

Langer, M. (2003) Nietzsche, Heidegger and Merleau-Ponty: Some of Their Contributions and Limitations for 'Environmentalism'. In Brown, C. S., and Toadvine, T. (eds.), *Eco-phenomenology: Back to the Earth Itself*. New York: State University of New York Press, 103–120.

Lepkoff, D. (2008) Contact Improvisation: A Question? http://daniellepkoff.com/writings/CI%20A%20question.php. Accessed 20 August 2018.

Little, N. (2014) Restructuring the Self-Sensing: Attention Training in Contact Improvisation. *Journal of Dance and Somatic Practices* 6(2): 247–260.

Macnaghten, P., and Urry, J. (eds.). (1998) *Contested Natures*. London: Sage.

Manning, E. (2009) *Relationscapes: Movement, Art, Philosophy*. Cambridge, MA: MIT Press. (Online book)

Manning, M. (2014) 5x10 Sharing at Teachers' Meeting. Contact Festival Freiburg, 5–9 August.

Merleau-Ponty, M. (1962) *The Phenomenology of Perception*. Trans. Colin Smith. London: Routledge and Kegan Paul.

Merleau-Ponty, M. (1968) *The Visible and the Invisible*. Trans. Alphonso Lingis. Ed. Claude Lefort. Evanston, IL: Northwestern University Press.

Monson, J. (2010) Interview with Jennifer Monson by Malaika Sarco-Thomas via Skype. 30 January.

Naess, A. (1973) The Shallow and the Deep, Long-Range Ecology Movement: A Summary. *Inquiry: An Interdisciplinary Journal of Philosophy* 16(1): 95–100.

Noë, A. (2004) *Action in Perception*. Cambridge, MA: MIT Press.

Pakes, A. (2009) Knowing through Dance-Making: Choreography, Practical Knowledge and Practice-as-Research. In Butterworth, J., and Wilsdschut, L. (eds.), *Contemporary Choreography: A Critical Reader*. London: Routledge, 10–22.

Parkinson, C. (2006a) Contemporary Technique. Class, P.A.R.T.S., Brussels.

Parkinson, C. (2006b) Folding the Field—Fielding the Fold. In De Belder, S., and Van Rompay, T. (eds.), *Ten Years of P.A.R.T.S.*. Brussels: P.A.R.T.S., 42–44.

Parkinson, C. (2009) Self Interview on Practice. https://vimeo.com/26763244 Accessed 20 August 2018.

Paxton, S. (1986) Steve Paxton's Description of Attention to the Small Dance in a Relaxed Stand. *Contact Quarterly* 11(1) (Winter): 48–50.

Paxton, S. (1987) Improvisation Is a Word for Something That Can't Keep a Name. *Contact Quarterly* (Spring/Summer): 15–19.

Paxton, S. (2003) Drafting Interior Techniques. In Albright, Ann Cooper, and Gere, D. (eds.), *Taken by Surprise: A Dance Improvisation Reader*. Middletown, CT: Wesleyan University Press, 175–184.

Proctor, J. D. (2001) Solid Rock and Shifting Sands: The Moral Paradox of Saving a Socially Constructed Nature. In Castree, N., and Braun, B. (eds.), *Social Nature: Theory, Practice and Politics*. Oxford: Blackwell, 225–240.

Rod, R. J. (2007) 'Playing Awake', dissertation, University of Copenhagen. Available at: https://www.academia.edu/28866745/Playing_Awake

Rolston, H. (1997) Nature for Real: Is Nature a Social Construct? In Chappell, T. D. J. (ed.), *The Philosophy of the Environment*. Edinburgh: Edinburgh University Press, 38–64.

Rothfield, P. (1994) Points of Contact: Philosophies of Movement. *Writings on Dance* 11(12): 77- 87.

Rudstrom, S. (2005) Action Theater Improvisation Training. Month-long intensive workshop, Aikido Dojo Südstern, Berlin, 1–27 August.

Rudstrom, S. (2015) Photos of sensing, feeling, action. Email correspondence. 6 March.

Sarco-Thomas, M. (2010) *Twig Dances: Improvisation Performance as Ecological Practice*. PhD. Dartington College of Arts and University of Plymouth.

Sarco-Thomas, M. (2013) Excitable Tissues in Motion Capture Practices: The Improvising Dancer as Technogenetic Imagist. *Journal of Dance and Somatic Practices* 5(2): 81–93.

Sarco-Thomas, M. (2014) *touch + talk*: Ecologies of Questioning in Contact and Improvisation. *Journal of Dance and Somatic Practices* 6(2): 189–204.

Sarma. (2018) SARMA: Laboratory for Discursive Practices and Expanded Publication. http://sarma.be/pages/About_Sarma. Accessed 20 August 2018.

Schama, S. (1996) *Landscape and Memory*. New York: Vintage Books.

Schechner, R. (2006) *Performance Studies: An Introduction*. London: Routledge.

Schechner, R., and Schuman, M. (1976) *Ritual, Play and Performance: Readings in the Social Sciences/Theater*. New York: Seabury Press.

Sheets, M. (1966) *The Phenomenology of Dance*. Madison: University of Wisconsin Press.

Sheets-Johnstone, M. (1979) *The Phenomenology of Dance*. 2nd ed. London: Dance Books.

Sheets-Johnstone, M. (1999) *The Primacy of Movement*. Philadelphia: John Benjamins.

Smith, M. (2001) *An Ethics of Place: Radical Ecology, Postmodernity and Social Theory*. Albany: State University of New York Press.

Soper, K. (1995) *What Is Nature? Culture, Politics and the Non-human*. Oxford: Blackwell.

Virilio, P. (1993) The Third Interval. Trans. Tom Conley. In Conley, V. A. (ed.), *Rethinking Technologies*. Minneapolis: University of Minnesota Press.

Whitehead, A. N. (1926) *The Concept of Nature*. London: Cambridge University Press.

Whitehead, A. N. (1969) *Process and Reality: An Essay in Cosmology*. Reprint. New York: MacMillan.

Wood, D. (2003a) ') What Is Eco-phenomenology?' In *Eco-phenomenology: Back to the Earth Itself*, edited by Charles Brown, Charles, and Ted Toadvine, Ted (eds.), *Eco-phenomenology: Back to the Earth Itself*. Albany: State University of New York Press, 211–234.

Wood, D. (2003b) What Is Eco-phenomenology? Adaptation of What Is Eco-phenomenology?, in Brown, Charles, and Toadvine, Ted (eds.), *Eco-phenomenology: Back to the Earth Itself*. Albany: State University of New York Press, 211–234. http://www.vanderbilt.edu/chronopod/phenomenology.pdf. Accessed 10 February 2015.

Zambrano, D. (2005) *Passing Through and Flying Low*. Workshop, P.A.R.T.S., Brussels. 5 January 2015–15 April 2005.

Zaporah, R. (1995) *Action Theater: The Improvisation of Presence*. Berkeley, CA: North Atlantic Books.

CHAPTER 10

RETHINKING IMPROVISATION FROM A DAOIST PERSPECTIVE OF QI-ENERGY

I-YING WU

One can say that, for the Chinese, everything in the universe, inorganic and organic, is composed of and defined by its Qi. Mountains, plants, and human emotions all have Qi. Qi is not so much a force added to lifeless matter but the state of being of any phenomena. For the Chinese, Qi is the pulsation of the cosmos itself.

(Ted J. Kaptchuk 2000: 43)

WHAT improvisation is about or how it is executed depends on the contexts in which it comes into being and is discussed. Different social and cultural contexts could determine how improvisation is thought about and embodied. Even in the same culture, improvisation may develop in diverse forms or ways based on different conceptions that might be chosen or adapted according to personal experiences or backgrounds. What cannot be ignored is the fact that different cultures might generate concepts of improvisation that appear similar because their cultural elements and thoughts have penetrated, mixed, and merged into each other or just somehow coincided; there might be certain subtle differences between them. For instance, American and European improvisation practices informed by somatic practices have similar inclinations to Asian meditative practices and thoughts, but it is possible to note that their ideas imply concepts of integration of the bodymind, in-between, and wholeness that are grounded on different epistemic framings.[1] Different modes of improvisation reflect how the body is thought or regarded and how the body gives rise to movement in diverse contexts. Since the philosophical and the cultural aspects of improvisation are interrelated, I suggest contexts that are significant enough to be either apparently mentioned or tacitly considered when talking about improvisation in any modes developed in any times, even if this essay focuses on the improvisation practices related to the bodymind or somatic movement.

I am a Taiwanese improvisation practitioner who has learned Chinese traditional advanced qigong (a meditative qigong)[2] and practised it as daily routine. Inherited from Chinese traditional culture and thinking, qi not only is a significant concept and practice in martial arts but also has been embodied in the daily language and Taiwanese culture in which I was born and raised. Qi is an internalized experience in my body, which influences my disposition—the ways I think, behave, move, and improvise. My improvised movement becomes prone to emerge from the inner awareness, such as a sensitive physical impulse in my body, and an implicit sense that is unknown and deep inside, fostered by training in qi.

After a long-term learning and exploring qi in meditative qigong as well as improvisation, I feel qi more as a particular sense of being than as a physical energy, just as Ted J. Kaptchuk (2000) addresses qi in his study of Chinese medicine. Qi is a sense 'somewhere in between, a kind of matter on the verge of becoming energy, or energy at the point of materializing' (43). Since qi has metaphorical and cultural meanings beyond energy in Chinese thought and is deeply embodied in life (Kaptchuk 2000: 43), it represents a Chinese perspective of being in the moment of the in-between in terms of energy, which shapes a specific awareness, consciousness, and understanding of the world. Qi as a sense of being is thereby a way of seeing and a way of coexisting with every thing and being in the cosmos.

Whilst regarding qi as a prevailing life philosophy in Chinese culture, one should not ignore that everyone has different sensations, feelings, and reactions with qi, depending on individual constitutions and dispositions. A sense of being 'somewhere in between' could vary from person to person. The subtleties could occur even at different stages, every day and every second in one's life. In other words, the 'state' of the self or being is never fixed but ceaselessly changing. For qi, 'state' is not still but dynamic, in a sense of being as becoming. Overall, qi is both an experiential and a philosophical, personal, and cultural phenomenon.

The in-between character of qi can be associated with the concept of *wu* in Daoism. Beyond its literal meaning of 'emptiness', *wu* is not the equivalent of absolute nothingness but something as nothing or nothing as something. In other words, *wu* is a state in which everything unidentified is still whole, whilst it might be felt or experienced as a 'gap' of empty or tranquil consciousness. Such a state is much more relaxed, heightened, and concentrated on a sense of being, as if in meditations, than is the release state in an improvisation based on somatics, so that it allows qi to emerge and circulate. This gap is indicative of a calm and meditative space containing infinite possibilities. Nothing (emptiness) means something (fullness).

Occurring in a state before or beyond things are identified or interpreted, an emergence of qi can be unexpected in an intuitive and spontaneous mode that we might call 'improvisational'. Distinct from a compositional mode of improvisation based on American and European dance contexts, Daoist spontaneity and intuition comes from a heightened, meditative consciousness of calmness or emptiness, that is, *wu*. Bringing a Daoist mode of heightened consciousness into action of improvisation, I realized that the contemplative state is the source of instantaneous inspiration, spontaneous emergence, and being present, allowing something unexpected to happen, which is just what improvisation in practice as well as performance requires. From this specific cultural and philosophical as well as experiential view of qi, the concept of improvisation needs to be rethought based on the Daoist notion of *wu*.

CONSIDERING IMPROVISATION WITHIN PARTICULAR CULTURAL CONTEXTS

The verb *ji-xing* (即興) means 'to improvise' in Chinese. Its literal meaning, *ji*, translates as 'instantly', whilst *xing* means to 'emerge' or 'arise', which occurs with the emergence of qi.[3] Daoist interpretation tends to conserve *xing*'s ritual character, based on its initial meaning in primitive times, instead of from Chinese poetry, developed afterwards. Originally, *xing* referred to a group of people's sounds arising when they collectively lift an object in a specific religious rite, implying an atmosphere of singing, dancing, and having a sense of being together in a sacred moment (Xiao 2012: 96; Chai 2012: 122). Thus, *xing* is related to praising the heavens, Earth, and the spell of Nature's power (Xiao 2012: 97–98). Thus, *xing* is a divine mode of emergence, a transcendental experience of being.

Since there is a particular meaning of improvisation inherent in the tradition of my culture, I have carried out research on the concept of improvisation from my own cultural context. Improvisation based on contemporary dance has been introduced to Taiwan through Japanese and Chinese artists and educators who followed the legacy of Japanese modern dance adapted from German expressionist modern dance and Dalcroze Eurhythmics since the 1930s and particularly in dance education during the 1950s–1980s (Chao 2008: 39, 44, 55; Lu 1995: 8; Wu 2006: 45). Owing to the fact that Taiwan has developed close political and strategic ties with America since Japan ended its control over Taiwan after World War II, American concepts of improvisation have made a more direct impact on Taiwanese artists' practices, especially improvisation in performance after the 1970s (Li and Yu 2005: 644; Wu 2006: 21).[4]

Given this intercultural history of adaptation and influence, I ask: Are there other ways of understanding improvisation, beyond applying or adapting American and European improvisation approaches or somehow fusing them with Chinese philosophy, even if the two diverse thinking systems have somewhat merged into the concept of improvisation?

Improvisation and its concepts have been related to somatic practices predicated on bodymind integration, within American and European dance contexts, in order to challenge Cartesian body/mind dualism (International Association for Dance Medicine and Science 2009: 1). Since the late 1950s and early 1960s, movement-based practitioners, influenced by Asian, African, Latin American, and American Indian cultures, have had a tendency to pay attention to sensation, spontaneous action, and inner awareness in their work (Foster 2002: 31, 34). This trend emerged from praxis of Grand Union , an improvisational performance group in the 1970s that is regarded as a reunion of the Judson Dance Theatre members all of whom were avant-garde artists in the 1960s (Steinman 1995: 78–80). Particularly inspired by African American jazz, experimental theatre, and contemporary dance, both Judson and Grand Union's practice was compositional and related to structure and instant decision-making as tools for improvising in a performance (Foster 2002: 27, 31; Hayes 2003: 106). Whilst the above examples show that improvisation can involve performance, the same cultural roots of improvisation also illustrate that improvisation may have nothing to do with performance, englobing rather spontaneous dance influenced by somatic experience, with little to no choreographic intention (De Spain 1997: 5; Foster 2002: 31).

Since the 1970s, many improvisation practitioners have drawn on ideas of somatics that could be beneficial to enhance reception and response and escape from habitual movements during improvisation (see International Association for Dance Medicine and Science 2009). In addition, some practitioners of improvisation have found that Asian meditative practices, such as martial arts, yoga, and qigong, also help to enhance perceptual experience and bodily awareness, just as has happened in the field of somatic practice. For example, Steve Paxton—one of the pioneers of contact improvisation—borrowed ideas of aikido in the development of his improvisation approach (Nugent 1998: 20). Moreover, Eva Karczag's improvisation method, informed by her experiences of somatic methods such as the Alexander Technique, ideokinesis, and Authentic Movement, was also inspired by qigong, t'ai chi ch'uan, and yoga (see Crow and Sager 2006). An even greater impact made by qigong and aikido can be found in Kirstie Simson's improvisation practice, which often stresses qi-like energy (see *Force of Nature* 2011). Owing to the influence of Asian meditative practices, the three practitioners all adopt a *wu-wei*-like or 'nonassertive action' attitude (Hall and Ames 1998: 52)[5] in order to allow a movement or phenomenon to emerge as needed, rather than creating it or making it occur with intention.

Compared with somatics, established in America and Europe, qi is a different bodymind experience: a mode of heightened consciousness and awareness that does not focus on the sensory system but on a more generalized sense of being, even if it still has a certain influence on proprioception. Qigong can be thought of as a somatic practice handed down or developed from Chinese tradition that works in a mode of energy and consciousness.

In Taiwan's dance field, artists such as Lin Hwai-min (林懷民), Liou Shaw-lu (劉紹爐), Lin Hsiu-Wei (林秀偉), Tao Fu-lann (陶馥蘭), and Lin Lee-chen (林麗珍) have borrowed traditional Asian philosophies and practices that have views or energy similar to those of qi—such as Daoism, Buddhism, Zen, Hinduism, T'ai Chi, or T'ai Chi Dao Yin, as well as other Chinese qigong methods—in order to explore the somatic aspect of dance by means of improvisation. This trend occurred in the 1970s, when Taiwan became mired in a severe political situation, withdrawing from the United Nations and breaking off diplomatic relations with the United States, which stirred and inspired Taiwanese choreographers to look back at their own roots in terms of cultural identification (Mo 2014: 52). They attempted during the 1980s and 1990s to innovate dance forms which represented the 'Eastern body' by combining the American concepts of improvisation, Chinese martial arts, Asian meditative practices, and local Taiwanese cultures (Wang 1994, my translation). This phenomenon prevailed not only in dance but in Taiwanese *little theatre* (a form of avant-garde theatre in Taiwan) as well, so the two fields were interpenetrated in terms of a common view and goal of an integrated bodymind state.

This tendency drew Taiwanese artists' attention to a united state of the body and mind in Chinese traditional thought, which somewhat resonates with the impact of somatic practices on improvisation practitioners in American and European dance contexts; yet the causes arising in the two diverse backgrounds are different. In the Taiwanese contexts, whilst bodymind integration was for returning to or getting back a cultural tradition (a holistic body), it was also a means for rebelling against a tradition (dualism) imported from the American and European contexts. Since the knowledge and practices of somatics did not prevail in the dance field until 2000 in Taiwan (via the Somatic Education Society of Taiwan [n.d.]), those artists' works which draw on Asian meditative thoughts and practices unfold a holistic bodymind state and quality distinct from those which carry out the view of American and European somatics based on a perceptual experience.

Take the director and choreographer of the Legend Lin Dance Theatre, Lin Lee-chen, as an example. For Lin, improvisation is a way to enhance bodymind awareness and explore concepts and approaches to draw forth a specific body quality or energy state from the inner self—a kind of 'internal tension'—instead of a physical skill (Mo 2014: 125–127, 236, my translation). Her practice of bodymind awareness focuses on deep breath into *dan tian* (the lower abdomen, where qi can be stored) to bring forth qi-energy along the spine to spiral through the body (118). Thus, most of the time dancers are asked during rehearsals to improvise and search for all possibilities of the body based on this concept, rather than practising set movement sequences (124).

Although Lin did not learn dance abroad, the trend of the Grotowski technique in Taiwan's little theatres had a great impact on her practice. Lin's concept and practice guides dancers to reach a Daoist state of *wu* via the pathway of Polish director Jerzy Grotowski's practice. Differing from the calmness required in Daoism, the Grotowski technique challenges the body in an unsecured situation to awaken a primal state of the self and make energy flow. Both approaches focus on a transforming process of detachment, a return, or an awakening for realization of the primal, inner self or life experience, which is Dao in Daoism, or Art as Vehicle in Grotowski's practice (Mo 2014: 116–121). All of her works explore Taiwanese rituals and identity, as other little theatres' works have done, with their tendency of 'digging the personal inner world or returning to one's own culture', influenced by Grotowski's practice (56, my translation). Combining the ideas and methods of the two systems, the dancers move in a calm, meditative state as well as in a sacred state of trance. In such a state, a particular aesthetic of slow walk is featured in her works (see Mo 2014).

There have been more improvisational performances in Taiwan since martial law was lifted at the end of the 1980s. Choreographer and improvisation practitioner Ku Ming-shen, a student of Lin Lee-Chen, was the influential artist who introduced contact improvisation to Taiwan and has promoted dance improvisation in performance since the 1990s. She followed Paxton in America and then established the Ku & Dancers, the first performing group featuring dance improvisation in Taiwan. (The company also produces performances without improvisation.) Unlike Lin, Ku does not aim to create an 'Eastern' form, drawing on material or ideas from local cultures or Asian meditative practices. Instead, her practice was inherited from the American and European tradition of dance improvisation.

Even so, Lin's practice has still had great impact on Ku's body when she is dancing. Taught by Lin in her childhood, before Lin developed her previously mentioned body-awareness practice, Ku began her experience of improvisation with great passion, valuing inner concentration and energy rather than physical skills in performance, as Lin's later dance practice emphasized (Mo 2014: 189). Through Lin's training, Ku's body grew to be relaxed, soft, and stable, particularly in the hips, with 'sustained and free and indirect' energy (190, my translation). Her movement thus has a flexible quality and relies on sensitive awareness.

Ku's improvisation practice basically looks at sensitive awareness which can focus inwards and expand outwards, with a sense of being based in the anatomical paradigm. She regards improvisation as a means of generating creative actions to explore the unknown (Ku 2013: 84–85). In performance, improvisation is an instant choreography, focusing on 'temporal and spatial decision-making at the instant a thought or an intention arises, in assistance with a phenomenon appearing from expression of movement qualities when movement is being executed' (8, my translation).

For Ku, as an improviser as well as a choreographer, improvisation and choreography are regarded as one, rather than opposites, in the aspect of improvisation in performance (Ku 2013: 7). Therefore, she thinks it is important to have a clear intention of movement so as to communicate with the audience in a certain expressive way, no matter whether the meaning is known or unknown. Moreover, in order to make an improvisation feel like a performance piece, a structure or score is a significant element of her approach, following in the American tradition of structured improvisation in performance, as in the Judson Dance Theater of the 1960s.

Even though not explicitly adapting Asian meditative methods or concepts in her approach, Ku still links her improvisation practice with her own cultural conceptual framework in a rather implicit way. She interprets the state of 'listening' that empties the subjective self for receiving and responding to stimuli from partners in contact improvisation with the Daoist notion of *wu*. She thinks a state of *wu* implies an intimate, very 'personal sense of being' rather than just nothing (Chen 1997: 52; Wu 2006: 16, my translation).

Moreover, Ku particularly emphasizes the idea of changing, considering it to be central to improvisation performance and associating some notions of improvisation with Daoist thoughts in her dance practice of contact improvisation and improvisational performance. For example, in her work *Decode 2010*, she relates the philosophical concept of changing in the Chinese classic the *I Ching* and in Daoist sage Lao-Tsu's *Daodejing* with the format of an open improvisation performance without a score (Ku 2013: 183–185).

Through examining diverse adaptions of Daoist notion of *wu* in improvisational training, practices, and performances in the Taiwanese, American, and European dance contexts, I ponder what improvisation means based on qi. What is the meaning of 'emergence' and its connection with 'improvisation' in Chinese from a Daoist perspective of qi? What if an improvisation is simply allowed to emerge in a state of *wu* that is beyond the compositional, scored, or structured intention that is characteristic in Western performance?

THE MEANING OF IMPROVISATION
IN TERMS OF DAOIST QI

Looking back on the meaning of improvisation (*ji-xing*) in Chinese ancient thought based on Daoism, *xing* signifies a divine mode of emergence (as discussed previously). Expanding from this original meaning, *xing* has been understood as 'inspiration'—a method of working during a creative process in the arts (Xiao 2012: 100, my translation). This Daoist thought stresses a particular mode of inspiration that may happen with a sudden awareness or understanding of Dao when the self and heaven are united as one (Xiao 2012: 103), which is just like the previously mentioned emergence of qi. This infers that *xing* is related to qi; both are spontaneous phenomena in connection with the self.

Parallel to the phenomenon of qi, *xing* is an implicit emergence from the self beyond thought or before recognition, by coincidence or synchronization, instead of in a cause-and-effect relationship (Xiao 2012: 92; Chai 2012: 125). For Daoism, this kind of preconscious experience is regarded as intuitive. The preconscious reaction emerges from a gap in consciousness as if caused by 'nothing', which connects with the notion of *wu-wei* (Wu 2014: 72). The Chinese concept and practice of improvising derived from a Daoist view thereby has characteristics of a distinctive ambience, a sense of togetherness, subtlety, implicitness, oneness, and preconscious intuition, which feature *xing* as well as qi. I suggest that the divinity, subtlety, and ingenuity of *xing* (Xiao 2012: 104) or inspiration emerging from qi imply Daoist creativity coming from the calmness of the *wu*-state.

On the grounds of the Chinese notion of *xing* relating to qi, the moment of emergence from qi can be thought of as the beginning of an improvised movement and even an improvisation. In other words, improvisation can be regarded as an extended phenomenon of the circulation of qi, expanding from the very point of the qi-mode emergence based on Daoism. The qi-mode of emergence can heighten a mover's state of consciousness and accelerate her intuitive reaction in the moment and so open her to all improvisational possibilities, such as imagery, kinaesthetic sensation, decision-making, structure, and score. Following qi, the occurrences of these possibilities spontaneously become an emergent mode instead of an imposed intention.

Therefore, improvisation based on the spontaneous emergence of qi is not imposed, like the compositional mode of improvisation rising in the American and European post–modern dance period. Following this heritage, dance scholar Michelle Heffner Hayes (2003) suggests that improvisation often concerns a reference to 'a "map" of possible choices determined by the structure of the form' as a means of instant composition for the mover to make a quick decision (106). An example of this is the improvisation work of both the Judson Dance Theater and of Ku. Hayes argues that improvisation is 'neither truly spontaneous nor fully choreographed' at the moment when the mover has to make a quick decision as a means of instant composition (2003: 106). This infers an in-between character of improvisation and somewhat corresponds with qi-mode emergence. As a feature of qi, emergence is an in-between experience beyond kinaesthesia, so the mode is not exactly like responding to sensation or stimuli of the inside and the outside in contact improvisation.

Susan Sgorbati also employs the term 'emergence' to describe a mode that is not 'externally imposed, composed, or directed' in her Emergent Improvisation practice (Sgorbati and Weber 2006: 5). Improvisation as 'a process of composing in the moment' is 'the spontaneous creation of integrated sound and movement by performers who are adapting to internal and external stimuli, impulses and interactions' in her approach (Emergent Improvisation [n.d.]; Sgorbati 2005). A piece of improvisation as a parallel with a complex system in Nature is shaped by the 'emergent form' that spontaneously comes into being as 'the products of dynamic, self-organizing systems operating in open-ended environments' (Sgorbati and Weber 2006: 5).

The sense of 'emergent form' in Sgorbati's improvisation practice, based on a scientific theory of a complex system, feels somewhat like the mode from which improvised movement arises from qi based on Daoism. The two thinking systems, that is, physics and Daoist philosophy, might be connected somehow concerning this phenomenon. However, the mode of emergence from a philosophical perspective of qi relies less on tangible stimuli in the physical world than does the mode of emergence from a scientific perspective of a complex system. One more difference can be revealed by Zen master and photographer John Daido Loori's description of how an image emerges by itself and flows with/as qi-energy in a creative process: 'as my sense cleared, images began to reveal themselves, gradually at first, the more and more intensely until they were rushing at me. I could not ignore them.... In the creative process, as long as the energy is strong, the process continues. It may take minutes or hours. As long as you feel chi [qi] peaking and flowing, let it run its course. It's important to allow this flow and expression, without attempting to edit what is happening—without trying to name, judge, analyze, or understand it' (2005: 90). Correspondent with the Daoist interpretation of *xing*, such

a mode of emergence as a creative approach is more like a transcendent or divine process of revealing an authentic state of being or self in the moment in terms of energy, and
the improvisational is inherent in being. The approach is as subtle as *wu-wei*, beyond
the intention of 'composing in the moment' and 'spontaneous creation' which Sgorbati's
Emergent Improvisation practice employs.

Even so, spontaneous emergence of qi is not entirely indeterminate. For instance,
when sensing a strong qi-energy in my left leg, I was aware that a thought about whether
responding to the sensation or not flashed through my mind. In a second, a movement
emerged. Suddenly I was conscious that something like a 'decision' to follow the sensation of movement was made quickly in a subtle way, neither merely by the brain nor
merely by the body. It may be more suitable to call the implicit and transcendent mode
of 'decision-making' a sort of sudden understanding of an inner disposition or awareness of a state of being or in terms of qi; that is, Daoist intuition, as previously defined.

The instant that something emerges via an articulation between qi and the self signifies the awakening of a certain awareness or rising qi-energy. During an improvisation,
my movements, images, texts, and sounds arise as my energy flows to the place where
these emergences can take place. All spontaneous emergences can be thought of as directed by a sense of qi, even though the sense of guidance from qi may be very subtle or
even beyond a perceivable experience at times.

Led by qi, an improvisation can also allow something like 'structure' to come into
being gradually by itself, through emergence, with a *wu-wei* attitude . Since Daoist intuition works beyond interpretation, I am aware that something is about to be known, yet
it just shifts to other states of the unknown before a meaning or tangible image is fully
recognized; however, these unknown states could somehow connect with one another
as an ethereal sense of 'story', 'structure', or 'composition' of poetic images. This experience might be associated with the phenomenon of 'self-organising' that can be observed
in Sgorbati's improvisation practice, based on a complex system, as well as in the work
of qi for Chinese traditional advanced qigong. If we were to term this as a Daoist intuitive mode of instant 'choreography', it is highly implicit and only amorphously present
during improvisations emerging from qi.

In Between Practice and Performance

Improvisation emerging from qi has an in-between character—being an authentic self
and a Daoist intuitive mode of instant 'choreography', as both were discussed in the
previous section. The two aspects unfold at the same time, or rather, are authentic at
the instant of Daoist intuitive 'choreography'. This is because Daoism suggests that the
'heart' (*xin*), which is prone to a state of consciousness rather than sentimentality, de-
cides how a person sees, thinks, or feels. The heart is the one that merges all 'activities
we would classify as thinking, judgment, and feeling' of the self before they are separately identified or named. Organization by the heart is necessary for the self, which is

an indivisible whole in traditional Chinese thinking (Hall and Ames 1998: 29). In a state of *wu* or during the circulation of qi, when the heart moves, the body moves, no earlier or later (Wilhelm and Jung 1929: 56). This signifies that a performer in an improvisation performance based on Daoism must be honest to his state of being or true to the depth of the self in the moment.

Since the heart is the most significant source, a learner can carry on the somatic process in the heart beyond physical sessions. In this case, a somatic practice would have no time and space limits. All times are for practising as a lifelong process. Consequently, a somatic practice does not mean just a learning process; instead it is an embodied experience that sustains or is inherent in the self. From a Daoist perspective, when a person pays attention to improvising, no matter how the movements function in the moment, in private or in public, in practice or in performance, he has commenced an individual session of practising and discovering the self.

Philosophical scholar Chang Chung-yuan's (2011) book *Creativity and Taoism: A Study of Chinese Philosophy, Art and Poetry* echoes the same feature of in-between practice and work in Chinese ancient painting and poetry, from a Daoist perspective of aesthetics. Chang says: 'Chinese painting is not merely a product of technical skill but it is basically an achievement of a high level of self-cultivation, without which creative intuition cannot emerge' (2011: 258, my translation). He points out that in Chinese thought the 'real meaning of art' is 'to reveal the artist's inner state of being', namely, the transformation of the self (267, my translation).

However, differing from traditional Chinese painting and poetry as productions reserved as visual, an improvisational performance is live and temporal. A traditional Chinese painting or poem reveals the artists' achievement of a heightened state of the self or qi, since its creative process is personal. In an improvisation performance, the practising process of the inner self and a moment of performing and improvising proceed simultaneously.

An improvisation performance offers a situation that propels me to be more involved in *wu*-state, for creativity, than does the situation of practising improvisation alone. The moment of being watched needs more concentration on a *wu*-state in order to keep calm and make higher energy spread up. Other people's being also allows a sense of sharing or togetherness to happen, as a characteristic of *xing*. Thus, for me each improvisation performance is an advanced practice of authentically being myself. I just throw myself into the moment of *wu*, allowing all phenomena to arise, and creativity and sincerity to emerge. In a *wu*-state, qi will flow.

In considering working with qi and the heart as essential practice for Daoism, it becomes clear that improvisation is about an attitude towards the bodymind or a bodymind state of being rather than an approach to movement. That is to say, an attitude or a state is the most important, rather than forms of movement in improvisation. Appearance, style, and creativity as expression will emerge by themselves, namely as qi flows or in a state of *wu*, from the inside out.

Under this conception, as improvisation becomes a performance, an issue arises: how can an introspective or contemplative improvisation beyond movement forms be performative? What is 'performative' in a Daoist aspect? Echoing Ku's considerations for improvisational performance, how to communicate with spectators has to be further considered.

To discuss this question, I would borrow English director Peter Brook's argument about 'the present moment' as 'the essence of theatre' (2013: 81). The reasons for searching for support from Brook's theory is that he has researched and often commented on Grotowski's works of Poor Theatre and that the Grotowski technique has had a great impact on Taiwan's little theatres. In addition, there are certain similarities between Daoism and Grotowski's practice, as my discussion of Lin's case highlighted. Brook emphasizes the recognition of the unknown of emptiness in the moment during performance, in order to 'allow the imagination to fill the gaps' (27). This sounds somewhat like my previous arguments that a state of *wu*, like a gap of the in-between or unknown, allows more possibilities to emerge. Brook asserts that presence in the moment is most significant for theatre and that 'each moment is the whole of all possible moments, and what we call time will have disappeared' (83). It is a contemplative state during a performance. In terms of Daoism, the 'moment' is timeless and holistic; in other words, it is an experience in a state of *wu*.

Furthermore, Brook (2013) suggests that performers have a responsibility to 'interest' the audience every moment. (Ku also has a similar idea.) For Brook, what 'interesting' means is making 'the first words, sounds or actions of the performance release deep within each spectator a murmur related to the hidden themes that gradually appear' (2013: 84). That is, the method of drawing the viewer's attention is to connect the themes with their inner depth. A big-scaled movement is not always necessary, nor is an apparently dramatic action. The present moment of every emergence, the sense of emptiness and its energy, can break the division between seeing and being seen and articulate the two sides as one (6). This openness and transformation of the performer-and-viewer relationship make the experience of theatre unanticipated, which is a requirement of theatre in Brook's opinion (95).

Brook's view on the essence of theatre can also apply to improvisation performance based on Daoism. As Brook recognizes, the moment of being in a state of *wu* is performative through the sharing of its energy. However, the energy qualities in Daoism and in Brook's theatre theory are different. The heightened concentration of Daoist qi is in a relaxed and calm mode; the theatrical energy of emptiness which Brook highlights is more intensive and immersed (2013: 10). Concentration on being the self along with other selves, that is, spectators, in the moment is a way to invite spectators to have a somatic experience together. An energy in the moment of being thus flows to and fro between the improviser and spectators, building a subtle connection, a sharing relationship, and an atmosphere of togetherness.

The difference between Brook's approach and mine is that improvisation is a mode of performance for my study. With the characteristic of *wu*, the 'performative' aspect of improvisation performance comes from the emergence from nothing to something; something in-between gradually growing from the unknown or nothing in a relationship beyond cause and effect.

I suggest that searching for the unknown could be felt as another invitation to do something implicitly together. It can raise spectators' curiosity, drawing them into the improviser's performing moment and subtly articulating that all people in the here and now are as one. . The curiosity of the unknown can interest spectators and make them follow an improvisational work according to the concept of *wu* in Daoism.

A poetic sense of gaps, that is, the unknown of the in-between, created by a meditative state thus features in my improvisational performances based on Daoism, since a state of *wu*, a Daoist contemplative state or a heightened, introspective concentration, is my key to allowing all possibilities to emerge by themselves during improvisation. Through practising *wu* during improvisation performances, I embody Dao, as Dao is change itself, a way to understand *wu* that cannot be named, shaped, and timed but is fluid beyond any form of restriction (Lai 2008: 14). Everything can grow in its own way.

Notes

1. Even if some of them are also influenced by Asian thoughts, many American and European practitioners' practices are based on the body's anatomical and physiological structure, that are different from Asian practices which consider a vital energy such as qi to be the most basic constituent of the body prior to tangible or perceivable sources of material organs. For instance, improvisation practitioner Steve Paxton (2008) explores movement via sensation of the spine in his practice of Material for the Spine; Eva Karczag researches on 'weight' of deepening sensation in her improvisation practice (Crow and Sager 2006: 9–10). The orientation towards physical matter in their approaches may make the body and movement look more 'grounded' than those based on qi, while the momentum is soft and flowing, like qi-energy. More elaborations follow in the next section.
2. Meditative qigong (Jing Gong) focuses on 'developing a clear, tranquil state of mind, alongside a deeper self-awareness and harmony with nature', based on Daoist and Buddhist concepts (Cohen 1997: 5). This differs from 'martial qigong' (Wu Gong), which works with fixed movement patterns realized externally in the space, although both forms of qigong practices elicit an embodied experience of being (6).
3. I made this connection thanks to my sister, Wu Yi-Chen, who has drawn on the idea of *xing* as a method of Chinese poetry in her PhD thesis, *Qi-arising Space: The Embodiment of Qi in Taiwanese Hypermedial Theatre* (Wu 2015). Her study theorizes hypermedial theatre from a Taiwanese context, drawing on a Confucian perspective of qi. With a standpoint different from hers, for articulating my embodied experience of qi in improvisation, I keep to a Daoist view to look at *xing*.
4. For a brief history of improvisation in Taiwan's contemporary dance field, see Wu 2006: 43–54.
5. *Wu-wei* is an attitude, as well as a way to move in a state of *wu*. According to Daoist scholar David L. Hall and Roger T. Ames, *wu-wei* is a kind of 'nonassertive action' or 'deferential response' that is not affected by learned or habitual knowledge but is instead 'unmediated, unstructured, unprincipled, and spontaneous' (1998: 52). I will give more examples of *wu-wei* throughout this essay.

References

Brook, P. (2013) *There Are No Secrets: Thoughts on Acting and Theatre*. London: Bloomsbury Methuen Drama.

Chai, Y. [蔡瑜]. (2012) Elaborating a Question of Interpreting Li Po's Poems in Terms of 'Emerging from Poetry' [從「興於詩」論李白詩詮釋的一個問題]. In Young, R.-B. (ed.), *Hermeneutic Tradition of Chinese Classics (3): The Volume of Literature and Daoism Classics* [中國經典詮釋傳統（三）：文學與道家經典篇]. Taipei: National Taiwan University, 109–139.

Chang, C.-Y. (2011) *Creativity and Taoism: A Study of Chinese Philosophy, Art and Poetry*. London: Singing Dragon.

Chao, C.-F. [趙綺芳]. (2008) Global Modernity, Nationalism and 'New Dance': An Analysis of Development of Modern Dance in Pre-1945 Japan [全球現代性、國家主義與「新舞踊」:以 1945 年以前日本現代舞發展為例之分析]. *Arts Review* [藝術評論] 18: 27–55.

Chen, Y.-P. [陳雅萍]. (1997) Find a 'Way Out' Together? Interviewing Ku Ming-shen [共謀「出路」？訪古名伸]. *Performing Arts Review* [表演藝術] 52: 51–53.

Cohen, K. S. (1997) *The Way of Qigong: The Art and Science of Chinese Energy Healing*. New York: Ballantine Books.

Crow, A., and Sager, P. (2006) These Dances Rise Up: An Interview with Eva Karczag. *A Moving Journal* (Summer): 7–12.

De Spain, K. S. (1997) Solo Movement Improvisation: Constructing Understanding through Lived Somatic Experience. PhD. Temple University.

Emergent Improvisation (n.d.) Practice and Performance. http://emergentimprovisation.org/home.html. Accessed 24 January 2007.

Force of Nature: A Performance Documentary with Kirstie Simson. (2011) Directed by Katrina MacPherson. Nairnshire, Scotland: Goat Media. (DVD)

Foster, S. L. (2002) *Dances That Describe Themselves: The Improvised Choreography of Richard Bull*. Middletown, CT: Wesleyan University Press.

Hall, D. L., and Ames, R. T. (1998) *Thinking from the Han: Self, Truth, and Transcendence in Chinese and Western Culture*. Albany: State University of New York Press.

Hayes, M. H. (2003) The Writing on the Wall: Reading Improvisation in Flamenco and Postmodern Dance. In Albright, Ann Cooper, and Gere, D. (eds.), *Taken by Surprise: A Dance Improvisation Reader*. Middletown, CT: Wesleyan University Press, 105–116.

International Association for Dance Medicine and Science. (2009) Somatic Studies and Dance. https://cdn.ymaws.com/www.iadms.org/resource/resmgr/imported/info/somatic_studies.pdf. Accessed 14 April 2012.

Kaptchuk, T. J. (2000) *Chinese Medicine: The Web That Has No Weaver*. London: Rider.

Ku, M.-S. [古名伸]. (2013) *Between Planning and Changing: Ming-shen Ku's Creative Collection Report* [在規劃與變化之間—古名伸創作報告集]. Taipei: Taipei National University of the Arts.

Lai, X.-S. [賴錫三]. (2008) *Contemporary Interpretation of Spiritual Glow in Zhuang-zi* [莊子靈光的當代詮釋]. Xinzhu, Taiwan: National Tsing Hua University.

Li, T.-M. [李天民], and Yu, G.-F. [余國芳]. (2005) *Dance History in Taiwan* [台灣舞蹈史（上）]. Vol. 1. Taipei: Da Juan Wen Hua.

Loori, J. D. (2005) *The Zen of Creativity: Cultivating Your Artistic Life*. New York: Ballantine Books.

Lu, J.-Y. [盧健英]. (1995) Dancing over a Half Century, Allowing the Body to Tell the History: Reviewing the Fifty Years of Taiwan's Dance [舞過半世紀，讓身體述說歷史－回顧台灣舞蹈五十年]. *Performing Arts Review* [表演藝術] 33: 7–21.

Mo, L.-L. (2014) *Interpreting the Aesthetics of Legend Lin Dance Theatre: Metempsychosical Phantasma in Theatre Performance of Two Works: Mirror of Life; and Anthem to the Fading Flowers* [解讀無垢式美學—《醮》與《花神祭》轉生心像之劇場演現]. Taipei: Hopscotch Movement Body Theater.

Nugent, A. (1998) Surfing with Steve Paxton (25 Years of Contact Improvisation Discussed via the E-mail). *Dance Theatre Journal* 14(1): 20–23.

Paxton, S. (2008) *Material for the Spine: A Movement Study*. Brussels: Contredanse. (DVD)

Sgorbati, S. (2005) Emergent Improvisation: Essay by Susan Sgorbati. http://emergentimprovisation.org/Essay-on-Emergent-Improvisation.html. Accessed 6 September 2014.

Sgorbati, S., and Weber, B. (2006) How Deep and Broad Are the Laws of Emergence? Presentation at International Conference on Complex Systems, Boston, 25–30 June. http://necsi.org/events/iccs6/viewpaper.php?id=46. Accessed 24 January 2007.

Somatic Education Society of Taiwan [台灣身心教育學會]. (n.d.) Introduction to Somatics [身心學介紹]. http://www.somatics.org.tw/chinese/?page_id=11. Accessed 30 January 2015.

Steinman, L. (1995) *The Knowing Body: The Artist as Storyteller in Contemporary Performance*. 2nd ed. Berkeley, CA: North Atlantic Books.

Wang, Y.-L. [王亞玲]. (1994) This Year, Wild Winds Have Blown Over the Dance Field—The Blooming Dance Field Has Two Phenomena: One Is the 'Wind of the Body' and the Other Is the 'Wind of Dance Theatre', Both of Which Are Greatly influencing New Development of Dance in Taiwan [今年，舞蹈界風了－「百花齊放」的舞蹈界今年有兩大現象一個是「身體風」另一個是「舞蹈劇場風」兩個都是深深影響著台灣舞蹈的新發展]. *Chinese Times* [中國時報], 30 December, 33.

Wilhelm, R., and Jung, C. G. (1962 [1929]) *The Secret of the Golden Flower: A Chinese Book of Life*. Trans. C. F. Baynes. New York: Harvest.

Wu, I.-Y. [吳怡瑩]. (2006) *The Development of Contact Improvisation in Taiwan: A Study on Ku & Dancers Company* [探討「接觸即興」在台灣之演變—以《古名伸舞團》為例]. MA. National Taiwan University of Arts.

Wu, I.-Y. (2014) *Being Formless: A Daoist Movement Practice*. PhD. University of Northampton.

Wu, Y. -C. (2015) *Qi-arising Space: The Embodiment of Qi in Taiwanese Hypermedial Theatre*. PhD. University of Exeter.

Xiao, L.-H. [蕭麗華]. (2012) Unity of the Heaven and the Self: Dao in Xing Poetry [天人合一：興詩中的「道」]. In Young, R.-B. (ed.), *Hermeneutic Tradition of Chinese Classics (3): The Volume of Literature and Daoism Classics* [中國經典詮釋傳統（三）：文學與道家經典篇]. Taipei: National Taiwan University, 87–108.

CHAPTER 11

....

EXPLORING UNCERTAINTIES OF LANGUAGE IN DANCE IMPROVISATION

....

LOUISE MCDOWALL

DANCE improvisation is a practice known experientially ('in the doing'); it generates understanding about the phenomena of being through 'presencing' a polyattentive body, conversing with ambiguity, uncertainty, potentiality, and choice. Knowledge of this practice is said predominately to be realized through movement; given this, to what extent can the generation of this experiential knowledge be found through processes of writing, 'languaging', and conceptualizing?

These provocations are what this essay sets out to explore: to reflect on ways language is used, functions, and constructs meaning in the practice(s) of dance improvisation, drawing support from dance writer and educator Candace Feck (2008) to establish a role that language might play. I position dance improvisation in this chapter as an existential practice, offering a discourse that confronts the rich complexity of knowing and its ambiguity, from a bodied perspective. Rather than seeking to dilute the complexity of bodily discourse and improvisation practice, I delve into the richness of discussing a polyattentive body, acknowledging the slipperiness of the bodily lexicons and vocabulary of dance improvisation practices. Doing so ventures towards understandings of the murky 'grey' areas of bodily complexity that hold no absolutes, and it is from there, in this position of teetering uncertainty, that I offer a perspective.

BEING IN THE MOMENT

....

The fear of ineffectually capturing experiences of dance improvisation and homogenizing its content and practice has left the communicating of dance improvisation somewhat bereft of ways to identify the discipline's 'insider' knowledge to those outside its community, with the result that misrepresentations of practice of dance improvisation have emerged. One such misrepresentation occurs through the term 'being in the moment', a complex dance improvisation expression to untangle. First is the issue of 'being' and what it might mean 'to be', whether multiple modes of 'being' exist simultaneously 'in the moment', and if 'being' implies a singular modus operandi. Second is understanding of 'the moment', which similarly contains the potential for several interpretations relating to when this specific moment occurs, and what the potential significance of 'in' may be for the term 'being in the moment'.

Amongst dance practitioners, various accounts exist regarding the experiencing of 'this moment', aided by descriptions such as 'feeling lost', 'disorientated', 'dazed', 'elsewhere', 'transported somewhere', 'a zen or zen-like state', or having a sense of 'presence/present-ness'. Yet due to the inherent subjectivity of experience and the ways this moment is experienced by dance practitioners, discrepancies continue to proliferate among understandings of this expression.

The intention of the word cloud shown in figure 11.1 is to begin to language understanding(s) of the conversations and word choice(s) which surround the particularities in the experiencing and communicating of 'being in the moment'. To look more closely, these experiences are collectively framed through a sense of journeying and transition, a loss of orientation, a loss of a sense of spatiotemporal locality, and a loss of control.

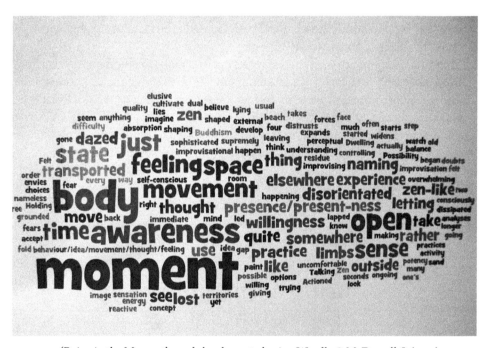

FIG. 11.1 'Being in the Moment' word cloud, created using Wordle © McDowall, L (2015).

This closer look leads to an understanding of 'being in the moment' as clustered around its being understood as a momentary sensate experience beyond the reference point of bodily habit(s), a vantage which points to knowledge as-yet-unknown. I identify the sense of loss that is illustrated through this language as the gradual dissipating of representation (of self, ego, body as fixed boundary), of the reality you have created for yourself within that very moment being given over to a harmonizing with environment, to an experiencing of being part of, rather than epicentre.

To unravel where the confusion in this term may stem from, it is useful to grapple with this idea of time, and 'moment'. Gary Peters (2009: 135) argues that the term's preoccupation with 'the moment' is indicative of a mediation which preferences a coming future over a past predating the future. Peters's point raises the question whether this perspective has arisen through use of the word 'present' by dance improvisers.

The existent perception (outside the dance improvisation community) of time as quantified may harm understandings of this dance improvisation phrase, through an insistence on dividing time into a past, present, and future, as isolated occurrences which are not assumed to inform or influence moments of time. Yet I argue, drawing support from the improvisers Shelley Marshall and Simon Ellis, that there is an implicit understanding within dance improvisation practice of temporality, cultivated through the medium's awareness of the body and its practice as a body-based art form. Whilst these understandings of temporality are not continually raised, or highlighted through the communication of improvisational experiences such as 'being in the moment', they nevertheless underpin its basis. Marshall acknowledges the issue of 'being in the moment' in an online conversation with Ellis and Norbert Pape, where she advises: 'we do not come to dances with only a 'present'. We come to a dance with histories, with bodies created through those histories and movement patterns inscribed by them, this much we can take for granted' (Marshall, Ellis, and Pape 2009a: 2).

Essentially, in this chapter I conceive the bodily archive of experiences, histories, and movement patterns that Marshall describes here as known to the improviser through an understanding of habit. I conceptualize habit as an internalized conversation that is occurring whilst improvising and is revealed through a bodily intensification that the improviser encounters through the conditions of habits becoming, via memory, flesh, perception, and repetition.

I position habit here as an 'act of understanding' (Merleau-Ponty 1945: 165) that unifies experiences through learnt, tacit knowledge, which functions through a progressive learning enabled by perception, proprioception, and memory. I explore habit as a bodily guarantee that offers a referential frame, or point of comparison from which other improvisational experiences/encounters can be understood, due to its facility to develop whilst maintaining a coherence and consistency. In this sense, habit facilitates a bodily preparedness for eventualities by introducing known knowledge into the arena of consciousness for the individual. The materialization of this process is evidence of the dance improviser cultivating a sense of interiority through the utility of habit as a practice of the self (to adopt Foucault's understanding of 'care for self'), as the means through which the self-constituting of the individual as a subject occurs through the emergent practice(s) of knowledge (Foucault 1981–82: 10–11).

Ellis situates the issue of communicating improvisational experience(s) as hinged upon location and space: 'I might pick up on this idea of presence invoking a sense of the spatial. To be present implies (whether we mean it or not) knowing where one is located. But, at the same time, we tend to refer to the temporal—of being in the now for example—as being a critical aspect of presence' (Marshall, Ellis, and Pape 2009a: 8). Ellis describes the unwitting cultivation of presence through its allocation by improvisers to that of locality and space. Recurring examples of a potential separateness of thinkings around space and time are reinforced through Anna Halprin and Deborah Hay's use of 'here' to delineate space and 'now' as signifier of time. In conversation with Janice Ross, Halprin says that her work with the San Francisco Dancers' Workgroup was 'part of the here and now philosophy of being present in the moment' (Ross 2003: 48, citing 1995 interview with Halprin). Deborah Hay (2000) offers an illustration of how the words 'here' and 'now' can be interpreted through the lens of an improviser's spatial and temporal locating of oneself: 'What if my whole body at once has the potential to perceive *Here*, spatially, including everything I see and everything I can't see, *now*, and *now*, and *now*? What if *Now* is my past, present, and future *here, here,* and *here*?' (2000: 104, my emphasis). The introduction of philosophers Gil and Lepecki (2006) and Casey (1996) offers another way to interrogate the spatial and temporal via presence as a bodily integration of space/time and their relatedness, by collapsing the need for articulations emphasizing separateness. Gil and Lepecki (2006: 26) argues that depth enables the discerning of the body from objective space, due to the capacity of depth (or 'spatium' in Deleuzian terms) to locate and tie itself to a place via the body. Casey builds on this understanding through his concept of 'emplacement' (1996: 24)[1] to illustrate an acknowledgement of place as coexisting with embodiment. Casey (37–38) understands space and time as dimensions of place, and it is place which brings together the joining of space and time, experienced as an 'event' that forges a spatiotemporalization of place. Applying these considerations of Casey's as an aid to understanding the depth which Gil discusses, and the presence to which Ellis refers, reveals this depth as a spatialization of knowledge, an emplaced knowledge of the body that is continually presencing itself through the particularity of the spatial relations encountered whilst improvising.

Philosopher Henri Bergson's (1913) theory of pure duration reveals presence as operating through an experience-continuum, as a conscious flow of memory, temporality, and attention. Assimilating Bergson's understanding of duration as a way of informing the conceptualizing of 'being in the moment' shifts an understanding of experience away from a designated moment in time, thought of in isolation as the 'now', and towards the potential elasticity of time.

An exploration of how this elasticity of time and understanding of presence unfolds for the dance improviser can be pursued through utilizing the referential relationship that coexists between habit and possibility, as a potential frame from which to understand 'being in the moment'. As improvisers, we deal with time's intensification rather than quantification. Erin Manning (2007) suggests an understanding of this process through the term 'lingering', which she ties to Gottfried Leibniz's concept of elasticity, describing it as the 'pure experience of experimenting with the almost' (38). She advises that by testing the point of inflection (or elastic point) experienced in 'the moment', the improviser teeters precariously close to an emerging sensed difference introduced by possibility, and the axial pull of the established (the known).

Habit and possibility evidence an example of the elastic exchange Manning refers to above through their affectation of one another spatiotemporally, through the concepts of elasticity, variation, exfoliation, rhythm, and folding. Affectations such as rhythm (activating the rhythming of a becoming-form) or the introduction of touch (folding experiences of possibility into habit) offer points of inflection created by habit and possibility, situating the body in a tangential relationship to itself (Serres 2008: 22), resulting in a process of subjectivation occurring for the improviser.

THE GAP

Nancy Stark Smith's description of 'the Gap' details the creation of an inflection point through which the elastic exchanges of habit and possibility are experienced, resulting in a process of subjectivation occurring for the improviser.

The threshold between the known and unknown knowing is a key area of exploration for improvisers, a space Stark Smith refers to as 'the Gap' (1987: 3). The lineage of this term originates with an editorial comment Stark Smith made in 1987 in *Contact Quarterly*. Stark Smith (3, cited in 2003: 246–247) explains improvisational experience(s) of 'the Gap' with the analogy of quitting smoking, whereby the desire for a cigarette is an action, or movement impulse, which if not granted creates a 'Gap'. The creation of this 'Gap' is understood as a moment which has not been automatically filled through a habitual response of patterned behaviour, thus breaking a 'momentum of being' (247), as it is a space left unfilled.

Stark Smith advises that this space, moment, or 'Gap' is punctuated by drawing 'attention and charge' (2003: 247) to something which would otherwise have passed unacknowledged. Concurrent with this idea of presence is the dual aspect of temporality functioning within the term, demonstrated through a space, 'Gap', or moment which is in transition, identified through the suspension of tacit knowledge, which rather than being carried forth into the next moment is held open.

Parallels can be drawn here with Kirstie Simson's 'suspension of active wanting' (Marshall, Ellis, and Pape 2009a: 5), explored through her 'No' exercise, which enables the improviser to cultivate an agency over desire through an exploration of delay. In doing so, desire becomes a resource at the disposal of the improviser through which listening (in a body-based context) is foregrounded above ego. An interpretation of Simson's exercise can advance when it is understood alongside the assertion of philosopher Alfred North Whitehead that 'all physical experience is accompanied by an appetite for or against its continuance' (1978: 32). Locating his statement through

Simson's 'No' exercise may aid an understanding of improvisational decisions as operating under the conditions of continuance ('yes') and inhibition ('no'). In this given context, 'yes' is utilized as a decision driven by a need for continuance, whilst 'no' is established as a decision which inhibits, disrupting the desire for continuance in offering opposition to this drive. A desire for continuance could take many forms in improvisation, one of which could be to adopt Csikszentmihalyi's (1990) idea of flow. Yet in the suspension of 'active wanting', a perceived rupture is forced into occurrence, disrupting the desired continuance through the improviser's decision to say 'no'. This act of suspension creates a 'Gap', or moment which widens, opening the improviser to the available existence of possibilities and potentialities. Albright's notion of 'dwelling in possibility' (2003: 260) affords an explanation as to how an improviser may inhabit this state of suspension. Albright notes: 'dwelling is a heightened experience of inhabiting—fully and consciously—such that a space becomes more than the sum of its parts, such that the space makes things happen. This conception of space is similar, I believe to what Simone Forti describes as a "dancing state," where sensations juice the body, encouraging imaginative connections that might otherwise be impossible' (260). Albright cites an understanding of 'dwelling' as informed by Martin Heidegger's ecological 'sense of space' as 'sparing and preserving' (Heidegger 1975: 149, cited in Albright, 2003:260–266). 'Dwelling', given this, could be conceived of as the ability to stay with something, be this a feeling or a movement action, to see what provision an integrated space offers for the exploration of possibilities.

   Understanding of 'the Gap' can continue to develop through Erin Manning's depiction of the term 'espacement' as 'mark(ing) the difference between spaces' (2007: 59). The etymology of 'espacement' is drawn from Jacques Derrida and his concept of difference (or *différance*). Derrida discusses 'spacing (espacement)' as 'the production of space' (1967/1978: 299), which functions simultaneously as a means of structuring and a movement, or producing of space, through the act of difference. The notion of space discussed by both Derrida and Manning is of a reflexive space of emergence, of a 'becoming-space' rather than a preexisting understanding of space, which cultivates subjectivity. Manning approaches an understanding of 'espacement' through touch, suggesting that 'touch embodies difference: through touch I ascertain the difference between bodies and surfaces. This espacement that marks the difference between spaces introduces my body to a becoming-space of time and a becoming-time of space. This becoming is the constitution of a subjectivity that is in movement … formed within the tactile hollows of difference' (Manning 2007: 59). To discern this concept, an appreciation of the body as qualifying space through providing not only form but also configurations of depth, spatial relations, infinity, and contemplation must be acknowledged. The body qualifies space by introducing the affectation of feeling into the spatial equation, from which the promise of transformation and potentiality can be harnessed. What possibility introduces into relations with habit is a means of interfacing with the world, an exposure to sensory qualities through an externalized contact (or engagement) that is 'other' to the self. Possibility is understood as the experience which establishes contact with the outside through touch, which it introduces into the body via the skin to inflect impressions of the sensate surroundings and extensive forces to which the improviser has been exposed. These in-flected impressions allow the permeating of feelings to filter from the skin into fleshy de-posits as feelings felt. In other words, flesh[2] 'gives being' to the information presented by the skin[3] of sensorial possibilities and impressions of extensive forces. The skin then rhythms this kinaesthetic information, activating a process of forgetting, resulting in its withdrawal as a 'becoming space of time' (59). The act of withdrawal facilitates the presencing of the flesh, presencing 'being' through a 'becoming time of space' (59).

Perhaps Hardt's position, proposed by the term 'becoming-flesh' (1997: 585) could now be accounted for as cultivating space for the withdrawal of flesh (or the embodied knowledge of improvisational remembering conceived of as habit) to occur. The with-drawal of fleshy knowing presences the sensuous encounter the skin affords for possi-bility, creating the emergence of a 'privileged spatial relation' (Gil 1998: 123) that defines and unifies relations so the relationality of habit and possibility is fostered through their proximity (in time, space, and relation).

Continuing the developing perspective proposed here, the sought relation between flesh (habit) and skin (possibility) is defined and unified through the created depth and sense of perspective that space facilitates. Thought through this perspective, habit be-comes the vantage point for understanding possibility in the establishing of proximity and spatial affinity between the two, for possibility can only develop and transform through connecting with habit. The reason for this is that possibility does not have the self-mechanizing corporeal system, which habit has, and as such lacks the facility to de-velop and mutate beyond itself. It is for this reason that understandings of possibility are approached as relational exchanges, creating ruptures of knowing and form to occur within the body, through the introduction of an as-yet-unharnessed potentiality, or unmovemented possibility.

To evoke a Kantian turn of phrase, this space of 'free play' (Kant 1892) or 'space of errancy' (Peters 2009: 122), created through a 'momentary suspension' or withdrawal, facilitates a 'becoming-space' (or time). This 'becoming-space' contains the potential of unmediated possibility, thought of as the play of the expected with the surprising, play that may be conceived as helping to build a relationship to the unpredictable. Through this hypothesis, play could be expressed through its ability to anticipate unknowns, ex-ploring the space existent between habit and its relation to possibility, the known and unknown knowing, or a feeling becoming felt.

The improviser has the facility to presence embodied memories of the flesh as a 'living remembering' (Marshall, Ellis, and Pape 2009a: 7), a perceptual chain of experiences emplaced through the process of a 'becoming-time of space' (Manning 2007: 59), which are reconciled through their generation as habit(s).

The practice of improvising also enables the improviser to engage with ephem-eral, discontinuous spatiotemporal experiences, positioned as 'momentary percepts' (Warren 1995: 264) revealed through the sensorial possibility of the skin rhythming a becoming-form. The skin is understood as activating a process of forgetting through this rhythming of sensorial experience which introduces the improviser to a 'becoming-space of time' (Manning 2007: 59), a condition cultivating a sense of possibility.

LANGUAGE: A SLIPPERY PROPOSITION

In the opinion of Ann Cooper Albright, writing in 2003, there has been an uneasy relationship between dance improvisation and academic discourse, caused by the elusiveness of improvisation practice. She supports the problematic nature of researching dance improvisation as a 'textual practice', noting her own reluctance to do so and highlighting the difficulty of finding a suitable frame and tone from which to conceptualize improvisation (2003: 260).

Albright identifies her own fears in conceptualizing improvisation, acknowledging 'the omnipresent fear of bruising the form of improvisation, pinning it down to static meanings, dissecting it for the sake of epistemological stability' (2003: 261). These are fears I share with Albright as a fellow 'insider' of this practice, and it has been important to honour the tacit understanding I have cultivated for this medium as a solipsistic practice. Yet the question remains of how to consider a practice that is continually in conceptual and physical flux, producing spaces of curiosity and discovery, without diminishing its complexity and heterogeneity?

To do so through language, I argue, should not seem paradoxical, if language is understood as a contributory feature of dance improvisation practice. The perceived difficulty of articulating embodied knowledge has meant that discourse surrounding the complexity, polyattentiveness, and 'languaging' of dance improvisation is underserved through literature, and quietly absent from discussions. Yet this inability does not detract from the value to be found by exploring ways to negotiate the struggle of expression.

Theatre and dance practitioner Ruth Zaporah describes the struggle to articulate embodied experiences through language, suggesting that 'the words one chooses are never quite right, because words are conceptualisations of a non-conceptual experience' (2002:53). In her attempts to illustrate embodied experiences, Zaporah falls into the all-too-familiar trap of separating by pitting these ways of knowing in opposition to one another, pitting 'the conceptual' (language) as relating to intelligence. Inadvertently, by doing so she situates dance improvisation as a 'nonconceptual' experience, as unintelligent, and the body as medium of this form is therefore relegated to the realm of the unintelligent. Yet the intelligence of dance improvisation is found through a knowing emanating through a conversing body (a fluid tripartite interconnected system of body, brain, and mind) simultaneously grappling physically and conceptually with understandings of habit, desire, spatiotemporalization, possibility, and choice, practicing survival whilst in continual flux.

There seems to be a reluctance to intellectualize dance improvisation, fearing that doing so takes practitioners away from the experience of simply doing. Yet I argue that this perspective is not coherent with the inherent conceptual complexity of improvisation practice, for practitioners to suggest that 'we switch our brains off and stop thinking' when moving. Lisa Nelson supports this perspective, as is demonstrated in her interview with Agnes Benoit where she suggests that 'when I improvise, there is a lot more that I'm deciding not to do, than I am deciding to do in my body' (1997: 67). Nelson highlights the agency of the improviser borne from an implicit bodily knowing; she indicates the emergence of a filtering process of choices occurring whilst improvising, functioning simultaneously through the inhibiting, and revealing, of decisions or desired decision-making.

An acknowledged rift between language and dance improvisation emerges through Zaporah's comments; however, she does identify the need for further exploration of this area, whilst to some extent inadvertently reinforcing a common dualistic habit. The continuation of this thinking is not the sole preserve of practitioners; it is evident scholastically in the ascribing of the body as a site of duality and conflict which is contested using binaries. Feminist Elizabeth Grosz (1994) proposes the existence of a philosophical blind spot when it comes to discourses surrounding the body; she supports the foregoing perspective, arguing that there is an evident dualistic and binary body/mind preference which takes effect.

Nancy Stark Smith suggests that it was the fear of being too prescriptive and policing the practice of dance improvisation (or appearing as the 'contact cops' (2005/2006: 3, para. 1) which led practitioners to move away from definitions of improvisation. Practitioners have sought to deliberately keep the 'languaging' of this practice looser, so as not to impede the content, practice, or future development of this art form. In a *Contact Quarterly* editorial from 1982 (and reproduced in 2003), Stark Smith reveals a conversation she accidentally overheard between students who were questioning the knowing of contact improvisation: 'they know what it is, but they just won't tell. That Steve Paxton has passed on a legacy of ambiguity that keeps everyone from saying what it is, but they know' (2003: 159). This astute comment conveys the problematic nature of a practice whose way of arriving at understanding is inscribed through the experience of doing, as a fleshy knowing that practitioners refuse to presence in conversation.

As a practice and discourse, dance improvisation seems far more comfortable describing itself through what it is not, what defies description (the embodied, the unknown), rather than the 'presencing' of what it is, and the knowledge and understanding we as practitioners have tacitly accumulated as living archives of this form. It is unarguable that traces of improvisational practice will remain embodied, discernible only though the knowing of the body moving in spaces language cannot reach, ascertain, or grapple with. The knowing discussed here is the body's alone; it is prelanguage, in its infancy of becoming-known sensorially to the improviser.

What I am interested in are those meanings which are knowable through language, those felt somatic markers which have stabilized into known, knowable entities for the improviser. It is here, through these anchored somatic demarcations, that language enables a further entry point and route into knowing for the improviser. Language in these instances functions as an enabler, facilitating a further means to sense and meaning-make our way around these experiences, the awareness we feel and sense yet lack the integrity of language to discuss and grow as a community.

It is interesting briefly to trace the emergence of discourse surrounding dance improvisation practice as cultivated through its absence, evidenced in the Dadaist-inspired
statement made by Yvonne Rainer (Judson Church Dance/Theater) in 1965 as she attempted to neutralize dance away from discussions of its representation or subjectivity
through 'an aesthetics of denial' concerning what dance is not (Banes 1987: 43). This attitude is reminiscent of Rainer's emerges in 1986 concerning the initial statements made
about 'New Dance' by Fergus Early (a member of the X6 collective). Similarly, he utilizes
a manifesto premised around what 'New Dance' does not involve, seeking to liberate it
from other dance forms through its attitude (Jordan 1992: 67).

Anna Halprin, in an interview conducted by Yvonne Rainer in 1963 and reproduced
in the 1995 text *Moving Towards Life*, advises that (for her) the intention of improvisation 'was not self-expression' but the attempt to 'eliminate stereotyped ways of reacting'
(1995: 77). Again, it is interesting to note the preference for discussion of improvisation through what it is not (in this case self-expression) and what it eliminates from
movement.

Central to these arguments posed by the practitioners Yvonne Rainer, Fergus Early,
and Anna Halprin concerns the documenting of an art form through what it is not, what
is missing or eliminated, rather than what is present. Yet it seems that this is precisely
how an understanding of improvisation practice unfolds, meaning the absence and
elimination of ideas and movement through its discourse functions to presence what
dance improvisation entails. Steve Paxton offers an example of this in his article *Drafting
Interior Techniques*, where he writes 'I have come to think of Contact Improvisation as a
physical event best described negatively' (Paxton 2003: 175).

It is precisely this position of absence which has spurred me to actively seek ways to
presence the known, and the becoming-known, of a relational practice and to value attempts to describe the supposedly indescribable, the embodied. Whilst improvisational
discussions are kept deliberately vague, sketchy, and absent of the rich complexity of
knowledge-known, and emergent-knowing, of this practice, the implied issue becomes
this: if practitioners are not talking about this practice, then who is, and how?

THE STAND

Steve Paxton in conversation with Peter Hulton articulates the linguistic challenges he
faced when teaching the 'small dance' (Hulton 1975: 9).[4] Figure 11.2 is an image I have
created to portray how Paxton languages his pedagogy: the 'small dance', emphasizing
key words to aid understanding of the language choices he makes when teaching.

Paxton describes the struggle he has with the translation of 'standing still' as a concept through words. He admits for ease, the adoption of a recognizable turn of phrase
as something that everyone could understand: what it is to be still. Yet it seems these
words are offered as a signpost, rather like a directional guide, a jumping-off point as it
were, from which the reality of 'standing still' is departed from and its understanding is

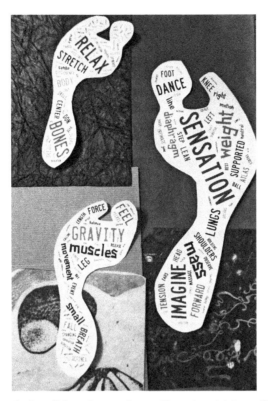

FIG. 11.2 Languaging the 'small dance', created using Tagxedo © McDowall, L (2014/15).

found for oneself. The key reason for this seems to be that linguistically, 'standing still' fails to capture the 'perceptual reality' (1975: 19) of this embodied yet living experience, for 'standing still' is thought to presuppose any movement occurring. Yet whilst linguistically this is fine and presents no problems as an 'objective reality' (19), in practice the 'perceptual reality' (19) of this experience is problematic. Linguistically, 'standing still' seems indicative of a motionless state lacking movement, impossible for the improviser to achieve. In practice, the improviser experiences an awareness of the active potential composing this state, in which the movement of breath and subtle micromanagement of the body shifts the configuring and reconfiguring of spatiotemporal bodily forms presencing this supposed state of stillness. It is interesting to briefly note that in a 1986 article by Paxton, reprinted in 1997, titled *The Small Dance, The Stand* (Paxton 2008), this issue of 'stillness' presented by the term 'standing still' seems to be erased, resolved by a term simply given as 'the stand'.

Paxton (2008a) offers an example of the evolving vocabulary inscribed from improvisation practice and the struggle and search for ways to language tacit understanding. It is interesting, then, given what has just been described, to draw on a 1993 article where he describes how he teaches 'the stand' through images: 'images were used to concentrate the mind and then give the mind foci within the sensations of the body. The words were to be unambiguous, unthreatening, informative, and generally understood' (2003: 183). The element I wish to pick up on from this quotation is Paxton's preference for the *unambiguous* when seeking words for teaching his pedagogy, particularly when he notes this very ambiguity existent within words as he struggles to articulate, when teaching, the image he requires. From my perspective, it raises the question: why attempt to language a heterogeneous practice homogenously? It is interesting to briefly note Paxton's unequivocal need for words to be unambiguous, shown in his 'languaging' of 'the stand', without affording this same ambiguity promoted through movement to be realized through the sense and meaning-making of the words which language this form.

Figure 11.2 depicts a worded image I produced to map the particularity in the language choices Paxton makes when teaching 'the small dance'; recurring words are detailed through size: 'relax', 'sensation', 'gravity', 'mass', 'imagine', 'bones', 'supported', 'muscles', 'feel', 'diaphragm', and 'stretch'. I created this image to signal that these words are open to multiple subjective interpretations, revealing that improvisation practice should language itself through multiplicity and embrace the uncertainty of words, rather than attempting to quell through language that which makes it distinct as a practice. However, in saying this, it is pertinent to establish that practitioners such as Steve Paxton never anticipated or agreed to scribe the legacy of dance improvisation, yet uniquely in terms of dance improvisation this is precisely what has happened, in part due to the lack of discourse surrounding this art form outside its practitioners. An example in point is the journal *Contact Quarterly*, which I would suggest remains the richest resource and topography we have of dance improvisation practice.

CONVERSATIONAL PRACTICE

I argue that it is the fear of being too prescriptive which has become a key gatekeeper preventing the sharing of improvisation practice, thus endangering its continued development. Albright concurs with this perspective, offering the consideration that 'by keeping improvisational work outside of current intellectual discussions we limit its influence' (2003: 261).

Support for challenging this reticence to 'language' within the field of dance improvisation appears to be gaining momentum amongst career-long practitioners, perhaps necessitated by the need to define and identify a practice whose canon continues to expand. This expansion, it could be argued, has been forged through the notable rise in pedagogical resources developed by career-long practitioners of this form, the wealth of improvisational jams and festivals happening globally (predominately with a contact improvisation focus), a proliferation in the teaching of dance improvisation in higher education, and continued expansions into other fields, most notably in the area of somatic practice.

Whilst the positives of this model denote a developing creative form which maintains currency through its continual changes, adaptations, and encompassment of other practices (particularly those within the somatic arena) and their concerns, there is growing concern in the improvisational community about the dilution of dance improvisation practices, as anything resembling the 'look' or technique becomes a substitute for the form itself (Stark Smith 2005/2006). Stark Smith notes 'that it is possible to practice contact improvisation without ever really improvising' (1985, cited in 2003: 165) through a practice more familiar as a 'how to' guide for learning steps and lifts. At the same time, Lisa Nelson, in conversation with Kent De Spain, suggests that 'a lot of what people call improvising, I call 'dancing.' I wouldn't put it in the category of improvising. When I think about improvising, it's already ... another phase of a dancing urge, and it has to do with making something' (De Spain 2014: 39); whilst Deborah Hay, also in conversation with Kent De Spain, states that currently she is *experimenting* and would not call the work she is doing improvising according to how she understands the life of that word (38).

This trend seems to have brought the emergence of high-profile publications detailing improvisational pedagogies by pioneers of the form, such as Steve Paxton's DVD-ROM *Material for the Spine* (2008) and Nancy Stark Smith and David Koteen's text *Caught Falling: The Confluence of Contact Improvisation, Nancy Stark Smith and Other Moving Ideas* (2008), which features 'The Underscore', depicted in print for the first time.

As a practice, dance improvisation holds a position it has never held before; it is no longer the revolutionary marginalized art form skating on the periphery of acceptance by the gatekeepers of dance. It has become accepted, familiar, and popularized not only as a practice in and of itself but also as a choreographic tool. Herein is the reason why there is a responsibility going forward to aid rather than stunt the development and appreciation of this practice, to get better at the way we, the improvisation community, articulate what it is that we do, the knowledge and understanding we have of and for this practice, and in doing so to cultivate the provision of a voice and language which is consistent with it.

One such example of the dissension in understandings of improvisation practice emerges through Anna Halprin, who, according to her understanding of improvisation, suggests the renaming of contact improvisation as 'contact exploration' (1987: 12). She feels that its intention (it is a practice around a specific theme, touch) and its developmental aspects are synonymous with exploration, a facility she does not regard improvisation to have because it is a practice of discontinuity. This begs the question whether contact improvisation, a practice synonymous with dance improvisation practice, is indeed improvisation at all, or whether it is more usefully conceived as a modulated form of improvisation.

Most movement considered to be improvisation derives from exploratory practices that inform the act of improvisation, rather than constituting improvising in and of themselves. It is helpful instead to appreciate these as preparatory practices which facilitate ways of sensitizing the body, acting as primers for the improviser, priming an awareness and responsiveness which is open to 'moments' when improvisation occurs.

My understanding of improvisation is that it is fleeting, it is a momentary experience which is unable to be sustained for a prolonged amount of time, as by its nature it is discontinuous. Therefore, I would counter that an entirely improvised performance is not possible, according to the way I understand this term. From my perspective, the act of improvisation occurs nestled in the betweenness of 'the Gap' identified by Stark Smith (1987: 3) and realized through the process of 'being in the moment'.

CONVERSATIONAL DYNAMIC

In the opinion of Candace Feck, language is 'one of the ways we communicate among each other and with those outside of the dance community' (2008: 42). It is important to appreciate both communication as a central organizing principle of improvisation practice and the role language occupies in the developing vocabulary (or 'insider speech') which surrounds improvisation practices. The vocabulary which dance improvisation employs evolves from its teaching and pedagogies to the sharing of improvisational experiences amongst fellow improvisers, and to the 'languaging' of experience(s) and knowledge to academics and practitioners outside the field.

Yet there is a reluctance on the part of the improvisation community to debate the inconsistencies in our 'languaging' of this art form, to identify and scrutinize the ways in which the complexities of improvisational experiences are being shaped through our uses of language. Therefore, it is important to readdress the significance language provides in the continued development of improvisation practice, and to recognize its contribution as a facet of dance improvisation practice.

In response to the need to reconcile these understandings of the experience of improvisation with its communication, I have cultivated an understanding of improvisation as a conversational practice functioning through an experience-communication continuum. This conception evolved through the search to track the ways in which experiences of habit, possibility, desire, space, and time are produced, and their potential to be reexperienced through the ways in which they are communicated.

'Conversational dynamic' (Belgrad 1998: 5) is explored as a developing methodology for embodied practices, as an offered mode of 'entering into improvisational dialogue with one's materials' (10), whilst also locating the researcher/practitioner as embroiled in a similarly emergent dialogical process with her own research/practice (Dils and Crosby 2001: 68). Exploring improvisation as a 'conversational dynamic' (Belgrad 1998: 5) exposes the inherent intersubjectivity of its practice and communication. My interest in this term concerns the implications it has for solipsistic forms of improvisation practice(s), as a potential model of subjectivation that enables a reengagement with one's practice to occur. The reflexivity this method offers provides a platform for the complexity of experiences improvisers interface with, and the facility to position these within a nexus of communication—a nexus that circulates exchanges between, and about, an embodied perceptual landscape, and an yet-to-be-known sensate territory, enabling the improviser to look at the existence of relationships experienced whilst improvising alongside the reciprocal exchanges of language as fundamental to the on-going communication of improvisation practice.

The use of 'conversational dynamic' serves not to extend a quality upon conversation as 'being dynamic' but to pinpoint conversation as having a dynamic of its own creation, manifest in conversations coming to be and dissolution of form. With this said, an understanding of conversation is involved in a process of becoming, of form taking, occurring between at least two perspectives or 'knowledges' evidencing a distinct coherence of thought, action, or concept. The adopted perspective utilizes 'conversation' rather than 'dialogue' because of the perceived elastic potential conversation holds which is unfounded in dialogue. *Dialogue* is considered as relating to a conversation of the particular, whereas *conversation* enables a more nuanced and complex lens to be utilized through a polyattentive approach that veers away from singularity and towards the simultaneous dialogues occurring in and around particularities.

'Conversational dynamic' (Belgrad 1998: 5) seeks to rhythm the emergent becoming-form of knowledge forms by engendering an understanding of 'other' through a process of 'territorialisation' (Deleuze and Guattari 1988: 11), enabling the cultivation of subjectivity as a reflexive tool. Developing upon this principle of reflexivity as a tool situates the 'territorialisation' (11) of improvisation practice as an establishing becoming-knowledge (possibility), 'deterritorialising' (11) an established cohesive knowledge (habit), to 'reterritorialise' (11) an established knowledge with the information presented by possibility. This process results in the forming of an emergent knowing borne of a conversational practice that is framed through both knowledges that proceeds as a 'line of flight' (23) tracking a renewed texture of relational knowing, which constitutes a subjectivity.

CONVERGENCE: CHOICE, UNCERTAINTY, AND LANGUAGE-IN-MOTION

In asserting a perspective which considers the coextensive relation between improvisation and language, it is hoped that understandings may be bridged, and may be considered for the influence improvisation and language exert on one another's practice. Erin Manning, whilst recognizing the shortfalls in communicating through language, concurs with this position, depicting the provision of language as 'able to convey a certain complexity of the concepts at work, bridging the worlds such that a dialogue between worlds-in-the-making can begin' (2008:2). So how can these 'worlds-in-the-making' start talking, engaging, and relating with one another? At least initially, the conversation needs to change, away from distinctness and separation and towards convergence around the three facets detailed below.

1. Choice

One of the ways we can do this is to build an understanding of the possibilities evident in language through 'word choice' (Feck 2008: 42, citing Maher 1983) and bring this into the arena of movement, to approach the prospect of choice as evident through improvisational practice through the words one chooses and also the movement options available when moving. It is in the provision of choice that language holds the ability to encourage a sense of play, to move with, to rupture, affect, and colour preceding ideas, to rhythm a passage through syntax, and to offer contrast to what has come before.

2. Uncertainty

What if our use of writing and language around improvisation practice was founded on uncertainty? In adopting this improvisational principle in our approaches to writing and language, would this instil an aliveness in our communications and enable a freedom from the constraints so often rubbed up against in the translation of this embodied form outside its given medium?

A potential solution offered here is to utilize writing as a method of inquiry, taking influence from theorists such as Sommerville (2007, 2008), Laurel Richardson (2000), and Deleuze and Parnet (2006). The latter suggest that 'writing as a method of inquiry carries us across our threshold, toward a destination which is unknown, not foreseeable, not pre-existent' (1977: 125).

What if we (the improvisational community) situated ourselves in a place of not knowing (or as Sommerville says, 'waiting in the chaotic place of unknowing' (2008: 211) and sat with uncertainty? How could this offer a renewed perspective of the relationship existent between improvisation, language, and ways to conceptualize dance improvisation practice?

To engage with uncertainty facilitates the creation of space(s). In its broadest sense, this includes the discerning of conceptual and metaphysical spaces. Derek McCormack would identify these as 'thinking-spaces' (2008: 2). The example utilized in this chapter has been Nancy Stark Smith's description of 'the Gap' (1987: 3). Both examples are producing spaces which stage intersubjectivities, confront ambiguity, reveal the interconnectivity of multiple foci, and confront notions of absence and presence.

3. Language-in-Motion

The relationship dance improvisation has forged with language is an attitude endemic across dance and body-based 'knowledges' where language is sought to represent experiences rather than as part of the process in arriving at understanding. Given this, let us change our understanding of language and see it as generating its own emergent experience of knowing, aiding our understanding of the becoming-known. Let us think of language as infinite, and let us preface language as a 'fluid construct' (Shildrick and Price 1999: 3) that is subject to change, nuance, indeterminacy, and potential.

Influenced by aspects of Margaret Sommerville's (2007, 2008) term 'postmodern emergence', I propose that the improvisation community adopt elements of *wondering, becoming,* and *generating* as approaches to formulating knowledge and enabling the cultivation of a mindset which is looser, fluid, and open to ideas and thoughts which are in states of transition. I suggest one of the ways this could be achieved would be to employ language as a verb ('languaging'), to appreciate the activity of language and its participation in meaning and sense-making for the improviser. Albright (2003) provides support for this stance by establishing that just as writing engenders change in the embodied experience of improvising, thinking and writing also have the potential to resituate an improviser's engagement with, and towards, embodied experience.

What needs attention and promotion in dance improvisation practice and its discourse is the space to arrive at understanding, the 'becoming-known' of knowledge and ways of knowing rather than a predetermined terminus of knowledge-known. It is this, and the search for transparency based in subjectivity, that my own research and practice continues to develop and explore, by enabling improvisers to access reflections and engagements with their fleshy practice whilst simultaneously acknowledging the conscious shaping of their practice through their language choices.

To write *with* rather than *about* improvisation practice situates the researcher/practitioner as a coproducer, a collaborator, in this emergent production of knowledge. By introducing the concept of uncertainty and choice into writing, a sense of hierarchy and authority can be diffused. Writing is then free to participate, to act as a vehicle of discovery, a way of knowing and of knowledge-generation.

I consider hybrid writings as producing practices related to the discovery of improvisational knowing, practices that reflect and consider the potentiality of words, reveal 'languaging' habits, and explore the presentation and spatialization of writings on the page. These include explorations with tracing paper, word clouds, drawing and doodles, creating and scoring conversations between texts, coding passages of text, cut-up and die-cut techniques, bookbinding, and origami. These strategies cultivate a conversational practice, elicited through an understanding of writing as a participatory approach which contributes to improvisational knowing. The knowledge generated through this conversational practice of improvising is embraced as a discourse of knowledge in and of itself.

In a sense, the hybrid writing practices explored throughout this chapter (i.e. the word cloud which wrestles with understandings of 'being in the moment', and languaging of the small dance through a collation of words depicted through feet and textures) converse with the academic writing of dance improvisation practice to create a sense of transparency within the text. Alongside the writing of this chapter (not evidenced visually) are stream of consciousness writings and origami-based explorations which also inform understandings of practice (i.e. possibility folding into habit). These examples echo the interplay between habit and possibility within dance improvisation practice, by rendering existent experience as a concurrent witness to that which is being experienced. Employing a conversational practice has enabled the repotentializing of conceptual understandings, through exposure to an emergent experiencing and attentional engagement within writing and improvisation to unfold.

This chapter seeks to provide encouragement for a sometimes reluctant field to broaden the possibilities of debate by establishing a platform to facilitate discourse regarding the exchange and 'languaging' of dance improvisation experiences. What seems to materialize from these 'languaging' efforts is an incessant falling back on binaries and dualisms as a means of explanation. It is almost as if language needs to wrestle itself away from binary dualistic tendencies, withdrawing from a sense of fixity and stasis assumed through rigid categorizations to create a space of inbetweeness which oscillates amongst these binaries. As any movement researcher/practitioner encountering bodily discourse will proffer, there is a need to source a vocabulary of uncertainty, of potential, of possibility, which is emergent. It is from this space of uncertainty that a processual becoming-language can emerge, introducing a conception of language as a 'site of potential', as 'fluid construct' (Shildrick and Price 1999: 3), rather than fixity. The provocation offered by this chapter encourages consideration and exploration of ways in which the availability of language as a tool for exploring uncertainty and ambiguity can be promoted through improvisation practice, offering the perspective that language should open itself to the possibility that indeterminacy affords.

Notes

1. Edward Casey, introducing an understanding of the concept of 'emplacement', notes that 'the living-moving body is essential to the process of emplacement', suggesting that 'bodies are never placeless' (1996: 24). He seeks a consideration which understands that 'bodies and places interanimate each other' (24), arguing that there is a binary dogma that pervades discussions of space and time instilled through the misunderstanding of place as that which separates the relation of space and time (37).
2. An understanding of flesh is framed through the theorists Michael Hardt (1997) and Maurice Merleau-Ponty (1945, 1968). Hardt contextualizes flesh through an exploration of Pasolini's poem 'Crucifixion', which Hardt reinterprets through an exploration of flesh and its exposure. He discusses flesh as promoting exposure to qualities of the world through possibility; he is clear to address the issue that whilst flesh is responsive to these qualities, flesh is not beholden to these qualities for definition. Hardt conceives of 'becoming-flesh' (1997: 585) as abandonment of something, to something. An interpretation of this abandonment considering dance improvisation may be to conceive of this as an abandoning of objectivity for subjectivity, or as indicating a sense of withdrawal rather than abandonment. Merleau-Ponty provides the perspective that 'flesh is not matter, is not mind, is not substance' (1945: 139), it is a generalized condition (or 'element') of being. He continues by describing flesh as an incarnate principle existing between the spatiotemporal individual and the idea (139). He understands flesh as a mode of communication, a 'facticity' (140) which bridges a processual understanding of experiences, recognizing, encompassing, affirming, and qualifying them. Flesh offers a sense of counterpoint in the understanding of what is thought of as other, because it has experienced this other, offering this perspective through a sense of 'reversibility' (144).
3. Michel Serres situates an understanding of skin as that which communes and interfaces with the environment, in effect positioning the skin as the initial port of call where

perception is concerned. He understands the connection of skin in contact with skin as emanating a consciousness that is specific to moments when the body is tangential to itself (2008: 22).

4. The 'small dance' (Hulton 1975: 9) originates from standing, working with a visualization of the skeleton through an understanding of bones stacked on top of one another. In this chapter I consider the 'small dance' to be a movement exercise in entraining a sensitization to bodily reflexes, as a tool to prime the infinitesimal impulses that catalyze movement.

REFERENCES

Albright, Ann Cooper, and Gere, D. (eds.). (2003) *Taken by Surprise: A Dance Improvisation Reader*. Middletown, CT: Wesleyan University Press.

Banes, S. (1987) *Terpsichore in Sneakers*. Middletown, CT: Wesleyan University Press. (Originally published 1977)

Belgrad, D. (1998) *The Culture of Spontaneity: Improvisation and the Arts in Postwar America*. Chicago: University of Chicago Press.

Benoit, A. (1997) *On the Edge/Créateurs De L'Imprévu*. Nouvelles De Danse 32/33. Brussels: Contredanse.

Bergson, H. (1913) *Time and Free Will: An Essay on the Immediate Data of Consciousness*. Trans. F. Pogson. 3rd ed. London: Allen and Unwin.

Casey, E. (1996) How to Get from Space to Place in a Fairly Short Stretch of Time: Phenomenological Prolegomena. In Feld, S., and Basso, K. (eds)., *Senses of Place*. Santa Fe: School of American Research Press, 13–52.

Csikszentmihalyi, M. (1990) *Flow: The Psychology of Optimal Performance*. New York: Quality Paperback Book Club.

Deleuze, G., and Guattari, F. (1988) *A Thousand Plateaus: Capitalism and Schizophrenia*. Trans. B. Massumi. London: Continuum. (Originally published 1980)

Deleuze, G., and Parnet, C. (2006) *Dialogues II*. Trans. H. Tomlinson and B. Habberjam. London: Continuum. (Originally published 1977)

Derrida, J. (1967/1978) *Writing and Difference*. Trans. Alan Bass. London: Routledge and Kegan Paul.

De Spain, K. (2014) *Landscape of the Now: A Topography of Movement Improvisation*. New York: Oxford University Press.

Dils, A., and Crosby, J. (2001) Dialogue in Dance Studies Research. The University of North Carolina at Greensboro (UNCG) library.http://libres.uncg.edu/ir/uncg/listing.aspx?id=3973. Accessed 13 July 2004.

Feck, C. (2008) Against 'ON': A Dance Writer Weighs In on Words. *Contact Quarterly* 34(1): 42–43.

Foucault, M. (1981–1982) *The Hermeneutics of the Subject: Lectures at the College de France 1981-2*. New York: Picador.

Gil, J. (ed.). (1998) *Metamorphosis of the Body*. Trans. Stephen Muecke (1985). Minneapolis: University of Minnesota Press.

Gil, J., and Lepecki, A. (2006) Paradoxical Body. *The Drama Review* 50(4):21 35.

Grosz, E. (1994) *Volatile Bodies: Toward a Corporeal Feminism*. Bloomington: Indiana University Press.

Halprin, A. (1995) *Moving towards Life: Five Decades of Transformational Dance.* Middletown, CT: Wesleyan University Press.

Hardt, M. (1997) Exposure: Pasolini in the Flesh. *Canadian Review of Comparative Literature* 24(3): 581–587.

Hay, D. (2000) *My Body the Buddhist.* Middletown, CT: Wesleyan University Press.

Hulton, P. (1975) Steve Paxton in Interview with Peter Hulton. *Theatre Papers the First Series 1977–78.* http://spa.exeter.ac.uk/drama/research/exeterdigitalarchives/theatre_papers/paxton.pdf. Accessed 16 September 2009.

Jordan, S. (1992) *Striding Out: Aspects of Contemporary and New Dance in Britain.* London: Dance Books.

Kant, I. (1892/1914) *Critique of Judgement,* Trans. J.H. Bernard (2nd ed. revised). London: Macmillan.

Manning, E. (2007) *Politics of Touch: Sense, Movement, Sovereignty.* Minneapolis: University of Minnesota Press.

Manning, E. (2008) Creative Propositions for Thought in Motion. *Inflexions* 1(1). http://www.inflexions.org. Accessed 22 February 2009.

Marshall, S., Ellis, S., and Pape, N. (2009a) Bouncing Off Each Other—An Online Relay. *Proximity* 12(1): 1–12.

Marshall, S., Ellis, S., and Pape, N. (2009b) Bouncing Off Each Other—An Online Relay. Extended version. http://proximity.slightly.net/blog. Accessed 15 January 2010.

McCormack, D. (2008) Thinking-Spaces for Research-Creation. *Inflexions* 1(1) http://www.inflexions.org. Accessed 22 February 2009.

Merleau-Ponty, M. (1945) *Phenomenology of Perception.* Trans. C. Smith (1962). London: Routledge.

Merleau-Ponty, M. (1968) *The Visible and the Invisible.* Trans. A. Lingis. Bloomington: Indiana University Press.

Paxton, S. (2008) The Small Dance, The Stand (1986). Reprinted 1997. http://myriadicity.net/ci36/satellite-events/the-small-dance-the-stand. Accessed 16 September 2009.

Paxton, S. (2003) Drafting Interior Techniques (1993). In Albright, Ann Cooper, and Gere, D. (eds.), *Taken by Surprise: A Dance Improvisation Reader.* Middletown, CT: Wesleyan University Press, 175–183.

Paxton, S. (2008) *Material for the Spine: A Movement Study.* Brussels: Contredanse. (DVD-ROM)

Peters, G. (2009) *The Philosophy of Improvisation.* Chicago: University of Chicago Press.

Richardson, L. (2000) Writing: A Method of Inquiry. In Denzin, N., and Lincoln, Y. (eds.), *Handbook of Qualitative Research,* 2nd ed. London: Sage Publications Inc, 923–948.

Ross, J. (2003) Anna Halprin and Improvisation as Child's Play: A Search for Informed Innocence. In Albright, Ann Cooper, and Gere, D. (eds.), *Taken by Surprise: A Dance Improvisation Reader.* Middletown, CT: Wesleyan University Press, 41–51.

Serres, M. (2008) *The Five Senses: A Philosophy of Mingled Bodies.* Trans. M. Sankey and P. Cowley. London: Continuum International. (Originally published 1985)

Shildrick, M., and Price, J. (1999) *Feminist Theory and the Body: A Reader.* Edinburgh: Edinburgh University Press.

Sommerville, M. (2007) Postmodern Emergence. *International Journal of Qualitative Studies in Education* 20(2): 225–243.

Sommerville, M. (2008) Waiting in the Chaotic Place of Unknowing: Articulating Postmodern Emergence. In *International Journal of Qualitative Studies in Education* 21(3): 209–220.

Stark Smith, N. (1987) After Improv. *Contact Quarterly* 12(3): 9–19.

Stark Smith, N. (2003) A Subjective History of Contact Improvisation. In Albright, Ann Cooper, and Gere, D. (eds.), *Taken by Surprise: A Dance Improvisation Reader*. Middletown, CT: Wesleyan University Press, 153–173.

Stark Smith, N. (2005/2006) Harvest: One History of Contact Improvisation. http://www.contactquarterly.com/cq/webtext/Harvest.html. Accessed 2 April 2011.

Stark Smith, N., and Koteen, D. (2008) *Caught Falling: The Confluence of Contact Improvisation, Nancy Stark Smith, and Other Moving Ideas*. Northampton, MA: Contact Editions.

Warren, W., Jr. (1995) Self-Motion: Visual Perception and Visual Control. In Epstein, W., and Rodgers, S. (eds.), *Perception of Space and Motion*. London: Academic Press, 263–325.

Whitehead, A. (1978) *Process and Reality*. New York: Free Press.

Zaporah, R. (2002) What's on My Mind Now: Frames, Listening and Expression. *Contact Quarterly*, 27(1): 51–56.

PART III

HABIT, FREEDOM, AND RESISTANCE

CHAPTER 12

....

IMPROVISATION AND HABIT

....

GARY PETERS

> The best we can do is to confront our inherited ... nature with our know-
> ledge of it, and ... inplant in ourselves a new habit, a new instinct, a second
> nature, so that our first nature withers away.
>
> (Nietzsche 1983: 76)

IN 2007 the Slovenian dancer Jurij Konjar, as part of the production *Fake It!*, conceived by Nataša Zavalovšek and Janez Jansa, began a series of reimprovisations of Steve Paxton's *Goldberg Variations,* originally performed in the 1980s. For me, having witnessed one of these reimprovisations in Copenhagen at the Dansehallerne on 21 May 2013, this essay constitutes a belated response both to the event itself and to a conversation with Jurij Konjar in an elevator at the University of Copenhagen the next day: also an event.[1]

STEVE PAXTON: The score for the *Goldberg Variations* was to not do what I have done before ... finding ways to trick myself. In '91, when I couldn't find ways to trick myself anymore ... I stopped.... Having worked on contact improvisation to see if I could figure out why this thing called improvisation has a reputation for not having a structure, I kept finding structure. At a certain point I decided that the structure was me. That I couldn't get outside of that. I couldn't continue the process because I kept running into myself, and my habit. (Konjar 2011: 16–17)

JURIJ KONJAR: I start planning and I fall back into my habits.... But it's a choice ... that I'm trying to avoid having habits. (Konjar 2011: 13)

JURIJ KONJAR: The NO Score ... is based on 'no-ing' many impulses.... This is like tricking myself.... I ask myself what is the 'me'? ... The 'me' is the dancer of 'I do', the self-conscious being of 'I want', the private life person of 'I am', and they all manifest through the body ... I ... exclude all of the above 'me's' from the process. (Konjar 2011: 20)

Paxton and Konjar appear to be engaged in a very similar process here, a shared commitment to the exposure and obliteration of habit as embedded in the very structure of the I, me, mine. But are they?

Here is Paxton's response on first hearing of *Fake It!*

> It is an amusing, serious and political proposal. I think you are doing formally what dancers have always done, to be influenced by other dancers. Usually the influence *slips into the body without public notice*, so this event brings to the front of the mind how dance, seeming to have a *life of its own*, transfers from one studio to another. (Konjar 2011: 20, my emphasis)

The manner in which the determining power of the other 'slips into the body' has everything to do with the unconscious accumulation of habits which are ultimately responsible for what Paxton might describe as the structural closure of the improvisational openness he explicitly sought in his *Goldberg Variations*: as he describes it, '[I was] trying open improvisation against a very formal music' (Paxton 2014).

For Paxton, as indicated in the foregoing passages, the event of improvised dance is for it to have a 'life of its own', an acknowledgement that, as *event*, dance infinitely exceeds the intentions, desires, and habits of individual dancers, himself very much included. The intentionality of the conscious self, constantly 'running into' itself as unwanted habitual structure, is for him the 'fictional' (2014) content that needs to be removed in order for the real 'non-conscious' content to be revealed: his postmodernist and modernist acts, respectively, just to problematize the crude and naive labelling of him as the 'father of postmodernist dance'.

Paxton's suspicious hyper-self-awareness can be contrasted with the greater neutrality of Konjar's more detached method of observing rather than attempting to outwit and outrun the very process by which the other 'slips into the body' of the 'I'.

Paxton, very much a man of 1960s counterculture, uses the idiomatic vocabulary of encounter and discovery. His is an intensive and intense language of an interiority that ultimately cannot be escaped—'I couldn't get outside'—but is endlessly stumbled upon as an habitual structure that, paradoxically, the very *openness* of the improvisation brings to the surface. 'I found the Bach brought out classical training in my nervous system, noting that once a style gets into the body-mind it is firmly entrenched' (2014).

With Konjar, very much a man of post-1960s spectacle and spectatorship, it is the exteriority of gesture and the sense of sight that predominate, and where observation displaces participation as the primary performative mode: 'it seems to me that the creator, performer, and analyst all start with—**observing**' (Konjar 2011: 9, bold in original).

> I'm looking at a recording of Paxton
> . . . looking at the form and copying
> and looking further . . .
> in order to be here . . .
> I need to find answers
> so I observe and embody beyond form. (5)

Paxton's *Goldberg Variations* are conceived as a *negative* act, a freedom-from: the desire to guilefully trick the habitual self through the performance of pure nonhabitual movement—'it's about movement that I *haven't* done before' (16, my emphasis).

Konjar's *Goldberg Variations* are conceived an *affirmative* act, a freedom-to: the desire to observe and then *preserve* both the habitual and nonhabitual movements of the self and other (Paxton), through a performative reserve or 'restraint' that, as Heidegger would see it, is active rather than passive. Konjar:

> I see Steve goes fully for it. The thing is, if I go fully for it, I start planning movement and I fall back on my habits. (Konjar 2011: 13)

For Paxton, the improvised act has an immediacy that momentarily integrates (or strives to integrate) interiority and exteriority in a pure virgin space without history or habits. To 'fully go for it' is to commit absolutely to the possibility of this moment. Lisa Nelson:

> Steve's attention and yours are very different, Steve's is more internal, and yours is more in the space. (16)

For Konjar, to *see* the space rather than *be* the space, to have the 'time to observe the outside *and* the inside' (2011: 21) is different. *Seeing* the space introduces a moment of delay into the improvised movement whereby the observation of the other (Konjar's endless observation of Paxton) and/or the observation of oneself is an enactment of 'lagging-behind' (2) that is not only historical but existential, even ontological. Yet Konjar, albeit differently, still echoes Paxton on habit:

> I'm trying to avoid having habits; and trying to avoid knowing; and get to a place where I don't know anything.... Go for things, but kind of just wait. (13)

Habit revolves around the witting or unwitting inheritance of given models or patterns of practice, whereby that which 'has a life of its own' (is unowned) is over time transformed into that which is thought and *felt* to be owned, and it is the latter which is in danger of becoming 'instinctual' in a bad sense—a 'first nature'.

The first step in the creation of what Nietzsche in this essay's epigraph calls a 'second nature' is to openly confront the historical dimension of both creation and preservation and to expose the moment of repetition by acknowledging that coming-into-being is also and always a coming-*back*-into-being.

Getting into the habit of recognizing and responding to the habitual acquires existential significance—Konjar is exemplary—as a heightened self-reflexivity or hyperawareness that introduces a delay into the moment of performance. Konjar:

> I've never tried doing things without seeing what they are before they happen. I realize I've always imagined what I will do a moment before doing.... And you're almost not involved ... you're observing. (Konjar 2011: 14)

Here the imagining 'I' and the doing 'I' are mediated by a splitting of the 'in the moment' moment into two: the moment and the 'moment before' the moment. This intraimprovisatory delay is articulated by Konjar as 'patience' (7–10). Martin Kilvady:

> held-back … observant … thoughtful … kind of marking … or testing. Looking at yourself. (11)

The philosopher Alain Badiou, writing on Nietzsche on dance, captures something of this moment in dance: 'The movement of dance can certainly manifest an extreme quickness, but only to the extent that it is inhabited by its latent slowness, by the affirmative power of restraint. Nietzsche proclaims the "the will must learn to be slow and mistrustful." Dance could then be defined as the expansion of slowness and the mistrust of the thought-body' (2005: 60–61). Such suspicious and mistrustful thinking maps well onto the performative predicament Paxton describes when explaining the eventual termination of his *Goldberg Variations*, but does it capture the restraint Konjar describes as patience? Is Konjar mistrustful at all?

One way of trying to answer this is to stay with Badiou a moment and consider the dialectic he proposes between restraint and vulgarity: 'Nietzsche writes that all vulgarity derives from the incapacity to resist an entreaty.… Accordingly, dance is defined as the movement of a body subtracted from all vulgarity.… Dance offers a metaphor for a light and subtle thought precisely because it shows the restraint immanent to movement and thereby opposes itself to the spontaneous vulgarity of the body' (2005: 60). Yes, but the issue for us and for Konjar is not vulgarity. There is no question of him resisting the entreaties of the spontaneous body, a body that, unless it is dancing, Badiou believes is 'constrained by itself' (60)—another way of saying habitual. There is no question of Konjar working through a dialectic of constraint-unconstraint any more than there is a requirement that the dancing body enter into a 'state of disobedience vis-à-vis its own impulses' (60). Indeed, perhaps it is this that distinguishes Paxton's improvisations from Konjar's reimprovisations. Whatever, the issue is not obedience or disobedience but observing and accepting. There is constraint in obedience but not in acceptance. Konjar speaks of acceptance, and such acceptance acknowledges, as it should, the vulgarity of the obedient or habitual body, here described as 'bad taste'. Konjar:

> Include the obvious, the yours, the already done
> Don't fall in love and don't criticize.
> Accept—that mistakes and things of bad taste will happen.
> Most of all, don't panic.
> (2011: 11)

No disobedience in evidence here, and it would be difficult to see, with Badiou, how such dancing could act as a 'metaphor for thought'. If there is thought here, it is a thoughtless thought that forgets itself on the threshold of the moment and *acts*, observes, and continues to act, accepting that the will to dance is one that must inevitably include the habitual (the 'obvious, the yours, the already done') and the vulgar.

Obedience, acceptance, restraint, habit: whatever happened to the *surprise* of improvisation? In fact, Paxton confirms that (in spite of his habitual self) he was frequently 'caught by surprise' when dancing the *Goldberg Variations,* and it is interesting to note that this was due not so much to the absence of habitual structures as to a recognition and fleeting occupation of the spaces *between* or *within* such structures. Paxton:

> In the **shifting between** movement elements and musical elements I could be caught by surprise. What I thought my body was going to do might be altered as it was happening. This was an experience I was looking for, a non-conscious evidence of the dance I had worked for decades to bring to mind. It was fragile and quick. (2014; bold in original)

And yet, as I have shown, the main reason for the cessation of his *Goldberg Variations* was that he could no longer surprise himself, on account of his evil twin the *habitual* Steve Paxton who insidiously imposed the structures of the deeply known on the surprising otherness of the unknown. But it is precisely this subjectivization of habit that is responsible for the subjectivized yearning for infinite surprise; one that, in turn, is all too easily translated into the similarly subjectivized experience of an expectant audience: all part of the same 'unspoken contract'. Paxton:

> So part of my work in developing the *Goldberg* was to work on lines of thought. My lines of thought did not include how to relate to the public. I thought the public and I had an unspoken contract.... So instead of being concerned with the public, I was concerned with what I was making ... what my body was making. In each moment, I felt like there was some place to go, some place to change from. To listen for a place I can change from is what I choose to choose.
>   So there's a choosing going on in this improvisation. Not that I know where I'm going, but I am very aware of what I'm *not* doing. (Konjar 2011: 17, my emphasis)

Again, there is a lot of I, me, mine here, and it is this that gets in the way of a more essential understanding of both the nature of habit and the surprise of the improvised event. Interestingly, it is Paxton *himself* who alludes to the surprise of the event rather than the mere event of surprise, when he suggests that it is not the tricking of the habitual self that is the issue but rather the experience of being *tricked by* the ingrained body-mind that is surprising for the dancer and, when witnessed, by the audience, too. Evidence, if evidence were needed, of Paxton's highly complex and constantly probing reflections on improvisation.

Similarly, Jean-Luc Nancy conceives of the event as being governed by the experience of surprise, but ... 'the 'surprise' is not ... an attribute, quality, or property of the event, but the event itself, its being or its essence. What eventuates in the event is not only that which happens, but that which surprises—perhaps even that which surprises itself' (1998: 91). Nancy is at pains to separate the surprising-ness of the event from the subjective and subjectivized experience of surprise in the face of what merely 'happens'. The post-*Goldberg* Steve Paxton would say that what is unsurprising is the product of accumulated habits, hence his desire to emancipate himself from them. It is this, the hegemonic conception of a 'force of habit' that is perceived as a threat by all subjectivized aesthetics of individual choice and freedom. For him, then, it is habit that obscures the event of dance which, as event, has a 'life of its own'. And yet more recently what might be called the post-post-*Goldberg* Paxton would seem to have recognized the surprising alterability of habit *itself*, one that situates improvisation within and between structures rather than outside them.

However, this 'mechanism' (Malabou 2005) model of (the force of) habit has recently (and not so recently) been challenged by a more affirmative perspective, one that recognizes the 'plasticity' of habituation and embraces the idea that habit is a 'disposition' rather than a brute determining force. In this understanding, habit is *responsible for* rather than *resistant to* the transformation of human action and the creativity associated with that. So, not so recently, in 1838 Felix Ravaisson writes: 'habit is ... a disposition relative to change, which is engendered in a being by the continuity or *the repetition of this very same change* .... Nothing, then, is capable of habit that is not capable of change' (2008: 25, my emphasis). More recently, Catherine Malabou, in her 2008 preface to the above, writes: 'if being was able to change once, in the manner of contracting a habit, it can change again. It is available for a change to come. Certainly, change generates habit, but in return *habit is actualized as a habit of changing*' (viii, my emphasis). Rather than being either a *universal* determining force that completely absorbs individual freedom in an undifferentiated mechanism or the *singular* mannerisms and idiosyncrasies of the creative performer/artist, habit actually mediates these binaries and in doing so makes possible the *liberation* of the self: a reversal of the improvisers' charter, where the desire is to liberate oneself *from* habits.

The word 'habit' derives from the Latin *habere*; 'habit is a way of "having," a kind of possession, a property' (Ravaisson 2008: viii). But possession signifies both the ownership of something (*having* property) as well as being possessed *by* something: the opposite of ownership. The liberating force of habit is that it frees the habitual self from both having and being-had. Moving this discussion into a more ontological vein: neither possessed nor dispossessed, the habitual self is the one most attuned to the essence of the event, which, in one of its most profound iterations (Heidegger's), is characterized by just such an *absence* of ownership.

In Heidegger's thinking of the event (*Ereignis*, often translated as 'appropriation'), it is never a question of the appropriation *of* or being appropriated *by* but rather of a 'strange ownership and strange appropriation': 'we must experience simply this owning in which man and Being are delivered over to each other, that is, we must enter into what we call the *event of appropriation.* ... [But] ... the term event of appropriation no longer means what we would call a happening or an occurrence' (Heidegger 2002: 36). The issue here is not the intentional acts of the ego/performer/improviser in pursuit of surprises and self-fulfilment but a desubjectivized '*comportment*' towards being which is not a thinking-about but more an act of orientation that, through a certain 'releasement' of the self, 'opens' (speaking with Heidegger) beings to the event of Being. If this can be described as an act and, as act, a 'new habit', it is an act or habit more of 'waiting' than of doing: something closer to Konjar's 'restraint'.

But what is being waited for here? Waiting to be surprised? Is this what Konjar is waiting for? Konjar:

> You are monitoring 'patience', not movement.
> You don't know what is coming ... but you can sense what is not 'it' yet ... so you wait, now. You don't remember ideas and you don't look for them (plan them), you just wait. (Konjar 2011: 8)

Mostly, improvisers wait for something to 'happen' or 'occur'; that, for many, is the essence of the improvised event. But if we follow Heidegger and get into the habit of ignoring happenings and occurrences, just as Nancy ignores the attributes, qualities, and properties of the event, then Konjar's comportment might be understood as a waiting for something other than a surprise.

Nancy certainly believes that the event has nothing to do with subjective experience: 'But it is not a surprise for the subject.... The surprise—the event—does not belong to the order of representation.... It coincides with this surprise; it is only this surprise that is not yet "its own"' (Nancy 1998: 101–102). Once again, it is belonging and ownership that comes to the fore as a reminder that it is not what we—as subjective I, me, mine—say, think, or do but the 'patient' *observation* of an opening of Being that we appropriate/disappropriate through what we might describe as the rehabitualization of our comportment. And this is the crux: there *is* no beyond or outside, there is no escape from habit; as Ravaisson recognized: 'habit is a general and permanent way of being'.

But even if habits *are* the product of past changes and always 'open' for future changes in the moment, nevertheless they still *enforce* themselves as forgotten habitual acts that one can either choose to combat (Paxton) or choose to observe and resign oneself to (Konjar); but, staying with Heidegger, choice is not the decisive thing: *decision* itself is decisive: 'What is decision at all? Not *choice*. Choosing always involves only what is pregiven and can be taken or rejected. *Decision* here means grounding and creating, disposing in advance and beyond oneself' (Heidegger 1999: 69). Now the locus of surprise changes: while the improvisatory nature of the improvised event has much to do with the choices made 'in the moment', some perceived as surprising, some not, the truth is we (especially the audience) *expect* to be surprised in this way and, indeed, *anticipate* witnessing the unforeseeable consequences of unexpected choices. At the performative level of choice, surprise is often the most unsurprising thing imaginable, so much so that it is more of a surprise when we are *not* surprised: a surprising boredom.

As Heidegger reveals in his famous lectures on the subject (1995: 78–164), boredom is not, ontologically speaking, the psychological/existential experience of boring things, one that, as an antidote, endlessly craves surprising events as a means of fending off such tedium. On the contrary, he *affirms* boredom as a profound 'attunement' to a particular 'limbo' that reveals both the absence or ontological insignificance of lived clock time and the more essential temporality of being, one that encompasses all time—past, present, and future. And the attunement to this is not a choice made in the moment before an audience but an a priori *decision* that 'constitutes the ground of the possibility of the subjectivity of subjects'. This disjuncture between the time of the performance and what we might call the temporality of the event is captured in this brief remark by Konjar:

> One cannot be completely concentrated for 10 minutes a day while improvising, and be like a young goat for the rest of the time. It's a decision that improvisation becomes a life. (2011: 8)

Remember where the epigraph to this essay comes from: Nietzsche's essay 'The Uses and Disadvantages of History for *Life*'. The life of an improviser is not a life dedicated to the mastery of improvisation as a performative strategy, any more than it is an improvised life made up on the spot; nor is the decisive moment the moment when the improviser announces: 'I have decided: improvisation will from this day onwards be my life'. No, for all of their importance, these remain a posteriori choices made as part of the actualization of decisions already made '*in advance*' of conscious self-knowledge and subjective commitment. Nietzsche's decisive decision before all else is the 'love of fate' (*amor fati*). Deleuze describes this as a primordial 'affirmation of chance', one that releases chance from contingency: a decisive moment. We become who we are by taking or not taking chances as they arise. The dancer becomes a dancer by taking different chances from those taken by the philosopher; it is this that separates Paxton and Heidegger; Konjar and Badiou; dancers and dance scholars.

Remembering the possessive/depossessive hybridity of the event, to *take* a chance is too voluntaristic, ignoring as it does the disappropriative moment of being *taken-by* chance (or *taken-by* surprise). We *do* take possession of what we are possessed-by, to the extent that we embark upon a life that is formed and transformed by the repetition of this evental moment in habitual acts that, in a reversal of our prevailing improvisatory *doxa*, end up 'canonizing *being's* improvisations' (Malabou 2005: 74) And the idea that *Being* improvises is, perhaps, the decisive moment in this essay.

Malabou describes 'being's improvisation' as follows:

> 'Plastic individuals' are those that synthesize in their very 'style' the essence of the genus and the accident which has become habitual. What in the beginning was merely an accidental fact—Plato's commitment to philosophy, Pericles' to politics, Phidias to sculpture—is changed through the continual repetition of the same gestures, through practice, achieving the integrity of a 'form'. Effected by habit, the singularity of the 'plastic individual' becomes an *essence a posteriori*. *The process of habit ends by canonizing being's improvisations on its own themes* [my emphasis]. The philosopher, the political man or sculptor, are determinations which could not have been anticipated just by the simple generic definition of man: they are destinies contained *virtually* in the genus 'man', but remain there as something unpredictable. By forming themselves, by undergoing repetition and practice, these determinations ultimately construct a state which is habitual and accordingly *essential*. Habit is the

process whereby the contingent becomes essential. (74, emphasis in original except where indicated)

After repeated readings of his *Chapbook 2*, it becomes clear that Konjar's repetition of Paxton's *Goldberg Variations* itself reveals a significant difference not only in their approaches to improvisation but, underpinning that, to repetition itself. As Paxton explains to Konjar, his primary aim was 'to not repeat myself' (Konjar 2011: 16), to which Konjar perceptively responds: 'if the score was not to do what you know you have done before, wouldn't the shows be very similar to one another?' (17). This essential question brings back into play the boringness of improvisation while also allowing us to call on Deleuze to help us consider a crucial distinction.

Paxton's apparent assumption is that it is the *avoidance* of repetition (the repetition necessary for habit formation and the repetition of the habitual acts themselves) that creates *difference*, whereas for Deleuze such a strategy can only produce *diversity*, a disguised form of same-ness. This, to be provocative, might help explain the boringness of so much improvisation that strives to be infinitely different but achieves only diversity: the same difference rather than a different sameness. The decisive concept for Paxton is clearly the self, the deep-structure of the habitual nonconscious 'me' that he constantly confronts and then attempts to negate through the creation, on the 'horizontal' plane of diversity (to stay with Deleuze's language), of nonhabitual gestures, which, however, ultimately 'fail' to recognize or sufficiently address the 'vertical' difference or 'excess' of the 'virtual' idea of the originary self *itself*. The result is a repetitive improvised gesture of difference that produces only a *diverse* perspective on an unchanging, undifferentiated, and ultimately static concept of the habitual 'me'. For all of his talk of choice and 'choosing to choose', Paxton often leaves unacknowledged the *decisive* moment in his own life as a dancer/improviser, one that renders all subsequent habit-breaking action secondary and, in fact, renders it testimony to the improvisatory essence of habit formation itself. What is *beyond* choice is fate, as Nietzsche (quoted with approval by Deleuze in *Difference and Repetition*) is at pains to remind us: 'there is something irreducible in the depths of the spirit: a monolithic bloc of Fatum, of *decision already taken* on all problems in their measure and their relations to us; and also a right that we have to accede to certain problems, like a hot-iron brand imprinted on our names' (Nietzsche 1973: 231, my emphasis). In a sense, it was Paxton's inability to develop a love (as opposed to a recognition) of fate that resulted in his final choice to give up the task of the *Goldberg Variations*. Paxton:

> So there is a choosing going on in this improvisation. Not that I know where I'm going, but I'm very aware of what I am not doing. And I am doing something. I'm really trying to do the dancing strategy that I have arrived at. Until it became too complex, until I had done everything. (Konjar 2011: 17)

But the *decisive* issue is not about *doing* but of *having* (*habere*), and of being-had-by.

In retrospect, it is clear that Konjar's 'NO score', although reverberating with Paxton's often negative language, is in truth much more affirmative than it sounds. While he

speaks of excluding 'all the "me's"' (I do, I want, I am), the very plurality of the concept reveals a more decisive multiplicity in the originary/virtual idea. But, more directly,
having made this exclusive gesture (in the spirit of his mentor) he immediately considers the circumstances by which they (the 'me's') are brought back into play. Konjar:

> If the flow itself becomes the focus, the other 'me's' can become active elements in
> the process; elements that can play or not, enter or exit, be observed.... They can be
> looked upon from some distance, and manipulated; instead of dogmatically limiting
> (through the 'no' logic) what the movement can or cannot be. (2011: 20)

This reference to the dogmatism of a 'no' logic suggests that Konjar is at the very least
aware of the space between himself and Paxton, and his proposal of a new 'YES dance'
compounds this, while at the same time confirming his commitment to a *vertically* differentiated model of the self that promises more than the familiar horizontal/successive
diversity typical of improvised performance. Konjar:

> A new score for GV—a YES dance of one hour.
> The movement does not need 'me' in order to be happening, but the flow of
> movement can be played with by *all I am* and able to observe. (20, my emphasis)

There is a subtle but real distinction here between the performative 'me' who takes ownership of the *horizontal/successive* improvisational space-time and the 'all I am' which
is in excess of this performative moment and, through restraint, observation, and re-
linquishment brings into view the decisive *vertical* difference that allows choice and
habit to *coexist*—the choice of habit/the habit of choosing. This is not some 'dizzying'
philosophical mystification; it is, rather, the crucial moment in any understanding of
improvisation, conceived (with Deleuze) as the endlessly open 'actualisation' of the
'virtual', where the infinite multiplicity of the 'all I am' ensures that the 'stumbled-upon'
structures of the self can always be undone and differentiated: if only Paxton had read
Deleuze!
    Konjar:

> Bottom line: There is more than just a moment, that's an illusion I've built for myself
> which was useful for a time. Now my mind tells me there are also habit, composition,
> and making choices. There is planning, assuming; and there are thoughts about an
> audience. (21)

Paxton at times valorizes the moment of choice in an effort (doomed, as he himself is
aware) to outrun the a priori presence of *decision*. Konjar recognizes that such choices
can only be made within an improvisatory 'flow' that is *already happening*. Paxton is
primarily, although not exclusively, concerned with what might be called the improvisation of *beings*: individual performers (himself) within a performative situation. We
might suggest that Konjar is more willing to accept what we've seen Catherine Malabou

describe as 'being's improvisations', improvisations only revealed through the formation and transformation of habit; hence the move away from the 'NO' of his mentor to the 'YES' of his own situation.

Near the end of the *Chapbook 2*, Konjar begins enumerating his 'own' habits (the habits that 'own' him):

> continuous turning ... a movement initiative from the spine ... the habit to use the hands in a sort of 'stay away' of 'I give up' gesture ... (Konjar 2011: 32)

The question he then asks again marks the distance he appears to have travelled from Paxton:

> My question to myself is not how to avoid these elements [these habits], but what to do with them when they appear. I could take a different approach and try to do something completely different, but actually I've done that too, several times, until it became another pattern [another habit]. (32)

Like Paxton, Konjar recognizes the futility of trying to outwit habit, which can only result in the habit of outwitting habit. But his response is subtly different; for him, it is not primarily a question of avoiding habits but of *doing something with them*. Perhaps Konjar has been listening to his friend Martin Kilvady:

> KILVADY: People come to me and say 'I want to change this habit of mine. I always do the same, I want to change, go to a place where I usually don't go'. I think it's a bit of a false direction. Why would you want to change what you do? You are good at it, you know how to do it, why change? (13)

Why indeed? But then one answer, perhaps Paxton's, would be that simply accepting our habits would be to leave them in place as what he would call nonconscious ingrained events. For him it is not so much a matter of removing the habitual structures that underpin what we do as of bringing them to consciousness, even if this results in the ultimate termination of the improvisation, as with the *Goldberg Variations*. For the Q & A at the end of his Walker Arts Center lecture, Paxton humorously and brilliantly poses his own list of questions: here are two of them:

> PAXTON: What is the ratio of quickest time of non-conscious events [*sic*] to conscious ones? How many non-conscious events can happen in the duration of one conscious one (a ballpark figure)? (2014)

To attempt to answer these questions is already to make a change, not from habit to nonhabit but from *within* the habitual as it attains to consciousness in the looking and listening of the improviser. Paxton's moment of surprise. In a sense what Paxton describes as nonconscious and conscious events both obscure *the* event of dance itself, just as the structure of language obscures the event of the 'Real' in Lacanian psychoanalysis, and no one could be more suspicious of language than Steve Paxton.

As for Konjar, how does he actually answer Kilvady's question: 'why change?' Konjar:

It's not 'things', though. It's patterns of thinking. (Konjar 2011: 13)

Paxton often makes the distinction between the speed of language and the slowness of thought. His continuing collaboration and dialogue with Konjar, while rooted in dance, is primarily about their own patterns of thinking, over an increasingly long time, on and around dance, patterns that are singular, different, infinitely mobile, and thankfully unresolved. If Konjar is explicit in his desire to change his habitual patterns of thought, which for a dancer and improviser means a change in his dancing and improvisations, then the implication is that, for him, the event of dance can be sensed within the nonmechanistic 'plasticity' of habit itself. While Paxton's avowed desire to 'trick' habit in the name of a nonhabitual improvisatory freedom, outside of the structures of the 'I', has here been counterposed to Konjar's more neutral stance, perhaps their continuing dialogue is partly responsible for the more nuanced account of the *Goldberg Variations* offered more recently by Paxton, where being 'caught by surprise' describes a moment of transition between 'registers', forms, and structures rather than something beyond them: who knows?

If, as both Deleuze and Badiou agree, the event has either always already happened or has yet to come (Deleuze 2004: 73)[2] then perhaps the event of dance—'the life of dance'—can be jointly sensed in the mental and muscle-memory of Paxton on the one side and the observant waiting, patience, and expectancy of Konjar on the other: or is that just too glib?

Notes

1. I would like to thank Steve Purcell and Bush Hartshorn for inviting me to this event, and Karen Vedel for arranging my talk at the University of Copenhagen. I would also like to thank Jurij Konjar both for his performance and for coming along to the lecture the next day, which, incidentally, was not about dance or about him.
2. 'The event ... in its impassibility and its impenetrability has no present. It rather retreats and advances in two directions at once, being the perpetual object of a double question: What is going to happen? What has just happened? The agonizing aspect of the pure event is that it is always and at the same time something which has just happened and something about to happen; never something which is happening'.

References

Badiou, A. (2005) *Handbook of Inaesthetics*. Trans. Alberto Toscano. Stanford: Stanford University Press.

Bogue, R. (2013) *Deleuze on Music, Painting and the Arts*. London: Routledge.

Deleuze, G., (2001) *Difference and Repetition*. Trans. Paul Patton. London: Continuum.

Deleuze, G. (2004) *The Logic of Sense*. Trans. Mark Lester. London: Continuum.

Deleuze, G., and Guattari, F. (1987) *A Thousand Plateaus*. Trans. Brian Massumi. London: Athlone Press.

Deleuze, G., and Guattari, F. (1994) *What Is Philosophy?* Trans. Graham Burchill and Hugh Tomlinson. London: Verso.

Heidegger, M. (1995) *The Fundamental Concepts of Metaphysics*. Trans. William McNeill and Nicholas Walker. Bloomington: Indiana University Press.

Heidegger, M. (1999) *Contributions to Philosophy: From Enowning*. Trans. Parvis Emad and Kenneth Maly. Bloomington: Indiana University Press.

Heidegger, M. (2002) *Identity and Difference*. Trans. Joan Stambaugh. Chicago: University of Chicago Press.

Konjar, J. (2011) *Contact Quarterly, Chapbook 2*, 'The Goldberg Observations: Unwritable Notes on an Unthinkable Practice: From the working diary of Jurij Konjar, with Steve Paxton, Martin Kilvady, Lisa Nelson, Natasa Zavolovsek and Sandra Noeth'. Vol. 36 (Summer/ Fall) (2): 1–36.

Luhmann, N. (2000) *Art as a Social System*. Trans. Eva Knodt. Stanford: Stanford University Press.

Malabou, C. (2005) *The Future of Hegel: Plasticity, Temporality and Dialectic*. Trans. Lisabeth During. London: Routledge.

Nancy, J-L. (1998) 'The Surprise of the Event'. Trans. L Festa and S Barnett. In S. Barnett (ed.) *Hegel After Derrida*. London: Routledge.

Nietzsche, F. (1973) *Beyond Good and Evil*. Trans. R. J. Hollingdale. Harmondsworth, UK: Penguin Books.

Nietzsche, F. (1983) 'The Uses and Disadvantages of History for Life'. Trans. R. J. Hollingdale. In *Untimely Meditations*. Cambridge: Cambridge University Press.

Paxton, S. (2014) Talking Dance. Lecture, Walker Art Center 13 November 2014. https://www.youtube.com/watch?v=_82Od5NM4LI.

Ravaisson, F. (2008) *Of Habit*. Trans. Clare Carlisle and Mark Sinclair. London: Continuum.

CHAPTER 13

UNPREDICTABLE MANOEUVRES

Eva Karczag's Improvised Strategies for Thwarting Institutional Agendas

DORAN GEORGE

To the sustained whimper of Malcolm Goldstein's barely changing violin tones, the generous arc in Eva Karczag's spine, extended by her head and neck, draws her effortlessly to the ground as her legs judiciously collapse beneath in agreement. We are at (the now canonized) Judson Memorial Church in New York's Greenwich Village, witnessing the end of *Wrapt Concurrence,* a twenty-five-minute improvised dance and live music collaboration. Rocking her pelvis laterally, Karczag sidles diagonally forward, building to a shake throughout her whole body till she finds what seems like a supine resting position. Between her small fists, held with bent elbows above her shoulders, tension gathers, ultimately flushing her body open into another arch that transits her backward across the floor of Judson's nave. With a counter-melody of flexing limbs, her retracting shoulders and hips, undulations of the spine, and delicate motion of digits all interrupt the rolling-and-opening-out. In an erratic inconstancy of speed, small and subtle jerks and slides punctuate Karczag's melting and fracturing, all of which she weaves into a seamless movement tapestry. Her kinetic complexity hinders my attempts to archive *Wrapt Concurrence* in words, a problem with which dance writers are familiar. Yet Karczag basks in motility's elusiveness, as she bewilderingly vacillates, with her capricious use of tempo, between fine motor movement and change in her spatial configuration. I sample here only traces of the final two minutes of her dance; and Karczag's motile contrariety, defies anyone to chronicle the other twenty-three. In figures 13.1 and 13.2 we see these qualities in Karczag's dancing as captured in the still image.

Wendy Perron, who like Karczag choreographed her own artistic vision after dancing for Trisha Brown, registers the same virtuoso subtlety I observe in Karczag's improvisatory dancing. Perron recounts 'something incredible' that Karczag conveys 'just twisting her hands'. Yet even while wondering if she should have chosen a similar aesthetic for

FIG. 13.1 Christian Kip, in taking this 2014 photograph of Eva Karczag performing an improvisation at the Coventry festival 'Summer Dancing', organized by Decoda, purposefully let the
dancers' movement blur the image. Kip thus gestures towards the unpredictable elusiveness that
Karczag often stages.

an upcoming show, Perron ultimately infantilizes Karczag's approach: 'I'm used to intimacy', she asserts, 'and I know I can always do inward sorts of things, but I'm trying
to be more grown up' (Perron in Goldberg and Albright 1987: 43). She is referring to
Karczag's dependence on audience proximity, not possible in larger spaces. Indeed,
Wrapt Concurrence's audience shared the dance floor, flanking three sides, no more than
a few rows deep, while the dancer was sometimes within reach of the front row. For its
legibility, the understated vocabulary relied on such immediacy, along with an overall
wash of 'work-light' that made the audience and dancer equally visible. However, Perron
sees artistic development as depending on progressing beyond such intimacy with vocabulary that is visible in large concert houses.

Perron belies Karczag's choice of salon-style performances and, by describing the
dance as 'inward sorts of things', points to but fails to grasp Karczag's negotiation of the
politics of theatrical spectatorship. Perron is in good company because, despite a substantial contribution to the professional and educational field, Karczag has received little
critical attention, probably because her improvising circumnavigates some institutional

demands that Perron reifies. Nevertheless, because Karczag also invests in some broadly held beliefs in contemporary dance, I am theorizing her marginality to help elucidate some wider issues. Karczag deploys a dominant discourse on the dancing body, which is that the sources for her motile efficiency and innovation are inherent in anatomical function. Yet through her elusiveness, she nevertheless rejects large concert house protocols and the prevailing pedagogy of most training institutions. Constructing the body as naturally unpredictable, Karczag conceives of improvisation as the logical means for performing corporeal authenticity, a practice that the demands of large spaces, to which dance training tends to direct itself, usually extinguish. Therefore, while sharing a dominant understanding of the dancing body with most contemporary dancers, choreographers, and educators, Karczag teaches and performs a 'slipperiness' that large theatres and dance training programs struggle to grasp.

To claim critical significance for Karczag's practice, I categorize and theorize distinct threads in her methodology, structurally eliding her trope of unpredictability. A recollection from my time as Karczag's student at the Dutch European Dance Development Center in the 1990s illustrates this problem. Referring to 'tensegrity' (Juhan 1987), Karczag used a small three-dimensional model of wooden beams joined by elastic to demonstrate how activity in any one locale of the body, as in the model, affects the whole structure. Yet replicating this idea would demand textual opacity, something like Peggy Phelan's 'performative writing' (Phelan 1993), which I fear would obfuscate Karczag's work for readers not already invested in such marginal practices—something that writing on improvisation can easily do (Novack 1990: 19). I have therefore opted to dissect rather than be caught in Karczag's methodological web. This chapter first positions her improvisation of a natural body sociopolitically and then explores how, along with other improvisers, she resists trends that resulted from the corporatization of late twentieth-century contemporary dance. Looking back on the lineage from which Karczag draws, I go on to theorize how improvising nature established itself as a strategy for claiming creative freedom. Looking closely at her methodology, I conclude that Karczag displaces the productivity that corporate dance culture commonly attributes to a natural body. With meandering elusiveness, she flouts the demand for efficiency and innovation.

IMPROVISING NATURE

Karczag concurs with large numbers of artists and educators in her insistence that dancers cultivate optimum capacity for movement execution, providing unlimited resources for creativity, by accessing the body's anatomical functional imperatives. She sees herself as 'disentangling the imprints of social, cultural influences, and genetic heritage, revealing the mechanics'. Imagining a precultural or essential body that releases dance from culture's impact, Karczag aims to access functional imperatives, such that 'movement choices are less obscured or impeded, and we have greater physical availability, in order to be able to express what lies in us all … our bodies can become more available and responsive'. When I talk of the natural body that Karczag constructs, I am thus referring to the her conviction about ideas such as these:

> the way a ball and socket joint moves, and how that's different from the movement of the structures of the skull; the fact that the diaphragm pulls down on the in-breath (no matter what culture, color, sexual orientation, kind of parents, schooling, religious upbringing one might have had); the way the multi-jointedness of the foot allows us to walk on uneven terrain and cushions our running (tho this can change thru wearing heavy, stiff-soled shoes at all times, or Nikes, or high heeled shoes, or having one's feet bound, or walking on concrete …), the way the shoulder blade is in the back, not the front of the body.… everyone, no matter who they are, or where they come from, needs to eat, digest, eliminate; our hearts beat, blood flows thru our system, we all breathe, sneeze, cough, fart.[1]

The uptake of such ideas accompanied the proliferation of regimens that broadly became known as 'somatics'. I am conceiving of somatics as a culture, held together by aesthetic and pedagogical alliances in which dancers implement biological and mechanical constructs as the logic for dance classes, claiming to uncover a more 'natural' way of moving (Gilbert 2014). Not all practitioners of these regimens will agree with this characterization, but I maintain that because the training is so central to the conception of the body in contemporary dance, its investment in 'nature' deserves deconstructing. In line with cultural studies scholars who show that the term 'nature' functions ideologically (Butler 1990; Foucault 1978; Foster 1986), I warn elsewhere that, with somatic ideas having achieved dominance in the professional field, the idea of naturalness conceals cultural specificity. Non-Western traditions, nonwhite bodies, and transgender expression risk marginalization through a process in which aesthetics gets stratified into groups who are thought to be more or less authentically natural (Gilbert 2014: 1).

Karczag's definition of improvisation exemplifies the problems with 'nature'. Constructing corporeality as in constant flux, she attributes to it unforeseen motile possibility, and thereby participates in an improvisatory tradition that enshrines early 1960s New York Greenwich Village as an artistic watershed. Brenda Dixon Gottschild defines this lineage, which she calls 'downtown dance' (referring to its association with lower Manhattan), as racially white (Gottschild 2003: 20). Indeed, for one example, the conception of improvisation as navigating the unknown contrasts greatly to Ghanaian dance, in which kinetic and rhythmic traditions are sustained through responsive improvisation between musicians and dancers (Cohen-Bull [Novack] 1997). This difference is far from benign because, as Dixon Gottschild points out, racism erases the roots of American culture in the African aesthetic legacies that survived the Middle Passage (Gottschild 1996). The rarely recognized influence of jazz music on early 1960s Greenwich Village dancers is a case in point (Banes 1993; Forti 1974). Moreover, like Ghanaian dance, African American improvisation sustains and extends black traditions, resisting cultural whitewashing (Foster 1998: 15). A discourse that claims the natural status of improvisational unpredictability thus erases its cultural specificity and positions Africanist traditions as less 'authentic' in their preservation of what is known.

Yet while Karczag risks participating in cultural dominance, her marginal position betrays how the institutionalization of somatics unevenly distributes its benefits to white as well as nonwhite artists. Through recourse to nature, a small group of 1960s and 1970s dancers initially used anatomical knowledge to care for their bodies rather than meet punishing aesthetic protocols, and they reconfigured their role from interpretive to creative artists with somatic procedures for generating vocabulary (Gilbert 2014). Choreographers capitalized on this shift by creating strategies for making dances that showcased greater diversity in vocabulary. But the new approach dovetailed with the corporatization of American concert dance, when programmers became increasingly dependent on businesses that sponsored the arts to gain visibility and respectability. Corporate funding engendered choreography that could guarantee audiences while appearing to be innovative, which pressured artists to establish recognizable signatures, in the face of shrinking resources for experimentation (Foster 2002: 131–139). Americans such as Brown, Bill T. Jones, and Petronio and Brits such as Siobhan Davies and Lloyd Newson developed strategies that were taken up more widely in which dancers created or improvised with their choreographers' signature vocabulary to create set compositions (Gilbert 2014: 370). Consequently, as somatics hit premier Western concert stages, the choreographer's visibility overshadowed the dancers' contribution even as the creative burden on dancers grew. The popularization of somatics thus neglects the 'liberation' that dancers had initially sought, even as these same concert dance works depended on the new procedures for making dance through which that liberation had been achieved decades earlier.

Karczag resists the changes in the significance of the 'natural body' that came with the institutionalization of somatic experimentation. Through improvisation's unpredictability, she stages the dancer's creativity rather than concealing it within the interpretive role. By insisting on the motile unpredictability of the body's natural flux, Karczag also improvises opposition to the growing corporate arts pressure for vocabulary that appears innovative, but also tried and tested. Against what she sees as the subjugation of dancers to the creative dicta of set choreography, she charges corporeality with elusiveness, insisting: 'institutionalization very often deadens and makes static the bodymind that is actually movement and constant change'.[2] With its apparent space for the unknown, improvisation thus emerges as the logical modality for accessing and performing the natural body as it theorized in Karczag's use of somatics.

Karczag has consequently failed to achieve institutional legitimacy not only because she resists dominant aesthetics but also because she does so with a theory of nature that has fallen into scholarly disrepute. Tracing her deployment of nature reveals how she contests patterns of subjugation in contemporary dance using the very idea of precultural corporeality that corporate arts culture has appropriated. Karczag thus stages resistance within contemporary dance's hegemonic characterization of the dancing body, that is, she works within a belief system that is widely considered the only reasonable option. This leads me to prioritize the ends for which the discourse on nature is used, rather than settling with a critique of the discourse alone. My approach parallels studies that observe how the category of 'diversity', designed to resist marginalization on the basis of race, sexuality, and disability, can be used to compound power imbalances in institutionalized dance cultures (Adair 2007; Albright 1997; Foster 2001). Nevertheless, to establish Karczag's critical importance, I articulate the ideological character of her natural body, contesting her core assumption of foundational truth. Yet by revealing how she wields her theory of nature, I restore her authorship and provide some of the critical visibility she has largely been denied. Prompts and procedures she creates, based on the assumption of essential movement capacity, cultivate a dancing body that eludes the reliability and productivity of the 'natural' body on which corporate dance culture depends.

Navigating Corporate Arts Culture

Karczag's participation in an institutionalized discourse on the natural body indicates a precarious position that she occupies in the professional field. Along with other solo improvisers, she capitalizes on the growth of choreographer-led companies based on a signature style, even while rejecting that model. Steve Paxton, Lisa Nelson, and Daniel Lepkoff, all of whom Karczag cites as influences, as well as Simone Forti, Laurie Booth, Kirstie Simpson, and Julyen Hamilton, all assert their individual bodies as inextricable from their artistic perspective and methodology. They stage vocabulary as not able to be emulated in the way that companies based on signature choreography depend. Yet while resisting dominant corporate arts protocols, these artists model and teach creative autonomy, securing positions as masters for training entrepreneurial dancers. As much as they critique the institutionalization of the dancer's autonomy in signature-company-culture, solo improvisers thus survive by contributing to their students' ability to compete for jobs in contemporary companies (Gilbert 2014: 157). They fill full-time or visiting positions at conservatories and universities and lead workshops for independent dance organizations and successful studios such as Brown's or Davies's. Furthermore, large theaters demonstrate their edginess by occasionally programming solo improvised concerts (307).

My association of Karczag with artists such as Paxton and Forti, who occupy a marginal position whilst at the same time having achieved canonization, exemplifies solo improvisers' contradictory position. Forti and Paxton both enjoy critical attention as veterans of 1960s experimentation (Banes 1980, 1993), and art institutions celebrate them in a turn of visual art towards movement. Art museums focus on Forti's minimal 1960s movement work, *The Dance Constructions* (Banes 1980: 26), and Paxton's central role in the creation of contact improvisation (Novack 1990: 52). Based on instructions that produce a recognizable event, museums frame Forti's work as conceptual and as signifying a history for which the art world is nostalgic (Lambery 2004). Meanwhile, as new training and vocabulary, contact improvisation achieved significance in its application to set choreography, including incorporation into ballet (Schaffman 2001). Similarly, Karczag enjoys a history of adulation for her dancing with Britain's Strider in the early 1970s, with Australia's Dance Exchange later that decade, and then with Brown into the mid-1980s, when the dance press lauded each of these companies as cutting edge. Renowned New York critic Deborah Jowitt, for example, describes Karczag as having 'graced' Brown's company, indicating the reverence with which her skills are viewed (Jowitt 1994).

Yet improvisation that foregrounds unpredictability fails to attract comparable attention from institutions which are relying on the dependability of a choreographic signature. The output of the early 1970s company Grand Union, whose members constitute a veritable who's who of 1960s experimentation including Paxton and Brown, has largely eluded institutional attention, with work that is harder to pin down than contact improvisation and Forti's early work (Foster 2002: 79–84). When the Los Angeles Getty Center hosted a retrospective of Yvonne Rainer (the initiator of Grand Union), rather than restage works, they used performance ephemera to represent the company (Rainer 2014). Meanwhile, long-term improvisation projects begun by Paxton and Forti in the 1980s—Paxton's work with J. S. Bach's *Goldberg Variations* and Forti's project using press clippings, *The News Animations*—have received little critical attention (Burt 2002).[3] Likewise, Karczag's improvisation inhabits the margins. Further research could also reveal the degree to which solo improvisers' income levels reflect their marginality relative to company choreographers. For example, Karczag left full-time employment at the European Dance Development Center after disagreements about pedagogy, and as full-time faculty at the University of Illinois, Simpson is a rarity. Karczag and other solo improvisers thus pursue their approaches despite experiencing greater economic and cultural precariousness than choreographers with signature companies do.

The value of the trouble that solo improvisation poses for institutions is that artists are able to invest in an idea of the dancers' creative agency as it was conceived independently from the corporatization of contemporary dance. For example, dancer-scholar Emilyn Claid characterizes Simpson as exceeding concert dance's dominant protocols. She does so in a way that references the uniqueness of her body by gesturing towards the dancer's exceptional height and rambunctious vocabulary. Claid describes her as a 'powerful physical presence that could never be contained within the constraints of contemporary dance' (2006: 74). Although some of the artists mentioned here distance themselves from somatics, they all connect improvisation and ideas about nature by performing the investigation of their singular physicalities (Gilbert 2014: 92, 101). Theorizing corporeal unpredictability through somatics, Karczag provides a blueprint for the role of a conceit of (belief in) the natural body for solo improvisation. While she was key to the dissemination of somatics, she remains committed to improvisation as the optimum means to stage natural capacity, an idea that lost traction as the creativity of the dancer came to be overshadowed. Even while somatics is now taught in many of the world's most venerable dance schools, Karczag lacks the visibility of some of her contemporaries, in part because she turned away from set composition.

In summation, for her precarious foothold in contemporary dance, Karczag relies on a ubiquity that the concept of the natural body has achieved. The foundational status of somatics in late twentieth-century dance training thus figures 'nature' as a privileged term for both embodying and critiquing dominant conventions. Constructing an unpredictable natural body provided Karczag with a powerful and legible counter-discourse to the marshalling of somatics towards producing choreographic signatures. This use of somatics within companies that are based on a signature vocabulary is evident, for example, in dancers' use of Klein and Alexander (somatic) techniques to meet the demands of dancing in companies like Brown's, which I have historicized elsewhere (Gilbert 2014: 140). But by the same token, many dancers find value in Karczag's insistence on the natural body's potency and her rigorous cultivation of kinaesthetic awareness. This has made her approach valuable for reconstructing Brown's repertory in dance education programs and for teaching in major cultural centres. However, with procedures underpinned by the conceit of naturalness, dancers contest as much as they serve institutionalization, both erasing and foregrounding cultural differences. For example, despite having defined downtown as white, Dixon Gottschild argues that somatics, which is generally associated with lower Manhattan's dance scene, afforded African Americans and others a way to resist the idealization of a white body (2003: 184). Karczag embodies these contradictions in somatics: she compounds the natural body's foundational status by insisting that the skills she teaches are corporeally inherent, and she contributes to the culture of the dancer as entrepreneur by cultivating autonomy. Yet by constructing bodily unpredictability, she throws a spanner in the works of corporate arts culture's call for set-signature-vocabulary and compliant dancers.

FOREGROUNDING THE DANCER'S CREATIVITY

By theorizing improvisation as a means to source each body's unique creativity, Karczag and other artists invested the dancer role with the creative agency previously ascribed to choreographers. They centralized 'bodily intelligence' in composition, building on a 1960s push for creative freedom that extended the midcentury avant-garde's concerns. Artists such as Merce Cunningham and Ann Halprin feared that the 1950s institutionalization of modern dance had resulted in 'artistic authoritarianism', stifling creative freedom as part of wider threats to social liberties (Morris 2006; Ross 2007). The idea that choreographers imposed styles on dancers met opposition in a link that this new generation made between nature, training, and compositional modalities— an approach for which they drew on somatic and Eastern philosophies such as Zen Buddhism (Gilbert 2014: 72–82). For the 1960s avant-garde, improvisation emerged as a key strategy through which, as Banes asserts, 'the dancer be not just a dancing body, but a thinking dancing body', by making explicit the 'free associative, improvisatory, decision making process in performance' (1993: 242). Artists such as Paxton, Brown, and Forti saw themselves as freeing creative capacity in performance by listening to impulses from within and between their respective bodies (Gilbert 2014: 279).

For early 1960s artists, improvisation effectively unearthed inherent bodily intelligence that had been subjugated by modern dance authoritarianism, a conviction that Karczag recycles to 'disentangle essential corporeality from culture's impact'. In Rainer's 1964 text *Some Thoughts on Improvisation*, Banes identifies the idea that 'compositional ideas or impulses ... have a purely physical nature,' concluding that 'consciousness for Rainer was formed in and by the material of the body' (1993: 242). Dancers thus contested Cartesian consciousness, associated with Martha Graham (Franko 1995: 40), in which intellectual volition drives a passive body (Thomas 2003: 34). By the 1970s, new techniques were claimed to access intrinsic physical capacity, replacing preexisting aesthetic ideals in training and choreography. An integrated and universal natural-artistic-identity emerged (Banes 2003), rejecting modern dance master narratives and the accompanying choreographer's authority. Approaches like contact improvisation and Anatomical Release work established nature as a source of creative uniqueness in each dancer by theorizing the embodiment of terrestrial forces (like gravity and momentum) in anatomical structure as a basis for kinetic decision-making. Dancers thus saw their movement as governed by a shared physical 'reality', performing unique in-the-moment reactions to a changing group endeavour, as an interdependent community of individuals.

By 'liberating' the dancer, collective projects of the 1960s and 1970s precipitated new ways of imagining dancing and choreography. For example, Banes theorizes both contact improvisation and Grand Union as asserting the dancer's creative agency by staging explicit real-time choices made by dancers (2003: 78–81). Paxton extended this focus on what he calls 'those who were seen to be the pawns in the game; the dancers', by exploring 'the source and processing of choreographic movement'.[4] Through attention to the minutia of the body's workings, he configured the labour traditionally associated with dancers (how to execute rather than compose movement) as a choreographic endeavour. He impacted the field profoundly, through what dancer and writer (and ex–company member with Brown) Lisa Kraus calls his 'methodical, curious trials' with how the body functions, which for her resulted in the 'cultivation of ... awareness–beyond any particular form'. She argues: 'whole generations of dancers ... have been made sensitive, curious and respectful of the body's sensations and delicate instinctual dances of balance which most often go unnoticed' (2014). Kraus's description recalls Perron's characterization of Karczag's detail as 'inward sorts of things', a connection that bespeaks how both Paxton and Karczag perform the dancer's intelligence as a choreographic endeavour.

Karczag's career trajectory exemplifies the ways dancers extricated themselves from the apparent tyranny of traditional company modalities. She ceased dancing for the London Festival Ballet precisely because of its size and hierarchical structure, recalling that some corps de ballet had been performing minimal movement to frame soloists for years. She sought creative satisfaction in 1970s collective improvisational projects to which the idea of individual natural authenticity was central. Strider, the collective Karczag joined after abandoning ballet, rejected the hierarchy its members had experienced in the classical and recently established Graham-based British modern dance establishments (Jordan 1992: 1). Credited with being Britain's first independent contemporary dance company (18), Strider differentiated dancer and choreographer roles more than contact improvisation and Grand Union, but rather than 'imposing' a style, choreographers 'facilitated' the dancers' creation of vocabulary.[5] Inaugurated along similar lines by ex-Strider dancers, Dance Exchange, which Karczag joined later in the 1970s, also relied on the dancers' creativity to generate choreography.[6]

Emphasizing the body's creative intelligence, the British and Australian outfits, much like contact improvisation and Grand Union, employed improvisational approaches, albeit in a distinct manner. Banes calls contact improvisation and Grand Union's approaches 'situation-response composition', because the dancers responded to the situation in which they were dancing with vocabulary that was not set prior to performing (Banes 2003: 79). By contrast, Strider and Dance Exchange collective members generated set material through improvisation, with which they then sometimes extemporized in performance. Artists such as Brown and Forti, as well Rosemary Butcher in Britain, used this collaborative creative approach, asserting the dancers' contribution no less than collective situation-response composition (Gilbert 2014: 313–331). With Karczag as a company member, Brown made some of the dances with which she established her choreographic signature, such as *Son of Gone Fishin'* (1981) and *Set and Reset* (1983). Brown and her dancers fulfilled tasks and improvised with material Brown taught. Banes argues that in 1980s downtown New York, such practices became increasingly important for composition (2003: 82). In contrast with ballet's division of creative labour between choreographers and dancers, Karczag, who also danced for Butcher, recalls sharing concerns and values with the artists for whom she danced, resulting in easier communication than at the London Festival Ballet.

Collaborative composition depended on new skills that dancers developed as they pursued what they saw as their liberation. Karczag made key contributions to the companies for which she danced by actively severing her training from set-choreography. Theorizing late twentieth-century contemporary training, Melanie Bales defines this process as a paradigm shift that began in Paxton, Forti, and Brown's 1960s artistic scene, when concert vocabulary, having reflected the forms learned in dance class (in both ballet and modern dance), ceased to do so (Bales 2008: 29). Unlike in the 1990s and beyond, when training offered dancers a dexterous capacity to create a range of material (Foster 1997: 253–256), the 1970s saw few independent regimens. While many dancers studied at Cunningham's studio, for Karczag this approach replicated a balletic line she sought to escape, and conflicted with the physicality she had developed in t'ai chi, Alexander Technique, and Anatomical Release work with Mary Fulkerson. She thus consolidated alternatives to learning by rote in explorative movement training. Collaborating with others, she drew from contact improvisation, Nancy Topf's Anatomical Release work, and Bonnie Bainbridge Cohen's Body-Mind Centering, as well as Andre Bernard's ideokinesis, which Eric Hawkins had used in his technique

(Gilbert 2014: 115). With skills in exploration that were honed for improvising new material, Karczag and her colleagues affirmed the creative value of a collaborative creative modality.

Improvisation and somatics, with their central role in collaborative choreographic processes, fuelled the development of new vocabularies, affirming the potential of dancers' creative agency. Strider and Dance Exchange softened Cunningham's vocabulary using the dancers' knowledge of anatomical function developed in somatic training, and they performed 'pedestrian movement' in Fulkerson's compositions for these companies (Gilbert 2014, chap. 2). Meanwhile, using related ideas and dancers' aptitudes, Brown synthesized complex, novel vocabulary that was thought to be more 'natural' to the body than classical and modern lexicons (Bales 2008: 160). Collaborative, improvisational processes thus signified not only dancers' liberation from authoritarianism but also new expressive potential for choreographers. Dancers also sought vocabulary that, with its claim of working with intrinsic physical capacity, seemed to engender greater autonomy. Karczag, for example, even before dancing for the company, saw potential in Brown's use of detail, while Kraus discovered the applied value of her somatic training in Brown's lexicon; an experience Karczag also recalls (118). The dancer's creative contribution subsequently extended its centrality to contemporary dance, when Brown's dancers began teaching the company repertory in new training and ultimately established their own companies (117–126).[7]

RESISTING THE DEMISE OF THE DANCER'S CREATIVE AGENCY

The very success of dancer-choreographer collaborations contributed to the demise of the dancers agency when 1990s training normalized the dancer-as-entrepreneur. Brown's transnational success saw her signature overshadow her dancers' contribution, a shift I have traced elsewhere in the staging and reception of the repertory (Gilbert 2014: 367–369): Late 1970s dancers enjoyed latitude in their execution, a uniqueness that critics lauded in Kraus, Karczag, and Brown. Yet as the twentieth century progressed, the dancers again became pawns, to borrow Paxton's term, both in rehearsals where they learned material by rote and in critical receptions of the work that ignored dancers' individuality. This pattern reflects how America's corporate arts culture sought star choreographers who had established themselves in New York's press with work that would read well in large theatres and was appealing to provincial audiences (Novack 1990: 224–227). Choreographers benefited from the collaborative strategies developed in the 1970s as they ascended within the new arts economy, even as funding for creative investigation dramatically diminished (Foster 2002: 139), To develop signature work without extended experimentation, younger choreographers depended on dancers who could improvise and take care of their bodies with the skills afforded by somatic training.

The visibility of the dancers' intelligence thus disappeared in two distinct but related ways. First, beginning in the 1980s, situation-response composition was too risky for programmers (Banes 2003: 81), contributing to the dissolution of groups like Grand Union. In a related manner, Strider lost state support in the mid-1970s when they began staging the somatic and improvisational practices they had learned from Fulkerson. Committed to respectable concert dance, and following America's lead, the Arts Council of England considered such experimentation to be detrimental to a contemporary British concert dance (De Wit 2000: 102). Second, the dancers' role within companies, of generating vocabulary, collapsed into old company hierarchies because choreographers advanced their careers as the 'creators' of work, while the dancers' collaborative role was naturalized as subordinate through the widely used phrase 'choreographed by ... with the dancers', which denies the dancers the cultural capital of choreographic agency that translates into a reputation that attracts financial and programming support (Reynoso 2011). Sharing Paxton's interest in the 'pawn in the game', Karczag left Brown's company in the early 1980s because, with its success, she felt her value as an innovator disappear. During rehearsals in large theatres, she also recalls watching the detail that she had so valued get lost, at a time when Brown was considering having a rehearsal director.

Solo improvisation solves a number of problems for artists such as Karczag, who remain invested in the dancers' agency despite the changes in contemporary dance's economy. By performing movement exploration as a 'situation-response composition' within a single body, solo improvisers stage the dancer's creativity in the nontransferability of their vocabulary. The low overheads of not running a company also brings relative economic independence and greater flexibility, even while artists who choose this approach are on the margins of contemporary dance's venue and training network relative to choreographer-led companies. However, although the marginal status of solo improvisation often means performing in smaller spaces, Karczag seeks such intimacy because it promotes the elements in Brown's work to which she was initially attracted. In the 1970s, the intimate New York venues in which Karczag first saw Brown's work confirmed what she felt watching Strider: 'the small details, the gestures were very visible', which for her meant that the dancers could be seen as human beings, in contrast with the distance and the orchestra pit's wall of sound that obscured them from the large concert house audiences for whom Karczag performed with the London Festival Ballet. Moreover, Brown didn't want audiences to be lulled into knowing what was going to happen, revealing to Karczag the potency of kinetic unpredictability. Yet when Brown's elusiveness gave way to a recognizable signature under the demand to project in large spaces, Karczag resuscitated unpredictability by improvising bodily flux in salon-style performances where the dancer's responsiveness achieves visibility.

Karczag ultimately asserted her creative agency by pushing idiosyncrasy beyond Brown's signature. It was by consolidating an aesthetic of beauty, recognizable in a certain ease, flow, and complexity of set material, that Brown met corporate arts culture's demands. Yet in smaller spaces that don't attract such sponsorship, Karczag flouts the demand to establish such a tried and tested vocabulary. Her pedagogy as faculty at the Dutch European Dance Development Center exhibited such aims. In a 1993 document, she comments on a new institutional directive for students to study 'complex movement', noting that the term 'usually means making movement material, remembering material, often in the form of phrases, and … with the remembered movement material … making … solos or … setting … group structures'. By contrast, in the same document Karczag conceives of complexity as 'moving that arises through improvisation, and the enrichment of each person's complexity of moving through the experiences of internal changes brought about: by touch; through the quality and intent of each person's looking and all that that can teach; through giving and receiving thoughtful feedback; and through … instructions that challenge each person to fulfil a task that has the potential of carrying them beyond habitual ways of moving'.[8] In her teaching as much as her performing, she privileged improvisation as a means by which dancers could invest in movement investigation as an aesthetic practice in and of itself rather than to produce vocabulary within the remit of a company.

METHODOLOGY

For Karczag, the creative potential of bodily logic resides in a fluctuating nature that can never be grasped in its totality by rational thought; situation-response composition represents the means to access this bodily intelligence, sustaining Rainer's insistence on corporeality's role in consciousness. For dancers to connect with their physicality, they must 'stay in the moment' by listening to the body. Karczag found the imperative of such responsiveness in t'ai chi's 'martial arts' readiness for the unexpected, and the integration into human volition of changes in anatomy's delicate balance at which Alexander Technique aims. For example, Alexandrian tactile feedback, commonly called 'hands-on', connects the receiver with his use of anatomical structure in what Karczag calls a 'reality check' (Dempster and Karzag 1996: 41). By 'putting yourself into the moment, not ahead of yourself, not behind yourself but right there', she believes that choreographic decisions can be made by cultivating an imaginative awareness of kinetic actions and responses (43). Karczag calls this 'non-composing composing', of which she says: 'while allowing material to unfold, I am also rooting myself in a compositional mind and the longer I work, the more aware I become of the skill and virtuosity it demands to be in both places at once'.[9] To understand Karczag as only focused on inner experience, as Perron seems to, thus fails to grasp her representation of the dancer's creative labour by consciously staging the immediacy of her unfolding kinetics through attending to the overall topography of her composition.

Karczag believes that attentiveness to bodily fluctuation affords the creative freedom she observed in, for example, Paxton's intense focus on being present, and in the myriad choices she saw Lepkoff make in the same dance for which she attended multiple performances. As a source for the unique and unlimited vocabulary of a particular dancing body, she cultivates kinaesthetic awareness (Dempster and Karzag 1996: 41). T'ai chi and the Alexander Technique promote 'released' muscle, 'not flaccid but ready', by reducing tension and facilitating movement's free flow. Along with many other dancers, Karczag uses this awareness to gain a heightened sense of moving in what she calls a 'lightness' of the body. She cultivates a consciousness, also influenced by Alexander training, of how movement choices are being made, aiming to move beyond motile habits, while t'ai chi and contact improvisation offer an image of the body's roundness and 360 degrees of spatial awareness, affording readiness in any direction. Karczag thus expands her motile possibilities by responding, with readiness, to multidirectional images and sensations of movement as they arise in the moment. Corporeality's capacity to process and execute an unanticipated constellation of kinetics thus constitutes for her the bodily intelligence with which she engages in situation-response composition; through kinaesthetic awareness of her bodily motion, she both witnesses (noncomposing) while authoring (composing) her dance.

In her diversification of vocabulary, Karczag participated in a burgeoning of somatics in downtown dance. An 'East Village' scene, emerging in the 1980s, put 'nature' to increasingly contradictory uses with the belief that anatomical function provides a carte blanche for unlimited movement possibilities. Contesting Reagan-era cultural conservatism and critiquing exclusionary ideologies such as whiteness, patriarchy, and heterosexuality, East Village dancers opposed the instrumentalization of

FIG. 13.2. Here we see Eva Karczag, improvising for Nienke Terpsma's lens in 1986, seemingly simultaneously experiencing (witnessing) the full weight of her torso opening into the floor, while she remains attentive with her head and limbs to the immediate and broader space around her, thereby composing the dance, listening for the next moment.

the body for an imposed vocabulary. They represented individuality as diverse socio-cultural experiences, still imagining inherent corporeal potential as their source for movement. Like the solo improvisers, who also contributed to the East Village scene, they aimed to bring their truth to composition rather than subjugate themselves to a choreographer's vision. Yet, as Sally Banes notes, this new generation questioned the precultural artistic identities of the 1970s by staging identity politics in an increasingly racially diverse community (Banes 2003: 81–82). Ishmael Houston-Jones and Bill T. Jones, for example, improvised black queer identities, inaugurating a critique of dance that claimed precultural status (Gilbert 2014: 292). Yet Houston-Jones attributed his ability to crash into walls, the floor, and other dancers to the facility Karczag claims for released muscle (129). With similar vigorous movement, Yvonne Meier, Jennifer Monson, and Stephanie Skura flouted feminine propriety (Gilbert 2014; Albright 1997). The East Village dancers thus engendered irreverence, embodying frustration and dismay at the eroding of reproductive rights and the blaming of the AIDS crisis on the sick and dying (George 2015, 2011, , 2017). Moreover, on the same off-off-Broadway types of stages, Jawole Willa Jo Zollar's company The Urban Bush Women claimed improvisation's African heritage and contested misunderstandings of African movement cultures (Gottschild 2003: 176–187).

White artists and audiences dominated the East Village scene at the time (Albright 1997: 20), a dominance which explains the continuing conception of improvisation as unpredictability. Nonetheless, although white artists rarely reflected on their racial specificity, many aligned themselves with and took inspiration from the critique articulated by black artists such as Houston-Jones. The unpredictability of improvising, and its' association with natural facility as a means to generate vocabulary, means that improvisation was viewed as means to tackle social exigencies. Techniques that combined training and creativity using improvisation, as Anatomical Release work had done, consequently thrived in the East Village. Skinner Releasing seemed to broaden vocabulary possibilities by supplanting anatomical images such as 'up the back and down the front' with poetic natural ones like 'the bone joints are sea sponges' or 'the legs are shadows falling from a bottomless well at the solar plexus'. Meanwhile, dancing with their eyes closed, students of Authentic Movement aimed to release the kinetic vicissitudes of their psyches.

Rather than staging explicit social themes, Karczag claims natural bodily unpredictability as her content, seeing herself as investigating pure movement, as she did in the 1980s. Yet I want to align her, and other solo improvisers who prioritize movement investigation over themes, with the East Village politicization of dance. For example, Claid saw Simpson as contravening concert dance's conventional femininity, describing her as having, 'no physical boundaries ... no feminine pretense, no primness; she is out in the open, free from constraint' (2006: 74). Similarly, in her decisive rejection of classical line and explicit concern with physical sensation rather than her appearance, Karczag resists conventional dancing white femininity. Furthermore, despite, and in fact because of, the different intent behind her dances, Karczag's choreography reveals the ways artists resolved some problems in representing social themes during a time when the discourse on a natural body achieved increasing ubiquity. She *performs* the methodology that dancers who were engaging political content left in the training studio.

Karczag's work thus provides insight into a contradiction Banes identifies in 1980s New York improvisation. Banes argues that the construction of social categories such as race, gender, and sexuality relied on essentialist rhetoric which 'postmodernism in the cultural/theoretical sphere denies' and which instead proposed a theory of the self as fragmented (2003: 81). Academic suspicion towards the idea of a natural body, which I noted early on in this essay, also rejects essentialism. To extend Banes's idea, I suggest that rather than achieving integration through recourse to nature, which 1970s artists felt they were doing, 1980s artists grappled explicitly with 'culture' by staging a fragmentation of the self. For example, to illustrate the conflict, Banes refers to John Jasperse's improvisation of a gay identity (an essential truth) through his simultaneous embodiment of masculine and feminine codes (the fragmenting affect of cultural constructions). She distinguishes his dance from the integrated self of 1970s androgyny that was understood to be continuous with nature (81) and was achieved by theorizing anatomical function as equivalent for both sexes, in contact improvisation and Anatomical Releasing, for example. Jasperse's dance reveals a contradiction between essentialist identity, as in the supposed foundational 'truth' of being gay, and fragmentation, as in the simultaneous embodiment of oppositional signs of gender that signify 'gayness' whereby essence is conveyed as a social theme. Karczag eschews explicit themes, yet her work reveals a similar shift from the 1970s to the 1980s in the deployment of functional anatomy with which artists such as Jasperse nevertheless worked in their training.

In her move from Brown's company to solo improvisation, Karczag exhibits the shift from an integrated to a fragmented embodiment of somatics. She refined her articulateness by investigating 'not moving, not making the logical choice'. In this sense, she configures an adagio-like flow as her 'particular habit in the Alexandrian sense'. Inhibiting the loose-limbed continuity that had characterized her dancing for Brown, Karczag postulated that new movement possibility resided underneath her habit, deeper within her body. Working with Authentic Movement, she cultivated an 'internal witness' to track her habit of flow and open up kinetic choices (Whitehouse 1999: 153–155).[10] Essentialist ideas thus endured in the notion of inherent creative resources deep in the body, yet she employed procedures aimed at kinetic fragmentation. Much like Jasperse, Karczag constructed a truth that entailed grappling with culture; with the Alexandrian concept of habit (culture) and what lies beneath it (nature), she resolves the contradiction that Banes identifies. The somatic idea of inherent capacity served as an essential foundation of identity, while moving beyond habit ignited the constant renewal of this essence. Meanwhile, by rejecting conventional feminine elegance, grace, and display, with kinetic fragmentation, Karczag grapples with cultural signs to which she is subject.

Karczag's choreographic modality exemplifies how the greater range of movement which dancers purported to access by focusing on the natural body concurred with identities built between essentialism and fragmentation. Tracking corporeal shift through kinaesthetic awareness, she theorizes an essential physical truth as fuelling her embodiment of an impressive range of seemingly contrary vocabulary. Notorious for her seamless moving between incongruous juxtapositions (Gilbert 2014: 309), she integrates kinetic flotsam and jetsam. For Karczag, this arises from somatic free flow in movement and imagination that integrates mind and body, facilitating speed and sharpness, like the vigour I have associated with Houston-Jones and others. Confounding any distinction between emotion and physicality, she researches layers of psychophysical possibility in 'dimensions of the body opening up, deepening into detail, opening-up bigger worlds'. With beliefs about the psyche that Authentic Movement inherits from Jung (Whitehouse 1999), Karczag imagines the dancer to be charting an unknowable territory of the self that is at once essential and fragmented, reconciled by listening to the sensory landscape of motile discontinuity. She theorizes spaces below conscious and subconscious thought, encouraging students to see where sensations take them as they access deep personal layers in exercises that include touch via hands-on partner working methods. Convinced that the body's capriciousness and depth manifest in finer movement (Dempster and Karzag 1996), Karczag privileges salon-style concerts in order to achieve legibility for her aesthetic.

Much like her treatise on teaching 'complex movement' at the Dutch European Dance Development Center, despite ostensibly relying on the idea of bodily nature for her compositional intricacy, Karczag carefully authors her layered body. She realizes corporeality's simultaneous immediacy and elusiveness by foregrounding basic truths about the body while insisting on the unimaginable dancing possibilities that such information can propel. For example, she works by 'tracing and defining, especially skeletal structure, feeling the true weight of parts—a return to the physical body that houses us' (Dempster and Karzag 1996: 34). After viewing multiple images of a bone or joint structure, Karczag and her collaborators or students might palpate said skeletal component through the skin, sensing its size, mass, relative placement, and heaviness. Yet Karczag convolutes the kinetic effects of receiving and giving tactile feedback by shuttling between writing, viewing, dancing, watching, giving and receiving feedback, and dancing in response to feedback or writing.

Fluctuation not only manifests in the intentional layering of successive dances but also by virtue of written imagery. After a 'hands-on' session with British dance-artist Miranda Tufnell in November 2012 l, Karczag wrote: 'slow surge of thick oil, a golden cascade of luminosity as light grows dim and fingers of twilight reach towards your outline. A moving shore, the ebb and flow of tides, a dampness of sinking sand, and your toes digging deep in search of flight and everyday joys'. Her writing between 2007 and 2014, in response to tactile feedback, dancing, and watching, exhibits a similar avoidance of transparent representations of the physical movement or anatomical and mechanical terms.[11] It thus parallels Joan Skinner's aforementioned replacement of anatomical image prompts with poetic ones in Skinner Releasing. Karczag's prompts for exploration still detail anatomy and its function, yet by refraining, as Skinner has, from codifying a language for her practice, Karczag invests more deeply in the idea of elusiveness. Nevertheless, both women insist on physicality as a gateway to unlimited imaginative possibility, which is reflected in their use of undirected writing or drawing following dancing, which for Karczag propels more dancing. This was how artist-educators like

Karczag and Skinner recalibrated somatics towards idiosyncratic vocabulary as part of the broader 1980s trend that contributed to the emergence of solo improvisation (Gilbert 2014: 133–137). They thus 'author' a concept of bodily nature, even as that entails the belief in a corporeal essence which they aim to access.

To insist on the critical creative role of the dancer, Karczag has deployed a physical and textual language of the natural body that is broadly legible within contemporary dance. Yet her contribution must neither be collapsed into a general dismissal of work that draws on essentialist notions nor configured as a practice that has failed to rise to the challenge of large concert houses. She resists the institutionalization of experimentation by replacing innovation with elusiveness: rather than repeatable signature vocabulary, Karczag (non)composes the body's ungraspable nature. Similarly, she cultivates bodily meandering against efficiency: rather than cultivating creativity that guarantees reliable choreographic product, the body which is constructed in her pedagogy and performance drifts evasively. Even while evading the productivity on which corporate arts culture depends, however, Karczag's work can't be dismissed as lacking in skill, because of the virtuosity with which she meanders elusively. This is precisely the dilemma in which Perron finds herself when she notes that, despite wishing that she were doing the 'inward sorts of things' in her own concert that she identifies with Karczag, she laments that it 'would never read' in the larger space in which she will work. But rather than characterize the different strategies in which Karczag and Perron engage in terms of artists' maturity, I propose that they are distinct value-laden ways of negotiating contemporary dance's economic and cultural economy.

NOTES

1. Email to the author, 13 June 2015.
2. Email to the author, 13 June 2015.
3. When I was researching my PhD dissertation (Gilbert 2014), a colleague who was focusing on Forti provided me with a comprehensive bibliography that contained very little on any work post-1970s.
4. Steve Paxton, email correspondence with author, 15 July 2014.
5. Strider's collective members, such as Nannette Hassall and Christopher Banner, choreographed for the company, along with guest artists, such as Mary Fulkerson; for a fuller history see Jordan (1992).
6. Nanette Hassall and Russell Dumas started Dance Exchange in 1976. Eva Karczag, interview with author, 29 December 2014. All following references to Karczag are from this interview unless otherwise indicated.
7. Along with Karczag and Kraus, company members such as Petronio, Diane Madden, Shelley Senter, Vicky Schick, and Irene Hultman used somatics to develop, execute, and teach Brown's and their own signature vocabularies.
8. Courtesy of the artist, sent by email 31 December 2014.
9. Email to the author, 20 June 2015.
10. In a methodological dyad central to Authentic Movement, a witness observes the mover. Karczag recalls internalizing the witness role in her work with Authentic Movement

practitioner Eileen Crow in New York in the mid-1980s. Interview with the author 29 December 2014.

11. Courtesy of the artist, sent by email 3 January 2015.

REFERENCES

Adair, C. (2007) *Dancing the Black Question: The Phoenix Dance Company Phenomenon*. Alton, Hampshire, UK: Dance Books.

Albright, Ann Cooper. (1997) *Choreographing Difference: The Body and Identity in Contemporary Dance*. Middletown, CT: Wesleyan University Press.

Bales, M. R. N.-F. (2008) *The Body Eclectic: Evolving Practices in Dance Training*. Urbana: University of Illinois Press.

Banes, S. (1980) *Terpsichore in Sneakers: Post-modern Dance*. Boston: Houghton Mifflin.

Banes, S. (1993) Greenwich Village 1963: Avant-Garde Performance and the Effervescent Body. Durham, NC: Duke University Press.

Banes, S. (2003) Spontaneous Combustion: Notes on Improvisation from the Sixties to the Nineties. In Albright, Ann Cooper, and Gere, D. (eds.), *Taken by Surprise: A Dance Improvisation Reader*. Middletown, CT: Wesleyan University Press, 77–85.

Burt, R. (2002) Steve Paxton's Goldberg Variations and the Angel of History. *TDR The Drama Review: The Journal of Performance Studies* 46: 46–64.

Butler, J. (1990) Gender Trouble: Feminism and the Subversion of Identity. New York: Routledge.

Claid, E. (2006) *Yes? No! Maybe—: Seductive Ambiguity in Dance*. London: Routledge.

Cohen-Bull (Novack), C. J. (1997) Sense, Meaning and Perception in Three Dance Cultures. In Desmond, J. (ed.), *Meaning in Motion: New Cultural Studies of Dance*. Durham, NC: Duke University Press, 269–287.

Dempster, E., and Karzag, E. (1996) An Interview with Eva Karczag., *Writings on Dance*, 4, Summer: 32–52.

De Wit, M. (2000) New Dance Development at Dartington College of Arts U.K. 1971–1987. Ph.D. Middlesex University.

Forti, S. (1974) *Handbook in Motion*. New York: New York University Press.

Foster, S. L. (1986) Reading Dancing: Bodies and Subjects in Contemporary American Dance. Berkeley: University of California Press.

Foster, S. L. (1997) Dancing Bodies. In Desmond, J. (ed.), *Meaning in Motion: New Cultural Studies of Dance*. Durham, NC: Duke University Press, 235–257.

Foster, S. L. (1998) Choreographies of Gender. *Signs* (24): 1–33.

Foster, S. L. (2001) Closets Full of Dances: Modern Dance's Performance of Masculinity and Sexuality. In Desmond, J. (ed.), *Dancing Desires: Choreographing Sexualities On and Off the Stage*. Madison: University of Wisconsin Press, 147–207.

Foster, S. L. (2002) Dances That Describe Themselves: The Improvised Choreography of Richard Bull. Middletown, CT: Wesleyan University Press.

Foucault, M. (1978) *The History of Sexuality*. New York: Pantheon Books.

Franko, M. (1995) *Dancing Modernism/Performing Politics*. Bloomington: Indiana University Press.

George, D. (2011) Propelled by Bewilderment: Dramaturgy, Reconstruction, and Improvisation in the Re-staging of THEM. Presentation at Society of Dance History Scholars 34th Annual

Conference, Dance Dramaturgy: Catalyst, Perspective and Memory, York University and University of Toronto, June 23–26.

George, D. (2015) The Unstable Flesh and Bones of Transcendence: Tracking Transformation in a Somatic Tradition of the Natural Dancing Body. Presentation at Open Embodiments: Locating Somatechnics in Tucson, University of Arizona, April 15–18.

George, D. (2017) The Hysterical Spectator: Dancing with Feminists, Nellies, Andro-Dykes and Drag Queens. In Croft, C. (ed.), Queer Dance: *Meanings and Makings*. Oxford: Oxford University Press, 83–108.

Gilbert, D. (2014) A Conceit of the Natural Body: The Universal Individual in Somatic Dance Training. PhD. University of California, Los Angeles.

Goldberg, M., and Albright, Ann Cooper. (1987) Roundtable Interview: Post-modernism and Feminism in Dance. *Women and Performance: A Journal of Feminist Theory* (3): 41–56.

Gottschild, B. D. (1996) Digging the Africanist Presence in American Performance: Dance and Other Contexts. Westport, CT: Greenwood Press.

Gottschild, B. D. (2003) The Black Dancing Body: A Geography from Coon to Cool. New York: Palgrave Macmillan.

Jordan, S. (1992) Striding Out: Aspects of Contemporary and New Dance in Britain. London: Dance Books.

Jowitt, D. (1994) By Deborah Jowitt. *Village Voice*, 8 March, 85.

Juhan, D. (1987) *Job's Body: A Handbook for Bodywork*. Barrytown, N.Y.: Station Hill Press.

Kraus, L. (2014) Thoughts about Steve Paxton on Viewing Four of His Dances at Dia:Beacon, *thINKing Dance*, http://thinkingdance.net/articles/2014/11/20/34/Thoughts-about-Steve-Paxton-on-viewing-four-of-his-dances-at-DiaBeacon/. Accessed 14 March 2015.

Lambery, C. (2004) More or Less Minimalism: Six Notes on Performance and Visual Art in the 1960s. In Goldstein, A and Mark, L.(eds.), *A Minimal Future? Art as Object 1958–1968*.Massachusetts: MIT 103–110.

Morris, G. (2006) A Game for Dancers: Performing Modernism in the Postwar Years, 1945–1960. Middletown, CT: Wesleyan University Press.

Novack, C. J. (1990) *Sharing the Dance: Contact Improvisation and American Culture*. Madison: University of Wisconsin Press.

Phelan, P. (1993) *Unmarked: The Politics of Performance*. London: Routledge.

Rainer, Y. (2014) *Yvonne Rainer: Dances and Films*. Getty Research Institute, Los Angeles, California, http://www.getty.edu/research/exhibitions_events/exhibitions/rainer/. Accessed 29 August 2018.

Reynoso, J. (2011) Economies of Symbolic and Cultural Capital Production and Distribution in Postmodern/Contemporary Dance Making: A Search for Egalitarianism. Paper presented at Dance under Construction Graduate Student Dance Studies Conference, University of California, Riverside, 16–17 April.

Ross, J. (2007) *Anna Halprin: Experience as Dance*. Berkeley: University of California Press.

Schaffman, K. H. (2001) From the Margins to the Mainstream: Contact Improvisation and the Commodification of Touch. PhD. University of California, Riverside.

Thomas, H. (2003) *The Body, Dance, and Cultural Theory*. New York: Palgrave Macmillan.

Whitehouse, M. (1999) *Authentic Movement*. Philadelphia: J. Kingsley.

CHAPTER 14

···

MOVEMENTS OF FREEDOM

Performing Popular Liberty in the Early Cancan

···

CLARE PARFITT

ON 10 October 1829, a nineteen-year-old milliner called Marie Sauve (elsewhere Angiolina Sauve or Marie-Angiolina Sauve) was brought to trial in Paris, charged with a 'public outrage to decency in dancing the *chahut*' (Anonymous 1829c). The *chahut* was a wilder version of the cancan, or rather, as Sauve's lawyer, Monsieur Genret, put it, 'the *cancan* is the *chahut purified*' (Anonymous 1829c: 1186, trans. CJ).[1] Sauve was arrested at the Elysée des Dames dance hall, and although she was apparently not the first female dancer to be arrested for indecent dancing at this venue, the majority of the many social dancers brought to trial between 1828 and the mid-1840s were male. The moves for which both men and women were arrested were far from the clichéd image of female dancers kicking in a line or revealing their underwear. Descriptions of the early cancan suggest that a wide range of movements were employed, using a variety of body parts. Sauve's prosecution, for example, includes a demonstration of her dancing by the prosecuting policeman in which he 'takes a step backwards, places himself in front of the court clerk, and taking up a dancing position, advances balancing his body on his hips' (1185, trans. CJ).[2] Monsieur Genret argues that Sauve danced the cancan rather than the 'repellent' *chahut*, but she is nevertheless condemned to three months in prison.

Sauve appeals the decision, and in Genret's defence at her retrial on 18 November 1829, he refers to another feature of the contemporary cancan: its improvisation. First, he concedes that the cancan's ambiguity and ephemerality render it legally 'reprehensible, because as fleeting a gesture as a *rond de jambe* or a *balancé* could not find favour with the rigours of criminal law' (Anonymous 1829a: 61, trans. CJ).[3] The cancan's transient movements evade the legal demand for evidence and appear to operate outside not only the criminal law but any law. This in itself, it seems, is grounds for its legal indecency. Genret then proceeds to argue that on the contrary, the cancan is not devoid of rule, regulations, and standards. He warns the appeal court: 'do not think, Gentlemen, that the *cancan* dance is a pure invention: it has its rhythms, like the *minuet* has its rhythms' (61, trans. CJ).[4] Genret's claim raises two important points. First, it suggests that in 1829, the cancan was already synonymous with individually invented movement; Genret's defence rests on challenging this assumption. Second, it points beyond the easy equation of the cancan with unregulated extemporization and towards a deeper tension in the dance between invention and 'rhythm', lawlessness and legality, improvisation and structure. This chapter argues that this tension connects the cancan's physical form to its political significance as an embodiment of liberty in a highly repressive context.

IMPROVISATIONS WITHIN STRUCTURE

With a few exceptions, like the example just presented, archival traces of the cancan and *chahut* in the 1820s and 1830s, the first two decades of their existence, make little mention of their improvisatory nature. During this period, the cancan's notoriety was based on the deviation of its movements from accepted norms of decency (embodied in the quadrille, for example) rather than on how these movements were devised. The improvisatory nature of these deviations from the graceful movements choreographed by the dancing masters seems to have gone without saying during this early period, as Genret's effort to counter this assumption implies.

From 1839 onwards, however, a body of literature on the cancan began to emerge, which explicitly described its improvisatory nature. This literature was penned by a generation of writers who documented the spectacle of Parisian life from the position of the *flâneur* (Gluck 2005: 65–107). They sought to describe in intimate detail the panorama of urban social types and practices, especially those that embodied the liberal energies animating modern life. The cancan and its improvisations provided excellent material for this emerging mass print culture.

A particularly detailed description of the cancan's improvisations from this period was written in 1841 by 'Paul Smith', a pseudonym for Désiré-Guillaume-Edouard Monnais, a journalist and playwright who was also codirector of the Paris Opéra at this time. Smith reflects retrospectively on the changes wrought to the 'old-fashioned' contredanse by social dancers who felt a 'lack of life and passion' (Smith 1841: 114, trans. AD)[5] in its set figures. It is worth quoting his description of these changes at length:

> So what did they do? ... Each dancer set about improvising a kind of mimed dialogue, with a very lively expression. Instead of dancing quite simply, with the most elegance and grace possible, with straight head, arms close to the body, and without departing from the catalogue of classical steps—the *assemblée*, the *six-sol*, the *entrechat*—they invented foot movements, arm movements, head movements; they attacked the *status quo* by dancing from all sides at once.... Gone were the conventional forms, the routine, the uniformity.... You could give yourself over wholly to your verve, to your fantasy. You could be yourself and copy no one. In short, here the contredanse is a dramatic form where each person improvises, following his or her flair, expressing his or her individuality. (Smith 1841: 114, trans. AD)[6]

Smith highlights the individual nature of these anticlassical inventions, based on personal fantasy rather than imitation. Louis Huart, a journalist and writer who played a key role in developing the literature of Parisian social types in the 1840s, places a similar emphasis on the absence of imitative movement: 'When the gentleman steps forward alone in the naive figure of the Pastourelle [a figure in the quadrille, successor of the contredanse], he gives himself over to a whole improvisation of his imagination, and among five hundred dancers, not one imitates his neighbour. Indeed, such is the spirit of inventiveness that the municipal officer is obliged to calm this excessive zeal' (Huart 1845: 54, trans. AD).[7] Smith and Huart portray the cancan as an embodiment of Romanticism: an anticlassical act of individual expression, motivated by fantasy, imagination, inspiration, and genius. Smith was opposed to Romanticism in music (Ellis 2007: 161–162), and although he welcomes the challenge the cancan had made to the 'cold' contredanse, he judges that 'in general dance improvisation has taken a deplorable turn' (Smith 1841: 114, trans. AD).[8] The Romantic lens Smith places on the cancan negatively affects his evaluation of it, but it may also influence his (and Huart's) descriptions of the cancan improvisations. Angela Esterhammer (2008: 78), in her study of the relationship between Romanticism and improvisation in the context of Romantic-era poetry, argues that Romantic ideology influenced the reception of the poetic improviser by providing the criteria (such as genius) by which improvisers were judged. Furthermore, Esterhammer implies that the Romanticization of the improviser led to a narrowing of the margins of interpretation for improvisation, so that improvisation could *only* be interpreted in a Romantic way: 'The poet who performs spontaneous composition now comes to function as a representation or a visualization of Romantic genius; the body of the improviser, that is to say, becomes the site at which the mechanisms of genius are manifested and observed' (78). In a similar way, the bodies of the cancan improvisers arguably become overdetermined by Romanticism in Smith's and Huart's descriptions, causing an overemphasis on individual, uninhibited, non-imitative movement, and a deemphasis on the dancers' engagements with the conventions, constraints, and movement landscapes of the real world in which they moved.

Danielle Goldman observes this issue in writings on improvisation more generally: 'a ... serious problem with many discussions of improvisation is that their emphasis on spontaneity and intuition often implies a lack of preparation, thereby eliding the historical knowledge, the sense of tradition, and the enormous skill that the most eloquent improvisers are able to mobilize' (2010: 5). I would argue that this difficulty is particularly trenchant in writings on improvisation in popular dance forms, which are often already framed as facile, trivial, and ahistorical or otherwise 'primitive', natural, and irrational, obscuring the complexity of the forms and the expertise of the dancers. Ramsay Burt (1998: 56) makes a similar argument when he points out that Josephine Baker's dance improvisations were not just 'made up' but drew from a 'specific and codified movement vocabulary' and were probably rehearsed. In this chapter, I seek to demonstrate that in the case of the cancan improvisations, dancers drew on specific movement repertoires and the particular improvisatory principles they embodied.

The cancan emerged as improvisations within the quadrille, a standardized version of the contredanse composed of set figures performed by four couples in a square formation using steps influenced by ballet vocabulary. The intricate patterns of interaction between couples and individuals produced by the dance normally relied on dancers accurately reproducing the choreographed steps and spatial trajectories prescribed by the dancing masters. The exceptions to this rule were the *cavalier seul* and *cavalière seule* or *dame seule* sections, in which the men (*cavaliers*) and ladies (*dames*) performed improvised solos for a set duration within the music. Ordinarily, dancers would draw from the range of ballet steps employed in social dance in these improvisations, and the more competent dancers would demonstrate their mastery of difficult steps, such as *entrechats, pas de zéphyr*, and *brisés* (Rogers 2003: 210). In the cancan or *chahut* improvisations, however, dancers would introduce steps from outside the legitimate repertoire. These included the 'national dances' featured in the ballet-pantomimes and melodramas of the popular theatres, such as the Spanish *cachucha* (Smith 1841: 114) and the Haitian *chica* (Luchet 1833: 42). They also included movements from street performance, such as the *saut de carpe*, in which dancers raised themselves from face-down on the floor to standing (Capello 1814: 145; Gardembas 1845: 75), and a form of street fighting called *savate* (Gautier 1847: 205). Steps such as the *grand écart* (splits) and high kick may have been influenced by the Commedia dell'Arte, which developed these movements as part of the *lazzi*, or set-piece physical tricks that the actors interspersed with their theatrical improvisations (Duchartre 19266 36). These movements would have been known to early nineteenth-century audiences through their influence on comic dancers such as Charles Mazurier (Winter 1962: 152–158, 131). Furthermore, Auguste Delaforest, in his 1853 dictionary definition of the cancan and *chahut*, adds that these dances distorted the contredanse 'by manners borrowed from market people and dockers' (Delaforest 1853: 337, trans. CJ).[9] The *cavalier seul*, therefore, seems to have provided a space for dancers to undermine the quadrille's choreographed elegance from the inside, allowing subversive movements derived from popular culture to be performed without disrupting the framework of the dance.

The principle of improvising within, rather than against, the structure of the quadrille was embodied by the *cavalier seul* but infiltrated other quadrille steps and figures, too, such as the *avant-deux*, and the finale, especially when performed as a wild gallop. Each step and figure offered different possibilities for experimentation by inserting moves or playing with the direction, energy level, and quality of the prescribed steps. Delaforest identifies improvised alterations made by individual dancers both to the prescribed steps (such as dancers crossing over back-to-back instead of face-to-face) and to the performative quality or attitude they bring to the movement. While acknowledging that the latter is easier to convey in an image than in writing, he gives this example:

> if this is what takes his fancy, the [male] dancer, instead of dancing, of jumping, will put his hands in the pockets of his trousers, of his coat, of his waistcoat, will take a few steps forward or will remain motionless looking at his female opposite in a haughty, imperious, or lascivious manner which he will attempt to make as satanic as he can,

in the manner of Frédérick Lemaître when he danced the waltz of Mephistopheles in the melodrama *Faust*; or, instead of glancing at his opposite dancer, he will turn his gaze from left to right to those present and will seem occupied by something entirely different. (Delaforest 1853: 337, trans. CJ)[10]

Importantly, however, these improvisations maintain a respect for the framework of the quadrille, in terms of its structure of figures and key points of reference, such as the periodic return of the dancers to their starting positions. This is made clear in an instructional article, published in 1829, detailing male and female cancan steps and attitudes:

> In the *chaîne anglaise*, for example, they [the female dancers] rush blindly in front of them, run seemingly indiscriminately; we would take them for escapees from Charenton [a mental asylum in southeastern Paris]; but seeing the art with which they return to their dancers, we soon recognize that their petulance is not without method. They lose no figure of the contredanse; and when in the disorder that often marks the end of an animated figure, they arrive at their place before the orchestra has completed the ritornelle [repeated musical phrase], their feet, strongly stamping the ground, and their heads swaying on their shoulders, mark the rhythm of the tempo that their legs were unable to accomplish. (Anonymous 1829b: 490, trans. CJ)[11]

This is a practice of improvisation-within-structure that, according to Smith, treats the contredanse 'like those *canevas* of Italian theatre which the actors embroider, following their wit and their talent' (Smith 1841: 114, trans. AD).[12] He is referring to the Commedia dell'Arte, in which actors improvised within outline plots and characterizations called *canevas* rather than following a script (Ravel 1999: 114). This improvisational form was central to Commedia dell'Arte, which Robert Henke describes as 'an art of improvisation that cannily negotiated flexibility and structure' or, as he states in his title, 'form and freedom' (2015: 22). The Commedia was present in France from the sixteenth century, and its influence in French theatre and popular culture was wideranging. Judith Wechsler (1982) traces the influence of its stock characters and improvisational tradition through Parisian fairground mime and acrobatic troupes, and then into the ballet-pantomimes and vaudeville productions of the popular theatres along the Boulevard du Temple. The cross-class audiences of the popular theatres also attended the carnival balls where the cancan was performed in the 1830s and 1840s. On the dance floor, these audiences embodied the Commedia aesthetic they witnessed at the theatre, by performing physical tricks such as the aforementioned high kick, and by donning Commedia-influenced costumes, particularly that of Pierrot, a character popularized by the pantomimic artistry of Jean-Gaspard Deburau. The presence of these other Commedia elements in the cancan's carnival ball context suggests that the cancan's principles of improvisation may have been influenced by, rather than coincidentally resembling, those of the Commedia tradition. The cancan dancers transferred and adapted this art of improvising between 'form and freedom' to a new context, that of social dance, at a historical moment in France when the relationship between freedom and control was highly politically charged.

DANCING LIBERTY IN 'TIGHT PLACES'

Historian Richard Terdiman (1993: 94) argues that the notion of liberty played an intensely conflicted role in the lives of the generation following the French Revolution. They both glorified the revolutionary *liberté* that had animated recent French history and feared the violent retribution of the paranoid postrevolutionary monarchies for any attempt to reignite its flame. In this situation, Terdiman contends, the children of the Revolution began to explore 'a pervasive set of deeper infrastructural constraints' (93) on freedom, present not just within the political system but also within each individual. Socializing structures such as education and language, he states, 'turned out to have a powerful capacity to determine and limit social behavior. And they did so all the more mystifyingly because they were not experienced as structures of oppression' (93). In his earlier work *Discourse/Counter-discourse* (1985), Terdiman examines how these internal structures were challenged in nineteenth-century France through various types of writing (journalism, academic tracts, novels, and prose poems) and through satirical caricatures published in mass-produced newspapers. What Terdiman and other nineteenth-century historians have overlooked, however, is that the postrevolutionary generation also recognized and confronted the limits on freedom in a different but crucial realm, that of the body.

The dancing body played a crucial role in rethinking liberty in French popular culture following the French Revolution and the subsequent nineteenth-century revolutions. This role is suggested in satirical form in *Physiologie des Bals de Paris*, a book published in 1841 by the pseudonymous Chicard and Balochard. These pseudonyms refer to male dancing characters enacted at the carnival balls, although they are often reified as real individuals in contemporary writings. Balochard writes ironically of the freedoms his friend Chicard is willing and unwilling to relinquish to the authorities:

> My friend Chicard clings to his freedom to think and to write about what he thinks. Suppress this right!
>
> Kill the liberty of the press, which, before dying, will make its will. . . .
>
> From concession to concession, you will thus get from him more or less all that you need to obtain.
>
> But my friend Chicard holds essentially only on to one liberty.
>
> But this one, how he holds on to it!!!
>
> He needs *the liberty of his legs!*
>
> And that is why my friend Chicard delights in the *danse aux barrières*.
>
> It is there that he can make immoderate use of his dear liberty.—I speak of that of his legs.

The *barrière* dance, that is what he loves! (Balochard and Chicard 1841: 33–34, trans. CJ)[13]

As other parts of the book make clear, the dance of the *barrières* (the pleasure zones surrounding the gateways in the city walls) is the cancan. In the face of the suppression of all other rights to freedom (freedom of thought, of speech, of the press), Chicard fights to retain the liberty of his body, specifically his legs, through the freedom of movement offered by this dance. As civil liberties are restricted by the Bourbon Restoration and the July Monarchy, the author suggests, the cancan becomes the last refuge of freedom. For some early performers of the cancan, many of whom were working class (predominantly men but also women), this danced refuge was an escape from the deprivations of poverty and repressive employment practices. For others, such as male students, who were not allowed to vote until at least the age of twenty-five, the dance provided an avenue for the expression of liberal, republican politics. As increasing numbers of women from across the class spectrum, but particularly working-class women, performed the dance in the 1840s, it offered (and sometimes delivered, though transiently) forms of financial and social independence that were otherwise unavailable. The cancan allowed individuals to imagine, perform, and embody forms of liberty that exceeded not only the liberties available in the repressive postrevolutionary context, but also the male, bourgeois definitions of liberty constructed during the French Revolution itself (Outram 1989).

The cancan of the 1830s and 1840s performed the role Goldman (2010) ascribes to a range of improvisatory dance forms, both popular and elite, of 'practices of freedom' in 'tight places'. Her notion of a practice of freedom is derived from Michel Foucault's later work, in which he theorizes explicitly the possibilities for resistance within the regimes of power discussed in his earlier writings. In 'The Ethics of the Concern for Self as a Practice of Freedom' (1997), Foucault makes a distinction between 'processes of liberation', which are wholesale reversals of power, such as wars of independence (or in the context of the present argument, the French Revolution), and 'practices of freedom', which are small-scale acts through which individuals redefine their relationships with themselves and with others. These acts are not invented anew by each individual but are chosen and adapted from a repertoire of practices available in the individual's particular cultural and historical context. Foucault argues that such practices are usually possible even in what he calls 'states of domination', where there is an 'extremely limited margin of freedom' (1997: 292). Goldman, in her application of this theory to dance, calls these states 'tight places'—a term she takes from African American literature scholar Houston Baker. 'Tight places', for Goldman, are spaces that are highly constrained, by, for example, 'race but also class, gender, sexuality, time, and even artistic conventions' (2010: 6). Goldman argues that improvisation emerges as an embodied response to, and negotiation of, such 'tight places'.

The early cancan might be considered a 'practice of freedom' in the 'tight places' experienced by the working classes, young people, and women across the class spectrum in the repressive contexts of the postrevolutionary monarchies. This place was 'tight' in several senses. In 1814, and again in 1815, the Bourbon monarchy was restored to power, and although it was a constitutional monarchy, as opposed to the absolutist monarchy that had been overthrown in the French Revolution, suffrage was restricted to property-owning men who paid over 300 francs per year in tax (Magraw 1983: 23). Freedom of expression and freedom to meet in public were both limited during the Restoration, and particularly under Charles X (1825–1830) (Hauser 1951; Kroen 2000: 161). The working class lost the benefits of association afforded them before the Revolution, and many were both poverty-stricken and powerless (Artz 1963: 270). Before the emergence of the cancan, the dance floor offered little release from the hegemony of elite culture. The civilized quadrille had dominated the dance floor since the Revolution, and the popularity across the social spectrum of its simplified form signified a democratization of the aristocratic performance of superiority rather than an escape from it. Nevertheless, the Restoration authorities quickly realized that dance halls were potential hotbeds of liberalism, and one of the first laws passed by the Restoration restricted opening hours for drinking venues and dance halls (Davidson 2007: 155). The Prefecture de Police established a large-scale surveillance operation to monitor dancing at the public balls, and police officers were instructed to arrest those suspected of indecent dancing under Article 330 of the Penal Code, concerning public outrages against modesty (The Penal Code of France 1819; Barlet 1831). French citizens excluded from the electoral franchise by their class, youth, or gender, therefore, may have found little respite from the Restoration's political, legal, and choreographic 'tight places'.

In response, cancan dancers attempted to prise open improvisatory moments within the otherwise fixed choreography of the quadrille. To evade the 'choreopolicing' (Lepecki 2013) of their movements by the municipal guards who patrolled Parisian dance venues, they carefully timed, spaced, and judged their improvisations to avoid detection (see, for example, Vanderburch and Langlé 1834). In these ways, their actions made corporeal incursions into the repressive structures of the Restoration regime, embodying the possibility of liberation within constraint and developing the cancan as a 'practice of freedom'. However, Foucault's theory of 'practices of freedom', articulated towards the end of his life, was left relatively undeveloped compared to the regimes of power, about which he wrote in extensive detail in the middle of his career. A corrective to this imbalance is offered by Michel de Certeau (1984), who builds on, and reverses the focus of, Foucault's work by shifting attention from the micropolitics of discipline to the micropolitics of antidiscipline. De Certeau's antidisciplinary 'tactics' provide a good model for the cancan as a 'practice of freedom'.

De Certeau makes a distinction between two types of practices operating in everyday life. The first is the 'strategy', which is enacted by 'a subject of will and power (a proprietor, an enterprise, a city, a scientific institution)' (1984: xix), based on the subject's occupation of a 'proper' place from which the subject can generate relations to external others, such as competitors, clients, or objects of research. These strategies might be considered to produce something like Foucault's discipline, although for Foucault the sources of power are not located in a 'place' but are dispersed. The second type of practice de Certeau discerns is the 'tactic', which is enacted by the 'others', who do not have a 'proper' place and therefore must cleverly use the available opportunities and resources to appropriate the landscape that has been created and occupied by strategies and turn it to their advantage. Tactics are the multitude of ways people use or consume the structures (such as built environments, products, and languages) necessary for everyday life, ways that are often 'against the grain' of these structures' intended purposes. He cites as examples 'talking, reading, moving about, shopping, cooking, etc.' (xix). For de Certeau, tactics constitute an antidiscipline, an everyday practice of opposition to the structures of power that shape ordinary lives.

By focusing attention on tactics rather than strategies, de Certeau highlights the ways disciplinary structures are transformed by their creative use, such that they diffuse the apparently irresistible power of strategies and the structures they produce. From this perspective, disciplinary structures become merely the framework for the play of tactical acts: 'carried to its limit, this order [of the strategies] would be the equivalent of the rules of meter and rhyme for poets of earlier times: a body of constraints stimulating new discoveries, a set of rules with which improvisation plays' (de Certeau 1984: xxii). This formulation is reminiscent of Smith's comparison of cancan dancers' treatment of the contredanse with the use of outline *canevas* by Commedia dell'Arte actors. The quadrille is no longer a power structure that, in Foucault's terms, disciplines 'docile bodies' (Foucault 1991) by imposing on them an aristocratic civility but becomes a loose script which can be appropriated, domesticated, repurposed, by those who now move within it.

De Certeau uses the creative acts of tenants, non–native language speakers, and pedestrians to exemplify this tactical habitation of given spaces and vocabularies: 'this mutation makes the text habitable, like a rented apartment. It transforms another person's property into a space borrowed for a moment by a transient. Renters make comparable changes in an apartment they furnish with their acts and memories; as do speakers, in the language into which they insert both the messages of their native tongue and, through their accent, through their own 'turns of phrase', etc., their own history; as do pedestrians, in the streets they fill with the forests of their desires and goals' (1984: xxi). De Certeau's image of tenants, speakers, and pedestrians inserting memories, accents, histories, and desires into spaces, speech, and streets provides a useful model for thinking about cancan dancers' improvisations within the quadrille, especially when combined with Foucault's notion of a 'practice of freedom'. It is important to note here that the contredanse and the quadrille were already embodiments of certain historical definitions of liberty and democratization during their emergence and early popularity. With its nonhierarchical arrangement of dancers as a social group, the contredanse had revolutionized French court dancing in the late seventeenth and early eighteenth centuries, embodying the decentralization of political and social power that was already taking place within the French aristocracy (Cohen 2000). In the postrevolutionary period, the standardization and simplification of the contredanse into the quadrille, making it accessible beyond the aristocracy to all levels of society while maintaining its civilized aesthetic, allowed the bourgeoisie to prove their civility as successors to the aristocracy while rejecting aristocratic elitism. But for the early working-class cancan dancers, the spread of the contredanse's civilized aesthetic was a process less of democratization than of creeping hegemony. To counteract that hegemony, they drew on an alternative history of embodied liberty, found not in aristocratic culture but in popular cultural sources. This history was not a continuous, intact tradition which they could easily take up and reproduce. Rather, it was an array of fragmentary practices distributed amongst a variety of popular performance contexts, including street culture (performance and fighting), the fairground, carnival (in its limited nineteenth-century form, having undergone a number of repressions; see Bakhtin 1984; Johnson 2001; Stallybrass and White 1986), the marketplace, and the popular theatre genres of melodrama, pantomime, and ballet-pantomime, particularly grotesque, comic movements from the Commedia dell'Arte tradition, and foreign national dance forms. Each of these carried its own histories and cultural memories of embodied opposition to 'authorised' culture (see Parker 2011) and notions of liberty defined 'from below' (on liberty in melodrama see Brooks 1976, chap. 2), forming a collection of repertoires (Taylor 2003) on which cancan improvisers could draw.

By inserting movements drawn from these practices into the quadrille, cancan dancers hollowed out the civilized aesthetic of the dance and gave the shell new historical, mnemonic, and political content. Experimentation with popular performance repertoires allowed those who had become disenfranchised by the postrevolutionary regimes to physically explore alternative ways of embodying liberty. Crucially, however, the structure of the quadrille, its figures and key steps, remained, so that the new content was grafted into a form that continued to carry a long history of embodying and democratizing the French body politic which stretched back to the contredanse (Clark 2002: 510–511; Smith 1841: 114). Significantly, the term 'quadrille', and even sometimes 'contredanse', continued to be used to refer to the cancan throughout the nineteenth century, and particularly at the fin de siècle. This continuity of the contredanse as a carrier of French national identity and memory may help to explain the rapidity with which—by the early 1840s—liberal French writers hailed the cancan as the new French national dance (Alhoy 1840: 4; Bourget 1842: 83; Philipon 1842–43: 382–383). The cancan was not, in fact, an entirely new national dance but the empty vessel of the old national dance, animated and transformed by postrevolutionary popular culture.

It should be noted that not all quadrille dancers chose to take advantage of the new improvisatory possibilities the cancan offered. The quadrille continued to be danced as a performance of bourgeois civilized sociality throughout the nineteenth century, and dancing masters continued to choreograph new figures. Indeed, the anonymous author of *Paris dansant, ou Les filles d'Hérodiade, folles danseuses des bals publics* (Paris Dancing, or the Girls of Herodius, Crazy Dancers of the Public Balls; Anonymous 1845) notes that 'at Mabille, at the Chaumière, at Valentino [public balls where the cancan was performed] we are free. There, everyone dances as they wish: you can walk, like in high society, you can also leap about and do a cartwheel during the *pastourelle* [quadrille figure] solos' (Anonymous 1845: 10, trans. CJ).[14] The quadrilles at these balls would have displayed a kaleidoscope of different embodiments of liberty, from choreographed performances of civilized sociality to individual improvisations consisting of isolations of the body's extremities and to deviations from 'grace' into the grotesque and the exotic. These heterogeneous expressions of liberty embodied deep divisions in French society regarding questions of freedom and equality that the Revolution had violently performed but not resolved. Cancan dancers would continue to improvise responses to these problems for the rest of the century, alongside and in between the repeated revolutions that engaged bodies more violently in such questions.

DANGEROUS RHYTHMS

The lawyer Monsieur Genret makes the claim, mentioned at the beginning of this chapter, that the cancan is not 'pure invention' but 'has its rhythms', pointing to the multilayered relationship between improvisation and structure in the dance. This relationship can be observed on a physical level in the improvisations that penetrated the quadrille's choreographic structure and replaced civilized sociality with popular cultural embodiments of liberty. The policeman's gaze also placed these physical improvisations within legal constraints, forcing dancers to time, space, and execute their moves tactically. The determination of the postrevolutionary monarchies to police these acts of insubordination suggests that they registered powerfully at a political level. The dancers' improvisations-within-structure made visibly present marginalized popular performance repertoires embodying liberty and opposition to authority and sutured these performances into the contredanse and quadrille, forms that embodied French national identity. In doing so, the dancers made a physical protest against the limited definitions of liberty developed prior to and during the French Revolution and played with alternative definitions on their own bodies. The improvised nature of this protest made it difficult for the authorities to police, while its use of the nationally resonant contredanse and quadrille structures made it impossible for those authorities to ignore. Monsieur Genret's assertion that the cancan 'has its rhythms' might have reassured the courtroom that it was not an excuse for anarchy. But the cancan dancers' improvisations were all the more subversive *because* they played with the rhythms of choreographic, legal, and political authority, finding ways of moving within and between those constraints to open up transient moments of resistance and liberty.

NOTES

The research for this chapter was supported by the University of Chichester; and the Arts and Humanities Research Council (grant number AH/L010879/1). I am deeply grateful to my research assistants on these projects, Dr Anna Davies and Dr Claire Jones, whose detailed translations and dialogues about interpretation have brought the material to life. Their translations are credited throughout using their initials, AD and CJ.

1. 'Le *cancan* est une *chahut épurée*' (Genret cited in Anonymous 1829c: 1186).

2. 'Fait un pas en arrière, se place en face du greffier, et prenant une position dansante, il s'avance en balançant son corps sur ses hanches' (Anonymous 1829c: 1185).

3. 'Répréhensible, puisqu'un geste aussi fugitif qu'un *rond de jambe* ou un *balancé* n'a pu trouver grâce devant les rigueurs de la loi pénale' (Anonymous 1829a: 61).

4. 'N'allez pas croire, Messieurs, que la danse *cancan* soit de pure invention: elle a ses rythmes, comme le *menuet* avait les siens' (Anonymous 1829a: 61).

5. 'Forme vieillie' 'absence de vie et de passion' (Smith 1841: 114).

6. 'Pour cela, qu'ont-ils fait? ... Chaque danseur s'est mis à improviser une espèce de dialogue mimé, d'une expression très vive. Au lieu de figurer tout uniment, avec le plus d'élégance et de grâce possible, la tête droite, les bras collés au corps, et sans sortir du catalogue des pas classiques, l'*assemblée*, le *six-sol*, l'*entrechat*, ils ont inventé des mouvements de pieds, des mouvements de bras, des mouvements de tête; ils ont attaqué le *statu quo* dansant de tous les côtés à la fois.... Plus de formes convenues, plus de routine, plus d'uniformité.. on peut s'y livrer à sa verve, à sa fantaisie: on peut être soi-même et ne copier personne; en un mot, dans ce système la contredanse est une forme dramatique, où chacun improvise, suivant son génie, et met en relief son individualité' (Smith 1841: 114).

7. 'Quand le cavalier seul va en avant dans la naïve figure de la Pastourelle, il se livre surtout à toute l'improvisation de son génie, et sur cinq cents danseurs pas un n'imite son voisin. Il en est même dont le génie s'allume tellement, que le garde municipal est obligé de venir calmer cet excès d'enthousiasme' (Huart 1845: 54).

8. 'En général l'improvisation dansante a pris une tendance déplorable' (Smith 1841: 114).

9. 'Par des allures empruntées aux gens de la halle et aux débardeurs des ports' (Delaforest 1853: 337).

10. 'Si cela lui passe par la tête, l'homme, au lieu de danser, de sauter, mettra les mains dans les poches de son pantalon, de son habit, de son gilet, fera quelques pas en avant ou restera immobile regardant son vis-à-vis féminin d'un air hautain, impérieux ou lascif, qu'il tâchera de rendre le plus satanique qu'il pourra, à la façon de Frédérick-Lemaître lorsqu'il dansait la valse de Méphistophélès, dans le mélodrame de *Faust*; ou bien, loin de jeter les yeux sur son vis-à-vis, il les tournera à droite et à gauche sur l'assemblée, et semblera occupé de toute autre chose' (Delaforest 1853: 337).

11. 'Dans la *chaine anglaise*, par exemple, elles se précipitant aveuglement devant elles, courent en apparence sans discernement; on les prendrait pour des échappées de Charenton; mais en voyant l'art avec lequel elles retournent vers leurs danseurs, on reconnait bientôt que leur pétulance n'est pas sans méthode. Elles ne perdent aucune figure de la contredanse; et lorsque dans le désordre qui marque souvent la fin d'une figure animée, elles arrivent à leur place avant que l'orchestre ait achevé la ritournelle [sic], leurs pieds, en frappant vivement la terre, et leur tête en se balançant sur leurs épaules, marquent le rythme des mesures que leurs jambes n'ont pu accomplir' (Anonymous 1829b: 490).

12. 'Comme un de ces canevas de pièce italienne que brodent les acteurs, suivant leur esprit et leur talent' (Smith 1841: 114).

13. 'Mon ami Chicard tient à son droit de penser et d'écrire ce qu'il pense.

   Supprimez ce droit!

   Tuez la liberté de la presse, qui, avant de mourir, fera son testament....

   De concession en concession, vous obtiendrez ainsi de lui à peu près tout ce qu'il vous plaira d'obtenir.

   Mon ami Chicard ne tient essentiellement qu'à une liberté.

   Mais celle-ci, comme il y tient!!!

Il lui faut *la liberté des jambes!*
Et voilà pourquoi mon ami Chicard raffolle de la *danse aux barrières.*
C'est-là qu'il peut faire un usage immodéré de sa chère liberté.—Je parle de celle des jambes.
La danse aux barrières, voilà ce qu'il aime!' (Balochard and Chicard 1841: 33–34).

14. 'On est libre à Mabille, à la Chaumière, à Valentino. Là, chacun danse comme il l'entend: il peut marcher, comme dans le grand monde; il peut aussi tricoter des entrechats et faire la roue dans les solos de pastourelle' (Anonymous 1845: 10).

References

Alhoy, M. (1840) L'Interrogatoire. In Alhoy, M., Huart, L., and Philippon, C. (eds.), *Le Musée pour rire* 3(126): n.p.

Anonymous. (1829a) Outrage public à la pudeur en dansant la chahut. *Gazette des Tribunaux* 1307 (17 October): 1185–1186.

Anonymous. (1829b) Outrage public à la pudeur en dansant la chahut. *Gazette des Tribunaux* 1335 (19 November): 61.

Anonymous. (1829c) *Journal des dames et des modes* 62 (10 November): 490–491.

Anonymous. (1845) *Paris dansant, ou les filles d'Hérodiade, folles danseuses des bals publics: Le bal Mabille, la Grande-Chaumière, le Ranelagh, etc.* Paris: J. Breauté.

Artz, F. B. (1963) *France under the Bourbon Restoration, 1814–1830.* New York: Russell and Russell.

Bakhtin, M. (1984) *Rabelais and His World.* Trans. H. Iswolsky. Bloomington: Indiana University Press.

Balochard and Chicard. (1841) *Physiologie des bals de Paris par Chicard et Balochard, dessins par MM. Lacoste et Kolb.* Paris: Desloges.

Barlet, Officer of the Peace. (1831) *Le Guide des sergens de ville et autres préposés de l'administration de la police.* Paris: L'Auteur.

Bourget, E. (1842) *Physiologie du gamin de Paris: Galopin industriel.* Paris: J. Laisné.

Brooks, P. (1976) *The Melodramatic Imagination: Balzac, Henry James, Melodrama, and the Mode of Excess.* New Haven: Yale University Press.

Burt, R. (1998) *Alien Bodies: Representations of Modernity, 'Race', and Nation in Early Modern Dance.* London: Routledge.

Capello, L. (1814) *Dictionnaire portatif piémontais-français: Suivi d'un vocabulaire français des termes usités dans les arts et métiers.* Turin: Vincent Bianco.

Clark, M. (2002) The Quadrille as Embodied Musical Experience in Nineteenth-Century Paris. *Journal of Musicology* 19(3): 503–526.

Cohen, S. R. (2000) *Art, Dance, and the Body in French Culture of the Ancien Régime.* Cambridge: Cambridge University Press.

Davidson, D. Z. (2007) *France after Revolution: Urban Life, Gender, and the New Social Order.* Cambridge, MA: Harvard University Press.

de Certeau, M. (1984) *The Practice of Everyday Life.* Trans. S. Rendall. Berkeley: University of California Press.

Delaforest, A. (1853) Cancan et Chahut. In Duckett, W. (ed.), *Dictionnaire de la conversation et de la lecture: Inventaire raisonné des notions générale les plus indispensable à tous* 4. 2nd ed. Paris: Aux comptoirs de la direction, 337–339.

Duchartre, P. L. (1966) *The Italian Comedy*. Trans. R. T. Weaver. New York: Dover.

Ellis, K. (2007) *Music Criticism in Nineteenth-Century France: La Revue et gazette musicale de Paris 1834–80*. Cambridge: Cambridge University Press.

Esterhammer, A. (2008) *Romanticism and Improvisation, 1750–1850*. Cambridge: Cambridge University Press.

Foucault, M. (1991) *Discipline and Punish: The Birth of the Prison*. London: Penguin Books.

Foucault, M. (1997) The Ethics of the Concern for Self as a Practice of Freedom. In Rabinow, P. (ed.), *Ethics, Subjectivity and Truth*. New York: New Press, 281–301.

Gardembas, A. (1845) *Almanach du crime et des causes célèbres françaises et étrangères, 1845: Contenant un choix des plus intéressants procès jugés cette année*. Paris: Librairie du Passage D'Harcourt and Leriche.

Gautier, T. (1847). Le carnaval de Paris en 1847. *Revue de Paris* 2: 202–212.

Gluck, M. (2005) *Popular Bohemia: Modernism and Urban Culture in Nineteenth-Century Paris*. Cambridge, MA: Harvard University Press.

Goldman, D. (2010) *I Want to be Ready: Improvised Dance as a Practice of Freedom*. Ann Arbor: University of Michigan Press.

Hauser, A. (1951) *The Social History of Art*. Vol. 3. *Rococo, Classicism and Romanticism*. London: Routledge and Kegan Paul.

Henke, R. (2015) Form and Freedom: Between Scenario and Stage. In Chaffee, J., and Crick, O. (eds.), *The Routledge Companion to Commedia dell'Arte*. New York: Routledge, 21–29.

Huart, L. (1845) *Paris au bal*. Paris: Aubert.

Johnson, J. H. (2001) Versailles, Meet Les Halles: Masks, Carnival, and the French Revolution. *Representations* 73: 89–116.

Kroen, S. (2000) *Politics and Theater: The Crisis of Legitimacy in Restoration France, 1815–1830*. Berkeley: University of California Press.

Lepecki, A. (2013) Choreopolice and Choreopolitics: Or, the Task of the Dancer. *TDR/The Drama Review* 57(4): 13–27.

Luchet, A. (1833) La Descente de La Courtille en 1833. In Ladvocat, C. (ed.), *Paris, ou Le livre des cent et un* 11: 29–55.

Magraw, R. (1983) *France 1815–1914: The Bourgeois Century*. Oxford: Fontana.

Outram, D. (1989) *The Body and the French Revolution: Sex, Class, and Political Culture*. New Haven : Yale University Press.

Parker, H. N. (2011) Toward a Definition of Popular Culture. *History and Theory* 50(2): 147–170.

Philipon, C. (1842–1843) *Musée ou magasin comique de Philipon: Contenant près de 800 dessins* 2. Paris: Aubert.

Ravel, J. S. (1999) *The Contested Parterre: Public Theater and French Political Culture, 1680–1791*. Ithaca: Cornell University Press.

Rogers, E. A. (2003) *The Quadrille: A Practical Guide to Its Origin, Development and Performance*. Orpington, UK: E. Rogers.

Smith, P. [Edouard Monnais]. (1841) Danses Prohibées. *La Revue et gazette musicale de Paris* 8 (21 February): 114.

Stallybrass, P., and White, A. (1986) *The Politics and Poetics of Transgression*. London: Methuen.

Taylor, D. (2003) *The Archive and the Repertoire: Performing Cultural Memory in the Americas*. Durham, NC: Duke University Press.

Terdiman, R. (1985) *Discourse/Counter-discourse: The Theory and Practice of Symbolic Resistance in Nineteenth-Century France*. Ithaca: Cornell University Press.

Terdiman, R. (1993) *Present Past: Modernity and the Memory Crisis*. Ithaca: Cornell University Press.

The Penal Code of France, Translated into English with a Preliminary Dissertation and Notes. (1819) London: H. Butterworth and Baldwin, Cradock, and Joy.

Vanderburch, L. É., and Langlé, J. A. F. (1834) *Le Procès du cancan, ou la chasse aux Pierrots*. Paris: Duvernois.

Wechsler, J. (1982) *A Human Comedy: Physiognomy and Caricature in Nineteenth Century Paris*. London: Thames and Hudson.

Winter, M. H. (1962) *The Theatre of Marvels*. London: Benjamin Blom.

CHAPTER 15

VALORIZING UNCERTAINTY

Chance, Totalitarianism, and Soviet Ballet

JANICE ROSS

> If at bottom all things proceed in accordance with the law, and if there
> is nothing that is accidental—causeless—it is clear there can be no such
> thing as an accident in history.
>
> Nikolai Bukharin (1921)

CHANCE. Improvisation. Uncertainty. During the Cold War, each of these words came to be freighted with a different and complex set of aesthetic meanings in the Soviet Union and the United States. These nuances in the usage of these terms, the kind of arts practice they made possible, and the ways they were linked, directly or obliquely, to each nation's political discourses, hold important insights into the politicizing of aesthetic practices and the aestheticizing of social revolutions. Avoiding an overly simplistic binary that positions chance and improvisation 'as good' and preplanned and controlled art as 'not good', this essay instead considers the affordances *of* constraints when paired with the selective use of improvisation in the work of Russian choreographer Leonid Yakobson. A close reading of the work of Yakobson, the leading modernist at the Kirov and Bolshoi Ballets throughout the years of Stalin's totalitarian rule and into the first decades of the Cold War, is a relevant case study. It reveals how, clandestinely in his rehearsal rooms, a degree of improvisation and the courting of chance carried unique aesthetic force and political risk.

Marxist theoretician Nikolai Bukharin's (1925) often quoted declaration above, from 1921, that 'if at bottom all things proceed in accordance with the law and if there is nothing that is accidental—causeless—it is clear *there can be no such thing as an accident in history*' (my emphasis) was intended initially in reference to a political system when he presented it as part of the rational for political legitimation of the Bolshevik social revolution. However, it quickly entered circulation as the abbreviated 'there is no such thing as an accident in history', effectively a declaration that chance did not operate under the new Soviet order. In subsequent decades, this came to resonate in other areas of culture, and especially Cold War literature, in which the 'no accident' ethos of

FIG. 15.1 Leonid Yakobson 'conducting' with his hands as he rehearses his Choreographic Miniatures Company, Leningrad, c. 1972. Photograph by Vladimir Zenzinov.

Communism has been the subject of considerable scholarship. Until now, dance has been left out of these analyses. Jacques Monod (1972) argued in *Chance and Necessity* that Soviet reality was an all-encompassing fiction which was visible as such because it denied the operation of absolute chance.

This essay addresses that oversight, arguing that dance was one cultural arena where these politicized meanings of accidents, chance, and improvisation played out with particular vividness during the Cold War. As such, I contend that dance offers a unique window onto the ideological battleground between the Soviet Union and the United States. Equally important, the ways the uncontrollable and unplanned were deployed, or deplored, as aesthetic strategies in each nation offer insights into the force and impact of the aesthetic discoveries they facilitated and the social structures they attempted to navigate. Beginning in the late nineteenth century, chance was linked in the United States with gambling, competition, and the conditions of liberal capitalism (Puskar 2012: 6–7). Healthy competition was viewed as a good way to train young men into capitalist ideology and give them practice in conscious striving to win as a recreational activity that also made them good competing workers. In contrast, the Bolshevik doctrine effectively refused to admit that important events can be accidental or contingent (Belletto 2012: 15). This was because contingency and accident ran counter to a political system that evolved to promise a planned and controlled authoritarian-ruled future.

Although the term 'improvisation' is generally used to refer to 'something composed or uttered without preparation or premeditation' and 'chance' designates 'the occurrence of events in the absence of any obvious intention or cause', Yakobson's embrace of uncertainty in the creation of his ballets played between these strategies without ever really settling exclusively with one or the other (Puskar 2012: 7). He used a range of aesthetic approaches to discover and conjure movement from his dancers, taking risks and valorizing uncertainty at times as he pushed the dancers he worked with into the unknown. I reference these definitions in the spirit of scholar Jason Puskar, who has written about the production of chance as a conceptual category in the late nineteenth and twentieth centuries. Puskar suggests that 'rather than ask what chance is, then, it seems more fruitful to ask what chance does' (8). Puskar extends this to claim that 'chance creates dynamic instabilities at many different levels—knowledge, ethics, identity, economics, power—that are not just disruptive but finally useful to a loosely allied set of progressive reforms' (7).

Chance in the ballet studio was an opening into a similar constellation of aesthetic and social concerns for Yakobson. The more topical and the less like traditional ballet the subject matter of his dances, the more resonant Yakobson's embrace of open movement prompts even in small moments in the dance. A case in point is his 1963 ballet *Hiroshima*. Elena Selivanova, who worked with Yakobson as he was making *Hiroshima*, recalled how he used structured improvisation inspired by metaphor to get the dancers to invent movement passages in this work.

> This miniature, set to Henryk Gorecki's music, required an especially poignant emotional expression on the part of the cast, which consisted of five dancers. We were so young and naïve that we laughed when Jacobson asked us to open our mouths wide and assume what then seemed to us anti-esthetic postures. During rehearsals Jacobson explained: 'Imagine yourself being consumed by fire, your skin peeling off your bodies; you feel unbearable pain—you are shaking with pain. You are racked by nervous tremors. Make me hear your hysterical screaming'.... [In a sense] Jacobson demanded that we display a dramatic skill using only pantomime. He even designed special make-up for this ballet. The members of a visiting delegation from Japan who were shown *Hiroshima* couldn't believe their eyes: through movement alone Jacobson managed to convey the horror and torments of people struck by a nuclear bomb. (Selivanova 2010: 124, Marina Brodskaya translation)

This use of metaphor as a prompt for the dancers to improvise their way from one more structured part of the dance to another in this instance pushed them to think about the physical toll on the body that resulted from nuclear warfare. It personalized the political, and it deployed ugliness or, as Selivanova phrased it, 'anti-esthetic postures', both of which went against the acceptable in the Soviet Union. Ethics, power, politics on a human scale can come into play for performers, and ultimately audiences, as a result of these discoveries through movement in the ballet studio.

Yakobson (1904–1975) is the paradigmatic case of an innovative choreographer who used improvisatory approaches like this at different points in his creative process during the Cold War as a means towards choreographic invention in Communist Russia (Selivanova 2010: 124). Almost always using a musical score as his basis, he structured his use of improvisation in rehearsal as a spontaneous response to the music for each ballet he was making, as he sought to discover movement possibilities within the genre of classical ballet. His dances were not classical in style. Rather, the ballet movement vocabulary that was the medium in which he made his 'what if?' discoveries certainly derived from classicism. Paralleling his use of improvisatory and aleatoric methods were those of the modern dance experimentalists in the United States who were also using improvisation or chance methods to open new politicized territory in dance during the decades of the Cold War, beginning in the 1950s.[1] For Yakobson, this was a risky foray into a practice deemed bourgeois, anti-Soviet, and subject to meddling. For the American artists who used chance, it was about nontraditional invention and an embrace of spontaneous free movement as an antidote to socialized obedience.

Yet within the frame of the Cold War Soviet Union, Yakobson's rehearsals made a spectacle of uncertainty. They positioned instability at the heart of Soviet cultural production, and they did this in the studios where classical ballet was birthed. Bounding about the studio as he exhorted a couple to try an impossible lift-into-a-drop manoeuver or as he coached a group of male dancers in how to appear invisible as they ferried a ballerina flying high above their heads in a racing run around the studio, Yakobson reconfigured the world of dance invention as having chance and discovery embedded in it. This could be seen as incendiary and antithetical to the Soviet concept of planned social order.

In fact, his very demeanour in the ballet studio might be considered more aligned with liberal capitalist values and their reflection of more tolerance for risk-taking and less valuing of steady labour and its conservation. Yakobson's dancers recount tales of how once he had his own company, Choreographic Miniatures, and was under less official oversight, he rehearsed them late into the night in marathon rehearsal sessions, losing his sense of time and the fact that he was depleting them to the point of exhaustion. Valentina Klimova Sergeyeva, one of the leading dancers in Yakobson's troupe and a fearless virtuoso, noted the following about how his fluid sense of invention could spill into a spontaneous sense of time and neglect of the limits of stamina in his dancers.

> The creative process, which was very dynamic, took place in the rehearsal hall. Jacobson knew what he wanted to accomplish but not how he would go about it. Just as a sculptor needs clay or an artist paints so did he need the body of a dancer, male or female. The entire troupe took part in the staging of a ballet. For example, when he staged a *pas-de-deux*, several pairs of dancers would be trying out a sequence of movements at the same time in the middle of the room. If one of them managed to execute a lift successfully, Jacobson—who may not have even known at the outset what that movement would look like, but now liked what he saw—immediately adopted it. We prompted his decisions through our movements and our plastic rendering [of the music].... Before every rehearsal I always felt very nervous. Jacobson created choreography extremely quickly, and in discrete small fragments. He would listen to an extremely short musical passage and immediately, while the sound still resounded in our ears, show us the movement. In order to grasp, memorize and perform it, one had to maintain absolute concentration. One had to attune oneself to the pace of his fantasy, which was as swift as lightning—if we failed to register a movement there and then Jacobson, who was constitutionally unable to visualize the same

pas twice, changed it in some way. This is why he always pleaded with us: 'Faster, faster—all of you, please, memorize; I won't be able to repeat this for you, but [what you just saw] was right: this is how it should be done'. [The movements,] born spontaneously and instantaneously in his imagination, vanished as rapidly—and this was the only weakness of his improvisation method. His choreography was impossible to get used to—it was always full of surprises. Neither could one tell how he would begin or end a piece. (Zozulina 2010: 131, Marina Brodskaya, Translation)

To better understand the risks Yakobson courted with his use of improvisation it is useful to explore how chance and improvisation were regarded in contrasting ways in the Soviet Union and the United States during this postwar period. Chance, which can be called 'the occurrence and development of events in the absence of any obvious design', was generally deemed by the Soviets to contradict the official concept of control over individual will. This has been presented by Cold War scholar Steven Belletto as so absolute that reality became managed to where even chance seemed to have disappeared (4). Belletto describes how the politicizing of the concept of chance during the Cold War, through literary works like Jerzy Kosinski's book *The Future is Ours Comrade*, led to its association with American democratic freedom, while the denial of chance became linked with Soviet-style totalitarianism. Further defining 'chance' according to its etymological roots, Belletto associated the word 'chance' with the idea of falling and 'the absence of design' (2012: 12). 'The Cold War encouraged Americans—and those sympathetic to American democratic norms—to mobilize the concept of chance in order to underscore the naturalness of American democratic freedom as opposed to Soviet-style totalitarianism', Belletto explains, by way of demonstrating how each side regarded chance and improvisation as either a welcome marker of naturalness and individual liberty (the United States) or unwelcome control by an unintelligible outer force (the Soviet Union) (16–17, 19).

Dance improvisation might be said to be what chance-in-action looks like in the dance studio. It celebrates accident and contingencies. It is moving spontaneously and freely, deliberately trying not to let the conscious mind direct one towards planned outcomes. Susan Foster says of it that 'rather than suppress any functions of mind, improvisation's bodily mindfulness summons up a kind of hyperawareness of the relation between immediate action and overall shape, between that which is about to take place, or taking place and that which will take place' (Foster 2003: 7). This prompting of alertness and a questioning state of mind would be understandably inimical to a political system built on minimizing options for the individual. The more one considers the social ramifications of chance, the more evident are the risks it might have opened for a choreographer in the Soviet Union.

The dance artist most frequently associated with chance and uncertainty in the twentieth century is the American choreographer Merce Cunningham. Because Cunningham courted the unknown within a set structure, he always avoided the term 'improvisation', using 'chance' instead to describe his processes. In his choreography of the post–World War II period, Cunningham pioneered aleatoric methods in the dance studio. Openly, and at times even theatrically, he used the structured incorporation of chance and objective procedures, such as throwing the *I Ching* to determine movement sequences or using a stopwatch to set the precise length of time for part or all of a dance. Thus, random external structures were used as a means of discovering new modes of collecting and assembling movement. Subsequently, scholars have associated Cunningham's use of chance and its link to the composer John Cage's use of aleatoric methods in music composition with these artists' having been inspired by practices of Zen Buddhism and its openness to the chaos and implicit order of the universe as a larger external system.

One of the best known photographic images of Cunningham in relation to chance composition is a 1962 photo by Jack Mitchell that depicts him smiling broadly at the camera, while the composer John Cage stands behind Cunningham holding a giant stopwatch in his outstretched hand, as if teasingly offering the mystery object that controls their chance operations. Instead of no control, they are using duration. For Cunningham, this meant a natural time arrived at usually through the trial and error of rehearsal to determine how long a given phrase of movement 'wants' for its performance. That the phrase of movement may well have been generated by Cunningham's use of chance structures in rehearsal makes the indeterminacy layered and the controlled, and not-uncontrolled, dynamically fluid.

Yakobson had no such opportunity to be so transparent in his use of improvisation—instead he deliberately described what he did as always anchored by the musical composition he had selected and what it inspired in him with a full group of dancers looking on. This was true, but also perhaps a strategy of evading direct responsibility. Alexander Stepin, one of his dancers, said of Yakobson's process:

> How did he go about staging [his ballets]? He never wrote anything down.... And the way he treated a music score was legendary. His way of counting was highly idiosyncratic ... something like this: 'One, two, three. One and, two and, three and, four and, five and, six, seven, eleven'. We memorized the emerging beat as if it were a prayer. Jacobson would demonstrate [movements for] several bars—he was a genius at that, especially as concerns pantomime—and all the while, out of the corner of his eye he would observe the dancers, in order to choose the best one. Then he would point at that person and say: 'Do as he does'. Having achieved what he wanted, he consolidated it [made sure that the dancer consistently reproduced a movement correctly]. And that was all. There was no [further] work [to understand and develop] the character. He gave a concrete form to [i.e., achieved] what happened to be in his mind's eye at that moment through demonstration and the impact of the music alone [by influencing us with the music]. Such was his style. (Zozulina 2010: 128, Marina Brodskaya, translation)

Indeed, Yakobson was performing his spontaneous passion and engagement, seemingly so unmediated that he used to shout at the dancers to repeat what he had done as quickly as possible so that it would not be forgotten and lost. Klimova said of Yakobson's speedy invention: 'We realized that he was being guided by some mysterious hand. He created simultaneously several astounding fragments, choreographically unbelievably difficult. Surprised at his own performance he asked: "In your opinion, where did it all come from—what I have just made up?" "How are we supposed to know, Leonid Veniaminovich," we replied' (131). Interestingly, it was the exact opposite sentiment—dispassion—that was often used to describe Cunningham's work, in part because his use of chance seemed to remove emotion and sentiment, or at least the communication of specific predetermined feelings.

Some scholars doing a queer reading of Cunningham's aesthetic of disengagement with these chance procedures have suggested that this avoidance of active choice and the deliberate absence of a conscious inscription of ego on his dances reflects a posture of non-self-disclosure by him at a time when homophobia was particularly virulent and career damaging in the United States. In the 1970s, the British art historian Moira Roth used the term 'an aesthetic of disengagement' to describe retrospectively Marcel Duchamp's courting of chance procedures in some of his visual artworks. These included works where he dropped strings from a height onto glass and preserved their patterns, as well as the cracks in a shattered plate of glass or, most famously, in his *Readymade*, where he chose a mass-produced object, like a urinal, as an object proffered for aesthetic contemplation.

Susan Foster (2003) and Danielle Goldman (2010) are two scholars who have both theorized improvisation as holding more complex identities as they have traced the psychological and political charge it carries. Foster, in a 2003 essay, argues for improvisation as a state of 'hyperawareness of the relation between immediate action and overall shape'. Although she is speaking primarily of dancers who improvise in the act of performing rather than exclusively in the act of choreographing, as was the case for Yakobson, who drilled his dancers in a standard rehearsal after the improvised material was learned, Foster addresses the mental state of improvising as 'entailing a vigilant porousness toward the unknown'. She continues: 'it demands a reflexive awareness of when the known is becoming a stereotype, a rut instead of a path and it insists upon the courage and wit to recalibrate known and unknown as the performance unfolds' (Foster 2003: 6–7). These are aesthetic choices, but they are just as readily social rehearsals that can prepare one to challenge the status quo.

It is this capacity of movement improvisation to, as Foster puts it, 'empower those who witness it as well as those who perform it', as well as its ability to impact our understanding of 'human agency' and 'the special identity of the body discovered through improvisation' that has the potential to make it a proxy for political consciousness raising. Danielle Goldman focuses on this quality when she frames improvised dance of the postwar period in the United States in particular as 'a practice of freedom', the subtitle of her book on dance improvisation (2010: 4).

There are no photographs of Leonid Yakobson with a stopwatch; rather, the image most emblematic of his improvisatory experiments was his animated presence in the midst of rehearsing with dancers, often with others at the perimeter of the studio watching. Foster's concept of improvisation 'empowering those who witness it' perhaps accounts, then, for the intense curiosity of the onlookers in the photographs of Yakobson rehearsing. Interestingly, it is these photos of Yakobson as an animated presence in the midst of rehearsals that are the most prevalent images of him from the years of his own company, extending from 1971 to his death in October 1975. They document how the moment he had the authority to open the customarily sequestered process of dance creation, he opened the doors of his studio wide, essentially allowing anyone who asked permission to watch, and photograph, uncertainty. Nina Alovert, a leading dance photographer working in the Soviet Union during this period, said of the many photographs of Yakobson in rehearsal that photographers were drawn to him because 'he was a persona in the ballet world'. Because his concentration was so intense while he was improvising, having a photographer in the room, which would have been disturbing for most choreographers, did not affect him. 'He let photographers take pictures during his rehearsals because the photographers did not bother him', Alovert said.[2] From the decades prior to these four years, when Yakobson worked at the Kirov Ballet and the Bolshoi Ballet, there are only a couple photos of him rehearsing, and these images all appear carefully staged. They are orderly, and facial expressions are relaxed. In contrast, the rehearsal photos of Yakobson working with his own company, when he was finally able to use only dancers who would willingly follow his wild improvisatory manner, are remarkable documents.

In these images Yakobson, dressed in casual yet stylish patterned shirts and loose jeans, gestures with his arms, torso, and head, often in the pose of an arrested action that looks like an exaggerated gesture in daily life. In one, he makes a gesture of welcome with his arms flung wide open, fingers wide, like a parent about to hug a child.

In another, he gestures like a conductor demanding silence, one finger raised to his lips.

FIG. 15.2 Leonid Yakobson gesturing as he works with the dancers in his Choreographic Miniatures Company, Leningrad, c. 1972. Photograph by Anatoly Pronin.

FIG. 15.3 Leonid Yakobson in rehearsal demonstrating for his Choreographic Miniatures Company dancers, Leningrad, c. 1972. Photograph by Anatoly Pronin.

While these images are most likely from the end of the improvisatory process, as he shaped his choreography, they still reveal his unabashed physical expressiveness. He gave experienced and amateur photographers easy access to watching these kinds of moments in his rehearsals. They snapped streams of images, as if documenting this wading into the unknown of improvisation were more fascinating than photographing the final polishing of a completed dance in dress rehearsal. What is de facto documented here is Soviet curiosity in even watching improvisation in messy action as a choreographic process.

In the Soviet Union, culture was used as a highly visible 'pragmatic tool of mobilization', according to scholar Matthew Lenoe (2004) in his study of Soviet newspapers. Officially the master narrative of Stalinist culture was about the glorification of a known, predictable, and centrally controlled future, 'a new master narrative Soviet history and a new Bolshevik identity for millions of novice Communists' (Lenoe 2004: 245). This erasure of accident as a reality, and chance as a possibility, in the shaping of this tale had profound implications for the arts. Anatoly Pronin documented Yakobson in the rehearsal studio beginning in 1971, when he created his own company. Pronin was among those young photographers who came to Yakobson and asked permission to memorialize his process of permissiveness. His photographs show Yakobson in the midst of clusters of dancers in rehearsals and grabbing people and showing them what to do or exhorting them to try something he cannot even begin to demonstrate because it lies so outside the realm of known possibilities. 'You could see in the photos the expression on his face [and] you knew the dancers knew what he was feeling', Pronin said. 'He was always inside the group on the stage the whole time with the dancers—showing them what he wanted them to do—jumping around'.[3]

Elena Volynina, another Yakobson dancer, also remembered the quality of breathless speed with which his improvisations unfolded and how he only rarely tempered this energy, even when he had to in the presence of a major star dancer like the Bolshoi's Maya Plisetskaya: '"Jacobson worked with Plisetskaya, who came to rehearse at Mayakovsky 15," Volynina recalled, naming the address of Yakobson's Company home. "Plisetskaya was slow and methodical, while Leonid Veniaminovich worked on impulse, improvising and staging his numbers at a breakneck pace. If anyone couldn't keep up, he would say: 'Step aside, you dolt! You are in the way!' However, even though Plisetskaya was obviously not quick enough for him, he never mentioned this to her and treated her extremely well. He liked talented people"' (Zozulina 2010: 137, Marina Brodskaya translation). The aesthetic of socialist realism might be thought of as the antidote to the uncertainty Yakobson relished—a visual system of representation that made certitude into an aesthetic strategy and the visualization and enactment of a predictable and centrally controlled future the only acceptable art style. So while the American artists who were using chance and uncertainty in their work were often considered radical and antiestablishment provocateurs by an American mainstream accustomed to a linear narrative and conscious shaping of art, viewed from the Soviet perspective they were predictably complicit in manifesting a bourgeois aesthetic of democracy.

Just as the Soviets deemed chance and courting the unknown in dance to be a politicizing act, several American interpreters of chance read it as far more than neutral disengagement. The dance critic Jill Johnston, writing for the *Village Voice* in 1962, made the following observation about chance procedures and dance in reviewing an evening of works by several postmodern choreographers at Judson Memorial Church: 'chance procedures are preliminary controls; the chance results are subjected to the control of performance and that means you always end up with a person expressing himself. Movement is not like sound in that respect. Movement is the person'. Johnston's comment, ironically, describes surprisingly well the spirit of Yakobson and his use of chance, perhaps better than it does the postmodern American dance-makers about whom it was initially written.

What is telling in Johnston's observation is that chance is in fact framed as a path into the personal rather than into the anonymity often ascribed to Cunningham's use of it. In an interview Yakobson once gave about his process of using improvisation, he spoke of just this quality of illuminating the person through movement as central to how and why he chose improvisation and the indelibility of the dancer herself in what gets preserved in the final choreography:

> The quality of dance design depends to a great extent on the artistic persona of the performer. It makes all the difference to me who I am rehearsing with, for I improvise using the qualities [material], both physical and spiritual, that the actor possesses.

If an actor is sensitive to music, has good plasticity and a rich inner world, he will direct the choreographer towards various possibilities even if he has no intention of doing so. A dancer who is mentally rigid, who is used to routine dancing, and who is insensitive to music and devoid of imagination and temperament is bound to break the choreographer's wings. Improvisation is first and foremost interaction between the choreographer, the music, and the performer. I take into consideration the actor's individuality; indeed, I cannot help doing so, since the insights and emotions the music engenders in me must be filtered through the actor's personality. My perceptions are expressed not as abstractions but through a concrete image. The point of departure for my improvisation is the actor's [plastic] physical and inner self. [The actor's] humor, energy, movement flow, elevation, tenderness, and precision—all of these leave their mark on the character. In my ballets, the parts are created together with the soloists. This, of course, does not preclude the possibility that their successors might perform them better and with more brilliance. (Akimov 1983: 9, Marina Brodskaya translation.)

Although Yakobson could not use chance procedures openly, his approach to choreography once he had his own company increasingly began with this improvisational testing of what the dancers' bodies could do that was beyond known territory in ballet. For example, In his *Mozart Pas de Deux,* made in 1970–1971, Yakobson strips back the pas de deux to the bare frame of an entrée for a man and woman, an adagio, solo variations, and a coda. He discards the predictability and balanced symmetry that customarily unfolds within this structure, containing the couple dance. Instead he replaces it with the very *un*-Soviet aesthetic of uncertainty and chance. The unfinished *Mozart Pas de Deux* is not an improvisation, but it does record the traces of how it was created—in a rush of free-form questioning—a series of 'what-if' encounters between Yakobson, the Mozart score, and his dancers' physical abilities. This marks it as the record of an incursion into free experimentation. At one point, the male dancer partners the woman from a semireclining position on the ground, and he later assists her in a turn by guiding her from her elbow. Every phrase in this brief work is unique. There is not a standard ballet step at any point where a dancer could simply cruise along—at each moment surprise lurks around the corner.

An archival 1960 film of this work, recorded as part of a Lenfilm broadcast about Yakobson's ballet miniatures, the term given to his short choreographies, captures Tatyana Kvasova and Igor Kuzmin in a sparkling performance of the adagio and coda, accompanied by Mozart's *Twelve Variations in C – on 'Ah, vous dirai-je, Maman'*. As the couple enters with a courtly air, she in a tutu like an abbreviated baroque ballgown and he in a black velvet courtier's jacket over white tights, their feet perform little skipping steps that offer a rhythmic intertext with Mozart's score. The music begins with deceptive simplicity, and then its tempo accelerates to a breathlessly fast speed as the notes and steps cluster more densely. At times, the dancers tuck quick little flourishes of the feet into the movement phrases so that their actions seem like visual music that is as logical a part of the score as the actual notes. Soon the woman is being spun in rapid supported turns on pointe, which she executes with deliberately soft bent legs while angling her head, arms, torso, and hands in gentle side-to-side twists, embellishments that have the quality of baroque ornamentation. He lifts and carries her, momentarily wrapping her across his back, without breaking the momentum of their partnering. The more difficult it becomes—she rotates in finger turns from a squat so deep she seems nearly to be sitting on the floor—the more confident and relaxed both dancers' smiles become. From her squat she keeps her feet fully stretched on pointe and walks forward, flicking her toes, as her steers her by her upraised arms as if he were driving a miniature horse and cart. Now she tosses herself to him, and he catches her, allowing her to recline against his arm. They seem to be dancing inside the music, so tight is their coordination with its rhythms yet so inventive are their movements, which look as if they might embrace classicism but instead swerve away to the modern at the last instant.

Deliberately avoiding the customary windup framing a virtuoso movement, virtually everything Kvasova and Kuzmin do in *Mozart Pas de Deux* is fresh and surprising. For example, instead of a vertical supported turn with her standing straight and tall, they complete a full turn as she tilts to the side and bends her standing leg just slightly as he slowly revolves her. Their conclusion is all subtlety and nuance, as she scampers up his leg and onto his back and off, ending with the offer of her toe-shoe-clad foot, which he kisses as if it were a gloved hand. Finally, posing with a flourish that suggests that they might be settling at last into a fish dive (*poisson* pose), they suddenly change, ending with a quirky virtuoso finish: Kvasova walks up and over Kuzmin's extended leg, pausing as he grasps her with her legs extended in a split jump, as if he had simply grabbed her out of the air in midleap. Their ease suggests that the unexpected gives them endless pleasure. In dispensing with the traditional big-drumroll notification that they are about to perform a special feat, Kvasova and Kuzmin showcase the felicity of the continually unexpected. Louis Pasteur's dictum 'Chance favors only the prepared mind' was always on display in Yakobson's working process, as he invested enormous amounts of time immersing himself in the music and researching and drafting a libretto of a work long before he arrived in the studio, in order to free himself to spontaneously improvise his way into the choreography:

> I improvise the outlines of a dance; I do not devise beforehand the transitions, groupings and mise en scenes, nor do I write down the sequence of movements. For me, to create a dance (sketch, outline) is to improvise. This method requires the ability to achieve inspiration during rehearsals. Under these circumstances, any chance occurrence becomes extremely important—[as are] the actors' psychological state, the choreographer's mood, his relations with the performers, and the rendering of the music by the accompanist.
>
> [Thus] the whole—the design of a dance—is born out of innumerable trivial details. The movements are superimposed on one another, ultimately forming a plastic theme with its distinct inner content and color. It is only when a dance piece (work) is complete that the meaning and purpose of its every detail, improvised by the choreographer, is revealed. (Akimov 1983: 9, Marina Brodskaya, translation)

Yakobson's description of his use of improvisation here as a way to 'achieve inspiration' suggests that it is a path of temporary wandering in order to arrive at a more deeply considered sense of self. He is not fleeing personal disclosure but tapping into his and the dancers' affective lives—and then sharing those onstage. This kind of personalization went directly counter to the grand scale of socialist realist art, which was supposed to reflect and advocate for an idealized socialist society through generic images, not messily individual ones such as Yakobson sought. 'Some spectators and critics believe my dance design to be excessively fragmented, elusive and shifting', he admitted. 'But I only do as the music tells me', he continued, explaining that his self-administered injunction was to make the music visible. This was a true statement but also one that slyly displaced the responsibility for whatever emerged improvisationally to the composer, effectively leaving the choreographer a mere broker of those meanings. 'I confine myself to the theme that the music states explicitly and to the mood it implies, but the concrete forms, lines and modes of expression come to me on the spur of the moment, that is, while a certain musical passage is being played and while the dancer [artist] is looking to me for a demonstration', he elaborated. The results were not always pleasant for the dancers, Yakobson confessed: 'this fragmentation of the composition, the detailing of the design, is at times resisted by the dancers, [since] it demands extra effort, as well as sensitivity and attention to music. [But] once the actor has fleshed out the choreographer's design, has merged with it, and has acquired a sense of freedom in the confines imposed upon him, he can no longer replace, discard, or modify any part of the dance. The actors get used to my understanding of music and to my method of extemporizing' (9). In the face of a Soviet system predicated on planned and controlled outcomes, Yakobson effectively used aesthetics as shield to 'not know', and he made this a social force. Valentina Klimova recalled the atmosphere in the initial rehearsals of Yakobson's company and the way freedom, contained by strict behavioural discipline, infused his choreographic inventions:

> the entire troupe took part in the staging of a ballet. For example, when he staged a pas-de-deux, several pairs of dancers would be trying out a difficult sequence of movements at the same time in the middle of the room. If one of them managed to execute a lift successfully, Yakobson—who may not have even known at the outset what that movement would look like, but now liked what he saw— immediately adopted it. 'We prompted his decisions through our movements and our plastic rendering [of the music]', Klimova said, recalling the heightened tension that was always part of Yakobson's rehearsals because of this. 'Before every rehearsal I always felt very nervous. Yakobson created choreography extremely quickly, and in discrete small fragments. He would listen to an extremely short musical passage and immediately, while the sound still resounded in our ears, show us the movement. In order to grasp, memorize and perform it, one had to maintain absolute concentration. One had to attune oneself to the pace of his fantasy, which was as swift as lightning—if we failed to register a movement there and then Yakobson, who was constitutionally unable to visualize the same pas twice, changed it in some way', she said explaining this was why in the midst of improvising Yakobson would often tell the dancers: 'Faster, faster— all of you, please, memorize; I won't be able to repeat this for you, but [what you just saw] was right: this is how it should be done'. Klimova candidly confessed

that this strength of speed was also the liability of Yakobson's improvisations. '[The movements,] born spontaneously and instantaneously in his imagination, vanished as rapidly— and this was the only weakness of his improvisation method. His chore-ography was impossible to get used to—it was always full of surprises'. (Zozulina 2010: 110)

While his finished ballets never left anything to chance in performance, Yakobson's method of building dance was filled with discovery.

The actual movements of Yakobson's choreography gave off an aura of invention. A film fragment, in his widow's possession, of his *Rossini Pas de Trois*—one of the pieces in the cycle *Classicism—Romanticism* (a cycle that included *Medieval Dances with Kisses, Bellini Pas de Quatre, Cachucha, Mozart Pas de Deux,* and *Taglioni's Flight*) and choreographed in this flood of new dances made in 1970–1971—documents ballet so daring that forty years later it would still be a significant challenge for dancers. *Rossini* opens quietly with the ballerina in a short white skirt with a wide black belt accenting her waist. Slowly she turns in an off-balance pose, one leg extended high overhead as her partner pivots her from a stance that is also deliberately off-center and unstable. As the music and the dancing accelerate, she walks up his leg and rolls across his back, accenting her descent with a swift flutter kick of her legs. The man's variation is also accented with crisp movement flourishes, all happening so quickly that nothing is highlighted as a big dance 'event'. The challenges multiply as the dancers tuck in more surprises—a whip-ping turn for the man that ends with a tricky landing on one foot rather than two, a zip-ping series of *piqué* turns for the woman that send her in one direction while she snaps her head and focuses the other way. Often the dancer's body suggests a counterpoint of forces within a single individual, as the arms and torso move with an ease while the feet and legs race through a thicket of steps, each one delivered with pithy neatness.

In the initial months of building his new company's repertoire, Yakobson worked in three studios simultaneously, switching not just steps but entire genres of dance from one room to the next. Larissa Yermolova, a Yakobson dancer, once described him as 'working on a creative conveyer, as it were. It defies imagination how he could switch from one of these ballets to another and produce a work of genius as the end result' (Zozulina 2010: 97). This was a strategy with a particular political resonance during the Cold War years in the Soviet Union, for his improvisatory quickness, excessive rehearsal times and capacity for fluid invention were seen as a decidedly Western and bourgeoisie aesthetic. This capacity to choreograph widely disparate ballets simultaneously also had a curious, mercurial stylistic variability that suggested what was potentially a politically perilous "rootlessness" in regard to his choreographic style. Yakobson's aesthetic home was deliberately not classicism or neoclassicism or modernism but a fluid circulation among these styles.

In the end, it may well have been his use of improvisation and chance that made it possible for Yakobson to work at all. Instead of negotiating internally what the author-ities might and might not allow in the form of ballets, Yakobson created a little docket of safety for himself by fashioning this space of uncertainty in the initial stage of his dance-making. We are all products of our cultural moment and its social constraints, and he certainly understood that. But to say to his dancers, 'I am improvising to the music, watch me and catch what you see!' was like passing a secret message and asking those who saw it to shelter it in their bodies and physical memories. The fact that Yakobson's ballets survived at all is a testament to how patiently they honoured that request and went for the ride of improvisation with him. Yakobson often claimed that as an artist he couldn't know precisely what the end result of a dance would be. In the process, he made uncertainty a virtue, a defence, a questioning, and a refutation of planning. For him it was the only conscionable means of cultural production in Soviet Russia.

NOTES

1. These include Anna Halprin and the choreographers and dancers associated with Judson Memorial Church and Robert Dunn's workshops.
2. Nina Alovert, email communication with the author, 20 August 2014.
3. Interview by the author and Marina Broniskaya, Palo Alto, California, 9 December 2014.

REFERENCES

Akimov, N. (1983) Secrets of Mastery. *Musical Life* 13 (July): 9.

Belletto, S. (2012) No Accident, Comrade: Chance and Design in Cold War American Narratives. New York: Oxford University Press.

Bukharin, N. (1925) *Historical Materialism: A System of Sociology.* New York: International.

Foster, S. (2003) Taken by Surprise: Improvisation in Dance and Mind. In Albright, Ann Cooper, and Gere, D. (eds.), *Taken by Surprise: A Dance Improvisation Reader.* Middletown, CT: Wesleyan University Press, 1–14.

Goldman, D. (2010) *I Want to Be Ready: Improvised Dance as a Practice of Freedom.* Ann Arbor: University of Michigan Press.

Lenoe, M. (2004) Closer to the Masses: Stalinist Culture, Social Revolution, and Soviet Newspapers. Cambridge, MA: Harvard University Press.

Monod, J. (1972) Chance and Necessity: An Essay on the Natural Philosophy of Modern Biology. New York: Vintage Books.

Puskar, J. R. (2012) Accident Society: Fiction, Collectivity, and the Production of Chance. Redwood City, CA: Stanford University Press.

Selivanova, E. (2010) 'Ni I stupay k svoemu Yakobsonu!' ['Then go to your Yakobson!'] In Zozulina, N. (ed.), *Teatr Leonida Yakobsona.* St. Petersburg: Liki Rossi.

Zozulina, N. (ed.). (2010). *Teatr Leonida Yakobsona: Stati Vospominaniya Fotomateriali* [The theatre of Leonid Yakobson: Articles, reminiscences, photographs]. St. Petersburg: Liki Rossi.

CHAPTER 16

....

THE EMANCIPATION OF
IMPROVISATION

....

LARRY LAVENDER

IMPROVISATION occurs when deliberative thought and habitual or expected processes are at least temporarily suspended in favour of spontaneous, intuitive, and nonroutine activities that may yield surprising results (Albright and Gere 2003; Belgrad 1999; Carter 2000; Sawyer 2000). In most cases, the suspended processes are soon reinstated in order to facilitate the calculated modification and development of freshly improvised material into products for practical/commercial use. Such uses are commonly held in view from the start and are implied, if not explicit, in instructions given to improvisers to seed their activity with a predetermined direction and, perhaps, a preferred form. In these cases, improvisation is assigned instrumental value: seen as a means for achieving a particular end but not as an end in itself.

Many dance choreographers crafting 'set' choreography rely on improvisation as a tool in the early stages of work and/or when creative flow is stalled. It is common for choreographers to devise personalized approaches to improvisation. Kloppenberg explains: 'working improvisationally in a studio is like abstract expressionism with an eraser—maybe even with a whole toolbox: the spontaneous laying down of "paint" engages dancers in improvisational tasks or scores from which the choreographer then selects movements or sequences to remake. After transforming improvised content into fixed movement patterns, a choreographer can mine that material, edit, rearrange, add, and fill in detail. The choreographer constructs a piece over time, recreating selected improvised moments or structural elements as building blocks' (2010: 189–190).

I suggest that the kinds of processes Kloppenberg describes enact a traditional Western conception of private property as involving the mixing of human purposes, in this case the desires of the choreographic mind, with appropriated natural or 'raw' material—that is, dancers' improvised movement (Leach 2007). That is, in authoring and imposing tasks or scores for improvisers to follow, and in selecting from improvised material certain movements or sequences to remake or 'set' into patterns and 'erasing' the rest, dance choreographers display ownership over dancers' labour and its products.

Not surprisingly, the capacity to deliver coordinated repeatable sameness in their exe-cution of movement gives dancers viability as commodities; once a dance is set upon bodies, viewers on different occasions of its performance may be said to have witnessed 'the same work'. In pursuit of this end, dancers typically spend hours practicing move-ment to perfection, or at least near enough to perfection to satisfy dance-market de-mands. It is generally not considered appropriate during these periods of practice for dancers to make up new movement; the aims of 'setting' a dance are at odds with im-provisation. Nevertheless, improvisation may resist the congealing of performers' la-bour into repeatable constructs. Witness the admonishment to a young saxophonist famously delivered by jazz great Charles Mingus: 'play something different, man; play something different. This is jazz, man. You played that last night and the night before' (Berliner 1994: 271).

Mingus's valorization of 'something different' notwithstanding, improvisation is often viewed with suspicion for resisting repetitive sameness. For example, Buckwalter ex-plains that improvisation's 'unpredictable nature and emphasis on process over product make it difficult for dance producers to sell in a market-driven arts world' (2010: 7). This difficulty may explain why, as Kloppenberg notes, many choreographers who include improvisation in their creative process proceed to 'mine' the movement material that emerges and 'transform' selected bits into images or patterns in a set work.

I find Kloppenberg's analogy between mining and dance-making useful in under-standing the capture and instrumentalization of improvisation by what I term the 'danced-choreographic', for the analogy crystallizes the common status of improvised movement as raw material whose value is that it may be designed into a set dance. I use the term 'danced-choreographic' to reference the traditional politics of institutionalized discipline and control that has long provided the rational bases for training movers in techniques for dancing; the body management practices—including instrumentalized improvisation—used by many choreographers to develop, set, and 'polish' dances for repeatable performances; and the commodity aesthetics of concert and theatrical dance. These variables hold privileged places in what Sparshott terms the 'basic hierarchy of theatre dance'. He writes: 'the creative choreographer devises the dances, specifying (or completing the specification of), what is to be danced' (1995: 374). It follows that in reactualizing a set work in performance, dancers should try to dance correctly what the work's author(s) have determined to be danced, censoring movements or qualities of movement not authorized as part of the dance.

I am making no sweeping universal claims; certainly dance choreographers nego-tiate in quite different ways, and many reject entirely, the entrenched power dynamic of the danced-choreographic. I challenge that power dynamic here not because it is uni-versal but because it is so firmly ensconced as 'normal' within theories and practices of training dancers and choreographers, and in the production and consumption of concert and theatrical dances. The normalcy of exercising authoritarian control over movers and their movement is my target, even as such control is often accomplished with a soft voice, in an ostensibly caring manner, and dancers may willingly submit to it. There is not time to develop the point here, but I suggest that one's willingness to submit to any kind of oppression (and perhaps to not even recognize it *as* oppression) is hardly a defence of that oppression. Similarly, the fact that we may find exceptions to any rule, or departures from any norm, does not grant the rule or the norm immunity from criticism.

Of course, the dance field is not alone in instrumentalizing improvisation. Writers in other fields, theatre and music especially but also painting and sculpture, and even management/organization theory, offer accounts of traditional or newly devised practical ends towards whose achievement improvisation is a valued means (Brown 2000; Drinko 2013; Leep 2008; Spolin 1963; Weick 1998). Instrumentalist accounts of the use and value of improvisation unite around the idea that improvisers must follow rules that are consistent with, or at least not a detriment to, such desired outcomes as an entertaining skit, an unusual interpretation of an existing musical score, an aesthetically pleasing dance, or an efficient business model. For example, Leep (2008) urges theatre improvisers to set up in advance and adhere in performance to rules concerning the focus or goal of the improvisation, the permissible and impermissible actions of players, and the permissible range of players' justifications for choices. For Leep, such rule-bound restraints mitigate the risk of players 'wandering around on stage having a good time' (2008: 13), a danger that entails boring the audience, whose spectatorial pleasure holds privilege in Leep's account.

Yet rule-governed improvisation carries its own risks. As Weick notes, business managers may elicit little more than a caricature of improvisation by grafting improvisational principles 'onto concepts that basically are built to explain order'—presuming to embrace improvisational approaches but 'without giving up the prior commitment to stability and order in the form of habit, repetition, automatic thinking, rational constraints, formalization, culture, and standardization' (1998: 551).

Despite its obvious instrumental value in achieving goals other than itself, improvisation may be assigned terminal value: cherished as a worthy end in itself, regardless of any use-for-profit imagined for its outcomes. I regard movement improvisation as possessing terminal value, and in promoting the emancipation of improvisation from the danced-choreographic, I imagine improvisers immersed in the 'now' of movement, experiencing a condition I term as 'body freedom', with no aesthetic obligations to the past or the future impinging on the present. Body freedom is a condition under which movers may find and explore movement afforded by moving, unfastened from habits and concerns about appearance.

Ironically, the illusion of body freedom, even if not actual body freedom, is valued by the danced-choreographic; performers of set choreography derived from earlier improvisations strive to retain 'a movement texture and performance tone that retains the active presence, impulsivity, and spontaneity of the initial improvisations' (Kloppenberg 2010: 189–190). Lepecki speaks to the latter point when he writes: 'choreography demands a yielding to commanding voices of masters (living and dead), it demands submitting body and desire to disciplining regimes (anatomical, dietary, gender, racial), all for the perfect fulfilment of a transcendental and preordained set of steps, postures, and gestures that *nevertheless must appear as spontaneous*' (2006: 9, my emphasis).

Elsewhere, in a passage that informs my critique of the danced-choreographic, Allsopp and Lepecki characterize choreography as 'a system of command' and an 'apparatus of capture' that 'seizes bodies in order to make them into other(ed) bodies—highly trained (physically, emotionally, artistically, and intellectually) variations of what Foucault once called "docile bodies"' (2008: 3). Roche offers similar ideas in discussing implications for dance of modernism/colonialism. For Roche, institutionalized dance training 'entails a relationship to the incorporation of "otherness" that could be considered, in the extreme, to reflect the colonizing process' (2011: 107).

In addition to glossing set movement with an artificial spontaneity, some choreographers allocate space within a set work for dancers' freshly improvised movement or embellishments to memorized movement (Carter 2000). Yet body freedom is frequently curtailed in these cases by the governing principles of a particular dance technique or style and/or by choreographic structuring imperatives aimed at realizing such traditional aesthetic values as coherence in part-to-whole relationships and repetition, development, and variation of visual and temporal motifs and/or narrative themes. Serving such aims requires improvisers to censor their attention and responsiveness to movement opportunities afforded by moving; movers are praised for appearing as the score deems it is correct to appear. In turn, authors of improvisation scores may earn praise for achieving values of aesthetic form typically attached to set choreography or denigrated for failing to achieve these values (Buckwalter 2010; Goldman 2010).

I suggest that a patriarchal value structure animates the everyday routines through which some teachers and choreographers plant, cultivate, and/or extract desired movement from bodies and privilege movers who are willing to give up body freedom in favour of self-surveillance and adjustment of their appearances in the face of external movement imperatives (Lavender 2014). Arnold (2000: 89) speaks to this point in describing the 'passive dancer' as one who serves as 'a willing and compliant vehicle in the hands of the choreographer'. The passive dancer is essentially 'a tool or an instrument to be manipulated. Individuality and initiative are neither wanted nor encouraged'. Interestingly, even in discussing the 'active dancer' as playing a much more collaborative role than the passive dancer in shaping new works, Arnold likens the dancer to a visual object; one who learns to watch one's self as if from outside. For without the corrective function of such self-produced 'objectification', Arnold suggests, a dancer may 'fall short of what is necessary', which is 'to embody what is required in a refined, accentuated, and vivified way without becoming overly self-expressive' (91).

With the aforementioned ideas in mind, I suggest that such ancient patriarchal dualisms as order/chaos, master/slave, reason/nature, human/animal, masculine/feminine, and especially mind/body both engender and reinforce a choreography/improvisation and a choreographer/dancer dualism. Lakes addresses some behavioural aspects of these dualisms when she notes: 'one of the great puzzles within the Western concert dance world is why so many artists who create revolutionary works onstage conduct their classes and rehearsals as demagogues. Such teachers are engaged in teaching practices that replicate and reproduce in the dance studio the very power relationships they are often critiquing as unjust and inhumane in their artwork onstage' (2005: 3).

The power relationships to which Lakes refers reflect the logic of dualisms: a privileged person, group, or idea exercises authority over subordinate persons, groups, or ideas whose instrumental use produces benefits for those above them in hierarchy.

Even as they take the form of simple binaries, dualisms differ from simple binaries, and from simple distinctions. A simple binary, such as *on/off* or *left/right*, identifies two components that make up a system. Importantly, the political implications of a binary may be zero; nothing in the description of *on* or *off* suggests that one of them may automatically hold privilege over the other. Similarly, to describe the location of an item as 'to the left' of another item is neither to valorize left-sidedness nor to impugn it for its negligence or native lack of ability in exhibiting right-sidedness. For simple binaries do not perform the political manoeuvre of positioning constituent parts in hierarchical relation. Dualisms *are* constructed to perform such work; even as they may wear the mask of simple binaries, dualisms create politically oppositional and exclusive categories. In assigning the 'lower' half of each pairing to a subordinate position relative to the 'upper' half, dualisms normalize fundamentally unjust relationships.

The history of patriarchal dualisms is a history of the inferiorization and subsequent instrumentalizing of the spontaneous, the unpredictable, the somatically intuitive, the animal, the primitive, and of course the female by rationalist and order-seeking power. In Plato, for example, we find a conception of universal causation that provides the roots of the dismissive and controlling attitudes I have heard expressed by dance teachers and choreographers towards improvisation. In explaining the source of all that is fair and good, and thus of all to which we should aspire, Plato (1965) privileges what he holds as the higher of two forms of causation: rational, universal, intellectual principles and procedures—that is, *cosmos*—which is masculine, brain-centred, and intended to operate over and against the 'lower' form of causation (*chaos*), which is irrational, instinctual, body-centred, and feminine. Viewed through the lens of the culture/nature dualism, nature and all associated phenomena are dangerous unless harnessed and developed under the civilizing hand of culture (Plato 1965: 46). In a later section I will elaborate on patriarchal dualisms in dance. Here, I turn next to a discussion of an improvisation practice, termed 'affordance-based movement finding', that I have devised to emancipate improvisation from the dualisms of the danced-choreographic.

AFFORDANCE-BASED MOVEMENT FINDING

Affordance is a concept which has been explicated most influentially by perception theorist James J. Gibson (1979) and is applied widely today in various design/engineering and product development fields. Briefly, an affordance is a relationship between the capacities of an organism and a feature of the environment. An organism perceives and pursues interactions with features of the environment which afford possibilities for the organism to flourish. A mouse in the house, for example, perceives that small cracks under closed doors afford an opportunity to move to the next room. Obviously, the small openings and passageways that mice perceive and utilize do not afford people (or, more important for mice, cats) the same opportunities. A doorknob, however, affords most people (but neither cats nor mice) the opportunity to grasp, turn, and push or pull, which opens the door and affords access to the space beyond. Mice and cats do not perceive the grasp-ability and turn-ability of doorknobs. But humans and other creatures with the capacity to grasp, turn, and pull or push on knobs, and with some need or preference to perform such actions, readily perceive doorknobs and the opportunities they afford. A creature's environmental niche is thus determined by the affordances in and of the environment for that creature; the proverbial fish out of water flops to death because a waterless environment affords nothing of use to a fish.

A creature detects and interacts with environmental features that afford it ways to pursue its interests and meet its needs. Within the environment of a movement improvisation, for example, one's own and others' *current* movements and positions afford many opportunities. Imagine improvisers walking randomly within a space, and imagine that they are free to follow body interests in shifting out of walking and into any movement they prefer, including the cessation of movement. Each mover is likely to make shifts in different ways, at different moments, and in response to perceiving different affordances from those perceived by the other movers. Affordance-based movement finding colonizes no portion of the movers' awareness with any necessity to adhere to or achieve any predetermined dance-technical or aesthetic values; there is nothing *choreographic* to remember to do, or to avoid doing. Each mover may attend entirely to the interests of the body in experiencing *what's next* in the interactions between her capacities and available movement opportunities. Configurations of others' bodies at any moment may afford some movers the opportunity to crouch, spring, and dive through small openings between others, even as such opportunities are not afforded to movers like me, because our brittle knees cannot safely accommodate the demands of crouching, springing, and diving. Movers like me may not even detect crouch, spring, and dive opportunities any more readily than we detect small branches in trees on which we might perch, because perching on small branches and diving through small openings are not afforded to us. Similarly, movers well suited to crouching, springing, and diving may not perceive movement affordances with which my body's interests and capacities are aligned.

The body freedom intrinsic to affordance-based movement finding runs counter to the traditional interests of the danced-choreographic: to control bodies and harvest for development and repetitive use some of the movements and images which bodies may produce. In performing set choreography, a dancer usually reenacts a single and preexisting path or journey of movement (trying to appear as 'spontaneous' as possible). She strives to hit her assigned marks through a well-practiced set of adjustments to her body's shape, flow, direction, facing, and so on. For example, if the choreographic imperative is to stand still facing stage left until a certain moment in the music and then collapse and crawl to centre stage, then rise and adopt a certain pose for three counts before collapsing again, the performer repeats just that sequence at the assigned moment in every performance, even as she is afforded at virtually every moment an infinite number of movement options, each of which is ignored.

Even in dance improvisation settings, the danced-choreographic routinely exercises control through the use of prompts or scores that privilege some range of choreographic variables: the movers' orientation to and interactions with space, time, energy, shape, direction, emotional tone, activation, deactivation, and use of body parts, specific movement qualities, and so on. Whenever choreographic imperatives launch and govern improvisation, movers' body freedom is vastly reduced by the necessity to hold in mind, attend to, and fulfil the imperatives. Roche underscores this point in sharing remarks made to her by a dancer: ' "What's my movement identity?" I don't have one anymore. All I can do is give on the outside of me what somebody else wants to see, remove the places that I've definitely wanted to go, and get rid of them and go somewhere else and it's like "none of this belongs to me." When I'm improvising maybe that's what I have to do, to find what me is, but it's like I've had plastic surgery' (2011: 114). Even as movers may be free to explore *within* the constraints stipulated by an improvisation prompt or score, they cannot experience anything approaching the full range of available movement affordances. For example, the imperative to 'remain disconnected' commands improvisers to quash any impulses they may experience to perform such actions as linking arms or sharing/exchanging their weight.

Multiple choreographic imperatives for improvisation are often clustered. For example, 'make sure one of you is always at low level' and 'never allow your body shape to be symmetrical' might be stacked on top of 'remain disconnected'. The more imperatives there are, the more energy a mover devotes to remembering the rules and avoiding acting on affordances that may contradict them. Improvisers with a highly developed ability for this self-censorship may be praised as skilled. Yet arguably the ease with which many movers exercise this so-called skill exemplifies Foucault's conception of docility in the face of productive and prohibitive power (Bartky 1998).

My research on movement affordances began in 2008 when four collaborators joined me in exploring body freedom by 'moving without dancing'. We wondered what might be interesting about unfastening from trained-in habits and concerns about appearance with which we had been saturated during years of dance training and performative involvement with the danced-choreographic. During one-to-two-hour 'convenings', we allowed our bodies to determine what was next. We called our sessions 'convenings' rather than rehearsals because we were unfastened from the standard dance rehearsal protocol of remembering, repeating, or improving our work from one session to the next. After some months, we chose to convene in the presence of others, both in studio and in formal performance settings. We came to call our work 'The Practice of Existence', after one visitor said 'it looks like you are practicing existing', and this seemed to fit. Figure 16.1 below shows how the work sometimes broke traditional boundaries between performer and audience.

I wondered how our activity might be introduced to newcomers who wished to experience it directly; how does one 'teach' this work? My coexister Caitlin Spencer and I identified the following specific 'operations' we detected in the work:

Shared pulse: physically connect with another exister to find and explore a shared motional and emotional path
Core finding: accept movement impulses from far below the skin surface and from the extremities, and far from languaged concepts

Detail tracking: follow with the eyes the physical movements of a body of another, keeping the eyes in close proximity to the source

Facework: activate an involuntary chain of face muscle actions

Joining: enter the kinaesthetic bubbles of others, making contact and forming fusions of mutual purpose

Perception sounding: make public through oral calls the movements, pathways, and qualities detected about oneself and others

Purpose sounding: signal through oral calls your intentions, desires, motives, and reactions

Roaming: roam the environment in any direction for any duration without accumulating obligations

Sponging: notice and adopt the movements of others either as a *replacement for* or as *embellishment of* your movement

Dynamic solitude: withdraw from social action for a chosen duration but remain in active readiness, scanning with all senses

Micro-repetitions: focus intently on small motions and repeat for extended durations

FIG. 16.1 Screenshot of Larry Lavender (centre) engaging with an audience member during Practice of Existence performance.

In sharing Practice of Existence operations, I encourage movers to explore any direction these operations may afford. This list is descriptive but not prescriptive: there is no need for a mover to carry an inner awareness about when, how, or why one or another of the operations may or may not be actualized. To remain still, fall asleep, or go home is no less or more appropriate than 'dancing'. The work honours *presence-ing* the body, as distinct from *past-ing* the body, as dancers do in repeating choreography set at an earlier time. A *presence-ing* body may continually *re-new* movement, free of any obligation to *re-old* preexisting movements, as is routine in dance class and on stage.

Its commitment to body freedom aligns affordance-based movement finding with Davies's (2004) conception of 'pure improvisation.' For Davies, pure improvisation 'neither specifies the performative constraints for a new work nor interprets an existing work' and is thus distinct both from 'improvisational interpretation' based on a preexisting work and from 'improvisational composition', in which a new work is produced under a set of performative constraints all of whose future instantiations count as a performance of 'the same work' (Davies 2004: 227–228). By foregrounding the interests of the improviser's body, unfastened from external imperatives, affordance-based movement finding is unmarked by the interpretive and compositional preoccupations of the danced-choreographic.

In addition to such distinctions as Davies makes among kinds of improvisation, and the uses to which improvised outcomes may be put, improvisers' dancing skill is a crucial consideration in dance. Choreographers often prize most highly the contributions of improvisers with demonstrated expertise in one or another codified techniques of dancing and/or whose improvised movements satisfy the choreographer's standards for 'good choreography'. Goldman, for example, praises as 'skilled' those improvisers who exercise 'a keen aesthetic sense of form' (2010: 141) as well as improvisers whose movement viewers find elegant, exquisite, noble, intricate, gorgeous, and stunning. Goldman deserves no criticism for representing with accuracy the predominance of these values in concert dance, but the ease with which improvisation may be instrumentalized by the presentational aesthetics of concert dance does warrant criticism. One might suggest, for example, that whether movement appears as, say, elegant and gorgeous or as awkward and clumsy is actually of no importance to improvisation. For improvisation grants no automatic privilege to any particular properties or qualities of movement, even as those who instrumentalize improvisation often do award such privileges. Moreover, improvisation grants no automatic privilege to any particular body type or previous body experience. On the contrary, to practice improvisation a mover needs no 'artistic' skills gleaned from any levelled curriculum of dance technique, nor must a mover highlight or suppress any previous body experiences, preferences, or movement skills learned elsewhere. A curiosity to experience *what's next* in movement is the only prerequisite for improvisation.

PATRIARCHAL DUALISMS IN THE DANCED-CHOREOGRAPHIC

As mentioned earlier, I find that a patriarchal dualistic value structure permeates the domain of concert dance, engendering both a choreography/improvisation dualism and a choreographer/dancer dualism. These dualisms manifest in the everyday routines through which many dance teachers and choreographers exercise authority over movers and movement works. Even in choreography classes, where one might expect students creating works to possess creative licence to challenge norms within the field and perhaps to expand its possibilities, patriarchal dualisms manifest through assignments and assessments that privilege the codes of order and repeatability on which the danced-choreographic prides itself. As if in fear of improvisational incursions into commodified performative terrain which they've been schooled to believe is exclusively their own, some teachers reenact an assumed superiority of choreography over improvisation, often characterizing improvisation as lazy; an attempt to 'get off easy' by privileging the expression of the body's interests in *this moment* over the ingestion, memorization, and repetitive reexpression of a choreographer/author's movement desires from some *earlier* moment.

I have witnessed choreography teachers dismissing as 'not a *real* dance' new works that transgress the compositional assumptions of concert dance by foregrounding body freedom in relations among bodies. Such works are often met with criticism in which the word 'just' sits pejoratively in front of the word 'improvisation': 'Oh, that is *just* improvisation'. It is not uncommon for such remarks to be followed by 'but you could develop that as choreography'.

These kinds of remarks bring to mind Foster's discussion of the ways in which the term 'choreography' serves to 'validate some forms of dancing while excluding others' (Foster 2010: 16). I am reminded, too, that within the Western cultural imaginary, the term 'develop' refers primarily to those processes through which the *natural* is instrumentalized and commodified by the rational/productive industries of the *cultural*; the natural has traditionally been construed as chaotic and disordered until 'developed'—that is, brought under control—by a civilizing and disciplining hand (Plumwood 1993). Untrammelled forest, for example, is regarded as 'undeveloped' until its trees and wildlife are removed and replaced with roads and buildings or rows of crops. Similarly, improvised movement is usually regarded as 'undeveloped' until refined by choreographic structuring devices delivered through overt imperatives or embedded within scores. Recall Kloppenberg's description of choreographers who, after selecting and editing dancers' improvised movements, proceed to 'mine that material' as they construct a dance, 'recreating selected improvised moments or structural elements as building blocks' (2010: 189–190). I suggest that such practices reenact colonialist/ imperialist master/slave relations and attitudes of superiority over the 'primitive other', whose personal and cultural identity is construed as 'raw material' for the production of 'civilization' (Hewitt 2005; Lakes 2005).

That patriarchal dualisms in dance so readily persist may be attributed to the fact that dualistic habits usually operate below conscious awareness and are enacted by people who do not necessarily wish to comply with patriarchy but are nevertheless trapped in its grip. Patriarchal dualisms operate below conscious awareness because their operations have been naturalized over time as defining positions occupied by people, regardless of which people occupy the positions. As people enter into the positions of choreographer, dancer, teacher, or student, the power or lack of power intrinsic to each position, as constructed by patriarchy, determines 'normal' attitudes, whether or not each person would otherwise choose them. Of course, some people make conscious efforts not to reenact the power relations bestowed by patriarchy on positions they hold. Many others do not think to challenge these power relations, and some revel in the power they hold and seek to cultivate it. My point is that if one makes no reflective choice, the default is to reenact dualistic power relations simply because they reside in positions we hold before we come to hold them.

Dualistic habits of thought have provided substantive shape and direction to the danced-choreographic. For example, Horst, the recognized father of systematized instruction in choreography, writes: 'Composition is based on only two things: a conception of a theme and the manipulation of that theme. Whatever the chosen theme may be, it cannot be manipulated, developed, shaped, without knowledge of the rules of composition.... The laws which are the basis on which any dance must be built should be so familiar to the choreographer that he follows them almost unconsciously' (1961: 23). As concerns teaching choreography, Horst (1949) asserts that the 'disciplinary period' required for learning is best considered as a period 'of law and order, and any art must demand it' (Coleman 1949: 128). Arguably, the ease with which Horst conjoins 'any art' with a 'demand' for 'law and order' reveals the heart and soul of the danced-choreographic: the ancient culture/nature dualism and its attendant drive to tame and civilize the wild through the imposition and enforcement of the 'laws' of civilization, which are represented in Horst's case by the preclassic and classical forms of Western music, which he advocates as compositional paradigms. Ideas similar to Horst's appear in writings by Margaret H'Doubler, a founder of dance curricula in higher education, when she writes (in a passage that foreshadows Horst's 'laws' proposition) that a dance, 'as much as any other work of art ... is subject to the general laws of unity or wholeness, and of organic coherence', and that 'only artistic form can do full justice to sincere and earnest feeling' (1925: 184). H'Doubler appears to reinforce the culture/nature dualism and to inferiorize the expressions of earlier peoples when she writes: 'with the savage, expressive acts could have been none other than random, impulsive movements that afforded quite unconscious outlet to his passing feelings'. H'Doubler reassures us, however, that the expressive acts of 'the savage' gradually 'became consciously and intentionally expressive' and that 'it was when thus modified that early man's expressive activities became art' (10). Arnold's (2000: 91) claim that the dancer must learn to perform what is required 'in a refined, accentuated, and vivified way without becoming overly self-expressive' echoes H'Doubler's ideas.

In holding that there are or should be 'laws' of choreography and in withholding the status of 'art' from 'random and impulsive'—that is, natural—expressions until they have been consciously and intentionally 'modified', Horst and H'Doubler recuperate ancient dualistic logic, setting up terms under which the danced-choreographic (as culture) may justify its exertion of developmental rule upon bodies and movements (as nature). Horst and H'Doubler's ideological manoeuvres bring to mind the infamous mind/body dualism, a sibling to the culture/nature dualism. The mind/body dualism is generally traced to the 'substance dualism' articulated by Descartes: the idea that the mind and body have distinct essences, one of thought and the other of spatial extension (Rodriguez-Pereyra 2008). Yet the logic of mind/body dualism dates back much further than Descartes: in *Phaedo*, for example, Plato privileges the mind and rejects dependency on the body, claiming that the body 'is of no help in the attainment of wisdom' and that the nearest approach to true knowledge comes with 'the least possible intercourse with or communion with the body' (Plato 1948: 204). In *Timaeus*, Plato remarks that the body—and nature as a whole—must always be mastered and controlled. Plato sees the body, as the site of 'lower passions', as needing control by 'commands' and 'threats' (1965: 70). Plato's sentiments foreshadow the denial of the mind's dependency on bodily senses issued by Descartes and other Enlightenment thinkers and their suspicion of bodily senses as sources of error.

THE ARTISTIC USE OF AFFORDANCE-BASED MOVEMENT FINDING

I turn now to two performance works in and for which affordance-based movement finding, and the values which nourish it, provided impetus and content. The work *Sociography* (2010) was commissioned by the Weatherspoon Art Museum in Greensboro, North Carolina, to accompany the opening of a retrospective exhibition of works by Leonardo Drew. For an hour before the gallery opened, the movers followed the movement affordances engendered by their body responses to Drew's works. As the public and the artist entered the space and dispersed among the paintings and sculptures, the movers mingled, introducing themselves and soliciting help in preparing the performance. Accompanied by 'scribes' with pen and paper, the movers asked members of the public to share verbal impressions of Drew's work. After about ten minutes of public interaction, the movers slowly shifted into 're-existing' as movement the public's verbal impressions, following the affordances of initial movement to create new movement. The performers also exercised at will the option verbally to 're-voice' verbal impressions gathered earlier from the public: 'Thick wavy lines ... garish complexity ... multiple reiterations'. The 're-existing' and 're-voicing' processes paralleled the manner in which Drew had created the works on display with found and discarded natural and synthetic materials. The photos in Figures 16.2 and 16.3 were taken from the same spot in the gallery, but facing in opposite directions.

FIG. 16.2 Jesse Morales moves between the two halves of the gallery space in *Sociography*. Photograph by Larry Lavender.

FIG. 16.3 Front to back: Jesse Morales, Emily Hatfield, Allison Rice, and Emily Bannerman perform *Sociography*. Photograph by Larry Lavender.

The movers gradually expanded the work's scope by exercising the option to voice memories of movement that had emerged during the hour spent alone with Drew's works: 'Caitlin's descent ... remembering Emily's hands ... watching Jesse roll'. The scribes roamed the gallery reading aloud images gathered earlier from the conversations between movers and the public: 'layered complexity ... absorbed existence.' From time to time a mover exercised the option to call out 'remind me', in response to which another mover, or a scribe, and sometimes a member of the public called out a remembered image, giving fresh impetus to the work.

Even as *Sociography* was made up of interactive activities that began an hour before the public arrived and included further options the movers could exercise, the movers possessed improvisational body freedom throughout the work (Lavender 2011). No movements or kinds of movement were privileged or marginalized, and no responses or ways of responding to verbal, visual, or somatic information were construed in advance as right or wrong or better or worse. The work also enfranchised the public's body freedom, and many members of the public shifted locations within the gallery during the work.

Affordance-based movement finding made up the content of the migratory/proscenium work *Hugs Destination* (2011). The work began at the start of a dance concert: lights came up on me 'dancing' to a bouncy pop song. Everything stopped on a dime after about thirty seconds, and I explained to the audience that the actual work I wished to share was a quarter of a mile away in another building, waiting to be invited to the concert. I took out my cellphone and called a performer in the other building and said: 'the audience and I invite you to migrate here and perform'. The dance agreed to come, so I reported to the audience that while they waited for the dance's arrival they could enjoy three other choreographers' dances, which were already in the building and waiting to inhabit the stage. During the first half of the dance concert, the *Hugs Destination* cast undertook an affordance-based movement finding migration across campus to the theatre. Figures 16.4 and 16.5 find the movers along their journey.

Witnessed only by passersby who may or may not have been interested, the movers spent an hour migrating through a park, past campus buildings, and across two roads before arriving at the theatre during intermission. They drifted peaceably through the crowd in the lobby and entered the theatre with the returning audience. They lined up with their backs to the audience, facing the stage as seen in fig. 16.6. They slowly shed the shoes, gloves, scarves, hats, and coats they had worn to protect themselves from the cold outside and stood quietly, considering whether or not to step across the line dividing the pedestrian world from the fictionalized world of the stage, where they would become objects of artistic display. The movers faced no pressure to cross over; the score of the work asked them only to engage in choosing whether or not to do so. They were free to remain un-staged by standing at the line forever or by leaving. But they all eventually crossed, and under stage lights, and boxed in by the rectangle, they resumed affordance-based movement finding.

When I discussed with the movers their choice whether or not to cross over the line, we agreed that the line signified a distinction between 'performing' movements specifically

FIG. 16.4 *Hugs Destination* movers during their migration towards the dance theatre. Photograph by Larry Lavender.

FIG. 16.5 *Hugs Destination* movers during their migration towards the dance theatre. Photograph by Larry Lavender.

FIG. 16.6 Having arrived at the dance theatre, *Hugs Destination* movers decide whether or not to cross the line and stage themselves for artistic display. Photograph by Bridget Lavender.

for others to witness and on the other hand 'being with' one's own and others' movements regardless of whether or not anyone witnessed the activity, and without concern about judgements any witness might make. We acknowledged that even as the performance tradition of the danced-choreographic confers status to any 'staged' movements, the highest praise is usually reserved for coordinated enactments of a specialized subset of human movements termed as 'dancing', and the concomitant display of bodies (preferably trim and well-conditioned) moving in patterns. We also acknowledged that with its commitment to affordance-based movement finding, *Hugs Destination* was unfastened from all but one of the expectations of the danced-choreographic: it occupied, for at least part of its life, the site and occasion of a traditional dance concert. In so doing, *Hugs Destination* 'performed' the emancipation of improvisation by disproving the implicit claim of the danced-choreographic that only dancers dancing dances belong at this site during this kind of occasion. Not only was *Hugs Destination* not 'a dance', most of it took place outside and away from the theatre and was therefore inaccessible to the dance concert audience.

A key feature of *Hugs Destination* was that no one was afforded visual access to the entire work, for a second way in which I wished to emancipate improvisation was to immunize it against the form-based choreography criticism to which dances are routinely exposed; one cannot criticize a dance one cannot view in its entirety. A third aim was to close the traditional gap between performers and audience. To achieve this, the work first established a vastly larger-than-usual gap between the two populations, but at the end each performer crossed back over the line separating stage and audience, said his or

FIG. 16.7 Having crossed the line to become 'art', *Hugs Destination* movers reinitiate affordance-based movement finding. Photograph by Larry Lavender.

her name out loud, and offered a hug to any audience member who wanted one. With these actions the gap was closed socially, and with each pressing together of an audience body and a performer body, the gap was closed literally. Each audience member who shared a hug with a dancer became a 'hug destination'.

Rehearsals for *Hugs Destination* were made up of sustained affordance-based movement finding sessions the standing prompt for which was to 'find a position your body likes, seek a state of present connection to your being, and decide what, if any, movements are next'. The principle of body freedom applied even to rehearsal. I had invited every mover who auditioned to join the work, and at the start I suggested that movers attend rehearsals and performances only if it was the best place to be with their bodies at that time. I said that if only one mover arrived, the work would be a solo. And if none arrived, I would tell the audience that the work did not wish to be seen, and the concert would proceed to the next work. There were never fewer than nine movers at any rehearsal, and as the concert drew near it swelled back to twenty-three, including several who arrived uninvited. Since I never knew who would actually perform, I listed all the movers' names as 'possible performers' in the program information I had to submit weeks before the performance. Nineteen movers participated in the performance for an audience. Figure 16.7 finds the movers engaged in the work after deciding to become staged performers.

Conclusion

In promoting affordance-based movement finding as an emancipation of improvisation from the danced-choreographic, I horizontalize power within one small corner of the domain of dance (Li 1997). Affordance-based movement finding, by offering its joys to any mover under any conditions, counters the systematic training and production of a privileged moving/dancing body that is valued primarily for enacting in front of paying customers identical replications of decided-in-advance movements. Obviously, during affordance-based movement finding, movers may constrain and modify their movements as they prefer, but the practice neither depends on nor values front-loaded constraints on movement choices or after-the-fact modifications of any movement that emerges. If the practice did promote such dependencies and values, it would not be emancipatory; movers would be recycled back into the self-surveillance and self-correction that characterize the danced-choreographic.

I characterize affordance-based movement finding as emancipatory because within the movement experience afforded by body freedom, one experiences a dissolving of the bifurcated self that is induced through traditional dance and choreographic regimens: half of this self engages in 'doing' as the other half engages in 'sensing/watching/judging myself doing'. Recall Arnold's (2000: 91) claim that dancers must see themselves as if from outside, for without such 'objectification' a dancer can 'fall short of what is necessary'.

I hold that the social and political value of improvisational body freedom at least equals, if it does not exceed, the value of movement practices valorized by the danced-choreographic. For the human urge towards the improvisational arguably comes from and reaches into the most profound reasons people need and want to be together moving, and embracing this urge provides as much as, if not more than, the danced-choreographic ever provides of what people need to thrive and to be happy. Certainly the danced-choreographic offers abundant somatic and visual pleasures, and occasional intellectual ones, and makes money for producers. But the production of choreographic commodities is too complicit with patriarchal suppressions of movement (Lakes 2005; Smith 1998). However, the emancipation of improvisation is not a call for a reversal of power between it and the danced-choreographic. Reversals of power whereby the sides of a dualism exchange places in an unequal power dynamic are no remedy for the pernicious effects of dualisms. Yes, such reversals may momentarily alleviate past injustices, but they inevitably promote future injustices by leaving untroubled the fundamental dynamic that legitimizes dualism-based hierarchy. Thus, rather than working to reverse power within dance hierarchy while leaving intact a reliance on hierarchy, I have unfastened my artistic work from hierarchical power-over relations and let that act of unfastening and my efforts to explain it effect a push towards the eventual atrophy and disappearance of the habits of thought that sustain hierarchical power-over relations in the first place. it is possible to create in our field a fresh ethics of being-with bodies, which is needed in the world; and in calling for the emancipation of improvisation, I encourage the danced-choreographic to forge a new identity through gentler means than commanding the movements and policing the appearances of bodies.

REFERENCES

Albright, Ann Cooper, and Gere, D. (2003) *Taken by Surprise: A Dance Improvisation Reader.* Middletown, CT: Wesleyan University Press.

Allsopp, R., and Lepecki, A. (2008) Editorial: On Choreography. *Performance Research* 13(1): 1.

Arnold, P. (2000) Aspects of the Dancer's Role in the Art of Dance. *Journal of Aesthetic Education* 34(1): 87–95.

Bartky, S. (1988) Foucault, Femininity and the Modernization of Patriarchal Power. In Diamond, I., and Quinby, L. (eds.), *Feminism and Foucault: Reflections on Resistance.* Boston: Northeastern University Press, 61–86.

Belgrad, D. (1999) *The Culture of Spontaneity: Improvisation and the Arts in Postwar America.* Chicago: University of Chicago Press.

Berliner, P. (1994) *Thinking in Jazz: The Infinite Art of Improvisation.* Chicago: University of Chicago Press.

Brown, L. (2000) 'Feeling My Way': Jazz Improvisation and Its Vicissitudes—A Plea for Imperfection. *Journal of Aesthetics and Art Criticism* 58(2): 113–123.

Buckwalter, M. (2010) *Composing While Dancing: An Improviser's Companion.* Madison: University of Wisconsin Press.

Carter, C. (2000) Improvisation in Dance. *Journal of Aesthetics and Art Criticism* 58(2): 181–190.

Coleman, M. (1949) On the Teaching of Choreography: Interview with Louis Horst. *Dance Observer* 16 (9): 128.

Davies, D. (2004) *Art as Performance.* Malden: Blackwell.

Drinko, C. (2013) *Theatrical Improvisation, Consciousness and Cognition.* New York: Palgrave Macmillan.

Foster, S. (2010) *Choreographing Empathy: Kinesthesia in Performance.* New York: Routledge.

Gibson, J. (1979) *The Ecological Approach to Visual Perception.* Boston: Houghton Mifflin.

Goldman, D. (2010) *I Want To Be Ready: Improvised Dance as a Practice of Freedom.* Ann Arbor: University of Michigan Press.

H'Doubler, M. (1925) *The Dance and Its Place in Education.* New York: Harcourt, Brace.

Horst, L., and Russell, C. (1961) *Modern Dance Forms in Relation to the Other Modern Arts.* San Francisco: Impulse.

Hewitt, A. (2005) *Social Choreography: Ideology as Performance in Dance and Everyday Movement.* Durham, NC: Duke University Press.

Kloppenberg, A. (2010) Improvisation in Process: 'Post-control' Choreography. *Dance Chronicle* 33(2): 180–207.

Lakes, R. (2005) The Message behind the Methods: The Authoritarian Pedagogical Legacy in Western Concert Dance Technique Training and Rehearsals. *Arts Education Policy Review* 106(5): 3–18.

Lavender, L. (2011) Sociography. *Brolga: An Australian Journal about Dance* 35: 17–26.

Lavender, L. (2014) Patriarchal Dualisms in Dance. In Proceedings of the *National Dance Education Organization* conference on 'The Art and Craft of Teaching', Miami, FL 10/26/2013, 174–182.

Leach, J. (2007) Creativity, Subjectivity, and the Dynamic of Possessive Individualism. In Hallam, E., and T. Ingold, (ed.), *Creativity and Cultural Improvisation.* Oxford: Berg.

Leep, J. (2008) *Theatrical Improvisation.* New York: Palgrave Macmillan.

Lepecki, A. (2006) *Exhausting Dance, Performance and the Politics of Movement.* New York: Routledge.

Li, J. (1997) Creativity in Horizontal and Vertical Domains. *Creativity Research Journal* 10: 107–132.

Plato. (1948) *The Portable Plato.* Harmondsworth, UK: Penguin.

Plato. (1965) *Timaeus and Critias.* Harmondsworth, UK: Penguin.

Plumwood, V. (1993) *Feminism and the Mastery of Nature.* London: Routledge.

Roche, J. (2011) Embodying Multiplicity: The Independent Contemporary Dancer's Moving Identity. *Research in Dance Education* 12(2): 105–118.

Rodriguez-Pereyra, G. (2008) Descartes's Substance Dualism and His Independence Conception of Substance. *Journal of the History of Philosophy* 46(1): 69–90.

Sawyer, K. (2000) Improvisation and the Creative Process: Dewey, Collingwood, and the Aesthetics of Spontaneity. *Journal of Aesthetics and Art Criticism* 58(2): 149–161.

Smith, C. (1998) On Authoritarianism in the Dance Classroom. In Shapiro, S. (ed.), *Dance, Power, and Difference.* Champaign, IL: Human Kinetics, 123–146.

Sparshott, F. (1995) *A Measured Pace: Toward a Philosophical Understanding of the Arts of Dance.* Toronto: University of Toronto Press.

Spolin, V. (1963) *Improvisation for the Theatre.* Evanston, IL: Northwestern University Press.

Weick, K. (1998) Improvisation as a Mindset for Organizational Analysis. *Organization Science* 9(5): 543–555.

PART IV

MEMORY AND
TRANSMISSION

CHAPTER 17

....

IMPROVISATION IN ARGENTINEAN TANGO

On Playing with Body Memories

....

SUSANNE RAVN

It is a while since I have been here—at this tango studio in Copenhagen. Tonight, the occasion is not even a milonga, but a practica.[1] Most people will come in couples to practise the tango for a longer time with their partner. No cortinas will signal the shift in partnering in between the tandas.[2] So I know it might be difficult to get dances. That is okay. I have been long enough on the tango scene to have found my way to sit, wait, and enjoy the music while watching the other couples dancing: looking for the good dancers, deciding for myself whom I would like to dance with, and trying to get eye contact with him in the small intervals between music. Depending on my mood: better few but good dances. Nevertheless, the strategy of sitting, waiting, and trying to get eye contact can also be hard. In some local milongas and practicas new to me, this 'art of wall-flowering' (Savigliano 2007) can go on for hours.

About half the couples tonight are still what I would think of as relatively new to the tango scene and busy with figuring out how to make the partnering work and their tango improvisation flow. To my experience, they have only a minor awareness of the movement of the other couples on the floor, tend to relate to the rhythm of the music, and are not really aware of dancing in relation to the melody and the characteristics of the different kinds of tango being played. They make me remember how hard tango dancing can be the first two or three years. The dance requires practitioners to have incorporated specific kinds of movement patterns and sequences of steps when embracing their dance partners, to improvise based on these movement patterns, and to deal with it all in a social setting—dancing in front of other tango enthusiasts, sitting down, waiting, and watching. Carl,[3] an experienced contemporary dancer, once told me: 'I have always trained my body—trained a lot of technique—including improvisation, but I have never really enjoyed social dancing. Tango has been a huge challenge to me—especially the social aspect. But then at a certain time I realized that even though it is difficult, the only way to learn to dance tango is to take it seriously and start joining the milongas'.

After about an hour, Simon asks me to dance. I know him from my hometown. Coincidentally, he is here as well. Normally, he would not ask me. In the implicit hierarchy within my local community of tango practitioners, I can chose to dance with more experienced leaders, but the practica here opens the setting of practicing. It invites us to meet each other anew.

Improvising the tango with Simon, I dance the follower role to his lead. I sense the embrace is a little stiff and I receive relatively weak, or partly unclear, intentions through the embrace. I try to shape the flexibility of our connection, but it is difficult. Simon does not seem to be all that aware of how to actively shape the way he holds me. Instead, he tends to lead by opening the embrace and then kind of waits until I have taken my step and moved my torso in front of his so he can close the embrace again to make sure I am right in front of him when he walks forward and I backward. In a sense, the improvisation flows, but it is as if he is concentrated on his feet and our placement in relation to each other in preference to nursing the flexibility of our embrace. I feel that I am invited to improvise on my own in the small intervals when Simon is standing still, waiting for me to get back in place in front of him. The improvisation flows in and out of these waiting moments.

Recognizing that I am dancing with a less experienced leader, I begin secretly to watch out for the other couples dancing. From former experiences (blue marks and sore bones), I know that if my partner is not aware (enough) of moving with the other couples' movements as well, I will most probably be the one to get hit by the high heels of another follower. At the same time, I realize that I begin to deliberately add possible ornamentations (extra small movements with my free leg) to the tango we dance. I sense he dances the rhythm in a quite straightforward way, and I begin using his relatively unclear invitations 'my way', in accord with my interpretation of the melody of the tango. It's a hot summer evening, and I am already wet with perspiration. This is my first dance at this practica, and I am interested in making a tango statement to the leaders watching. I am dancing to get dances . . .

. . . Finally, I get eye contact with this guy in red shoes. His name is Thorkill, I learn after the first dance. I have tried to catch his eyes all night. I really like his posture and his way of being concentrated in the embrace and on his partner's movement. In the first tango we dance, the figures he leads are relatively simple while we shape our connection within the embrace and find a shared sense of pauses and timings. I need to feel that I am here in this dance with him and deliberately insist on some of the pauses. He listens and shares the pausing. The elasticity and changes of tensions in our embrace shapes our movements—including our pauses—and thereby how tango figures find their form during the improvisation. I adjust and reshape my movements in the embrace with him just as well as my way of moving becomes part of the way he leads. My feet seem to find their way on their own, while I can focus my awareness on the tiny nuances of tensions and suggestive directions for how to move with him. Only afterwards,

I realize that I was led into dancing complicated combinations of movement patterns which I did not know of before dancing this tango with Thorkill. Nursed through the sharedness of the embrace, we not only recreate recognizable movement patterns of the tango repertoire but explore how these figures might take shape as they come to live in this improvisation.

THE Argentinean tango can be characterized by its specific steps and repertoire of figures, which refer to specific, recognizable structures of the couple's movement patterns. However, and as I intended to illustrate in the introductory description of dancing at a *practica*, it would be a mistake to think of the tango dancing as if unfolding as an improvisation of how the sequences of tango figures are put together. Rather, figures are constantly reinvented and unfolded anew in each dance. For the best dancers, every step and movement are given life in the moment as this moment is shared through the connection established in the embrace.

In this essay, I aim to explore how embodied memory as related to tango is constantly nursed, recreated, and reshaped in the interaction of the couple improvising the dance. Drawing on recent phenomenological research, I argue that improvising can be thought of as playing with body memories. In that connection, the introductory auto-ethnographical description of my visit to a *practica* in Copenhagen is also intended to set the scene for the exploration and to illustrate and remind that the social events where the tango is danced entail implicit rules and expectations: before being on the dance floor ready to dance the tango, you first have to improvise your way through the tango event to 'get' dances, and then, while you are there on the floor sharing the embrace with a partner, histories and ideals of tango influence expectations and preshape the improvisation of the dance. The introductory description is thus also intended to emphasize the contextual premises of the tango improvisation—that the unfolding of *body memories* and the phenomena of *playing* are attuned to the tango as a social event. Accordingly, I begin the exploration by focusing more explicitly on the way different ideals and training backgrounds form part of the dancing and then continue to focus on the ways in which different kinds of body memories come into play in the interaction of the couple improvising a tango together. Throughout these explorations, I draw on analyses of both auto-ethnographically based descriptions and interviews with tango dancers (Ravn 2013, 2016) as well as descriptions, analyses, and discussions presented in recent work on tango practices.

THE DIVERSITY OF DIFFERENCES IN TANGO EMBRACES

As philosopher Erin Manning (2007, 2009) and sociologist Brandon Olszewski (2008) have indicated, in their different ways, the flow of improvisation in tango is fundamentally connected to how the intimate kinetic connection works. While Olszewski, through his analysis of ethnographical fieldwork and interviews, emphasizes that tango dancers strive for the 'good dances' where everything flows, Manning (2009) uses her experiences of tango dancing as a crystal to reflect philosophical argumentations on 'relationscapes'. In that connection, she specifically emphasizes that the ideal is for the dancers to move in a breathing and flexible embrace. Among tango practitioners and enthusiasts, the ideal kind of intimate kinetic connection formed in the embrace has also been characterized as the creation of 'a four-legged creature' (e.g., Westergaard 2011). As the description of my dances with Simon and Thorkill hopefully illustrates, the intimate kinetic connection unfolds very differently depending on who you are dancing with. Obviously, part of the difference has to do with training background. That is, the flexibility and breathing characteristics of the connection is based not only on the dancers' embodied engagement of the here and now and their deliberate and focused attention but also, and not least, on the ways they have trained to be aware of the tiny nuances of this intimate kinetic connection. When Simon *waits* for my movements and the improvisation comes to flow in and out of these waiting moments, the tango is far from the ideal of how the improvisation ought to flow as described by Manning. In comparison, *sharing the pausing* when improvising with Thorkill presents a kind of tango dancing that seems to come much closer to the ideal Manning presents of how to form part of a breathing and flexible embrace (2007, 2009).

Different tango styles—for example *salon, milonguero*, and *nuevo*—in their different ways can be characterized with regard to the closeness and flexibility of the embrace, the specificity of how you are to walk and to handle the leader and follower roles, how the music is listened to (or not), and which kind of tango music the tango dancers involved prefer (e.g., Merrit 2012; Savigliano 1995). Descriptions of styles blend with tendencies and different opinions on how you are to nurse your posture, train your walking, and shape the kinetic connection. Further, as Carolyn Merrit makes us specifically aware, within the last decades other movement disciplines have facilitated a rethinking of the art of leading the tango and how tango can be taught (2012: 54). Staying abroad for longer periods has, for example, forced (and still forces) Argentinean tango teachers to rethink their way of (re)presenting tango (79). Influenced by the conditions of a globalized world, the ideas and opinions of how to dance tango are constantly in process at each local milonga event (Merrit 2012; Savigliano 1995). The senses of movement and movement skills that dancers bring into their dancing differ and mix different ideals of what Argentinean tango is—and can be. Thus, through descriptions and analyses of tango dancing, Merrit and Savigliano in their different ways also indicate that tango is danced in very different ways and according to relatively different ideals of how the intimate kinetic connection is to be nursed.

As a tango practitioner, I lean towards the ideal of the intimate kinetic connection unfolding in a breathing and flexible way as described by Manning (2007, 2009). However, as part of the analytical process, 'fighting' my familiarity with tango practices and ideals (Hammersley and Atkinson 2007: 79; Thorpe and Olive 2016), it becomes central also to acknowledge the diversity of the ways tango can be thought of and danced. Descriptions and explorations of how embodied memory is at play when improvising the tango are, in that sense, to be based on an understanding of tango dancing as a field of practice in which different interpretations of ideals mix and blend. Tango is not only danced differently depending on, for example, whether the dancers are more or less experienced and more or less capable of creating a flow in the improvisation. Differences change when ideals change. When improvising with a partner whom you have just met at a *practica* or *milonga*, you do not only engage in handling and exploring the differences of a practice while improvising. You also, whether it is implicitly or explicitly realized by the dancers, engage in the diversity of how these differences can unfold (Ravn 2012). Improvising the tango with a partner can therefore also be perceived as a meeting of possible versions of what tango can be. The improvisation of tango comes to live both in and through the practices of the dance as a social event and with the many different folds of passions, interests, and experiences that are shared in the embraces and the striving for the good dance. On the one hand the recognizable structures of tango movement, the tango figures, form a basis for how the tango is improvised. On the other hand, recognizing the diversities of the ways tango can be danced, the figures are at the same time no more than suggestable templates for variations and possibilities which are used and given life through the different ways in which the flexibility of the embraces unfold.

Incorporating and Training the Steps and Figures of Tango

Many tango teachers present tango as simply a matter of walking together. However, any tango enthusiast knows that you are subsequently expected to give years to learning to walk together in a proper tango way. In the beginning, couples experiment with how the shared walking may contribute to how the intimate connection is established through the embrace. The first challenge is often to sense how the leader can initiate a shared walking from his torso by actively pushing down into the floor and letting the follower receive the initiation of movement through the embrace. The tango leaders I have interviewed have emphasized that at the beginning of their tango careers, they specifically faced the challenge of learning how to both coordinate the steps of the figures and handle the timings and sensations of how these steps are connected to the leading from one's torso (Ravn 2013, 2016). In other words, they first of all struggled to incorporate an embodied sensation of how the flexibility of the embrace could nurse the dynamic of the figures danced—including the dynamics of their steps (see fig. 17.1).

After one has incorporated basic movements and steps, one's training often continues. Tango dancers join classes and workshops both to learn new figures and to train in how tango steps and figures can invite certain movements in different ways. Still, and as explicated by Carl in the introduction, joining the social events—the *milongas* and the less formal *practicas*—is central to really developing and exploring

FIG. 17.1 'Nursing the flexibility of the embrace'. Daniel Carlsson and Anna Solakios, professional tango teachers and dancers, at the Summer tango festival in Malmø, Sweden, 2014. Photograph by Lars Kårholm.

the improvisational potentials of each tango step. These social settings offer the opportunity to explore and be surprised by the many ways steps and figures can be recreated, rearranged, and dissolved through the embrace. Figures are broken down, played with, and reinvented at the same time. As formulated by Merritt: 'The steps were familiar, but their execution, the music shaping them, the space surrounding them, and the bodies enacting them were anything but' (2012: 15). By taking part in these social events of dancing, you come to know about the implicit timings related to how steps feed into each other and figures unfold and dissolve. The differentiation between waiting and pausing—and, not least, the appreciation of the pausing—becomes embodied within the complex web of interactions unfolding at the *practicas* and *milongas*.

Philosopher Bruce Ellis Benson makes us aware that improvisation is defined as a process in which one 'fabricates' something out of 'what is on hand' (2003: 32).[4] As already argued, what is 'on hand' for the tango dancers are the embodied memories of steps, figures, and parts of figures—as well as ways to possibly perform figures and steps differently. Significantly, Benson emphasizes that when improvising, we also participate in a performance tradition: we are part of a connection that allows the tradition to build on itself. Drawing on Husserl's work, Benson describes how the implicit knowing of timings and preferences of 'what to do next' when improvising is part of a process of sedimentation related to the artistic tradition in relation to which we perform (100). In other words, the tradition of *how* to use the tango figures as templates for the improvisation, and *how* to use, for example, pausing, is also to be considered central to how steps and figures become incorporated: pauses are to become pauses in the proper tango way. This process of sedimentation both presents and represents the connection of a tradition which tango dancers form part of when dancing. The sense of pausing both belongs to the tango couples dancing and represents the sedimentation of a tango tradition.

DIFFERENT KINDS OF EMBODIED MEMORIES

The immediate adjustments nursing the flexibility of the embrace and the silent embodied knowing of the steps and pauses obviously present bodily ways of knowing how to move in the moment. However, it should be emphasized that it would be a mistake to think of embodied memory as if it were entirely intuitive and outside the psychological realm. As philosopher John Sutton and his colleague Kellie Williamson (2014) recently emphasized, any kind of memory, including the explicitly autobiographical kind of memory, is embodied. That is, recalling, for example, the experience of a specific tango danced at a *practica* is fundamentally based in one's embodied being. Already a century ago, philosopher Henri Bergson made us aware that recollection (Bergson's conceptual reference to autobiographical memory) makes no sense without the incorporated and implicit knowing of the 'how to do'. However, at the same time, recollections of the past unfolding 'here-and-now' like a camera focus on the possible real and actual movement taking place (Bergson 1911: 210). Representational and nonrepresentational kinds of memories are, in this sense, to be considered as acting between and 'of' each other and lending each other mutual support (89–90). As is further emphasized in Sutton's work (2005, 2014), we should not only recognize that there are different kinds of body memories but also recognize that they are working and feeding into each other at the same time.

As is implicitly exemplified in my introductory description of my dancing with Simon and Thorkill, when playing with steps and parts of figures, I do not have to be intentionally aware of what my feet are doing. I can choose to *submit* to my incorporated expertise of performing the tango steps (Colombetti 2014: 130) and to direct my awareness towards other facets of the dancing—for example, the flexibility of our embrace or the melody of the tango music. In that sense, I can deliberately shift between using different kinds of embodied memories to inform my movements. At the same time, the movements unfolding in the improvisation also revitalize sensations and former experiences of dancing tango which feed into the way I use my intentional awareness.

My field notes and the post hoc descriptions presented in this essay could not have been produced without me having some kind of bodily self-monitoring going on in the dancing (Colombetti 2014: 113; Legrand 2007). Thinking back on the dancing, I can, for example, recall the kinaesthetic sensation of performing a *boleo*. In the *boleo*, the leader uses the elasticity of the embrace to create a sharp twisting movement of the follower's torso, which then affects her hip and leg movement in a successive twisting flow of movement through her body. As she keeps her knees aligned with her torso, the lower leg ends up performing a swing in the knee joint. Recalling my sensations, I realize that the kinaesthetic sensations of my swinging lower leg are closely related to the way my sense of a vertical axis in my body forms a reference for this movement. I am also reminded that I have an irritating tendency to speed up and force the timing of the *boleo*. When back at a *practica*, reflections like these come back and direct my attention. Thus, my reflections on the logic of the *boleo* and my embodied sensations blend. Reflections become part of how I move.

Finally, sharing the embrace with different dance partners, I also engage in emotional aspects closely connected to my experience of, among others, different smells and the softness and warmness of my partner's hands. These affective aspects add flavours to the improvisation and the ways our embodied memories unfold in the present. In other words, the body, by virtue of its history and accumulated experiences, has acquired tendencies that are not only sensorimotor but also affective. Self-monitoring, reflections, recalled experiences, sensations, and not least incorporated movement patterns feed into how movements unfold in the present improvisation. However, the way I inhabit these experiences with my feelings and affections, often invoked by smell, softness, and intuitive attraction (or lack of attraction), also animates my movements. Obviously, as closely connected to emotions, the affective aspects of our body memory can strongly influence which partners we prefer to dance with and how the sharedness of the tango becomes shaped. Forming part of our body memories, affectivity specifically highlights the recognition that the different forms of body memories should not be misunderstood as if they are a set of dispositions ready to be played with in the improvisation. Rather, the different kinds of body memories should be understood as forming part of a *present condition* that affects every moment of our existence (Colombetti, Dylan, and Ravn 2014).[5]

A Microcosm of Interaction

The descriptions I have presented of the flexibility of the embrace already imply that the tango dancers' sense of movement neither begins nor stops at the skin but goes beyond the physical surface of the body. That is, the leader leads by the way in which he[6] senses the relaxation and resistance in the follower's body, and the follower closely interacts with the movement of the leader based on how she senses the intention and direction of his lead. As a tango leader described it, 'all her steps, I feel here [in the torso]—and if she steps out of line I can feel it here immediately'. He also explains that the way he finds out 'if the communication works is via her body—her reactions' (Ravn 2016: 126). In other words, the flexibility of the embrace involves the tango dancers sensing their movements as *extended* through their dance partners. This sense of extension is somehow comparable to the way a blind person's stick works as an extension of her physical body. However, the connection is not fixed, as is the case when using a stick to become aware of the environment. As is clarified and discussed by phenomenologist De Jaegher and her colleagues, there is a continuous coordination of the kind of connection that exists between two subjects moving together, one that is comparable to a microcosm of interactions (De Jaegher and Di Paolo 2007). During the course of interaction, two 'centres of gravity' oscillate between activity and receptivity (Fuchs and De Jaegher 2009). The intentionality of the movements does not belong to the one or the other (for example, the leader or the follower) but is given life and direction in the flux of interaction. In other words, while the stick can be thought of as physical prolongation of the perception-action loop of the blind person, a partner's movement forms an interactive part of a shared perception-action loop. De Jaegher and Di Paolo's and Fuchs and De Jaegher's phenomenological clarifications suggest that the improvised tango is not to be reduced to being based on a certain tango-specific dynamic of actions and reactions playing back and forth between two bodies but finds its form through an interactive flux of microcoordination. Accordingly, movements come to be shaped and directed not only because of but also *through* the movements of the other. When one takes a closer look at tango dancers' descriptions, one sees that their experiences strongly indicate that the interactive setting goes beyond and 'is more' than the sum of several first person perspectives (Ravn 2016). When dancing the tango, my sense of my body moving is also part of a sense of our bodies moving in connected ways—and vice versa.

Consequently, in the interactive flux of microcoordination, my movements become directed and shaped before I am aware of it. To be more precise, De Jaegher and her colleagues also specifically indicate that within the sharedness created by the interactional shaping of the embrace, meaningful connections have already been formed at the level of a prereflective intentionality. Merleau-Ponty specifically describes how a prereflective intentionality, which he refers to as our operative intentionality, is to be considered the precondition for any judgmental-related intentionality, also referred to as an intentionality of act (1962: xviii). Drawing on Merleau-Ponty's phenomenological work, the explicit gain from De Jaegher and Di Paolo's (2007) and Fuchs and De Jaegher's (2009) work is the emphasis that the operative intentionality is not per se centred *in* the subject but can unfold in the intersubjective realm of interaction. As indicated in their work, this prereflective kind of intentionality can unfold in a connection that is in a state of flux. When the interactive oscillation of the two 'centres of gravity' is in sync, the subjects experience the interaction process as gaining an intentionality of its own (Fuchs and De

Jaegher 2009: 471). In tango dancing, the connection being in sync corresponds to the experience 'that "it dances me" ... and anyway, these movements are at the same time also me [mine]', as one of my tango fellows described it in an interview (Ravn 2016).

However, that movements unfold in the interactive oscillation of intentionalities does not mean that the tango practitioner sacrifices her intentionality with respect to her body as a singularized body. The tango dancer can at any time focus her awareness on, for example, her sense of her axis and the kinaesthetic dynamic of her movement while forming part of the embrace (as I, for example, described in relation to performing the *boleo*). However, the phenomenological descriptions of how interaction becomes co-ordinated indicate that the *process of playing* is to be understood as a mutual affair of revitalizing and shaping different kinds of body memories. Based on the condition of the way the social event frames the tango dancing, body memories feed into the dancing moment as they are brought to life in the interactive microcosm of the couple improvising the tango together.

THE TRIO OF PRIVATE LESSONS

A few days after the *practica*, I had made arrangement for private lessons with Pablo Fidanza and Julia Marini,[7] an Argentinean couple with whom I have taken classes during the last five years when they have been in Denmark. Similar to the practice in most private lessons, I dance with Pablo while Julia watches my movement and uses her experiences of the same kind of movement to supplement Pablo's feedback on how he senses the movement of my body in the embrace. The feedback takes place as a combination of Pablo's feeling and Julia's seeing of my dancing.

Julia and Pablo are teaching me the movement patterns and timings of the backward *saccada* (displacement) as performed by the follower. The saccada version we train is part of a rather challenging figure where the follower has to keep the contact of the embrace with the leader while twisting her lower body maximally (to the left) so that her (right) foot (heel first) can be placed between the leader's feet in her backward step. Julia mentions that she remembers how difficult the backward *saccada* was in the beginning and explains to me: 'When we recognize the movement we add something more ... Like in the *giro* [turn]. He leads the turn but we know it, so we add something extra'. Pablo continues: 'It is not the saccada which is important, it is the posture and the technique of the backward step of the saccada. I mean, when we are in a more difficult situation when it happens we lose ... so it is about the control of our body. What is interesting is that we really need to know the step—how to project ... how to place the foot. ... Let's try once more'.

We continue ... I sweat and swear and we laugh. Julia hums with the tango music, sings a little with the singer, while I continue to explore how to cope with the timing of the step, pushing my torsion to a maximum, experimenting with how I can use my 'feel' of my axis while letting my movements form part of the impulses and timings of Pablo's lead. At the same time, I am painfully aware of all the unnecessary anticipations I built up. I try to let go of the tensions by focusing on resting in the sense of my axis. I know that Pablo is aware of nuances of my tensions in ways which I only have a glimpse of. Based on his experiences of variations and nuances of the saccada figures, he nurses the pauses and invites me to be with his timing. By tapping into the timing of his movements, I am invited into dancing the figure.

When taking classes in both contemporary dance and ballet, I have the possibility of watching my own body moving. The mirror enables me to combine the look and the feel of my body and to involve myself in processes of internalizing the external eye and externalizing the internal sensation in an interwoven process (Ravn 2009: 236–246). When dancing the tango, I cannot establish the same connection between looking and feeling. My visual field is physically constrained by my partner's body and is set by the premises of our embrace: the way I hold my head in extension of my torso will immediately influence the dynamic of our embrace. By turning my head just a little bit, I change the interaction that I wanted to scrutinize by using the mirror.

In these private lessons, Julia becomes my eyes. She is the third dancer of our tango. I become aware of the look and the feel of my movements through the embodied experiences of both Pablo and Julia. We establish a trio in which we share the look and feel of the two of us dancing together. Accordingly, the sharing and exchange of embodied memories are guided by perception-action loops, which actively involve the three of us. Reshaping and expanding my tango expertise requires me to experiment with how my embodied memories can be used in process and exchange. Within the scene of tango dancing today, forming an active part of such a triplex of perception-action loops presents a highly kinaesthetic way of—so to speak—tapping into the expertise of more experienced dancers.

CONCLUSION

Through my dances with Simon, Thorkill, and Pablo, I have exemplified the way the tango improvisation of today in Northern Europe unfolds in different ways and situations. Drawing on recent phenomenological research on improvisation, body memory, and interaction, I have argued that different kinds of body memories are in operation—and played with—at the same time when improvising the tango. Accordingly, I have emphasized that body memory is not to be reduced to some kind of silent embodied disposition. It does not belong to the inner realm of the subject but comes to live through the interaction of the embrace, and through the way this embrace is further shaped by the interactions and implicit negotiations that characterize the tango as a social event. When describing tango improvisation, we are, from the outset, to be aware that the locally inhabited versions and ideals of tango which are at play at *milongas* and *practicas* influence the ways dancers bring body memories to life in the constant recreation and reshaping of incorporated steps and parts of tango figures. Self-monitoring, reflections, recalled experiences, sensations, affectivity, and not least the incorporated movement patterns themselves feed into how movements unfold in the present tango improvisation. In doing all this, dancers are actively involved in embodied meetings with what tango can be like—and thereby in reshaping and possibly transforming their embodied memories of tango.

As an example of a particularly intricate kind of interaction, tango exemplifies how we can sense movement not only because of but also through another subject. My descriptions of how I have made the improvisations with Simon, Thorkill, and Pablo work exemplify phenomenological conceptualizations of the way in which perception-action loops can extend to include the other and, accordingly, exemplify the insight that prereflective intentionality can unfold in a connection that is in a state of flux. In this way, the intentionality of the improvised tango movements does not belong to the one or the other. However, nor do the tango dancers sacrifice the intentionality of their bodies. Descriptions accordingly suggest that tango dancers can use their awareness strategically to influence the way perception-action loops extend and the way intentionality becomes shared. As I argued in the latter part of this essay, the practice of tango improvisation also indicates how the microcosm of interaction can include three dancers. That is, the description of how private lessons in tango dancing can unfold specifically reveals how perception-action loops can dynamically extend and be shared through the reciprocal interactions of two dancers dancing and, possibly, a third dancer intensively watching.

Improvisation in tango can be understood as a playing with body memories—body memories that are, first of all, to be understood as a present condition of the bodies dancing. Accordingly, this essay has indicated that in the kinaesthetic meeting established in the tango embrace, body memories are both revitalized and transformed, based on how the intentionality of the playing is given life through the microcosm of interaction.

NOTES

1. *Milonga* refers to places where tango is danced, while *practica* is often used for more informal settings where tango can also be practiced for training. That is, the exchange of dance partners and the flow of the couples moving on the floor is, in a relative sense, less predictable compared to a *milonga,* and couples can, for example, make small stops to try out certain tango figures more times in a row.
2. The *cortina* refers to a splice of nontango music played in between the *tandas,* which is a 'set' of three or four tangos with the same kind of style of tango music, for example, tango-waltzes, tango-*milongas,* or the musical style of a specific tango orchestra.
3. For the sake of privacy, names are fictional.
4. Benson focuses his phenomenological exploration on the improvisation of a musical dialogue. However, in the first chapters of his book (2003), his clarifying description of the improvisation process is presented as a general epistemology of improvisation.
5. The discussion of how body memory is more than dispositions is presented in Colombetti's contribution to this book review.

6. In traditional Argentinean tango styles the leader role is danced by a male and the follower role by a female dancer.

7. Pablo Fidanza and Julia Marini have given me permission to use their names in these descriptions.

References

Benson, B. E. (2003) *The Improvisation of Musical Dialogue—A Phenomenology of Music.* Cambridge: Cambridge University Press.

Bergson, H. (1911) *Matter and Memory.* London: Allen and Unwin. (Originally published 1896, in French)

Colombetti, G. (2014) *The Feeling Body—Affective Science Meets the Enactive Mind.* Cambridge, MA: MIT Press.

Colombetti, G., Trigg, D., and Ravn, S. (2014) Book Review: *Body Memory, Metaphor and Movement. Memory Studies* 7(3): 393–400.

De Jaegher, H., and di Paolo, E. (2007) Participatory Sense-Making—An Enactive Approach to Social Cognition. *Phenomenology and the Cognitive Sciences* 6: 485–507.

Fuchs, T., and De Jaegher, H. (2009) Enactive Intersubjectivity: Participatory Sense-Making and Mutual Incorporation. *Phenomenology and the Cognitive Sciences* 8: 465–486.

Hammersley, M., and Atkinson, P. (2007) *Ethnography—Principles in Practice.* 3rd ed. London: Routledge.

Legrand, D. (2007) Pre-reflective Self-Consciousness: On Being Bodily in the World. *Janus Head* 9(2): 493–519.

Legrand, D., and Ravn, S. (2009) Perceiving Subjectivity in Bodily Movement: The Case of Dancers. *Phenomenology and Cognitive Science* 8: 389–408.

Manning, E. (2007) *The Politics of Touch: Sense, Movement, Sovereignty.* Minneapolis: University of Minnesota Press.

Manning, E. (2009) *Relationscapes: Movement, Art, Philosophy.* Cambridge, MA: MIT Press.

Merleau-Ponty, M. (1998) *The Phenomenology of Perception.* London: Routledge. (Originally published 1962)

Merritt, C. (2012) *Tango Nuevo.* Gainesville: University Press of Florida.

Olszewski, B. (2008) El Cuerpo del Baile: The Kinetic and Social Fundaments of Tango. *Body and Society* 14(2): 63–81.

Ravn, S. (2009) *Sensing Movement, Living Spaces—An Investigation of Movement Based on the Lived Experience of 13 Professional Dancers.* Saarbrücken, Germany: VDM Verlag Dr. Müller.

Ravn, S. (2012) Interacting Spaces in Argentinean Tango. In Ravn, S., and Rouhiainen, L. (eds.), *Dance Spaces: Practices of Movement.* Odense: University Press of Southern Denmark, 99–118.

Ravn, S. (2013) Tango, interaktion og bevægelsesgrunde—Om den sanselige bevægelsesoplevelse. In Ravn, S., and Hansen, J. (eds.), *Tics, træning og tango—bevæggrunde for bevægelse.* Odense: Syddansk Universitetsforlag, 93–118.

Ravn, S. (2016) Embodying Interaction in Argentinean Tango and Sports Dance. In DeFrantz, T., and Rothfield, P. (eds.), *Choreography and Corporeality—Relay in Motion.* London: Palgrave, 119–134.

Savigliano, M. E. (1995) *Tango and the Political Economy of Passion.* Boulder: Westview Press.

Savigliano, M. E. (2007) Wallflowers and Femme Fatales: Dancing Gender and Politics at the Milongas. Paper presented at Agassiz Theater, Harvard University, Radcliffe Institute of Advanced Study, Cambridge, Massachusetts, 27 October.

Sutton, J. (2005) Moving and Thinking Together in Dance. In Grove, R., Stevens, C., and McKechnie, S. (eds.), *Thinking in Four Dimensions*. Melbourne: Melbourne University Press, 50–56.

Sutton, J. (2014) Memory Perspectives (Editorial). *Memory Studies* 7(2): 141–145.

Sutton, J., and Williamson, K. (2014) Embodied Remembering. In Shapiro, L. (ed.), *The Routledge Handbook of Embodied Cognition*. London: Routledge, 315–325.

Thorpe, H., and Olive, R. (2016) Conducting Observations in Sport and Exercise Settings. In Smith, B., and Sparkes, A. C. (eds.), *The Routledge Handbook of Qualitative Research in Sport and Exercise*. London: Routledge, 124–138.

Westergaard, M. (2011) *Tango Passion—and the Rules of the Game*. Stuttgart: Abrazos.

CHAPTER 18

DANCING LIFE

NORAH ZUNIGA SHAW

In 2001 Richard Linklater's breakthrough animation and live action film *Waking Life* gave us a character travelling through a series of philosophical conversations, chance meetings, and public lectures that may or may not be happening in reality. In the film, we are both in the main character's 'head' and in the world, and we remain unsure whether he is alive or dead or dreaming. In the character's search for meaning, reality becomes memory and memory a fiction pushing at notions of self, mind and body, and time. Although the film is carefully scripted and edited, it also gives the sensation of immediacy, of improvisation and the stream of impulses, ideas, and images that cycle through our lives. I have taken this idea as the leaping-off point for this essay, in which I use the story structure and conceptual framework of *Waking Life* to conduct my own search back into the improvisation teachings of those who have influenced my dancing life and the lives of so many others.

As an improvisation artist, I am acutely aware of the way lineage, both actual and adopted, operates in the present and the many voices that are in my dancing body each time I enter the studio. To write these voices—Simone Forti, Nancy Stark Smith, Thomas Hauert, William Forsythe, Nik Haffner, and Alana Shaw—I have chosen an approach more akin to magical realism and memoir, or perhaps historical fiction. I have combined interview transcripts of my own; sources available in print and online that I have edited, abbreviated, adapted, and sampled from as desired; and my own impressions and memories to create a fictional account that is grounded in these masters' actual practices, thinking, and contributions. In the notes to the chapter, I offer short sketches of the real professional biographies of all the voices included, and I indicate the sources of each voice's statements. But in the end, as Nancy Stark Smith says, 'there are many histories of the same moment. This, naturally, is my version of the story'.[1] And my memories of moments real and imagined are already changed because they are filtered through my perceptions. As in *Waking Life* and in the moment of deep flow that sometimes happens in improvisation, the line between self and other, real and unreal, is hard to locate, and perhaps we are only dreaming.

ATTENTION IS DESTINY

Five women, dancers. One is over seventy; the others are younger, maybe twenty-something; one of them is Main Character. They are in Simone Forti's sparsely furnished apartment in West Los Angeles, where stacks of books serve as the legs of a makeshift plywood table in a manner that is surprisingly pleasing and communicates a simplicity and elegance of taste.[2] The windows are open, letting in the soft air and the mingled smell of jasmine and car exhaust.

> SIMONE FORTI: Notice what you notice.
>   Take a walk with a partner in silence and notice what you notice.
> MAIN CHARACTER: Do we just walk or do we dance?
> FORTI: Notice what you notice, stay connected to yourself and your partner, and let yourself be silent. Maybe you will dance, maybe it is a walk. See what happens.
>   But before we start, prime your mind and body with something. Read the paper, read a poem or a quote, touch something, and notice what you notice, start from there.
>   And with this experience, try to be a little less compositional.
> MAIN CHARACTER: What do you mean? Do you want it um …
> FORTI: Less directed.
> MAIN CHARACTER: From where?
> FORTI: It doesn't always need to be the choreographer on stage. Try letting go of the composing mind.
> MAIN CHARACTER: Isn't that what improvisation is? It is composing on the fly, spontaneous selection and decision-making, working with what's there to create order or chaos but to create.
> FORTI: Not today. Today be present. Think with your body. Let's take a walk.

URSA MINOR

Main Character is driving on the 405 freeway in Los Angeles in an old black Honda Civic with the windows down. She parks outside Union Station in Los Angeles. The main lobby of the train station is almost empty; its high ceilings and 1940s furnishings have been updated with cheap polyester upholstery. She enters a train and rides for a while, her body rocking with the rhythm of the train. She steps out into a train station in Frankfurt, Germany, and calls her friend. There's a man there, and she sees him but doesn't stop.

Phone call:

> MAIN CHARACTER: Hallo! I've arrived. The flight was fine. The train too. All easy. I'm ready to work. Can you come get me? Um. Sure, but I don't know the way from here. Frankfurt am Main. There's a Starbucks. I'll figure it out. OK, danke. Super. Alles klar. Bis gleich …

(A polar bear lumbers down the busy Frankfurt street in front of the main station, with a woman who looks like but is not Simone Forti, on its back.)[3]

FORTI: Get on, let's go, anchors aweigh, Ursa Minor, steady on. Need a lift to the next shelter?

MAIN CHARACTER: I'm meeting someone.

FORTI: Come on up, don't cross a bear! When I started today I sat like this and I felt like yes, that feels good that's right. To be aware of impulses, in life it takes a lot of being aware of impulses. OK I'm here, I see that, I remember that dropping, what do I want to do now, I think I want to sit down. Yes, I like this and I might get on this bear here and take a ride, maybe this impulse will bear fruit.

Do you like this ride? What do you think? This ain't no dumb animal. This is an elder. She outranks us. She protects her young. You gotta show respect for that. There is a bear in all of us that the elders say we need to tame. I kind a like to move with it. I've been crawling a lot lately. And watching. Watching her move, the swing of her gait, the easy power, you can feel it even just sitting here can't you. Just get on and take a ride with me, follow your impulses or tame them, that's the ride. When to say yes. You know what I mean? There are land bears too you know. Imagine how they flow. Don't have our slick wet power. But they aren't running out of ground to stand on. Imagine that. Soon we are gonna have nowhere to stand. The ground is melting underneath us and crashing in big sheets making salty splashes that scare the seals away. Calves they call them, the sheets coming off the icebergs. Chunks really. Armageddon. What's that movement feel like, when the ground drops out from under you and there is no ground left to stand on. Don't leave me hanging. We're not landlocked we're water locked. So what's your plan? Go with the flow? Follow the impulse, tame it? Where do you want me to drop you?

MAIN CHARACTER: Me? I don't know. It all feels too far away. I can't quite get a hold on the scale. Anywhere is fine.

FORTI: You gotta tell me where, you're going in some direction? What's your plan, what's your score, where's your map?

A man sitting behind her on the bear's rump speaks up now.

MAN: I know. Wait five beats, then go the direction that comes to you. Not the first impulse, wait at least a few more impulses before the next turn. Stop when you feel a full body yes.

MAIN CHARACTER: Where will I be?

FORTI: Well I don't know, but it's somewhere, and it's going to determine the course of the rest of your life. All ashore that's going ashore. Ha ha ha ha ha. Toot, toot.[4]

THREE LIFE LESSONS

Main Character gets off the bear and catches a note that flies by in a cold breeze. It says 'look down', and the ground she stands on calves off in a cacophony of sound, completely obscuring her in an immense glacial landscape. She wakes up and seems to feel OK. She brushes her teeth, dresses, sips tea, and spills it. Goes to a dance class in a studio on the upper floor of a boathouse at Smith College, where a woman, Nancy Stark Smith,[5] is talking and moving, demonstrating her point, her long braid falling over her shoulder as she tips to the side. Sketched symbols appear around her as she talks.

Make Body Time

NANCY STARK SMITH: So that's what we will explore today, this *Underscore*. It didn't have a name for the first ten years of its existence. We used to just call it 'the score'. It came to me in 1990 after a crisis in my teaching. I rebelled. My rebellion came in the form of open space. I found myself prolonging open, structure-less sections of class during which I would suggest things to focus on—through language and my own movement. As we danced, I would continue to add images and concerns but never stop to form the activity into specific exercises or scores. It dawned on me that what I was experiencing as a random selection of materials was a very consistent score operating all the time, informing my choices. What was this inner *Underscore*?

Nancy closes her eyes and breaths deeply for a minute, softening the tone in her body and listening gently. Then she begins to speak again.

So let's move into the room and start to arrive here together. Bringing your attention, your presence, and also your will into the room.
Arriving energetically.
Arriving into the present moment.

It is quiet in the space as people move gently, some walking, some rolling a bit on the floor or stretching, breathing. Many have their eyes closed.

Focus your attention on physical sensations …
The textures and locations of sensation throughout the body …
The rise and fall of your breathing …
The sensation of muscle tissue stretching, the action inside the joint, the touch of your body against the floor, your weight …
You might bounce a little and imagine the globe is a ball that you are bouncing with your body.
Arrive into sensation.
Maybe it is useful to think of Steve Paxton's image of 'using the mind as a lens into the body'. Magnifying sensation with attention.
We are arriving into 'body time', where there is enough time to register your sensations and absorb their information and 'nutritional value' into your system (rather than just accomplishing a physical task).
Good. Let the sensations be nourishing to you.

And before we transition, just let a question arise in your practice. What seed do you want to plant for our practice today?[6]

Leave a Trace

Two women are walking across the campus of Smith College, talking, and we enter into their conversation in midstream.[7]

STARK SMITH: Yeah. That's the cycle we have talked about before. In embodied research we need a trace, but the trace is not the end. How does dance create knowledge, and on the other side of that question, how are our ideas experienced? How do we put language to experience, and create 'traces', like you say, that communicate? We've been working with this for years at *Contact Quarterly*. The journal was first and foremost about communicating. Then that communication became a document of what we were all working on at the time, the conversation, and the scores for moving, the ideas … and they created other ideas.

MAIN CHARACTER: And this is important again now. It is important in the larger discussion of cultural heritage in dance, especially in Europe but in the US too, and what happens to the traces we create and how do these trace (text, scores, audio, video, images) remain an active element of the ongoing creative process?

STARK SMITH: Right.

MAIN CHARACTER: And this cycle … starting with the body, then observing, or writing, or drawing, or talking, and then moving again. Cycling from question to embodiment, embodied investigation I guess, to trace, and looking at that trace, analyzing it, bringing it back to the body. And then the idea is that the traces help us discover a wider range of ideas and questions that are contained within a dance that can be moved, traced, transmitted, communicated, and used to catalyze new creativity, and of course that's what scores should be, are, were. Generative scores. The musical score is not the end, even the reading and performing of the score is not the end. The work is in dialog with the trace. Traces record or capture or articulate, but they also generate. Your symbols and names for stages of your *Underscore* are not only a set of parameters for motion but also a trace. I think this relates to your notions of prescriptive and descriptive. I think you make your hieroglyphs and glyphs in order to communicate but also to initiate, yes?

STARK SMITH: The glyphs and the hieroglyphs are different. The glyphs are more like symbols that I developed for the *Underscore*. They are used for communicating a dancing state, a particular organization of priorities and references, and they are a playful element for describing the score to people who are going to do it, probably. Most of the time when I'm describing the score, it is in preparation for actually doing it. So that's my intention, is to convey enough of a reference so people can go into the score and have an experience without worrying about what they are doing. The phases are articulated as names, and for each one there is also a glyph, like stereovision or something, two different means for getting a sense of the same thing. Maybe people get the energy of it from the glyph and they soften their ideas around the words. In making the glyphs, I'm sourcing from an experiential place to bring something to the page.…That's similar to the hieroglyphs I guess, but unlike the glyphs, the hieroglyphs have no content. The glyphs of the *Underscore* have content and they point to a range of experiences within certain parameters.

MAIN CHARACTER: What are the hieroglyphs then?

STARK SMITH: Hieroglyphs started as an attempt to bridge dancer's experience to a physical piece of paper, to language, and it was an effort to try to relax a dancer's relationship to the actual act of writing, of putting pen to paper and making a mark. So instead of marking it with a word, which is a huge jump into language, I said, let's … I started with doing a physical relaxation … with a piece of paper nearby and a pen, talked through a whole relaxation … take the pen, with your eyes closed at a certain point, put it down on the paper and try to move the pen. Let the energy that's moving in your body move out through your hand into the pen onto the paper and just make that translation. It doesn't have to mean anything. So we did that and sort of came out of the physical focus and looked at what's on the page. Then we did that again, put the pen down and make a move, just move it and stop. So they became these individual hieroglyphs, discrete units. So that they were the equivalent, sort of, of words, in that it wasn't a drawing, it was an individual move that came from the body onto the page. And people could move up to down, or across.

MAIN CHARACTER: Like writing?

STARK SMITH: Yeah, like writing. And so then we started to share with each other, like reading, and to see what's transmitted with these marks. So that's its own trajectory … but there is really no content. Whereas with the glyphs for the *Underscore,* they developed very differently, and they really don't change. I've really never conflated the two, but I suppose there is something again about trying to match experience with something that's on the page.

MAIN CHARACTER: So that's description.

STARK SMITH: Yeah, but like if I am travelling through the room and I am overlapping kinaespheres with other people in the room, I'm moving close and far away but I'm not touching them yet, and I'm having an experience of that that is very specific, I can make a mark that represents something vividly and quickly about what I'm doing, so it contains it conceptually and helps us talk with one another about it. So it is also about communicating.

But the prescriptive use of it, aside from relaying it to prepare a group for doing the *Underscore,* or aside from having it on the wall and now we're going to do it, can also come through in more micro ways. For example, sometimes there are very tricky transitions between parts of the *Underscore,* like moving into travelling … so one technique sometimes or strategy I use is I sort of throw a seed out for myself or for my experience, which is like 'we're going towards traveling'. And then I notice how my body reorganizes for that. And I sometimes have to throw in a little will or a little discipline in certain ways but it is not like 'OK, let's get up and start travelling', you know? I think that's too much. Almost like an antibiotic or something, it kind of wipes out too much, you know the ecology of the small little things that are starting to develop there. You want to keep that ecology and start to direct it, add a little tone in the body and more interactive things in the space and with the other people. So that's pretty curious, to start to intend something that is already prescribed you could say. Part of my desire personally and what I hope for others is that you experience a genuine impulse to

move. I mean the question of 'why move?' really definitely comes up. So playing
with that also, issues of will and intention and discipline are also very interesting
to me. When do you exercise exertion to go in a certain direction and why? I really
like inviting people into the pleasure of seeing composition in life and inviting
pleasure at the coincidences.

MAIN CHARACTER: I like thinking that way, too, like the way I've learned to see
alignments and counterpoint all around me and when I 'notice what I notice' the
world jumps into focus in a different way. I remember being so surprised when
Simone suggested we stop composing so much during an improvisation … that we
stop 'making a dance' and instead do the dance that is there. Those aren't quite her
words but that's how I've carried her ideas forward in my life. It's like what you say
about … what is it … ? Just 'being with something as it is'.

STARK SMITH: Yeah, 'being with something as it is' is a contemplative practice.
There are so many different threads to improvisation, to why we are doing it and
what for and when and with whom. But Simone really is so skilled at creating
particular forms that *are* the composition. I mean priming the situation. Her
dances are primed with very specific ways of working that are already formal.
I think contact improvisation is that as well. It's almost like a perfect form, and
there are others of course, in the sense that it will illuminate whatever is put into
it. Even if the form, like the spiral roll, even if the roll itself doesn't change, you
can activate it differently internally with your own vitality. I'm interested lately
in ambiguity, how open a structure or a form or an idea can be … yeah … and
still keep returning to an articulation bringing it in lightly but with direction,
going into a thing and going a little bit more, penetrating it in order to open it up
more … keeping it streaming. Yeah, you know, it's something … something about
creating and sharing states of deep intelligent ambiguity.

Simone Forti is dancing and talking amidst scattered sections of a newspaper. She seems
lost in her own reveries. A critic for the *Los Angeles Times* is in the audience and starts
talking in a hushed voice.

DANCE CRITIC: You see dances, especially improvisations, are always in the act
of disappearing. So we critics, by putting language to them, are part of what gives
them duration, a voice, permanence even, something that can be returned to and
reflected on. You didn't see this piece, but I am seeing it. I can describe it for you in
words and images that create the possibility of motion for you. Look at her, listen,
she's busy with something. The tone of her voice is almost childlike but shakes a
bit through aging windpipes. There is an impish quality to her speaking, maybe
a little mischievous but focused and committed to the task and intent on it, that's
Simone Forti you know? Here, just read it: 'scattering sections of the *Times* across
the stage of Highways Performance Space in Santa Monica on Sunday, postmodern
matriarch Simone Forti scans them with a flashlight and walks on them as if they
were stepping stones to some undetermined destination—'maybe Hawaii,' she says.
She then arranges them to suggest global land masses—'Let's make the Persian
Gulf here'—and traces 'the estuary of the Tigris and Euphrates' from the stage floor
up through her body onto the back wall and ceiling.[8]

Two women are talking in a large room somewhere in New York City: Simone Forti and dance journalist Claudia La Rocco.

> FORTI: There's a connection between language and movement ... I started taking the news as the ground from which I was improvising, from which questions and speculations, bits of information, were floating up and connecting together in different ways. Even as I said, 'were floating up', as we were talking, I kind of spread my fingers and my hands came up and I hadn't planned to do that. It's something we do—some of us more than others—use our hands and our whole bodies as part of our expression. And I find that it's not only part of the expression, but it's part of understanding, it's part of the original thought or image or feeling about something, finding the words for it; the kind of energy you feel in your body....
> When I started working with the news—
>
> LA ROCCO: What year was that?
>
> FORTI: Around 1984. I would do things, like spread newspapers on the floor and make them into maps and talk about what I was reading. Playing it through my body helped me understand where there were tensions, where something maybe was about to change, how it might change something somewhere else. I was talking, also, and there were certain phrases in the newspapers, like 'the dollar in freefall', or 'Lebanon a slippery slope'.
>
> LA ROCCO: The pieces in which you're talking about the news and, particularly when you were responding to developments in the government that you find dismaying are obviously explicitly political. Have you always considered yourself a political artist?
>
> FORTI: No, I haven't. That really started with the news. It started late.[9]

Simone Forti stands next to a metal stool on a small makeshift stage at an arts college somewhere in California.[10]

> FORTI: I had the good fortune of finding a teacher who very much inspired me and that I could completely focus on working with for four years and that's Anna Halprin, who—

An image appears of a woman, Anna Halprin, sitting and smiling on a porch surrounded by redwood trees. She looks comfortable in her ageing body and is speaking softly.

> FORTI: —now in her early nineties, is still travelling all over the world and giving lectures and teaching ... When I came across her she was just stopping doing what was known as modern dance and getting completely focused on improvisation. And this was in 1955. That's quite a while ago ... A few of us kind of became her laboratory. She had a beautiful studio, which was a wooden deck out in the woods ... in Marin County at the foot of the mountain. One thing I learned from her is that any movement has its mood.

Forti picks up the stool, turns it on its side, and with intention tosses it with her right hand, sending it crashing and rolling along the tiny stage. She watches it, her right hand still in the position it ended in after swinging through, her attention focused until it stops moving.

> FORTI: You see? Any movement has its mood, its nature, its quality. I don't know if
> you can all see this but if you can't see it, you can imagine it. You have to just watch
> things. Cars. People walking. Wind in the trees. And um, I don't have to copy
> that. But I can sense its form and the roundness about it. And I find shapes and
> movements that out of the tradition of dance I wouldn't have access to. I get into a
> completely different mood.[10]

Dance Critic is sitting in the audience listening to Simone talk and speaks directly to us again in a hushed voice.

> DANCE CRITIC: That's how Forti sees human beings: physically connected to the natural
> world and deeply aligned with its contours and processes, whether she stretches out
> to encompass the cradle of civilization or scrunches up to depict the sharp angles of
> the Alps. 'Sometimes I feel like a hair on the head of the Earth', she says.[11]

Main Character is sitting in a mall somewhere in a suburban North American city. She writes a line in her notebook: 'Destiny is the quality of your attention. What is the nature of your attention?' and draws a picture next to it: Simone balancing gently on one foot, with her arm extended and her wild white hair falling around her face.

Play Tricks and Stay Alert

A dancer sits erect in a chair in street clothing backlit by a window that places him in shadow and obscures the details of his face. He speaks gently but firmly, his English slightly accented, his hands gesturing very deliberately and specifically to describe each point. He is Thomas Hauert.[12]

> THOMAS HAUERT: I mean. Listen, the body will keep finding solutions to the most
> complex and unpredictable cocktails of forces and directions imposed on it. As an
> artist this is liberating.
> To improvise in performance is to choreograph with all eventualities. Yes?
> So then for performing improvisation, it is spontaneous, but it doesn't come out
> of nowhere.
> We devise methods for rehearsing improvisation.
> For me, it comes from a desire to maximize—is that the right word? It comes
> from the desire to maximize the creative possibilities of the body in motion and go
> beyond habits in training, in the mind. The mind and body. Body/mind. The words
> are very bad for this.

But basically, improvisation is the interaction between our focus, attention, conscious command, sensual feedback, reflexes . . . and the body has the tendency to follow known paths. In order to increase our movement vocabularies, we have to surpass the movement patterns that have become habitual.

Somehow it comes down to tricking the body into inventing new movements rather than following inscribed patterns.

With practice, the body can learn to continue movement even if the conscious attention is not with it any more. I like to play with this. Sometimes it helps to have a partner or 'assistants' who can decide about the chain of places where changes are to happen for you. So it is like a solo, only you have others giving you inputs. In my company we call these 'assisted solos'. In addition to the awareness of the great variety of places available to initiate movement, a great side effect of 'assisted solo' is that the attention constantly skips and scans and zigzags through all the regions/places of the body, creating an 'alive' presence, a 'full' quality in the performance that I really like. You get the experience of spontaneous and unpredictable strings and combinations of movements, and it puts you in a really alert state of attention that is constantly travelling through the body.

With practice, this alert attention and unpredictable coordination can be continued without the assistants. It gives you a new set of eventualities.[13]

Disaster

Main Character enters a house. Next, we see her taking off her jacket and sitting on the floor. Then she leans back on the rug and stairs up at the ceiling, which appears to be covered in hieroglyphs. She looks at an analog clock above the fireplace mantel, and the hands don't seem to move in a regular rhythm but swing around erratically forward and back and settle unexpectedly. She closes her eyes, and we hear the noise of wind and the groan of large structures shifting as if there are giant glaciers or ocean liners outside, and Main Character begins to hover above the floor, and then higher and higher and through the roof, and over a dense urban landscape that is slowly filling up with water. Structures break off and slide away in the now gushing water. Fires burst up from explosions under the water. There are no people, just water and fire and the debris of a suburban landscape rapidly submerged. She opens her eyes and slides suddenly down from the sky. As the water drains, she lands on the ground amidst disaster and starts running.

Space of the Mind

A polar bear wanders into downtown Frankfurt near the opera house. The bear looks into the windows of a large, spacious dance studio on the second floor, where a man is dancing and talking and seems to be lost in a question of some kind: Nik Haffner.[14] Main

Character is sitting on the studio floor near him, and we enter into their conversation midstream.

NIK HAFFNER: Well I think you can see it in the performance quality and in how they work together on stage. But also that's what our work at the Ballet Frankfurt was about in the 1990s and with the Improvisation Technologies project, if you take what is really an imagined line or point or plane performed by the dancer and make it visible with a little simple animation, that little simple animation can be, especially for people from outside, a little revelation to see: 'Oh my God they're not just moving around they're actually working with an idea of a line, of a certain shape, of an object that they remembered'. Why keep this a secret, because there's good reason to share this.

MAIN CHARACTER: So it's sort of a philosophical standpoint, sharing; using or sharing scores for improvisation not as a finished thing but using them as a way of thinking, a way of working?

HAFFNER: Really it's not about results but about how, with tools, you can make many different things and you can also destroy things: like you can take a hammer and make a chair or destroy a chair or build a house or do many, many things with that one hammer. But once you understand how that tool—the hammer— functions, you might be able to invent your own little tool. If you learn how to use tools, you have plenty of possibilities to find ways to build or rebuild or unbuild.

And also this is an invitation, if you make some inside knowledge accessible and available and also in a way that it is kind of fun to explore, people let go of the idea that 'Oh it's dance. I have no idea how they do this, this is such a different world'. And only because some ideas then are out on the table, all of sudden a lot of other disciplines realize 'that's exactly what we've been dealing with'. And all of sudden you feel much closer in terms of collaboration or realize that communication with one another seems rather rewarding for everyone involved.

MAIN CHARACTER: Yes. And the processes, the ways of working.

HAFFNER: Right, I was amazed, especially in the first years I was in the Ballet Frankfurt, that Bill Forsythe would usually create a full evening piece in no more than six weeks. You could roughly divide the process of making the piece into two parts within those weeks. The first part was improvisation, a lot of it. We were stirring up material in terms of movement, research, and finding a shared pool of material that is available from then on to use and reuse. This might include text or video or any other sources that came into that particular piece. Then the second part was the process of organizing the material. He took all these bits of sources into the space, onto the stage, along with the other elements that were then becoming part of the stage space: the lights or any objects or the sound. Often Bill would keep trying out and reorganizing the whole piece a matter of days before the premiere, but the foundation was there from the first weeks. He became very good at knowing what he has to reset, and quite quickly and easily everyone would understand what each person had to do to organize it differently. If there was a new piece or a new proposition going through many versions, Bill would get closer and closer to where he wanted to go. I was always amazed by how quickly the reorganizing of that vast amount of material happened. But because everybody was comfortable shifting things around, it worked. He prepared everyone to do this. And maybe on top of that, there's the kind of engagement that this creates in every person: because I am not just doing the choreography I learned by heart and I can just repeat it, but I have responsibility to really pay attention to not missing the cue I'm getting and being prepared to clearly give my cues. Basically to communicate on stage and, when it comes to improvisation, to be very clear with the decisions I have to make in that moment. And you can see that engagement in the dancers and in their movement and physical presence. For me this created a kind of excitement, of never having the feeling 'Oh, here we go again'. At times Bill would make a very clear decision that the company had become too comfortable in a piece, so he would change it. He would be interested in still investigating, in reorganizing and reshaping, the piece even years after the premiere. And that would keep the piece alive and keep excitement within the company performing it alive as well. Sometimes he would give out a task, and some people would come up with some movement and other people would come up with movement that is completely different. And it turns out they misunderstood the task completely but maybe they made something really interesting. Bill would almost invite these accidents and these misunderstandings. Because this was also an 'Aha!' There was the same beginning of an idea that was put into the space, but how it was understood by the people in the space already was different, so how they translated the idea back into movement brought very different results. He was interested in how do you find a solution, what did you find, and how did you find it. He'd often say, 'What did you just do there?'

I use this now. There are so many situations where I find it is just easier and more fun to remind each other or yourself of that one question, 'What do we have here?' It's that practice to relook at even the same thing and wonder what else you can see or do. Once you understand that, it's so much easier to put your cards on the table, because you will not be held to your opinion for the rest of your life. Maybe you will be convinced at that table where you put your cards that maybe something else might be where you go: 'Oh, interesting. Maybe I will try that'.

MAIN CHARACTER: Ralph Lemon says that. He's an American choreographer, a really interesting maker, and when I met him in Los Angeles a few years back, he had this practice that every time he made an emphatic statement, he would follow it by saying: 'Or not'.

Or not …

HAFFNER: Just leave that space. Your mind is of that space.

Crisis

A woman with red face in jail is screaming and ranting about violence, about the persistence of fear, fear of the body, fear of women, control, rape, patriarchy, and the coming doom. She glows with rage.

THE HOLY MOMENT

Main Character hikes up a mountain. The landscape is dry and parched, but tiny wildflowers are blowing in the wind and slight damp of an alpine summer rain.

A woman is sitting meditating on a large outcropping of lichen-covered granite rocks. She opens her eyes. She is Alana Shaw.[15]

ALANA SHAW: You are here.
MAIN CHARACTER: Yeah I guess so.
SHAW: Take a journey with me?
MAIN CHARACTER: I already am.
SHAW: Take a different kind of journey. Start dreaming. Start finding, creating, inventing, practicing, and committing to a new way of standing on the earth, one that is connected to every living thing on the earth and driven absolutely by a deep and loving 'YES'. You already know everything you need to know about living a joyful, easeful, peaceful life. There is no external system that can tell you how to thrive or be happy or manifest. Your body has all that information and you are ready. The only question you need to ask is are you willing to recognize and express who you are at your deepest most expanded level in a way that supports and celebrates your unique and absolutely crucial gifts. The very survival of our earth depends on the manifestation of those gifts. Fall in love with yourself over and over again, gently and easily move on your way to manifesting more and more. The vibrations from your loving integrity move out into the collective unconscious of the world in circles of healing energy. Your magic is crying out to be brought forth. It has been there for a long time, waiting for your conditioned story to surrender. Let's just skip the old stuff and try something else why don't we?

Main Character sits on a rock nearby and gazes down at her shoes, noticing that she has stepped on a tiny mountain bluebell, crushing it. She touches the flower gently, changes positions, and leans back on the warm rock.

SHAW: I know you can create your own story, your own future, and your own happiness. You are not limited by your old stories, only blessed ultimately by their wisdom and the ways in which they deepen your own compassion for others. We do not have to be stopped or stuck anywhere. Our very dynamic brains and our ever changing, moving bodies will keep us dancing into the next moment. We are constantly in a state of becoming, moment by moment, body to body. Your body is your most fundamental mechanism of change. When we are moving, we use every single part of our brain—it all lights up. But move from choice. Life is choice. Life is really just one long series of improvisations. And improvising reflects your life in present time, where anything is possible. As you improvise, following your body into the space, you literally activate your preferences, curiosity, timing, senses, rhythms, pace, habits, stories, longings, feelings, creativity, intelligence. Every one of these moments is the next incredible opportunity for life to unfold. Just as we are reflected in nature, our bodies and our stories are reflected and played out in our spontaneous movement. All the skills we develop in improvisational movement integrate our ability to make choices about how we want to live our lives. Freeing up our movement, breath, and sound all develop our ability to respond in the moment—activating our creativity, and allowing us to live more fully. Begin your journey through the healing cycle and see what happens moment to moment little one, you are grown now. Ask yourself: 'What do I notice right now, in this moment, in my body?' The body now. My body now. Scan your body for sensations, or vibrations. Notice how and where in your body you are breathing right now. This choice to be curious about your body signals and to consciously listen to your body, is the beginning and the end, as the body is a dynamic, moving, energy field and is therefore always changing. Get up! Go on. The wheel of your life is turning. Get moving. Feel great. I'm here with you. We all are.[16]

Trapped in a Dream

Main Character is running down a residential street in downtown Frankfurt. The ground is wet, as if after a storm and she slows to a stop. Polar bears are lounging in a park. Simone Forti sits on a bench, gazing softly around her. Nik Haffner is quietly talking with Nancy Stark Smith, Bebe Miller and Alana Shaw under an old, old tree. Main character approaches a man who is pointing out architectural forms around him: William Forsythe.[17] Together they look carefully at a line of buildings across the street, noting old and new, modernist and baroque. There is a flash of movement as Thomas Hauert passes by, lost in thought, with the strings of a bunch of colourful balloons clasped in his hands.

WILLIAM FORSYTHE: It is not law. It isn't. Must they be used? These received notions of how to practice? There are a lot of received notions. You're talking to someone in rehearsal and they are perfectly normal people and then they get on stage and they think it is obligatory to sustain their ballet persona. But you don't have to do that. You don't have to sustain this artificial better self, so to speak. It doesn't have to be like that. That was one of our mottos. In this world we all assume things and these assumptions we make about things are dramatic. It doesn't have to be like that ... It finally boils down to the nature of attention. It doesn't matter what the method is, it's your relationship to the method and it's the quality of attention that you pay. If you go hear a great musician play what you're going to hear is the quality of their attention to an idea. It has to do with, it is ontological, it is state of being, it is a way of being. He's obviously in the position of a translator. We look at the page and we see black marks on a white page. And the musician says oh that is actually something that sounds like this. So you are going from one domain to another. From the visual domain through his body to the domain of tactility and then motor and he's moving through this inert object and creating things that go back into your auditory system. And it's the quality of attention. You don't want to hear him 'OK'. You want people to obliterate themselves with their attention, even if you are paying attention to not paying attention. There is no way you can escape this moment of presence. These are behaviors. The point is the state you're in.[18]

MAIN CHARACTER: And can it be a shared state, not just me on my own?

FORSYTHE: Sure, group unison is a state. But so is counterpoint and there are
moments in which we share some attributes but not others, forms of relationship,
isometries, alignments. It is a matter of attention again and intention.
MAIN CHARACTER: Attention to counterpoint?
FORSYTHE: Counterpoint emerges when some properties of unison are shared,
but not all and not always. What is striking are the moments when each different
attribute intermittently reverts predominantly to unison. Unison functions as a
base state from which to compare all further change. It is a complex organizational
task to create alignments and it comes back to attention. Dancers 'feel' the
organization dynamically. They are bound up in a system of connections that both
drives them and is driven by them.[19]

Lines of connection begin to draw out, between Main Character and Forsythe, the trees
and buildings and passersby, the others in the park. The lines are fleeting; they dissolve
and reorganize as people move, thoughts change, gazes shift. A web of pulsing lines of
light begins to accumulate in the space above the heads of everyone there, getting deeper
and deeper as new spatial and temporal and energetic relationships are formed and dissolved. They all rise up as a mesh of light, the lines pulsing, moving together but in their
own ways, coming together at times but only partially and at irregular intervals.

WAKE UP!

I am in the studio. I can just barely grasp an image of Main Character in my mind's eye.
Polar bears are on my mind, climate change, melting ice. I go into the studio for my
morning practice—'just twenty-five minutes of improvisation, at least make the space
for that', I tell myself. And each day it is strangely hard to get there, to get into the studio.

Thinking of Simone Forti, I have brought with me the day's newspaper and some climate change data and images I've printed out from sources online. It is the photo cap-
tions that stand out. A man kneels on the ground with his hands and arms raised. I skim
the headlines. Threats. Disasters in differing scales of time and space, Greenland is
melting, there are fires again in California, dwindling bees ... a globe in crisis while I sit
in relative peace and comfort, 'like a hair on the head of the earth'.

Simone would say: Move from there. Speak from there.

Moving into body time, as Nancy would invite me to do, and remembering my
mother's call to scan the body for sensation, I listen to the signals and say Yes! Notice
what you notice. As I walk, I notice the strips of tape on the floor, and I revel in the
autumn sunshine outside the windows. Sound and patterns are amplified by my silence. Outside, students are sitting on the grass. I think of pesticides on the grass,
Rachel Carson. I look up, noticing long trajectories more than I normally do, repeating
architectural patterns, lines mostly, a lighting grid. I stop and listen for a while, feel the
warmth of light through the window on the specific patch of skin and cheekbone I've

offered up. Breathing. I need somewhere to start. Sensation is nice, but I want a tighter container. I think of Bill Forsythe, and I start imagining points in my body and the lines between them and then stretching and bridging and matching and dropping and extruding those lines and points. I push harder at the cognitive habit of coordination itself. Thomas Hauert's body echoes in mine as I bend and straighten joints in irregular patterns, trying not to do the same thing on both sides of my body.

After awhile, I break free into a kind of boneless shaking movement state that brings other voices into the room from other improvisations: Noa Zuk's Gaga classes and Ohad Fishof's punk aesthetic of using what's near at hand, Eiko Otake's fierce but gentle cycles of unfolding states, Bonnie Bainbridge Cohen's cellular awareness, which brings Deborah Hay into the room, too, and of course Irene Dowd and her spirals are always present, Bebe Miller's genius for creating 'risky weight', 'weight at risk', and Nik Haffner's quiet voice calms me, tells me to work hard but not strain, and as the room fills up, I tumble through space and look behind me, just as the studio door opens one last time and gently, quietly, a polar bear wanders in.

NOTES

1. Stark Smith (2006: 46).
2. I met and worked with Simone Forti at the University of California, Los Angeles, where I did my graduate work in dance. I have borrowed the 'notice what you notice' score from Simone's practice, and she may have borrowed it from someone else, but it has become a valued strategy in my teaching and presenting. This and the next section are entirely fictional, drawing from memories of her classes and conversations with her in Los Angeles and my own relationship to her work and her sense of mischief and philosophical clarity. Simone's biography on the UCLA website describes her as coming of age in the 1950s and 1960s and points to her role in the explorations at the Judson Dance Theater that were very influential in the development of modern dance: '"from her early minimalist dance-constructions, through her animal movement studies, land portraits and news animations, Forti has had a seminal influence on her field. For the past two decades she has been developing *Logomotion*, an improvisational dance/narrative form' (Simone Forti Bio n.d.). She lives most of the time in Los Angeles.
3. Starting in the 1960s, Forti began spending time watching and engaging with animals at the zoo and exploring these experiences in her improvisation practices and teaching. She often referenced her observation of bears in the classes I took with her at UCLA. For more information, see Bryan-Wilson 2015.
4. This line is a direct quote from Chapter Two of the transcript of the film *Waking Life* (2001).
5. Like many in dance, I have known of Nancy Stark Smith and her work for years. She is a major figure in the field and is widely recognized for her participation in the invention of contact improvisation with Steve Paxton and others, as well as her many years developing the form through her work as a teacher, performer, writer, editor, and publisher of the journal *Contact Quarterly*, which she cofounded in 1975. Nancy was an athlete and gymnast first, coming to dance in the early 1970s. She travels and teaches

worldwide, and in addition to *Contact Quarterly*, her voice appears in the book *Taken by Surprise: A Dance Improvisation Reader* and in numerous online interviews. Nancy came into my life directly in 2005, when she brought me in to help edit her autobiographical book project *Caught Falling*. She has since become a valued friend, teacher, and collaborator. She lives with her partner, musician and composer Mike Vargas, in western Massachusetts.

6. Text excerpted from Stark Smith and Koteen (2008: 90–99). I am drawing specifically from Nancy's *Underscore*; I have changed some of the language to put it in a speaking rather than a written voice.

7. This section is adapted from numerous conversations Nancy and I have had in the context of developing a workshop on embodied research, and in particular from transcripts of discussions during our research residency together at The Ohio State University, Columbus, in April 2015.

8. From Segal (1998).

9. The La Rocco/Forti dialogue here consists of direct excerpts from La Rocco (2010).

10. The statements from Forti that follow are excerpted from Forti (2010).

11. Dance Critic's statement is excerpted from Segal (1998).

12. Thomas Hauert is a Swiss-born choreographer and dancer based in Brussels; he directs the ZOO Company. After dancing with Anne Teresa De Keersmaeker, David Zambrano, and others, Thomas founded ZOO in 1998 to explore performance improvisation specifically. They tour extensively and have received many European awards. Thomas is always developing his methods and is a gifted teacher who gives workshops internationally and has created pieces for many companies including the Zurich Ballet and Candoco Dance Company. He is the academic director of the bachelor degree in contemporary dance at the school La Manufacture in Lausanne. I met Thomas through mutual friends at PACT Zollverein Choreographic Center in Essen, Germany, and I was immediately excited by the specificity and rigour of his engagement with improvisation as a way of researching embodied cognition in performance. We collaborated to create the online dance score TWO for Motion Bank (Palazzi et al. 2013).

13. This text is taken from interviews I conducted with Thomas Hauert between 2011 and 2013 and from writing he did during our collaboration on TWO, the online dance score for Motion Bank (Palazzi et al. 2013), of which I am co–creative director. I have rewritten some of the language slightly to sound more like the way he speaks than more formal writing. Some of this material is available online at the project's website, http://scores.motionbank.org/two.

14. Nik Haffner was a dancer with William Forsythe in the Ballet Frankfurt from 1994 to 2004. While there, he was a key figure in the creation of the now well-known project Improvisation Technologies. Nik studied art history at Giessen University and dance at the Australian Ballet School in Melbourne. He is now a media artist and choreographer and serves as artistic director of the Inter-University Centre for Dance in Berlin. Nik and I met during the creation of Synchronous Objects, an online choreographic visualization project I co-created with Maria Palazzi and William Forsythe that premiered in 2009, http://synchronousobjects.osu.edu/. Nik and I have taught movement workshops together on improvisation technologies and other methods developed from Synchronous Objects. To write this section, I drew on a series of conversations Nik Haffner and I recorded together at The Ohio State University, during his residency in February 2009 (in my possession), in which we explored connections between our work.

15. Alana Shaw is the founder and executive director of Turning the Wheel, a nonprofit organization that creates intergenerational performances and teaches empowerment through movement improvisation and the arts in schools, organizations, and communities across the United States. She is a master teacher and guide who is known for her ability to facilitate joyful and healing movement modalities for people from all walks of life. With over four decades of experience, her work is influenced by her years of study in community dance practices with Liz Lerman, Nancy Spanier, and others; in dance therapy with the many wise teachers at the Naropa Institute; and in modern dance and visual art at the University of Colorado, Boulder. She is the author of two books including *Dancing Our Way Home,* a book of exercises and stories for dancing in community. She is also the mother of seven free-spirited grown-up children. I am her daughter.

16. The text in this section combines my own musings and my adaptations of excerpts from Shaw (2017).

17. William Forsythe is an American-born choreographer who was director of the Ballet Frankfurt from 1984 to 2004 and the Forsythe Company, also based in Germany, from 2004 to 2014. He is now working independently and is the Claude and Alfred Mann Professor of Practice in Dance and Artistic Advisor to the USC Choreographic Institute at the Glorya Kaufman School of Dance at The University of Southern California. He is celebrated as one of the great artists of our time and recognized for having completely reimagined the boundaries of classical ballet. He works extensively with improvisation in his process and at heart is a researcher. I met Bill first in graduate school at the University of California, Los Angeles, when he was there as a Regents' Lecturer and then again in 2005 when he was looking to collaborate on a new media project that would focus on counterpoint and visualizing choreographic structures in one of his dances. That became our collaborative online project Synchronous Objects. I have many interviews and transcripts of our conversations.

18. This monologue is adapted slightly from Forsythe and Sulcas (2014). This lovely excerpt made the most sense to me for this chapter.

19. Forsythe's statements in this dialogue are adapted from excerpts from his commentary in the "Process Catalog" for the Counterpoint Tool on Synchronous Objects, http://synchronousobjects.osu.edu.

REFERENCES

Bryan-Wilson, Julia. (2015) Simone Forti Goes to the Zoo. *October* 152(1): 26–52.

Forsythe, William, Palazzi, Maria, and Shaw, Norah Zuniga. (2009) Synchronous Objects. http://synchronousobjects.osu.edu. (Online choreographic visualization project)

Forsythe, William, and Sulcas, Roslyn. (2014) Forsythe Lectures: William Forsythe and Roslyn Sulcas. deSingel Internationale Kunstcampus, 2 April. https://www.youtube.com/watch?v=Mbe4VavLuLI. Accessed 10 March 2015.

Forti, Simone. (2010) Otis Visiting Artist: Simone Forti. Public Talk, Otis College of Art and Design, 13 April. https://www.youtube.com/watch?v=29VCs5TBY5I. Accessed 10 February 2015.

La Rocco, Claudia. (2010) Dance: In Conversation: Simone Forti with Claudia La Rocco. *Brooklyn Rail,* 2 April. http://www.brooklynrail.org/2010/04/dance/simone-forti-with-claudia-la-rocco. Accessed 31 January 2015.

Palazzi, Maria, Shaw, Norah Zuniga, Bebe Miller Company, and Thomas Hauert/ZOO Company. (2013) Motion Bank: TWO. http://scores.motionbank.org/two/. (Online dance project)

Segal, Lewis. (1998) Forti's 'Logomotion' Connects Humans, Nature. *Los Angeles Times*, 17 February. http://articles.latimes.com/1998/feb/17/entertainment/ca-19916. Accessed 31 January 2015.

Shaw, Alana. (2017) *The Body Now: Birthing the Yes Collective*. Bloomington: Balboa Press.

Simone Forti Bio. (n.d.) Website of University of California, Los Angeles. http://www.wacd.ucla.edu/lecturers-visiting-and-adjunct-professors/40-faculty/lecturers-visiting-and-adjunct-professors/63-simone-forti. Accessed 18 March 2015.

Stark Smith, Nancy. (2006) Harvest: One History of Contact Improvisation, a Talk Given by Nancy Stark Smith at the 2005 Freiburg Contact Festival. *Contact Quarterly* 31(2): 46.

Stark Smith, Nancy, and Koteen, David. (2008) *Caught Falling: The Confluence of Contact Improvisation, Nancy Stark Smith, and Other Moving Ideas*. Northampton, MA: Contact Editions.

Waking Life. (2001) Dir. Richard Linklater. (Video)

Waking Life. (2001) Online transcript http://wakinglifemovie.net/transcript/. Accessed 05 January 2015.

....

CHAPTER 19

DANCING KEYSTROKES, EXCAVATING MEMORY

....

ROBERT BINGHAM AND STEPHANIE HANNA

THIS is a long-distance improvisation centred on the authors' memories of a shared past. In the summer of 2013, Robert travelled to Berlin to establish a two-month artists' laboratory called the Migration Project. Eight dance and visual artists from six countries, including the authors, met twice weekly to conduct experiments in perception and movement.

These experiments eroded commonplace boundaries among dance, writing, drawing, and sound through instigations of brief and extended improvisations that poured through bodies and splashed across pages. After two months, the physical remains of these improvisations—pages of drawings and words written in many languages—were sifted and sorted. The group's favourites, chosen collectively, were displayed in a street-level art space that Stephanie runs in an unused department store window in Berlin's Neukölln district.

This exhibit was named *What Remains*.

A year later, in the spring of 2014, Robert was invited to write about this experience, and he asked Stephanie to join him. Rather than theorizing the improvisatory nature of the Migration Project, they decided to improvise their memories of a shared experience through the medium of email. They entered the process with an orientation to open-ended questions: How would they engage writing as a mode of dancing? What experiences would emerge from remembering through spontaneous writing? What would this reveal (if anything) about the nature of improvisation practice itself?

Robert's and Stephanie's approaches to the dance were different. For Robert, the kin-aesthetic enactment of writing was itself the dance. His intention was to unsettle nascent memories through the movement of keystrokes, leaving traces on the screen.

On the other side of the Atlantic, visual artist Stephanie searched for her memories by entering her imagination as a nonphysical space.

At first, Robert and Stephanie were unaware of this difference in approaches. Only later, as they sorted and curated the writing, did the distinction become obvious. They decided to highlight the nonequivalency of their experiences by organizing the writing into two columns.

The creative process was itself improvised, and its structure clarified midstream into three phases. One: improvise memory through the medium of email. Two: curate the material through layout, selection, re-ordering, illustration with Migration Project sketches (figures 19.1 to 19.3), and introduction. Three: edit the curated text, making additions and subtractions explicit for the reader.

In this final phase, Robert and Stephanie added comments and reflections relating to their distinct backgrounds in dance and visual arts. These interventions took the form of brackets and strikethroughs whose purpose was to make transparent the shifts between immediacy and reflection and between temporalities in the writing. Compared to live dance, the relative permanence of writing enabled transparency around the various phases of editing. What follows are the remains, in two parts, of a duet that played out in movement, writing, reflection, memory, and flesh over the course of four years.

Part One: Prelude

Robert, Philadelphia

My approach is phenomenological; I am aiming consciousness towards memory and describing the contents that arise. As I dance fingers across keyboard, the net of my consciousness gathers not only memories and their conversion to text, but a wholebody process: movements, sensations, sounds, and images manifesting as 'somatic resonances' (Sklar 2001: 193) within the experiential flow of the dance. Though I am alone, I imagine being seen by Stephanie, and this lashes me to the dancing; I cannot space out, exit, start over, edit, or delete. In improvisation there are no second takes. What is happening here-now *is* the dance; 'choreography' is not a script that exists apart from this moment.

Though unscripted, the dance is leaving, in its wake, a *post*script. This is the dance's remains. ~~The script's posteriority is necessary, because an improvisation, even if structured (though this one isn't particularly), cannot be prescribed.~~

Stephanie, Berlin

Improvising is my way to stay present, to relate to my surroundings and to activate my intuition, whether I am working with hidden meaning in found, inherited, and discarded objects, with people when intervening in specific social situations, or with video, documenting everyday surprises. Improvising makes me as aware as I can possibly be, and it invites the presence of coincidental outside impulses into my artistic work.

Usually, when I make a planned artwork of improvised encounters, I preserve my impressions in a recording of some sort. In this collaboration with Robert, the only recording I had was my subjective memories of the Migration Project. I recalled these memories at a significant distance, as one year had passed between the original experience and its recall through the emails. Then, two years passed between the first, rather immediate editing of our email conversation and its second work-over.

This dance is a greedy dance. It devours its freedom from prescription, yet, at the same time, it craves the (appearance of) solidity that a postscript provides. That script, as the dance's object remains, is lasting evidence that the dance happened, even long after its cellular reverberations have passed. More importantly, the script is a vehicle by means of which the dance will become 'available beyond my body to be shared with you' (Midgelow 2013: 13) through time and across space.

What kinds of memory are operative in this dance? Deidre Sklar identifies, within different categories of memory, different felt qualities of bodiness. Citing Edward Casey's distinction between body memory and memory of the body, she writes that 'the first works primarily through feelings-in-the-body, the second through representations of the body as an object of awareness' (2006: 98). Similarly, she distinguishes between remembering, which is 'imminent' within the body, and recollection, which holds the past at what Casey calls a 'quasi-pictorial distance from myself as a voyeur of the remembered' (99). Through the dance of keystrokes, I press towards imminence and discover memory and imagination folding into a single tissue ~~of "vitality affects"~~ (102).[1] I find myself unsure of the distinction. Alone as well as together, Stephanie and I 'steer the canoe of the text', as she once wrote in an email. Our oar-strokes fall into and out of a common rhythm.

Usually, I let my work find its form through intuitive collecting, sorting, and assembling of a given—circumstance, material, recording, and so on. In this process, being in separate physical spaces, in separate time zones, and from different artistic backgrounds shaped this cowriting in its form as well as in its content. Robert and I rarely responded directly to each other~~, as we would have done in a polite conversation~~. In our improvisational writing, more often, we ~~rather impolitely~~ reacted to singular aspects of an email that triggered a memory for us, spinning forth on that. In one shared space, for example in an improvised performance, this coincidental approach to interpersonal contact would maybe seem more familiar than it does here, now, laid out in two parallel columns.

~~In this writing, both of us seem to exist in separate worlds, searching our memories individually, parallel-ly.~~ Sometimes, our cowriting seems to be drifting apart while at other times, we synchronize, unexpectedly. And this is what I find most interesting in any improvisation: the unpredictable connections.

Part Two: Remembering What Remains

On Wed, Jul 9 2014 at 12:07 PM CEST, stephanie hanna wrote:

My experience of migration, ~~in the first months in the Netherlands in 1996,~~ being outside of my known surroundings and networks of friends, was a specific awareness of being alone with my experience and perception~~, being cut from my roots and habits~~.

Movement has been essential in these times, preventing me from closing up in a defensive and limiting way by exposing myself to new discoveries and new connections.

In [physical and spatial] movement, I experienced that this standing alone can transform into a grounding for new horizons, offering new possibilities of perception and action. ~~Which might be also this impulse many people experience in Berlin, in creative grounds where everything seems to be possible.~~

The situation of the performer is in a way similar:
Lonely by exposure. ~~The exposure is of a different kind, but~~ [In it,] I experience a similar, energizing effect.

On Thu, Jul 10 2014 at 4:00 PM EST, robertkbingham wrote:

~~MOVEMENT becomes a way to sidestep closing down when you are outside the familiar mode of habit?~~ This resonates with me. I'm jumping back into the studio at Tanzfabrik and thinking about the qualities of movement that were happening. There was a time, or it took time, to begin to feel the temperature of the group, to hear its voice. It was quite minimal, at least that was my early impression, and I remember thinking: is my desire to tear around the studio eating up space an American desire to eat space that my body has assimilated through my American-based training? Or was it an aesthetic interest in contrast: when there is a stillness or minimalism, is my habit to contrast that with something else to make it stand out? Was that my defensive stance, my comfort zone, which dissolved as I exposed myself to new connections and discoveries as you said?

I'm interested to know if you remember any specific moments during the project when you felt either liberated from habit or locked into it?

On Mon, Jul 14 2014 at 9:02 AM CEST, stephanie hanna wrote:

~~From the time of the Migration Project,~~ I do remember ~~very clearly~~ how different it felt to work with my body for four hours a day, twice a week, something I do not do usually. Perceiving the world through my body made thoughts and actions flow more easily.~~lighter~~.

Although I had not written down these thoughts and discoveries in those moments. I like to trust that these will integrate and manifest themselves in my experience and behaviour in the future. I like to let the material take over and decide where to go next.

For instance, both our impulses steer the canoe of this text, developing direction in exchange. Who is steering? Neither of us, really—but then, are we letting the text take over? I am following where its rhythm and its interest takes me, so are you. We are parallels. The text is aiming to be one, ~~to parallel points of view,~~ [yet] two parallel memories [are] swirling around a shared experience.

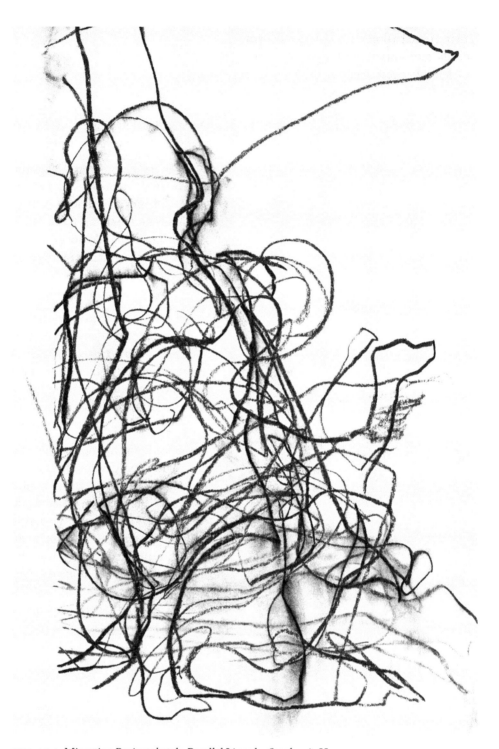

FIG. 19.1 Migration Project sketch: Parallel Lines by Stephanie Hanna, 2013.

[returning to your original question]
Through creating, I connect and become
more whole, ~~me~~. In painting and drawing,
most familiar activities to me, this feeling
of connection sets in immediately—I
am at ease with myself, focus inside. In
performance, my awareness is outside,
simply by being perceived. ~~So~~ This to me
is challenging, focusing in- and outside
simultaneously: connecting in exposure
(for a long time, my performing was
spiked with inhibition triggers).

Is it the more you delve into
this inward gaze,
the stronger the connection becomes?
And is it at the same time, the more you
delve into your audience, the stronger that
connection becomes?

On Mon, Jul 14 2014 at 3:36 PM EST,
robertkbingham wrote:

~~Opening up, alone in one's work: painting,~~
~~writing, composing, and then opening up for~~
~~another. And the opposite: going into the box.~~
~~And I remember it now, of course.~~ Rahul had
just left, it was a Thursday, I had ridden the
subway to the airport station with him, seen
him get on the bus, and then I reversed the
trip, went back to the flat, empty again. And
then, later in the day, at Tanzfabrik, we created
short solos, and that is when I climbed into
the wooden box in the corner and shut the lid.

On Tue, Jul 22 2014 at 11:40 AM CEST,
stephanie hanna wrote:

Rolling in the sun on the wooden floor of
Tanzfabrik. ~~Filming what I perceive.~~
I perceive feet moving carefully, slowly.
They are carrying another person filming.
The view through the camera is
determining the movement of the body.
Unconscious moving.
Then focus on movement, the view
through the lens becoming a surprise
determined by this movement. Then
balancing back and forth
between both impulses.

On Thu, Jul 31 2014 at 3:56 PM EST,
robertkbingham wrote:

I am inside this box and I surrender. I slow down,
soften and listen, my ribcage pooling against the
bottom. This pooling makes me think of pools,
water, the lake in Friedrichshagen. Marcela and
I are riding around the edge, we stop to swim;
Marcela removes all her clothes. I am shy about
this; my American body unable to reveal itself bare
in so public a place. I watch her back disappearing
as she walks toward the deep of the lake.

I shift in the box. My chin drops towards the chest.
I have impulses to move, to thrash, to telegraph
a story to you all, sitting outside the box, but this
time I simply watch the impulses pass by, like
dark clouds and distant lightning strikes. This is a
delicate dance, moving towards the heartbeat of
the earth. I really want to be underneath and to feel
the cool soil, to worm through. Outside, you sit,
maybe scratch.

[new paragraph]

Today is a sunny day, the light pouring through
the window making shadows of its panes along the
floor. Ahhhh! I am allowed to do this, to ride the
descent and melt into it, not always to push against
it. My American body. The body of America
pushing against descent, not yielding, rising up
and fighting. Always fighting. Always.

[new paragraph]

Out on the street, Kottbusser Damm, a junkie sits
on the bench just across the street from the park.
A can of beer sits next to him, he has headphones
on, marks run along his bare forearms. His head
is drifting towards his knees, but I can see a faint
movement or an echo of movement. Inside himself
he is dancing to a song pouring through his veins.

Finally, I push myself up, my head hits the roof of
the box, I send -

On Thu, Jul 31 2014 at 8:33 PM CEST,
stephanie hanna wrote:

I remember looking at the box from
the outside. It was very exciting,
nothing happening yet expecting
something to happen [every
second]. What is [might be] going
on inside?

Bundled concentration is
focused on
muffled sounds coming out of
the box.

Still no perceivable movement.

Suspense.

(doing the right thing sometimes
means doing nothing)

I imagine your ribcage as a pool,
spreading out on the floor
like water in a skin.

On Fri, Aug 1 2014 at 3:57 PM EST,
robertkbingham wrote:

I slowly shift in the box, consider reversing my
orientation: head where feet are. Not possible.
I can only shift slightly to my back. I knock on
the wall just to feel its rebound. I need to feel the
walls, the floor, to find my strength.

On Fri, Jul 18 2014 at 9:31 AM CEST,
stephanie hanna wrote:

Looking into sand.
Seeing a couple of feet on the edge of
the image,
reaching towards the sky.

Waiting.

On Sat, Jul 19 2014 at 5:07 PM EST,
robertkbingham wrote:

~~I'm waiting for the entrypoint.~~ Hanging off the
ledge, Viktoriapark. Upside down, watching
legs going by. Some fast, some slow. Then it's my
turn, I am the possessor of a pair of legs being
observed upside down. I ~~remember~~ [am] trying
to be compositional, instead of just letting myself
ride my legginess. I ended up on the sand, where
I leaned and fell. That was fun—I imagined
the view: me falling and disappearing under
the plank.

[It was fun, you falling out of my
picture frame. I loved you being
compositional.]

Earlier, on another part of the plank, I hung
upside down for a long time. I saw the park
sloping down to the street, and the row of
buildings, about six stories high. Above them,
the sky, blue, with some clouds. The sky didn't
change, but I changed. The sky became my
floor. I became someone for whom the sky was
the floor.
[Should I switch to present tense?]

What to do? Just observe. Move?
Observe, move, [these are]
opposites, it seems.
How do I observe while moving?
~~How do I move when nobody is
around to observe my movement?~~

There is not much impulse coming
from the sand,
or [maybe] I'm deaf to it.

I let my head drop over the edge
of the wooden platform.

On Sat, Aug 2 2014 at 10:10 AM EST,
robertkbingham wrote:

My American body that pushes against just
being. That worries and says to itself: No, there
must be more. Something has to be risked, a
scab has to be peeled off to reveal the rawness
underneath. ~~This was challenged again and again
in Berlin: the quietude in the studio, the twenty
minute wait for the server to bring me my menu.
It was a test, a challenge. Settling into this-ness,
not making it something else. Feeling the long
stretch of an hour—how many things can get
done in an hour? But letting the doing-ness fall
away from the vine. Not doing, but feeling the
impulses to do pulsing through my veins.~~

[This] feels good in my shoulders,
stretches and relaxes the muscles
that [so often] hold on so tightly.

Letting go of the weight of the head.
Just be. Observe observing.
Time passes. I let it pass by,
what else could I do?

On Mon, Jul 28 2014 at 1:33 PM,
robertkbingham wrote:

I am in the immediate midst of this world, with
dog, coffee table, leaves rustling in leaves, but
I am also moving into this other world of text
on computer screen—or, to be precise, the
world that the text is evoking. Two orders of life-
world ... the here-now and also the imagined
or remembered [and textual]. But of course the
walls that separate them don't really exist, they
aren't things, only conceptual walls. ~~How I am
living this moment includes how memory and
imagination are playing out in my body.~~

These different orders of reality that keep barging
in on each other, just as the reality of language's
linearity disrupts or alters thought.

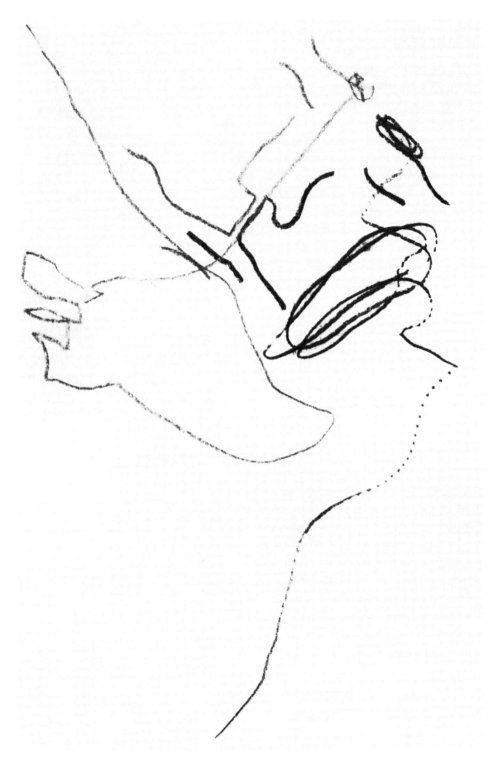

FIG. 19.2 Migration Project sketch: Footface by Stephanie Hanna, 2013.

On Mon, Jul 28 2014 at 9:47 AM CEST,
stephanie hanna wrote:

I was on the Tempelhofer Feld yesterday.
I saw my feet walking,
so I knew that I must have been inside
this body.

Almost unbelievable I was inhabiting
this body:
such a small body in such a vast space.

[I love this line]

I stretched out my arm, offering a direction,
entering into action.
My body was taking part of
what was forming the outside.

[I spent a lot of time at
Tempelhofer Feld
disappearing into my loneliness]

Where am I? Where is my memory?
Why do I feel lost the moment
the memory lane is taking over,
sucking me into a reality
that maybe was, a year ago?
Although maybe it was different?
Do I remember or do I imagine?
[Is this reality or is this a fantasy?]

In words, I am able to trace my thoughts.
I sort my thoughts into this required linearity.
But do they really make more sense that way?

In words, I delay my action. I saved my answer
to you a couple of days, returning to it now.
Doing this, delaying, my inner movement was
unperceivable to you. Or maybe not?

[I had no way of knowing]

How do I sense you, [even if we would be]
on the other side of ~~the~~ [one] room,
other than through my eyes?
How do I sense that you sense me?

On Sun, Jul 27 2014 at 3:45 PM EST,
robertkbingham wrote:

~~How can I know that the witness is~~
~~engaged? There is a vulnerability.~~
~~Vulnerability is energy. If I lean into it,~~
~~it takes me somewhere.~~
One day, when I arrived at Tanzfabrik,
we began our session together in pairs.
I was Katelyn's partner. I had my eyes
closed, and she was moving my body,
so gently. I could feel her presence, her
seeing me through her whole body.
It was palpable. My sadness was a
great weight that day, pulling me into
another ~~shape~~—[can't think of the
right word]

Katelyn put her arms around me and
said quietly: it's OK.

[I am remembering Katelyn now:]

Brown paper on the floor in Tanzfabrik,
cameras.

At first, the ~~beauty of the~~ setup drew me into
a retinal ~~perceptive~~ mode [of perception].
My eyes, [being located] in my head, [bring]
seeing so close to [interpretation]. ~~my cerebral~~
~~understanding~~ [Yet in my ongoing movement
research, I train to see unconditionally],
entering the space of ~~discoveries,~~ wondering
[and experiencing].

The sounds of the paper and the sensuality of
the material, the sight of bodies rolling onto the
paper, wrinkling it and lifting one corner, drew
me in. They offered a three-dimensionality
to my experience. The paper started to move
onto people. Soon I found myself standing
with paper over my head, in a small and private
world in the midst of a much bigger world.
Other planets were moving around me. Which
worlds were theirs? I wanted to see them, took
off the paper, and reconnected to my sense of
vision, ~~my main source of connecting to the~~
~~outside world, it seems.~~ I put the paper onto my
neighbor, thus trying to share my experience.

On Sun, Aug 3 2014 at 8:49 AM EST, robertkbingham wrote:

Back in the box. It is a place I can go, a portal to memory.

I pause for a very long time.

When I pause, my body returns, and my memory. I am reminded of the angles of the ceiling in my 6th floor walkup in Kreuzberg, the two windows just above the futon on the floor, the many plants lining the windowsill. There are no curtains. The sun goes down so late and arises so early. I wake up at 6 AM each day, the room flooded with light.

This box is the opposite, totally dark, except for a very thin sliver of outside light coming in where the lid rests on the walls. I train my eyes on that sliver. It seems to dance. The others are sitting mere feet away, yet theirs is another world. *Lebenswelt.* ~~Life-world~~ (Abram 1996). The world of darkness and a slim sliver of light that begins to fill with anxieties and imagination.

[new paragraph]

~~These are all ghosts, which I feed by relaxing into, yielding. Why do these dances always seem to be about settling and yielding? There's another part of me that wants to shatter the walls, to crash outside myself.~~

~~In the first meeting~~ When you were telling us about your ideas for this project, one idea especially caught my attention:

Tracing dance into doodling and vice versa, migrating one approach to understanding and expression into the other:

What remains [in this process]?
What is captured?
What is lost?

Later, we are sitting along the windows. Each of us does a solo. Sharon, standing near the back, faces us. Her arms are slightly out to the sides of her body, fingers clearly sensing the air. My gaze moves to her eyes; I see her seeing us seeing her. Something cracks, a small sliver forms in my heart, and I dissolve into seeing.

[By recalling and reviewing our memories of these experiences, we continue this practical research, migrating through form and time.

The form not only transports the content, it frames the experience of the receiver.

Strikethroughs might reveal developments of our thoughts—too often though I find them to be distracting, so I cheat and decide to use them only occasionally.

I am remembering a painting teacher in my first year at the art academy who answered my frustration about the ongoing gap between my paintings and the reality I wanted to depict simply by making me aware that the viewer of my paintings will never see this reality I see, ~~anyways.~~
~~Never will anyone see~~ as I can see it from my perspective.

Little did he know of how my practice would evolve. Today, it is exactly this drive to share my perspective, and have a look into the perspective of the other(s) I engage with, that keeps me going.
Yet still, even though I often do share my production process directly, this formality is not the most important aspect of the immediacy
I try to achieve in my work.]

On Sat, Aug 2 2014 at 4:26 PM EST, robertkbingham wrote:

[Switch to present tense]
In one of the sessions I led, I had the group free-write based on 'I saw' and 'I did'. Later, I had piles of pages with writing in different languages. I found myself reflected in one: 'dancing with Robert I see a surplus of expression'. Even though I did not know who wrote this, I could picture it: dancing in the quietude, a thump in my chest, the urge to make something happen, to feel a dam break, to smash through to something powerful and transformative and to have that rush pouring out into the space, causing bodies to hurl push, jump, pound shatter the air and to keep going until muscles begin to blend into fire, to become fire, heat, burning and then to drop back into the quiet, to float calmly like ash that needed the fire to become what it is.

I revisit that moment now with no surplus of expression. I am the softness of ash.

FIG. 19.3 Migration Project sketch: Oneliness by Stephanie Hanna, 2013.

On Fri, Aug 1 2014 at 9:06 AM CEST,
stephanie hanna wrote:

I remember the time we were pairing up
to learn a simple dance of each other's
with eyes closed and no speaking. Just one
touch on the hand was allowed to correct
the learner if a movement was wrong. ~~I
do not remember the dance I came up
with, but~~ I do remember trying to find my
way into Saori's dance just by sensing her
from a distance. She made me repeat the
exercise again and again, and for a very
long time, with my eyes closed, I did not
get what was wrong or missing.
When I finally looked at her dance, I saw it
was a smile on her face.

On Sun, Aug 3 2014 at 8:51 AM EST,
robertkbingham wrote:

Why not wrestle and fight?

[Were you addressing me here? Did you
want me to push and fight against the
boundaries your text offered rather than
staying self-involved and polite on my
side, reacting from a distance?

[No I was giving into what was burning
me up]

If so, then why was I hesitant to answer
this call? Was I simply too worn out
to continue producing out of a state of
emergency, in a constant struggle for
survival and acknowledgement?

On Mon, Aug 4 2014 at 11:41 AM EST,
robertkbingham wrote:

This process is for me about
groundlessness—not knowing where
I'm going, not knowing what I'm going
to write, ~~an improvisational mode that
is coming to seem less and less unlike
improvisational dancing.~~ I keep checking
into my soma as I write, the press of my
body into the cushion of the couch beneath
me. I am leaning slightly backward into the
seat back, with my

Was I done with this *Verausgabung*
people seemed to expect from artists, this
exhaustion ~~in the name~~ for the sake of art?
Did I just long for a space to be,
without any need for explanations?

Did I maybe even long for an opportunity
to heal in a soft reflection
of my own shortcomings?

head tilted forward. Birds chirp outside, and the reflection of the tree outside the window behind me dances across my computer screen.

~~So I am doing this to go to the place of groundlessness to relax into it and see what it yields. This is practice. But~~ I am ~~still~~ oriented in my groundlessness towards the experience of last summer that resides within my body. If I change my facing, will I remember differently? Or what if I, as in Galiya's workshop, hang upside down for a while. What will I remember?

~~That was a fail.~~ The dog ~~was~~ [is] not happy that I ~~was~~ [am] upside down, hanging off the couch. Nipping and scratching and pacing. Now she's lying down again, peaceably, ~~but I will not be able to continue with my experiment.~~

If I sit on the box, rather than go into it, where will my dance go? I feel more hopeful, like all the time and space that feels lonely and oppressive is now opportunity. I can get on the train, go to Wannsee,

But the feeling passes, the walls, the windows return.

~~Oppressive was the wrong word. Maybe heavy. And even.~~

So I jump off the box and pour tear rip shred my way into the furious middle of a furious dance but just for a second. Nope again: today is not about settling it's about striving and pushing and thrusting and continuing and not stopping and long phrases of movement that keep going beyond their natural endings not even natural

Did I just now remember my failure in learning Saori's dance as a metaphorical stand-in for the expectations I wanted to meet so desperately when I was a young child, but that were continuously too high to achieve?

Did I just see my father's face in yours?

Did I just recognize my neo-liberally subjectivated self in this struggle, trying to fulfill projected expectations?

Do I continue this old story still now? Is this text a legitimate means of healing? Could it be that this would be the only reason to produce art, or culture?]

~~[And can this production be reflective on itself?]~~

unnatural endings and they pop up
and lift a bit higher and become this
LONNNNNNNNNNNNNNNNNNNNG
decrescendo towards curiosity. New
seeing, hearing, tasting,

Quickness at this point is light sharp
heaviness is a distant dream, I am ~~now like~~
~~the~~ light itself.

NOTE

1. Sklar defines vitality effects, a concept term, attributed to psychologist Daniel Stern, as 'the complex qualities of kinetic energy inherent in all bodily activity' (2006: 102).

REFERENCES

Abram, D. (1996) *Spell of the Sensuous*. New York: Vintage Books.

Midgelow, V. (2013) Sensualities: Experiencing/Dancing/Writing. *New Writing: The International Journal for the Practice and Theory of Creative Writing* 10(1): 1–17.

Sklar, D. (2001) *Dancing with the Virgin: Body and Faith in the Fiesta of Tortugas, New Mexico*. Berkeley: University of California Press.

Sklar, D. (2006) Qualities of Memory: Two Dances of the Tortugas Fiesta, New Mexico. In Buckland, Theresa Jill (ed.), *Dancing from Past to Present: Nation, Culture, Identities*. Madison: University of Wisconsin Press, 97–122.

CHAPTER 20

IMPROVISATIONAL PRACTICES IN JAZZ DANCE BATTLES

JANE CARR AND IRVEN LEWIS

DURING the late 1970s and 1980s, a generation of British youth created new styles of improvised jazz dancing. Many variations in style emerged, based around clubs in different cities, as the dancers in each *scene* developed their own variations in vocabularies and practices that drew upon diverse sources, ranging from steps they learned from their parents and friends to dance seen on television and in martial arts films. While some of the jazz dancers also trained at established dance schools, the majority of training for these jazz dancers took place informally through practice at home and hours of dancing in clubs.

The dancing that developed in this way has become collectively known as *UK jazz dance* or sometimes *Old School jazz dance*.[1] In clubs, this dancing has been overshadowed by hip-hop and house dancing, but it is still practised today in cities as far apart as London, Tokyo, Seoul, Moscow, and Amsterdam, while the influence of its fast, improvised, rhythmic footwork can be seen to have been incorporated into more recent house dancing.

One of the styles that emerged from this period, usually called bebop, was developed by three dancers, Wayne James, Irven Lewis (see fig. 20.1), and Trevor Miller, who called themselves Brothers in Jazz. The danced challenges or battles between Brothers in Jazz and IDJ, the foremost proponents of another jazz style, fusion, at the WAG (Whiskey-A-Go-Go) club in London have become something of a legend.[2] However, the few video recordings of their dancing that are available are of choreographed events for television or stage shows and hence do not capture the improvisatory practice that was so important.[3]

The following account of this improvised dancing developed out of a series of discussions between the authors, Irven Lewis and Jane Carr, which explored Lewis's experiences of both dancing bebop and teaching a younger generation of dancers who have

FIG. 20.1 Irven Lewis, Self-Portrait. Photograph by Irven Lewis with thanks to Frank Wilson, 2017.

come to it in formal lessons.[4] These discussions also drew upon Carr's previous investigations of dancers' embodiment (2013, 2014) and the history of this jazz dancing (2012, 2017), and an earlier interview with Lewis (Lewis 2010). The comments on the practice of jazz improvisation (in italics) are Lewis's words captured from the discussions so as to place his lived experience of dancing at the centre of this text, in order to ensure that his particular perspective shapes this account of dancing UK jazz. The remainder of the chapter aims to represent the results of our shared reflections and discussions on this practice and its wider significance. The writing process, while it utilizes theoretical perspectives that draw on Carr's academic research, required collaboration between both authors, so what follows is aimed to be a synthesis of our different perspectives. We consider some of the issues we raise to be pertinent not only to jazz dance improvisation but also to a range of improvised dance practices in which neither conscious intention nor a tacit grasp of habitual patterns of movement seem to fully account for those often surprising moments of creativity that are appreciated for their innovation.

BEBOP JAZZ DANCING

Bebop, along with other forms of UK jazz dancing, such as fusion, developed informally, drawing on practices that, for many of the dancers, were established from a very young age. While those who developed jazz dancing in the club scenes of the late 1970s and early 1980s came from a variety of backgrounds, a significant proportion identified themselves as Black British, with strong family connections to Africa and the Caribbean.[5] Many amongst this group were the children of immigrants to Britain who had brought with them the music and dance practices of their previous homes that continued to play an important role in social activities. Dancing at family and social gatherings at home or at the local community centre was an important part of everyday life. Children were encouraged to dance and in this way gained the confidence to demonstrate their dance skills while absorbing the rhythms of popular dance music, such as ska. At parties, they gained an understanding of the format of a dance challenge that took place between two dancers within a circle of people watching. They also developed a sense of how to become immersed in the music. As they grew up, watching their parents and friends, they learned dance steps along with ways of improvising, particularly by playing with the musical rhythm.

Once they were old enough to go to clubs, the dance knowledge of this group of young people made an important contribution to the dancing. For all those dancing in the clubs that played jazz music, watching other dancers and copying their moves was a means to further develop a dance vocabulary or 'syllabus' that could be drawn on in improvisations.[6] In Lewis's home town of Leeds, reggae, lovers rock, dub, funk, jazz funk, and disco, and later on other styles of jazz music, including soul jazz, Latin jazz, and fusion, were all influential on the dance styles that emerged in clubs in the late 1970s: over a number of years, the rhythms of each style of music engendered changes in the dancing, so that the dancers developed a wealth of dance skills along with the ability to respond to a wide range of music. In addition, new moves that were seen at other clubs, on television, or on film could be incorporated into each dancer's own style. For example, Lewis remembers how, after a showing of the film *West Side Story* (1961) on television, many jazz dancers enjoyed showing off their knee spins. Moves seen in martial arts films and even ballet also inspired the jazz dancers, so that acrobatic leaps and balletic turns were also part of their palette of moves. In Leeds, the practice of scoring points in a dance challenge by touching your opponent, in a practice known as 'contact/no contact', encouraged the use of arm movements which were expected to fit in with the overall style and which became an important part of the dancers' vocabulary, even when they were not participating in a contact challenge.

On coming down to London, Lewis and fellow Leeds dancer Wayne James further developed their style in response to the demands of the local club scene. While they remained very committed to the street sensibility of club dancing, they also studied dance formally and thus were confident in drawing on the balletic moves they had previously copied from television. Inviting a third dancer, Trevor Miller, to join them, they formed Brothers in Jazz. The group's bebop style incorporated all Lewis and James had practiced when based in Leeds, including the faster footwork of fusion, which they now embellished with additional beats adapted from *batterie* as practiced in ballet. The bebop style is thus both rhythmically complex and technically difficult, demanding quick subtle changes of weight and complex coordination. For example, in *ties*, the dancer seems to glide effortlessly while executing quick stepping actions interspersed with jumps in which a gesture of the lower leg circling diagonally backwards and around momentarily throws the dancer off balance. In *canon steps,* the dancer's lower legs cross over each other very quickly, while in performing *airport* the dancer demonstrates the ability to shift and slide using all surfaces of the feet. However, in addition to knowledge of such steps, key to this style is the ability to improvise in response to jazz music and the demands of a dance challenge.

BASIC PRINCIPLES

> *People think that club dancing has no training involved. This is a misconception—It takes three to four years of training to become an efficient club dancer (street dancer).*

The foundations for any jazz dancer are a grasp of a dance vocabulary based on stepping patterns and an ability to improvise in response to both other dancers and the music. For many of the jazz dancers of the 1980s, the ability to improvise developed alongside their accumulation of a wider and increasingly complex vocabulary. However, Lewis advises those starting to improvise jazz dancing to focus on the basics.

> *Improvisation—It's easier than you think. The trick is to start simple. Most people, when they first improvise, become overwhelmed by all the choices. Instead of worrying about all those choices, let's make some of those choices for you—Stick to the side step and master this first. Your first experience of dance movement will be doing a simple side step (side-to-side). Within that movement, you are learning the basics: the rhythm of the music; phrasing of the beat; harmonies of the song; and, by observing your peers, you are also learning the style of movement of the specific dance genre.*
>
> *After three to four years of training and repetition, it becomes second nature, to do that same movement to any beat/music genre without thinking. Once you have mastered that simple side step, in all its intricacies, rhythms, harmonies, phrasings, and beats you can use that original sidestep to develop different variations from it.*

As is the case when practicing any form of dance, repetition builds up habitual movement patterns (or motor schema) that can be repeated without the conscious attention to every detail that is necessary when learning them. If these patterns are to be used as a source for creative improvisation, the dancer's skill in creating variations needs to be developed alongside the building of habitual movement patterns. Such variations may be achieved through choices of tempo and dynamic qualities, but changes may also be made to the movement patterns themselves, in terms of their spatial content or by combining elements in a different order.[7] Dancers thus need to develop the ability to shift between different modes of attention towards their movement so that they can rely on habitual movement patterns while also developing the capacity to bring conscious awareness to different details in order to effect changes in how they are performed. Here the development of the dancer's kinaesthetic awareness is important since it is through a kinaesthetic perception of their actions dancers are able to bring conscious awareness to habitual movement patterns in order to adjust them.[8] As they develop the ability to switch between different levels of conscious awareness of movement, the capacity to find new variations may be experienced as a form of creativity or individual agency.[9] Lewis, however, also emphasizes how, for jazz dancers, an important stimulus for improvisation is always the music.

> *That same side step, when you listen to a different song, with a different rhythm, will mean the original movement will change. You will learn to adapt that same movement to a different beat. You are beginning to create movement by listening and understanding the music. It becomes your own. You rely on the music to make you move—The music totally dictates your movement. Practicing steps over and over again and adapting them to the beat in this way you begin to learn to improvise.*

Learning how to respond to the music is all-important in jazz improvisation. While musical structures constrain the dancer's actions and how they are performed, this response is not simply a matter of following the music but of developing an understanding of musical rhythms so that the dancing is related to them in a more sophisticated manner.

> *You are always listening to the music and learning to interpret the music. You start putting in beats in your movement that relate to the music like you are a drummer. You learn different ways of playing with the movements to the musical beat.*

Polyrhythms, in which different rhythms play against one another. are an important part of an African Caribbean heritage (Dixon-Gottschild 1996). Nevertheless, for all dancers, whatever their cultural background, the ability to use the rhythmic precision of jazz dance footwork to play with musical structures takes years of practice, and listening to the rhythmic sound of their steps as they dance is all-important to jazz improvisers as they work to refine their skills.

Alongside their ability to respond to the music, jazz dancers also develop the skills required to respond competitively to another dancer in the challenges that are an important part of the jazz club scene and through which each dancer's range of movement, technical skills, musical knowledge, and creative imagination are tested against an adversary. To prepare for these contests, it is important to practice how to draw quickly on different moves without stopping to think about how to make a transition from one to another.

> *Putting different steps together is also a basic form of improvisation, although this is more like 'dancing by numbers'. To learn to do this, try giving each move a number and*

get someone to call out the numbers randomly so that you have to find ways of going from one move to another without stopping to think.

To understand how these basic improvisational skills are further developed in the *battling* that contributes to the development of jazz dance styles, it is important to consider how this form of improvisational dance was framed by the club context in which the dancing took place.

Jazz Dancing in the Club Scene

During the period this style of dancing emerged in clubs, anyone wanting to participate had to negotiate the social structures of the particular scene. In the clubs in many northern cities, particularly in Leeds, the most respected dancers would stay at one end of the club, and the newest would have to start dancing right at the other end. The only way to progress was to take part in challenges or battles, one dancer against another. By gaining recognition in a challenge, a dancer could move up the room, one battle at a time. Dancers needed to be able to copy others' moves, since in a dance battle the participants were expected to take on each other's actions, ideally performing them better than the other dancer or with a creative variation on the other dancer's moves. Those watching judged the dancing in terms of the creativity of the dancers: new and virtuosic moves could be incorporated, but they were required to be appropriate to the context and to work with the music and style of dancing. Dancers who frequented particular clubs thus developed a shared sense of style alongside an individual flair. Through hours of practice, they improved their dance skills and knowledge of musical structures, while regular challenges enhanced their ability to respond quickly to another dancer. Only those reaching the coveted far end of the room were deemed good enough to travel to other cities to challenge the dancers there. In an era before the Internet, it was not as easy as it is today to find out how people were dancing in another location, but through the practice of battling, the styles of dancers from different cities influenced one another. Setting off on a coach together to the 'all-dayers', dancers would get to clubs early and commit themselves to the dance floor, eschewing drinking and even socializing as they focused on honing their skills. When the dancing took the form of a battle, the two dancers pitting their skills against each other were surrounded by a circle of dancers and enthusiasts following their every move. Newer dancers would be matched against similarly skilled dancers from other cities and would perhaps only participate in a challenge for a few minutes at first. More seasoned dancers would know who their main rivals were, and a challenge between two key dancers would be a highly anticipated event. These challenges could become very competitive, yet along with the combative energy, there was also a sense of a shared creative endeavour and excitement when dancing reached a high standard.

This competitive emphasis may seem contrary to many of the assumptions regarding the democratic and communal aims that tend to be valorized in much literature on dance improvisation. Many dance improvisational practices in America and Europe have been inspired by the Judson Church dance artists of the 1960s and the performances of the Grand Union collective of dancers and choreographers in America the 1970s. In seeking to challenge traditional elitist ideas about technique and hierarchic approaches to choreographic structure and control, the dance experiments of American 'post-modern' dance are often thought to be 'symptomatic' of the concerns and ideals of the time (Reynolds and McCormick 2003: 394), and it is telling that a key text on the Judson Dance Theater is titled 'Democracy's Body' (Banes 1983).[10] However, the cultural theorist Gary Peters suggests that improvisation as a mode of performance 'is much more combative and competitive than the majority of discourses on improvisation are willing to admit' (2009: 51). Scrutiny of the debates between key players in the development of contact improvisation suggests that the commonly found assumption that the dancing 'espouses democracy and community' (Jarrett 1997/1998: 7) glosses over concerns, among the early developers of the form, regarding whether hidden, and not so hidden, hierarchies existed in the collective effort (Brown 1997[1977]; Novack 1997[1988]; Paxton 1997[1989]). Steve Paxton, one of the originators of contact improvisation, sums up the complex relationship between collectivist ideals and the dynamics of actual practice. Commenting on an article by the dancer and anthropologist Cynthia Novack, Paxton interrogates the assumption that contact improvisation is democratic:

> Contact Improvisation could not have 'embraced values of individualism equality, and anti-hierarchical relationships', because CI cannot do anything.
>   It is something to be done . . .
>   If liberty and equality are chosen then at the moment of choice they exist.
>   What happens the next moment is something for all of us, anthropologists especially, to ponder. (Paxton 1997[1989]: 166–167)

In addition to their very different movement styles and vocabularies, what distinguishes jazz traditions from improvisational practices such as contact improvisation is the former's more ready embrace of competition as a positive force. In contrast to improvisational aims in which 'the "I" is sacrificed to the "we"' (Peters 2009: 52), Peters draws on an account of a tap challenge, which he recognizes as part of an American jazz culture. In 'the "pushing and pulling" of improvisation', he finds 'the dialectic of negative and positive freedom . . . played out in full view of the audience' (53). In a similar manner, through their competitive interactions on the dance floor, jazz dancers may be understood as not only testing the possibilities of their style but entering into a dialogic relationship, not only with each other, but with the constraints of the form itself. In this way their improvisations may also be seen as at times exploring the boundaries of jazz style and, in so doing, negotiating the parameters of what constitutes the identity of jazz dancing. In the particular cultural context within which this dancing emerged, wider issues of personal identity may also have been at stake.

EMBODYING NEW IDENTITIES
THROUGH JAZZ DANCING

In developing their style of dancing jazz, the dancers might be said to draw on a particular *habitus* (Bourdieu 1984) that is important to their sense of identity, informing their choices of clothes, their social interactions, and their ways of moving.[11] Hours of practice ensure that a feel for appropriate bodily organization and rhythmic and spatial patterns are ingrained into habitual actions that reinforce a sense of habitus, so as to ensure that the dancer always maintains an appropriate style. Moreover, a tacit grasp of appropriate responses in a dance challenge allows for immediacy in dance interactions. Yet, as Wendy Bottero (2010) describes in relation to the sociological analysis of identities, the habitus can also be productive.[12] If the habitus is understood within a framework that emphasizes intersubjective experience as part of a reflexive process that can instigate change, improvisatory contests may be considered to have the potential to generate shifts in the habitus that may contribute to changes not only to the dancers' style of movement but to a sense of shared identity.

Although it is not something the dancers considered at the time they developed their dance style, Carr (2017) has argued previously that the habitus of the dancers in groups such as Brothers in Jazz may be understood to embody changes in a sense of British identity. Given the contribution of young Black British dancers to the development of jazz dancing in British clubs, it is important to recognize how a pan-African sensibility that informed aspects of the developing styles was a source of much controversy during the period when this form of jazz dancing became established in Britain. The sociologist Christian Joppke (1999) argues that in the transition from empire to commonwealth, the British government's immigration policy reinforced a sense of British identity as being defined by 'race'. During the 1980s, as Paul Gilroy (1987: 59) has observed, the Conservative Party promoted the idea that the loss of pan-African identity was required in order to successfully fit into British society. Yet Thomas DeFrantz (2001) describes how a common experience of oppression provides a sense of commonality that is a part of black people's pan-African identity in the Diaspora. This sense of identity was valuable in the 1980s to many people of Caribbean parentage who were born in Britain (and thus had full British citizenship) but did not feel fully British as a result of the racism they encountered. While some pan-African identities draw on a sense of an historical African past, the jazz dancers lived very self-consciously in the present. Although they recognized the importance of their cultural heritage, in their openness to a whole range of movement styles, they seem to have embodied a sensibility that is close to Stuart Hall's concept of 'new ethnicities' (1992), which looks forward, to a weakening of boundaries between different ethnic identities, and which also recognizes how a play of differences that include gender and sexuality contributes to a sense of identity. The jazz dancers' openness to different dance traditions and bodily styles was, however, fuelled less by a political reflection on postcolonial identities than by a desire to develop a competitive edge while not losing their sense of style.

In the context of the above discussion of the identities embodied in bebop jazz dancing, it is important to note that the jazz club scene in Leeds was open to people from a range of cultural backgrounds. The club environments within which this improvised jazz dancing developed were, at least initially, viewed as 'underground' venues and were frequented by many of those affected by the increasing unemployment that was a product of the economic changes overseen by Margaret Thatcher's Conservative government in the early 1980s. In this period, what many of the clubbers shared was poverty, youth, a sense of distance from the 'mainstream', and a lack of many other opportunities to assert their sense of self-worth. Few of the young people dancing in clubs were employed, and even fewer found jobs that were anything other than menial. Hence, for those who could excel, dancing provided a sense of individual status, while the skills of local dancers were a source of a collective pride attached to belonging to a particular city.

When they moved to London, determined to gain recognition for their skills, Lewis and James pioneered a new British dance identity that drew on their wealth of different dance and musical knowledge, ranging from skanking to mambo and ballet. Bringing together aspects of a complex cultural heritage, they challenged the binary polarization of African and European cultures while celebrating pan-African practices, including improvisation.

Developing Improvisational Skills within the Context of the Dance Challenge

The skills required for UK jazz dancing are informed by the context within which they emerged. Hence, this form of jazz dancing demands not only a feel for how to integrate a range of moves into a recognizable style, but the self-confidence and determination to dance in a highly competitive environment, a good level of fitness and coordination, a grasp of the conventions that shape the format of the danced challenge, musical understanding, and knowledge of and skill in combining different steps.

To excel in a dance challenge in a circle also requires the ability to respond creatively and seemingly instantaneously to both the music and the moves of an opponent while retaining an individual flair that nevertheless is situated within a shared understanding of an appropriate style. While in the 1980s many jazz dancers from African Caribbean cultural backgrounds were advantaged by their early experience of improvised dancing in related styles, the necessary improvisational skills can be developed by any dancer who practises them.

After three-four years everything that you have learnt (the phrases, steps, improvisation, and interpretation of the music) means you are ready to put it into practice. All the knowledge and experience you have mastered will go into the circle. This is where you will compete against someone else and where your skill at improvisation will be put to the test in a competitive arena. By the repetition of basic steps, you progress to a 'second nature' response, and this becomes a part of you, just like breathing air. You create your own dance language that is a part of you, and you can then adapt that language to any conversation—that is, to any music—to freestyle. You can relax and let go. You let go by understanding the music—the music becomes part of you and you become the music.

The jazz dancers in a dance challenge have to be able to 'let go' to 'freestyle' (improvise) yet be confident that their knowledge and understanding guides their actions, so that the responses they make in the moment not only fit an overall sense of style but gain the advantage against other dancers. A sense of habitus provides not only for this underlying feel for the style but for what are tacitly understood as appropriate responses in a specific context.

The danced interactions that take place in a battle may also be the result of more consciously recognized strategies. Dancers study each other over extended periods of time so that they know each other's moves. One way to unsettle an opponent is to perform one of that opponent's moves, if possible judging when the opponent is going to go into it and then to perform it ahead of the opponent. Or one dancer might repeat another's movement after the other dances it but perform it better or perhaps with a new variation added. Other strategies might be to manoeuvre someone who excels at dancing in a big space into a corner, or to make someone who prefers to stay in one small place engage with a large expanse of floor. Yet in spite of these more explicit tactics, what are most valued in a dance challenge are those moments that generate new movements that appear to be the product of neither conscious strategy nor habitual danced responses.

When you enter the circle you will dance for about twenty to thirty minutes. For the first ten minutes or so you will be doing standard moves and after that you will start to improvise upon those standard steps. As the dance competition gets more elevated, the DJ plays records to intensify the battle and you will, in turn, elevate the moves you have learned and then you will have to draw on improvisation. That is when people in the crowd can see you are dancing in the moment. It's not been learned, it's pure freestyle. This is the moment everyone has been waiting for—you are creating movement, a story of your own. This is when you have to lose yourself as your opponent will reply with a better story (dance style).

In part, this capacity for creativity is dependent on a training which encourages dancers to vary actions alongside learning them. However, it is also important to consider how such 'moments' may also be understood as created through the dynamics of the interpersonal interactions taking place. Here it is useful to further explore the role of the habitus in the production of dancing and, by drawing on the work of the philosopher

Maurice Merleau-Ponty, to emphasize intercorporeality as an intrinsic element of the intersubjective relationships that shape the habitus.

DISRUPTING THE HABITUS

The jazz dancer relies on the habitus to provide a tacit sense of style, a source of known movement patterns and of ways to vary them, together with a feel for appropriate responses to others' moves and the music. Dancers' habitus is, however, dynamically related to the 'field' in which their dancing is situated and as such may be conceptualized in ways that consider the interconnectedness of the experience of self and others. In developing the concepts of habitus and field, Bourdieu was influenced by the philosophy of Merleau-Ponty to 'rethink the subject-object dualisms' of conventional social analysis (Bottero 2010: 3). Merleau-Ponty (1968) challenges the very basic philosophical foundations from which the notion of individual, bounded consciousness is derived, so as to explore the reciprocity of the relationships between self and other and between consciousness and world.[13] Drawing upon her reading of Merleau-Ponty's work, Carr (2014) has previously proposed that dancers, and those actively engaged in watching them, may experience an intercorporeal transitivity that provides for a sense of connection between dancers and between dancer and spectator.[14] Hours of practice of improvisation in a club not only serves to heighten a jazz dancer's embodied perceptual sensitivity but also develops awareness that is reciprocally related to the environment and the people within it. Jazz dancers participating in a dance challenge within a circle might thus be thought of as immersed in a complex system of interrelationships in which consciousness of their actions is reciprocally related to the actions of others rather than as a separate intention emanating from a preconceived idea. In this context, if the DJ plays more obscure or complex tracks, or an opponent makes an unexpected move, the security of the dancer's habitus may be disrupted. Challenged by opponents and enlivened by the crowd, the dancers are pushed beyond their habitual movement patterns to find new variations in their dancing. In so doing they may experience the apparent paradox of both a sense of a loss of self and a heightened individual awareness 'in the moment' that is experienced not as a point in time but as being in the flux of time.

> *You are now having an out-of-body experience, you are no longer there, you are there for the ride, you have no control, your subconscious free spirit takes over completely. The crowd is absorbing your creativity at its ultimate level. Your opponent will mirror your response now, so you will have to go even deeper to win the battle. This is where the real improvisation kicks in. For me this is highest form of pure improvised dance, you see the true essence of the dancer in performance. This is core creativity, it is just your pure being.*

The association of improvisation with freedom and a transcendent metaphysics, while common within Western aesthetics and narratives of American jazz history,[15] may be criticized for a naïve assumption of subjective autonomy (Peters 2009). However, it is important to recognize how a transcendent, spiritual experience of dance is an important element in pan-African culture (DeFrantz 2002) and that this account of dancing accords with the perspective of an Africanist aesthetic.

Notwithstanding the influences of Africanist perspectives on British jazz dancing, the specific intracultural context within which this dancing developed suggests how it can also be important to consider other discourses within which this aspect of the dancer's experience might be understood. Improvised jazz dancing may be rooted in the dance practices of the African Caribbean (hence some of those brought up in those traditions may have an advantage), but it is also the product of contemporary British culture. Moreover, while in the context of many European dance practices today, improvisation tends to be regarded as the province of the avant-garde, or as part of popular culture, this is, and has not always been, the case. According to the dance historian Anne Daye, improvisation was important to the social dancing in the ballrooms of France and England from the sixteenth to the eighteenth century (email to Jane Carr, 5 August 2014). Within Western music practice, the turn away from improvisation coincided with the introduction of copyright and the emphasis on individual, authorial creative genius (Montuori 2003: 248). This was also the era dominated by a mechanistic view of the world that focused on breaking down knowledge of the material world into its smaller constituent parts. In dance, this period saw the development of detailed approaches to regulating the dancer's movements, both technically and choreographically, in a manner that served to reinforce the distinction between European dance forms and many of the dances practised in Europe's colonies in Africa and the Caribbean, where improvisation has a long tradition. In contrast to the polarization of Western and 'non-Western' dance forms during the nineteenth century and much of the twentieth, the incorporation of moves into bebop from very different cultural traditions can be understood to signal the resistance of this style of jazz to being identified within the boundaries of different national cultures.

The philosophy of Merleau-Ponty may offer an alternative to a pan-Africanist aesthetic as a framework for understanding the jazz dancer's experience of a transcendent loss of self. Merleau-Ponty's analysis of the doubleness of human embodied experience as both object and subject allows for the dancer's actions to be considered as reciprocally related to others while also being the product of one's sense of (creative) agency focused on the act of dancing. Indeed, it is the double aspect of embodied experience that provides for play between the sense of a loss of self and a heightened sense of creativity. Through this doubleness of embodied experience the improvising dancer avoids both a lapse into a formulaic responsiveness or to individualist virtuosity. From the perspective of Merleau-Ponty's existential phenomenology, during the most intense and creative moments in a battle, jazz dancers might be thought of as experiencing a renewed engagement with the world as lived in a manner that revitalizes perceptual awareness as if to (almost) regain a sense of that initiation into the (cultural) world understood as 'the opening of a dimension that can never again be closed, the establishment of a level in terms of which every other experience will henceforth be situated' (Merleau-Ponty 1968: 151). It is through such moments that established patterns of behaviour—and the related modes of engagement with the world that form the habitus—momentarily slacken their hold on the dancer. Hence, through the dance battle a creative process of intercorporeal transactions has the capacity to refashion the habitus and so develop the style of dancing.

CONCLUSION

To participate in improvisation in styles of UK jazz dancing, such as bebop, requires a process not only of learning the moves but also of developing a sense of habitus, which informs a grasp both of the style and of the practices that are central to a dance challenge, or battle. While many years' practice are required so that jazz dancers can perform dance steps with ease and improvise variations with an assured style and musicality, jazz dancers also have to be willing to 'let go' of their individual sense of control over those same habits they have built up with such effort. In the dance battle, it is the moments when the security of the habitus is disrupted that engender new responses that are felt to transcend a dancer's stock of moves and responses. Taking place in a circle of people focused on the dancing, shared understanding facilitates intercorporeal engagement between dancers and between them and those watching, so that the circle fosters creative exchange that is driven by the competitive drive of the dancers. While the habitus provides for a shared sense of practice, the stimulus of the unexpected—in terms of an opponent's moves or the DJ's playing a new record—engenders shifts in practice that are not fully the product of an individual dancer's habitual patterns of action or conscious strategy, though these play an important element in shaping the dance. It is the intensity of intercorporeal exchange that drives shifts in the complex interplay between consciousness, learned movement patterns, and the orientation of the self to the world, a world which opens up in new, unexpected ways. Such moments are recognized by those watching and—if accepted as legitimate moves in the context of a shared sense of jazz style—may contribute to changes in style and hence, reciprocally, even to the habitus that informs the dancing.

The relationship of habitus to a sense of both personal and group identity suggests that the significance of such changes may be understood to relate to a wider social context, particularly when, as during the period of the late 1970s and early 1980s in which this dancing developed, identities are the focus of political debate and social tension. As the jazz dancers battled on the dance floor of 'Thatcher's Britain', they improvised new British identities into being.

Where this dancing now takes place in many varied geographic locations, it is the dialogue between existing traditions/habits and the movement practices developed in response to a different environment that will engender creativity in new styles of jazz dancing. As this jazz dancing is taken on by younger dancers, whether they dance in Seoul, Moscow, or London, their improvisations will embody still newer identities.

Wherever they dance jazz, young dancers today need to feel the music to find their own sense of Soul and Heart.

NOTES

1. The DJ Mark Cotgrove ('Snowboy') charts his perspective on the history of the jazz clubs in Cotgrove (2009).
2. These styles of jazz dancing are discussed further in Carr (2012), in the context of a televised battle between Brothers in Jazz and IDJ.
3. Something of the jazz dancing of this era can be seen on film in *Temple* (1986), which features the Jazz Defektors. A choreographic representation by Irven Lewis of this dancing can be seen in Lewis (2001). In addition, a number of clips from pop videos and concerts that feature Brothers in Jazz or IDJ can often be found posted on YouTube.
4. Lewis taught regularly at Morley College South London for many years, and he has led workshops for many projects in the UK and when on tour in Amsterdam, Russia, and Japan.
5. The term 'Black British' is used by Lewis in respect to his identity and is thus used in this essay to refer to British people of African/African Caribbean heritage.
6. The term 'syllabus' is used by Lewis to emphasize how, while it developed informally, there is now an identifiable vocabulary that dancers learn. The steps he and others created have gained names, so that what was an informal body of knowledge is becoming codified.
7. Ivar Hagendoorn describes how motor schemas can be broken down and/ or recombined to create new movement patterns in Hagendoorn (2003: 221–228).
8. Although there is sometimes confusion over its precise definition, dancers tend to use the terms 'kinaesthesia' and 'kinaesthetic' to refer to all the felt sensations relevant to the body in dance. More specifically, Maxine Sheets-Johnstone refers to kinaesthesia as 'a sense of movement through muscular effort' (2009: 164). However, the term is also sometimes understood to include proprioceptive awareness of the body's position in relation to space and gravity.
9. Carrie Noland (2009) explores how a sense of agency is linked to changes to habitual bodily experience. Noland also suggests that 'kinesthetic experience, produced by acts of embodied gesturing, places pressure on the conditioning the body receives, encouraging variations in performance' (2009: 2–3). Jane Carr explores the relationship between kinaesthetic experience, culture, and agency further in relation to dancers' experiences in Carr (2013).
10. The accuracy of describing the Judson dancers and Grand Union as 'post-modern' and the relationship of this dancing to postmodernism more widely is the subject of much debate. For a discussion of dance in relation to postmodernism see Connor (1997).
11. See Bourdieu (1984). Bourdieu describes the habitus as a 'disposition that generates meaningful practices and meaning giving perceptions' (1984: 70). Experienced as a set of tacitly understood predispositions to act in certain ways, the habitus is both product of and productive of a shared culture belonging to a social group. A 'bodily hexis', or sense of bodily organization, forms an important part of the habitus.

12. See Bottero (2010). Recognizing that there is a tendency for Bourdieu's theories of habitus and field to be interpreted as supporting views in which the involuntary aspect of behaviour is overly limiting of the capacity for individuals to exert agency, Wendy Bottero suggests how Bourdieu's theories may be developed to emphasize the potential of intersubjective experience to provide for ways in which 'practices necessarily extend beyond agent's predispositions' (2010: 10).

13. See Merleau-Ponty (1968). Merleau-Ponty advances a radical decentring of consciousness to propose his concepts of 'flesh' and 'intercorporeity', so as to consider the ways in which physical being may be experienced as woven into the fabric of a feeling-thinking world.

14. See Carr's (2014) discussion of intercorporeal experience in relation to dance practices. Significant to this context is that Carr, while acknowledging criticism of Merleau-Ponty's seeming indifference to 'difference', proposes that an investigation of intercorporeal relationships can be developed to recognize the effect of inequalities based on differences such as gender and ethnicity.

15. See McCormack (2012). Ryan McCormack situates the narratives that construct jazz improvisation as an expression of freedom within an American cultural context that sustains a belief in individual agency transcending the limitations of an individual's position in society.

References

Absolute Beginners. (1986) Dir. J. Temple. Goldcrest Films International.

Banes, S. (1983) *Democracy's Body: Judson Dance Theater 1962–1964.* Ann Arbor, MI: UMI Research Press.

Bottero, W. (2010) Intersubjectivity and Bourdieusian Approaches to 'Identity'. *Cultural Sociology* 4(1): 3–22.

Bourdieu, P. (1984) *Distinction.* Trans. R. Nice. London: Routledge. (Originally published 1979)

Brown, B. (1997) The Politics of Contact. In *Contact Quarterly: Contact Improvisation Sourcebook.* Northampton, MA: Contact Editions, 18–21. (Originally published 1977)

Carr, J. (2012) Re-remembering the (Almost) Lost Jazz Dances of 1980s Britain. *Dance Chronicle* 35(3): 315–337.

Carr, J. (2013) Embodiment and Dance: Puzzles of Consciousness and Agency. In Bunker, J., Pakes, A., and Rowell, B. (eds.), *Thinking through Dance: The Philosophy of Dance Performance and Practices.* Hampshire: Dance Books, 63–82.

Carr, J. (2014) LandMark: Dance as a Site of Intertwining. *Journal of Dance and Somatic Practices* 6(1): 47–58.

Carr, J. (2017) Researching British (Underground) Jazz Dancing c. 1979–1990. In Adair, C., and Burt, R. (eds.), *British Dance: Black Routes* London: Routledge, 35–54.

Connor, S. (1997) *Postmodernist Culture: An Introduction to Theories of the Contemporary.* 2nd ed. Oxford: Blackwell.

Cotgrove, M. (2009) *From Jazz Funk and Fusion to Acid Jazz.* London: Chaser.

DeFrantz, T. (2001) Forward. In Fischer-Hornung, D., and Goeller, A. (eds.), *Embodying Liberation: The Black Body in American Dance.* Hamburg: Lit, 11–16.

DeFrantz, T. (ed.). (2002) *Dancing Many Drums: Excavations in African American Dance.* Madison: University of Wisconsin Press.

Dixon-Gottschild, B. (1996) *Digging That Africanist Presence in American Performance Dance and Other Contexts*. Westport, CT: Praeger.

Gilroy, P. (1987) *There Ain't No Black in the Union Jack: The Cultural Politics of Race and Nation*. London: Hutchinson.

Hagendoorn, I. (2003) Cognitive Dance Improvisation: How Study of the Motor System Can Inspire Dance (and Vice Versa). *Leonardo Music Journal* 36(3) (June): 221–228.

Hall, S. (1992) New Ethnicities. In Donald, J., and Rattansi, A. (eds.), *'Race' Culture and Difference*. London: Sage, 252–259.

Jarrett, L. (1997/1998) Contact 25: Making Contact. *Total Theatre* 9(4): 6–7.

Joppke, C. (1999) *Immigration and the Nation State: The United States, Germany and Great Britain*. Oxford: Oxford University Press.

Lewis, I. (2001) Ignite, Article 19. http://www.article19.co.uk/sdvideo/irven_lewis_ignite.php. Accessed 27 March 2017.

Lewis, I. (2010) Heritage Highlight: British Jazz Dance 1979–1990. *Hotfoot*. (Currently being archived by OneDance UK) ://www.onedanceuk.org/resource/hotfoot-online/.

McCormack, R. (2012) Outside of the Self: Subjectivity, the Allure of Transcendence, and Jazz Historiography. *Critical Studies in Improvisation* 8(1). http://www.criticalimprov.com/article/view/1682/2556. Accessed 5 March 2017.

Merleau-Ponty, M. (1968) The Intertwining—The Chiasm. In *The Visible and the Invisible*. Evanston, IL: Northwestern University Press, 130–155.

Montuori, A. (2003) The Complexity of Improvisation and the Improvisation of Complexity: Social Science, Art and Creativity. *Human Relation* 56(2): 237–255.

Noland, C. (2009) *Agency and Embodiment: Performing Gestures/ Producing Culture*. Cambridge, MA: Harvard University Press.

Novack, C. (1997) Egalitarianism and Hierarchy in Contact Improvisation. In *Contact Quarterly's Contact Improvisation Sourcebook*. Northampton, MA: Contact Editions, 140–141. (Originally published 1988)

Paxton, S. (1997) Higher-Visibility. In *Contact Quarterly's Contact Improvisation Sourcebook*. Northampton, MA: Contact Editions, 166–167. (Originally published 1989)

Peters, G. (2009) *The Philosophy of Improvisation*. Chicago: University of Chicago Press.

Reynolds, N., and McCormick, M. (2003) *No Fixed Points: Dance in the Twentieth Century*. New Haven: Yale University Press.

Sheets-Johnstone, M. (2009) *The Corporeal Turn: An Interdisciplinary Reader*. Exeter, UK: Imprint Academic.

West Side Story (1961) Dir. by R. Wise and J. Robbins. United Artists.

CHAPTER 21

··

TEN DAYS IN TARBENA

An Evolutionary Approach to Moving through Silence and Sound to Speech

··

ROBERT VESTY

Ten Action Theater™ Exercises

Throughout this essay I share a small sample of exercises taken from a ten-day Action Theater™ training in Tarbena, Spain. My aim is to give the reader an impression of the practice. These exercises were interspersed with discussion, further instruction, clarification, and demonstration. The daily sessions were organized in such a way that participants were responsible for their own bodily preparation (warmup), followed by a gathering in a circle to talk/reflect on the previous day's work, a series of exercises, and a twenty-minute rest break, followed by more practice, which typically ended with a sharing of work (set up as improviser(s)/watchers).[1]

It is a Sunday morning in June 2014. We are in Tarbena, a village located a little inland in the mountains of Valencia, Spain. It is around twenty-five degrees Celsius, and I can smell jasmine and hear exotic-sounding birds which sing incessantly. Twenty or so people have gathered from across the world to participate in a ten-day improvisation training in Action Theater™ led by its creator, Ruth Zaporah. We are in the Casa de Cultura—a building at the highest point of the village—in a large asymmetrical room. It has a municipal feel; good light, a white polystyrene ceiling, and a hard-tiled floor. Here we will work from 10 a.m. to 2 p.m. each day. I arrive to people milling, chatting, warming up—some are lying down on mats. People are wearing loose clothes; some wear trainers, some are barefoot. We gather to sit in a circle and introduce ourselves. Zaporah asks who is 'coming at' this improvisation practice from a 'movement/dance background' and who from an 'acting/theatre background'. I put my hand up both times. In the hours and days that follow I will engage in solo, duet, and ensemble improvisation practice. It will see us variously making movement, and making sounds which are at times reminiscent of a children's playground. Eventually, we will be vocalizing words, and ultimately strings of words, as 'narrative'. This will become the basis of our improvised performance.

The aim of this essay is to draw on this instance of Action Theater™ training and expand on how, as an interdisciplinary improvisation performance practice, Action Theater™ asks performers to feel their way through three modes of expression: silent movement, vocal sound and movement, and speech and movement. Action Theater™ training encourages performers to pay attention to a tactile-kinaesthetic awareness so that they can achieve what Zaporah calls an 'embodied presence'. For Zaporah, this relies on performers being equipped to remain in touch with their experiences by paying attention to 'feeling states'—the term Zaporah uses to describe the experience of sensation, mood, and emotion in the act of improvising. Because Action Theater™ is pedagogically structured to reflect this journey from silence to speech, I look at silent movement in this essay as a strategy for developing sensory awareness in Action Theater™ and as a scaffold for developing sound and speech. I argue that the journey from silence to speech that is embedded and codified by Zaporah can be viewed in evolutionary terms. There are two ways in which I maintain this evolutionary theme. One is by reflecting on the studio practice of Action Theater™ training itself; the other is by drawing on Maxine Sheets-Johnstone's work *The Primacy of Movement* (2011). Through a phenomenological approach, she considers the way in which the whole animate form must be understood in its evolutionary context if we are to begin to understand the development of human perception and how this is mirrored through learning in infancy and beyond.

I also briefly touch on how the Feldenkrais Method˚, a somatic education method, can be seen as a useful companion approach to Action Theater™, insofar as it invites the participant to reenter a kind of pseudo-early-developmental state in order to develop experiential knowledge.

Exercise: Ensemble walking to a pulse. Sharp shifts in direction. Add breath/pant. Can pause. Can walk half/double time. Can copy.

My analysis of any evolutionary dimension to Action Theater™ is also inspired by a working assumption that for many improvisers, including myself, moving from a silent mode of movement expression to one where speech is used can be inhibitive. It can produce feelings of fear. I need to feel-my-way, or get-a-feel-for-using, vocal sound and speech. An Action Theater™ performer's experience of flow[2] can be interrupted by using words, because their moment-by-moment experience can become too semantically charged; I develop this idea in more detail below.

Throughout the essay I draw on research I collected while participating in this specific training in Tarbena—research that remain within my bodily experience and memory, alongside other records, such as personal journal notes and interview transcripts. I also refer to other published material, particularly Zaporah's (2014) *Improvisation on the Edge: Notes from On and Off Stage*. In reflecting upon this material, I speak from the perspectives of participant and observer, improviser and researcher, which manifest in multiple registers, mostly, and unabashedly, in the first person.

ACTION THEATER™—A SHORT OVERVIEW

Action Theater™ is both an established training and a performance form honed by Zaporah over forty years through self-practice and collaboration.[3] It codifies silent movement, sound and movement, and speech, or what Zaporah refers to as 'physical narrative', in a pedagogy that ultimately aims towards a less codified and more open form of improvised performance. Action Theater™ produces an interdisciplinary performance aesthetic, in that it appears to fuse dance and theatre and is sometimes described in terms that occupy space between these disciplines, although Zaporah appears to more readily refer to the practice as 'physical-theatre improvisation'.[4]

Given the context in which Zaporah's work developed, however, it could be said that Action Theater™ represents an offering from the discipline of dance to the discipline of improvisational theatre. Zaporah's early background was in ballet and contemporary dance, but in 1973 she was invited to teach movement to a group of actors in Berkeley, California. Through this fertile period for improvisational performance in the United States often characterized with reference to key figures in US post–modern dance,[5] Zaporah developed both her teaching and her performance work out of a 'desire to speak, (and) an urge to break free of the soundless gestures of dance' (Morrow 2011), such that she formed collaborations with theatre artists.[6]

> *Exercise:* Solo then duet. Sustain a slow, slow, slow (and smooth) movement. Add sharp, sudden interruptions. Replace slow with pause.

Since the 1970s, Zaporah has developed her work as a performer and teacher. She has run trainings at her home studio (Santa Fe, New Mexico) each year and taught internationally. She has been able to trademark the practice and ally it with an accredited teacher-training programme, which she runs informally as a system whereby students qualify as teachers by building up studio hours of practice over time with an accredited teacher, some of which must be spent with Zaporah herself. As it stands, there are twenty-eight teachers worldwide who are legally qualified to teach the form.[7] Outside Tarbena, my experience of Action Theater™ has also been informed over the past five years by two of these teachers, Kate Hilder (UK) and Sten Rudstrøm (Germany), whose workshops I have participated in.

MOVING THROUGH SILENCE

To understand the processes of Action Theater™ and to view them in the evolutionary way I am proposing, we need to pay attention to the way the form draws on sensation as a stimulus for action. But what does 'action' mean in an Action Theater™ context?

According to Zaporah, 'all activity, no matter what its formal content, is experienced as equal and as part of a non-stop continuum. Silence is this auspicious sound. Stillness is as delicious as action. No preferences. All action is experienced, as a manifestation within a spacious silence' (2014: 41).

Exercise: Duet. A sounds, B moves in response. Then B moves, A sounds in response. Swap.

Action Theater™ encourages a performer, first and foremost, to develop a capacity to pay attention to sensation in order to be able to differentiate the quality and texture of the present moment through silent movement; and to cultivate a view of action which can manifest as stillness or silence. At the beginning of each day, Zaporah invited participants to gather up to thirty minutes before each session to do their own preparation, in which she proposed that participants pursue any 'warmup' task or exercise in a mode of curiosity and liveness. In my case, this would likely see me lying on the floor to pay attention to the contact my body was making in relation to it at that moment; attempting to draw qualitative distinctions through the movement. Inflected by my experience of the Feldenkrais Method°, I made small movement enquiries, perhaps of the pelvis, or vertebrae, all the time attempting to enact a mode of curiosity. Perhaps I would be wondering how I might notice more or less tension in some parts of myself at that moment, or how I might begin to differentiate the quality of feeling that one part of myself might have compared to another. My emphasis here was not on answers, or at least not at arriving at conclusions, rather to merely notice what I notice, or feel how I feel—a way to get in touch with sensation as a ground through which to become aware of the 'feeling states' in which the improvisatory content will later be rooted.

For Zaporah, a 'feeling state' is processual and therefore ever-changing. The focus on silent movement in Action Theater™ practice is thus a useful and necessary exploration aimed at nurturing a quality of attention, which can emphasize its processual nature. Using the continuous form, *attending*, honours this processual and qualitative nature of attention. Noting the etymology of the verb *to attend* as deriving from the French *atendre* (to stretch), the notion of expanding or stretching attention takes on its temporality as one that is experienced qualitatively. In this way, a feeling state is concerned with sensory perception and how a performer might move through the world, or how the world might move through the performer, in order to sense its changeability moment by moment—feeling its quality of altered temporality. Thus, by engaging in silent movement I can begin to cultivate a practice of attending, through sense-making and making-sense; what we might call a heightened kinaesthesia. In Tarbena, Zaporah asked us to begin moving slowly, locating attention in one part of the body, such as elbow, back of the neck, or forehead. The instruction was given to encourage a frame of movement through which we could immerse. In this mode, it began to feel as if the movement was emerging—its direction, texture, and quality had a feeling that it was being discovered, or listened to. Eventually, performers in Action Theater™ must develop their own self-movement so that they can remain ready to react to other stimuli in the space, while keeping intact a heightened kinaesthesia, which then goes on to inform the content of an improvised performance.

Movement exploration, in Action Theater™, is perception-based groundwork that later vocalization is built on. This developmental approach can be further illuminated if we turn to Sheets-Johnstone, for whom the primacy of movement is fundamental to the function of perception: 'the dynamics essential to our progressive sense-makings of ourselves and of the world are intrinsic to and inherent in our primal animation and in our being the particular animate forms we are' (2011: 453).

> *Exercise:* Solo. Sound and movement together. 50 percent still. Add changes in direction of eyes. Add high and low tension.

Sheets-Johnstone's thesis is aimed at repositioning movement as the primary mode through which an organism evolves its powers of perception and asserts that this stretches back through the evolutionary journey of all animate forms. For a human being, for kinaesthesia to develop, it must be practiced at some point through movement in silence: 'to be mindful of movement asks us first of all to be silent, and, in our silence, to witness the phenomenon of movement—around self-movement and the movement of all that is animate or animated in our surrounding world' (xix). Similarly, Action Theater™ training develops in a performer a skill in heightened kinaesthesia. By going slow, and being in silence, I get to practise, time and again, the simple process of relaxing my attention into the moment as it emerges. Yet in its simplicity there is a seeming paradox, and according to Zaporah, although 'to relax our attention into the present moment is extraordinarily simple . . . it demands a lifetime of practice' (1995: xx). The updating of this skill is a continuous process and not one simply acquired. Indeed, this kind of silent enquiry was the predominant mode of practice for the first few days in Tarbena.

The conception of a heightened kinaesthesia as a kind of skill in Action Theater™ can be seen as having some synergy with so-called enactive theories of perception expounded by some working in the field of cognitive studies. For example, in *Varieties of Presence*, Alva Noë argues that the world is always present in the way that it is always available, but that one 'achieves' presence through a complex and skilful utilization of oneself as an organism (2012: 12). Noë's case is predicated on the basis that 'the perceiver's movements produce changes in the character of the standing motorsensory relation' (22), so that perceptual consciousness is movement-dependent: 'perception as a movement from here to there, from this place to that. We ourselves (whole persons) undertake our perceptual consciousness of the world in, with, and in relation to the places where we find ourselves' (5). Although Sheets-Johnstone appears to take exception to enactivism's emphasis on action above experience (2011: 477), I suggest that in an improvisatory moment in Action Theater™ practice, there is no such debate—action and experience are placed on a continuum and bear equal footing. Indeed, they happen at the same time but are differentiated by the degree of their expressivity. In one improvisatory moment practised in an ensemble I recall lying face down on the floor for many seconds, maybe more than a minute, inspecting flecks of colour in the detail of the tiles, while all around me bigger and louder things were no doubt happening in the composition. My experience of movement was through a relative stillness but must still be construed as action. For Zaporah, the experience of an embodied presence, in this instance, cannot be differentiated from action except by the degree of its expressivity.

Through this, a theme emerges in Action Theater™ practice which is about resisting dualistic ways of thinking about perception as internal/external, better/worse, from here to there, and so on. It's a theme which Sheets-Johnstone also illuminates, because she invites us to think less about beginning with sensory perception in order to arrive at deeper understandings of the motor end of movement and instead to think of working backwards by thinking of movement as the primary mode for accessing perceptual information. Doing this re-places the kinetic in a field of perception and puts it central to the way we get to know the world around us—what she calls an 'epistemological gateway' (2011: xxi). Sheets-Johnstone elevates not just movement but the human being as an animate form by pointing to its immanence. Likewise, in Action Theater™ practice, Zaporah's insistence that I embody a 'feeling state' also calls on me to consider movement as *already* a part of (neither inside or outside) myself; *already* interlaced in my evolution as human being/animate form. A democratizing of the embodied experience again upsets the duality of thinking through the notion of exteriority and interiority— that an object exists outside a body experiencing it but that a body experiencing it can only experience it through itself.

If what is available to an Action Theater™ performer is felt for, it may not be very helpful to think of the object of that feeling being merely or solely outside myself. One clear and literal example of how this idea can be said to have manifested as practice in Tarbena was through one Action Theater™ exercise that asked participants to move and sound as phenomena such as rock, electricity, silk, or snow. Zaporah's instruction was not that we represent what these phenomena might look like but that we embody the feeling of them. We were compelled to internalize a connection to certain environmental phenomena through processes of imagination.

In Tarbena, the role of imagination was often discussed. At one point Zaporah spoke about imagination as a fictive world and its relation to the so-called real world, saying: 'we're stepping inside a new world in an improvisation—an imaginal world. Real life is the hard world' (*Personal Journal Notes*). On the face of it, it could appear that Zaporah's imaginal world is another place, which exists somehow separately. But this notion troubles another apparent duality—the imaginal/real—that might be better thought of or practised as somehow continuous. Just as a view of *minding* may no longer accept a body through which it happens as separate from a brain it collaborates with (hence the proliferation in some quarters of the term *bodymind*), it may be just as useful to think of the imaginal world (of atmospheres, colours, fictions, characters, etc.) as simply coextensive of the more or less mundane real of the hard floor in the Casa de Cultura. While I might readily speak of the real as immediate and concrete, my sensing, as an improvising performer in Action Theater™, through this environment serves as a crucial window through which to access, integrate, and in turn express a more vibrant kind of life which, in practice, resists a real/imaginal duality. In this way I see these supposed two-worlds integrated explicitly through Action Theater™ practice.

Exercise: Duet. Sit forward on chair. Neutral position, legs planted, hands on knees.
A sounds until B interrupts. Sound contrasts (shifts), or develops (transforms).

I want briefly to take a small, but relevant, detour which may add further insight to this slipperiness between the real and imaginal. In Tarbena, I taught three group Feldenkrais Method® lessons (known as Awareness Through Movement or ATM lessons)[8] to participants (including Zaporah) over the duration of the course—two before the training session and one on a rest day. The method's focus on small, slow, repetitive movement offers a structure through which to develop awareness, and its relation to spontaneity means it offers one modality through which to notice habitual patterns of movement. It is, I believe, complementary to Action Theater™ practice in many ways. For example, the Feldenkrais Method® focuses on spontaneity and the need to cultivate awareness of ourselves in the moment; it also invites us to remember and somehow revisit some of our earliest infant-like movement explorations. But particularly germane here is the Feldenkrais Method®'s use and understanding of imagination and how it can be conceived as action, which again resists an imaginal/real dichotomy. For example, in one lesson, I asked students lying on their backs to imagine their closed eyes moving left and right. The arc of the lesson invited students to eventually imagine this movement extending to a roll sideways and to imagine, gradually, arriving in a sitting position. By the end of the lesson, students were likely to be rolling to one side and back repeatedly, so that the exploration of the eyes' movement began to be integrated in movement that is functional. In an ATM lesson, the use of imagination in this way is well established. The movement that is performed in imagination is therefore done for 'real', and the imagined movement is conceived as a rehearsal for the real, which has a direct and tangible impact on a person's ability to perform that action in a smooth and easy way. As I have said, this idea of the imaginary being embodied can suggest that the imaginal world exists someplace else and needs somehow to be brought in to one's experience of one's sensory apparatus, yet by making explicit the link between imaginary and real movement, the Feldenkrais Method® integrates the experience of these modes as concrete action because it casts the act of imagining *as* movement, even if that movement is conceived as interior action.

Exercise: A speaks 'STOP' or 'WALK' with a particular quality/rhythm/tone/texture; B/others either stop or walk embodying quality etc. 'Walk how I say walk, and stop how I say stop'.

Through this lens, the imaginary becomes concretely integrated in action because the act of imagination is viewed as another form of animation. Only by lingering in silent (and slow) movement for a while am I able to feel my way towards this mode of action as embodied presence.

Exercise: Duet. A moves a phrase to a rhythm, leading with different body parts, B repeats phrase with same rhythm but different body part.

The notion of feeling-around or getting-a-feel-for-things suggests a gentle and gradual practice, as I have suggested, but in Action Theater™, feeling's processual nature is also made explicit. While *feeling* as a term has multiple registers, identities, and meanings, Zaporah's use of the term 'feeling state' has a specificity which was emphasized in Tarbena time and again. Zaporah told us: 'I do not use the word "emotion"; I use "feeling state", "inner state", "sensory awareness" ' (*Personal Journal Notes*). By focusing on feeling state, Zaporah invites a performer to live through transformation—for flux to be enacted. Thus, here, 'feeling state' serves as a carrier term—a container where some of us in the training might well have also placed notions of sensation, mood, or emotion. 'Feeling state' emerges as a key term for Zaporah's communication of what it means to be engaged in improvisation. She says that 'to touch the world we go through it' (*Personal Journal Notes*). I understand 'touch' here not just in its haptic sense but as a heightened kinaesthesia where a feeling of perception is experienced as a kind of fully fleshed and vibrant kind of life—Zaporah's imaginal world.

Thus, Action Theater™ practice encourages performers to root their improvisatory work in sensory ground in a holistic way, through an emphasis on the body in kinesis. In Action Theater™ there is a clear pattern to the processes at work, so that sessions allow performers time to engage in the kind of slow, attentive movement which is likely to encourage a deepening of performers' ability to perceive what is available to them in the improvisatory moment.

Moving through Sound

Despite my emphasis above on silent movement, in Action Theater™ the practice moves an improviser quickly into making vocal sound. Zaporah tells us: 'in classes we often make only sounds and avoid words for a while. The voice calls forward states that are nameless, preverbal, and that draw from our animal nature and lift spirits to lofty planes' (2014: 99).

> *Exercise:* Ensemble. Four stand with backs to watchers. One turns with an impulsive sound, which develops into words/narrative continues until interrupted by another. Only one person facing forward at a time. Play with length of time between interruptions.

Action Theater™ can be a noisy business—a lively playground of maybe twenty people making vocalizations that are variously quiet, loud, low, high, percussive, guttural, flitty, breathy, or bold. Using voice can feel like crossing a threshold that involves social permission, and a practice in daring. It can produce feelings of nervousness, anxiety, and doubt. The moment before the silence is punctured, when the idea of making sound feels like a big step, can feel like an intrusion on space. It can feel like I am expending too much energy ushering in this sound. But then sound comes. At this early stage in sound-making, my palette of sounds can feel limited. I desire more range. As my practice develops, it feels as if the sounds-make-me, and before long I begin to feel like these sounds take me by surprise.

The process of arriving at the voice, in practice, is incremental because Zaporah's pedagogy scaffolds the learning so that to touch sound happens through a gradual process of playing with breath. One exercise asked us to be in movement half the time and stillness half the time. After a while we were invited to add breath to the moving part, such that the breath could encounter its different qualities; it was not yet sound, but through playing with intensity, and the shape of our mouths, the channel through which the breath passed could take on a tone or texture which began to bring a particular feeling state into clearer view. Eventually, the breath was given voice. For me, the familiarity I had found in the short time with breath made audible allowed me to move into sound with a feeling of ease.

The use of voice in Action Theater™, for my purposes, serves as a useful site for enquiry into what happens with a feeling or perception when this faculty is more fully activated in the sensory apparatus, and I want to extend Zaporah's assertion that this mode draws on human beings' animal nature. To speak of an evolutionary quality to this improvisatory work, especially in my presentation of the gradual movement from silence to sound as embedded in its pedagogy, presents something of a paradox, because there is also a regressive quality to the processes at work. I have suggested that the sound emanating from the Casa de Cultura in Tarbena might have reminded some of a children's playground and in allowing an unfettered voice to give expression to my experience, there were certainly times when I felt as if I was getting in touch with a more childlike and playful experience of myself.

> *Exercise:* Duet. A sits. B stands behind. B touches A, who sounds with words in response (physical narrative). Quality of sound matches quality of touch, e.g.: touch low on back = low pitch sound; firmer touch = higher volume; staccato touch = staccato sound. No touch, no sound.

Brian Massumi's book *What Animals Teach Us about Politics* (2014) sheds useful light on the way some animals engage in play, and given Zaporah's invocation of *animality* above, it seems pertinent to draw on this. Massumi's aim is to articulate how ludic gestures might help us think about engaging with concepts, and especially how they might be conversational. For Massumi, this requires 'replacing the human on the animal continuum ... in a way that does not erase what is different about the human, but respects that difference while bringing it to new expression on the continuum: immanent to animality' (2014: 3).

> *Exercise:* Duet. A speaks an image in one sentence. B adds with another. A adds another. B begins with a new image with contrasting feeling/atmosphere/mood. Back and forth, on and on.

Massumi goes on to draw on Gregory Bateson's ideas to do with ludic gestures signalling their belonging to the arena of play, in such a way that play's mimicry of reality enacts a gap which is paradoxical. The example Massumi gives is that 'in play, you don't bite, you nip. The difference between biting and nipping is what opens the analogical gap between combat and play' (2014: 5), allowing for a conditional reality which is, crucially, a site of learning through communication with another, and that this is in some ways conversational.

It is useful to think of the practice of making vocal sound in Action Theater™ similarly—as *vital play*; and, in line with Massumi, to think of it on an animal continuum. For Massumi, 'when we humans say "this is play", we are assuming our animality', and 'animal play creates the conditions for language' (8). This thinking is particularly useful because it prepares a way of conceiving of spoken language in the form of speech in such a way that it can be cleaved from any understanding of it as simple semantic meaning-making. Instead, it invites me to consider the gestural quality of making vocal sound as action; and this in turn helps explain how Action Theater™ practice follows a similar pattern, which also prepares an evolutionary ground for thinking of speech-making as ludic sound gestures.

Crucially, the use of sound in Action Theater™ exists on a movement continuum. Sound becomes another gateway for what can appear to be a more playful mode of attention—one that might access, more readily at least, Zaporah's allusion to animality. At the same time, situating sound on this movement continuum further resists the kind of thinking that separates body and voice, or movement and sound, as activities. It is worth stating the obvious: that vocal sound is already movement, given that the use of voice activates complex movements of breath, mouth, tongue, muscular tension, and so on, which are all deeply corporeal. There is often a perception that the activity of sound-making is closer in relation to speech-making than in relation to movement. I suggest that the Action Theater™ pedagogy challenges that idea explicitly and necessarily but in doing so presents its performer with a very particular challenge.

MOVING THROUGH SPEECH

Moving through silent movement and again through the vocalization of sound brings us eventually to the practice of words in Action Theater™. According to Zaporah, 'language carries a heavier weight than movement or vocalization' (2014: 78), and this can represent a clear challenge for an Action Theater™ performer; and in Tarbena, this domain of physical narrative was certainly a more difficult skill to practise. This difficulty implicates the question of how we grapple with markers of language as semantic, and this is particularly pertinent to questions around feeling and emotion which become central themes in this section. But first it is necessary to offer a little detail about how language features in Action Theater™.

Advertising a recent (2015) workshop in London titled *Ta(l)king Your Head Off!*, Action Theater™ teacher Sten Rudstrøm invited participants to enter the 'explosive, colorful, absurdity of experiential speech', telling us: 'once you discover that language is a

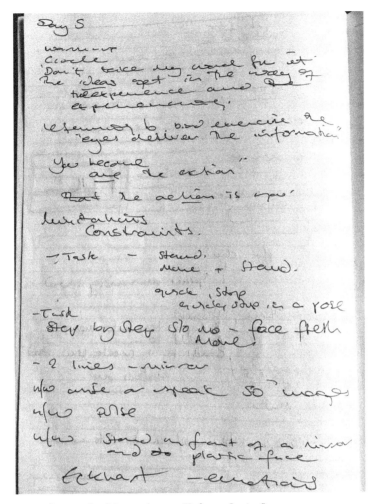

FIG. 21.1 Extract from author's journal notes, Tarbena, Spain, June 2014.

visceral experience, that words are not purely mental constructs but actual body experiences, your improvisations crank up. You are no longer limited by what you think you should say or believe should be said. You are being led by the experience. Each word, each vowel and consonant, on the tongue, in the mouth, teeth, air leads the improvisation. Awareness of the sensations becomes the driving force for language not thought. Thought and imagination are assistants on the path of language, not the directors.[9] In a typical Action Theater™ training, words are strung together with a kind of physical muscularity which emphasizes the sound, shape, and feel of them as much as it attends to any normative ideas about linear narratives or 'life-like' meaning-making. In this way, there is a certain physiology of word, and although this may well add up to create full-blown narratives, the emphasis remains, for a performer, less on creating tidy stories and more on investing and committing to moving through words.

Sheets-Johnstone draws attention to research which highlights the sensory way in which sound is perceived; that 'gestures producing phonemes are co-articulated in complex ways such that speech perception cannot be explained by general auditory principles' (2011: 322). The gestural quality of speech, for Sheets-Johnstone, undergirds the progression of her argument for speech being an animate practice. Crucially here, the use of speech is a marker of perception, simply changed by degree, and not as a higher order of consciousness. This would appear to be in line with Zaporah's call that we see *all* experience in the improvisatory moment—regardless of whether it is encountered in silent, sound, or speech modes—as having equal value.

This evolutionary way of thinking about speech is supported further when Sheets-Johnstone suggests 'that rather than speak of the period before language as the *pre-linguistic*, we should speak of the advent of language as the *post-kinetic*' (2011: xxxi). This reprioritizing of the kinetic in linguistic processes aligns with the pathway to physical narrative in Action Theater™ practice, which has been practiced too through movement. Yet it is important to draw attention to the way speech in Action Theater™ practice appears to have the potential to disrupt an experience of kinetic flow. A central concern in Action Theater™ remains: how can I maintain a state of *embodied presence* when using language? This experience chimes with Sheets-Johnstone when she says: 'what moves and changes is always in excess of the word—or words—that tries to name it' (434); and that in turn, words can all too easily enter the domain of ideas and a habit of wanting to make those ideas make sense in some literal or consciously logical way. Certainly, for me, in Action Theater™ practice, the gateway, or transitional space, between sound and word can appear more expansive and insecure than that between silent movement and sound. Yet Zaporah's teaching, and the Action Theater™ form, takes account of this fear implicitly, by scaffolding the learning. The pedagogy allows for gradual transitions. Even the term 'physical narrative' itself appears to facilitate this, because of its suggestion of the shape, feel, size, and quality of a word. A word's movement in this practice can be elongated, de-formed, and shrunk. Narratives in turn emerge not out of a will to create story, though stories can and often do emerge, but out of a will to stay in touch with the somatic ground of sensation of words or strings of words. In this way, physical narrative is explained through its dynamic action as process, severed from any insistence on representation. Action Theater™ practice therefore trains a performer to displace the need to make clear sense of a narrative in literal ways or for words to have any obviously literal link to the movement that is happening. I could say perhaps that my Action Theater™ practice demands that I shift to being somatically rather than semantically hooked into words.

However, any semantic dominance in the way we use language cannot be easily dismissed. Indeed, I suggest that this challenge to the semantic dominance of language forms a key tension in Action Theater™ practice. A semantically bound reflection on feeling is discouraged during the improvisatory moment in Action Theater™ practice, because it refers to experience which is no longer relevant—the moment has passed. It is remarkable that in a watcher/performer setup, there is a decided lack of explicit reflection on the quality of the improvised material in Action Theater™ after the performance of it is over. To enter into a critique or to engage in value judgements about what the improvised material might have meant, signified, or evoked, or indeed how good/bad the improvisation was, appears to be resisted in the practice, because once again it would shift a performer (and a watcher) into a use of words which are more likely to operate in an overly semantic rather than somatic domain. It is as if any attempt to describe what emerges from a feeling state, either inside or outside the improvised content, is regarded as a futile and no longer relevant gesture. Words, somehow, are not good enough.

Zaporah expands this territory: 'suppose we could climb in between perception and identification. Suppose we could romp around in that no-man's land of the unnamed, unknown terrain. Suppose within that romp our imagination could reassemble the world into a fresh existence' (2014: 71). Zaporah may well be advocating here a reconnection with a prenoetic state not unlike that which Sheets-Johnstone suggests when she talks about thinking through movement rather than using words that might reduce experience because of a postkinetic conditioning: 'the actual dynamic kinetic event is not reducible to a word or even to a series of words. We all have knowledge of just such physical events just as we all have non-linguistic concepts of their dynamics. We have this knowledge in these concepts because we have all been nurtured by an original capacity to think of movement, a capacity that does not diminish with age but merely becomes submerged or hidden by the capacity and practice of thinking in words' (2011: 434). In Action Theater™, an improviser must practice an appreciation of words, first as containers of knowledge that may not always be explicable, and second as working in tandem with movement and its capacity to also speak.

As I mentioned, Zaporah's insistence on attending to a feeling state as the ground for language invites questions to do with the place emotion has in this conception of feeling. For Zaporah, if a feeling state is overidentified with and named, it loses its potency. The concept of emotion remains such a contested term for Zaporah because it presumes identification with a fixed idea of feeling. This problem of identifying the content was tackled in Tarbena time and again. Zaporah insisted that an experience be accepted for what it was, and not named. In Action Theater™ the act of naming experience fixes it. Thus, because the training encourages performers to pay attention to a tactile-kinaesthetic awareness so that they can achieve Zaporah's notion of *embodied presence*, it would appear to challenge any habitual tendencies towards fixing a feeling by adding semantic markers or naming it as an emotion. The experience of physical narrative is bound by an imperative to accept and commit to the feeling state such that it can give rise to new or unfamiliar experience.

Further distinctions have been made between feeling and emotion in the field of neuroscience. In *The Feeling of What Happens*, Antonio Damasio suggests: 'feeling an emotion is a simple matter. It consists of having mental images arising from the neural patterns, which represent the changes in body and brain that make up an emotion. But knowing that we have that feeling, "feeling" that feeling, occurs only after we build the second-order representations' (2000: 169). This more tacit conception of knowing feeling is perhaps closer to Zaporah's position. Through the Action Theater™ form, she similarly rejects any focus on second-order identification with emotion and asks us to stay connected to our feeling states, not simply because the aesthetics of the practice appear to resist the explicit composition of emotional landscapes but also because the practice as improvisation, as process, absolutely demands of us as improvisers that we be located in our experiential, embodied, animate self which cannot be reduced to representations of emotion.

Action Theater™ practice can appear, however, fraught with representations of emotion. In Tarbena, Zaporah cited psychologist Paul Ekman's (1992) studies in emotion where he identifies several basic, but apparently universal, emotions found to be expressed through facial expression—a reduction of emotions, at least in their exteriority, to either *fear, anger, disgust, joy, sadness, or surprise*. In Action Theater™ practice, this identification of feeling as emotion cannot account for the nuance exacted by the fluidity of an ever-changing improvisatory landscape, despite the practice's quite explicit utilization of facial expression. For me, once a mental process of naming a feeling state as emotion is ushered in, I can feel an experience of disruption in the flow of physical narrative. Such mental processes promote a feeling of rupture or hesitation that interrupts the flow of experience. An improvisatory frame gets stuck and cannot move out of the emotional landscape that I have identified it as. This process runs the risk of ossifying an idea of what is being experienced, instead of the experience itself being embodied as the kinetic and ever-changing moment-by-moment dynamic that it is. For Zaporah in Action Theater™ practice, the eyes and face keep a constant track of the inner feeling state as it emerges so that the face expresses a feeling state's processual quality. Avoiding solidifying emotions by fixing them on the face or in the eyes, so they too can stay dynamically expressive is a key part of the Action Theater™ practice. In this way, Action Theater™ demands that I think of physical narrative corporeally, kinetically, playfully, animally … without identifying the improvised content as emotionally represented. What this presents to the improviser is a challenge to remain aware of an ever-changing feeling state from which the physical narrative springs.

SUMMARY

Zaporah's Action Theater™ training attempts to place *all* experience, regardless of whether it is felt through silence, vocalization, or verbalization, on an equal footing. This democratizing feature of the practice may seem at odds with my schematization of these three modes in my analysis above, yet it is through this schematization that, for me, Action Theater™'s evolutionary quality becomes explicit and its pedagogical structure and challenge become clear. While Action Theater™ remains formal in its structure, there is a way in which the modes of working—silent movement, movement and sound, physical narrative—are integrated in a far less delineated way than my analysis might suggest, but by presenting the development of the form in this way, my aim is to have shown that it is possible to see how central to the practice this evolutionary way of thinking through movement is. Action Theater™ practice challenges ideas about silent movement being merely preverbal and invites a reconsideration of speech as a postkinetic endeavour, dependent on moving through silent movement, so that we can ultimately feel the movement of words first as sound; and as the practice evolves, we can be empowered as Action Theater™ improvisers to feel a fuller-fleshed perceptivity as an embodied presence. Physical narratives produced through Action Theater™ are revealed in turn as having a fuller affective potential which ultimately invites us to think of words as being somatically, rather than semantically, charged.

Notes

1. Readers can readily access much more detailed explanations of Action Theater™ exercises. See in particular Zaporah (1998).
2. In Mihalyi Csikszentmihalyi's conception of it; see Csikszentmihalyi (1990).
3. Although relatively little has been published on Action Theater™, there are much fuller descriptions of what it is—how it looks, its form, its pedagogy, etc.—to refer to. Zaporah (1995) details a notional twenty-day training, with each day including a selection of exercises or forms, with a commentary from Zaporah; she has self-published an exercise-per-page handbook (1998) for the more 'experienced improviser'; and she has coauthored a recent prose work (Zaporah, Eckert, and Roshi 2014). Susanna Morrow (2006, 2011) aims to establish Action Theater™ pedagogy as 'a vital and unique contribution to the field of improvisational training' (2011: 99–113). More recently, Kent De Spain counts Zaporah among Steve Paxton, Simone Forti, Lisa Nelson, Deborah Hay, Nancy Stark Smith, Barbara Dilley, and Anna Halprin in his collection of interviews (2014), around which he thematizes an analysis. A film by De Spain, *A Moving Presence* (2010), explores Zaporah's pedagogy, with footage of an intensive training in her studio in Santa Fe. See also De Spain (1995) and Zaporah (2003).
4. Action Theater™ has been described as 'body-based improvisational theater' (Zaporah 1995: xx); 'movement improvisation' (De Spain 2014), and 'a physical theatre improvisation pedagogy' (Morrow 2006: iii)—all terms that might sit happily under dance or theatre rubrics.
5. Noting the influence of dance on the development of her practice, Zaporah's Action Theater™ can be situated in relation to the development of twentieth-century dance in context (1960s/1970s East and West Coast, US) with which many readers may already be familiar. Zaporah tells us: 'most of everything, I have today in the way of improvisational "chops" comes from the years between 1969–1976 spent evolving out of Yvonne Rainer's "Continuous Project Altered Daily" into The Grand Union, that great circus of improvisational performance. Steve Paxton, Trisha Brown, David Gordon, Nancy Lewis, Douglas Dunn, myself, and others from time to time began the extraordinary saga of making it up as we went along, over and over again' (Zaporah 1995: xvi).
6. See Morrow (2006), who traces in some detail how Zaporah, like many of her contemporaries, was 'helped along by her collaborations with theater artists, principally Bob Ernst of the Jerzy Grotowski influenced Blake Street Hawkeyes and secondarily Ken Jenkins, a Joe Chaikin trained director and actor' (2006: 133). This interdisciplinarity continues to be reflected in the demography of the participants who are drawn to the practice today. Of the

twenty participants in Tarbena, although several were dance or theatre artists, just as many were from backgrounds in other disciplines, such as law and finance, for example.

7. See   http://www.actiontheater.com/teachers.htm—information   last   accessed   18 February 2015.
8. I am a practitioner of the Feldenkrais Method®, certified by the UK Feldenkrais Guild.
9. Sten Rudstrøm, email to the author, received 13 February 2015.

References

Csikszentmihalyi, M. (1990) *Flow: The Psychology of Optimal Performance.* New York: Cambridge University Press.

Damasio, A. R. (2000) *The Feeling of What Happens: Body and Emotion in the Making of Consciousness.* Boston, MA: Houghton Mifflin Harcourt.

De Spain, K. (1995) A Moving Decision: Notes on the Improvising Mind. *Contact Quarterly* 20.1: 48–50.

De Spain, K. (2014) *Landscape of the Now: A Topography of Movement Improvisation.* Oxford: Oxford University Press.

Ekman, P. (1992) An Argument for Basic Emotions. *Cognition and Emotion* 6(3–4): 169–200.

Massumi, B. (2014) *What Animals Teach Us about Politics.* Durham, NC: Duke University Press.

Morrow, S. (2011) Psyche Meets Soma: Accessing Creativity through Ruth Zaporah's Action Theater. *Theatre, Dance and Performance Training* 2(1): 99–113.

Morrow, S. R. (2006) *Action Theater: Divine Play for the Stage.* PhD.

Noë, A. (2012) *Varieties of Presence.* Cambridge, MA: Harvard University Press.

Sheets-Johnstone, M. (2011) *The Primacy of Movement.* Philadelphia, PA: John Benjamins.

Vesty, R. (2014) *Personal Journal Notes.*

Zaporah, R. (1995) *Action Theater: The Improvisation of Presence.* Berkeley, CA: North Atlantic Books.

Zaporah, R. (1998) *Action Theater: The Manual.*

Zaporah, R., (2003) "Dance: A Body with a Mind of Its Own." In Ann Cooper Albright and D. Gere (eds.), *Taken by Surprise: A Dance Improvisation Reader.* Hanover, CT: Wesleyan University Press, 21–26.

Zaporah, R., Eckert, R., and Roshi, J. S. (2014) *Improvisation on the Edge: Notes from On and Off Stage.* North Atlantic Books.

CHAPTER 22

....

INTENTION AND SURRENDER

....

STEPHANIE SKURA

IN over thirty years working professionally as a performance-maker—with my own company, when fulfilling commissions, or doing solo work, theater directing, or experiments in my living room—improvisation has always been a key element in the process. My ever-evolving understanding of improvisation as a critical skill in both life and dance, and the methods I've assembled to inspire others in rehearsals as well as classes, have been drawn directly from my own dancing and directing. Sometimes the performed work is completely set; sometimes it consists of structured improvisations. These improvisations are not always mine; they often develop from collaborative research with participating performers. Rather than teaching steps from my own dancing, I've generally preferred to find movement from diverse movers working with similar concepts, interpreted and realized in different ways. This is not due to laziness! Choreographing, refining, and structuring movement from improvisations of collaborators is tough, focused, demanding work for all concerned.

This chapter aims to illuminate some of the methods I've evolved to teach improvisation and to guide performance-making. I include concrete descriptions of activities and, importantly, elucidation of purposes and underlying concepts. For both facilitators and participants, understanding and embracing underlying concepts is necessary for the various methods to catalyse results. In a larger sense, these methods for improvisation and performance-making constitute a framework for how creativity can operate. And perhaps because in our Western worlds we tend to become accustomed to mostly analytical ways of finding form and even content, these methods often focus on accessing the wealth of information that lies below conscious and intentional forming. As creators of all stripes eventually discover, navigating below consciousness and intention, in partnership with more familiar analytical methods, is a necessary ingredient for inspired creative process, and can catalyse revelations not only about content but also about structure.

And now it all comes together. No doubt, no fear, a figurine gone wild, slinging herself off the countertop, perpetual movement without any windup. Fabulous panting, ambiguous and loud and penetrating.

The pedagogy I've developed to teach improvisation grew from a choreographic rehearsal process rather than from any learned methods of improvising. I discovered that improvisation, sensitively guided, could be a potent pathway to performers' transcendence. Motivated by a powerful desire to witness powerful performers, I also realized that performers are the most charismatic, astounding, and magical when they've participated in creating their material, conceptually and physically. And in my search to enliven and activate the whole being of each performer, I learned that opening pathways to each one's subconscious life is vital. To manifest powerful content and enlightened performance relationships, everyone needs to be a creator. This collaborative rehearsal process has given rise to a pedagogy for teaching improvisation.

A whole-being approach to creation seemed to also necessitate working interdisciplinarily, even though we were oriented *from* dance and much of our training was in the realm of dance. All performance takes place in a specific environment, all humans naturally think, move, and make sound (and also, it seems, draw!), and there is always a visual element, whether it's a 'set' or lighting design or just the layout of the venue. And I realized that when audiences comprehend performance with their whole beings—rather than only their thinking brains—they have the most powerful experiences. I wanted to get to the magical roots of performance, to a time when dance, music, storytelling, visual art, and poetry were as one; when performance was a way to feed our social, artistic, and spiritual lives in a participatory way; when people and communities enacted their visions and dreams, and were thus empowered to make enlightened decisions about their future.

To involve the whole being and subconscious life of each participant, my improvisational pedagogy often includes free-associative writing, drawing, and speaking, as well as movement. Working with these approaches can lead to refreshed perceptions of movement itself: as a metaphorical yet direct language and as a potent activator—of ideas, thoughts, imagery, and methods.

The key sections of the chapter elucidate these topics:

- Underlying values I aim to evoke in improvising movers
- What I consider the basic forms of improvisational response
- Several workshop practices to illuminate each of these responses
- Methods to activate relationships between moving, writing, and drawing
- Ways of working with scores and how they support both improvisational and choreographic practice
- Teaching composition in a way that empowers individual creative freedom

A bit of a waddle, but no—let's go there, jumping for awhile till tentativeness takes over. A thrill that lasts about a second. False ending, zigzag wandering: precise, long-legged, multidirectional, coughing, looking up at the corner, covering your ears. Let's start over.

Desperation creeps in. You pull yourself together, bending over as if to find a lost something on the ground, touching the fronts of your thighs, your ribs, your back, then letting your arms hang low. A determined walk to download more information. Sit,

FIG. 22.1 Stephanie Skura performing the structured improvisation 'Sacrilege Is Needed. Competency Is Hell.' Here she is working with the score, 'loose flings into stillness, initiated by the spine.' Photograph by Ian Douglas.

lie, spread, rock, no need to ever move any faster than this. Sensation of smoothness, of stillness with breath. End. Get up. More info, fall-forward, pointing, arms, shoulder, the arrow, the business. This could be the beginning of a corny dance, but only the begin-ning, and then it disappears. Crawling backwards, enjoying the diagonals, the turned-out hands and feet, hair hanging, not gloating. Even a bit facile. Small diagonal runs looking over your shoulder, as if. Compact and stumbling, no terror, no children, no decorations.

Inserted throughout this chapter are samples of what I've named 'writing from wit nessing'. Witnessing each other moving and possibly vocalizing, participants describe what they see, while documenting their 'mental landscape' during the describing.

Mental landscape is anything that flashes through one's consciousness, directly related or not. It might include words the mover is speaking, memories, dream fragments, bits of overheard conversations, bits of films remembered, mundane thoughts about practical life concerns, comments about any of it, voices of other people within oneself, or any seemingly unrelated images or thoughts. There is rigour involved in this kind of writing! With no attempt to be clever, poetic, funny, dramatic, or entertaining, we go off on tangents, then keep coming back to describing what we perceive. Truly a document of one's mental terrain, it's also an interesting practice that helps get at subconscious meaning, rather than writing with a theme decided beforehand. This kind of writing can also help us hone and specify the richness of our perceptions as we witness movement. I am continually fascinated by what dancers see when they witness dance, by the circuits that are stimulated in their inner lives. When this perceptual richness is made apparent, it seems to deepen both the movement and the perception of movement. In addition, the writing can be used in myriad ways: for instance, as spoken word alone or in relation to movement activity, or even as a score for further movement. The material revealed in the writing provides a way of including all of our insides as well as our outsides in our improvisations and compositions.

I wrote all the inserts in the chapter while witnessing Alex Crowe and Vanessa Dewolf during ongoing process sessions.

Sometimes, like a feather. The edge of opportunity, a slipping away. An almost heavy arm, the uncertainty of air. Left leaning, left alone. Leaving a trace. Say nothing. Feel the imbalance. Fall, a little. The feet are thinking. The hands, now and then, coming alive. Fill the bag almost to the top. She too used to get scared before those medical procedures, think she was going to die.

A savage loss, shrugged off, again, with hope of a future win, again. The moles underground are unaware of all this, as they dig their tunnels.

Lying on our sides, with wild eyes.

When I began choreographing, I brought various strategies into rehearsals to evoke each performer's power, wildness, and individuality. Some strategies articulated processes I was doing myself. Some were ideas I tried out on the intrepid dancer-souls who trusted me. Later, when I started teaching, a pedagogy began to take form, one that keeps evolving now thirty years later. During the past ten years, my ongoing research has included radical approaches to language and an athletic approach to the voice, with experiments integrating moving with writing, speaking, and drawing. Importantly, the pedagogy involves underlying essential concepts that continue to define themselves.

(As I write this, I get out of the chair and improvise in my living room between each paragraph. My poetic writing usually happens in conjunction with movement, so why not expository writing as well?)

WHAT I AIM TO EVOKE
IN IMPROVISING MOVERS

I've called it 'psychic boldness'. It's a strong, convicted presence, a deep immersion in and fascination with one's own created material. It's lack of inhibition. It's an ability to perceive our actions as they occur and bravely immerse in this specificity while letting our physicality lead us into unknown territory. It's an appetite for integrating intuitive and analytical, a willingness to invite the mind to collaborate rather than control. It's trust in deeply personal material. It's a desire to express complexities of consciousness with movement. It's a readiness to manifest the many layers of our being, and not just the seemingly normal, acceptable layers. It's a high degree of consciousness without self-consciousness. It's a profoundly implicative interest in diverse humans connecting with each other without always doing the same thing. It's a desire to avoid cliché. It's courage to free-associate, without fear of seeming weird or neurotic. It's open-mindedness about organic forms of structuring rather than geometric forms. It's tolerance of seeming messiness, of chaos. For me, dance is not about the physical body; it's about the

FIG. 22.2 Susanna Hood, John Dixon, and Yvonne Ng in a moving/writing practice. Photograph by Stephanie Skura.

complexity, excitement, and athleticism of our multilayered consciousness. When we integrate body with consciousness, the body *is* our being and our soul.

SOME BASIC FORMS OF IMPROVISATIONAL RESPONSE: WORKSHOP PRACTICES

It's reassuring and useful to consider all improvising as only responding. Sometimes we feel pressure to invent when in fact there's so much to respond to, and so many responses already going on inside us. We can just tune in and act on any one of them. Even a seeming initiation is a form of response. In teaching, I find it essential to isolate and practice each of several basic forms of response, even though in our dancing and lives they're all happening simultaneously.

> *Disclaimer! These are methods I've created to practice specific awarenesses. Other teachers and artists may adapt and change them in response to their situations and needs, or create their own methods. I tend to avoid 'how to' approaches, because what's essential is not the method itself but the spirit and understanding driving it. If you experiment with these methods, focus on underlying ideas and how they change outer forms. We can let go of the desire, possibly out of hunger for seeming purity, to hold outer form in a fixed position. Outer forms inevitably need to be re-created in response to changing circumstances and a changing world.*

Energy Responses

We start simply, experiencing our own and each other's movements as if we were ghosts with no bodies—not as people or even shapes, just sheer energy. If a ghost were to run across the room and leave an energy trail, what would be its direction, rhythm, quality? Beginning along the edges of the space, our options are walking or running. (We discover along the way: there are infinite forms of walking and running.) You can enter and stay as long or as short as you wish. Those who are witnessing practice seeing only energy. Additional awareness: notice organic relationships amongst the energy trails. Energies coming towards us might push us away. We might spin off circular energies, be drawn in by energies moving away from us, or experience other seemingly logical or personal energetic responses. After awhile, we add sitting and rolling. Near the end, we add any kind of movement, experienced and perceived as pure energy.

This is an entirely natural way of responding to movement. Animals do it, and non-dance-trained humans do it. As dancers, we get so accustomed to perceiving shape that we can forget this primal way of relating.

Start from where you are! This is a guideline for all improvisational practices. No need to try to move differently than we feel, be it heavy, buoyant, jagged, messy, ragged, clean, tentative, bombastic, sluggish, loose, or otherwise. We might be surprised by how our energy transforms and how much more energy we have when we let go of internal struggles to be other than wherever and however we are.

Energy Duets

These are very fast energy responses to a partner's movements. There's no call and response; both move simultaneously, quickly, thoughtlessly. Every movement is a palpable force in space—pushing, pulling, sending us into the floor or into the air, turning, diving, rumpling, quivering, curving, or any other energetic response. It's helpful to do this with vocalizing, both on inhale and exhale, after a vocal warm-up. Sound is riding on the breath, rather than invented. Speed and vocal sounds are ways of bypassing the mind's inhibitions. Once things are going fluidly, the duets can include smaller, slower movements. After awhile, movement can continue without sound, just with breath. It's interesting how, after sound is removed, dancers want to include it, even those who were previously uncomfortable with sound. Vocalizing begins to feel like a natural part of the movement, and it is.

Enhancing

Enhancing is all about saying yes to what's happening by helping it become more of what it already is. It can be done with a single partner, or with a duet, trio, or group. It can provide a coherence option when people are doing vastly different things. Both physical and a state of mind, it's about being supportive. It can take myriad forms, from literal weight support to counterbalance support, subtle hands-on alignment support, framing your partner's movement with stillness, responding to its energy patterns, subtly reflecting the movement, having supportive thoughts, or helping move your partner in a way they are already moving. Enhancing is a dance in itself, tuning in and intuitively amplifying what we perceive.

In teaching, enhancing works best preceded by specific weight-sharing and touch activities; palpable support then becomes an available option in the enhancing duet. It's useful to begin with clear roles: the mover moving simply and the enhancer simply tuning in. The mover moves independently though is affected by the enhancement. After awhile, the duet continues by changing roles, once again allowing time to tune in and adjust to the new role. After another while, I suggest the roles might reverse at any time as an aspect of each duet, and there might be some time during which our role is ambiguous, and we can enjoy this ambiguity.

Subtext

Working with subtext is about responding to what's underneath the outer form. We focus on underlying qualities, rather than shape, and use them as starting points to develop physically. Though subtext is rarely talked about in dance, it's a natural way humans and animals interact. Children do it easily, and adults can rediscover it as a rich mine of potential improvisational responses.

We've all probably done the exercise in which we face our partners and mirror their moves. Subtext work is nonliteral mirroring, reflecting a quality we sense underneath. It can even be an underneath quality of a still person. Some qualities are overtly physical; some border on psychological. It's essential to work physically with all qualities, even psychological ones, rather than focus on the emotional. The physical is a metaphor for the psychological, and an effective doorway into exploring states of being.

I introduce subtext with a trio practice. Partner A does a ten-second spontaneous movement event: start large, end small, no repetition, and change tempos. Partners B and C immediately respond by noticing any one subtextual quality that jumps out for them and develop it for ten seconds. B and C might be working with two different qualities or the same one. Then B does a new ten-second movement event, and A and C immediately respond with an underneath quality developed for ten seconds. Then C does a new ten-second movement event, and A and B immediately respond with a subtext. The subtext might be something seemingly movement-related, or not. There are an infinite number of these. Examples: efficient, juicy, watery, dry, metallic, percussive, gushing, hesitant, curvy, bombastic, wispy, smoldering, fiery, slippery, brittle, messy, rigid, overenthusiastic, fearful, with a sense of urgency, with a sense of loss, like a tidal wave, like you just woke up, glib, sneaky, deluded, awkward, fanatical, regretful, as if every move has a coded significance.

If the group is comfortable with vocalizing, a fascinating variation is to respond three times to each ten-second movement event: first developing a sound version of the subtext, then a movement version, then both together.

Eventually, subtext responses can be brought into group improvisations and extended longer. We can also include the perceived *opposite* of a subtext. Juxtaposition of opposites creates a rich form of coherence, countering the default impulse to do what everyone else is doing.

Free-Associative Response

Rigour in free association might seem like a contradiction in terms, but free association can be a highly skilled practice rather than a free-for-all. Possibly more familiar as writing technique than movement practice, it can be applied to any art form. One method I've used involves giving a single word to begin. Examples: fall, light, blurt. You write your immediate associations, becoming a chain of associations, until one arises that lends itself to movement. Anyone can enter the space and move from that association, in relation to others moving from their own associative worlds. At any time you can return to the edge of the space and write associations on what you are witnessing, and then reenter when an association lends itself to movement. If the group is familiar with reading and speaking, they might also read from their writings. This becomes a world of internal and external consciousness, all intertwined. Everybody's subconscious is right out there, with each able to relate to the others' intensely personal universes.

Since developing this exercise, I've researched additional ways of integrating personal associative text with movement, and of honing the speaking voice to express ranges of nuanced physicality that carry the energy of imagery.

> Note: These energy response, subtext, and free association practices were instigated by Joan Skinner's descriptions of improvisation techniques she created.

MOVING AND WRITING: SOME APPROACHES

Wow, that makes my childhood seem almost—Well, I think if he could do THAT (elbowing his way in and out of the room, capturing sound with the flat of the hand, the fists). Amplitude of shoulder fantasy, then PLOP—fingers askew, inside a second skin, stove-top, avenue, like there's a ring-side seat. SLAP. All ready to go, ready to go. This one's mine—the cavalcade of your back leg, caught in a trap, staying up all night worrying. Wait, did it move? The pubic hopping god-like effluorescent shower-stampede of a better brother.

Are these platform boots, or—? Sidling is just a stylistic matter. The story is, as always, reliable. Until, one day, hunched over himself, fingers twisting, he's driven out of town. Straight arms whipping, impeded, gasping with surprise, walking deliberately towards nothing. Don't run away! Don't run away! Your adorable palpitations, how they hover and arrange themselves. Surely someone is in charge.

But eggplants always have this effect (as somebody knocks on the door). Heave-ho, my darling, you've picked all the flowers. Catching a glimpse of his brother out of the corner of his eye, stinking like a swan's wing.

Twentieth-century surrealists practiced 'automatic writing', unmitigated by conscious thought. I began borrowing some of their methods and integrating them with movement. Finding pathways to the subconscious, and giving equal weight to conscious and subconscious realities, are integral aspects of art-making.

It's incredibly useful to apply physical qualities not only to movement but also to vocalizing and writing. There's no need to start with a theme; a quality can drive us, be it punching, slippery, hard-edged, tentative, perfunctory, sticky, delicate, resolute, illuminated, spiffy, infantile, matriarchal, surprised, panicky, overly decorative, flinging, floating, easily distracted, urgent, presentational, wild, contained, confrontational, clean, or any one of an infinite variety of dynamics. In writing, vocalizing, and moving, various textures interact within us and in relation to others, as individuals work with similar or radically different qualities. Themes can emerge from this practice, often surprisingly relevant and deep.

> *She is the slippery developing one, gravelly, tossing her thoughts, her hair, her head, her arms. Reconsidering by allowing moments of . . . just breath. Those arm dances, they're the initiation—for spine, legs, pelvis. Turn off the light, leave it off, the bulb burned out, the bit of mold in the bathroom.*

Messy, Clean, Etc.

A. Begin with a free-associative writing project. An easy-entry first one: Describe the room. Go into details. As you describe, include anything you flash on, free-associate to, or remember. Go off on tangents, then return to the room description. Use full sentences or fragments, rather than a list of nouns, or adjectives and nouns. Make no attempt to be interesting, clever, funny, dramatic, or poetic. The writing is a document of your mental landscape as you describe the room. Refrain from editing. Refrain from going back and reading what you've written so far. Just keep writing. Feel free to be mundane, irrelevant, dark, or not nice. Write legibly, then place your writing on the edge of the space.
Guideline: Our detailed personal associations are valid, valuable, and resonant for others.

B. Give four different qualities for improvising, one at a time. Each is explored all together by the group, first with movement and vocalizing, then going to the edges and reading the room descriptions with that quality. In reading, the body is active but not travelling in space; the voice is dancing. Speak directly to someone on the other side of the room.
Guideline for reading: no need to focus on the meaning of words. We already know what these words mean. Practice focusing on the quality. Though not entirely divorced from meaning, we let our inner connections with the words be fluid and less conscious as we focus on the physical quality.
   The four ways of improvising are:
   1. *Messy*: Your idea of what messiness is. Begin quickly, with a quick pulse underneath, while allowing some slower moves and some pauses. Messy sound too.
   2. *Clean.* Your idea of what cleanliness is, both movement and sound. Again, begin with a quick pulse, allowing some slower moves and pauses.
   3. *Large energies that quickly dissolve and reverberate for a long time.* Emphasize the reverberation; what are we left with once that largeness dissolves? (We don't need to name it to be immersed in it.) Sound can be nonverbal or words.
   4. *Delicacy.* This means easily broken. Not necessarily slow or smooth, any kind of movement can be done with delicacy. Maybe the air feels delicate, or our seeing is delicate.

C. Once the four qualities have been explored, we do a group improvisation in which
everyone moves and sounds with any one of the four qualities for as long or as short
as they want or need. With awareness of relationships that already exist between
movers/sounders, we allow relationships to develop from awareness: rhythmic,
energy-directional, juxtaposition of opposites, triggering, or spatial. One person
at a time can move to the side and bring the quality he's been moving/sounding
with into reading their text. Reader sees and responds to movers, as movers hear
and respond to reader (see fig. 22.8).
Guideline: Allow silence. Allow stillness.

The four qualities in this list are useful as an introductory writing/moving activity, but
there are many options. It's important that the qualities cover a range of states of being,
and jog people loose from their inhibitions.

There are lots of other writing approaches that work well in mapping our mental landscapes. Describing the room effectively gets at personal material without approaching it
head-on. After all, we're only describing the room! The same goes for writing based on
found objects. Or for 'list writing', in which every sentence starts with the same words,
such as 'I remember…'.

Partners Writing from Moving

This is a duet practice. Partner A moves while Partner B, on an edge of the space,
writes from witnessing Partner A. The mover might include sound or free-associative

FIG. 22.3 Marisol Salinas and Susanna Hood in a moving/writing duet. Photograph by
Stephanie Skura.

speaking, and be guided by a specific focus, or not. One guideline I like is taking the psychic time to be aware of the inner life of your movement. The writing witnesses describe in detail their perceptions of their movers, along with their mental landscape while witnessing. The text ranges from physical description to perceived images to wildly free-associated material, always returning to witnessing the mover. If the mover speaks, the mover's words can enter into the witnessing text. Partner Bs then transition from writing to moving, sourcing from something in their writing that lends itself to movement. Partner As transition from mover to witnessing writers. Guideline: Allow permeable membranes between witnessing and participating, with gradual transitions. Movement can begin while still with your page, and overlap with your partner's movement, creating a movement duet. Then Partner As transition from writing to moving, and Partner Bs transition to reading their own texts in relation with Partner As' moving. Then, Partner As read while Partner Bs move. These duets can continue with fluid transitions without cuing from me, (see fig. 22.3).

> *Guidelines: Allow silence as well as sound. Allow stillness as well as movement. Focus on textural and rhythmic relationships between movement and text. When transitions become more fluid, some might speak as they're moving.*
>
> *Pole-jumping, or the equivalent. A sore foot, a waddling walk, wings floating, heels wobbling. I turn my back, no offense, sniffing. Slow, slow, side-side, did you drop something? Whoa! Staggering backwards, back still turned. Let's just experiment, no need for specific results. Hold tight, that nearly knocked me over! Hand on chest, hand probing air to the side, splayed for a moment—fingers, legs—weaving, singing to self. Inching towards, quick reverse.*
>
> *The clutching of nothing, the night air, his coat after he died, his smell. Yes I know, this is funny, this is the ground we crawl on, when we worship, when we flap our hands rhythmically.*
>
> *Swift descent, air singing, a sound nobody recognizes but everybody remembers. You who devote your life to a small unexplored subject, studying and writing. How shall we make a mark? The lion who runs up to embrace the man, snuggling and licking. That would be enough for anybody I should think.*

SCORES: SOME APPROACHES

A score is a set of instructions to be carried out in a personal way. Containing images, drawings, and/or words, it might be a description of potent aspects of an improvisation, or the score itself might *be* the improvisation. Scores can be tools for accessing, developing, and clarifying subconscious meanings. They can help us find specificity by honing in on qualities, images, and even processes—rather than always repeating exact outer forms (see fig. 22.4).

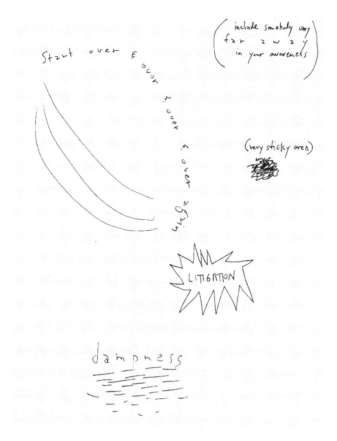

FIG. 22.4 Score made for a partner. By Stephanie Skura.

I've worked with scoring practices since I began making dances. But it was in teaching composition that I named and formalized the practice, using visual scores on paper, rather than score-like ideas in my head. I created a class called 'Finding Forms', to guide others to find structure by integrating intuitive and analytical faculties. I very much wanted to help dance-makers find their own processes, rather than teaching how I make work. I wasn't suggesting that people always create with scores; rather, I sensed that working with scores would catalyse them to find their own methods. And this indeed is what happened.

Score-making hones intuition when working with structure. Form can be derived from content, rather than something imposed on content (see fig. 22.5).

Scores can consist of drawings, words, or both. I generally set a rule that scores be specific and physical, with a broad definition of 'physical', and not include narrative or emotion. When emotion is decided beforehand, it tends to stultify inner life. For fluid inner life, alive in the moment, I advise scoring physicality, quality, exact image, colour, energy quality, texture of environment, chronology of landmarks, even possibly the process.

FIG. 22.5 Score made for a partner. By Stephanie Skura.

A score can be made from an improvisation. It doesn't need to include everything, just what seemed important. Thus, intentionality leads to form. The score asks 'What happened that seemed resonant, potent, significant?'

There are myriad ways to approach score-making. 'Score, dance, score, dance' is one method: each time we work, we work with our previous score, then make a new score based on what just happened. Or we can work with the same score each time, possibly refining it. Some have made scores during performance while witnessing what others are doing and then entered working with the score they just made. There are an infinite number of ways to work with scores, depending on individual needs, imaginations, and comfort levels with knowing and not-knowing (see fig. 22.6).

Guideline: Each score element is a starting point, rather than goal. It's a way of being specific, while being open to what develops when we go on a physical journey with an idea. Our bodies are resources for intuitive knowing. When scores lead us on physical pathways, we travel to places we couldn't have discovered purely through analytical thought. We may not know what the material means at the outset, but we discover meaning as we go.

Working with scores develops a mind muscle that helps us improvise, whether we're working with visual scores or not. This 'score muscle' articulates—in words or sensing— what we're doing as we're doing it, helping us be specific and develop our ideas. Even if what we're doing is a squiggle on the page, we know we're working with that squiggle, and we are more inclined to be fascinated by it, see how it develops, and really go there. Immersion in physical specificity also expands our movement vocabulary, so we're not always doing versions of the same thing. Another benefit of the score muscle: we go deeply and develop ideas, rather than leaving things before they develop and looking for the next idea.

Scores are also useful in practicing a key aspect of improvisation: *every moment is both intention and surrender.* At every moment, we know what we're doing, yet we're

FIG. 22.6 Susanna Hood working with a score. Photograph by Stephanie Skura.

entirely open to how this intention may develop and how we respond to each other and our environment. A score gives us intention. The practice, which is lifelong, is staying with the score while remaining open.

Energy Drawings as Scores

Once improvisers experience movement as pure energy, a further dimension of this awareness is drawing energies they witness. This can become an in-and-out-of-the-centre activity, beginning with some people moving while witnesses draw energies that are vivid for them. At any time, a drawing witness can enter the space, working with the drawings as visual scores—springboards for physical explorations. Textures of the lines, their directions, pathways, locations on the page—are all open for interpretation. A spidery squiggle may become a spatial pathway. A black square might become dense movement, or a hole to fall into. As movers explore their scores, they are also aware of relationships among themselves (see fig. 22.7).

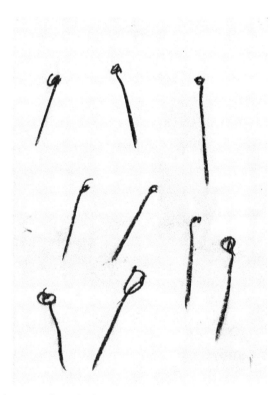

FIG. 22.7 Energy drawing of another's movement, providing score for my own movement. By Stephanie Skura.

Score Made from Witnessing Alex Crowe

Unready, jittery
Curving expansiveness
Stillness
Labyrinthine
Determination
Large steps, bent arms, often move from elbows
In and around oneself, breathy
Fall sideways
The descent
Quiet observance
Chugging walks with lots of homolateral-ness

Scores Made from Witnessing a Partner

We can make scores based on witnessing a partner: describe several things we perceive. The description is physical, with a broad definition of physicality. Though not exact descriptions of movements, the describing is specific, including images, qualities, rhythm, size, spatial patterns, or other kinds of physicality. It can be in the form of a list. It can be chronological, or not. Partners change roles, then give each other the scores they made, and work with those given scores. After developing a relationship with their scores, they can work together as a duet. Or they may choose to make solos. As with other scoring practices, a good score provides various kinds of variety and contrast (see fig. 22.2).

Scores Made by Describing Our Own Movements

We can also make a score from our own improvisations, notating what seemed important with words and drawings. Location on the page is significant, as well as textures of words and drawings, pathways, chronologies, or any other instructions that find their way onto the page. As a next step, we work with the score freely, not necessarily interpreting elements as originally intended. For instance, the word 'light' may have been intended as the quality of lightness, but we might interpret it as locating something in a square of light on the floor coming from a window. It's interesting that this way of freely interpreting language relates to the kind of logic in our dreams, which are often full of puns and anagrams. By freely interpreting scores we've made for ourselves, we may get at deeper meanings than consciously intended.

Recently, I've been working with a process of moving for a few minutes, writing a description of what I was doing, going back to moving, writing a description of that movement, and so on, resulting in at least four different movement descriptions. I often do this with a partner who's doing the same, though we may not be directly relating to each other. We then each improvise with our respective scores, physicalizing one description after the other, while the other writes from witnessing. Then we reverse roles.

Describing My Movement

1. *Curves and lines that pause.*
2. *Loose flings into stillness, initiated by the spine (see fig. 22.1).*
3. *Tiny seeds of movement initiated deep inside the torso.*
4. *Random relatively large sudden moves. Emphasize randomness.*

1. *Minimal disjointedness, and being open to where it leads.*
2. *Quick chugging steps, finding repetitive moves of body parts, and repetitive ways of travelling that are awkward in their inefficiency.*
3. *Enliven tissues between ribs. Spacious. Sporadic.*
4. *Stop-motion: very fast, with long stillnesses.*

1. *1000 curves/1000 lines*
2. *Loose, authoritative, and falling on the horizontal plane.*
3. *Quickly change location, find yourself there, then sharply change one thing, then another, e.g., an angle, a limb, focus, aspect of line or plane.*
4. *Messy and flingy with sounds like bottled laughter.*
5. *In a chair, both clear and tentative.*

Scores Made for a Particular Person

A score can be an improvisation in itself created for a particular person, considering what would be interesting and challenging to bring out of this individual. It can result in a duet, with partners making scores for each other and working with those scores simultaneously. It can also be a solo form.

Score for Giuseppina Turra, Actor-Dancer

1. *Tell a story with your spine while muttering.*
2. *Confrontational moves, moving gradually downstage.*
3. *Move vigorously but don't dance, with vigorous sounds that aren't musical.*
4. *Strong curvy rhythmic moves with stillnesses, against a wall.*
5. *Small and awkward.*
6. *Entrances and exits—each with a different specific theme, including grandiose and presentational—with increasing desperation, never quite hitting the mark.*

FIG. 22.8 Alex Crowe, John Dixon, and Susanna Hood working with individual scores. Photograph by Stephanie Skura.

7. *Express the inexpressible with gestures.*
8. *Repetitive and obsessive.*
9. *Tell a personal intimate story involving a chicken, that's not entirely true, with no attempt to entertain or be funny.*
10. *Again, this time with back to audience, tell a story with your spine.*

Score for Paige Barnes, Dancer-Choreographer

1. *Like you just woke up.*
2. *Sharp sudden angular movement at low altitude on diagonal path.*
3. *Small off-balances without moving feet.*
4. *Ask practical questions.*
5. *Repetitive and obsessive.*
6. *Small and psychologically awkward.*
7. *Grandiose and presentational movement that gradually loses control and becomes chaotic.*
8. *Press flatness.*
9. *Trapped at window.*

ISSUES OF COMPOSITION AND SPACE

I find it vital to experiment with improvisation as an expressive form before stressing composition as a goal. When composition is emphasized before enough focus is given to movement expression, improvisation becomes 'instant composition', with content sacrificed to structure. If humans are structural elements without expressing their humanity, that's a statement in itself.

Spatial, rhythmic, directional, energetic, and textural relationships are aspects of responding that organically create structure. Though some might assume content comes to us intuitively and structure analytically, they can be fruits of a fertile marriage of intuitive and analytical faculties. *Structure becomes a revelation of content* (after Denise Levertov).[1]

And so I don't usually approach spatial relationships as a distinct type of response. Spatial impulses are integral aspects of how we relate to each other and our environment, with personal and psychological resonance. And sometimes our impulses are 'architectural'. Viewing the whole moving picture even as we're kinaesthetically inside it, we see ourselves somewhere else, and we act on that spatial impulse.

Playing with different ways of creating and using scores greases the wheels of our form-making imagination. We shed preconceived notions about what structure is supposed to be—Newtonian concepts of geometric shapes, or music-derived ideas about theme and variation, or ABA structures—and allow forms to emerge that are unique to the content and process of each project.

In this time of the early twenty-first century, there's an ever-greater need to appreciate how to support individual creative process. This is a different kind of learning from acquiring skills. Though people are becoming ever more proficient in specific areas of expertise, what is not, so far, widely understood is how to look within to access the wealth of ideas and impulses in each of us. Our culture, looking increasingly outward for information and stimulation, has yet to balance itself and train us to look inward.

I often call composition workshops 'Finding Forms'. Once we've researched approaches to score-making, each participant keeps an idea journal. We discuss what ideas are; rather than having to hunt for them, they come to us, often unexpectedly while we're doing other things. I encourage people to write down all ideas, whether or not they seem possible to realize. Sometimes an idea comes from an activity we find ourselves doing and then identify in words; sometimes it's yet to be explored. I suggest choosing ideas that feel adventurous to pursue. They could be qualities, particular sites, ways of working with light or objects or text, specific costumes, an ordeal of sorts, an intriguing process. It might be as simple as a skirt that obstructs movement. Or a structure that involves multiple beginnings, middles, and ends. Or an accumulation of movements and actions we add to each day. It could be a way of working with scores—asking a colleague to create a score for us, or making a score from something we wouldn't ordinarily associate with scores: a group of objects, or photographs, or an etching from a sidewalk. It should be something that beckons, that we don't yet know the meaning of, something that will lead we know not where.

When students source performances from their own ideas, they have an infinite amount of energy for their projects. The atmosphere of excitement and discovery is contagious, whether or not people are working on the same projects. Showings along the way, during which more discoveries are made, benefit from the energy of an intimate, supportive audience.

A rigorous and supportive creative work atmosphere can lead to performance work that lives and grows for years to come. Whole careers have begun in such fertile situations. The Judson era originated with a similarly fertile and challenging composition class, one that changed the very definition of dance for years to come.

Just at the end, something happens. It took all that time to engage, and then rhythm inflates words. Like a bird singing for its life, for its world to exist at all. And in the last moment, a flare of tail and display of colors we never knew were there, hidden in the under-feathers.

NOTE

1. 'Form is never more than a revelation of content' (Levertov 1965: p. 424).

REFERENCE

Levertov, Denise. (1965) Some Notes on Organic Form. *Poetry* 106(6): 420–425.

PART V

AGENCY AND TRANSFORMATION

....

CHAPTER 23

TRANSCENDING BOUNDARIES

Improvisation and Disability in Dance

....

SARAH WHATLEY

THIS chapter will explore the shifts and turns in the relationship between disability and improvisation in dance in recent years. Drawing from disabled dancers' own views about the place of improvisation in their making and performance practice, the discussion will reference work that deliberately incorporates improvisation as a device to blur the boundaries between the 'fixed' and the fluid in dance. Moreover, examining the writing *about* improvisation in relation to the writing *through* improvisation offers another way of recognizing the labile nature of the practice, which can never be fully captured in writing alone. In tracing, and recounting, these different journeys and artist recollections, I hope to demonstrate that improvisation can be a means to be able to transcend the borders between 'disabled' and 'nondisabled' in dance. I do this also to argue that these labels ('disabled' and 'nondisabled') are also not meant to be fixed, reflecting the fluid and inherently fragile nature and status of the human body as it naturally ages and may become impaired or disabled and so resists fixed categories.

DANCE AND DISABILITY IN CONTEXT

....

It is more than a decade since Adam Benjamin's book *Making an Entrance* (2002) entered the world and offered an important resource for anyone interested in inclusive dance practice and particularly for those wanting to teach dance with disabled and nondisabled dancers. Emphasizing the positive role of improvisation within a variety of dance contexts, Benjamin offers a range of strategies to support teachers, students, and artists in integrating improvisation within the dance studio. Benjamin's considerable experience, accumulated in part as cofounder and codirector of the UK-based Candoco Dance Company until 1998 and as an improviser himself, affords this text authority and wisdom 'from the inside', and it continues to have relevance today. Perhaps a disappointment is that we have seen so little real change in how dancers with disabilities access dance training in the years since the book's publication, although Benjamin has continued to combine improvisation and inclusion in his own performance work.[1] Improvisation may now be more firmly embedded within the training and education of dancers more generally, and within the community dance sector, but few inclusive training opportunities exist, and consequently only a small professional independent disabled dance community exists in the UK, and the dancers in that community have varying experiences of improvisation within their practice.

A handful of other texts provide a valuable overview of the role of improvisation within dance teaching and practice, frequently including a range of exercises and activities to bring attention to improvisation as a vital aspect of a dancers' experience (Blom and Chaplin 1988; Nagrin 1994; Albright and Gere 2003; Hagendoorn 2008; Biasutti 2013; Schwartz 2000). Because of the openness and freedom that is associated with improvisation, it is a practice that is often enjoyed by differently-abled dancers.[2] On the positive side, improvisation is inherently emancipatory, embodying values that enable disabled dancers to participate on more equal terms with nondisabled dancers. As an approach to artful moving with its own distinctive and underpinning principles, improvisation values human diversity and variation and so finds a place in many corners of the dance sector.

Less positive is that there is often an assumption that improvisation is the only dance practice that can be relevant for differently-abled dancers because it allows for individual 'free expression', thus avoiding the difficulty of adjusting other technical dance practices to accommodate a range of bodies and abilities. Consequently, differently-abled dance artists have understandably had an uneasy relationship with improvisation, yet improvisation has at the same time enabled the disabled dancer to find her own movement 'voice' and a means to be fully involved in the dance. This paradox has meant that on the one hand improvisation is the 'best tool' for inclusion and has provided an entry for disabled dancers into the dance profession (as set out in Benjamin's book), and on the other hand this inclusion means that disabled practitioners can feel marginalized by the very method that enables them to fully participate.[3] However, the increased inclusion of improvisation within the working methods and performance outcomes of established nondisabled choreographers and dance artists[4] has shifted the collective perception of improvisation within professional dance practice, and consequently the previous tension between improvisation and 'technique' within disability dance has been diluted.

Improvisation is now playing a more positive role in disabled dancers' daily practice, as well as within performance, which grows as much out of the dancer's individual body and movement patterns as the choreographer's vision or intention. As I will discuss later, the disabled dancers who have contributed reflections on their experiences for this chapter testify to the positive role that improvisation plays within their daily practice as well as, for some, within performance.

In addition to Benjamin's text, which not only offers tools for teaching but also provides a vivid insight into his own practice, several other texts offer a useful context for considering the extent to which improvisation is incorporated in the teaching and/or practice of differently-abled dancers (Morris et al. 2015; Cheesman 2012; Davies 2010; Kuppers 2011; Whatley 2010). In particular, Albright and Gere (2003) bring together a number of essays with a distinctly North American perspective from practitioners and theorists to counter the view that to improvise 'is to engage in aimless, even talentless, noodling' (Gere 2003: xv). In *Taken By Surprise* and elsewhere (Albright 1997), Albright has written of the 'intriguing possibilities of interdependence' (1997: 262) that mark out improvisation and in particular contact improvisation (CI), which she has taught and practiced for many years.

CONTACT IMPROVISATION AND DISABILITY

As a particular duet form of improvisation, CI has played a significant role in validating the work of disabled dancers since its wide uptake within the dance sector over the last four decades. Contact improvisation prioritizes interaction with different bodies, evolving an aesthetic based on sensory adjustment and accommodation. It calls for a revised gaze that makes space for physical disorientation, disrupting the privileging of the upright, Apollonian, and vertical line of ascension in the dancer.[5] Consequently, CI has been crucial in making it possible for disabled dancers to join the dance community because 'it widened the range and definition of acceptable dance bodies, and it fashioned a movement practice that parallels certain experiences of physical disability' (Davies 2010: 44). Furthermore, as CI has become more embedded in dance training,[6] it has been taught in increasingly codified modes, resulting in it being bound within recognizable and somewhat limited aesthetic territories. It might be argued that through practising CI, disabled dancers 'force' a return to the initial values of the form as a way of bridging the divide between its origins and contemporary approaches.

Steve Paxton, the American dancer who initiated CI in 1972, talks about CI as prioritizing responsiveness and the emerging, 'becoming' nature of the practice (2003: 90). Paxton is the subject of extensive writing about CI, and his own words reveal a lifetime's practical research into improvisation.[7] He writes about the borderland between two aspects of physical control that are accessed in CI—conscious control and reflexive control and claims that when we linger in the borderland on purpose we become our own experiment (Paxton 2003: 177). Conventional dance techniques may be useful—though not necessarily, in his view—for examining the gaps in consciousness during unexpected movement (178). As an alternative to the specific physical or aesthetic goals that are core to conventional dance techniques, CI emphasizes the play with the unexpected and the relinquishing of control and desire for completion. Improvisers may find the play with the unexpected appealing even if it may induce a concurrent fear of the unknown, which can be destabilizing at different moments, whilst ultimately liberating. It is perhaps a different dimension of the 'borderland' that Paxton refers to, where CI can elicit the sensations of either fear and freedom, or both.

Over the years, Paxton has worked with many disabled practitioners, and although the practice was not conceived to bring disability into dance, CI does seem to have 'disable[d] conventional notions of the body in classical and modern dance techniques' (Davies 2010: 45). Contact improvisation also became the primary practice for a programme in the United States, DanceAbility,[8] which has brought together disabled and nondisabled dancers to fulfil the promise of postmodern dance in the 1960s in the United States and to promote access and the egalitarian, democratic idea that dance is for everyone. Regarded as a radical site for questioning ability and disability in dance (Albright 1997: 84), CI has also been a regular part of the practice of AXIS Dance Company, based in San Francisco in the United States. This company is an ensemble of performers with and without disabilities, performing what they describe as 'physically integrated dance'.[9] Performance and disability studies scholar Telory Davies discusses how AXIS employs CI in their work with choreographers Bill T. Jones and Stephen Petronio, describing the role of falling in CI and how 'the prostrate position of the dancer's body in a contact fall places all bodies in a non-hierarchical movement framework' (Davies 2010: 46). Davies also observes that AXIS incorporates CI so as to redefine all body surfaces and external object surfaces as dance sites; thus the wheelchair and other assistive technologies are as valid a dance partner as another human body (48).

Contact improvisation is characterized by its emphasis on using weight and momentum and on freedom, disorientation, friction, vulnerability, and spatial conditioning (Smith 2003: 166). Contact improvisation can be gentle and quiet, and very physical as well. For example, the aikido roll is one of the skills traditionally taught as part of the training. It therefore can be virtuosic and spectacular as well as casual and individualistic. Such contrasting qualities might suggest that CI can be inaccessible for dancers who are unable to participate in such physical spectacle. These contrasts are observed by Albright, who recognizes that within the larger CI community there are two kinds of dancing: 'one that emphasizes virtuosic movement skills and one that emphasizes movement communication that is accessible to any body' (2003b: 210). But these two kinds are perhaps more properly seen on a scale that readily accommodates variation and diversity, thus reconciling the extremes of the virtuosic and the pedestrian. Albright goes on to argue that the CI aesthetic focuses on the process of the dancing communication between two bodies, pointing out that more than any other genre of dance, 'Contact Improvisation has nurtured and embraced dancing that can integrate multiple abilities and limitations' (210).

In relation to scale, Albright speaks from her own experience of CI about the empowering experience of being passive when in the continuum from active to passive in the CI duet (2003a: 264). She discusses how improvising with differently-abled dancers provided a means back into dancing for her during a period of temporary disability (265). It may be that it is this mode of engagement continuum that is so appealing to disabled dancers who are able to negotiate in equal terms with a dancing partner, secure in the knowledge that passivity is as generative as activity, revising the frequent assumption that disabled dancers are always necessarily passive (and thereby dependent on others).

Conversely, the equalizing properties of CI might be seen to 'smooth over' the disorder and involuntary motion that disabled dancing bodies offer as a reconceptualization of the acceptable aesthetic in dance.

In the same collection by Albright and Gere, Bruce Curtis discusses his somatic experience of spinal cord injury and its impact on his dancing in a wheelchair that he states has become a part of his body (2003: 14). He describes his early encounters with CI and how for the first time he 'felt truly equal in the creating of the dance' (15). He talks of the conversation when improvising with another and his recognition that CI enables him to feel supported against the flow of gravity, not afraid to let go of holding on (16). Curtis points to the liberation and joy he feels when improvising in contact with another, and the pleasure in the intimate communication and vulnerability that CI gives him. What Curtis draws attention to is the potential for improvisation, and specifically CI, to unfix identities, in his case a wheelchair user 'bound' to a particular spatial, dynamic, and relational contact with the world, and thus CI becomes a political act of emancipation.

Curtis's journey into CI and his wider performance practice was a significant influence on British multidisciplinary performer and choreographer Claire Cunningham.[10] Cunningham began her performing career as a singer, gradually discovering an affinity with dance and acting that is now core to her work. She describes her formative experience with Curtis, and with dance and improvisation, as 'a "road to Damascus" that all dancers should experience'.[11] She talks of CI providing her 'with a new way of thinking about my body that began with honing my proprioception; with eyes closed, how do I know where my arm is?' This investigation brought her into dance from a sensory place, 'from the inside out'. She describes how 'for the first time, I left my crutches at the side of the studio space and moved without them. At the same time, Curtis was intrigued by the way I incorporated my crutches in everyday movement—sitting on them, hanging from them, often to relieve the pressure I felt on my back due to my impairment—and he asked me to improvise a pathway across the floor'. This opened up new possibilities for how Cunningham could use her crutches in performance 'as pivot points, for shifting my weight', and enabled her to recognize that her impairment was core to the work she makes; 'my crutches became my route to creativity and virtuosic performance'. No longer, she realized, did she need to transcend or 'overcome' her disability to be a dancer; her developing virtuosity in its own terms enabled her to rethink the boundaries between ability and disability, and the language of disability, which is continually fraught with debate about the discriminatory nature of terminology. As Albright points out, '[t]he politics of naming are, needless to say, fraught through and through with the politics of identity' (1997: 59). More particularly, Cunningham's individualistic 'crutch dancing' vocabulary shows that whilst her crutches become an extension of her own body, much as the wheelchair becomes part of the expressive wheelchair dancer's body, she uses them as part of the dramaturgy and to confront the gaze,[12] drawing attention to her unique physicality and her own history of exclusion.

THE ROLE OF IMPROVISATION IN DANCE

As an improviser myself, I am fully aware of how improvising dance forces me, willingly, into a physical awareness which I rarely find elsewhere. Contact improvisation enables me to confront a fear of 'losing control', and I enjoy the dizzying feeling of falling and flying in the fluid and mobile exchange with another. But I am also aware that CI can induce a fear of the unknown, which can be uncomfortable. As a dancer I am all too aware of how improvisation reflects back to me the changing abilities of my aging body; what is liberating for me might be terrifying for a disabled dancer who is more used to contact with another person being about control, restraint, and support to prevent falling. But not for wheelchair dancer and choreographer Caroline Bowditch, who describes her first experience with CI as 'the first time in my life that I felt like I had landed in my skin. I discovered what this strange and awkward body, that had felt so wrong in the world for so long, could do, rather than worrying about what it couldn't do'.[13]

Not all improvisation involves contact with another, whether framed as CI or not, but all improvisation does require training to open the body to new possibilities, to develop trust and curiosity. The physical and conceptual demands of improvisation may not be so apparent to the outsider. As Albright observes, 'improvisation often creates an awareness of aesthetic priorities, compositional strategies, and physical experiences that may, at first, be less visible or less easily discernible' (2003a: 261).

Dance improvisation also fulfils several functions. It can be a method for seeing what happens, between the dancers and between the dancers and the dance (Marks 2003: 135). It encourages an acute awareness of awareness—what Susan Foster describes as a 'hyperawareness of relationalities' and 'playful labor'—bound up in the space/time of the dance itself rather than directed toward the origin of the work prior to the artist and the artwork' (cited in Peters 2009:29). It can be a tool for finding dance material or an end in itself (De Spain 2003: 27).

Improvisation is also principally a marking of the space. Drawing on philosophical readings of the dance artist's occupation and mobilization of space through improvisation also indicates that the space of, or created by, the dance is hardly neutral. As cultural theorist Gary Peters claims in his philosophical account of improvisation, the 'interdependence of the artist and the artwork, ensures that the marking of the unmarked space is not a singular, momentary act but the initiation of a process that ties the artist not to this or that work, each with their own beginnings and endings, but to the *working* of the work that produces both the artwork and the artist' (2009: 13–14; italics in original). However, whilst Peters's argument that the work and the artist are created through the *working* of the work is plausible, it may not be the case that the differently-abled dancer begins in the same 'unmarked' space as does the nondisabled dancer.

Disability tends to mark the space before the dance begins. It marks the audience's expectations as well as the performer's history. It also marks the marketing and preperformance statements that together establish the general milieu in which the performance takes place. As it happens, Peters later acknowledges the problematic of the 'unmarked' space, stating: 'clearly, all spaces are in reality marked by the presence of other works, not least the artist's own, which implies that the ingenuity of origination must find ways to erase or forget the presence of the given in order to both avoid imitation (including self-imitation, perhaps the most common form) and open up the path to be followed' (Peters 2009: 37). The difficulty with the privileging of origination, though perhaps desirable for a 'successful' improvisation, is that it calls for erasure, which implies the need for neutrality. In dance, where the body is both materially representative and physically present, physical difference is made very visible—to cover up disability would be to negate the richness of diversity and difference (Albright 1997: 58). However, when the disabled dancer enters the 'nondisabled' space, as in the main stage theatre,[14] difference can result in unqualified or unfair discrimination. Bowditch recalls when she was touring with Scottish Dance Theatre and performed in *The Long and the Short of It*: 'it was once written up as a community dance piece, obviously based on the fact that I have a disability ... it's not seen as the same quality, it's therapy ... and the reviewer was kind of saying "is it right to have it sit alongside such a professional dance company?"[15] The potential richness provided by Bowditch's different physicality and her queering of the mainstream theatrical space, marked as preserved for the able and virtuosic, seemed to be lost on the reviewer.

The potential for difference and diversity to be source material for improvised performance seems to be a key concern in Adam Benjamin's recent work. In his FATHoM Project, a collective of disabled and nondisabled artists, he explores a range of improvisational strategies that ensure that the individual performers retain agency within the work, free to inhabit the work according to their own abilities. In particular, improvised tasks are given to the performers, and choreographic structures are devised to fully incorporate the wheelchair of Bowditch. Bowditch and her chair are in many ways a central focus for one of the project's works, *Slight* (2008). Much of the movement seems to be sourced from Bowditch's unique habitation of the collaborative theatrical space. Movement focuses on surface, on changing levels (Bowditch raises and lowers her chair to shift her relationship with other performers), and on the exploration of 'seated' movement. Benjamin's other improvised performance practice similarly develops out of his deep interest in integration in dance, the dialogue between different and unfamiliar bodies and an ongoing commitment to ensuring the equal contribution of all performers onstage.[16]

Improvisation is thus part of processing, of making the 'work', and improvisation might be 'the work', and if so, then whilst it may be fluid it will still conform to some ontological conditions of 'work', in that it has at least some structure (and/or intent) and context, which might be determined or decided by a director or might be collectively established. Each instance will thus be different, but subsequent iterations will be connected through title or structure or intent. However, it may not always be clear in performance whether a dance work is improvised, or includes some elements of improvisation. One such work that has a clear theatrical presentational form and choreographic structure but is largely improvised is Thomas Hauert's *Notturnino* (2014),[17] commissioned and performed by Candoco Dance Company.

Candoco Dance Company is a repertory company that tours works commissioned by a wide range of choreographers. Their repertoire and artistic policy has been the focus for many in writing about inclusive/integrated/mixed ability dance and has attracted both praise and criticism for positioning itself within contemporary dance's mainstream. But their consistent commitment to inclusion has made an important challenge to the 'corporeal homogeneity and exclusivity' (Smith 2005: 75) that characterizes the mainstream, 'through their rewriting of the dominant dance manual that insists on the exclusivity of a limited physicality' (75).

Improvisation has not been a particular feature of Candoco Dance Company's work thus far, so *Notturnino* represents something of a departure. Hauert's work has required the dancers to 'be in a specific head—and body—space' and 'bring[s] some of the private processes that happen in the studio to the stage.'[18] Hauert talks about the dancers needing total alertness and presence and how the resulting creative unity produced a kind of utopia.[19] His interest in improvisation is what allows the dance to be more complex if the dancers can invent without consciously commanding movement. He talks about his curiosity in seeing how methods devised for his own normative body worked differently on different bodies. The dancers were required to tune in to each other and to narrow and consider the choices available to them to drive on through the piece.[20] Pedro Machado, previous co–artistic director of Candoco Dance Company, refers to the demands that *Notturnino* also made upon the audience, stating how improvisation gives a new dimension to the unspoken agreement between performers and audiences, who are asked to make sense of some aspects of the theatrical experience, to sense a different mode of performance.[21]

Notturnino is performed by a range of bodies, both nondisabled and disabled. The improvisational structure is informed by the particularities of the dancers' bodies and gives agency to the dancers and so produces an equalizing, collaborative manner of performance. However, there are moments in the dance that are memorable for the focus on the particular physicalities of individual dancers. For example, one dancer, Tanja Erhart, has one leg (although as she says herself, when dancing with her crutches, she also has three legs);[22] in one section she is standing, balancing on her one leg without crutches, surrounded by the other dancers, who are lying on their backs 'doing an exercise for hands and feet' with their legs floating in the air towards her. The image of an abundance of legs set against an absence emphasizes difference whilst also creating an abstracted 'leg dance'. The other dancers' legs and hands are a support for Erhart to assist her in balancing. Together they help to bring more attention to the unique expressive physicality of her dancing as well as the (different) effort involved in what is a familiar challenge for dancers: standing on one leg. Although retaining an improvisational element and quality, the structure at this point is determined.

The unique nature of Erhart's body contributes a particular dynamic and expressive register to the whole dance, which might then appear to be dependent on one dancer's unique contribution. Writing when David Toole was dancing with Candoco Dance Company, Albright proposed that the work of Candoco Dance Company upheld the distinction between the classical (virtuosic) and the grotesque (passive) bodies in the company because of its focus at that time on one exceptional performer (Toole) (1997: 78).[23] The improvisational form in *Notturnino* manages to avoid a similar criticism by emphasizing a democratic, collaborative performance mode (as permitted within the narrative structure) and thereby softening the attention on Erhart. But it is probably unavoidable that a dancer who is visibly *more* different will draw more attention or curiosity and thus be more prominent in the work.

Elsewhere, Erhart's singularity becomes a source for an ensemble section in which all the dancers improvise with crutches, to modify the difference between her and the other members of the company (which includes Rick Rodgers, a wheelchair dancer). The attention switches away from the corporeal to the mechanics of the crutches and the new aesthetic that is created through the way the crutches become extensions of all the dancers' limbs. Erhart believes that the work enables the dancers and the audience to be aware of the changing body and how we may all become disabled. She regards disability as an everyday issue, reminding us all of our own fragility.[24]

Writing through and between Improvisation

The slippery nature of improvisation (Albright 2003a: 260) makes it particularly difficult to talk about and write about, but the growing corpus of writings and reflections that emerge from the practice of dance improvisation are particularly valuable in helping to build a discourse and a theoretical framework for the practice. The contribution of differently-abled dancers to this discourse is valuable and as demonstrated in the writing of those referred to earlier, can bring new insights. But not all appear to welcome the emerging discourse of improvisation. Though not talking specifically about dance, Peters's view is that 'for the last four decades the discourses of improvisation have become increasingly submerged in a collective language of care and enabling, of dialogue and participation, a pure, aesthetically cleansed language of communal love' (2009: 23–24). He refers to improvisation as an exercise in healthy living, claiming that 'the cultural turn toward the spirituality of the East, the self-sufficiency of the land, the concern for peaceful coexistence with the Other 'man', the concern for the ecosystem, the concern for the downtrodden and silenced, all of this has left its indelible mark on the dominant discourses of improvisation as they can be found today' (Peters 2009: 23). Whether or not the specific discourses of *dance* improvisation are part of Peters's critique, dance artist-researchers have acknowledged the challenge in writing through and alongside an embodied practice and have understandably resisted a theorization of improvisation whilst acknowledging the need to find a language for it if it is to be fully included in intellectual discussion.[25] One such practitioner, Kent De Spain, has been concerned with thinking about how to extract meaning from the experience of dance improvisation, describing improvisation as a movement based somatic state (2003: 28–29). His work in exploring the role of language and literacy in dance improvisation acknowledges that language has limits and argues that improvisation is primarily an attentional practice (29). He recognizes that it is important to find a language about the experience but is mindful that what is recorded by each dancer is affected by conscious awareness of proprioception (30), which is a highly individualized condition. Nonetheless, including the voices and experiences of differently-abled dancers is important for expanding our taxonomies of improvisation and the textual reflections on experience.[26]

Building on De Spain's project, I hope that the documenting of some of the experiences of differently-abled dancers working within this sphere of practice who are mentioned in this chapter will contribute to the growing discourse of dance improvisation. Kate Marsh, independent dance artist, researcher, and former performer with Candoco Dance Company, describes an uneasy relationship with improvisation. She says that 'there is often a view of improvisation as "easy" and "accepting" of difference whilst "set" dancing is "challenging" and "proper."' She reports that throughout her career she has been involved in many debates about improvisation being the 'best tool' for inclusion, which can convey the feeling that 'disabled practitioners are limited to improvisation'. Conversely, she believes that the wider incorporation and acceptance of improvisation within the context of the UK professional dance industry has shifted the collective perception of improvisation, and it is now included more readily in dance teaching, blurring the boundaries between 'technique' and improvisation in class. During her time working with Candoco Dance Company, improvisation was often the way in to the creative process, which in practical terms allowed for better access for all the dancers (although she wasn't sure whether the same choreographers would use improvisation for their own choreographic processes).

In her own work, Marsh 'uses improvisation as a way of generating and exploring movement material and rarely as a performance mode'. However, in a recent duet project, she incorporated an improvised solo within a set spatial parameter, so 'timing and spacing were constant but the movement material changed every time and was influenced by various factors; my own movement, the audience, the other dancer and so on'. Her choice to explore improvisation and CI in her practice is based on her belief that 'improvisation and CI offer a greater equality of participation' and therefore offer her greater integrity as a performer: 'there is less emphasis on body specificity, which means that as a dancer with a disability I can explore ways of moving that are more organic for my own body'. As a dance-maker, she explains, she 'is interested in what improvisation offers in terms of allowing each dancer to explore on her own terms, finding it exciting that improvisation affords space for individuality, for change and is less static as a creative form'.[27] Stasis is not a condition readily associated with dance, but what Marsh seems to be referring to is a different kind of relationship with the compositional process. By retaining fluidity in the devising and performing process, improvisation allows for equality in each dancer's contribution, thereby resisting the veneration of virtuosic and augmented disabled bodies that can unintentionally reinscribe the classical body within the body of difference.

Caroline Bowditch also incorporates improvisation within her creative process as a choreographer. Aware of her own very particular physicality and the individual ranges of movement of each of her dancers, she has developed a method that elicits movement from her performers as a response to tasks or concepts that she asks her dancers to perform or reflect in their movement. From this raw material she creates the work. Whilst not unusual as a method, it is informed by a deep awareness of her own nonnormative body and the strategies she needs to develop to direct her company performers. Bowditch has also worked with Fiona Wright as Girl Jonah, and their website explains their working process, referring to improvisation as part of their workshop's offering: 'we will use simple improvisation scores to include dance and text to develop individual inclinations and collaborative structures'.[28]

Artists who blog often share their working process, providing a more informal way of contributing to the discourse of improvisation. For example, StopGap Dance Company provides a very full blog that records the experiences of company members, who post frequently. In documenting reflections on Artificial Things, a creative residency project in 2013 at Pavilion Dance, the National Dance Development Organisation for the South West of England, Lucy Bennett, the artistic director, describes a rehearsal session in which the participants devised a movement-making system developed from 'improvisation that involves quick fire adaptations'. She continues:

> I ask Laura to 'stream' from one end of the studio to the other exploring and repeating a sensation—the other dancers look for alternative adaptations. They take a close look at rhythm, eye line and details such as hand shape and arm line; they quickly dive in and offer their movement translations. Streaming from one side of the studio to the other. If I see something that works, connects or is unusual—we pause and all try it and Laura often finds an adaptation of an adaption of her original movement ... There is a buzz in the studio when we are catching a language—the dancers love to throw ideas into the melting pot, experiment and capture the results. The quick-fire energy aids the instinctive reactions and often the best adaptations.

Laura Jones, to whom Bennett refers here, is a long-standing company member and wheelchair dancer. Jones also blogs about her developing duet with David Toole in the same project, in which they experiment with moving in and around each other, pushing into body parts. She adds: 'we then involved my chair, dismantling it, giving more opportunities for improvisation. This was a more difficult task than expected as we were both so used to moving in our chairs rather than out. However, after investigating further it came together rather quickly'.[29] These blog entries tell us something about the continual investigation that is not only about movement selection and choreographic structure but the additional processes of translation, adaptation, and negotiation of different bodies and physicalities that enrich the practice of improvisation for differently-abled dancers. These other considerations also present the company dancers with additional challenges in and pressures on their creative process.

Catherine Long, a disabled performer, has actively sought writing from those she im-provises with.[30] To support her own development as teacher and dance-maker, she in-vited dancers to give her feedback about being part of a movement group in the United States with a diverse range of experiences, movement ranges, and abilities. Long was the only person in the group with a visible impairment. In particular, she wanted responses to improvising with her visibly different body,[31] and about the awkwardness and fear when entering a space and moving with people one is not familiar with. The workshops were focusing on CI, so most of the responses refer to dancing in contact with Long.

One dancer talks about the warmth, strength, and power exuding from her contact with Long, which shocked this dancer in its intensity. The same respondent shares how she observed others treating Long as a 'fragile being' and reflected on how she realized that by contrast she herself was seen by others as having strength, neither breakable or fragile. These and other responses talk of 'problem solving', 'movement dialogue', and 'intermingling' with Long. Another member of the group talks about her excitement at working with 'another skilled dancer with a different set of tools and ways of moving'. She continues: 'I actually found it much easier to move with you because you were so consistently conscious of the movement decisions you were making, it forced me to slow down and become more conscious as well. There is also an ease, simplicity and efficiency in the way you move—perhaps the way you need to move . . . I didn't see you as someone who 'lacked a limb' but rather a dancer who had learned how to move without a limb—such an interesting skill set'. Some recognized that Long's openness and honesty about her physical condition ('my knees didn't fully develop') put them at ease but also recog-nized that having to explain herself was probably a burden for Long.

Long's own response to the workshop is also revealing. She acknowledges how she 'felt apologetic and awkward when working with some', believing that her body made her partner feel uncomfortable. But she also recognizes that the question about discom-fort is very often present for her, regardless of who she is partnering, so she tries 'to be present with the full experience and go into it'. But when she feels huge discomfort, 'it can result in a sense of almost paralysis', so she does what she can. She talks of 'trying to experiment with how the feeling could be more embodied' but instead resisting it and pretending to do something else, and 'this doing is something else, not reflective of the fear or paralysis, so it feels fake, like I am pretending'. However, Long has also talked about how her process has developed since that time, enabling her to incorporate her experiences into a later solo, *Impasse* (2014). She explains: 'in *Impasse* I performed the awkwardness and incapacity with which my body tends to be associated. The dance included losing balance; stumbling; seeming to be paralyzed, frustrated or debilitated; moving with rigidity or exploding from constraint'.[32]

The discourse of improvisation rarely acknowledges or records the awkwardness that is about discomfort and pain. Although CI can lead to injury, the rhetoric favours the positive impact of freedom, play, collaboration, and democracy, much as Peters argues. Long's approach involves her being honest and clear about her physical impairment and functionality. As she asks: 'if one person has a significantly different range of mo-tion to the other, how is that worked with without it "restricting" one or highlighting the "limits" of one? With essencing/mirroring, is it appropriate for one dancer to not use their left arm? Or reference the fact that they are using it in relation to my absent one, and I reference their "two limbs" with my singular one? (when creating a duet). Do we directly bring the issue in or not?' In these comments, Long reveals what for her is the awkwardness of partnering. She acknowledges the fakery that sometimes results in partnering, which is refreshing and introduces a necessary recalibration to balance the positive, life-affirming rhetoric that might in itself exclude those whose experience is 'other'.

CONCLUSION

This brief survey of the meeting between disability and dance improvisation indicates that improvisation has enabled greater participation in dance by differently-abled dancers and on more equal terms with their nondisabled coperformers. Improvisation enables dancers to find ways of negotiating physical difference and to confront the realities of the moving body. This reality includes accommodating physical and mechanical movement aids and recognizing the actual effort involved, what Davies describes as 'actualism' in her examination of AXIS Dance Company (2010: 44). The integration of CI as a particular strand of improvisation seems to have had a significant impact on extending movement ranges and choreographic strategies for disabled dancers, expanding the possibilities for integrating wheelchairs, crutches, and canes as part of the topological, spatial, and theatrical dance landscape. Contact improvisation is a source of validation and teaches how to interact with different bodies. It also provides space for honest responses to the discomfort of moving, as well as the positive, liberating aspects of improvisation.

The inclusive philosophy that underpins improvisation and has infused professional dance practice as much as community dance practice has enabled more disabled dancers to find a route into dance that has largely shaken off its assumed relationship with therapeutic practice that is based on a medical model of disability, which stigmatizes it as something to be cured, casting 'people with disabilities as "patients", a role that is often infantilizing, pathologizing, and disempowering' (Sandahl and Auslander 2005: 129). Yet there is still more to do before disabled dancers and their presence in dance are no longer a novelty and become the norm. Improvisation enables disabled dancers to find their own movement voices, uninhibited by the external demands of a codified technical practice. But this can reinforce the view that the disabled dancer needs another way of participating in dance, which is separated from the rigours of a professional company process. The division between the 'hard' work of set choreography and the more accessible process of improvisation is now softening, with appropriate respect being afforded to the challenge of improvisation as a performance mode. The incorporation of improvisation with mainstream dance, including within the repertoire of inclusive dance companies (such as Hauert's commission for Candoco Dance Company) has helped to support this shift. As a consequence, dance improvisation is much richer for adopting disability in its shifting physical aesthetic.

Dancers are now finding more platforms for writing through and about dance improvisation. The increasing number of artist blogs and websites has helped to extend the means by which dancers can share their experiences and reflections on or about improvisation. My intention in this chapter has been to highlight the value of these records whilst also bringing attention to UK dance artists who may have received critical attention through performance reviews but have not been the focus of scholarly writing thus far. I hope I have shown that improvisation can be a powerful tool in reducing the binaries that have long plagued disabled dance—between ability and disability, fixed and fluid, active and passive, and so on. At the same time, disabled dancers have forced a revision in traditional ways of working, moving, thinking, and looking at dance.

Notes

I am grateful to the dance artists who have openly shared their experiences with me, thereby providing very valuable information for this chapter: Kate Marsh, Catherine Long, Claire Cunningham, and Caroline Bowditch. I am also grateful to my colleagues in the InVisible Difference; Dance, Disability and Law project, who have helped with the collection of some this data. For more on this project, see https://invisibledifferenceorguk.wordpress.com/, accessed 25 March 2017.

1. See Adam Benjamin's website for a chronology of his improvisation work: http://www.adambenjamin.co.uk/home.html, accessed September 20, 2014.
2. I use both the terms 'disabled' and 'differently-abled' in the chapter but no distinction is implied. I incorporate 'differently-abled' because some dancers with disabilities prefer this term.
3. The dancers who comment in this essay make reference to this tension. Another example of the problem that can ensue when 'improvisation' is assumed to be the best way of accessing dance for disabled people is captured in a published conversational essay between performance practitioners Petra Kuppers and Neil Marcus. Reflecting on a contact improvisation festival, Marcus comments: 'I am not easy with the word crip. Still. But I'll use it here as shorthand.... We were crips at this contact festival. They were thrilled to have us as some of their focus was 'mixed abilities', an awful term in my mind. Reminds me of dog breeding. They were very interested in being sensitive to the needs of crips ... but they ended up being so 'careful' and 'sensitive' it was very irritating. And I felt very insulted. yuck! and excluded anyway' (Kuppers and Marcus 2009: 146).
4. For example, in the UK such choreographers/companies include, amongst others, Siobhan Davies, Russell Maliphant, Motionhouse, Charlie Morrissey.
5. See Smith (2005) for more reference to disability in relation to the Apollonian frame.
6. A quick glance at course content indicates that most university and conservatoire dance programmes in the UK include improvisation in the curriculum, either as a focused studio-based practice or woven through other activities. Improvisation also features in most of the prominent dance training institutions across Europe and in North America. A more extensive survey of the place of improvisation worldwide is beyond the scope of this chapter.

7. The journal *Contact Quarterly*, founded in 1975 and coedited by Nancy Stark Smith and Lisa Nelson, is the principal publication about contact improvisation, presenting 'the artist's voice in the artist's words'. Paxton is a supporting editor, and his work features regularly in the journal. 'Mixed-abilities dance' is specifically mentioned in the description of the practices that are presented within the journal. See http://www.contactquarterly.com/cq/cq_contactq.php, accessed 27 September 2014.

8. DanceAbility International states that it 'continues to pursue its vision of using art as a means to change people's preconceived ideas about disabilities through performances, workshops, educational programs, teacher training and choreography in the U.S. and throughout the world'. The cofounder and artistic director is Alito Alessi. See http://www.danceability.com, accessed 20 September 2014.

9. See http://axisdance.org/about-us/, accessed 20 September 2014.

10. See http://www.clairecunningham.co.uk, accessed 17 September 2014.

11. All these comments are taken from an interview with Claire Cunningham by the author, 18 July 2013.

12. There isn't space here to discuss the different ways the disabled dancer is looked at, but Cunningham's performance work confronts the ways both women's bodies and impaired bodies are looked at. A number of theorists discuss the gaze in relation to disability, notably Garland Thomson (2009).

13. See interview with Caroline Bowditch by Victoria Wright published on 15 September 2014 in Disability Arts Online, a website showcasing arts and culture: http://www.disabilityartsonline.org.uk/caroline-bowditch-falling-in-love-with-frida, accessed 15 February 2015.

14. By 'main stage' I refer to traditional, proscenium arch Western theatre venues. In dance, large and middle-scale companies, including repertory companies, are generally those programmed in these venues. Few disabled dancers have the opportunity to perform in them, one notable exception in the UK being Candoco Dance Company.

15. See interview with Caroline Bowditch by Victoria Wright published on 15 September 2014 in Disability Arts Online, a website showcasing arts and culture: http://www.disabilityartsonline.org.uk/caroline-bowditch-falling-in-love-with-frida, accessed 15 February 2015.

16. For example, Benjamin's work *5 Men Dancing* (2004–present).

17. Thomas Hauert is a Swiss-born choreographer who is particularly interested in improvisation-based processes.

18. Pedro Machado, previous co–artistic director of Candoco Dance Company, in his blog 'Candoco's improv dance brings the spirit of rehearsal to the stage', *Guardian*, 27 February 2014, http://www.theguardian.com/stage/dance-blog/2014/feb/27/candoco-improv-dance-rehearsals-stage, accessed 2 April 2014.

19. Hauert speaking on the film, 'Notturnino – Candoco Dance Company' Candoco Dance Company website, http://www.candoco.co.uk/productions/repertory/current/new-company-work/ accessed 26 September 2014.

20. Hauert speaking on the film, 'Insight: Making of Notturnino by Thomas Hauert: Candoco Dance Company' Candoco Dance Company website, http://www.candoco.co.uk/productions/repertory/current/new-company-work/, accessed September 20, 2014.

21. Pedro Machado, previous co–artistic director of Candoco Dance Company, in his blog 'Candoco'simprovdancebringsthespiritofrehearsaltothestage',*Guardian*,27February2014,

http://www.theguardian.com/stage/dance-blog/2014/feb/27/candoco-improv-dance-rehearsals-stage, accessed 2 April 2014.
22. Erhart speaking on the film 'Notturnino – Candoco Dance Company' Candoco Dance Company website, http://www.candoco.co.uk/productions/repertory/current/new-company-work/, accessed 20 September 2014.
23. David Toole was born without legs. He danced with Candoco Dance Company until 1999 and has since performed in his own work, with other companies, and as part of the 2012 Summer Paralympics opening ceremony in London, 29 August 2012.
24. Erhart speaking on the film, 'Notturnino – Candoco Dance Company', Candoco Dance Company website, http://www.candoco.co.uk/productions/repertory/current/new-company-work/, accessed 20 September 2014.
25. Albright speaks to this point in her own writing (2003a: 260–261).
26. The lack of writing documenting the work of disabled dancers is one of the areas of study conducted by the research team in the Arts and Humanities Research Council funding project InVisible Difference; Dance, Disability and Law. See http://www.invisibledifference.org.uk, accessed 26 September 2014.
27. Kate Marsh, email communications to author, July–September 2014.
28. Girl Jonah website, http://www.girljonah.org/workshops.html, accessed 26 September 2014.
29. 'Artificial Things – An Insight from the Artistic Director Lucy Bennett' Stopgap Dance Company blog, posted 12 February 2013, http://stopgapdance.com/blog/artificial-things-creative-residency-at-pavilion-dance, accessed 26 September 2014.
30. The comments from Long and her workshop attendees were shared with me by email, September 2014.
31. Long is very clear with her respondents about her disability, describing to them the nature of her physical impairment.
32. Email correspondence with author, September 2014.

REFERENCES

Albright, Ann Cooper. (1997) *Choreographing Difference: The Body and Identity in Contemporary Dance*. Middletown, CT: Wesleyan University Press.
Albright, Ann Cooper. (2003a) Dwelling in Possibility. In Albright, Ann Cooper, and Gere, D. (eds.), *Taken By Surprise: A Dance Improvisation Reader*. Middletown, CT: Wesleyan University Press, 257–266.
Albright, Ann Cooper. (2003b) Present Tense: Contact Improvisation at Twenty-Five. In Albright, Ann Cooper, and Gere, D. (eds.), *Taken by Surprise: A Dance Improvisation Reader*. Middletown, CT: Wesleyan University Press, 205–214.
Albright, Ann Cooper, and Gere, D. (eds.). (2003) *Taken by Surprise: A Dance Improvisation Reader*. Middletown, CT: Wesleyan University Press, xii–xxl.
Benjamin, A. (2002) *Making an Entrance; Theory and Practice for Disabled and Non-disabled Dancers*. Abingdon, UK: Routledge.
Biasutti, M. (2013) Improvisation in Dance Education: Teacher Views. *Research in Dance Education* 14(2): 120–140.
Blom, L. A., and Chaplin, T. (1988) *The Moment of Movement: Dance Improvisation*. Pittsburgh: University of Pittsburgh Press.

Cheesman, S. (2012) A Dance Teacher's Dialogue on Working within Disabled/Non-disabled Engagement in Dance. *International Journal of the Arts in Society* 6(3): 321–330.

Curtis, B. (2003) Exposed to Gravity. In Albright, Ann Cooper, and Gere, D. (eds.), *Taken by Surprise: A Dance Improvisation Reader* (Middletown, CT: Wesleyan University Press, 13–20.

Davies, T. (2010) Mobility: AXIS Dancers Push the Boundaries of Access. In Henderson, B., and Ostrander, N. (eds.), *Understanding Disability Studies and Performance Studies*. Abingdon, UK: Routledge, 43–63.

De Spain, K. (2003) The Cutting Edge of Awareness: Reports from the Inside of Improvisation. In Albright, Ann Cooper, and Gere, D. (eds.), *Taken by Surprise: A Dance Improvisation Reader*. Middletown, CT: Wesleyan University Press, 27–40.

Garland Thomson, R. (2009) *Staring: How We Look*. Oxford: Oxford University Press.

Gere, D. (2003) Introduction to Albright, Ann Cooper, and Gere, D. (eds.), *Taken by Surprise: A Dance Improvisation Reader*. Middletown, CT: Wesleyan University Press.

Hagendoorn, I. (2008) Emergent Patterns in Dance Improvisation and Choreography. In Minai, A., and Bar-Yam, Y. (eds.), *Unifying Themes in Complex Systems IV: Proceedings of the Fourth International Conference on Complex Systems*. Berlin: Springer-Verlag, 183–195.

Hauert, T. (2014) *Notturnino*. UK: Candoco Dance Company.

Kuppers, P. (2011) *Disability Culture and Community Performance: Find a Strange and Twisted Shape*. UK: Palgrave Macmillan.

Kuppers, P. (2014) *Studying Disability Arts and Culture: An Introduction*. Basingstoke, UK: Palgrave Macmillan.

Kuppers, P., and Marcus, N. (2009) Contact/Disability Performance: An Essay Constructed between Petra Kuppers and Neil Marcus. *Research in Drama Education: The Journal of Applied Theatre and Performance* 14(1): 141–155.

Marks, V. (2003) Against Improvisation: A Postmodernist Makes the Case of Choreography. In Albright, Ann Cooper, and Gere, D. (eds.), *Taken by Surprise: A Dance Improvisation Reader*. Middletown, CT: Wesleyan University Press, 135–140.

Morris, M. L., Baldeon, M., and Scheuneman, D. (2015) Developing and Sustaining an Inclusive Dance Program: Strategic Tools and Methods. *Journal of Dance Education* 15(3): 122–129.

Nagrin, D. (1994) *Dance and the Specific Image: Improvisation*. Pittsburgh: University of Pittsburgh Press.

Paxton, S. (2003) Drafting Interior Techniques. In Albright, Ann Cooper, and Gere, D. (eds.), *Taken by Surprise: A Dance Improvisation Reader*. Middletown, CT: Wesleyan University Press, 175–184.

Peters, G. (2009) *The Philosophy of Improvisation*. Chicago: University of Chicago Press.

Schwartz, P. (2000) Action Research: Dance Improvisation as Dance Technique. *Journal of Physical Education, Recreation and Dance* 71(5): 42–46.

Smith, O. (2005) Shifting Apollo's Frame: Challenging the Body Aesthetic in Theater Dance. In Sandahl, C., and Auslander, P. (eds.), *Bodies in Commotion: Disability and Performance*. Ann Arbor: University of Michigan Press, 73–85.

Stark Smith, N. (2003) A Subjective History of Contact Improvisation. In Albright, Ann Cooper, and Gere, D. (eds.), *Taken by Surprise: A Dance Improvisation Reader*. Middletown, CT: Wesleyan University Press, 153–174.

Whatley, S. (2010) The Spectacle of Difference: Dance and Disability on Screen. *International Journal of Screendance* 1(1): 41–52.

CHAPTER 24

....

ARTFUL HUMANIZING CONVERSATIONS

Improvisation in Early Years Dance

....

KERRY CHAPPELL AND LIZZIE SWINFORD

'ARTFUL humanizing conversations' describes the way in which we have come to think about both our dance and our research practice. In debating our thoughts about improvisation in early years dance, we have grown and developed three themes in these conversations which have helped us to understand and articulate the dynamics of this practice: *knowing yourself in your body, dialogues with children*, and *making and being made*. These themes are particularly significant for the children featured in this chapter as they are experiencing the beginnings of their life and relationships; they are at the start of knowing who they are and how they relate to others. The children we talk about are aged two to four years. They are engaging in artist-led workshops, some in a mainstream UK state preschool setting and some in a weekly independent dance and storytelling session which they attend with a parent. These children are learning to dance and are learning life skills through dance, as a creative and aesthetically driven exploration, as opposed to a practice of watch and do. The pedagogies we discuss are giving them experience in relationships through dialogue.

In considering improvisation in early years dance, we have found it especially fruitful to frame our thinking in terms of the theory of wise humanizing creativity (WHC). This idea has been lead-developed by Kerry with a team of researchers at the University of Exeter and Trinity Laban in the period up until 2016 (e.g., Chappell, Rolfe, Craft, and Jobbins 2011). This theory involves attending to the ethics of creativity; what matters to the community within which new ideas and movements are being created is entwined within the creative process. At its heart, WHC is driven by the dialogic connection between creativity and identity; creators are both making and being made. This kind of creativity sees people going on journeys of becoming.

In terms of WHC, we see the children with whom we work learning to work as a group and becoming themselves. This draws strongly on the three themes of *knowing yourself, dialogues with children*, and *making and being made*, which we will discuss. This kind of improvisational dance practice means that children are active in creating and expressing themselves in a personal way. It seems to uniquely give children space for this learning process because it is embodied—so inextricably 'me'. At the end of the chapter, we will go on to connect the idea of WHC and the three early years themes to wider debates within education about how creativity might be positioned and how important improvisational, aesthetic, and embodied (or 'soma'-based) practice is in understanding how to do so, set against more rationalist, marketized views of education and adult day-to-day existence.

Origins of the Ideas

Our analysis and discussions, which we present thematically here, have developed recently as part of ongoing work we have been doing, together and separately. This includes collaborative action research within the Devon Carousel Project (Chappell, Pender, Swinford, and Ford 2016), a mentored solo action research process, and action research for M-level study, all connected in some way to explorations of the WHC idea. Our ideas about improvisation in early years dance have emerged from an overarching analysis of data and writing across these projects.

Both of us are mixtures of dance practitioner, researcher, and mum, the latter of which has perhaps been the driver for us dipping our toes into movement and dance work in the early years. Kerry is an education/dance education academic and dance artist specializing in creativity and educational futures. She has worked increasingly in the last ten years to develop more flattened hierarchies within her research and has developed with Anna Craft the practice of Living Dialogic Spaces (Chappell and Craft 2011). This practice is about using creative learning conversations to bring academics, practitioners, and children and young people into as equal a research experience (offering potential for everyone's contribution) as is possible and appropriate within a particular project. Shared curiosity and passion for the research area are key, with different research partners using the research practice for their own developmental ends, as well as the research team aiming to find common ground through both research process and product (e.g., Chappell, Rolfe, Craft, and Jobbins 2011). Issues of quality, trustworthiness, and rigour in these kinds of research relationships are complex and challenging. We are all constantly involved, sometimes individually, sometimes collaboratively, in making informed decisions about analysis and the ensuing representations of outcomes that are differently manifested in different contexts.

Lizzie is a dance practitioner based in Exeter with a background as a dance artist and teacher, working with children and adults in further and higher education. In the last few years she has focused on dance with early years children. Her work has been influenced by the interdisciplinary context of the Devon Carousel Project, where, working with visual artists, she has developed her approach to involve play and exploration rather than a more traditional teacher-led strategy.

Kerry initially became involved with Lizzie in the Devon Carousel Project (http://www.thecarouselproject.org.uk) as a mum taking two young children along to drop-in sessions at her local children's centre. But Kerry quite quickly found common questions with the Carousel artists, about creativity, early years arts practice, and children's experiences. This led to us developing a collaborative action research model in which Kerry mentored the Carousel team and we all took part in creative learning conversations within Living Dialogic Spaces. The research asked two questions: What is the approach of the Carousel artists? What are the children getting from the Carousel approach? The activity was being facilitated by three Carousel artists in a local nursery school once a week for six weeks. Their theme was circles. The research team used observation schedules, research photography, film, creative artefacts, and reflective journaling to collect data. Thematic analysis was carried out with triangulation across the data and between researchers, and the project resulted in a short research film (http://www.thecarouselproject.org.uk/playing-with-circles/).

The mentored solo action research process was part of a 2013 scheme (hereafter the UoE Catalyst/DNA project) run with Dance Network Active (DNA) (http://dancenetworkactive.wordpress.com) and funded by the University of Exeter Catalyst Scheme. This provided two funded six-month action research bursaries to dance practitioners/researchers who were local to the university, one of whom was Lizzie. Her action research asked the question 'What is the adult's role when using play in early years creative dance?' The research took place over six weeks at a preschool setting, with contact with the children and practitioners twice a week during that time, and was mentored by Kerry. It used observations, reflections, photographs, and film to collect qualitative data that were analysed inductively, using a grounded approach: looking at the data with an open mind to see what themes emerged rather than using existing theories to interpret it. Analysis was triangulated both between data sources and between Lizzie as the researcher and Kerry as research mentor.

The action research for M-level study was focused around Flim Flam (https://www.facebook.com/flimflam1234)—a weekly dance and storytelling session that Lizzie runs for two-year-olds and their families, which Kerry was attending at the time with her young son. Most weeks centre on a story, which we tell together in dance. Lizzie's aim is to draw out movement ideas from the children, stimulate their imaginations, and celebrate their individuality. There is always a strong element of play and exploration, which enables her to develop the ideas initiated in the UoE Catalyst/DNA project, but this element is structured alongside more teacher-led time, as Lizzie is always aware of balancing parents' expectations with a flexible child-centred approach. It is a drop-in session so she has to work to ensure people will come back! Lizzie chose this group to work with as part of her master's degree in education at the University of Exeter (http://socialsciences.exeter.ac.uk/education/graduatestudies/masters/maeducation/), investigating how dance and mark-making can contribute to children's awareness of themselves. This work is also a continuation of a piece of action research initiated during a collaboration with an artist-printmaker (the Devon Carousel Project's Arts Council England-funded Round and Round You Turn Me research; see https://www.thecarouselproject.org.uk/round-round-turn/

As our paths continually crossed within these projects, we kept stumbling into the question of what it was the children were doing when they were exploring so physically. Was it dance, and what were Lizzie, as a practitioner, and Kerry, as a parent with a background as a practitioner and researcher, doing in relation to it? In focusing our thinking on early years dance improvisation, we decided to go back and review all of the data from the projects detailed above, analysing through the new lens of asking two questions: What is improvisation in early years dance? How might it be connected to WHC? This has involved a conversation between inductive and deductive analysis which has allowed us to find answers to this question, which we offer thematically below. Italicization across the following sections indicates quotes from the three original data sets, which we reanalysed. Other nonitalicized text hereafter indicates our shared opinion as a result of the analysis, unless we name ourselves separately.

Knowing Yourself in Your Body

The first answer emerged, in our discussions and analysis, as children being able to 'know themselves in their body'. It became apparent that the aesthetic and artistic

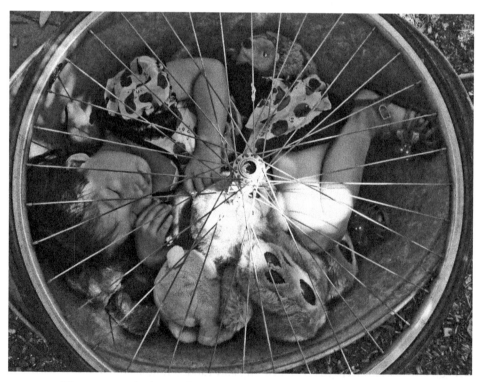

FIG. 24.1 Closeness, enveloping, enclosing, wrapping, covering, Sian feeling safe and snug.

part of this is vital to the children's experiences. This is dance—the children are not arbitrarily exploring their physicality. Their movements may not replicate adult dance gestures and may challenge our ideas of what dance is. But they flow from their own independent creativity and imagination. They are expressive of their inner impulses and exhibit the purposeful dynamic actions and body shapes of dance. They are playing, exploring, and problem-solving within a dance space which is explicitly and intuitively created and held by Lizzie with all her dance artist's knowledge and experience. It is a particular and special kind of knowing yourself which we discuss next, beginning with a close-up insight into Sian's world. Sian is a little girl at nursery with English as an additional language who really showed us how crucial physical and aesthetic experiences can be in children coming to know themselves.

Clare (early years practitioner, observations and reflections on fig. 24.1):
Closeness, enveloping, enclosing, wrapping, covering, feeling safe and snug.

FIG. 24.2 Being safe.

Flying Away, Being Safe

Clare (early years practitioner, observations and reflections):

Sian likes to feel close, and Lizzie enabled her to be very intimate and physically closer to an adult in the nursery than she may usually be. This is seen in fig. 24.2. The time with Lizzie has facilitated relationships with other adults, especially me. On both occasions, Sian has involved me in the exploration by creeping up on me, passing me animals, tickling me even though I am on the outskirts as an observer.

I wonder if she likes to be close and snug with her family at home. How we can share our observations with her school and family? This has made me wonder how her life is, because we saw an insight into her that we would never have seen before.

Sian was a monster, [she] fed Lizzie then she was a bird. fig. 24.3 shows she was playful, active and very, very engaged.

FIG. 24.3 Sian being playful, active, and very, very engaged.

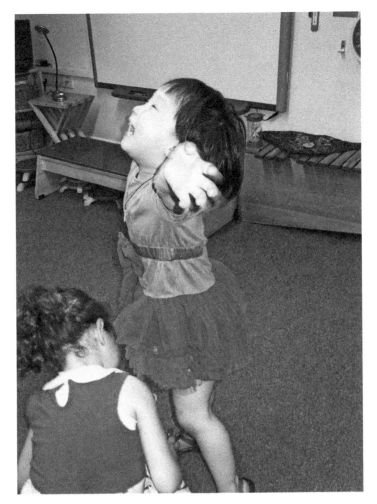

FIG. 24.4 Sian feels enjoyment, excitement.

Clare (early years practitioner, observations and reflections on fig. 24.4):

Laughing, giggling, copying, watching, flying. Sian feels enjoyment, excitement, freedom, and fun. I wonder how much the language barrier impacts on provision for Sian. I wonder how much we really know her.

Clare (early years practitioner, observations and reflections on fig. 24.5):

Sian gets deeply involved in the activities with Lizzie. She appears to feel safe. She enjoyed the modelling game. She didn't shy away. It was also wonderful to hear the children discover new skills about their peers and possibly see them in a different light. Children who may often take a step back from such an activity, particularly the children with English as an additional language, were totally involved and having fun.

FIG. 24.5 Sian deeply involved with Lizzie.

Lizzie (visiting dance practitioner, reflections): Before Clare mentioned her interest in Sian, I engaged with her as with any other lively four-year-old. We didn't say much, but that wasn't unusual—after all, we were dancing, not talking. Clare mentioned that Sian didn't speak English at nursery. She felt she was consequently often on the edge of things. Clare was thrilled to see her fully engaged and in the centre of the action.

When I looked back at one of the session films, I could see that Sian was not listening to my explanations. She joined in as she saw what was happening, responding entirely to movement with movement. She was open and alert to physical cues, diving in and entering the activities in a nonverbal but fully immersed way. As her confidence grew and relationships were secured, she took a lead role in the play and improvisations.

As we have analysed and reflected on the exploratory adventures of young children like Sian, we have started to see more clearly how improvisational dance manifests with a group of children who are still mainly driven by their physicality. Kathy Nutbrown (2013) has talked about the role of the arts in early years education being so vital because pre-school children experience the world through their 'aesthetic-incunabula' (Dissanayake 2001: 336)—a kind of aesthetic enveloping which makes the emotional effects of the arts discernible from early on and dominates their interactions with the world. In understanding the notion of the children 'knowing themselves in their body', a physical perception of themselves that encompasses the mind and is not separated from it, Nutbrown's ideas are important. She cites how Clough (2002) refers to the human need to experience the world through the aesthetic as 'aesthetic attending'; Clough suggests that we innately attend to the objects and people we encounter through our senses. The children in the sessions detailed above seem to be exploring the world via their aesthetic attention in their improvisations and so coming to learn about and through themselves.

This kind of improvisational learning about self through the body has also been identified by Jasmine Pasch, a highly experienced UK early years dance practitioner (LeVoguer and Pasch 2014). Writing with LeVoguer about children's creeping and crawling, she draws on Walsh (2004), who states that 'autonomy, assurance, and resilience are experienced through repeated opportunities for children to wrestle with problem solving and to independently follow their own desires' (LeVoguer and Pasch 2014: 98). We see this in our example, as children in the sessions experience both the world and the way they themselves interact with it through physically improvising with ideas and problem-solving. Moments where Sian curls her body inside a barrel, emerges from fabric, or uses touch in her play are resonant with what LeVoguer and Pasch refer to as 'companionable movement' (104) and with Sherbourne's Developmental Movement method, where activities stimulate the tactile sense and develop children's awareness of themselves and their bodies (Sherbourne 2001: 111).

Greenland also affirms this succinctly on the basis of her own work with Jabadao (the creators of DMP—Developmental Movement Play) in the early years, when she says 'the body is our first home' (2009: 9) and the value of movement is to 'support children's natural ability to embody the whole of their lives' (8), making a link between the use of the body and life itself. Writing about Italian Reggio Emilia practice, the words of Malaguzzi are useful here, too, as he explains that the use of creativity and the arts help children find ways to express their 'me-ness' (1987: 47). Where Sian was perhaps at a disadvantage because of her lack of English, her 'me-ness' becomes increasingly evident to her teachers in their reflections, as they watch her move and move responsively with her.

Following on from this, we would argue that early years dance improvisation is a practice in its own right because of the way early years children are living in their bodies and the experiences they have had to date. They are in the early stages of language development. Embodied communication with few words is more significant day to day and is the key to their interaction with the world and others. Shusterman's (2008) concept of the 'soma' is helpful here; he discusses this as the body and mind working together as an embodied whole. In the early years we see the operation of the soma very clearly—the body and mind integrated together as the child responds to the sensory world in a direct and fluid way through means of physical rather than verbal expression. This integration is perhaps more easily accessible than in the average adult. And it may even also be more accessible than for a professional dancer/improvisers who, it might be said, have to work to find this body-mind interconnection in the studio, away from the different body-mind balance of their day-to-day existence.

Shusterman sees the soma as 'a locus of sensory-aesthetic appreciation and creative fashioning' (2004: 51), so in improvisation the body-mind can work in a unique combination of discovery and creation. In a very young body-mind, existing via the soma is very close to a child's default day-to-day way of being, and perhaps, we might argue, coupled with the fact that they are relatively unhindered by dance knowledge and conventions, means that they are able to improvise in dance in a way that is extremely difficult to access for an adult. For the practitioner, one's role becomes more about finding ways to foreground this innate physicality and the operation of the soma. This often involves following in the slipstream of the flow of this embodied creativity, witnessing and facilitating before stepping forward.

We can also find connections between the notion of knowing yourself in your body and the way in which professional dance practice highlights empathy within improvisation. Ribeiro and Fonseca are alert to this. Where we have observed Sian relating to others through movement, we can see resonance with how Ribeiro and Fonseca describe improvisation as how we put ourselves in another's position and try to predict future interactions. Interestingly, they connect this to work in neuroscience which argues that 'mirror neurons allow this connection between the self and the other' (2011: 78). They talk about how this helps to understand other people and their intentions through 'kinesthetic empathy' (79) where 'movements are observed and performed in a continuous process of action and reaction based on the sharing of intentions' (80). We've also seen this responsive, equal communication without words in movement activities with babies. This turn-taking and mirroring dance is a significant way in which babies initiate and build relationships with adults and their peers. We have seen these movement conversations starting as early as four months, with mutual shifts of weight, supporting, pushing against, wriggling, and allowing space.

For young children to get to know themselves through their bodies, they are attending aesthetically, empathetically, in an embodied way; as Smith has suggested in relation to professional dance improvisation, they are becoming 'attuned to self' and 'giving and receiving of each other through lived movement experiences' (2002: 128); yet they do this within an especially embodied body which we adults find more difficult to access than our more dominantly verbalized everyday experience of the world. This idea of 'giving and receiving of each other' brings us to our next theme, where adults can perhaps have their embodiment reawakened via *dialogues with children*. We introduce this idea with an excerpt from one of Lizzie's reflective journals.

DIALOGUES WITH CHILDREN

Lizzie (reflections):   I wonder a lot about how I'm working with the children. I feel I'm in conversation with them; there's dialogue. In this situation, then, I wonder what is my role as an adult? Is it any different to theirs?

Am I a model for them? This is tricky to identify. Although it happens, I'm more often conscious of it not happening successfully. This is part of the reason for developing my work towards a more improvisational interactive approach. I aim to improvise with them; finding relationships and modeling using my whole body with a sense of focus and freedom.

FIG. 24.6 Andrew exclaims 'I'm flying'.

Andrew exclaims: 'I'm flying!'
They do often seem to be experiencing freedom. The lycra web structure (fig. 24.6)
encouraged high-energy movement. It provided an environment for the children's
improvisations but allowed them to step in and out as they chose. They used it like a
climbing frame, jumping over and under, enjoying getting tangled up and rescuing
each other. Some were very inventive in how they found different ways and body parts
to push against the threads.
I observed a delight in working on a large scale and enjoyment of being enveloped.
Their play was mostly based not in imitation but in enjoying physicality.
But if there is this freedom, how do I offer a useful structure? When do I need to
step in? I remember two girls making the web into something completely different—
constructing a 'Kieran trap' using a pulley system connecting the tree with the web.
This was not what I envisaged. I deliberated—should I intervene and try to return
them to the web theme? I didn't want to because what they were doing looked really
interesting and fun. I loved their creativity and autonomy.
I asked myself—was it dance? Even movement? Did that matter? What they were doing
was shaping the space, which in a sense is what dance does. Wasn't the learning experience
more important? This is something I find so exciting about using play in movement
work—it enables the physical starting point to bleed into different learning areas.
Clare has talked about waiting for the cue to join in with the children's play. When
they made the Kieran trap, I didn't have an invitation so I decided to just watch and
see where it led.

FIG. 24.7 Adult as anchor.

> *Knowing when to step back and when to interact with them is difficult. Laura-Jane, another early years practitioner at the setting (fig. 24.7), has explained that you can support children 'just by being with them'.*
>
> *I experienced this myself at the nursery. Bob was engaged with Andrew in leaning back on the lycra. Others were busy in the web we had made. They seemed to be playing and moving independently of me. I wanted to take a photo and found what I thought was a good moment to nip off and get my camera when they wouldn't notice. I came back after only about ten seconds. Everyone except Sian was leaving; they had lost interest. It seemed I was helping them to stay engaged somehow even though I didn't feel that I was doing much.*

Here we can see early years dance challenging leaders' ideas about what dance is. The children's creativity crosses media; they express themselves and their ideas with their bodies, by building, vocalizing, mark-making, and sometimes all at once. Adult responses need to be flexible and intuitive, demonstrating an expansive view of children's capability that stretches boundaries between art forms. We need to be able to observe and follow as well as lead.

Sometimes, as with Laura Jane and Lizzie here, we did not need to feel we were 'doing much'. Tina Bruce has identified how an adult can be an 'anchor' (2004: 25) for a child's creative involvement. With 'sensitive companionship' we can provide the security and confidence which allows children to concentrate, experiment, and let their ideas 'flow' (25). This is a role it can take confidence to inhabit as a practitioner, as from the outside it can seem to involve doing very little.

A sensitive companion will know when to support, suggest, and encourage. As the foregoing reflections reveal, questions of how and when to become involved arise frequently. To mirror or respond to a child's movement can initiate a dialogue. To introduce a new provocation or dynamic can take a conversation in a new direction. Throughout our dancing with the children, the notion of active dialogue has been very important. This is the nature of our involvement; a kind of dialogue that spirals through question and answer, and questioning again. The Reggio idea of the 'pedagogy of listening' seems key here; this is learning that takes place between adults and children through relationships and the encountering of new ideas and different points of view (Vecchi 2010: 2). Through observation and interaction in movement, there is an embodied communication, empathy, and 'silent agreement between improvisation partners' (Ribeiro and Fonseca 2011: 80). In duet and group improvisations, we can work within a system of exchange where gestures and ideas are shared. Again, Reggio practitioners have recognized this idea. Bonilauri and Filippini have observed that 'the systems of giving, exchange ... nourish a child in a sense of belonging' (1987: 173), enabling them to operate as a responsive and active part of a community or indeed part of a dance experience. The question and answer and question in this kind of active dialogue allows improvisations to occur which feed both the children and the practitioner, connecting back to the idea of *knowing yourself through your body*, but also extending it to emphasize the importance of that knowledge being embedded in a communal experience.

Lizzie thinks that this is why she finds the idea of being a model difficult, as it does not necessarily involve dialogue. However, you can model an attitude of responsiveness and freedom, which is what she aims to do with the children. Nutbrown writes of adults as 'models of users and makers of art' (2013: 240). Perhaps this is a more open and democratic idea; we 'use' and 'make' dance together. Similarly, Shagoury Hubbard (1996) talks of teachers as mentors—being active, 'making and doing as well as instructing' (1996: 47). She also mentions the children's ability to 'apprentice themselves to other learners' (151). This web of models or mentors across the group creates a kind of community: a safe place to improvise and share ideas.

We have come to the conclusion that for an equal dialogue to occur, children must feel free to discover what it is they want to communicate. Greenland asserts that 'children are biologically programmed to seek out the optimum experiences to provide them with the required stimulation' (2009: 12). Lizzie, especially, feels that they do not need constant direction but at times need to be left to explore, to improvise. But in a teaching situation, the line between freedom and disorder is a subjective one. For some, the tipping point into anarchy comes almost immediately when physical freedom is offered. For others, the children's sense of agency and empowerment is paramount.

Halprin is a relevant example here. Ross records her sense that 'a certain amount of chaos didn't bother the children, why should it bother me?' (2003: 50). However, Ross also notes Halprin's desire to find a 'balance between structure and freedom' (42) and her use of structures that told the children what to do but not how to do it (50). Her aim was to provide frameworks, ideas, spaces, and opportunities but not to dictate how the children should respond to them or what their movement choices should be—to be, as Greenland has advocated, 'helpful adults' who 'step aside' and 'stop telling children what to do and how to do it' (2009: 9). In the example above, the web introduces a physical structure, a possible theme, and a challenge to the children. The adults can step aside, having offered a freedom that has a basis in an idea and presents something new on which the children can exercise their own creativity. How they do this is up to them.

Although in some ways, for Lizzie, this is an appealing model of child independence and autonomy tempered by a wise framework, in practical situations she is also aware of the question of how and when to 'stand back' or 'step forward' (Craft, Matthews, and McConnon 2012: 60). Tuning in to the children so that we know when to leave them to it and when to interact requires a relationship which can be built and tested through dialogue. It is important to stand side by side with the children, ready to interact when they give the cue (Vecchi 2010: 31) as well as to offer them triggers to develop their own creative ideas. Perhaps the role Craft and colleagues identify as 'meddling in the middle' is particularly apt here. They define this as 'co-constructing alongside and with the children' (2012: 58), which helps to explain what improvising in dialogue with the children means.

The term 'meddling' sounds deceptively easy . The research question for the UoE Catalyst/DNA project, from which the above data are drawn, asked 'what is the adult's role?' and grew out of Lizzie's experience of learning to meddle. She realized that it was a skill that required wisdom and a child-centred view. As we looked at the data, we hoped to discover what that skill entailed. It seemed the following were important: tuning in, offering provocations, embodied communication, and having a playful attitude.

When adult 'meddling' attempts to change children's ideas into adult's ideas, there is a danger it can obvert and obstruct the flow of children's creativity (Bruce 2004: 103). Tuning in to children's interests and allowing them to be the focus allows their creativity to take centre stage. When the children are placed 'at the centre of the action' (Anttila 2003: 96), they can generate their own ideas, which are valued by adults. They can explore movement preferences, experiment with new qualities, embody invented characters or imagined scenarios. The choices they make and ideas they express may emanate from physical or emotional responses, or from their own innovations, but are deeply personal and are an expression of who they are. They are linked to identity. In the movement that arises in improvised dialogue, the children are 'the physical substance of the ideas' (Chappell et al. 2012: 20). This link between creativity in movement and identity opens up opportunities for them to make and be made, which is the final theme that emerged in our analysis and discussions. We introduce this theme here through our combined reflections on improvising with Kerry's son and fellow participants in Flim Flam.

MAKING AND BEING MADE

Kerry (observations and reflections):   *I come into the room with Hal. We nod to Lizzie. I see the lycra web strung out and after a little nudge from Lizzie suggest to Hal that we attach some more strands to build the web. I stretch a piece of lycra to a table leg and tie it on. Hal glances at me and smiles. He gets another strand and starts his own part of the web. He's always been fairly independent—not a little boy who wants to hold hands much—he seems to have the confidence to do his own thing here.*

Lizzie (observations and reflections):   *I leave Kerry and Hal to it. They don't need me for this. Rory, another little boy in the group, is busily engaged running in the web, carrying a bundle of lycra to add to it. His mum isn't joining in—she's occupied with her baby. Rory jumps and turns at a fast pace with a grin on his face, continuing his solo exploration. A child asks 'What are you doing?' He says 'I'm trying to get out!' He's not always this forthcoming or engaged. Why has the web drawn him out like this? Is it the physical adventure, the sense of independence, or the image of the web and the spider who built it?*

Kerry (observations and reflections):   *I'm kneeling back from the web and Hal is wiggling through the strands. It's great to watch him testing out what's possible, Lizzie suggests we 'fly and stick'. When she shouts 'fly', we are flies around the web. When she shouts 'stick', we get stuck on the web. Hal is finding it tricky to negotiate his way through the web—I can see he's getting in a bit of a tangle. He gets frustrated and pulls at a lycra strand round his middle. I unwind him and he carries on ducking under the strands. I can see him concentrating on feeding his legs and arms through the holes made by the lycra. I would love to have his low centre of gravity that makes it look as easy to move on all fours as it does to walk through the web.*

Lizzie (observations and reflections):   *As I get stuck to the web, Hal comes to stand beside me and holds a piece of lycra to the back of his neck. He begins to spin as we did earlier. He isn't mirroring me, he has absorbed the idea of his body getting stuck on the web and is using it in his own way, completely differently to me. In spinning he is returning to Rory's ideas from earlier in the session and playing with them independently. To me this is wonderful—embodied and thoughtful improvisation from a two-year-old—but there is not much uniformity or following from Hal or the group as a whole.*

I lead everyone in rolling under the web, lying underneath and feeling the web with our feet. A few children and adults join me and there is an increase in the pace and amount of activity from everyone. Greg and Rory stay standing and jump around. I think they're enjoying the view of looking down on everyone. I announce 'One last climb before we say goodbye to the web'.

Kerry (reflections):   *We all start to speed over and under the lycra strands. The energy builds. I feel slightly guilty—is this class about me moving or Hal moving? Or maybe it's a combination of the two? Hal laughs and squeezes in a few final spins—I join him and roll under the lycra. Lizzie brings this final flurry to an end and we all start to untie the web to put it away.*

For Kerry especially this is a pertinent episode. She has spent considerable time unpacking what we mean by 'creativity' in education, especially in young people's dance. This has led to the conclusion that more needs to be understood about the motivations for creativity. Craft (2005) questioned the ethicality of creativity framed in education in terms of marketization—an individualized, competitive, workforce-developing framing of creativity that pays little attention to its more humane implications. This prompted Kerry to explore whether the arts had more to offer and, with a team of researchers, she found that the dynamics of creativity in dance education demonstrated a more 'humanising' practice (Chappell, Rolfe, Craft, and Jobbins 2011: 99–100). More specifically, the group empirically researched and conceptualized WHC in dance education, which is described in the introduction.

In working to better understand early years improvisation, we chose to reflect on this episode because it seemed both to offer us an insight into the dynamics of improvisation within early years dance involving children and their families and, for Kerry especially, to have something of WHC in it as a means of understanding the improvisation. Hal and Rory interacted with us in their improvisations; they were 'making'—and Kerry certainly knows from ongoing close interactions with Hal that he was 'being made' by his actions. Kerry watched him build on these ideas at home; these imaginative, physical interactions and explorations in the world shaped who and how he is. In the episode, the idea of embodied dialogue is incredibly important. Lizzie reflects on how Hal is not copying her but how their responses build like a physical conversation, with Hal and Rory both leading at different times. From being in it but also seeing it from the outside, it seems apparent that we were all immersed in the moment in moving in the web and figuring out what we needed to do with ourselves to navigate it and the other people in it. This kind of in-the-moment immersion can be difficult to achieve (Csikszentmihalyi 1996) in our future- and results-oriented education system, yet it is another defining feature of WHC which forms the basis for embodied dialogue, and which was alive and well in our web improvisations.

The quality of our interaction in building and physically navigating the web mattered to our group that week in Flim Flam. We all invested in building the web's flexible structure and moving through it, exploring its dynamics, at times enthusiastically but never destructively. We were all creating together in a humanizing way, trying to be wise, even if only on a small scale. This connects to what LeVoguer and Pasch identify as 'everyday morality' (2014: 102). Citing Gill (2007), they discuss how social skills can be practiced as children negotiate and observe others, seeing something of what draws them out or leaves them cold. They can feed off each others' ideas and negotiate space when doing so. We can recognize the development of everyday morality in our creativity that day.

For Lizzie, there are also strong connections to our discussion earlier of *dialogues with children*. It is wonderful to see those moments of immersion—total engagement and absorption in the 'now'. Smith notes that this takes place in 'embodied experience', when we enter Merleau-Ponty's 'field of the present' (2002: 135). Lizzie aims to build in lots of time in the sessions for independent exploration where children are developing their own voices. But as the teacher, she is constantly aware of the context of the whole class—the other children who want to move on, or the importance of balancing the needs of the babies and toddlers in the room against those of the older children, who may be relishing a moment of crazy speed and dizziness. At its best, the group is like a small community; it is intergenerational and embedded in life—practicalities and emotions can dominate. Sleep-deprived parents, potty-training toddlers, and feisty four-year-olds ready for school dance side by side. The session needs to meet all these individuals' needs and build what Kerry has referred to previously as a 'shared creative group identity' (Chappell 2011: 12), working with a communality within WHC that holds everyone's ideas—no mean feat!

CONCLUSION

So in trying to understand what improvisation in early years dance is, and how it connects to WHC, we can say that it is about children and adults moving aesthetically and artfully to know themselves better in their bodies; it is about doing this in relationship and in empathetic dialogue, and it is about understanding the connection between the creativity inherent in improvisation and our developing embodied identities. We are engaging together in artful, humanizing conversations.

In the examples above, we see children getting to know themselves better in their bodies when they are able to work in a self-determined way, led by personal interest and sensory stimulation. Sensory exploration is central to our understanding of the aesthetic and the arts in this early years context. Eisner describes the arts as a 'supermarket for the senses' (2004: 9), and it is through this that early years children discover themselves, the world, and their place in it. Improvisation as a form taps into this way that the under-fives experience the world. It is immediate and fluid, offering permission for intuitive movement, as well as space for reflection and the deliberate choices that shape our identities. In our early years practice, we are giving children opportunities for immersion that are tailored to their innate physicality and capacity to inhabit and discover. We do this by creating environments, using images, and encouraging stories, movements, and characters to unfold.

In dance improvisation, children are able to fashion their own responses using their 'soma' as an embodied whole (Shusterman 2008). In this way, they can find and exercise their preferences and in so doing discover their identities, how it feels to be in their bodies, and maybe begin to imagine what it might be like to be in someone else's—to develop empathy. This opens the door to dialogue with others. In an enabling environment where children know their ideas are valued and feel free to share them, they can work in relationship with others in an embodied, empathetic dialogue. Here they meet new perspectives and creative ideas that may be absorbed by them and form part of their growing identities.

This is the process by which they are 'making and being made' and which Chappell 2011: 96) describes as coming from the interplay of the inside of themselves stretching into conversation with what is on the outside and vice versa. In the examples above, young children are able to bring themselves and their embodied ideas into conversation with those of other children, their families, and the dance practitioners in the group. Writing about professional dance, Briginshaw highlighted the potency of the 'inside/outside interface', which she argues has the 'potential for new world views' (2001: 18). The new world views of the under-fives detailed above are fresh for them and in our experience can also challenge adults and family members dancing with them to experience and see the world in a different way, too.

Stepping back to the wider context, the existence of this kind of perspective shift for both adults and children via embodied, communal activity responds to concerns expressed by, for example, Tobin, that children's lives are 'increasingly disembodied', as educational cultures, and indeed our lives more generally, focus on rationality and risk avoidance (2004: 124). It therefore seems important now more than ever to value the capacity for change that is rooted in embodied, communal understanding as a means for thriving, not just surviving, in everyday life (Ross 2003). By embedding our discussions of early years dance improvisation within the conceptual home of WHC we want to bring in arguments made by Chappell and Craft which are pertinent here (e.g., Chappell and Craft with Rolfe and Jobbins 2011). This kind of creativity, evident in early years dance improvisation, can challenge globalized, disembodied, marketized understandings of creativity.

Chappell and Craft with Rolfe and Jobbins (2011) argue that despite a deceptive rhetoric from some policy-makers, we do have a choice regarding our children's educational futures, and indeed their futures per se, and how we change them. There are alternatives (Fielding and Moss 2010). As demonstrated above, through a WHC lens we can see them coming to know themselves and developing their identities as part of the improvisational creative process. When this is considered within the collaborative and communal dynamics of the early years settings, there is a further capacity for communally driven change, what Chappell and Craft with Rolfe and Jobbins (2011) refer to as 'quiet revolutions'.

The discussions in this chapter offer us snapshots in time of the process of becoming, rather than the bigger ongoing incremental and cumulative communal changes that make up full-blown quiet revolutions. But we can see the children in these snapshots showing the potential to be the creative, empathetic, responsive, and responsible adults of tomorrow. They are already the possible change-makers of the future. Through our practice and research in this area, we are coming to the conclusion that we have a responsibility to further equip them with the kind of informed creative skills and intuitions that will allow them to continue to be just that. In return, they can help us to access our own 'new world views', which are similarly embodied and empathetic and continue to grow through dialogue.

ACKNOWLEDGEMENTS

We would like to thank Gill Holmyard, Clare Farion, and Laura-Jane Wright at the nursery and all the families who come along to Flim Flam and the Devon Carousel Project. We also acknowledge the support of the University of Exeter and Dance Network Active in the Catalyst Bursary Scheme. We affirm that all the research was carried out subject to the British Educational Research Association's Ethical Guidelines (2011). This means that pseudonyms have been used as appropriate.

References

Anttila, E. (2003) *A Dream Journey to the Unknown, Searching for Dialogue in Dance Education.* Helsinki: Theatre Academy

Bonilauri, S., and Filippini, T. (1987) In Malaguzzi, L., *I cento linguaggi dei bambini: The Hundred Languages of Children: Narrative of the Possible Proposals and Intuitions of Children from the Infant and Toddler Centers and Preschools of the City of Reggio Emilia/Educational Direction of the Exhibition Loris Malaguzzi.* Modena, Italy: Reggio Emilia.

Briginshaw, V. (2001) *Dance, Space and Subjectivity.* Basingstoke, UK: Palgrave.

Bruce, T. (2004) *Cultivating Creativity in Babies, Toddlers and Young Children.* London: Arnold.

Chappell, K. (2011) Journeys of Becoming; Humanising Creativity. In Chappell, K., Rolfe, L., Craft, A., and Jobbins, V., *Close Encounters: Dance Partners for Creativity.* Stoke on Trent, UK: Trentham Books.

Chappell, K., and Craft, A. (2011) Creative Learning Conversations. *Educational Research* 53(3): 363–385.

Chappell, K., Craft, A., Rolfe, L., and Jobbins, V. (2012) Humanising Creativity: Valuing Our Journeys of Becoming. *International Journal of Education and the Arts* 13(8): 1–35. http://www.ijea.org/v13n8/. Accessed 11 January 2013.

Chappell, K., and Craft, A., with Rolfe, L., and Jobbins, V. (2011) Not Just Surviving but Thriving. In Chappell, K., Rolfe, L., Craft, A., and Jobbins, V., *Close Encounters: Dance Partners for Creativity.* Stoke on Trent, UK: Trentham Books.

Chappell, K., Rolfe, L., Craft, A., and Jobbins, V. (2011) *Close Encounters: Dance Partners for Creativity.* Stoke on Trent, UK: Trentham Books.

Craft, A. (2005) *Creativity in Schools: Tensions and Dilemmas.* Abingdon, UK: Routledge.

Chappell, K., Pender, T., Swinford, E., and Ford, K. (2016) Making and Being Made: Wise Humanising Creativity in Interdisciplinary Early Years Arts Education. *International Journal of Early Years Education.* DOI: 10.1080/09669760.2016.1162704.

Clough, P. (2002). *Narratives and Fictions in Educational Research.* Buckingham: Open University Press.

Craft, A., Matthews, A., and McConnon, L. (2012) Child-Initiated Play and Professional Creativity: Enabling Four-Year-Olds' Possibility Thinking. *Thinking Skills and Creativity* 7: 48–61.

Csikszentmihalyi, Mihalyi. (1996) *Creativity: Flow and the Psychology of Discovery and Invention.* New York: Harper Perennial.

Dissanayake, E. (2001) Aesthetic Incunabula. *Philosophy and Literature* 25: 335–346.

Eisner, E. (2004) What Can Education Learn from the Arts about the Practice of Education? *International Journal of Education and the Arts* 5(4): 1–13.

Fielding, M., and Moss, P. (2010) *Radical Education and the Common School: A Democratic Alternative.* London: Routledge.

Gill, T. (2007) *No Fear: Growing Up in a Risk Averse Society*. London: Calouste Gulbenkian Foundation.

Greenland, P. (2001) *Movement Play*. Leeds: Jabadao Centre for Movement Studies.

Greenland, P. (2009) *Jabadao Developmental Movement Play—Final Report on a Ten Year Action Research Project*. Leeds: Jabadao Centre for Movement Studies.

Hubbard, R. S. (1996) *A Workshop of the Possible: Nurturing Children's Creative Development*. York, ME: Stenhouse.

LeVoguer, M., and Pasch, J. (2014) Physical Well-Being: Autonomy, Exploration, and Risk Taking. In J. Manning-Morton (ed.), *Exploring Well-Being in the Early Years*. Maidenhead, UK: Open University Press.

Malaguzzi, L. (1987) *I cento linguaggi dei bambini: The hundred languages of children: Narrative of the possible proposals and intuitions of children from the infant and toddler centers and preschools of the City of Reggio Emilia/educational direction of the exhibition Loris Malaguzzi*. Modena: Reggio Emilia.

Nutbrown, C. (2013) Conceptualising Arts-Based Learning in the Early Years. *Research Papers in Education* 28(2): 239–263.

Ribeiro, M., and Fonseca, A. (2011) The Empathy and the Structuring Sharing Modes of Movement Sequences in the Improvisation of Contemporary Dance. *Research in Dance Education* 12(2): 71–85.

Ross, J. (2003) Anna Halprin and Improvisation as Child's Play: A Search for Informed Innocence. In Albright, Ann Cooper, and Gere, D. (eds.), *Taken by Surprise: A Dance Improvisation Reader*. Middletown, CT: Wesleyan University Press.

Sansom, A. (2009) Mindful Pedagogy in Dance: Honoring the Life of the Child. *Research in Dance Education* 10(3): 161–176.

Sherbourne, V. (2001) *Developmental Movement for Children*. London: Worth.

Shusterman, R. (2008) *Body Consciousness: A Philosophy of Mindfulness and Somaesthetics*. Cambridge: Cambridge University Press.

Smith, M. L. (2002) Moving Self: The Thread Which Bridges Dance and Theatre. *Research in Dance Education* 3(2): 123–141.

Tobin, J. (2004) The Disappearance of the Body in Early Childhood Education. In Bresler, L. (ed.), *Knowing Bodies, Moving Minds: Towards Embodied Teaching and Learning*, vol. 3. Springer.

Vecchi, V. (2010) *Art and Creativity in Reggio Emilia*. London: Routledge.

Walsh, D.J. (2004) Frog Boy and the American Monkey: The Body in Japanese Early Schooling. In Bresler, L. (ed.), *Knowing Bodies, Moving Minds: Towards Embodied Teaching and Learning*. Dordrecht: Kluwer Academic.

....

CHAPTER 25

INSTINCTIVE CONNECTIONS

Improvisation as a Research Methodology in Health and Care Settings

....

LISA DOWLER

THE joy of dance improvisation for me is dancing the unknown into being. Whether dancing solo or with another, the delight is in the lived experience of heightened awareness, attuning to others and/or space whilst at the same time paying attention to your own sensations and how you are feeling, moment to moment. It is an incredibly rich process; one where preconceptions dissolve and possibilities multiply. Then you have choice, to be open, to be specific, and all of the spaces in between. As an approach to relating to another in creating movement and dance, for me dance improvisation is the most inclusive and is therefore, I believe, especially appropriate for dance artists working in health and care settings. As an approach to movement practice, which facilitates person-centred inquiry, improvisation can engender creativity and self-expression, whilst at the same time providing a framework for phenomenological approaches to data collection, through reflective description of experiences. In this way, improvisational processes can support or become a research methodology as experiences of improvisation are gathered to offer insight into the practice and our perceptions.

This essay draws on current discourse on dance improvisation, merging and revealing concepts central to its practice (De Spain 2003, 2014; Buckwalter 2010; Tufnell and Crickmay 1990; 2004). It outlines the means by which these concepts and processes are applicable to health and care settings, utilizing my experience in paediatric and dementia care settings as instances where improvisation is a seemly suitable or appropriate approach both to creative practice and to research. Throughout this essay, I will discuss the relevance of improvisation primarily as a resource for creativity and art-making, as opposed to as a therapeutic method, with the belief that the context of the creative encounter should not necessarily create the framework for the dancing; rather, the participant holds the privilege to decide the content of the duet through a process of co-creation and language which may be verbal or nonverbal. For me this is a matter of agency; when we are under medical care, we hand over our bodies and therefore our-selves to the medical establishment. This can be life saving and life enhancing in many ways, but it can also disrupt one's sense of self. In this situation we are no longer able to make choices about what is going to happen to us and we are not considered experts of our own bodies. Interactions with professionals will consist of therapeutic intervention, oriented towards a desired outcome or goal.

I believe that improvisers can have a vital role to play in the midst of this, in meeting and listening to the whole person, seeing beyond the condition for which they are being treated or cared for. By widening the lens to see the whole person you empower the in-dividual, by moving with them you bring them into bodily sensation and awareness, by improvising with them you allow the person to fully live the present moment (fig. 25.1). These beliefs are supported by my experience in, and the philosophy of, Contact Improvisation, an improvised duet in which each dancer, regardless of experience, shares and develops the possibility of the dance; as De Spain explains, 'whether you are a beginner or an expert, improvising puts you on a level playing field with everyone else in one important sense: none of us knows what will happen next' (2014: 4).

Intriguingly, this acknowledgement of uncertainty creates a significant overlap and opening in the medical field for dance improvisers. The uniqueness of human beings ensures that outcomes from injuries, illness, and disease cannot be predicted with any certainty. As medical doctor Richard Baron states, 'prognosis is always statistical and in that sense rarely tells a particular person what will happen to him or her' (1985: 609).

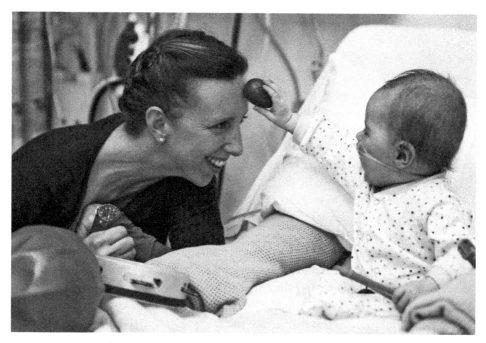

FIG. 25.1 Lisa Dowler improvising with a nine-month-old infant on the Cardiac ward at Alder Hey Children's Hospital. Photograph by Leila Romaya.

During the past decade of working as a dance artist in health settings, I have witnessed an element of the unknown in the medical treatment of illness and injury. Clinicians have the knowledge and experience that care needs are individual; and therapy and treatment are a dialogue between interventions and responses. There is a process whereby assessments are made and appropriate responses are explored, and the most successful treatment of injury, illness and disease happens when these responses are tailored to the individual.

Therefore, for patients existing in a vulnerable place of the unknown, improvisational practices offer the opportunity to have influence, make choices and be heard. This can play an important role in empowering the individual and fostering a sense of self, in a situation whereby it is often external forces which shape their future, for example, diagnostics and treatment. In such contexts, improvisation can enhance a sense of holistic or personalized care, offering a space to explore aspects of who we are outside of our illnesses, shifting the focus from experiencing our limitations to experiencing our possibilities. Despite this, improvisers working in health and care settings are thin on the ground. This is in part due to the lack of evidence of the benefits of dance in health settings in comparison to other art forms in health care.

Writing from the Body

So how can we create the evidence? The process of documenting and researching a practice that responds to context and continually shifts can be tricky. Therefore, this essay is peppered with reflective writings in the present, which enable me to track and explore my perceptions of my experiences whilst in the process of writing. This exemplifies how we can share the subjective experience of our practice to offer insight and disseminate its impact. This practice of reflective writing is accessible and is widely used by professional dance practitioners and is akin to the veracity of embodied research. Phenomenologist Linda Finlay cites Anderson (2001) as she explains this process: 'rather than being an academic exercise, the writing-up stage of research needs to be an embodied lived experience in itself. . . . When I write a sentence and read it back, I find that I play with it, dance with it; I tune in and ask my sensing body to tell me if the words I have chosen are good enough' (Finlay 2013: 10). Therefore, as I practice the lived experience of writing, as well as sensing in my body my past experiences of improvisation and the dances I have shared in various contexts, I am also with the sensations I am experiencing at that moment. This layering of experiences, I feel, is essential to writing about improvisation: as a process of flux, it provides a context, an anchor, for my embodied experiences, both past and present. It gives me permission to be moved to write as I am that day, and in that way I sense the freedom of improvisation, that which maybe I offer to others: to move as they are.

A great silence overcomes me, and I wonder why I ever thought to use language. (Rumi 1995: 20) (fig. 25.2)

FIG. 25.2 Lisa Dowler with her daughter, Siena Dowler-Mercer, during a rehearsal for improvised performance *A Moment in Time*, Walker Art Gallery, Liverpool. Photograph by Emmer Winder.

Dance and movement are most often a nonverbal language; even in stillness we move. Our breath travels to each and every cell, a constant exchange and flow, the continuum of the fluid system as it shifts from one quality to the next, the muscular and skeletal shifts as we balance our weight in response to gravity; the living body perpetuates it all. This essay locates my experience in improvisation at the nucleus of my practice as a dance artist and also in my existence as a human being. Like the nucleus of the cell, improvisation is the place of regulation of my activity, at the core, guiding, nurturing, and holding me, as I navigate the unknown, in terms of both the physical context in which I work and the creative and imaginative happenstances. As an 'attentional practice', it is both a process of discovery of aspects of myself in relationship with others and a mode of communication for those where verbal language is not available.

Thursday 24 July 2014, Contact Improvisation session led by Wendy Thomas, TILT studio, Liverpool

I am lying down on the floor. A band is rehearsing in the room underneath, I can hear it and feel the vibration through the floor ... Wendy gives us permission to let our attention be there ... whilst at the same time we are exploring a score, something about creating space inside the body ... I am only with snippets of what she says ... my mind is still spinning with thoughts about this chapter which I began to write this morning ... idea after idea ... they keep coming ... like any creative process ... there isn't an on/off button ....

Also Siena, my nine-year-old daughter, has come to class with me ... she is on the edge of the space reading ... but part of me is with her ... expanding ... opening ... I'm more in my periphery ... my membrane ...

Then Wendy offers a specific invitation to us, to say 'no' to ourselves in our moving ... to inhibit ... to pause at a place where we wouldn't usually pause ... SCHOOOOM ... I zoom in ....I'm inside my moving now ... It is very clear, the shift in my attention ... everything else dissolves and I'm with my sensation, in that moment I begin improvising (fig. 25.3).

FIG. 25.3 Lisa Dowler, Siena Dowler-Mercer, Paula Hampson, and Niamh Mcardle. Rehearsing for improvised performance *A Moment in Time*, Walker Art Gallery, Liverpool. Photograph by Emmer Winder.

So what exactly is improvisation? Buckwalter offers a simple explanation: 'improvisation is about just that, the experience of moving and not knowing, finding the next thing, and learning about what is becoming in the process' (2010: 4).

It is the learning part for me that refocuses improvisation as a potential research method. Drawing on the conception of the practitioner-researcher model, whereby according to arts and health pioneer Shaun McNiff, arts-based practice can be considered 'as a life-long mode of research' (1998: 63). Therefore, the active process of improvisation is not in the pursuit of theory but in a fluid and evolving growth of embodied knowledge through praxis. By means of rigour in paying attention to this moment and that, we are able to create new knowledge about ourselves as human beings, about our creativity, and about the form itself. Therefore, overlaying improvisation with a phenomenological method enables an embodied research process, which is at the same time practitioner and participant centred, dissolving hierarchies as they, too, dissipate in the improvised duet. By adopting a practitioner-researcher role, one is able to offer insight into one's practice from both first-person reflection and the experience of others through phenomenology (Nelson 2006: 110). As dance phenomenologist Maxine Sheets-Johnstone contends, for dance improvisers who 'dance the dance as it comes into being at this particular moment at this particular place', a phenomenological account through first person description is essential to understanding 'the incarnation of creativity as process' (2009: 29, 30).

Research in Practice

Since 2006 I have been a dance artist-in-residence at Alder Hey Children's Hospital in Liverpool. From the outset this was an experiment, a research project, an improvisation. I was invited to be the first dance artist to work at the hospital, so neither the hospital nor I had preconceptions of what I might do or what the outcomes could be. In addition, I had not trained specifically for this setting, although I had been involved in projects related to health before, for example, with pregnant women, older people, unaccompanied minors seeking asylum, disabled children. However, this was completely new to me. I had to let go of thinking about what I 'could' or 'should' do and really trust that my practice and experience in improvisation would enable me to create dances in unusual spaces with children and young people with life-limiting and life-threatening conditions.

On my first day on the neuromedical ward, Julie Sellers, then senior play specialist, said to me: 'anything is a bonus here, Lisa, any response or movement is a bonus'. Again there was no expectation that I should do 'something'; there was an open invitation to explore, and I feel very privileged to have been given that opportunity. Julie knew the patients well, and she, or fellow play specialist Helen Traynor, stayed with me in a supportive role throughout the first few years of my work. The clinical needs of the patient were supported by the multidisciplinary team of care around that patient; I was there as an artist to instigate movement, play, and creativity.

This is attributable to the vision of Dr. Jane Ratcliffe, the chair of Alder Hey Arts and consultant in paediatric intensive care, and the support of the arts coordinator, Vicky Charnock. I owe them both a great deal; their understanding and value in the transformative nature of the arts has created a vibrant and progressive arts-for-health department, which continues to flourish.

On the neuromedical ward, I was working one-to-one with children with acquired brain injuries and complex and multiple disabilities. As at the beginning of any improvised duet, I 'tuned' in to my partners, their breathing, rhythms, tones, movements, emotions, and I made a connection wherever I could. This was the starting place, the beginning.

One of the children I met was Jake, aged two, who had endured a serious head injury that caused spasticity and dystonia; he was no longer able to communicate verbally. He had recently come to the neuromedical ward from the Intensive Care Unit. He had a tracheostomy and was receiving oxygen, and his overall tonal state, or residual muscle tone, was very high. He had some movement of one of his arms, which was very jerky and disconnected from the rest of his body, and the clinical team were unsure whether he could see or hear. My intuition was to offer him reassurance and a sense of being supported where he was. I began with what in the somatic practice of Body-Mind Centering is known as 'cellular touch' (Bainbridge Cohen 2008: 70). It is a 'being with' touch rather than a 'doing to'. It is restful and nondirective and offers a steady presence. I noticed that in response to this touch Jake's tone softened, he became more relaxed, and his breathing became less laboured. Over the following weeks, I continued to work in this way and to offer other touch qualities. I worked with the early developmental pattern of navel radiation that develops in utero, whereby the navel is the organizing centre of movement. Through gentle touch with Jake, I explored connecting the movement he had in his extremity to his centre (see Hartley 2004; Bainbridge Cohen 2008). At a later stage, I began to work with gently stimulating his reflexes (flexor withdrawal and extensor thrust), which again underlie developmental movement. I found that once he was relaxed through touch, he was able to respond by withdrawing or extending into stimulation, with my support. This meant that he had the choice of moving into flexion, as his usual state had been one of extension. I also stimulated his rooting reflex, and he responded by turning his head; I supported this by moving into rolling and prone positions.

This very gentle, child-centred approach was successful immediately. Given the creative space to explore and a companion to support, often children found new movements and ways of expressing through movement. In 2008, with the support of Edge Hill University and Alder Hey's Research Department, Small Things Dance Collective's first research project at Alder Hey was initiated. Phenomenologist Linda Finlay offers some insight into the attributes necessary for embodied research: 'researchers, I argue, require a critical, embodied self-awareness, a capacity to reflect on their own (inter-) subjectivity, processes, assumptions and interests both during the data collection encounter and after' (2014: 8). I believe that these qualities are readily available to improvisers who have sharpened their awareness on multiple levels throughout the evolution of their practice. Therefore, in terms of a phenomenological approach to research, it is simply a matter of framing the practice with a research question. I had been experimenting with improvisation and somatic approaches to dance in Alder Hey for two years. I was having positive experiences, and the effect of the work was benefitting patients on multiple levels. This was new work for Small Things and for the hospital. We were equally excited and eager to research what was happening both for us as artists and for the patients, as well as the implications for the medical setting.

We consulted with the Research Department, in particular the director of research, Dr. Matthew Peake, and created this protocol and focus for our enquiry: 'an investigation of measures to evaluate the practice of dance improvisation, on the neuromedical and oncology wards of Alder Hey Children's Hospital'.

This open-ended framework enabled us to gather accounts of personal experiences of participants in our sessions, as well as those witnessing, including parents and hospital staff. We also wrote our own reflections immediately following each session, and these multiple layers of experience were intertwined through Interpretative Phenomenological Analysis (For a full discussion of this approach and research findings see Dowler [2013].)

In summary, the findings of this research were that improvisation for these patients transformed their experiences of their hospital stays in a positive way. The shift in the perception of their experiences supported them in finding new movements, expressing themselves creatively, and reducing anxiety. This was recorded by the patients: 'That was really good fun, it was cool!' (Matthew, aged seven, oncology ward); 'I really enjoy making the dances up!' (Sarah, aged eleven, neuromedical ward). Parents responded as well:

'before the session Chrissey was apprehensive and didn't really enjoy physio, so didn't want to take part in the session. She is embarrassed that she has weakness and she is very frustrated with her limbs that do not work in the way they did before. During the session she needed to leave for hydrotherapy, she did not want to leave, she was having a good time. This was emotionally good for her as she has been depressed since she moved to the ward. Lisa was very adaptable and listened to me as a parent when I asked her to encourage certain movements. She was very approachable and friendly with the children; Chrissey can't wait to see her next week!' Mother of Neuromedical patient, aged 12. (Dowler 2013: 171)

The improvisation sessions also supported clinical and play specialists in their roles and offered respite for parents and caregivers during a difficult time in their lives. Dr. Jane Ratcliffe summarized: 'the dance programme was described by patients as something which was fun and provided welcome distraction from clinical routine (fig. 25.4). Parents and carers were very keen for their children and young people to be involved ... because of the benefits they observed. The impact on healthcare staff was threefold. In addition

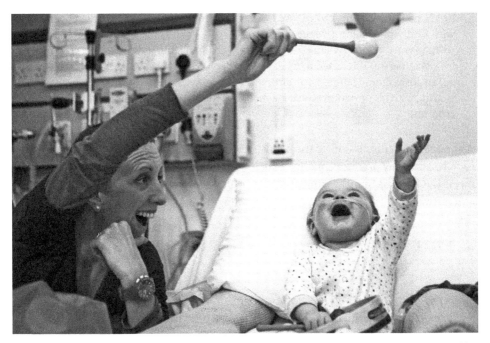

FIG. 25.4 Lisa Dowler improvising with a nine-month-old infant on the Cardiac ward at Alder Hey Children's Hospital. Photograph by Leila Romaya.

to reduced requirements for analgesia and more rapid mobilisation, they saw how the ward environment was altered in a positive way by the multi-dimensional approach of the dancers' (Ratcliffe 2010).

Following the success of this research, two further stages of research were formulated with improvisation at the heart, supported primarily by Arts Council England and Edge Hill University. These included *Invisible Duets* a film and performance installation which included patients in the creative process, and a mixed-method study involving twenty-five children and young people experiencing acute pain on the neuromedical, cardiac, and orthopaedic wards of the hospital. This study utilized a descriptive qualitative approach to help the participants and witnesses verbalize/record their experiences of the improvised somatic dance sessions, and pain scores were assessed before and after the sessions using validated pain assessment tools. We found that 92 percent experienced a reduction in their pain or their perception of their pain, and all participants expressed a greater sense of well-being. The following is a vignette from a session on the orthopaedic ward.

> Kevin, aged thirteen, accidental stab wound to his thigh while playing. His doctor identified Kevin as a potential participant in somatic dance as he was anxious and his pain seemed to be increasing.
>   'Kevin talked and chatted to us about his accident as we worked. He often became quite anxious. At one point the pain in his left leg he described as very intense, then

he seemed to relax and smiled. We worked with touch, breath and gentle movement with Kevin for an hour.' (Dance Artist)

'It was nice because when I sat or stood before it hurt but now it doesn't.' (Kevin)

'His nurse was interested in what we had been doing because there had been such a transformation. Half an hour after our session, we saw Kevin working on weight bearing with his physiotherapist. He managed this very well.' (Dance Artist) (Dowler 2016: 20)

Although a full discussion of these investigations is beyond the scope of this chapter, each has held my practice equally in such a way that it has not been compromised. For me, this is because improvisation and Contact Improvisation are inherently acquiescent and the methodology is responsive to the context.

SHIFTING SETTINGS, DISTINCTIVE PRACTICE

I experienced the flexibility of an improvised approach when I later explored my practice in a dementia care setting. I had experienced working with older people for several years; however, I had never experienced working with movement and dance with people with dementia and again had had no specific training in this area. I was invited to work as project artist in a Breathing Space residency at Ashlar House in Epping in the summer of 2013. This was a collaboration between Dance Art Foundation, Nordoff Robbins, and Barchester Healthcare and was funded by the Barchester Healthcare Foundation.

This project became research into my practice in a specific context; how would I improvise here? How would I engage with people who had lost much of their ability to communicate in the later stages of their dementia? I experienced entering this new space in the same way as when I began at the children's hospital seven years earlier: I trusted my practice and my ability to form connections instinctively.

There was another layer to this investigation, in that I was invited to work specifically with music therapist and improviser Roddy Skeaping, who had been working at Ashlar House for several years. Manager Emma Bryer explains: 'I was approached by Nordoff Robbins as we've had a music therapist here for a number of years, and we've seen the positive interactions and the benefits to the residents to their well-being. So it was looking at taking that to another level and incorporating dance, to see if that improved the well-being of the residents' (Bryer 2013). So the project was designed with a sense of enquiry; it was a process whereby we could investigate ways in which Roddy and I could collaborate, support, and enhance each other's practice in engaging residents in creative practice. Roddy shares his perspective: 'it was an experiment we went into just to see what happened. How we could use music and the idea of dance together. I think the way we played it in the end was not to try and over co-ordinate our activities, but to just match each other appropriately in our different fields' (Skeaping 2013). This idea of 'appropriate matching' seems to be relatively obvious. However, Roddy has considerable skill and many years of practice as an improviser and collaborator. There was very little verbal discussion; rather, we communicated through our respective art forms, music and voice with movement and touch. What we created through the layering of our processes was further choices for the residents as to how they could engage. This multisensory approach was incredibly effective, and we made new discoveries about our own practices and how we could engage with individuals in later stages of dementia. Both Roddy and I felt that improvisation as a shared method of investigation enabled us to immediately work together, although I think the ease with which this happened, as with two old friends with a shared history and way of being, was equally surprising, powerful, and joyful for both of us.

As a dancer in health and care contexts working with others, specifically one-to-one, as I most often do, I have found my experience in Contact Improvisation to be fundamental. It provides a framework for creating a relationship through movement and touch with another person that is nonhierarchical, nondiagnostic, and not goal oriented, attributes that differentiate it from a therapy encounter. That is not to say that there are not therapeutic benefits—finding movement and flow for people who are unwell, recovering from illness, or with diminishing neurological function can be deeply therapeutic; but it can also be artistic, fun, and inspiring (fig. 25.5).

Karen Schaffman states: 'CI is a physical metaphor for trust, risk taking, unpredictability, spontaneity, collaboration, cooperation, and an array of emotional relationships'

FIG. 25.5 Lisa Dowler, Siena Dowler-Mercer, Paula Hampson, and Niamh Mcardle rehearsing for improvised performance *A Moment in Time*, Walker Art Gallery, Liverpool. Photograph by Emmer Winder.

(2008: 44). I would argue that working with children in any context relies on all these things and that in a hospital they are equally important. For medical reasons, there is very little freedom for anyone in hospital, yet children even in the most difficult situations never cease to amaze me with how they can transform their experiences through their imagination and play.

Notes, neuromedical ward, 6 August 2014

I met Leon today, he is seven years old and six days ago had a stroke. He had little use of his right side, and I said to him that we could do anything he wanted to do. I had lots of objects, and we decided just to explore together the things I had. After going through a few different objects, a guiro, wooden sticks, some feathers, he became particularly interested in a pink squishy creature with a big hole in the bottom. I sensed his curiosity and followed and supported him in his exploration. This creature devoured pretty much everything it could, we pushed koosh balls, toy snakes, and frog castanets inside him. We created sound effects with our voices (even though Leon's speech had been impaired due to his stroke), rescuing and pulling out his meals, only for them to be attacked and eaten again.

Leon used all of the movement and sound he had available to him; I supported where there was difficulty. We co-created a story, and he laughed and played in spite of his current condition.

His parents said he had started to become depressed and were so happy to see his spirits lifted and his energy change, they asked if I would come back.

The simplicity of what Leon and I did belies the complexity of improvisation. I agree with Mike Vargas that 'the rigor in improvisation lies in the agility and versatility of both body and mind' (2013: 24). Therefore, being at ease with not knowing what a session will include and being available to follow and respond to another are essential qualities when working in health and are intrinsic to improvisation as well. Being able to choose whether to participate and to decide on the content of the improvisation is vital for a child in hospital (fig. 25.6).

When talking about her early experiences in working with children, Anna Halprin states: 'I was captivated by the unpredictability of what the kids would do' (quoted in Ross 2003: 43). As an improviser, this is the ground in which you flourish, in the unpredictable; it is in the unknown spaces that your dance exists. As Buckwalter conveys it, 'improvisation is more about the thrill that comes from *not knowing* what it will be in the next moment or the next time. That dare is its lure' (2010: 3).

My own experience in developing my approach to this has been enhanced by somatic studies in the experiential anatomy of Body-Mind Centering. This has opened doorways in my perceptions of my own and other people's body systems and given me more choice in how I may enter into a relationship. For example, in Body-Mind Centering we learn to touch from the different qualities of the body systems and how to listen to

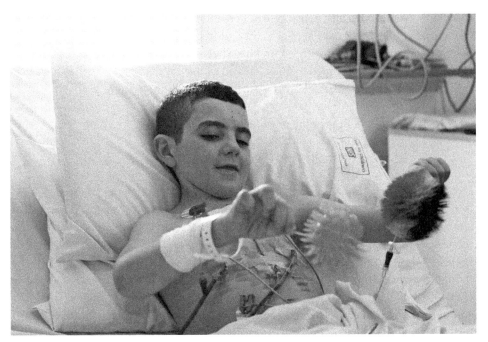

FIG. 25.6 Lisa Dowler improvising with objects with a boy following major surgery on the Cardiac ward at Alder Hey Children's Hospital. Photograph by Leila Romaya.

the quality of another's body system through our touch and visual perceptions. A more specific example could be how I initially approach working with a child or young person who has experienced an acquired brain injury. In my experience, there is often dystonia, that is, sustained muscle contractions throughout the body. There is generally no verbal communication, and facial expressions may offer the impression that the person is in pain. So I would enter into relationship with them through my voice and through touch, a listening touch, to which I have been introduced in Contact Improvisation class.

An extension of this is what in Body-Mind Centering we call 'cellular touch', which is specifically nondirective and about presence and being with as opposed to doing to (Bainbridge Cohen 2008). I have found this quality of touch to be a safe beginning for many encounters, as it is open, generous, and nonjudgemental. It is not searching for anything but allowing what *is* to be present and acknowledged. Generally I have found the response to this specific touch quality to be a release in muscular tone, which I perceive as an invitation to move on.

This shifts me back into a Contact Improvisation duet of listening, responding and co-creating moment by moment. My experiences of Body-Mind Centering and Contact Improvisation are layered and entwined and inform each other; they are interconnected. For me, Contact Improvisation is a site of cross-pollination, whereby individual practitioners can connect layers of their praxis within a form, which continues to evolve. In speaking about Contact Improvisation, Nancy Stark Smith states: 'each individual who engages in the dance is an essential ingredient in its present and its future—his or her choices as a dancer, teacher, artist, researcher, and human strongly influence the work' (2009: 3). For me, this equally applies to the children in the hospital setting and the older people in dementia settings with whom I have been privileged to share dances. Through these dances, I have continued to question and evolve my own practice: they have been my teachers, as I yield to the unknown spaces of dance improvisation.

> Be grateful for whoever comes,
> Because each has been sent
> As a guide from beyond (Rumi 1995: 109)

Frequently this process of yielding into the unknown and following an essence which is indefinable is referred to in a way that suggests that something magical is happening, almost as if another force is guiding, or at least an aspect of you which you are less conscious of. Ruth Zaporah describes this experience this way: 'I always think that the fairies—I don't know what else to call it—magic—these are the responses that feel as though they are coming from beyond my imagination; I don't know where they are coming from. They're a mystery' (2013: 29). In my experience in working with children and older people in health and care settings, this approach has been instinctive and effortless. The immediacy of the ability to connect and relate through my practice of improvisation has been one I have never had to question. It is about being with someone and gently inviting a connection, nothing forced or imposed, just opening up a space where you both can enter.

Notes, 3 June 2013, Ashlar House

I began with Sarah with a yellow feather; she responded to this, she spoke ... 'oh ... oh ... yes!' I stroked her arms and hands. Her hands were curled tight, and stroking them encouraged a softening and opening. Roddy was playing the accordion, supporting the touch. I stroked her face with the feather, and the tickle made her shiver; it was really lovely to see. I did it to myself and shivered too, and then she laughed.

After working with touch and skin for a while her hands had opened. I offered the keyboard on my iPad as Roddy had told me she was a pianist. She could move her fingers slightly as I held the keypad, and Roddy beautifully supported the notes she made with his accordion. We improvised like this for a while.

Roddy and I worked with Sarah each week exploring different approaches, including large balloons and different touch qualities. In an interview he explains how valuable this process was to him:

> one of the most meaningful things for me was working with a lady I've worked with for a long period of time and who's been slipping further and further into dementia, who I've ceased to be able to work with. A lovely lady with a great sense of humour, who was originally quite a fine pianist, although she's lost the capacity to play some

time ago ... and seeing how she responded, as I was always aware that she was listening to what I was doing, but she was unable to respond ... and the use of the ball
and the feathers and Lisa's whole approach really enlivened her. (Skeaping 2013)

What became apparent as we explored our relationships with each other as artists and
with the residents was that we were working instinctively. There were not any specific plans or ideas we had or any preparation in going to work with a resident, just our
many years of experience and practice in improvisation. We trusted this, and it was all
that was needed to tap in or make a connection with someone who was increasingly
disconnecting from his or her environment and the people who shared it. Manager
Emma Bryer reflects on this:

> And what I have seen and what staff are reporting to me, is that the level of engage-
> ment especially with those residents who are more locked in in their dementia, they
> are being reached on a much more sensory level.

> Residents who can engage who can sing, get up and dance have always benefitted
> greatly from the music therapy, however those residents who are more locked in, it's
> difficult to always interpret whether they are benefitting from it, but we are seeing
> from the touch, from using sensory objects, these residents do seem fully, fully en-
> gaged. (Bryer 2013)

In coming to understand why this approach may be bridging those spaces and making
connection with or engaging someone who is at an advanced stage in dementia, I am
brought back to my studies in somatic practice and learning about the nervous system.
I have consistently found touch, especially the specific qualities of a listening touch,
has elicited responses in both children I have worked with in neuro rehabilitation and
older people with dementia. These responses can be on multiple levels, body felt, verbal,
emotional—and can be very subtle or more obvious.

So why is touch so powerful—how can something so peripheral resonate so profoundly through the whole body? Deane Juhan encapsulates this fundamental theory of
why touch is so meaningful: 'the skin is no more separated from the brain than the surface of a lake is separate from its depths; the two are different locations in a continuous
medium. "Peripheral" and "central" are merely spatial distinctions which do more harm
than good if they lure us into forgetting that the brain is a single functional unit, from
cortex to fingertips to toes. To touch the surface is to stir the depths' (2003: 43) (fig. 25.7).

Furthermore, memories are not stored in single nerve cells; different aspects of
memory are stored in different cells and tissues in the body as we sense or absorb our experiences in our living body (Davis Bastings 2009: 15; Pearsall 1998: 116). Touch is a way
of awakening tissues of the body and creating pathways for streams of information and
responses to flow from the periphery to the internal landscape of the body, potentially
accessing memories stored within abundant spaces in the body. These are the spaces
that incubate creativity, which can emerge from places we may not fully understand and
can be accessed through improvisational practices and refined touch.

FIG. 25.7 Lisa Dowler and Siena Dowler-Mercer rehearsing for improvised performance *A Moment in Time*, Walker Art Gallery, Liverpool. Photograph by Emmer Winder.

Nancy Stark Smith and Bonnie Bainbridge Cohen discuss this concept of unknown spaces from which creativity flourishes, with Bainbridge Cohen articulating this space as 'generative space': 'there is a generative force that actually takes over. It drops below. I don't think its been identified as a place; I think its probably space ... where space is generative itself.... When we're inspired and when we have this generative power, or when we're creative, we are in space ... it's instant. It's all of a sudden—it's there. You don't know how you got there.... You're here and then you're there' (Bainbridge Cohen 2013: 34). The idea that improvisation accesses space is particularly exciting when those with who you are working have limited access to physical space through their movement, such as those with brain injury or in the later stages of dementia. Perhaps we are also practising at a metaphysical level, whereby we are creating spaces that are not material and through our imagination are transforming our perceptions and experiences of the here and now and thereby eliciting responses that are beyond our habitual ones. There is much more to research and develop in terms of how improvisation can be utilized in health and care contexts; however, it already appears that this inherently generous and generative form is capable of creating spaces where instinctive connections can be made. Improvisation as an experimental approach to movement that willingly mutates into a research methodology can enable multifarious approaches to documentation and research. In health contexts this attribute of improvisation is especially valuable, as it holds at the centre the practitioner alongside the participant, with each contributing equally to creating new knowledge—for themselves and their communities, as well as towards a continually evolving form.

REFERENCES

Bainbridge Cohen, B. (2008) *Sensing, Feeling and Action: The Experiential Anatomy of Body-Mind Centering.* Northampton, MA: Contact Editions.

Bainbridge Cohen, B. (2013) Bonnie Bainbridge Cohen on Cellular Imagination and Generative Space: Excerpt from interview with Bonnie Bainbridge Cohen by Nancy Stark Smith for CQ, July 7, 2011, NYC. *Contact Quarterly* 38(1) (Winter/Spring): 33–34.

Baron, R. (1985) An Introduction to Medical Phenomenology: I Can't Hear You While I'm Listening. *Annals of Internal Medicine* 103(4): 606–611.

Bryer, E. (2013) Interview by Lea Gratch, Juju Films, on Behalf of Dance Art Foundation at Ashlar House, Epping, UK, 8 July. https://vimeo.com/108160471

Buckwalter, M. (2010) *Composing While Dancing: An Improviser's Companion.* Madison: University of Wisconsin Press.

Davis Bastings, A. (2009) *Forget Memory.* Baltimore: John Hopkins University Press.

De Spain, K. (2003) The Cutting Edge of Awareness: Reports from the Inside of Improvisation. In Albright, Ann Cooper, and Gere, D. (eds.), *Taken by Surprise: A Dance Improvisation Reader.* Middletown, CT: Wesleyan University Press, 27–38.

De Spain, K. (2014) *Landscape of the Now: A Topography of Movement Improvisation.* New York: Oxford University Press.

Dowler, L. (2013) Improvising on the Ward: Exploring Somatic Dance and Potential in Paediatric Health Care. *Journal of Applied Arts and Health* 4(2): 163–178.

Dowler, L. (2016) Can Somatic Dance Practices Reduce Acute Pain for Children and Young People in Hospital? *Nursing Children and Young People* 28(9): 20–25.

Finlay, L. (2014) Embodying Research. *Person-Centered and Experiential Psychotherapies* 13(1): 4–18.

Hartley, L. (2004) *Somatic Psychology: Body, Mind and Meaning.* London: Whurr.

Juhan, D. (2003) *Job's Body: A Handbook for Bodywork.* Barrytown, NY: Station Hill Press.

McNiff, S. (1998) *Art-Based Research.* London: Jessica Kingsley.

Nelson, R. (2006) Practice-as-Research and the Problem of Knowledge. *Performance Research* 11(4): 105–116.

Pearsall, P. (1998) *The Heart's Code.* New York: Broadway Books.

Ratcliffe, J. (2010) Email interview with author, 10 November 2010.

Ross, J. (2003) Anna Halprin and Improvisation as Child's Play. In Albright, Ann Cooper, and Gere, D. (eds.), *Taken by Surprise: A Dance Improvisation Reader*. Middletown, CT: Wesleyan University Press, 41–51.

Rumi, J. (1995) *The Essential Rumi*. Trans. Coleman Barks. San Francisco: Harper.

Schaffman, K. (2008) Still Moving: Contact Improvisation and Its Influence on Contemporary Dance Practice. *Contact Quarterly* 33(2): (Summer/Fall): 43–49.

Sheets-Johnstone, M. (2009) *The Corporeal Turn: An Interdisciplinary Reader*. Exeter, UK: Imprint Academic.

Skeaping, R. (2013) Interview by Lea Gratch, Juju Films, on Behalf of Dance Art Foundation. Ashlar House, Epping, UK, July 2013.

Stark Smith, N. (2009) Celebrating and Cerebrating Contact at CI36. Editorial. *Contact Quarterly* 34(1) (Winter/Spring): P3.

Tufnell, M., and Crickmay, C. (1990) *Body, Space, Image: Notes towards improvisation and performance*. London: Dance Books

Tufnell, M., and Crickmay, C. (2004) *A Widening Field: Journeys in Body and Imagination*. London: Dance Books

Vargas, M. (2013) Notice and Contribute: Collaborative Negotiations between Improvised Music and Dance. *Contact Quarterly* 38(1) (Winter/Spring): 24–27.

CHAPTER 26

SOMATIC SENSING AND CREATURELY KNOWING IN THE UNIVERSITY IMPROVISATION CLASS

ALISON (ALI) EAST

> You cannot decide direction, you can only live this moment that is available to you. By living it, direction arises. If you dance, the next moment is going to be of a deeper dance. Not that you decide, but you simply dance this moment.
>
> Zen master Osho, *Intuition: Knowing beyond Logic* (2001: 188–189)

As an educator, choreographer, and performance improvisor over more than forty years, I have become interested not so much in what we might teach our students as in how we can invite them to access movement possibilities that lie dormant deep within their core consciousness (Damasio 1999) and cellular memories.

I call this process of somatic sensing *creaturely knowing* or *biological backtracking*. How, I ask, might an intuitive tracing beneath one's acquired behaviour patterns to a place of pure sensory response influence students' deep sensing of self? How might they dredge their 'creaturely knowing' (Sheets-Johnstone 2009: 182) as they perform their lives through their spontaneous dance? Richard Shusterman, borrowing from Merleau-Ponty, advocates practice in 'lived somaesthetic experience' (2008: 63) but also suggests the 'fruitful possibility of ... lived somaesthetic reflection ... of body consciousness' (63). I address the latter idea in the final section of this chapter. In Shusterman's view, by practicing somaesthetic awareness, one's proprioceptive consciousness and sensory system become better tuned to one's performing of life. This way of moving is individualistic and sensuous yet is ultimately connected and interrelational (East 2011b). Its motivational impulse dwells beneath movement memories that have been culturally inscribed or externally learned as codified techniques. Sourcing movement through this improvisational approach has, I contend, the potential to heighten and broaden students' sense of self-identity from that which is ego-centred and to that which is more merging, empathic, and relational. Art philosopher Suzi Gablik refers to an ecolological identity of 'self plus other plus environment' (1993: 307). This form of identity is, however, at the same time, highly individualistic, self-determining (autopoietic), and constantly evolving. In the process, students' creativity (and ultimately sense of artistry) is also stimulated as they come to understand their integral relationship with, and connection to, the ecology of the classroom community and, by inference, world ecology. An explicit alignment with the principles of ecological holism validates and reinforces the interrelationship between all life forms, ideas, processes, energy systems—planetary and cosmological, conscious and unconscious, intentional and spontaneous.

In her detailed research study *The Intuitive Experience,* Claire Petitmengin-Peugeot observed that 'at the moment of the intuition, the sensation of being an "ego" distinct from the world vacillates and even dissolves' (1999: 71). If she is right, then the act of deep sensory improvisation or *creaturely knowing* has the potential to enhance a deep connection with our fragile planet.

In order to theoretically ground a practice in *creaturely knowing,* I draw on ideas from somatics, neuroscience cognitive biology, biochemistry, eco-perception psychology, evolutionary aesthetics, education, and dance, so as to underpin and recontextualize dance improvisation—both in educational and performance-based practice. At the University of Otago, New Zealand, where I teach, the dance studies programme, while a core component of the Performing Arts degree, is housed in the Division of Sciences. Here, a broad spectrum of the aesthetic, somatic, philosophical, educational, cultural, psychological, and neurophysiological subject matter are pursued across a variety of dance studies courses. This relationship with the sciences, however, requires ongoing justification and nurturing, even within our multidisciplinary School of Physical Education, Sport, and Exercise Sciences. In 2010 I presented a paper proposing a role for dance researchers (particularly those interested in improvisation) in transdisciplinary research within the university (East 2011a).

Specific links with the biological and neurological sciences and the artistic and educational practice of improvisation within the university setting are espoused here. In the process-oriented movement research within an improvisation classroom, it is possible, I contend, to link theoretical concepts from a variety of disciplinary areas as *poetic word-scape* into the sensed/intuited action-scape of the dance. When the language of improvisation is carefully considered (East 2006, 2011b), new knowledge may be assimilated into the dancer's consciousness as part of the organic somatosensory process without unduly disturbing the deep individual intuitive movement investigation. I include examples of word 'prompts' in order to stimulate a language for this purpose. As a result of combining ideas from the disciplines of the biological sciences with creative movement exploration, the ecology of the classroom becomes enlivened and the student's somatic investigations deepened. When the usual disciplinary boundaries are dissolved, students' understanding of the subject of 'dance' is broadened. My prompts suggest a further interweaving of scientific, somatic, and sensory imagery into the dance improvisation classroom. I am building here on two earlier texts in particular. In their book *Body Space Image,* Miranda Tufnell and Chris Crickmay (1990) unpack the body's skeletal architecture in a series of improvisational prompts designed to help students understand the structural interconnecting mechanisms of body and external world. Likewise, Andrea Olsen's text *Body and Earth* (2002) offers exercises of connection in order to link the internal workings of the human body with those of the planet. However, the improvisational journey of *spontaneous biological backtracking* may initially lack a verbal language of description, as such, for young students. It is here that a conundrum may arise within the academic setting, where written and verbal expression is required for assessment and accountability. I discuss this aspect later in the chapter as I address the academic rigour implicit in the work.

MERGING VOICES—DANCE AND THE NATURAL SCIENCES

Studies by cognitive biologists Francisco Varela (1999) and his colleague Renaud Barbaras (1999) have led to a new awareness of cognition as a whole body activity and new understanding of how sensory experience might be processed as a complex holistic set of responses—something we dancers know intuitively to be true. Mabel Todd knew it also when she wrote *The Thinking Body* (1937). Barbaras refers to 'behaviour as an expression of ... totality ... that can no longer be grasped as an encounter between a living being and an already constituted world, but as an expression' (1999: 532–533) making and unmaking itself from moment to moment as it makes contact with the world or operates within it. In other words, we and the world are shaped and reshaped each moment by our actions and interactions in a continually evolving dance.

> Prompt: *We shape and re-shape ourselves and the world in a continually evolving dance—each moment making and unmaking itself.* (Barbaras 1999)

> Prompt: *Organism and environment enfold into each other and unfold from one another in the fundamental circularity that is life itself.* (Varela, Thompson, and Rosch 2000: 217)

Varela, Thompson, and Rosch define this form of sensuous contact with the environment as 'a form of rapport between the senses and their objects, a matching of sensitivity between a sense and an object ... a dynamic process giving rise to emergence ... both a cause and an effect ... a coming together where there is potential for awareness' (119). These authors reject the notion of a need for self-consciousness, preferring instead the term 'emergence'.

> Prompt: *How might we explore the idea of emerging (while merging) presence?*

Among the various writers on dance improvisation, Melinda Buckwalter usefully surveys the strategies, processes, and applications for improvisational dance-making through a study of a number of key artists. They include her description of Monson's 're-negotiation of the boundaries between the human and natural worlds' as 'both immersion and translation at work' (2010: 140) and of Susan Sgorbati's investigation of 'complex self-organization', inspired by the work of evolutionary scientists and complexity theorists (135). Sgorbati has named her dance 'emergent improvisation' (2013: 2). Susan Foster discusses the ways the practice of dance improvisation may be considered empathic: it is affirming of both separateness (a re-inforcing of identity) and connectedness with the world (through kinaesthetic sensation) and is 'undertaken by one's entire subjectivity' (2011: 127). In her site-responsive improvisatory art, Pam Woods (2013) combines memories of people and place and sound resonances with detached self-witnessing. There is an increase in the number of academic writers who are exploring processes of somatic attunement and spontaneous performance practice which seeks to explore a more sensitized relationship with self and environment (Fraleigh 2004; Olsen 2002; Olsen and McHose 2014; East 2011b). Andrea Olsen suggests that 'as we open our senses to the world outside and to the world inside, we come to recognise them as one. From this perspective, without changing anything else, we are dancing in a new place. And there is no prescribed response: new forms, new visions, will emerge' (2014: xix). Each of these writers and dance artists promotes the sensing, holistic dancing body/mind as part of the living, breathing fabric and rhythmic expression of the self-regulating organism of Earth.

Merging, Evolving Identities

A number of writers and educators have written about identity and self-discovery through art-making. This is also true within dance. Marrying theories of self psychology with the practice of dance improvisation, one of these authors, Carol Press, advocates for practice in sensory awareness, exploration, and self-assertion (2002: 184). In her words, 'through interactions with functioning selfobjects, our sense of self evolves as our subjective patterns and organising of our experience creates self-structures—our intrapsychic ways of being in the world and interacting with it' (70). Taking a broader-than-human perspective, biochemist Mae Wan Ho describes the ceaseless emerging, submerging and reemerging of new patterns in the universe from the energy substrate. I might encourage the same continuous energy flow and transforming from the students, acknowledging that the sensory act of movement is itself its own meaning (Ho 2003: 249).

> Prompt: *From this place in the bedrock where you have lain still for millennia, begin to unpeel the layers of substrate, to evolve as a new form, a new configuration of energy.*
>
> ['The active now connecting "past" and "future," real with ideal' (248).]

Prompt: *Allow a ceaseless emerging, submerging and re-emerging from the energy sub-strate of new patterns in the universe.* (Ho 2003)

Ho suggests that as (human) space-time structures, we shape and reshape ourselves and our actions from moment to moment as we choreograph ourselves in and as part of the world. I make a direct link here to students' evolving self-identity, as Ho states: 'the positing of 'self' as a domain of a coherent space-time structure implies the existence of active agents who are free. Freedom in this context means being true to 'self', in other words, being coherent. A free act is thus a coherent act' (245). But individual identity can only exist within a community of diverse others, and thus Ho describes 'a nested hier-archy of individuals and communities ... truly a participatory creative universe' (248), which aligns with the classroom community of improvising dancers.

Prompt: *As diverse species in an old forest, allow yourself to exist in accordance with your truest nature, yet amongst others.*

Through guided 'danced' endeavours, teachers can plant the seed of identity into this 'energy substrate' of which Ho speaks, allowing original movement to evolve from a core rootstock of individual somaesthetic consciousness (Damasio 1999; Shusterman 2008; Sheets-Johnstone 2009). Antonio Damasio describes 'a transient core-self' (1999: 171) that is shaped and reshaped by contact with objects in the environment. From the mem-ories of this contact, an autobiographical self constructs itself. Maxine Sheets-Johnstone refers to the most fundamental level of somatic consciousness as 'creaturely knowing', which is simply to do with 'surface recognition sensitivity' (2009: 182). She suggests that corporeal consciousness may have evolved from these tactile sensuous interfaces into conscious movement. (I have appropriated her term here to describe my particular teaching approach.)

This deep investigation of oneself, finding one's 'authentic' movement patterns, via danced responses, is a difficult place to bring students to—especially those in their freshman year and still burdened with either their codified dance training or with no dance training at all, and almost certainly struggling with their identities as young adults. Theirs is not so much a search for choreographic expression as a search for the essence of themselves and an affirmation of their place within the current global youth culture, which includes knowing the 'moves'.

Prompt: *Evolutionary patterns of action re-emerge: Mutuality—enclosing, protecting, covering. Engagement—enclosing, surrounding, engulfing, supporting.*

When students truly explore this new kind of material, they leave behind the conven-tions of modernist choreographic practice, as well as the various kinds of aesthetic values, the various kinds of evaluations of product, and the presumption of theatrical presentation. I am, however, conscious that there is a component of unmediated and uncensored performativity involved in moment-to-moment intuitive movement

FIG. 26.1 Surface moving over surface. Improvisation in a Container (Dunedin Fringe Festival, 2013) with Ali East, dancer Hahna Briggs, and musicians Trevor Colman and Nick Cornish. Photograph courtesy of Ali East.

exploration that interested viewers may find absorbing or empathically engaging, and therefore I am not excluding the viewer as active witness. Revealing self to self or self to others (a tenet of Mary Starks Whitehouse's Authentic Movement practice) is an important educational classroom practice. Students can be carefully familiarized with working while being observed (witnessed) by each other.

Students of *somatic sensing* and *creaturely knowing* are encouraged to 'dig down' beneath the intellect to a place so instinctual, so beneath any strategy or rationale, that a move may happen as or before one becomes aware of it as an event. During such a moment, within my own improvising, I don't ask myself why, for instance, I am licking the leg of my co-dancer (this did happen once), grazing across the floor like some primordial starfish or sea urchin, or reaching my arms towards the light as a tendril searching for support. I am, as the epigraph to this chapter suggests, simply living this moment as it becomes available to me—I am dancing the moment—or the moment is dancing me. I am simply present—highly attentive to this moment *now*. Cognitive biologist Francisco Varela (Varela and Shear 2002) calls this act of being in the moment 'now ness', which he describes as 'pre semantic in that it does not require memoration (or in Husserl's terms, "presentification") in order to emerge' (118). The somaticist Fraleigh also describes a state of 'now' which is 'increased in awareness and a potential already present in the world' (2004: 119).[1]

We read from scientists such as Varela, Ho, and Fraleigh a different way of discussing time, space, intention, memory (past action), now-time (nowness), and expressivity, which may serve to recontextualize the study of dance within broader academic fields that include the cognitive sciences.

To allow students to move beyond self-consciousness and into 'a truly timeless-spaceless state which is almost certainly beyond our comprehension' is, according to Ho (2003: 242), to allow a glimpse of states of pure aesthetic inspiration akin to what some may call a religious experience or altered state. As an organism interacts with the environment, changes occur on a deep level of sensory perception. Leading students in experiencing this 'performing' of their fundamental selves offers them, I suggest, crucial personal insight. They may not quite achieve a Zen state of 'no mind', but they can certainly experience a lack of self-consciousness and a shedding of old habits and learned movements. According to dance educator Larry Lavender, 'they are dancing their "present-ness" as opposed to their "past-ness"' (2012: 63). While I am not suggesting that this coming to terms with self might be all that happens in the choreography class, it does nevertheless add another educational value and another dimension to dance within the university—in this case merging the disciplines of dance, psychology, and philosophy. For Fraleigh, sensory experience informs our understanding both of ourselves as conscious organisms and of the expressive energies of dance. She states: 'at an experiential level, somatic movement explorations and dance are related' (2000: 60).

> Prompt: *Like a plant moving towards the light the sensuous soma approaches, without judgement or expectation. There is curiosity with innocence.*

As this prompt suggests, my interest in plants also informs this work. I like their egoless yet determined reaching into the world—their searching, spiralling movement towards the light (see Chamovitz 2012).

> Prompt: *How is my 'vegetal intelligence' experiencing gravity and verticality?* (Chamovitz 2012: 137)

Authors such as Chamovitz, and Tompkins and Bird (*The Secret Life of Plants*, 1974), and naturalist filmmaker David Attenborough remind us of our shared DNA with plants and of their sensory awareness, un-self-consciousness, and self-determining searching and growing. I recall once finding myself face-downward on the floor with one outstretched arm and claw-like spread and arched fingers, feeling the floor around me before withdrawing, arching, twisting, and spiralling, only to repeat the same move in another direction several more times. A friend who witnessed the performance described one moment when I adopted an insect-like action that hovered and swayed, multilimbed and fragile. Meanwhile, my animal ears were tuned to the musical sounds and vocal utterings of other participants. I was conscious of, yet unconcerned by, those watching. The postshow feeling was of exhilaration and complete emptiness of mind. In his book *Your Inner Fish*, evolutionary historian Neil Shubin (2008) proves our direct ancestral links with fish, frogs, and sharks and even insects and worms. We learn that our brains, olfactory system, and jaws were formed from former gills, our ear was once our jaw, and our eyes were light-sensitive cells contained in our skin. Not only are we related to fish and reptiles but we know that during our foetal development, we re-peat those evolutionary phases of our history. It is possible to *re-member*, to put these memories of our past back together, to practice *biological backtracking* within the intuitive and sensuous moment of our dance.

> Prompt: *Re-membering the inner fish,*
>
> > *Jaw listens,*
> >
> > *Gills give voice to memory*
> >
> > *Seeing skin senses light.*

Educational Values of Practice in Somatic Sensing and Creaturely Knowing

The kind of purposeful yet intuitive sensing and searching through the world which I am promoting resonates with that of educator Edith Cobb (1895–1977), who described the way children learn naturally through spontaneous creative play as 'world-making' (1977: 66). Here students are 'worlding' (Heidegger's term) each moment into existence or, more accurately, engaging wilfully in a practice of psycho-somatic merging with the world. Cobb describes world-making as 'learning in the widest sense, but it is also an adaptation to environment as nature, a search for higher levels of synthesis of self and world' (66).

> Prompt: *Animal voices surface and disappear, morph and change.*

Press comments that 'fundamentally the mission of education is the development of individuals who can meaningfully engage the world with exploration, self-assertion, vitality and reciprocity, for the enhancement and transformation of sense of self, group self and the evolution of significant culture' (2002: 175). Similarly, Adam Curle (1973), cites noncompetitiveness, empathy, and the promotion of awareness as major aims of education. A university dance improvisation class, through its interactive, practice-based, and socially sensitive (empathically concerned) methodologies and ideologies, is well placed to play an important role in fostering these (still current) educational aims.

So what do I see as the value(s) in inviting students to explore movement improvisa-tion guided by their somato-sensory intuitions rather than learning someone else's external expectation of 'the danced-choreographic' (Lavender 2012: 63)? Perhaps I am simply tired of seeing whole classes using the same lifts, holds, turns, and steps within what they consider to be different dances but which in fact look like the same one. Even within the improvisational dance setting, it is difficult to move students beyond familiar learned skills and vocabularies and to see them genuinely explore a time/space of delicate and new movement—to invest all of their consciousness (and sub-consciousness) in this somatic searching. In this place, as the Zen master Osho attests, one simply dances each moment, each new direction as it arises.

R. G. H. Siu, in his classic *The Tao of Science*, describes a form of intuitive knowing which he calls 'no-knowledge' or 'non-being' (wu), which is transcendent of shape and time and deals with the sensory aspects of the world, or 'sensate truth' (1976: 79), as opposed to the 'rational truth' which is largely the focus of university learning. In this state of consciousness, the world and all of human action and thought are perceived as an 'undifferentiated aesthetic continuum' (81) and 'grasped as an immediate total apprehension' (75). Siu suggests that 'what is essential in education is a receptiveness to intuitive extrapolations into the totality of nature and a communion with her in the realm of no-knowledge.... Implementing techniques of transferring this superrational knowledge must be devised' (99). It would appear that when the motivation for movement is simply moving itself, there can be no end goal, no final academic outcome, and no particular standard to attain. Improvisation is a moving investigation that does not attempt to shape students in any particular way. It is a practice that requires no conscious symbolic expression or learned movement patterns. Students simply enter into a spontaneous *searching, surfacing,* and *sensing* of their environment, each other, and themselves. Nevertheless, as I hope to convey, there is important sustainable educational value implicit in this approach.

> Prompt: *SEARCHING—through air, reaching, spiralling, opening/closing, rolling, slithering, upwards, along, around, between.*
>
> *SURFACING—walls, floor, another body, own body.*
>
> *SENSING—smell, taste, texture, temperature, listening, seeing.*
>
> *MUSICIANS—Is there a sound-scape beneath or outside of learned, regular tonal range and rhythmic structure that might be a response to these images?*

I contend that Siu's sentiments (of almost sixty years ago) in urging a refocusing of academic education that validates knowledge gained through intuition and the senses is still valid today. Siu also reminds us that the educational 'procedures' and knowledge bases of the sciences and the arts are indeed 'not two distinct methods but one simultaneity' (92).

The following are some further key educational values as I perceive them.

First, this approach to teaching dance improvisation promotes less self-consciousness amongst the students and a deeper concentration on the unperformed/enacted moment. It is not that the students are not aware they are being witnessed but that their

FIG. 26.2 Plant-like searching of the air as tendril. Photograph by Molly Mitchley (with permission).

directed energy is more deeply in the action—time, space, and memory are interacting intuitively and unhesitatingly.

Second, there is transformative value in this educational practice. Davis Hutchinson and Sandra Bosaki (2001) include intuitive practices as a valid aspect of holistic, experiential and transformative education. While describing intuition as 'a cognitive process unmediated by rational analysis' (: 179), they suggest that there might be a form of reflection that is 'a state of being unto itself, a vehicle for encountering the richness and depth of the universe' (181). I suggest here that this practice can itself bring about new or transformative understanding for students. Action and reflection, memory and immediate perception, meld into one in the moment of being/doing. This, I contend, is the new leading edge of experiential education—in simply acknowledging the value of conscious presence and absolute awareness in the unobstructed moment of doing.

Other defining values of this kind of holistic and transformative education emphasize 'personal integration, as well as sociocultural and ecological awareness' (Hutchinson and Bosaki: 182). This value connects with an empathic concern with care and belonging (Gablik 1993; Foster 2011), a sense of community, relationship, or oneness with the world and its peoples—nature and culture combined and experienced as one interrelated process. (Geographer and environmental planner Janet Stephenson [Stephenson et al. 2010] coined the term 'nulture' to express this relationship.) In other words, this kind of learning activity nurtures a sense of ecological identity (Naess 1989; Sewell 1999;

Gablik 1993) that sees self as part of and not separate from others and the environment. A self-plus-other-plus-environment. Here I reference J. J. Gibson's (1979) ecological basis for perception, an interconnected self and world that is a seeing into self and the world—an actively and mutually receptive exchange between self and world.

Third, in its valuing of first-person intuition and tacit understanding, this method belongs within a somatic approach to teaching and learning. As such, it is self-directed, self-activated, self-determining, and self-reflexive (Fraleigh 2004). Fraleigh suggests further educational value from experiencing this spontaneous merging, or 'matching' as she calls it, as 'open[ing] up perception in non-competitive, non-judgemental ways' (2004: 122).

Fourth, there is value for the university research community as the dance improvisation class becomes a collaborator in transdisciplinary research, cognitive thinking, intuition, perception psychology, creativity, and more. In the same way that Varela and colleagues (2000: 33) advocate for mindfulness meditation as a link between the cognitive sciences and direct experience, I advocate the improvisational practice of *somatic sensing, creaturely knowing*, and *biological backtracking* as a way to help forge this link.

Finally, to quote Foster on Novack, this kind of educational dance experience can bring about 'a reconceptual[lizing of] the body's movement as a potential conduit to new ways of perceiving and orienting oneself in the world' (2011: 116). This approach to teaching improvisation has the potential to engender a deeper sense of the world ('a deepening world image'; Cobb 1977: 67), which involves an overlap of the arts and sciences.

ACADEMIC RIGOR, ASSESSMENT, AND REQUIRED GRADUATE ATTRIBUTES

It will be obvious by now that in this improvisational teaching and learning approach, there is no required acquisition of any complex movement technique, no wrong or right way to proceed, and no anticipated prescribed outcome. We are simply opening up the possibility of sensory engagement through which 'knowledge production' (Foster 2011: 218) (of self and other) may take place. Assessment is largely achieved through autoethnographic research essays and reflexive journal writing. Students define their progress in *creaturely knowing* in their own terms as they reflect on their sensory experiences and encounters; their intuitions of self-coherence, connection, or disconnection to others and the environment; and their sustained immersion in what Lavender (2013) has referred to as 'the interests of the body'. They are encouraged to make connections with the literature of somaesthetics, eco-perception psychology, and the biological and cognitive sciences, along with recent writing by other innovators of the improvisation class. Following the practice, students may take time to share thoughts and revelations and to either draw or write their immediate reflections, which feed into a report. Claire

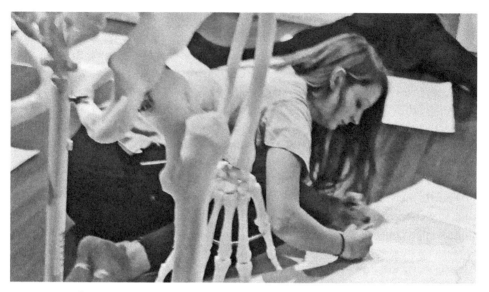

FIG. 26.3 Reflecting on somatic experience in the improvisation class. Student Lucia McEwan, 2014 (with permission); photograph by Ali East.

Petitmengin suggests that there is another level of academic understanding to be gained from reflecting on the nature of description itself: 'the description of the very process of becoming aware and describing [in this case, one's intuitive somato-sensory experience] is an essential condition for understanding, refinement, and evaluation of introspection methods as well as for the reproducibility of their results' (Petitmengin 2011).

This is not to unduly privilege verbal or written language over the knowledge and freedom gained from the deep intuitive sensing itself. However, finding a language for such experience allows collective sharing, thereby expanding each individual's perspective on perception even further and providing an easier fit with the university setting.

> Prompt: *Writing, drawing as dancing*
>> *Allow the mind to track back, surge forward.*
>> *Doesn't need to make sense—might be a poem, a list, a sketch.*
>> *Might be a memory a sensation, an encounter.*
>> *In what ways do I encounter the world?*
>> *Who is this 'I' who encounters?*

I concur with educationalist Patricia Broadfoot when she suggests that 'some of the most powerful ingredients of effective learning, that may be non-assessable by standard means, are excluded from curriculum .... We pay a high educational price for our obsession with measurement' (2000: 200).

If we consider self-awareness, and creative self-reliance, problem solving, and intuition, as essential attributes for surviving in an ever-changing and unpredictable

FIG. 26.4 Examples of first-year-level student journals (with student's permission). Photograph by East (2014)

transdisciplinary world, then we can make a strong case for the kinds of self-determining and self-reflexive improvisational practices of intuitive *somatic sensing* that I am promoting here. Broadfoot suggests that there has been 'a relative lack of scholarly attention' (2000: 202) to intuition in university research. Some of us who do have this interest may be to blame for working to make our creative pedagogies fit into an outmoded model of nineteenth-century assessment requirements. But can we simply sidestep academic assessment because it no longer suits our subject matter? Not yet, I think.

Microbiologist René Dubos suggests that free will, or one's ability to make choices based on one's experiences, is crucial to one's advancement and to one's creative and intellectual health and development. He states: 'the ability to choose among ideas and possible courses of action may be the most important of all human attributes; it has probably been and still is a crucial determinant of human evolution' (1970: 98). The freedom to determine the direction and shape of one's movement in an instinctual and unpredetermined manner is in direct contrast to the kind of prescribed, syllabus-based, standardized curriculum content that has been commonly taught in the dance class— and may be easily assessed and ranked by examiners. Is this the kind of educational experience that allows individuality to emerge and identity to evolve? I don't think so. The *creaturely knowing* classroom makes human freedom an explicit educational outcome. In the current world climate, such that the individual freedom of whole nations is at stake, this objective takes on an even greater significance.

In Conclusion

A program of *creaturely knowing, somatic sensing,* and *biological backtracking,* as I have named these improvisational provocations and practices, can help students discover deeper aspects of their individual selves, and understand shared qualities and capacities of human-ness. For in the end, it is the discovery and affirmation of ourselves as vibrant empathic, par-ticipatory, and connected human beings that may be the most important facet of all learning. By reorienting the course goals and learning outcomes, the university-based improvisation class has the capacity to make a strong contribution here. The resulting 'naturally aesthetic behaviour' (Dissanayake 1995: 71) or 'immersion in the interests of the body' (Lavender 2013) or what I have previously termed *intuitive movement practice* (East 1999) and more re-cently *creaturely knowing* can be validated as an important part of the dance studies curricu-lum. As such, it can make an important contribution both to the consolidation of student self-identity and to cross- and transdisciplinary research within the university. I conclude with a comment by developmental psychologist Joan Erikson: 'wisdom belongs to the world of actuality to which our senses give us access' (1997: 7).

FIG. 26.5 Ali East dancing with students and musician (2013). Photograph by Molly Mitchley (with permission).

NOTE

1. Drawing together perceptual experience and the temporalizing experience of 'now', Sondra Fraleigh refers to the way both Merleau-Ponty and Heidegger 'link perceptual experience and the temporalizing present, a "now"' (2004: 119).

REFERENCES

Barbaras, R. (1999) The Movement of the Living as the Originary Foundation of Perceptual Intentionality. In Petitot, J., Varela, F. J., Pachoud, B., and Roy, J.-M. (eds.), *Naturalizing Phenomenology: Issues in Contemporary Phenomenology and Cognitive Science*. Stanford, CA: Stanford University Press, 525–538.

Broadfoot, P. (2000) Assessment and Intuition. In Atkinson, Terry, and Claxton, Guy (eds.), *The Intuitive Practitioner: On the Value of Not Always Knowing What One Is Doing*. Buckingham, UK: Open University Press, 199–219.

Buckwalter, M. (2010) *Composing While Dancing: An Improviser's Companion*. Madison: University of Wisconsin Press.

Chamovitz, D. (2012) *What a Plant Knows; A Field Guide to the Senses*. Brunswick, Australia: Scribe Books.

Cobb, E. (1977) *The Ecology of Imagination in Early Childhood*. Dallas: Spring.

Curle, A. (1973) *Education for Liberation*. London: Tavistock Publications Limited.

Damasio, A. (1999) *The Feeling of What Happens: Body and Emotion in the Making of Consciousness*. New York: Harcourt, Brace.

Dissanayake, E. (1995) *Homo Aestheticus: Where Art Comes From and Why*. Seattle: University of Washington Press.

Dubos, H. (1970) *So Human an Animal*. London: Sphere Books.

East, A. (1999) Intuitive Movement Practice (IMP) as a Valid Teaching and Learning Tool within the University. Unpublished paper. University of Otago, Dunedin, NZ.

East, A. (2006) Teaching Dance As If the World Matters: A Design for Teaching Dance-Making in the 21st Century. Thesis. University of Otago, Dunedin, New Zealand.

East, A. (2011a) The Role of Dance Studies in a Transdisciplinary University Research Environment. *Brolga: An Australian Journal about Dance* 35: 49–56.

East, A. (2011b) *Teaching Dance As If the World Matters: A Design for Teaching Dance-Making in the 21st Century*. Saarbrücken, Germany: Lambert Press.

Erikson, J. (1997) *The Life Cycle Completed*. New York: Norton.

Foster, S. L. (2011) *Choreographing Empathy: Kinaesthesia in Performance*. London: Routledge.

Fraleigh, S. (1999) *Dancing into Darkness: Butoh, Zen, and Japan*. Pittsburgh: University of Pittsburgh Press.

Fraleigh, S. (2000) Consciousness Matters. *Dance Research Journal* 32(1): 54–62.

Fraleigh, S. (2004) *Dancing Identity: Metaphysics in Motion*. Pittsburgh: University of Pittsburgh Press.

Gablik, S. (1993) Towards an Ecological Self. In Hertz, R. (ed.), *Theories of Contemporary Art*, 2nd ed. New Jersey, NJ: Prentice Hall, 301–309.

Gibson, J. J. (1979) *The Ecological Approach to Visual Perception*. Boston: Houghton Mifflin.

Ho, M. W. (2003) *The Rainbow and the Worm: The Physics of Organisms*. 2nd ed. Singapore: World Scientific Publishing.

Hutchinson, D., and Bosaki, S. (2001) Over the Edge; Can Holistic Education Contribute to Experiential Education? *Journal of Experiential Education* 23(3): 177–182.

Lavender, L. (2012) The Emancipation of Improvisation. In Elkins, Lesley (ed.), *Conference ProceedingsNational Dance Education Organization of America*. Los Angeles: National Dance Education Organization of America, 62–70.

Lavender, L. (2013) Email conversation with Ali East, 26 March

Naess, A. (1989) *Ecology, Community and Lifestyle: Outline of an Ecosophy*. Trans. D. Rothenburg. New York: Cambridge University Press.

Olsen, A. (2002) *Body and Earth: An Experiential Guide*. Middlebury Bicentennial Series in Environmental Studies. Middlebury, MA: University Press of New England.

Olsen, A., and McHose, C. (2014) *The Place of Dance: A Somatic Guide to Dancing and Dance-Making*. Middletown, CT: Wesleyan University Press.

Osho. (2001) *Intuition: Knowing beyond Logic*. New York, NY: St Martins Griffin.

Petitmengin, C. (2011) Describing the Experience of Describing? The Blindspot of Introspection. *Journal of Consciousness Studies* 18(1): 44–62. (Abstract)

Petitmengin-Peugeot, C. (1999) The Intuitive Experience. In Varela, Francisco, and Shear, Jonathan (eds.), *The View from Within: First-Person Approaches to the Study of Consciousness*. Bowling Green, OH: Imprint Academic, 43–77.

Petitot, J., Varela, F. J., Pachoud, B., and Roy, J.-M. (eds.). (1999) *Naturalizing Phenomenology: Issues in Contemporary Phenomenology and Cognitive Science*. Stanford, CA: Stanford University Press.

Press, C. (2002) *The Dancing Self: Creativity, Modern Dance, Self-Psychology and Transformative Education*. Cresskill, NJ: Hampton Press.

Sewell, L. (1999) *Sight and Sensibility: The Eco-psychology of Perception*. New York: Tarcher/Penguin Putnam.

Sgorbati, S. (2013) Preface: Emergent Improvisation. On the Nature of Spontaneous Composition Where Dance Meets Science. *Contact Quarterly Dance and Improvisation Journal*. Chapbook 4, 38(2), Summer/Fall.

Sheets-Johnstone, M. (2009) *The Corporeal Turn: An Interdisciplinary Reader*. Exeter, UK: Imprint Academic.

Shubin, N. (2008) *Your Inner Fish*. London: Penguin Books.

Shusterman, R. (2008) *Body Consciousness: A Philosophy of Mindfulness and Somaesthetics*. New York: Cambridge University Press.

Siu, R. G. H. (1976) *The Tao of Science*. Cambridge, MA: MIT Press.

Stephenson, J., Abbot, N., and Ruru, J. (eds.). (2010) *Beyond the Scene: Landscape and Identity in Aotearoa New Zealand*. Dunedin: Otago University Press.

Todd, M. (1937) *The Thinking Body*. Trenton, NJ: Princeton Book Company.

Tompkins, P., and Bird, C. (1974) *The Secret Life of Plants*. Victoria, Australia: Penguin Books.

Tufnell, M., and Crickmay, C. (1990) *Body Space Image: Notes towards Improvisation and Performance*. Alton, Hampshire, UK: Dance Books.

Varela, F. (1999) Present-Time Consciousness. In Varela, Francisco, and Shear, Jonathan (eds.), *The View from Within: First-Person Approaches to the Study of Consciousness. Journal of Consciousness Studies* 6(2–3). Thorverton, EX. UK: Imprint Academic, 111–140.

Varela, F. J., and Shear, J. (2002) The View from Within: First Person Approaches to the Study of Consciousness. *Journal of Consciousness Studies* 6(2–3). Reprint. Thorverton, EX. UK: Imprint Academic. (Originally published 1999)

Varela, F. J., Thompson, E., and Rosch, E. (2000) *The Embodied Mind: Cognitive Science and Human Experience*. Cambridge, MA: MIT Press.

Woods, P. (2013) 'The Resonant Body'. In edited by Reeve, Sandra (ed.), *Ways of Being a Body: Body and Performance*. Axminster, UK: Triarchy Press, 53–66.

CHAPTER 27

IMPROVISING HAPPINESS

Belly Dance's Evolution through Improvisation

BARBARA SELLERS-YOUNG

What is most critical about improvisation is that the past is always already manifest in the embodied techniques that ground it; equally important, improvisation is never an exact reproduction of the past. The practices performers embody are resources, or capital, for transaction and transformation in the very process of doing. In this way, improvisation is an interpretive strategy for negotiating the present as well as embodiment of skills and techniques that have withstood the test of history. Improvisations are thus synthesizing practices that apply embodied knowledge to new situations. They are hybrid and nomadic.

Margaret Thompson Drewal (2003: 120)

IT is March 1973 and I am in a living room in Eugene, Oregon, with six other women in a circle, taking my first belly dance class. The teacher, Scylla, is guiding us through a set of movements in which our hips curve in circles and eights or punctuate the space with sharp direct gestures. After an hour of practice to the rhythmic beat of a recorded drum, Scylla puts on a version of the Greek traditional song 'Misirlou' and tells us to go ahead and improvise to the music using the three or four movements she has taught us. Feeling slightly uncomfortable, I find a corner and begin to try to combine circles with figure eights, hips with circles, and consider what I should be doing with my head, arms, and hands. I seem to know my body as parts and not as an expressive whole. I keep repeating each movement searching for the connection between pelvis and spine, torso and arms, torso and legs. Finally, Scylla brings us back to the circle and suggests this is the period in which we share what we learn with the class by performing our improvisations for each other. I am terrified. I cannot imagine performing with so little movement vocabulary. However, I am pulled into the centre of the circle by the warmth and generosity of Scylla's presence, which seems to spread around the room and to the other women. In the end, the class, which was going to be a one-time-only experience to begin to get in shape following the birth of my second daughter, becomes a weekly event to which I look forward.[1]

My experience of improvisation as a central component of a belly dance class is not unique. As belly dance has become part of the global popular culture, improvisation has been a central component of classes, as students of the form from Toronto to Singapore, from London to Cape Town, from Paris to Beijing, seek to discover their self-expressive potential. This essay considers improvisation with the framework defined by Margaret Thompson Drewal: 'an interpretive strategy for negotiating the present as well as embodiment of skills and techniques that have withstood the test of history' (2003: 120). As such, the essay considers the nomadic positioning of improvisation in belly dance, from the dance's presence at family celebrations in North Africa, the Middle East, and related diaspora to its inclusion in the second wave of feminism in North America and Europe, and to the development of new hybrid styles of the dance and theatrical representations of the form that have grown out of improvisations that have united the vocabulary of belly dance with other dance forms.

Although the focus of the essay is on the role of improvisation in constructing the movement vocabulary and therefore the evolution of belly dance in the United States, the global history of belly dance, as previous essays have noted (Shay and Sellers-Young 2003; Jarmakani 2008; Maira 2008; Deagon 2015), is consistently infused with what Edward Said (1978) termed 'Orientalism', a perceptual framework that imposes an interpretation on the improvisational dances of North Africa and the Middle East that ranges from the erotic to the spiritual. The consequence is that the improvisations associated with the evolution of belly dance, regardless of geographic location, are performed with orientalism as a psychic backdrop. In essence, the dancer is improvising self through the known construction of the orientalist lens in a desire for personal agency either within an orientalist construction or in opposition to it. Dancers are therefore improvising from an assumed known, orientalism, to discover the unknown of the improvised self. This essay thus demonstrates the pivotal role of improvisation and the individual explorations of what Susan Foster states is a central tenet of improvisation: an ongoing exploration of *known* and the *unknown* through the immediacy of the self (2003: 3).

THE ROOTS OF IMPROVISATION

Lois Ibsen al-Farqui (1978) identified solo improvisational forms, such as the Egyptian *raqs sharqi,* that managed, along with combat, group, and religious dances, to survive both medieval Islam's and Christianity's discomfort with dance as a mode of expression. Embedded in the tenets of Islam are concerns with human representation that Wood and Shay (1976) note are part of Islamic attitudes towards the performing arts in general. It is an attitude Shay in his 1999 study on dance in Iran and its related diaspora labelled 'choreophobia'. This term encompasses a wide range of prohibitions on physical behaviours, based on gender, age, social status, religiosity, context, and individual personality traits that impact a dancer or a dancer's reception in a particular context. Shay's model demonstrates how the complex set of relationships that contribute to dance is a component of social celebrations yet also is a mode of expression that needs careful regulation to prevent transgressions of accepted gender relations.

Al-Farqui (1987), Anthony Shay (1999), and Najwa Adra (2005) all describe the movement vocabulary and related aesthetics of North African and the Middle East. Al-Farqui writes: 'aesthetic beauty was intuitively conceived as that which stylized and disguised nature, or avoided it completely in abstract designs' (1978: 7). Shay (1995) suggests that the movement vocabularies of the various solo improvisational dances tend to be patterned on abstraction and Islamic visual arts such as calligraphy. This is kinaesthetically realized in a dance vocabulary that is inclined towards small, intricate movements of the head, hands, torso, or hips. The legs are used to augment the movement of the head and torso; the arms are used to frame the movement. Often the dancer accentuates the movement of the hips and torso with the rapid-fire accompaniment of brass finger cymbals. The dance's structure is based on improvised movements that evolve into a series of minicrescendos that reflect the complexity of the music.

Adra describes this improvisational form as social play that is part of the discursive framework of celebratory events. Those attending a wedding, birthday, or other social gathering are encouraged to express their joy in community by getting up to dance and then inviting another to dance: 'the dancer will then improvise, sometimes turning her attention inward, sometimes playing at flirtation with a spectator of either sex. The dancer might move toward a spectator with shoulder shimmies, or execute a back bend directed toward a spectator's lap, stopping short of touching the person. The spectator may be a friend, a favoured relative or an honoured guest. At a family gathering, this normally would not be a prospective spouse or anyone with whom a serious flirtation could legitimately occur' (2005: 33). Adra further points out that the dance in the subtleness of its movement vocabulary is embodying the psychophysical representation of the daily negotiations individuals make between the valuing of individual autonomy and the context of social mores. As she phrases it:

> the dance form is very much the ideal of self-expression. By encouraging individuality and competition while controlling its contexts, the cultural message is that there is considerable leeway for a person to do what she (he) wants so long as it is done away from the public gaze.... In a society that values community and autonomy, the authentic self is less important than the multiple roles each person is required to play. The negotiation of the rules of appropriate behaviour inherent in amateur belly dancing events, the current isolation of various body parts, and the continuous improvisation, all replicate the negotiation skills necessary for daily life in this society. (43)

These amateur performances are engaged, as Sherifa Zuhur points out, in the aesthetic quality of *tarab*, or enchantment. *Tarab* is a 'quality that causes enjoyment,

reciprocation of emotion and communication between performers and their audiences'
(2000: 1) that is learned from improvisational participation in community celebrations.
Ethnomusicologist A. J. Racy expands on this concept of enchantment and describes
tarab as a transformational experience of ecstasy related to improvisation: 'the nuances
and connotations of the word *tarab* as commonly used today are consistent with the
concept of ecstasy as explained in standard English sources. Accordingly, ecstasy, like
tarab, implies experiences of emotional excitement, pain or other similarly intense emotions, exaltation, a sense of yearning or absorption, feeling of timelessness, elation or
rapturous delight. Moreover, the term ecstasy tends to fit the various conditions associated with *tarab* as a transformative state, for example those connected with intoxica-
tion, empowerment, inspiration, and creativity' (2003: 6). The depth of emotional state
related to *tarab* is brought about by the music's aural representation of a deep cultural
matrix of interconnected relationships between religious, social, and cultural forces and
invocation of them in memory.

Dance scholar Candace Bordelon explains in an essay on the aesthetic dimensions of
performance that the dance as a revelation of *tarab* is a 'merger between the music and
emotional transformation' (2013: 33); phrased another way: the dancer sings the music.
Amateur and professional dancers engage an improvisational mode through a depth
of listening and related musical understanding to portray a series of emotional portraits that are a revelation of the music and its association with the audience's cultural
framework. In Egypt, this could be a rendition of a popular song, a village *baladi* tune, or
one of the compositions created for the most popular singer in Egyptian history, Umm
Kulthūm. Bordelon suggests that dancers pick classical compositions of composers
such as Farid al Atrash because the music's complex interweaving of different rhythms
and musical phrasing brings forth 'images, ideas and feelings associated' with a specific
emotional context for the audience 'that are transcendent because they are not limited to
a specific time and place' (42).

As Racy, Zuhur, and Bordelon note, an important portion of the dance is conveyed
through improvisation that is deeply engaged with the music and that in its immediacy
connects the performers and audience in mutual enjoyment. Dancing in the context
of a family or community celebration, the individual dancer is participating in a wedding or other life-cycle ritual in which the dancer is performing a set of movements to
a music for which the dancer has an entire cultural history that integrates the style and
quality of the movement with the music and the context of performance. With each new
movement, the dancer improvises a set of gestures that is reminiscent of the members of
the dancer's community. As these are events in which more than one family or community member will be performing, the dancer has an opportunity to investigate through
improvisation the movement style and vocabulary of more than one person and to
evolve a personal improvisational style. In an increasingly globalized world, these intimate points of contact between music and performer share the imaginative space with
public venues in which the cultural values of *tarab* may or may not be an important aesthetic component of the performance, as native and nonnative performers and choreographers create dances that may include Western aesthetics (Shay 2002: 126–162).

BELLY DANCE IN THE DIASPORA

Within the Arab diaspora, the dance has retained its improvisational focus in communities throughout the globe. In a series of articles for *Arabesque*, Lebanese dancer Ibrahim Farrah (1939–1998) described learning the dance his mother referred to as the 'happiness dance' from his male relatives at family celebrations. His memories of his male relatives dancing are grouped into three categories. The first he refers to as 'expressionist', in reference to the dancer's deep connection to gravity and space: 'they would stamp their feet on the ground, and one could feel the entire weight of their body and strength push through the earth. With a slow shift of weight and a wave of arms, their energy would suddenly transfer from weighing on the earth to floating in air, giving the appearance of someone about to take flight' (1992: 15–17). He described a second style as 'conservative' in its reliance on simplicity and a limited movement vocabulary and saw it as similar to a feminine style in its limited use of space. He wrote: 'step patterns in the men's dance had a touch of heaviness as opposed to the light footedness of the women's style. While women shook their shoulders softly and loosely, the men's shoulder motions were those with rhythmic sharpness and more defined accents. Their shoulders would pulse up and down or thrust forward and be released in a honed fashion. Although extremely graceful, they used few decorative arm patterns, moving their arms rhythmically from pose to pose (and gesture to gesture) with a musicality and poetry that can only be described as extraordinary' (15–17). The third category he defined as 'freer': 'men moved with more freedom of motion. Their dances were decorated with more turning patterns, a quick shuffling of feet that could send them scurrying across the room and through space, unconstrained: shoulder shakes were loose: arms were more decorative; a little hip action; and an emotion of sheer exuberance' (15–17). Farrah's dance style evolved as an integration of these masculine styles that united the movement vocabulary of hips, torso, and head with a clear delineation of the strength of a male body's command of space, delineated by the use of feet, hips, and shoulders outlined by the position of the arms.

Learning the dance from his male relatives, Farrah engaged a form of mimêsis, a direct transmission from the body of the dancer to the body of the observer. In this approach to the dance experience, the performer and observer are performing a set of movements to a music for which they have an immediate cultural history that integrates the style and quality of the movement with the music and the context of performance. With each repetition of the performer's movement, the observer increasingly takes on the nuances of the performer's body—the shifts of weight, the adjustment of the spine and torso, the turn of the head, the placement of the arms and hands—until the observer's entire being embodies not only the movement phrasing but the entire emotional ethos attached to the movement.

Ultimately, the improvising dancer has transformed the experience of the dancer's 'lived-body' through an intensive engagement with the body of another, a transformation in which the body of the performer, through imitation, becomes the object of the learner's subjective identity. In this instance, the dancer becomes through personal improvisation an extension of the performer and any cultural metaphors embedded in the movement vocabulary of the technique. The dualistic subject/object field is united in their embodied consciousness via the total engagement of all sensory modes in a transmission process of intersubjectivity that culminates in the body of the observer becoming a moving image of the body or bodies of those the observer has imitated. Ultimately, the experience for the dancer is a unification of multiple senses within a single action. The result is an integration of technique and cultural knowledge in a single act of the dancer's improvised embodiment of a specific cultural consciousness in which the known of the everyday becomes deeply embedded in the dancer. Improvisation in this context becomes a means of continuing tradition and a means of self-discovery as self within this cultural milieu.

In the United States following World War II, a number of Middle Eastern themed restaurants and clubs developed. These venues were, according to ethnomusicologist Anne Rasmussen, 'an outgrowth of the community music events of Arab Americans' (1992: 355) and an extension of the commercial aspirations of this community. While a Middle Eastern American community-based event would not include orientalist decor reminiscent of a Hollywood film set, many restaurant and nightclub venues did embrace the prevailing melting pot philosophy and adopted a fantasy version of the Orient to appeal to a diverse clientele (Rasmussen 1992). Rasmussen points out that the restaurant musicians came from throughout North Africa and the Middle East. As Egypt was the centre of the entertainment industry, the majority of the music played was by noted Egyptians, such as Farid al-Atrash and Mohammed Abdel Wahab. At the same time, the musicians who were used to improvisation as a component of the music integrated the 4/4 and 4/8 rhythms of Egypt, the 9/8 rhythms of Turkey, and the 6/8 rhythms of North Africa. The musical styles and instruments of Greece, Turkey, Egypt, Lebanon, Syria, and elsewhere in the Middle East mingled with the saxophone, electric guitar, and drum set.

Musicians in these venues played while patrons of the restaurants participated in group dances, most often the *dabke*. But there were also solo performances, referred to as *raqs sharqi*, by professional dancers from the Middle East. In New York's Middle Eastern restaurants, these performances were contemporary versions of the performances of twentieth-century dancers of Cairo and Istanbul, made famous internationally by the Egyptian film industry. In these restaurants, each belly dancer improvised a performance in correspondence with the musicians that was her version of *raqs sharqi*, based on traditions from the Middle Eastern country where she grew up. This dance vocabulary was combined with the movement vocabulary that the dancer picked up by watching the other dancers in the restaurant.

Over time, musicians and dancers integrated the folk rhythms from throughout North Africa and the Middle East, and a dancer from Egypt would not only be familiar with the 4/4 and 4/8 rhythms of Egypt but also the 9/8 rhythms of Turkey and the 6/8 rhythms of North Africa. As Rasmussen describes them, the restaurants were 'adventurous, creative, polyethnic, electronic, and commercial. The music reflected interaction both with other immigrant groups and with American society and music culture as a whole' (1998: 47). As Rasmussen points out, these sites held some emotional ambiva-lence for the musicians and other performers: 'although the trademarks of Orientalism helped these musicians to achieve success, the racist bias of this European belief system served to enhance the foreignness of these Arab and other Middle Eastern immigrants and their families, placing them in an imaginary world that was exotic—even to them-selves' (1992: 345–365). The Middle Eastern immigrant patrons of these restaurants, who were from Greece, Turkey, Egypt, Palestine, Syria, Lebanon, and elsewhere, were forced to individually negotiate and enact an identity through the integration of music and dance styles that reflected not the specificity of their personal backgrounds but a popular conception of the Orient.

With the popularization of such dance in restaurants, there was an increased demand for entertainers. American dancers who had watched the movements of the Middle Eastern dancers on the restaurant stages found work through an improvised copy of these staged representations. One of these early dancers, Morocco, describes their per-formances: 'dances were improvised to live music for at least half an hour, often more, using what was considered the "expected" format at that time: fast opener/*magensi*, slow/*rhumba*-like tempo, heavy *chiftetelli* or *wahada debria*, drum solo and fast end or fast *karsilama*. Later, another upbeat section was added between the rhumba and the *wahada* or heavy *chifititelli*. We all used what we'd seen, learned and felt inspired to try. We learned to think on our dancing feet, since there was no guarantee as to who would play what nor when' (2000). Unlike the members of the North African and Middle Eastern diaspora who as children had used improvisation as a component of their imi-tations of their friends and relatives, the American restaurant dancers integrated imi-tation and improvisation of an unknown but desirable and erotic other. With a limited understanding of the cultural context, their improvisational mode was a replication and personalization of belly dance's movement vocabulary. In order to give meaning to the form, they began to combine their personal improvisations with new versions of history.

IMPROVISING SELF

American actor, dancer, and poet Daniela Gioseffi, along with other American dan-cers of the second wave of feminism in the 1960s and 1970s, engaged in a new nar-rative for the dance. Gioseffi improvised her feminist narrative in a one-woman show titled 'The Birth Dance of Earth: A Celebration of Women and the Earth in Poetry, Music and Dance'. Her improvised performance was a scored narrative of an Etruscan priestess who entered the performance space covered by a veil that floated around her and subtly revealed her face, torso, and pelvis as she moved to the beat of the drum. Ultimately, she revealed her 'body to the community of women and men. They watched, enthralled by her flowing motions, her spectacular garments, the mes-merizing stare of her eyes above her veiled face, the even contained rhythms of her walk' (1980: 22). In Gioseffi's imagined rendition of the dance and the mythology she evolved for it, the men looked on in awe and the women with reverence as they saw in the movement an image of the primordial mother goddess, as she dropped to the floor and, with a series of belly rolls and stomach flutters, mimed giving birth. In this mythic depiction's focus on woman as life giver, Gioseffi's performance celebrated the potential of a woman's body to discover and express the joy of the relationship between the internal kinaesthesia of the spirals and circles of the pelvis and spine that moved from inward to outward projection, from individual self-revelation to mutual discovery in performance with an audience.

In the studio, in rehearsal, and onstage, belly dancers of the 1970s embraced the image of the goddess and negotiated through improvisation the intersections between self, society, and the perceptual awareness of their dancing bodies to create a style referred to as American cabaret. The dancer's body in performance increasingly became an act of mediation between the physical vocabulary of the dance form and personal conceptions of identity. For many women during the second wave of feminism, belly dance was an erotic site of power and transcendence. Dancing their internalized version of the oriental feminine derived from films such as *Salome* (1953), featuring Rita Hayworth, or *Salomon and Sheba* (1959), with Yul Brynner and Gina Lollobrigida, the women who embodied media representations of the feminine that, prior to performance, were only mental fantasies. In a variation of group therapy and its role-playing model, the women improvised these internalized images in classes and small recitals. Their self-perception changed as the movements of the dance engaged them with 'the wholeness of the deeply and subtly minded body-of-action' (Fraleigh 1987: 30). Feeling empowered by the experience of the dance, women described the dance and subsequent performance as giving them a sense of ownership of their bodies.[2]

In its embrace of a woman's body through the image of an ancient goddess, belly dance celebrated the sensuality of a woman's body, the innate ability of women to give birth, and the meditative qualities of movement. This kind of performance thus incorporated several themes that were an extension of the search for free expression of the female form sought by early modern dance pioneers Loie Fuller, Isadora Duncan, and Ruth St. Denis. Contemporary belly dancers often reference the early modern dancers as models.

American Tribal Style: Choreographic Improvisation

Carolena Nericcio-Bohlman is a dancer from the lineage of those who engaged the image of the goddess. She is a personal physical trainer as well as a belly dancer who shares Gioseffi's interest in women's ownership of their bodies. Even so, she defines physical ownership differently than Gioseffi. Nericcio-Bohlman correlates physical with psychological strength and relates both to dance. Her version of belly dance is a style referred to as American Tribal Belly Dance. This style of belly dance is an expression of the innate strength of a powerful and confident female body that is developed in the gym, physically refined in the dance studio, and aesthetically focused on the stage.

Classes at Nericcio-Bohlman's San Francisco studio or in the DVDs she has produced are an example of this philosophy. Would-be dancers stand in staggered lines behind her and carefully imitate her upright body posture and carefully orchestrated movement vocabulary of hip and arm gestures. The unity of form among the students is created through the consistent repetition of the same movements in unison with other dancers. This format disregards improvisation as a primary mode and replaces it with repetition to create a kinaesthetic engagement with the other students in the course of which the dance form becomes a concrete language. Individual expressiveness is subsumed within the physical form and aesthetic style of Nericcio-Bohlman's version of American Tribal Belly Dance, in which heads are held high, backs arch, arms stay lifted, and hips swivel so as to convey strength of the body in motion.

Nericcio-Bohlman's version of American Tribal Belly Dance is achieved to a degree through a common movement vocabulary and costume. Yet the power of its presentation is realized onstage through a form of improvisational choreography. The performance of American Tribal Belly Dance relies on a set of visual and aural cues from a designated leader. Physical cues are subtle gestures that suggest a change in movement. They can be a rise on the toes to indicate a level change or a lift of a wrist to signal a turn. With recorded music, there could be a change in the music that points to a change, or the lead dancer could use her finger cymbals as a break between movement phrases. There is, however, at all times a designated, rotating leader. In fact, one of the primary tenets is that every woman is both leader and follower in a process of ongoing surrender to and reliance on each other.

The company's staged performance is influenced by the demand, imposed by this method of improvised choreography, that all dancers must be able to see the leader. Thus, stage use is restricted to combinations of half circles, triangles, or staggered and diagonal lines. Within these stage configurations, the dancer, under her layers of costume and make-up, wears a smile that engages yet distances her from the audience. Her attention is not on creating a relationship with the audience but on the interplay between dancers that signifies the ongoing interdependence of the tribe; or as Nericcio-Bohlman suggests 'in tribal style, the dancers are surrendering to their fellow dancers. Everyone has to cooperate or the show falls apart' (Alexis 2002: 52). Unlike a cabaret belly dancer, a dancer of American Tribal Belly Dance is not improvising a set of internalized Hollywood images in an attempt to come to a state of transcendence. Instead, she has (re)defined the feminine image and is presenting it in conjunction with her tribal sisters. This is a sense of tribe that extends beyond the stage to create a community in which dancers come to identify one another as members of an extended family that provides the support system typically associated with blood relatives, a tribe that presents itself through its improvised choreography not as performing for the audience but performing for one another with the audience observing.

The tribal or extended family component of American Tribal Belly Dance is the enduring centre of this fast-growing variety of belly dance. Variations of the American Tribal Belly Dance company have developed in the San Francisco Bay Area and elsewhere around the globe. These companies imitate the form and costume style of American Tribal Belly Dance while at the same time creating an identity that reflects a local version of the concept of being a tribe. As such, they could reproduce images from the *National Geographic* and other media and from the videos of gypsy life *Latcho Drom* and *Gacjo Dilo*. There is also a belief that the tribe impacts participants' personal identities as women.

American Tribal Belly Dance, with its emphasis on group identity and related expression of that identity, is a variation of the improvised self-expression that cabaret dancers espoused in the earlier phases of belly dance's history in the United States. With its clearly recognized movement and costume style, the form is not a rendition of the Hollywood/television image of the Middle East. The women performing it are not attempting to allay an internalized version of the oriental *femme fatale*. They are instead creating an alternative image of the erotic power of a woman existing in her communion with other women, onstage as performers and offstage in the emotional support they provide to one other. Within this improvised staged identity, the power of media images of women over a woman's subjective experience of self is challenged.

IMPROVISING THE GLOBAL IN THE LOCAL: TRIBAL, FUSION, GOTHIC, AND OTHER FORMS OF BELLY DANCE

American cabaret and American Tribal Belly Dance are not the only versions of belly dance that have been removed from belly dance's specific cultural moorings in North Africa and the Middle East. In fact, belly dance has consistently transformed and changed to create new styles and vocabularies that reflect a social cultural context and associated historical moment. This includes new forms of American Tribal Belly Dance that integrate improvisation in the class and on the stage. Paulette Rees-Denis, director and founder of the Gypsy Caravan Dance Company, is an example (see fig. 27.1). An artist and musician as well as a dancer, Rees-Denis traces her dance background to San Francisco and her life as teacher and performer to the Pacific Northwest and Portland, Oregon. At the centre of her goals as a dance teacher is transmitting a sense of expanded self-image through empowerment. In a recent course, she encouraged students to explore what empowerment meant to them by asking 'What does the word empowerment mean to you? How does it differ from the word power? Where do you feel empowered in your body? And when do you feel empowered?'[3] Such personal questions are asked within the context of an environment of emotional and psychophysical safety for the students. For Rees-Denis's primary goal is to encourage students to get in touch with the depth of their own experience, or what she refers to as the 'intuitive self'. Thus, the class begins and ends with a group circle of acknowledgement of self and one another and proceeds through a focus on breath, guided meditation, and warm-up that combines yoga with the circles and spirals of belly dance, followed by the introduction of a new dance movement and an opportunity to integrate the new vocabulary into an evolving individual style of movement through improvisation. There are also opportunities within the course's structure for dancers to participate in improvisational explorations in which they mirror or respond to each other's movement in pairs and in larger groups. Music by the affiliated music group, also called Gypsy Caravan, provides much of the rhythmic backdrop and phrasing for the improvisations. Global in its composition, the music blends musical styles from North Africa, the Middle East, and around the world.

From twenty years of teaching students, Rees-Denis has witnessed how life-changing her course is for students as they make discoveries through the integration of personal safety, breath, focus, movement and improvisation, and expanded sense of self. Kent De Spain unites this heightened skill set with embodied cognition. He writes: 'one such skill is a heightened sensitivity to what is happening during the improvisation, a layered, synchronic process of embodied cognition that I refer to as 'improvisational aware-ness' (2011: 26). Esther Thelen and Linda Smith (1996) discuss this expanded self as a consequence of an increased neural plasticity of the dancer's cognitive structures that

FIG. 27.1 Dancers: Christine Haviland (New Zealand), Cinzia DiCioccio (Italy), Karen Hunt (US), Paulette Rees-Denis (US), Deirdre McDonald (UK), Amanda Richardson (US), Nina Martinez (Australia). Photography by Carrie Meyers/The Dancer's Eye (2015)

develops as the result of focus initially on the breath and one's own body and ultimately through improvisation with the bodies of others. As Thelen phrases it: 'to say that cognition is embodied means that it arises from bodily interactions with the world. From this point of view, cognition depends on the kinds of experiences that come from having a body with particular perceptual and motor capacities that are inseparably linked and that together form the matrix within which memory, emotion, language, and all other aspects of life are meshed' (2001: xx). Thelen and Smith further argue that the relationship between individual cognition and the environment is a dynamic system in which a variety of the body's forces interact to integrate information. This is an ongoing process in which new activity of the body in relationship to the environment integrates past information with the new experience so as to evolve new forms of embodied consciousness, which results in new behaviours. These dynamic cognitive processes are also lifelong. These consciously engaged new patterns often become what Antonio Damasio in *Self Comes to Mind* (2010) refers to as unconscious behaviour, as they become embedded into the neural structure of experience. Rees-Denis's anecdotal observation is that the students in her courses have an increased level of awareness that opens avenues of problem-solving that they apply to their lives outside the studio.

TRIBAL FEST AND THE IMPROVISATIONAL FUTURE

Sitting in the main auditorium of the Sebastopol Community Center in May 2014, I watched three days of performances at *Tribal Fest 14: From the Root to the Fruit*. Watching performance after performance, I was reminded of the history of belly dance, from its inclusion within the family and community celebrations in North Africa and the Middle East to its arrival at the Chicago World's Fair in 1893, and to the evolution of the form as it exists today in global popular culture. Dancers who are creating their professional lives through the form continue to use improvisation to push the boundaries of the form's vocabulary. This includes studio courses by belly dance teachers who continue to use improvisation as part of their pedagogical method but purposely integrate belly dance vocabulary with other forms. One such example is Toronto-based dancer-teacher Yasmina, whose classes include special workshops in what she terms 'advanced dance artistry', which incorporate choreographers in contemporary dance, hip-hop, Japanese, ballet, African, and flamenco' to 'unlock new horizons and potential' for those who attend (Yasmina 2014).

Other dancers create thematic staged performances at the intersection of the vocabulary of belly dance and other forms. One such example is Jillina, former artistic director of the international touring company Belly Dance Superstars, formed by rock music producer Miles Copeland. In 2009, she created Belly Dance Evolution, a company that states its mission as to explore, celebrate, and reimagine 'Middle Eastern dance for the

21st century. By fusing belly dance with dance forms more specific to the West, Belly Dance Evolution takes you on a spectacular journey that will excite both mainstream audiences and belly dance enthusiasts' (2014). Although the company's dancing is based on a fusion of belly dance with other dance forms evolved from the improvisational framework of the studio, the final performances are choreographed. In this regard, Jillina is following in the footsteps of early twentieth-century dance promoter Badi'a Masabni. Through her Cairo Opera House, she integrated the tradition of improvisational performances by the public dancers—referred to as Ghawazee—with Western staging and vocabulary borrowed from ballet, so as to provide entertainment for the elite of Egyptian society. Two noted dancers who worked with her, Tahia Carioca and Samia Gamal, brought this style to Egyptian films of the 1940s–1950s and thus to the global community (Sellers-Young 2013: 5).

Bellydance Evolution has used an integration of the Internet and the practice of the festival—a type of event that occurs often in belly dance communities—to bring Jillina's version of belly dance to a global community. Using specific stories or themes, such as 'Alice in Wonderland', murder and deceit within a mythical kingdom ('Dark Side of the Crown'), and stories of passion, jealousy, and love ('Immortal Desires'), the company creates a production that they present initially in Los Angeles, where they are located. This production is marketed to the global belly dance community through an online casting competition in which dancers from an urban centre are cast in conjunction with a core group of dancers affiliated with Jillina. The dancers chosen are sent videos of their roles one month prior to performance and go through an intensive weeklong rehearsal the week of performance. The company members who travel to the site of the performance also provide workshops that are open to all dancers in that area. Thus far, Bellydance Evolution has brought this style of production to over twenty countries around the world.

Arjun Appadurai (1996) has observed that the social imaginary of the global community is negotiated through the impact of five global flows: ethnoscapes, mediascapes, technoscapes, financescapes, and ideoscapes. Sydney Hutchinson suggests (2013) that Appardurai's concept be expanded to include the choreoscape, which references dance forms and their relationship to a combination of the global flow of images and the cultural life of a specific community. As choreoscape, these flows converge with the social imaginary and impact the evolution of a dance form. Within the framework of belly dance history, the subtext of the flow of images has been improvisation. An improvisational mode is found in the versions of belly dance that take place in communities in North Africa and the Middle East and related diaspora. This includes the performances on the stages of ethnic restaurants. A version of improvisation is encouraged in belly dance classes when dancers are given the opportunity to take the movement vocabulary and make it their own. Another version takes place in the highly visual and kinaesthesia-reliant improvisational stage choreography that has been developed by Carolena Nericcio Bohlman and has been incorporated into the work of dance companies around the globe that practise derivatives of it. In addition, there is the improvisation that takes place when a dancer improvises between forms and integrates the belly dance vocabulary with other movement forms and from this creates the thematic productions of such groups as Bellydance Evolution.

Tribal Fest is fourteen years old (having started in 2000); the moving global dialogue that it represents is over a hundred years old, and somewhere in the process, belly dance, in whose movement and costuming the belly features so predominantly, is no longer a dance of North Africa and the Middle East but a dance of popular culture shared by people across the globe. People who have found joy, creativity, meaning, and identity within the improvising possibilities of belly dance have followed it in a personal integration of self and dancing body in such a way as to evolve new movement images. This process of improvisation and integration has led to new dance styles that have been themselves 'played' with through improvisation. Although the styles, costumes, and locations of performance have changed, the role of improvisation as instigator of the embodied *known* to the improvisational *unknown,* as referenced by Susan Foster (2003), is still the motivating force.

In its ongoing global transformation, belly dance has moved further and further away from a dance that historically was an improvisational visualization of the complex community and musical ethos of North Africa and the Middle East. Although the derivative forms of belly dance, such as tribal, have expanded around the globe, they have not become part of the dance context in the area of belly dance's historical origin. Instead, *raqs sharqi,* in Egypt and Lebanon, and *oryantal dansoz,* in Turkey, have entered into very specific internal dialogues associated with the social/cultural dynamics and politics of their individual countries. Examples are the impact on *raqs sharqi* of the Islamic purposeful art movement and the increased influence of Islam in Egypt (Van Nieuwkerk 2008) and the impact of the neoliberal gentrification of Istanbul on *oryantal dansoz* in Turkey, as discussed by Potuoğlu-Cook (2011). As such, solo improvisational dance in Egypt, Lebanon, and Turkey provides an example of the limits of globalization's influence and affirms the role of the local context in which improvisation, as Thompson Drewal suggests, is rooted in the history of 'the embodied techniques that ground it' (2003: 120).

NOTES

1. This essay is based on my experience as a student, teacher, and performer of belly dance from 1973 to 1990; since then I have focused on belly dance as an area of research and attended classes, festivals, and performances in the United States, Canada, Egypt, Australia, Turkey, and Greece.
2. Judy Alves-Masters discovered in her 1979 study that participation in belly dance classes enhanced women's self-esteem (Alves-Masters 1979).
3. Paulette Rees-Denis, online course material incorporated into email to author, March 2014.

REFERENCES

Adra, N. (2005) Belly Dance: An Urban Folk Genre. In Shay, Anthony, and Sellers-Young, Barbara (eds.), *Belly Dance: Orientalism, Transnationalism and Harem Fantasy*. Costa Mesa, CA: Mazda Press, 28–50.

Alexis, I. (2002) A Dance of Her Own: FatChanceBellyDance Proves That the Female Figure, No Matter What Size, Can Be Sexy. *Dance Magazine* 76(11): 52–53.

Al-Faruqi, Lois Ibsen. (1987) Dance as an Expression of Islamic Culture. *Dance Research Journal* 10: 6–17.

Alves-Masters, J. (1979) Changing Self-Esteem of Women through Middle Eastern Dance. Doctoral degree, University of Georgia.

Appadurai, A. (1996) *Modernity at Large: Cultural Dimensions of Globalization*. Minneapolis: University of Minnesota Press.

Belly Dance Evolution. (2014) http://bellydanceevolution.com/about/the-company/. Accessed November 26.

Bordeon, C. (2013) Finding 'the Feeling': Oriental Dance, Musiqa al-Gadid, and Tarab. In McDonald, Caitlin, and Sellers-Young, Barbara (eds.), *Belly Dance around the World: New Communities, Performance and Identity*. Jefferson, NC: McFarland, 33–47.

Damasio, A. (2010) *Self Comes to Mind: Constructing the Conscious Brain*. New York: Pantheon.

Deagon, A. (2015) Orientalism and the American Belly Dancer: Multiplicity, Authenticity, Identity. In Shay, Anthony, and Sellers-Young, Barbara (eds.), *Oxford Handbook of Dance and Ethnicity*. Oxford: Oxford University Press, 367–390.

De Spain, K. (2011) Improvisation and Intimate Technologies. *Choreographic Practices* 2: 25–42.

Drewal, M. T. (2003) Improvisation as Participatory Performance: Egungun Masked Dancers in the Yoruba Tradition. In Albright, Ann Cooper, and Gere, David (eds.), *Taken by Surprise: A Dance Improvisation Reader*. Middletown, CT: Wesleyan University Press, 119–134.

Farrah, I. (1992) A Dancer's Chronicle: Growing Up in Dance: Vis a Vis the Masculine Motif. Part 1. *Arabesque* 18(5): 8–10.

Foster, S. (2003) Taken by Surprise: Improvisation and Dance in the Mind. In Albright, Ann Cooper, and Gere, David (eds.), *Taken by Surprise: A Dance Improvisation Reader*. Middletown, CT: Wesleyan University Press, 3–12.

Fraleigh, S. (1987) *Dance and the Lived Body: A Descriptive Aesthetics*. Pittsburgh: University of Pittsburgh Press.

Gioseffi, D. (1980) *Earth Dancing*. New York: Stackpole Books.

Hutchinson, S. (2013) *Salsa World: A Global Dance in Local Contexts*. Philadelphia: Temple University Press.

Jarmakani, A. (2008) *Imagining Arab Womanhood: The Cultural Mythology of Veils, Harems, and Belly Dancers in the U.S.* New York: Palgrave Macmillan.

Maira, Sunaina. (2008) Belly Dancing: Arab-Face, Orientalist Feminism, and US Empire. *American Quarterly* 60: 317–345.

Morocco. (2000) Personal interview by the author, March.

Potuoğlu-Cook, Öykü. (2011) *Night Shifts: Moral, Economic, and Cultural Politics of Turkish Belly Dance across the Fins-de-Siecle*. PhD. Northwestern University, ProQuest: UMI Dissertation Publishing.

Racy, A. J. (2003) *Making Music in the Arab World*. London: Cambridge Press.

Rasmussen, A. (1992) An Evening in the Orient: The Middle Eastern Nightclub in America. *Asian Music* 13(2): 345–365.

Rasmussen, A. (1998) The Music of Arab Americans. In Zuhur, Sherifa (ed.), *The Images of Enchantment*. Cairo: American University Press.135–156.

Said, E. (1978) *Orientalism*. New York: Pantheon Books.

Sellers-Young, B. (2013) Interplay of Dance and the Imagined Possibilities of Identity. In McDonald, Caitlin, and Sellers-Young, Barbara (eds.), *Belly Dance around the World: New Communities, Performance and Identity.* Jefferson, NC: McFarland, 3–16.

Sellers-Young, B. (2016) *Belly Dance, Pilgrimage and Identity.* London: Palgrave Macmillan.

Shay, A. (1995) Dance and Non-dance: Patterned Movement in Iran and Islam. *Journal of Iranian Studies* 28: 61–78.

Shay, A. (1999) *Choreophobia: Solo Improvised Dance in the Iranian World.* Costa Mesa, CA: Mazda.

Shay, A. (2002). *Choreographic Politics. State Folk Dance Companies, Representation.* Conneticut: Wesleyan University Press.

Shay, A., and Sellers-Young, B. (2003) Belly Dance: Representation, Orientalism, and Harem Fantasy, with Anthony Shay, *Dance Research Journal* 35/1 (Summer): 13–37.

Shay, A., and Wood, L. (1976) Danse du Ventre: A Fresh Appraisal. *Dance Research Journal* 8: 18–30.

Studlar, Gaylyn. (1995) Out-Salomeing Salome. *Michigan Quarterly Review* 34: 487–510.

Thelen, E., and Smith, L. (1996) *A Dynamic Systems Approach to the Development of Cognition and Action.* Cambridge, MA: MIT Press.

Thelen, E., Smith, L., Schoner, G., and Scheier, C. (2001) The Dynamics of Embodiment: A Field Theory of Infant Preservative Reaching. *Behavioural and Brain Sciences* 24: 1–34.

Van Nieuwkerk, K. (2008) 'Repentant' Artists in Egypt: Debating Gender, Performing Arts and Religion. *Contemporary Islam* 2: 191–210.

Yasmina. (2014) Website of Yasmina. http://www.arabesquedance.ca/yasmina/index.php, Accessed December 2014.

PART VI

INTERCONNECTIVITY, EMERGENCE, AND TECHNOLOGIES

....

CHAPTER 28

DANCING THE INTERFACE

Improvisation in Zones of Virtual Exchange

....

THOMAS F. DEFRANTZ

DANCING the interface involves creating physical movement in relationship to data stored and manipulated by electric charges. Dance improvisers who work in the area of technology constantly face challenges of nonhuman interaction and the risk of mechanical failure. In addition, improvisers working with computer interfaces endure an overwhelming sense of nonempathetic indifference to questions of social identity that provide the warp and woof of physical imagination. This chapter offers commentary on and analysis of these processes as they were realized by SLIPPAGE: Performance|Culture|Technology, a performance research group in residence at MIT from 2003 to 2011. The case studies under consideration here include teaching tap dance to students in Singapore from a teleconference studio in Cambridge, Massachusetts; dancing improvised house music choreography while fitted with a wireless Miditron system that fed data that could control pitch, tempo, and playback for preselected audio files; creating motion-capture files of house dancing for use in a stage performance; improvising tap dancing on responsive floors that issued sound and video depending on the performer's improvised step; and improvising with Wii controllers that repurposed photographic images onto specially constructed surfaces in real-time performance. In each of these encounters, the terms of physical comprehension expanded and contracted, suggesting an every-where-ness and not-really-here-ness that deserve exploration. Exploring methods of improvising towards empathy, the essay suggests ways in which dancing bodies redistribute energy in relation to impossible connectivities that are often not human and insistently nonempathetic.

To paraphrase Isadora Duncan, as a performer, I often work as a soloist, but seldom do I dance alone. For me, the ghosts of sensation and the traces of light that surround being in time animate my approach to gesture, space, energy, emotion, and presence. I move by impulse, an impulse shaped by desire and ambition to fulfil, or extend, a sense of capacity. These are abstract motivations, in a way, but they also allow me to imagine a sexualized, sensual, gender-becoming person at once inside and outside motion.

I work most consistently as a gestural improviser in particular narrative circumstances, responding in real time to motivations provided by electronic interfaces designed by collaborating artists of SLIPPAGE. For me, moving with purposeful presence in modes of immediate discovery generates a sense of honesty about dancing that feeds my ethical sense of performing. If performing might be about sharing and expanding capacity for discovery among gathered witnesses, including the performers themselves, I've worked to develop strategies for mobilizing energy and gestural impulse in these performances. Thinking physically and striving to respond immediately, I work to combine lingering questions about race, class, gender, and sexuality with the choices of the moment.

My shift into improvisation as a method arrived alongside my work in interface design. SLIPPAGE collaborations feature digital archives manipulated in response to the physical gestures of the performer. As we mobilized these interface designs towards performance, it became important to match the spontaneous generation of the digital interface with movement choices conceived to be dialogic. An ethic of responsibility to engage the interfaces at hand inspired me to work in immediate responsiveness to the present condition, even as that condition changed, and the interfaces provided unexpected information for the emergent performance. As I often narrate for students of performance and technology, finding an abiding method to 'be present in the moment' encourages physical, social, and intellectual flexibility that might be important for many of us in various circumstances of life. Ultimately, this is my quest as an improviser: to engage and model social flexibility as a mode of art-making.

SLIPPAGE artists often consult theoretical writings to better understand ideologies that circulate in their performance projects. Engaging with theory is an embodied practice, and in time, these writings become foundational concepts for the development of research into performance. In addition to helping us understand how social relations have been made manifest, concepts of psychoanalysis, cultural memory, physical empathy, and social subjection offer points of entry to the organization of energy in space and time. We take it for granted that the continual interplay between theoretical writing and work in the studio enlivens dance, as well as the process of devising performance interfaces.

Tapping into a Twenty-Millisecond Delay: Lacan and the Problem of Latency

Psychoanalyst Jacques Lacan wondered at the way in which time might be situated in experience that extends beyond calculations of rhythmic meter. In his paper 'Logical Time' (1945), Lacan articulated a concept of time that follows a dialectical structure: seeing, understanding, and concluding. As in Suzanne Langer's theory of aesthetic perception *Feeling and Form* (1953), the intuitive, neurobiological 'seeing' stage is followed by the processing of material in an 'understanding' phase of time, which leads to the interpretation and 'concluding' that surrounds experience and meaning. Notably, the central *understanding* phase of time might be stretched or compressed according to circumstance. The mediating process of the understanding phase allows for the recognition of retroaction and anticipation in time; retroaction, as a reconceptualization of events that occurred before, and anticipation, of events yet to come.

Considered alongside realities of computer data processing, Lacan's concept of the pliant *understanding* phase of time corresponds to issues of latency in video streaming. Latency is a continual bugaboo for performance involving live feed video design. When digital image processing lags far behind what humans typically experience, we note, with discomfort, the uneasy fit. This is the annoying and sometimes confusing lag between live gestures in the room, augmented by sensory signals of smell, sound, and sometimes touch, that arrive sooner than projected live-feed imagery. At rock concerts, or in technology-driven performances, audience members sense the time-lag disconnect between the performer on stage and the often-oversized image of that performer, typically projected overhead or behind the action. While some artists try to build latency into the creative visual design of a live-feed project, the fact remains that networked latency has not been solved to a threshold of zero or even imperceptibility, and the time of *understanding* that Lacan theorized remains an unavoidable truth in execution for dance technology projects.

On 14 September 2004, SLIPPAGE participated in a networked dance event, Moves across the Water. Staged at MIT, the event networked tap dancers at MIT with hip-hop dancers at the National University of Singapore (NUS) (see fig. 28.1). Working at 8 a.m., SLIPPAGE-affiliated artists and MIT student dancers in Cambridge, Massachusetts, collaborated with NUS hip-hop dancers at 8 p.m. in Singapore.[1] I taught a series of tap dance movements to the NUS students; in turn, we engaged the hip-hop styling of choreographer Patrick Loo. Sponsored by the Singapore-MIT Alliance, the event offered an example of Internet2 network capabilities in commensurate conference spaces refitted to allow for dance movement.[2] Steven Lerman, professor of computer science at MIT, provided technical oversight to the project.

Lerman promised that the Internet2 infrastructure would allow for the most diminished latency possible at the time: nearly twenty-one milliseconds. This represents a big advance over forms of streaming, which might range from two to ten seconds. Yet in the context of a session in dance, the latency arrived entirely palpable and present. We all constantly felt the lag between what I said, the sounds that I made with my tapping feet, and the movements performed by dancers at NUS.

Dance teaching always involves a human latency, as students try to anticipate and match movement that has not yet materialized and engage it simultaneously with the instructor's effort. Over time, this lag in response is reduced, as teachers and students come to predict movement impulses together. After studying with a teacher for a time, students can anticipate movement enough to create credible versions of dance material even as it is first demonstrated.

But in this case, as with many dance technology experiments, the Moves Across the Water event was conceived as a one-off phenomenon, in which MIT and NUS dancers

FIG. 28.1 Thomas F. DeFrantz in Moves Across the Water (2004)

played with Internet2 networking without any serious plan for development or follow-up. Teaching an improvised movement phrase to student dancers 9,500 miles away in a first encounter, and then learning a movement phrase from their instructor, offered frustrating and odd shifts of time. Confronted by a large monitor, without the possibility of touch or smell, we foundered in my attempts to match movement. I struggled to offer movements in tap dance—a form the NUS dancers did not practice regularly—via the camera interface. Worst of all, I physically winced as I realized that the time between my call and execution of a tap movement could never match the execution I witnessed on the monitor. While the timing was surely closer than it might have been in other setups, we could never dance in recognizable tandem. The twenty-one-millisecond latency was enough to force me to recalibrate my movements, and leave even more time for *under-standing* what happened in the digital processing of movement. As Lacan predicted, a distinction between the flexible logical time of my movement production and the fixed chronological time of the processing system led to a rupture in communication. In this instance, improvisation in hip-hop or tap dance could not bridge the misunderstandings surrounding gestures in formation.

I also often work in concert with technologies that simultaneously emphasize the presence of spectral haunting, while they diminish the elusive, taste-able scent palpable in moving alongside of others. I feel tension as I work with the constant sixty herz hum, barely perceptible but always there, as my collaborating dancers emerge from electrical currents, all-too-typically underresourced. Electricity becomes my partner-in-crime, and programmers and technicians its agents. I dance with fragments of time repurposed via media. Something surely shifts in this transference, from a dance of engagement with an unprecedented Other of a person to the dance within the complex, but bounded, algorithmically prescribed interface. Could tap dance improvisation provide a method of suggesting or realizing an empathetic possibility in interface? SLIPPAGE addressed this question in the project Monk's Mood: A Performance Meditation on the Life and Music of Thelonious Monk.

SOURCING THE ARCHIVE FOR THE LYRICISM OF THE SURPLUS: MONK'S MOOD AND THE DIGITAL ARCHIVE OF THE INFORMATION AGE

See, black performance has always been the ongoing improvisation of a kind of lyricism of the surplus—invagination, rupture, collision, augmentation. This surplus lyricism ... is what a lot of people are after when they invoke the art and culture—the radical (both rooted and out there, immanent and transcendent) sensuality—of and for my people.... Blurred, dying life; liberatory, improvisatory, damaged love; freedom drive.

(Moten 2003: 26)

Performance theorist Fred Moten suggests that a resistance to objectification, a certain 'freedom drive', is carried at the heart of black performance. This drive is a resistance to fixity; and it is an aural capacity that is surely perceptible, even in visual materials, as a remnant of black voice. Moten's complex rendering of radical traditions in black artistry creates an unprecedented space for lyrical surplus: performance that exceeds by augmentation, collision, rupture, or even invagination to create something unexpected and imbued with the desire to somehow break free. This resistant drive confirms a sounding of radical aesthetics that persistently exceeds limitations or expectations of form. For Moten, the surplus of this aesthetic formation is conceived as an encounter with lyricism; an elegance of performative execution that confirms a capacity for improvisation to answer a political quest towards freedom.

When SLIPPAGE decided to explore the life of composer Thelonious Monk with a dance and theater work in 1999, our first approach focused on the narrative contours of Monk's biography as it had been understood to that time. Monk's unimpeachable place among creative artists needed none of our attention; but we were struck with the ways that Monk danced when he performed his music. His improvised dancing—visible in several documentaries—was a puppet-ish off-step stumble; a forging of weight towards impact without bounding recovery. Dancing, Monk often appeared to be out of his own control

and more than a little lost within his own physicality. At times, movement seemed to surprise him, even when he generated the motion in response to the music that he wrote.

Research for the project also embraced the expansive mediated archive of materials
related to Monk's career. Over the course of six months, we were able to 'read' Monk's recorded catalogue: the entirety of music captured over the course of his professional lifetime as a musician. This astonishing access to sonic information offered a huge archive
of materials to evaluate. The many versions of compositions that Monk wrote and recorded represented an unwieldy and provocative assortment of sources; finding our
pathway towards a coherent collection of musical inspiration forced us to face the lyricism of surplus in the very archive of Monk's creative output.

The first version of Monk's Mood extended this concept to involve an experienced
puppeteer collaborator. Lead visual artist Eto Otitigbe and puppeteer Noelia Ortiz-
Cortés created several avatars for Monk's family and his bandmates: from a tiny mar-
ionette of Monk himself that played a tiny grand piano; to clothing that represented his
wife, animated by the puppeteer in plain sight; and to oversized sculptural constructions
of cardboard and wood of musicians playing outsized instruments. I danced with and
among these puppets and in response to selected video imagery created by Otitigbe that
drew on documentary sources (see image of Monk's Mood below, fig. 28.2).

My tap dancing meditation on Monk began at the end of his life, flashed back to his
youngest days of creating music by himself and with his small ensemble friends, and
worked its way through events in his life embodied in various relationships with his
wife, children, and chief patron, Baroness Pannonica de Koenigswarter. Because the
piece began at the end of things, with an older man testing the state of his memory and
his ability to still 'do' as a creative artist, the work arrived imbued with a sad feeling of
melancholy. Gearing myself towards performance in this work always involved summoning a state of detachment that allowed for the expressive physical imagining of off-
centre music like 'Ruby, My Dear', 'Epistrophy', 'Monk's Mood', and ''Round Midnight'.
As a whole, the work explored the potential of tap dance as a lyrical form of storytelling.

As the work developed, it became clear that we needed to make more space for improvisation in its very structure. No matter the amount of dance improvisation set into the
work, with its prepared media and expert puppetry, this first draft felt too carefully arranged. We went back to the drawing board to imagine a method that could make space
for the surplus lyricism to which Moten alludes; to develop something that could embed
improvisation in the staging of the memory of Monk's life and work. Lead designer Eto
Otitigbe worked with two Stanford University colleagues to repurpose the platform of
the popular video game Dance Dance Revolution.[3] By rewiring the platform and creating a software interface run by Max/MSP,[4] we were able to create a step-platform
that triggered theatrical event by the pressure placed on areas of the platform. The
performer's step triggered event. We created a map of Monk's activities in the performance area: stage right for musical memories; stage left for memories driven by image.
We separated bits and pieces of his piano recordings to create an archive of sounds that
could be triggered by step during performance; we recast the prepared video in segments that could overlay or play in various tempi according to the triggering gesture of

FIG. 28.2 Thomas F. DeFrantz in Monk's Mood: A Performance Meditation on the Life and Music of Thelonious Monk (2002)

step. These archives, enlivened by the performer's step, became an instrument ready to play and improvise.

In performance, I worked to leave space for the unexpected arrival of sound or image according to step. Without knowing what sound or video document might come from any particular region of the platform, I could create a performance built on the improvisatory instinct that begged a surplus lyricism; one that somehow intended to demonstrate the freedom drive. Several sections of the forty-five-minute performance made use of this newly crafted interface, allowing me to choose my way through the fragments and respond in emergent improvisation to the sound and image released.

In this case, the interface responded literally to my foot-touch, and seemed navigable and sturdy. Over time, we jettisoned the bulky platforms surrounding the actual 'hot spots' of the interface and replaced them with small copper pads that were tethered to a control computer, typically located stage right of the performance area. These copper plates made the touch-trigger nature of the interface more obvious to the audience and reduced the questions surrounding causality that often overshadow interactive technology performance. The fact that the floor-step triggered events aligned well with improvised tap dancing as a retelling of Monk's life and music. The conceit of the work became an improvised solo tap dance performance augmented by an interface that accessed a large digital archive in an unpredictable, improvisatory manner.

Dancing this interface, I appreciated its clarity of intention and effect. My step was rewarded by sound or image; this correlation allowed me to construct a performance that participated in the surplus of lyricism that Monk's playing always approached. Performances of this work stretched from 2002 to 2012 and offered a sustained engagement with the trigger-step interface as an instrument employed in the service of theatrical storytelling. Visual imagery and fragments of piano sounds became reliable partners to my creation of a performance, and I looked forward to their unexpected arrival, triggered by my step, in each performance circumstance.

INTANGIBLE CONNECTIONS
AND EMPATHETIC RAPPORT

The House Music Project

> To 'choreograph empathy' thus entails the construction and cultivation of a specific physicality whose kinesthetic experience guides our perception of and connection to what another is feeling.
>
> (Foster 2011: 2)

> Are there techniques of knowledge production that invite us to imagine the other without presuming knowledge of the other?
>
> (Foster 2011: 14)

Dance theorist Susan Foster offers a historicizing methodology to examine 'how bodies feel and how they feel about each other' (2011: 14). In seeking out correspondences between choreography, kinaesthesia, and empathy, she explores how changes in these concepts over time have contributed to changes in a general capacity for understanding what movement does, and how it can feel to movers and their witnesses. Foster encourages her readers to note how choreography can provide clues to the specific experience of the physical in the ways that it 'records or documents movement, and also in the ways that it sets forth principles upon which movement is to be learned and crafted' (175). Empathy, as a concept of great interest for contemporary neuroscientists, offers a most 'fundamental capacity of our minds, foundational to the very way that knowledge is acquired' (178).

   The important distinction between movers and those watching (or not moving) becomes manifest in wearable technology work that correlates gesture to effect without visible means of connection. Many artists have engaged wireless or camera-tracking technologies to distribute image or sound according to the movement of the dancers onstage. Yet watching a wearable technology work is quite different from performing in one. Somehow, we still might imagine that these technology-driven works can generate some sense of empathy for viewers. Working on the House Music Project, from 2002 to 2007, I enjoyed dancing a custom-designed interface that predicted the X-Box Kinect interface in its ability to allow my movement to influence audio cues. Wearing the interface, which was a series of sensors connected to a wireless Miditron pack, I imagined sharing the sense of flow and movement impulse with gathered witness who could sense the connection between movement and sound.[5]

With the House Music Project, SLIPPAGE wanted to explore a history of house music, a widely distributed but little discussed idiom of black popular culture. House is a black American musical form from the late 1970s, born of its predecessors disco and funk and contemporaneous with the emergence of hip-hop. House gave way to techno and rave events before splitting into the myriad forms practised today: jungle house, trip house, hard house, acid house, chill house, and so on. House began in queer, LGBT black and Latino sites of celebration, as music that kinetically connected Sunday morning gospel music and worship traditions with Saturday night imperatives of partying. In house settings, a DJ mixes snatches of prerecorded gospel-styled vocals over pulsing, regularly metered drum and bass foundations. Many house DJs add live musical accompaniment to their mixing efforts, typically with small keyboard synthesizers connected to a dual-turntable setup. House is an electronic form of black popular music, built around the circulation of electricity for its production.

SLIPPAGE artists originally imagined the work as a performance/installation developed from a large and ever-expanding archive of historical materials related to house music.[6] We wanted to create an interface that would allow the performer to operate as a DJ of sorts, as dance movements would trigger events in various media directed at a physical environment setting that represents a literal 'house'. After a few years of casual research and imagination sessions, the project moved towards realization in a month-long residency at the University of Texas at Dallas in January 2006. At the university, we were able to make use of a large, fully functional motion-capture laboratory to generate data streams based on house dance movements and to play with the wireless Miditron setup in a theatrical space.

House dancing involves a full physicality of relentless flow in its execution—house dancers rarely stand still. For the dance interface of this work, we turned to the commercially available Miditron and worked to create a robust wireless version that could function with sensor readings from different areas of a dancing body in motion. We placed a variety of small sensors at different points of the body—accelerometers along the shoulders; tilt-sensors along the ankles; a button-sensor in the right hand. These sensors fed a stream of information to a Max/MSP setup that determined various events related to sound. Sound sequences, selected from an archive of house music created for the project, could be accelerated, slowed to a zero tempo, or played in reverse; sound could be equalized according to gesture, with a raised hand triggering an audio equalization (EQ) that sounded only high tones, while a foot stop triggered an EQ that emphasized low, bass tones. Particular shimmies of the shoulders could trigger the looping of particular sound fragments; combined with other motions, fragments could be layered on top of each other by the performer.

The project also involved motion capture. Working with engineers at the university's lab, we caught sequences of house dancing and mapped them to a stick figure drawing.

Clips of this manipulated material were fed into a computer running Isadora software;[7] these images were released onto the stage environment as certain aspects of the performer's movement triggered them.

Dancing this interface, I always wondered when the connection would work and when it might fail. The wireless Miditron infrastructure—created with Max/MSP programming—was not nearly so robust or reliable as we might have hoped. While the interface worked much more often than it did not, and probably produced the hoped-for outcome in nearly each performance application, I never felt sure that it would. Thus, my performances with the bodypack attached were never as free-flowing or fully engaged as I might have liked. In sequences that involved actively controlling sound via gesture, I rarely felt free to move and assume that my dancing partner—the Miditron—would keep up with my movements.

The short amount of time available to actually work with the interface affected the way the performance could be realized. While we developed the context for the project across several years, the actual implementation phase of the project was quite short—only three months. This accelerated timeline was not conducive to in-depth experimentation or achievement. As with many technology-driven projects, the diminished amount of tech time profoundly influenced what happened on stage. We do plan to return to this project in the near future and work with camera-based technologies of gesture processing. In that revised version, we might hope for an empathy of trust between performer and interface; a way to allow the dancer and the interface to share information, improvisationally, without presuming to 'know' what the other will do, when, or precisely why.

HAUNTING THE SHADOWS: *CANE* AND REPURPOSED WII CONTROLLERS

Performance can never be entirely new or entirely volitional, as all performance repeats prior nonoriginal substitutions, even if those substitutions are invisible, forgotten, buried, or ignored.

(Bhana Young 2006: 24)

To be black is to have accrued a subjectivity haunted by the spectral traces of a social, political and ideological history.

(Bhana Young 2006: 25)

In her provocative study of an African diaspora that is always already bound up with gender, performance theorist Hershini Bhana Young wonders at the historical injury and collective wounding wrought by slavery and colonialism. She works to delineate a diaspora that is 'much more than global patterns of flows and resistances'—'or even systems of cultural exchanges'—to consider one that might be 'embedded in the dense structures of memory' (Bhana Young 2006: 1). This memory includes the hauntings of violence done not only to individuals but also to groups of subjugated black people who have been cast as the ghosts of modernity, the 'indispensible coerced mechanisms of labor, the Other against whom the whiteness of the imperial Subject was formed' (47).

Sometime in 2005 it became clear that we wanted to think about how environments hold history, and how particular locations tell their own tales of human trauma and survival. Bhana Young's 2006 text *Haunting Capital: Memory, Text, and the Black Diasporic Body* offered a framework for thinking about the complex ways trauma and violence circulate across geographies. Poet Jean Toomer's experimental text *Cane* (1923) inspired an exploration of the lives of women and men circumscribed by violence, as African Americans living in the South during the height of sharecropping. In *Cane,* the various exchanges among people are always witnessed by an uncompromising natural surround.

In 2007 we started work on CANE, inspired by Toomer's text and influenced by Bhana Young's writings (see fig. 28.3). The sugar cane fields figure prominently in Toomer's work; we decided to develop a responsive cane field environment, to act as mirror and witness to the movement of a man and woman. Constructed of the tubing that usually surrounds fluorescent lights, the cane field included microphones and speakers, miniature cameras, and images that were released onto the tubing structures via short-throw projectors. We worked to create a cane field that breathed, animated by sound and light according to random algorithms at all times and by specific setups at some times during performance. According to what the microphones in the cane fields 'heard', they would release sound into a soundscape at irregular intervals. The sounds included musical cues pulled from the score by composer Tara Rodgers and clips culled from the Library of Congress recordings of slave narratives from the Federal Writers' Project of 1936–1938.

The two responsive stands of synthetic cane allowed for movement alongside, in front of, and behind their vertical rods. Imagery distributed onto the stands ranged from archival materials of African American sharecropping lives to newly created film imagery of the performers. One area of the performance space represented a small cabin with a makeshift cot; this area of the stage had no mediated connection to the electronic cane field. Rather, the cane field, with its various devices of surveillance and reportage, held visual and sonic memories of events that had taken place in outdoor spaces.

One interface developed for this workshop production involved an Isadora patch created for a repurposed Nintendo Wii controller. The patch written for Osculator, and readily available online, allows for data from the various sensors that operate within the controller to be processed by Isadora. We created a setup that allowed the motion of the controller to influence the scale of a portrait image displayed on one of the cane fields. The portrait displayed in any performance of the work was chosen by the program at random from an archive of several available images. Waving the controller, like a magic wand, changed the size of the image along horizontal or vertical axes, or both axes in tandem. Dancing with the controller in hand, the performer could manipulate the size and shape of a child's face that seemed to gaze impassively at the dance performance under way.

Created to suggest possibilities of shimmering, mediated histories mixed in real time via a specially constructed responsive environment, CANE reveals itself through an

FIG. 28.3. Thomas F. DeFrantz in CANE workshop (2007)

interface that responds to the dancers, offering sound in response to sound, image in response to motion, and adjustments of sound or image in response to what the interface perceived. Dancing the interface—and especially in the setup that involved the Wii controller and the oversized portrait—forced my attention to the point of contact: my hand holding the device. Disguised as a discarded cane stalk, in a wooden, reed-like enclosure, the controller demanded my creative attention in motion. The interface between its movements and the image on the cane field correlated to my own visual attention to the image. My movements became inordinately driven by my hands: the amount of force needed to effect width; the shifts in velocity or angle that adjusted simultaneous x and y calibration. As any video game fan knows, the Wii controller offers a robust platform, with reliable data streams that are not difficult to learn to manipulate. But dancing with the disguised controller raised other performance concerns. Turning towards the ground, I worked to maintain the vertical horizon of the controller so as to only adjust the projected face slightly during this manoeuvre. Tilting my torso, while raising my arms, I stayed attentive to the angle of my hand holding the controller, so that the overall size of the projected image would shrink and expand in time with my movement. In total, these attentions to the limb and hand most responsible for the control of the interface strongly adjusted my movement choices towards a delicacy and sense of minutiae that were not present in other portions of the performance.

Dancing improvisationally in the electronic cane field, inspired by the potent poetry and storytelling of Jean Toomer, embodying imagined women's lives probably too real by half to be drawn as fiction, I felt a traumatic return to rage and confusion. My usual cool modes of movement—which typically aligned well with technologies still in development with various SLIPPAGE projects—failed in this circumstance; they felt awkward and incomplete, flimsy, mechanical. My movement couldn't respond to the emotion released by visiting this scene of subjection, even though we created scenes of our own volition. Bhana Young asserts that 'performance ... always carries the ghostly traces of a history that is always violent' (2006: 24); CANE confirmed this trace even in its first workshop iterations of 2007.[8]

A truism suggests that technological intervention will not surpass or equal the variety of stimulation that personal interplay provides; in many ways, these examples confirm this assumption. Improvising in these environments, I wonder how I feel. This wondering is an active component of my performance research; it is the process of assessment that allows me to make improvisational movement choices as I dance, and it feeds choices that we make as we develop technologies for dance interface. These four examples offer a range of responses to dancing an interface: frustrated by the latency of an Internet2 connection; enlivened by a reliable step trigger in a tap work; unsure of the capacity of my electronic partner in a sensor-on-the-body setup; enthralled by the attentive response of a wand that creates an easily perceptible connection from hand to electronic image.

While these four SLIPPAGE projects employed technologies as means towards an end, we developed their interfaces to answer particular questions of historiography in terms of dance theater. As an interdisciplinary research group steeped in the American educational academy, SLIPPAGE sources contemporary theory, historical research, popular culture, African American folklore, gender and sexuality studies, dance, theater, and performance studies to imagine alternative histories for underexplored topics. As this essay demonstrates, these academic modes of analysis inspire theatrical projects that tilt towards the creation of danceable interfaces, preferably projects that realize themselves with improvisatory modes of moving at their core.

Narrated in this way, the ambition to explore alternative histories through dance takes precedence over the development of the interface. This seems only fair to me. For me, this alignment of technological research that aids in the development of theatrical storytelling predicts a potential for development that centres an ambition to communicate. While these interfaces sometimes felt chilly and left me craving palpable human connection, they arrived in response to a need for physical augmentation, precipitated by the project at hand. They allow a connection across distances that is otherwise impossible. Perhaps they predict an alternative sort of empathy, a different way of feeling across space-time that we will come to develop and understand in time. Improvising dance in these interfaces and according to our agreed-on narrative constraints, I often thought of the engineers, technologists, researchers, and collaborating designers as I attempted to manipulate a tone wearing the Miditron or stretch the face of a young woman with the Wii controller. By themselves, the interfaces seldom allowed for the spark of empathetic recognition, as another improvising performer might have done. In the end, these human relationships, and all the missteps and accomplishments that led us towards performance, were the material that fed my ability to compose while dancing.

NOTES

1. Special thanks to Charmian Wells and to all SLIPPAGE collaborators involved in this research.

    The MIT student dancers included James Tolbert, a senior majoring in computer science, and Bradford Backus, a graduate student in the Harvard-MIT Program in Health Sciences and Technology. Patrick Loo led six NUS student dancers.
2. Internet2 is a research consortium that tests emergent hardware and protocols for speedy data transmission. was The Singapore-MIT Alliance is a program that engages MIT, the National University of Singapore, and Nanyang Technological University in a collaborative graduate education and research program. This specific collaboration was facilitated by Alan Brody, MIT provost for the arts, playwright, and novelist, and Edwin Thumboo, poet and director of the Center for Fine Arts at NUS.
3. These Stanford University colleagues were Luigi Castelli and Bert Scheittecatte.
4. Max/MSP is a visual programming language for music and multimedia developed and maintained by San Francisco–based software company Cycling '74.
5. The Miditron is a board that allows artists and inventors to experiment with electronics and programming and create new forms of time-based robotic and interactive works. Invented by engineer-artist Eric Singer, the Miditron allows you to use a Mac or a PC as a primary control platform and programming platform and to use the Miditron board as a coprocessor, handling sensor inputs and outputs and interfacing these to a variety of software and user environments.
6. Collaborating artists included project designers Eto Otitigbe and James Tolbert and visiting artists Venus Opal Reese and Edoni Fleitas. Performers included Jeff Senita, Webster Heffern, Yang Ruan, Tilly Whitney, Edward Lim, Stephen Steger, Kim Tapp Jackson, Matthew Breton, and Jonathan GNO White.
7. Isadora is a proprietary graphic programming environment for Mac OS X and Microsoft Windows, with emphasis on real-time manipulation of digital video. Designed by Mark Coniglio, it offers support for Open Sound Control.
8. CANE continued its development to a final form in 2013, created in collaboration with Wideman-Davis Dance Company, Tanya and Thaddeus Wideman Davis, directors. Video of the work can be seen at www.slippage.org.

REFERENCES

Foster, Susan Leigh. (2011) *Choreographing Empathy: Kinesthesia in Performance.* New York: Routledge.

Lacan, Jacques. (1988) Logical Time and the Assertion of Anticipated Certainty: A New Sophism. Trans. B. Fink and M. Silver. *Newsletter of the Freudian Field* 2(2): 4–22.

Moten, Fred. (2003) *In the Break: The Aesthetics of the Black Radical Tradition.* Minneapolis: University of Minnesota Press.

Young, Hershini Bhana. (2006) *Haunting Capital: Memory, Text, and the Black Diasporic Body.* Lebanon, NH: Dartmouth College Press.

CHAPTER 29

....

PROGRAMMED IMPROVISATION INSPIRED FROM AUTONOMOUS HUMANOIDS

....

AMY LAVIERS

THIS essay will outline the use of the mathematical machinery used to program auto-mated systems as a way to describe a form of structured improvisation. Moreover, this way of thinking is equivalent to posing the idea that users interacting with machines are *improvising* along the affordances provided by the interface. Examples of such auto-mated systems range from simple devices like a remote control to complex automation governing the status of a high-security building. The essay will point out the connection of the mathematics governing these systems to the movements induced in users of such automated systems and will delve deeply into how such objects describe a whole class of possible movement sequences, or choices, in a given structured improvisation. In a world where such programmed devices are ubiquitous, this type of embodied explor-ation from artists is essential in understanding how these devices are changing human movement and, thus, human lives.

Improvisation is often characterized by its lack of structure or called an opportunity for free-form, unprepared movement. The notion of 'programmed' improvisation, thus, seems like an oxymoron, as such an act would seem to be prechoreographed and deter-ministic. However, the word 'programmed' simply implies the existence of a discrete set of instructions to be followed at various junctions. Similarly, structure is often inserted into improvisations via a guiding image, sensory prompt, or movement challenge. This structure can be critical in removing the overwhelming sense of choice an improviser is confronted with in completely free-form improvisation. It also helps break a mover out of default movement patterns and can help inject randomness, rather than predictable choice, into dance work.

During such an improvisation, movers might be given particular prompts—as from an instructor or collaborator—or be given (or choose for themselves) a particular set of music (which may change throughout) to which they should respond. It may be the case that a mover will write words or images surrounding a particular theme onto note cards and have these words read or posted around a room, through which the mover will respond by generating movement according to this theme. These various structure options may be arranged in an almost limitless set of options—and, surely, other chapters in this book may describe some particular, novel options. It is an open area of research to create new structures and understand what uses they may have (including practical uses, e.g., in physical therapy). This essay will lay out another version of such structured improvisation, one that has particular use in the context of grappling with the role of technology in human life today.

The Nature of Programmed Devices

Recent technological devices work in a way that is fundamentally different from natural settings. This difference has been ushered in by—and these devices enabled by—the advent of the transistor. The transistor is not a continuous object (for example, the sunset contains a continuous array of colours as it fades from blue to fiery red); it is, instead, discrete. It is like a light switch, either on or off. There is no gradation of choices between on or off (whereas in the sunset, you can see many shades of colours between blue and red). This lack of gradation produces objects that interact in a fundamentally different way from natural things. Another way to think of this difference is the difference between a hill and a set of steps. Walking up the steps, you are always at a discrete, predefined height from your original level (until you ascend to the top). On the other hand when walking up a hill, you have, in theory, an infinite choice of heights at which you can be. Thus, technological devices create completely different interactions from natural ones.

 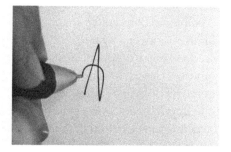

FIG. 29.1 A discrete versus continuous representation of movement as afforded by different tools. In the image on the left, writing occurs via discrete buttons. In the image on the right, writing occurs in a continuous way, with many gradations of options possible.

As another example, consider writing on a sheet of paper with a pen. This act requires continuous movements to draw the curves of the letters. When typing on a computer, however, you are aiming for the discrete location of letters on the space of the keyboard, and then you've either pressed them hard enough to activate the little sensor beneath, which switches a circuit from off to on, letting the computer know which letters to type when, or you haven't. This form of writing can thus be well described with the adjective 'discrete' (as shown in fig. 29.1).

This difference can be explored in the realm of improvisation as well, particularly via a structured improvisation that forces discrete choices on the mover. Rather than allowing the mover to revel in many continuous options, prompts might specify a discrete set of movement options at a certain moment. This is akin to the type of writing experience one has on a computer: a computer user is never, meaningfully, in the middle of drawing an A—the user either has the A button pressed or not. In this form of improvisation, a mover would similarly never be selecting options in the middle of a single movement. The mover would instead complete discrete movements, based on a predefined set of movements, and be offered choices based on the structure of a finite state machine (or automaton), a structure that I will discuss in the next section.

Another way to think about structured improvisation, and to motivate its relevance, is to imagine a person flipping around through screens and apps on an iPhone. Each screen presents a discrete set of images that portray a set of available movements the user can employ to navigate through the device functionality. This is an inherently discrete improvisation with the device. This similarity between using a programmed device and improvisation will be discussed in further sections, with emphasis on relevance to modern life.

MATHEMATICAL MACHINERY
BEHIND PROGRAMMED DEVICES

Programmed devices must bridge a gap between the seemingly continuous experience of our lives and the discrete nature of the fundamental building block of today's electronic devices: the transistor. The transistor is best thought of as an electronic switch. This switch, just like a light switch, may be on or off. This status is abstracted in engineering as a 1 or a 0, respectively. Finite state machines, or *automata*, are mathematical objects that can easily be represented graphically (see fig. 29.2) and allow for high-level behaviour of a device to be translated into low-level behaviour of transistor switches (0s and 1s).

Finite state machines, or automata (or a single automaton), have three major components: a set of states (the circles in fig. 29.2), a set of events, or transitions, (the arrows in fig. 29.2), and an arrangement, given by a mapping function, of how these two connect (depicted in fig. 29.2). The machines also typically name an initial state (indicated by the arrow terminating, but not originating, in a state in fig. 29.2) and a 'marked' state with a double circle, which indicates when a sequence through the machine may terminate.

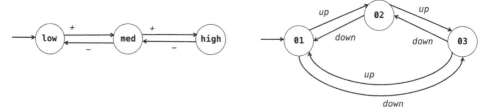

FIG. 29.2 Two examples of finite state machines governing the behaviour of a basic remote control. On the left is a hypothetical structure of a simple volume button; on the right, in contrast, is a channel button on a TV with three channels. Any of these states are a feasible terminating state; hence, none are marked with a double circle Note how quickly the complexity of this machine will increase as we take into account the many settings of modern TVs.

FIG. 29.3 Snapshots of the movements a user employs to use a programmed device. These movements only occur in a very specific sequence—as governed by the underlying automaton.

Take the example of a TV remote that allows a user to adjust the volume or flip between three TV channels. This is the scenario shown in figure 29.2. The user may press the volume '+' or '-' button or the channel 'up' or 'down' button on the remote, as in figure 29.3. We call these options 'actions' or 'events'. This causes the TV to change its channel or state. 'State' is a central concept in engineering—it allows for control of engineered systems by defining the fundamental essence of the system. In the case of automata, we have a *discrete* set of options for the state of the system, called a 'state space'. The state space of the systems in figure 29.2 may be written this way:

$$X_1 = \{low, med, high\} \qquad X_2 = \{01, 02, 03\}$$

Similarly, the event spaces, shown in figure 29.3, are as follows:

$$E_1 = \{+, -\} \qquad E_2 = \{up, down\}$$

Note that this is similar to the discrete action representation in figure 29.1. The structure in figure 29.2 specifies how the device moves between these states based on the actions of a user. This structure allows engineers to translate this behaviour right down to the circuits, the transistors, of the remote control (and TV).

'Improvisation' with a Programmed Device and 'Programming' Performance

The technological machinery discussed in the previous section results in devices with which interactions are fundamentally different from humans' interactions with other humans or more physically rooted technology, like the shovel, ax, knitting needles, or rolling pins. These objects also constituted technological advances and allowed for more comfortable living spaces, but they are, in a sense, *analog*—not digital. They are continuous, not discrete. Thus, they *afford* a different way of moving.

In the field of human factors, the word 'affordance' has technical meaning (Gibson 1977; Gaver 1991; Norman 1999). It is the notion that engineered systems lead their uses to move or act in a particular way. For example, in interface design, a bright red round button is usually used for something like an 'Emergency Stop'—in order to facilitate its ease of use in an emergency, designers make the button big (so it's easy to press) and red (so it's easy to see and is associated with urgency). However, a reset button is usually very tiny and hard to find. This is because you do not use the reset function often and do not want to accidentally press it; thus it is created with a different affordance. In Norman (1999) the notions of perceived and physical affordances are introduced. In the previous example, the physical buttons of the remote are physical affordances (which cannot be changed by a digital circuit) and the reprogrammable behaviour of each button is a kind of perceived affordance.

As programmed devices have progressed, their affordances have changed. The iPhone has a very different set of affordances (physical and perceived) from its predecessor phones. In fact, its affordances are much more aligned to our natural motion. Simple swiping gestures enable many of the interactions, whereas the touchtone phone used buttons that had to be pressed, and the rotary dial had these funny little circles cut out and required swiping around a circle for each new action. All these devices afford and induce very different sets of movements in their users. Advances in more complex gestures as paradigms for interaction have also been explored (Hong et al. 2000; Bauckhage et al. 2004; Natarajan and Nevatia 2008). This afforded, or forced, movement has been written about in several contexts. Haraway wrote: 'by the late twentieth century, our time, a mythic time, we are all chimeras, theorized and fabricated hybrids of machine and organism; in short, we are cyborgs' (1991: 150). The image of programmed devices inducing movements in their users is a powerful one that warrants artistic exploration that requires knowledge of the technical interworkings of these devices.

Such a notion of 'forcing' movement has also been used to generate novel movement. This can be seen as similar to some of the choreographic devices employed in Cunningham's work. He employed discrete influences in his work to create his distinct style of movement; for example, the use of random chance as infused by choreographic choices made based on the outcome of rolling dice (Copeland 2004). Such a strategy can be used to 'program' or force previously foreign movement patterns in our bodies.

FROM DEVICES TO MOVEMENTS:
APPLICATION TO ROBOTS

We are in an exciting time for robotics: robots are good at doing things. They make precise and powerful spot welds, providing a new level of quality in metal frame assembly; they move large warehouse shelves to factory workers, reducing load on workers and improving efficiency; and they can even vacuum living room floors, offloading an arduous task to a simple, repeatable behaviour. However, outside these repeatable tasks, results have been less exciting. Robotic tour guides, chefs, and hospital assistants are envisioned in a myriad of instances of each relevant context. These hopes are distinguished by a lack of a one-size-fits-all solution and a need for high-level behaviour that can be crafted by users.

Thus, tools are being developed to study and develop tools for crafting such high-level behaviour. A common trend in this area is to work at the level of *motion primitives*, which in some contexts may be modulated, that is, executed and sequenced in slightly different ways. These tools leverage the capability of sophisticated low-level controllers, which utilize feedback design to execute a specific motion, in order to focus on the supervisory control of predefined motion primitives or autonomous modes.

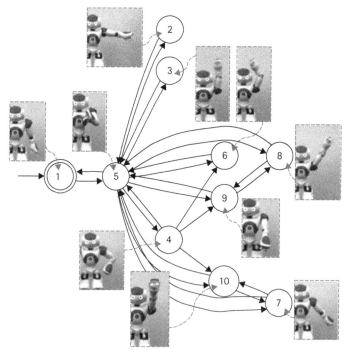

FIG. 29.4 A depiction of one arm moving with two different styles of movement sequencing (a and b) and a visualization of how the same arm 'movement' may be performed with different quality, or style (c). *Source:* (a) and (b) from LaViers and Egerstedt (2012: 43 and 30), where (a) represented a 'disco' style of sequencing and (b) represented a 'cheerleading' style.

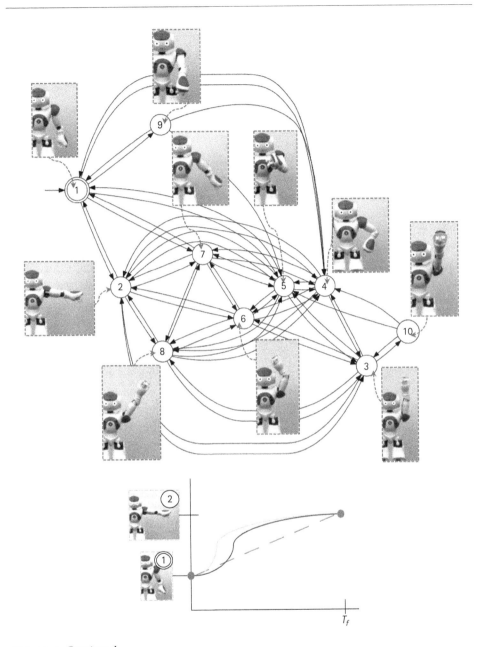

FIG. 29.4 Continued

I have developed a finite state machine description of robot behaviour, using supervisory control tools to control the output of behaviour built up from smaller primitives, as shown in figures 29.4a and 29.4b (see also LaViers and Egerstedt 2011, 2012; LaViers et al. 2011a, 2011b). In this framework, we think of motion primitives, like the arm motions given to a robot by a user, as being scaled by appropriate parameters (as in figure 29.4c; see LaViers [2012]) and then sequenced by these supervisory control operators. In particular, I view this framework as a notion of what I term *style* that relies on three parameters: (1) a transition system describing a set of movement primitives; (2) knobs in a supervisory controller that determine logical and temporal rules for the sequencing of motion primitives; and (3) weights in a cost function that modulate the trajectories between poses. This framework can be implemented on a computer controlling a robot's actions by reading in the measurements on the robot's sensors and sending commands to the robot's actuators. In this way, the quantitative description of style generates complex movement. Importantly, it is not one single motion sequence that is defined by this quantitative framework but a family of motion sequences.

In other words, the series of images in figure 29.4 depicts a framework that can be used to program a distinguishing quantity of high-level behaviours and a method for generating families of sequences in a device like a humanoid robot. First, the finite state machines in figures 4a and 4b determine the structure of the order of poses allowable for the robot. Moving from circle to circle via connecting arrows, these machines describe many different sequences of poses that are allowable. Each circle contains a pose of the robot, and arrows indicate a movement between two poses. In an improvisatory mode, the robot controller will select at random from among the arrows leading away from its current state, that is, the machine executes a selection from a set of available movements at discrete time points in its evolution. Moreover, combinations of basic machines can produce more complex movement sequences, for example, with two arms. For human improvisers, the removal of the notion of infinite choice from a given structured improvisation could lead to exciting discoveries about the intersection of technology design and human movement as well as humans' own default movement patterns.

Optimization-based modulation schemes allow for different executions of each movement, determining the motion quality. As shown in figure 29.4c, there are many exact trajectories that a given joint angle may take on its way between one pose and another. By setting up a cost function and thus defining an optimization, this trajectory can be modified. In LaViers (2012) these modifications are mapped to the language of Rudolf Laban's notion of 'Effort'. Seeing this quality as separate from the order of movements produces a notion about movement that can be explored through improvisation by human movers as well.

In robotics, this work has been an important advance in a key way: it creates movement that *qualitatively looks different*, with a generative, quantitative model backing it up. Thus, we can tell the difference between two styles with labels such as 'disco dancing' or 'cheerleading'. While these labels may be subjective, the differences in movement are not, and there is quite a range of movement styles that can be generated with this framework.

PROGRAMMED IMPROVISATION

An alternate automaton is offered in figure 29.5. This automaton illustrates how the same machinery governing the remote control in figure 29.2 can describe the movements of a dancer. Figure 29.5 contains a graphical depiction of what this automaton's

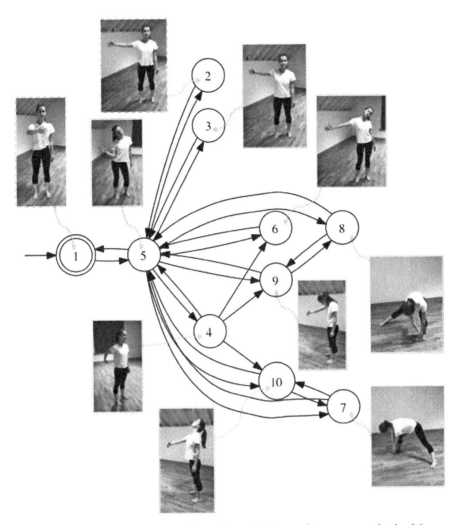

FIG. 29.5 Example of a sequencing style machine. In this machine, we may think of the movement of a dancer as being described by the discrete, sequencing structure of an automaton. *Source*: LaViers (2013b: 81–82).

states correspond to: the shape of a human body. However, these states may also contain more information than just body pose, such as intention, dynamic quality, some aspect of context, and so on. In an improvisation through this nondeterministic machine, a dancer would only transition between the set of states named, according to the presence and absence of allowable transitions or events.

This notion of improvisation aligns with the notion of style I have laid out in three previous technical veins of research: one on the sequencing of robotic movements (La Veirs et al. 2011a, 2011b; LaViers and Egerstedt 2012), one on the generation of exact trajectories endowed with a notion of quality (LaViers and Egerstedt 2012), and one leveraging these generative techniques for interpretation of real human movement data (LaViers 2013b). The goal of the work in 2011 and 2012 was to produce distinct movement behaviours that were generated in a principled way yet were still rooted in movement experience, and in the later work in 2013, the goal was to interpret human movement in a principled way using the kinaesthetically inspired tools. This quantitative definition of behaviour is inspired by dance theory and practice. It also relies on a separation of movement ordering and execution and provides templates for using that definition to extract features from real human movement.

For a robot, this framework *defines* improvisation. For a human, this framework *can facilitate* improvisation. These style machines may be seen as a guiding image for structured improvisations. As in a more traditional structured improvisation where, for example, notecards with guiding images or words written on them may be strewn around the dancer's space to be used in moments of needed prompt, when a human is moving under the influence of this guiding image, it may be seen as a both a source of movement inspiration and a limiting of choice in sequence, such as to produce opportunity to play with execution or effort. Dancers in such an improvisation would use an image like the one in figure 29.5 to determine their options for movement. In the case depicted in figure 29.5, the structure is easy to remember (though the machine may look complex, it boils down to only a few key movements, all of which return to a basic starting pose, represented by state 5); however, for more complex machines a printed poster or a motion recognition system could be used to display the dancer's options in real time.

This scenario produces one where the improviser is given a concrete problem to solve—that is, follow the available sequence of poses—that has many, many solutions. Indeed, the terms 'discrete' and 'continuous' are simply abstractions meant to help understand and make sense of the world. For example, using the machine in figure 29.5, the mover may focus on the how and the why of getting from pose to pose, opening up a range of diverse narratives and dynamic choices. This concept was applied to the creative process for an original piece of choreography, *Automaton*, presented at the Georgia Institute of Technology with a cast of four dancers and a small humanoid robot (LaViers 2013a). In this performance, dancers improvised alongside an autonomous humanoid robot; their movements were 'programmed' via this framework. In the final section of the piece, dancers and a small humanoid robot stood in a line, each performing a particular 'style program'—an allowable sequence through the dancer's or robot's defined machine. In this vignette, each agent was given a movement sequence developed through exploring a specific finite state machine description of allowable actions (given in LaViers and Egersted 2014).

In another performance, *A Dance Score for the Downtown Mall*, in Charlottesville, Virginia, this structure was used to denote a movement score as described in Halprin (1969), and a performance in April 2014 that included structured improvisation was generated from this. Figure 29.6 shows the movement score. It is also in the form of a finite state machine and utilizes a high-level language of actions (verbs) that movers could interpret for themselves, adhering to the guiding sequencing structure specified by the score. The following description was included with the score and was provided to the audience so that they, too, could explore these instantiated movement patterns.

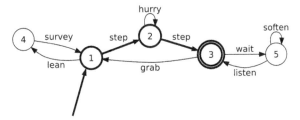

FIG. 29.6 A movement score written for a performance at the Charlottesville Downtown Mall that gives dancers in the performance, as well as audience members, instructions on how to move through a staircase near the Charlottesville Transit Center.

Use the image to guide your actions. For example, each performance of this score will begin with a 'step' (this is the transition from State 1 to State 2). Now you are presented with a choice: you may either 'hurry' or 'step' again. To finish, another 'step' will bring you to State 3, where you may end or choose to continue. Thus, the simplest version of this score is just two steps—and this path is bolded in the image above. (Note that infinitely long paths through the automaton like 'step, step, grab, step, step, grab, step, step, wait, listen, grab . . .' exist too. I hope you will seek out one of the many options in between!)

An automated system could be set up to facilitate this process. You would first have to give the system recorded data of what each movement looks like via some sensor (like a Kinect or other motion capture system). Then, a matching scheme would be set up such that a computer algorithm analysed a dancer's movements until it had a reasonable match to its library, and then, through a visual interface, the system could display representations (either recorded motion or images to symbolize these motions) of what options were available next.

Besides sequencing parameters, we could also have quality, or execution, parameters. For example, the same movement might be executed with different intentions: an extended arm could be thrust out suddenly with directive direction, or it could be eased out cautiously without a clear sense of spatial intent. These differences were studied by Laban when he laid out his system of Effort (Laban and Lawrence 1947). The library might include some generalized method of measuring Effort in movement, or it might contain movements generated with a specific set of prerecorded qualities.

MOVEMENT IN THE TWENTY-FIRST CENTURY

Using technology in the performing arts is not a new endeavour, dating back to Anna Pavlova's pointe shoe, Loie Fuller's fantastical lighting effects (Brown et al. 1998), and Merce Cunningham's explorations in electronic music and computer-aided choreography (Copeland 2004; Calvert et al. 1991; Calvert et al. 1993), and performing robots

(Breazeal et al. 2003; LaViers et al. 2014). Instead, the ideas described here are ones that might be infused with somatic taxonomies, such as Laban/Bartenieff Movement Studies, which aims to codify a whole canon of kinaesthetic experience by examining the behaviour of humans and the structure of programmed devices (Laban and Lawrence 1947; Laban 1956, 1966, Bartenieff 1980; Maletic 1987; Newlove and Dably 2004; Moore 2009; Studd and Cox 2013). Extensions in other directions will deal with generating diverse high-level behaviour in robots in a great variety of human-envisioned tasks.

Thinking of movement improvisation in this way opens up an important dialogue about how programmed devices influence our movement. For example, you may feel in control of your movement when playing around with your iPhone, but you are not entirely. Your body is responding to the embedded automaton, or finite state machine, of the iPhone's software structure. On a given screen, the phone dictates the movements available to you. Thus, we all know what it feels like to move as governed by a finite state machine; translating this experience to dance improvisation in general, as this essay has done, is a reasonable, even timely, extension that can facilitate critical artistic conversations surrounding our relationship with technology.

As technology is involved in more and more of our lives (more peoples' lives and more amounts of time per individual life), it is important for artists to explore and consider this type of movement; so structured improvisation, informed by the exact set of principles and guiding equations that builds, runs, and brings to life these devices, is not only an interesting pursuit but a needed one. Moreover, it's an open question whether today's quantitative tools are capable of describing the complex phenomena involved in generating human movement. This question needs to be explored in not only technical research but also somatic practice and artistic expression. While these tools currently seem reasonable for generating machine behaviour, their application to describing human movement is more conjectural.

In this essay, I have endeavoured to bring to light the types of concepts that do govern this world in an accessible manner such that artists can begin to explore these concepts. Artists need to make these explorations so as to help society grapple with what consequences or effects this type of technology may have. Such exploration can lead to better digestion of how we do move, contextualizing common movement sequences and bringing to bear a new way of seeing our relationship with digitally controlled systems. Even more, it can lead to the design of better devices. Is this the right way to do things? Do we want something different? These are the kinds of questions that artists are uniquely equipped to handle and engineers need help answering.

REFERENCES

Bartenieff, I. (1980) *Body Movement: Coping with the Environment*. New York, NY: Psychology Press.

Bauckhage, C., Hanheide, M., Wrede, S., and Sagerer, G. (2004) A Cognitive Vision System for Action Recognition in Office Environments. *Proceedings of the 2004 IEEE Computer Society Conference on Computer Vision and Pattern Recognition*, CVPR 2: II–827–II–833.

Breazeal, C., Brooks, A., Gray, J., Hancher, M., McBean, J., Stiehl, D., and Strickon, J. (2003) Interactive Robot Theatre. *Communications of the ACM* 46 (7): 76–85.

Brown, J. M., Mindlin, N., and Woodford, C. H. (1998) *The Vision of Modern Dance: In the Words of Its Creators*. Hightstown, NJ: Princeton Book Company.

Calvert, T. W., Bruderlin, A., Mah, S., Schiphorst, T., and Welman, C. (1993) The Evolution of an Interface for Choreographers. In *Proceedings of the INTERACT'93 and CHI'93 Conference on Human Factors in Computing Systems*. Amsterdam, Netherlands, ACM. 115–122.

Calvert, T. W., Welman, C., Gaudet, S., Schiphorst, T., and Lee, C. (1991) Composition of Multiple Figure Sequences for Dance and Animation. *Visual Computer* 7(2–3): 114–121.

Copeland, R. (2004) *Merce Cunningham: The Modernizing of Modern Dance*. New York: Routledge.

Fothergill, S., Mentis, H., Kohli, P., and Nowozin, S. (2012) Instructing People for Training Gestural Interactive Systems. In *Proceedings of the SIGCHI Conference on Human Factors in Computing Systems*, ser. CHI 12. New York: ACM, 1737–1746.

Gaver, W. W. (1991) Technology Affordances. In *Proceedings of the SIGCHI Conference on Human Factors in Computing Systems*. New York: ACM, 79–84.

Gibson, J. J. (1977) The Theory of Affordances. In Shaw, R. E., and Bransford, J. (eds.), *Perceiving, Acting, and Knowing*. Hillsdale, NJ: Erlbaum, 127–143.

Halprin, L. (1969) *The RSVP Cycles: Creative Processes in the Human Environment*. New York: Braziller.

Haraway, D. (1991) A Cyborg Manifesto: Science, Technology, and Socialist-Feminism in the Late Twentieth Century. In *Simians, Cyborgs and Women: The Reinvention of Nature*. New York, NY: Routledge, 149–181.

Hong, P., Turk, M., and Huang, T. (2000) Gesture Modeling and Recognition Using Finite State Machines. In *Proceedings of the Fourth IEEE International Conference on Automatic Face and Gesture Recognition*. Grenoble, France: IEEE, 410–415.

Laban, R. (1956) *Principles of Dance and Movement Notation: With 114 Basic Movement Graphs and Their Explanation*. London: Macdonald and Evans.

Laban, R. (1966) *The Language of Movement: A Guidebook to Choreutics*. Boston, MA: Plays, Inc.

Laban, R., and Lawrence, F. C. (1947) *Effort*. London: Macdonald and Evans.

LaViers, A. (2013a) *Automaton*. Clough Undergraduate Commons, Georgia Institute of Technology, 6 April. (Dance event)

LaViers, A. (2013b) *Choreographic Abstractions for Style-Based Robotic Motion*. PhD. Georgia Institute of Technology.

LaViers, A., and Egerstedt, M. (2011) The Ballet Automaton: A Formal Model for Human Motion. *American Control Conference, Proceedings*.

LaViers, A., and Egerstedt, M. (2012) Style Based Robotic Motion. *Proceedings of the American Control Conference*. San Francisco, CA, 4327–4332.

LaViers, A., and Egerstedt, M. (2014) Style-Based Abstractions for Human Motion Classification. *ACM/IEEE 5th International Conference on Cyber-Physical Systems*. Berlin: GER, 84–91.

LaViers, A., Chen, Y., Belta, C., and Egerstedt, M. (2011a) Automatic Generation of Balletic Motions. *ACM/IEEE Second International Conference on Cyber-Physical Systems*. Chicago, IL, USA, 13–21.

LaViers, A., Chen, Y., Belta, C., and Egerstedt, M. (2011b) Automatic Sequencing of Ballet Poses. *IEEE Robotics and Automation Magazine, IEEE* 18 (3): 87–95.

LaViers, A., Sheng, Y., Heddy, J., Bashiri, A., and Bai, L. (2015) Abstractions for Design-by-Humans of Heterogeneous Autonomous Behaviors. *Dance Notations and Robot Motion Springer Tracts in Advanced Robotics (STAR)*. Heidelberg, New York; Dordrecht, London: Springer, 237–262.

LaViers, A., Teague, T., and Egerstedt, M. (2014) Style-Based Robotic Motion in Contemporary Dance Performance. In *Controls and Art: Inquiries That Intersect the Subjective and the Objective*. Heidelberg, New York; Dordrecht, London: Springer, 205–229.

Maletic, V. (1987) *Body, Space, Expression*. Berlin: de Gruyter.

Moore, C. L. (2009) *The Harmonic Structure of Movement, Music, and Dance According to Rudolf Laban: An Examination of His Unpublished Writings and Drawings*. Lewiston, NY: Edwin Mellen Press.

Natarajan, P., and Nevatia, R. (2008) Online, Real-Time Tracking and Recognition of Human Actions. In *IEEE 2008 Workshop on Motion and Video Computing*. Copper Mountain, CO: WMVC, 1–8.

Newlove, J., and Dalby, J. (2004) *Laban for All*. New York, NY: Nick Hern Books.

Norman, D. A. (1999) Affordance, Conventions, and Design. *Interactions* 6(3): 38–43.

Oniga, S., Vegh, J., and Orha, I. (2012) Intelligent Human-Machine Interface Using Hand Gestures Recognition. In *Automation Quality and Testing Robotics (AQTR), 2012 IEEE International Conference on*. IEEE, 559–563.

Sheng, Y., and LaViers, A. (2014) Style Based Human Movement Segmentation. In *IEEE International Conference on Systems Man and Cybernetics*.

Studd, K., and Cox, L. (2013) *Everybody Is a Body*. Indianapolis, IN: Dog Ear Publishing.

CHAPTER 30

CONTACT IMPROVISATION AND EMBODIED SOCIAL COGNITION

APRIL FLAKNE

AGAINST familiar theories of social cognition, recent phenomenological alternatives argue that attention to embodied interaction can help solve intractable puzzles of inter-subjectivity and social understanding (see Gallagher and Zahavi 2008). Exemplifying such interaction, dance has often offered convenient models or metaphors to such theorists.[1] But might certain dance practices go beyond mere illustration and act as a kind of laboratory to provoke and expose the sorts of embodied interaction that these phenomenological approaches to social cognition and ontology seek to defend?[2]

In truth, the rule-governed forms of social and/or couples dance these theorists often invoke to defend their views are a poor fit. These forms often tempt us to accept a conservative hermeneutic where social interaction always refers to and reentrenches existing patterns of communication or understanding. Contact improvisation, by contrast, allows us to catch sense-making and mutual understanding in the act of occurring—a goal compatible with one of the most radical and promising versions of the new embodied social cognition theories: participatory sense-making (De Jaegher and Di Paolo 2007). By destabilizing proprioception, together with marked, habitual, and socially mediated gestures, contact improvisation has the capacity to tap into the intercorporeal origins of even instrumental and communicative gesture, offering special access to the presubjective, affective, and social processes that constitute the deepest layers of social ontology.

In contact improvisation, the body of the other(s) is 'taken up' through processes of intercorporeal discharge, combinatory potential, and reappropriation of kinaesthetic energies, putting bodies into immediate and vital interaction with other bodies. Contact improvisation heightens awareness not only of kinaesthesis and proprioception but equally of what I will call *alloception*—an enactive bodily receptivity to the sensory and kinaesthetic processes of others that arguably underlies anything like 'mind reading'. Despite its name, social cognition theory has so completely neglected this crucial alloceptive dimension that it even lacks a distinctive name for the range of phenomena associated with bodies' natural attunement to other bodies—from contagious yawning to mimicked postures or expression to other-induced pheromonal and heart rate adjustments.[3] Contact improvisation's approach to 'contact' plumbs this neglected alloceptive depth, which can in turn (as I discuss in the following section) help embodied social cognition theory interrogate the space where meaning-making unfolds beneath and beyond the formal/social and the conscious/intentional levels. I argue (in the section after that) that this beneath or beyond points to intercorporeity as the ontogenetically and ontologically primary resource for fundamental sense-making—a resource that is revealed in the nature of contact improvisation as a *praxis* that disrupts more rigidly constituted sense and supports meaningful gesture and movement through space, whether in dance or in the quotidian lifeworld/habitus.[4] Contact improvisation takes us to the heart of intercorporeal processes of 'kinesthetic agency' (Nolan 2009) and affectivity between bodies.[5] These intercorporeal processes exceed their socially constructed forms, though they are not a product of autonomous individual activity either. They are at once subpersonal and impersonally shared, profoundly affecting the genesis of mutual understanding.

WHAT IS CONTACT IMPROVISATION?
INTERPRETATION AND
SELF-INTERPRETATIONS

In a 2012 Ted Talk, Itay Yatuv presents a film of himself and his two-and-a-half-year old daughter practicing improvisation'. The interplay between the experienced dancer and master of contact improvisation and the toddling child amuses and charms, but it does more than that. It furthers a hunch that contact improvisation might hold ontogenetic keys to Merleau-Ponty's elusive ontological concept of intercorporeity: 'like a toddler taking her tentative first steps, the self and its 'proper' body are not to be assumed in advance; nor are they the result of mastery and technological self-fashioning. They are instead nothing but an ever-improvised centering in contact with the improvisations of others in an open, dynamic space: choreography as contact-improv(isation)' (Flakne 2007: 48). Yatuv likewise suspects a profound 'connection between the principles used in contact improvisation and infant development, both motor skills and in the way an infant physically communicates with his or her parent' (2012). The theoretical perspective and the practical application aim at the same primary ontogenetic layer where motor and communication skills intertwine and mutually enable each other. The question is how the 'principles' of contact improvisation might help unearth this layer and perhaps reveal its ongoing significance for all intersubjective understanding.

Contact improvisation grew out of choreographer Steve Paxton's work in 1972 and has branched wildly from there. Paxton claimed he originally wanted to pursue 'an energetic state of physical disorientation, trusting in one's basic survival instincts. It is a free play with balance, self-correcting the wrong moves and reinforcing the right ones, bringing forth a physical/emotional truth about a shared moment of movement that leaves the participants informed, centered, and enlivened' (1997). Unpacking Paxton's words in light of dance theorist Carrie Noland's (2009) concept 'kinesthetic agency' might help us understand what is at stake here. Paxton sought an 'energetic state of physical disorientation' not for its own sake but as it moves towards 'survival' while encouraging participants to emerge 'informed, centered, and enlivened'. In *Agency and Embodiment*, Noland seeks to rescue an embodied sense of agency from the two extremes of social construction as outlined in Bourdieu's concept of habitus or Butler's semiotics of the body on the one hand and traditional dualisms that cast the body as a mere puppet of an autonomous and controlling rational mind on the other. In 'kinesthetic agency', she discovers an excess sense of 'I can' that is present in every performed gesture, no matter how ritualized, habitual, or even reflexive. This 'I can' refers to a movement possibility projected from past acts of motility towards the needs of a present situation, for example standing on tiptoes to retrieve a light chain that has snapped with too energetic a tug. The breaking of the chain would create an interval between the achievement of pragmatic tasks in the world. In the interval, the sensation of (over)exertion just deployed in the tug might bristle along the biceps recoiling from the slack chain in the fingers, while a possibility of gingerness splays the fingers and prompts a fluid reaching from the ribcage instead of the upper arm. The 'I can' dips into a latent repertoire of movement, and the body feels its readiness and its power in motor recollection and intentionality as it faces the unexpected and redefined task.

Such 'I cans' are mostly unconscious—'I can' reach for the coffee cup, and also the q key—but they may, on Noland's account, become subject to reflective, bodily focus of the sort that Paxton exploits when he pursues disorientation as an 'energetic state'. In such cases, the body in its possibilities beckons: to master the light chain I must achieve maximum height, perhaps balancing on one leg in *demi pointe* as I reach for the broken bit of chain to *gently* engage it. To 'survive', I must be able to balance in this pose and still control the movement of an arm stretched maximally. If I lose balance, I will inevitably tug too hard or even fall forward. The decentring and recentring that emerge by way of prompted survival instincts thus involve a body that is 'informed and enlivened'. I sense what my body has done and what it *can do*; I calibrate balance and muscle tension in dialogue with the situation. In terms of 'kinesthetic agency', such 'information' induces the moving body to articulate its own possibilities, calling up resources it may not have known it possessed, or combining capacities that might belong to distinct effort contexts (tiptoes v. *demi pointe*). The 'enlivening' occurs alongside this information, issuing from focused and intensified bodily energy as it is engendered, dispensed, restrained, and so on, in moving within an environment. In the case of contact improvisation, however, the whole process occurs not just in interaction with more or less inert environmental objects but also with other active, kinaesthetically agential bodies. This places 'kinesthetic agency' in the vicinity of Arendtian praxis: contact improvisers engage plural kinesthetic agencies to *create* a space for action, rather than relying on an already constituted one.

Paxton's way to contact improvisation began with solo kinaesthetic experimentation to inform and enliven, but it did not stall there. In his self-summary, Paxton emphasizes 'bringing forth a physical/emotional truth about a *shared* moment of movement'. What has come to be viewed primarily as a duet form emerged initially out of Paxton's own solo experimentation—a component maintained in the practice of the 'small dance'—coupled with his interest in setting the piece *Momentum* on a group of young male dancers. Paxton envisioned *Momentum* as capturing multiple bodies colliding like 'atoms' in space. Longtime collaborator and contact improvisation innovator Nancy Stark Smith compared the debut of *Momentum* to a 'fountain of male dancers' (2005). This fascination with atomic or elemental interaction led Paxton to discover that his medium was nothing less than the 'possible' within movement itself, unlimited by the techniques and habits structuring single dancers' bodies. *Momentum* allowed Paxton to explore 'what a body can do' through what *bodies*—conceived as 'atomic', or molecular systems entering into more or less stable configurations, drawing energy from each other or depleting it, blocking it or expanding its flows—might be able to do.[6] With this attention to movement possibilities *between* bodies, we shift from an individual, personal, or subjective conception of kinaesthetic agencies as bodily intentionalities to *the affective engendering* of movement possibilities that are, in a Deleuzian sense, *impersonal*, belonging neither to you or me but unfolding in and shaping the space between us. To participate in this affectivity is to experience kinaesthetic agency, not only through recombinations of movement possibilities that are personally experienced and bodily archived, but also as an experience of kinaesthetic possibilities through *alloception*, opening the moving self to intimate interventions from the gestures, body parts, and bodily energies of moving others.

Paxton had come to see classical dance—primarily ballet—as a discipline that deployed micro- or *subpersonal* techniques within individual (and sometimes partnered) bodies to maximize energies, but always towards very specific, preset, and delimited goals—often resisting gravity or carefully manipulating inertia. Because such genre-based 'technologies' were aimed at narrowly defined outcomes through patterned movements and predetermined muscular strategies, Paxton viewed them as ultimately restricting the very possibilities they unleashed through rigorous training and breaking down of quotidian movements (Paxton 2009). Contact improvisation, by contrast, meant to disinhibit these energies, these possibilities, which had been discovered only to be prematurely reharnessed, and to put them instead into a free play where the forces of disorientation and subsequent survival (the body emerging as informed, centred, and enlivened) were a-telic: after all, no one knows what resources challenged, interactive bodies might draw on or create to reorient themselves. Paxton's method of experimentation going forward was to be two-pronged—'contact' and 'improvisation'.

The only goal and constraint of 'contact', Paxton (1998) insists, is 'to stay in touch'. The focus is 'on the skin'. But Yatuv is quick to clarify that the skin as point of contact is not a boundary or a limit of a self-contained individual body but an energetic relay of 'weight-sharing, losing and regaining balance, momentum, and other surprises'. In other words, the skin is the medium of alloception as an 'intense flow of information' (Yatuv 2012), a current that runs between bodies and brings them into communication. Unpredictable transfers of subpersonal energy take place, allowing, for example, smaller, frailer bodies to accept the weight of larger ones without deploying premeditated techniques. Even in relative stillness, proximate bodies communicate a wide range of energies (breath, pulse, involuntary or reflexive response), with kinaesthetic counterparts felt deep in the bodies of the dancers. But whose energies and in which dancer? Between bodies destabilized, improvisation enters the breach of alloception and proprioception that is motivated by the contact.

For Yatuv, the 'improvisational element' both discovers and demands 'immediacy', a 'complete two way communication', and an ability to 'react intuitively' to an 'abundance of intensity' (2012). Nor is such discovery trivial. From the point of view of recent theories of embodied social cognition, it may well advance current thinking on three fronts. It may: (1) augment recent attempts to escape the logic of analogy when confronting the problem of 'other minds' by focusing directly on bodily affectivity; (2) allow us to explore how mutual understanding transpires *below* the level of individual intentionality; (3) provide missing links between preestablished pragmatic and semantic contexts of social interaction *against which* bodies are always already legible (as in Bourdieu's habitus) and the ability of interacting bodies to *generate* meanings through their interactions.

CONTACT IMPROVISATION AND EMBODIED THEORIES OF SOCIAL COGNITION

Philosophical inquiries into social cognition generally focus on two related questions. First, the famous enigma of other minds, namely how, if I only have immediate reflexive access to my own mind, I might ever be able to *know that* there *are* other minds in the bodies that I perceive around me, that they are not mere zombies or automata. For present purposes, this thorny metaphysical question can be set to the side. The second, related question, often treated empirically, assumes that other such minds exist and asks how I might understand them or know *what* such other minds think (the so-called mind-reading question). Until very recently, theorists interested in the mind-reading problem mainly relied on some sort of argument from analogy to address it. My body, they reckoned, is to my mind as that body over there must be to its mind.[7] This turns the behaving body of the other into a rubric according to which its mind might be read. Contemporary social cognition theories that rely on analogical approaches are often grouped into two camps: theory-theory[8] and simulation theory.[9] Theory-theorists think that we observe the behaviour of others and make inferences from it to others' 'hidden' beliefs and desires. These inferences gain their plausibility from self-observation of our own states and their bodily expression. We predict future behaviours based on these inferences, and we check and correct our inferences according to what we observe.

Simulation theorists, by contrast, look to neural resonance systems and argue that we can access the feelings of others because our neurons automatically and subpersonally 'mirror' their gestures. Their gestures evoke corresponding emotions in us. Empathy spreads from body to body, dragging affective registers in its wake. Using these registers as felt through our own neural systems, we can feel our way into another's affective state.

However plausible theory-theory may initially seem for certain limited (and probably highly artificial) cases where we must puzzle out surprising behaviour, it seems like an extraordinarily clunky way to pick up on the intentions of others in everyday life. Contact improvisation's provocation of an 'intuitive' and 'immediate' communication gives the lie to such deliberate processes of inference formation and testing, isolating instead a current running directly between bodies and needing no mediation by minds and mental states to act as masters and commanders of kinaesthetically agential bodies.[10]

This seems to prop up the plausibility of simulation theory by default for attentive dance theorists. Yet while attention to intimate bodily mirroring and response to other active bodies is certainly a step in the right direction, contact improvisation reveals more than an empathetic replay of the body I see within the body I live. Even more than theory-theory, simulation theory remains trapped in the notion that bodies and their mental and emotional states are independent, separate yet *analogous* to each other, as though we somehow rely on corresponding coordinates when we interact with others. For theory-theory, this analogy occurs on the level of beliefs and desires as these attach to outwardly observable bodily behaviours. For simulation theory, it relies on proprioceptive feedback prompted by the bodies of the others, but still occurring *within my interior stage*: when I see you hunch your shoulders, I feel the gesture within my own kinaesthetic repertoire, along with associated sets of attitudes and dispositions, whether I actually mimic the gesture or not.

But the practice of contact improvisation sketched above should make us question the picture of discrete minds trapped within self-contained body-boxes that need to be bridged through cognitive or affective analogies. Recent phenomenological alternatives, such as direct perception and interaction theory,[11] may get us closer to the contact improvisation experience by proposing that we recast subjectivities as embodied agencies acting within a shared, meaningful situation or lifeworld. We understand intentional actions—our own and others'—through mutual interaction *in the space between us,* that is, in shared intelligible contexts of concern and action. Only when this shared context and its attendant prompts and expectations break down do we need to resort to the sort of specialized mind-reading feats that theory-theory and simulation theory posit as basic for social understanding.

The relevance and felicity of such phenomenological approaches for dance are ample. They allow a thoroughgoing shift in emphasis from enclosed, merely mediating bodies to bodies that *do* and *can* enact intelligibly in space and with each other. For Gallagher and Zahavi, bodies are not merely mutually deciphering each other by comparing internal affective and cognitive coordinates; they are also and primarily grappling with space and with each other in overlapping sets of opportunities and concerns. De Jaegher and Di Paolo agree with this focus on exterior interaction between bodies but go further to focus on the sub- and supra- individual processes that drive these interactions. They call their specifically *enactive* approach to embodied social cognition 'participatory sense-making'[12]—a name that happens to go to the heart of what goes on in contact improvisation as well.

According to enactivism, perceptive organisms are in constant goal-oriented exchange with their environments. De Jaegher and Di Paolo endorse a view of enactivism in which the telos of each system and subsystem is 'autopoiesis', or the achievement of (relative) autonomy and sustainability. De Jaegher and Di Paolo reject methodologically individualist versions of autopoietic enactivism, however, claiming that enactive organisms constantly interact to create new systems that generate sui generis autopoietic tendencies. These tendencies can place new or additional opportunities and constraints on the individual organisms participating in the newly formed systems.

Familiar forms of couple or group social dance, such as tango, might initially appear to provide excellent examples of this sort of system interaction. In such forms, the logic of the dance directs the intentions of the individual dancers while still making room for individual decision-making and virtuosity (see van Alphen 2010). Maintaining the dance system is paramount, such that swapping out individual partners need not disturb the logic of the dance. At the same time, the specific character of the dance will be determined by the movement capacities and vocabulary of individual participants in their responsive interactions with other participants. Such individual variations are built into the very structure of the dance (see van Alphen 2010). However, in these forms of dance, the general parameter of exchange and meaningful gesture structure any innovation. Sense can only evolve incrementally. The question is whether participatory sense-making can help dance theorists grasp the kind of upheaval in meaningful movement patterns and habits that contact improvisation precipitates and, correlatively, if the sort of 'thinking in movement' that emerges as a result of this upheaval in contact improvisation[13] can help demonstrate the strength of participatory sense-making as a comprehensive theory of social cognition.

Contact improvisation indeed provides ample evidence of such collaborative system-forming rather than system-reliant sense-making. While participants are surely not stripped bare of their prior training and habits, their gestures are decontextualized along with the anticipated systemic gains for each participating individual—gains such as balance, range of motion, and so on. This clears the way for 'sense'—Paxton's 'survival'—to be made not *within* (proprioceptively) but *between* (alloceptively) the individuals. The dominance of the interactive system relative to the individual participants will, of course, modulate, depending on the tasks and the individuals involved in a given contact improvisation scenario. This fits with participatory sense-making, since it favours neither individual agents or pregiven supraindividual rules or processes but draws attention to complex and dynamic combinations that focus on 'the coordination of intentional activity in interaction, whereby individual sense-making processes are affected and *new domains of social sensemaking can be generated that were not available to each individual on her own*' (De Jeagher and Di Paolo 2007: 497; emphasis in original).

In other words, participatory sense-making centres on the 'autonomy' of social sense-making processes, not necessarily *in lieu of* but certainly *in addition to* the autonomy of the agents involved, and on how these generate new action possibilities and contexts for the participants. This means that for participatory sense-making, (1) there are multiple and differential autonomous centres, from individual organisms to interactive systems and subsystems, each with its own dynamics; (2) such autonomous centres can co-exist and be mutually affecting without necessarily cancelling or overriding other such centres; and (3) the interaction of such autonomies may in some circumstances radically alter and even increase possibilities for further autonomous activity on the part of each participating agent.

While any partnered dance would demonstrate premises 1 and 2, contact improvisation exposes the operation of the third and most radical premise. Contact improvisation shows not only how bodies may interact with other bodies in rule-bound and implicitly or explicitly structured and structuring environments but also how, through interaction, *'new domains of social sensemaking can be generated that were not available to each individual on her own'.* This opening of new, potentially transformative ways of interacting helps participatory sense-making escape the potential hermeneutic drag threatening related phenomenological models of embodied social cognition, and assures its relevance for improvisational praxis.

Recall that according to interaction theory and direct perception (Gallagher 2008), embodied agents need not, for the most part, engage in explicit acts of mind-reading because they have 'primary and pervasive' direct access to each other's intentions through the embodied comportments within and towards a shared environment of concern.[14] But notice that the shared environment of concern is already significant to each agent as both agents move through and towards it in conscious and unconscious ways. When they encounter another comporting agent, they already ('directly') *perceive* the movements of these others as meaningful, intentional, or significant, insofar as they are concernfully directed to a shared action context. In other words, they perceive the others' movements as specifically *gestural,*[15] as expressive and/or instrumental according to the assumptions of the shared background context. Such gestures naturally lie on a semantic continuum, from articulate parts of an abstract symbol system (sign language, choreographic conventions) to culturally and/or biologically ingrained emphatic or emotive signals (smiles, tears) and to 'unconscious', habitual, or even very nearly reflexive bodily movements (blinking, squinting).

Direct perception accounts construed in this way must assume that movements become gestures by virtue of their legibility against a shared backdrop of significance. But how can this explain improvisational practices that precisely aim to destabilize that significance, uprooting, in the case of contact improvisation, even the most basic proprioceptive functions that distinguish and give sense to self and other, self and environment? Participatory sense-making can surpass background assumptions essential to other embodied social cognition models by viewing gestures not as those movements that are 'always already' intentional and significant but as those movements that present as *opportunities to be taken up*—in whatever fashion—by other kinaesthetic agencies striving towards collaborative sense. Here the gestural movements themselves—and not just their preformed semantic or intentional content in a given context—are taken up as saliences and affordances for another kinaesthetic agent. This is done immediately through the agents' bodies; my body forms a response to your bodily movements in our shared—that is, action-orienting, not necessarily semiotically or semantically structured—space long before I get around to thinking about or analysing any intentions 'behind' our gestures.

Like the other phenomenological proposals, participatory sense-making breaks directly and decisively with analogical approaches to others. While immediate bodily responsiveness to other bodies may sound something like simulation theory and its application to 'kinesthetic empathy' (see Foster 2010)—one's ability, by way of resonance systems, to 'mirror' another's movements in one's 'own' neurological network—it is no passive neurological effect. Instead it is the *activity* of perceiving the other through movement that *creates* a connection and sense between us: alloception. Empathetic processes may well be an important *part* of my ability to respond actively to your gestures, but they do not tell the whole story. While I feel your gesturing within myself, your gestures enable or awaken a sense of bodily possibilities that I could not have 'possessed' before our interaction. Alloception as enactive 'responsiveness' to the other's moving body means that gestures—which need not be intentional and can include subconscious, reflexive, and 'meaningless' bodily processes like breathing and pulse rate—become occasions of manifold opportunities to intervene in situations that include them. I participate in, impinge upon, encourage, deflect (and so on) your survival and sense-making activity as bodily enacted through your gestures as you move through the environment we share, and you do the same with my gestures, which become responsively wrapped up in your own. The dynamics of our gestural interaction go quite beyond anything we as agents intended or sometimes are even capable of intending independently, setting up their own logics and demands, opportunities and constraints, while reaching out towards a newly instituted, collaborative sense.

Could it be that the 'intuitive reaction', immediacy', and 'complete two way communication' (Yatuv's articulation of the improvisational element of contact improvisation) just is this capacity for alloception—a ontogenetic survival mechanism even the youngest infants possess?[16] And could it be that it is now coming to the fore under new systemic demands? I think this and more. Pushing past preestablished gestural vocabularies and rules, for example, signals for transition, contact improvisation exceeds formal partnering and 'couples social dance' to reveal the ontological condition of possibility informing the interactive processes that participatory sense-making strives to capture empirically: intercorporeity.[17] When contact becomes the only telos, the 'meaning' and 'appropriate uptake' of familiar gestures is suspended, put in 'brackets'. This means that the body does not 'know' how to respond, either through conditioned, habitual action or thought-out inferences and strategies. Instead, the body needs to 'wing it', to improvise. In this way, contact improvisation exceeds formed, intentional agency and rule-governed intelligible gesture within an already constituted action context or environment of concern to glimpse the body-to-body alloceptive origin of gestural significance in its process of emergence.

Having laid out the self-understandings of contact improvisers in relation to the neglected faculty of allocetion, I have explored here how contact improvisation can join forces with recent phenomenologically inspired social cognition theories to challenge analogical approaches to social cognition. In particular, participatory sense-making can attend to how allocetive openness can generate fresh sense where existing contexts are destabilized or challenged. Contact improvisation can help catch this sense-making in the act of occurring. In the next section, I will draw on a recent ontological interpretation of improvisation to show how contact improvisation's invocation of allocetion can press even further past questions of social cognition to illuminate an underlying social ontology rooted in intercorporeity.

Contact Improvisation
as Intercorporeal Sense-Making

Contact improvisation often begins with participants, unengaged. They might move individually through the 'kinaesphere', feeling space as an arena for movement, perhaps drawing special attention to Nancy Stark Smith's 'skinesphere' as the moving body in various velocities plays with the flesh's contact with the air and with different available solid surfaces (Stark Smith et al. 2008). Perhaps each mover individually initiates the 'small dance', Paxton's method of experimenting with mass, gravity, and a range of proprioceptive and kinaesthetic sensations through exercises deploying mindfulness and metaphor (see Paxton 2008). Such exercises can be understood in phenomenological terms as inducing a kind of kinaesthetic epoche, drawing attention to habitual processes built into to an ordinary act of, say, standing, by suspending them. First to go is talk of 'centre'—which in dance means many things, according to Paxton, including not only 'the mass of the pelvis' but also the centre axis 'of the tube of the body', or the 'nonconscious mental activity which maintains balance' (i.e., proprioception). Against such centre talk, Paxton insists that the small dance provokes a 'body-field event, centerless' (2008).

The epoche that is the small dance can prepare each participant for contact, but even if one skips this step, the contact itself will soon enough provoke similar bracketing effects. The participants approach each other. Proximity creates sensitivity and opportunity. If the only goal is constant contact between two (or more) moving bodies, and the medium is the surface of the body, intentionality surrenders to motor imperatives. The body of the other becomes a sort of prosthetic, an extension of the body that confuses 'proper' and 'alien' in acts of integration and surrender.[18] Under such conditions, proprioception merges with allocetion—that intimate sense of another's bodily processes as opportunities for engagement—through a growing interdependence as what belongs to me and what belongs to the other enter into dynamic interplay. 'My' balance depends on 'yours', our velocities interconnect, you communicate your readiness through vital signs of breath and muscular tension transferred to 'me' through 'our' skin.

While the purpose of the small dance may be to catch the body in the act of proprioception by interrupting and resuming it, contact reaches a deeper level where the 'proper' of proprioception is itself dismantled. The continuation of the movement between the dancers will depend on their ability to be in a nonpremeditated responsive relation to each other. This means, among other things, that habitual gestures will be interrupted or resumed by the other partner, transfiguring intentional structures at the same time that bodily boundaries are challenged through information exchange. This information exchange will exceed the proprioceptive and kinaesthetic, which are directly acted upon in the movement, and intrude upon other interoceptively oriented faculties such as breathing, heart rate, body temperature, and so on.

'Contact' awakens 'alloception' on a wide variety of registers, of which simulated 'kinaesthetic empathy' is only a fragment. I am not just mirroring my partner's enacted gestures within myself; I am taking them up as my own, but also as a dis-ruption of my own. My bodily trajectory, the sense it marked in space, is ruptured and dis-placed, but also resumed in a new space and place. As I move with my partner and respond to her, and as contact initiates information about and interventions into her anticipations and inertias, respiration, pulse, and so on, I feel all of this within my body as an occasion for the future projection of 'my' body. Just as the small dance played with proprioceptive habits to try to capture proprioceptive energy in the act with respect to environmental features of gravity and mass, so now proprioception is challenged as a constant dialogue between itself and an other who invades it, alloceptively encourages it, augments it, or blocks it, all the while placing it in radical question: if the proper is what it is only in response to what is other, creating kinaesthetic response-ability, in what way can it be 'proper' at all? This is the question that builds an existential and ontological element into the improvisation prompted by contact.

Improvisation certainly means, etymologically, what is 'un-provided-for'. In the case of familiar art domains, this can mean simply what falls outside the providence of a composer, choreographer, playwright, and so on. Yet my discussion of participatory sense-making suggests that we might extend the meaning of improvisation to any action context in which the expectations or organism-based needs of the involved agents mesh poorly with the expectations or needs of other involved agents, or with elements of the action context itself. In such a situation, the involved agents cannot 'survive'. They are un-provided-for and forced to 'make new sense' in a collaborative way, where constraints and opportunities from the situation and/or the other participants might open 'new domains of social sensemaking ... that were not available to each individual on her own' (De Jaegher and Di Paolo 2007: 497).

The novelty implied in this quote, however, need not be overstated. As G Peters warns, any understanding of improvisation as simple innovation, or chasing after the new, can mislead. The task of improvisation, on his plausible Heideggerian interpretation, attends to 'the manner in which the given is given in ever new ways' (2009: 120). This strange phrase must be carefully parsed. According to Peters, if modernism exhausts itself in the illusory chase after the new, certain varieties of postmodern pseudoimprovisation simply repeat the old in ever new contexts (e.g., sampling, mash-ups). Rather than returning to an origin, this 'borrowing' from the past risks effacing and flattening historicity altogether. While admitting that such 'recycling' activity has its pleasures—say the surprise juxtaposition of two beloved familiar tunes, or even focusing our attention on a continuity of the present with a comforting (and therefore not really past) past, as in the case of nostalgia, this does not get to the heart of improvisation, properly conceived.

For Peters, genuine improvisation is best conceptualized as a return to origins in order to release potentials that were silenced or abandoned in the actualization of an artwork (or action-context), and doing this for the sake of opening up avenues of exploration for the future. This leads him to critique the self-interpreted temporality of many improvisers—including contact improvisers—as being 'in the moment' or 'immediate'. This is only right, Peters maintains, if we understand 'the moment' to be punctured by the essential absences of past and future. Improvisation, on his account, needs to be viewed as a return to an already actualized 'past' for the sake of releasing a future, at least in what he calls an 'existential' register or, perhaps better, a 'lived experience' register. For him, the past always contains possibilities that were never realized/actualized—say a range of harmonics, a shift in key or tempo, or a kinetic series—and retrieving these can transform the work, sometimes into something that 'works' very differently. This process casts into relief what worked in the past, and why it might have done so, while allowing perplexity to provoke a different approach to a problem that may have even ceased to be viewed as a problem at all.

In the case of contact improvisation, this sort of improvisation is glimpsed operating even at the level of the small dance, where standing proprioception itself becomes problematic and we must retrieve kinaesthetic possibilities long suppressed in our habits of standing and walking. It becomes even more pronounced when multiple dancers interact. Here gestures that might be habitually 'read' or received as inviting predictable counter-movements, such as erotic or aggressive, are transfigured into 'mere' movement opportunities in the course of each body groping towards contact-based sustainability. The movement, along with the kinaesthetic energies and attendant sensations, is opened to novel sequences and dynamics, suspending and/or accelerating routine or technical gestural intentionalities, and opening them up to redeployment and resignifications *between* the improvising dancers, who will each need to contribute to make the context actionable.

If such reworking of the gestural and agential possibilities of the individual dancers expresses the 'existential' or 'lived experiential' register, Peters also wants to unearth an 'ontological' register of the improvisation. The ontological level aims to expose the 'gifting' of the given and the gift. In contact improvisation, we might say that a well-known technique or familiar gesture embodied through habit is the 'given', while the cultural production, for example a choreographic sequence around familiar aspects and predictable (provided) variations of it, would be the 'gift'. The work of improvisation exposes the coming-into-being of the gift—the presencing of what is now present—so as to witness the re-birth, the repotentializing, of the gift in its giving. Consider for example a series of lifts in a ballet pas de deux. These lifts will follow ballet conventions while incorporating constraints protecting each dancer, maximizing a given effect, and emerging out of prior sequences while setting up subsequent ones in the phrase. If two trained ballet dancers embark on a contact improvisation exercise, they will almost certainly embody the presuppositions of their craft, given as built into their bodies through rigorous training and habit. Then, through the process of the improvisation, they may begin to vary these givens with a sloped shoulder or arched back, a roll, a rejection, or a role switch, all throwing off their carefully developed techniques. Neither dancers nor nondancers can ever enter the improvisation ex nihilo, in search of what has never been done before. Improvisation starts with and moves through and away from the givens, stretching them to see the solutions they provided (the gift), as well as what puzzles they raise, which can be raised and solved anew with each embodied effort of 'survival' for the disoriented participants.

In contact improvisation, then, the gift is nothing other than significant gestures, whether these are the familiar gestural vocabularies of established dance genres, as in a choreographic exercise, or the quotidian gestures and postures of everyday life. On the existential or lived experience register, such contact improvisational practices can be illuminating and even therapeutic, as bodily habits that ingrain character traits and/ or power relations, even regimes of injury or self-harm, are taken up through the interactive, lived body—shyness, selfishness, distrust, domination—and reworked. But the 'giving' of interactive gestures in their emergence points to a deeper, ontological register: the level of intercorporeity running beneath the alloceptive-proprioceptive call and response, making it possible. At its most efficacious, contact improvisation brings this intercorporeity itself to the fore as the very possibility of social cognition or intersubjective understanding between self and other caught in the act of coming to be.

CONCLUSION: RECREATING SENSE THROUGH INTERCORPOREITY

In Merleau-Ponty's essay 'The Philosopher and His Shadow', intercorporeity is presented not just as variety of but as the very condition of possibility for anything like intersubjectivity. In its thinnest sense, intercorporeity simply names bodies' ability to affect and be affected by other bodies. Bodies are in continual and constant 'communication', best understood through the Kantian category of 'community', that is, 'the reciprocity of agent and patient'. Rather than involving causal, instrumental, strategic, or metaphysically hierarchical relations, intercorporeity indicates a multidirectional call and response that brings agencies into being by making them response able. Bodies are enmeshed in such multidirectional communication at all times, affecting each other 'beneath' other more explicit forms of culturally and symbolically mediated forms of communication or influence, whether the latter be implicit or explicit, conscious or un-conscious. Signifying gestures will at once participate in established regimes of sense while overrunning them on the intercorporeal level, setting into motion their own sub- and suprapersonal dynamics and systems. Contact improvisation stages and allows us to glimpse this undercurrent between bodies, bringing it to the fore as the condition and motor of any social cognition whatsoever.

At the deepest level of intercorporeal communication, sense can be made—and unmade—due to the fluidity of bodies themselves in their ability to affect other bodies in multiple ways and on multiple levels, thereby affecting the systems of coher-ence that register for each organism as sense. Participatory sense-making elaborates a theory of autopoiesis in which an organism is enactively engaged in an environ-ment that impacts it and that it impacts. Such an organism continually strives to make (poiesis) itself (auto) stabile and viable out of this interactive flux. Intercorporeity adds to this organism-environment dynamic a direct organism-organism dynamic. If the organism-environment relation is well named as an (auto)*poiesis*, the organism-organism interaction is rightly conceived as an Arendtian *praxis*—a plurally motivated creation and recreation of action(able) contexts where the prevailing sense or system is questioned and a new one comes into being. But Arendt surely missed the extent to which intercorporeity enables her strictly political praxis. Bodies can affect and be af-fected by each other because they are in a constant process of destabilizing and reconsti-tuting themselves, each other, and the shared environment that their interaction brings about: Paxton's disorientation and survival rendered plurally intercorporeal exposes organisms capable of making and remaking sense through active participation and en-gagement with the bodies of others.

This interpretation makes body-to-body affectivity prior to the proprioception that some recent phenomenological theories take to be fundamental for selfhood (see Gallagher and Zahavi 2008) and takes intercorporeity, as supraindividual while its elem-ents and energies are subindividual, to be the really primary and pervasive element in all social cognition. Indeed, it makes of proprioception a constantly projected *achieve-ment*, rather than a presupposition, and an achievement that always already involves *alloception*, the active material affectivity though which the bodily processes of others are enactively perceived as part of any collaborative sense-making project. Contact im-provisation forces us to attend to alloception, thereby glimpsing intercorporeity in the act of making us mutually intelligible to each other.[19]

Let me conclude, then, as I began, with Yatuv's fascination with the often-falling toddler and the world of adults who would rush to 'save' her while her father looked on. When Yatuv spotted the affinity between his own praxis of contact improvisation and the progress of his toddler towards upright motility, he was entranced by her grasping towards proprioceptive control in an environment populated by objects and others that served not simply as isolated models to emulate but as various enticing, enhancing, and hindering prostheses. Movement and communication were tightly intertwined. For the infant never embarked on her developmental journey alone; even prenatally she was striving for proprioception against a backdrop of radical and swiftly altering terms of intercorporeity—which only became more complicated and plural at birth. The infant was nurtured through the bodies of others, continually protected or exposed to a more or less built environment through which she enacted her sense, her 'survival', together with others, using all evolving alloceptive and proprioceptive information amid continual developmental and environmental disorientation. Her 'self' as a relatively autonomous and defined system developed its contours in embodied response to others, who also responded to her. Contact improvisation retrieves this fundamental ontogenetic and ontological origin of intercorporeity by putting into question our individualized bodily accomplishments and intentionalities in order to release them into new possibilities beyond constrained vocabularies and habitual gestures, including any reified habitus that limits, secures, and simplifies bodies' sense-making potential and chances of 'survival'. In doing so, contact improvisation releases the potential of kinaesthetic agencies towards a plural, participatory goal of sense-making that never forgets its origins in, and the promises of, embodied improvisation.

NOTES

1. Uses of dance metaphors are rife in social cognition literature, for example, early facial imitation between infant and caretaker is often described as a 'dance'. Gallagher refers to dance when he wants to show how body schemas extend to include environmental features, in some cases even the bodies of others. See Gallagher (2006: 35-37). De Jaegher and Di Paolo, meanwhile, discuss couples dance to get at the tensions between an individual system and a joint or joined system. See De Jaegher and Di Paolo (2007: 495–496).
2. Maxine Sheets-Johnstone makes a move beyond the metaphorical when she proposes improvisational dance as a *paradigm* of 'thinking in movement' rather than just an illustration of it. See Sheets-Johnstone (2009: 28–63).
3. 'Empathy' is sometimes invoked to do this work, but because this term itself is so imprecise, it confuses more than it clarifies. Is empathy a cognitive or an affective process? Is it part of a judgement, or the judgement itself? Does it refer to neurological resonance systems, or is it the result of these? While empathy is an extremely important concept for social cognition theory, the processes involved need to be carefully disentangled and conceptually clarified. Dan Zahavi (2001) does a good deal of this work. Most problematically, current conceptions of empathy too often rely on a model of analogy where each of us is a closed box to the other. Empathy is then brought in to bridge the boxes. Finally, empathy is too passive a process in many constructions. My term 'alloception' means to deny a closed-box model and get at our fundamental, (en)*active* bodily connection to each other. Alloception indicates a perception that takes up the bodies of other as affordances or possibilities.
4. I use the term 'praxis' in its Arendtian sense to get at a necessarily plural—person to person, rather than person to artifact or world—action oriented towards change or rupture in a stable or inert state of affairs. See Hannah Arendt, *The Human Condition* (Chicago: University of Chicago Press, 191958).
5. I borrow heavily from Carrie Noland's notion of 'kinesthetic agency' as developed in Noland (2009). However, I disagree with her narrowing of affect theory to emotions

facially expressed, as well as her emphasis on the individual. I turn to affect to indicate embodied yet impersonal—i.e., nonsubjective, nonindividual—attunements to other bodies in space.

6. 'We know nothing about a body until we know what it can do, in other words, what its affects are, how they can or cannot enter into composition with other affects, with the affects of another body, either to destroy that body or to be destroyed by it, either to exchange actions and passions with it or to join with it in composing a more powerful body'. Deleuze and Guattari (1987), 284.

7. The more I rely on analogy, the more I (1) insist on a special reflexive self-access as the standard of truth about what it means to be minded, and (2) take my own mind as paradigmatic, thereby making all other minds alter egos or versions of my own mind, deflating in the process what we most assume other minds to be: spontaneous and sui generis centres. For more on this, see Flakne (2017).

8. There is a great deal of philosophical and cognitive science literature on this topic, but Gopnik and Meltzoff (1997) is considered seminal, while Churchland (1994) and Carruthers (1996) provide helpful overviews of the topic. Finally, Baron-Cohen (1997) has probably done the most to popularize this view.

9. As in theory-theory of mind, the literature is vast and expanding. Gallese and Goldman (1998) remains influential, while Rizzolatti, Sinigaglia, and Anderson (2007) charts developments in the field.

10. Sheets-Johnstone (2009) is helpful in this context.

11. For a combination and summary of the phenomenological alternative to social cognition theories, see Gallagher and Zahavi (2008).

12. See De Jaegher and Di Paolo (2007). Gallagher accepts their insights as offering less a challenge to than an empirically rooted confirmation of his own 'interactive theory' alternative to theory-theory and simulation theory. Indeed, the extent of his commitment to methodological individualism seems to vary, especially when he writes about embodied intersubjectivity and dance at the end of chapter 3 of Gallagher (2006).

13. Maxine Sheets-Johnstone famously articulates the idea of 'thinking in movement'. Michelle Merritt (2013) has recently updated these findings with insights from enactive cognition.

14. Questions have been raised about just how 'direct' direct perception really is; maybe microinferential process of a theory-theory or simulation theory sort are mediating or propping up such context-driven gestural practices all of the time. See Jacob (2011). Phenomenological and enactive accounts of perception, however, are in an excellent position to answer such worries, as do Krueger and Overgaard (2012). Under the enactive version of this paradigm, perception should not be viewed as a processing of raw, isolated data but as grounded in affordances and saliences for the organism as it moves through its environment. These affordances and saliences govern what we are able to see, hear, feel, smell, taste. The organism projects a coherent sensory environment, which it responds to and, in responding, alters. In-coherencies are assimilated, rejected, or altered according to the needs and interests of the agencies involved. This projection of coherence and alteration of incoherence just is the cognitive act of 'sense-making'.

15. I reserve the term 'gesture' for movements that are registered and taken up by other bodies, whether or not they have a traditional semantic sense.

16. This is the 'dance' of the caretaker-infant, observable in the first moments after birth, as discussed by Meltzoff and Moore (1977).

17. For De Jeagher's own take on the connection between participatory sense-making and intercorporeity, see De Jeagher and Fuchs (2009).

18. I discuss this process as a way to understand Merleau-Ponty's equation of my right hand touching my left hand to a handshake in Flakne (2007). De Jeagher and Fuchs (2007) also speak about this phenomenon as one of 'mutual incorporation'.

19. Where we began with Noland's kinaesthetic agency (2009) as an 'I can' that exceeds every 'I did', with intercorporeity we grasp a collective enabling of bodies in direct interaction with other bodies into a 'we can'. The 'I can' is released from its proprioceptive moorings and alloception awakens, repotentializing forgotten modes of social understanding rooted in intercorporeity.

References

Arendt, H. (1958) *The Human Condition*. Chicago: University of Chicago Press.

Baron-Cohen, S. (1997) *Mindblindness*. London: MIT Press.

Bourdieu, P. (1990) *The Logic of Structuring Practices*. Trans. Richard Nice. Stanford, CA: Stanford University Press.

Carruthers, P., and Smith, P. K. (eds.). (1996) *Theories of Theories of Mind*. Cambridge: Cambridge University Press.

Churchland, P. M. (1994) Folk Psychology (2). In Guttenplan, S. (ed.), *A Companion to the Philosophy of Mind*. Oxford: Blackwell, 308–316.

Contact Collaborations, Inc. (2014) 'About Contact Improvisation' Website of *Contact Quarterly*. http://www.contactquarterly.com/contact-improvisation/about/cq_ciAbout.php. Accessed 30 July 2014.

De Jaegher, H., and Di Paolo, E. (2007) Participatory Sense-Making: An Enactive Approach to Social Cognition. *Phenomenology and the Cognitive Sciences* 6: 485–507.

De Jeagher, H., and Fuchs, T. (2009) Enactive Intersubjectivity: Participatory Sense-Making and Mutual Incorporation. *Phenomenology and Cognitive Science* 8: 465–486.

Deleuze, G., and Guattari, F. (1987) *A Thousand Plateaus*. Trans. Brian Massumi. Minneapolis: University of Minnesota Press.

Flakne, A. (2007) Contact/Improv: A Sunaesthetic Rejoinder to Derrida's Reading of Merleau-Ponty. *Philosophy Today* 5: 42–49.

Flakne, A. (2017) Is Direct Perception Arrogant Perception? In Fielding, H., and Olkowski, D. (eds.), *Future Directions in Feminist Phenomenology*. Indianapolis: Indiana University Press.

Foster, S. (2010) *Choreographing Empathy*. New York: Routledge.

Gallagher, S. (2006) *How the Body Shapes the Mind*. Oxford: Oxford University Press.

Gallagher, S. (2008) Direct Perception in the Intersubjective Context. *Consciousness and Cognition* 17: 535–543.

Gallagher, S., and Zahavi, D. (2008) *The Phenomenological Mind*. London: Routledge.

Gallese, V., and Goldman, A. (1998) Mirror Neurons and the Simulation Theory of Mind-Reading. *Trends in Cognitive Sciences* 12: 493–501.

Gopnik, A., and Meltzoff, A. (1997) *Words, Thoughts, and Theories*. Cambridge, MA: MIT Press.

Jacob, P. (2011) The Direct-Perception Model of Empathy: A Critique. *Review of Philosophy and Psychology* 2(3): 519–540.

Krueger, J., and Overgaard, S. (2012) Seeing Subjectivity: Defending a Perceptual Account of Other Minds. *ProtoSociology: Consciousness and Subjectivity* 47: 239–262

Meltzoff, A. N., and Moore, M. K. (1977) Imitation of Facial and Manual Gestures by Human Neonate. *Science* 198: 75–78.

Merritt, M. (2013) Thinking Is Moving: Dance, Agency, and a Radically Enacted Mind. *Phenomenology and the Cognitive Sciences* 14: 95-110.

Noland, C. (2009) *Agency and Embodiment: Performing Gestures/Producing Culture.* Cambridge, MA: Harvard University Press

Paxton, S. (1998) Jacob's Pillow Interview. In *Jacob's Pillow Dance Interactive.* http://danceinteractive.jacobspillow.org/dance/steve-paxton. Accessed 25 July 2014.

Paxton, S. (2008) The Small Dance, the Stand. Class notes from February 1977 reprinted in Ken Manheimer, *Myriadcity* website https://myriadicity.net/contact-improvisation/contact-improv-as-a-way-of-moving/steve-paxton-s-1977-small-dance-guidance   Accessed   25 July 2014.

Paxton, S. (2009) Steve Paxton Interview. Website of *Contact Quarterly.* http://www.contactquarterly.com/contact-improvisation/webtexts/view/paxton-talk-at-ci36 Accessed 25 July 2014.

Peters, G. (2009) *The Philosophy of Improvisation.* Chicago: University of Chicago Press.

Rizzolatti, G., Sinigaglia, C., and Anderson, F. (2007) *Mirrors in the Brain. How Our Minds Share Actions, Emotions, and Experience.* Oxford: Oxford University Press.

Sheets-Johnstone, M. (2009) Thinking in Movement. In *The Corporeal Turn.* Exeter, UK: Imprint Academic, 28–63.

Stark Smith, N. (2006) Harvest: One History of Contact Improvisation. In CQ 31: 46-54.

Stark Smith, N., Koteen, D., and Paxton, S. (2008) *Caught Falling: The Confluence of Contact Improvisation, Nancy Stark Smith, and Other Moving Ideas.* Northampton, MA: Contact Editions.

van Alphen, F. (2010) Tango and Enactivism: First Steps in Exploring the Dynamics and Experience of Interaction. Integrative Psychological and Behavioral Science 48(3): 322–331.

Yatuv, I. (2012) Contact Improvisation: An Intuitive, Non-verbal and Intimate Dialogue. (Video) http://www.youtube.com/watch?v=Gi-OaiQvnTU. Accessed 8 August 2014.

Zahavi, Dan. (2001) Beyond Empathy. *Journal of Consciousness Studies* 8(5–7): 151–156.

CHAPTER 31

....

MODELLING IMPROVISATION AS EMERGENCE

A Critical Investigation of the Practice of Cognition

....

COLLEEN DUNAGAN, ROXANE L. FENTON,
AND EVAN D. DORN

SINCE the early 1990s, the concept of emergence has resurfaced to become influential in many scientific disciplines, philosophy, teaching, even city planning and public policy. (See Sawyer [1999: 447] for a relatively brief but detailed recounting of the history of the term.) Emergence theory seeks to identify and explain the development of complex systems or behaviours (involving novel, higher-level patterns, organization, or collective action) that cannot be reduced to the functions of their individual parts. The lens of emergence provides an opportunity to look at improvisation in various ways: to continue a dialogue with science, to emphasize the action of dancers as bodyminds (both at the individual level and in group performance), and to reexamine the teaching of improvisation. Further, emergence offers a way for practitioners to understand thinking in dance as a bodymind activity, rather than one solely of the rational intellect. Or even to see dancing *as* thinking, rather than something opposed to it.[1]

While much of the existing work on emergence and dance deals with emergence as a model for the ensemble, we believe that emergence theory in improvisation can also be applied to a second level: how the behaviour of each individual emerges from that individual's 'parts', including sensory perception, habitual and automated decision-making, and the multiple mental aspects that constitute higher-level consciousness (e.g., subjective, abstract, and reflective thought, each of which also emerges from smaller processes in the brain).

Because these two levels of emergence interact (see fig. 31.1), employing theories of emergence, complexity, and dynamical systems theory with attention to both levels allows us to reexamine how the field of emergence might provide conceptual models that support improvisational dance practices and their pedagogy in a manner that

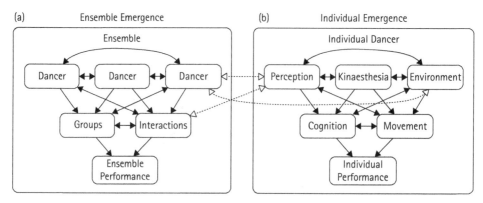

FIG. 31.1 Two 'levels' of emergence in improvisational dance. Prior work has focused primarily on how ensemble performances emerge from the movements and interactions of individual dancers (a). The performance of each dancer may also be seen as an emergent phenomenon resulting from the dancer's intentions, movements, perception, cognition, etc. (b). (Both diagrams are simplified; in reality, many more aspects influence the performance than the few shown here.) The dotted arrows illustrate how the two levels of emergence interact: for example, each dancer's movements are influenced by her perceptions of other groups and interactions in the ensemble, and the locations of other dancers constitute parts of her environment.

embraces the bodymind as a basic premise. While we focus our discussion primarily on two specific improvisational dance practices, Susan Sgorbati's Emergent Improvisation and contact improvisation, we recognize that a range of improvisation practices employ conceptual models that foster the emergent, regardless of whether or not this connection has been previously identified. Consider, for example, Authentic Movement, Nina Martin's Ensemble Thinking, Richard Bull's structural improvisations, William Forsythe's Improvisational Technologies, and the work of Judith Dunn, Dianne McIntyre, Susan Rose, and many others who have practised improvisation in and for performance (Buckwalter 2010; Foster 2002; Goldman 2010).

This focus on emergence and multiple levels of cognition enables an important evaluation of how conceptual models employed in dance pedagogy play a central role, not only in disciplinary instruction but also in developing and promoting approaches to dance education and dance's role in culture. Too frequently, discussion of improvisation in concert dance (among dancers, dance audiences, teachers) is still tied to modernist and even Romantic conceptions of the self and of the artist, focusing on individuality, interiority, and inspiration. This issue is not unique to dance. As Keith Sawyer points out in the introduction to his book *Group Genius*, both research into creativity and popular-press writing about it have tended to focus on the individual (2007: n.p.). Such discourse has various effects. We argue that when dance is so tied to interiority and identified with emotion, it is perceived as opaque to rigorous discussion and analysis (see Albright 2003; Gibbs 2003). A focus on inspiration diminishes the perception of improvisation not only as a skill that can be taught but also as one that must be practised. It ignores the roles of craft and knowledge in improvisation, choreography, and creativity more generally and obscures some of the benefits for all dancers in studying improvisation.

We support the notion that the study of improvisation and its validity as subject of scientific enquiry must of necessity include both doing and observing. Viewing perspective matters to the exploration of emergence within dance improvisation. Within our author group of two improvisers/dance scholars and a computational neuroscientist, we have seen how watching from the outside provides a perspective and experience of emergent behaviour, patterns, and systems that is, at times, distinct from what the participant noticed during the same improvisation. (Not surprisingly, training in dance informs and shapes the nature of this external observation.) Some improvisational forms make moments of emergence more readily visible to observers; this happens in contact improvisation due to the often precarious nature of the improvised contact between bodies. Differences in perception between watching and doing have the potential to both negatively and positively impact scientific studies of cognition and emergence.[2]

Examination of dance improvisation, at the levels both of the body and of the ensemble, offers an opportunity to study emergence and cognition within practices that train cognitive development (abstract thought, self-reflective observation, motor skills, awareness) and foster emergence. In order to look more closely at how the study of emergence in cognitive science aligns with the study of dance improvisation and its discoveries, we turn first to the concept of emergence itself.

A BRIEF HISTORY OF EMERGENCE

Emergence is a cross-disciplinary framework for studying the concept colloquially expressed as 'the whole is more than the sum of its parts'. Emergence, and the debates surrounding it, can be dated back to at least the mid-1800s (Kim 1999). Arguments for emergent structures can be found in nonlinear dynamics, connectionist modelling, chaos theory, complexity studies, artificial life, quantum mechanics, philosophy of mind, education, and the arts. In many fields, the study of emergence draws on dynamical systems theory and its concern with nonlinear systems (Silberstein and McGeever 1999: 184).[3] Several aspects of the broad subject of emergence particularly interest us:

- *Complexity from simplicity*: familiar from the scientific subjects of chaos theory and dynamical systems theory, the idea that complex behaviour can emerge from simpler components has obvious applicability to ensemble improvisational dance.
- *Constraint*: across theories of complex systems and emergence, the notion of constraint plays a vital role; without constraints the interactions of individual parts lend themselves not to emergent organization but to randomness. Dynamical systems theory suggests that the limitations of the individual parts, the relative simplicity of their functions, and the limitations of the environment in which they operate are crucial ingredients for novel forms of complex organization.

- *Criticality*: the emergence of a complex behaviour from smaller components also relies on a 'point of criticality' in its development. In other words, it is the moment in an improvisation when the behaviour of the dancers has generated enough potential material and the dancers are maintaining a sufficient state of awareness of each other that the improvisation can move from seemingly randomness and chaos to manifesting recognizable patterns and organization.
- *Self-organization*: on one level, self-organization simply refers to the lack of external guidance. In emergence theory, 'self-organized criticality' refers to systems that self-organize so as to remain near the cusp of criticality, thus enabling emergent behaviour. At the individual level, the human brain is seen as one such system (Beggs and Plenz 2003; Ouelette 2014). At the ensemble level, self-organization points to the ability of dancers to consciously influence the dance in a way that facilitates improvisational goals.

The key effort in studies of emergence is to identify jumps in structure (our scientist author likes 'phase transitions' and 'criticality avalanches') from the simple to the complex and to understand structures that arise out of numerous interactions occurring simultaneously in time and space (Johnson 2010: 843). Each of these aspects of emergence theory parallel the kinds of events and relationships that practitioner-researchers in dance improvisation (and jazz music) have investigated and developed intensively since the early twentieth century. In recognizing this connection, we acknowledge an aspect of cognitive science that has the potential to support dance concepts, while also reinforcing the vitality of dance as a field of intellectual study.

EMERGENCE OF THE ENSEMBLE: SUSAN SGORBATI AND NINA MARTIN

The idea of considering emergence theory in relationship to improvisation first occurred to us in response to our own experiences practising and teaching both contact improvisation and ensemble-focused improvisation for performance.[4] Over the course of twenty years, we encountered structured ensemble improvisation in three shared dance experiences: (1) structured improvisation in the heritage of Richard Bull, as taught by Susan Leigh Foster; (2) the work of Nina Martin, as introduced by graduate school colleague Karen Schaffman and encountered elsewhere; and (3) learning to teach improvisation (as part of composition or on its own) within U.S. university dance departments. We also studied contact improvisation with Caroline Waters and others. Emergence came to our attention more recently as a result of its growing visibility. As part of this trend, scholars, artists, educators, social scientists, and others have recognized connections between emergence and collaboration that relate directly to how the concept operates within improvisation. When we began actively researching improvisation's relationship to emergence, we discovered the work of Susan Sgorbati.

Emergence theory has obvious applicability to an improvisational ensemble, as performers' simpler individual actions combine to form a complex, self-organized collective performance. There is no central organizing agent: all members of the ensemble are simultaneously creating and performing. Even performances structured by a score emerge differently each time. A score provides one source of constraint, but there are countless others: from the environment, social context and expectations, the condition of individual bodies in a given moment, training, memory, previous performances, and so on. To address the ways emergence relates to improvisation, we begin by introducing Nina Martin's ensemble training practice of Ensemble Thinking.

Ensemble Thinking aims to introduce what she calls 'rigour' to improvising, often through exercises that simplify choices, enabling performers to think/act quickly, yet towards common compositional goals. 'Ensemble Thinking enables the performer to produce clear choices and avoid the bane of improvisation: "mush" (when there are no primary compositional concerns being articulated/recognized by the group, and complexity overwhelms everyone's efforts.)' (Martin 2007: 10). Martin does not use the language of emergence herself, but we would argue that her practice fosters the emergence of a dance (intended to be interesting to the audience) out of the complex system of the ensemble. This happens through the rigour imposed by constraints, including a lack of time for deliberation. Martin's Ensemble Thinking bears much in common with Sgorbati's work with emergence and improvisation.

Susan Sgorbati developed an improvisational practice with her students at Bennington College over the course of two decades that exemplifies the applicability of emergence theory to dance. After collaborative dialogue with scientists studying complex systems (particularly evolutionary biologist Bruce Weber, neuroscientist Gerald Edelman, and complex systems theorist Stuart Kauffman), she recognized direct parallels between her practice and emergence theory. Sgorbati calls her practice Emergent Improvisation. In her 2013 chapbook *Emergent Improvisation: Where Dance Meets Science on the Nature of Spontaneous Composition*, as well as in other essays in *Contact Quarterly* and on her website, she has done substantial work on identifying conceptual overlaps between complex systems theory (including emergence and self-organization) and dance improvisation.

Emergent Improvisation includes both a solo and ensemble practice. Sgorbati divides the solo practice into four areas of exploration: embodiment-sensory work, discovery of movement vocabulary, attention to spatial environment, and focus on the particular. These practices work to enhance the dancer's awareness of the dancer's own body, in relation to itself and to the surrounding space, in order to build a unique and individual technique and vocabulary (2013: 20–22). For Sgorbati, the goal of these techniques is to enable the emergence of a personal vocabulary for each dancer, one that, because of its emergent nature, moves beyond the dancer's existing technical vocabulary and training. She sees the solo practice as 'a microcosm of building on organic structuring principles within an ensemble' (20). Sgorbati has identified four emergent structures, or patterns,

that tend to occur during the solo practice as dancers develop a movement vocabulary: theme and variation, accumulation, initial conditions, and excavation (23).[5] These
terms apply to compositional principles that are familiar within dance and occur within
the solo practice as tactics for developing and building complex movement vocabularies
and phrase work on the solo body.

While Sgorbati explicitly connects these aspects of the solo improvising body to theories of complex systems and emergence, other dancers working intensively with structured improvisational forms also train the solo body in ways that we see as promoting
emergence. For example, in her ReWire: Dancing States practice, Nina Martin has developed scores that force rapid, spontaneous movement generation by diverting the
dancer's efforts to control, edit, or design the movement. In fact, she notes, 'one element
of improvisational performance that can frustrate efforts toward coherent composition is "personal vocabulary," or focusing on the body's movement vocabulary within
its kinesphere.... It is difficult, though not impossible to simultaneously work on the
microlevel of vocabulary while maintaining awareness at the macro level of the group's
compositional goals' (2007: 12). The goal is training dancers to think on their feet during
an improvisation. As a result, Martin's training for the solo body facilitates emergence
at the level of consciousness rather than individual vocabulary. Likewise, Martin and
Sgorbati differ in terms of the vocabulary they use to describe their ensemble practices,
but ultimately they engage in similar strategies.

Sgorbati refers to her ensemble practice as a 'complex system in which the dancers'
personal movement vocabularies are embedded within compositional patterns or
structures, and emergent structures are embedded within larger organizational patterns' (2007: 33). She identifies four key aspects of the practice: assessment/reflection,
compositional exercises for entering an ensemble practice, compositional tools, emergent structures, and communication (33–38). However, as hinted in the quote above,
smaller, more localized 'emergent structures' often surface within the group; these
structures create associations and effects. For example, 'tableaus,' 'pathways,' and 'waves/
eddies' describe particular ways of relating bodies in space that also might evoke particular associations with nature or social relations (37). At times these structures remain
localized, while at others they develop into larger organizational patterns, or forms (33).
Thus, Sgorbati envisions the ensemble as a self-organizing system in which the structural principles, the dancers' choices, and their bodies provide layered constraints that
allow larger structural forms or organizational patterns to emerge.

By developing the dancers' awareness on multiple levels (awareness of one's body, its
actions, and possible actions; awareness of the immediate environment; and awareness
of the larger space), as well as skills with, collaboration, attention to development, and
pattern recognition, Sgorbati's improvisational practice prepares dancers to build towards, recognize, and embrace moments of criticality, enabling emergent structures to
manifest within the dance.[6] Improvising dancers must also pay attention to patterns in
time and must develop good recall, because the development of an ensemble improvisation as a dynamic system and the possibility of self-organization within the dance
relies on the already complex system of human memory. In a given improvisational

performance, memory facilitates emergence because dancers are able to track, repeat, and develop material and structures over the course of the dance.[7]

Within ensemble improvisation, individual behaviour informs the action of the social group, and because the individuals function as independent units, they inform the action of the group in unpredictable ways. However, these individuals are not singular identities working in isolation, a dynamic that challenges approaches to improvisation that focus primarily on notions of individual exploration and inspiration. Correspondingly, we argue that the behaviour of each individual emerges from that individual's 'parts', such as sensory perception, habitual and automated decision-making, and higher-level consciousness (subjective, reflective thought), to which we turn, shortly, through an examination of contact improvisation. Thus, ensemble dance improvisation demonstrates the ways complex systems or behaviours (involving novel, higher-level patterns, organization, or collective action) cannot merely be reduced to the functions of their individual parts, because the dancers (or parts) are themselves self-organizing and their behaviours emergent and thus unpredictable. Acknowledging this concept can provide students with a pragmatic entryway into improvisational practices because it alleviates the pressure on students to see innovation as an act of individual creation. While moments of patterning and group organization emerge out of collaborative interactions during contact improvisation jams, this dance form also offers key evidence of complexity and self-organizing principles at the level of the individual body and cognition.

EMERGENCE WITHIN THE INDIVIDUAL PERFORMER—PERSPECTIVES ON COGNITION, AWARENESS, AND CONTACT IMPROVISATION

Contemporary approaches to cognitive science such as complexity theory, emergence, and embodied cognition emphasize the importance of the brain's position as part of a larger system that includes the body and the environment (Batson 2014: 71–86). Shapiro contrasts this understanding with older approaches to cognitive science that modelled cognition as symbolic computation focused on the study of the mind as an isolated function of the brain. His preferred approach, modelling the brain-body-environment as conjoined dynamical systems, in effect describes the bodymind as an emergent phenomenon of those three entities (2010: 126).

Applying the concept of emergence to human cognition suggests that it arises as an apparently unified, yet complex whole from the many (simpler) aspects of the bodymind: perception, memory, cognition, kinaesthesia, and so on. Within the brain itself, function and cognition arise through cooperative action of series of components at many scales (ion channels to synapses to neurons to neuron clusters and to entire brain regions), with new complex behaviour emerging at each level (Kelso 1995 227–283). Paul V. Fusella's discussion of dynamical systems theory addresses emergence and its relationship to cognition: 'psychological capacities are viewed as emerging as more complex forms from prior simpler states, moving from chaotic to more stable trajectories in a theoretical state-space that culminate in the manifestation of a specific thought in real-time or a developmental phenomenon over ontogenesis' (2013: 1). This approach to cognitive studies recognizes the human brain and mind as complex compositions of a whole series of neurological systems (neurons, nuclei/brain regions, groups of regions, the hemispheres of the brain, and other subcomponents of perception and cognition) that, to greater or lesser degrees, work independently of one another. It is through their communication and connections that the 'mind' as a construct emerges. However, embodied cognition expands this notion to include the body and its sensory mechanisms as a part of this self-organizing consciousness (Shapiro 2010). Thus, in its widest definition, emergence, as applied to embodied cognition, seeks to account for both the emergence of consciousness (what we perceive as a whole, a consistent 'I') from semiindependent brain structures and the intersections between those structures and sensory data gathered throughout the body. This understanding supports the concept of a self-organizing consciousness informed by lived experience, a notion that posits that consciousness emerges out of neural processes that occur below our awareness level and across a range of neurological components and systems (see Singh 2003).[8]

The model of self-organizing consciousness, including the interplay between automatic (biological processes and reflexes, but also habitual movement developed through repetition) and nonautomatic processes, offers one way to explain the relationship between cognition and motor skills that occurs in a contact improvisation duet. Psychologists Pierre Perruchet and Annie Vinter summarize the prevailing concept of automatic processes in studies of cognition.[9] They note that these often unconscious processes do not interfere with or receive interference from 'attended' or conscious activities. They can 'be triggered without a supporting intention (strategies, expectancies, etc.) and once started, cannot be stopped intentionally'. Finally, processes that begin under conscious control become automatic with training and practice (Perruchet and Vinter 2002: 321). Automaticity can describe many of the nonintentional actions that take place in a contact duet; however, it fails to account for the fact that a dancer must *allow* for the body to respond automatically to the phenomenal sensory data being received during the dance and the fact that a dancer still possesses the ability to stop the automatic response, though doing so might disrupt the dance or create a potentially precarious situation.

In their critique of automaticity, Perruchet and Vinter offer examples from studies that refute or question aspects of the theory. One key challenge offered by Logan (1988) suggests that the 'withdrawal of attention that characterizes automatization is not a cause, but a consequence of a change in the nature of the operations performed by the learner. The change is described as a transition from performance based on a general algorithm to performance based on memory retrieval' (Perruchet and Vinter 2002: 322). However, the notion of a reliance on memory is an inadequate explanation for the process that occurs in contact improvisation. While dancers' training in the technique includes the practice of movement patterns, sequences, and tasks (e.g., handstands and rolls) that provide the body with the skills necessary to negotiate the flowing, weight-sharing encounter of a contact improvisation duet, when the body finds its way in the middle of a dance, it does more than simply fall back on what dancers call 'muscle memory'.

Both self-organizing consciousness and automaticity are still debated in cognitive psychology and neuroscience, and indeed, the phenomenological experience of contact improvisation appears both to align with them yet suggest the need for alternative models (or at least further investigation) informed by the concept of embodied cognition. Literature about cognition and learning often focuses on the conversion of deliberative processes into memorized or automatic ones. On the other hand, much of dance training, and certainly ensemble improvisation and contact improvisation, strives to heighten awareness in ways that bring attention to what might otherwise be automatic processes and to develop sophisticated cognitive processes to the point that they become almost automatic. Steve Paxton's teaching and writing about contact improvisation frequently references training or developing 'reflexes'. According to Buckwalter, Nina Martin discovered that her improvisational training exercises that are focused not on contact improvisation but on dancers' reflexes produced better contact improvisation skills than when students copied experienced practitioners of contact improvisation (2010: 96). Ultimately, these skills point to the necessity of shifting how dance practitioners and teachers conceptualize 'thinking' within dance and how they convey the relationship between 'thinking' and 'dancing' to students.

We suggest that contact improvisation demonstrates the emergence of self-organization at the level of the solo bodymind because of the ways it employs automaticity in conjunction with self-reflective observation. Each individual's movement must arise from a combination of that person's sensory and conscious interactions, while simultaneously being shaped by the constraints of maintaining a continuously moving point of contact with a partner. In mutually allowing the point of contact and momentum to inform the direction of movement and the forms of weight-sharing that arise, both dancers place themselves in a situation in which they must give up some conscious decision-making so as to allow the bodymind to negotiate the changing terrain. Simultaneously, they must maintain an active awareness of what is happening and where the dance *might* go. Dancers must both allow their bodies to make choices based on the physics of any given moment, especially gravity and momentum, and be prepared to make conscious, deliberate choices on only a moment's notice should the need or opportunity to do so arise.

In a video filmed at Earthdance (an artist-run workshop, residency, and retreat centre) in Plainfield, Massachusetts (January 2010), Blake Nellis and Aaron Brandes dance an extended duet of fluid, calm exchanges of lifts, balances, and sustained contact. Watching the video, we can track the point of contact and see the moments of initiation arise—sometimes out of momentum and sometimes out of the placement of weight—as the dancers seem to allow their bodies to determine how best to proceed. At other times, the dancers make visibly intentional or conscious choices. For example, Brandes kneels on the ground with both hands on the floor as Nellis leans over him. Nellis chooses to slide his hands down Brandes's back until his hips come to rest on Brandes's right shoulder.[10] The back is there, a surface offering itself as a potential point of contact and support. Out of this sliding action and the way it brings Nellis's hip into contact with Brandes's shoulder, the opportunity for a moment of shifting weight and support arises. At this point, he releases his hands and hangs for a moment, floating on the shoulder as Brandes shifts his body to verticality. Both men have tracked, or followed, the interaction between their two bodies. This moment emerged from a combination of the performer's conscious, intentional movements and the constraints provided by gravity and their prior body positions. Brandes was able to meet his partner's hips and take on a weight-bearing role, while Nellis easily accepted his new position, suspended atop Brandes's shoulder (see fig. 31.2).

As Brandes then shifts forward, Nellis's feet come to floor; however, the two do not separate. Instead, as Nellis begins to stand, he tracks his arms along the sides of Brandes's body, and Brandes anchors his hands behind Nellis's knees. As Nellis is rocked back onto his feet to stand, he allows this action to happen and simply finds his footing at the appropriate moment; he does not appear to have aimed to arrive there. Both dancers continue to follow the weight and momentum so that as Brandes kicks his legs into the air, sinking his weight into Nellis's thighs, Nellis catches his hips and walks backwards as he supports Brandes's slide down his body and their mutual descent to the floor (see fig. 31.3).

'Following', as distinct from purely intentional (and conscious) choice, might better be understood as a process that combines conscious self-reflection, or observation, with the body's 'automatic' actions as it draws on its 'knowledge' to respond to evolving physical situations. In contact improvisation, following entails conscious awareness and attention without necessarily indicating that the dancer is making a choice to shape or

FIG. 31.2 A moment of emergence. Brandes's prior movement to a kneeling position and Nellis's (probably conscious) decision to slide his hands down his partner's back (a) are intentional inputs. Constraints are provided by physics and the shape of the dancers' bodies. When these elements combine to place Nellis's hip in contact with Brandes's shoulder in a direction opposite gravity (b), a point of criticality emerges—the opportunity for a lift (c). © Aaron Brandes 2010.

FIG. 31.3 Nellis's apparently unconscious foot placement is generated by his downward move-ment and a constraint—contact with the floor. The dancers remain aware of each other in order to maintain the hip-to-shoulder contact from the previous lift. When Brandes chooses to kick his legs up (a), these elements combine to allow the emergence of another lift (b) and a carry-through to a dramatic slide to the floor (c). As with figure 31.2, the performance is not planned but arises from a mix of intentional and subconscious movements, the partners' awareness of each other, and constraints of physical limitations. © Aaron Brandes 2010.

guide the action in a particular way. This distinction is important because cognition is neither a singular whole nor an unembodied process, and the relationship among con-sciousness, unconsciousness, and awareness is complex. We expand on the nature of this relationship within contact improvisation in the following discussion and example.

In 'Drafting Interior Techniques', Paxton describes the initial explorations that were part of his dance work *Magnesium* (1972), out of which contact improvisation devel-oped. Paxton looks back on those explorations from the perspective of having spent years physically researching the form and describes the practice of what came to be known as the Stand (also sometimes called the Small Dance). 'What gets exercised in there, inside the standing body, is the habit of observation; a noticeable movement of consciousness through the body.... It clearly seems to be one subsystem, conscious-ness, examining others. The other subsystems are not obviously connected to the wan-dering consciousness, except that the encounter happens in what one calls "my body." The consciousness-as-observer regards the other subsystems as separate from itself' (1993: 176–177). What Paxton describes here is (from a scientific perspective) actually a composite of different cognitive activities, but his description accurately captures the phenomenal experience of the 'hard problem of consciousness'.[11] While many studies of human cognition have focused on cognitive processes such as reading or performing mathematical calculations, Paxton's description points to the phenomenon of human cognition that allows us to reflect on our own behaviours and thought processes. As he points out, contact improvisation dancers train to bring self-conscious awareness (self-reflectivity) to bodily processes that would normally occur automatically or habitually and without conscious awareness. Dancers learn to track what might otherwise become 'unconscious' moments.[12]

Examining the practice of contact improvisation highlights issues of attention and the focusing of awareness. Cognitive studies and neuroscience research suggest that we can, particularly in perception and motor responses, process multiple things in parallel (Sigman and Dehaene 2008). However, these studies also suggest that attention is a specific neural mechanism that allows us to pick one focal point for our conscious awareness and process it more rapidly and with greater detail. Attention operates in all senses, from vision (Carrasco 2011) to proprioception and motor planning (Brown et al. 2011), and integrates across multiple senses (Talsma et al. 2010). This attention mechanism is fundamentally serial, even though lower-level cognitive processes are thought to be nonlinear (Pashler et al. 2001).[13]

The relationship between awareness and the 'whole' of cognition speaks to how awareness appears to function within contact improvisation. Concepts of embodied cognition that posit the body's sensory and motor mechanisms as an essential aspect of cognition are better able to account for the complexity of cognition within contact improvisation. In contact improvisation, we seek to allow ourselves to find the next initiation or response within the distribution of weight, the direction and flow of the momentum, and the structural possibilities in each moment. We dancers must *listen* to the movement and to both our own and our partners' bodies (Brandstetter 2013; Albright 2013). Thus, while *attention* may reside in only one place (point of contact or activity) at a time, we must maintain a more global awareness of the bodies, as well as the ability to quickly shift our attention from one focal point to another as the need arises. Often when dancing, we discover the movement as we go, and in its most thrilling incarnations, we *observe* the body finding its way through the movement from one configuration to the next.

As Paxton's description of the Stand suggests, the very act of observing one's own responses implies multiple selves, or the self as a construct that arises out of the interaction of multiple singularities (parts)—an actor and an observer work in concert, making the whole action of self-reflexivity itself fundamentally emergent. This form of self-observation and the form of emergence it suggests points to how the solo body of contact improvisation might prove to be a valuable site of study for cognitive science. As seen in the above description of Brandes and Nellis, dancing in a contact improvisation duet requires ongoing multiple levels of awareness and decision-making, while at the same time requiring openness and a willingness to respond to possibilities that may emerge from the interactions between two bodies in a duet. In any one moment, one of the dancers may initiate an action with a clear intent, but the partner's response to that action is unknown. Furthermore, these initiations and responses occur in an ongoing flux or exchange, so that intentional actions will sometimes find an unexpected resolution.

As the practice of contact improvisation demonstrates via the apparent multiple selves at play within the form, memory is vital, and the bodymind clearly falls back on patterns it knows; however, in doing so it must still assess the phenomenal sensory data to determine what is possible. It must modify and integrate that information with the memory of related movements in order to effectively act, and it completes this decision-making process just a hair faster than the dancer's conscious awareness of the choice can occur (Kaiser and Willingham 2002: 342–343). Thus within a contact improvisation duet, we suggest, much of the dancers' movement can be viewed as emergent as the result of self-organizing aspects of cognition, because consciousness operates on multiple levels simultaneously. The body's cognition of movement (at a neural and proprioceptive level), one's self-reflective awareness of what is happening, and one's focal attention (awareness) work in coordination to navigate the terrain of the contact improvisation dance. This coordinated effort is what we offer as evidence of self-organizing consciousness within contact improvisation. And it is this form of self-organization that we identify as emergent within the practice. With this understanding of both levels of emergence in hand, we invite readers to examine this quote about contact improvisation by Torrence et al.: 'therefore, the unit of this dance is not the individual but the system formed by the two dancers. However, this system is not the sum of the motor actions of both dancers, as the relationship between the dancers creates a new system, which generates new movements. These principles would explain the feeling of dancers during improvisation, when they are surprised by the new movement patterns that suddenly appear, or the impression that each partner produces a new and different style of dancing' (2010: 2). Having mapped the forms of emergence found in Emergent Improvisation and contact improvisation and their relationship to cognitive science and its investigations into emergence and self-organizing consciousness, we turn now to how this knowledge might best inform shifts in dance pedagogy.

Pedagogical Argument and Conclusion

We argue that the language of emergence and its use as a conceptual framework at both the ensemble and intrapersonal levels offer a useful and much-needed model for the study of improvisation within concert dance training. At the ensemble level, we believe it is particularly useful for dancers to come to understand the concepts of points of criticality and constraints (understood by Sgorbati as 'embeddedness') that shape the group performance. The resulting increased awareness of the process will promote their engagement with critical thinking and problem solving, encouraging them to actively seek out, manipulate, and employ an understanding of structure and relationship as a means to creating better and more fluid performances, whether improvised or traditionally choreographed. Improvisational groups that understand criticality can *actively* and consciously self-organize in order to maintain the level of movement and the quantity of interactions at a point of criticality. This would keep the ensemble in a state conducive to the spontaneous emergence of visually engaging group behaviour.

On the individual level, incorporating a greater awareness of self and how one's own performance arises from many contributing factors will allow dancers (student or otherwise) to understand their own improvisational movements (and contributions to the ensemble) with more depth. In particular, the meta-awareness of a dancer's self-observation during the performance and the incorporation of self-observation as a fundamental function of the bodymind present an exciting pedagogical opportunity to help students understand their dancing as thinking. Understanding dancing as thinking opens up the possibility for students to see their physical practice as a conceptual form and a mode of decision-making. It breaks down distinctions between body and mind that encourage students to discount the value of thinking within dancing or to view their physical practice as divorced from critical thought. In turn, it facilitates their development as dancers by helping them understand how to think in/through action in performance contexts at both technical and compositional levels. Dance becomes a problem to be solved through the bodymind (Batson 2014, 36–37; Fraleigh 1987; Sheets-Johnstone 2011). By incorporating concepts of emergence arising within cognitive science in our dance pedagogy, we better prepare students for understanding dance as an active participant in cultural discourse.

As we have framed it, emergence also offers a way of introducing students to improvisation from a perspective that rejects the notion of the individual as a lone creative spirit, relying on a stroke of inspiration. Instead, it invites dancers to recognize how creativity involves listening to what is already happening and then actively following connections and making associations. In his essay 'Improvisation in Teaching', Sawyer argues for placing improvisation at the core of music curricula (2008). We would extend that argument to dance curricula in the U.S. university and conservatory setting. While improvisation has always been at the centre of dance training in some teaching lineages (for example, Wigman-Holm-Nikolais) and has played a vital role in the work of some contemporary choreographers (for example, Trisha Brown, Bill T. Jones, and William Forsythe), it is by and large not situated at the core of dance education in the United States and has not been as highly valued in the professional world as technical virtuosity. Paraphrasing Sawyer's words for dance echoes a discussion we have had many times: dancers trained extensively in improvisation would be better able to think physically, to understand movement and interpret choreography, and to pay attention to other dancers and respond with understanding in ensemble performance (Sawyer 2008: 1).

Studying improvisation, with its emergent nature and creation of forms and movement across and between bodies, also trains dancers in the skills necessary to participate in improvisation as a part of a choreographic process, whether in their own work or the work of others. In his research with Wayne McGregor's company Random Dance, David Kirsh notes both the importance of 'distributed creativity' to McGregor's choreographic process and the value of studying choreography for understanding distributed cognition and creativity (2011: n.p.; Kirsh et al. 2009: 188). Kirsh defines distributed creativity as 'the mechanisms by which team members harness resources to interactively invent new concepts and elements, and then structure things into a coherent product' (2011: n.p.). As is the case with many other contemporary choreographers, McGregor's decisions about movement vocabulary and choreographic structure are made through interactions between him and the dancers in rehearsal.

Sawyer points to the study in cognitive science of 'the mental structures and processes underlying expert performance' and the type of knowledge underlying it. He lists four key features: deep conceptual understanding, integrated knowledge, adaptive expertise, and collaborative skills. In other words, experts connect new knowledge to existing knowledge and conceptual frameworks. They can adapt and combine concepts and problem-solving approaches when they encounter new situations, and they are able to collaborate with others in loosely defined working situations (2008: 2). By citing the work of Robert Florida on the 'creative class', he also implies that these will be the kinds of important skills required in a knowledge economy of the present and future. Sawyer's four features of expert performance and Florida's concept of the creative class support our emphasis on the educational value of improvisation.

The constraints employed in improvisation games/exercises/structures introduce participants to the kind of thinking Sawyer details in his analysis of expert performance. In order to produce a dance from within the constraints of a game-like improvisation score, students must collaborate with each other as they work to adapt and combine prior knowledge and problem-solving approaches. As the work of Sgorbati, Martin, Bull, and others demonstrates, structures and limitations serve other roles as well, because they purposely split the focus/awareness of the dancers, asking them to pay attention not only to their own desires, or the movements they are performing, but also to how those things fit the structure, relate to the rules, and intersect with the choices of the ensemble. Gradually, they learn to treat rules or structures as puzzles to be solved. By investing in the puzzle, while simultaneously tracking their own performances, dancers in an ensemble are forced to develop the ability to allow for consciousness of the dance and of themselves, thus encouraging the development of a split consciousness or layered awareness. As their attention becomes multifocused and attentive to a wide array of phenomenal data, cognition must happen on multiple levels simultaneously, to the point that the choices they enact are required to be emergent, rather than preplanned, in order to work successfully within the given improvisation.

Thus the conceptual frameworks used to teach improvisation can play a pivotal role in helping students to move from imagining novelty and creativity in improvisation as an expression of something already inside them and towards understanding novelty and creativity as something that emerges out of the ever-evolving relations between themselves, the structure, the space, and the other dancers. The goal in teaching improvisation, in many ways, is to eliminate student's innate, unthinking resistance to emergence, which occurs often as a result of the desire to maintain habits and hold onto what is known. Breaking habits is critical, because critical thinking, collaboration, problem solving, and creativity require that we let go of what we know in order to embrace possibilities that are unknown. In other words, by learning to break habits, we, and our students, learn how to be better able to embrace difference and live in a world that requires interaction much more than it does isolation.

NOTES

1. Emergence is certainly not the only potentially fruitful way to draw together these concerns.
2. For general challenges to studying cognition in dance, see Batson with Wilson (2014: 55–58). For one example of how moving contributes to the choreographic process differently from watching, see Kirsh (2012).
3. In nonlinear systems, the effect of an event is out of proportion with the event itself. In other words, the effect of a given event will be to some degree unpredictable, whereas within a linear system, the effect of a given event will be in proportion to the event and so will be predictable when the operation of the subcomponents of the system is known.
4. In relationship to practising dance improvisation, 'our' refers to authors Dunagan and Fenton.
5. Sgorbati defines initial conditions as the development of new movement vocabulary from an aspect of the initial improvised phrase. Excavation, according to Sgorbati, is similar to initial conditions because it too begins with an initial movement phrase; however, in excavation new material is developed by looking to the 'subtext' or associations generated by aspects of the phrase and generating new movement in relation to those.
6. Again, these skills are found in many ensemble improvisational practices.
7. For examples of improvised dances requiring virtuoso levels of memory from performers, see Trisha Brown's *Accumulation Plus Talking with Watermotor* and Bull's *Making and Doing*.
8. Singh briefly introduces Marvin Minsky's theory of the mind as emergent, arising out of the interaction of smaller components and systems as follows: 'Minsky introduces the term *agent* to refer to the simplest individuals that populate such societies of mind. Each agent is on the scale of a typical component of a computer program, like a simple subroutine or data structure, and as with the components of computer programs, agents can be connected and composed into larger systems called *societies of agents*. Together, societies of agents can perform functions more complex than any single agent could, and ultimately produce the many abilities we attribute to minds' (2003: 522).
9. Their purpose in summarizing this concept is to refute it, and we find their refutation unconvincing. However, their summary is useful.
10. This 'choice' may have been unconscious for Nellis, but it was not required by the gravity, the momentum, or the distribution of weight between the two dancers.
11. The question of scientific investigation into self-observation is widely agreed to be the most difficult problem in neuroscience, according to Chalmers (1995: 200–219).
12. This somewhat meditative bent in contact improvisation points to the interest among many contact improvisation practitioners throughout its history (including Paxton) in yoga, Buddhist meditation traditions, and Asian martial arts, which are other practices in which participants seek to develop similar types of awareness.
13. You can listen closely to what someone is saying on your cell phone, or you can pay close attention to the road while you're driving, but you can't do both.

REFERENCES

Albright, Ann Cooper. (2003) Dwelling in Possibility. In Albright, Ann Cooper, and Gere, D. (eds.), *Taken by Surprise: A Dance Improvisation Reader*. Middletown, CT: Wesleyan University Press, 257–266.

Albright, Ann Cooper. (2013) Feeling In and Out: Contact Improvisation and the Politics of Empathy. In Brandstetter, G., Egert, G., and Zubarik, S. (eds.), *Touching and Being Touched: Kinesthesia and Empathy in Dance and Movement*. Berlin: de Gruyter, 263–273.

Batson, G., with Wilson, M. (2014) *Body and Mind in Motion: Dance and Neuroscience in Conversation*. Chicago: University of Chicago Press.

Beggs, J. M., and Plenz, D. (2003) Neuronal Avalanches in Neocortical Circuits. *Journal of Neuroscience* 25(35): 11167–11177.

Brandstetter, G. (2013) 'Listening': Kinesthetic Awareness in Contemporary Dance. In Brandstetter, G., Egert, G., and Zubarik, S. (eds.), *Touching and Being Touched: Kinesthesia and Empathy in Dance and Movement*. Berlin: de Gruyter, 163–179.

Brown, H., Friston, K., and Bestmann, S. (2011) Active Inference, Attention, and Motor Preparation. *Frontiers in Psychology* 2: 218.

Buckwalter, M. (2010) *Composing While Dancing: An Improviser's Companion*. Madison: University of Wisconsin Press.

Carrasco, M. (2011) Visual Attention: The Past 25 Years. *Vision Research* 51: 1484–1525.

Chalmers, D. J. (1995) Facing Up to the Problem of Consciousness. *Journal of Consciousness Studies* 2(3): 200–219.

Foster, S. L. (2002) *Dances That Describe Themselves: The Improvised Choreography of Richard Bull*. Middletown, CT: Wesleyan University Press.

Fraleigh, S. H. (1987) *Dance and the Lived Body: A Descriptive Aesthetics*. Pittsburgh: University of Pittsburgh Press.

Fusella, P. V. (2013) Dynamic Systems Theory in Cognitive Science: Major Elements, Applications, and Debates Surrounding a Revolutionary Metatheory. *Dynamical Psychology* (January 15): 1.

Gibbs, Jr., R. W. (2003) Embodied Meanings in Performing, Interpreting, and Talking about Dance Improvisation. In Albright, Ann Cooper, and Gere, D. (eds.), *Taken by Surprise: A Dance Improvisation Reader*. Middletown, CT: Wesleyan University Press, 185–196.

Goldman, D. (2010) *I Want to Be Ready: Improvised Dance as a Practice of Freedom*. Ann Arbor: University of Michigan Press.

Johnson, B. R. (2010) Eliminating the Mystery from the Concept of Emergence. *Biological Philosophy* 25: 843.

Keisler, A. S., and Willingham, D. T. (2002) Unconscious Abstraction in Motor Learning. Response to 'Self-Organizing Consciousness'. *Behavioral and Brain Sciences* 25: 342–343.

Kelso, J. A. S. (1995) *Dynamic Patterns: The Self-Organization of Brain and Behavior*. Cambridge, MA: MIT Press.

Kim, J. (1999) Making Sense of Emergence. *Philosophical Studies: An International Journal for Philosophy in the Analytic Tradition* 95(1/2): 3–36.

Kirsh, D. (2011) Creative Cognition in Choreography. Paper presented at Second International Conference on Computational Creativity. April 27-29, 2011 at La Universidad Autónoma Metropolitana in Mexico. http://adrenaline.ucsd.edu/kirsh/Articles/CreativeChoreography/Creative_Cognition_in_Choreography_Final.pdf. Accessed 20 April 2015.

Kirsh, D. (2012). Running It through the Body. *Proceedings of the Annual Cognitive Science Society*, 34. Lawrence Erlbaum, 539–598. http://adrenaline.ucsd.edu/kirsh/Articles/Running/Running.pdf. Accessed 15 March 2015.

Kirsh, D., Muntanyola, D., Jao, R. J., Lew, A., and Sugihara, M. (2009). Paper presented at Choreographic Methods for Creating Novel, High Quality Dance. Proceedings of the 5th International Workshop on Design and Semantics of Form and Movement. October 26-27,

2009, National Taiwan University of Science and Technology, Taipei, Taiwan. http://adren-aline.ucsd.edu/Kirsh/Articles/Interaction/kirshetal2009.pdf. Accessed 15 March 2015.

Logan, G. D. (1988) Towards an Instance Theory of Automatization. *Psychological Review* 76: 165–178.

Martin, N. (2007) Ensemble Thinking: Compositional Strategies for Group Improvisation. *Contact Quarterly* 32(2): 10–15.

Ouelette, J. (2014). A Fundamental Theory to Model the Mind. *Quanta* (3 April). http://www.simonsfoundation.org/quanta/20140403-a-fundamental-theory-to-model-the-mind/. Accessed 15 March 2015.

Pashler, H., Johnston, J. C., and Ruthruff, E. (2001) Attention and Performance. *Annual Review of Psychology* 52: 629–651.

Paxton, S. (1993) Drafting Interior Techniques. In Albright, Ann Cooper, and Gere, D. (eds.), *Taken by Surprise: A Dance Improvisation Reader*. Middletown, CT: Wesleyan University Press, 175–183.

Perruchet, P., and Vinter, A. (2002) The Self-Organizing Consciousness. *Behavioral and Brain Sciences* 25: 297–388.

Sawyer, R. K. (1999) The Emergence of Creativity. *Philosophical Psychology* 12(4): 447–469.

Sawyer, R. K. (2007) *Group Genius: The Creative Power of Collaboration*. New York: Basic Books.

Sawyer, R. K. (2008) Improvisation in Teaching. *Critical Studies in Improvisation/Études critiques en improvisation* 3(2): 1–4.

Sgorbati, S., with Climer, E., and Haas, M. L. (2013) Emergent Improvisation: Where Dance Meets Science on the Nature of Spontaneous Composition. *Contact Quarterly* Chapbook 4 38(2): 1–58.

Shapiro, L. (2010) *Embodied Cognition*. New York: Routledge.

Sheets-Johnstone, M. (2011) *The Primacy of Movement*. Expanded 2nd ed. Philadelphia: John Benjamins.

Sigman, M., and Dehaene, S. (2008) Brain Mechanisms of Serial and Parallel Processing during Dual-Task Performance. *Journal of Neuroscience* 28(30): 7585–7598.

Silberstein, M., and McGeever, J. (1999) The Search for Ontological Emergence. *Philosophical Quarterly* 49(195): 1.

Singh, P. (2003) Examining the Society of Mind. *Computing and Informatics* 22: 521–543.

Talsma, D., Senkowski, D., Soto-Faraco S., and Woldoff, M. G. (2010) The Multifaceted Interplay between Attention and Multisensory Integration. *Trends in Cognitive Sciences* 14: 400–410.

Torrents, C., Castañer, M., Dinušová, M., and Anguera, M. T. (2010) Discovering New Ways of Moving: Observational Analysis of Motor Creativity While Dancing Contact Improvisation and the Influence of the Partner. *Journal of Creative Behavior*,

CHAPTER 32

A COGNITIVE THEORY OF JOINT IMPROVISATION

The Case of Tango Argentino

MICHAEL KIMMEL

MODELS of improvisational cognition have been pioneered by musicologists (Sudnow 1978; Pressing 1988; 1998; Sloboda 1988; Nettl and Russell 1998; Johnson-Laird 2002; Kenny and Gellrich 2002; Iyer 2002; Berkowitz 2010; Biasutti and Frezza 2009; Norgaard 2011). Yet the mechanisms are not particularly well understood beyond solos, despite some overtures on studying jazz duets, string quartets, flamenco ensembles, and improv theater groups (Schögler 1999; Glowinski et al. 2013; Badino et al. 2014; Sawyer 2001; Mendonça and Wallace 2004; 2007; Seddon 2005; Seddon and Biasutti 2009; Maduell and Wing 2007; Magerko et al. 2009; Walton et al. 2015), as well as recent studies on creativity in contact improvisation (Torrents et al. 2010; Torrents, Ric, and Hristovski 2015; Kimmel, Hristova, and Kussmaul 2018).

My aim is to elucidate from a skill-related standpoint what enables and constrains *embodied* improvised interaction, while highlighting the various cognitive resources adept pair dancers must integrate. My case study of tango argentino[1] will partly generalize to other body interaction skills and highlight aspects generally relevant to collaborative creativity (Sawyer 2003, 2012) and interaction research (Fogel 2006; Oullier and Kelso 2009; Passos, Davids, and Chow 2016). Bear in mind, however, that tango is an unusually structured kind of improvisation with a strict general 'grammar', an enormous but finite 'lexicon' of forms, and a clear role distribution, thus differing from, for example, contact improvisation.

1 Introducing the Tango

The hallmark of enjoyable tango is joint improvisation while transducing the music into bodily expression and harmoniously blending with the overall flow on the dance floor. Tango is a system allowing for perfectly connected joint action on the spur of the moment. A typical dance fluidly connects two to five modular interaction elements per second, notably steps, circling, invasions, and leg crosses/wraps/swings. This may go on for three to twenty minutes and generate hundreds of nonscripted combinations. Improvisation lies in the couple's ability to combine elements in variable ways and occasionally discover new systemically permissible elements. Tango improvisation unfolds within formal constraints; it exhibits tremendous rapport, precision, and virtuosity in complementary roles: A leader 'incorporates' offerings of the music and the dance floor in real time, while a follower responds with almost imperceptible delay. The leader signals 'invitations' to the follower, who responds by active locomotion or by providing postural neutrality and grounding when moved passively, for example in pivots, with some leeway for precise step timing or flourishes, but without impairing the lead. The follower may also request slowing down and time for an ornament. By and large, in traditional tango, followers shape the 'how' but not the 'what'. Their creative contributions dominantly concern accentuation and ornamentation. Followers are nonetheless integrally important by ensuring dynamic stability, relaxation, and precision that enables joint improvisation to begin with and, on occasion, by subtle suggestions.

1.1 Defining improvisation

Improvisation necessitates 'combined behavioural and cognitive activity that requires serial creativity under tight time constraint in order to meet performance objectives' (Mendonça and Fiedrich 2006: 350). Improvisers make use of readily available, 'good enough' rather than optimal resources in closest proximity between planning and execution.

On a milonga venue—the prototypical tango setting—the dance trajectory is created step by step (or nearly). Dancers respond to momentarily arising perceptual *affordances* (Gibson 1979) provided by the partner and the dance-floor situation. Leader movements create invitational affordances for a follower, who creates a matching co-action; the resulting configuration suggests affordances for the leader again to choose from for the subsequent action. This real-time choice always matches up the momentarily perceived affordances with possible improvisational ideas. Creative choices are constrained *and* driven by an interactive situation, such that unforeseen external pressures may also solicit inventive solutions.

1.2 Modalities

Improvisation is one *production principle* among several for generating serial tango structure. Others include full choreographies, for example, for stage shows, and serially executing 'ready-mades' (scripts) that precompose multiple action units ahead of time. Improvisation isn't an either-or; it can be partial: dancers employ sketch plans (Norgaard 2011), scripts with sensitivity to rerouting options (Kimmel 2012), or general event-templates (Pressing 1984) like 'start with a quick passage, then vary, repeat an earlier theme, but make it more difficult, and end with an aesthetic pose'.

Creative improvisation is an end in itself in tango. Most creativity is *combinatoric* and *serial*: it creates variable combinations of familiar interaction elements. Dancers also extemporize *micro-creatively* by adding ornamentations, new accentuations, or the like. Although dancers progressively enlarge their personal repertoire, *essential* creativity concerning never-tried-before elements is less frequent, especially spontaneously 'invented' forms. (We bracket out *genre* creativity here, for example, hybridizing tango with salsa.)

1.3 Constraints

Dancers learn early on to understand how constraints common to all movement skills, notably safety, spatial continuity, and dynamic stability, play out in tango. Many discipline-specific constraints add well-formed-ness to these fundamentals, notably uprightness, geometry, and strict separation of linear and circular movements. Tango is a rigorously structured improvisation system, with many movements being off limits, for example, side-bending. Quick and confident dancing works only when partners adhere to a precise intrabody organization, posture, and balance, while cultivating a sensorial attitude. Both individual 'presettings' and interpersonal enabling patterns are conducive to ceaseless information flow and responsiveness (see section 2 and subsection 3.5). Dancers who strategically reduce degrees of freedom (Bernstein 1996) render signal transmission fast, precise, and unambiguous, while also ensuring action-readiness and enabling joint feats quite impossible alone.

A couple gains freedom of joint creative expression precisely through rigour in these fundamental respects, which ensure dynamic stability, safety, and communication. Respecting these constraints channels movement creativity into something tango-like and a fortiori enables the jointness without which creativity would fail at the execution stage. Overall, a leader's creative options are delimited by bodily, interactive, spatial, and musical constraints, as well as, frequently, by self-imposed constraints issuing from thematic interests. Skilful solutions must satisfy this multiplicity in context-intelligent ways. To beginners, the simultaneity of sensorimotor and interactional constraints poses a major challenge (Baillieul and Özcimder 2012: primary v. secondary control structures), as does fitting creativity with the music and available space. The multiconstraint field frequently requires prioritizing, too. The ethos of togetherness, fluid interaction, and musicality will almost always take precedence; it may demand restraint in creative experimentation to respect these (and tango etiquette, with loss of social capital imposed as penalty for dance-floor collisions).

1.4 Improvisational Systems

Its precise structuration lends tango its unmistakable 'style' and geometry (Kimmel and Preuschl 2015). Like all improvisational systems, tango incorporates tacit rules, springing from deeply internalized repertoires (Csikszentmihályi and Rich 1997). We might even think of tango as a language system, despite the incomplete analogy: the serial deployment of joint moves is akin to word combinations, constrained by well-formed-ness principles akin to grammar. Generativity, after Chomsky (1957), is rooted in a structured and tagged lexicon and compositional rules. Tango displays a motion lexicon and syntax, from which a set of allowable transitions results, hence a movement *system*. In principle, compositional dance rules are learnable, like a linguistic grammar (Opacic, Stevens, and Tillmann 2009). Improvisers familiar with system elements and combinations are adept at 'finding paths through the knowledge base' (Berkowitz 2010: 80).

This reflects dance research positing a hierarchy of within-unit forms, transitions, and chained structures (Opacic, Stevens, and Tillmann 2009; Orgs, Hagura, and Haggard 2013). Possible combinations of serialized dance 'movemes' have been modelled for ballet poses on the warm-up barre (LaViers, Chen, et al. 2011; LaViers, Egerstedt, et al. 2011) and for swing dance (Gentry and Feron 2004). Mathematically, generativity can be expressed as a *finite state machine*, where each state can link to several others further down the line and is visited repeated times from varying entry paths. The degree of interconnectivity in the machine's make-up determines how much committing to a move restricts subsequent choices.

To chart tango in this way we can represent a couple's combinatory options on a matrix (Castro 2004) with linkages, decision points, and bifurcations. Figure 32.1 illustrates a submatrix of the tango system, the so-called parallel system. It sets in from the larger oval, a neutral 'both-partners-opposite-same-weight' stance, and shows bifurcations and reentry links with moves as small as a half step or a simple weight shift. If 'crossed system' options (red arrows) and rotations were added, the matrix would include hundreds of further states. This matrix is immediately suggestive of how tango's systemic constraints, together with the biomechanics of human gait, spawn a set of optimal decision-making and rerouting points, each with multiple affordances. A finite number of trajectories and forms results, which gives tango its geometrical appearance. Meanwhile, what we conveniently summarize as matrix here does not imply that improvisations exclusively result from linkages and nodes that a leader internalizes.

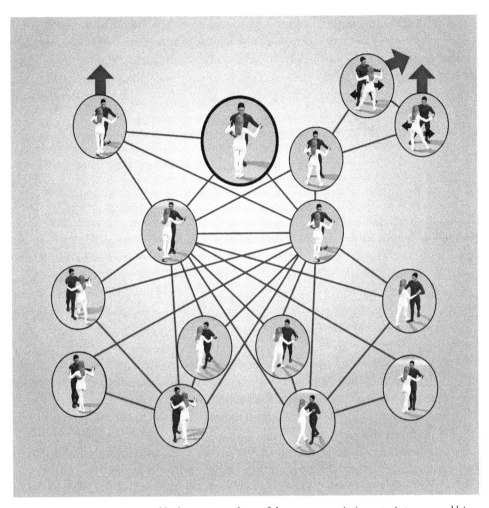

FIG. 32.1 Decision points and linkages as a subset of the tango matrix (constraint: opposed hips, parallel weights).

This Chomskyan model of generativity suggests excessive fixity, though. Dynamic systems research provides a more state-of-the-art metaphor of an *attractor landscape* which the agents traverse (Tschacher, Schiepek, and Brunner 2002; Passos, Davids, and Chow 2016; Chow et al. 2011). Attractors are thought of as energy-optimal system states, best visualized as troughs within a terrain that a ball easily rolls into. We may thus think of dancers' improvisatory efforts as exploring this landscape of available interaction patterns. Serial improvisation navigates between attractors of varying prominence. Over time, new attractors appear, and weak attractors increase their pull, as improvisers widen their options. Importantly, skill and repertoire determine the current attractor landscape. As will become apparent, dancers may slightly tune and develop this landscape through their interactive dynamics. The precise landscape further depends on what the leader currently prioritizes: experimentation, 'leaving the beaten path', precision, organic movement, rapport, or virtuosic music interpretation. Thus, the landscape actually comes into being because couples skilfully create facilitative conditions—ideally as a network of cross-catalysing (*self-organizing*) elements (see section 5.4). This suggests that the tango matrix is relatively permanent but not set in stone or impervious to microskills.

2 A Mixed Bag of Skills

Tango is a 'multiskill' (Kimmel 2016)—dancers must train many different abilities, and modelling improvisation requires a profound prior analysis of these skills. We may contrast improvisation-specific with more generic capabilities one would have to master even in choreographed modes. The generic skills enable and inform extemporizing, while not explaining improvisational abilities as such. They primarily supply basic sensorimotor and interaction capabilities but also contribute a *metastable* body organization, poised for improvisation and surprise:

- A set of body habits should kick in when entering the dance floor (see section 3.5): postural uprightness, bone alignment, core-stability, and efficient distribution of tone for fatigue minimization, balancing in a neutral action-ready state ('being in axis'), and configuring arms and torso muscles to connect the embrace to the body-centre and legs.
- Motor skills: precise walking demands a measured use of controlled lability to generate step energy. Pivoting requires minimizing resistance by aligning the axis and lengthening the body, keeping hips level, slightly bending the knees to ensure grounding ('rotating into the ground'), and closing the heels in time.
- Communication skills: dancers must competently issue signals and read them. For example, the follower must distinguish the onset threshold for initiating her step from the degree of the leader's weight shift. General intersubjectivity skills for feeling and being felt add to this: knowing how to calibrate the embrace, how and where to touch to gather information, how to maximize feedback for the partner's benefit, and how to maintain advantageous dyadic configurations.
- Perceptual skills: dancers cultivate an attentional focus on 'what counts' by tracking functionally relevant body-parts or relations. Skills for 'smart perception' (Runeson 1977) allow for feeling through the embrace where the partner's weight is and in which step-phase the partner is. Whole-body information is perceived integrally. Attentional 'marking' of functional areas is equally crucial. For example, by monitoring hip points one knows a dancer's current movement direction; monitoring the length of their torso diagonal (i.e., hip-chest dissociation) reveals how loaded with energy the 'body-coil' is.

- Imagery skills: dancers imaginatively enhance percepts (e.g., by reading the centre of gravity or body-axis into the perceived silhouette), use axis-imagery to track trajectories and configurations, or summarize good coordinative habits in simple didactic images.
- Music skills: transposing music into motor commands requires dexterity and timing skills, while knowing possible patterns by which to implement different beats or melodies is a cognitive skill in its own right.

Items from this rich toolbox need to be integrated into contextually appropriate synergies. Typical tasks require proper alignment, a particular interbody geometry and sensory alertness before starting, action techniques, and lead signals, together with the right musical timing. Meanwhile, some operative tango 'tricks' crosscut many skill types, notably a good tango axis. Axial alignment kills several birds with one stone (*simplexity*; Berthoz 2012) by being conducive to dynamic stability qua uprightness, to motility by providing neutrality, to aesthetics by elegance, to motor efficiency because elongated core muscles minimize fatigue of weaker peripheral muscles, and to reliable signal transmission by recruiting muscle chains that pass on impulses.

3 TOGETHERNESS

Improvising as a couple crucially depends on interaction skills, since any idea not executed *jointly* fails immediately. The cognitive demands of joint improvisation considerably exceed those of solos (Monson 2006). While solo improvisation is a 'closed skill' that relies only on self-produced stimuli (Pressing 1988: 134), interactivity-based improvisation is partly driven by external information (partner, dance floor, music) and, what is more, depends on joint physical and informational structures.

3.1 Creating 'the Beast of Four Legs'

Basic togetherness is the precondition of even moderate improvisation, while fully effortless togetherness unleashes creativity, safe exploration, and serendipity. Thus, I will now look at facilitative interpersonal factors that underlie *participatory sense-making* (Fuchs and DeJaegher 2009; van Alphen 2014) and *collaborative emergence* (Sawyer 2012) between the dancers, and which are as demanding as creativity itself.

The tango's basic mediating structure is the embrace. It creates a resonance loop between partners and allows coordinating the invitation-response dynamic in real time. Mutual resonance exemplifies *coregulation* (Fogel 1993), meaning that dancers are bidirectionally linked in reciprocal causation, mishaps and all! With good rapport skills, dancers move 'as one'. A state of dynamic mutual entanglement results (Froese and

Fuchs 2012), the proverbial 'four-legged tango beast'. Followers exhibit a phasing delay of merely twenty to thirty milliseconds between their body centres and their leaders' body centres (Kimmel and Preuschl 2015). This synchronized energy flow permits staying on the beat together—the sine qua non of fluent, fast dancing.

How do precisely coordinated, synchronized, and functionally complementary co-actions arise? Part of the explanatory burden is carried by consensual *interaction frames* (Fogel 1993), that is, the wish to tango together, to respect etiquette (Becker 2000) and the basic motion grammar. Any deeper explanation should, however, elucidate (1) higher-timescale physical structures that couples create, and (2) task-specific rules of microsteering, microcorrection, or microcompensation between partners that demonstrate how role-bound strategies result in coordinated interaction patterns.

3.2   Physicality and Sensorial Interpenetration

Dancers talk a lot about tango as a dialogue (Tateo 2014) where the leader issues convention-based 'requests' that the follower picks up and autonomously executes. While there is some truth to this metaphor, a merely cue-based (Maduell and Wing 2007; Seddon 2005) and symbolic *interactional semiotics* (Sawyer 2003) underspecifies tango: first, mechanic push-pull connections add to informational cues. Second, stable musculoskeletal chains between bodies allow leaders to feel and 'remote control' followers' legs incrementally without touching or seeing them. Through this sensorial interpenetration, leaders gain closed-loop control of the whole dance-unit. Agents literally experience 'expanding into the other body' (van Alphen 2014: 327; also see *extended bodies* in Clark 2008 and *mutual incorporation* in Froese and Fuchs 2012). Third, a collective weight system arises. As dancers 'meld' into each other's embrace, they share two kilos of weight, as force-plate measurements indicate. Systemically speaking, individual autonomies merge in a joint, lower-dimensional structure that makes the couple a single functional unit. Different kinds of joint physical structures underlie off-axis techniques (leaning or pulling), stabilizing rotations with circular energy in the embrace, and even satisfactory joint walking.

Interestingly, these push-pull, shared-structure, and sensorial-interpenetration effects imbue cue-based information exchange with some physical causation. A leader's shoulder opening or chest dissociation have immediate biomechanic consequences, provided these movements impinge on a follower body that is sufficiently organized in its degrees of freedom to channel the information. The lead's motion energy now prefigures the desired response. The need to *interpret* behavioural cues is diminished to the extent that followers do what feels organic and energy-efficient within the constraints of their postural and dynamic habits.

3.3   Feedback Awareness

Even though the leader's motor planning ostensibly unfurls in chunks (basic action units; see section 4.1), movements are seldom executed in 'blind-flight'. Feedback sensitivity matters. Only ceaselessly interpenetrating action and feedback streams between dancers allow minute coordination down to the finest increments. Real-time monitoring of follower coactions enables leaders to correct against deviations on the fly (see Braun, Ortega, and Wolper; 2011; Wolpert, Diedrichsen, and Flanagan 2011), adapting, or switching tasks. Followers themselves learn to complete steps only when sanctioned by the resonance loop with the leader. Autonomous completion frequently opens a gap to the leader. Thus, followers master finely calibrated responses to microinvitations, generate motor commands with utmost phase-sensitivity, and collect the leaders' energy, while providing only measured additions to it. Followers do well not to set off 'prepackaged' motor commands lest they overshoot the lead. Anticipatory task-alignment (Sebanz, Bekkering, and Knoblich 2006) results in bad timing or contact loss and sometimes in incorrect anticipation. Overzealous responses also deny the leader improvisatory options such as 'feints', reversals, or slowing down. Elements such as leg whips (*boleos*) work effortlessly with the follower unaware and just attempting to walk normally. Feedback-sensitive coaction creates much greater potential for creativity, which often emerges from subtle interbody synergies (see section 5.4). Anticipating instead of sensing is detrimental for all these reasons.

3.4 Microcoordination

Able tango dancers coordinate even the briefest standard elements minutely via the resonance loop, to respect phase-by-phase action dependencies. Even a forward step demands a well-connected joint weight transfer and avoiding leg collisions. This requires complex microcoordination between different body parts *across* the couple. Both torsos and free legs are successively initialized in an interlocking sequence, beginning with the leader's gradually increasing weight shift (fig. 32.2, left):

1. {*Forward weight projection of leader: controlled lability informs the follower of incipient intention*} →
2. {*Follower 'loads up' torso but stays put, while channelling the information to the free leg, which extends backwards*} →
3. {*Sensing the follower's torso-leg stretch, the leader releases his weight fully while the follower activates supporting leg to generate thrust*}

To achieve this coordinative feat, dancers take guidance from the partner's phase-specific sensory feedback: the follower feels the leader's incipient weight shift via resistance, tension changes, and diagonal forces in the embrace. The leader feels how far the follower's leg extends via tension on her shoulder blade and diagonal forces. In steps, the leader's continuous weight shift must elicit a well-timed suite of microresponses from the follower.

Other 'movemes' even contain marked intraunit changes of movement quality or direction. The lead changes actions midway when a specific sensory trigger is actuated

FIG. 32.2 Left: temporal scheme of forward walk; centre: direction reversal trigger in leg-swing (*boleo*); right: enabling breastbone opposition.

(Kimmel 2012). For example, the *boleo*—a crisp leg swing the leader induces in the follower—requires a sharp direction reversal of the follower's rotating torso (fig. 32.2, centre). Done correctly, the *boleo* interrupts a back step midway and may surprise the follower. The leader uses the tensile feedback from the followers' diagonal muscles connecting leg and shoulder to time the reversal at the maximum stretch or simply make the follower 'rebound', a sort of self-structuring biomechanic dynamic.

In all types of microcoordination, the coordinative pattern arises from criss-crossing microtriggers, with onsets of micro-actions somewhat like interlocking cogs on a wheel (A-B-A-B-A). A perfectly coordinated unfolding of the 'moveme' is ensured by task- and phase-specific microtriggers and microresponses, that is, perception-action linkages movement researchers might formalize through *control laws* (Warren 2006). Tango practice trains both dance roles in specific dynamic sequencing 'algorithms' from which complementary coactions arise, hence a truly joint technical execution.

3.5 Readiness, Order, and Rapport

Good basic tango habits are equally instrumental to joint improvisation. Activating a set of enabling 'precalibrations' on entering the dance floor does a large part of the work for all later tasks by sufficiently narrowing the initial degrees of freedom.

First, each dancer respects the *basic postural 'grammar'*, for example, a long torso, but relaxed knees, chest, and navel moving as one, deep-muscle activity, and relaxed breathing. Notably, axial alignment affords a neutral position between all four cardinal directions, subject to minimal centrifugal forces in pivots. A good axis provides for stability at the brink of moving (*metastability*). These individual skills work to mutual benefit. Good alignment and optimal muscle organization heighten receptivity and communication clarity: Well-organized followers detect immediately whether subtle nudges are intended as an actual step invitation. Similarly, a well-aligned leader eliminates any vagueness for the follower. Bursts of step energy versus 'locking into' balanced alignment are felt as 1 and 0. Step onsets become crisp and render the communication unambiguous both ways.

Second, proper *interpersonal 'grammar'* creates permanent order parameters, which enable communication and keep the couple a compact, action-ready unit. Thus, establishing musculoskeletal channels from A's legs to B's torso and vice versa benefits information flow, as do proper geometries: by pointing the breastbone vectors towards each other, dancers ensure optimal kinetic transmission (fig. 32.2, right). This configures the embrace into a force parallelogram that allows maximal biomechanic leverage and enhances sensitivity to minute signals. Followers feel effects of impinging force immediately, whereas at a critical deviation angle this sensation begins to slip. Some interpersonal rules like 'share weight in forward direction' actually multiply lead choices: when the leader rotates in opposite open stance, this makes the follower rotate within her body by default and backwards only when the leader adds peripheral energy. When followers share no weight, a follower rotation within cannot be easily led. Something similar applies to staying opposite to leaders with the hips unless forced to do otherwise. Thus, expert dancers monitor and keep enabling interpersonal *relations* in an acceptable range, such as geometry, distance, or delay. They deal on-the-fly with glitches through small 'repairs' and reciprocal compensation (Riley et al. 2011) that kicks in, for example, when the partner *begins* to compromise the joint axis, overshoots, or anticipates. For example, one may counterbalance a slightly overshooting partner through one's own weight centre.

Finally, a suite of enactive *microskills for optimizing information flow* are reported. When noticing something going awry, dancers collect their attentional focus on the partner's chest and switch to enhanced receptivity. When communicative clarity is lacking, they may actively focus on the embrace's quality, adapt its height or rigidity, seek out the partner's shoulder-blade ridge, or actively meld into the partner's counter-body motion to amplify incoming signals. Inversely, a dancer will amplify signals for the partner's benefit by providing a clear hand barrier in the embrace, initiating rotations from the core-body, 'three-dimensionalizing' the lead, or simply calm following.

4 COGNITIVE-PERCEPTUAL BASES

We now move to improvisation-specific foundations that leaders employ to be creative. Leaders must acquire a repertoire, organize it cognitively, and find pathways through it. This knowledge base involves elements, collocation, junctures, compositional rules, and perceptual principles.

4.1 Elementary Motor Repertoires

One hallmark of growing improvisational expertise is a modularized knowledge base of small 'movemes'. Dancers must master—and, when needed, isolate—increasingly finer motor units. Learning motor repertoires usually begins with the rote repetition of standard patterns, which are progressively subdivided as dancers gain in flexibility. They deconstruct scripts into primitives and reshuffle these.

Specifically, motor control is thought to rely on units called *basic action concepts* (Bläsing, Schack, and Puttke 2010; Schack 2010; Bläsing 2010), goal-directed motor programs which leaders envisage at a 150-to-500-millisecond timescale for microplanning the next movement.[2] They recruit such units to form a microintention and initiate action. Only after each unit is executed is a new choice needed. Although skills for improvisational choice differ from motor enskilment, the boundaries of ideomotor modules coevolve with the discovery of 'natural' transitional points. Even their first improvising attempts challenge leaders to match motor commands with points where safe stopping or rerouting is possible on the tango matrix, for example, when another couple suddenly blocks the way. Repertoire memory is inherently *hierarchical*, with action concepts at several nested levels:

1. *Individual*: single-body action concepts include elementary steps and pivots. From each centred (torso-above-leg-support) position, there are four cardinal directions for stepping, including two leg-crosses, four diagonal steps, and two pivots (fig. 32.3, upper panels).
2. *Dyadic*: dyadic concepts are—via combination—numerous. In fig. 32.3, the central lower tier shows an elementary interaction concept: {*partners in open-legged stance, knees facing each other*}→ *ROTATION, WEIGHT SHIFT TO RIGHT LEG* → {*crossed legs*}. These involve role-specific point-of-view representations. Dancers possess multimodal imagery of their own motor commands and proprioceptive feedback, together with external feedback imagery of their partner (whose motor commands and feedback control remain opaque). Expert dancers also mentally simulate interpersonal causal contingencies, that is, 'if I do X my partner reacts with Y'.

Both types of action representations are temporally subdivided. Dancers frequently imagine small ideomotor pegs for incremental control, for example, the origin, midpoint, and endpoint of a rotation (fig. 32.3, lower left panel). They acquire the whole gestalt when developing automatized modular routines but also break it down to increments.

Furthermore, dancers learn to dissect full-body actions into *dynamic primitives* (Hogan and Sternad 2013). Tango primitives include shoulder opening, chest rotation, controlled lability ('weight projection'), and weight transfer (Milite 2007) (fig 32.3, lower right panel). Interpersonally, something similar happens: as dancers loosen their ties to 'prefabricated' interaction concepts, they discover generalized functions of primitives like weight shifting, what they do for regulating the lead, and how they enable or constrain other primitives.

4.2 Composite Repertoires

Leaders enrich elementary actions with bigrams, trigrams, and larger collocations, analogous to multiword formulaic speech. Although repertoire learning frequently

FIG. 32.3 Upper tier: elementary single-body productions (left: various directional steps; right: leg crosses). Lower left tier: sequencing points of a single-body production, a rotation into body-space, and the corresponding elementary dyadic production of a joint rotation. Lower right tier: dynamic primitives for a single body.

starts with such *miniscripts* and progressively breaks them down, even in experts miniscripts continue to play a role (see section 5.1). Frequent variation builds memory variants of these miniscripts (e.g., ABC, ABD, ABE, AFC; AFD, and so on) stored as *prototypes* or *exemplars*. Multiple transitions and variations form part of *hierarchical memory* (Pressing 1984), knowledge of which benefits fluid cross-linkages under varying conditions (Pressing 1998; Berkowitz 2010) and preparations one or two steps ahead. Another reason for variation training is to adapt transition timing to fit different music styles like tango *vals* and 'architectural' constraints of an expected musical phrase.

4.3 Node Representations

Improvisers are aware of recurrent decision points (bifurcations of the behavioural matrix) and may internalize them. These *nodes* represent a transitional pair configuration, a 'keyframe' located at the boundaries between 'movemes', and, frequently, possible entry paths towards and continuations from there. Nodes arise from a trajectory-related perceptual analysis of bifurcations within the tango system one has learned to use. Nodes afford possibilities for rerouting and creative springboards. They furnish a cognitive grid to build the improvisation around and provide recurrently used 'homebases'. Interruptions, reversals, shortcuts, and creative inserts (inlays, reshufflings of elementary 'movemes') typically set in here.

Node repertoires are refined with experience. A seasoned *tanguero* might be able to perceive and use two or three nodes within a step cycle, where a beginner perceives one. Nodes are usually salient in memory and recognized as potential bifurcations even when not actively exploited. Many nodes also provide biomechanic benefits: every torso-above-supporting-leg position affords settling into a perfectly balanced stop. Partners can 'collect themselves' and reconsolidate the couple before beginning something new. Important choices are easiest to initiate at such points.

4.4 Perceptual Analysis of Interbody Invariants

Another powerful resource for specifying available continuations involves directly perceived *body-configurational* cues: at every step boundary, the torso-above-supporting-leg position leaders recognize that they can initiate a pivot, shift weights, stop, reverse, or reroute. Similarly, a partner in midstep position inherently allows a *sacada* (invasion). Thus, every tango moment has geometric-dynamic signatures with a particular feel that indicate continuation possibilities.

How this works is highlighted by ecological psychology: experts 'educate their attention' by attuning themselves to meaningful perceptual affordances (Gibson 1979; McArthur and Baron 1983). Proprioceptive-kinaesthetic, balance-related, and visual cues signal possible task-relevant continuations. Incipient micromovements often additionally clarify these affordances. Invariants imply that affordances relate to a *functionally equivalent class* of situations and extrapolate what similar configurations share. This liberates advanced dancers from memorizing interactions in their full specifics. They strip away situational information that makes little difference in terms of choice. Through perceptual analysis of invariants, leaders needn't memorize what different situations look like; they can kinaesthetically *feel* their options.

Invariants also capture the gist even of novel situations. For instance, they discriminate the so-called parallel and crossed walking systems, that is, whether the follower is on the mirroring leg, by exploiting the embrace's inherent pressure differential: a diagonal geometry of 'body-columns' and dominant pressure on the contact point opposite to one's weighted leg indicates crossed status (fig. 32.4). Feeding subtle force into the partner provides further information, with a circular or rhomboid microresponse indicating crossed status and linear responsiveness indicating parallel status.[3]

This refined perceptual awareness requires simultaneous sensitivities to pair geometry, movement vectors and distances between partners, parallel or crossed weights, where body-fronts are pointing and how much chests are aligned with hips, distance to nearby couples, and more. Advanced experts learn to integrally interpret this multidimensional mix of interpersonal dynamic primitives to evaluate their options relative to it. They perceive the dance in terms of its *generic functional logic* (Zeitz 1997).

FIG. 32.4 'Crossed system' invariant: +/- indicate the felt pressure differential of the partner in the embrace diagonal to the dancer's weighted foot.

5 IMPROVISATIONAL MODES

Improvisational variation can apply to elementary units, their composition, or style and dynamics. Leaders use (and *mix*!) various generative modes. Each mode extends one of the aforementioned cognitive bases which furnish the 'stuff' for compositional variation, microcreativity, and, sometimes, for creating novel forms.

5.1 Script-Based Creativity

Dancers may memorize A-B, A-B-C, or more complex chains of elementary 'movemes' to solve the combinatorics challenge. Scripting thus draws on stored collocations; it means planning and fluidly executing up to six or eight elements (somewhat like 'licks' in jazz), while bracketing out potential rerouting affordances in between.[4]

- Some dancers use scripts as a reference frame for memorizing frequent step types and progressions (*paso básico*, fig. 32.5, upper panel).
- Known scripts can provide a secure basis for gradually augmenting or deconstructing patterns. Especially certain multistep 'loops' (forward-backward, *cuadrado, cadenas*, etc.) furnish material to play with. Scripts also provide spring-boards for local variation. Microcreativity, albeit without tremendous compositional novelty, arises when adding embellishments or when varying accentuation or execution style.
- Chaining *small* scripts also allows a certain compositional variability. Suppose a leader typically combines trigrams—this would provide considerable variation potential over a three-minute tango piece. Seasoned leaders frequently employ scripting; bigram and trigram collocations in particular are a useful 'package size' and allow preparatory adjustments for an upcoming element concerning details of geometry, embrace, or dynamics. Moreover, there are certain elements one tends not to initiate unless it is in preparation for some follow-up element. For example, pivoting the follower into a T position tends to happen in deliberate preparation for eights (*ocho*), invasions (*sacada*), circulating (*giros*), or related sequences.
- The scripting mode gains power by truncating and reassembling miniscripts on-the-fly, or creating shortcuts into neighbouring scripts (fig. 32.5; see matrix skills in section 5.2).

Barring the last qualification, exclusive reliance on scripting generates richly varied tango productions if, and only if, the leader commands a huge *exemplar*-based repertoire. Available scripts must start from the myriad junctures in the tango matrix. However, juggling around many hundreds of *exemplars* may overstretch memory capacities. Moreover, while reliance on miniscripting might work out regarding creativity, its disadvantage is that it lacks flexibility in response to unexpected events. Even with an impeccable follower, scripting is not always feasible on crowded milongas, because imponderables like crossing couples require midscript rerouting. Consequently, leaders with a scripting preference must be capable of hybrid modes.

One such mode employs *non-enforced scripts* that preplan several units, while retaining utmost sensitivity to real-time feedback in execution. Immediate rerouting to another option remains possible when a continuation affordance remains absent or an alternative tickles one's fancy midway. Another hybrid mode is to pre-plan a *contingency bundle*, that is, a Plan B to the preferred continuation, possibly Plans C, D, and E. (see Gobet 1998). Contingency bundles provide fallback options and prepare the motor system for likely events, although this mode is cognitively costly: with a certain 'move depth'—as in chess—it becomes impracticable to map out bifurcations. A third hybrid between scripts and elementary units is to sketchily plan the approximate trajectory, for example, circulation around the partner, but leave specifics to real-time selection.

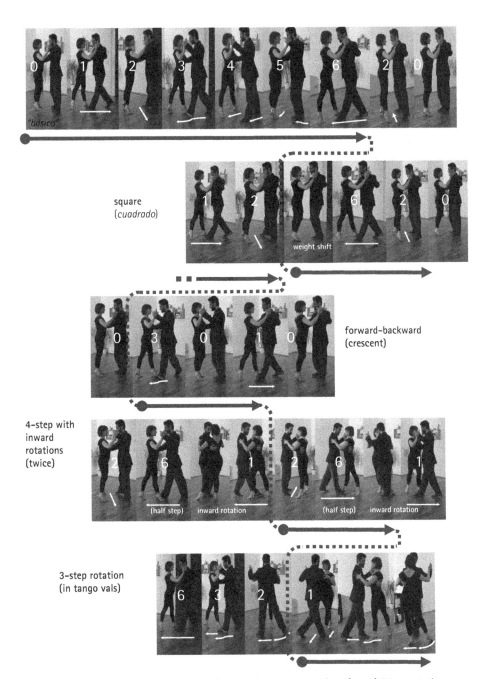

FIG. 32.5 Switching between loops (numbers: reference steps taken from *básico* script).

5.2 Element-Based and Matrix Creativity

In a more fine-grained generative mode, leaders select and chain modular elements in real time, that is, 'movemes' of 150 to 500 milliseconds (see section 4.1). Motor commands for each 'moveme' are executed without planning ahead. Only as the next decision window arises are continuation *affordances* picked up. Action choice happens with the barest minimum of planning, minimally before or just as the ongoing element ends. Either leaders may have memorized the range of continuation options at a node (see section 4.3), or they perceptually analyse the current configurational constraints and systemically licenced degrees of freedom to detect possible continuations (see section 4.4). Furthermore, since many triggering configurations are spatially adjacent (for example, the follower's forward *ocho* and back *ocho*), the leader can adapt to the interpersonally most fitting alternatives. The leader accommodates when the partner reacts unexpectedly or with a delay, when miscommunication occurs, or when a dance-floor path is suddenly blocked. The strategy is to reroute on–the-fly when a dynamic repair is considered too disruptive or forceful. Leaders opportunistically exploit—or through micronudges create—alternative affordances (Kimmel and Rogler 2018), an essential leading skill. Doing this smoothly enough not to disrupt the dance flow and to remain unnoticed by the partner is one hallmark of advanced improvising.

Complementarily, leaders can creatively navigate between nodes, especially when internalized together with entry paths and continuations. Node representations provide springboards and targets. Leaders begin a 'moveme' by steering towards a familiar node; then they choose and prepare the next 'moveme' shortly before reaching it. Again, adepts excel at opportunistically exploiting unexpected nodes rather than enforcing their original intention. Moreover, they may think up new improvisational pathways between nodes, try inserts, reshuffle, or backtrack. 'Surfing' the node matrix can be a powerful intuition pump. For example, node transitions that have never been attempted can be explored. Leaders might envisage a remote position in the matrix and infer multiple intermediate steps to get there. They might think something like 'I'm in a full frontal position in crossed-weight system and want us to get to the *American* position. I therefore need to (1) change the relative weight system (by staying put while shifting the partner or by shifting myself while holding the partner in place) (2) pivot us both ninety degrees and open outwardly, and (3) shift weight onto the free leg to do a mirror-like step until both partner's legs touch at their tips'. This online problem solving is used to infer steps towards a goal-node, often by inserting rote-learned 'fitting pieces'.

5.3 Generic Creativity

Recall that using moment-to-moment perceptual analysis of geometric and dynamic invariants is a powerful resource for inferring continuations on-the-fly from a situation's essential properties. The same sensitivity for multidimensional invariants (see section 4.4) arguably also shapes creative exploration and discovery of novel patterns. Genuine creativity must bring several further abilities into play, though.

Adepts learn to flexibly combine sets of semi-abstract structures (see modal model: Sawyer 1996), the *generic logic of tango*. This incurs the double benefit of tailoring responses to nonstandard contexts and of generating novel continuations far beyond any previously experienced exemplars. Mastering this generic logic may largely liberate leaders from ready-mades and stored continuations and allows developing new material. Putatively, such high-level generativity operates in a force field of:

- *General constraining principles,* such as 'seek full frontality when possible', 'act on the centre of gravity', or 'follow the kinetic vector of least resistance'.
- *Scenario-based best practices,* for example, 'in off-axis *colgadas* sit backwards, weight on toes, remain tall, with balancing counterweights'.
- *Technical contingency representations,* such as 'when in T position, chest opening/torso rotation will trigger a forward step of the partner, and if I initiate my own forward step a split second later to replace the partner's position, this will create a *sacada* (invasion)'. Awareness is needed of effects that particular actions have on partners within a given configuration.
- *Semi-abstract categories of action configurations,* for example, topological sets of possible force-vectorial interaction configurations (opposite, parallel, T, etc.).
- *Creativity heuristics,* such as 'most interaction patterns can be mirrored from left to right'.
- *Dynamic primitives*: advanced perceptual analysis breaks tango productions into semi-independent control dimensions (distance and interpersonal geometry, relative body-front orientation, parallel versus crossed weight systems, etc.) and thereby generates dynamic primitives.

In experts, each control dimension can figure as a semi-independent production system to play with, each with its relative freedom and control laws. Dancers may, for example, combine dynamic primitives, graft them to atypical circumstances, try to blend microelements observed in others into their dance, transpose principles to new tasks, or blend principles. Besides knowing contextual tolerances and critical thresholds (Warren 2006) for each control dimension, leaders must be capable of anticipating enabling and constraining cross-influences between them (e.g., 'from what point on does spinning away from a partner with a loose embrace impact her orientation?'). Based on this *synergistic* expertise, leaders may, for example, blend compatible subactions into hybrid 'movemes', such as inserting a quick flourish into a step. As leaders mesh control dimensions into creative mixes, they must ensure integral motor synergies. What advanced dancers presumably do here closely reflects the dynamic systems viewpoint that motor solutions are *softly assembled* from a pool of variably recruited, functionally not strictly prespecified control tools (Kelso 1995; Kello and Van Orden 2009).

Hence, generic creativity involves a perceptual analysis of relevant control dimensions, realizing what their current parametrization affords doing, matching this with an improvisational/exploratory interest, meshing selected control tools into context-adequate synergies, and dynamically homing in on a novel movement. Future work will have to address whether mature experts always end up using generic creativity and perhaps verify traces of soft assembly in other creative modalities.

5.4 Interactive Creativity and Emergence

Mentally simulating a viable mix of primitives in advance and executing it is one basic option. Alternatively, online feedback can augment semi-specified intentions. In other words, although dances are led by one partner, a purely internalistic view of tango creativity would be misguided. *Interactivity-based creative resources* (Steffensen 2013; Kirsh 2014; Kimmel, Hristova, and Kussmaul 2018) can be utilized. Leaders may envisage an approximate trajectory and assemble the details as they go along using cues from the (self)-generated dynamic (Kimmel, Irran, and Luger 2015). Any process might start in a gradually probing fashion, for example, by initiating a risky micromanoeuver in one control system, checking if other systems adapt favourably, and if so, completing the synergy on the go, guided by a sensitivity for functional fit. Or suddenly arising 'easy paths' may suggest a direction, and certain micromovements may suggest playing with or further augmenting them. Chance occurrences, small mistakes, ad hoc repairs, nudges, or microfluctuations may prove not only constraining but inspirational (Barrett 1998). When followers 'play', for example, in creating leg flourishes, leaders can join in this play, for example, by surprisingly redirecting the follower's energy. Furthermore, all this fits with the idea of *soft assembly* in a field of multiple constraints: interactivity-based nudges can disambiguate attractive from lesser options, a point emerging in motor control theories that emphasize environmental coupling (Thelen and Smith 2004).

Another key idea is that bodies and interbody systems can spontaneously self-organize into new states (Torrents et al. 2016; Harrison and Stergiou 2015). Brief moments of spontaneous emergence occur (including disruptive emergence ensuing from miscommunication, rapport loss, mishaps and dwindling attention, or excessive risk-taking). Positive emergence—the odd 'magic moment'—is reported when partners boost each other towards unpremeditated forms and even surprise themselves. Especially when bodies are organized in *metastability* (see section 2), partners 'click' effortlessly without disrupting fluency. This interpersonal synergy may allow a difficult technique to be executed effortlessly; at other times even a novel pattern emerges. Both are cases of a self-organizing system. While many tango attractors (see section 1.4) are cognitively known and deliberately steered towards by leaders, fully relaxed couples 'going with the flow' may spontaneously discover subjectively unknown energy-optimal states. The dancers' time-locked coactions spontaneously gravitate to a yet unvisited attractor when entering its vicinity. These 'magic moments' emerge through multicausal catalysing, contingent on a well-prepared ground: a favourable attractor landscape must be present which deepens previously shallow quasi attractors. This is the case when all fundamental degrees of freedom are optimally organized through precise postural and body organization, functional interpenetration of partners, mutual stabilization, relaxation, and emotional security. The music's rhythmical entrainment may enhance this interpersonal catalysis. Under such conditions even micromovements or chance fluctuations can be cross-catalytically magnified, increase an attractor's 'gravitation', and make unlikely interaction patterns suddenly appear easy and natural. Thus, multiple factors may conspire to convert a dimple in the attractor landscape to a sizeable trough that exerts attraction when entering its vicinity.

Meanwhile, the most radical kind of emergence is nearly absent in tango, principally because tango evolved to allow speed and musicality aims, which requires constraints: a strict role distribution keeps followers from any active explorations that might disrupt, whilst 'grammar' preordains rather definite windows for rerouting and task transition. By contrast, dances like contact improvisation offer possibilities of genuinely 'interenactive' negotiation of decisions, with microimpulses of both dancers meshing all the time. Interaction patterns arise by genuinely superindividual agency, describable as cumulative emergence and sometimes experienced as 'third mind' deciding for you (Kimmel, Hristova, and Kussmaul, 2018).

5.5 Discussion

In sum, scripts have their benefits and provide a creative starting point, but within limits. A break-down to modular 'movemes' and affordance recognition after each 'moveme' makes leaders far more flexible and responsive to dance-floor situations. Furthermore, to move beyond merely combinatorial and towards genuinely essential creativity, experienced leaders restructure their knowledge base. They extract principles, dissect complex movements into flexible primitives, and combinatorially generate new material from these; they pick up on interactivity-based nudges, specify sketchy ideas dynamically, and merge constraint-based exploration with serendipity.

Due to a hierarchically organized memory, multiple creative modes can peacefully coexist in the same dance(r). Improvisers likely recruit them depending on attentional resources, mood, personal preference, and momentarily emphasized aims (rapport, aesthetics, organicity, playfulness, virtuosity). Future scholarship needs to address what mode occurs when, what the benefits and limits of each are, and how modes fluctuate. For example, a moment of scripting may free attention for ideal rapport or for enhanced sensory acuity and thereby create a springboard for special creativity the very next moment.

6 Conclusion

The skill of collaborative improvisation is defined by the core criteria of low planning range, remaining flexibly poised, and respecting emergence—all fundamental aspirations of tango dancers. Openness to every moment's fancy *and* emergent adaptive pressures characterize joint improvisation. Inherently, a certain tension exists between 'wanting to improvise', that is, creative intention on the spur of the moment, and 'having to improvise' to deal with ecological pressures in an interactive field (dance-floor contingencies, mishaps, etc.). While these types are not precisely distinct, they remind us that discussing creativity as divorced from interaction is an idealization.

In both cases, tango improvisation mainly manifests as compositional chaining of elements.[5] The possibility of serial creativity emerges because dancers are poised in a semi-open task space where multiple paths begin wherever one is located. Some microcreativity and occasional widening of the lexicon or even essential creativity 'in the act' add to this.

Functionally, the feat of joint improvisation requires multiple constraints to be concurrently satisfied by integrating the respective skill sets. This boils down to matching a knowledge-base with present affordances summarily emerging from the interaction, music, available dance space, and—often—a leader's interests (fig. 32.6).

- Tango creativity and adaptivity are *enabled* by improvisation-unspecific skills, which set the scene. By respecting 'grammar'-sanctioned restrictions on movement, posture, and movement geometry, dancers ensure that a maximum of improvisational affordances will manifest to select from.
- By a similar token, enabling constraints of togetherness are respected, including permanent ones like proper embracing. This interaction 'grammar' has historically evolved to afford optimal kinaesthetic interconnectivity, dynamic stability, and efficient joint movement.
- Furthermore, skills for microcoordinating elements, situated interaction management, communicating clear intentions, and letting the partner do his or her part will ultimately facilitate joint improvisation, and—by virtue of seamless information transmission and optimal mechanical leverage—relax the couple into a generativity-prone state.
- Improvisation in the narrower sense requires an internalized generative system with a basic 'grammar' and specific repertoires. I concur with influential approaches on solos (Pressing 1984; Johnson-Laird 2002; Berkowitz 2010) which suggest that improvisers build a rich, partly redundant knowledge base ('movemes', scripts, nodes, dynamic primitives, principles, best practices, etc.) and acquire perceptual analysis expertise along the main control dimensions of 'tango logic'.
- The tango case suggests moderating recent views that downplay representational resources (Schiavio and Høffding 2015), although interactivity-based resources do matter in subtle ways (and they'd matter more if tango were a symmetric negotiation system like contact improvisation dancing).

In sum, joint improvisation requires, *all at once*, deeply entrenched individual and interpersonal habits, interactive-dynamic microskills, and—for leaders—complex knowledge resources. Only with this present may interpersonal self-organization occasionally augment the leader's deliberate creativity.

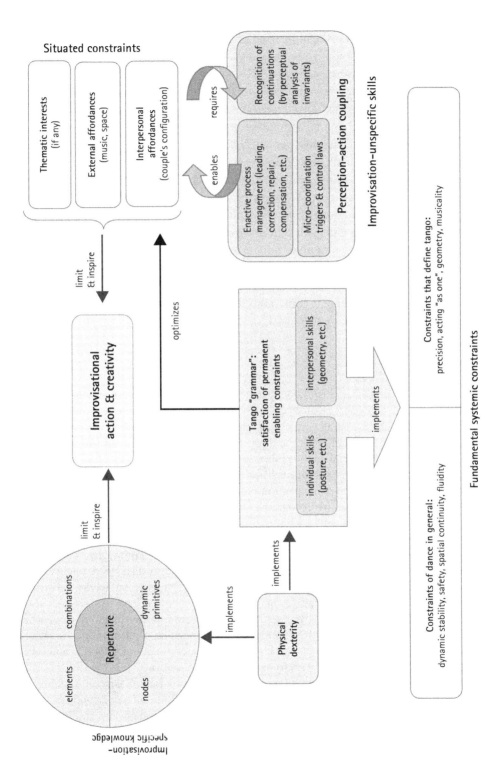

FIG. 32.6 Factors governing improvisational choice (light grey boxes refer to skills).

It is misguided to reduce tango to a single cognitive skill in yet another way: expert improvisers command a host of improvisational modes, including the chaining of elementary 'movemes', planning scripted bigrams, trigrams or larger collocations, moving between particular nodes and experimentally combining dynamic primitives. These resources may be combined in complex ways. Putatively, the dancers' maturity, improvisational interests, and situational demands all shape the improvisational mode that is preferred, although much remains for future investigation here.

Finally, tango suggests a twofold general conclusion about closely coupled embodied improvisation. (1) To explain coordinated interaction *execution*, physical interpenetration and a collective, low-dimensional structure supervene on classical cognitive posits like anticipatorily shared goals. 'Presencing' skills enacted within joint embodied structures provide a functionally powerful alternative mechanism. A tango embrace affords a resonance loop and push-pull connections, making joint actions quicker and communication more reliable than anticipatory alignment ever could (often facilitated by musical entrainment). (2) In contradistinction, explaining leader *decisions* requires internalistic resources, albeit with concepts that can be sketchy or tentative and that must mesh with emergent constraints and allow constant tuning, updating, and morphing in execution.

NOTES

1. I draw from a phenomenological study done with microgenetic interviews, think-alouds, a six-year diary of my participatory experience as a *tanguero*, as well as, in smaller proportion, a motion capture study with eleven tango teachers. This research was supported by the Austrian Science Fund (FWF) under grant P-23067. I wish to thank Germano Milite for his continued support with the project and the graphic art, and Floor van Alphen, Paul Rössler, and Dayana Hristova for feedback. My gratitude also goes to many anonymous interviewees and to eleven participants in a motion capture study.
2. As further background, see neurocognitive work on general motor theory (Bläsing, Schack, and Puttke 2010; Sevdalis and Keller 2011; Bläsing et al. 2012) and tango specifically (Brown, Martinez, and Parsons 2006; Limb and Braun 2008; Amoruso et al. 2014).
3. Dancers may also rely on short-term memories of what was led immediately before. For example, when both partners were on the same track and one just changed weight and the other not, 'crossed' status can be inferred. Although such inferencing works, experts are typically able to diagnose the status ad hoc.
4. Note that leaders occasionally engage in multi-'moveme' action planning even when envisaging something never tried before. A novel combination suddenly flashes up, which they plan and execute as a nonstandard script. Hence, scripting understood as a novel ad hoc idea planned in time is different from using standard scripts.
5. I hesitate to make creative novelty a core criterion for improvisation. One can combinatorially improvise really well yet pick familiar elements. In addition, adaptivity and novelty are logically orthogonal: real-time flexibility is possible without true novelty, and inversely, a leader might envision a novel series of steps ad hoc but script it mentally so as to execute it without further flexibility after that point.

REFERENCES

Amoruso, L., Sedeño, L., Huepe, D., Tomio, A., Kamienkowski, J., Hurtado, E., Cardona, J. F., Álvarez González, M. Á., Rieznik, A., Sigman, M., Manes, F., and Ibáñez, A. (2014) Time to Tango: Expertise and Contextual Anticipation during Action Observation. *NeuroImage* 98: 366–385.

Badino, L., D'Ausilio, A., Glowinski, D., Camurri, A., and Fadiga, L. (2014) Sensorimotor Communication in Professional Quartets. *Neuropsychologia* 55: 98–104.

Baillieul, J., and Ozcimder, K. (2012) The Control Theory of Motion-Based Communication: Problems in Teaching Robots to Dance. In *American Control Conference (ACC) 2012*. IEEE. 4319–4326.

Barrett, F. J. (1998) Creativity and Improvisation in Jazz and Organizations: Implications for Organizational Learning. *Organization Science* 9(5): 605–622.

Becker, H. S. (2000) The Etiquette of Improvisation. *Mind, Culture, and Activity* 7(3): 171–176. doi: 10.1207/S15327884MCA0703_03.

Berkowitz, A. L. (2010) *The Improvising Mind. Cognition and Creativity in the Musical Moment.* New York: Oxford University Press.

Bernstein, N. (1996) On Dexterity and Development. In Latash, M. L., and Turvey, M. T. (eds.), *Dexterity and Its Development.* Mahwah, NJ: Erlbaum. 1–244.

Berthoz, A. (2012) *Simplexity.* New Haven: Yale University Press.

Biasutti, M., and Frezza, L. (2009) Dimensions of Music Improvisation. *Creativity Research Journal* 21(2–3): 232–242.

Bläsing, B. (2010) The Dancer's Memory: Expertise and Cognitive Structure in Dance. In Bläsing, B., Puttke, M., and Schack, T. (eds.), *The Neurocognition of Dance: Mind, Movement and Motor Skills.* New York: Psychology Press, 75–98.

Bläsing, B., Calvo-Merino, B., Cross, E. S., Jola, C., Honisch, J., and Stevens, C. J. (2012) Neurocognitive Control in Dance Perception and Performance. *Acta Psychologica* 139(2): 300–308.

Bläsing, B., Schack, T., and Puttke, M. (eds.). (2010) *The Neurocognition of Dance: Mind, Movement and Motor Skills.* New York: Psychology Press.

Braun, D. A., Ortega, P. A., and Wolpert, D. M. (2011) Motor Coordination: When Two Have to Act as One. *Experimental Brain Research* 211(3–4): 631–641.

Brown, S., Martinez, M., and Parsons, L. M. (2006) The Neural Basis of Human Dance. *Cerebral Cortex* 16(8): 1157–1167.

Castro, M. (2004) *Tango Awareness.* Buenos Aires.

Chomsky, N. (1957) *Syntactic Structures.* The Hague: Mouton.

Chow, J. Y., Davids, K., Hristovski, R., Araújo, D., and Passos, P. (2011) Nonlinear Pedagogy: Learning Design for Self-Organizing Neurobiological Systems. *New Ideas in Psychology* 29(2): 189–200.

Clark, A. (2008) *Supersizing the Mind.* Oxford: Oxford University Press.

Csikszentmihályi, M., and Rich, J. G. (1997) Musical Improvisation: A Systems Approach. In Sawyer, K. (ed.), *Creativity in Performance.* London: Ablex, 43–66.

Fogel, A. (1993) *Developing through Relationships. Origins of Communication, Self, and Culture.* Chicago: University of Chicago Press.

Fogel, A. (2006) Dynamic Systems Research on Interindividual Communication: The Transformation of Meaning-Making. *Journal of Developmental Processes* 1: 7–30.

Froese, T., and Fuchs, T. (2012) The Extended Body: A Case Study in the Neurophenomenology of Social Interaction. *Phenomenology and the Cognitive Sciences* 11(2): 205–235.

Fuchs, T., and DeJaegher, H. (2009) Enactive Intersubjectivity: Participatory Sense-Making and Mutual Incorporation. *Phenomenology and the Cognitive Sciences* 8(4): 465–486.

Gentry, S., and Feron, E. (2004) Modeling Musically Meaningful Choreography. In *2004 IEEE International Conference on Systems, Man and Cybernetics*. The Hague, Netherlands, 3880–3885.

Gibson, J. J. (1979) *The Ecological Approach to Visual Perception*. Boston: Houghton Mifflin.

Glowinski, D., Mancini, M., Cowie, R., Camurri, A., Chiorri, C., and Doherty, C. (2013) The Movements Made by Performers in a Skilled Quartet: A Distinctive Pattern, and the Function That It Serves. *Frontiers in Psychology* 4, Article 841, 1–9.

Gobet, F. (1998) Expert Memory: A Comparison of Four Theories. *Cognition* 66(2): 115–152.

Harrison, S. J., and Stergiou, N. (2015) Complex Adaptive Behavior and Dexterous Action. *Nonlinear Dynamics, Psychology, and Life Sciences* 19(4): 345.

Hogan, N., and Sternad, D. (2013) Dynamic Primitives in the Control of Locomotion. *Frontiers in Computational Neuroscience* 7, Article 71, 1–16.

Iyer, V. (2002) Embodied Mind, Situated Cognition, and Expressive Microtiming in African-American Music. *Music Perception* 19(3): 387–414.

Johnson-Laird, P. N. (2002) How Jazz Musicians Improvise. *Music Perception: An Interdisciplinary Journal* 19(3): 415–442.

Kello, C. T., and Van Orden, G. C. (2009) Soft-Assembly of Sensorimotor Function. *Nonlinear Dynamics, Psychology, and Life Sciences* 13(1): 57–78.

Kelso, S. (1995) *Dynamic Patterns*. Cambridge, MA: MIT Press.

Kenny, B. J., and Gellrich, M. (2002) Improvisation. In Parncutt, R., and McPherson, G. E. (eds.), *The Science and Psychology of Music Performance*. New York: Oxford University Press, 117–134.

Kimmel, M. (2012) Intersubjectivity at Close Quarters: Shared, Distributed, and Superindividual Imagery in Tango Argentino. *Cognitive Semiotics* 4(1): 76–124.

Kimmel, M. (2016) Embodied Micro-skills in Tango Improvisation—How a Collaborative Behavioral Arc Comes About. In Engel, F., and Marienberg, S. (eds.), *Out for a Walk. Das Entgegenkommende Denken*. Berlin: de Gruyter, 57–74.

Kimmel, M., Hristova, D., and Kussmaul, K. (2018) Sources of embodied creativity: Interactivity and ideation in Contact Improvisation Dancing. *Behavioral Sciences*, 8 (52), 1–37

Kimmel, M., Irran, C., and Luger, M. (2015) Bodywork as Systemic and Inter-enactive Competence: Participatory Process Management in Feldenkrais Method and Zen Shiatsu. *Frontiers in Psychology for Clinical Settings* 5, Article 1424, 1–23.

Kimmel, M., and Preuschl, E. (2015) Dynamic Coordination Patterns in Tango Argentino: A Cross-fertilization of Subjective Explication Methods and Motion Capture. In Lachaud, J.-P., and Abe, N. (eds.), *Dance Notations and Robot Motion*. Berlin: Springer, 209–236.

Kimmel, M., and Rogler, C. (2018) Affordances in Interaction—the Case of Aikido. *Ecological Psychology*, 30 (3), 195–223.

Kirsh, D. (2014) The Importance of Chance and Interactivity in Creativity. *Pragmatics & Cognition* 22(1): 5–26.

LaViers, A., Chen, Y., Belta, C., and Egerstedt, M. (2011) Automatic Sequencing of Ballet Poses. *IEEE Robotics & Automation Magazine* 18(3): 87–95. doi: 10.1109/MRA.2011.942118.

LaViers, A., Egerstedt, M., Chen, Y., and Belta, C. (2011) Automatic Generation of Balletic Motions. In *Proceedings of the 2011 IEEE/ACM Second International Conference on Cyber-physical Systems*. IEEE Computer Society, 13–21.

Limb, C. J., and Braun, A. R. (2008) Neural Substrates of Spontaneous Musical Performance: An fMRI Study of Jazz Improvisation. *PLoS ONE*. Special issue, Edited by E. Greene 3(2): e1679.

Maduell, M., and Wing, A. M. (2007) The Dynamics of Ensemble: The Case for Flamenco. *Psychology of Music* 35: 591–627.

Magerko, B., Manzoul, W., Riedl, M., Baumer, A., Fuller, D., Luther, K., and Pearce, C. (2009) An Empirical Study of Cognition and Theatrical Improvisation. In *Proceedings of the Seventh ACM Conference on Creativity and Cognition*. ACM, New York, 117–126.

McArthur, L. Z., and Baron, R. M. (1983) Toward an Ecological Theory of Social Perception. *Psychological Review* 90(3): 215.

Mendonça, D., and Fiedrich, F. (2006) Training for Improvisation in Emergency Management: Opportunities and Limits for Information Technology. *International Journal of Emergency Management* 3(4): 348–363.

Mendonça, D., and Wallace, W. A. (2007) A Cognitive Model of Improvisation in Emergency Management. *Systems, Man and Cybernetics, Part A: Systems and Humans, IEEE Transactions on on Systems, Man, and Cybernetics, Part A: Systems and Humans* 37(4): 547–561.

Mendonça, D., and Wallace, W. A. (2004) Cognition in Jazz Improvisation: An Exploratory Study. In *26th Annual Meeting of the Cognitive Science Society, Chicago, IL*. 956–961.

Milite, G. (2007) Die fünf Elemente des Tango. *El tango* 4: 16–19.

Monson, I. (2006) *Saying Something: Jazz Improvisation and Interaction*. Chicago: University of Chicago Press.

Nettl, B., and Russell, M. (eds.). (1998) *In the Course of Performance: Studies in the World of Musical Improvisation*. Chicago: University of Chicago Press.

Norgaard, M. (2011) Descriptions of Improvisational Thinking by Artist-Level Jazz Musicians. *Journal of Research in Music Education* 59(2): 109–127.

Opacic, T., Stevens, C., and Tillmann, B. (2009) Unspoken Knowledge: Implicit Learning of Structured Human Dance Movement. *Journal of Experimental Psychology: Learning, Memory, and Cognition* 35(6): 1570–1577.

Orgs, G., Hagura, N., and Haggard, P. (2013) Learning to Like It: Aesthetic Perception of Bodies, Movements and Choreographic Structure. *Consciousness and Cognition* 22(2): 603–612.

Oullier, O., and Kelso, S. J. A. (2009) Social Coordination from the Perspective of Coordination Dynamics. In Meyers, R.A. (ed.), *Encyclopedia of Complexity and Systems Sciences*.Berlin: Springer, 8198–8212.

Passos, P., Davids, K., and Chow, J. Y. (eds.). (2016) *Interpersonal Coordination and Performance in Social Systems*. New York: Routledge.

Pressing, J. (1984) Cognitive Processes in Improvisation. In Crozier, W., and Chapman, A. J. (eds.), *Cognitive Processes in the Perception of Art*. North Holland: Elsevier, 345–363.

Pressing, J. (1988) Improvisation: Methods and Models. In Sloboda, J. A. (ed.), *Generative Processes in Music: The Psychology of Performance, Improvisation, and Composition*. Oxford: Oxford University Press, 129–178.

Pressing, J. (1998) Psychological Constraints on Improvisational Expertise and Communication. In Nettl, B., and Russell, M. (eds.), *In the Course of Performance: Studies in the World of Musical Improvisation*. Chicago: University of Chicago Press, 47–67.

Riley, M. A., Richardson, M. J., Shockley, K., and Ramenzoni, V. C. (2011) Interpersonal Synergies. *Frontiers in Psychology* 2, Article 38, 1–7.

Runeson, S. (1977) On the Possibility of 'Smart' Perceptual Mechanisms. *Scandinavian Journal of Psychology* 18: 172–179.

Sawyer, K. (1996) The Semiotics of Improvisation: The Pragmatics of Musical and Verbal Performance. *Semiotica* 108(3–4): 269–306.

Sawyer, K. (2001) *Creating Conversations: Improvisation in Everyday Discourse*. New York: Hampton Press.

Sawyer, K. (2003) *Group Creativity: Music, Theater, Collaboration*. Mahwah, NJ: Erlbaum.

Sawyer, K. (2012) Individual and Group Creativity. In Kaufman, J. C., and Sternberg, R. J. (eds.), *The Cambridge Handbook of Creativity*. Cambridge: Cambridge University Press, 366–394.

Schack, T. (2010) Building Blocks and Architecture of Dance. In Bläsing, B., Puttke, M., and Schack, T. (eds.), *The Neurocognition of Dance. Mind, Movement and Motor Skills*. New York: Psychology Press, 11–40.

Schiavio, A., and Høffding, S. (2015) Playing Together without Communicating? A Pre-reflective and Enactive Account of Joint Musical Performance. *Musicae Scientiae* 19(4): 366–388.

Schögler, B. (1999) Studying Temporal Co-ordination in Jazz Duets. Special issue, *Musicæ Scientiæ* (1999–2000): 75–91.

Sebanz, N., Bekkering, H., and Knoblich, G. (2006) Joint Action: Bodies and Minds Moving Together. *Trends in Cognitive Sciences* 10(2): 70–76.

Seddon, F. A. (2005) Modes of Communication during Jazz Improvisation. *British Journal of Music Education* 22(1): 47–61.

Seddon, F., and Biasutti, M. (2009) A Comparison of Modes of Communication between Members of a String Quartet and a Jazz Sextet. *Psychology of Music* 37(4): 395–415.

Sevdalis, V., and Keller, P. E. (2011) Captured by Motion: Dance, Action Understanding, and Social Cognition. *Brain and Cognition* 77(2): 231–236.

Sloboda, J. A. (ed.). (1988) *Generative Processes in Music: The Psychology of Performance, Improvisation, and Composition*. Oxford: Oxford University Press.

Steffensen, S. V. (2013) Human Interactivity: Problem-Solving, Solution-Probing and Verbal Patterns in the Wild. In Cowley, S. J. and Vallée-Tourangeau, F. (Eds.), *Cognition beyond the Brain. Computation, Interactivity and Human Artifice*. Berlin: Springer, 195–221.

Sudnow, D. (1978) *Ways of the Hand: the Organization of Improvised Conduct*. Cambridge, MA: Harvard University Press.

Tateo, L. (2014) The Dialogical Dance: Self, Identity Construction, Positioning and Embodiment in Tango Dancers. *Integrative Psychological and Behavioral Science* 48(3): 299–321.

Thelen, E., and Smith, L. (2004) *A Dynamic Systems Approach to the Development of Cognition and Action*. Cambridge, MA: MIT Press.

Torrents, C., Castañer, M., Dinušová, M., and Anguera, M. T. (2010) Discovering New Ways of Moving: Observational Analysis of Motor Creativity While Dancing Contact Improvisation and the Influence of the Partner. *Journal of Creative Behavior* 44(1): 53–69.

Torrents, C., Hristovski, R., Coterón, J., and Ric, A. (2016) Interpersonal Coordination in Contact improvisation Dance. In Passos, P., Davids, K., and Chow, J. Y. (eds.), *Interpersonal Coordination and Performance in Social Systems*. Abingdon, UK: Routledge, 94–108.

Torrents, C., Ric, Á., and Hristovski, R. (2015) Creativity and Emergence of Specific Dance Movements Using Instructional Constraints. *Psychology of Aesthetics, Creativity, and the Arts* 9(1): 65–74.

Tschacher, W., Schiepek, G., and Brunner, E. J. (2002) *Self-Organization in Clinical Psychology— Empirical Approaches to Synergetics in Psychology*. Berlin: Springer.

van Alphen, F. (2014) Tango and Enactivism: First Steps in Exploring the Dynamics and Experience of Interaction. *Integrative Psychological and Behavioral Science* 48(3): 322–331.

Walton, A. E., Richardson, M. J., Langland-Hassan, P., and Chemero, A. (2015) Improvisation and the Self-Organization of Multiple Musical Bodies. *Frontiers in Psychology* 6, Article 313, 1–9.

Warren, W. H. (2006) The Dynamics of Perception and Action. *Psychological Review* 113(2): 358–389.

Wolpert, D. M., Diedrichsen, J., and Flanagan, J. R. (2011) Principles of Sensorimotor Learning. *Nature Reviews Neuroscience* 12: 740–751.

Zeitz, C. M. (1997) Some Concrete Advantages of Abstraction: How Experts' Representations Facilitate Reasoning. In Feltovich, P., Ford, K. M., and Hoffman, R. (eds.), *Expertise in Context: Human and Machine.* Menlo Park, CA: AAAI, MIT Press, 43–65.

PART VII

ECOLOGY AND ENVIRONMENTS

CHAPTER 33

IMPROVISATION AND THE EARTH

Dancing in the Moment as Ecological Practice

TAMARA ASHLEY

In this chapter, I draw upon artistic practice research to discuss the construction of improvisation scores as a deeply site-sensitive, time-sensitive, and person-sensitive process that leads to the construction of specific microrelations that connect specific practitioners to specific places on the earth. These microrelations manifest as mindful actions in the detailed cultivation of the earth as a score, where the artists can become concerned with the relational dimensions of their actions in terms of sustainability. I propose that the cultivation of mindfulness and explicit intention of each and every gesture as a contribution to the cultivation of the earth as score is where the ethical work of the artists resides.

The chapter offers a broad, questioning, and critical perspective on how the practices of improvisation might contribute to the development of a future dance ecology that is both sustainable and interconnected. Dance improvisation is thus proposed as an activist and applied practice that enables the experiential examination of ecologically sensitive relations, and I assert that the future of the dance ecology is entwined with how we relate to and embody the places in which dance is made.

MOVING WITH THE EARTH

The sky opens, and rain starts to come down in stair rods. Visibility drops, winds pick up, and our northwesterly facing receives the full force of the Atlantic weather arriving onshore as it meets the mountains. We are in the clouds. I am glad for the reasonable grips on my boots, but my feet still slip inside them. I am coleading a group of students down a fairly steep path to Buttermere in the English Lake District. I am hot inside, and

I am not sure if I am wet from sweat or the rain leaking through my clothes. It is a precarious thirty minutes. We are on a path, but it is rocky and extremely slippery. We reach the valley floor, a road, and the possibility of calling a taxi or waiting for a bus. We poll the group. Does anyone want to stop, go back, or find shelter? With the sky still releasing all of its water, I am surprised at the unanimous vote to continue our planned walk around the lake. And then I find myself running and screaming with several others as we speed across the flat expanse of the lake's floodplain. A rush of adrenaline and shared euphoria. I feel alive. I am saturated: wet inside and out.

The sky changes the walk. Rapidly descending clouds in mountain terrain transform this gentle traverse of a hillside into a deeper call on inner resources; wit, energy, persistence, and greater attentiveness. Where dry rock offers traction and support, wet rock turns each transfer of weight into an in-depth investigation of balance and maintaining grip that considers angle of foot placement, downward pressure to be exerted, speed of weight transfer, and sequence to the next step. The taken-for-granted action of stepping is visited anew in such conditions. Here, the step is given an attention to detail similar to that given in dance and body work, and it is on this hillside that I find my dancing body in a most useful conversation with the ground.

Cultivating an Ecological Practice through (Contact) Improvisation

It was my practice as a contact improviser that led me to be on that hillside in the first place. Explorations that included tuning to the weight of another body, moving through touch, weight flow, support and momentum in a shared dance of partnership had encouraged me to foster not only a sensitivity of alignment to others but also a sensitivity to the earth and my relationships with it. In contact improvisation, there is opportunity to develop a living ecology of movement with other dancer(s), and I wondered if one might one move with the earth in similar ways. Through the cultivation of sensitive, in-the-moment responses that draw upon an integration of senses, intuition, and rapport between the participants, the contact improvisation duet values attunement to change. This core value in the practice of (contact) improvisation enabled me to reconceptualize my relationship to the world as one being in dynamic movement; an ecology of relationships and continual flow. Others in the field recognize qualities of an ecological movement practice in similar ways. For example, in *Nine Ways of Seeing a Body*, Sandra Reeve describes her definition of an ecological body as 'a body-in-movement-in-a-changing-environment' (2011: 48) and goes on to articulate that 'an ecological body is situated in flux, participation and change' (51).

Development as a contact improvisation practitioner involves not only refining perceptual awareness of one's expressive, sensual, and physical limits but also cultivating awareness of how one responsibly engages others within the limits of that awareness. These boundaries shift and evolve with the changing experiences of the practitioner. Contact improvisation offers practitioners opportunities to explore their ways of being in the world from a physicalized experiential perspective. Susan Leigh Foster describes her view on the formation of subjectivity within the practice this way: 'it offered an intriguing new experience of subjectivity wherein dancers became defined by the contact between them. Rather than two separate entities coming together, they merged with the momentum generated by both bodies, a momentum that took on a life of its own' (2002: 132–133). In its pure form, where two dancers commit to follow the point of contact shared between them, this merging of subjectivity suggests blurring of boundaries between self and other where, during the dance, the identity of the participants is merged in the completion of the task of moving together.

Foster's observation of this seemingly merged agency, manifesting as momentum, invites further reflection. What is going on in the dance that enables the observer to perceive a moving between the participants that is so seamless that it appears merged? Students of the form will be familiar with exercises that focus on exchanging the roles of leading and following. Dancers follow their own movement impulses when in the leadership role and create responsive movements when in the following role. This practice can be layered and built up in such a way that it develops trust, rapport, and an empathy that eventually enables the dancers to let go of thinking about who is leading and who is following and allow their senses to lead and respond in the coevolution of the dance. This emphasis on sensing and working with the present moment is common across improvisational practices, but in contact improvisation, the present moment is brought into focus by the negotiation of the dance between one or more dancers, usually through touch.

The dialogue of leading and following offers a context for analysing the potential of the form to develop ecological awareness. A common hindrance to the practice of leading and following exercises are students' fears and insecurities about themselves and others. Will the dance be good enough? Am I strong enough? Am I doing it right? Does my partner want to dance with me? Am I valued here? Such questions are common and surface from a world in which we are judged, in which competition and survival of the fittest is a harsh reality, and in which our value is often placed in a hierarchy of economies, class, identity, ethnicity, and social standing. Interestingly, ecologists Fritjof Capra and Pier Luisi would place such questions and concerns in an economic paradigm, where 'economics emphasizes competition, expansion and domination; ecology emphasizes cooperation, conservation and partnership … nature sustains life by creating and nurturing communities' (2014: 355). By encouraging cooperation, partnership building, and the nurturing of connection in the exchanges between leading and following, the contact improvisation teacher, according to the definition of Capra and Luisi, can be seen to be cultivating an ecological paradigm.

One of the characteristics of an ecological paradigm is the emphasis on emergent and unfolding knowledge. In ecology, knowledge is made through encounters of active interactions of players in the system. The process of working improvisationally, without a predetermined design, locates in improvisers a responsibility for working that emphasizes paying attention to what is arising in their perceptions. Working mindfully without a predetermined design also locates in the performers an attitude of activism, in that the performer does not bring preconceived knowledge to the process; rather, the performer activates knowledge by perceiving in the present moment and by creating responses to those perceptions. It is my experience that the practice of contact improvisation can open a transitional space where the experience of the body can traverse the inclusion of the other, the divergent, and the different.

Economic paradigms have politicized perception to an extent where to be asked to simply listen to oneself, to perceive the movement impulses and ideas that might emerge spontaneously from a human being's wealth of lived experiences, can require courage in order to let go of external preconceptions about value, competition, and 'doing it right'. Being unafraid of difference and of the unexpected is a prerequisite for improvised dancing that is truly opening and transformative as a practice. Choices are made in terms of what is perceived and what is not perceived, and desires, projections, and previously formed intentions can come to inform the dance. Improvisation calls on the practitioner to offer an idiosyncratic, in-the-moment response, to draw upon the resources of self in order to resist reproduction of known forms from the outside, and to add to the diversity of infinite movement possibilities. From an ecological perspective, much is at stake in these micromoments of negotiation between self and other, between perception, intention, action, and affect in the world. The evolution of the dance holds within it the potential for embodying ecological values through dialogue, listening, rapport, sensitivity, and honesty, as much as it has potential for embodying economic values through imposition, domination, and control of one dancer over another. While both may be interesting as performance, ecologists might suggest, as Satish Kumar does, that a solution to some of the current crises in the economy and in the environment is 'to put ecology before economy' (2009: 62).

Kumar's point is not necessarily to create a binary between ecology and economy; his purpose is to point out that the relationship between economy and ecology is so out of balance that radical action is needed to bring 'economy within the parameters of ecology' (2009: 65). It is Kumar's view that these imbalances are 'rooted in the mind itself' and that 'when we are able to transform our mindset and cultivate a relational worldview, then we can return to a state of equilibrium' (68). The open-ended and creative play of an improvisational dance enables exploration of these tensions, crises, and potential solutions in individual expressions. Moreover, the improvisational imperative to respond with as much openness and presence as possible to the moment offers practitioners a rigorous discipline in coming to know themselves, as artists, movers, thinkers, and doers, through the practice. The development of ecological awareness through improvisation is an enquiry that begins with the self.

Mindfulness, Ecological Thinking, and Improvisation

As long as we understand ourselves as a closed system, we feel we must hold all our 'stuff' in our own small bodies, for we have denied ourselves access to any other place to put it. We are also less present, less grounded, less available to ourselves, to others and to the powerful currents of the practices that we undertake.

Klein (1998: 146)

It is interesting that Western scholars researching the nature and quality of mind through the disciplines of neuroscience, cybernetics, and embodied cognition are proposing explanations for the ways human beings perceive and come to know in the world that resonate not only with the relational paradigms of action called for by ecological thinkers but also with the mindfulness traditions in Eastern philosophy. In yoga, for example, the body is sometimes thought of as a microcosm that reflects the macrocosm. Yogic scholar Feuerstein writes that 'we can access the cosmos by going within ourselves because objective and subjective realities always co-evolve and subsist in the same reality' (1998: 61). Gregory Bateson asserts that 'mind is immanent in the larger system—man plus environment' (1972: 322), while Andy Clark asserts that humans are natural-born cyborgs because they have developed 'thinking and reasoning systems whose minds and selves are spread across biological brain and non-biological circuitry' (2003: 3). Clark articulates a thesis of the extended mind in which the boundaries between the individual and the tools that the individual uses for thought are blurred. What enables this, he argues, is that we are 'incomplete cognitive systems' (190) and that as such our biological brains are flexible and cocreate with our environments. That the mind is immanent to not only the body but also the environment radically deconstructs any notions of environment as other, as separate from and different from me.

That being said, perceptions of nature, of self, and of relationship are very much contingent upon one's experience and situation in the world. Rosi Braidotti usefully articulates that 'we actually inhabit a nature culture continuum which is both technologically mediated and globally enforced' (2013: 110). We are in and of nature, and our perceptions reflect these relationships that traverse the individual, social, environmental, and global. Becoming an ecological being is a process of navigating one's evolving understandings of nature and culture, individually and globally. How one might become an ecological being was a key interest in the research that led me to work with dance artists who were exploring similar questions of how to practice and live in ecological ways.

ALIGNING WITH NATURE: EARTH AS SCORE

I offer two portraits of practice, focusing on the work of Tim Rubidge and Nala Walla, artists whose improvisation practices ground their entire approaches to living, where the artists apply and extend the values of their art practices to their questions about how to live an ethical life that contributes to being part of a healthy world ecology, as well as a healthy dance ecology. When interacting with these artists, I began to think of the earth as a score, with which we can duet in many different ways, while the quality and care of that duet will come to inform perceptions and states of mind that emerge between practising beings and the earth. These two artists' contributions to the disciplines of dance, performance, and theatre can also be understood in the context of their respective commitments to the cultivation of an evolving score, rather than of an art object, as practice. As performance studies scholar Philip Auslander writes, 'theatre's complicity with the anti-ecological humanist condition has to be of critical concern to us' (2003: 299). Auslander's critique of theatre's complicity in the antiecological humanist condition rests on the fact that artworks often stay in the world longer than anything else and, in so doing, transcend the worldliness of things. The development of ecological choreographies is concerned with aligning the qualities of such endeavours with the immanent, adaptable, and evolutionary qualities of nature.

NATURE, MIND, AND MOVEMENT IN
THE WORK OF TIM RUBIDGE

Tim Rubidge is a dance artist based in rural Northumberland who focuses much of his practice at his home and rural arts centre, Burnlaw, drawing upon it as an artistic resource: 'Burnlaw provides me with the privilege of supporting and retaining my own sense of place—where I live and how I live' (Tim Rubidge, personal communication, 15 March 2017). Since 2006, Tim and I have undertaken several collaborations that have included improvisation in performance, walking practices, and movement research. For Tim, walking is analogous to improvisation, and he regularly walks in the landscape around Burnlaw as part of his daily practice, viewing the practice as a rich creative resource: he says that he finds that 'for me, my most interesting thoughts have come out of walking or dancing' (Tim Rubidge, personal communication, 12 June 2009). On moving and walking in the landscape, he reflects that he 'is not looking to find nor answer questions' (personal communication, 3 April 2009). Tim discusses his responsiveness to the land and his concern with being open to what emerges in the practices of walking and moving:

I am pretty sure that despite countless walks that have criss-crossed the land here-abouts, I have never placed a foot where I had placed a foot before. Meaning, it always feels new. Leaving me still curious—about what it is; what I notice, whether moving or standing still; what I see or hear; the smells, the feel, the rigour and the changing contours of the land. Allowing movement to emerge out of the walk and beyond the walk. Sometimes developing this, and sometimes not. Unpredictable like the weather—and this part of the world gets plenty of that—in from the east coast, or the more prevailing from the west, the Atlantic and the Irish Sea. (personal communication, March 15 2017)

Tim's responses are shaped by the weather as much as by the ground, and he also highlights the specificity of place, perception, and response. A wall of wind is a weather feature regularly encountered in the upland moors of Northumberland and can be so strong that it requires physical effort to work outside in it.

When discussing his work, Tim articulates the potential of the body as a locus of community and shared dialogue: 'I really was taken with the body, that one could be expressive, imaginative and bring people together' (personal communication, April 2009). Tim views the body as a 'connective tissue' that can be developed to bring ideas, people, and landscapes into relation. For Tim, the development of this connective tissue is embedded in processes of embodiment that emphasize sensing, instinct, and trust, where there is 'no construct that I am aware of that we are filtering things through' (personal communication, November 2009). The body is a resource to be listened to, trusted, and worked with in the development of work. Tim further explains: 'connective tissue is fibre that forms a framework and supportive structure for body tissues and organs. I am working with the body as a connective tissue between our inner world of ambition, reflection and imagination, and the outer world of our surroundings, the place where we find ourselves. A supportive structure that can listen and notice; that can receive, feel, hold, embrace, and respond. It is through the body that we meet the world, explore our place in it and grow our knowledge of it' (email communication, 9 November 2009). For Tim, participating ecologically means paying attention to how the individual body creates connective tissues, and more recently he has come to consider the land as a muscle (personal communication, 15 March 2017). He considers the qualities and resonances of the tissues made, whether they are human to human or human to nature. In one of our dances, Tim and I work on sharing weight. As we build trust, the sensation of support goes deeper through skin to soft tissue to bone level. The depths and contours of our bodies become a shifting geology of a dance in formation. The body navigates change in gradient, shape, and form moving within and without, inside and outside, in dialogue. The dialogue literally creates a connective tissue of muscle memories and physical patterns of support that we can return to and build on. This connective tissue is built not only from physical work but also from the multiple dimensions of emotion, trust, sensitivity, and rapport that constitute participation in a dialogue.

When discussing our collaborative performance process, Tim highlights how watching and moving together, as solos and separately, contribute to the development of trust, rapport, and honesty: 'when we first started working together physically, we were soloing and witnessing each other's solos and then we got to a stage where we went into contact. We had to do a lot of finding out and in that finding out there were sensitivities, there was a tentativeness as there is and can be in any situation of finding out. We were very supportive of each other's tentativeness and then in that support, what was grown in that support, was trust, confidence' (personal communication, 9 November 2009). As we worked together, Tim and I chose to improvise together and apart as the moment took us, both in the studio and outdoors on long walks through the landscape. We let both body and earth guide and support us, while also trying to be respectful of what we were yet to find out. We were interested to discover what kind of connective tissue we could form. During our process, we added sessions in order to allow for the completion of processes and cycles that we had initiated. The improvisational nature of our approach meant that some tasks took more time than anticipated if they were to be finished in ways that felt complete to us.

As a performer, who works through improvisation, my research process is usually concerned with the devising of a score for performance, a baseline from which to work, but not necessarily to follow, and from which to depart if the improvisation develops that way, but I generally formulate concepts as holding structures. Tim's approach is to develop a score that is based in rich experiential explorations, which creates a resource field from which to draw in the performance. In our walks, we negotiated our differences as performers, and we developed memories in muscles and minds of the contours and weather of the land, and of the conversations and journeys between us. With the shared experiences of walking and moving in the studio, I realized that we would not need to agree on a score for the performance and that we would approach it from our respective experiences, thoughts, and memories.

Tim and I discussed this moving between landscape and theatre-based performance in terms of improvisation. For Tim, the attention on how the body is inspired to move in the moment is connected to a 'truth and integrity of the body', and he is interested in the performer communicating that 'some humanity with arms and legs is making sense of itself having had landscape as some sort of early reference' (personal communication, 9 November 2009). This integrity and truth is a value I share; as such, to be able to enter into the dance as two unique beings coming to share a series of movements, to find moments of connection and rapport, meant that we agreed on very broad frames for the performance of time, sound score, and basic lighting. Tim describes how in the performance, to be truthful to his embodied experience is to be in attentive relationship to it. He wants to be true to the nature of the body and offer that as an appropriately sensitive response to the theatre space. He reflects: 'truth is connected with integrity and integrity is connected with nature. So, that's why I preferred our approach to remain in the realm of embodying because there isn't then any construct' (personal communication, 9 November 2009). What I experienced in working with Tim was that by making a series of shared memories, we created the body as a connective tissue between ourselves, ourselves and the landscapes, and then between ourselves and those we invited to see the work in the theatre. In the theatre, the connective tissues of memory in mind and muscle became resources through which we could reconnect as each moment unfolded.

The Improviser as Ecological Actor in the Work of Nala Walla

In 2009–2010, I undertook a series of collaborations with Nala Walla, an ecologically concerned dance artist based in Washington state in the United States. A ten-day visit to Nala's homestead enabled me to join her in her extended practice of improvisation that includes permaculture, activism, performance, and stewardship of the environment. The garden is the central feature of Nala's land. The buildings on the land organize around it, and there are gates in the deer fence in several places to allow access from the outdoor kitchen, the house, and the yurt. This garden is one of Nala's main improvisational scores, which she tends to with sensitivity and responsibility. The garden is organized on permaculture principles and, to me, seems abundant and rich. Every day we have harvested more than enough leaves for salad and berries for dessert. This abundance is underpinned by hard work, commitment, and devotion to developing an ecologically sensitive way of life.

Prior to settling on her land, Nala's journey took her in search of ways that exemplified ecologically sound living. She initially moved to Seattle to study freshwater ecology and dance at the University of Washington. Seeing dance and ecology as interwoven and connected through creative processes and living systems and wanting to explore these interdisciplinary connections in her work, Nala encountered resistance to her ideas within academia. She recalls: 'it was all too theoretical. I was testing water samples in a fluorescent lit laboratory and I was thinking that this was not really ecology' (personal communication, 9 July 2009). She left, feeling that it would be more fruitful to explore her questions on her own. Her subsequent journeys took her on a two-year boat trip to Alaska and to the eventual acquisition of her land.

Nala has striven to cultivate a self-sufficient, off-grid way of life informed by the integration of permaculture principles and dance improvisation, and she recognizes many parallels between the two practices: 'when I started hearing about permaculture it immediately rang true for me … it's the exact same language as improvisation. The exact same concepts, slightly different language—working with nature, going with the flow, respecting edges in an ecosystem as the place that has the most productivity and the most diversity' (personal communication, 5 July 2009). Nala believes that 'we can have a relationship with the environment where we are actually enhancing the environment, creating more abundance for everyone. That is one of the main principles in permaculture; that everything gardens' (personal communication, 9 July 2009). A key idea in permaculture is to apply understanding of natural ecosystems, particularly in terms of their sustainable and self-sufficient qualities, to the design of a garden. A forest, where all different kinds of plants grow together, for example, provides good inspiration to a permaculture practitioner. As found in many permaculture gardens, the beds in Nala's garden all contain several species of plants that might come to function as a miniecosystem in the bed—potatoes and other root vegetables in the ground, lettuces and strawberries at the ground level, kale and beans that grow to a midlevel, and small apple trees to a higher level. Permaculture practitioners respect the diversity of nature, so weed killers and pesticides are not used. In permaculture, the role of gardener is to use nature's design as a guide.

Gardening and the garden guide Nala's movement practices. It is through gardening that she weaves permaculture and improvisational dance practice. The cultivation of a garden enables her to work on a score that brings her into close relationship with the earth, in terms of sustenance and moving towards integrated systems of movement, body, and earth in one place. These integrated movement, body, and earth systems arise from practical need as much as artistic vision. Nala states that one of her goals is not to ever 'leave this spot, except for where I can walk' (personal communication, 9 July 2009). The off-grid way of life Nala and her partner are cultivating is a time-intensive, as well as physically intensive, way of life. Living without running water, for example, means that rainwater is collected and each day jugs for water needs are filled. Living without electricity means ensuring that there is enough firewood cut for the burner and that the woodshed is well stocked before the winter. Such tasks are physically strenuous and offer invitation for exploration in terms of movement practice.

Nala is mindful of her movement when she can be and takes opportunities to stretch, move, dance, and express through movement as and when she can, and feels inclined. The work on the homestead means that there is no time that can be specifically set aside for art practice, yoga, or meditation, and because Nala has no space to function as a studio, she uses the garden. Things happen as and when they need to, according to season, weather, health, and well-being. Nala is deliberately resistant to compartmentalizing her time. She reflects: 'most people who are living in a village would not have time to devote six, four, or two hours to separate a practice'; and she questions cosmetic applications of body-based practices for the purposes of aesthetics and beautification (personal communication, 5 July 2009). Nala integrates body awareness into her daily tasks and researches the somatic aspects of gardening, foraging, and the other physical tasks that are undertaken on her land. She is interested in how these tasks can be completed as a somatic practice, not only in ways that prevent injury but also in ways that allow for a healthy evolution of the body. The garden itself embodies the scale of a pedestrian body. The plant beds are designed on the African keyhole concept, which means that no place in the bed is beyond arm's reach. I am slicing brassica plants. It is interesting how the task becomes the focus of all of my energy and I forget about my posture. I reach into the plants without thinking about my movement. Nala offers feedback on how I am moving. We analyse, codify the stages of moving, and create repetitions. As each plant is unique, there are no exact repetitions, but Nala emphasizes the development of a robust rhythm and mindful alignment of breath, movement, and relationship to the plant. For Nala, body-based practices allow her to propose gardening as a somatic practice that nour-ishes both body and earth.

To participate in this way with the earth is to work with local resources with under-standing, sensitivity, intuition, care, and skilful means. Nala is interested in learning from indigenous practices that model local, sustainable, and in-place ways of living: 'so what would it be like, to be a native person, to be an indigenous person, within this land-scape.... What would that look like, if I were to be native? There are cultures all around the world that have a small little cabin, that collect their rainwater off the roof. I'm trying to create a little model of what that might look like—to be a neo-indigenous person. My footprint is small and I'm developing those techniques' (personal communication, 9 July 2009). Over the years, her commitment to engage in what she describes as a process of *re-indigenization,* to access the wildness within and to cultivate more self-reliant and first person relationships with land, has become a core principle of her approach: 'our ability to respond creatively and decisively to rising sea levels, to civil wars, to nuclear meltdowns, is directly dependent upon our ability to recognize this inner Wildness and tap into its rich wisdom. The patient seeds of our indigeneity are lying somewhere within our bodies, waiting for us to simply step outside our double-insulated, climate-controlled routines, into the nourishing rain and soil so our seeds can sprout once again' (Walla 2013, para. 1). Nala believes that improvisational practices enable the develop-ment of creative skills that are needed to navigate processes of re-indigenization. She believes that the healing potential of improvisational practice lies in the co-created structures of dancing together and participating in open-ended processes of moving that, like natural processes, allow for growth, death, and decay. It is through the sharing of such processes that, Nala believes, a healthy functioning of communities can be developed wherein creative practices enable 'the conversion of the stresses of life into growth' (2008: 31). As a forum of storytelling, Nala describes how improvisation can also develop 'bonds, which hold the group together in times of stress' (31) and com-munal practices of storytelling, art-making, and ceremony are important to individual, communal, and ecological health. That ecological practice should have a robust social aspect is important to Nala. Her idea that 'everything gardens' is envisaged throughout her relationships with the world, the garden, her home, and people.

CHOREOGRAPHY AS CIVIC GESTURE

Nala and Tim are creating spaces of action in which alternatives can be envisaged. Might the work of these two artists be thought of as (improvised) choreographies of civic gesture? When considering their work as civic gesture, one can read and interact with their practices as contributions to public discourse. These two artists' choice to position their work as performative situates them in a public role and invites reflec-tion upon their work as propositions to the development of civic and social organiza-tion. In articulating their practice as performance, both of these artists create gestures that matter to themselves, to the earth, to the public, and any others they deem to be participating as audiences, which might include microorganisms, plants, animals, and people. While improvised and unfolding, the accumulation of gestures contributes to a choreographic design that is concerned with ecological health in a context of environmental change, crisis, and challenge.

Civic gestures point towards the future and the evolution of civic society. Nala's invitation to *reindigenize* practice calls for a critical reflection on how the earth is approached through gardening, dancing, and farming. Gestures that propose alternative ways of conceptualizing life, performance, art, and social organization offer trajectories that afford the potential for the development of social and ecological justice. Much of the work of Nala and Tim is concerned with the cultivation of their own microrelations of participation as embedded in their lived locales. These microrelations manifest as mindful actions in the detailed cultivation of the earth as score, where the artists are concerned with the relational dimensions of their actions in terms of sustainability. There is a daily-ness in the quality of the artists' actions that defines a person-sensitive, place-sensitive, and time-sensitive ethical orientation. This notion of finding out along the way while holding particular intentions in mind, however these intentions might evolve and change, suggest an approach to ecological activism that is responsive, open-ended, and inclusive.

Being Present: Dancing in the Moment as Ecological Practice

A loss of focus when navigating a steep slope on a Lake District mountain is dangerous. The terrain and weather conditions channel focus and problem-solving skills into a moment-to-moment navigation of each step down the mountain. It is an apt metaphor for the collective focus that might be needed to deal with environmental change at local and global levels. Working improvisationally enables artists, such as Nala and Tim, to synchronize with the fluid and evolutionary qualities of nature, where certain rhythms, such as the seasons, give structure, but where what is working today might not work tomorrow. Tim's approach to *building connective tissues* assumes a synchrony with the patterns of nature, in the body and in the environment. If, as Nala asserts, 'everything gardens', then cultivation, growth, building, harvesting, and tending are the indicative actions for the person who takes the garden as a score. As the earth as score is continually cultivated by the artists, they yield uniquely earth-sensitive approaches to working with the body, with the earth, and with the community. The earth as score opens the dialogue through which relationships form, and it is these relationships of body, earth, and community that might suggest that an integration of mindfulness, ecological thinking, and improvisational practice could enable dancing in the moment to cultivate an ecological practice.

Aligning with nature, improvising within and without, creates space for the release and opening of in-the-moment perceptions to self and surroundings as well as for past experiences that might be brought into awareness. What is revealed in your perceptions in practice may be ruptures, dislocations, and dis-ease as well as well-being, joy, and harmony. Elizabeth Grosz writes that 'art is the most direct intensification of the resonance, and dissonance, between bodies and the cosmos, between one milieu or rhythm and another' (2008: 24). While it may be an ecological imperative to align our beings, to cooperate with one another and with the earth and to cultivate interconnected relations, paying attention to mind through improvisation reveals resonances and dissonances. There is not an end point to this improvisation. Alignment is momentary, but the search for it places a practitioner on an ethical path where one can do the best with what one knows. This is the ethical dimension of improvisation, where one responds to the present moment in the best ways one can.

The alternative ways of life to the consumerist mainstream that Nala and Tim propose participate in a larger transdisciplinary discourse of ecological concern and environmental activism in which there is an ongoing search for sustainable ways of living. As these sustainable ways of living are sought, the work of Nala and Tim illustrates how dance and movement practices have much to contribute to larger cultural, institutional, and political transitions of society. Not only do they offer models of sustainable ways of life but also they offer tools for individuals to manage change and navigate the complexity of an earth in transition. Such tools include the physical partnering exercises, games, and communal movement practices that build trust, understanding, and rapport among participants. Moreover, art practices offer opportunities for expression of individual and group experiences in forms that can be received and made sense of by others and thus contribute to the evolution of individual, communal, and social understandings. The expressive dimension of moving with the earth can be acknowledged and integrated into the cultivation of the earth as a score and in the development of new choreographies.

In such a context, the artists might be understood as mediators of emergence through sensitive working, with sustainable ecological perspectives, as best as they know them in any particular moment, and, through working with others, activating a coming-to-terms with self-organizing dynamics in the nature of participation. The honouring of first person perception, intuition, and in-the-moment response also seems to me to be a valuable contribution of each of the artists to the cultivation of an ethical and ecological point of view. By giving time to fully perceiving the present and attending to feeling states, phenomena, and qualities that arise as knowledge emerges, the artists endeavour to encounter their emergent selves as *becoming* more ecological and sustainable. Such an approach enables the ideals of philosophical and ethical paradigms to be lived through and adapted to the conditions of the unfolding and emergent life.

Ideas about ecology, improvisation, sustainability, health, and well-being will evolve and change. In each moment a moving dialogue unfolds with gravity and air, ground and sky; and within that dialogue there are potentials for changes, transformations, and transitions to new ways of knowing. Our potential to know this dialogue shifts and changes, but we can attend to it and cultivate a mindfulness that might contribute to movements with the earth that sustain. How might we support one another and the earth through these continual processes of change and adaptation? Artists can offer ways of knowing in which inspiration might be found, but if the nature of improvisation as ecological practice articulated in this chapter is to be taken up, each individual must find out for herself or himself along the way. The work is to practise, to become present, to align, transform, and begin, again and again.

References

Abram, D. (1996) *The Spell of the Sensuous*. New York: Random House.

Abram, D. (2003) Earth in Eclipse. Alliance for Wild Ethics. http://www.wildethics.org/essays/earth_in_eclipse.html. Accessed April 2011.

Abram, D. (2010) *Becoming Animal*. New York: Pantheon.

Albright, Ann Cooper. (1997) *Choreographing Difference: The Body and Identity in Contemporary Dance*. Middletown, CT: Wesleyan University Press.

Anon. (2006) Teacher's Wisdom: Nancy Stark Smith. *Dance Magazine*. http://findarticles.com/p/articles/mi_m1083/is_6_80/ai_n16484487.

Ashley, T., and Kenyon, S. (2007) *The Pennine Way: The Legs That Made Us*. Newcastle Upon Tyne, UK: Brief Magnetics.

Auslander, P. (2003) *Performance: Critical Concepts in Literary and Cultural Studies*. London: Routledge.

Bateson, G. (1972) *Steps towards an Ecology of Mind*. Chicago: University of Chicago Press.

Berry, T. (1991) *The Ecozoic Era*. UK: E. F. Schumacher Society.

Braidotti, R. (2006) *Transpositions*. Great Barrington, MA: Polity Press.

Braidotti, R. (2013) *The Posthuman*. Cambridge, UK: Polity Press.

Burrows, J. (2010) *A Choreographer's Handbook*. Cambridge, UK: Routledge.

Capra, F., and Luisi, P. (2014) *The Systems View of Life: A Unifying Vision*. Cambridge: Cambridge University Press.

Clarke, A. (2005) *Situational Analysis*. London: Sage.

Conrad, E. (2007) *Life on Land*. Berkeley, CA: North Atlantic Books.

Creswell, J. W. (1998) *Qualitative Inquiry and Research Design*. Thousand Oaks, CA: Sage.

Feuerstein, G (1998) *Tantra: The Path of Ecstasy*. London: Shambhala Publications.

Foster, S. L. (2002) Danced Interventions. *SubStance* 31(2 and 3): 125–146.

Grosz, E. (2008) *Chaos, Territory, Art*. Chichester, UK: University of California Press.

Halprin, A. (1995) *Moving towards Life: Five Decades of Transformational Dance*. Ed. Rachel Kaplan. Middletown, CT: Wesleyan University Press.

Hanlon, Johnson, D. (1980) Somatic Platonism. *Somatics* (Autumn): 4–7.

Hanlon, Johnson, D. (1995) *Bone, Breath and Gesture*. Berkley, CA: North Atlantic Books.

Hanna, T. (1993) *The Body of Life*. Rochester, VT: Healing Arts Press.

Harding, S. (2006) *Animate Earth: Science, Intuition and Gaia*. Dartington, UK: Green Books.

Hiles, D. (2001) Heuristic Inquiry and Transpersonal Research. Psychology department De Montfort University. http://www.psy.dmu.ac.uk/drhiles/HIpaper.htm.

Hillyer, C. (2010) *Sacred House: Where Women Weave Words into the Earth*. Dartmoor, UK: Seventh Wave Books.

Jensen, D. (2004) *Listening to the Land: Conversations about Nature, Culture and Eros*. White River Junction, VT: Chelsea Green.

Johnson, D. (1995) *Bone, Breath and Gesture*. Berkeley, CA: North Atlantic Books.

Keogh, M. (2008) 101 Ways to Say No to Contact Improvisation. Martin Keogh. http://www.martinkeogh.com/resources/101WaystoSayNotoContactImprovisation.html.

Kim, J. (2006) Min Tanaka's Butoh. Trans. Kazue Kobata. *Theme*, iss. 7 (Fall). http://www.thememagazine.com/stories/min-tanaka/.

Klein, A. (1998) Grounding and Opening. In Friedman, L., and Moon, S. (eds.), *Being Bodies: Buddhist Women on the Paradox of Embodiment*. Boston: Shambhala, 139–147.

Kumar, S. (2009) *Earth Pilgrim*. Dartington, UK: Green Books.

Kwon, M. (2002) *One Place after Another: Site Specific Art and Locational Identity*. Cambridge, MA: MIT Press.

Lawrence-Lightfoot, S., and Hoffman Davis, S. (1997) *The Art and Science of Portraiture*. San Francisco: Jossey Bass.

Lovelock, J. (1979) *Gaia: A New Look at Earth*. Oxford: Oxford University Press.

Massumi, B. (2002) *Parables for the Virtual*. Durham, NC: Duke University Press.

Moustakas, C. (1990) *Heuristic Research: Design, Methodology and Applications*. London: Sage.

Moustakas, C. (1994) *Phenomenological Research Methods*. London: Sage.

Novack, C. (1990) *Sharing the Dance: Contact Improvisation and American Culture*. Madison: University of Wisconsin Press.

Olsen, A. (2002) *Body and Earth*. Middlebury, VT: Middlebury Press.

Plumwood, V. (2002) *Environmental Culture: The Ecological Crisis of Reason*. New York: Routledge.

Quincey, T. (2006) Swarm Bodies. www.BodyWeather.net/press/swarmbodies.pdf.

Reeve, S. (2011) *Nine Ways of Seeing a Body*. Bridport, UK: Triarchy Press.

Schaffman, K. (2001) *Contact Improvisation and the Commodification of Touch*. PhD. University of California, Riverside.

Soper, K., and Thomas, L. (2006) *Cultures of Consumption*. Institute for the Study of European Transformations, London Metropolitan University. (Working paper)

Steinman, L. (1995) *The Knowing Body: The Artist as Storyteller in Contemporary Performance*. Berkley: Atlantic Books.

Tufnell, M., and Crickmay, C. (2004) *A Widening Field*. London: Dance Books.

Walla, N. (2008) The Embodied Activist. *Contact Quarterly* 33(2) (Summer/Fall): 28–32.

Walla, N. (2013) The Farmer and the Witch: Reclaiming the Seeds of Indigeneity. http://bcollective.org/ESSAYS/farmer&witch.wp.may2013.pdf. Accessed 18 March 2017.

CHAPTER 34

....

DANCING THE LAND

An Emerging Geopoetics

....

MELINDA BUCKWALTER

WHAT makes a mountain sacred? How do spirits come to dwell in rock or forest? Which rituals are performed to bring rain? Traditional cultures formalized relationship to the land. In this essay, I consider the work of contemporary dance-makers Jennifer Monson, Eiko Otake, and Suprapto Suryodarmo, who use experiential approaches, including improvised movement, to investigate the environment—whether urban or rural, from courtyards to local parks. I argue that in so doing, these dance-makers create a contemporary geopoetics, propositions of relationship between the human body and a changing twenty-first-century landscape.

Regarding *geopoetics*, I borrow the term from the field of dance anthropology, for instance as used by Andrée Grau (2010) in her inaugural address on the Tiwi of Australia at the University of Roehampton. By *geo-*, I mean relating to the earth, and by *poetics*, an active artistic practice of knowing through making in one's chosen medium, such as performance studies theorist Ric Allsopp (2014) proposes in his lecture 'Performing Poetics'. By dancing the *land*, I mean to include rural, suburban, and urban areas and their built environments, also referred to as sites.

How do I, a person of the industrialized world who regularly passes over the land encased in steel, buffered by concrete, and cocooned in artificial light, develop a sense of physical place? Features of landscape are homogenized in shopping malls and connecting highways where it is always noontime. I travel the world almost instantaneously through search engines and social media, further affecting my sense of space and time. From this experience, a dichotomy of natural versus humanmade often arises. I position myself outside my environment. Through their work on site, these dance-makers disrupt this binary and suggest instead a continuum. By including human doings in their geopoetics, they help us to refind relationship within, offering a sense of integration with or embeddedness in the environment.

REFRAMED

In 2009, at an immersive workshop with Jennifer Monson, I had an experience which made me realize that her investigations weren't simply compositional in the strictest sense. This workshop introduced a practice new to me that travelled beyond my understanding of dance-making: the reframing of the activity of dancing to include a more broadly conceived sense of my body through interconnectivity with the environment.

Jennifer Monson, a New York City–based dance-maker originally from California, has helped define the field of dance as it relates to environmental concerns. Currently a professor of dance at the University of Illinois Urbana-Champaign by an initiative of the Environmental Council, she began work in the field of dance and the environment with BIRDBRAIN (2000), a durational dance project that followed the migration paths of various animals. She later expanded her work into urban migration and watershed studies. She says: 'these projects have radically reframed the role dance plays in our cultural understandings of nature and wilderness. By bringing the work into outdoor settings and creating a framework for viewing the work through workshops, panel discussions, and community involvement, I have found ways to re-engage the general public in a heightened physical and sensory experience of the phenomena and systems that surround us' (Jennifer Monson: Professor 2014). In 2004, Monson formed iLAND (Interdisciplinary Laboratory for Art, Nature, and Dance), which, through artist residencies and conferences, 'investigates the power of dance in collaboration with other fields to illuminate our kinetic understanding of the world' (Jennifer Monson: Professor 2014). In its residencies, iLAND fosters a community of collaborators who integrate movement exploration in the study of environmental issues.

Initially, I had regarded Monson's work as a comparative study. In my book *Composing While Dancing: An Improviser's Companion*, I discuss her work—along with that of twenty-six contemporary artists who work with improvised materials—in relation to how migratory species might 'choreograph' their travels. For example, Monson investigates how arrivals and departures from moving flocks and herds are analogous to a dancer's experience of entering and exiting a moving ensemble. Her migration studies inform improvising dancers, suggesting innovation in practice as well as the honing of ensemble awareness. Her approach also encourages interspecies empathy, a quality helpful in the development of ecological awareness.

My shift in understanding came about at the workshop Along the Watershed at SEEDS: Somatic Experiments in Earth, Dance + Science, an arts and ecology festival, which was held at Earthdance, an artist-run dance retreat centre based in rural western Massachusetts, and was copresented by Monson and Wales-based interdisciplinary movement artist Simon Whitehead (Monson and Whitehead 2009). A trained geographer and dancer, Whitehead's artistic practice focuses on the pedestrian; his works are made and often experienced at a walking pace. For example, his long-term performance practice *Locator* is 'an active exploration of ecology and perceptual being through a process of walking and wandering, witnessing, gathering, moving in site, rising and falling with the sun, getting lost, drawing, fasting, and making' in the Preseli hills, Wales (Whitehead 2006). Along the Watershed was part of a longer collaborative exchange between Monson and Whitehead which had begun earlier that June in New York City when the two artists hiked the East River watershed and littoral (Whitehead 2009). We workshoppers entered in the midst of this collaborative process—not only of two experts in the field but also of two very different landscapes. As Whitehead observed, 'the workshop engaged with studio practice and fieldwork, which was pursued in the vastness of the mature forest and valleys nearby. It was interesting to apply strategies that had been developed in a completely different landscape' (2009). Our activities confounded my notion of dance-making and awakened a physical sense of environment.

During the week, we took a daylong hike in the wooded mountains guided by nothing more than the water flowing downhill and the angle of filtered light (see fig. 34.1a). This hike pushed the edges of both my endurance and tolerance. We were constantly tracking and losing track. Due to an ice storm the previous winter, the woods were strewn with

FIG. 34.1A Clambering along the watershed; participant Cynthia Stevens and workshop coleader Simon Whitehead, Earthdance, Plainfield, Massachusetts, June 2009. Photograph by Melinda Buckwalter.

downed trees, adding an element of obstacle course. On the way up, we broke for an Authentic Movement session in the middle of the woods. A familiar go-to score in my local dance community, Authentic Movement, created by dance therapists Mary Starks Whitehouse and her student Janet Adler, is usually practised in the studio in pairs, a mover and a witness. The movers close their eyes and follow inner impulses for movement. Witnesses watch and afterward may offer nonjudgemental feedback. In our case, the witnesses also played a more active role in keeping the movers safe in the bumpy and pokey environment.

We continued for most of the day but never quite made it to our destination, a lake called Plainfield Pond, the source waters of the stream we followed. (We did discover a road, a waterfall, and an idyllic pasture of grazing horses and a mule.) The light turned low as we began to pick our way back through the forest, tired and struggling to find our way. Then, a dawning of recognition—that tree with the odd crook looks familiar; I had been here before, danced by it, during our Authentic Movement break on the way out. Though comforted, the feeling of found, I discovered, is relative. Where is *here* in the middle of the woods? Pushing against my limits, my sense of body attenuated, reaching for the vaguest of handholds: incidental memories that proved to be trail markers for the return trip (see fig. 34.1b).

Later that week, after a day's fast during a pitch-black night hike, my blood sugar was so low that my legs didn't feel attached to my body. I knew which direction to head, but I couldn't see to avoid the black-on-black outcroppings and drop-offs or the

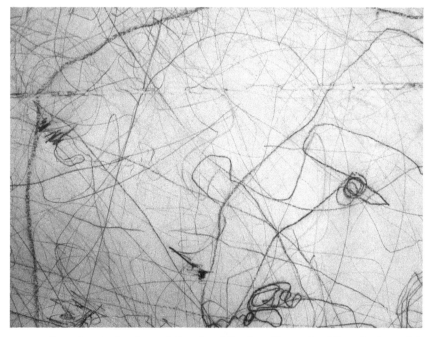

FIG. 34.1B Eyes-closed drawing of the day hike by Along the Watershed participants, Earthdance, Plainfield, Massachusetts, 2009. Photograph by Melinda Buckwalter.

fallen-tree jungle gym that blocked the path. The vegetation persisted, giving body to the darkness. And then, a perceptual aurora borealis—I experienced the flickering, ghostly transition to night vision, which Monson and Whitehead had discussed with us before the walk. Pushed beyond my familiar range and feeling desperate, I birthed a latent faculty.

Though intrigued by my experiences, I was flummoxed on day 5 when we were asked to make and show dances in the woods. What did our outings have to do with making dances? Beside some scores for movement exploration, we hadn't practised the arranging or composing of material; it seemed to me that we had simply hiked.

Then, Olive Bieringa, friend and cocurator of SEEDS, suggested: 'you've been making a body'. I had never before thought to consider what body I was improvising with. Previously, my studies in dance had centred on the practice of improvisation: which investigation, methodology, or pedagogy will I follow? But of course! The process I choose affects my bodily understanding of myself. Now, with this reframing, I let go of the need to make and track my process. Rather, I focused on the enjoyment of wielding my newly expanded phenomenological body in a dance (Buckwalter 2010b: 5).

For my performance, I chose a downed tree. I took off my glasses and mobile, hung them in its branches, and then dance-climbed through it, eyes closed. To create an attenuated sense of space that was so much part of my experience, I called my spectator-participants to me through the woods—find me! Thus embedded in the forest, I danced the land. Or had the land danced me?

The Lay of the Land

Just as I birthed latent capacities throughout this workshop, I believe that Monson, Whitehead, and other dance-makers who choose to work in outdoor spaces are sprouting novel methods that expand our notion of our bodies and increase connectivity with the environment. In this essay, I track a single problematic, the horizon line, and the response to it through improvised movement studies by three artists—Jennifer Monson, Eiko Otake (Eiko), and Suprapto Suryodarmo (Prapto). I consider in what ways these artists' dance practices promote a sense of embeddedness in the environment—as I see it, an emerging contemporary geopoetics.

Information from the disciplines of neuroscience, dance anthropology, and performance studies illuminate my discussion. For example, neuroscience offers clues to connections that arise between body and place. In their book *The Body Has a Mind of Its Own: How Body Maps in Your Brain Help You Do (Almost) Everything Better,* authors Sandra and Matthew Blakeslee (2007) explain investigations into nervous system plasticity, one of which concerns how humans map peripersonal space. Peripersonal space is similar to the idea of kinaesphere in dance terminology, the sphere of reach of our limbs. Peripersonal space is mapped in the brain in great detail and expands to include the tools we wield. For example, the driver's peripersonal space expands to include the car, which explains how an experienced driver can quite accurately judge a tight parking space. (Blakeslee 2007: chap. 7). In the instance of Along the Watershed, my peripersonal space was remapped in interaction with the environment to include not only physical limbs but also navigational limbs of sight and memory.

Anthropological enquiry helps us make sense of and expand notions and possibilities of body and place relationship. For instance, Andrée Grau (2005: 204) speaks of *emplacement* when describing the relationship of the Tiwi people to their ancestral land. The Tiwi dance their kinship relations, which are mapped to body parts. They remember both contemporary and ancestral relations in this way. By facing ancestral lands and calling out relatives or places from memory and dreams, a complex web of correlates develops that allows a kinaesthetic working out of relationship on the dance floor (191–192, 196, 204). Grau insists that the Tiwi relationship is more than metaphorical: 'this is why the Tiwi can say they *are* the land' (205). Grau uses the term *geopoetics* to describe this interwoven relationship of body and land (Grau 2010).

Poetics, a knowing through making in an artistic media such as dance, is also helpful in understanding environmental embeddedness. Allsopp, cofounder and joint editor of *Performance Research* and head of dance studies at Falmouth University (formerly Dartington College) in England, Ric explains in his lecture 'Performing Poetics': 'poetics privilege the openness and indeterminacies of enactment.... Dance tends to enact something rather than explain it; choreography is a means of finding ways to transmit the forms of such enactments' (2014). Through this process of knowing through making, dancers *bring into being*. For example, we create interconnectivity with the environment through the act of moving in it, and sometimes 'invent worlds to come' (Gore in Grau 2016: 248).

Finally, from the vantage of performance studies, consider the ramifications of site as stage space. A prominent feature of postmodern theatre and dance is the breaking of the fourth wall, often referred to as the 'distancing effect'. In the moment when the wall is broken, the audience, released from the theatrical spell, begins to critically question the action. A felt sense of distance emerges. However, in a site-specific work, the fourth wall is much more porous than the proscenium. Often the audience has experience of the site through prior engagement or through participatory elements like walking through or around the space at performance time. Instead of a distancing effect, we experience, rather, a familiarity effect. The audience is *drawn into* the dance space. This reverse effect, which often occurs in site dance, is quite useful for creating a shift of attention to the environment.

With these tools of peripersonal space, emplacement, enactment, and familiarity in mind, consider the horizon studies of Monson, Eiko, and Prapto. What geopoetics emerge from these dance-makers' practices? How are ties to the environment revealed, and to what affect?

JENNIFER MONSON: SYSTEMS/SCORES,
PRACTICE/PROCESS

In the summer of 2014, I again had the opportunity to work with Jennifer Monson, this time in an urban environment. As part of the MELT series produced by Movement Research, Monson offered a workshop called Systems/Scores: Practice/Process, at St. Marks Church in-the-Bowery, New York City (Monson 2014). The horizon line had become a prominent feature for Monson and her collaborators during research for her dance *Live Dancing Archive* (2013) (see fig 34.2b), which included watching many hours of video footage from her migration project BIRDBRAIN's Osprey Tour (2002) along the migration path of the osprey, from Maine to Florida, Cuba, and Venezuela. The collaborators designed a reflective white strip for the set, which shaped the performance space (Monson 2015). After moving from New York City to the Midwest, Monson continued her work with the horizon line in In Tow residencies in Urbana, Illinois (see fig. 34.2a). It was scores developed from these residencies that Monson adapted for the MELT workshop (Monson 2015).

Our first task was to draw a favourite horizon with charcoal on paper, eyes closed. We worked in duos. One partner watched while the other drew. A lot of variation resulted from these simple instructions. For example, some chose to draw a section of horizon typical of a landscape painting, while others included a panoramic 360 degrees.

FIG. 34.2A Jennifer Monson and the horizon line set piece from Monson's *Live Dancing Archive*, performed at the American Realness Festival, New York City, January 2013. Photograph by Ian Douglas.

FIG. 34.2B Jennifer Monson, eyes closed, drawing the horizon line of a familiar place, joined by Rose Kaczmarowski (background), during an In Tow residency, Urbana, Illinois, 2014. Photograph by Valerie Oliveiro.

The horizon line was also represented by varying amounts of texture available in the charcoal medium. We noted this differentiation in our duo as well as from a quick look around the room. The initial task of drawing the horizon, which I had conceptualized as a line, exploded on my page and on the many pages of participants. Chatter filled the air; immediately there were narratives behind these images. Which horizon did you draw? What is that little dip, feathered plume, or darkened swirl? In this first exercise, we began the process of decoding a remembered environment into embodied components, deconstructing our emplacement.

Next, we drew our horizons in the air, eyes closed, in a defined space, either between the columns of the church or on the wall. Our partners observed and then played back what they remembered of the tracing. This correlation of visual image and movement in space was a first invitation to physically enter the landscape. Having chosen my child-hood horizon, I quickly noticed emotional components—darker memories from that clump of trees on the western side due to a conflict with a neighbour, or magical times spent playing in a gully in the northeast. These memories affected my line, which developed in texture and depth.

Then, we were invited to move our horizon in space, with our partners tracing and playing back our movements. Another exponential leap in embodied detail emerged in our horizon studies; places were reentered through memory and were felt physically, and narratives were enacted. Whatever movement vocabularies or embodiment techniques a person knew were brought to bear on the task. I saw my partner's horizon translated through a lens of—was that Doris Humphrey–based modern dance technique with its dramatic breath and sweep? She received my Release Technique–enhanced vision. Around the room—contact improvisation and Cunningham, expressionism and postmodernism—a thick forest of stylistic influence threatened to cloud our horizons. Or was that the point? The landscape of our bodily trainings became visible in relief. As we dug deeper into our associations, our horizons revealed physical particularities through enactment.

Our last instruction was to consider our own interests arising from our study so far, and to come up with a score—a set of instructions to apply to the horizon dance—to pass on to another duo. My duo exchanged scores with a nearby Contact Improvisation couple who spoke their landscapes aloud as they danced. We offered them our hybridized score, a mash-up of our interests—move in relation to your remembered horizon while simultaneously finding resonance with your partner. Receiving an outside duo's score brought with it a healthy influx of new perspective to our dancing. For us, the invitation to touch offered its own anatomical landscape, while verbalizing afforded a broadband channel for reporting memory. These hybrid scores were the final layer of paint in our horizon study for the day.

Leaving that evening, I felt like I had received a gift. I was closely tied to my family's farmland, but we had relocated for employment when I was a teen. These movement studies gave body and personality to my childhood horizon with its solitary round mountain. I felt I had renewed an acquaintance with an out-of-touch friend. By bringing the horizon into movement, I had thrown my body along the skyline, creating a panoramic homunculus of sensory and motor memories. Here I wasn't working on embedding myself in the landscape as much as I was discovering the degree to which I was already emplaced. This recognition speaks to Monson's geopoetic: though these sensory connections to our environments are often subconscious, they are present whatever the environment—urban or wild.

It was in dancing with my partner, tracing her horizon as she moved, and then playing it back to her that I did something akin to breaking the fourth wall. At first an interloper in a private reverie, I entered my partner's remembered landscape tentatively, not sure what I could possibly decipher. However, as we repeated the score, small details returned. If nothing else, I could count on that swirl to show up—whether it was a sway in her hips or spiral in her shoulders and arms. A terrain emerged. Yes, she later reported, there is water up there. Each repetition was an outing that revealed a detail of place in her landscape. These short forays into her territory felt like reconnaissance missions— I was cartographer, ethnographer. No surprise, ultimately, that a roomful of dancers could translate a horizon into movement and find detail. Tracking and paying attention to this kind of detail in movement is, after all, what we are trained to do. In this exercise, the poetics of enactment are in play. I received information of another's environment through the medium of movement rather than the culturally familiar media of speech and vision.

We started the next day with a reprise, a microdance of our horizon line. Monson asked us to dance our horizon physically on top of our original drawing, an eleven-by-seventeen-inch rectangle. At first, it hardly seemed possible to fit the dance back onto the page after exploding the line through the exercises of the day before. However, this condensing also proved quite potent. We returned to it later in an exercise outdoors.

Before our afternoon on the city streets identifying biological systems at work in an urban landscape and building scores to investigate them, we revisited the horizon work for a warm-up, which took place in the courtyard of the church, a liminal zone, outside, yet sheltered from the hustle and bustle of the street. Now Monson asked us to choose a portion of the horizon around us—the church roof, leafy August trees, the brownstone skyline across Tenth Street—and translate it through directed touch along the bones of a partner's arm. As a trained body worker, I was initially put off by the idea of what I perceived to be random information pressed into my bones. So I was happily surprised to find that my body was highly interested by this touch. I had no idea what portion of the view my partner was transcribing . However, the abrupt textural changes, as well as the flavour of the details themselves, made me pay close attention. It was a combination that proved to be very relaxing—to be pressed and impressed, digitized and engraved, to have the horizon injected into my bones. Reversing the previous day's flinging out of the body across the sky, these compression exercises plugged the horizon data back into my tissues, perhaps for future retrieval. In the process, peripersonal space was playfully exploded and contracted. The amplification of sensory detail through expanding and condensing is one of the techniques Monson employs to engage participants in a heightened physical and sensory experience of the surrounding environment.

Monson is influenced by study with Joan Skinner, creator of Skinner Releasing Technique, a dance and movement training she developed in the 1960s and 1970s. With an institute now based in Seattle, Skinner Releasing Technique uses poetic imagery to activate underlying movement patterns, which effect change in inefficient habitual movement. Besides imagery-invoked improvised movement exploration, in Skinner Releasing Technique 'tactile exercises are used to give the imagery immediate kinaesthetic effect' (Welcome to Skinner Releasing 2009). This hands-on component helps focus the image work in the physical body rather than remaining untethered in the blogosphere of mind.

Monson has a feel for this process. In this exercise, the horizon line acts like the poetic image of Skinner's work. Once activated, the image, perhaps a bit like a homeopathic remedy, has an arc of potency, which continues to manifest through movement and unfold through time as it works its way through the body. There are dormant periods in which the image inhabits the tissues (e.g., the drawing and pressing exercises) and active periods where the image is mobilized (e.g., our horizon dance scores). Through the work, a degree of emplacement in the landscape is revealed. In bringing this inscription to consciousness, subaltern sensory experiences are supported and then released back to the subconscious, newly enlivened. Skinner Releasing Technique and other movement education approaches, such as Bonnie Bainbridge Cohen's Body-Mind Centering® and Moshe Feldenkrais's Feldenkrais Method, suggest that the senses thus enlivened inform kinaesthetic pathways, offering new options for movement. For participants, Monson's work excavates how, despite a lack of formal ritual, we are already embedded in the land. She shows us that the work is to awaken—rather than create—connection.

Her geopoetics is a key shift from that of human beings dwelling in humanmade spaces separate from the natural world to one of reciprocal relationship in continuum.

Eiko Mountain

With the understanding that landscapes are encoded in our bodies through interactions with the land, what happens when our environment is radically altered in our lifetime? Dance-maker Eiko Otake and historian William Johnston examine, through lecture, discussion, and movement practice, the extreme altering of the horizon due to the strip mining technique mountain top removal (MTR).

Eiko Otake, who has worked for four decades as the duo Eiko & Koma, began coteaching a course in 2006 called 'Japan and the Atomic Bomb' with Johnston at Wesleyan University in Middletown, Connecticut. For spring semester 2013, Johnston asked Eiko if she would join him in teaching 'Perspectives on Mountain Top Removal Mining', regarding the coal-mining technique, an extreme form of strip mining. Eiko accepted the challenge and adapted elements of Eiko & Koma's Delicious Movement Workshop, usually taught in community settings, for the purpose. Though I didn't participate in the class, having previously studied with Eiko & Koma, I was eager to find out how Eiko adapted the Delicious Movement Workshop scores for this environmental concern. Fortunately, Eiko and Johnston wrote about their collaborative teaching process in 'Experiment and Experience: An Historian and a Dancer Co-teach Courses on The Atomic Bomb and Mountaintop Removal' (Otake and Johnston 2014, 2016). Elements of the class were also documented on video (Johnston and Otake 2013).

Eiko, originally from Japan, met life and dance partner Koma as members of the company led by Tatsumi Hijikata, the erotic-grotesque surrealist pioneer of the dance/theatre form butoh. Eiko and Koma also studied with Kazuo Ohno, the famous butoh dancer and collaborator with Hijikata. Eiko and Koma quickly developed an experimental partnership and left Japan to study nonverbal theatre with modern dance expressionists in Europe (Manja Chmiel of Mary Wigman's School in Germany and Lucas Hoving of the José Limon Company in the Netherlands). They gave their first U.S. performances in 1976 and have since become permanent residents, regularly performing internationally (Otake 2015; Buckwalter 2010).

Site-specific dances with simple titles that evoke the place of performance are integral to Eiko & Koma's repertoire. For example, *River* (1995), originally created in Schoharie Creek, a river in New York state, is based on a simple score in which Eiko and Koma literally float down the Schoharie Creek river, pausing to dance, before floating out of view. The piece has since been performed in many rivers, as well as lakes and ponds, and as *Water* (2011), it was performed in the reflecting pools at Hearst Plaza in Los Angeles and Lincoln Center in New York City (Otake 2015). They choreograph works by reflecting on a place and developing themes of interest. Their choreography leaves room for spontaneous decision-making. In teaching Delicious Movement Workshops, Eiko encourages students to improvise by offering prompts that range from 'conceptual to tangible, such as delicious, hungry, dream, yawn, bloom, and wilt' (Otake 2015). At first, it seems hard to imagine the theme of MTR as delicious.

In the 1990s, Johnston began following the MTR process, which leaves whole mountain ecologies destroyed in its wake. The process of MTR is what it sounds like—a literal removal of the top portion of the mountain. First, the mountaintop is dynamited; it is then bulldozed to expose coal, which is shipped to market. The remaining debris is indiscriminately pushed into the surrounding valley, filling up existing watersheds and finally is covered with grass (Otake and Johnston 2016: 22). As a faculty fellow at Wesleyan's College of the Environment, Johnston was given the opportunity to teach a new class. Though neither he nor Eiko had tackled an environmental studies issue before, the topic had resonances with the destructiveness of the atomic bomb. They relied on the strength of the collaborative teaching process they had developed in their atomic bomb course, in which they used a weaving of experiential techniques, including meditation (Johnston is a practising Buddhist) and Delicious Movement, as well as traditional discussion of readings. In the MTR course, Johnston says: 'our approach combined history, social theory, environmental and public health science, fiction, music, reportage, and more. By reading several general pieces on environmental justice and the concept of slow violence, the students had some theoretical and conceptual tools to analyze the historical development of MTR' (2016: 24).

In contrast to Monson, who often brings people into the environment, in this instance Eiko worked in the studio to awaken a sense of the environment through the metaphor of the body and its interior as landscape. When Eiko introduces Delicious Movement, she often invites people to lie down on the floor (see fig. 34.3a). She says: 'when we lie

FIG. 34.3A Eiko moves with students in the 'Perspectives on Mountain Top Removal Mining' class, spring semester 2013. Photo courtesy of Wesleyan University Information Technology Department.

down, we are closer to inchworms and fallen dead leaves. That closeness is transformative. We feel the earth under the studio floor. Body parts and their relationships to one another are freer than when standing; they have less of a sense of destiny and purpose. Body weight can be supported by many body parts rather than simply by the feet as in standing. Face and hands can be free of greetings' (2016: 25).

First, she demonstrates the movement herself—lying down and initiating small movements with head, spine, and limbs that reach and flex but never conclude, as if in a dream. As both movers and watchers, we are invited to savour small details: the hand brushes the face, an armpit stretches, flesh presses into the floor. This demonstration gives people a chance to adjust to the movement's speed and scale—slower and smaller than everyday task-based movement and without obvious purpose—yet pleasurable. It also allows watchers to observe the body from a less familiar perspective. Eiko says: 'seeing a body on the nearby floor, one notices small details, which can be a revealing experience' (2016: 25).

Eiko often uses the context of the class to suggest images and a storyline for the movement. In this case, Johnston reports that Eiko crawled to the centre of the space on the tatami mat of the East Asian Studies Seminar Room, entreating softly: 'ple-a-se come clo-ser so I can almost touch you,' setting up the radical intimacy—in comparison to the typical academic classroom—of the dance studio (2016: 23). Once they had found a pathway to the floor, Eiko gave the students the prompt 'to forget their names and be useless' (23). Eiko says: 'humans are less harmful while resting and sleeping. When people stand up and move purposefully, human actions can harm other lives as well as the environment. The atomic bombings and MTR represent some of the worst such human behaviours' (23). Johnston adds that the task allowed students to reflect on the unspoken mandate of purposefulness and productivity in college education (23). In their classroom, Johnston and Eiko set up a balance of logics—based in reading, lecture, and discussion—and a poetics based in experiential knowledge through the medium of the body in movement.

From one perspective, many mountains can be seen as empty and unused space. What does empty and unused feel like? In terms of body experience, might nameless or useless be the state of an infant or aged grandparent, or a state of sleep, play, or forgetfulness. Are these indeed useless states? The exercise offered students the opportunity to ponder an existential dilemma through an immediate experience of their bodies. Eiko says: 'of course, we don't want the students to remain helpless and nameless throughout the semester, but it was a good place for us to start, especially when learning about environmental issues' (2014: 6). Indeed, the issues of environmental degradation and global climate change can leave an individual feeling quite helpless to effect change.

'Survey' is a basic Delicious Movement exercise in which dancers lying on the floor slowly roll across the surfaces of their bodies in all directions, tracking bony ridges and depressions as well as muscular mounds, as if surveying the land. As always, dancers are invited to enjoy details. The exercise develops microcoordination in adjusting the angle and amount of pressure required to follow the edge of a shoulder blade, ankle bone, or kneecap, while bearing the rolling weight of the body. What was once an insignificant bump becomes a landmark: it takes time to traverse the flat plain of the sacrum—'oh, there's that ridge again'. Metaphors of mountains and valleys arise; the body becomes a landscape. Effort is exerted in order to 'hike' this landscape, albeit on a very different scale from a mountain. Heightening and articulation of sensory experience are developed in the exercise.

Eiko extended the exercise, for the purposes of the MTR class, 'to being a mountain and then a river' for an hour (2016: 25). Through rolling, students remapped the familiar upright image of their bodies while integrating knowledge acquired in lectures and readings about mountain formation and lifespan. Eiko explains:

> when I ask students to be a thing—a marshmallow, a piece of popcorn, a mountain, or a river—it is not that they imitate these shapes. Instead they become mindful of the movements and textures of these things. It gives them time to think about other beings—their details and particulars. When one explores the essence of a thing, one discovers the differences and commonalities between oneself and that thing. This means one recognizes both the distance between two existences and the space, undercurrent, and the air that the two existences share. In becoming a thing, that distance—though it does not disappear—changes, which gives a strong sensation of discovering and knowing. (25)

Eiko then asked the students through their imagination and sensation to consider what happens in MTR. In this extended Survey, students practice enacting rather than fact-finding as a way of discovery regarding the process of MTR.

Eiko often splits dancers into groups in order that half may watch while the others move. She finds that watching supports the appreciation of detail. In the MTR class,

FIG. 34.3B Seeing mountains in bodies: a student draws during the 'Perspectives on Mountain Top Removal Mining' class, Wesleyan University, spring semester 2013. Video still courtesy of Wesleyan University Information Technology Department.

she had watchers draw 'whatever they see and are attracted to' (2016:26) on newsprint with charcoal during the Survey practice, while keeping their eyes on the moving body. Drawing became an extension of seeing; Eiko says: 'seeing does not have to arrive at or produce words' (26). The drawings, which resembled mountain ranges, were then displayed on the studio walls (see fig. 34.3b). Through Survey and the drawing exercise, Eiko set up a potent analogy of body to mountain for the course.

Along with topical in-class study and movement practice, the course included travel (for some during spring break) to West Virginia to see the effects of MTR and to attend meetings of the activist group Mountain Justice. On their return, the students held a Mountain Top Removal Awareness Festival on campus. For the final class, Eiko asked students to slowly melt down, taking no more time than was necessary, from their sitting meditation posture to the floor, enacting a change in state. Eiko says: 'melting down without obviously changing one's posture is not a natural movement and requires patient negotiation between conflicting directions while resisting momentum' (2016: 26). The meltdown exercise invoked a corporeal resonance with inexorable processes: gravity, the passing of time, mountain erosion, the aging process, and the long march of human civilization. The exercise also reflects a practice from the movement education world: fluidity in movement invokes a fluid state of mind, which may bring about a shift in attitude, in this instance in relationship to the land.

Next, students crawled to view a blowup of a fifteen-foot-long high-definition panoramic photo of an MTR site that Johnston had taken during the trip to West Virginia (see fig. 34.3c). The photo showed pristine mountains, an active mining site, and a postmining wasteland. Finally, Eiko lay down, explaining that she was not only Eiko but, as Johnston had dubbed her during the semester, Eiko Mountain. She called students by name, inviting each to visit her in order to say goodbye to their dying grandmother. Creating a mourning ritual for 'grandmother' allowed students to also express feelings for the destructive treatment of the land they had witnessed and was probably not a usual subject for mourning in their current cultural setting. Students entered Eiko's ritual space as participants-players. Each improvised an appropriate response to the dying Eiko Mountain (2016: 26). Because of the experiential nature of the class, they were able to dance their knowing of the situation—a practical final exam that balanced written components.

The importance to emotional health of marking loss through mourning is recognized, for example, by cultural anthropology in the practice of memorial-making in the wake of tragedy or atrocity and in diaspora. To not recognize a loss is to lose connection—to

FIG. 34.3C Mountain top removal in progress since 1986. Kayford Mountain panorama, Kayford, West Virginia, 2013. Photograph by William Johnston.

be distanced from. Without a means to mourn the loss of familiar or heritage land-scapes, which are sometimes drastically altered during a lifetime and from which some have been forcibly moved, we create an epidemic of separation and dis-placement from our environment.

Could the practice of movement be a remedy for this disconnect? In dance, experiential knowledge is amplified through the confluence of physical body as artistic instrument. Eiko says: 'I think one problem is that many students feel that their relatively comfortable lives give them no experience from which they can draw and relate to the extreme situations that the course on the atomic bombings or mountaintop removal expose them to. Since pain is so subjective, some writers suggest that without first-hand experience of, say, the atomic bombings, it is impossible to understand the pain of those who did experience them. I think we should honour that distance, but at the same time approach it as malleable' (2014: 15). Through expanding our sense of peripersonal space, we may come to regard the unfamiliar as approachable. Taking time to make physical links between body and land through artistic practice in movement creates a deepened sense of knowing through doing—a familiarity affect. 'When we somehow cross the boundaries of distance through empathy or imagination and feel even a little closer to the experiences of another person or thing,' says Eiko, 'then we have swallowed a piece of the other, which makes us look at history and understand catastrophe differently.... We can measure physical distance both in time and in space, but the distance to and from the subject can be radically changed, or even obliterated, by walking to or bringing home the subject.... This is my mantra: distance is malleable' (15). In Johnston and Eiko's geopoetic, the body becomes a site for understanding. By introducing a human scale through experiential enactments, students encounter what at first seemed too big, beyond, or outside them, finding that the ability to engage literally exists inside themselves.

Prapto: Land, Ocean, Sky

Indonesian dance-maker Suprapto Suryodarmo (Prapto) practices in sites that have cultural and historical significance. For example, he often holds workshops in the vicinity of the temple Samuan Tiga in the village of Bedulu, central Bali, where the confluence of three religions (Bali Aga, Hinduism, and Buddhism) occurred around the year 1000 (Butler and Suryodarmo 2008). These particular contexts are integral to Prapto's Amerta Movement practice, which he sees as, more than an improvisation technique, rather as a way of cultivating an attitude towards life (Suryodarmo 2007; Buckwalter 2010: 54, 182).

Instead of copying his exercises or repeating them in the same way they happened in the past, Prapto asks his students to *re-member*. Prapto (Suryodarmo 2015) says: 'starting from re-member, there is an understanding that we have body parts such as the palms of the hands, feet, legs, arms, a head, a torso, and so forth. These are the members. Remembering gives awareness again of these parts as members'. Through dancing, I re-member my body in movement in the context of a particular place, with attendant associations and memories. 'This re-member movement and re-membering are a process for transforming memories in the body to become a vocabulary for dance movement—not just memory and not just the body'. I know a place by moving in it. I allow the present moment and its circumstances to interact with my formulations of the past, refreshing previous impressions. My bodily experience is integral in this process. I find that this practice of re-membering makes both the environment and its social context an active partner in my dancing. The field of my surroundings allows for the interplay of physical and associative connection to take place through movement. My sense of peripersonal space becomes fluid, sipping from past and present influences.

As a young man, Prapto loved to move but found the traditional dances of his Javanese culture weren't the right form of expression for him. Instead, in the 1970s, he began a practice of free movement. He was drawn to study Vipassana and Javanese Sumarah meditation, which develop awareness while attending to simple action. This led him to create *Wayang Buddha* (Buddha's Shadow-Puppet; 1975) and other new ritual artworks that combine elements of religiosity and art. He places his Amerta Movement in a context of nature, sacred space, and cultural exchange. Amerta Movement has been practised by people from many disciplines, including but not limited to dance, in settings around the world. For example, through Web Art Garden, a worldwide network of artists and presenting organizations, Prapto has initiated annual cultural events around the world to celebrate the World Environment Day held yearly on June 5 (Suryodarmo 1997; Buckwalter 2010: 55–56).

I first corresponded with Prapto via email in 2007, while writing my book on methods of composing through improvised dance. Though I hadn't experienced his work, I was keen to include it in the book. I had read a 1994 *Contact Quarterly* article by Andrea Morein, a student of Prapto, which included a 1985 interview with him by Christina Stelzer and Jose Mulder van de Graf at Aryatara Buddhist Institute in Germany. In both these writings, I was struck by Prapto's language, which captured various states in improvisation that I hadn't previously heard described. This email dialogue with Prapto regarding my writing led to my first experience of his work in the nine-day workshop The Prayer of the Butterfly at the SEEDS Festival in 2008. We worked indoors and out, in solos and groups, dancing, discussing, and meditating. Prapto had a way of teaching that rubbed me up against an unconscious habit until I took notice. Out of that gnarly awareness, I was then able to shift my response—at first through movement and then in my attitudes. I felt a deep, multidimensional growth taking place in myself as well as in my friends who attended the workshop.

I was eager for a second opportunity to study with Prapto, which finally came in 2011 during his teaching tour in the United States. For his Being Blossoming workshop, participants practised in Jefferson Hall beside the chapel of the Unitarian Society of Santa Barbara, California; in the chapel's courtyard; and in a large public park with a pond across the street. We used the indoor space to practise, among many things, *not leaving*. In not leaving, we sat in and moved in and around our chairs but never left them. Even if we stood up to shift position, our attention was to stay focused on the chair. The chair was our *anchor*. In this exercise, we situated our sense of peripersonal space through focused attention on the chair. This proved a difficult practice for busy Americans, always on the run. Prapto mimicked, to hilarious effect, how we moved from one thing to another with our minds already on the next spot—where we are going rather than in the transit (Buckwalter 2014: 281).

In the park across the street, we practised *stopping in not moving, stopping in no moving*, and *stopping in moving*. Ducks were our mentors. We practised with them on a little island in their pond at the park (see fig. 34.4a). Stopping in not moving was when they slept, beak tucked under wing, oblivious. Stopping in no moving was their habitual paddle—lazing about, nibbling at the water, and throwing in a preen. Stopping in moving was when they took off after something, a rival duck or proffered breadcrumbs, darting with single-mindedness. This one-pointed focus during the duck's dart created the stopping effect—the dart translated as a kind of stillness of purpose. We observed, then practised. I often got it backwards. Nevertheless, I practised something, blindly, finding faith in the process (2014: 280). Here we identified a particular quality of attention while shifting states of movement.

In the courtyard, we gathered around the day lilies. Prapto discussed *being blossoming* with us, along with a short description of the Lotus Sutra—the Buddha's final and, many feel, ultimate teaching on enlightenment. During our sitting meditation, we were to use the practice of not leaving in order to stay inside the lily bud, where we would *show our face* rather than buzz around the outside of the flower with our busy minds. Somehow,

FIG. 34.4A Prapto stopping in no moving while the ducks rest among the lily pads, Santa Barbara, California, 2013. Photograph by Hugh Kelly.

after our hours of movement practices, when it came time to sit, we knew what to do. We were outwardly sitting, but inwardly we were showing our faces, basking in our blossoming, finding our stopping, not leaving to plan the next and the next and the next. Through this Lily Bud Sutra, Prapto showed me how to stop looking for something—new vocabulary, a fancy segue, the developing theme, emerging forms—and thus to stop leaving the dance (2014: 281). In this way, I stumbled on the holy grail of dance—embodiment. By enacting various states of attention through movement, I was later able to access them abstractly in sitting meditation.

Finally, it was beach day. Prapto often works on the beach at his home in Java, and in Bali, and I was thrilled to have the opportunity to practise with him in Santa Barbara. We carpooled and arrived at Butterfly Beach in the early afternoon, squeezed into the last few parking spots, and clambered down the stairs onto the sand. We immediately ran to the water's edge, dipping our toes, making overtures to the waves to let us in like little kids on holiday. Prapto gathered us together and admonished us not to lose ourselves. He then showed us how to find the horizon and ourselves *in relation*. That day, we danced our *human measurement* amid this infinite backdrop of land, ocean, and sky (2014: 282).

In doing Prapto's work, I find there is a point at which I simply must jump in and start with some movement—anything. It only begins to make sense in the doing. He demonstrates a little bit and then the dancer picks up a small piece and works with it, trying it

FIG. 34.4B 'Please come': Prapto, Tim Wood, and Melinda Buckwalter dancing on the beach, Butterfly Beach, Santa Barbara, California, October 2008. Photograph by Katya Bloom.

on, wearing the movement—much as a dancer might work in the creation process with a choreographer. In this instance, Prapto indicated the horizon line where the ocean met the sky, moving his arms along it, and catching sight of it while dancing. There were also small cliffs opposite the ocean, a very different horizon line. He suggested that we use this horizon as well to find our human measurement. Prapto described human measurement in terms of putting on clothing. He demonstrated with his T-shirt, sticking an arm partway in the sleeve, poking his head through the hole. Our body has proportion; our movements are a way of measuring, of knowing these proportions. In the terms of this essay, measuring our bodies in relation to the land includes the environment in our self-image, shifting our sense of peripersonal space. Indeed, is it that I measure myself against the land? Or is it the land impressing dimensionality on me? My perspective is inverted, and I find myself emplaced.

'Please come,' Prapto said, over and over, calling us to dance in duos and trios, in and out of the water, on and in the sand, with and without Prapto, who often sings or plays a drum in accompaniment (see fig. 34.4b). My attention struggled and flagged in the hot sun, grit, and beach gnats. What was I doing? I would find some strand of a dance to hang onto, only to have it drift away. The tide shifted around us. I felt a familiar sense of being lost, at sea in my improvisations (2014: 283). Prapto reminded us: 'find your stoppings, then you can recognize your composition'. The experience of being lost is necessary in the process of finding myself in relation.

As the sun set, I made my goodbyes to the group, feeling unresolved. The next morning, as I sat in a brief predawn meditation before a full day of flying, I felt, quite unexpectedly, the ocean moving. It was a physical echo, like a sailor experiencing land sickness. Slurping, slapping, rocking, laughing, washing. I felt myself in relation to the ocean, and for a moment, in my stopping, it all made sense: the endless movement, the ducks, coming and going, the not leaving. In finding my human measurement against the ocean, in pointing to that vastness, I had been reflected back—myself, ever-changing yet always right here. Then, the ocean of activity swallowed me, as it does every day. But for that moment of stopping, I could feel its gentle caress: I am here, I am here, I am still here (2014: 283). The slim anchor of attention we had cast during our exercises created a still point for the taking of a positional reading. I was able, however briefly, to get my bearings and *feel* myself reflected in relation to my ever-changing surroundings, as I had felt the fluidity of the ocean the day before.

In Prapto's work, dance is a means of articulating experiences of being. With a touch of humour, Prapto introduces us to ourselves through enactments such as re-membering, measuring, not leaving, stopping, and blossoming that take place in everyday settings. These exercises have the effect of bringing perceptual habit patterns to consciousness. We practise not getting stuck in the field of our experience, and instead, through movement, we learn to feel the ebb and flow. In doing so, we break a kind of fourth wall of self as doer and find ourselves—blossoming.

In our work with Prapto, the environment is a vast mirror. While dancing in the environment is key, it is our embeddedness in the landscape that makes the perceptual switch from foreground to background possible. Rather than agents acting within a landscape, we find ourselves defined in relationship to the landscape.

An Emerging Geopoetics

Composition: rather than placement inside a frame, emplacement. The emerging geopoetics is an experience of integration with environment. All of these dance-makers use their art to call attention to our embeddedness by raising environmental awareness, but in singular ways. Speaking from my experience in the specific case of the horizon studies and using the language of embodied enactment, in Jennifer Monson's work we *unearth*. By heightening physical and sensory awareness, Monson exposes an underlying interconnectedness with the environment, which is relayed through movement. Her geopoetics addresses an important shift in collective thinking if we are to change the current pattern of unsustainable overconsumption and wastefulness and realize the reciprocal nature of our actions.

Through attention to and heightening of internal awareness, Eiko's dancers *situate* themselves, using metaphoric prompts and in analogy to interdisciplinary study. This shift in interior landscape implies relationship and a sense of distance. This distance can be felt to grow closer through engagement of the metaphor. Eiko's geopoetics of the body, which empowers individual engagement, speaks to environmental crises and other survival issues facing humankind today, which have roots in denial (nonrelationship).

Through engaging with our environment in movement, Prapto's students *reflect* qualities of attention and being that we may not initially identify as our own. In doing so, we expand our sense of self, often accompanied by a feeling of wholeness and healing. Prapto's geopoetics orient the participant towards embodiment rather than continuous striving to accomplish, which pits us against our environment rather than supporting mutuality.

All three of these dance-makers use their artistry in unique ways to pull us across the boundary of self and towards a fresh experience of integration of self and environment. In so doing, they suggest paths to a needed sea change in attitude towards the environment.

References

Allsopp, R. (2014) Performing Poetics. Lecture at Live Legacy Project, Dusseldorf, Germany, 7–12 July 2014.

Allsopp, R. (2015) Performing Poetics. *CQ Unbound* 40(1). https://contactquarterly.com/cq/unbound/view/performing-poetics#$. Accessed: January 16, 2015.

Blakeslee, S., and Blakeslee, M. (2007) *The Body Has a Mind of Its Own: How Body Maps in Your Brain Help You Do (Almost) Everything Better*. New York City: Random House.

Buckwalter, M. (2010a) *Composing While Dancing: An Improviser's Companion*. Madison: University of Wisconsin Press.

Buckwalter, M. (2010b) Giving Body to a Body. *Contact Quarterly* 35(1): 5.

Buckwalter, M. (2014) Re-membering Butterfly Beach. In Bloom, K., Galanter, M., and Reeves, S. (eds.), *Embodied Lives: Reflections on the Influence of Suprapto Suryodarmo and Amerta Movement*. Charmouth, Dorset, UK: Triarchy Press, 277–283.

Butler, D., and Suryodarmo, S. (2008) Email correspondence with the author, 12 May 2008.

Eiko & Koma. (2014). Website of Eiko & Koma. http://www.eikoandkoma.org. Accessed 3 December 2014.

Grau, A. (2005) When Landscape Becomes Flesh: An Investigation into Body Boundaries with Special Reference to Tiwi Dance and Western Classical Ballet. *Journal for the Anthropological Study of Human Movement* 13(4): 189–210.

Grau, A. (2010) Geopoetics: Art, Dance, and Ritual among the Tiwi of Northern Australia. Inaugural Address 2010, Roehampton University. http://vimeo.com/56594759. Accessed 1 May 2014. (Video)

Grau, A. (2016) Why People Dance—Evolution, Sociality and Dance. *Dance, Movement & Spiritualities* 2(3): 233–254.

Jennifer Monson: Professor. (2014) Website of Dance at Illinois. www.dance.uiuc.edu/people/faculty/jennifer-monson. Accessed 24 August 2014.

Johnston, W., and Otake, E. (2013) Mountain Top Removal Class. (Video) Wesleyan University Informational Technologies Department. In Otake's personal collection.

Monson, J. (2014) Systems/Scores: Practice/Process. Workshop organized by Movement Research, St. Marks Church, New York, 4–8 August 2014.

Monson, J. (2015) Email correspondence with the author, 12 March 2015.

Monson, J., and Whitehead, S. (2009) Along the Watershed. Workshop at SEEDS: Somatic Experiments in Earth, Dance + Science Festival, curated by O. Bieringa, M. Buckwalter, and M. Galanter, Earthdance, Plainfield, Massachusetts, 14–18 June 2009.

Morein, A. (1994) A Practice Called Road: studying 'Movement in Meditation' with Suprapto Suryodarmo in Central Java. *Contact Quarterly* 19(1): 24–34.

Otake, E. (2015) Personal communication, 22 February 2015.

Otake, E., and Johnston, W. (2014) Experiment and Experience: A Historian and a Dancer Co-teach Courses on the Atomic Bomb and Mountaintop Removal Mining. Unpublished paper, author's personal collection.

Otake, E., and Johnston, W. (2016) Experiment and Experience: A Historian and a Dancer Coteach Courses on the Atomic Bomb and Mountaintop Removal Mining. *Contact Quarterly* 44(1): 21–26.

Suryodarmo, S. (1997) Web Art Garden—An Idea. *ACE: Art Culture Environment*. Cheltanham, Gloucester, UK, 1999.

Suryodarmo, S. (2007) Email correspondence with the author, 4 September 2007.

Suryodarmo, S. (2008) The Prayer of the Butterfly. Workshop at SEEDS: Somatic Experiments in Earth, Dance + Science Festival, curated by O. Bieringa, M. Galanter, et al. Earthdance, Plainfield, Massachusetts, July and August.

Suryodarmo, S. (2011) Being Blossoming. Workshop organized by K. Bloom, Santa Barbara, CA, 25–30 October 2011.

Suryodarmo S. (2015) Email correspondence with the author, 25 March 2015.

Welcome to Skinner Releasing. (2009) Website of Skinner Releasing Institute. Welcome to Skinner Releasing. [online] Available at: http://www.skinnerreleasing.com/. (Accessed 20 January 2015.

Whitehead, S. (2009) Whitehead, Simon: Field Work by Simon Whitehead. Website of Wales Arts International. http://www.wai.org.uk/north-america/usa/1690. Accessed 8 March 2015.

Whitehead, S. (2006) Locator: Excursion Wales. *Contact Quarterly* 31(2): 39.

CHAPTER 35

SCORING AND SITING

*Improvisatory Approaches to
Site-Specific Dance-Making*

VICTORIA HUNTER

SITE-SPECIFIC dance performance encompasses a number of presentational forms and choreographic practices that present artists and audiences with opportunities to engage with real-world locations differently, through the medium of dance. Choreographic processes differ greatly from one artist to another; however, a common thread of devising and employing movement scores as an investigative and curatorial tool can be witnessed in the work of many contemporary site-dance practitioners. In the wider field of contemporary dance practice, movement scores are employed by artists in a myriad of ways. A number of resources provide tangible examples of this type of approach, such as the online www.motionbank.org, which features score-based work developed by artists such as Jonathan Burrows, Deborah Hay, and William Forsythe, and a 2014 issue of the journal *Choreographic Practices* (that includes a reprint of Anna Halprin's RSVP cycles and reflexive writing by dance artists on scores and their implications).[1] Whilst these examples present a range of differing score-based methodologies, the artists engaging with this way of working share a common interest in opening up movement possibilities from a clear framework that incorporates an artistic choreographic curiosity or a specific question, such as: how might I know more about ... ? How can I explore ... ? What approach might work here?

This chapter is not concerned, however, with movement scores and dance notation systems, such as Benesh and Labanotation, that are frequently employed as tools for documenting, recording, and subsequently reconstructing dances for performance. The term 'movement score' will refer here to a set of instructions employed in sited dance improvisation tasks and exploratory dance 'episodes' that either exist as movement experiences in their own right or function as a mechanism for explorations that develop and produce material to be included in a dance composition at a later stage.

I explore here approaches to designing and utilizing improvised movement scores in site-specific dance-making. Drawing on my own practice-based research and the work of site-dance choreographers and movement/performance artists associated with processes of 'scoring', I consider the nature of improvisatory scores and their creative potential when applied in the site-dance context. In particular, the chapter explores how score-based improvisational practice imposes creative restraints and, through doing so, guides movement exploration towards 'things in particular' in a phenomenological sense.[2] The chapter questions what scores 'do' in the site-dance context and considers how they are designed, applied, and managed by practitioners. Furthermore, I explore how scores might lead us towards and divert us away from specific site components and question how they facilitate the management of architectural, spatial, and sensory 'data' in site-dance processes.

Informed by an interdisciplinary theoretical framework that employs ideas drawn from human geography, nonrepresentational theory, phenomenology, and spatial theory, the chapter explores how scoring approaches develop creative methods through which the body might enter into a spatial 'dialogue' with the site and effectively 'translate' the site into movement. Through this critical approach, I consider how movement scores might bring us closer to space and place and, through doing so, develop understandings of being-in-the-world. Through this perspective, I explore how scores might facilitate this process by enabling choreographers to 'dig away' at material and immaterial site components through the employment of methods that prioritize bodily knowledge, processual knowing, and understanding.

Contemporary understandings of scores and 'scoring' practised by artists and choreographers are informed by a lineage of experimental arts practice that can be traced back to the innovative experiments of the postmodern artists of the 1960s and early 1970s. The New York–based Judson Church group of choreographers, for example, were committed to developing approaches that engaged dance with real-world environments, both in terms of subject matter and as a site of performance. Steve Paxton's score for *Satisyin' Lover* (1967) famously employed pedestrian acts of walking, pausing, sitting, and standing as the key ingredients for his performance work, providing a democratized score that could be performed by anyone, anywhere. Similarly, Trisha Brown's rooftop and gallery performances and her many 'equipment pieces' employed a range of pedestrian instructions and pragmatic tasks that involved performers in the construction of movement material and performance environments. Brown in particular was interested in developing the use of movement scores in her work, for the creation of dance performed in both site-based and proscenium arch environments. The origin of her well-known 'cube' score is described by Marianne Goldberg: 'in *Locus*, Brown developed a spatial score based on a set of instructions for the dancer moving within her own kinesphere, the immediate space surrounding the dancer's body. Brown imagined the kinesphere as a cube defined by 27 points distributed along its sides. The dancer related to a sequence of points with modular gestures, each with its specific spatial obligation. Through this method, Brown began to perform clusters of separate gestures that were articulated simultaneously. This system gave Brown the means to three-dimensionally graph erratic, multi-directional movements' (1986: 154). Emerging from this period of innovation and experimentation, the work of California-based movement artist Anna Halprin is most relevant to the discussion developed in this chapter. In collaboration with her architect husband, Lawrence Halprin, she devised a method for developing movement content and dance events that were known as the RSVP cycles. Drawn from their own personal commitment to the development of an authentic mode of life-art practice in which body, world, and environment engage in a coconstitutive relationship, the RSVP process encouraged participants to foster an awareness of themselves within the environment and in relation to other bodies, objects, and elements in the sites where they worked. Hirsch (2011) provides a comprehensive overview of the practice that is worth quoting at length:

> RSVP, in this case stands for Resources, Scores, Valuaction and Performance. Although they conveniently correspond to the French acronym, which invites response or feedback, these four components are meant to occur in any order and in a cyclical on-going fashion rather than a linear one. 'Resources' refers to the pre-existing site conditions and the act of inventorying them in order to determine their potential for influencing the design or the structure of the Scores. Resources are both 'objective', including physical features and demographic data, and 'subjective' including biases, fantasies, and hidden agendas. 'Scores' are temporal-situational guidelines that structure the unfolding Performance. A closed score implies choreographic control and an open score invites participation by allowing for a range of response. 'Valuaction' (conflating the words 'value' and 'action') is a term Halprin and Burns coined for the dynamic feedback process that leads to the consistent revision of the scores or the workshop activities.[3] Because scores are intended to be 'non-judgemental', Valuaction embodies the analytical or judgemental component of the process. Finally, 'Performance' represents the acting out of scores. (Hirsch 2011: 128)

The RSVP cycles were employed by Lawrence Halprin in his 'Take Part Process', a series of public planning projects pioneered in the 1960s and 1970s in which workshop participants were encouraged to explore and experience urban areas and use their collective enquiry to inform subsequent architectural planning processes. Anna Halprin employed the technique in her own life/art teaching and movement practice at the San Francisco Dancer's Workshop, where she aimed to develop 'a common basis of experiences from which we can communicate, explore techniques of collective creativity, maximise diversity, create rituals and myths out of common experience, fulfil individual expectations within the group experience, develop group awareness to the environment and recycle the experiences of the workshop into daily life' (Anna Halprin 1974: 13). For Halprin, the employment of the RSVP cycle facilitated the development of a practice in which she championed the integration of the individual's physical, spiritual, and emotional experiences with their lived encounters with the environments in which they moved. Libby Worth and Helen Poynor, in their book that chronicles Halprin's life and work, observe: 'just as Halprin had refused to inhibit movement exploration by limiting what could be included under the term "dance" or by controlling

who could dance, similarly she expanded where dance could take place' (2004: 33). They
reflect on Halprin's work *Citydance* (1977) as a pertinent example, a multidisciplinary
dance-artwork that responded to the murder of local mayor George Moscone through
the creation of a day-long promenade movement intervention performed as an iconic
example of her dance-life-art approach: '*Citydance* travelled through contrasting environments and neighbourhoods, including woodland, a ghetto playground, a sky-
scraper, a formal plaza in the city centre, a graveyard and the cable car terminus. The
focus was on interacting with the environments, spaces and people of the city through
simple scores which facilitated spontaneous expression and individual participation'
(28). Halprin's approach to her movement practice eschewed the codified techniques
practised by the American modern dance pioneers and alternatively centred on improvisation as the primary mode of exploring the life/art experience. As her movement
research developed to include a focus on environmental practice and outdoor work
performed in nature spaces in the 1960s, the exploration of nature and natural forms
continued to feed and develop her improvisatory practice further: 'the underlying principles that guide her work in nature are based on three beliefs: that "the human body is
a microcosm of the earth," processes of nature offer aesthetic guidelines and nature is a
healer' (32).[4] In particular, Halprin's notion of movement 'exploration' implied a pointed
and focused and directed approach to dance improvisation, akin to a subjective process
of 'phenomenological reduction', a concept stemming from the philosophical ideas of
Heidegger and Merleau-Ponty, to describe 'a narrowing of attention to what is essential
in the problem while disregarding the superfluous and accidental' (Algis Mickunas and
David Stewart in Fraleigh 1987: 6). I propose that this type of scoring, by reducing our
perceptual and sensorial field through the application of restraints and boundaries, facilitates the engineering of this process, enabling an immediate and direct through-line
of connectivity to develop between body-self and world. In conversation with Nancy
Stark Smith, Halprin discusses her approach: 'What I called "dance explorations" was
different, because we would take a specific idea—you might take space or you might
take time, you might take force and we would work with a very specific focus and then
we would explore what are all the possibilities around working with space for example.
And in the process of exploration, we would come up with information that then later
on I began to call "resources." But "exploring" was much more focussed and controlled
than "improvising"' (in Kaplan 1995: 191). Halprin's approach illuminates a specific form
of guided improvisatory practice in which the movement researcher attempts to explore
something in particular and presents a form of practice that is housed within a clearly
defined set of parameters. Whilst the parameters are clearly defined, when working the
improviser is free to explore the specific phenomenon or kinetic concept according to
the improviser's own individualized movement style and corporeal responses. However,
the guiding framework described by Halprin here, manifested either through a specific
'exploratory' task or (subsequently) through the framework of the RSVP cycles, effectively prohibits the dancer from drifting off into a self-reflexive reverie and demands a
focusing of attention towards things in particular. Through this process, which has subsequently been adopted and developed by contemporary dance artists and practitioners

engaging in site-dance work, individuals become active participants in a dance with their surroundings and with others, as their awareness of both themselves and the environments in which they operate is prioritized.

SCORES: ARRIVING, CLOSING, AND OPENING

Arriving

When considering what scores can 'do' in the context of site-specific movement exploration and dance-making, a useful place to start is through observing the work of a number of practitioners who employ scores as initial introductory or 'grounding' devices. Frequently, scores are employed with the primary aim of encouraging individuals to stop, notice, arrive, and engage with their environment in a corporeal and sensorially attuned manner not usually afforded through our fast-paced and often frenetic lives. Dance artist Julia Handschuh has described her process of participation in an environmental dance workshop led by the American site-dance artist Jennifer Monson as part of her series of workshops in Manhattan titled Sustained Immersive Process/Watershed. Monson has been making site-dance work since 2000 and sustains a practical approach based on embodied knowing; she considers choreography an 'archival practice for environmental phenomena' (www.ilandart.org). Her approach proposes that choreographic practice and movement exploration can serve to highlight and 'curate' environmental phenomena and associated issues through corporeal means, and her works have explored themes such as regeneration, animal navigation, and environmental sustainability. The following score extract is accompanied by Handschuh's commentary on her own experiential encountering of a workshop task designed to facilitate a process of 'arriving'.

Score extract:

> There is a familiarity, a sense of willingness in my body and desire for physical release. I am circulating my arms towards my core as we stand witness to the movement of the gray waters in front of us and the expanse of silvery gray sky stretching out from side to side.

Commentary:

> A grounding of the feet, a centering of the breath, a circling motion of the arms, movement inspired Qigong; arriving here in this body, in this space, connecting breath to body to ground to landscape. (Handschuh in Besel and Blau 2014: 148)

In Handschuh's essay 'On Finding Ways of Being: Kinesthetic Empathy in Dance and Ecology', she describes and reflects further on the sited movement explorations she experienced and reflects on them as an approach that presents 'the possibility of forming an empathetic exchange between body and place, an exchange that could subsequently lead to a reorganisation of how we value each other and the environment' (2014: 151).

This approach to body-site engagement, instigated through a process of arriving and 'grounding' oneself in the site, resonates with my own movement-based approaches to developing site engagement, in which scores are designed to develop one's sense of awareness of oneself in a specific environment, in a present and 'attuned' manner. The following score provides an example of this method and was employed whilst leading a site-dance workshop in a specific built environment, the Centre Nationale de la Dance in Paris—a former concrete factory and a stunning example of 1960s brutalist architecture. The 'arriving' score aimed to encourage participants to observe, notice, and take

FIG. 35.1 Site-dance workshop, Paris, 2007. Photograph by Victoria Hunter.

in their physical surroundings whilst developing an awareness of the energies and phenomenological resonances emerging from being in the site:

Arriving

Walk around the space, feel the space through your feet.

Feel the space through the front, side, back of the body, feel '3D' in the space.

Send your awareness out into the space and acknowledge the entire space, encompassing the formal features, architecture, sound, light and the presence of other bodies, acknowledge their presence bodily, feel the disturbance of air caused by the flow of bodies.

Acknowledge your attention outside and inside the body, internally through an awareness of the sensations of the space upon the body, externally through the effects of the others' energies, movements and presence in the room, become aware of the internal /external exchange between your body and the space.

As the walking practice develops begin to find within your journey moments of 'arriving' in the space—arrive at a place and be present in the space. Become aware, present, engaged in the exchange between self and site—notice—avoid analysing/ thinking/ describing—take the time to be present.

Follow the body's impulse to leave and re-locate, move through space to discover another moment of arrival. (Hunter 2007).

From this score, participants engaged in a wide range of explorative actions, movements, and activities, including running and rolling down the smooth concrete surfaces of the site's corridors, performing headstands, or simply sitting and observing the view from the building's expansive windows (see fig. 35.1). These approaches, actions, and interventions, in a sense, presented individuals with opportunities to familiarize themselves with the site, explore potential movement possibilities, and try out initial movement ideas with/in the site.

The importance and significance of 'arriving' as a situating practice that prepares the body for real-world movement interactions is exemplified in the work of dance artist-researchers Chris Crickmay and Miranda Tufnell, who devote an entire chapter to the practice in their publication *A Widening Field: Journeys in Body and Imagination* (2004). The chapter, 'Arriving-Preparing to Work', includes a number of scores that encourage the development of sensory awareness and individual processes of 'tuning in' to both self and world. The following score provides an example of their work Tufnell and Crickmay 2004: 5).

Landing .... time to be still

Lie comfortably on the ground
Feel the shape and form of your body
From the soles of the feet to the crown of the head .... let the length of the spine open
   this should all be one line

Let go of the need .... to do .... anything
Let go of the chatter of your thoughts .... be empty
Rest .... take time to breathe

Let the weight of each part of your body give way .... settling .... gentle as snowfall
   this should all be one line
     feel the support of the earth rising under you
Let the whole body .... rest and fall
      small world of the body .... resting on the great world of the earth this
        should all be one line
feel the resonance of the body with the earth
      mountains ... valleys ... deserts ... rivers ...pools ... seas

What is soft .... fluid? .... What is hard .... dense?
What is fragile? .... What holds pain?

Let the field of your attention .... soften and spread out
Sense the temperature of the ground ....of the air
Sense the time of day .... season of the year .... weather
Open .... your ears .... listen .... let in the sounds around
Let each eye soften and rest .... sensing light .... shadow

Let breath come in .... opening space .... inside the body .... opening inside to out
   this should all be one line

The notion of 'landing' evoked through this score is particularly relevant to a discussion of site-based movement exploration, as it demands a physical grounding of the body as it connects with the earth and a metaphorical grounding of mind and soma as the experiencer is encouraged to listen to and sense the surroundings.

Performance practitioner and academic Mike Pearson suggests a more pragmatic and functional approach to arriving in and 'scoping' a location in which he encourages the experiencer to consider the context and conditions of a site. His work draws on notions of performance as a form of archaeological practice in which the explorer excavates the many layers of a site, consisting of numerous geological, historical, environmental, and geographical elements. In his publication *Site-Specific Performance* Pearson presents a number of scores and exercises 'to inspire and stimulate practical initiatives by the reader'; his score for visiting 'an island, or a forest, or a disused steelworks' includes the following directives (2010: 131).

- Use your own body—stride, orientation, range of site and hearing—as a device of measurement for surveying the location. What is recorded, what excluded?
- At five points write texts of fifty words to describe the place: topography, sky, flora, fauna, weather.
- Take two photographs. What do you choose to record?
- Recover one object.

- Use the data gathered to create a map of the location in another medium at another scale elsewhere. What is its symbolic order?
- How might you describe the location for an audience, using the records generated if desired?

This approach starts with an initial 'scoping' exercise, in which the improviser collates site-based information, and the score acts as a 'marker' or starting point for subsequent processes of site excavation that may (or may not) involve more subjective consideration of the site's affective qualities. If Tufnell and Crickmay's 'arriving' score prepares the body for site-exploration through an introspective approach, Pearson's method encourages a process of moving outwards and away from subjective reflection as the first mode of experiencing and towards an objective engagement with tangible site-components and their contextual situation. This score also invites the experiencer to consider the subsequent, potential re-construction of the site-experience through a process of re-telling the site to an audience at a later date in a different location and through doing so raises questions of selection and omission, authenticity and interpretation.

Closing

Whilst I have proposed here that scores in themselves present the choreographer with a useful tool from which to possibly direct the improviser's attention towards things in particular, it is also useful to identify further distinctions that can be made between scores or sets of instructions. In relation to the devising and development of site-specific dance work in particular, I make a distinction here between 'closed' scores, a series of instructions that focus on tangible, formal, or singular site components in a very directed and perhaps prescriptive manner, and 'open' scores, which encourage the improviser's exploration of broader site themes, atmospheres, and affects.

Directed or 'closed' scores can be equated to a process in which the choreographer identifies a particular problem or question to be explored and subsequently devises a score-based task through which the particular site component might be interrogated. Anna Halprin discusses the potential benefits of providing parameters for dance improvisation: 'the more you set on yourself, the more you have to push the edges out to get at more material. See, if I were just improvising I'd go to a certain point and I might just leave it and go to something else. An exploration requires that you stay on that particular path, focused on dealing with a particular element, for a given length of time. And that you can't just run off. Or you can't just move into some more familiar way of doing things' (in Kaplan 1995: 192). Here, Halprin captures the essence of the creative constraints often imposed on the dance improviser through closed scores that necessarily demand a focused and detailed exploration of things in particular. The creative constraints of site-based closed scores can, in this sense, act as catalysts for new discoveries

FIG. 35.2 Site-dance workshop participant, Denmark, 2011. Photograph by Victoria Hunter.

and, in my own work, often facilitate the development of new movement pathways and instigate creative solutions as new site discoveries are made and an associated process of subsequent questioning arises. The following extract exemplifies this type of approach and is drawn from a practical site-movement workshop I led at the conference Dancing Space, Spacing Dance in Odense, Denmark, in January 2011. The task described here encouraged participants to effectively 'measure' the site through their bodies and aimed to invoke a sense of proportional relationship between body and site:

Measuring

Find a site/space that interests you.

Walk around the space, notice its lines, contours, shapes and dimensions.

Take time to acknowledge the proportions of the site.

How does the site's dimensions and proportions resonate with the dimensions of the body?

How might we measure and 'map' this space through the body?

How many paces between x and y?

How many arm spans between here and there?

Explore how the measuring potential of arms, legs, torso, fingers, head and rib-cage might enable you to cover this space and map it through your physical proportions.

Explore measuring this site through the body, allow a dialogue to develop. ()[5]

The emerging movement improvisations arising from this score involved participants in a very close and tactile exploration of the site in which they attempted to span the length and proportions of the site and, in some cases, literally 'fit' themselves into the building's contours, corners, doorways, and ledges (see fig. 35.2). To return to Halprin's notion of movement 'explorations' (in Kaplan 1995: 191) versus a free-ranging improvisatory approach, the participants' responses observed here demonstrated a clear sense of focused engagement with specific site elements and things in particular.

In a similar manner, Australian-based choreographer Paula Alexandra Lay describes the employment of movement scores whilst making her site-specific work *10,000 Small Deaths* (2013), a work that explored the disused buildings of Cockatoo Island in Sydney Harbour. As a dance artist, Lay is interested in the immediacy of the body in improvisatory practice and its relationship to lived environments encountered through site-dance and dance film work. In an account of the creative process for *10,000 Small Deaths,* she describes employing a score based on exploring the linear design of the buildings that included instructions such as these:

disrupt and interrupt the lines,
reflect the lines and travel down one spatial, linear path from one end to another,
reference the lines present within the architectural design within the emerging
    movement.

(Lay 2014)

From this scored investigation, a movement phrase emerged containing linear arm gestures, stepping actions, bends of the knees, and angular leg and arm patterns that traced linear pathways in the dancer's immediate kinaesphere. The repetition of actions and pathways was also evident as Lay visited, processed, and revisited the spatial and architectural information manifested in prodding and jabbing arm gestures as she retracted and repeated the action in a mechanistic manner. This movement vocabulary was later translated into a proscenium-based performance dance work that recalled the themes of the original space and Lay's lived experience of the site, echoing notions of decay, decline, and the passing of time and reinvoking traces of the past. Other scores employed in Lay's project focused on explorations of the site's textures, the performer's associated site memories, and subsequent imagined landscapes invoked by the body-site interaction. Whilst identifying these as 'closed' scores, Lay also acknowledges the malleability of their parameters and describes how each exploration was open to the performer's embellishment emerging in the moment of execution informed by sensorial information and internally experienced responses to the unfolding improvisation (Lay 2014).

In a similar manner, in my own site-based work, I have often employed closed scores as a means of 'digging' into an environment through focused movement improvisation. In the development of my coastally located site-dance explorations (2011, 2013),[6] the use of closed scores proved particularly useful when attempting to 'frame' the performer's exploration of site-responses encountered at Flamborough South Landing and West Wittering beaches. In these projects, scores were used to develop the movement responses of five dancers who worked at the beach sites over a one-week period. In each instance, the beach sites contained a surfeit of natural elements, weather components, and geological features that, combined together, could prove potentially overwhelming for the site-based improviser. Through employing closed scores at both locations, it became possible to select specific site features for individual dancers to explore each day, from which a jigsaw of their total site experience could be pieced together. Here is an example of one score.

Horizon Line and Perspectives

Find a location from where you can clearly view the horizon line.

Beginning with the centre of the body explore the notion and feel of the horizon line as it plays along and is emulated through your own 'horizon' line. Play with this relationship.

Open up this exploration and begin to play with

perspective, begin to shift your focus from the far to the near, explore the interplay between 'here' and 'there', develop your movement exploration to include:

> Noticing other dancers close to and far away from you, echoing/mirroring/contrasting their movements with your own, connecting across space.

> Explore the horizon line versus the floor below.
> Explore the sky above and the scale of the surrounding cliffs.
> Explore the grains of sands and pebbly surfaces.

This score aimed to direct the dancers' attention towards developing a sense of relationship between their own bodies and the beach environment through suggesting a reciprocal relationship between the physical horizon line and a kinaesthetically imagined 'horizon line' situated in the body just below the ribcage. Through presenting the dancers with this provocation, the score challenged them to consider and play with a developing site-body duet in which a process of phenomenological reversibility might develop and a sense of body-world entwining might ensue. The design of this score is informed by the phenomenology of Merleau-Ponty and his notion of being-in-the world in which body-world relationships are coconstitutive. Through this approach a particular understanding of 'environment' is engendered; as Merleau-Ponty observes, 'the environment is that living connection, or rather identical with the existing parts of my body itself' (1962: 205).

Reflecting on the outcomes of this movement score witnessed whilst observing the dancers' improvisations on the beach, I became mindful of the fact that whilst providing an initial starting point for exploration, trained dancers and experienced improvisers often reaches a point where the original directions become subsumed in their developing, intuitive site-exploration. Responding to the body-self's experience of site-based qualia, the sensorial body began to provide its own score as it became open and porous, accepting of and responsive to the various dynamic qualities, felt experiences, rhythms, and refrains encountered through 'tuning in' to the beach-site experience. In a sense, the body-self's own 'score' began to emerge as the duration of the dance improvisation developed. The directed focus of the initial score became too prescriptive, and the body-self took the dancer off on its own exploratory pathway, selecting what to respond to on a moment-by-moment basis.

Opening

The notion of an open score in its widest sense is perhaps exemplified by the experiments undertaken by the situationist group of artists and activists of the 1950s and 1960s. Guy Debord's ideas involving the practice of the *derivé*, or 'drift', as a means of engaging in processes of psychogeography encouraged participants to experience the world anew through becoming lost and adrift in the world and invited new ways of thinking about space, place, and environment. Conceptual artist and author Sophie Calle extended the themes and philosophies of the early situationists through her work *Suite Venitiene* (1979), in which she (covertly) followed a man she met at a party in Paris to Venice and recorded her experiences of surveillance, subterfuge, and getting lost as key elements in an experiential, living artwork-experience. These psychogeographic approaches are often reflected and extended in contemporary site-based performance practice through the work of performance companies such as Wrights and Sites and Dreamthinkspeak and through the work of site-dance artists such as Susanne Thomas, the Quay Brothers, Katie Green, and Carolyn Deby. Resonances of this approach are also evident in methods of audience management employed by the site-based performance company Punchdrunk, in which audience members are free to navigate and reorder the sited performance work, an approach that effectively presents an 'open score' for audiencing. Psychogeographic influences resonate with the work of Manchester-based choreographer Anna MacDonald's performance *This is for you* (2010–2014), in which she employed an open score as an organizing structure for her improvised site-generic dance work. In this work, one audience member at a time is guided to a chair placed in an urban viewing location, often a shop window or a table at a café. Once in situ they are 'offered' an improvised dance by the performer (MacDonald) situated in the street outside. On her website she describes the dance: '*This is for you* is a site-specific public artwork designed to be seen through a window, by one person at a time. They watch a dancer, who performs in the street opposite them amidst the mundane and unpredictable space of the everyday. The work is about the pleasure of being seen. It explores communication across a distance and the complexities of sharing something of your self with another person'.[7] As the work is improvised, an organizing score is employed to set out the rules of the encounter, including simple instructions, such as:

- Viewer is guided to their seat by the host
- Host talks them through everything that will happen

(MacDonald 2014)

These instructions draw on the protocols of Authentic Movement practice, which engages a 'performer' with a 'witness', employed here to demarcate and organize a safe space in which the improvised encounter can take place and be contained. Following the placement of the audience member in her or his viewing space, the dancer performs an improvised dance in the street outside in which the dancer explores the material features and forms of the site. Macdonald (2014) describes this as a mapping process in which the dancer explores a 'measuring/meeting point' between body and site, marking out key points and features in the street space through the touch of the dancer's skin on specific site features. In this work, therefore, the open score sets out the rules of the encounter and acts as an organizing structure to contain the improvisation whilst ensuring a level of consistency between each iteration of the performance work. Macdonald's approach exemplifies how, as a method of improvised site-based performance-making, open scores can help us to discover things we didn't necessarily know we were looking for; often they provide starting points from which forays into the unknown ensue.

The work of US-based dance artist Hope Mohr provides a further example of open scoring practice employed in sited dance practice. Notions of 'listening' to the city and moving in urban environments in a sympathetic manner are explored in Mohr's account of The Language of the Listening Body (2007), an artistic project she conducted in collaboration with composer Michelle Nagai in New York in 2006 as part of a residency supported by the iLAND research organization, which Jennifer Monson founded. Usually based in San Francisco, Mohr turned her attention for this project to the city of New York and developed a project involving a core group of dancers in a two-week residency that explored locations in midtown Manhattan and Long island City, Queens. Moving from an initial interest in sonic engagements to embodied encounters with the city, the project engaged participants and members of the public in a series of 'soundwalks' in which they listened to the city's sonic landscapes and developed movement responses accordingly. As the residency progressed, the artists employed open scores to develop their engagement with the urban environment. Mohr describes one of the scores: 'on day 3 we explored specific methods of reacting physically to sound, from unconscious to intentional responses. From the unconscious mode, we progressed to exploring two "conscious" modes of responding to noise: "mirroring" and "paralleling." In "mirroring," we attempted to represent various sounds with our dancing. With "paralleling," we considered the implications of a sound: what information or message did the sound convey? We then tried to represent the message of the sound through movement' (2007: 191). Mohr describes here how the processes or 'scores' of mirroring and paralleling facilitated the participants' movement exploration of site-soundscapes as they embodied aural responses and amplified them through abstract improvised dance. She recalls that during the project's second, performed sound walk, participants were asked to travel in duets around Long Island and were given scores that explored listening and moving with another person:

> Notice how listening affects your moving
> Notice how moving affects your listening
> Look at the space between things.
> Play with closeness and distance between you and your partner while listening
>   together.
> Notice how the group moves through space.
> See the space between things
> Notice how the sound environment changes as you move down the street.
> Notice the space between you and your partner change as you travel down the street.
>
> (200)

This design of this score promoted moments of group collectivity and intersubjectivity as the duet couples exchanged movement ideas and worked collaboratively towards the development of an interactive duet dance that incorporated shared site responses. Towards the end of the essay, Mohr reflects on the outcomes of the creative processes and scoring methods and their efficacy as site-exploratory devices: 'we spent all week participating in the environment, listening for relationships, placing ourselves in context. Because of these choices, we were able to model a deep level of engagement in the land/ soundscape. There was no need to 'present' an active, creative relationship with the environment, because we already had one. We were used to 'sounding back' and 'dancing back' to the soundscape' (201). The notions of 'sounding' and 'dancing back' (201) to the environment encapsulate a form of improvised site-dance practice developed through and with the evolving open score framework. Mohr's observations regarding the residency's final presentational mode reflect a sense of knowing the site-world 'well' achieved through this practice. By articulating her lack of desire for the construction of a final performance product incorporating a representational portrayal of the body-site relationships developed, she alludes to a more preferable, organic form of relationship comparable to a form of osmosis as an outcome of this practice informed by the openness of the score's structure.

Furthering this notion of organic relationships between body and site, it is useful here to consider the work of US-based dance artist Andrea Olsen and her 'gestalt' approach to site-dance improvisation. Olsen explores a holistic approach to body-site relation-ships through her employment of ideas drawn from gestalt psychotherapy in her design of movement scores that explore a whole-person approach to engaging with space and place. She observes: 'place is emotional, based on your past history and associations. A gestalt dance in a specific place creates one mood and image, saturating every aspect of the dancing (2014: 118). She proposes that her score for a site-based gestalt dance should take place over two hours or several days, enabling a gradual process of body-site osmosis to develop:

- Find an unusual place to dance (hallway, closet, beach).
- Through moving, identify a feeling state or emotional image that calls your atten-tion. Allow it to permeate your body and guide every movement choice—creating a gestalt, a singular form and shape creating a wholeness.
- Make a dance based on this feeling state; note how the place informs your movement.
- Let your vocabulary be idiosyncratic—unique and true to your state.
- Decide your relationship to viewers before showing this work. Where will they stand or sit, and for how long? How do you cue the beginning or ending?
- Show this work. Discuss with your viewers.
- Write about your experience: what did you learn?

(118)

Olsen's gestalt approach refers to a totality of whole-person experience incorporating personal memories and experiences that inform and shape encounters with site in the present moment. This position reflects existential phenomenological perspectives that suggest that we exist in a constant state of becoming informed by a sense of present-ness in which 'the present does not cancel its past, nor will the future cancel its pre-sent' (Merleau-Ponty 1962: 82). A gestalt approach to experiencing sites acknowledges the body-self as an active participant in the world possessing an embodied sense of his-toricity, whilst at the same time acknowledging the dynamic nature of space and place proposed by spatial theorist Doreen Massey (2005), in which personal and place-based 'intersecting trajectories' converge and 'stories so-far' entwine. This approach fore-grounds the body-self as both a place of embodied knowledge and an activator of site-based epistemologies revealed during movement improvisations through which the individual comes to know the site-world well.

CONCLUSION

This chapter has explored how scores are designed, applied, and managed by prac-titioners and, through questioning what they might 'do' in the site-dance context, has reflected on how scores might lead us towards and divert us away from specific site components. Through a consideration of scores as enabling devices that facilitate the management of a range of site 'data' explored through corporeal means, the discussion positions the body-self as both a container of and a producer of knowledge. Closed scores enable us to employ the body-self as an investigative tool focused on specific site-related tasks in order to bring the improviser closer to an understanding of site. Open scores enable us to key in to the body-self's intuitive knowledge of the world in a more open format that enables the body's wisdom and sensory attunement to lead into an improvisation with a site in an intuitive manner, as dance phenomenologist Maxine Sheets-Johnstone observes: 'a dynamically attuned body that knows the world and makes its way within it kinetically is thoughtfully attuned to the variables of both its own movement and the movement of things in its surroundings' (2009: 61). Movement scores enable practitioners to focus on things in particular and to acknowledge the body-self's capacity to reveal site-based information in an embodied manner that is unique to the skills and expertise of the trained dancing body. Through articulating this tacit knowledge in the form of abstract improvised dance performance, this information can be employed and presented in a more structured performance format or can remain as a private, subjective practice employed by the experiencer as a means of knowing the world differently through the moving, sensate body. The array of improvised practices and approaches discussed here supports the assertion that however this resulting material might be employed, score-derived movement improvisations can invoke sited encounters that bring us closer to an embodied experience of the world, presenting a unique and often ineffable means of accessing and 'knowing' the site-world well through corporeal means.

Notes

1. *Choreographic Practices* 2(1) 2014.
2. Whilst this chapter addresses the use of scores in site-based work, it is perhaps useful to refer the reader to recent initiatives that engage with the use of scores in contemporary dance practice more broadly—see the Motionbank project: http://motionbank.org/.
3. Jim Burns was an associate of Lawrence Halprin at the Lawrence Halprin and Associates architecture practice in California.
4. The quotation 'the human body is a microcosm of the earth' is from Halprin 1995: 214.
5. This workshop is described in detail in Hunter (2015).
6. Both these projects are discussed in detail in Hunter (2015).
7. This is a quote from the website of Anna MacDonald, http://annamacdonaldart.co.uk/ http___www.annamacdonaldart.co.uk/Forecast_dance_home.html www.forecastdance.org.

References

Besel, R. D., and Blau, J. A. (eds.). (2014) *Performance on Behalf of the Environment*. Lanham, MD: Rowman and Littlefield.

Fraleigh, S. (1987) *Dance and the Lived Body: A Descriptive Aesthetics*. Pittsburgh: University of Pittsburgh Press.

Goldberg, M. (1986) Trisha Brown: 'All of the Person's Person Arriving'. *Drama Review* 30(1) (Spring): 149–170.

Halprin, A. (1974) Life / art Workshop Processes. In Halprin, L. and Burns, J. *Taking Part: A Workshop Approach to Collective Creativity*. Cambridge MA: MIT Press.

Halprin, A. (1995) *Moving Towards Life: Five decades of Transformational Dance*. Hanover NH: Wsleyan University Press.

Hirsch, A. B. (2011) Scoring the Participatory City: Lawrence (and Anna) Halprin's Take Part Process. *Journal of Architectural Education* 64(2): 127–140.

Kaplan, R. (ed.) (1995) *Moving towards Life: Anna Halprin, Five Decades of Transformational Dance*. Middletown, CT: Wesleyan University Press.

Handschuh, J. (2013) On Finding Ways of Being: Kinesthetic Empathy in Dance and Ecology. In Besel, R.D., and Blau, J. (eds.), *Performance on Behalf of the Environment*, Lanham MD: Rowman and Littlefield.

Hunter, V. (2007) 'Arriving Score' PaR Site-Dance Workshop, CORD Conference, Centre Nationale De La Danse, Paris.

Hunter, V. (2015) Revealing the Site through Phenomenological Movement Inquiry. In Brauer, F., Humm, M., and Shaw, D. B. (eds.), *Radical Space*. London: Rowman and Littlefield, 65–85.

Lay, Paula Alexandra. (2014) *Acts of Embodiment and Imagination in the Practice of Movement*. Unpublished conference presentation at World Dance Alliance Global Summit, Angers, France, July 6–11.

Macdonald, A. (2014) Containing the City in 'This Is for You'. [Unpublished conference paper] presented at conference Performance, Place, Possibility, University of Leeds, 4–5 April.

Massey, D. (2005) *For Space*. London: Sage.

Merleau-Ponty, M. (1962) *The Phenomenology of Perception*. London: Routledge and Kegan Paul.

Merriman, P. (2010). Architecture/Dance: Choreographing and Inhabiting Spaces with Anna and Lawrence Halprin. *Cultural Geographies* 7(4): 427–449.

Mohr, H. (2007) Listening and Moving in the Urban Environment. *Women and Performance: A Journal of Feminist Theory* 17(2): 185–203.

Sheets-Johnstone, M. (2009) *The Corporeal Turn: An Interdisciplinary Reader*. Exeter, UK: Imprint Press.

Tufnell, M., and Crickmay, C. (2004) *A Widening Field: Journeys in Body and Imagination*. London: Dance Books.

Worth, L., and Poynor, H. (eds.). (2004) *Anna Halprin*. London: Routledge.

CHAPTER 36

....

THE DANCER, THE
PHILOSOPHER, AND
THE TRAMP

....

HILARY ELLIOTT

THE aim of this chapter is to share with readers the pragmatics and attendant philosophy of a model of practice and discourse for the field of solo movement/dance improvisation that I call *withness*. I discuss this particular approach to unaccompanied, studio (or otherwise indoor)-based improvisation through a set of intertwined strategies or organizational anchors: *reading space*, its very specific subset *reading the words of space,* and *inhabiting an imaginative landscape.* These strategies, drawn on as and when desired, enable the solo improviser to channel and structure the creative experience of spontaneous, instant composition—understood here as the seeding, harnessing, and shaping of material as one process—in ways that are relational, responsive, and interactive. In withness, solo improvisation is calibrated as an ongoing dialogue or interchange between the improviser and the physical space—the material aspects and affective reverberations of the built environment—that the improviser is occupying; and the material that emerges, the specific content that is felt, moved, spoken, imaged, is a consequence of a self-aware perceptual interfacing with/in the delimitations and discovered freedoms of the given studio-environment. In short, improvisational material emerges in this practice as a consequence of the improviser's dynamic participatory attitude; an attitude that I will explore as both a pragmatic compositional operational mode and an embodied philosophical stance.

Laced through the pragmatic and attitudinal way of being that infuses withness is a key interest in the role vision can play amidst tactility and kinaesthesia as an attentional tool—a way of projecting oneself into and establishing direct contact with the space that contains and informs the work, and opening the improviser (and spectator) to the immediate presence of what is around her. Withness thus claims vision as a significant sense within the dynamic interplay of multiple perceptual systems in improvised dance, but it is a particularly fine-tuned visual attentiveness that is of interest here; one that invites visual impressions to impact the body/mind in order to catalyse a spontaneous response that reflects the improviser's experiencing of and *with* the space itself. Accessing and tapping into the imagination—which in this model of practice encompasses visual/mental or kinaesthetic images that are vivified and embodied, and includes shards of memory that are then fleshed out in the present moment—also functions as a dynamic avenue for spontaneous, transformative play; a way of conjuring up, as I explain later, landscapes or worlds that are seeded by attending to the idiosyncratic details, material aspects, and suggestive resonances of the immediate space but in unfolding take on additional, wider reverberations.

The opening section of the essay offers a reading of American novelist and Jazz critic Albert Murray's account of Charlie Chaplin's Tramp walking down a street with a lemon meringue pie (1998) as a charming illustration of an improviser's spontaneous corporeal responsiveness to his environment's idiosyncrasies. The parable also serves to introduce some of the philosophical ground that has informed my thinking and practice: the Tramp and French philosopher Maurice Merleau-Ponty (1908–1961) both articulate exemplars of phenomenological understandings of individual/world interdependence and embodied understandings of perception as active interfacing and interplay with and within our environs. The Tramp thus silently (and eloquently) illuminates the condition of withness, whilst the phenomenological ideas embedded in Merleau-Ponty's philosophical outlook, couched in the allusive poetic language for which he is renowned, supply part of the rationale, logic, and language of the strategies. His philosophical writings on the active and participatory nature of perception—to perceive is to 'render oneself present to something through the body' (Merleau-Ponty 1964c: 42)—interlaced with his calibration of the porousness of individual and world—the entities of the world 'pass into' me (1964b: 166), and I 'exist within' and 'emigrate into' them (1968: 139)—open a pathway through which to reflect on and with which to pinpoint and articulate the participatory attitude that is practised and highlighted throughout the strategies.

In order to give the reader a sense of how withness manifests in training/research and performance, I employ a number of different registers of writing—all postimprovising reflections: analyses, in which the philosophical underpinnings of the work are especially stressed; 'voicings' of my inner processes as a way of tracking the strategies at work in particular instances; and distillations of attitudes, actions, or emergent images—fragments of improvisational experience that (re)emphasize some of this practice's characteristic pragmatic and attitudinal ways of being or capture snippets of content that stayed with me and resonated in my memory after an event.

THE TRAMP

Serving as an exemplary, if fictional, illustration of withness, here is Albert Murray's account of Charlie Chaplin's Tramp walking down a street with a lemon meringue pie. Murray begins by introducing another figure 'who is in control of everything':

He's the guy who wears a top hat, he's got a cane; he's kind of a caricature of J. P. Morgan back in his heyday. He walks down the street, and he's in charge. Folks are on the sidewalk, and they're looking. He's the lord of all he surveys. He doesn't see that banana peel under his foot. Steps on a banana peel and breaks his crown. On the other street, here comes a tramp, Charlie Chaplin in his raggedy-butt pants, flat shoes, toes almost out, cutaway coat that looks somewhat pretentious, a bowler hat, and with the nerve to sport a boutonniere.... But instead of striding like he owns everything, he prances and dances like he's *related* to everything, like it's there *for him*. The other guy owns it, but Charlie Chaplin is *of it*: he's *of it* and *with it*. So he's dancing up, and he's obviously earning his living because someone has told him to deliver a lemon meringue pie. He's got his stick in one hand, he's swinging down the lane. And he's so busy looking, following a pretty girl, that he steps on a banana peel; but he's already hanging loose, so he just dances all over the sidewalk and finally re-trieves the pie and continues prancing on down the street with his fancy walking stick (Murray 1998: 577, emphasis in original)

'Hanging loose', we see that the Tramp is proximal to, not distanced from, the things and people around him; he is related and relating, connected and connecting. Living as a part *of* the world and explicitly striding/prancing/dancing *with* it, the Tramp makes ex-plicit his, and our, interrelationship and interdependence with our environs.[1]

He is clearly, in the words of Merleau-Ponty, 'in the world', and 'only in the world does he know himself' (1962: xi). More specifically, the Tramp knows the world through improvisation—his is an ability to extemporize dance in response to the world's vicissitudes, a capacity that for Murray suggests 'an exaggerated image of what we mean by resilience' (1998: 577). This is a point also made by Susan Foster when she cites the story in *Dances That Describe Themselves: The Improvised Choreography of Richard Bull* as part of her discussion of ensemble improvised dance (Foster 2002). For Foster, the Tramp illustrates and embodies adaptability to the world as it shifts, a way of being that is characteristic of ensemble dancers for whom separateness and 'potential conflict' dis-solve as they interact with each other in a fluid, ongoing exchange (Foster 2002: 240). Translated to the exigencies of solo, studio-based practice, ability to accommodate and respond to the world's surprising incursions serves to illustrate how the condi-tions of a particular physical space—even the outwardly static nature of a studio or indoor venue—can act as an influential and determining context for improvisational action. In this solo practice, individual and (built) environment are also enmeshed, and in the absence of the variables introduced by a moving ensemble, it is the physical space that becomes cocreator, perhaps even a duetting 'partner', in the kindling of in-stant composition. Explicitly influencing, organizing, even 'composing' the improviser, the architectural and spatial environment is inhabited as a place of performative pos-sibility, of creative opportunity, in which inclinations—familiar or fresh, recognizable or surprising, habitual or revitalizing—can emerge, be noted, sifted, curiously followed through, or discarded.

Returning briefly to the parable, it is implied that some time passes before the Tramp 'finally' retrieves his pie and 'continues prancing on down the street', and I like to imagine that he has spent the time revelling in the free play of his dancing/danced impulses; lingering in, playing with/in, the circumstances in which he unexpectedly finds himself. Unlike J. P. Morgan—the 'person who gets tangled up with the rigid thing'—the Tramp is 'ready to encompass more experience' (Murray 1998: 577); embodying a corporeal and attitudinal disposition towards fulsome participation in whatever his environment affords. In recognizing possibilities for extended exploration, discovery, or play within his immediate spatial context, the Tramp also serves as a reminder that the fundamental improvisational element of time—specifically time as duration and/or timing—can be creatively manipulated throughout any given improvisation. I pick up later on the durational aspect of vision (both rapid glances and extended moments of looking serving as efficacious tools in this model of improvisation) but note here that in the gap between stepping on the banana peel and 'finally' retrieving his pie, we can read the Tramp's extended (and presumably pleasurable) improvised corporeal engagement with his street, sidewalk, and fancy walking stick.

> Stick in one hand
> Swinging down the lane
> Busy looking
> Following
> Step
> Slip
> Off-balance
> Suspend
> Drop
> Rise
> Intake of breath
> Swing of an arm
> Turn
> Swivel
> Delight

Dialoguing or conversing with the surrounding environment—taking time to see (or in the case of The Tramp selectively see), touch, and navigate it—cultivates a felt knowledge of relationality, responsiveness, and interconnectedness. I also understand the Tramp's processes of inhabiting and corporeally responding to his environment's idiosyncrasies through Merleau-Ponty's phenomenology of embodied perception; the improviser 'inhabits', even 'haunts', space, improvising, in a 'wholly animated' way, his relationship to the things around him (Merleau-Ponty 1964a: 5). When spontaneously composing, applying myself to the particularized space I am in—'like a hand to an instrument' (5)—what unfolds is sensorial free play with/in the space of my surrounds, play that, like the Tramp's, is grounded in the phenomenological appreciation of perception as occurring through action: through active, sensory experiencing of and orientation to the entities around me. Figure 36.1, for instance, taken during a Spontaneous Combustion performance in Huddersfield, captures a moment in which the axial extension of my spine reflects the straight, vertical lines of the lighting tower. In line with the work of J. J. Gibson—whose groundbreaking study on perception *The Senses Considered as Perceptual Systems* (1966) was published two years before Merleau-Ponty's last, post-humously published work, *The Visible and the Invisible* (1968)—the exteroceptor senses here are systems for perception. Looking and touching (and more widely, listening, smelling, and tasting) are 'ways of seeking and extracting information about the environment' (Gibson 1966: 5), information which might then seed, infuse, loosely anchor, or explicitly shape the emergence of moments of improvised dance.

The sensory network is also to be understood, after Gibson, as interwoven; a fact that, despite being renowned for his ocular-centrism, Merleau-Ponty gauged and labelled 'the rule' of 'synaesthetic perception', in which the senses 'intercommunicate' (1962: 229). Thus in my practice I am aware of the senses as interwoven but different channels of information, and, crucially, I can choose to differently prioritize them throughout any given improvisation.[2]

FIG. 36.1 Sensorial free play with and with/in this space/place of my surrounds. Photograph by Mike Thresher.

A Collocation of Strategies

I am sitting at the edge of a small university dance studio, attending to the wider architectural and spatial environment I am in and how I am in it. Cross-legged, I feel the right edge of my right foot and the left edge of my left foot against the floor, palms of hands cupped around my knees, weight falling from my spine through the pelvis into the floor. Noticing this kinaesthetic information, I simultaneously slowly turn my head, visually scanning the architectural features. A smattering of small silver dots on the lower folds of the black drapes in the rear left-hand corner of the room catches my interest, sparking what Merleau-Ponty would deem 'a certain motor intention' (1962: 317), a corporeal impulse that occurs without any intervening mental processing. I walk to the corner and lie down on my left side, putting my head on my outstretched left arm, snuggling my body into the thick drapes. I spend some moments lingering in the sensation of my left ear squished against my left arm, just above the elbow, the contact of my left hip with the floor, the surface contact of my right heel on left heel. My right hand grabs folds of the thick curtain and slowly moves them as my eyes linger, close up, on the silver dots that are level with my eye-line. Maintaining a grip on the curtain, I begin to shuffle my weight so that I am lying on my back, simultaneously shifting the direction of my head so that I am looking up at the ceiling. Still aware of the feeling of the curtain in my right hand and the sense of giving my back's weight to the floor, I also notice a word, APOLLO, written in small capital letters, upside down from my viewing angle, on one of the lanterns above. Beginning a more deliberate rolling of weight from side to side, letting go of the curtain but feeling it brush against me as I brush against it, I allow images and imaginings to bubble up from the nuanced combination of these particular physical circumstances. Attending to my fluid, tactile relationship with the floor and curtains and, concomitantly, allowing the name APOLLO and the silver dots to begin to freely associate in my imagination, puts into play a logic of solo dance improvisation as active participation in and with/in my surroundings and a collocation of *reading space, reading the words of space,* and *inhabiting an imaginative landscape* as mobile, anchoring stratagems.

> *Rendering myself present to what I see/touch/feel*
> *Drinking silver dots*
> *Imaginings of starry skies*
> *Spacecraft*
> *Long-lost love*

Reading Space

Turning now to an illumination of each strategy in turn, with the aim of pinpointing the nuances that differentiate them as attitudinal and pragmatic ways of being, I stand still on one spot, roughly in the centre of the empty playing area, turning my head and eyes together. I am aware of my breath and the feel of the wooden floor underneath my feet, and I have a kinaesthetic/tactile sense of leaning slightly to the right. Although I am aware of this kinaesthetic/tactile information, I choose to background it and pay more attention to—foreground—what my eyes tell me about the space I am in. I note the specificity of visible architectural details and objects or props that also inhabit the space—a plastic carrier bag partially hidden behind a curtain, a water cooler with no cups, a pile of books in one corner, red roof tiles outside the uncurtained window, and in one surprising encounter, a pigeon.

Deliberately wielding vision as a tool of awareness, noting the visible details and idiosyncrasies of the physical space, allowing them to 'pass into' me (Merleau-Ponty 1964b: 166), functions as a means of tuning in to my body/mind/environment as it manifests today—or rearriving, if I find that during the course of an improvisation my processes of initiation and response have become habitual and unimmediate. Carrying in me the phenomenological material I have read, I understand this purposive 'seeing', what I call direct looking, through the lens of Merleau-Ponty's 'exploratory gaze' (1962: 315) and 'questioning' vision (226). It is a way of using the act of looking as a means of opening myself to the wider environment, extending my body/mind into the surrounds, and in establishing direct contact with the things around me also revitalizing my own felt sense of the immediate and present moment.

Visually following the outward contours, colours, and surfaces of the things around me (an image of a searchlight sometimes comes to mind), *reading space* gives me visual information about the context I am in, but I am also attuned to what the 'interesting bits' that 'draw' my visual attention may be (Gibson 1966: 260) and what that 'interesting' information might spark by way of kinaesthetic response and mental imagery. The strategy thus operates in a kind of hinge zone, tessellating what I see or choose to visually focus on (through and with different spatial positioning), and equally what draws my attention, with how the visible is experienced in terms of kinaesthetic sensation or mental image. The partially hidden plastic bag sparks curiosity, a mind/body impulse to further investigate it; the pigeon arrests my breath in surprise and delight; the pile of books brings to mind Prospero in *The Tempest*. (It is beyond the scope of this essay to examine why certain associations and impulses might be triggered by particular visual stimuli, but I mention it here to share the significance of cultivating an awareness that impulses and inclinations do arise and recognizing the generative potential that is then open of making choices about whether and how to pursue them.)

Vision is thus wielded here as a tool that invites proximity and closeness between self and the wider spatial environment—establishing a dynamic connection between interior and exterior—in a different way, but in tandem with, the proximity garnered through touch. Understood through a phenomenological lens, it is 'the same body (that) sees and touches' (Merleau-Ponty 1968: 134), and objects in the environment present themselves to the 'gaze/touch' (317); vision, like touch, happens 'among, or is caught in, things' (1964b: 163). Rather than instigating distance and separateness then—as Mark Paterson notes, 'the optic is supposedly associated with distance and transcendence'

(2007: 84)—vision in this practice exists in proximity because it is the combined dynamic of deliberately looking and/or consciously registering where my interest is drawn, letting what I am seeing 'pass into' my body/mind and cultivating attunement to the minutiae of kinaesthetic response to what is seen that seeds and begins to direct emergent material. Perhaps I have a sense of muscular tension or claustrophobia engendered by the (to me) oppressive whitewashed walls and low ceilings of a studio—I am reminded here of David Abram's comment that the 'superstraight lines and right angles of our office architecture ... make our animal senses wither' (1996: 64)—or a sensation of physical ease suddenly washes over me as a shaft of sunlight appears, radically altering the mood of the space and my own rapport with it. By tracking the felt correspondences between direct looking and these kinds of kinaesthetic impulses, improvised composition becomes firmly grounded in a felt sense of proximal, embodied relationality and space as it is phenomenally experienced; with the merging of outer visible stimulus with inner response or impulse operating as the guiding dynamic of the emergent choreography.

> *Taking in the far*
> *Textured wall*
>
> *Leaning forward*
> *Intake of breath*
> *Heels light*
> *Run*
>
> *Marks and lines*
> *Filigree the paint*
> *Like fissures*
> *Hairs*
> *Or veins*

The temporal dynamic is important to note here in relation to the use of direct looking as an attentional tool that locates me in the space and as a compositional pathway that can spark imaginative and corporeal impulses, as it can take place very quickly. Drew Leder notes that vision 'gives us in one glance a more comprehensive survey of the surrounding world, more detailed information about any particular object, more knowledge concerning the stable attributes of a thing, than does any other sense' (1990: 117), a point reiterated by Lisa Nelson when she comments that 'the eyes are the fastest sense to name things' (Movement Research n.d.) and 'the eyes are the first to know' (Dance-Tech n.d.).[3] Acknowledging our ability to 'see in a snapshot' (Dance-Tech n.d.), *reading space* can be effected very quickly, at a glance, through scanning or skimming the surroundings and attending to potentially equally rapid corporeal and/or imaginative responses.

Nelson also makes the useful point, however, that 'we don't often take the time to actually look at something' (Movement Research n.d.). In the context of Nelson's interest in decision-making processes at work in ensemble dance, 'taking the time' to look at movement facilitates a process of unearthing particular interests and proclivities so that the dancers can then begin to name and make explicit their compositional desires.

In *reading space,* I can also take time: maintaining a precise point of visual interest for longer than the few seconds that it takes to register that it is there. As I follow with my eyes, head, and body the movements of the pigeon darting about the rafters, a kinaesthetic image of loose arms gently rising and lowering in a soft breeze occurs; as I inspect a pair of pink shoes that have been tossed towards me by an audience member, a mental image of a young girl nebulously forms; as I move my eyes, fingers and hands amongst dust motes caught in a shaft of sunlight create a sense of intimacy. In all these instances, taking time to linger with/in a visual impression creates an extended, concentrated attunement to the conditions of the physical space and cultivates a sensitivity to the ways in which imaginative inclinations or images might gestate in the body/mind.

So a lightning glance may lead to a corporeal response that is quickly felt and/or swiftly enacted: I look at and move towards a window in a unified action that feels essentially seamless or, as Merleau-Ponty snappily phrases it, 'I want to go over there, and here I am' (1964d: 66). But once at the window, I see moths rhythmically spiralling around a street light in the darkness of early evening and choose to linger with them. In doing so, I gear into the physical space quite differently, remaining open and porous to images or imaginative fancies as they begin to gather more slowly into the shape of my response (aware, too, that a spectator may simply see me standing still by a window, an activity potentially imbued with choreographic or theatrical effect but in this case a vehicle for a different compositional agenda). Taking time to actually look at something animates Merleau-Ponty's dictum that the gaze 'gets more or less from things according to the way in which it questions them, ranges over or dwells on them' (1962: 153), as surprising notions or impulses—those that do not immediately present themselves—begin to emerge and crystallize.

> *Drink with my eyes*
> *Absorb what I see*
> *Vision becomes gesture*[4]
>
> *Moths*
> *Butterflies*
> *Small flaps of wings here*
> *Lead to*
> *Massive shifts there*

Letting in what I see—absorbing the shapes, forms, and textures of the wider architectural space so that there is a sense that I temporarily 'exist within' and 'emigrate into' them (Merleau-Ponty 1968: 139), and being receptive to corporeal and imaginative associations that bubble up, facilitates a process of finding consanguinity between what I see, how I see (in terms of duration and timing), and how what I see makes me feel. Impulses for instant composition are rooted in the affective relationship that emerges between my wider spatial environs and me, the lived experience, in the evocative words of Yvonne Rainer, of 'the body in the place, in the space of the place' (Rainer 1974: 298). Figure 36.2, for instance, taken during a Spontaneous Combustion performance in Huddersfield, captures a strong impulse to push upwards away from the floor.

FIG. 36.2 A lived felt connection between body and environment. Photograph by Mike Thresher.

At this stage I want to briefly note that *reading space* is a useful strategy to pick up and drop in relation to working with peripheral vision. Oscillating between direct looking and a softer focus (reminding myself that the eyes are situated deep inside the skull; only one-sixth of the eyeball is actually visible from the outside) refreshes, even rests, the eyes. When working with peripheral vision, I notice that the wider environs still act as an influence on movement choices, such as where I choose to be in space, and continue to subtly affect the qualities of my movement, but the galvanizing influence of the surroundings on my compositional choices is softened or tempered. Concomitantly, my eyes are still receptive and noting, taking in, but they are no longer seeding and directing the emergent composition by directly interfacing with the wider environment, seeing/seeking into it, traversing its contours.

Soft vision
Rolling locomotion
Low body architecture, in contact with the floor
Feel the floor through the back surface of my toes
Feel the back surface of my toes through the floor
Touching/touched
Rhythms regular, shapes soft

Something is at the edge of my vision

READING THE WORDS OF SPACE

Here are some words that I have encountered in different spaces:

On a water cooler: *jazz*
Upside down on a lantern: APOLLO
On a myriad first aid boxes: *First Aid*
A charcoal drawing on a wall: *There are more than 30,000 slaves in the world*
On a poster blue-tacked to a wall: *Raffle*
A handwritten notice on a wall: *still chill relax calm*
On a Post-It note on the floor: *Kate*

This subset of *reading space* draws on visible text as a stimulus for composition, an avenue for corporeal and imaginative play. *Reading the words of space* shifts into making danced and/or spoken material through a process of noticing any associations, correspondences, or resonances sparked by a word and then generating/allowing the promulgation of further impulses—corporeal and/or spoken. Similar in compositional structuring to Keith Johnstone's techniques of 'Associating Images' and 'Automatic Writing', in which students respond verbally or on the page to an initial image, triggering an ongoing flow of spontaneous responses (Johnstone 1981: 120–121), building associatively in this strategy enables the improviser to be surprised by nuggets of suggestion or layers of significance that appear. If I choose, I can imaginatively pursue any associative details; further material—such as the pictorial details of a fictional topography, the narrative details of a story or expressions of a character's inner landscape of psychology or emotion—can be harnessed and shaped as it emerges (segueing into *inhabiting an imaginative landscape*).

This very literal reading carries interesting ramifications for the inhabitation of space in improvised work. Enacting the strategy, the improviser fleshes out the two-dimensional manifestation of the word, enveloped in a particular (often mundane) everyday context, transforming it into an embodied concept, loosened from the specific connotations of the space in which it is inscribed. In doing so, the word becomes a dynamic part of the improviser's experienced external/internal environment. The word may trigger a wealth of associative images that I primarily choose to verbalize—and thus I continue to locate myself improvisatorially in a linguistic operational mode. Or I may choose to enter a nonverbal plane, one that is coloured by or laced through with the images and associations of the personal and collective significances of the word but in which I am able to suppress some of the more conscious verbal processing. There might be an amalgam of the two modes of moving and talking, so different amounts of conscious linguistic processing might be in play, since in my general approach to dance improvisation, moving and talking have equal status as expressive vocabularies. I conceptualize them as separate but interwoven activities in the process of composing pieces and utilize them as ways of differently inhabiting and articulating the emerging material. So in responding to words, the potential interplay between talking and moving functions as a shifting kaleidoscope that illuminates different facets of the transformation and fleshing out of the given text of the spatial environment.

> *Let in what I see*
>
> *Jazz*
>
> *Flappers*
> *Flouting convention*
> *Flaunt*
> *Move with disdain*
> *And cigarettes*

INHABITING AN IMAGINATIVE LANDSCAPE

Overlapping with and also extending the first strategy and its subset, particularly in longer-form improvisations over twenty minutes long, *inhabiting an imaginative landscape* stems from what is experienced in the immediate space of practice/performance—such as emergent kinaesthetic sensations, visual/mental or kinaesthetic images, or emotions sparked by visual information. Instant composition then rests on the improviser's investment in and engagement with an imaginary landscape as it emerges and unfolds. The strategy is thus infused with a desire to engage in associative, transformative play; to use the material givens and affective reverberations of the immediate environment as stepping stones towards the authorship of new imaginative spaces.

This impetus towards invention, towards the creation of new cosmologies, is in line with what Danielle Goldman calls the 'world-making potential of improvisation' (2010: 142). In her discussion of improvisational creativity, Goldman cites Bill Dixon's important differentiation between the ambiances that exist 'whether one wanted their presence or not' and those 'that one made oneself, that had more to do with what one wanted to have oneself surrounded by' (Dixon in Goldman 2010: 142). Honouring the profound ontological and sociopolitical significance that Dixon attached to creating through improvisation 'a more desirable setting in which to live' (Goldman 2010: 143), *inhabiting an imaginative landscape* shares an awareness of the powerful creative agency involved in bringing the hitherto unrealized into existence.

Beginning an improvisation in a bland, small, furnished room on a hard floor at a conference in Wales, for instance, I attend to the sight and sound of a ceiling fan, as it has caught my interest (Improvisation as Performance 2010). Watching it—letting it 'pass into' me—I am struck by a mental image of a typically hot day in Australia, when air conditioning is a common and necessary phenomenon. This surprising moment of recall—occurring in and because of the details of the here and now of the performance context—then becomes the foundational material of the ensuing improvisation, the platform for an unanticipated exploration of 'home', family, and identity.

The imaginative landscape may thus reside outside the body, somewhere in the studio/performance space, but alternatively or simultaneously a rich interiority may be experienced, an emotional texture suffusing the improviser's choices from within.[5] I use the word 'landscape' to encompass both a literal geography and an emotional terrain. In either case, it is both by immersing herself in this landscape, allowing it to function as the cog or driver of the material, and by simultaneously moulding that material by making choices about its articulation, that the strategy can enable a useful generativity and illuminate the momentum of the improviser's engagement in the textures of a newly conjured world.

The improviser may choose to silently inhabit a landscape, expressing emotion or situation purely corporeally. Specific corporeal choices such as speed, degrees of strong or light weight, isolation of particular body parts, or oscillations between locomotion and stillness in space will in this case be filtered through whatever character, emotion, or scenario is informing the emergent material. The spontaneous choreography—what Merleau-Ponty would call 'the ensemble of my body's routes' (1968: 247)—is a reflection and filtering of the improviser's involvement with the imaginative realm.

Another compositional avenue is the extemporizing of text, offering a first or third person perspective on an unfolding scenario. Here the improviser functions as storyteller—a stance in keeping with Chris Johnston's understanding of the generative energy of the imagination in dramatic improvisation. In his work, ideas and images are inhabited and cultivated so that they can 'spawn' their own world within the world of the improvised event itself (2006: 227). As with the purely corporeal enactment, the improviser here remains connected to the logic and momentum of this newly created 'world', perhaps building verbal material associatively, as I described earlier.

Whichever modality she chooses to embody, the improviser will simultaneously orient herself to two different uses of the space. She will occupy (and be seen in performance to occupy) the visible surroundings of the architectural space and will continue to orient herself within these actual parameters. She will also occupy an alternative landscape, the imaginative dimension, which will infiltrate her decisions within that physical space. To the extent that I fulsomely engage with the logic of the landscape that I inhabit,

I will find a dynamic momentum to my occupation of the space. Equally, to the extent that I attend to my external articulation of this imaginative realm, there will be a specificity and concreteness to my actions and utterances, a making visible of a reimagined experiencing of self and surrounds.

The corner enables me to give weight
To slide, rise and lower
I lean sideways, pressing my left shoulder, my left hip into the wall
I fall
Smooth, cold, white

An image of a frozen landscape appears
Engulfs

Conclusion

Reading space, reading the words of space, and *inhabiting an imaginative landscape* practise a commingling of improviser and surrounds—in which the improviser's felt sense of corporeal and imaginative engagement with/in her architectural and spatial surroundings is revitalized—in order to ground solo dance/movement improvisation in a relational, dialogic interplay between improviser and studio-environment. A rekindled visual acuity forms a core part of the attentiveness to mechanisms of sensing that underpins this participatory approach, establishing the compositional efficacy of moving/speaking/imagining with what and how I see; using emergent kinaesthetic sensations, visual/mental or kinaesthetic images or emotions sparked entirely, or in part, by visual information, as the wellsprings of spontaneous composition. When coupled with an imaginative fleshing out of (visual/tactile/kinaesthetic) sensory information, withness functions as a fecund resource for instant composition with and within the material realities and less tangible reverberations of the particularized space that infuses and delineates the work.

Inspired by the Tramp's corporeal articulation of individual/world interdependence and embodied understanding of perception as active interfacing and interplay with and within our environs, withness gives form to the improviser's lived experience of inhabiting and spontaneously responding to the physical conditions, idiosyncratic details, and affective reverberations of what is around her. Tessellated with Merleau-Ponty's intricately poetic phenomenology, withness offers a unique perspective on the experiencing, structuring, and framing of solo movement/dance improvisation; an improvisational model and discourse for the field that is both a pragmatic compositional approach and an embodied philosophical stance, in which interactivity, relationality and a dynamic participatory attitude take precedence.

Open your eyes
What do you see?
Let the visual impression
Fall into your body
A lived, felt connection between body and space

He prances and dances like he's related to everything

Surrendering to seeing
Moving with/in
Moving in relation

He's of it: he's of it and with it

This movement is a dialogue
Leading and following
My body and imagination instigate and respond

He just dances all over the sidewalk

Notes

1. Coincidentally, but revealingly, his improvisatory and ontological status is drawn in the same italics that Merleau-Ponty uses to situate the rest of us '*in* the being' and '*of* it' (Merleau-Ponty 1968: 248, italics in original). In this respect, the Tramp also parallels Merleau-Ponty's philosophical rubric in which individual and world gear into one another through the individual's corporeal participation, itself based on a foundational philosophical attitude of interdependence. I am touching here on the dynamic and motional construct at the heart of Merleau-Ponty's philosophical matrix, the 'me other exchange', of the chiasm (Merleau-Ponty 1968: 215), in which there is an active entwinement of individual and world, poetically expressed as 'a relation that is one of embrace' (271). The chiasm is variously described (and translated) as a 'me other exchange' (215); an 'overlapping or encroachment' (123); 'encroachment, infringement' (134); 'the intentional encroachment' (239); 'reversibility' (263 and 264) and 'Ineinander' (268)—German for 'into one another'. Merleau-Ponty's use of the term is a linguistic theft from physiology; the optic chiasm is the site in the brain where one set of nerve fibres from each eye crosses over and joins with the noncrossing fibres from the other eye, forming two optic tracts, each with information from both eyes.

2. There are further useful clues and cues to my treatment of improvised dance to be gauged by an etymological dissection of the word *perception*, understandings then reinforced through Merleau-Ponty's philosophical outlook. The Latin stem *percipere* means to seize or to grasp thoroughly, entirely (*per*, thoroughly; *capere*, to grasp). The root stem suggests motion and motor activity as well as a purposive, open, and receptive attitude. It also suggests directness and completeness. Extrapolating from this, perception can be understood—phenomenologically and in relation to improvised dance—as direct corporeal engagement with and participation in the world; it is the sensorial encounters of Merleau-Ponty's 'actual body' (Merleau-Ponty 1964b: 160).

3. Lisa Nelson has developed an ensemble training practice, 'Tuning Scores', which engages strategically with vision and kinaesthesia in order to make individual choreographic proclivities explicit.

4. Musing on the 'philosophy' that animates the painter, Merleau-Ponty distinguishes between painting as an expression of the artist's 'opinions about the world' and the vitality of 'the instant when his vision becomes gesture, when, in Cezanne's words, he "thinks in painting"' (Merleau-Ponty 1964b: 178).

5. I want to distinguish this use of the imagination from the use of imagery in dance work, as illustrated in the writings of Eric Franklin, for instance. His writings are geared towards the use of imagery as a means of enhancing dancers' technique and expressivity, and particular images may be determined before work begins, or they may arise spontaneously. There is, however, a passage in his *Dynamic Alignment through Imagery* that is relevant to my point about the physical location of the imaginative landscape. Franklin notes that in dance, 'you can place your image inside your body, on the surface of your body, in the near or intimate space surrounding you, in your slightly larger personal space, or on the whole stage, even in the entire world' (Franklin 1996: 52).

References

Abram, David. (1996) *The Spell of the Sensuous*. New York: Vintage.

Dance-Tech. (n.d.) http://www.dance-tech.net. Accessed 25 June 2014.

Foster, Susan. (2002) *Dances That Describe Themselves: The Improvised Choreography of Richard Bull*. Middletown, CT: Wesleyan University Press.

Franklin, Eric. (1996) *Dance Alignment through Imagery*. Champaign, IL: Human Kinetics.

Gibson, James J. (1966) *The Senses Considered as Perceptual Systems*. London: Allen and Unwin.

Goldman, Danielle. (2010) *I Want to Be Ready: Improvised Dance as a Practice of Freedom*. Ann Arbor: University of Michigan Press.

Improvisation as Performance and Immediate Writing. (2010) Workshop at Theatre and Performance Research Association Conference, Cardiff, Wales, September.

Johnston, Chris. (2006) *The Improvisation Game: Discovering the Secrets of Spontaneous Performance*. London: Nick Hern Books.

Johnstone, Keith. (1981) *Impro: Improvisation and the Theatre*. London: Eyre Methuen.

Leder, Drew. (1990) *The Absent Body*. Chicago: University of Chicago Press.

Merleau-Ponty, Maurice. (1962) *Phenomenology of Perception*. Trans. Colin Smith. London: Routledge.

Merleau-Ponty, Maurice. (1964a) An Unpublished Text. Trans. Arleen B. Dallery. In *The Primacy of Perception: And Other Essays on Phenomenological Psychology, and Philosophy of Art, History and Politics*. Evanston, IL: Northwestern University Press, 5.

Merleau-Ponty, Maurice. (1964b) Eye and Mind. Trans. Carleton Dallery. In *The Primacy of Perception: And Other Essays on Phenomenological Psychology, and Philosophy of Art, History and Politics*. Evanston, IL: Northwestern University Press, 160–178.

Merleau-Ponty, Maurice. (1964c) The Primacy of Perception and Its Philosophical Consequences. Trans. James M. Edie. In *The Primacy of Perception: And Other Essays on*

Phenomenological Psychology, and Philosophy of Art, History and Politics. Evanston, IL: Northwestern University Press, 42.

Merleau-Ponty, Maurice. (1964d) *Signs*. Trans. Richard McCleary. Evanston, IL: Northwestern University Press.

Merleau-Ponty, Maurice. (1968) *The Visible and the Invisible*. Trans. Alphonso Lingis. Evanston, IL: Northwestern University Press.

Movement Research. (n.d.) http://www.movementresearch.org. Accessed 7 May 2014.

Murray, Albert. (1988) The Function of the Heroic Image. In O'Meally, Robert (ed.), *The Jazz Cadence of American Culture*. New York: Columbia University Press, 569–576.

Paterson, Mark. (2007) *The Senses of Touch: Haptics, Affects and Technologies*. Oxford: Berg.

Rainer, Yvonne. (1974) *Work 1961–73*. Halifax, Nova Scotia: Press of the Nova Scotia College of Art and Design.

CHAPTER 37

....

AUDIENCE IMPROVISATION AND IMMERSIVE EXPERIENCES

The Sensuous World of the Body in the Work of Lundahl & Seitl

....

JOSEPHINE MACHON

Art is a state of encounter.

Nicolas Bourriaud (2002: 18)

ALERTNESS, intuition, instinct, sensitivity, control, action, reaction ... attending ... waiting ... *being* ...

Not a checklist for the performer but terms that describe states of audience involvement in an immersive experience. The conventional expectation of an audience member at a theatre production is that of sitting, listening, and spectating. In contrast to this, immersive performance has evolved the idea and the *practice* of audience into spontaneous-decision-making participants within the work. Audiences in immersive theatres might continue to observe, listen, and be receptive, yet now through direct involvement and active, embodied engagement, physically as much as intellectually charting their own journey through the event.

This chapter analyses the audience member as improviser in immersive practice. Beginning with an overview that outlines what I understand to define immersive theatre experiences in general terms, I will identify some of the opportunities for audience improvisation established within immersive contexts. To illustrate, I will consider the way the improvised dance—a unique, tactile exchange between audience and artist—operates in the work of Lundahl & Seitl. Recollections of my own improvisations in these events will be documented in the first person to reflect the immediate and subjective nature of interaction. Correspondingly, my subsequent critical stance ranges across the first and third person. This is deepened by original interview material with the artists and supported by reference to Susanne Ravn's phenomenological analysis of movement (2009), Miranda Tufnell and Chris Crickmay's embodied approach to imagination and improvisation (2001, 2004), and Stephen Di Benedetto's ideas around 'attendance' in theatre practice that stimulates the full human sensorium (2007, 2010). These theories address and explore the sensing body in/as lived experience as much as artistic practice. Ravn's approach explores 'movement as a fundamental condition for being a body-subject acting and interacting in the world' (2009: 5), while Crickmay and Tufnell identify how 'improvisation is a way of shifting the boundaries within which we experience our world' and highlight the importance of 'being receptive to the immediate moment … tuning in to our own sensations, feelings, dreams', which opens up the imagination (2001: n.p.). Di Benedetto's thinking unpacks how 'the provocation of the senses' in performance events that 'create an in-between state of experience and awareness' exercise 'perception, consciousness, and attention' (2010: 1–3). Our combined critical approaches survey the ways the sensual and physical experiences of an audience member during a Lundahl & Seitl event might find affinities with improvised dance. In light of this, my concluding thoughts open up a consideration of the opportunities offered by immersive practice for repositioning audience involvement in performance as a creative activity. Overall, this analysis considers new protocols of engagement that have emerged as a consequence of the rise of immersive performance. My aim is to offer an approach to audience appreciation as embodied philosophy; performance theory that evolves from improvisatory practice.

IMMERSIVE PERFORMANCE

> Artists who harness more than our eyes and ears encourage us to wake up, to be alert to the world around us, and to interact actively with the objects and creatures around us. It is an invitation to live, to feel, and to be part of a larger community.
>
> Stephen Di Benedetto (2007: 134)

The term 'immersive', once only applied as an adjective in regard to performance, is now often used by way of defining 'a genre'. Though a contestable term, it is applied to diverse events that broadly share commonalities in approach; in short, that blend a variety of forms and seek to exploit 'the experiential' in performance. Although immersive practice shares common features with qualities of affect to be had in other visceral performance work, including many staged and studio-based contemporary dance pieces, immersive theatres are different in form, primarily in relation to audience interaction and consequently in the nature of experience undergone.[1] As much as such practice may well display qualities of the immersive and trigger embodied responses, in simple terms, it is the separated auditorium/stage, audience/performance, that prevents other kinds of visceral performance from being wholly immersive in terms of formal aesthetics.

Immersive performances are interdisciplinary, involving varied art forms alongside pedestrian activities, elevating the latter within/as the artistic encounter. The works of companies such as dreamthinkspeak, Lundahl & Seitl, Punchdrunk, or Shunt are exemplary of this practice. Events created by these companies are testament to the fact that for a performance to be immersive it must establish an 'in-its-own-world'-ness, achieved through a deft handling of space, scenography, sound, duration, and action. The bespoke worlds established, into which the audience is physically inserted, are material as much as imaginative realms in which the audience-participant is incorporated in concept and form. Physical engagement is central to this practice. Given this, bodies are prioritized in these worlds, sometimes performing and always perceiving bodies, the latter belonging to the audience members, whose direct insertion in and interaction with the world shapes the outcomes of the event. Where technologies are employed to evoke or alter the world, these will accentuate a sensual connection with(in) the world, rather than serving to distance the participant. An important feature attributable to this work is that some kind of 'contract for participation' will be shared between audience-participant and artist in order to allow full immersion in the world. This may be explicit, in the form of written or spoken guidelines shared prior to entering the space; or implicit within the structures of the immersive world, unfolding for individuals as they journey through the performance; or a combination of the two. These codes of conduct, once 'inside' the immersive world, serve to encourage varying levels of agency and participation according to the parameters of the event. These 'contracts' are vital in terms of facilitating willingness to participate on the part of the audience member as much as ensuring the safety of both participant and artist.[2]

In immersive performance, the audience-participant is fundamentally complicit within the concept, content, and form, a living part of the aesthetic. In the very act of requiring playful interaction, full immersion involves degrees of improvisation on the part of audience member as much as artist. As a consequence, acts of immersive participation have nurtured a particular type of audience member: one who is attracted to unusual approaches to active engagement with(in) a work of art. In live performance this has seen to an *evolvement*, through *involvement*, of audience encounters and expectations. What I intend by this is, immersive performance has evolved the idea and the *practice* of audience or spectator beyond the conventional attitude and action shared between one or other or both of these terms, that is, as listener-to or watcher-at a production. The audience member in immersive theatre maintains the skills and audio-visual desires of the audience-spectator yet additionally takes on responsibilities of active participation, becoming improviser-performer-collaborator at any given moment, in various given structures. This is as true of intimate one-to-one performances, of which Lundahl & Seitl's work is exemplary, as it is of the large-scale productions of companies such as Punchdrunk.[3] Immersive performance combines the act of immersion (as in, submergence in a medium that *feels* unusual and requires a different mode of being to that of our regular environment), with a deep involvement in the activity within that medium, where all the senses are engaged and manipulated. This activity involves an invitation to the audience member to improvise, and it is this invitation to improvise that often holds the key to the form and theme of the work.

IMMERSION AND AUDIENCE IMPROVISATION

We improvise the moment we cease to know what is going to happen.
Miranda Tufnell and Chris Crickmay (2001: 46)

Audience improvisation in immersive experiences involves an imaginative journeying through themes and narratives. It can often incorporate a physical journey, which may be covertly signposted for you via such means as lighting or sound in the distance drawing you on, or overt guidance such as audio instructions through headphones, with the movement of the dancers leading you around the space or stewards, in role, steering you onwards. In addition, there are more intricate improvisations that are required in order to engage with the idiosyncrasies of the worlds created. The audience-adventurers in Punchdrunk productions can involve themselves deeply by interacting as they choose with the scenographic detail of the space; to pull open drawers and rootle around for clues to the story; to sniff the faded scent in perfume bottles and understand the personality of the character. The improvisation may entail you influencing the performers' actions, taking on multiple roles, as with Kate Bond and Morgan Lloyd's *You Me Bum Bum Train,* where you might become a teacher to a class of rowdy teenagers and then gee up a soccer team as you are cast as its coach. Your role may be set online in advance of your arriving at the venue for the event, to be developed by your actions and reactions as the piece progresses, deciding the fate of your collaborators amongst your community, as with Coney's *A Small Town Anywhere.* You may find yourself taken into a bizarre world via video goggles and headphones, where you respond in the moment to audio instruction and physical manipulation, as the world's sights, scents, sounds, and spatial effects become palpably present, created by unseen performers around you, as in Il Pixel Rosso's work. Alternatively, your improvisational skills as part-author, part-gamer will be tested when you construct the theme, narrative, and imagined space around you with the artist, as in Seth Kreibel's *The Unbuilt Room,* snap decision-making as you become aware that the fifteen minutes granted you are ticking by on the stopwatch under his chair. For some audience members, such improvisations are a pleasurable play in the performing moment. For others, the invitation to interact and choreograph their way through the performance is intimidating, disturbing, or simply irksome, in the onus it places on one to take responsibility for one's part in the work.

As these examples suggest, immersive performance is always interactive and relies on its audience to engage instinctively with the experience. Each composition, shared between creators, designers, performers, and audience, activates a sensory relationship in the experience of the piece, which embraces the play between choreographed and improvised moments. Intimate immersive performances, whether a one-to-one, a small group piece, or one's individual involvement with the sceno-graphic installation in a large-scale production, magnify the shared responsibility and respect for the work that must be shouldered by artist and audience-participant. As this outline indicates, although context and forms may change from one immer-sive production to another, a constant feature that defines an experience as totally immersive is the fact that the audience are integral to the *experiential* heart of the work and central to the aesthetic of the event. The participant shapes form, influ-ences function, and transforms possible outcomes. Consequently, immersive prac-tice creates a space for reinvigorating human interaction and exchange, however 'fictionalized' the encounter might be. Significantly, it encourages audience members to *attend* to the interaction occurring in the moment.

Unplanned action and reaction in any immersive performance underscores the ex-change of energy and feeling between the work and the audience-participant. As a con-sequence, the 'presentness' of human perception is given prominence in this practice. Here 'presence' directly correlates to its etymological roots, from *praesens*, 'to be before the senses' (*prae*, 'before'; *sensus*, 'feeling, sense'). Further to this, the Latin root form of 'present' accounts for a state of *being* or *feeling* and demonstrates the tactile proof of this being, when *praesent* is understood as 'being at hand', a 'being before' (from *praeesse: prae*, 'before', and *esse*, 'be'). By emphasizing these meanings of presence and present, in the immersive context, the state of stirring *praesence* felt by a participating individual in such events refers back to this full meaning and usage. In immersive prac-tice, it is the *praesent* body that interprets the performance, within which imagination and instinct are key components.

Arguably, one of the reasons why immersive practice has infiltrated the main-stream is because it exploits this vitality of form and, consequently, cannot be wholly replicated or fixed. It cannot be fixed because it relies on the improvised participa-tion, a singular response, of each individual audience member in order to realize, and give meaning to, the experience. It requires a revitalized relationship between artist and audience member that, in turn, establishes new protocols of perception and appreciation that are shaped by the unrepeatability of each improvisation within the event. Lundahl & Seitl's work is exemplary of the invitation to improvise in im-mersive practice. It is especially relevant to this handbook, as it can lead to the audi-ence member becoming dancer, extemporizing—imaginatively and physically—her way through the artistic journey.

EMBODIED ENCOUNTERS: AUDIENCE IMPROVISATION IN THE WORK OF LUNDAHL & SEITL

Improvisation is a negotiation with the patterns your body is thinking.

Jonathan Burrows (2010: 27)

Martina Seitl and Christer Lundahl formed Lundahl & Seitl in 2003. Based in London, the company produces work across Europe. The research process that underpins the company's work investigates space, time, and perception and involves multifarious collaborations, including with practitioners and researchers of architecture, classical music, cognitive neurology, critical theory, dance, fashion, and more recently environmental science and astrophysics. To date, all of Lundahl & Seitl's productions in the United Kingdom have incorporated binaural soundscapes through headphones coupled with a distinctive choreography. The combination of movement and sensual technologies establishes an unusual interplay of the real and the imagined for 'the visitor' (Lundahl and Seitl's term for audience members): a fusion of interiority and exteriority that is subtly manipulated to establish the world of each event.

Lundahl & Seitl's practice is firmly rooted in a haptic methodology that relies on tactility and sound to activate imagination.[4] Seitl's choreography involves the most delicate interplay of touch between performer and visitor; hand to hand, fingertip to fingertip, palm to palm, hand to shoulder, palm to back. The overriding experience of this gentle contact creates a whole-body sensation of floating in the space while being anchored through the body, tethered by the feet. The visitor's physical participation is facilitated by a highly sensitive response from the performer, a relationship that is developed from the dynamic initiated on first contact and then nurtured through a balance of coaxing and offering trust, shared between guide and visitor. It relies on the potency of hand-holding as a primitive and authentic means of communicating.[5] It is an embodied negotiation made possible by the dancers being open to the unpredictable as they advance the hand-to-hand, hand-to-shoulder, hand-to-arm, hand-to-back contact that, in turn, keeps the visitor (literally and figuratively) on her toes. This shared spontaneity requires a 'split focus', which Seitl has identified as coming close to parenting, in that it merges and questions 'the practical and the emotional … sometimes they're in conflict and sometimes coexisting; how to stay open and empathic within that.… Like parenting, you may have a plan and then you have to let go of that plan and respond to the child' (Seitl 2014). Seitl has developed her method from early investigations with dancers involving long rehearsal processes that 'took the performers into a deep state of *being*—within the self' (quoted in Machon 2013a: 174, emphasis in original). Seitl realized that for the audience to feel that same quality of experience, they needed to participate in the process rather than watching the performance. Seitl's investigations into 'meeting the body of the visitor' (Seitl 2014) led her to reverse the traditional theatre relationship by blindfolding audience members, who then, partnered with a dancer, would be taken through similar exercises, resulting in the audience 'visiting the experience' facilitated by the performer (quoted in Machon 2013a: 176). The term 'visitor' thus emerged from these early explorations as much as it is attributable to the visual arts, as in visitors to exhibitions (fig. 37.1).

This hour-long piece for six at a time is sited in a museum or gallery, my most recent experience being at the Royal Academy of Art in London. As one of the six visitors, an assistant gives me clear instructions regarding the technicalities of the event and the fact that I will always be kept safe. This assistant then leads us to an older, male guide who instructs us to seat ourselves on one of the stools that are placed equidistantly in the room and to focus our attention on a canvas hung on the far wall. Headphones are

FIG. 37.1 Lundahl & Seitl, *Symphony of a Missing Room*, National Museum Stockholm, 2009. Performer: Rachel Alexander. Photo credit: Tony Ahola. Image courtesy of Lundahl & Seitl.

put over my ears, and a prerecorded soundscape merges with the ambient sound of the space. Through these headphones a dreamy, Scandinavian voice instructs me to notice artworks, to attend to my ways of seeing in that space. The voice points out another assistant, standing towards the front of the space, instructs me to follow her. Along with the rest of my group I am led to an adjacent room, where I am blindfolded by whiteout goggles and, still led by the voice in my wireless headphones, placed in the care of disembodied, delicately dancing hands. This invisible dancing guide and her audio companion take me physically and imaginatively on a journey that traverses space and time, a series of subtle effects and scenarios created by the sensations of movement, sound, and (unbeknownst to the visitor) white light shone onto these goggles. This work engages me in a dialogue between the sensual, the recollected, and the imagined in a musing on my individual relationship with art, reawakening my ability for whole-body perception.[6]

> *Goggles are placed over my eyes and my vision is replaced with a milky-white opacity that attunes me to listen more closely as my headphones are returned. I'm instructed to reach my hand out in front of me, and there . . . is the welcoming hand of a disembodied guide. The size, shape, and softness of the hand suggests this guide is also female; an assumption that I trust to my tactile intuition. She's gently holding my palm, upper hand and fingers in both her hands as a reassuring, care-taking gesture of first contact. She leads me, walking carefully, then faster, eventually running, the bolder I become, while soundscape, narration and playful shifts in the light outside of the goggles accompany us to enhance the sensation of moving me from one location to the next; a tunnel through which I crawl; the edge of a cliff over which I peer and feel the sensation of height, rain all around; a wall on which my hands are placed so that I tactually search for a frame,*

for the textures of a painting, but I only find the solid surface of the wall; a lift where I feel the bodies of others pressed shoulder to shoulder, hip touching hip, that takes us up in a rumbling fashion; a ballroom where I twirl to the soaring, spinning music of violins; downstairs, outside to a courtyard with dappled light and a pond with a fountain, by which sits a silent, old man (and immediately the face that emblazons itself on my inner eye is that of my earlier, physical guide); through a watery vault that plunges me into the sensation of evolutionary time, time before time, all on a journey towards 'the missing room', where the memories of the Royal Academy are stored, along with all the artworks that have been exhibited or not yet displayed. (Machon 2014)

Lundahl & Seitl's collaborators spend a long time in workshops honing these skills of being open and empathic to the visitor, open to the unexpected. The technique is underpinned by Seitl's ongoing investigations into embodied experience and benefits from the synergetic philosophies of her collaborators' practice. Seitl's interest in Vipassana, which involves deep observation of sensation and perception, has enabled her to understand 'the type of movements that can happen in stillness' (Seitl 2014). Trained in different disciplines, including ballet, butoh, Feldenkrais, Laban Movement Analysis, Movement Therapy, physical theatre, and Land to Water Yoga, all the performers are 'very receptive to different physical states', with 'a broad perspective on dance and what the concept of dance is ... an openness to what movement can be. They are not interested in being seen; the ego is small, the interest in the research is bigger than their desire to be seen as dancers on stage' (Seitl 2014) (fig. 37.2).

FIG. 37.2 Lundahl & Seitl exploratory workshops, 'tacit knowledge'. Training week, April 2014. Performer: Rachel Alexander. Image courtesy of Lundahl & Seitl.

The company explore exercises related to hand contact and hapticity, including visualizing, describing, and drawing the sensations experienced in order to find ways of articulating the sensuality of the improvised exchange and of utilizing individual perception, unpacking the fundamentals of 'the most sensitive part of yourself as a guide and allowing that to respond ... looking at the different senses that we have and [questioning] with which sense do you proceed, which is your window to the outside world, your most sensitive tool' (Seitl 2014). Bearing in mind the individuality and training of each dancer, these 'windows' and 'tools of sensitivity' are different for each guide, which ensures that there can be no fixed technique as such in establishing trust and negotiating the exchange between dancer and visitor. Instead Seitl sets and focuses her own method as a way to internalize sensation and osmose this through physical contact. The dancers then use this to 'find their own way' to intuit with the visitor (Seitl 2014).

Illustration 2: *The Memory of W. T. Stead*, by Lundahl & Seitl (2013)

This was an intimate piece for six people that took place at Steinway Hall, London. I am seated on a stool at a piano, where assistants set me up with the wireless headphones and the whiteout goggles. My audio narrator is an elderly male, the voice of William Thomas Stead, the investigative journalist and short-story writer who uncannily anticipated his own death on an ocean liner in his 1892 story *From the Old World to the New*. (Twenty years later, he boarded the *Titanic*.) His narration is accompanied by an evocative soundscore: echoes of piano music, the creaking of ship timbers, all underscoring the gentle hand-to-hand guidance which leads me through rooms, and up stairs, and places my fingers on a keyboard, and the metal strings of the piano. Often I am left to stand still, feeling the sway of my body aboard ship, the rhythm of temporality itself flowing through me between past-present-future. Goggles at times are removed, so that I might engage with my environment, and then returned for the journey to my destination, to be finally removed when I reach it: a darkened room with the rest of the group, seated haphazardly in close proximity to the classical pianist Cassie Yukawa. She and her piano are the only objects in the room that are illuminated. She begins to play György Ligeti's Etude *Pour Irina*, slowly, slowly, becoming progressively frenetic. As the music builds to its crescendo, the light narrows in, until only her hands and the keyboard are visible. Isolated in this way, her hands become inhuman, mechanical, blurring in the light at the speed with which she plays. The piece dramatically ends, and we are in darkness, listening to the vibration of the final notes suspended in space and time.

> *My hand glides over softly enticing piano keys, play this note, just one, then zings against the cold, metal, percussive mechanics ... she places my hand on, what I believe is, a mirror and I feel like it might pass through my—internally perceived—reflection, through that hard surface, through this looking-glass into another world, to the icy*

depths of Stead's watery grave… The goggles are removed and I share glances with my group as we ride up together in an elevator. Later the removal reveals (what I assume have been) our dancing guides as a ghostly mirror reflection of us through the doors of this elevator, now a mysterious portal from the room in which we stand looking across to them; evoking both the shadowy depths of a memory aboard ship and a premonition of its wreckage on which our reflections now rock, enigmatically to and fro, ebb and flow. Their rhythm, transferred haptically to my body, meets the still present buoyancy of that floating, tactile dance.

I draw many connections with Ravn's analysis of dancers' movement (2009), alongside Tufnell and Crickmay's offerings on body, imagination, and improvisation (2001, 2004), and the work of Lundahl & Seitl. The dynamics of gravity, weight, space, time, sense awareness, kinaesthetics, and proprioception, commonly exercised in dance improvisations, are all vital elements of the experience for the visitor. Each physiological and emotional journey involves an embodiment of theme and recasts the visitor as medium of the work.[7] 'The [audio] suggestions trigger the visitor's archive of lived experience … images in their minds, but equally in their muscles, bones, nervous system and proprioceptive sense of the relations between their different body parts moving in space in certain positions, with a certain movement quality' (Lundahl in Machon 2013a: 178). The audio narrative and instructions together provide a template; a template that encourages the visitor's imagination to improvise within and across the parameters it sets —sensual descriptions and philosophies that elicit a spontaneous summoning of one's own store of images and perspectives on art, memory, time, and space. The haptic engagement with the surroundings, as much as the dancing guide, encourage the visitor to become aware of the edges of the body fusing with the kinaesphere. My journeys through each of Lundahl & Seitl's encounters have involved a series of improvised physical and imaginative actions and reactions in response to my guides. The sensation that runs through me, both during and following each event, is similar to that I am left with after a massage or a yoga session. I become aware of the pleasurable qualities of movement in my responses, of attention to this movement. I am aware that I invest my deportment directly after the encounter with these same qualities. During and immediately following a Lundahl & Seitl experience, I can *feel* how the sensuous world of my body has been the material of the work and the manifestation of its themes; a state that lingers as a corporeal memory in any subsequent recall and interpretation of these events. This resonates with Tufnell and Crickmay's observation: 'To move out of our heads and into our sensory world of the body awakens us not only to sensation but also to a slower, deeper landscape beneath the surface of everyday awareness, a landscape of feeling, memory, impulse and dream' (2004: 3).

As part of their research, dancers spend time on-site observing, noticing people and/with artworks, and then moving in the space. The responses of the collaborators here help to form the journey taken in each new version of *Symphony of a Missing Room*. The improvised physical and perceptual interactions of the guides with the theories, themes, and narratives of the piece in each new building become a foundation for the piece's reinvention. From the outset, the process establishes an engagement with the visual, spatial, and sonic arts in a multidimensional, multisensual manner. It is these early, investigative danced improvisations that uncover what exists in a building, in a story, in a musical philosophy, in a scientific theory, which is in turn translated through the danced improvisation with the visitor: 'dance performances are not based on the relation between a subject and an object but on physical *inter*actions between subjects through behaviour, gestures and physical action. Dance can ... actualise and question the body as situated in an intersubjective world ... art (here, dance) is a highlighter of what is paradigmatically in the shadows but could be highlighted in various ways' (Ravn 2009: 75, emphasis in original). In this way, there is a layered exchange between artistic concept, dancer, and audience member in regard to how the arts might be perceived. This results in an immersive form and methodology that functions *as* and with(in) the content. The duets with my dancing guides reawaken my wider perceptual field and open up my imaginative interiority. There is a 'sensory correspondence' between us; a 'kinaesthetic sensing in correspondence' (Ravn 2009: 122). It is a keenly felt blurring of boundaries between myself and/as the form and theme of the work. I am subject/object, audience/performer, and message/medium. I am the vessel that holds content and the vehicle through which comprehension of the ideas underpinning the work is reached. I experience each piece as an internalized landscape that shifts and blurs between impulse, feeling, memory, and dream.

ILLUSTRATION 3: *ROTATING IN A ROOM OF MOVING IMAGES*, BY LUNDAHL & SEITL (2011)

This fifteen-minute performance for one audience-participant at a time, programmed in studios or galleries (in this iteration, at Battersea Arts Centre in London), is a meditation on the pleasures of art; invoking the archive of artworks stored within—in order to question how they are perceived by—the body. The piece employs the audio instructions and the disembodied, invisible dancing hand, this time disorientating rather than guiding me, playfully twirling me, always in artful conjunction with the childlike voice in my ear. Ivory drapes are suspended from the ceiling to the floor; scale is manipulated. These drapes create corridors and screens, which change each time the piece shifts from total blackout to film projections and to a surprising live encounter with performers; a ghostly tableau vivant reminiscent of baroque artworks. The dimensions of the room are further manipulated by these shifts between the live and mediated image, accentuated by repeated fluctuations in lighting, from chiaroscuro states to total darkness.

> *I'm instructed to hold my hand out and it is immediately—gently and precisely—taken hold of by a seemingly disembodied, graceful, trustworthy hand. I am both captured*

and captivated by the playful, tactile interaction; her fingers to my fingers and palm; delicately dancing hands causing me to float, twirl, my body buoyant, not traversing an area but swirling in space' (Machon 2013b: 199; emphasis added).

IMPROVISING, ATTENDING, *BEING*

> Improvisation provides us with a means to excavating layers of experi-
> ence, sensation, character, feeling that we normally rush through or
> suppress—to travel deeper and deeper into an ever enlarging and chan-
> ging moment.... As a strategy for discovering and developing images it
> both demands and creates a whole range of skills, the most important
> of which is an ability to be still and open one's attention to the present
> moment.
>
> Miranda Tufnell and Chris Crickmay (2001: 46)

Lundahl & Seitl's works stimulate an awareness of *being* in the visitor. The sense of 'becoming my body anew' (after Ravn 2009: 25) is keenly felt through the patterns shaped
in my body at every stage of my journey; attending to this in the moment as much as
in retrospect. The hand-to-hand interchange brings me to a heightened awareness of
embodied mindfulness. The removal of sight enables the 'predisposition of my materi-
ality' to be transformed (51). My modes of perception shift from a reliance on external
sight and sound to a prioritization of proprioception, kinaesthetic awareness, and
an intensifying of inner sight, all of which influence my external interaction with my
physical surroundings. The spontaneity lies in my body and its desire to move through
the event. I set a pace and rhythm influenced by my audio instructions. I initiate the
unprompted reaching for and letting go of my guide. The choreography comes from
the charting of each step and each extension through my arm to my fingertips to establish contact with my guide in accordance with my audio instructions. An osmotic
exchange of sense awareness occurs between my invisible dancing guide and me. This
quality of movement inspires attentive *being* within me, involving a subtle awakening
of the senses within each evolving encounter, alongside an attending to the anticipation of the movement, as much as to the movement itself. Congruently, this movement quality arouses a strange temporality, a feeling of being suspended in time while
engaging in an ongoing present. Each physical interaction with guide, space, and object activates 'a heightened sense of presence, the kinesphere around the body' (Seitl
in Machon 2013: 180), which underpins this state of being with(in) myself.

In each of Lundahl & Seitl's productions, Di Benedetto's notion of becoming
'attendant ... implying presence and participation' (2007: 126) occurs by *giving*

attention to the bodily ways in which perception comes to bear. A reciprocal, sensual relationship is established between the self, the space, other bodies in that space, and the performance event itself. Becoming attendant incorporates being aware of one's presence and participation *in the moment* rather than simply being in attendance as in, in servitude, to the work. This is initiated at the start of the piece, where the audio design instigates a gentle submergence into the world of the event. This acclimatization, a subtle pulling you in via the soundscape, encourages you to notice space, scent, texture, story, in a whole-body fashion. It carefully prepares the imagination and proprioceptive senses to engender a heightened sentience through the performance. As described above, it is the quality of movement that is shared during the hand-to-hand exchange that inspires attentive *being* within the visitor. The moments of suspension in time and space exaggerate the ongoing present, increase expectancy, encourage the visitor to experience being within and between her own body, another's body, and the artistic encounter. The guide plays with the potentiality of absence and anticipation, the desire for the return of the disembodied hand. My spontaneity is thus charged by this sensation of *praesent*-absence, which in turn remains in any embodied recall of the work: 'my state of readiness involves a tangible sensation of waiting for that physical connection in the absence of that touch; always there in the pitch dark, always in artful conjunction with her childlike voice in my headphoned-ears. . . . It remains with me now, like the visual traces of a dream, just as that fleeting touch lies present, a corporeal memory in my hands and limbs' (Machon 2013b: 200). This intense inhabiting of the world of the event causes architectural space and objects to merge with the visitor's imagination; 'in that moment of suspension you're experiencing space around you, an interior architecture of that space' (Lundahl in Machon 2013: 180). Here it is the merging of art and architecture with my imaginative space, enlarged by the 'physical resonance' that occurs within my haptic improvisation, that gives the impression of my 'expansion into space'; altogether opening out 'the three-dimensionality of geometry' (Ravn 2009: 178). The whole-body, improvised interaction is the basis of Lundahl & Seitl immersive events; 'it's that sense of *presence* that we want to activate within the visitor' (Seitl in Machon 2013: 178–179, emphasis in original), shifting perception of the visual and sonic arts away from the eye and the ear so that it is felt through the whole body. Individual attendance to the moment becomes vital to the work and textures the quality of experience to be had, the interpretations that arise. Here 'embodiment forms part of the shaping of cognition' (Ravn 2009: 66), during and following the encounter. The distinctive nature of the touch reminds the visitor that the perceptual capacity of the body as a whole is haptic and that hapticity is a fusion of internal and external sensation. Sense memory and subjectivity are paramount, as is the process of becoming aware of one's own sensual responses in the improvised moment, all of which foreground the visitor's *praesence* within the performance.

CONCLUSION

> It is through the sensuous world of the body, through our eyes, ears, skin, muscles, and organs, that we see, feel and respond to all that happens. The body is the ground from which all knowing of the world begins. It is within our bodies, in our instinctual and sensory responses, that we discover the changing field of what is happening to us.
>
> Miranda Tufnell and Chris Crickmay (2004: 3)

My accounts here document how participation-as-improvisation in practice, where the participant is the audience member, encourages a symbiotic exchange between various aspects of the event on a number of levels. I observe myself from inside myself during this work as much as I comprehend and interpret the piece itself. Insight, in all its variations, is exercised as a consequence of the improvisations that occur without vision. The theories within the themes as much as the methods involved in the form of each work support this looking-in-to-look-out: embodied introspection that leads to embodied interpretation. The philosophies surveyed within the themes of the performance allow for an objectivity to be borne out of this subjective experience. My own response to Lundahl & Seitl's work has become a 'process of elaborating, analysing, categorising and condensing' practice (Ravn 2009: 128); a physical enquiry into affect and agency in participatory aesthetics.

My role as audience-collaborator within many such interactive events has led me to the conclusion that immersive performance positions the audience member as a practitioner. It opens up opportunities to explore the audience-participant's contribution to immersive performance as practice-as-research. The *practice* of audience as improviser allows for an implicit partnership to emerge in collaboration with the artist. Experiencing the performance in the moment, thinking beyond the performance in the moment, or thinking *in* the performance *beyond* the moment, in order to analyse attributes, impacts, and outcomes from the audience perspective, invites future practice-as-research projects that investigate the extensive potential of this work.

Notes

1. I discuss the experiential nature of such works in Machon (2011), which includes examples of contemporary dance such as the practice of Akram Khan Company, Bodies in Flight, Maxine Doyle's work with Punchdrunk, and Pina Bausch's Tanztheater Wuppertal.
2. See Machon (2013a) for a more detailed explanation of immersive theatres and the 'scale of immersivity' from which these features are summarized, alongside a wider examination of critical and creative approaches to the practice.
3. One-to-ones (or one-on-ones) are performances made for one recipient at a time that explore the direct connection between performer, performance, and individual audience

member, and usually encourage that individual's solitary and sentient interaction with(in) the space.

4. I use 'haptic' and 'hapticity' (from the Greek *haptikos* and *haptesthai*, to grasp, sense, perceive, 'lay hold of') in relation to the performing/perceiving body, alongside 'tactile', as the latter tends to connote only the surface quality of touch. 'Haptic' emphasizes the tactile perceptual experience of the body as a whole (rather than merely the fingers) and highlights the perceptive faculty of kinaesthetics (the body's locomotion in space), which involves proprioception (stimulation produced and perceived within the body relating to position and movement of the body). Haptic perception encompasses the sensate experience of an individual's moving body and that individual's perceptual comprehension of the moving bodies of others.

5. Coincidentally, at the time of writing, A. L. Kennedy (2014) offers an insightful contemplation of the power of hand-holding.

6. A version of this experience has been adapted for BBC Arts Online (see Lundahl & Seitl 2014b). I discuss this piece in greater depth in Machon with Lundahl and Seitl (2017).

7. 'I see the work as almost having no content at its core because the content is the visitor's to fill. The content is the visitor's core and response. Their inner images and experiences make the work' (Seitl 2014).

REFERENCES

Bourriaud, N. (2002) *Relational Aesthetics*. Trans. Simon Pleasance and Fronza Woods with Mathieu Copeland. Dijon: Les Presses du Réel.

Burrows, J. (2010) *A Choreographer's Handbook*. London: Routledge.

Di Benedetto, S. (2007) Guiding Somatic Responses within Performative Structures: Contemporary Live Art and Sensorial Perception. In Banes, Sally, and Lepecki, André (eds.), *The Senses in Performance*. London: Routledge, 124–134.

Di Benedetto, S. (2011) *The Provocation of the Senses in Contemporary Theatre*. London: Routledge.

Kennedy, A. L. (writer and presenter). (2014) *Holding Hands*. Produced by Kate Bland. A Cast Iron Production for BBC Radio 4. First broadcast 13 July; rebroadcast 10 September. http://www.bbc.co.uk/programmes/b04754xq. Accessed 24 August 2018.

Lundahl & Seitl (artistic dirs.). (2011) *Rotating in a Room of Images*. Martina Seitl, choreographer. Produced by Battersea Arts Centre. Dance work presented at One-on-One Festival, Battersea Arts Centre, London, 29 March.

Lundahl & Seitl (artistic dirs.). (2013) *The Memory of W. T. Stead*. Rachel Alexander, assistant dir. Laura Hemming-Lowe, Sara Lindström, Genevieve Maxwell, Colin McLean, Lucía Montero, and Pia Nordin, collaborators. Produced by Nomad, London. Supported by Mont Blanc and Arts Council England. Dance work presented at Seinway & Sons W1, London, 3 April.

Lundahl & Seitl (artistic dirs.). (2014a) *Symphony of a Missing Room*. Martina Seitl, choreographer. Dagmara Bilon, Lisette Drangert, Laura Hemming-Lowe, Catherine Hoffman, Genevieve Maxwell, Colin McLean, and Pia Nordin, collaborators. Jula Reindell, costume designer. Emma Leach, project manager. Dance work presented at Lift Festival, Royal Academy of Arts, London, 5 June.

Lundahl & Seitl. (2014b) *Symphony of a Missing Room—An Extra Sensory Journey around the Royal Academy of Arts, An Interpretation for BBC Arts Online.* http://www.bbc.co.uk/programmes/articles/4QLmql9rFDD7Vr1CwyS5PsQ/an-extra-sensory-journey-around-the-royal-academy-of-arts. Accessed 24 August 2018.

Machon, J. (2011) *(Syn)aesthetics—Redefining Visceral Performance.* Basingstoke, UK: Palgrave Macmillan.

Machon, J. (2013a) *Immersive Theatres—Intimacy and Immediacy in Contemporary Performance.* Basingstoke, UK: Palgrave Macmillan.

Machon, J. (2013b) (Syn)aesthetics and Immersive Theatre: Embodied Beholding in Lundahl & Seitl's *Rotating in a Room of Moving Images.* In Shaughnessy, Nicola (ed.), *Affective Performance and Cognitive Science: Body, Brain and Being.* London: Methuen, 199–216.

Machon, J. (2014) Blind(fold)ed by Light in Lundahl & Seitl's *Symphony in a Missing Room*: Thinking Out Loud in the Dark. Audio-installation paper presented at symposium Theatre in the Dark, University of Surrey, SeedPOD Nodus Centre, 12 July.

Machon, J., with Lundahl, C., and Seitl, S. (2017) Missing Rooms and Unknown Clouds: Darkness and Illumination in the Work of Lundahl & Seitl. In Alston, Adam, and Welton, Martin (eds.), *Theatre in the Dark—Shadow, Gloom and Blackout in Contemporary Theatre.* Mark Taylor-Batty and Enoch Brater, ser. eds. London: Bloomsbury Methuen Drama, 147–168.

Ravn, S. (2009) *Sensing Movement, Living Spaces: An Investigation of Movement Based on the Lived Experience of 13 Professional Dancers.* Saarbrücken: VDM.

Seitl, Martina (2014b). Unpublished interview with the author via Skype, 28 August.

Tufnell, M., and Crickmay, C. (2001) *Body Space Image—Notes towards Improvisation and Performance.* London: Dance Books.

Tufnell, M., and Crickmay, C. (2004) *A Widening Field—Journeys in Body and Imagination.* London: Dance Books.

PART VIII

TECHNIQUES, STRATEGIES, AND HISTORIES

....

CHAPTER 38

LOST IN THE FOOTLIGHTS

The Secret Life of Improvisation in Contemporary American Concert Dance

....

KENT DE SPAIN

FIRST steps. False steps. Step-by-step. Stepsisters. In our world of walking two-legged creatures, we are surrounded by steps both real and metaphorical. This essay concerns dance steps, a colloquial way to refer to the movements in a dance. Specifically, it is concerned with 'choreographed' steps and 'improvised' steps, and with investigating whether there is any actual or theoretical or pragmatic difference between them. This essay is also interested in unpacking the role that improvisation plays in the process and particularly in the performance of contemporary concert dance in the United States.

How and why might dance-makers choose between these two creative approaches: 'setting' movement so it looks essentially the same in each performance, or structuring brief or extended passages of improvised movement that might *feel* similar but, by definition, use different movement each time? Is it for the benefit of the dance-maker? Does choosing one path or the other alter the experience of creating movement in ways that make it simpler or more exciting or more effective? Is it for the benefit of the dancers? Does it make them more comfortable or more invested? Or is it for the benefit of the audience? Is there an assumption that choosing predetermined versus improvised movements affects the viewer in different ways or conveys different meanings?

While there have been diachronic and synchronic divergences and fluidities in the concepts of choreography and improvisation, our dualistic, literate culture tends to view them in opposition, and often privileges the idea of choreography while pushing improvisation to the margins (where the marginalized have often explored and mastered it in ways that are eventually reappropriated by the choreographic mainstream). But the dividing lines are not so clear. Even the most inveterate improvisers can set rigorous structures that guide their work, while choreographers who set every movement for performance may use improvisation extensively to create those movements. Because of the legacy of many groundbreaking artists over the past several decades, there is a vast middle ground where contemporary dance-makers can and do choose either path as needed. But, in my experience, even when both choices are present in a performance, the improvisational elements tend to live in the shadow cast by the power of the choreographic paradigm, so much so that audiences of my improvised works often assume that everything they have seen is set. So, in addition to investigating the reasons to set or improvise movements, I want to know how often dance-makers who are known primarily as 'choreographers' make the improvisational choice. Is the continued dominance of the paradigm of the choreographer obscuring the presence and importance of improvisation and the real-time creative contributions of dancers?

This essay will examine these questions in three steps. First, it is important to define our terms by looking at the words 'choreography' and 'improvisation' and the ways they (fittingly) have moved their meanings across time and space. Next, by looking at what critics and theorists have to say about the nature of improvisation, we can speculate about what it might bring to 'choreographed' dance. Finally, I place my usual value on documenting the thoughts and practices of artists themselves by asking two respected American 'choreographers'—Joe Goode and Bebe Miller—how and why and how often they choose to use improvisation in their performance works. This is a small sample but will hopefully open up interesting avenues for future study.

WHAT'S IN A NAME?

I should begin this section by managing some expectations. The words 'choreography' and 'improvisation' are understood and used in a variety of ways, often, but not always, as opposing processes of movement creation, specifically 'created over time and set' versus 'created in the moment of performance, then forgotten'. But the reality of dance-making in America is much more complex, so no matter how much some definitional clarity might seem helpful here, you will not find it forthcoming. In fact, I will likely make things worse. Even if I could structure a poignant and articulate elucidation of these concepts, it would probably be out of date by the time this essay makes it into print. We are an active culture, and these terms are constantly being reconfigured and recycled to fulfil our needs of the moment. The best I can offer is to look at some examples of what these terms have meant in the past, both to verify their impalpability and to shed some light on how we arrived in the present.

In her 2011 book *Choreographing Empathy*, Susan Foster does some scholarly heavy lifting in thoroughly tracing the etymology and use of the word 'choreography'. True to its Greek roots (*choreia*, dancing, and *graph*, writing), the earliest use of the term in English—in the late eighteenth century—referred to the process of 'writing' movement using notation systems such as the one popularized by Raoul Auger Feuillet (Foster 2011: 17). The person who taught and sometimes created dances was not yet a choreographer but a 'dancing master', a role of increasing responsibility as the country and court dances of the sixteenth and seventeenth centuries in Europe became the elaborately produced story ballets of Jean-Georges Noverre, Filippo Taglioni, August Bournonville, and Marius Petipa. These men were part of what Foster calls the 'gendered division of labor' in ballet, where the male dancing masters were 'empowered as creators and producers' while women, such as Fanny Elssler, Carlotta Grisi, and Marie Taglioni, were the star performers (42). In a too familiar way, men appeared to be the mind and women the body of nineteenth-century ballet, but the terminology, if not the gender bias, was beginning to change.

Locked into our day-to-day experience as we are, it is easy to forget that language is alive; that it is responsive and fickle. Somewhere in the fervour of the fin de siècle, 'choreography' shifted its definitional stance, morphing from 'writing movement' to 'the art of dancing', and then finally, with the advent of the radical innovations of Ballet Russe, becoming the go-to word for the process of creating and organizing movements into a dance, with all appropriate bragging rights (and, sometimes, copyrights). The previously crucial role of dancing master (or ballet master) was demoted to 'staff', training the dancers but not creating the works. Creativity in movement was now the domain of a choreographer. Interestingly, Foster points out that the term was more slowly adopted by and applied to the burgeoning modern dance of Denishawn and others (Foster 2011: 43). But by the height of midcentury modernism we found ourselves in the era of the Choreographer, writ large, with luminaries like Martha Graham seen as creative geniuses responsible not just for making movement but also for a grand philosophy (one might, with tongue lightly in cheek, say a religion) of dance as an art form. As Foster says, 'the choreographer was one who could synthesize the knowledge gained through the study of compositional craft with a unique, inspired vision, a process that replicated and reinforced the mandate for a dance to fuse personal and universal concerns' (52).

The Judson revolution (and similar experiments elsewhere) seriously complicated this choreographic grandeur. Were Yvonne Rainer's rules about where to move mattresses in *Parts of Some Sextets* to be considered 'choreography'? Or Trisha Brown's instructions to the audience to yell at her in *Yellowbelly*? More to the point, what did we call the fluid mix of 'choreographed' movement, instructions for movement/interaction, and invitations to the dancers to include their own material that made up Rainer's constantly shifting *Continuous Project—Altered Daily*? These radical interventions broke down the door of the church of modern dance, making possible almost any creative choice, although 'choreography' still managed to survive for some dance artists—as exemplified by the intricately patterned work of Lucinda Childs or the detailed movement style and sassy bricolage of Twyla Tharp, or even the deceptive dances of Trisha Brown (think *Son of Gone Fishin'*), whose released movement could look somehow improvised but be beautifully, immutably set. Judson left no last will and testament, so artists had to choose for themselves whether to go back to the future in the older model of choreography or to pick and choose from a broad range of potential structures as desired or needed. The ways each new generation of dance-makers navigates those choices determine this year's model of the changeable concept of 'choreography'.

Like 'choreography', the word 'improvisation' has a slippery past. Variants were first used in English in the sixteenth century as pejoratives—*improvisitlie* or *improvision*, meaning imprudent, without forethought. The modern spelling (with slightly more positive associations) first appeared in print in the same decade (interestingly) as the word 'choreography' (Oxford University Press 2015). While it has always meant accomplishing or creating something extemporaneously, the whys and wherefores of that creative process have constituted their own kind of linguistic improvisation, although the shifting meanings have not followed any kind of linear path (as with the word 'choreography'). Rather, they have advanced and receded with the dominance of the preset notion of composition/choreography, and have been (as Grove Music Online [2015] puts it) dependent 'on the stability and perceived identity of the "fixed musical work," which varies widely according to musical culture and historical period'. Replace the word 'musical' with 'dance' to make an important point here: improvisation is a shifting concept for a constantly shifting ground, and the more we try to 'fix' the identity of a dance 'work' (i.e., document it and make it repeatable and identifiably separate from any other works), the more we privilege the preset idea of choreography and weaken improvisation.

This is not to say that the creativity at the root of improvisation is not appreciated, but the language (and the meanings underlying the language) may still subtly disparage the practice, particularly in relation to choreography. As an example, 'to improvise' sometimes means 'to make do' with what is available, but that also carries the connotation that you are working with inadequate or inappropriate materials. 'Improvisation' can also mean doing something 'without preparation', which can also mean a kind of 'faking it'. In a dance or musical context this is an ironic thought, since consistently successful improvisation requires intense preparation—years of developing technical skills, engaging with the process, and becoming savvy, adept, and responsive in real time. Be it Ornette Coleman or Steve Paxton, there is some serious practice underlying such 'unprepared' performance. But compare this language with off-label use of the word 'choreography'. The 'choreography' of the planets or insects in flight implies an elegant and thoughtful organization of motion that is pleasing to the eye. This is a long way from 'making do'.

Dance critic Curtis L. Carter sees three distinct roles for improvisation in theatre dance, only one of which lives beyond the dominant world of 'set choreography'. There are 'embellishments left to the individual artists where a set choreography persists; improvisation as a process of spontaneous free movement to invent original movement intended for use in set choreography; and improvisation for its own sake that is brought to a high level of performance' (2000: 182). Sally Banes also mentions the historical role of embellishment—'we know that the choreography in nineteenth century ballets was loose enough for star ballerinas regularly to embroider their own solo variations upon set choreography' (1994: 341)—so it appears that the dancing masters were not the only creators, after all.

How can we resolve this definitional dilemma so it is not a zero-sum game—choreography versus improvisation? What conceptual structures will help us find a fluidity, or at least a broader range of choice, that matches the Judson legacy? First off, the idea that choreography and improvisation are somehow opposing processes needs to be dispensed with. This is in no way a dichotomy. It is a spectrum, a continuum.

And while the extremes at the ends of this spectrum are possible choices, most contemporary dance-makers drift around in the vast territory between. So where is the common ground?

First, choreography and improvisation are both, at times, rooted in the process of composition (even if that composition is happening, in the case of improvisation, in real time). Keith Sawyer, discussing ethnomusicologist Bruno Nettl, points out that 'Nettl viewed this continuum as representing "rapid composition" at the improvisational end, and "slow composition" at the compositional end' (1996: 273). Questions of progression, spacing, timing, facing, interaction with other dancers, connection to the music or the ambient sounds, and finding movement appropriate to the moment are the same, or at least very similar, whether you are answering them prior to performance or in the moment of moving.

Choreography and improvisation are also both, at times, reliant on the process of inviting and capturing creative magic that occurs in the moment. In improvisation, that moment must occur in the crucible of performance. In choreography, that moment can come almost anywhere/anytime. It could conveniently come in rehearsal, when the dancers are there to help reify it into movement, but it might also come on the subway or in the semi–dream state before sleeping or waking.

Even when blessed by creative magic, both processes have to navigate the flow and resistance of real bodies engaged in actions, so that moment of insight that leads to a new pathway for investigation may turn out to be a dead end. Whether in real time or rehearsal, dance-makers must then choose to adapt or abandon the product of that insight, as appropriate. And since magic is sometimes a fickle partner, there are times in both choreography and improvisation when dance-makers must make choices of necessity or expedience. An improviser learns to love those choices and build unexpected worlds on their backs. A choreographer has the theoretical luxury to return later and edit, tweak, or discard, but telling dancers to throw out something they have worked hard to master never feels luxurious.

If, as it seems, set choreography and improvisation share more similarities than differences, what sets them apart? What do dance-makers or performers or audiences gain from a moment of improvisation that is not present or as strong in set choreography?

In Theory

The last twenty years have seen a real growth in the documentation and analysis of movement improvisation, and in the examination of the cultural climate in which improvisational practice has, to some degree, thrived. Several important cultural studies (e.g., Daniel Belgrad, *The Culture of Spontaneity*, ; Foster [2002], *Dances That Describe Themselves*; and Goldman [2010], *I Want to Be Ready*), compilations (*Taken by Surprise*, edited by Ann Cooper Albright and David Gere), and process documentation studies (e.g., *Composing While Dancing*, by Melinda Buckwalter, or my own *Landscape of the*

Now) have both broadened and deepened our understanding of contemporary practice. In addition, several more essays have been published in various journals, some of which probe the question at hand: how is improvisation different?

In one of the most thorough attempts at framing the difference, Annie Kloppenberg identifies a range of issues but stops short of applying them to performed improvisation. Instead, she examines the increasing role of collaboration and improvisation in the development of contemporary set choreography. Her interest is, in essence, the power and politics of creative process in the era of what she shrewdly terms 'post-control' choreography. Suggesting that post-Judson dance artists have absorbed such 1960s values as 'collective authorship within a democratic community, attention to process, exchange, or dialogue, and an aesthetic that embraces imperfection and reflects human fallibility', Kloppenberg posits that using improvisation to develop set movement allows choreographers to 'unearth a particular kind of vitality' and 'the freshness of an emergent idea' (2010: 184, 188). Curtis Carter concurs that 'theater dance in some of its developments has moved from the mainly hierarchical systems of earlier centuries to collective participatory practices' and 'greater freedom and responsibility for those who actually perform' (2000: 181).

But what does movement developed through improvisation and collective authorship look like? Is it noticeably different from movement created in a more hierarchical structure by a single choreographer? And doesn't this create yet a third category in performance: 'Choreographed' movement, improvised movement, and now previously improvised movement that has been selected, edited, and set by the dance-maker for later use in performance? Does this last category of movement preserve Kloppenberg's 'vitality' throughout the editing and setting process? She maintains that as a choreographer 'recreates selected improvised moments' it brings 'a movement texture and performance tone that retains the active presence, impulsivity, and spontaneity of the initial improvisations' (2010). Does this 'active presence' look different from a more typical 'stage presence?' Can we see the impulsivity and spontaneity, and how does it affect the overall energy or look of a dance? Does improvisation somehow become an entropic spectre in this otherwise choreographed world? Is there a kind of stigmergic trace of the liveness of former choices that still influences the dancers or the viewers? And what else can improvisation access or express that may differ from set choreography?

Although there are many answers to this last question, the cultural and historical context of the improvising helps determine what we might see. In the 1940s and 1950s, Anna Halprin, like her mentor, Margaret H'Doubler, used improvisation as a kind of Swiss army knife. First, it was a tool of individual movement exploration through which she was 'finding out what our bodies could do, not learning somebody else's pattern or technique' (quoted in Ross 2007: 86–87). This was a strong (perhaps even revolutionary) counterpoint to the dominant, stylized modern dance techniques of Martha Graham or Doris Humphrey or José Limón. In this conception, a dancer uses improvisation to explore her own anatomy, moving uniquely 'like herself', rather than as a trained and integrated stylistic part of a larger ensemble whole. A work full of such dancers would inevitably look very different from *Appalachian Spring* or *Passacaglia*. In the words of

Halprin biographer Janice Ross, 'in the postwar conservatism of the time this was a crit-ical sequencing, leading the dancers gently into the radical act of dancing about oneself' (2007: 88).

For Halprin, there was more than anatomy on display. True to her lineage, from John Dewey through H'Doubler, Halprin's improvisation was also dance as 'experience', not in raw form but crafted and expressive of inner states. We would be expected to see the dancer as 'a craftsman as he uses his kinesthetic sense, and a creator as he thinks with it. He will improvise as a way of unleashing inner experiences, and will shape and define this experience with his creative intelligence' (Halprin 1955: 11). In Ross's words again, Halprin 'shaped [improvisation] as discovery within parameters where movements ori-ginated in an intuitive union of feelings with actions' (2007: 89). Such dancing was no slick illusion like a trompe l'oeil painting. With Halprin's improvisation you could not only see the brushstrokes but the painter worrying about what colour to choose from the palette. To see a different manifestation of individual action, expression, creative thought, and anatomically based movement from each performer in an improvisa-tion was a quiet West Coast dance revolution, one that started a sea change and quickly spread east.

In the 1960s, the Judson artists (some of whom had studied with her) brought Halprin's improvisational aesthetic into a new, more political era. According to Sally Banes, the now 'postmodern' improvisation embodied values like 'freedom, abundance, and community' (2003: 77–78). It also brought an informality—in unplanned move-ment and everyday clothing and makeshift performance spaces—that stuck a thumb in the eye of a previous generation of choreographers who approached the 'art' of dance with the utmost reverence (Banes 1994: 342). Banes also offers a surfeit of possible names for the process of including improvisation in Judson performances: 'indeterminate choreography' or 'open choreography' (as opposed to determinate, 'closed' choreog-raphy), 'situation-response composition' or '*in situ* composition' (2003: 78). Each of Banes's terms for the use of improvisation in performance strives to maintain a com-positional/choreographic orientation, rather than to carve out an alternative space for real-time movement creation.

Perhaps the improvisation of 'freedom, abundance, and community' reached its pin-nacle in the early 1970s in the cultivated madness of Grand Union. According to Banes, the group 'explored movement interaction and social intercourse in various 'keys' of reality; fictional, dramatic, metatheatrical, and everyday … and everything was com-mented upon in an ironic mode that made the group's antics resemble a surrealistic vaudeville' (2003: 79–80). Curtis Carter suggests that the members of Grand Union might even have been free (or perhaps freed themselves) from a typical choreographic constraint, that of making work for audience consumption. He says: 'dance in certain improvisational contexts became more an object of satisfaction to the makers, with less attention to dance as an object of satisfaction for the viewers' (Carter 2000: 188). If we saw a sample of movement from Grand Union selected and repeated for us today, would we still sense the freedom and community? Do these qualities inhere in some way, still there within the movement, or the choices, or the bodies, or the social interactions? Or can we only say, 'I guess you had to be there?' Did they really have freedom? Was it there for anyone who improvised? Or is that kind of freedom a fleeting social construct, or just an illusion created by a romanticized ideal of improvisation?

In her excellent book *I Want to Be Ready*, Danielle Goldman examines this popular idea of improvisation as an expression of freedom—you can choose to do anything in this moment, right?—but smartly recognizes it as more a practice of navigating and negotiating with constraint. Goldman is focused on political/cultural limitations, particularly in African American culture and performance forms, but constraints are imposed from every direction in an improvisation: from culture and body and mind and partners and predetermined structures and, of course, from the invigorating and maddening context of the now. Improvisation is, in Goldman's words, 'exquisite in that [it reveals] bravery, and choice, and surprise, and trust, and often a keen aesthetic sense of form, all of which are particularly poignant when understood as erupting out of, and in relation to, a variety of tight places.... It is an incessant preparation, grounded in the present while open to the next moment's possible actions and constraints' (2010: 141–142). Music theorist Philip Alperson echoes that idea: 'we appreciate improvisation, therefore, as spontaneous achievement within the constraints of the possible' (2010: 274). Freedom, while perhaps visible in many of the improvisations of the mostly white Judson dancers or Daniel Nagrin's Workgroup or Grand Union, was somehow both countercultural and privileged at the very same time, and might have read very differently if viewed on bodies more inscribed.

The landscape of improvisation shifted again in the 1980s and 1990s in response to changing times. The 'self' of the 1950s, and the 'freedom, abundance, and community' of the 1960s became 'nostalgic notions of the past'. According to Banes, 'postmodern culture in the eighties and nineties declared that there is no singular, authentic self ... cultural critics in the eighties and nineties questioned the meaning of freedom and community—even the community that identity politics might promise' (2003: 81). Improviser Jennifer Monson noted at the time: 'the times are so different. The world we're living in is harsher. We're responding to tragedy and hopelessness. People then were willing to take more time with their explorations' (1994: 346). In an essay for *Dance Ink*, Banes refers to Monson's 'fierceness and urgency', two qualities incongruous with the improvisations of earlier eras (1994: 346).

By tracing this shifting history, I do not intend to imply that improvisational movement could be seen only one way at any one time, rather that improvisation has been and continues to be uncannily nimble and responsive, quickly adapting to changing circumstances and new demands, even at the level of day-to-day social and political events. Set choreography is also adaptive but, by its nature, never as quickly. Alperson (speaking of musical improvisation) addresses this quality directly: 'there is another dimension of improvised music that extends into the social.... It is not just that improvisation provides a vivid instance of human shaping or even that it offers, in some sense, a model of thinking and action. Particular improvisations may have an import derived from concrete historical situations.... The social commentary here is an integral part of the performance, and attuned listeners hear it this way. This kind of "hearing as" is underwritten in part by the music and in part by the context in which the performance is realized' (2010: 279). A dancing example will be instructive here.

Ruth Zaporah, creator and practitioner of the Action Theater form of movement and spoken improvisation, travelled to Croatia, Bosnia, and Serbia during the ethnic conflicts of the 1990s. Reading about the violence and the complexity of the politics, she wrote, could not truly prepare her for the conditions endured by the people she encountered. She says: 'a few days into the tour, it became clear that our "show" ... the one we had spent hours designing and refining, the one that was intelligent, universal, playful and compassionate, turned out to be completely inappropriate for the camps'. She had to adapt her improvisations on the fly. 'After a day in the refugee camps, I longed for silence, for my body to respond to the horrendous experiences that I had been witnessing. I longed for beauty. Dance came forward with one transformation after another: Vulnerability became strength. Strength became weakness. Weakness became grace. Grace became grief. Grief became strength and on it went' (2014: 70). If dance is only a performance, then a predetermined gift of set choreography can be accepted or rejected by the viewer. The performative aspects of set choreography may be able to adapt in the now, but only as far as the fixed framework of the movement will allow. Improvisation may have a greater chance to be a conversation through art (rather than a performance), responding in real time, even to its own reception, sometimes changing radically or referencing anything available within the social context. *Punakawan*, the clown-servant characters who often poke fun at real-life local figures and events during specific performances of Indonesian Wayang Kulit, are an example of how the nimbleness of improvisation can help it connect to viewers in ways that set choreography cannot.

This sense of real-time responsivity is just one aspect of what is probably the most unique and compelling characteristic of improvisation in performance: seeing agency in action, humans navigating a complex and changing landscape, making the choices that both meet the challenge of the present moment and determine the circumstances of the next. Good actors (or dancers) can often make the same decision feel fresh and real in each performance of a play, and that is one way to bring a sense of improvisation into set material. But there is an assumption here that there is also a significant distinction between such performance skills and real-time solutions to a completely new set of circumstances.

What are we seeing in such movement? Alperson references Richard Barney, who coins the excellent term 'improvisational subjectivities' (2010). Barney, a scholar of eighteenth-century literature, was examining the development of the modern sense of the individual through the way we experience literary characters navigating choices in difficult circumstances. Alperson applies this notion to viewing improvisation: 'part of the attraction, I believe, is the sense that we are actually witnessing the shaping activity of the improviser. It is as if we in the audience gain privileged access to the performer's mind at the moment of creation' (2010: 274). If improvisation has shifted, yet again, from the 'fierceness and urgency' and the identity politics of the 1980s and 1990s, is this not, perhaps, where it has gone: that it grants us 'privileged access' to ourselves (and others) as we construct and survive a moment of the world?

Curtis Carter, speaking of Anna Halprin, says: 'her aim was to use improvisation to break the traditional division between performers and spectators and to make the dance experience more accessible to dance audiences and the public. Halprin's methods extend the notion of subjectivity, which had conventionally focused on the choreographer's explorations in modern dance, to include the individual dancers whose free and spontaneous movements also contribute to the dance process' (2000: 185). Improvisational subjectivities resist the viewer seeing movers as mobile objets d'art, as kinetic sculptures organized and manipulated by an unseen force (the 'choreographer'). They are, instead, persistently human, each distinct from us and from each other.

The late Richard Bull, an intensely clever and creative dance artist who has been called 'the father of choreographic structured improvisation', playfully tweaks this idea of the unseen choreographer with his piece *The Dance That Describes Itself* (Miller 1999; Foster 2002: 3). In an ongoing self-aware narration, a mysterious voice comes on what in theatre is known as a 'God mic' and takes credit for every movement and idiosyncratic moment of the improvisation and surrounding performance process as it is unfolding. Subjectivity and individual agency, what appear to be the hallmarks of contemporary improvisation, are appropriated, framed for us, and suddenly subsumed into a masculine, even paternalistic (the voice knows what the dancers need to do and what we need to see) creation myth. The improvisational creativity that is right in front of us becomes conceptually elided through this sleight-of-voice. This layered irony somehow both lauds and lampoons the subtle force of this centralized concept of creativity and uncovers the possibility that, caught in the aura of the 'choreographer' in concert dance, we may have failed to recognize powerful moments of improvisation all along.

Even after more than sixty years of exploration and incorporation of improvisation into almost every inch of the creative spectrum in dance, to distribute creative authority away from a choreographer, to place it in the individual choices of movers in a culturally and structurally constrained environment, or in the interstitial creative space between such movers, rather than in the creative instincts and craft of one uber-artist, still feels like a subtly radical act because of the weight of responsibility we lay on the shoulders of choreography. So the last act in this play is to examine, in their own words, the reasons why dance-makers do or do not take that radical stance.

IN PRACTICE

It is easy to be so focused on the Romantic ideal of artistic creation that we overlook the practical side of practice, but dance-makers, in the best of circumstances, are doing a job, and a hard job, at that. Sometimes their choices are more pragmatic than aesthetic, and they must weigh the advantages and disadvantages of using improvisation in process or performance. In the early 1970s, Trisha Brown was deeply involved with improvisation as a performance form. As a member of Grand Union for five years she toured widely in the United States and beyond, participating in what is perhaps the best known example of collaborative improvisational dance performance in the postmodern era. But she left Grand Union before their final season to dedicate herself exclusively to her choreographic work (Ramsay 1986: 79). Looking back in 1991, Brown explained that decision this way:

> I moved away from improvisation because you can't put it in the bank. You cannot recall it, and it began to break my heart that absolutely miraculous events were not repeatable.... I just reached an age when I needed to support myself and my son, and I needed to make dances that could be shown in theaters and be accepted by the network of dance presentation which our touring supports. And so, little by little, I moved away. But I took my precious improvisational form, because it is still my metaphor for magnificent movement. Then, little by little, I tried to improvise and then reiterate it to create a style of movement. Where I am is what I was able to do with that. (Brown 1991)

I have always found this to be a haunting statement. While the cultural aesthetics and economics of dance companies are always complex, that the improvisational luminaries involved in Grand Union (Brown, Steve Paxton, David Gordon, Barbara Dilley, Douglas Dunn, Yvonne Rainer, and others) couldn't 'put it in the bank' on a par with more traditionally choreographic companies speaks volumes about the relative power of the two paradigms. It is also a demonstration of the pragmatic risk undertaken by dance artists who are choosing to improvise in a choreography-dominant world.

But pragmatism swings both ways. After many years of living and working out of New York, choreographer Bebe Miller found that she and the dancers she wanted to work with had spread out all over the United States. Instead of long periods of daily rehearsal, she needed to restructure her creative process to maximize just a few intensive residencies where everyone could come together. A more 'choreographic' process—slowly building fragments of set material into phrases and sections—became more difficult with the long layoffs between residencies. Improvisation offered one practical solution. She says:

> if we have to spend a lot of time trying to remember what we had made at the last residency, we have less time to move forward. So the shift of strategy was very specifically about finding some improvisational scoring devices that we can hone in on and use those for the performance, in and around set material. (Miller 2012)

So, aside from any aesthetic considerations, improvisation saves time and effort for Miller and her company. In a different kind of pragmatic choice, choreographer Joe Goode, who does not use improvisation very often in performance, finds it a crucial tool in rehearsal to facilitate the kind of productive interaction he wants to have with his dancers:

> as a youngster my understanding of choreography was that you had a vision and you pooped it out and other people just kind of fit into it or learned it, and that was

enormously unproductive and unsatisfying. Trying to make people dance like you or think like you or be you in some way is just really fruitless, and you realize that that can never happen, and I think many of us quickly came to that conclusion.... So I don't ever give [my dancers] steps or ask them to do a particular thing, rather I ask them to solve a problem or to answer a question through movement or through voice or through spoken word. (Goode 2012)

Pragmatism may make some aspects of creative process easier, but pragmatic choices have aesthetic consequences, and it is unlikely that dance-makers would compromise too far just for ease. If they use both set and improvised structures in process and/or performance, they are probably comfortable in both worlds. That can lead to choices that look a bit like no choice at all, a liminal place near the middle of the set-to-improvised spectrum where dance-makers try to have their choreographic cake and eat it improvisationally, too.

Bebe Miller says that sometimes 'it feels like we've set some things that look improvised, and we've improvised some things that look set' (Miller 2012). This statement interests me because it implies both that there may be some recognizable qualities of set or improvised movement that a dance-maker may choose to access and that there is more than one way to elicit such qualities. One of those pathways is to seek the freshness, the real-time presentness, of every performative moment, whether the underlying movement material is set or new. For Joe Goode, the answer to the set/new debate is both, and neither:

this is where we get into a deep philosophical discussion because I would say that every moment is improvised on a certain level because I never come to it with the same frame of mind. I never come to it with the same state of being, or the same amount of energy. So every time I perform, even a very set, regulated movement, I'm still improvising. I'm a big believer in that. And the way that I set up the works, often there's a vocal component, a physical component, and the kind of emotional dynamic that I have to have with another person, with an object or something. So it's an obstacle course. Every time I approach those things they're going to be a little different and the vocal is maybe going to be more important this time, and the physical more important next time, and the relationship with my partner more important the third time. So it's always changing. And over the course of performing the same work many times it evolves massively. I mean, things really change. And yet, the obstacles that we're overcoming or encountering are always the same, so in a way that material is set, but the outcome can be very different. (Goode 2012)

Bebe Miller has a similar concern:

even in structuring something that feels more like set choreography, there is that moment of putting your foot down on the floor, or whatever body part that is, and that it's unknown, and everything forms around that, which is improvisational.... I feel as a director I am instigating or interrupting what maybe is flowing more kinetically from the performers and trying to expand on the nature of that interruption. And that feels like that is improvisatory. (Miller 2012)

Ironically, even in this era of 'post-control choreography', another important consideration for both Miller and Goode is the ability to control, or 'craft', the material of their dances, although their definitions or methods of crafting lead to two different outcomes for improvisation in performance. Goode has his doubts about the details of improvised moments:

> because I like to make work that's *about* something, that's topic driven, and definitely content driven within that meditation on a topic, I want there to be a wide variance of materials. I want something that's going to be very visual and organized in space, just as a texture.... That organization that I crave, and that kind of visual layering of organized material, I need set material to get there. And it satisfies my eye, and it satisfies my need for a kind of craft, a knitted, quilted fabric. So that's always something I crave, in different dosages in different pieces. I'm also a bit of a wordsmith, so I like to craft language. While I think there are moments when language can be discovered and found in the voice, in the body, and in the state of one's being, I don't trust it for the duration of a performance. (Goode 2012)

Bebe Miller sees another way, where she can craft intention rather than specific movements:

> even though the detail of movement has always been very important to me, there seemed to be kind of a development [where] the specifics didn't matter quite as much. I mean, I want it to be very specific, but rather than crafting from the specifics, it was trying to hone it on what the essence of the intention was, and that felt more improvisational, or investigative, differently investigative. (Miller 2012)

It is clear from these descriptions that the use of improvisation in process or performance is not about 'freedom' for either of these dance-makers (or their dancers). Goode seeks to capture the improvisational qualities of carefully crafted set movement that was originally derived through improvisation, while Miller carefully crafts intentions in a way that produces very specific improvised movements. The choices of the dancers are tightly controlled in either process. For Goode, set movement is the meat in an improvisational sandwich, whereas Miller directs an episode of *Iron Chef* in which she challenges the dancers to make a movement meal in real time, but only with the ingredients she provides. Because the hand of the dance-maker is so evident in either process, it is easy to see how a viewer might overlook the presence of improvisation altogether. But there are three more crucial roles that improvisation plays for these two dance-makers that might be more clearly improvisational to that viewer.

The first, and perhaps most obvious, is to incorporate the audience themselves into some aspect of the live performance of the piece. They can see their own ideas or desires played out in real time, see the process in performance. In his work the *Human Kind Series*, Joe Goode dips into that well:

> we actually, in the performance, solicit little messages from the audience.... An individual performer will go out and talk to somebody, privately, not in a public way, but sit beside them and say, I want to ask you this question and would you mind answering it. And let me take notes or you can write the notes. And then at a later point in the piece that conversation or that response that they got, they encounter it with, again, a narrow scope of how they're going to approach it, but it's an improvisation for sure, in the classical sense. And of course, depending on what the person is giving them, it changes dramatically.... It's something I would only entrust to a company that I have worked with for a very long time, because I feel like I'm not going to get just some kind of virtuosity or some kind of showoff nonsense, but I'm actually going to get an investigation that feels honest and real. (Goode 2012)

Another option pursues the opposite of what Goode earlier referred to as 'trying to make people dance like you or think like you'. What if, instead, you wanted your dancers to move and think uniquely like themselves? Bebe Miller, in her piece *Necessary Beauty*, creates a choreographic space for this kind of solo improvisation:

> I feel that I pretty much designed a way for Kathleen [Hermesdorf] to do Kathleen. The piece ends with Angie [Hauser] doing Angie. Not in any way, you know. There are landmarks. But one of the things that both of those women do extraordinarily beautifully is arrive in a new world that has a dynamic that they are riding. It's a psychic world. It has a personality. It's not just a physical form. It's happening to them or with them, and then they kind of evolve into the next aspect of that state.... So how do I shape the piece so they can do that, and so that then, choreographically, the timing of that element solves something overall? (Miller 2012)

The last use harkens back to Halprin, and has echoes throughout the history I have traced here, and that is the power of improvisation to allow the viewer into the creative body/mind of the performer in the now, to experience her encountering what is present in the moment and being forced to choose how and when and where to move. This encapsulates both the risk and the reward of allowing improvisation a seat at the choreographic table. For Miller:

> we're watching somebody solve something.... we're looking at a situation where somebody has to make a choice, and that's compelling, even if they've made that same choice the day before. And I think it's taken a while for me to get to that, and to trust that, and then kind of figure out where that's going to go, rather than panicking over it. Because I think there's something about the theatrical experience, there's a complexity to the visual picture that I'm presenting. It's not only movement. It's not just the music. It's also temporal. It's visual, where the light is, how the light evolves, and "ping," something happens—and then there's an image. All of that is in motion. So I think I'm choreographing the space, not just the body.... There's a thickness to

the flow of a theatrical moment that is crafted of many different things, and there's less importance to the completion of the cool move on its own. (Miller 2012)

A FINAL WORD

As a researcher who has dedicated a significant amount of my life to documenting the process of movement improvisation, I probably have an axe to grind when improvisation is (to borrow Brenda Dixon Gottschild's term from Africanist critical theory) 'invisibilized' within the dominant choreographic paradigm of modern and post–modern American concert dance. But I hope that this process of uncovery (as opposed to discovery) is worth the journey for more reasons than to right that slight.

It is not surprising to me that the answer to many of this essay's foundational questions is 'yes (in certain circumstances)'. I have presented pragmatic and aesthetic reasons for dance-makers to incorporate improvisation into their process of creating a work. I have also shown that the collaborative aspects of 'post-control choreography' are designed to increase the creative participation and investment of dancers within both process and performance. Both theorists and artists have talked about the ways improvisation offers viewers greater access to the experience and individuality of the performers, and allows us to see beyond the sometimes slick surface of live dance. But it is not my intention to suggest that improvisation replace set movement. There is value to both. The only real change I recommend is linguistic. Increasing awareness of the role and presence of improvisation in contemporary dance will, perhaps, continue a process of erosion on the idea of a choreographer as a lone artistic genius who controls all aspects of a work. Making dances at the professional level is a monumentally difficult task, and fraught with (among other perils) the dangers of ego and the limitations of self. Contemporary 'choreographers' do not have to use improvisation in process or performance to make good dances. But it seems clear that opening up that toolbox (Pandora's box?), even a little, can offer them access to creativity and movement and choices beyond their familiar ground and convey a compelling sense that this dance is happening now, and only now, just for you. Considering the seamless ways choreographers such as Joe Goode and Bebe Miller weave together the set and the improvised, the life of improvisation in contemporary American concert dance is perhaps only secret because it has become so thoroughly integrated into what we just think of as dance.

REFERENCES

Alperson, P. (2010) A Topography of Improvisation. *Journal of Aesthetics and Art Criticism* 68(3): 273–280.
Banes, S. (1994) *Writing Dancing in the Age of Postmodernism*. Middletown, CT: Wesleyan University Press.

Banes, S. (2003) Spontaneous Combustion: Notes on Dance Improvisation from the Sixties to the Nineties. In Albright, Ann Cooper, and Gere, D. (eds.), *Taken by Surprise: A Dance Improvisation Reader*. Middletown, CT: Wesleyan University Press, 77–87.

Brown, T. (1991) Personal interview.

Carter, C. L. (2000) Improvisation in Dance. *Journal of Aesthetics and Art Criticism* 58(2): 181–190.

Foster, S. L. (2002) *Dances That Describe Themselves: The Improvised Choreography of Richard Bull*. Middletown, CT: Wesleyan University Press.

Foster, S. L. (2011) *Choreographing Empathy: Kinesthesia in Performance*. New York: Routledge.

Goldman, D. (2010) *I Want to Be Ready: Improvised Dance as a Practice of Freedom*. Ann Arbor: University of Michigan Press.

Goode, J. (2012) Personal interview.

Grove Music Online. (2015) http://www.oxfordmusiconline.com:80/subscriber/article/grove/music/13738pg2. Accessed 10 January 2015.

Halprin, A. (1955) Intuition and Improvisation in Dance. *Impulse* 10–12.

Kloppenberg, A. (2010) Improvisation in Process: 'Post-control' Choreography. *Dance Chronicle* 33: 180–207.

Miller, B. (2012) Personal interview.

Miller, G. W. (1999) Regarding Richard. *Contact Quarterly* 24(1): 23.

Oxford University Press. (2015) Oxford English Dictionary Online. http://www.oed.com/

Ramsay, M. H. (1986) *Grand Union (1970–1976), An Improvisational Performance Group*. PhD. New York University.

Ross, J. (2007) *Anna Halprin: Experience as Dance*. Berkeley: University of California Press.

Sawyer, R. K. (1996) The Semiotics of Improvisation: The Pragmatics of Musical and Verbal Performance. *Semiotics* 108(3–4): 269–306.

Zaporah, R. (2014) *Improvisation on the Edge: Notes from On and Off Stage*. Berkeley: North Atlantic Books.

CHAPTER 39

....

IN THE MOMENT

Improvisation in Traditional Dance

....

ANTHONY SHAY

IT is widely thought, even among some dance scholars, that traditional dances constitute a part of ancient tradition, in which dances, like heirlooms, are lovingly and dutifully passed down from generation to generation as static, unchanging objects. This can indeed be true for dances of a ritual nature in which the dance is carefully repeated as exactly as possible in order for the ritual to ensure the correct order of the universe, or provide crops and rain, or promise the success of a hunt. The Japanese court dance bugaku provides us with an example of an important ritual dance, perhaps the oldest dance in the world that can be documented. In the PBS series *Dancing*, in the *Dancing in the Court* sequence, a master teacher and performer of *bugaku* tells the audience that the dance has been carefully handed down in his family from father to son for over thirty-nine generations and that the exact repetition of the dance is necessary to ensure the proper order of the cosmos. (*Dancing in the Court*, sequence 2: Japan).

Most individuals experience and view traditional dance in the form of what I call ethnoidentity dances, that is, dances that are prepared for stage, for tourism, for concerts, and for purposes of the representation of ethnic and national identities. For example, more people have experienced Irish step dancing through appearances of Riverdance than in Irish village pubs. In my own experience, the difference between staged dances performed by Lado, the Croatian State Folk Ensemble, in which every performance of a dance is the same, and dances 'in the field' in which villagers might improvise is great.

For over fifty years, I studied and staged many forms of traditional dances, and I researched the dances in the field to learn them. Part of that learning, was learning how improvisation occurred, and how to improvise. At times, as in staging dances from the Persian Gulf or Greek taverna dances, I built improvisation into the staging in order to demonstrate how important the element of improvisation is in that dance genre.

Unlike ethnoidentity dances, many social and what are called 'traditional', 'ethnic', or 'folk dance' traditions include improvisational elements that constitute a crucial element of their performance. By the term 'improvisation', I mean a spontaneous, in-the-moment performance of steps, figures, and movements that flow freely during the dance performance and are generally never again repeated in the same way. Improvisation, that is, the heuristic selection of movements and gestures, differs in process and form from genre to genre, context to context, and culture to culture. It is important to stress that improvisation is governed by expressive intention, structural elements, and rules.

In addition, many people think that only certain forms of dance, such as contract improvisation and modern dance, have elements of improvisation. But this is far from the case; most dance traditions contain elements of improvisation, and some, such as Iranian solo improvised dance or belly dancing, are almost entirely improvised, particularly in informal settings such as social parties or wedding celebrations.

In this essay, I will demonstrate that, in fact, improvisation constitutes the very lifeblood of many choreographic traditions throughout the world. Taking examples as far afield as Iran, Serbia, Greece, Ireland, Argentina, and India, I will show the ways improvisation can be observed. I suggest that the ways a dancer shapes the dance during the improvisational process can inform and reveal to the viewer the aesthetic bases of many other forms of artistic production, including architecture, music, storytelling, visual art, and theatre. The dance scholar, through observation and analysis, identifies the parameters and how the individual dancer negotiates the aesthetic bases in order to create movement combinations that keep the ongoing tradition fresh and alive.

CHARACTERISTICS OF IMPROVISATION

Among all of the aspects of dance that scholars attempt to describe and analyze, improvisation most frequently proves to be the most elusive and complex. Above all, I suggest that improvisation is a complex process. For instance, Iranian solo improvised dance might at first appear to the viewer as a series of chaotic or unformed movements. In fact, upon close viewing, the analyst can observe and note certain types of patterns and sequences based on geometric patterns, consistent with Iranian aesthetics.

The relatively few readings about improvisation, which largely serve as 'how to' guides, often convey a sense to the reader that improvisation is a formless, shapeless, chaotic process that occurs when the performer 'feels' a certain freedom and then lets his or her instincts take over in a kind of mental free fall. As dance scholar Danielle Goldman observes: '"freedom" is a persistent fixture in discussions of improvisation and the arts—and yet its precise meaning is rarely examined' (2010: 2). In this chapter I assert that the performance of improvisational elements can require more alertness and focused concentration than even the most complex rehearsed steps. As modern dancer Laurie Cameron observed about her years in a professional dance company that performed largely improvised work in concert settings: 'it was during the improvisational process that we had to be most attuned and focused. No one just performed free form, that would have gotten you tossed out of the group' (interview with the author, 2

December 2011). In fact, improvisation is not 'free', it is a highly constrained practice, worked out within physical, contextual, aesthetic, and cultural parameters.

Other dancers, as Goldman notes, have claimed that improvisation was 'free', giving the impression that improvisation was arbitrary and 'anything goes'. One writer of one of the several 'how to' books on improvisation states that 'it is possible for anyone with or without experience to enjoy dance improvisation' (Mettler 1975: 13). Jazz musicians and players of baroque music would not make such a claim; they would insist that to improvise requires years of practice. Only the performer who has total control over his or her tradition, its movements and gestures, and aesthetic underpinnings can successfully innovate when dancing 'in the moment'. I have selected several examples of how improvisation occurs in a variety of traditions because some improvise exclusively using changing foot patterns, others use change of direction, some change hand and arm gestures, many feature syncopated steps, and some use a number of these elements as they improvise. For this reason I wanted to provide an array of improvisational possibilities.

IRANIAN SOLO IMPROVISED DANCE

For several semesters, I taught students how to develop techniques for improvising: how to select and perform a series of movements in order to dance within the stylistic and aesthetic structure of Iranian solo improvisation. The goal of this exercise was to ensure that the students who attended the class, if they learned well, would be accepted and admired by Iranian viewers for their stylistic correctness and dancing abilities.

This goal required that students understand the nature of Iranian dance events, including proper etiquette, so that they could understand in which contexts improvisation is practiced most frequently, how improvisational practices change in different contexts, an understanding of the aesthetic structure of the specific genre, the process by which performers make choices, what types of choices are available in this specific genre, and very importantly, how outstanding performers are evaluated over others. These questions become important, in Iranian solo improvised dance, because if the viewer does not know exactly what comes next, in certain social contexts, the potential for transgression can occur. This transgressive potential is embedded in congeries of social, class, and gendered conditions. Elsewhere, I have described several other contexts in which individuals transgressed through their dancing, resulting in either temporarily or permanently damaging their reputations (Shay 1999: 116–150).

In my study of Iranian solo improvised dance as a social form, I note that women tend to display more innovation, and more often through detailed movements of the hands, arms, torso, and facial features, than do men. Dance for women is a primary form of expression, and as young girls, many women spend a great deal of their free time practicing different movements. For men on the other hand dance is a secondary activity, as their lives are largely dominated by sports and all-male social gatherings. Nonetheless, men sometimes enjoy sharing the dance. Iranian choreographer Jamal reveals that when he was a soldier, dance became an important free-time activity in the barracks during the evenings when there was nothing else to do, and the young men learned new movements from each other (personal communication with the author, 8 January 2012).

The improvisational elements observed in Iranian solo improvised dance can be likened to Claude Levi-Strauss's concept of 'bricolage'. The 'bricoleur', Levi-Strauss's model for the way individuals in traditional societies solve problems, is an itinerant peddler who travels around the French countryside fixing and repairing household and farmyard implements and vessels by taking items from a box he carries with him that is filled with a large number of items, odds and ends known as bricolage. Just as the bricoleur is limited to the items in his box, the dancer is limited to the movements and gestures in his or her tradition. Thus, as the bricoleur selects items from his bricolage to meet the purpose at hand, the dancer selects movements and gestures with which he or she is familiar; in other words, both the bricoleur and the dancer are selecting the items and the movements from a fixed range of possibilities and improvising with them. In this way, the dancer strives to find fresh ways to create choreographic expression. During the process of improvising, the Iranian dancer selects from a well-known collection of movements learned through her lifetime and arranges them as she proceeds through the dance.

A second concept I used to describe the process came from the model provided by Alfred Lord (1970) in his study of Balkan bards (*guslari*), who have the mental map of a narrative drama that they chant to the accompaniment of a one-stringed fiddle-like instrument. To fill in the spaces between the events they narrate, they interpolate details from a collection of well-known descriptive devices, for example, 'the wine-dark sea'. I used this model to show how dancers in an Iranian context use parallel strategies of composition of movement phrases and formulae to elaborate, develop, and embellish their dancing during performances. For example, if a dancer innovates a movement with her right hand, she will repeat it to her left, filling in the space, which constitutes an important aspect of Iranian aesthetics. She will have a fixed three-step pattern and will interpolate a series of movements—her version of the 'wine-dark sea'—into a basic pattern that is familiar to her viewers.

I have also discerned certain patterns from which the dancer selects the elements of his or her improvised performance, which I call the 'the principles of a logic of choice'. I identify three large, overarching categories that characterize the types of choices made by the dancer in that cultural and stylistic genre: (1) alteration, (2) opposition, and (3) simultaneity. Typically, the dancer when using the alternation will move the hands and arms across the chest, first to the left side of the body and then to the right. Or the dancer might turn once to the right and once to the left. In opposition, the dancer might raise the left hand and rotate the wrist, while she lowers her right hand in opposition to the raised right hand. In simultaneity, the dancer, instead of alternating the rotating of first the left hand and then the right, will move them together, creating a slow arc above her head as she brings her arms slowly up along the body in a circular movement, simultaneously rotating both wrists. Thus, the observer can begin to see patterns emerge which the dancer uses during the process of improvisation and to observe how she develops new movements and ornamentation as she moves with the flow of the moment.

This model also serves to show how dancers in many genres of folk and social dance select from known elements but combine them in new ways that result in keeping the dance fresh and ever-changing.

IMPROVISATION IN THE BALKANS

It is through the practice of improvisation that innovation expands the stylistic characteristics of a particular genre. In more traditional societies, an individual recognized as an outstanding dancer can introduce a step, a variant, or a new gesture that others will aspire to learn, and eventually that new movement or step becomes part of the general dance repertoire. Throughout the Balkans, traditionally line and circle dances prevailed over couple or solo dances, and these dances accompanied observances of the life and seasonal cycle, weddings, and other celebratory events.

The pioneering dance scholars Ljubica and Danica Janković, who began to observe, notate, and analyze dances of the Serbian Orthodox populations of the former Yugoslavia in the early twentieth century, noted this improvisational characteristic throughout this large region. They noted that there were two types of individual who could be identified as those who improvised frequently. It is the first type that is of interest in this chapter: 'in one type falls the folk dancer who has creative ability. The majority of these creators are in the position to improvise new figures in the spirit of the collective folk style and technique as they ornament and expand the dance, from which new dances and variants are created' (1949: 161). Throughout their eight-volume study, the Jankovićs discuss several of these creative individuals at length, noting that they always keep the dances fresh and interesting, provided that they stay within the stylistic parameters of the native form.

Most people who dance in the various Balkan societies look to the dance leader as the best or most exceptional dancer. He, or more rarely she, can carry a great deal of social weight. Croatian dance scholar Ivan Ivančan notes: 'kolo-leaders (*kolovođa*) or dance callers had an important role in dance and dance parties. They concerned themselves over the execution of the dance, and in some places like southern Dalmatia, they determined whether or not a dance could be held at all' (1996: 325).

Expanding on this discussion of improvisation in the Balkans, one can note two types of improvisation: one in which the leader alone improvises while the rest of the dancers in the line perform the basic step, although sometimes the last dancer can also improvise special figures. This is common in many popular Greek dances such as the *syrto*. 'The person in the second position, has the most important place in the dance, for it is he or she who must keep the basic step so that the other dancers will not be confused while the lead dancer performs special figures' (Taylor 2014). In this case the lead dancer, if he is excellent, performs highly athletic, showy figures. My memory of Greek dancing is of frequently standing in place, 'in order to give the lead dancer a chance to perform those improvisations that are usually executed in place such as squats, somersaults, leaps, and foot or leg slaps, etc.' (Torp 1990: 72). This can last several minutes before the basic pattern is resumed. Sometimes the leader pays the orchestra for the privilege of leading the dancing.

The second type of improvisation occurs in dances from the region of Northern Serbia, with its former mixed population of Serbs and Croats in dances like *malo kolo, veliko kolo*, or *Bunjevačko momačko kolo*. Each man (the women typically keep the basic step), performs intricate footwork with clicks of the heels and the rapid movement of the feet, creating small circles, stamps, and kicks as he ornaments the basic steps.

As an example I will describe how a dancer might improvise in the popular Serbian *u šest* ('in six'). Participants can all improvise at various points during the dance. Beginning the dance, the dancer steps right on the right foot, steps to the right on the left foot, steps on the right (closing the left foot to the right), steps on the left (closing the right foot to it), steps on the right foot (closing the left foot, but not taking the weight in preparation to stepping left). This pattern is repeated to the left stepping on the left. As the music quickens, the dancers begin to ornament the basic pattern. One of the most popular ways of doing that is following what I call 'the rule of three'. Instead of simple steps with closing steps in place, the dancer may perform the step right, step left, but instead of the step close then stepping right on beat 1 and then bouncing on both feet instead of closing on beats 3 and 4. The dancer may step right and cross the left foot in front to perform the same pattern. The popularity of *u šest* over the past century resides in the capacity of dancers to perform many variations of this simple pattern.

Gender, too, can have an impact on the degree of improvisation that one can perform. In Iranian solo improvised dance, women are generally regarded as superior improvisers. In Croatian and other Balkan dance traditions, the men demonstrate a wider range of virtuosic improvisational techniques and movements.

In a good example of gendered improvisational structure, in Romanian folk dance the men and the women often have different patterns: 'the man's kinetic pattern includes such movements as leaps, hops, heel clicks (on the ground and in the air), stamping, stamping-steps, turns (under 90°) and active hand and arm movements to lead the woman. The woman's movement vocabulary consists of gliding steps, turns (over 90°), and a great many simple and double pirouettes on both heels with and without hand connection' (Giurchescu and Bloland 1995: 114).

SEAN-NÓS: IRISH IMPROVISED
STEP DANCING

All of the step-dancing traditions in Ireland go back to what is today called *sean-nós*: Gaelic for 'old style'. The dance tradition has several important characteristics: the informality, the individual styles of the dancers, and the traditional old style. These characteristics set *sean-nós* apart from the more formally learned dancing-master tradition.

The dancing masters described by Catherine Foley in her two studies of dancing in Kerry may well have taken their steps from an already existing store of step-dance patterns in the same way as the bricoleurs whom Levi-Strauss (1966) described in the French countryside improvised uses for the bricolage they brought with them. I suggest that the dancing masters took their creations from already preexisting rhythmic footwork, since most rural Irish dancing masters emerged from the same peasant class as those whom they taught. Step dancing has regional styles that are coloured by the placement of the feet and other elements. What has characterized step dancing from the outset are the inventive ways the dancers combine steps to create intricate rhythmic interpretations of the music. In many ways, the dancing masters who emerged as early as the seventeenth century, through their efforts of creating new steps and rhythmic patterns, appear to have practiced their art at a higher level of professionalism than the average sean-nós dancer, who mostly danced for fun and amusement.

Improvisation also sets sean-nós of western Ireland apart from the dancing master and from dance learning in the performance traditions of the other parts of Ireland. In dance-master learning, the student begins by copying the teacher's movements exactly, and only when one has acquired several years of experience does one begin to improvise. Improvisation is entirely missing from competition dancing and *Riverdance*, which are choreographed for presentational—that is, ethnoidentity—dance purposes. Nevertheless, viewing the popular theatrical presentation, *Riverdance*, the observer can see an extremely virtuosic version of sean-nós and can grasp the ways the dancers interpret the rhythms of the dance.

Catherine E. Foley, an Irish dance scholar, characterizes step dancing this way: 'these movements consisted of foot and leg movements such as weight transfers, batters, tips, toes, heels, stamps, cuts, jumps, hops, leaps, rocks, drums and toefences. Particular combinations of these movements and others, structured within eight bars of the accompanying traditional dance music, produced a step, or step dance. These step dances were performed in a close-to-the-floor style with precision, discipline, neatness and rhythmic timing on the feet in dialogue with the accompanying music' (2013b: 95). Sean-nós qualifies as a folk dance not only because of the way it is learned—that is in a folkloric fashion of face-to-face learning from those around one—but also because of the contexts and variations of its performance. Dance scholar Helen Brennan notes that it was often done for fun and for amusing its performers and viewers: 'some dancers had party tricks. For instance, a Michael Tully of Baliiebro could dance and play the fiddle at the same time.... Comic or grotesque dances were also highly popular at a time when notions of political correctness were not a consideration' (1999: 78). People danced at crossroads, country fairs, house parties, and ritual events and to celebrate weddings and harvests, which constitute typical European settings in which people, especially country inhabitants, perform folk dances.

Helen Brennan makes the crucial point that, above all, solo step dancing is a form of competition: 'the solo dance tradition in Ireland is essentially a virtuoso affair. The purpose is to amaze, to intrigue, to invite wonder and respect. In a word it is exhibitionistic. .... Occasionally, rival dancers would challenge one another to a form of endurance test, and such an event could become part of the folk memory of the area' (1999: 74, 75). I assert that it is this competitive aspect of Irish step dancing that has resulted in and driven the highly stylized, increasingly virtuosic and spectacularized style of dance that characterizes the current competitive style of dancing, right up to and including showpiece productions like *Riverdance* and *Lord of the Dance*.

The improvised dancing, shown in Kieran Jordan's outstanding film *Secrets of the Sole* (2008), which features traditional sean-nós dancer Aidan Vaughan, demonstrates the style of dancing and indicates that step dancing is used both in solo improvised dancing and in set, or group, dances. Vaughan hails from western Ireland, centered largely in the Connemara Gaeltracht of West Galway, where Gaelic is still spoken and sean-nós preserved. There is currently a large revival of the style, and people from all over the country are beginning to perform it, since 'many local people began to see the sean-nós as a badge of cultural identity and a source of pride' (Vaughan 2008). Vaughan demonstrates the dance, which is lower to the ground and uses more parts of the body than the other three styles that appear to be derived from sean-nós. Vaughan calls it a 'heel and toe' that he learned through 'watching and absorbing ... I can't break down the steps, I do it by watching and envisioning the rhythm' (Jordan 2008). He describes the steps, which he uses in both of the solos he performs, and the set dances that he demonstrates with three other dancers in *Secrets of the Sole*, including Jordan, who is also an accomplished step dancer.

Irish dancing, in general, is a highly desexualized genre. Messenger says: 'there is considerable evidence to suggest that the rigid body and arms of the step dancer is an early nineteenth century product of Jansenist doctrine in the church, which attempted to desexualize dancing. Most of the movement is below the hips of the dancer, and it is the feet of the performer which are watched intently by the audience, at least openly. Inis Beag men move their upper bodies and arms more than is customary on the mainland, and they are not as graceful as other Irish dances' (1969: 120). Interestingly, as Messenger observed of the Inis Beag dancing, and as I observed Vaughan dancing in *Secrets of the Sole*, I noticed that Vaughan generally looks down at the floor as he performs. Vaughan's demeanour underscores Messenger's point that Irish step dancers in western Ireland display a shy, nonsexual demeanour during their performances.

Helen Brennan notes: 'beneath the words is another sound: the echo of tapping, stamping, drumming feet. They reverberate down the centuries and resound from the floors and walls of deserted cabins, the timbers of emigrant ships, the stages of cities of American and Britain, the platforms of roadside "dancing decks": from tables, barrel tops, half-doors: indeed from any surface which could amplify that most insistent beat of Irish life—the rhythm of the dance' (1999: 14).

Improvisation in Argentine Tango

The tango can appear to be a very simple dance to the uninitiated viewer. Tango scholar María Susana Azzi tells us that in the 'Golden Age of the Tango', the 1920s-1990s, 'the man walks the tango, moving always counter-clockwise. He presses gently on the woman's back to indicate the figures and poses. [the *marca*]. The woman adds adornment through her footwork. It is all simple and elegant, a stylized tango, not the spirited and exuberant tango of the *barrios*' (1995: 155). Azzi describes the smooth, social tango found in contemporary Buenos Aires. Earlier tangos were more rambunctious. Marilyn Grace Miller points out: 'in its earliest form, the tango was more lively, more "black" than white—an image distant indeed from the consecrated versions later popularized in film and television' (2004: 83). This consecrated version is the *tango de salón*; the smooth *tango liso* was cleaned up and made safe for upper-class society in Paris before the elite classes of Argentina accepted and began to dance it.

Meanwhile, back in lower-class Buenos Aires, Salessi says, 'in wine shops and brothels men compete with each other in the creation of the most intricate filigrees of the tango, acquiring thus their own style of erotic exaggerations' (1997: 164).

The tango, in fact, is a complex of forms. Azzi notes: 'since the 1700s "tango" has referred to many different forms of dance and music (in chronological order): *tango de negros, tango americano* or *habanera, tango andaluz* or *tango español, tango criollo, tango rioplatense*, and *tango argentino*' (1998: 91). In addition, *tango canyengue, tango orillero*, older and faster, as well as later iterations of the latter form, have been developed since the turn of the century: *tango liscio* or *liso, tango fantasía*, and *tango de salón*, among others. Simon Collier states: 'it seems fairly clear that the milonga actually *was* the embryonic form of the tango before the new dance was finally given a name' (1995: 40; emphasis in original). The tango most probably originated from folk forms of dance, such as the milonga and the polka, combined with the exciting Afro-Cuban habanera rhythm.

Thus, pulling together the many rhythmic and choreographic strands of African and European making, from around 18801–910, the tango has been woven into a fabric that can be recognizable as the contemporary dance. However, as in many improvised dance genres, there is always the possibility of transgression, dangerous or sexy. Ethnochoreologist Jürgen Torp characterizes it this way: 'tango, unlike other popular dances, uses not only variations appearing in a short opening moment within a larger set of fixed movements. Also tango is not a free improvisation in the sense of inventing formally "unbound" movements as in some modern dance forms like "Contact Improvisation." Tango functions rather like common speech, improvised by the speakers in every moment, but within a concrete formal language system. That is why tango is often perceived (from the outside) as a fixed dance form, being (from an inside point of view) essentially a highly structured system of formal improvisation' (1998). Among all of the aspects of dance to describe and analyze, improvisation most frequently proves to be the most difficult, because the viewer never knows what the outstanding dancer will attempt. This is particularly true in a couple dance in which one, usually the man, known as 'the lead', makes the improvisatory movement, and the partner, 'the follower', responds. Each of these responses to the music and the moment require great skill if one is to be evaluated as a gifted dancer.

Improvisation lies at the heart of tango and provides the performers with endless possibilities for creation.

A viewer of films like *The Tango Lesson* can see the power of individual tango dancers employing a range of movements, within the specific Argentine aesthetic framework: throughout the film, the primary dancer, Pablo Verón, can be seen pushing the edges of that framework. By providing the basic figures of the tango, Mauricio Castro (2000) attempts to demonstrate the innumerable ways one sequence of movements and steps can lead to the next improvised moment.

Besides elegance in style, knowledgeable viewers award kudos to those who can improvise in the most innovative fashion. They judge innovative changes in direction, and the way in which the follower executes small, rapid kicks in and around the lead's legs, as the lead pauses. Tango scholar María Susana Azzi notes one of the aesthetics of the tango: 'the posture, the embrace, and the ability to place one's foot "just so" defines the good dancer' (1998: 93). During the improvisational process, the follower also contributes: 'with an attitude that is creative and active rather than passive or submissive, the woman intuits the movements her partner desires. She plays and adorns with her feet and must know how to turn and twirl.... If he only makes figures, he cannot pause, which is when the woman plays' (92). Mario Casillas, a longtime tango dancer, states: 'improvisation, and not knowing what is coming next, inevitably produces tension between the partners in the tango. It is one of the aspects of tango that few seem to notice, but I think that tension is one of the most characteristic elements in the dance' (interview with the author, 17 October 2013). Thus, in tango, improvisation introduces anxiety in the follower, because she (also increasingly *he* in the case of queer tango) never knows what is coming next.

Improvisation in Indian Classical Dance

According to the notes to *Symphony Celestial*, a recent set of DVDs (2003), there are now ten genres of classical Indian dance. Because of the ways the classical traditions of these dances are presented as ancient and unchanging by many writers and dancers, it is important to note that these traditions have changed, sometimes radically, through time. Today's Bharatanatyam, as dance scholar Janet O'Shea observes, is a sanitized version of its predecessor, *sadir*, which was 'a primarily solo dance form practiced by devadasis, courtesans affiliated with temples and courts as performers and ritual officiants' (2007: 2).

Improvisation constitutes an important element in at least the two most popular and well-known genres of Indian classical dance, Bharatanatyam and Kathak. I will use these two genres to point out the ways improvisation informs these traditions, for which claims of antiquity abound. (On the history of the radical transformations of today's classical dance forms, see Knight 2010; O'Shea 2007; Soneji 2012.)

According to the highly respected Indian dance historian and scholar Kapila Vatsyayan, prior to the tenth or eleventh centuries, 'there was a common art tradition in the country', and it was found to 'flourish in the precincts of the temples. The dance-style prevalent in north India was akin to the Bharatanatyam or Orissi—at least the sculptural evidence points toward this conclusion' (1992: 84). Certainly, that changed dramatically following the Mughal invasion and under the dominion of that Muslim dynasty. Dance in the Islamic world, in general, is an abstract art, not a narrative one. However, in Java, India, and other Muslim courts, the rulers often supported dance traditions that were in place in pre-Islamic times; in some cases they doted on them. In northern India, dance became an art form rather than an open form of religious expression. 'In the court, the Kathak virtuoso gave up the literary content in preference to a demonstration of sheer technique. Somewhere, in the unsaid part of the performance, the Hindu myth and legend still remained and communicated itself in the interpretive portions of the dance' (88). However, in an Islamic environment, the Hindu elements became more muted in favor of the spectacularized dance technique.

Improvisation and techniques of improvisation are taught to the advanced students as part of their training. 'Normally, the dancer is taught to improvise on a 16 beat pattern in such a manner that all the other *talas* [rhythmic structure] can be set to the basic 16 beat pattern. The dexterity and precision of the dancer lies in her [or his] absolute synchronization with *sama* [beginning of a cycle of meter] of the original metrical pattern' (Vatsyayan 1992: 93). Thus, in Kathak, one of most important improvisational elements the dancer utilizes is the rhythmic, lightning-fast footwork variation of the rhythmic pattern.

In contrast to Kathak and its dominance of technique, Bharatanatyam contains a crucial element of spirituality. Balasaraswati's biographer Douglas M. Knight Jr. notes: 'Balasaraswati herself commented, "Bharata natyam, in its highest moments, is the embodiment of music in visual form, a ceremony, and an act of devotion"' (2010: 128). In this system, the dancer has a teacher/mentor. It is 'a learning process that constituted the traditional *gurukula* arrangement, in which a student lives with the teacher to pursue long-term immersion in dance study through both formal lessons and informal tutelage' (O'Shea 2007: 41). Improvisation was an important aspect of that teaching. Rather than constituting a static dance form, dancers in these traditional forms had to learn the skill of improvisation. 'In fact every traditional dancer "improvised." There was no concept of fixed or composed narrative dance; dance masters would teach the art of generating interpretive dance in numerous varieties' (Knight 2010: 128).

As part of both Kathak and Bharatanatyam, in order to improvise, the dancer and her musicians, particularly the percussionist, must work together and play off one another. Balasaraswati, one of the two most important figures in the development of Bharatanatyam (the other was Rukmini Devi), was famous for her improvisational prowess. Knight states: 'Bala credits Chinnayya Naidu [her guru] with teaching her "to develop improvisation, by singing short phrases and with very few cues, [and asking] me to state which *nayika* [heroine] was appropriate"' (2010: 77). Thus, in this narrative dance tradition, histrionic talent, combined with the ability to be in the moment, constituted an important aspect of a successful dance performance, and in particular the ability to improvise the histrionic qualities of the characters differently in each performance was an asset. Even after she had obtained fame, she continued to learn from a guru how to improvise (140). Thus, as Knight notes, 'the parts of the performance that involved *abhinaya* [the part of the dance in which the dancer performs the dramatic content] were never rehearsed. So all of the collaboration of music and dance in javalis [musical forms] and padams [songs], the lyrically interpreted portions of the varnam, sloka, and viruttam [musical and vocal forms] would emerge, sometimes in unexpected ways, during performance' (212). It is important to note that the musicians improvised with melodic lines, verses, and rhythmic patterns.

Janet O'Shea notes that Balasaraswati

> argued that the dancer's original input into the form came not through incorporating new pieces into the bharata natyam repertoire but through the expressive opportunities offered by improvisation, especially in the abhinaya aspect of conventional performance.... She emphasized improvisation rather than composition, achieving renown for her inventive and evocative *sanchari* bhavas, or elaborations of the sung poet text of a piece [and] such was her skill at improvisation that, according to the American ethnomusicologist Robert Brown, Balasaraswati performed the same piece fifteen times during a concert yet rendered each version anew by deploying a wide range of references and poetic tropes in improvised sections. (2007: 484–9)

O'Shea's observation here underscores how the unique capacity to improvise can almost certainly become the most crucial element that can set a brilliant dancer apart from other, lesser performers. Balasaraswati's career emphasizes the importance of improvisation on a number of levels in Indian traditional classical dances. For the connoisseur, familiar with these dance genres, the improvisational portions found in an evening concert have the capacity to offer perhaps the most satisfying aspect of a performance.

CONCLUSION

In this essay, I have attempted to demonstrate that improvisation can be found in a wide variety of traditional dance forms. It can take place in the form of movement and gesture, foot patterns, dramatic elements, interpretation of song lyrics, ornamentation and augmentation of rhythmic patterns, adding athletic skills, making dramatic changes of direction, and innovative histrionic elements—by the dancers and often on the part of the musicians as well.

References

Albright, Ann Cooper, and Gere, David (eds.). (2003) *Taken by Surprise: A Dance Improvisation Reader*. Middletown, CT: Wesleyan University Press.

Azzi, Maria Susana. (1995) The Golden Age and After: 1920s–1990s. In Collier, Simon, Cooper, Artemis, Azzi, María Susana, and Martin, Richard, *Tango! The Dance, The Song, The Story*. London: Thames and Hudson, 114–168.

Azzi, Maria Susana. (1998) Tango. *International Encyclopedia of Dance*. Oxford: Oxford University Press, 91–94.

Breathnach, Breandán. (1971) *Folk Music and Dances of Ireland*. Dublin: Mercier Press.

Brennan, Helen. (1999) *The Story of Irish Dance*. Lanham, MD: Roberts Rinehart.

Castro, Mauricio. (2000) *Tango: Estructura de la danza: Los secretos del baile revelados*. Buenos Aires: Cesarini Hnos, Editores.

Collier, Simon, Cooper, Artemis, Azzi, María Susana, and Martin, Richard. (1995) *Tango! The Dance, the Song, the Story*. London: Thames and Hudson.

Dance Sean Nós: Steps for Irish Traditional Improvised Dance with Tutors: Ronan Regan and Maldon Meehan. (n.d.) Eyelight Media. (Video)

Dancing. (1993) Dir. David Wolff. New York: WNET Public Television Station. (Video)

Foley, Catherine E. (2011) Dance. In Vallely, Fintan (ed.), *Companion to Irish Traditional Music*, 2nd ed. Cork University Press, 180–200.

Foley, Catherine E. (2012) The Notion and Process of Collecting, Recording and Representing Irish Traditional Music, Song and Dance. In Smith, Thérèse (ed.), *Ancestral Imprints: Histories of Irish Traditional Music and Dance*. Cork University Press, 107–117.

Foley, Catherine E. (2013a) *Irish Traditional Step Dancing in North Kerry: A Contextual and Structural Analysis*. Listowel, County Kerry, Ireland: North Kerry Literary Trust.

Foley, Catherine E. (2013b) *Step Dancing in Ireland: Culture and History*. Farnham, Surrey, UK: Ashgate.

Giurchescu, Anca, and Bloland, Sunni. (1995) *Romanian Traditional Dance: A Contextual and Structural Approach*. Mill Valley, CA: Wildflower Press.

Goldman, Danielle. (2010) *I Want To Be Ready: Improvised Dance as a Practice of Freedom*. Ann Arbor: University of Michigan Press.

Ivančan, Ivan. (1996) *Narodni Plesni Običaji u Hrvata*. Zagreb: Hrvatska Matica Iseljenika I Institute za Etnologiju I Golkloristiku.

Janković, Ljubica S., and Danica S. (1949) *Narodne Igre*. Vol. 5. Belgrade: Prosveta.

Knight, Douglas M., Jr. *Balasaraswati: Her Art and Life*. Middletown, CT: Wesleyan University Press.

Levi-Strauss, Claude. (1966) *The Savage Mind*. Chicago: University of Chicago Press.

Lord, Alfred. (1970) *Singer of Tales*. New York: Athanaeum.

Messenger, John C. (1969) *Inis Beag: Isle of Ireland*. Prospect Heights, IL: Waveland Press.

Mettler, Barbara. (1975) *Group Dance Improvisation*. Tucson: University of Arizona Press.

O'Shea, Janet. 2007. *At Home in the World: Bharata Natyam on the Global Stage*. Middletown, CT: Wesleyan University Press.

Salessi, Jorge. 1997. Medics, Crooks, and Tango Queens: The National Appropriation of a Gay Tango. Trans. Celeste Fraser Delgado. In Fraser Delgado, Celeste, and Muñoz, José Esteban (eds.), *Everynight Life: Culture and Dance in Latin America*. Durham, NC: Duke University Press, 141–174.

Shay, Anthony. (1999) *Choreophobia: Solo Improvised Dance in the Iranian World*. Costa Mesa, CA: Mazda.

Soneji, Davesh. (2012) *Unfinished Gestures: Devadasis, Memory, and Modernity in South India*. Chicago: University of Chicago Press.

Tango. (1998) Dir. Carlos Saura. Sony Picture Classics. (Video)

Tango, Our Dance. (1988) Dir. Jorge Zanada. Facets Videos. (Video)

Tango, the Obsession. (1988) Dir. Adam Boucher. Adam Boucher Films. (Video)

Taylor, Mady. (2014) Lecture, 29 March.

Torp, Jörgen. (1998) Tango: Improvisation in a Couple Dance. In *The Proceedings of the 20th Symposium of the Study Group on Ethnochoreology*. (CD-ROM)

Torp, Lisbet. (1990) *Chain and Round Dance Patterns: A Method for Structural Analysis and Its Application to European Material*. Copenhagen: University of Copenhagen/Museum Tusculanum Press.

Vatsyayan, Kapila. (1992) *Indian Classical Dance*. 2nd ed. New Delhi: Ministry of Information and Broadcasting.

(2003) Notes to *Symphony Celestial*, Gold ed. Kerala, India: Invis Multimedia. (Video)

....

PLAYING WITH THE BEAT

Choreomusical Improvisation in Rhythm Tap Dance

....

ALLISON ROBBINS AND CHRISTOPHER J. WELLS

IN his autobiography *Savion!: My Life in Tap*, internationally renowned rhythm tap dancer Savion Glover describes his craft in musical terms.

> I know my feet, all about them. It's like my feet are the drums, and my shoes are the sticks. So if I'm hearing a bass sound in my head, where is that bass? Well, I have different tones. My left heel is stronger, for some reason, than my right; it's my bass drum. My right heel is like the floor tom-tom. I can get a snare out of my right toe, a whip sound, not putting it down on the floor hard, but kind of whipping the floor with it. I get the sounds of a top tom-tom from the balls of my feet. The hi-hat is a sneaky one. I do it with a slight toe lift, either foot, so like a drummer, I can slip it in there anytime. And if I want cymbals, crash crash, that's landing flat, both feet, full strength on the floor, full weight on both feet. That's the cymbals. (2000: 19)

For Glover, the sound often takes precedence over the 'look' of his dance, and he presents himself as a percussive musician. So do many rhythm tap dancers, whose sounding movements collapse the space between music and dance.

This chapter explores layers of connection between rhythm tap dance and jazz music, emphasizing aspects of their shared history, aesthetics, and improvisational structures. Afrocentric approaches to improvisation have always been a fundamental aspect of both art forms. The scholarly work on African American dance traditions elucidates the improvisatory processes and aesthetics of rhythm tap, and not surprisingly, so too does the ethnomusicological literature on jazz music. Here, we seek a closer dialogue between these literatures by applying the work of Ingrid Monson and Paul Berliner, two pioneering ethnomusicologists working in jazz studies, to improvisatory performances by modern tap virtuosi Michelle Dorrance and Jason Samuels Smith. This chapter thus explicates the choreomusical improvisation of rhythm tap and, more broadly, provides one model for how music studies might contribute more substantively to scholarship on dance improvisation.

Rhythm Tap as Music

Rhythm tap, also referred to as jazz tap, differs from other styles of tap dance in its emphasis on sound and on African diasporic aesthetics. Terry Monaghan differentiates it from 'Showtap,' a Broadway style that incorporates movement vocabulary from ballet and other European dance forms. In his account, rhythm tap focuses more on rhythmic patterns, regardless of whether one is a 'heavy hitter' or a 'class dancer' (2002: 21). Constance Valis Hill defines jazz tap in relation to music, describing it as 'the most rhythmically complex form of jazz dancing, setting itself apart from all earlier forms of tap dance by matching its speed to that of jazz music' (2010: 388). Notably, neither Monaghan nor Hill explicitly define rhythm tap as improvisatory; nonetheless, rhythm tap largely shapes current conceptions of tap improvisation.

The origins of rhythm tap reside in the late nineteenth and early twentieth centuries, when African Americans syncretized African and European percussive folk dances, but over the next few decades, the techniques and styles that would define 'rhythm tap' crystallized into a specific percussive dance tradition. 'If there were two traditions of tap dancing that had flourished since the turn of the century—one being the jig and clog, the other black rhythm tap', Hill explains, 'by the 1930s, these two rhythmic dance traditions were becoming ever more different' (2010: 99). Rhythm tap prospered in Harlem at the Cotton Club and at the Lafayette and Apollo theatres as well as in less public spaces like the Hoofers Club, where tap dancers met informally in jam sessions and cutting contests. Oral tap histories identify John W. 'Bubbles' Sublett (1902–1986) as the father of rhythm tap. His contributions were technical—he dropped his heels and added toe taps, in contrast to Bill 'Bojangles' Robinson's 'up on the toes' style—but also musical. Marshall and Jean Stearns write: 'in dancer's terminology, Bubbles changed from two-to-a-bar to four-to-a-bar, cutting the tempo in half and giving himself twice as much time to add new inventions' (1979: 215). In doing so, Bubbles followed the general shift in jazz music from the 2/4 syncopation popular in the 1920s to the 1930s' 'four-on-the-floor' swing. In the four-to-a-bar approach, Bubbles also added what Stearns and Stearns refer to as 'unusual accenting' (217), syncopation that was dependent on Bubbles's down-in-the-heels technique. 'When he started dropping his heels', Charles Honi Coles explains, 'he could get an extra thud whenever he wanted it' (quoted at 217).

The technical and musical changes attributed to Bubbles would shape the improvisatory bop style associated with the 1940s and 1950s, when once again, changes in tap dance paralleled changes in jazz music. 'As Swing gave way to Bebop in the late 1940s', Hill writes, 'tap inspired its first inward-looking artists. They were willing to explore their own pioneering rhythmic inventions, to create percussive accents that were implied, but not bound to, the underlying beat' (2010: 174). Baby Laurence (1921–1974), born Laurence Donald Jackson, is a key figure in the exploration of the bebop idiom through tap. He studied the recordings of Dizzy Gillespie and Bud Powell, imitated the rhythmic complexity of Charlie Parker's improvisations, and was inspired by the phrasings of pianist Art Tatum, with whom he worked New York's jazz clubs (200). Not surprisingly, Laurence and other tappers who danced to and, in their account, shaped bebop described themselves as musicians. Leon Collins claimed: 'tap is music. We use our feet to get the same sound as an instrument' (quoted at 176). Typically, rhythm tappers described themselves as drummers, a fitting comparison given that many jazz drummers had experience tap dancing and that bebop drummers like Max Roach, Art Blakey, and Dannie Richmond frequently accompanied jazz tappers (Malone 1996: 94–96). As Hill observes, however, tappers and drummers from the era rarely admit the others' influence, and who influenced whom remains a point of contention (2010: 215–217).

The majority of African American rhythm tappers active in the late 1940s and 1950s—dancers like Laurence, Collins, Teddy Hale, Jimmy Slyde, and Bunny Briggs—had a difficult time finding enough performance opportunities to sustain careers and worked more or less underground, frequently engaging in cutting contests in jazz and tap clubs. Their relative invisibility in mainstream culture led to their rediscovery at jazz and folk festivals in the 1960s, where they were heralded as masters of a dying art (Hill 2010: 199–204). Tap, of course, did not die, and many of the older generation of rhythm tappers became the sought-after mentors of the tap revival in the 1970s, 1980s, and 1990s. Their bebop aesthetic, with its focus on rhythmic complexity, musicality, and competitive improvisation, became the standard for a new generation of tappers, who attended tap jams at nightclubs like New York's La Cave. Here, under the guidance of Slyde, Chuck Green, Lou Chaney, and Buster Brown, what Hill calls 'instructional improvisatory performance' took hold: 'relatively inexperienced tap dancers were welcomed to the onstage circle to improvise solos and trade choruses with dancers and musicians, while being observed by a nonjudgmental drinking "audience" sitting at the bar and at small tables' (302).

The influence of the bebop tappers is especially apparent in the way dancers schooled at the 'University of La Cave' describe and practice their art.[1] Michelle Dorrance and Jason Samuels Smith, whose improvisations we discuss later, focus on tap as a musical art form and frequently discuss musicality. In other dance forms, musicality typically refers to a sensitivity to music, which a dancer communicates in the precision of her movement. Tap dancers complicate this generalized notion of musicality, for as Cheryl Willis writes, tap dance is defined by the 'music which accompanies the dance, but also the music that the dance creates' (1994: 146). This complex, layered relationship between a tap dancer's style and the concept of musicality raises many questions. Thomas DeFrantz asks: is a tapper's musicality 'embedded in the musical accompaniment and the dancer's relationship to that, or is it actually in the rhythm performed by the dancer? Is musicality a quality that can be detached from rhythm, or is this "visual musicality" actually an element of style?' (2002a: 20). As a community, tap dancers do not answer these questions so much as contribute to this ongoing, multilayered conversation by creating sounding movements that invite multiple interpretations.

In addition to promoting a bebop-derived positioning of tap-as-music, many contemporary tappers continue the longstanding tradition of cutting contests. Hill argues that tap improvisation occurs primarily during a challenge, which she defines as 'any competition, contest, breakdown, or showdown in which dancers compete before an audience of spectators or judges' (2003: 90). In this competitive atmosphere, dancers interact with each other, musicians, and audience members to showcase innovative rhythms and virtuosic steps that surprise and in some cases parody their opponents. Hill acknowledges that dancers draw from previously rehearsed materials in the heat of the battle; nonetheless, the challenge is perceived as extemporaneous, produced on the spot in real time. The tap challenge is certainly one of the more public performances of tap improvisation, but it is not the only setting in which tap improvisation takes place. Informal jam sessions allow dancers to improvise without the pressure of an official competition, trying out new steps as they learn—and steal[2]—from one another. Group choreography may feature individual soloists, who improvise short sections. And, following the jazz tradition, many tappers engage in improvisation alongside musicians, taking a chorus like any other member of the band.

Afrocentric Improvisation in Dance and Music Studies

Given the history, aesthetics, and structure of their art form, rhythm tappers in the twenty-first century clearly partake in an Afrocentric improvisatory tradition, whether or not the dancers themselves identify as African American. Historically, European and Euro-American observers have misread improvised African American dance as instinctual rather than learned and failed to understand the rigorous training that occurs in its ostensibly informal social spaces (Malone 1996: 28). Even outside Afrocentric aesthetic practices, a racialized hierarchy frequently maps itself onto discourses of improvisation and contributes to its relatively low status; improvisation, associated with spontaneous, corporeal expression, is marginalized relative to choreography, in which the temporal distance between creation and performance suggests a studied and cerebral process. In an American context, this Cartesian division between action and thought carries an implicit black-white coding that sublimates and exoticizes improvised performance. Within this fraught discursive space, scholarship on Afrocentric dance improvisation performs a delicate balancing act as it seeks to validate the complexity of these traditions without reinforcing the very Eurocentric system that creates the need to advocate for black improvisation in the first place. The ethnomusicological literature on jazz, we suggest, can aid this negotiation by explicating the craft of improvisation in terms legible to Eurocentric aesthetic systems while simultaneously challenging these systems' epistemological cores.

Scholarship on African American vernacular dance has long focused on linking its improvisatory aesthetic explicitly to Africa. Marshall and Jean Stearns's *Jazz Dance*, one of the first published histories of African American dance traditions, lists improvisation as one of six characteristics that connect black dance in the United States to its African heritage (1979: 15). Likewise, Katrina Hazzard Donald describes how West African dance, like African American dance, features improvisation, polyrhythm, and 'mimetic performance' (1990: 18). Emphasizing the African roots of improvisation risks subsuming the great diversity of West African dance into a singular improvisatory style and obscuring the uniquely African American contexts that shaped art forms like tap. Nonetheless, detailing retentions of African paradigms of improvisation in African American music and dance forms remains important, for as Thomas DeFrantz writes, these characteristics 'provide a theoretical framework for identification and interpretation of diasporic traditions of art-making' (2002b: 15).

In addition to identifying the Afrocentric improvisatory system underlying African American dance, dance scholars have challenged the idea that improvisation in black dance is entirely spontaneous and unstructured and thus of lesser artistic value than European and Euro-American forms that privilege choreography and composition. 'Contrary to popular opinion', Jacqui Malone explains, 'black idiomatic dancers always improvise with intent—they compose on the spot—with the success of the improvisations depending on the mastery of the nuances and elements of craft called for by the idiom' (1996: 34). *Compose, mastery, craft*—these words present improvisation as a process that relies as much on preexisting knowledge and training as on spontaneous, moment-to-moment decisions. Framing Afrocentric improvisation in these terms places it on equal footing with choreography by emphasizing the rigorous practice and preparation the two modalities share. Indeed, Jonathan David Jackson argues that 'in African-American vernacular dancing improvisation *is* choreography' and, further, that differentiating improvisation from choreography and privileging the latter 'runs the risk of being ethnocentric' (2001/2: 42, 44, italics in original).

Jackson understands improvisation in black dance forms as inextricably linked to the ways African Americans experience dance as individuals and how they negotiate social change within their communities. Individual dancers, he writes, typically *repeat* movement to intensify an aesthetic experience; *braid* movement to 'produce complex, interwoven dynamic contrasts'; and *layer* steps to 'create a sense of flow, juxtaposition, overlap, or continuity between actions'. At the community level, which Jackson refers to as 'ritualization', dancers participate in the interactive processes of the *battle*, in which they compete; *call-response*, in which they respond to an engaged chorus or audience; *precision-work*, in which they dance together to create a feeling of shared showmanship; and *jamming*, in which there is 'ecstatic, continuously changing, unpredictable group interaction' (46). These categories, when applied to specific examples as Jackson does in his research, encourage one to place improvisation within a particular social context and to identify who is improvising, how they are doing so, and for what purpose.

Two foundational works of ethnomusicological scholarship on jazz music reinforce the central claims of Jackson's research and the other scholarly work in dance studies that advocates for the artistic, cultural, and social value of Afrocentric improvisation: Paul Berliner's *Thinking in Jazz* (1994) and Ingrid Monson's *Saying Something* (1996). Berliner's *Thinking in Jazz* methodically unpacks the formal and informal apprenticeship system through which jazz musicians learn to improvise and portrays successful improvisation as the result of a lifetime spent assimilating the sensibilities of jazz. His thick descriptions of jazz music further clarify how Afrocentric improvisation in dance is, as Malone and Jackson contend, composition in real time, an act that relies on experience and knowledge to underwrite the corporeal labor so often read as 'pure' spontaneous creativity. Extending this work beyond Berliner's focus on jazz soloing, Monson's *Saying Something* explores the sociality of improvisation within the jazz rhythm section. The concepts she develops in this study, most notably intermusicality and participant framework, offer additional insights into the individual and group improvisatory processes Jackson describes in vernacular African American dance traditions. As we explain below, the ideas offered by Berliner and Monson apply particularly well to rhythm tap, given its emphasis on sound and musicality.

Berliner frames jazz improvisation as deeply engaged with history, grounded in a dialectic tension between past practices and current innovations. Improvisations, he explains, are built from the musical and stylistic vocabulary a musician acquires through years of deep, dedicated listening to recordings and live performances by other improvisers. As members of a community with a sense of shared history, jazz musicians who wish to be respected must comment upon and innovate within the shared musical knowledge that forms a cohesive jazz tradition.[3] Berliner terms this corpus of knowledge a musician's 'storehouse', which encompasses both the ideas and the embodied processes from which an improvising jazz musician draws:

> the improviser's evolving storehouse of knowledge includes musical elements and forms varied in detail and design: jazz tunes, progressions, vocabulary patterns, and myriad features of style. Performers can draw faithfully on their assorted materials, as when they treat a formerly mastered phrase as a discrete idea and play it intact. Soon, they realize the infinite implications of their knowledge, for virtually all aspects can serve as compositional models. Pursuing subtle courses, musicians carry over the inflections and ornaments of particular phrases to embellish other phrases. Venturing further, they may extract a figure's salient characteristic, such as a melodic shape or rhythmic configuration, and treat it as the rudiment for new figures. (1994: 146)

Implicit in this process is a system in which rote memorization and recapitulation give way to recombination and ultimately the innovative development of new contributions.

During improvisation, Berliner emphasizes, a musician's cerebral invention and physical dexterity are equally important, and he outlines a relationship between unconscious spontaneity and precomposition, in which a musical idea precedes its realization by anywhere from seconds to months or years, as an interaction between the 'singing mind' and the body. Performers must develop a 'singing mind' in order to translate material from within their storehouse into something that sounds 'musical' within the jazz idiom (1994: 181). The musician's body can be either a constraining force or a generative source of creativity in this process. In an improviser's early development, her ideas are necessarily limited by what her body can capably realize on her chosen instrument. However, as a musician achieves mastery, a player's embodied 'storehouse' jumps in front of his conscious mind as it 'interprets and responds to sounds as physical impressions, subtly informing or reshaping mental concepts' (190).

Perhaps we might riff on the idea of a 'singing mind' and propose that rhythm tap dancers possess a highly attuned 'scatting mind', one that relies on embodied steps and rhythmic patterns to craft effective musical phrases in the moment of performance. To be sure, jazz music and rhythm tap improvisation are different. Jazz soloists improvise melody over a repeating harmonic progression, and pitch is a central concern. Tappers, by contrast, are not bound to specific chords so much as to metric and formal structures, and rhythm remains the primary focus. Still, tappers can and do use steps to suggest melodic contour. If musicians learn tunes and melodic gestures, tappers learn steps that use different parts of their shoes to suggest pitch through subtle timbral shadings, and the scat vocables they speak or feel internally while they dance reveal a nuanced sense of timbre and phrasing. To create idiomatic improvisations, then, tappers do not sing so much as scat as they recombine the steps from their storehouses into convincingly 'musical' phrases that demonstrate their mastery of a complex art form.

These storehouses, built from the music's history, create a shared vocabulary that, as Monson explains, facilitates social interaction among jazz musicians in the act of collective performance. Her work on the sociality of jazz improvisation within rhythm sections resonates with the interactions that occur between improvising dancers and musicians. 'Interacting musical roles are simultaneously interacting human personalities', she writes, 'whose particular characters have considerable importance in determining the spontaneity and success of the musical event' (1996: 7). Adapting the work of sociolinguist Marjorie Goodwin, Monson describes the interactions that facilitate jazz improvisation as a 'participant framework' forged between an improvising soloist and a supporting rhythm section. This framework, Monson argues, encourages improvisation by grounding it within a regular structure that maintains both a consistent tempo and a steady groove (83–85). Here, there are clear parallels with Jackson's improvising individual, who repeats, braids, and layers movement, and the community event, which provides the affective structure in which to improvise.

Monson's concept of intermusicality provides insight into how the braiding and layering of movement might function in a rhythm tap improvisation. She argues that the historical nature of musicians' storehouses encourages jazz improvisers to access intermusicality, which she defines as 'something like intertextuality', as 'music and, more generally, sound itself can refer to the past and offer social commentary' (1996: 97). Musicians might 'quote a particular musician's solo, play a tune with a particular groove, or imitate a particular player's sound' to demonstrate their knowledge of jazz history and solidify their place within it by commenting upon their shared musical tradition. Rhythm tap dancers participate in a similar process when they braid and layer well-known steps, rhythms, and movement styles in their improvisations. Like jazz musicians, most rhythm tappers are invested in their tradition's past and actively build their storehouse from an archive of steps and movements—the bebop generation's mentorship during the tap revival fostered this tradition's continuity, as have YouTube and other online video sites that provide access to tap's filmed history. The braiding and layering of movement in rhythm tap improvisation thus draws meaning from the social and cultural resonance, we might say 'intermusical' resonance, that the chosen steps have for the dancers and their audience.

Hereafter, we analyse specific rhythm tap performances, applying Berliner and Monson's perspectives to improvisations by Michelle Dorrance and Jason Samuels Smith that were filmed in 2013 at the Stockholm Tap Festival's Faculty Showcase (Dorrance 2013; Smith 2013). For Dorrance's improvisation, we focus on the tapper's storehouse and Berliner's concept of the singing mind. Our analysis of Jason Samuels Smith's improvisation emphasizes the sociality and communicative dynamics between dancer, musicians, and audience through Monson's concepts of intermusicality and participant framework.[4]

Michelle Dorrance

Michelle Dorrance (b. 1979) has been a professional tap dancer since the late 1990s. She joined Gene Medler's North Carolina Youth Tap Ensemble as a teenager, later toured in the off-Broadway show *Stomp!*, and in 2004 danced with Savion Glover's company Ti Dii (Hill 2010: 350–351; Dorrance n.d.). Her work with Dorrance Dance, a company she founded in 2011, has resulted in numerous awards, including the Jacob's Pillow Dance Award, a Herb Alpert Award in the Arts, and most recently a MacArthur Foundation fellowship. In her solo improvisations, Dorrance carefully attends to the rhythmic and melodic contour of her phrases. The consistency with which she innovates familiar steps and rhythmic patterns suggests that Dorrance's 'musicality' is strikingly similar to Berliner's singing mind.

Like a jazz musician, Dorrance opens her performance at the 2013 Stockholm Tap Festival by performing a *head*, a choreographed (or composed) chorus that introduces the stable formal and metric structure that will shape her subsequent improvisation (Dorrance 2013: 0:15–0:35) (see fig. 40.1). Here, she presents phrases of ten beats rather than the standard eight. Within this unusual structure, she creates anticipation for the downbeat of each phrase by performing a flurry of sounds at the end of each ten-beat phrase. Two steps create this increased rhythmic activity: in the first three phrases of the head, it is a seven-sound *brush heel toe heel* step, similar to the Shirley Temple (0:18–0:20), and in the fourth and final phrase of the head, it is a five-sound *flap heel heel* step (0:33–0:35).[5] The component parts of these movements are staples of any rhythm tap dancer's storehouse and are not particularly unusual. What makes them exciting musically is the way Dorrance uses them to elucidate the nonstandard ten-count phrase structure.

Dorrance continues to manipulate these two steps in subsequent choruses as she places them in dialogue with more virtuosic movements. In one chorus, she crosses her right leg behind the left in a pretzel-like motion and touches her toe taps together (2013: 0:43–0:46); in another, she stands on the heels of her shoes while clicking her

FIG. 40.1 Michelle Dorrance, accompanied by a three-piece band, performs at the Stockholm Tap Festival, 2013.

toes in the air (1:17–1:22); in yet another, she performs a series of wings (1:08–1:13). In between these technically challenging steps, the Shirley Temple and the flap-heel step fill out the ten-count phrases, though never in a way that is monotonous or repetitive. Dorrance's movement is guided by her physical memory of these storehouse steps as she varies them slightly, adding or dropping a sound or initiating them at different moments in the phrase structure.

The third chorus of Dorrance's performance (2013: 0:54–1:13) illustrates her singing mind's manipulation of her storehouse. In the first phrase, Dorrance returns to the seven-sound Shirley Temple step, executing it at the end of count 4. The step returns again in counts 6 and 7, although the rhythm is altered as she inserts a hesitation in the middle of the pattern. In count 9, she tacks on yet another Shirley Temple to fill out the phrase. In the next phrase, the flap-heel step returns. When she first performed this step in the head, Dorrance initiated it on count 7 and repeated it twice more before landing on the downbeat. Here, she begins the flap-heel step at the very end of count 7, repeats it once, and abbreviates the third iteration in order to complete the phrase in time with the downbeat. These moments suggest that Dorrance falls into her storehouse steps spontaneously, her feet tracing familiar, embodied patterns while her singing mind shapes them into an effective musical phrase.

In the final phrase of the third chorus, Dorrance similarly adapts a series of single wings, a flash step she repeats in order to create intensity and anticipation (2013: 1:08–1:13). The first few wings feel accidental, but Dorrance quickly harnesses the repeating movement and moulds it into an interesting rhythmic pattern. Each wing consists of four sounds: the three sounds of the right toe scraping out, brushing in, and landing on the ball of the foot, and the final sound of the left foot stamping solidly with both toe and heel. In this series of wings, Dorrance displaces one from the next by a sixteenth-note rest, a momentary hesitation that confuses the existing metric structure. Only in the final count of the phrase does she realign metrically with the musicians, adding four heel drops so that she hits the downbeat of the next chorus together with the musical accompaniment. It is one of many satisfying moments in which Dorrance takes the audience away from the musical structure only to return to it just before the downbeat. Her singing mind plays with the beat, weaving familiar steps and rhythmic patterns into an innovative and exciting improvisation.

Jason Samuels Smith

An Emmy award–winning choreographer, Jason Samuels Smith (b. 1980) is among the most influential tap dancers of his generation. Smith rose to prominence in his teens through performances on *Sesame Street* and as understudy for the lead role in Savion Glover's *Bring in Da Noise, Bring in Da Funk*. From these formative experiences to more recent collaborations with hip-hop and jazz musicians as well as master Kathak musician Panjit Chitresh, Smith has long approached his craft as an act of music-making (Divine Rhythm Productions n.d.). Smith's performance at the 2013 Stockholm Tap Festival (Smith 2013) makes apparent this fascination with tap dancing's relationship to music. As he performs alongside a funk/jazz trio of a drummer, bassist, and keyboardist, Smith's improvised performance displays a striking ambivalence towards his own role as a featured solo performer. He explores the fluid sociality of the jazz rhythm section by playing with different roles in the ensemble and skilfully drifting between layers of the musical texture (see fig. 40.2).

The performance begins with Smith improvising over a repetitive funk riff produced by the bass player. As Smith begins developing simple patterns into more complex combinations, the bass player's riff creates a stable participant framework to ground Smith's improvisations, articulating a series of eight-bar phrases in 4/4 time that Smith will largely follow, and occasionally distort, for the performance's duration. The most crucial element of this musical pattern is its final bar, which ends with a two-note gesture that emphasizes beat 2 of the musical measure. This ending creates space: each time the bassist or, later, the pianist plays the motive, he allows Smith to perform on his own for a few counts, creating a balance between the familiar phrase ending and Smith's propulsive energy, which drives towards the next phrase's downbeat. This give and take reflects

FIG. 40.2 Jason Samuels Smith engages with the band at the Stockholm Tap Festival, 2003.

Monson's description of the stable participant framework that rhythm players create for improvising soloists (1996: 81–82).

The two-note phrase ending quickly becomes the centrepiece of a more intricate musical conversation between Smith and the keyboard player. Shortly after the keyboardist takes over this motive, Smith incorporates it into his improvisation, creating a moment for the pair to 'lock in' before Smith ventures into his own rhythmic explorations. This first occurs when Smith emphasizes the motive with two toe slaps on his right foot (2013: 0:43) and again when he elaborates the gesture with a single pull back (0:58–59). Their most striking synching moment occurs shortly thereafter when Smith hits the motive with a staccato landing on both feet (1:25–1:26). He lands in this split-weight position from three spins, which visually accent the music's growing rhythmic intensity. To finish the phrase, he silently slides his feet past each other in contrary motion, a movement that aligns with the decay of the keyboard's sound.

While the pair abandons this game for a time, it returns and expands during an extended period of stop-time (2013: 3:20–5:40). Stop-time, common in tap performances with a jazz combo, occurs when the rhythm section articulates only the initial beat of each musical measure, leaving the rest of the space for the soloist and encouraging him to reach for greater virtuosity. This particular stop-time section is divided into four-bar sections, with the ensemble emphasizing the downbeat of the first three measures and then marking the phrase ending in the fourth measure with the aforementioned two-note motive. Here, Smith initially fulfils standard expectations for a tap soloist as he performs rapid and rhythmically complex movements with crescendoing intensity. But he eventually transitions into a subtler musicality, adjusting his role within the ensemble's texture (4:46). No longer powering through the space created by the musicians, he quiets his rhythms and sets himself apart from the stop-time phrasing, executing a slow deliberate rhythm that works against the musicians' phrase structure. Music scholars identify this kind of temporal ambiguity as a core tenet of African diasporic aesthetics (Wilson 1983; Floyd 1995; Keil 1987).

The sociality in Smith's performance is not limited to his interactions with the other musicians; it extends off the stage and into the crowd. While the crowd is vocally appreciative throughout, there are two moments where simple figures elicit a loud response. First, during the stop-time section, a simple pair of *heel brush steps* (a step one could learn in a first tap lesson) elicits knowing laughter from Smith's audience. What these audience members are likely responding to is a rhythmic quotation of the signature motive from Dizzy Gillespie's bebop anthem 'Salt Peanuts'. Even without pitched melody, it is recognizable (2013: 4:56–5:02). The pleasure in this moment of intermusicality comes from the way Smith's simple gesture simultaneously honours Gillespie and affirms his own participation in a community where musical connoisseurship is highly valued. In doing so, he invites audience members to affirm their own sense of membership in this community. Smith's second intermusical quotation is both sonic and visual: he lowers into a squatting posture to perform Tack Annies (6:10), a step featured prominently in the Shim Sham routine and frequently taught to beginning tappers. This gesture affirms Smith's commitment to the dance form's rich history and its early pioneers—a high cultural priority amongst contemporary tap dancers. It also reveals the roots of his virtuosic improvisation, which, while on a level unachievable for most, builds from a foundation of movement patterns available to all.

Conclusion

The impetus driving our analytical approach to tap improvisation is not unusual; many dance scholars recommend applying musical concepts to African American dance forms. Jonathan David Jackson incorporates Albert Murray's writing on blues music, and the title of Jacqui Malone's book, *Steppin' on the Blues: the Visible Rhythms of African American Dance*, indicates how intertwined she understands dance and music to be. Even Marshall Stearns had his feet squarely in both music and dance studies. His initial interest in jazz began with record collecting, a musical interest that clearly colours his approach to dance. Jazz dance, he writes, 'can, of course, be performed without any accompaniment but even then, it makes jazz rhythms visible, creating a new dimension' (1979: xiv).

Even given this scholarly consensus, questions remain. How useful, for example, are ethnomusicological studies of jazz improvisation to Eurocentric dance traditions that incorporate improvisation? Brenda Dixon Gottschild argues that Afrocentric improvisatory forms in popular dance shaped improvisation in Euro-American art dance, as many modern and postmodern dancers valued and appropriated African American aesthetics (1996: 49, 53). Rhythm tap in particular, she reasons, served as a model for postmodern dance: both dance forms privilege a smooth, mellow state, so much so that descriptions of jazz tappers and postmodern dancers read in strikingly similar ways.[6] If there are connections between rhythm tap and postmodern dance, it follows that the principles behind tap and jazz improvisation might also illuminate forms of Eurocentric concert dance improvisation. Yet mapping the work of Berliner, Monson, and other jazz scholars onto traditions not steeped in African American culture still feels forced. As Jackson notes, sociocultural concepts and aesthetics are inseparable, and although 'aesthetic theory in dance studies has often separated discussions of creative process from cultural interpretation' (2001/2: 42), there are clear pitfalls to such an approach. Our analysis of rhythm tap improvisation suggests that music and dance scholarship best illuminate each other when the music and dance in question share a cultural history.

There remain gaps and holes, fuzzy edges that we have avoided in our examination of rhythm tap's choreomusicality. We deliberately chose dancers whose phrasing and rhythms are clear, who are invested in tap's cultural history and their place within it, and who explicitly describe their work as musical. Other tappers may approach improvisation differently: they might dance to music that is not jazz, they might follow the music in their bodies more than the music they hear, they might not be particularly invested in the rhythms of tap's past. These dancers force the question posed by Thomas DeFrantz: in rhythm tap, can musicality be detached from the actual rhythms produced by the dancers? If it can, where does that leave the dialogue we seek between music and dance studies? In this chapter, we have focused on what music studies might offer dance scholars, but perhaps the issues raised by these questions are best served by the ideas that dance studies can offer music scholars. The musicologist's understanding of musicality remains limited, tied to how notes sound with less consideration for how they look on the performing bodies of dancers and musicians; the idea of an artist's body as a tool of analysis is far less developed or accepted among musicologists.[7] We await future studies that show us not only how to hear dance but also how to more clearly see and feel music.

NOTES

1. Jimmy Slyde explains why the La Cave tap jams were referred to in academic terms: 'the kids used to call it The University of La Cave, and I like that because that implied there was some learning going on. Not that you learn steps, not that you learn combinations, but that you learn how to handle yourself, while finding yourself the combinations. And not being afraid to venture now and then. Ad lib, not improvise, ad lib' (quoted in Hill 2010: 302). Tap dancers have long appropriated academic terminology to recognize prestige within their art form and also to critique tap's marginality within institutions.

2. Anthea Kraut argues that improvising and stealing steps 'proves the most effectual protection device against theft' (2010: 187).
3. This sense of a 'jazz tradition' as a shared 'storehouse' of musical material that serious performers are expected to know is distinct from, but related to, the canonic historical narrative of 'the jazz tradition', described by Scott DeVeaux in his landmark historiographical essay 'Constructing the Jazz Tradition' (1991).
4. Specific moments from these improvisations are indicated in the text above by minute and second markings. Our analyses use the names of common tap dance steps; definitions for these terms can be found in Knowles (1998) and in the glossary to Hill (2010).
5. In tap dance, the word 'step' has varied meanings. Here, we mean a combination of sounds that forms a short, identifiable phrase of one to two counts. 'Step' can also refer to a simple transfer of weight from one foot to the other, and the term is also used to refer to a longer combination of tap steps that make up an eight-bar, sixteen-bar, or thirty-two-bar phrase.
6. Musicologist George Lewis (1996) makes a similar argument about Eurocentric avant-garde music traditions that recast black improvisatory practices as new, innovative developments in the Western art music tradition.
7. Two notable exceptions are Le Guin (2005) and Cusick (1994).

References

Berliner, P. (1994) *Thinking in Jazz: The Infinite Art of Improvisation*. Chicago: University of Chicago Press.

Cusick, S. (1994) On a Lesbian Relationship with Music: A Serious Effort Not to Think Straight. In Brett, P., Wood, E., and Thomas, G. (eds.), *Queering the Pitch: The New Gay and Lesbian Musicology*. New York: Routledge, 67–84.

DeFrantz, T. (2002a) 'Being Savion Glover': Black Masculinity, Translocation, and Tap Dance. *Discourses in Dance* 1(1): 17–28.

DeFrantz, T. (ed.). (2002b) *Dancing Many Drums: Excavations in African American Dance*. Madison: University of Wisconsin Press.

DeVeaux, S. (1991) Constructing the Jazz Tradition: Jazz Historiography. *Black American Literature Forum* 25(3): 525–560.

Dixon Gottschild, B. (1996) *Digging the Africanist Presence in American Performance: Dance and Other Contexts*. Westport, CT: Greenwood Press.

Dorrance, M. (2013) *Michelle Dorrance at Stockholm Tap Festival 2013*. Jonas Fogelström, videographer. (Online video) YouTube channel of Jonas Fogelström. https://www.youtube.com/watch?v=yVzmyl9D5rE. Accessed 31 January 2015.

Dorrance, M. (n.d.) Michelle Dorrance—Bio. http://michelledorrance.com/bio.html. Accessed 31 January 2015.

Floyd, S., Jr. (1995) *The Power of Black Music: Interpreting Its History from Africa to the United States*. New York: Oxford University Press.

Glover, S., and Weber, B. (2000) *Savion: My Life in Tap*. New York: Morrow.

Hazzard-Gordon, K. (1990) *Jookin': The Rise of Social Dance Formations in African American Culture*. Philadelphia: Temple University Press.

Hill, C. V. (2003) Stepping, Stealing, Sharing, and Dancing. In Albright, Ann Cooper, and Gere, D. (eds.), *Taken by Surprise: A Dance Improvisation Reader*. Middletown, CT: Wesleyan University Press.

Hill, C. V. (2010) *Tap Dancing America, a Cultural History*. New York: Oxford University Press.

Jackson, J. D. (2001/2) Improvisation in African-American Vernacular Dancing. *Dance Research Journal* 33(2): 40–53.

Keil, C. (1987) Participatory Discrepancies and the Power of Music. *Cultural Anthropology* 2(3): 275–283.

Knowles, M. (1998) *The Tap Dance Dictionary*. Jefferson, NC: McFarland.

Kraut, A. (2010) 'Stealing Steps' and Signature Moves: Embodied Theories of Dance as Intellectual Property. *Theatre Journal* 62(2): 173–189.

Le Guin, E. (2005) *Boccherini's Body: An Essay in Carnal Musicology*. Berkeley: University of California Press.

Lewis, G. (1996) Improvised Music after 1950: Afrological and Eurological Perspectives. *Black Music Research Journal* 16(1): 91–122.

Malone, J. (1996) *Steppin' on the Blues: The Visible Rhythms of African American Dance*. Urbana: University of Illinois Press.

Monaghan, T. (2002) Narratives of Rhythm Tap. *Dancing Times* 92: 21, 23, 25.

Monson, I. (1996) *Saying Something: Jazz Improvisation and Interaction*. Chicago: University of Chicago Press.

Smith, J. S. (2013) *Jason Samuels Smith at Stockholm Tap Festival 2013*. Jonas Fogelström, videographer. (Online video) YouTube channel of Jonas Fogelström. https://www.youtube.com/watch?v=-usEiqjkxNw. Accessed 31 January 2015.

Smith, Jason Samuels. (n.d.) Website of Divine Rhythm Productions. http://www.divinerhythmproductions.com/JasonSamuelsSmith.html. Accessed 31 January 2015.

Stearns, M. and J. (1979) *Jazz Dance: The Story of American Vernacular Dance*. New York: Schirmer Macmillan.

Willis, C. (1994) Tap Dance: Manifestation of the African Aesthetic. In Welsh-Asante, K. (ed.), *African Dance: An Artistic, Historical, and Philosophical Inquiry*. Trenton, NJ: Africa-World Press.

Wilson, O. (1983) Black Music as an Art Form. *Black Music Research Journal* 3: 1–22.

CHAPTER 41

....

MOVING SOUND

New Relationships between Contemporary Dance and Music in Improvisation

....

ANA SÁNCHEZ-COLBERG AND DIMITRIS KARALIS

INTRODUCTION

THIS essay revisits the relationship between music and dance, sound and movement, in contemporary dance and music in improvisation. The discussion evolves from the premise that much of the history of twentieth- to twenty-first-century approaches to dance and music in improvisation—notwithstanding, or perhaps due to, the Cage-Cunningham collaborations—has been one of diverging pathways, parallel and coexisting in some respects but, primarily, separating. Dance improvisation generally has reflected trends towards a 'somatic turn' that has promoted emancipation from music and its perceived theatricality and formal narrativity. Consideration of dance and music in improvisation has remained the domain of vernacular forms such as tap, flamenco, or Indian dance (Albright and Gere 2003). This study proposes that after such period of mutual 'emancipation', much is to be gained from bringing the knowledge discovered to inform the search for new relationships between the two art forms, both in the process of improvisation as well as in performance. The main philosophical thrust for the discussion draws from Gary Peters's book *The Philosophy of Improvisation* (2009). Peters argues that true improvisation, rather than being a performance of risk-taking and abandonment in pursuit of 'freedom' (what he describes as a 'glorified love-in dressed up as art'), requires 'a powerful memory, memory of the parameters of an instrument, of the body, of available technology, the parameter's of a work's structure, and one's place within it at any time, the parameters of an idiom, a genre and its history, its possibilities' (2009: 82). This idea, of the need to set parameters, to understand rules and structures, as well as one's positions within an improvisational process, will be central to this discussion.

In this discussion, we propose that in order to enter into a complex improvisation process between dance and music we need to consider the particular 'given-ness' of dance and music: what are its 'figures' (features), its ground (contexts), and its field (its coexistence/correlations in time and space). In the discussion, 'figure' will refer to the analogical analysis of movement and musical structures; 'ground' will refer to the *context of each discipline* (where it 'stands' conceptually in relation to the notion of improvisation) at the moment that the two disciplines come into collaboration; finally, 'field' will refer to the proposed new 'synthesis'. In a study of kinematics and sound, Haga suggests that 'it should be noted that the term *similarity* refers to phenomena that bear a resemblance to each other. This implies that correspondences are basically not a study of *sameness*; it is a study of *similarities*' (2008: 10). Therefore, analogies between music and dance are reviewed through a 'postformal' lens, which is aligned to a complex thinking that involves 'openness, dialectical process, contextualization and on-going re-evaluation' (Montouri 2003: 252). Seen from this perspective, what have been considered 'formal structures' (historically perceived to alienate the subject's awareness from the 'here-ness' of the moment—central to most understanding of improvisation) are returned to their 'bodily-ness'; what previously had been considered opposites are hereby taken to be poles of a continuum at the moment of improvisation.

We will discuss the project *Moving Sound*, a collaboration between ourselves choreographer Ana Sánchez-Colberg, and music director Dimitris Karalis, with composer-saxophonist Yannis Kassetas, as a case study. The project, which has undergone a series of R & D stages since 2007, elaborates a common ground for practitioners of both genres, in order not to coexist through synchronic monologues but to engage in actual dialogues. The project has two interrelated strands: an exploration of the function of composition and its role in 'free improvisation' between dance and music. For this discussion, we will focus on the work on 'free improvisation'. The practice that supports the discussion involved a rich and varied group of dancers and musicians who gathered for six consecutive days in April 2014: ten professional dancers, members of Compañia de Danza 21 (CoDa21), one of Puerto Rico's premier dance companies, four musicians, and the project leaders. The dancers were mostly 'veteran dancers' who started their careers as ballet dancers (all have reached soloist status in their careers) and in later years have expanded their work to include contemporary forms of dance as well as other body-based therapies (yoga, Pilates, etc.). Significantly for the collaboration, the dancers had an understanding of music coming from their classical training as well as skills in movement-based improvisation, as the company's repertory includes regular devised work with guest choreographers. Some of them also have professional experience in other dance forms, for example jazz dance and salsa, a local vernacular form of dance/music. The project involved five musicians: four of them were the members of Guess Who, a local jazz group composed of one flutist, one percussionist, one piano player, one bass player, and the fifth was Kassetas, the composer, playing saxophone. The dancers have worked with 'live music' innumerable times; this was the first time the musicians of Guess Who were working with contemporary dancers. However, they had experience in jazz improvisation. One of the musicians—the bassist—also played in local bomba jams, a local Afro-Caribbean form of dance that involves improvisation between dancers, singers, and percussionists.

OPENING THOUGHTS ON MUSIC AND DANCE

We often see music and dance together without questioning their coexistence. As listeners, we are culturally predisposed to attend to rhythm and thematic melody. (For more on the relationship between music, power, and culture, see Cox and Warner [2004]). We assume that it is natural to listen to the beat and to move. However, in this understanding we are not talking about a real unity between music and dance, an interchange of ideas and cocreation between the two, music is one closed system and dance is another. As in the Cage-Cunningham collaborations, two individual practices happen at the same time but are not intrinsically connected. Most of the time, if a type of unity is seen, it is based only on external elements or happens arbitrarily. Even though the interconnections that might appear each time on the basis of chance might be interesting, we can explore other more intrinsic connections, for example, structure.

Our urge to question the historically given relation between dance and music came from our observation of jazz bands during improvisation. In jazz, improvisation can happen only because there is a common 'language' containing a complex set of rules based on detailed elements that the participants share. In *Jazz Theory* (1995), one of the most influential books on jazz improvisation, Mark Levine describes how these common elements serve as the ground that allows musicians to exchange specific roles and, most important, to establish communication. Levine's analysis of improvisation is founded on the examination of structure—that is, sequence, patterns, and phrasing. Rhythm, scale, intonation, articulation, nuance, and intensity are only a few of the elements that are shared amongst jazz musicians. Jazz musicians, unlike contemporary dancers, bring not only technical knowledge but also knowledge of the 'standards' of the jazz canon, as well as a wide variety of musical patterns and phrases (licks), segments of which are brought into the improvisation, embellished, transformed, and reconsidered: 'licks and patterns should become part of your musical unconscious, kind of like an inner library you can draw upon. At the same time they should not be your musical be-all and end-all' (Levine 1995: 250). In this way, improvisation remains entirely open, yet through the potential use of structured phrases, the participants can understand, cocompose, and anticipate the next movement of the leading instrument. This allows for a 'productive interpretation of origination and regeneration as the new and the old are engaged with simultaneously' (Peters 2009: 2).

Significantly, the musical structures (and history) that *Moving Sound* brings into dialogue with contemporary dance are those of contemporary jazz—a musical form that, not unlike dance improvisation, has pursued 'independence' from the 'constraints' of classical composition and performance. Speaking of the early jazz improvisers, David

Bogo (2002) notes that 'the primary musical bond shared between these diverse performers is a fascination with sonic possibilities and surprising musical occurrences and a desire to improvise, to a significant degree, both the content *and the form* of the performance. In other words, free improvisation moves beyond matters of expressive detail to matters of collective structure; it is not formless music-making, but *form-making music*' (2002: 167). It is important to note that this definition of free improvisation engages directly with notions of structure and form, whereby the main aim is not collective expression (Peters's 'love-in') but actual form-making. Peters goes as far as to suggest that the fundamental relationship in improvisation is between 'improvisor and improvisation, not between improvisor and improvisor' (2009: 3).

In utilizing the idea of 'dialogue', the discussion moves beyond what has been referred to as 'listening with the eye'—the conventional call and response of much improvisation involving music—where interlocutors 'are always looking for an opening in which to respond' (Peters 2009: 123) and moves on to an understanding of dialogue as a 'listening of the ear', whereby participants listen to 'what is there' at the beginning of improvisation, in which the 'given is given in ever-new ways' (120). Furthermore, Bradlyn suggests that 'the first step in learning to listen is stopping still and opening our ears, first to *figure*, next to *ground*, next to *field*. The field, the aggregate soundscape is the most difficult to perceive.... There must be a constant flux, a never fully focused shifting among figure, ground, and field.... One performer's playing may suddenly emerge as a stark figure against the ground of another's only to just as suddenly submerge into the ground or even farther back into the field as another voice emerges' (cited in Bogo 2002: 177). It is important to note that amongst the aims of the project and related to improvisational frameworks is the creation of an ensemble. We choose this word precisely because of its literal meaning: '[musical] interconnectedness makes an ensemble more than just a collection of individuals. Interactions in jazz involve the spontaneous and improvised musical reactions of one musician to what another musician in the ensemble has performed. Interactions can either be an isolated incident in which one musical statement elicits a simple response or it can be an ongoing process in which one musical idea triggers a response that prompts yet another response.... It can also be multi-dimensional, interaction can involve all members of the ensemble' (Rinzler 2008: 28). If music and dance have developed apart for a long time, Moving Sound takes them back to their roots.

THE GROUND ON WHICH WE STAND

The history of dance's 'emancipation' from music en route to establishing itself as an 'independent' art form is well established—from the avant-garde experiments of the German expressionists (Wigman, Laban, Jooss) to Merce Cunningham and John Cage. It is commonly understood that the Cage/Cunningham inheritance that has shaped contemporary dance improvisational landscape is marked by a desire to resist a perceived 'mimeticism' between music structures and movement vocabularies in the classical and modern dance traditions. Furthermore, this legacy has been marked by a search for a democratic art-making, with an emphasis on collective creation and collective authorship which stands in opposition to the hierarchical structures embedded within a classical score. There is a clear move away from the invisible supremacy of the composer and choreographer that places performers are `instruments, to interpret movements, `notes' mirroring the musical score in a chain of representation and narrativity.

Besides the Cage/Cunningham collaborations, there is evidence of other exploration in sound and movement in improvisation. In the essay 'We Insist! Seeing Music and Hearing Dance', Danielle Goldman brings to the fore the work of Judith Dunn and Bill Dixon, whose work throughout the 1970s was based on jazz improvisational modes: 'musicians and dancers were working as equals, meaning that the music was not an accompaniment to the dance, and dancing wasn't just an explanation of the music. The idea that they were both running parallel and interacting, was a key element of their work' (2010: 65). Dianne McIntyre founded the dance company Sounds in Motion in 1972. Her work grew out of Dixon's and Dunn's and considers improvisation primarily in its capacity to act a practice of freedom and protest. Little is known of the actual methodology; fragments of reviews refer to McIntyre's ability to translate 'the rhythms into different parts of her body' (87). For reasons that are cultural and political and touch upon issues of class, race, and gender at the time these collaborations were taking place, critical response was not very positive, and the work of Sounds in Motion has gone into oblivion. There is little left behind of their actual processes that can contribute significantly to our methodological considerations in this essay. However, what is significant about Goldman's examination of these two cases of improvisation to jazz music is her conclusion that a pervasive bias remains that dance is an art of the body and music is an art of the mind, which goes some way to explain the continuing separation of these two arts in the general zeitgeist of 'contemporary dance'.

It is safe to generalize that in recent years, in cases when music/sound enters into improvisation with dance, there is a marked preference for 'sounds landscapes' and sonic environments. The abstract and formal nature of musical structures seems to be at odds with the actuality and physicality of the body in movement and the body's presence on stage. Work with 'music' exists primarily in the domain of 'choreographer'-led work, the work of Anna Teresa Keersmaker and Steve Reich, Davies and Gavin Bryars, and Mark Morris stand out. Therefore, it seems that music and dance in improvisation not only suffer from the bias of a perceived body/mind dichotomy; their collaboration has suffered from what David Gere defines as an ongoing divide between improvisation as a 'reflection and private discovery' and composition (hence choreography) with its demands for a rigour that goes against individual expressiveness and freedom (Albright and Gere 2003: xv). This position seems at odd with the definitions of improvisation in general, as previously discussed.

Consequently, dance improvisation has been approached primarily from a perspective that prioritizes a movement-based somatic state guided by proprioception. This

approach favours the focus on a 'world-inside' based on the 'improviser's aesthetic reactions to their own moving', a listening 'within skin' (De Spain 2003: 31). This perspective is supported by another factor: a recurrent reference to a prelinguistic state, one of
pure presence in the moment. Recent studies of presence in performance strongly argue
against this prelinguistic state as a precondition for such presence (a position normally
underscored by misreading or partial readings of phenomenology), as any act of 'presence is always encoded with cultural intertexts that complicate the experience of the
present' (Power 2008: 205).

Foster suggests a different approach to improvisation, one that chimes with Peters's
position previously discussed and opens up the path to a more complex engagement
with music, as proposed in *Moving Sound*. Foster suggests that improvisation requires
a state of 'bodymindfulness' that 'rather than suppress any function of the mind summons up a kind of hyperawareness [a word also used by Peters] of the relationship between immediate action and overall shape, between that which is about to take place
and that which has and will take place' (1994: 7). She goes on to suggest that it is a careful
'back and forth between the unknown and the known'—a known that includes 'any
overarching structural guidelines that delimit the improvising body's choices, such as
a score for performance, or any set of rules predetermined in advance.... The known
includes any allied medium with which the performance is in collaboration, such an improvisation among musicians and dancers' (4).

It is this 'possible allegiance', in Foster's terms, that *Moving Sound* explores in detail: how do we bring music structures and dance to work together again? Can musical
structures be aligned to 'bodily' structures so that they present themselves as part of the
bodymindfulness suggested by Foster? What will happen if the notion of 'form-making'
as it is understood in free jazz improvisation is brought to bear on movement and sound
improvisation?

The 'allied' relationship suggested by Foster and evolved in *Moving Sounds* begins with recent developments in the understanding of sound, motion, and 'the body'.
These underpin the methods of the project. In the essay *Cognition and the Body*, Wayne
Bowman discusses the ways in which 'sonorous experience is invariably corporeal, and
it is distinguished from other semiotic experience by its links to muscle, movement
and action' (2004: 17). Bowman argues that musical properties which many consider
as 'structural devices' are in fact bodily constituted: tension and release, dissonance and
consonance, volume, balance are all consonant with the reflective language of body-
based improvisation. Therefore, music material, rather than appearing as an alienating
force in improvisation, actually has the potential to return focus to the body 'actively
guiding, shaping, facilitating, enabling' (26) both dancers and musicians. Bowman notes
that the relationship between sound and body is reciprocal: structures move the body,
and equally there is a 'human capacity for cross modal transfer, a natural gift for mapping structures, patterns and gestures from our embodied experience and action onto
inviting sonorous material' (19). There is already a reciprocity that invites a common
ground to be established in order to achieve a *synthesis*, not parallelisms: a synthesis in
which motion and sound participate equally, as performing elements *of one common*

system. Within 'moving sound' we can compose movements of bodies and instruments practically on the same score, and thus enrich the ways we understand and achieve the interrelation between motion and sound, movement and dance.

FIGURES IN A LANDSCAPE

In our project the process of improvisation began by questioning (and then establishing) a *field* of common 'knowns' across dancers and musicians. What do musicians bring into the improvisation? What do dancers? We began by looking at what musicians bring into an emergent 'common system'. We selected basic music structures in order to start the collaboration in such a way that dancers would become familiar with the 'knowns' of a jazz ensemble, the musical structural elements of jazz improvisation, in order to evolve the common system. These were rhythm, pitch, volume, articulation, and phrasing. These musical 'knowns' were cross-mapped to fundamental 'knowns' in dance. The primary tool we chose was Labananalysis, in particular the four effort factors. It is well documented that Laban's studies in movement harmony were highly influenced by music harmony: 'between the harmonic components of music and those of dance, there is not only an outward resemblance, but a structural congruity, which although hidden at first, can be investigated and verified, point by point' (Laban cited in Moore 2009: 189). In a manner that echoes Haga's discussion of similarities, Carol Lynne Moore proposes that Laban seemed to have been employing 'an analogic metaphor ... [that] combines analogic modelling with the imaginative function of metaphoric thinking' (2009: 189). She clarifies further: 'an analogic metaphor is a controlled comparison in which the analogue model (in this case dance) shares with the original model (in this case music harmony) the same structure and pattern of relationships' (189).

The first element of structuring the audible in relation to the kinetic is *rhythm*, which Stephanie Jordan considers to be 'a principle of organization common to music and dance' (2005: 23). Arguably, in dance improvisation this organizing capacity of rhythm is more prevalent in forms such as flamenco, tap, Indian dance, and other vernacular forms, where the connection between the beat and gesture (step) is the fundamental motivation of the dance form. Speaking of flamenco, Heffner-Hayes comments: 'in Flamenco, the shape of the improvisational event is contained by the rhythmic structure and a dynamic of building complexity' (2003: 112). Heffner-Hayes points to the important fact that 'flamenco improvisation demands that the internal structure and the outer appearance of the event resemble established flamenco' (114). However, in contrast, in our work we aimed to cultivate the ability in the mover to hold onto an esoteric sense of duration, which contradicted the exoteric. In order to achieve this, we began exploring simple structures: a walking pattern done to the shifting of duration of movement from 2/4 beat to ¾ to 4/4, stepping only on the first quarter note of each time signature, proceeding to step in the second note of each time signature and so on in order to activate the ear and connect the exoteric audible stimulus to the esoteric (inner) sense of duration of movement. After exploring the consonant relationship between rhythm and movement, we explored counterpoint; for example: step on the first quarter note of a 4/4 beat when the audible beat is in 3/4. With these exercises, the dancers began to move independently, but also with a complete awareness of the whole: musical/rhythmical structures, counterpointing/dissonant moving bodies in space.

Pitch, the next foundational element of music, was defined in the vertical axis—high level for high pitch and low level for low pitch. Although there is ample discussion of the phenomenology of pitch and motion (e.g., Pratt 1930; Shove and Rep 1995), the discussion seems not to have transferred to dance and even less to dance improvisation. We began to address this by mapping pitch onto two complementary spatial axes. During the early improvisations, the vertical plane of the body was divided into three zones, each mirroring an octave: feet to hip joint, hip joint to shoulder, shoulder to the space reached by an extended arm (the edge of the vertical plane in the kinaesphere). In other instances, pitch was mapped onto a general space axis, where movements up and down the scale were not determined by a body axis but by relative positioning of body parts in the space grid. Towards the final stages of the work, dancers could shift from one axis to the next. The pitch figure was mapped onto the movement factor of *weight*, as there is correlation between the high and low tones (in relation to rising and falling tension) in pitch and the 'increasing and decreasing pressure' quality of weight (Moore 2009: 151).

Pitch is organized into intervals. The mathematical analogy of *intervals* in the eight-tone/twelve-tone scale, the musical scale that is organized on tones and semitones as we understand it in Western musical theory derives from the Pythagorean music theory, is interestingly connected to the analogy of the parts of the body,, akin to the mathematical concept that led to the creation of the Golden Measure in figurative arts. We therefore used the same analogy in order to establish the 'steps' or 'intervals' of the basic subdivisions of tones and semitones connecting each tone of the scale to a specific level of movement. We started with a simple task, mapping ascending and descending scales to movement from a lower to a higher level. We exercised on chromatic scales (semitones, smallest steps), major/minor scales, whole tone scales, cadences, and so on. Although it seemed simple at first, there was an inherent performance challenge, inasmuch as dancers had to learn to modulate their range of movement within a continuum, with clear indication of the subdivisions that span from the highest to the lowest tone of the scale. After establishing the connections of the basic subdivisions of the musical scale to the body (on the vertical axis), we practiced interval variation—triads, arpeggios, and patterns—commonly used in jazz improvisation.

In the explorations of pitch, an important difference had to be established: the metaphoric spatial rising and falling of pitch in music can become an actual rising and falling of the body in the vertical axis. However, if the movement is only manifested in an axis (two-dimensional), we quickly enter into music mimicry. We had to rethink the mapping of pitch onto a vertical *plane*, rather than an axis, as the lateral tension contained within a plane of movement allowed for more variety in the movement response.

In music, 'volume' refers to the fullness or intensity of a sound. It is defined within the piano/forte continuum: the energy it takes to produce a sound. We cross-mapped this to the movement factor of 'flow'. Although in music the term 'flow' is connected to phrasing, in movement terms 'flow' refers to the amount of energy that gives definition to a given movement. Normally it refers to the ability to stop or not the movement. However, flow can also be perceived as how energy is contained within muscle and tissue. For example, a bound movement is defined by the tension of energy within, a bound movement projects into space, that is higher sonic volume. In actions that are free, the energy is unbound within; it is a movement that does not project. Therefore, free flow was made analogous to *piano*.

Phrasing in music leads us to consider 'articulation', defined by the contrasting factors of staccato/legato (separated/connected), to which in movement terms the closest but not identical correspondence is the movement factor of time. The movement quality of 'sudden' is defined by Laban as 'movement sensation of a short span of time' (73) and was related to staccato. Furthermore, in staccato the sense is of instant occurrence, which goes some way to understand its possible connections to Laban's 'quick', a word which is also used in connection to 'sudden'. The quality of 'sustained', 'a movement sensation of a long span of time', was mapped to legato.

After we had familiarized ourselves with the basic elements, the explorations became more complex as we began to deal with the embodiment of these structures in combinations. For example: we used a simple musical phrase of ten notes containing alternating variables: the pitch phrase remained the same (repeated x times), but with each cycle of repetition, changes happened in articulation; for example, the three first notes staccato, the rest legato. In the next cycle of repetition, we added the factor of volume, ending up with combinations of staccato/forte followed by legato/piano and so forth until all combinations had been explored.

We chose not to work with either music or Laban notation, as in the context of this work they represent quite closed systems of notations. Rather in keeping with more recent trends in the use of scores for improvisation and composition, we worked from a graphic score in which the key musical structures of pitch, volume, articulation, and phrasing were depicted. This facilitated various aspects of the process of setting up the analogies: it was an effective shorthand way for dancers to encounter the elements of the audible; it helped to guide phrasing in both music and dance terms; and significantly to the moment of 'free improvisation', to safeguard both dancers and musicians autonomous creative and physical response to the 'figure':

> at first the score, how to read it, how to be creative was difficult, particularly the silences, where you realized it did not mean that you should stay still, but that in that moment your choices were totally open. It was interesting this negotiating of total freedom and very precise restrictions within the same improvisation. (Joshua Rosado, dancer)

Similarly:

> The score seemed to demand a lot of material, more variation. The limits were at first difficult, but interesting, in time, I was able to use my whole body. (Tania Muniz, dancer).

EXPLORATIONS FURTHER AFIELD

The project gave the opportunity to the musicians to open up their artistry and see its effect on a broader scale. It was not an easy task. In order to participate in this project, the musicians had to break the 'box' of the musical sheet and be able to go beyond perceiving the world aurally; to see different aspects of their very art by witnessing the transformation of music into another art form:

> I had not played with dancers before, this was very different, You find yourself in a very different relationship with the instrument and the dancers. (Edward Ortiz, Jr., flutist)

In the same manner that dancers were introduced to musical structures, musicians were introduced to movement factors. We explored various tasks, as follows.

In the first improvisation, we asked each musician to follow one dancer's whole body movements. The musician could choose which elements of the body in movement to respond to musically. The aim was to establish an improvisation motivated by a palindrome of stimuli. From the perspective of the dancer, music offered the aural, for the musicians the visual, both shaping their art separately and at the same time as one. It was clear that this task was too broad and could easily lead to what we were trying to avoid—superficial interpretation of movement in sound. The movement of the body was so dense that the musician did not know how to deconstruct and respond to it musically:

> it is funny for us, the words rhythms, pitch, groove have immediate practical meaning, we can perform them, we can 'notice' them when performing with other musicians, no problem, but ask me to 'understand' what the leg is doing, or an arm … that is hard. (Edward Ortiz, Jr., flutist)

At the same time, we recognized that the dancers did not address the task of offering something 'clear' to the improvisation, as they were very focused on their own sensations of movement.

Hence in the early attempts, we ended up in two parallel monologues. Clearer restrictions were needed. In the next set of improvisations, we assigned one instrument to one specific body part (i.e., flute follows right hand). The flute was following the hand, in a way not unlike following a conductor, looking for changes in direction, energy, and flow as stimuli for the musical response. In another instance, the bass followed the legs. For one musician:

> I compare it with bomba, we have rhythms we have melody ... and understand your intention, legs were easy, arms harder. (Richard Pena, bassist)

The musicians found it easy to work with what the legs could offer; however, if the dancer was proposing using the core area of the body, (torso, hips) this proved more challenging, as the subtleties of motion in that part of the body were not immediately accessible:

> the core is hard, not so easy to see, it will need lots of practice, the movement is very subtle, but the thing that comes out musically is very interesting. (Yannis Kassetas, saxophonist)

It was a slow and detailed improvisatory process—each dancer improvising to each instrument, so that the commonalities and differences across each could be identified, perceived, and worked on:

> in the group improvisation there is a challenge, you establish something with one dancer, you 'get it', and then another dancer comes in with a different proposal, you have to reestablish the connection. (Edward Ortiz, Jr., flutist)

The ability of the body to offer a multiplicity of projected movements is what makes the construction of the dialogue between dancer and musician so dynamically interesting.

> When I am moving my hand (for example) I am still aware that I am moving with the whole body, to support the hand. I think that I am sending the intention 'hand' to the musician, that he can pick up the signal, but I will still move the rest of the body to the side, then I have the doubt, of whether the musician can 'read' this. (Omar Nieves, dancer)

The musician of a monophonic instrument (i.e., flute, saxophone) has the ability to address one moving element at a time. The same movement in this way, in its complexity, can be interpreted by the musician in innumerable variations, which yet remain systematically identical (or coherent). This additionally offers the chance to two or more musicians to respond in dialogue between them (according/dis-cording) to the same kinetic stimulus offered by one dancer. Thus, the improvisation is generated by structured layers upon layers of propositions.

On the other hand an instrument that is polyphonic (like a piano) is able to address synchronically more elements of the kinetic stimulus. Thus the dialogue can be structured on what we call in music vertical harmony. Simultaneously, the dancer is responding each time to a different aspect of her very action and therefore reinterprets the dynamic implications of it.

Therefore, *Moving Sound*, in congruence with current understanding of improvisation, offers a process of openness that can only happen through the establishment of a coherent system, with commonly shared rules. In the particular case of *Moving Sound*, instead of creating two systems of separate discourse, we have created the conditions of constructing one, establishing the parameters of communication between dancer and musician in the 'present moment' of any improvisation. *Moving Sound* has pursued the creation of a more versatile instrument, in which not only the simultaneous exchange of the same notions are possible but also the creation of a new, more complex polyphony, within which sound and movement function as intrinsic elements. The recursive system of *Moving Sound* allows for the cocreating musician and dancer to construct improvisation in the sense of an instant composition, in which parts of what could be movements in dance, or notes in music, are roles that can be interexchanged, creating melodic lines or 'chords' of vertical harmony. By interweaving motion and sound, we can achieve a common polyphony (instead of two polyphonic systems monophonically arranged), only this time with even more voices, more nuances, more artistic perspectives, more possibilities—achieving ultimately a more complete and complex engagement of the senses; even reaching complete audiovisual substitution: hence, reconsidering the musically arranged dance in silence. Choreographing from the lens of musical structures although there is no actual sound heard, the sound is seen in the arrangement and quality of the movement.

REFERENCES

Albright, Ann Cooper and Gere, D. (eds.). (2003) *Taken by Surprise: A Dance Improvisation Reader*. Middletown, CT: Wesleyan University Press.

Bogo, D. (2002) Negotiating Freedom: Values and Practices in Contemporary Improvisational Music. *Black Music Research Journal* 22(2) (Autumn): 165–188.

Bowman, W. (2004) Cognition and the Body: Perspectives from Music Education. In Bresler, L. (ed.), *Knowing Bodies, Moving Minds: Toward Embodied Teaching and Learning*. Dordrecht, The Netherlands: Kluwer Academic Press, 29–50.

Cox, C., and Warner, D. (2004) *Audio Culture: Readings in Modern Music*. Continuum Books.

De Spain, K. (2003) The Cutting Edge of Awareness. In Albright, Ann Cooper, and Gere, D. (eds.), *Taken by Surprise: A Dance Improvisation Reader*. Middletown, CT: Wesleyan University Press, 27–38.

Foster, S. L. (1994) Taken by Surprise: Improvisation in Dance and Mind. In Albright, Ann Cooper, and Gere, D. (eds.), *Taken by Surprise: A Dance Improvisation Reader*. Middletown, CT: Wesleyan University Press, 3–10.

Goldman, D. (2010) *I Want to Be Ready: Improvised Dance as a Practice of Freedom*. Ann Arbor: University of Michigan Press.

Haga, E. (2008) *Correspondences between Music and Body Movement*. PhD. University of Oslo. https://www.duo.uio.no/bitstream/.../music-movement-Haga-final.pdf.

Heffner-Hayes, M. (2003) The Writing on the Wall: Reading Improvisation in Flamenco and Postmodern Dance. In Albright, Ann Cooper, and Gere, D. (eds.), *Taken by Surprise: A Dance Improvisation Reader*. Middletown, CT: Wesleyan University Press, 105–116.

Jordan, S. (2005) Musical/Choreographical Discourse: Method, Music Theory. In Morris, G. (ed.), *Meaning in Moving Words: Re-writing Dance*. London: Routledge, 14–24.

Levine, M. (1995) *Jazz Theory*. Petaluma, CA: Sher Music Co.

Montouri, A. (2003) The Complexity of Improvisation and the Improvisation of Complexity: Social Science, Art and Creativity. *Human Relations* 56(2): 237–255.

Moore, C. L. (2009) The Harmonic Structure of Movement, Music and Dance According to Rudolf Laban: An Examination of His Unpublished Writings and Drawings. *American Journal of Dance Therapy* 33(1): 78–81.

Peters, G. (2009) *The Philosophy of Improvisation*. Chicago: University of Chicago Press.

Power, C. (2008) *Presence in Play: A Critique of Theories of Presence in Theatre*. Amsterdam: Rodopi.

Pratt, C. (1930) The Spatial Characters of High and Low Tones. *Journal of Experimental Psychology* 13: 278–285.

Rinzler, P. E. (2008) *The Contradictions of Jazz*. Lanham, MD: Scarecrow Press.

Shove, P., and Rep, B. (1995) Musical Motion in Performance: Theoretical and Empirical Perspectives. In Rink, J. (ed.), *The Practice of Performance: Studies in Musical Interpretation*. Cambridge: Cambridge University Press, 55–83.

CHAPTER 42

AN AGILE MIND IN AN AGILE BODY

IVAR HAGENDOORN

INTRODUCTION

DANCERS and choreographers have developed numerous improvisation techniques to facilitate the real-time composition of movement sequences, from simple behavioural tasks, such as drawing imaginary figures with different parts of the body, to problem-solving tasks that require the dancer to translate a word or a phrase into movement, such as 'separate the wheat from the chaff', 'make angels out of devils', 'spicy', and 'water'. A key difference between these techniques and other approaches to dance improvisation is that these techniques involve the exercise of one's *cognitive* capacities. In contact improvisation, for example, the impetus for a movement is physical and may originate in the pull of another dancer or the removal of support. Another key difference is that the dancers typically need to know and be able to explain what they do. Ideally, different observers should be able to agree on whether a task has been accomplished, and different dancers should arrive at comparable results; otherwise, the connection between task and result would be lost. There should be a difference between 'water' and 'frozen'.

I am aware that following rules and employing techniques is anathema to many dance improvisation practitioners. Doesn't this take the spontaneity out of improvisation? Isn't improvisation about freedom? However, improvisation is not as free and spontaneous as it may seem. Habits, mannerisms, and behavioural dispositions may lead one to unconsciously make the same choices repeatedly and lapse into stereotypical movements. As the French author Raymond Queneau once wrote: 'the sort of inspiration that consists in blindly obeying every impulse is in reality a kind of slavery. The classic writer who composes his tragedy by observing a certain number of rules that he knows is freer than the poet who writes whatever comes into his head, and who is a slave to other rules that he doesn't see' (2007: 36).

The 'other rules' to which Queneau refers in this passage are the hidden laws and unconscious inclinations that guide our behaviour and the aesthetic preferences and cultural biases which have become embedded in our mind.

There is, however, no need to revert to the classical rules of composition to achieve the artistic freedom to which Queneau aspires. Any odd rule will do, as Queneau himself demonstrated in his *Exercises in Style* (1947), which is both a catalogue of literary genres and style figures and a display of the freedom one attains when one masters them all. In improvisation, too, familiarity with different styles and genres leads to increased freedom of mind. One reason Keith Jarrett is such a phenomenal performer is his intimate knowledge of various musical traditions, from the entire canon of Western classical music to jazz, blues, and pop.

I would like to argue that, in improvisation at least, freedom cannot only be achieved through knowledge and experience, but also through understanding. For if we could gain a better understanding of the workings of the mind and brain and make the implicit rules that guide our behaviour explicit, we could transcend our behavioural dispositions and attain a new degree of freedom: what was unconscious has now become a conscious choice.

In the following sections, I will show how some familiar dance improvisation techniques have their roots in properties of the motor system. I will also show how experimental findings from cognitive neuroscience and psychology may inspire improvisation techniques that may be new to some readers.[1] I will not dwell here on the question of what happens where in the brain, as this is of little direct relevance to the practice of dance improvisation.[2] I will also forgo an analysis of why dancers may get stuck when improvising.[3] The emphasis is on practical techniques that can be easily performed by dancers and nondancers alike.

From Theoretical Concepts to Experimental Techniques

Let's start with a simple experiment. Take a piece of paper and a pen, draw a square and a triangle, and sign it by writing your name underneath. Next, hold the pen in your nondominant hand and repeat the exercise. Now place a piece of paper on the floor, hold the pen between your toes, and do it again. You have just demonstrated a classic finding in neuroscience known as motor equivalence. From an anatomical point of view, there are a number of differences between the movements involved in writing with one's hand and one's foot and writing on a piece of paper and a blackboard. Drawing a small circle on a piece of paper requires fine control of the thumb and index finger, while drawing a giant circle on a blackboard requires control of the arm and shoulder. Despite these differences, the result looks more or less the same. This suggests that the central nervous system encodes movements in terms that are more abstract than instructions to specific muscles. It also suggests that circles, squares, letters, and more complex shapes, such as Chinese characters and one's signature, are encoded as abstract memory structures, which are translated into an action sequence once the limb or end effector, to use a technical term, is selected.

Motor equivalence forms the basis for a well-known improvisation technique whereby the goal is to draw imaginary figures with different parts of the body. This technique goes by various names and has been reinvented by many dance practitioners. For example, in *Improvisation Technologies* (1999) William Forsythe refers to it as 'writing'. As Forsythe emphasizes, when practising this technique you should take care not to stop at using the hand, finger, foot, and elbow but also experiment with the shoulder, head, hip, and so on. This technique can easily be extended to circumscribing two- and three-dimensional shapes and figures. For example, you can outline the shape of a ball or a vase with your hands and arms. In my own work, I use architectural drawings and data visualizations, which the dancers then translate into movement. I should add that the goal is not for the audience to be able to guess the figure the dancers are drawing: the goal is to generate movements. You can stop at any moment and continue with doing something else.

Let's do another experiment. This time it involves reaching for an object, say a glass of water. Depending on the distance between the glass and your body, you can do so by extending only the arm or by bending forward and rotating around the waist. By carefully examining video recordings of just this task, researchers found that when one reaches for an object, the fingers already begin to shape as the arm extends towards the object's location (Jeannerod 1981). It was also found that the preshaping of the fingers depends on the shape of the object one is reaching for. This may sound obvious, but it isn't. After all, you could also first extend the arm and then open the hand, or the other way around, the way one might program a robot to grasp something. Now suppose that it is a glass that has a stem and is upside down on the table. When grasping the glass in order to fill it, most people will turn the hand during reaching; otherwise, the hand would end up in an awkward position upon turning the glass upside down. This shows that one's grasp is shaped not only by the object but also by what one intends to do with it (Rosenbaum et al. 2012).

As I'm sure many readers will have recognized, these experimental findings are easily put to creative use: find as many ways of reaching for an object by varying the form and dynamics of the movement, the starting position, the distance to the object, its location, and so on. As a matter of fact, this could be the basis for a dance performance, *Glass on the Table* (2017). All we need to do is select the costumes, determine the lighting, add a soundtrack, and we are done.[4]

Suppose that you want to drink from the glass in the previous experiment. You could, of course, just grasp it and bring it to your mouth. However, if the glass is too full it would be wise to bend forward and sip from it in order to prevent spilling its contents, as indeed many people do. In the first instance, the head stays in the same position and the glass is transported towards the head; in the second instance the glass stays in the same position and the head is transported towards the glass. This observation provided the inspiration for an improvisation technique, which I have termed 'fixed point technique' in a playful homage to the Dutch mathematician L. E. J. Brouwer (1881–1966), who is best known for his fixed point theorem, a basic result in the mathematical field of topology (Hagendoorn 2003). The technique draws on the observation that the position of an object (and a part of the body) can be defined both in an *intrinsic* frame of reference, which is relative to the body—to one's left, at hip level—and in an *extrinsic* frame of reference, which is relative to other objects, on the desk, next to the dictionary, or as coordinates in an abstract space.

With this distinction in mind, the first thing to observe is that one can establish an intrinsic relationship between two or more parts of the body and maintain that relationship while moving through extrinsic space. For example, one can stretch an arm and lie down while keeping the arm stretched, that is, while maintaining the intrinsic relationship between arm and chest. Obviously, there are always some intrinsic relationships between different body parts that remain constant as one moves. For example, when walking, the arms remain in more or less the same position next to the torso. But remember that we are trying to raise these unconscious patterns to a conscious level in order to make them a conscious choice. Once you are aware of the position of your arms while you are walking, you can decide to change the way you hold your arms.

The next thing to observe is that there are essentially two ways by which one can reestablish an intrinsic relation between two body parts. For example, extending one's hand from one's chest to a point in extrinsic space changes the intrinsic relation between one's arm and the rest of one's body. To reestablish the starting position (between the hand and the chest) one could either reverse the movement by bringing the hand back to the chest *or* move the chest towards the hand. If one were standing, one would do so by stepping forward. In the first case, the chest is fixed in extrinsic space; in the second, the hand. I probably make it sound more complicated than it is, but once you get the idea you will notice that this way of varying the parts of the body that are held fixed in intrinsic and extrinsic space gives rise to a great multiplicity of movements. Breakdancers will instantly recognize this technique as one of the fundamental components of popping. To give another, practical, example, you can scratch your left arm by moving the fingers of your right hand across your left arm, holding the left arm fixed in extrinsic space, and by keeping your right hand fixed in extrinsic space and running your left arm underneath.

Let's return to the glass on the table one more time. Suppose that you are standing in front of the table and are about to reach for the glass. As you extend your arm, the muscles in your legs and feet contract to maintain the body's centre of mass within its base of support. If you stand further away from the table, you may have to bend forward and stretch your arm to reach the glass. This in turn may force you to extend your other arm backwards and possibly even a leg so as to keep yourself from tipping over.

Let's call the arm that is extended towards the glass the primary, acting, or leading limb or movement, and let's call the movements of the leg and arm that are engaged to maintain balance the residual movement. The primary purpose of this distinction is to draw attention to the parts of the body that are not directly engaged in an action.

Instead of just leaving your left arm dangling as you extend your right arm, you can hold it behind your back, and when the hands are not engaged, you can ball your hand into a fist or shape your fingers in the form of a *hasta*, one of the single hand gestures from Bharatanatyam. This distinction can also be turned into a technique for generating movements, for example by changing the leading movement, left arm, right leg, left shoulder, and so on or by alternating the leading movement. Possibly the best real-world example of this technique is the triple jump in athletics, which consists of a hop, a step, and a jump (in that order), whereby the athlete lands first on the same foot as that from which she has taken off and then makes a step landing on the other foot before making the final jump.

As the foregoing examples show, one can analyse the fundamental properties of the motor system so as to develop an improvisation technique. I used drawing imaginary figures as an example of a technique based on motor equivalence, but with this principle in mind one could also design a different technique.

The key to developing an improvisation technique is to find some discernible regularity and to formulate the concept or the rule that best describes it. The advantage of knowing a rule is that you don't have to memorize the individual cases: once you understand the rule for adding and subtracting fractions, you can add any fractions (without having to grab a calculator). Similarly, once you grasp the idea behind what I termed fixed point technique, you can apply it at all times, and once you are aware of which limbs are acting and which are residual, you can decide to change the leading movement (or not).

To give one more example, a technique I find very useful draws on a distinction between global and local movements. Local movements are movements that span a small region in space, such as flexing a finger or rolling a shoulder. They are what in Cunningham technique are referred to as 'isolations'. Global movements span a large region in space and typically involve stretched arms and legs. However, what counts as global or local is in part determined by the previous and subsequent movements. Keep this at the back of your mind when you are improvising, so that you can alternate between global and local movements or consciously decide to keep your movements local for an extended period of time.

Motor Schemas

A central concept in the cognitive neuroscience of action is that of motor primitives (Wolpert et al. 2011) or motor schemas (Arbib et al. 1998).[5] A motor schema is an abstract representation of a movement such as a tennis stroke or an arabesque and only represents the structure of a movement. A forehand, a backhand, and a serve look quite different, but they are all variations on a tennis stroke. An arabesque remains an arabesque whether it is performed slowly or quickly, clumsily or gracefully. Motor schemas can be thought of as neural control modules that can be modulated and combined to generate an extensive repertoire of movements. They are recursive, in that they can be combined with other schemas to form a new, higher-order schema or, alternatively, can be taken apart into smaller schemas. Together the collection of all motor schemas constitutes one's motor vocabulary. Ballet, breakdance, and Bharatanatyam can thus be thought of as particular sets of motor schemas. The module that gets uploaded to Neo's brain in *The Matrix* (1999) presumably consists of the schemas for a collection of martial arts moves. If only the mind would work that way. It would save considerable rehearsal time!

Many everyday actions involve a tool or an object. Since the schemas for each of these movements are part of one's motor vocabulary, one can easily mimic any of these movements in the absence of the actual object. You could imagine picking up a large ball, carrying it over to another location, squeezing it, dropping it, and kicking it away. As a way of generating novel motor schemas, during rehearsals you can use an actual object and explore different ways of engaging with it. You can then take out the object and keep the movement, although you may have to repeat it several times before the temporary schema assemblage is fixed into a schema of its own. You will find that even an object as simple as a broomstick can give rise to a wide range of movements.

While the concept of a motor schema is thought to underpin motor behaviour in general, it can be used as a framework for generating movements. One could start with a collection of simple movements and explore the different ways in which they can be combined into a larger assemblage. As a matter of fact, starting from a collection of movements or poses, one could simply concatenate the movements and poses to create a performance. In the late eighteenth century, Emma Hamilton (1765–1815) made a name for herself with her 'Attitudes', a series of mimes and poses representing figures from antiquity, classical literature, and history. Her repertoire consisted of around two hundred poses and included such characters as Medea slaying her child and reinterpretations of scenes depicted on the antique Greek vases from the collection of her husband, Sir William Hamilton. As she moved from one pose to another, audiences would try and guess the names of the characters and scenes she portrayed. Her act became a big success and drew audiences from across Europe to her home in Naples.

Instead of starting with a collection of simple movements, one could also start with a choreographed, composite movement sequence, take it apart into its constitutive elements, and recombine them into a new configuration. One need not stop here, for instead of merely concatenating a series of movements, one could create variations on each building block or movement segment. One could reverse left and right or transpose a movement from the leg to the arm or vice versa, so that extending an arm becomes extending a leg. If the original movement is small (think writing on a piece of paper) one could enlarge it (think writing on a wall) and vice versa. A transformation can be applied to the primary movement and the next operation to the resulting residual movement, turning what was residual in the previous movement into the primary or leading movement.

In principle, any dance style or genre can be recreated by varying the vocabulary and the rules and restrictions that describe how the individual motor schemas can be recombined. This method for engendering movement lends itself particularly well to minimal dance, with its shifts and variations on a basic movement repertoire. In my own work I use a combination of choreographed phrases, which change for each performance, and an ever-growing collection of everyday movements. At any moment during a performance a dancer can isolate a particular sequence of movements and use that as a composite motor schema to be taken apart and recombined. As dancers become more familiar with this concept, they will also notice that applying transformation X to movement A results in the same movement as applying transformation Y and Z to movement B.

For *Self Meant to Govern* (1994) and *Eidos: Telos* (1995), of which *Self Meant to Govern* is the first section, William Forsythe, in collaboration with the dancers, created a collection of about 130 movements. Each movement was given a name, such as 'brick', 'pizza', 'bottle', 'oyster', or 'rabbit'. During the performance, the dancers could perform the movement connected with the word 'pizza' and subsequently perform 'atlas', which begins with the last letter of the previous word, or they could perform 'honey', because it is also food. The dancers could also notice that, while performing one movement, say 'oyster', the elbow and knee might be in the same configuration as in another movement, and then continue with this movement. In this case the overlapping body positions create an anatomical bridge between two movements. In addition, the dancers could transform a movement using any of the dance improvisation techniques Forsythe had developed over the years (Forsythe 1999). During the actual performance, clocks, with letters instead of digits, were dispersed across the stage and served as word/movement cues; in addition, invisible to the audience, banners with the names of the various improvisation techniques were displayed on both sides of the stage.

Metaphors and Analogies

When working on a new production, Pina Bausch famously handed the dancers a list of keywords, questions, themes, and instructions, which the dancers then interpreted in the form of movements. But how do you dance a wing, bay leaves, the moon, dead feet, expectations, or like a king? How do you console an object or resist temptation, in dance, that is? And what does it mean to pull your bones in or to alternately dance like you push the earth and like the earth pushes you, to cite some instructions from a class in Gaga, the dance improvisation technique developed by Ohad Naharin?

When asked to dance like a king, one would first imagine what it is like to be a king, what a king does, and how one might recognize a king. One might imagine the demeanour of a king to be grand and stately if not pompous, so one might move accordingly. To dance water, one might examine the properties of water, for instance that it flows, and create flowing movements. In each of these examples, an analogy is sought that could be rendered in movement. Of course, water is wet, but that doesn't readily translate into movement.

According to the cognitive scientists Fauconnier and Turner (2002) the ability to create analogies relies on a core human cognitive capacity which they refer to as 'conceptual integration' or 'blending'. Conceptual integration is a mental process that combines the elements from two different mental spaces into a new configuration or blend. Mental spaces can be thought of as some kind of temporary thought assemblies that are constructed as one thinks and speaks. For example, when you think of a circus, a mental space is activated which includes clowns, acrobats, a marquee, and whatever your personal memories of a circus encompass.

Conceptual integration is best understood when the process is visualized. In figure 42.1, mental spaces are represented as circles, their respective elements as points, and the connections between elements in different spaces as lines. A partial cross-space mapping connects the elements in the two input spaces, represented by the solid lines. The elements that both input spaces have in common are contained in the generic space. The blended space, or blend for short, contains a projection of *selected* elements from the two input spaces and may also contain some elements not found in either of the input spaces, represented by the small circles. The blended space has a structure of its own and is not contained in any of the input spaces, as is represented by the solid square in the diagram.

When two mental spaces are combined or integrated, the resulting blend can take over the structure of the input spaces or acquire a structure of its own. For example, Picasso's cubist portraits combine features from a profile and a full-face perspective, but the organizing frame is that of a face. In its most complex form, which Fauconnier and Turner (2002) call double-scope blending, the two input spaces have different and possibly clashing organizing frames. The blended frame is a projection of elements of both

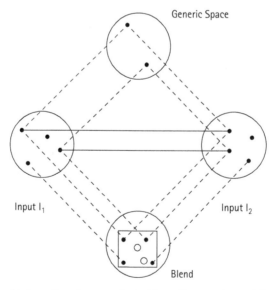

FIG. 42.1 Conceptual integration. *Source*: adapted from Fauconnier and Turner (2002: 46).

input frames but also has a structure of its own. The trashcan on your desktop is an example of such a double-scope blend. It combines elements from the frame of everyday life (throwing trash away) and from the frame of computer commands (delete).

One of the most famous classical ballets, *Swan Lake*, offers an excellent example of conceptual integration in the form of Odette. Odette's movements do not aim to imitate those of a swan but try to capture a swan's grace and essence transposed onto a human body, thus creating a blended figure with a structure of its own. Gregory Bateson perfectly captures Odette's dual nature in his 'Metalogue: Why a Swan?' As the father explains to the daughter: 'I get confused when I speak of the "swan" and the dancer as two different things. I would rather say that the thing I see on the stage—the swan figure—is both "sort of" human and "sort of" swan' (2000: 33).

Conceptual integration is governed by several principles that describe the various conceptual relations that can obtain between different mental spaces, such as change, identity, time, space, cause-effect, part-whole, role, property, category, and intentionality. For example, when one says of a sweater that it is warm, the fact that it keeps one warm is translated into a property of the object. Obviously, the sweater is not warm the way a cup of tea or a fire is, unless, of course, it has just been removed from a tumble dryer.

It is an open question whether the mind operates according to the principles identified by Fauconnier and Turner (2002), but it is a useful paradigm for analysing what dancers do when they translate a metaphor into dance. When consoling an object or separating the wheat from the chaff, the dancers of Pina Bausch Tanztheater Wuppertal unconsciously looked for the conceptual relations that might obtain between the instruction and their postures and movements. *Oblique Strategies,* developed by Brian Eno and Peter Schmidt, which I sometimes use in my own work, relies on the same principle. Originally designed in 1975 as a deck of cards, *Oblique Strategies* consists of a set of cards/phrases which offer cues for generating new ideas. How would your best friend do it? What went wrong the last time? Give way to your worst impulse. Decorate. Don't be afraid of clichés. Make it big/small. Lighten up.

Pina Bausch used her lists of questions and keywords only during rehearsals for a new production, but one can imagine employing the same concept in a live session. One could, for example, place monitors on stage displaying a random slide show of phrases, pictures, and film sequences, to serve as cues for the dancers. Some improvisation purists might consider this cheating, but the dance would still be improvised, and besides, who cares if it makes for an interesting performance?

SPATIAL AND TEMPORAL ORGANIZATION

Dance improvisation and dance in general do not consist in twisting the body in every conceivable way. One of the things I noticed when I first attended a dance improvisation session was that the dancers tended to stay in the same place and kept on moving at more or less the same pace. There is nothing wrong with this if it is a conscious choice, but to make it a conscious choice one needs to be aware of the existence of alternatives. In much the same way as one can formulate rules and techniques for generating movements, one can design rules for their spatial and temporal organization.

In general, patterns emerge from the arrangement of repeated or corresponding parts, so to create a spatiotemporal pattern, all one has to do is repeat a movement. Repeating the same movement creates a temporal pattern; repeating the same movement at a different location creates a spatiotemporal pattern. Repetitions need not be identical; mirroring a previous movement also creates a pattern; they don't need to be evenly spaced either; what matters is that there is a discernable regularity within the stream of movements.

A simple rule for breaking a constant stream of movement is to freeze and remain within the same position for X seconds. If you are performing for an audience, this will also give the viewers a moment of respite to catch up with the ongoing stream of sensory stimuli. I know that this isn't exactly rocket science and that these ideas will be familiar to anyone with a passing knowledge of dance improvisation, but having these four concepts—freeze, repeat, slow down, accelerate—at the top of your mind when you are improvising will make it easier to vary not only the form but also the dynamics of your movements.

In a choreography, the dancers follow the directions of the choreographer. In the absence of a choreographer who designs the spatial organization, the dancers will have to determine their own itineraries. Without a destination, deciding on a trajectory can be a challenge. A concept from mathematics that is also employed in psychogeography as a strategy for exploring a city can be of use in this respect.[6]

Imagine randomly selecting one of four cards after every step: clubs you step forward, diamonds you step backward, hearts you turn left, and spades you turn right. These instructions result in what in mathematics is referred to as a *random walk*, a path that consists of a succession of random steps. It is used, among other things, to model the movements of bacteria, foraging animals, and stock prices. As a computer simulation might show, if you were to strictly adhere to the above rule, you might end up moving around in the same area. It is, however, fairly straightforward to extend this concept to more choices. Imagine throwing a die and moving one step forward at one, one step backward at two, five steps forward at three, and so on. In practice you can just move around and remember to turn into a different direction every now and then, to vary the number of steps and to alternate moving forward, backwards, and sideways. There is no need to confine your movements to a lattice either, and should you bump into a wall or leave the stage, you can turn around and continue in any direction.

Another strategy for organizing movements in space is to divide the stage into different sections: two halves, a grid, and so on. This concept, too, will be familiar to most readers, and I only mention it for the sake of completeness. One section of *Communications from the Lab* (2004), a production I created for the Ballett Frankfurt, consisted of multiple lanes and the rule that no two dancers could occupy the same lane. Since there were more dancers than lanes, this simple rule forced the dancers to jump lanes. Another section was set on a grid. The dancers had to imagine they were moving through narrow corridors, and their movements were constrained accordingly. I had listed the events that could happen when two or more dancers would meet, and together with the dancers, I worked out some schematic solutions. Thus, if two dancers met in the same lane or corridor, they could either block each other's way or figure out a way to get past each other while maintaining the idea of the narrow corridor. If two, three, or four dancers met at a crossing of two lanes, they could get past each other using a combination of choreographed movements, which formed the basis for an impromptu duet, trio, or quartet.

CONCLUSION: LEARNING TO IMPROVISE

Anyone can improvise. There is nothing to it. Just do whatever comes to your mind. But sometimes the mind goes blank. Overwhelmed by the infinite number of possibilities, the mind may even shut down altogether. With practice, one can improve one's improvisation skills. Keith Jarrett did not become a virtuoso overnight either. But which type of practice is going to make you a better improviser? And how do you know whether you are making progress?

Motor learning in general can be defined as a process which leads to long-term changes in the capacity to perform certain motor tasks as a result of training and exercise. When learning to play baseball, one's sensorimotor control improves to the point where one can hit the ball deliberately and repeatedly and not just by chance. When learning an existing choreography, the dancers rehearse the movements until they closely resemble the choreographed movements. But what does learning mean in the context of dance improvisation? And how does one assess whether a dancer fully grasps and masters the present or any other improvisation techniques?

Psychologists commonly measure creativity by asking participants to list as many interesting and unusual uses of, for example, empty cardboard boxes or tin cans within a given timespan. Participants are then evaluated by fluency (number of responses), flexibility (variety of responses), and originality (unusual responses). In much the same way, one could rehearse the aforementioned improvisation technique and evaluate the progress one is making. One could list the number of different instances of a particular technique a dancer can generate or measure the number and variety of different phrases a dancer can construct from a few motor schemas.

The goal in dance improvisation is not to produce a random sequence of movements, although it might make for an interesting performance. Dance improvisation, like choreography, involves structure as much as variation. The difference between an improvised and a choreographed performance is that in the latter the movements are designed in advance, whereas in the former they are designed in real time. This difference is becoming increasingly blurred, as choreographers such as William Forsythe, Ohad Naharin, and Emanuel Gat incorporate different forms of improvisation in their work, and dance improvisation practitioners employ games as a structuring principle.

The dance improvisation techniques considered in this chapter serve the dual purpose of creating variation in structure and structure in variation. They can be applied in dance but also in skating, snow boarding, synchronized swimming, and so on. They can be used to generate movements, which can subsequently be laid down in a choreographed sequence. They can be a means to an end and used to realize the artistic vision of a particular individual, and they can be used to break out of established patterns and challenge one's implicit aesthetic preferences. They are conceptual tools as well as physical exercises. As such, they are a way to enhance one's physical and mental agility. For dance improvisation requires not only an agile body but, first and foremost, an agile mind.

EPILOGUE: BEYOND THE HUMAN BODY

The past few years have seen a dramatic increase in computer capacity. At the turn of the century, self-driving cars were the stuff of science fiction; now they are driving the streets of Silicon Valley. Humanoid robots, too, are becoming increasingly sophisticated, and one can only imagine what they will be capable of twenty years from now. Although myriad technological challenges would still need to be surmounted, in principle most of the ideas described in this chapter could be implemented in robotics or using a three-dimensional avatar. But what does this mean for how we look at dance improvisation? Most people would consider improvisation a creative act. But if a robot were to improvise, would that mean the robot is creative? And if one doesn't consider the robot itself creative, but for example its developers, why would one consider a human dancer creative? Only because he or she is human? It won't be long before these questions become pertinent. One thing is certain, though: the advent of improvising robots and avatars will alter the choreographic landscape and enrich our aesthetic experience.

NOTES

1. Disclaimer: this is a systematic, not a historical, overview. I first outlined some of the techniques described here in Hagendoorn (2003), but I do not claim to have invented any of them. Evidently, the work of William Forsythe has been an invaluable source of inspiration for my research. I had the great fortune of being able to witness rehearsals and join in the discussions at the time when *Eidos: Telos* (1995) was created and *Improvisation Technologies* (Forsythe 1999) was produced.
2. A number of neuroimaging studies have investigated the neural correlates of improvisation in music (e.g., Bengtsson et al. 2007; Limb and Braun 2008). Depending on the experimental paradigm, these studies report increased activity in some brain regions and decreased activity in other regions. While these findings may be of interest to neuroscientists, for example because they shed light on the similarities in neural processing between music and language production, it is unclear how musicians might benefit from this knowledge.

3. The reason dancers (and musicians) get stuck when improvising is not much different from creative block in general. The difference is that a writer, composer, or choreographer can spend hours contemplating the next phrase. When improvising, one does not have this luxury: one has to decide in real time what one is going to do next. And whereas a writer or a composer can review what he or she has done and even gain a helicopter view of the entire project, when improvising one has to rely on one's memory, which is both limited and faulty.

4. And find funding, of course.

5. The term 'motor primitive' suggests that it is the most basic unit of movement, which is why I prefer the term 'motor schema'.

6. Throughout this chapter I have silently assumed that we are moving in an empty studio or on an empty stage. In parkour, which can also be considered a form of dance improvisation, the entire city becomes a stage.

REFERENCES

Arbib, M. A., Érdi, P., and Szentágothai, J. (1998) *Neural Organization: Structure, Function, and Dynamics*. Cambridge, MA: MIT Press.

Bateson, G. (2000) Metalogue: Why a Swan? In G. Bateson, *Steps to an Ecology of Mind: Collected Essays in Anthropology, Psychiatry, Evolution, and Epistemology*. Chicago: University of Chicago Press, 33–37.

Bengtsson, S. L., Csíkszentmihályi, M., and Ullén, F. (2007) Cortical Regions Involved in the Generation of Musical Structures during Improvisation in Pianists. *Journal of Cognitive Neuroscience* 19: 1–13.

Fauconnier, G., and Turner, M. (2002) *The Way We Think: Conceptual Blending and the Mind's Hidden Complexities*. New York: Basic Books.

Forsythe, W. (1999) *Improvisation Technologies: A Tool for the Analytical Dance Eye*. Karlsruhe, Germany: Center for Art and Mediatechnology.

Gazzaniga, M., Ivry, R. B., and Mangun, G. R. (2013) *Cognitive Neuroscience: The Biology of the Mind*. New York: Norton.

Hagendoorn, I. G. (2003) Cognitive Dance Improvisation: How Study of the Motor System Can Inspire Dance (and Vice Versa). *Leonardo* 36(3): 221–227.

Hagendoorn, I. G. (2011) *Dance, Aesthetics and the Brain*. Tilburg, The Netherlands: Tilburg University.

Jeannerod, M. (1981) Intersegmental Coordination during Reaching at Natural Visual Objects. In Long, J., and Baddeley, A. (eds.), *Attention and Performance* IX. Hillsdale, NJ: Erlbaum, 153–168.

Kandel, E. R., Schwartz, J. H., Jessell, Th. M., Siegelbaum, S. A., and Hudspeth, A. J. (2012) *Principles of Neuroscience*. New York: McGraw-Hill.

Limb, C. J., and Braun, A. R. (2008) Neural Substrates of Spontaneous Musical Performance: An fMRI Study of Jazz Improvisation. *PLoS One* 3: e1679.

Queneau, R. (2007) What Is Art? In *Letters, Numbers, Forms. Essays, 1928–70*. Trans. Jordan Stump. Champaign: University of Illinois Press, 33–37.

Rosenbaum, D. A., Chapman, K. M., Weigelt, M., Weiss, D. J., and Van der Wel, R. (2012) Cognition, Action, and Object Manipulation. *Psychological Bulletin* 138: 924–946.

Wolpert, D. M., Diedrichsen, J., and Flanagan, J. R. (2011) Principles of Sensorimotor Learning. *Nature Reviews Neuroscience* 12: 739–751.

CHAPTER 43

....

EMBODIOLOGY

A Hybrid Neo-African Improvisation-as-Performance
Practice Distinguished by Dynamic Rhythm

....

S. AMA WRAY

INTRODUCTION

....

DYNAMIC Rhythm is at the core of Embodiology®, my theoretical and practical concep-
tualization of how improvisation, as a form of performance, is realized in West African
performance practices. Embodiology® was developed through practice in the field.
Consequently, my praxis translates this knowledge into strategies and techniques that
contemporary dance and music artists can apply to generate improvised performance.[i]
The neologism particularizes an understanding of West African practices of improvisation by focusing on interrelated sensory and cognitive processes.

Improvisation is a critical dimension of performing Africa's dances, serving as a vehicle for creativity, edification, civic engagement, social interaction, spiritual communion, and aesthetic innovation, among other advances. It is a collaborative communal
practice that yields knowledge production and circulation. Performance studies theorist Margaret Drewal explains that from a Yorùbá perspective, 'improvisation requires
a mastery of logic of action and in-body codes . . . together with the skill to intervene and
transform them' (1991: 43).

From this perspective, improvisation-as-performance is dependent on expertise
that builds on recognized information. Embodiology enables these values to come to
the fore and conceptualizes aesthetic processes that are evident across a broad range
of performance environments. These processes are deeply intertwined with music
and are adaptively applied in order to generate contemporary performance practices.
Concomitantly, Embodiology's model of improvisation-as-performance can also be
used as an analytical schematic to identify generative strategies deployed within African
diasporan or 'Neo-African' performance practices at large (Euba 2003). The latter aspect

of Embodiology, however, is not the subject of this essay; rather, the focus is on Dynamic Rhythm, henceforth the metagenerator of improvisation-as-performance, which leads the first of its six generative principles.

MODEL OF EMBODIOLOGY

First, I will briefly outline Embodiology as a whole, which consists of six components that interweave aesthesis, evident in Ewe and Yorùbá cultures. Similarly, they also reflect African diasporan values that distinguish my own dance history.[ii] Embodiology praxis furnishes individuals and groups of performers with the ability to generate and sustain high-level performance. Its six generative components create an autopoietic system, capable of maintaining and recreating itself. At the helm is Dynamic Rhythm, Embodiology's metastructuring component, which impacts all outcomes through its consciously sustained invocation. Then, I elaborate on how my fieldwork in Ghana propels Dynamic Rhythm to the core of my studio practice through my work with a group of dancers and musicians brought together as the Embodiology Research Group (Gwen Jones, Bless Klepcharek, Ingrid Mackinnon, Corey Mwamba, Martin Pyne, Johanna Sarinnen, Lauren Segal, Chiara Vinci, and Noelle White).

SIX-COMPONENT MODEL OF IMPROVISATION

Figure 43.1 represents the relationships between Embodiology's six components: Dynamic Rhythm, Fractal Code, and Inner Sensing and Balance, Collaborative Competition, Play and Decision Making, and Audience Proxemics. The first three are primary (found in all contexts) and the latter three secondary (found in all contexts, but with greater variance), collectively these make up the tenets of Embodiology.

Component 1: Dynamic Rhythm

Dynamic Rhythm represents temporal dimensions of improvisation-as-performance, which most often are represented as music-based interactions. It is evident that during various types of performance that participants—Ewe, Fanti, Yorùbá, for example—perspicaciously listen, identify, and honour the value of the layered tonally-based patterns highlighted in their musical repertoires. To be musically responsive, the entire body must be engaged in qualitative listening so as to understand how time is musically configured. This is not in the mechanical sense but as a grounded development of kinaesthetic alliteration where absorption of sound takes place.

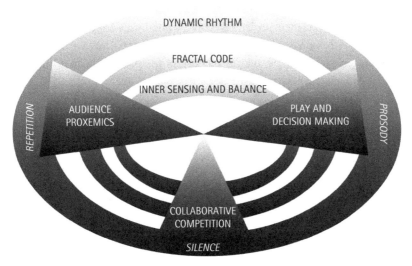

FIG. 43.1. Model of Embodiology.

Dynamic Rhythm contains three subfeatures: repetition, prosody, and silence. These (noun-like concepts/components/ideas) are important to define because general conceptions of rhythm in dance are insufficient and do not account for particular gradations. I will explain these subfeatures in greater detail after I present the overview of the model, scoping these features through illustrations of them as encountered in my fieldwork. To complete the transference of knowledge from theory and fieldwork to contemporary dance practice, I will also show examples of Dynamic Rhythm's subfeatures reconfigured as tasks, animated by the dancers and musicians who make up the Embodiology Research Group, demonstrating these features' generative capacity to produce improvisation-as-performance. Developing the responsive skill to detect how communication is carried through tone, cadence, duration, and pitch is tantamount to informing a sensory-knowing performer, one who can equitably inform those playing the music how it might develop its tonal qualities and inspire further participation. While being able to identify and generate patterns spontaneously, the tacit and sensory values of silence must accurately be felt.

Component 2: Fractal Code

Each site of performance has a history, customs, custodians, protocols for participation, potential new enthusiasts, reservoir of lived memories, and repertory of previous events that make up its Fractal Code. This term conceptualizes repetitious formations (Eglash 1999), based on particular constraints manifested at varying scales, both temporally and geographically. A performance form can geographically migrate with a people. While some aspects of that form remain consistent, certain characteristics are altered to accord with local social and economic currents. Novelty emerges out of the event's Fractal Code, its existing knowledge projected anew, whereupon continuity is evident. This temporal concept, though aurally and kinaesthetically based, has similarities to the way a scholarly exegesis takes shape, taking account of the past while creating opportunity for new perspectives to emerge.

Component 3: Inner Sensing and Balance

Performers' interior sensory and cognitive landscapes produce impulses that inspire interventions whereby participants' actions create emotional connections with others, be they 'informed audience' members or others who are dynamically shaping the unfolding action (Dortey 2012: 57). For example, the intentional use of eye contact leads to definite recognition of another participant, a haptic intensification of in-the-moment awareness for both the viewer and that connection's initiator. Other modes of sensory awareness invoked within this concept include the imagination, kinaesthesia, synaesthesia, and intuition, which can coalesce to produce exaggerated impulses that heighten the emotional surges as a performance unfolds. The performers' 'intersensory' (Sacks 2003: 233) worlds, as this extends outward, invokes the presence of joy as an aesthetic value, an enduring concern.

Component 4: Play and Decision Making

With the intensity of new information that is present in a performance, where improvisation shapes the proceedings, performers make conscious in-the-moment decisions. Such actions demonstrate the role that executive function (Diamond: 2011) plays in harnessing responsivity and flexibility. Revealing new ideas out of familiar material is invoked by a commitment to discover novelty through intensive investigative play, leading to dramatic redrafting of repertoire, which in turn can reinspire the undercurrents of the performance. Executive brain function integrates the use of deductive reasoning; short- and long-term memory make it possible to deploy an extensive range of interventions that may also include irony, as well as nonaction. Courage is displayed through daring to make provocative choices, demanding that others use their reflexes to respond. For the audience such surges of surprise produce affect, which in turn create durable memories that go well beyond that of the performance duration.

Component 5: Collaborative Competition

Seemingly an oxymoron, this clause is used to represent a type of competition similarly found among members of the same sporting team. In such cases, an individual's efforts towards excellence propel others within their group to achieve greater levels of acumen and skill. In this way, individuals collectively energize and sustain performance through overtly challenging each other, themselves, or even the audience in a series of brinkmanship activities where parody, copying, and outmanoeuvring are common tactics, enabling levels of unforeseeable virtuosity to be on display. In broader West African and African diasporan contexts, we can see that improvisation engenders competition among expert dancers (Jackson 2001; Daniel 1995). Competition is not only to show movement mastery but also to critically demonstrate innovation through rhythmic perspicuity despite existing constraints of movement, vocabulary, or style. In this way, musical distinction creates higher and higher levels of competitiveness that yields a collaborative mode of instantaneous learning and reinvention, where individuals observe each other closely, using skills of mimesis, satire, and ironic play (Daniel 1995; Drewal 1992). An informed audience's attentiveness to this communicative jousting brings critical attention to cocreators' innovations, and with this interaction they affirm their community's cultural values.

Component 6: Audience Proxemics

The audience is not assumed to be a fixed entity that is made up solely of static observers. They are stratified participants (in age, experience, expertise, and even mood) and, in a dance-drumming context, they may only engage on a subtle level of head nodding or foot tapping; there could be those among them who are leaders and who could emerge as physical or vocal performers. The physical space where the performance takes place is also porous, an entity through which action can flow in or out (Ajayi 1998). At any given moment, performers can direct their focus towards a particular section of the audience, or indeed the viewers can simultaneously be the performers, as in a procession performance. Moreover, it is expected that the audience contains those who have expert knowledge; it is they who deem a virtuosic performance worthy of praise or dismissal through their palpable diminished engagement.

DETAILING DYNAMIC RHYTHM: FROM THE FIELD TO THE STUDIO

Returning to Dynamic Rhythm, I now give further credence to its three subfeatures: repetition, silence, and prosody. Each creates specific pathways to generate action that transmits to and interacts with others. After defining them, I will show how I turn the concepts into techniques to ground improvisation practice. Preliminary aspects of this translating process are evident in the deep autoethnographic excavation of Dynamic Rhythm, which I undertook in Kopeyia village, an Ewe district in Ghana that borders Togo, known worldwide for its practitioners and teachers of Ewe dance-drumming.[iii] While based at the Dagbe Center of Ewe Arts, the prolific nature of music and dance throughout village life was abundantly clear. Locating myself here, I invested my improvisation inquiry through reflective practice across a broad range of activity, ranging from formal repertory-learning activity to social interactions and privileged access to attend a spiritual festival. Through conversing with local experts and leaning into life alongside practice to comprehend the interstitial aspects of their prolific dance-drumming lives, I understood more precisely what skills, modalities of awareness, and values lead to improvisation competencies.

In my case, situated in a context of learning Ewe dances, the first and greatest challenge was to learn the intertwined relationship between speech, song, drum, and movement (Agawu 1995). Beyond the formal space of learning codified Ewe dances at Dabge Arts, I also experienced the communicative nature of song, drum, and dance while attending a funeral, observing a Breketé spiritual festival, and participating in a regular *Kinka* (community meeting). Through participatory-experience, I learned that (1) each musician can expertly demonstrate dance movements, coordinating the reception of sound proprioceptively, which stands above visuality; (2) where there is dance, then the music exists to serve it; (3) individuals may choose to redirect you if you are dancing without adequate understanding of appropriate bodily emphasis; (4) improvisations or embellishments are a requirement only after competency is achieved; and (5) there is an audience for individual contributions, be it as subtle as a head nod or a foot tap. Overarching my experience, I learned that participation affirms the value of communicative interaction at a variety of intensities. My initial academic tendency toward separating these entities caused a delay in recognizing and thus synthesizing them, which is the goal in understanding Dynamic Rhythm's movement-music syntax.

Repetition, Dynamic Rhythm's first subfeature, affirms the significance of movement; intensification through repeating is highlighted in Kariamu Welsh-Asante's work outlining aesthetic properties in Africa's dances (Welsh-Asante 1985). Thus, while improvising a movement's reinscription leads to its transformations, moreover, we can see that whereas pattern generation, recognition, and iteration are critical to human development, it is the capacity to introduce difference, bringing about something new, that makes repetition valuable. The act of repeating a movement phrase while improvising allows the performer to fully explore it proprioceptively; in parallel they also transmit its kinetically, allowing others to kinaesthetically empathize with it (Reason and Reynolds 2010). In addition, this act of repetition commits the action to short-term memory for later recall by themselves or others participants. Musicians also deploy repetition in the use of their sensorimotor skills when making the many different types of African music. Ethnomusicologist Ruth Stone points out that multiple layers of asymmetric pattern are performed as 'polychronic time' (1985: 44), meaning 'many-things-at-time'. Such polycentricism is similarly experienced by dancers who perform dances that reflect a symbiotic relationship with the music's polyrhythms, thus displaying polycentric movement, in which time is displayed variously through different limbs at the same time (Gottschild 1996; Welsh-Asante 1993).

In the Ewe contexts, repetition-with-a-difference manifests as cyclical movement patterns, evident in the practice of their dances, ranging from simpler forms, such as *Kinka* and *Agbadza*, which support high degrees of individualized elaboration, to the very demanding and highly specific *Togo Atsiã*. Only once knowledge of this music and dance phrases is achieved, then the pathway for sensitized dancers to extemporize is laid open. The repetitive aspects of this presentational dance, successfully performed, require dancers' maintenance of the integrity of each rhythmic movement statement in an ongoing fashion without knowing necessarily for how long that particular motif will last; the choice to change the movement-music variation, in Ewe cases, is completely within the lead drummer's jurisdiction. What this means for the dancers is that they must continue to unreservedly commit to repetition, thus being decidedly in the moment, while also listening acutely for when the drums call for change, a shift into a new pattern; this must be precise and lock into the pocket of the new musical expression immediately.

There are implications for improvisation practice here. Foremost, the dancer must consistently invest in the relationship with the music; performing is not a solo pursuit. Second, the music enters into the body not only via the ears but also through other membranes that conduct energy waves: the body's surfaces have varying degrees of porosity; consequently, vibrations that fill the environment are transferred into the body. In addition, different regions of the body correspond to distinctive tones (Zbikowski 2002). Third, this ability to recognize and value patterns of repetitious phenomena through immersion consciously utilizes cognitive and somatic intersensory processes. Vibratory feedback from the music reinscribes the communication, affirming what is presented; in effect, repetition is not mechanical movement or music but presents new opportunities to represent the material's full dimensions, becoming an interactive entity through which to communicate with the audience and other performers. Applied, these dexterities enable performers to serially navigate the changing dynamics of musical time's subterranean divisions; these 'multilogics' (Drewal 1992: 90) are the first rule of embodying time with acuity.

I specifically draw from my Ewe experience to develop this listening acuity in contemporary dancers. Expert Ewe performers who display movement show musical perspicacity through all of their communicative transactions, which takes place through maintaining a prioritization of recursive repetition-driven exchange. These transactions are all grounded by the music's primary, centripetal timekeeping instrument, known locally as the *kangokoui*, commonly referred to as the bell. Apprenticeship in dance-drumming begins here with learning to play its seven-beat bell-pattern amidst the density of the many other layers of timing. Essentially, until its asymmetric pattern is fully embodied, there can be no definite progression in Ewe dance-drumming. I make use of this easily portable iron duo-toned instrument, both symbolically and practically, in the studio to support the dancers' process of assimilating to its polychronic duple and triple time-feels. Figure 43.2 shows two people playing the bell together, making the challenge to maintain its steady representation even greater.

FIG. 43.2 The bell-pattern played simultaneously by two people during an *Adzogbo* event, an Ewe cultural practice. Afloa, Volta Region, Ghana, July 2013.

FIG. 43.3 *A* seven-beat Ewe bell-pattern, approximately recreated on a Western music stave by composer Derek Bermel, who has studied Ghanaian music. The recreation exemplifies the two different signatures or time-feels.

The bell-pattern contains seven beats within one cycle; it can be thought of as containing two rounds of a triplet pattern or a continuous ambulatory 2/4 pulse, even and steady, like walking. While playing their instruments, Ewe musicians interchange between the two time-feels without disrupting the music's integrity. Figure 43.3 represents these two different time signatures on a Western stave, showing how they overlay and interstice to make one pattern.

To explore this embodied musical perspicuity, I work with a group of contemporary trained dancers in the United Kingdom. As part of the analysis, I use their expert voices to highlight moments of learning, and revelation, which points towards deeper levels of inquiry. First, together we form a circle—a rhythmic circle (a spatial organization we return to often) to assist in apprehending anew, the motor skills we use in embodying the bell-pattern. Conceptually, circles in African aesthesis are significant in a number of ways: they are predominant in musical structures; movements have curvilinear form; and they are visible in the architecture of performance spaces, and symbolically representing democratic nonhierarchical unified structures (Anku 2000; Welsh-Asante 1995). I participate in our rhythmic circle alongside the dancers because my experiences in Ghana confirm that I, too, am still learning. In addition, partaking supports my kinaesthetic alignment with the dancers' experiences, promoting my discovery of new skills alongside theirs.

From the open view of the circle, we clap the bell-pattern. I identify the triplet pattern that repeats itself twice in one cycle of the motif. Then, on beat 1, I step to the side with the left foot; n the next beat I transfer weight on the ball of the right foot; and then on beat 3, I transfer again with the whole left foot. A simple, somewhat simple foot pattern is what we use to demonstrate the ongoing triplet cycle, illuminating itself through a pendulum weight shifts, reciprocating from side to side. This seems like a straightforward undertaking of 'dual task interference', where there is a distinction between the spatial and temporal motions of two different movements (Hagendoorn 2003), in this case dancing the triplet while clapping with the bell-pattern. However, it is not as direct as putting two initially independent actions together; there are more overlapping layers within this process.

The steps of the triplet do not fall in synch with the bell-pattern's asymmetric phrasing. This phrase contains seven beats, which with the slightest lapse in concentration feels disruptive. In addition, the strong downbeat of each triplet does not coincide with that of the bell-pattern's beginning, because it takes two cycles of triplets to complete one cycle of the bell-pattern. The symmetrical form of the triplet sits uncomfortably with what now feels like ever-increasing asymmetry in the bell-pattern. Dance scholar Brenda Dixon Gottschild calls this inhabitation of differing modes of time 'embracing the conflict' (Gottschild 1996; DeFrantz 2004: 64–81). However, we seek to go beyond restive tolerance and enter into a state of holistic confluence.

Moreover, continuing on, we layer in the second time signature the 2/4 ambulatory march (found within the 6/8). This alternate time-feel is tantamount to slowing down the pace and experiencing a significant gap between the even steps. This contrasts significantly with the former, more dominating, 3/4 time that is comparatively incessant, requiring less motor control to achieve accuracy. The 6/8 walking time seems abstract and disconnected—that is, until our fibrous body breathes and consciously registers change, so that we sensationally recognize that we are not in discord or hanging ambiguously without a relationship to the existing pulse. Moving between these subtly intertwined modes of time is 'polychronic', as Stone suggests (1985). Conceivably, for dancers, this experience of time-flow is also poly haptic. By this I mean that an understanding of time is deduced through multiple sensory interpretations (kinaesthetic, cognitive, visual, and haptic), which relay qualitative information. Excelling in this application of

Dynamic Rhythm certainly goes beyond differences in the spatial and temporal motions of two different body parts, rather entering into more advanced states of cognitively embodied presence.

The purposes of developing rhythmic dexterities are ultimately to build intersensory awareness and to strengthen communicative performance skills while extemporizing for an unknown public. Including additional stimulus from the outside world, we add the gaze of an audience by moving this rhythmic training to a public space. Both attentive viewers and passers-by provide us with variance in the audience-gaze. Practice in uncontrolled public spaces requires a sharp internal focus, providing a gateway to allowing more finite sensory connections to enter into the body, a definitive requirement to blend these differentiated inhabitations of time. Such experimentation creates an entryway for dancers to connect their experience to onlookers' tacit inquiries. Onlookers' unconscious identification with rhythmic patterns signals participatory impulses, and dancers recognize the potential to engage with Audience Proxemics in modular ways through their direct or indirect responses to this public attention.

An example of this is evident in another exercise to understand the bell-pattern and its internal rhythms, to create a networked, simultaneous polyhaptic experience of its subpatterns. While outdoors, working in groups of three, we transfuse the bell-pattern's three prominent layers into each other's bodies through physical rhythmic patting on the body so that the rhythmic layers are simultaneously felt. Through tactile application, each of the rhythmic tiers can be identified singularly or experienced as confluence. The formation of the haptic-transfusion is as follows: the first person of three is the central receiver, and she stands in place, but is not still; she claps only the main bell-pattern. The second stands behind her and takes the duple (2/4) rhythm, patting this on outside the receiver's hips. The third person taps out the triplet (3/4) rhythm lightly on her head or the back of her shoulders. The idea of locating the resonance of the sound in different parts of the body also relates to the polycentric aspects of movements found in many West African and African diasporan dance and music forms, mentioned earlier. This task directs the receiver towards being able to explicitly feel time being shared across different bodily locations—with specificity—while also identifying the rhythmic conglomeration. This experiential understanding of being able to sense rhythm transfers directly into practical knowledge of how to perform isolations and how to create a synthesis of several rhythmically distinct isolations into one polyhaptic combination.

Continuing on, to amplify the haptic sensation, we all magnify our vibratory fields, enlisting another oscillating pattern through singing the rhythms aloud. Deep listening begins as a 'polychronic', immersive investigation into sound and its sensory location in the body. The task demands patience and perseverance. Recurrently, each person's embodied cognition falters, and loss of participation in the rhythmic network occurs. A rhythmic network is when musical movement patterns are generated and developed conversationally by two or more participants, and if this falters, to regain access we must listen strategically—inwardly and outwardly. When one loses one's place, this creates a separation, causing what philosopher Henri Lefebvre calls

FIG. 43.4 Highbury Green, August 2013. A London public space where the Embodiology Research Group practices the bell-pattern.

FIG. 43.5 The three-person rhythmic transfusion.

'arrhythmia' (2004: 17), which is a moment of disequilibrium and in this case awkward embodiment.

Conversely, when actively immersed, there is a distinctive feeling of connection and 'kinaesonic' holism (Wlison-Bokowiec and Bokowiec 2006). As a result of rhythms being played on our bodies, vibrations interact internally and coalesce. The interior meeting of rhythmic patterns produces a haptic experience of their overlapping relationship. By tapping specific parts of the body, the vector receiving knowledge, accessing formerly hidden or submerged tripartite rhythms becomes attainable. Figures 43.4 and 43.5 show this tactile immersion. In other words, by adding touch and vocal sound to assist deep listening, these multiple senses produce a state where exploratory associations between layers of time are possible because their absorption—haptically, sonically, and collaboratively—provides the receiver with intersensory dimensionality.

From this foundation of deep communicative listening, the next day we return rhythmically wiser to the studio, joined by the two instrumentalists, playing kit drums and vibraphone. We form the rhythmic circle, where we reassume the bell-pattern. Unapologetically, with our rhythmic confidence on display, we share our seven-beat bell-pattern, with our understanding of its components. Together we build short pieces by layering and posing rhythmic statements, which are short patterns that are repeatable, and these build into sophisticated rhythmic networks.

In combined tasks with the musicians, the dancers are required to concentrate on sustaining *rhythmic network,* thereby actively using memory and producing patterns in three distinguishable ways: (1) creating clear discernable patterns, adding to an existing composition, (2) enabling the learning of phrases created by others while simultaneously performing one's own, and (3) being able to produce new unique patterns that are different discernibly different from those created by others. To achieve this insertion, it is necessary to see the space in another person's movement or sound, to observe space and *feel* silence, which is the final feature of Dynamic Rhythm on which I will elaborate. Layer by layer, we build a performance from a simple clapping rhythm, and it develops into full movement and use of space. Tactics of inventing, capturing, and sustaining rhythm are at the fore. Reflecting on the final phase of foundational rhythmic games, Bless Klepcharek reports on his experience as follows: 'I felt that finally we started to move forward, everyone enjoying themselves. At the end of the day we created a piece which we could already perform. All of us put effort into doing something together. If you are working as a group it is much stronger than just one single person' (2013). Klepcharek's testimony asserts that the challenge of being responsively attentive, as a concern for improvisation, occurs automatically with this activity of rhythmic exchange and invention. Moreover, joyfulness arises as the group creates together, a default benefit that co-opts stamina. In addition, the other dancers describe the activity as addressing 'unity', 'connection', 'sensitivity', and 'multisensory listening'.

My full participation to develop these initial foundational exercises is important for two additional reasons: first, it supports the realization of trust and parity between myself as a researcher and my expert subjects, since we are tackling tasks with the same restraints, and second, it gives me a more precise reading of what the challenges are as they arise. Consequently, I am in flow, effective in my ability to intuit what the investigation's next intervention needs to be, without disrupting the performers' momentum.

Leading on from Dynamic Rhythm is the next feature, Prosody. 'Prosody' is a linguistic term referring to poetic qualities inherent to language—the cadence, pitch, and melody essential in the carriage of meaning when words are spoken (Nketia 2002). West African languages such as Ewe and Yorùbá are syntactically tonal in nature, which means that changes in speech cadence transform meaning.

In Ewe music, drums are designed as linguistic membranes. When played expertly, the tonality in the drumming corresponds directly with pitches and patterns in their spoken language. There are grammatical structures in Ewe drumming. Identified verbally in conversation by master Ewe drum teacher Emmanuel Agbeli, he articulates a system as follows: 'TOE; TE; GA; GI; DEY-GI; TO; GA-DRA—those are the notes we use in drumming'. Furthermore, he states: 'When we are playing, these are the notes we put together to make words as a variation' (2013). Note that by 'variation' he means improvisation. Overarchingly, speech, poetics, and communication between musicians, singers, dancers, and participatory observers are realized by perspicacious listening. For the dancers to interact effectively, they must register the 'melo-rhythm' of the music (Nzewi 1974), discerning its tonal registration in order to inform the amplitude of the movement. In developing such agility, 'kinaesonic' mapping techniques—physical renderings of sound as body movement (Bokowiec and Bokowiec 2006)—are deployed to observe musical gradations, charting these across the body with specificity.

Prosody—Examining Musical
Textures of Speech

Adapting the concept of Prosody with the Embodiology Research Group, I develop a distinctive syntax of movement method in order to graft motion onto speech and vice versa. Taking the prosodic, often melodic, lilt found in English speech as the starting point for furnishing the improviser with a wealth of opportunity to develop syntactical movement, we begin with a body-vocal exploration. The task has several generative stages of evolution, and outcomes include a recalibration of the dancer's perception of risk-taking and access to an unending source of novelty. In the first phase, I speak aloud, extemporaneously, and task the dancers' to move (stepping or isolating a body part) according to the cadence of my speech. I speak with clear annunciation and affirm that their locomotion should be precise—each shift must be a visible enunciation of each word, paying deference to the syllables that give each word its rhythmic arc.

To give an example of the second phase of Prosody development, I use a local Ewe proverb and translate it into English: 'Nobody knows tomorrow' (Tsra 2005: 27).[iv] Using this as a fixed sentence, it is possible to repeat it with variation in cadence, speed, volume, and inference. We break it down by number of words and also by syllable. Performers then generate the corresponding number of physical steps or movements to correspond with the words and their syllabic breakdown. This method does not indicate the qualities that these actions may have, since these temporal actions are influenced by the aural textures and tones of these words, impelling the dancer to move responsively and not simply mechanistically. When this sentence—'Nobody knows tomorrow'— is spoken naturally, in each of its syllables and the phrase overall there are changes in pitch, both upward and downward, as cadences transition. These characteristics propose qualitative weight change from syllable to syllable; how the dancer embodies the tonal motion is presented as potential for variation with each sound.

After identifying that the phonology of 'tomorrow' contains three syllables, the dancers must articulate each syllable by flexing, extending, or isolating a different part of the body, or by moving and using the same part but to a greater or lesser degree, simultaneously as I speak the phrase aloud. Symbiotically, dancers comprehend that connecting with the speaker's breath pattern results in greater precision. As dancers steer away from mimetic gesture, their reflexes produce movement that visually appears as vocal and physical simultaneity. An iterative challenge is set is to stringently detect the syllabic breakdown of a speech in a storytelling context. This time with a partner, the dancers use each other's narratives to produce simultaneous bodily articulations. Overall, this syllabic articulation presents greater challenge than merely tracing movement that flows with the melodic contours of storytelling speech. It requires rigorous concentration since narrative comprehension, as well as tonal and syllabic filters, are at work.

After achieving a level of actualization, the next iteration is applied, in which the dancers speak aloud while moving in tandem, creating their own prosodic textures. The entire body is in locomotion, while expressive stillness represents punctuation. To expand the range of movement articulations, we exaggerate the use of our voices; and together these stringent detections of the syllabic and tonal make-up of our speech produce simultaneous bodily articulations. Once established, performers can go beyond normal tonal range of speech: elongating words, intentionally stammering and changing the pitch (sometimes artificially—even within one syllable), exceeding the realms of everyday speech or even song. These utterances now present greater colour and texture, and the expressions of movement follow. These syllabic movement articulations are similar in character to 'Africanist' movement modalities identified in African American and Caribbean forms in which fast isolations and counterpoising coordination are prominent (Gottschild 1996; DeFrantz 2004).

In addition, underlying speech patterns exists a subterranean tempo, a hidden pulse carrying the voice and likewise the motion. These iterative cycles of exploration show ancillary potential in achieving the simultaneity of aligning movement with speech poetics. Insofar as making words comprehensible, it engenders an automatic coordinated use of breath that informs and differentiates each person's subterranean pulse. By making this breath control intentional, we distinguish both our tonal range and our punctuation. Refracted, these voice modulations in movement produce notable gradations in motion and gesture. Each iteration of this task serves to demand more of the dancers' attention to emerging detail; the challenge is to attend to this exercise with increasing precision; it is not impressionistic, as their performances show direct relationships between movement, sensation, and speech poetics.

To illustrate use of a short spoken phrase danced with these finite modulations, Gwen Jones, working intensively in this laboratory setting, deploys a simple clause, uttering: 'I feel great in this space'. She uses repetition of this sentence with a range of modulations, including pitch, volume, and speed. Notably, her actions reveal that, at times, her voice is altered by the movement's momentum. These consequential changes in cadence demonstrate how motion can impact linguistic carriage of meaning. Jones, on hearing these vocal changes, is affected and makes immediate, definite choices to respond to these cadences. At one point, she chooses to increase volume in her voice, and the movement develops into much bolder gestures, which challenges her balance, but instead of pushing her to lose control, her movement expression becomes virtuosic and surprising.

GWEN JONES EXPLORES PROSODY

What Jones shows in Figures 43.6–43.9 is common among the group—textured, repetitious use of a short statement that leads to unusual movement pathways, placing bodies at extremes of physical range, but with virtuosic ease.

FIG. 43.6 Gwen Jones's prosody exploration.

FIG. 43.7 Prosodic pronouncements.

FIG. 43.8 Prosodic conviction.

FIG. 43.9 Prosodic abandon.

On discussing where the experiment might go next, a turn is taken to explore whether the same effect might occur without speaking out loud. In other words, can we internalize Prosody and will this still produce movement differentiation? Astonishingly, equal fluidity and virtuosity does occur when the dancers recite their statements (with prosodic variation) only in their minds. Imagined manipulation of sound creates vivid bodily articulations that demonstrate strong individuated aesthetics. Ingrid MacKinnon, reflecting on the development of her prosodic articulations, surmises: 'when you speak and you're trying to make your point and you're not sure of what you are saying, you pause to make sure that you are being articulate and make sense. When you transpose that onto movement, you take pauses to make sure to make your movements make sense or translate into *something*; rather than just constantly moving, and never really making a point' (MacKinnon in group interview, 2013).

Speech syntax requires the use of pauses, brief suspensions of time; these are intervallic punctuations, necessary for comprehension. Transferred into movement, these silences translate into an array of punctuations—halts, dramatic level changes, and recalibrations of energy. Similarly, group member Noelle White confirms that the Prosody technique makes it possible for her to remain in the moment and create with greater differentiated qualities. Uncharted patterns of movement that enable florid cadence to unfurl are accessible using this strategy; the mind is visibly expanded as cognition distributes across the body. Movements appear radically free, at times, almost abandoned. However, the performers visibly remain in firm control, demonstrating a responsive awareness of environmental factors—sound, space, and the presence of others.

Within these 'kinaesonic' body-mind phenomena, where a sequence of events appears linear, with the speaking voice conterminously determining the movement, upon close examination, one discovers a dynamic multidirectional loop. Through use of voice, dancers take increased risk with their movement, and more technical skills (balance, coordination, range, speed, level, and multiples uses of directional change) are co-opted in their handling of seemingly precarious and multifaceted movements. Prosody explorations, informed by the linguistic base of Ewe drumming, create unique routes towards complex arrangements of novelty and dexterous control, not revealed by other processes. However, further elaborations of voice and movement relations, beyond what is described here, can be iterated. Precision is of utmost importance in Prosody, affirming that movement can inform language. Though other ways of interweaving voice and movement exist, this approach is founded on syntactical actuality, resonating in the body, and not on allusions to sonic hues.

In this exploration of spoken language, one of the important features we encounter in speech are silences, or pauses. Silence is the third feature of Dynamic Rhythm. It is these suspensions within speech that deliver meaning and enable comprehension in the listener; the use of punctuation enables meaning to be deciphered. It has a number of connotations, depending on whether it is a referencing term for sound or physical movement, which may more accurately be thought of as suspension, because micromotions continue and these too are expressive; in both cases, sound or motion pertain to occupying physical space. As I have established, rhythm is identifiable through the presence of repetitious forms or patterns. These organized time-shapes work across micro- and macrospaces. Patterns realized have discernable shapes; they make impressions through non-expressions, thus giving form to space; the way that space differentiates regularity and asymmetry creates their characteristics and ultimately their communicative affect.

Fundamentally, to sustain a pattern requires the use and observance of silence and space; this creates form, legibility and comprehension. Where the dance is concerned, Welsh-Asante points out that 'attention must be directed at the silence and the stillness if one is to appreciate the full complexity and beauty of the polymultiple [*sic*] experience'

(Welsh-Asante 1985: 81). Paul Berliner, scholar of both Zimbabwean music and North American jazz, classifies parts of rhythm that are absent, calling them nonstrokes that are felt to be 'inherent'. Furthermore, Agawu's argumentative essay 'Structural Analysis or Cultural Analysis? Competing Perspectives on the "Standard Pattern" of West African Rhythm' points out the significance of silence on several occasions. At one point he states that 'a metric cycle may also employ silence as a marker of the regulative beat' (2006: 23) and 'armed with the cultural notion of play ... silences are just as likely to mark beats as sound' (26).

The entry point of silence comes from aural resonance that furnishes rhythm with entryways back to connecting with the next tone. The feeling of space is in itself generative, it is not emptiness (Thiong'o 1997); it is visual, spatial, and tactile, a metadirectional connector of events, and this interweaving of actual and implied timing holds implications for improvised interactions. This attentional directive towards space amplifies the conceptual significance of silence as a tactile entity, following time's viscosity. This aesthesis, or in other words tacit process, suggests ways for timing dynamics to be examined in the dance studio setting. The subtleties of the spaces between rhythm and timing are a critical part of polyphonic dance-drumming music. Its microsuspensions, in conjunction with the surrounding kinetic activity and sensory-cognitive awareness, makes Embodiology's deployment and examinations of rhythm unformulaic.

It could be argued that silence is the leading feature of rhythm, since the other two aspects, Prosody and Repetition, cannot exist without it. I, however, chose to represent these three features in the specified order, ending with silence, as a way to arrive at this place of coalescence whereupon emphasis on a sensory mastery of space, silence, and suspension creates undeniable facility. It is possible to identify space, silence, and suspension at the core of our being, through our breath. When we breathe, we observe suspension between the inhalation and exhalation; when one exhales, one's lungs can be considered empty, but in another sense that suspension hails the moment of expectation when the lungs are ready to be filled.

Conclusion

While constraints exist in Dynamic Rhythm through practical and theoretical study of concepts—including rhythmic network, kinaesthetic alliteration, and repetition-with-a-difference—it is possible to achieve a level of embodied acuity. In this way, practitioners' abilities to spontaneously create, in groups or individually, exceed conscious competence. Moreover, these distinctive neo-African laws of improvisation become clear. When later recombined with the other five constitutive parts of Embodiology, Dynamic Rhythm fulfils the role of the metagenerator. Emerging from the essence of breath, from this place Dynamic Rhythm encompasses various sensory and cognitive states of awareness. To practice improvisation with deference to Dynamic Rhythm requires the cultivation of whole-body listening to discern internal patterns, to generate external, legible forms, to transform them collaboratively, and to sustain them with the proprioceptive wisdom that supports interactivity. By working with the Ewe bell-pattern to infuse the body with simultaneous multiple time-feels creates gateways for experientially registering different resonances of time across the body that coalesce to become one unifying vibration that promotes musical flow and readiness to interpret musical phrasing offered by others. The rhythmic network is always active, communicating to participants in accordance with their level of acuity and activity. The relating of rhythmic pattern to speech poetics, through deploying Prosody strategies, makes the relationship between movement polycentrism, isolation, and unyielding inventiveness clear, a reality that brings with it nuances of tonally informed, individually virtuosic movement, but without loss of connectedness with others who are participating.

This paradigm for generating performance stems from improvisation practices found in West Africa; Diaspora dance styles have subsequently extended out from the continent through an implicit deployment of these six generative laws, and many also have African foundations—to name a few: tap dance, dancehall, lindy hop, house, vogueing, breaking, salsa, flamenco, and tango. These dance cultures emerged in conjunction with specific types of music; therefore, to research and practice improvisation with African-centred logic it is necessary to approach it holistically. This interdisciplinary and intercultural fact is woven into Embodiology praxis, which offers West African aesthetics as bountiful alternative strategies to inform and enrich contemporary dance practices, wherein improvisation-is-performance.

NOTES

i. Embodiology* is a registered trademark and as such demonstrates my commitment, as an action researcher, to return a royalty payment to the Ewe community in Ghana each time its principles are shared in full or in part.

ii. My multimodal methodology combines adapted strategies from autoethnography, Practice-as-Research, action research, and grounded theory. My journey toward Embodiology stems from a fascination with improvising, traceable to my formative years of dancing at home with my mother, learning 1950s and 1960s Jamaican social dances. In this informal yet performance context, with family members watching, blue beat, ska, calypso, and reggae, interchanged with US rock and roll, rhythm and blues, and Motown, inspired hours of original dancing based on combined musical interactivity of instrumentalists and singers. Fast-forward into the latter years of my formal studio-based dance training in the late 1980s and 1990s, I revisited the social context, vigorously participating in club dancing, and this brought with it a musical awareness of jazz-funk, bebop, Latin jazz, fusion, and breakbeats. So, despite performing challenging repertory, in London Contemporary Dance Theatre and Rambert Dance Company, by choreographers including Jane Dudley, Ohad Naharin, Robert Cohan, and Anthony Tudor, I remained inspired by improvisation, which, I contend, uniquely emerges as inventive, self-actualized performance.

iii. Other researchers, such as influential American ethnomusicologists David Locke (1992) and James Burns (2009), have also undertaken research residence at this site. Despite Ewes being one of the country's minority ethnic groups, dances and 'musics' (Lomax 1980) from this region are a central part of the National Dance Company of Ghana; furthermore, across the African Diaspora, Ewe songs and dances are also widely practised.

iv. A proverb is a short sentence in common circulation that declares an accepted wisdom. This proverb means: no one knows what will happen tomorrow, so we need to be careful in life. Further interpreted, it cautions those 'who make plans without submitting them to the will of God' (Tsra 2005: 26).

REFERENCES

Agawu, V. K. (1995) *African Rhythm: A Northern Ewe Perspective*. New York: Cambridge University Press.

Agbeli, E. (2013) Interview by the author. 18 July.

Ajayi, O. S. (1998) Yoruba Dance: The Semiotics of Movement and Body Attitude in a Nigerian Culture. Trenton, NJ: Africa World Press.

Anku, W. (2000) Circles and Time: A Theory of Structural Organization of Rhythm in African Music. *Music Theory Online* 6(1). http://www.mtosmt.org/issues/mto.00.6.1/mto.00.6.1.anku.html?q=mto/issues/mto.00.6.1/mto.00.6.1.anku.html

Barber, K. (2000) *The Generation of Plays: Yoruba Popular Life in Theater*. Bloomington: Indiana University Press.

Berliner, P. (1978) *The Soul of Mbira: Music and Traditions of the Shona People of Zimbabwe*. Berkeley: University of California Press.

Burns, J. (2009) *Female Voices from an Ewe Dance-Drumming Community in Ghana: Our Music Has Become a Divine Spirit*. Burlington, VT: Ashgate.

Chernoff, J. M. (1979) *African Rhythm and African Sensibility: Aesthetics and Social Action in African Musical Idioms*. Chicago: University of Chicago Press.

Daniel, Y. (1995) *Rumba: Dance and Social Change in Contemporary Cuba*. Bloomington: Indiana University Press.

DeFrantz, T. F. (2004) The Black Beat Made Visible: Body Power in Hip Hop Dance. In Lepecki, A. (ed.), *Of the Presence of the Body: Essays on Dance and Performance Theory*. Middletown, CT: Wesleyan University Press, 64–81.

Dortey, M. (2012) Kplejoo of Nungua and Tema: An Integrative Performance Study of Music, Dance, Ritual and Drama. PhD. University of Ghana, Legon.

Drewal, M. (1991) The State of Research on Performance in Africa. *African Studies Review* 34(3): 1–64.

Drewal, M. T. (1992) *Yoruba Ritual: Performers, Play, Agency*. Bloomington: Indiana University Press.

Eglash, R., (1999) *African Fractals: Modern Computing and Indigenous Design*. New Brunswick, NJ: Rutgers University Press.

Euba, A. (2003) Concepts of Neo-African Music as Manifested in the Yorùbá Folk Opera. in Monson, I. T. (ed.), *The African Diaspora: A Musical Perspective*. London: Routledge, 207–241.

Fenton, D. (2008) *Unstable Acts: A Practitioner's Case Study of the Poetics of Postdramatic Theatre and Intermediality*. PhD. Queensland University of Technology, Australia. http://eprints.qut.edu.au/16527/1/David_Fenton_Thesis.pdf.

Fiagbedzi, N. (2005) *An Essay on the Nature of the Aesthetic in the African Musical Arts*. Accra: Royal Crown Press.

Friedson, S. M. (2009) *Remains of Ritual: Northern Gods in a Southern Land*. Chicago: University of Chicago Press.

Gallagher, S. (2005) *How the Body Shapes the Mind*. Oxford: Clarendon Press.

Geurts, K. L. (2002) *Culture and the Senses: Bodily Ways of Knowing in an African Community*. Berkeley: University of California Press.

Geurts, K. L., and Adikah, E. G. (2006) Enduring and Endearing Feelings and the Transformation of Material Culture in West Africa. *Sensible Objects: Colonialism, Museums and Material Culture* 35: 35–60.

Goldman, D. (2010) *I Want to Be Ready: Improvised Dance as a Practice of Freedom*. Ann Arbor: University of Michigan Press.

Gottschild, B. D. (1996) *Digging the Africanist Presence in American Performance: Dance and other Contexts*. Westport, CT: Greenwood.

Gottschild, B. D. (2000) Stripping the Emperor: The Africanist Presence in American Concert Dance. *European Contributions to American Studies* 44: 273–288.

Hagendoorn, I. (2003) Cognitive Dance Improvisation: How Study of the Motor System Can Inspire Dance (And Vice Versa), *Leonardo*, 36 (3): 221–227.

Hall, E. T. (1969) *The Hidden Dimension*. Garden City, NY: Doubleday.

Haseman, B. (2007) Rupture and Recognition: Identifying the Performative, Research Paradigm. In Barrett, E., and Bolt, B. (eds.), *Practice as Research: Approaches to Creative Arts Inquiry*. London: I. B. Tauris, 147–157.

Hendrickson, H. (1996) *Clothing and Difference: Embodied Identities in Colonial and Post-colonial Africa*. Durham, NC: Duke University Press.

Iyer, V. (2002) Embodied Mind, Situated Cognition, and Expressive Microtiming in African-American Music. *Music Perception* 19(3): 387–414.

Jackson, J. D. (2001) Improvisation in African-American Vernacular Dancing. *Dance Research Journal* 33(2): 40–53.

Lefebvre, H. (2004) *Rhythmanalysis: Space, Time, and Everyday Life*. London: Continuum.

Linn Geurts, K. (2005) Consciousness as Feeling in the Body. In Howes, D. (ed.), *Empire of the Senses: The Sensual Culture Reader*. Oxford: Berg, 164–178.

Locke, D. (1992) *Kpegisu: A War Drum of the Ewe*. Tempe, AZ: White Cliffs Media; distributed by Talman.

Lomax, A. (1980) Appeal for Cultural Equity. *African Music* 6(1): 22–31.

McNaughton, P. (2008) *Bird Dance Near Saturday City: Sidi Ballo and the Art of West African Masquerade*. Bloomington: Indiana University Press.

Melrose, S. (2005a) *Out of Words*. Centre for the History and Analysis of Recorded Music, Middlesex University.

Melrose, S. (2005b) *Towards Tomorrow? International Gathering 2005*. Aberystwyth, Wales: Centre for Performance Research.

Nelson, R. (2013) *Practice as Research in the Arts: Principles, Protocols, Pedagogies, Resistances*. Palgrave Macmillan.

Nketia, J. H. K. (1974) *The Music of Africa*. New York: Norton.

Nketia, J. H. K. (2002) Musicology and Linguistics: Integrating the Phraseology of Text and Tune in the Creative Process. *Black Music Research Journal* 22(2): 143–164.

Nzewi, M. (1974) Melo-rhythmic Essence and Hot Rhythm in Nigerian Folk Music. *Black Perspective in Music* 2(1): 23–28.

Reason, M., and Reynolds, D. (2010) Kinesthesia, Empathy, and Related Pleasures: An inquiry into Audience Experiences of Watching Dance. *Dance Research Journal* 42(2): 49–75.

Rye, C. (2003) Incorporating Practice: A Multi-viewpoint Approach to Performance Documentation. *Journal of Media Practice* 3: 115–123.

Scott, M. (2014) A Study of the Power of Club Jazz in 1980s London. In Guarino, L., and Oliver, W. (eds.), *Jazz Dance: A History of the Roots and Branches*. Gainesville: University Press of Florida, 261–267.

Speca, A. (2001) *Hypothetical Syllogistic and Stoic Logic*. Leiden: Brill.

Stone, R. M. (1985) In Search of Time in African Music. *Music Theory Spectrum* 7: 139–148.

Thiong'o, N. W. (1997) Enactments of Power: The Politics of Performance Space. *The Drama Review: TDR* 41(3): 11.

Thompson-Drewal, M. (2003) Improvisation as Participatory Performance: Egungun Masked Dancers in the Yoruba Tradition. In Albright, Ann Cooper, and Gere, D. (eds.), *Taken by Surprise: A Dance Improvisation Reader*. Middletown, CT: Wesleyan University Press, 119–144.

Tiérou, A. (1992) *Doople: The Eternal Law of African Dance*. Philadelphia: Harwood Academic.

Tsra, S. W. K. (2005) *Some Ewe Proverbs and their Literal Meaning in English*. Accra: GertMash Desktop Service.

Turner, T. S. (2012) The Social Skin. *HAU: Journal of Ethnographic Theory* 2(2): 486–504.

Wacquant, L. J. D. (2004) *Body and Soul: Notebooks of an Apprentice Boxer*. Oxford: Oxford University Press.

Welsh-Asante, K. (1990) Philosophy and Dance in Africa: The Views of Cabral and Fanon. *Journal of Black Studies* 21(2): 224–232.

Welsh-Asante, K. (ed.). (1993) *The African Aesthetic: Keeper of the Traditions*. Westport, CT: Greenwood Press.

Welsh-Asante, K. (1996) The Zimbabwean Dance Aesthetic: Senses, Cannons and Characteristics. In Welsh-Asante, W. (ed.), *African Dance: An Artistic, Historical, and Philosophical Inquiry*. Trenton, NJ: Africa World Press, 202–220.

Welsh-Asante, K. (1985) Commonalities in African Dance: An Aesthetic Foundation. In Asante, M. K., and Welsh-Asante, K. (eds.), *African Culture: The Rhythms of Unity*. Westport, CT: Greenwood Press, 71–82.

Wilson-Bokowiec, J., and Bokowiec, M. A. (2006) Kinaesonics: The Intertwining Relationship of Body and Sound. *Contemporary Music* Review 25(1–2): 47–57.

Zaporah, R. (1995) *Action Theater: The Improvisation of Presence*. Berkeley, CA: North Atlantic Books.

Zbikowski, L. M. (2002) *Conceptualizing Music: Cognitive Structure, Theory, and Analysis*. Oxford: Oxford University Press.

Index